## TREASURY FUNCTIONS

## PERSONNEL FUNCTIONS

## CORPORATE DEVELOPMENT

## ADMINISTRATIVE

## GOVERNMENT REPORTING AND REGULATIONS

## MANAGEMENT LIAISON FUNCTIONS

## INDEX

# CORPORATE CONTROLLER'S MANUAL

*Editor*
**Paul J. Wendell, CPA**

**WARREN, GORHAM & LAMONT**
Boston • New York

# Contributing Authors

**C. Richard Baker**
*L.F. Rothschild, Unterberg, Towbin*

**Martin Benis**
*Professor of Accounting,*
*The Bernard M. Baruch College of the City University of New York*

**Edward M. Bixler**
*Vice President and Corporate Controller, Monier Company*

**Max Block**
*Founder-Partner (retired), Anchin, Block & Anchin;*
*Editor (retired), The CPA Journal*

**Gilbert D. Bloom**
*Partner, Peat, Marwick, Mitchell & Co.*

**Robert A. Bonsack**
*Principal, Peat, Marwick, Mitchell & Co.*

**David P. Boxer**
*Assistant Technical Director, Public Oversight Board,*
*SEC Practice Section—AICPA*

**Steven A. Braun**
*Partner, Alexander Grant & Co.*

**William H. Bryan**
*Credit management consultant, writer and speaker;*
*Retired credit manager, Alton Box Board Company*

**Charles J. Cater, Jr.**
*Manager, Internal Auditing, South Central Bell Telephone Company*

**Robert L. Collins**
*Controller, Corporate Operating Services, McGraw-Hill, Inc.*

**Anthony J. Curley**
*Professor of Finance, The Pennsylvania State University*

**James W. DeLoach, Jr.**
*Manager, Arthur Andersen & Co.*

**Gary Dudley**
*Manager, Touche Ross & Co.*

**David E. Finkler**
*Director, Management Information Systems, United States Filter Corp.*

**Jerry L. Ford**
*Vice President of Finance and Treasurer,*
*Poppin Fresh Pies, Inc., a Pillsbury Company subsidiary*

**Robert Ford**
*Vice President, Corporate Cash Management,*
*Manufacturers Hanover Trust Co.*

**Thomas C. Franco**
*Account Executive, Georgeson & Co.*

**Charles H. Gibson**
*Professor of Accounting, University of Toledo*

**Vincent C. Hennessy**
*Division Manager, Exxon International Co.*

**Franklin R. Johnson**
*Partner, Price Waterhouse & Co.*

**Maureen Conners Kessler**
*Associate, Kelley, Drye & Warren*

**Michael F. Klein**
*Manager, Touche Ross & Co.*

**Richard Lancioni**
*Professor of Logistics and Marketing, Temple University*

**Matthew Lenz, Jr.**
*Chairman, Property-Liability Insurance Division,*
*The College of Insurance*

**Mel Levine**
*Manager, Touche Ross & Co.*

**Leslie N. Masonson**
*Assistant Vice President,*
*Cash Management Consulting, Citibank, N.A.*

**Richard J. Melucci**
*Associate Professor of Management, Adelphi University*

**Edward Mendlowitz**
*Partner, Siegel & Mendlowitz, P.C.*

**Donald E. Mitchell**
*Vice President and Controller, Cyclops Corp.*

**Donald J. Moulin**
*Partner, Peat, Marwick, Mitchell & Co.*

**Winthrop C. Neilson**
*Principal, Georgeson & Co.*

**Harry H. Ness**
*Vice President, Standard Research Consultants*

**Frederick L. Neumann**
*Professor of Accountancy, University of Illinois at Urbana-Champaign*

**Anthony C. Paddock**
*Vice President, Standard Research Consultants*

**Stanley H. Pantowich**
*Partner, Arthur Young & Company*

**James W. Pattillo**
*Manager, Crowe, Chizek & Co.*

**Arthur D. Perrone**
*Vice President and Controller, Ameron*

**Felix Pomeranz**
*Partner, Coopers & Lybrand*

**G. Edward Powell**
*Partner, Price Waterhouse & Co.*

**James R. Ratliff**
*Associate Professor of Accounting, New York University*

**Robert O. Redd**
*Partner, Seidman & Seidman*

**Robert F. Reilly**
*Manager, Internal Audit, Huffy Corporation*

**David N. Ricchiute**
*Assistant Professor of Accounting, University of Notre Dame*

**Richard R. Rosen**
*Partner, Anchin, Block & Anchin*

**Arthur J. Schomer**
*Partner, Eisner & Lubin*

**Harold B. Shapiro**
*Vice President and Controller, Diversified Industries, Inc.*

**David R. Shelton**
*Director of Corporate Financial Planning, Trans Union Corp.*

**Gilbert Simonetti, Jr.**
*Partner, Price Waterhouse & Co.*

**Hugo J. Standing**
*Senior Vice President and Director, Alexander & Alexander, Inc.*

**Martin G. Strieter**
*Vice President, Alexander & Alexander, Inc.*

**S. Bleecker Totten**
*Senior Vice President, Consulting Division,*
*Edward S. Gordon Company, Inc.*

**Alan D. Yohalem**
*Controller, The Economics Press, Inc.*

# Preface

When I was asked to prepare an outline for this book, I took the normal first step of going to the library and checking the available controller reference books. I found useful books on accounting functions, preparation of financial statements, cost accounting, treasury functions and other specialized areas such as budgeting and taxes, but no one book that covered the full range of controllership functions in a practical and fully up-to-date way.

The publisher and I decided that this book should be written so that it would be useful both to experienced controllers who require guidance in specialized areas that they usually do not encounter, such as mergers and acquisitions or divestments, and to recently promoted controllers who also need help in handling complicated accounting problems, such as LIFO or leases.

Authors and compilers of reference books in the accounting area find that changes in pertinent laws, regulations, and accounting rules rapidly render most publications out-of-date. Warren, Gorham & Lamont will update this book as it does its other reference books, by publishing periodic supplements as they are needed, but at least annually, rather than issuing "revised editions" at longer intervals. The supplements will also contain new material in developing areas or material that could not be included in the basic book. For example, this volume does not contain a chapter on foreign exchange translation accounting because during the period the book was in preparation, the FASB was still trying to revise its unsatisfactory rules in this area. A chapter on the new foreign exchange accounting rules will be included in the first supplement. The periodic supplements should increase the usefulness and value of this manual.

We decided to prepare this volume on a multi-author basis because: (1) we wanted to take advantage of the broad perspective and expertise of an experienced author group with practical hands-on experience in their respective areas; (2) no one person is really expert in the variety of topics covered; and (3) we were able to persuade busy controllers, academicians, accountants and lawyers to write a single chapter on a topic within their expertise who were not willing to undertake an entire book or even a major section. Although this book was written by many authors, we have tried to achieve a unity of style and structure, and have, in each chapter, directed the reader to areas of related interest in other parts of the book.

Since no book can cover the many topics we selected in an exhaustive way, each author has added a list of suggested readings at the end of his chapter for readers who require additional information.

The contributing authors were carefully selected for their background and expertise, and my associates and I have enjoyed working with them and learning from them. To each of them I offer my sincere appreciation for their contribution to this book.

Editing the work of fifty-three authors and keeping track of the status of each chapter and the necessary tables and other reference material is a vast administrative job. This book could not have been produced without the efforts of my managing editor Naomi Weinberg. She not only handled the administrative details but she also conformed the editorial format of each chapter so that the varying styles of writing could be blended into a cohesive and uniform style. I am sincerely grateful for her contribution.

I also want to thank Alan Huisman, Victoria Mathews, and Kevin Callahan for their very professional copyediting of the manuscripts. And finally, I want to thank Eugene Simonoff for sharing his experience with me. This is my first multi-author book, and I am indebted to Gene for getting me started with a minimum of fumbling.

One final note. I am aware that women are rapidly assuming important roles in corporate management. To simplify the textual material, however, the editors have used the pronouns *he*, *his*, and *him* generically to refer both to men and to women.

January 1981 PAUL J. WENDELL

# Contents

## Part I   The Role of the Controller

## Part II   Financial Functions

## Part III   Management Decision Functions

## Part IV   Internal Control Functions

# Part V    Treasury Functions

# Part VI    Personnel Functions

# Part VII    Corporate Development

# Part VIII    Administrative Functions

# Part IX    Government Reporting and Regulations

# Part X   Management Liaison Functions

# Index

## Part X Managerial Decision Making

Index

# Part I

## The Role of the Controller

# 1

# An Overall View

*Paul J. Wendell*

## DEFINITION OF A CONTROLLER'S DUTIES

The Financial Executives Institute (the national organization for controllers and treasurers) has published a statement that outlines responsibilities for both positions. The following list of a controller's functions, while quite general, provides a good starting point for discussing his corporate role.

1.  *Planning for control.* To establish, coordinate, and administer, as an integral part of management, an adequate plan for the control of operations. To the extent required by the business, this plan would provide profit planning, programs for capital investing and for financing, sales forecasts, expense budgets and cost standards, and the necessary procedures for effecting the plan.

2.  *Reporting and interpreting.* To compare performance with operating plans and standards and to report and interpret the results of operations to all levels of management and to the owners of the business. This function includes the formulation of accounting policy, the coordination of systems and procedures, the preparation of operating data and special reports as required.

3.  *Evaluating and consulting.* To consult with all segments of management responsible for policy or action concerning any phase of the business that relates to attainment of objectives, effectiveness of policies, organization structure, and procedures.

4.  *Tax administration.* To establish and administer tax policies and procedures.

5.  *Government reporting.* To supervise or coordinate the preparation of reports to government agencies.

6.  *Protection of assets.* To assure protection for the assets of the business through internal control, internal auditing, and proper insurance coverage.

7.  *Economic appraisal.* To continuously appraise economic and social forces and government influences and to interpret their effect upon the business.

The FEI list of treasurership functions should probably be added to the controller's listing because, for all but very large companies, these functions usually fall within the controller's responsibilities. A list of the principal categories of treasurership functions should be sufficient to indicate the broader responsibilities of most controllers.

-   Providing capital;
-   Investor relations;
-   Short-term financing;
-   Banking and custody;
-   Credits and collections; and
-   Investments.

## The Expansion of the Controller's Role

A review of current literature on the functions of the controller indicates that most authors believe the controller's role to have been vastly expanded in the past decade or two. Sam R. Goodman, in describing the changing scope of the controller's function, states:

The controller is being increasingly cast as an internal quantitative consultant who, through various techniques, discipline, and objectivity can assist many other areas of the company to optimize their programs. It is the controller who is in the best position to advise the marketing area of levels of geographic and customer profitability, and the efficiency or inefficiency of media and promotion policy. The controller is also in an ideal position to advise the manufacturing area relative to the efficient use of directly applied manufacturing costs as well as the utilization of manufacturing period expenses.[1]

Writing in somewhat the same vein, A. Carl Kotchian notes:

For the modern financial executive the tools of the function now commonly include linear programming, simulation, queuing, sampling theory, decision theory, game theory, and probability theory or risk analysis. The financial executive does not have to acquire the skills to perform these tasks himself, but he should be knowledgeable to the degree that he understands how these tools may be profitably applied to his operations. Additionally, discounted cash flow or present values are widely used to measure the relative worth of competing investment projects. With the theory and tools now at hand, the financial executive's role is today more rapidly expanding than ever.[2]

**What Really Increased the Controller's Role?** The comments of both authors attribute the controller's expanded role in the corporation to the controller's technical ability and to his use of more sophisticated tools. Neither of these comments, however, seem to explain adequately the expanded role of the controller in management decisions. At one time, the controller was simply a source of financial data. He did not participate in management decisions because he lacked an operations background and, according to the management of those days, could not properly evaluate operating decisions. Although it is true that the controller's status and role in management have continuously expanded during the past two decades, this expansion has not been a result of the reasons cited above, but has generally paralleled the growth of government regulation of business.

As the management of corporations realized that their net income was becoming increasingly subject to complicated laws, rules, and regulations of the Internal Revenue Service, the Securities and Exchange Commission, the accounting profession (which we consider to be an outgrowth of government regulation), the Cost Accounting Standards Board, and other government regulators, management was forced to turn for guidance to those who understood these laws, rules, and regulations—the controller and corporate counsel. As top corporate executives increasingly included the controller in planning meetings so that he could interpret the effect of government rules on contemplated changes in operations, they found that his advice was also valuable in other areas. Management discovered that although

---

[1] Sam R. Goodman, "The Changing Scope of the Controller's Function," *Controller's Handbook*, Sam R. Goodman and James S. Reece, ed. Homewood, Illinois: Dow Jones-Irwin, 1978, p. 24.

[2] A. Carl Kotchian, "An Overview," *Financial Executive's Handbook*, Richard F. Vancil, ed. Homewood, Illinois: Dow Jones-Irwin, 1970, p. 9.

the controller was not an operating person, he knew as much or more about the business as any of the operating executives. He could pinpoint excessive costs, determine which operations were efficient or inefficient, and find the possible flaws in new plans.

This realization of the controller's knowledge of the business, with the increasing growth of government regulation, has spurred the advancement of the controller in the corporate management hierarchy. A great many controllers have come up through the finance ranks, to become chief executives of large publicly held companies.

### A Definition Applicable to This Book

This book is generally designed to aid controllers of corporations with less than 1,000 employees or less than $50 million in revenues. In such firms, the controller generally has responsibility that is far removed from his basic financial functions. Either no one else in management wants the assignments or the chief executive officer believes that the controller's competence and knowledge of the business can be applied to areas such as personnel, risk management, real estate management, or energy conservation. Because we recognize how diverse the controller's responsibilities may be in medium-sized and smaller companies, we have broadened the scope of the controller's duties beyond that described by the FEI. Briefly, the controller acts as the chief financial and administrative officer of the corporation. He is an integral part of management and participates in all corporate planning. He establishes, coordinates, and administers all financial systems, internal controls, and related areas. He prepares reviews, appraises budgets and forecasts, and monitors the operating results. He establishes and administers tax policies and procedures, as well as other government reporting requirements. He reviews and appraises plans for mergers, acquisitions, divestments, new ventures, and capital expenditures. He maintains a working relationship with the audit committee, the outside auditors, bankers, creditors, and corporate counsel. Finally, but probably most significant, he advises the chief executive officer on all important matters.

## THE CONTROLLER'S FINANCIAL FUNCTIONS

No matter how broad a controller's role may become in a given situation, his primary responsibilities are in the financial area. We therefore commence our overall view of the controller's role with a discussion of his financial functions.

### Setting Accounting Policies

One of the more important phrases in the controller's vocabulary is *generally accepted accounting principles* (GAAP). Financial statements issued by a corporation to investors, bankers, and others must conform to GAAP. When an independent certified public accountant issues a report on a company's financial statements, whether audited, compiled, or reviewed, he is required to note any material deviation from GAAP. If the accountant is issuing an audited report, he is required to either qualify his opinion, issue an adverse opinion, or disclaim an opinion, depending on the materiality of the deviation from GAAP in the financial statements.

Since the financial statements are expected to conform to GAAP, the controller must make sure that the company's accounting policies conform to GAAP. Problems arise because GAAP is not a straightforward list of accounting rules. Acceptable alternative principles are available, depending upon what is preferable in the circumstances and whether the corporation is in a specialized industry such as real estate, banking, construction, and others.

The controller should be aware of the use of preferable alternatives within the concept of GAAP and the factors that should be considered before a choice is made for a new enterprise or revised for an existing corporation. The controller must also understand the requirement to disclose all significant accounting policies and any changes in such policies in the notes to the financial statements.

**Big GAAP Versus Little GAAP.** The controllers of nonpublic companies and their outside accountants have complained for the past several years that the increasingly complex GAAP is primarily applicable to public companies and that nonpublic companies should be able to follow a simpler set of rules. The Financial Accounting Standards Board (FASB), the standard-setting body for the accounting profession, has reviewed this problem, but to date, nonpublic companies have been relieved of only two requirements: reporting earnings per share and disclosing business segment data. While most financial statement users would agree that nonpublic companies should have less burdensome accounting rules than public companies, the difficulties arise in agreeing on specific changes. Should nonpublic companies have different lease accounting rules or less disclosure of pension liabilities? Controllers and accountants who believe that there should be a different standard of GAAP for nonpublic companies should make their views known to the FASB and the American Institute of Certified Public Accountants (AICPA) and, if possible, offer specific suggestions for change.

### Selecting Appropriate Accounting Methods

While GAAP offers alternatives within certain areas of accounting, the alternatives are not supposed to be freely chosen. Theoretically, a company should choose the accounting methods that clearly reflect income within its own particular circumstances. As a matter of practice, a business is usually able to select advantageous accounting methods, for either financial or tax reasons. It then formulates the reasons that make its selections preferable in the circumstances. The controller must weigh the advantages and disadvantages of alternative methods and select those which will advance the objectives of management, will be simple to apply, and will be suitable for the company's operations. In order to make such a choice, the controller must understand the alternative methods and how they would affect the company's financial position and net income. The two most significant areas where alternative accounting methods are available are:

- Inventory valuation; and
- Depreciation.

The choice of the FIFO or LIFO inventory valuation method or straight-line or accelerated depreciation can have a significant effect on the corporation's profit picture. Before management makes the final decision on which alternatives to use, the controller must inform management of both the short-term and long-term effects of each method.

Cost accounting is another area in which several alternatives are available. In this area, however, the significant factor is not the effect on net income (although there can be some effect), but selecting the cost method that is not only applicable to the type of business, but will be most effective in helping management understand the true cost of production.

Accounting methods that have recently been revised and/or are difficult to implement present additional problems for the controller. Lease capitalization accounting and accounting for foreign exchange translation are examples of these.

The effective controller will fully understand the alternatives offered by GAAP and will guide his executive management in making intelligent choices. Such a controller will master the current changes in accounting methods so that the financial statements he prepares are accepted by the financial community as being in conformity with GAAP.

## Management Reports

A basic financial function of the controller is the timely dissemination of reports to management. The variety and format of such reports are as diverse as the imagination of the controller and the requirements of management.

The major considerations in all financial reporting are:

- Usefulness,
- Accuracy,
- Timeliness, and
- Comprehensibility.

While reports to stockholders do not always meet these goals (particularly the goal of comprehensibility) because of regulatory requirements and accounting rules, reports to management must. If not, the controller is not performing satisfactorily. Since the controller's reports to management are not bound by GAAP or any other rules, he can choose whatever format best serves his purposes of informing management and highlighting problems. There is, however, one basic principle that controllers generally follow in preparing management reports. The complexity of reports and the amount of detail included in them should vary inversely with the level of responsibility and authority, with each higher level of management receiving less detail on a larger segment of the business.

**Other Factors to Consider.** In developing an efficient management reporting system, the controller must also consider the form of report best suited to his management: narrative, statistical, graphical, or some combination of these. The distribution of reports should be limited to those requiring the information, and the frequency of reporting must relate to the levels of management and their ability to react to the information.

**Inflation Accounting.** While the FASB and the financial community argue about which type of inflation accounting best suits the users of financial reports, many controllers are already preparing management reports on either a price-level or current cost method. To properly report to management on the operations of the business, the controller should use a method applicable to his company. The method chosen should factor out the effects of inflation on financial results.

### Stockholder Reports

The FASB is committed to developing a framework of accounting that will determine the form and direction of future accounting principles. These fundamentals of financial accounting and reporting standards are being issued in a series called "Statements of Financial Accounting Concepts." The first statement in the series is entitled "Objectives of Financial Reporting by Business Enterprises." Some of these objectives, which should be considered by the controller in preparing stockholder reports are as follows:[3]

- General purpose external financial reporting is directed toward the common interest of various potential users in the ability of an enterprise to generate favorable cash flows.
- The role of financial reporting in the economy is to provide information that is useful in making business and economic decisions, not to determine what those decisions should be.
- Financial reporting should provide information that is useful to present and potential investors and creditors and to other users in making rational investment, credit, and similar decisions. The information should be comprehensible to those who have a reasonable understanding of business and economic activities and are willing to study the information with reasonable diligence.

The basic information for stockholder reports of public companies is prescribed

---

[3] Statement of Financial Accounting Concepts No. 1, Stamford, Conn.: *Financial Accounting Standards Board*, November, 1978.

by Rule 14a-3(b) and by Regulations S-X and S-K of the SEC. Most companies provide information beyond the basic requirements, and the controller should review the objectives of financial reporting with management before deciding on the overall format of the report. Of course, the controller should have a reasonable understanding of the SEC reporting requirements and should rely on the outside auditor and corporate counsel to make sure that the corporation complies with all the requirements. Penalties for noncompliance can be quite severe.

Nonpublic companies are often required to issue financial reports to bankers, creditors, or for other special purposes. The controllers of such companies should understand the requirements and objectives of external financial reporting so that the financial statements will be useful to those receiving them, but will not reveal details that management would rather not disclose about company operations.

Two requirements for stockholder reports are applicable only to public companies: earnings per share and segment reporting. The controller should fully understand the accounting rules covering both of these areas because of their importance to security analysts and potential investors.

Another area in which an alert controller should be involved is the cost of producing the annual stockholders' report. The controller should prepare an analysis of the various factors that determine the cost of the report—the type of paper, use of color, photographs, charts, number of pages, and the use of an outside financial public relations firm. He should review the analysis with management to ensure an informed decision on the report's size and format.

### Using EDP for Financial Accounting and Reporting

It would be unusual today to find a controller, even among the smaller companies, who does not have a basic understanding of computers and their use in financial accounting and reporting. The controller has a significant role in the planning and operation of the company's information processing facility. The range of currently available hardware and software is so large that the controller is faced with complex and difficult decisions when choosing the best system for his company. In addition to hardware and software, he must consider physical and personnel requirements, as well as future financial and reporting requirements.

Many controllers turn to a service bureau to help them solve their data processing problems. However, even in choosing a service bureau, the controller must consider various criteria to make sure that the service bureau performs satisfactorily.

**Using Outside Experts.** The controller is the prime source and user of the computer facility output and should have management control over the software applications and the timing and format of reports. When the controller does not have adequate knowledge of computer operations, he should seek outside expertise rather than depend on manufacturer representatives and the in-house data processing manager and programmer to design the computer system. Many auditing firms have data processing experts who can work with the controller in designing a computer-based system. Whether the controller uses the audit firm or other experts, he must be sure that he fully understands the system's input, output, and internal accounting controls. The controller who does not have this understanding of the computer system is not fulfilling his responsibility and will find himself at the mercy of the data processing manager.

## THE CONTROLLER'S MANAGEMENT DECISION FUNCTIONS

The controller's input to the management decision process is evident in his responsibilities in the following areas:

- Preparation of budgets;
- Preparation of forecasts;
- Inventory management and control;
- Pricing decisions; and
- Monitoring for management control.

The controller's role in each of these areas goes beyond just compilation of information. His direct effect on management decisions in these areas is discussed below.

### Preparation and Use of Budgets

Many executives, including controllers, confuse budgets and forecasts. A budget is the process by which costs are assigned to specific functions or activities planned within a designated upcoming period, usually one or more years. A forecast, on the other hand, is a prediction of future corporate performance, in one or more areas, based on certain underlying assumptions or premises. Part of the reason for the confusion of the two terms is that a budget, when approved, is management's plan for future operations and at *that point in time* would agree with a forecast. However, as operations develop, changes in various factors may ultimately make the budget quite different from the forecast.

**The Controller's Role.** The controller should establish budget objectives, based on management's perspectives, and determine methods of presentation that will highlight these objectives (e.g., reduce marketing costs, increase research and development). Budgets are a means of establishing management's plans and goals and should be used as an instrument of performance measurement and control.

In addition to coordinating the flow of information from operating management, the controller should evaluate each manager's budget in relation to prior performance, plans of interrelated functions (manufacturing should not budget for increased production if marketing is budgeting for decreased sales), and overall management objectives.

### Preparation of Forecasts

Inasmuch as forecasting predicts future corporate performance, it may be an integral part of the planning process, particularly when the forecast is used as a basis for budget preparation. Generally, however, forecasts are used to alert management to weaknesses in various operations or profit centers so that remedial action may be taken as soon as possible. Forecasts may be prepared for any aspect of corporate activity, but they usually cover operations and cash flow.

**The Controller's Role.** In addition to his basic role of compiling information and preparing the forecast, the controller must test the validity of the assumptions underlying the forecast. Successful forecasting starts with valid assumptions. The controller is in a good position to evaluate the assumptions used by operating managers; he can test them against historical results, seasonal trends, and the logic of interrelated factors.

The controller is responsible for periodically reviewing the forecasting system to ensure that the assumptions or premises used in forecasting continue to be valid, that the data used in the forecast is still reliable, and that the forecast methods used are still correct. Changes in any of these factors would require new forecasts. The controller is also responsible for monitoring the accuracy of forecasts and taking necessary action to adjust the forecasting process when forecast performance is unsatisfactory.

The SEC has encouraged the dissemination of forecasts by public companies by providing a "safe-harbor" rule. This rule eliminates corporate liability, under the securities acts, for incorrect forecasts if they were prepared in good faith and in a valid manner. The controller should prepare a list of the pros and cons of publishing forecasts of sales and earnings as an aid to management in deciding this matter. At present, very few public companies provide investors with forecasts of operations. Even with the "safe-harbor" provision as protection, we do not expect many more firms to start publishing forecasts because of the poor publicity resulting from inaccurate forecasts.

### Inventory Management and Control

Inventory control has always been an important area for management supervision because inventories have a direct effect on profits, cash flow, production levels, and customer service. Only during the past decade have controllers become involved in inventory management; this is due primarily to the development of computer decision models for optimum inventory levels and the use of the computer for inventory recordkeeping and control. The controller, through his supervision of the data processing function, his understanding of computer techniques, and his overall knowledge of the business, has become a significant addition to the inventory management team.

The management team arrives at policy decisions which are submitted to the chief

executive officer for approval. Some typical areas for policy decisions include product mix, market areas, and customer service levels. Once policy has been approved,
the controller, in addition to his normal recordkeeping responsibilities, is responsible
for implementing and monitoring the policy decisions.

In larger companies, computer decision models are used to determine reorder
points, economic order quantities, and the quantities required to meet the desired
customer service levels. In small companies, the controller's department may manually compute these decision levels.

The controller is responsible for reporting to management on the success or failure of an inventory management program. Success can be measured in terms of
increased cash flow, reduced costs, and reduced inventory write-offs. Other reporting techniques include a schedule of variances between actual inventory levels and
planned quantities, inventory ratios, exception reporting, and forecasts. Reports to
management should be accompanied by comments from the management team
regarding the reasons for deficiencies in results as well as plans for clearing up problem areas.

### Pricing Decisions

The prime role of the controller in pricing policy is to evaluate the estimated economic effect of alternate pricing decisions. The controller can provide management
with financial data relating to return on investment for prior successful product
introductions, the opportunity cost of corporate resources, the estimated inflation
rate, and the internal rate of return required for different payback periods. This
information will enable management, or the board of directors, to determine a corporate pricing policy that can be used to evaluate the potential of new products, as
well as the profitability of current products.

**Evaluation Techniques.** The controller should be familiar with computer modeling techniques that compute optimum price-unit sales combinations. By taking
advantage of efficient production runs, a return on investment that falls within management's acceptable parameters can be provided.

**Management Reports.** The controller is also responsible for reporting to management on the results of its product decisions and the adherence by line management to overall pricing policy. The usual methods of reporting include:

- Actual compared to budget;
- Analysis of variance from budget and comparable periods;
- Return on investment in constant dollars; and
- Comparison with industry statistics.

The controller should be familiar with each of these reporting methods. The
reports submitted to management should provide at least the following information:

- Variances from plan;
- Reasons for the variances; and
- Responsibility for the variances.

The controller who goes beyond mechanical arithmetic calculations that determine pricing, to factors such as competitive pressures, loss leaders, and cash flow considerations, can have an expanded role in the management decision-making process.

### Monitoring for Management Control

Even in medium-sized companies, the amount of financial information available to management is generally more than it can understand or digest. It is the controller's function to concentrate management's attention on matters which require action. To this end, the controller must highlight significant variances from budget, early indications of unsatisfactory profit or cost trends, and projected deficiencies in cash resources.

**Monitoring Techniques.** The controller can use a variety of monitoring techniques to isolate variances from the norm. The more common methods used include comparison reporting, ratio analysis, five year or longer trend analyses, and graphs.

Each of these techniques can be used in a variety of ways. For example, comparison reporting can be used for the following:

- Actual versus budget;
- Current period versus prior period;
- Actual versus forecast; and
- Actual versus industry statistics or competitors.

There are many different ratios that can be used to indicate areas of weakness or strength in both the balance sheet and the income statement.

The controller must select the proper tools for highlighting significant variations and trends in an efficient manner. If too many monitoring methods are used, the results may become as difficult to interpret as the basic financial figures. The efficient use of monitoring techniques will allow the controller to isolate, with a minimum of effort, the variances that require management's attention.

**Interpretation of Variances.** Once variances have been identified, the controller must find out why performance differs from plan by interviewing the responsible line managers. The controller's next step is to check the explanations with applicable records or interviews with other managers. The controller must ensure that the explanations reported to management have been verified to the extent possible. The controller should also provide suggestions for improvement, either from line management or his own sources.

## THE CONTROLLER'S INTERNAL CONTROL FUNCTIONS

The controller has always been responsible for preparing and implementing internal control systems, both accounting and administrative. The methods of monitoring (reviewed in the preceding section) are examples of administrative controls supervised by the controller. However, the current emphasis is on accounting controls, particularly since passage in 1977 of the Foreign Corrupt Practices Act (FCPA).

### Internal Control Systems and the FCPA

The FCPA mandates an adequate system of internal accounting control for public companies subject to the Securities Exchange Act of 1934. However, the publicity given to disclosures of foreign and domestic bribery cases has caused the effect of the law to filter down to many nonpublic companies. Banks and other major creditors often seek assurance that a company has an adequate, workable system of internal accounting control. The outside auditors are now emphasizing review of internal accounting control and the reports to management of material weaknesses in the system.

**Management Responsibility.** Management is basically responsible for maintaining an adequate system of internal accounting control, but the job is generally delegated to the controller. He should review the present system for areas of weakness and also request a review by the outside accountants. Based on such reviews, the system should be upgraded or revised as necessary. Management should be kept informed of planned changes in the system and its active support solicited. Such support could take the form of communicating to all employees management's policy on maintaining strong internal controls and prompt investigation and correction of discovered weaknesses in the system.

**Internal Auditing.** In the past, only very large companies used internal auditors. Today, however, internal auditors are found in many medium-sized companies because of the need to monitor compliance with the internal control system. While the prime reason for instituting an internal auditing function may be compliance monitoring, companies have found that auditors often pay their way through operations audits that result in suggestions for cost cutting or improvement of operating efficiency. The internal auditor also often reduces the outside auditor's fee by doing certain audit work or preparing audit workpapers for the independent accountants.

The controller should avoid direct supervision of the internal auditor, except in unusual circumstances, because the internal auditor reviewing the work of the controller's department should be independent of any operations being audited.

## THE CONTROLLER'S OTHER FUNCTIONS

The Financial Executives Institute's list of controller and treasurer functions reproduced earlier in this chapter includes many nonfinancial functions. The extent to which the controller gets involved in such areas as debt financing, mergers and acquisitions, tax administration, and government reporting depends partly on the size of his company and partly on his aggressiveness in expanding his areas of responsibility.

### Treasury Functions

Controllers in all but the largest firms are generally responsible for handling treasury functions such as cash management, financing, investment of surplus funds, and credit and collection. The high cost of money that developed in the late 1970s as a result of high inflation rates puts a premium on efficient management of these functions.

**Working with Bankers.** The controller's knowledge of his company's financial strengths and weaknesses and its future profit plan makes him the ideal person to deal with bankers, factors, and other major creditors. To the extent that the controller can adequately explain his company's financial structure and management's future plans to bankers and other creditors the easier it will be for the firm fo obtain financing. The controller must not only be fully prepared to answer all questions relating to finances but must be able to communicate this knowledge. When meetings with lenders are held to discuss a large financing or credit line, the chief executive or another top executive should be available to discuss business plans, and the controller to explain financial matters.

**Public Offerings.** The use of public offerings to raise long-term debt or equity capital expands and contracts with the state of the market. A public offering is nevertheless a good method of obtaining financing, particularly now that costs have been reduced through the SEC's efforts to simplify registration requirements, especially for smaller offerings.

The controller of a company that intends to file a registration statement for a public offering should not attempt to handle the matter himself. A registration statement, even a simplified one, requires the services of an accountant and attorney experienced in security laws and regulations.

### Corporate Development

The controller's role in corporate development encompasses mergers and acquisitions, divestments, capital expenditures and new ventures. The controller's ability to function knowledgeably in these areas may often make the difference between the success and failure of the company.

**Mergers and Acquisitions.** The controller should participate in a thorough investigation of a prospective acquisition. He must see that management obtains the needed information regarding the prospective acquiree in order to arrive at a fair price, to determine that the business fits the company's long range operating plans, and most important, to ensure that no unpleasant surprises will surface after consummation. The controller should use his outside accountants, if they have experience in this area, for guidance and assistance.

The controller's other function in an acquisition is to integrate the accounting methods of the acquiree with those of the acquiror. This is easier in theory than it is in practice. The task must be carefully planned, with the understanding that the controller and staff of the acquiree can be helpful if they are properly approached and motivated.

**Divestment Factors.** It might appear that the controller dealing with the sale of a subsidiary or division is in the same position as the seller in an acquisition, but this is not so. While the tax rules are similar in many respects, there are special accounting rules for disposal of a segment of a business, as well as financing and other problems that are unique to divestments.

The controller's role in a divestment is to provide management with a reasonable idea of the market value of the business unit being sold and favorable and unfavorable factors that are not on the balance sheet, such as tax loss carryforwards or contingent liabilities. The controller should also advise management regarding the financial accounting and tax effects of the divestment. This is another area that calls for experience and expertise, and the controller should use his outside accountants for guidance and assistance.

**Capital Expenditures.** This area of corporate development is most familiar to controllers. Management will usually be faced with more capital expenditure proposals than the corporation can finance. It is the controller's job to rank the proposals on the basis of payback periods, return on investment, and current cost so that management can allocate budgeted capital funds efficiently.

From a systems standpoint, the controller should prepare capital expenditure proposal forms and related forms for evaluations and endorsements. This will ensure that line managers submit proposals in a standard format.

### Taxes—Planning and Control

**Developing Proper Planning.** There is virtually no corporate activity that does not involve some tax effect. The controller must know enough about taxes to recognize a problem in present or planned operations. He should then call on the outside accountant or corporate counsel for advice and suggested actions.

The controller must develop a tax awareness within the organization so that no significant actions are contemplated or commenced without a review of the possible tax implications.  The need for such a tax review must be communicated to all levels of the organization, including the board of directors.

The controller, as chief accounting officer, should advise management of the financial effects of planned tax reduction transactions, such as the adoption of the LIFO inventory method or new pension or medical plans.  In some cases, tax savings plans are not feasible if they reduce financial income subject to debt covenant restrictions.  The controller should also dissuade management from adopting tax schemes that are not in line with the company's business strategy or that do not make economic sense.

**Tax Administration.**  The controller is responsible for the timely preparation of all required tax returns and the payment of taxes when due.  Even if the tax returns are prepared by the outside accounting firm, the controller should have a tax calendar and tickler file to alert himself to the due dates of tax returns and tax payments.

If the tax returns are handled in-house, the controller or his assistant should handle a tax audit.  If the returns are prepared by the outside accountant, it would be best to have him deal with the tax agent, but the controller should be kept informed of progress and should approve any proposed deficiencies with advice of the accountant.

Most executives and controllers are aware of the need for planning and control for federal income taxes.  However, the principles of planning and control are applicable to all tax levels: federal, state, local, and payroll taxes.  Many of these secondary taxes, particularly payroll taxes, have reached a significant level in recent years and merit close attention in order to reduce costs.

## Miscellaneous Functions

In most smaller companies there are a number of nonfinancial responsibilities which become part of the controller's workload because volume is insufficient to require hiring a specialist, and line managers are not interested in these areas.  Examples of such miscellaneous functions include:

- Risk management;
- Real estate matters;
- ERISA reporting; and
- Other government reporting.

In some areas, such as risk management, the controller should seek expert advice.  A mistake in risk coverage can be quite expensive.  Also, the costs are complex, and an expert may be able to save more than his fee.  In other areas, such as ERISA or other government reporting, the controller should be able to handle the problems in-house with some assistance from the outside accountant or counsel.

## FUTURE TRENDS

### Specialization Versus General Strategies

In the past two decades, the trend in developing financial executives has been toward specialization. In many companies, the controller is restricted to financial accounting matters. Other matters are supervised by tax specialists, EDP specialists, cash managers, distribution cost specialists, and other similar specialists. The controller's responsibilities have been fragmented because of the increasing proliferation of laws and rules that make it impossible for any one person to keep abreast of developments and changes in more than one or two areas. This trend toward more complicated rules and specialization seems to be continuing into the 1980s.

Nevertheless, the successful controller must be a generalist who has the ability to use and control the specialists. In smaller companies, he may call on outside specialists as needed; in larger companies these specialists would be part of his staff. The controller must be an integral part of the management team and must understand management's viewpoint and business strategy. From that vantage point he can coordinate the work of the specialists and make sure that their actions are in line with corporate business strategy. The trend toward the business-manager controller has already started in the largest companies. It is expected to expand to the medium-sized companies during the 1980s.

### Decision-Making in the Computer Era

The office of the future is now becoming part of the present. The reduced cost, increased abilities, and reliability of micro and minicomputers have made it feasible to install a computer terminal in a manager's office that can communicate with other managers in the company, people outside the company (electronic mail), and that can extract information from a central or regional computer.

This arrangement provides the controller with the ability to review such financial data as cash resources, sales, and accounts receivable collections on a daily basis so that opportunities and problems can be brought to management's attention faster. The computer can handle various administrative tasks such as tax return preparation, tax payments, and accounts receivable agings, releasing the controller from a flood of details and giving him time to consider ways to increase profits and to manage the financial area.

**Computer Communications.** The widespread use of computers for managerial communications and various administrative tasks has taken much longer than predicted, but it appears that it will finally occur in the 1980s. We expect that before 1990 the use of computer terminals will spread to most companies that use computer processing. Even companies that use a service bureau will have terminals tied to the service bureau computer. These will perform the same functions as an in-house network.

## The Controller's Future Role

There is no danger that the corporate controller's role will diminish in the future. While the trend toward specialization has reduced his responsibilities in some situations, the need for a controller who is a generalist, accompanied by the spread of computer capabilities, will increase his role in management. It is interesting to note that many recent chief executive officer appointments in large companies have come from the financial ranks. This trend should continue as the controller's role grows in management.

# Part II

## Financial Functions

# 2

# Accounting Principles

*Anthony J. Curley*

## INTRODUCTION

The accounting process records, classifies, and reports the financial impact of business transactions. It is an art and not a science. Contrary to popular belief it is not exact, and it is not necessarily meaningful. Accountants can easily produce many different "correct" answers under the alternative procedures that are currently available without violating *generally accepted accounting principles* (GAAP). This lack of precision, the so-called gap in GAAP, is a difficult problem for managers, shareholders, analysts, regulatory authorities, and others who rely on financial statements. For that reason, GAAP requires that the corporate controller adopt accounting policies that are applied uniformly and consistently from one year to another.

# DOUBLE-ENTRY ACCOUNTING

## Financial Accounting Objectives

Accounting operations include *financial accounting*, which involves the preparation of financial statements for external use, and *managerial accounting*, which provides internally generated data for the use of management. Financial accounting measures the performance of a firm in achieving its goals and objectives. This performance is summarized in the *annual report*—the balance sheet, income statement, and statement of changes in financial position—constructed under a rather loose set of guidelines (GAAP). In contrast, managerial accounting has only one guiding principle—to help managers make better decisions. Accounting data can be manipulated internally in any useful manner, but they must conform to accepted practices when they are used for external reporting purposes.

Financial accounting serves far too many masters; management, shareholders, analysts, tax authorities, and others all have a different purpose and a different use for accounting data. As a result, it was inevitable that conflict would arise in the establishment and maintenance of valuation principles and reporting standards. Nonetheless, the key role is exercised by corporate officers who are responsible for preparing statements that measure their own performance.

Management faces the dilemma of requesting the controller to minimize taxes under applicable statutes while fully recognizing that minimizing taxes may also minimize reported income. The controller is responsible for consistently reporting results in accordance with GAAP, but he must also, for obvious reasons, be aware of management's responsibility to maintain good investor relationships. Faced with a choice of alternative acceptable procedures, some that make operating results look better, others that make them look worse, the controller must balance corporate interests with the long-run interests of shareholders, who have entrusted management with their savings. The controller must cope with accounting rules that may influence management decisions directly. For example, in the past some multinational companies denominated some of their debt in foreign currencies or paid to hedge currency risk in the futures market because the accounting procedures adopted by the Financial Accounting Standards Board (FASB) reflected currency revaluation in operating income—the "bottom line"—immediately and directly. (These rules have recently been tentatively revised to mitigate the direct effect of unrealized foreign exchange gains and losses.)

For these reasons, and in recognition of their fiduciary responsibility to shareholders, the objectives of financial accounting have traditionally been focused inward, toward the firm's management team. From this viewpoint, shareholder and analyst needs were considered secondary, with external requirements satisfied by adequate disclosure of details in footnotes to the annual report. Recently, this approach has been seriously challenged. An opposing viewpoint argues that management, with access to records that are not available to stockholders, should adopt reporting standards that are helpful in evaluating the cash consequences of the decisions they have made. The argument has not been settled, and the identification of specific objectives, aside from general agreement on the measurement of performance, is still very controversial.

## Accounting Procedures

Financial accounting seems a very simple process consisting of two operations: (1) transactions are observed and recorded as they occur and (2) recorded transactions are then periodically summarized and reported. In fact, however, there are serious problems, in both theory and practice, at that very basic level. Problems arise because there is no consistent framework for accepting or rejecting alternative accounting principles. The FASB is currently spending a great deal of time and effort in an attempt to identify and define a conceptual foundation that is acceptable to a majority of financial statement users.

**Underlying Principles.** No one invented the double-entry accounting system. Instead, it simply evolved, adapting to current problems as they occurred. The first accounting records were descriptive journals that listed transactions as they happened. In time, the need to summarize events in a monetary format led to the inclusion of a money column on the side of the journal—so-called *single-entry* accounting. As commerce developed and expanded and merchant families and joint ventures grew, it became necessary to measure the equity interest of all parties to a transaction. This led, in turn, to a second monetary column, and *double-entry* accounting resulted. The first accounting text, published at the end of the fifteenth century, simply recorded the many practices that had evolved and been passed down over hundreds of years through the master-apprentice system.

Early financial statements are similar to modern ones, with such common features as a depreciation allowance that offsets the cost of buildings and equipment (and livestock and slaves). There were no stock option procedures in the fifteenth century because there were no stock options at that time; if someone had invented options, someone else would have developed a procedure to account for them. Industrialization increased the complexity of commercial operations, and accounting procedures, accordingly, became more complicated as well. Unfortunately, nonuniform procedures were developed because no common framework existed for establishing accounting principles. The introduction of the income tax in 1913 resulted in far more detailed and defensible records. Over the years, new legislation allowed a number of different tax procedures, and many of these alternatives are reflected in current accounting standards. The problems caused by accounting alternatives were recognized as early as World War I, when the Federal Trade Commission attempted to audit cost-plus-fixed-fee military contracts. As a result, a strong plea for uniformity was issued in the November 1917 Federal Reserve Bulletin, but it went unanswered despite repeated pressure during the depression-ridden 1930s. By the beginning of World War II, standardized *auditing* procedures had been adopted in place of standardized *accounting* procedures, and nonuniformity increased as increasingly difficult and complicated transactions developed.

Accounting procedures evolved and adapted to a changing business climate, but there was never any general agreement on the basic purpose of accounting. As a result, lacking a foundation that could be used to evaluate different proposals, differences of opinion could not be settled, and alternative practices were common. Recent efforts to develop a broad conceptual framework are promising, but the search, if it succeeds, will take years. In the meantime, financial accounting generates variable outcomes, obscuring the meaning of accounting numbers.

**Recording Transactions.** In order to record transactions, three problems must be solved: recognition, measurement, and classification.

*Recognition.* When has a transaction occurred? Should a transaction be recognized, for example, when an airline company signs a noncancelable, long-term lease for a fleet of jet aircraft? Until 1977 the answer was no, although footnote disclosure was required to help shareholders and others who read and evaluated financial statements. Since 1977 the answer is yes—the cost of those aircraft must be recorded by the controller as a depreciable asset, and the present value of the stream of lease payments must be recorded as a liability (see Chapter 4). Recognition is a difficult problem in such areas as real estate sales, franchise operations, consignment sales, installment sales, product warranties, and revenue received on long-term construction contracts.

*Measurement.* When a transaction has been recognized, it must then be quantified. Accounting values are based on the *historical cost* convention, in which monetary cost is used at the time of recognition. But this fails to solve the problem of multinational transactions that are denominated in a foreign currency. The current rules for currency translation are very controversial, and the FASB was in the process of amending them when this chapter was written. Inflation is another serious problem, because conventional procedures do not distinguish between historical costs and current costs (in which the dollar has less purchasing power). Under experimental rules effective in 1980, certain corporations are required to report three sets of numbers: (1) historical costs, (2) constant dollar values, for which historical costs are adjusted by the consumer price index, and (3) current values for specified items, measured by estimated replacement value. The usefulness and relevance of this type of disclosure has yet to be determined, but the initial reaction has been great skepticism.

*Classification.* This is accomplished by the controller under double-entry accounting, as shown in Figure 2.1. Every transaction includes at least one debit (Dr.) entry and one credit (Cr.) entry. Debits reflect an increase in an asset or a decrease in either a liability or an equity account. Credits reflect the opposite—a decrease in an asset or an increase in a liability or an equity account. Changes in equity include, among other things, expenses (Dr.), dividends (Dr.), and revenue (Cr.). When wages are paid in cash, for example, equity (expense) is debited and cash is credited. The scheme is a very simple one, but the problem of classification is not.

| *Debit (Dr.)* | | *Credit (Cr.)* | |
|---|---|---|---|
| ┌─ Asset | + | Asset | − |
| │  Liability | − | Liability | + |
| │  Equity: | | Equity: | |
| │    Retained Earnings | − | Retained Earnings | + |
| └─→  (Expense) | | (Revenue) | |
|    (Dividends) | | | |
|    Stock | − | Stock | + |

FIGURE 2.1   DOUBLE-ENTRY ACCOUNTING

When a machine is overhauled, with a corresponding credit to cash, the debit entry may be an asset or it may be an expense (a decrease in retained earnings). The same problem exists for many different kinds of expenditures, including interest costs, mineral exploration costs, and preopening costs before a new plant becomes operational. In theory the problem is solved by capitalizing (recording as an asset) any expenditure that promises benefits or services in the future. The cost of overhauling the machine would then be capitalized if it extended useful life or lowered future operating costs; otherwise it would be expensed. In theory this is very easy, but in practice it is often very difficult.

Research and development expenditures are a case in point. An efficient R&D program is expected to generate future benefits for the corporation. Nevertheless, under Statement of Financial Accounting Standards (SFAS) No. 2, effective in 1975, R&D costs must be expensed as they are paid. The reason is practical—the extent and duration of R&D benefits cannot be estimated. Mineral exploration costs are another important example. The treatment of expenditures that result in dry holes, in which no new reserves are located, is very controversial. Some people argue that there is no service potential in this case, and that payments should therefore be expensed—*successful efforts accounting*. That was the original position of the FASB before political pressure forced the board to postpone the effective date of its SFAS 19 in 1977. Others argue that all efforts, successful or not, are part of the entity's general search, and all exploration costs should therefore be capitalized—*full cost accounting*. The argument has not been settled, and it is an important threat to the prestige of the FASB; this will be discussed later in this chapter.

Disagreements about classification are more than an academic exercise; they have serious economic, political, and legal overtones. From one perspective, an asset can in theory be described as a property right, a "thing of value owned," something that will someday benefit the company. But from a different perspective, from a manager's point of view, an asset might better be called *an expense waiting to happen*. Capitalization delays the recognition of expense, increasing current reported income (revenue less expense). Moreover, the delay is sometimes permanent. That was possible when the purchase price exceeded the fair market value of a company or division purchased prior to November 1970. The excess cost, sometimes loosely referred to as *acquired goodwill*, was allowed to stay on the balance sheet indefinitely. In 1970, GAAP was prospectively changed to require amortization of such excess cost over forty years or less. Most firms have adopted this minimum required annual rate for transferring (amortizing) goodwill to expense. With amortization, assets are reduced and the debit becomes an expense.

**Period Reporting.** Transactions that have been recorded—recognized, measured, and classified—must then be summarized by the controller and reported in financial statements. This also requires simplifying assumptions that increase the number of acceptable accounting alternatives. In the process, the controller is guided by:

- The *realization principle,*
- The *matching principle*, and
- The *period allocation principle.*

*The realization principle.* The realization principle recognizes revenue at the point of delivery, when no significant remaining service or contingency exists. Sales are therefore recorded when the product or service is received by the customer, not when cash is received. Although easily applied in the case of credit sales, the principle is often difficult to apply in other areas. In the case of long-term construction contracts, for example, some people argue that delivery takes place when the project is completely finished; under this assumption, the *completed-contract* basis, all receipts and expenditures are capitalized until the date of completion. Others, following the *percentage-of-completion* method, recognize both revenue and expense during interim periods, with income measured proportionally on the basis of total costs to date as a percentage of total estimated costs. Most controllers and accountants follow the latter method for both internal and external financial reporting. The completed-contract method is often used for tax reporting.

Accounting for real estate and land sales, characterized by mortgage payments over an extended period, is another issue that led to severe criticism of accounting in the late 1960s and early 1970s. Under GAAP, revenue must be recognized at the point of sale, with expected defaults provided for as an allowance for doubtful accounts. This results in a substantial timing difference between the recognition of income and the realization of cash flow, and it was a major element in the troubles Penn Central faced in the late 1960s. Accounting for franchise contracts also came under heavy fire at that time for the same reason.

*The matching principle.* The matching principle is used to recognize expense. Under this principle, expense is associated (and recorded concurrently) with the revenue it generates. This is fine in theory, but in practice it may or may not be possible. Expenses are classified as *product costs* or *period costs*. Product costs—labor, material, and overhead—are inventoried and capitalized until the product is sold and the revenue is recognized. Period costs—for the most part general and administrative costs—are expensed in the period in which they are incurred. Unfortunately, some product expenditures cannot be matched directly, and in those cases some assumption as to the flow of costs becomes necessary. Inventory is an important case in point. Some inventoried items cannot be identified specifically as they are sold, so it is necessary to assume some flow of goods in order to distinguish between costs that are allocated to cost of sales and costs that remain unmatched on the balance sheet. The most common assumptions are the average cost, the first-in, first-out (FIFO), and the last-in, first-out (LIFO) methods. Under LIFO the oldest costs remain on the balance sheet; in periods of inflation, with current costs flowing through to the income statement, both income and income taxes are thereby minimized. By choosing LIFO, management increases current cash flow, which they should, but they also decrease reported income, which they would prefer not to do. In the recession period of 1974-1975, some controllers were forced to change from LIFO to FIFO, thus accepting a larger tax liability, in order to protect management's already depressed profit levels.

*Period allocation principle.* Some expenditures do not fit the period-product cost classification and must be allocated among reporting periods in some other manner. The most important of these are governed by the period allocation principle, in which costs are distributed over the life of the asset in some rational and objective manner. Period allocation is used for estimating the depreciation of tangible fixed assets and the amortization of the costs of a number of intangible assets. Allocation is necessary because the period in which the transaction is recorded does not coincide with the financial accounting reporting period. It is impossible to measure the exact contribution of some piece of equipment to the revenue generated in any particular accounting period during the asset's useful life. Instead, the cost for each period is estimated by the controller in advance, and the capitalized cost is then transferred to expense in accordance with that schedule. (Depreciation methods are considered in detail in Chapter 5.)

### Accuracy of Accounting Data

Specific problems of revenue recognition, expense matching, and period allocation are addressed in GAAP. In the absence of agreement concerning the underlying purpose and objectives of financial accounting, basic agreement on these procedures is also lacking, and GAAP allows certain alternative procedures in recording, summarizing, and reporting transactions. Procedural alternatives create diverse outcomes: they allow more than one "correct" answer. In the case of inventory, for example, both income and assets will be different if LIFO instead of FIFO valuation is used; here two "correct" answers result. In the case of depreciation, the straight-line (SL) method results in numbers that are different from the numbers generated by the sum-of-the-year's-digits (SYD) method, and two more alternative answers result. Combining LIFO, FIFO, SL, and SYD, there are now four possible "right" answers—and the allowable variations of inventory and depreciation have not yet been exhausted. On the basis of a comprehensive "inventory" of GAAP published in 1965, it has been estimated that more than 30 million "correct" answers are possible! That is, of course, clearly a gross exaggeration, because some variations are trivial, others apply to only a few companies (e.g., rules for construction contracts), and still others have been tightened in the interim. A realistic estimate is probably closer to forty or fifty, but this is still very bothersome because of the adverse impact of variability on managers and shareholders. The controller has the responsibility to select and use a consistent set of principles so that comparability is maintained from period to period.

Some firms compensate their executives on the basis of reported return on assets (ROA), the ratio of income to assets. If two divisions of a corporation have identical streams of cash flow and identical managerial performance, but one is capital intensive while the other is research (R&D) intensive, the R&D manager will appear to be superior, because R&D must be expensed and it never enters the asset base. Other things being equal, the R&D division would show an inflated ROA, because of the cumulative effect of expensing on a depressed asset base. In these situations, the controller must explain to management the difference in accounting treatment and devise a compensation measurement plan that recognizes economic performance on a basis that is applicable to different divisions.

Variability in reported outcomes also creates severe problems for analysts and shareholders, especially with respect to rate-of-return comparisons among firms with different accounting procedures. No amount of disclosure is adequate to the task of adjusting values for one firm so that it can be compared to another that uses significantly different procedures. In this important application of accounting data, the gap in GAAP is far too wide to be bridged externally.

**Consistency.** In the absence of standardization and uniformity, accounting authorities have adopted the principle of consistency, which requires a firm to use the same set of procedures from period to period as far as is possible, clearly disclosing the impact of any changes that are made. The auditor's opinion specifically recognizes and affirms consistent treatment, and the auditor must indicate agreement or disagreement with any changes in accounting principles or methods that a company makes. Some critics have viewed consistency as a vice instead of a virtue, claiming that it implies acceptance of error, allowing a company "to be wrong, as long as it is wrong the same way, from period to period." Notwithstanding criticism, the consistent application of one set of procedures is very useful to analysts and others who judge trends in managerial performance.

**Conservatism.** Another widely followed principle is the rule of conservatism which prohibits the recognition of unrealized appreciation in value while a permanent loss in value can be recorded. This has resulted in the common adoption of *lower-of-cost-or-market* valuations, and it specifically prohibits the recognition of unrealized capital gains. Conservatism has also been criticized—on the basis that it is acceptable to be wrong "as long as it is wrong in only one direction"—but the rule has prevented firms from recording unrealized and potentially unattainable paper profits while probable losses are recognized.

Nonuniformity in accounting data is a very serious problem, but it cannot be solved until a basic conceptual foundation is defined and accepted. Until that is accomplished, managers and other users of financial statements must recognize the severity of the problem, and they should view accounting values with at least some degree of skepticism. In the interim, consistent and conservative treatment of accounting alternatives is both useful and logical.

### Search for a Conceptual Framework

When the FASB was first organized in 1972, it adopted a technical agenda that included an attempt to establish broad and qualitative standards for financial reporting—a search for an encompassing foundation, which largely had been ignored to that point. The project was viewed realistically, with the recognition that no comprehensive and acceptable foundation is likely to result from any short-run single effort. The search was originally directed to an unbiased reexamination of the basic assumptions underlying the current practice of accountancy. A ten-member task force was formed in December 1973 to study the most central issue: the objectives of financial reporting.

**Bases for Valuation.** A discussion memorandum published in June 1974 proposed five valuation bases that could be defended, depending on the circumstances, in a given instance. This recognizes that no valuation basis is necessarily applicable for every firm at every point in time. The five possibilities are:

1. *Historical cost*—the currently used and conventional procedure;
2. *Current cost*—the estimated replacement value of a firm's assets;
3. *Current exit value*—the estimated value of assets in the event of immediate liquidation;
4. *Expected exit value*—the estimated resale value of assets in the normal course of business; and
5. *Present value of expected cash flows*—a measure of the expected benefits to be realized from cash flows to be generated by the company's assets.

In December 1976 the FASB issued its conceptual framework discussion memorandum and, following comment and discussion, divided the search into six distinct phases:

1. Objectives of financial reporting;
2. Elements of financial statements;
3. Measurement of the elements of financial statements;
4. Qualitative characteristics;

5. Recognition problems; and
6. Earnings presentation.

**Ongoing efforts.** In November 1978 the board issued its first Statement of
Financial Accounting Concepts, *Objectives of Financial Reporting by Business En-*
*terprises,* which FASB Chairman Donald J. Kirk described as "the cornerstone . . . ,
a constitution for financial accounting and reporting." In July 1979 the discussion
memorandum, *Reporting Earnings,* addressed industry segment and expense
reporting; criteria for identifying irregular revenues, expenses, gains, and losses;
income statement formats; and the difficult question of publishing managerial forecasts. In May 1980 the FASB issued the second concept statement, *Qualitative*
*Characteristics of Accounting Information,* which addressed the characteristics that
make acounting information useful. SFAC No. 3, *Elements of Financial Statements*
*of Business Enterprises,* issued in December 1980, defined eight financial elements
—assets, liabilities, owners' equity, comprehensive income, revenues, expenses,
gains, and losses. In December 1980 the board also issued SFAC No. 4, *Objectives*
*of Financial Reporting by Nonbusiness Organizations.* All of these efforts are part
of the ongoing project to define a conceptual framework.

The project is ambitious and complicated, and it will not be completed in the near
future; discovery of a comprehensive and acceptable foundation is a very difficult
and possibly unattainable task. But the FASB has recognized the basic deficiency in
GAAP, and it has adopted the practical but time-consuming approach of exposing
its opinions to critical review and restatement prior to release.

**Critical Obstacles.** The framework project must overcome two critical obstacles.
First, the major question of perspective must be resolved. Should accounting adopt
an internal view, focused on management, as it has for many decades, or should it
adopt an external view, one that looks to the objectives of users in evaluating the
cash consequences of managerial decisions? At this time, sentiment seems to favor
the external focus. Second, should accounting assume an asset-liability perspective,
which may lead to some form of value accounting, or should it continue to be based
on a matched revenue-expense approach, which is consistent with current practice?
There appears to be some sentiment in favor of a radical change to a value-based
foundation, but the issue is far from settled, and the most informed opinion continues to be very speculative. In the FASB statements issued to this point, there is
some evidence of opposition to the "dangling debit" (the tangible or intangible
expense waiting to happen), which provides some support that the board is leaning
toward a valuation framework. This is suggested by such pronouncements as SFAS
2, which requires the expensing of R&D costs. However, in 1980 the board agreed
to allow the capitalization of certain interest costs, so the jury is still out, and the
focus remains to be settled.

The search for a generally acceptable conceptual framework is difficult and hazardous, and it will not be completed easily, especially because accounting is becoming increasingly politicized. But the gap in GAAP cannot be closed without a
framework, and the problems arising because of accounting alternatives cannot be
solved unless the search is successful.

## ACCOUNTING AUTHORITIES

As accounting evolved and then adapted to current practice, authoritative opinion also evolved and became increasingly codified. Financial accounting principles currently range from nonexistent in the Soviet Union and its satellites, where attention is directed entirely to managerial accounting, to strict and formal legal requirements in West Germany and Scandinavia, where principles are based on tax and fiscal policy and published reports are merely a by-product. In the United States, codification developed in the private sector, largely through agencies of the American Institute of Certified Public Accountants (AICPA), but the process is moving rapidly to legislative and bureaucratic control in the public sector. Some would argue that accountancy in the United States is already dominated by the public sector, and the argument has a great deal of merit.

The primary responsibility for the preparation and accuracy of financial statements rests with management. The controller, as the representative of management, selects accounting policies within a framework established and administered jointly by the FASB and the Securities and Exchange Commission. (Even nonpublic companies are eventually affected by SEC pronouncements.) Accounting statements are the representation of management concerning its discharge of stewardship responsibility, including an independent auditor's opinion as to compliance with the rules within the context of available alternative procedures. At the same time, management's role is limited by standards that are established by others, and as the rules are tightened the role of management will continue to be lessened. In fact, a study of authoritative pronouncements in the 1960s and 1970s paints a picture of some innovative controllers who recognized loopholes in GAAP and applied creative accounting practices, especially in the calculation of earnings and earnings per share. In some cases, there has been something of an adversary relationship between the controller and management on one hand and the accounting profession on the other. This was a major factor in the increasing activism of congressional and regulatory authorities and in the loss of prestige of the private sector, especially during the 1970s.

### AICPA

The AICPA (originally the American Institute of Accountants) was founded in 1887 by a group of accountants and auditors. During the next forty years the institute became very prominent and influential, and the practice of public accounting became synonymous with the expression "the accounting profession." During that period, attention was concentrated on the balance sheet, which attempted to report the value of the firm, and the role of the auditor was to "certify" its accuracy. The practice of conservatism spread rapidly, mainly as a hedge against the certification of value that did not exist. By the 1930s, at the start of the Depression, the AICPA was firmly established as the authoritative accounting body in the United States.

The stock market crash of 1929 and the catastrophic losses of some investors had two effects that proved to have a profound impact on today's accounting profession.

The first was the establishment of the Securities and Exchange Commission, which was required by the Securities Exchange Act of 1934. Although the SEC was relatively powerless during its early years, reporting requirements for publicly held firms were legally assigned to the public sector. The second effect was the outcome of a joint effort by committees of the New York Stock Exchange and the AICPA to establish standards for published financial statements. The focus shifted from the balance sheet to the income statement, with the balance sheet reduced to a subsidiary statement of remaining residual values after the books are closed each year. The significance of this shift in emphasis would be reflected later in such things as LIFO, justified in terms of the impact on reported income despite the problem of severe understatement of the value of inventory in the balance sheet. More importantly, efforts to standardize accounting practice were defeated, and standardized auditing practices were developed instead. As the focus shifted from the balance sheet to the income statement, the auditor's "certificate" changed to an "opinion" as to conformity within a growing body of increasingly nonuniform GAAP.

### Committee on Accounting Procedure (1939-1958)

In 1939 the AICPA formed the Committee on Accounting Procedure (CAP) to study current problems and to issue authoritative opinions on accounting practices and procedures. Between 1939 and 1958, CAP issued 51 Accounting Research Bulletins. The first 42 ARBs were summarized and codified in Bulletin 43 (1953). This was the first authoritative statement of accounting principles in the United States, and it remains in effect except for areas that were subsequently amended by successor authorities.

Unfortunately, CAP never addressed the question of a basic foundation for accounting practice; instead, bulletins were directed to current problems and developing issues. Accounting alternatives continued to multiply, and accounting principles continued to reflect the time-honored process of evolution and adaptation. CAP opinions never enjoyed complete popular support, even within the AICPA, and the committee gradually lost prestige.

### Accounting Principles Board (1959-1973)

In 1959, in an effort to reestablish its influence, the AICPA formed the Accounting Principles Board (APB) and the Accounting Research Division. The research group was formed to study basic issues and assumptions and to provide input to the APB as it struggled to resolve accounting controversies. The APB was charged with establishing accounting principles. It is interesting to note that no enforcement procedures were provided for APB opinions because it was assumed that the board, backed by output from the research division, would have sufficient prestige to enjoy enforcement by persuasion. Unfortunately, both groups were destined to fail.

During its tenure the APB issued 31 opinions; these statements, some of which amended ARB 43, continue in force unless they have been superseded. The board also issued four statements with recommendations and comments on unresolved issues.

### Financial Accounting Standards Board (1972-     )

Faced with the loss of a great deal of prestige and influence, the AICPA formed two groups, the Trueblood Committee and the Wheat Commission. The former was asked to study the objectives of financial accounting. Their report, issued in 1973, had little immediate impact, but it has become an important element in the search for a conceptual foundation. The second group, chaired by former SEC Chairman Francis Wheat, examined the process of determining accounting principles. It resulted in the formation, in 1973, of the Financial Accounting Standards Board (FASB), the current private sector accounting authority.

The FASB has seven full-time members (partly because of charges of conflict of interest on the part of members of the part-time APB), and they are backed by an advisory council consisting of government and corporate accountants, auditors, professors, analysts, and others who are interested in accounting issues and controversies. The board follows a very deliberate policy of seeking counsel and advice. The politics of the process are clearly recognized—general acceptance is sought before rather than after the fact. Proposed statements are widely circulated in draft discussion memorandums (DMs), public hearings are held, and comments are solicited before the release of revised statements. The controversy surrounding some issues has led to reference to the DMs as the "DMZ," an accounting demilitarized zone.

Through late 1980 the FASB had issued 42 Statements of Financial Accounting Standards and 33 Interpretations, which are, together with unamended opinions surviving from CAP and APB, the body of generally accepted accounting principles. Given the complexity and breadth of the problems that have been addressed and the trail of rules that can be traced back to ARB 43, accounting principles are now summarized in loose-leaf services, such as the one prepared by the staff of the AICPA and published by Commerce Clearing House.

### Securities and Exchange Commission

The SEC was formed to ensure adequate disclosure of financial and other data to keep investors fully informed about publicly held corporations. Currently, more than 11 thousand companies that are listed on one of the organized exchanges or traded in the over-the-counter market are required to file with the Commission. Regulations S-X and S-K govern the form and content of financial statements, and relevant accounting principles are defined in the Accounting Series Releases (ASRs).

Registration statements are required for new issues; these contain detailed information as to the extent and cost of distribution, financial statements and exhibits, and other data concerning the firm, its management, special agreements, and any notable risk that investors should recognize. Most publicly held firms must also file an annual Form 10-K with detailed information concerning the business, its properties, executive renumeration, legal proceedings, and, in addition to financial statements, other detail that is of interest to investors.

In addition to the annual 10-K form, firms are required to file unaudited quarterly 10-Q forms and occasional 8-K forms for such unscheduled events as bankruptcy, merger, or a change in auditors. Controllers must be familiar with SEC rules, regulations, and interpretations in order to be able to prepare the required periodic reports. (See Chapters 10 and 22 for discussions on SEC reporting requirements and public offerings.)

Although the basic role of the SEC is to ensure disclosure and to oversee the standard-setting process, the Commission has the authority to require compliance in annual and quarterly filings, and no publicly held firm can afford to jeopardize its position by resisting SEC rules. As a result, the SEC has enormous power, which it has recently started to use. Accounting has become very political, and it would be difficult for the Commission to resist congressional pressure to become more active, because concern can be addressed through some other agency if the SEC fails to meet political objections. It is reasonable to expect the influence of the SEC to continue to grow as the trend of standard setting continues to move from the private sector toward the public sector.

### International Authorities

The search for standardization and uniformity is also taking place internationally. The International Accounting Standards Committee (IASC) was formed in 1973 to reconcile differing practices among members of the 53 countries that are represented. The IASC issued 13 statements through 1979, many of them addressing basic principles that are already accepted in the United States and the United Kingdom. At present the IASC is not especially influential, but this may change as multinational corporate growth continues. In 1973 representatives from more than 50 countries formed the International Federation of Accountants (IFAC), a group that is complementary to IASC, to coordinate the international accounting profession, especially with respect to auditing practices and professional ethics. Controllers with international operations or investments should be familiar with IASC statements, if only to recognize the differences from U.S. GAAP.

## REPORTING STANDARDS AND DISCLOSURE

Accounting alternatives may obscure the meaning of accounting numbers. As a result, it is important that every possible assistance is available to the users of financial statements. A number of procedures have been recommended for identifying principles that have been selected and for tracing the effect of principles that have been changed.

## Summary of Significant Accounting Policies

APB Opinion No. 22, *Disclosure of Accounting Policies* (1972), recommends that significant accounting principles and methods should be identified and summarized in a separate statement attached to financial statements. These include such policies as amortization of intangibles, basis for consolidation, depreciation methods, inventory valuation procedures, mergers and acquisitions, treatment of investment credits, and treatment of unfunded pension costs. In addition, methods that are peculiar to a given industry should also be specified, as in the case of net realizable value (selling price less expected selling cost), which is used for inventory valuation in the meat-packing industry, and the allowance for returns in the publishing and record industries.

It is important for the controller, in consultation with management, to select accounting policies and methods that will be applicable over the long term, because of the requirement for consistent application from period to period and the need for auditor concurrence with the change. In fact, the SEC has a requirement that the auditor must write a letter stating that the change in accounting principle is "preferable in the circumstances."

The AICPA has published a number of pronouncements concerning specialized practices and procedures in CAP bulletins, APB opinions, and, more recently, in four industry accounting guides (on motion pictures, franchising, retail land sales, and real estate) and, through 1979, 29 Statements of Position. The FASB intends to address specialized procedures in the normal course of its business; it published a temporary list of specialized principles that it considers to be generally acceptable in SFAS 32. In the interim, firms are not required to change the principles they are currently using, but may justify a change to any of such principles as being preferable in the circumstances.

## Accounting Changes

As noted, principles should be applied consistently from period to period in order to discourage the manipulation of values. APB Opinion No. 20, *Accounting Changes* (1971), provides guidance when changes are made. The opinion identifies four general types of adjustment: change in (1) *principle,* (2) *estimate,* (3) *entity,* and (4) *error correction.*

**Change in Principle.** This is a change from one generally accepted principle to another. If assets that were being depreciated on an accelerated basis are then depreciated on the straight-line basis, it is a change in principle. But care must be exercised; when a firm that uses accelerated depreciation chooses straight-line for a newly acquired plant, leaving the method for existing assets unchanged, it is not an accounting change. Under APB 22, the different methods would be identified in the summary of significant accounting policies.

In general, the controller should account for changes in principles currently, with the cumulative net-of-tax effect reported separately in the income statement as a nonextraordinary item but after the caption "Net income." The cumulative effect is the difference between the opening balance in retained earnings and the balance that would have resulted if the changed principle had been adopted in all prior periods. Comparative statements from prior periods are presented as previously reported when they are included for comparative purposes. The impact on both income and earnings per share should be disclosed.

In some cases retroactive treatment is preferred because of the potential impact on earnings. These are change from LIFO to another inventory method, change to or from the full cost method in the extractive industries, and change in the method of accounting for long-term construction contracts. In these cases the impact is shown retroactively, with financial statements of previous periods restated, as far as possible, to a basis consistent with the change. The effect of the change on income before extraordinary items, net income, and earnings per share should be disclosed. The beginning balance in retained earnings would be adjusted, with appropriate disclosure.

**Change in Estimate.** Controllers often rely on estimates, especially for income tax liability, warranty costs, and bad debts. In time, an estimate may prove to have been wrong, and it must be corrected. This correction is classified as a change in estimate, which is to be accounted for prospectively, without adjustment of previous data. If the remaining useful life of a fixed asset is now believed to be seven years, whatever the old estimate, the undepreciated balance would be expensed in each of the next seven years. Depreciation expense for prior years would not be restated.

**Change in Entity.** When the accounting entity changes, the controller must restate financial statements of prior periods in terms of the current entity. The most important cases here are changes in the firms that are consolidated, a change in the method of accounting for subsidiaries, or the addition of a new firm as a result of a stock-for-stock merger. Data for different entities are clearly confusing, especially for sales and earnings per share, and restatement is very useful to investors.

**Error Correction.** Accounting errors include arithmetic mistakes, oversights, incorrect classifications, and the use of procedures in violation of GAAP. Error corrections are prior-period adjustments, with prior statements redrawn to show the correct values. Material errors should be identified by the controller in the financial statements, especially the statement of retained earnings, and full disclosure is appropriate.

### Information Overload

Disclosure rules are intended to help shareholders cope with the many accounting alternatives possible under GAAP. But the complexity of disclosure rules and the amount of data provided in annual reports and 10-K forms may, counterproductively, add to the problem. Annual reports are a serious challenge even to trained accountants and analysts who are familiar with the terms and trade jargon contained in financial statements. With training, it is possible to read between the lines, but even here the amount of information provided overloads the system. The average reader is in a much worse position, and disclosure is as likely to confuse as it is to enlighten.

Disclosure developed because accounting objectives focused on management. Disclosure is a symptom of the problem; it is not a solution. With the attention that has been directed to investors' needs recently, disclosure may begin to give way to simplification as alternatives are narrowed and the accounting "GAAP" is closed.

## SUGGESTED READING

American Institute of Certified Public Accountants. *Accounting: Current Text.* Chicago: Commerce Clearing House, Published annually as of July 1.

Brilloff, Abraham J. *Unaccountable Accounting.* New York: Harper & Row, 1972.

Curley, Anthony J., and Bear, Robert M. "Accounting Data," Chapter 7 of *Investment Analysis and Management.* New York: Harper & Row, 1979.

Horngren, Charles T. "Accounting Principles: Private or Public Sector?" *Journal of Accountancy*, May, 1972, pp. 37-41.

Kieso, Donald E., and Weygandt, Jerry J. *Intermediate Accounting.* New York: Wiley, 1977.

Miller, Martin A. *Comprehensive GAAP Guide.* New York: Harcourt Brace Jovanovich, 1980.

Norby, William C. "The SEC Decision on Oil and Gas Accounting." *Financial Analysts Journal*, November-December, 1978, pp. 13-16 and 77.

Runser, Robert J. "The Conceptual Framework and Inflation Accounting." *Financial Executive*, April, 1979, pp. 30-38.

# 3

# LIFO Inventory Accounting

*James W. DeLoach Jr.*

## THE LIFO INVENTORY CONCEPT

In recent years many companies have adopted a last-in, first-out (LIFO) costing method for inventory valuation purposes. The use of LIFO eliminates higher replacement cost from the inventory during periods of rising prices, and as a result reduces reported income. LIFO assumes that the goods most recently acquired or produced are those currently sold to customers. This assumption of cost flows is very rarely true of actual physical flow, but LIFO is a cost concept, not a physical-flow concept. Under LIFO, costs are more appropriately matched with current revenues, because costs reported on the income statement are relatively current costs. At the same time, inventories valued using LIFO are not satisfactorily stated on the balance sheet in a period of changing price levels. During a period of rising prices, LIFO tends to state inventories at substantially below current cost.

### LIFO Versus FIFO

Both the LIFO and FIFO (first-in, first-out) methods are acceptable under generally accepted accounting principles. Under FIFO, inventory is priced at its most recent cost. This procedure frequently coincides with the actual physical movement of the inventory. Although FIFO is the more traditionally followed method, inflation has forced businessmen to recognize that illusory profits result from its use. In periods of rapid inflation, the use of LIFO eliminates the inflationary profits that are recognized under FIFO and yields results that more closely approximate the economic facts.

In the following illustration of the LIFO concept, assume XYZ Company is in the sugar business. The company purchases 30,000 pounds of sugar for $0.10 a pound. It sells the sugar for $0.16 a pound in the marketplace, realizing a profit of $0.06 a pound, or a gross profit of $1,800 before fixed costs, taxes, and other expenses. When the company returns to its sources of supply to replenish its stock, it finds that the purchase price for sugar has increased to $0.15 a pound. Because its revenues exceed costs of replacement by only $0.01 a pound, the company has realized a gross profit of only $300 in the economic sense. The company's management understands the economics of their business. What they often do not understand is the accountant's figures. In this example, XYZ Company's income statement and cash-flow picture using FIFO and LIFO might appear as follows:

|  | Inventory Valuation | |
| --- | --- | --- |
|  | FIFO | LIFO |
| Revenues (30,000 @ $0.16) | $4,800 | $4,800 |
| Costs and expenses: | | |
| Cost of sugar sold | | |
| FIFO (30,000 @ $0.10) | 3,000 | |
| LIFO (30,000 @ $0.15) | | 4,500 |
| Depreciation | 500 | 500 |
| Various out-of-pocket costs | 300 | 300 |
| Total | 3,800 | 5,300 |
| Earnings (loss) before taxes | 1,000 | (500) |
| Taxes (using 50% rate) | 500 | — |
| Earnings (loss) after taxes | 500 | (500) |

| | Inventory Valuation | |
| --- | --- | --- |
| | *FIFO* | *LIFO* |
| Net earnings (loss) | 500 | (500) |
| Add back depreciation | 500 | 500 |
| Net cash flow as reported under inventory valuation method | $1,000 | $ –0– |
| Excess of actual replacement cost over cost of sugar sold reported under inventory valuation method | (1,500) | — |
| Actual net cash flow | $ (500) | $ –0– |

As seen above, LIFO eliminates $1,500 of gross profit, because the cost of sugar is $0.15 a pound, the cost of the last purchase. Under LIFO, XYZ Company doesn't pay the $500 in taxes it would pay under FIFO—taxes on income that the company did not realize from an economic standpoint.

The figures above for FIFO tell a story of $500 of net earnings and $1,000 in positive cash flow. In this particular case, the earnings and cash flow reported under FIFO are illusory. The company recognizes this problem when it replenishes its stock. In an inflationary environment, the replacement cost for goods sold can increase so rapidly that the company may be continually faced with a shortage of cash with which to operate and pay taxes. Ultimately, it might have to raise additional capital, borrow money, or discontinue the business.

If a firm uses the LIFO method, it can preserve for use in its business the cash that would have otherwise been paid to federal and state governments for income taxes on the difference between FIFO and LIFO costs. The current cost of maintaining inventories at normal levels is matched with current revenues—a determination of income that addresses the practical economics and realities of the business environment.

One of the key principles under the LIFO concept is that a business maintains a relatively stable supply of goods as long as it is in business. A basic supply of goods is regarded as a nondepreciable fixed asset having a reported value that should remain constant except for actual physical impairment or actual physical increase in the volume of goods on hand. Volume increases are valued at current prices in the period of addition.

## FACTORS AFFECTING THE LIFO DECISION

At one time or another, most companies have considered adopting LIFO for valuing all or part of their inventory. Management must decide whether LIFO would be beneficial over the short and long term, basing its decision on a careful analysis of all relevant factors, including current and expected price levels, inventory levels, productivity changes, technological improvements, and other factors. In other words, management must decide whether the LIFO inventory method more accurately reflects income. There are several advantages and disadvantages that may be important to a given company when it considers adopting LIFO.

## Advantages of Using LIFO

Some of the advantages of using LIFO are:

1. *Increased cash flow.* In an inflationary environment, LIFO provides a potential permanent tax deferral and, as a result, more cash flow than the FIFO method. The greater the rate of inflation, the greater the cash-flow benefits under LIFO.
2. *Improved reporting of earnings.* LIFO provides a better matching of costs and revenues through the reduction or elimination of inventory profits and losses during periods of changing price levels. The elimination of inventory profits reported using the LIFO method in a period of inflation results in what many financial analysts regard as higher quality earnings.
3. *Recognition for tax purposes.* Although not a substitute for price level accounting or current value accounting as a way of accounting for inflation, LIFO does partially mitigate the effects of inflation in reporting results of operation and, at the same time, is allowable for tax purposes. Price level and current value accounting are not allowable for tax purposes at the present time.
4. *Encourages better inventory control.* The strict standards of the tax regulations imposed on a company adopting LIFO necessitate improved inventory management and controls. The fact that a company uses the LIFO method might encourage it to develop improved business practices in the areas of inventory and production control, and to dispose of excess and obsolete stock on a current basis.

## Disadvantages of Using LIFO

Some of the disadvantages of using LIFO are:

1. *Impact on balance sheet.* LIFO reports lower inventory valuations on the balance sheet, making it less useful as a financial analysis tool. This problem is partially mitigated through disclosure of current cost inventories in the footnotes to the financial statements.
2. *Full cost requirements.* LIFO is a full cost method for tax purposes. As a result, it requires the restoration of all market valuation reserves and inventory write-downs previously deducted for tax purposes and the adoption of full absorption costing. From a tax standpoint, the impact of these two factors could offset the tax deferral otherwise available under LIFO in the initial or early years of its adoption.
3. *Impact on market values.* The use of LIFO in an inflationary period with stable or increasing inventory levels reduces reported earnings and earnings per share.
4. *Increased cost and effort required.* Typically, LIFO is costly and time-consuming in the initial year of adoption. Although the cost and effort required may be reduced in subsequent years, in some industries the burden may be an ongoing problem. The mechanics of LIFO are sometimes very difficult and may require extensive time to implement.

5. *Impact on interim reporting.* Interim reporting under LIFO is not easy. Depending on the method used for interim reporting, net income reported in an interim period can be distorted. Because of inaccurate interim estimates, LIFO can result in significant year-end adjustments, which can create a credibility problem for a company's interim reporting. In many cases, interim accounting under LIFO is difficult for both management and shareholders to understand.

6. *Impact on company agreements and incentive compensation plans.* Loan agreements, profit-sharing plans, stock option plans, and so on, must be reviewed to determine whether a change to LIFO is allowed and whether any waivers or amendments are needed. Since the continued use of FIFO earnings under these various plans could present a problem under the IRS conformity rules, the company adopting LIFO should seek technical advice. In addition, it should determine (a) the effect of lower earnings, (b) the lower net book values and ratios on loan covenants, and (c) the effect on incentive plans resulting from lower earnings. Some of these problems have been eased by proposed IRS regulations (see Financial Reporting below).

7. *Adherence to rules and regulations.* A company must comply with the rather technical and complex tax regulations relating to LIFO adoption in order to protect its LIFO election from a tax standpoint.

8. *Impact of decrements.* A substantial decline in the volume of inventory will usually produce significantly higher profits under LIFO. Under IRS regulations, a decline in volume is permanent in that subsequent restoration to normal volume levels must be treated as a new increment and priced at current costs in the year of replacement. If management considers the decline in volume temporary, this treatment may not make sense from a financial reporting standpoint; however, under the conformity rules, the IRS does not allow a charge to reported financial earnings offsetting the profit derived from the liquidation in the LIFO base.

9. *A change back to FIFO.* Once adopted, LIFO must be used for both book and tax purposes. A change back to FIFO requires advance IRS approval. Although the IRS has generally permitted changes in the past, approval is not automatic, especially if the change might be advantageous to a taxpayer. LIFO is adopted for financial reporting primarily because it more appropriately matches costs and revenues. A subsequent accounting change back to FIFO requires explanation and justification under the accounting rules (and an accountant's preferability letter under SEC rules for public reporting companies).

## WHO CAN USE LIFO?

Under federal income tax law, any company (corporation, individual, partnership, or trust) with inventories may use the LIFO method. In order to justify the use of LIFO from a tax standpoint, a company must demonstrate that goods or merchandise are *inventory* under the Internal Revenue Code, which defines the term as:

- Goods or merchandise held for sale in the ordinary course of business; and
- Goods in the process of being produced or consumed in the production process.

Not everyone can use LIFO. The following points help a company determine whether its goods and merchandise are inventory for LIFO purposes from a tax standpoint:

1. The company must have title to the goods. Merchandise purchased under a consignment arrangement is not inventory.
2. Upon sale, title to the merchandise must pass to the purchaser. Hence, products manufactured or held for lease rather than sale are not part of inventory.
3. Supplies are considered general and administrative items rather than inventory, because they are not sold to customers.
4. A business is not eligible to use LIFO if it is involved in service-oriented activities as opposed to the sale of a product.
5. The IRS has held that costs incurred on long-term contracts are not eligible for LIFO; however, companies having long-term contracts may use LIFO for goods or merchandise held for sale if the goods are purchased for purposes other than meeting long-term contractual commitments.

## IMPLEMENTING LIFO

In practice, because accounting records vary greatly in design and the nature of each business tends to be unique, many questions arise in connection with applying LIFO. This section addresses many of these questions and explains many of the problems encountered in applying the LIFO method of inventory valuation.

### Formal Adoption of LIFO

Unlike most accounting changes, adoption of LIFO does not require prior IRS approval; however, important tax elections must be made in the initial year of change.

**Filing.** To elect LIFO, a completed Form 970 is attached to the tax return for the year of change. Although the tax return for a calendar tax year may be filed as late as September 15th of the following year, in practice an earlier LIFO election date is better for most companies. The tax law and regulations prescribe that annual financial reports to shareholders, creditors, and others must also meet LIFO criteria. Consequently, the operative deadline for election of LIFO coincides with the issuance of the annual financial statements.

The official application, Form 970, is relatively simple, but it must be completed and filed carefully. If a company fails to file the form, its right to use LIFO could be invalidated.

**Elections.** Important elections on the form must be indicated when the form is initially filed. Because a company may be "locked in" to its elections in the future, it must consider the various elections carefully in terms of its needs and the nature of its operations. Further, the company must disclose on the form the existence of write-downs or reserves as of the close of the prior year. In a multicorporate enterprise, a separate LIFO election is required for each company, and each company's inventory must be accounted for separately.

## Election Choices

These are the elections to consider when a company adopts LIFO:

1. *LIFO method.* The company may select either the specific identification method (referred to as Unit Method on Form 970) or a dollar value method. (The various LIFO inventory methods are discussed later.)
2. *Pooling of items.* If the specific identification method is used, identical items would be combined in a separate pool. Under the dollar value method, similar items may be pooled depending on the company's specific election. (This important area is discussed further under Definition of Pools.)
3. *Method for computing LIFO (if a dollar method is selected).* There are a number of alternative dollar value methods available. These methods include the *full double-extension* method, *index* method, and *link-chain* method. Retailers may also adopt the LIFO *retail method.* (The mechanics of each of these methods and some of the ramifications involved are discussed under LIFO Inventory Methods.)
4. *Method for pricing increments.* Under the double-extension method, the quantity of items in the inventory at the close of the taxable year is extended at both the base-year unit cost and current-year unit cost. The index is then computed to price out the current-year increment. Since base-year unit costs are constant depending on the year LIFO is adopted, the key to determining the index for pricing out the increment is the current-year unit cost. Under IRS regulations, current-year unit costs may be determined using (a) actual cost of the goods most recently purchased or produced (sometimes referred to as *latest cost*); (b) actual cost of the goods purchased or produced during the taxable year in the order of acquisition (sometimes referred to as *earliest cost*); (c) average unit costs equal to the aggregate of all the goods purchased or produced during the taxable year divided by the total number of units purchased or produced; or (d) any other unit cost that in the opinion of the IRS clearly reflects income. The use of earliest costs as opposed to latest costs can increase the cash-flow benefits under LIFO.
5. *Inventories that will not be subject to LIFO.* Under some circumstances a company may conclude that certain inventory costs should not be valued under the LIFO method. For example, a division might not have adequate records to support the LIFO calculations. Such inventories may be specifically left out of the LIFO election.

## Definition of Pools

Items in inventory can be pooled for LIFO purposes on the basis of either the *natural business unit* or *multiple pools.* A company considering LIFO must understand the significance of choosing the appropriate method of pooling inventory items.

**Natural Business Units.** The IRS regulations define a natural business unit as "the entire productive activity of the enterprise within one product line or within two or more related product lines including (to the extent engaged in by the enterprise) the obtaining of materials, the processing of materials and the selling of manufactured or processed goods." For example, a manufacturer producing refrigerators and freezers at several locations would be considered to have a single pool. If he also manufactured small hand tools, a separate pool would be established for the tooling business. Segment reporting and line-of-business disclosures in accordance with generally accepted accounting principles and the SEC guidelines could provide a basis for determining natural business units.

**Multiple Pools.** Each pool must consist of a group of items that are substantially similar. All companies other than manufacturers or processors must elect multiple pools. If a manufacturer or processor elects multiple pools, raw materials of a substantially similar nature may be combined within a similar pool. Finished goods and work in process must be included in pools according to major classes or types of goods.

*Raw material content* pools are another option available to manufacturers or processors. These pools consist of raw materials only, including the raw material content of finished goods and work in process. Under this election, labor and overhead costs are not on LIFO.

Wholesalers, retailers, jobbers, and distributors pool by grouping items by major product line and class of goods. If a wholesaler or retailer also engages in manufacturing operations, goods in the manufacturing stage may be pooled under the natural business unit concept, multiple pool concept, or raw material content pooling concept. Goods in the wholesaling or retailing stage of the operation must be grouped in multiple pools by major product lines and classes of goods.

## Market Valuation Reserves

LIFO is strictly a cost method for tax purposes. Reserves and write-downs that might have been appropriate under the FIFO method must be restored to income to properly state the base inventory at cost in the initial year of adopting LIFO. Amended tax returns must be filed and income tax paid on the increase in income.

Over the years, the IRS has issued rulings indicating that LIFO inventories should not be reduced for inventory write-downs of *any* kind, including provision for excess stock, obsolescence reserves, and market valuation reserves. From a tax standpoint, this simply means that companies having LIFO inventories should aggressively pursue their excess and obsolete stock policies on a current basis rather than solely at year-end or at the time physical inventories are taken. Management should carefully review excess stocks to determine whether operating, customer service, and other requirements demand the maintenance of such inventories. If these actions are not taken by company management, tax benefits that otherwise would currently be available to the company will have to be deferred to future tax returns. Under a recent Supreme Court decision, a write-down of excess stocks will not be allowed under the FIFO method either.

## Maintenance of Records

Under LIFO it is difficult to maintain adequate records to support the LIFO calculations. However, if LIFO is properly evaluated and implemented, most of the significant cost and effort will occur when LIFO is first adopted. Annual maintenance cost is ordinarily not as significant but nevertheless requires consideration when management evaluates the decision to adopt LIFO.

**Maintenance of Base Inventory.** The regulations specifically require that base-year unit costs be permanently maintained, no matter which method of valuing inventories is used. Under the double-extension procedure described later in this chapter, the company will use these unit costs in making LIFO calculations for future years. Under the index and link-chain methods, the base-year unit costs are either less significant or not needed at all in future years. However, a company may be called on to justify LIFO calculations under these methods by recomputation of the year-end LIFO inventory using actual base-year unit costs. Failure to perform these recomputations because available base-year information is not available can result in an IRS challenge to the LIFO election.

**New Additions to Pool.** Under the double-extension method, a base unit cost must be ascertained for each item entering the pool for the first time subsequent to the beginning of the base year. In such cases, the base unit cost of new items will be the current-year cost of that item, unless the company is able to reconstruct a cost at the time of the base period.

It is important to understand that, whenever possible, new items should be valued at a reconstructed base cost instead of a current cost, because a company will realize greater LIFO benefit when it uses reconstructed base-year costs. There are several possible approaches to reconstructing a base-year cost:

- The relationship of base unit cost to current unit cost of similar items can be considered and applied to the current cost of the new item.
- Reference can be made to vendor price lists and other material in effect at the time of the base period.
- An overall index can be used to compute base-year unit costs.

**LIFO Computations.** For all years for which the LIFO method is used, there should be complete documentation for the LIFO computations. This is important not only in the event the IRS examines the company's tax return, but also to ensure that the calculation is performed consistently from year to year and that decrements arising in future years can be appropriately applied against prior-year increments.

**Full Absorption Costing.** Records should be maintained to support compliance with the full absorption costing regulations of the IRS.

## LIFO INVENTORY METHODS

There are several methods that are available to value inventories using LIFO. These methods are:

- Specific identification method, and
- Dollar value methods:
  - Full double-extension method,
  - Index method,
  - Link-chain method, and
  - Retail method.

This section will provide a brief overview of the methodology followed under each of these methods.

### Specific Identification Method

Under the specific identification method, the value of inventory is normally measured by using the physical quantities of the product, for example, number of pounds, linear feet, cubic yardage, and so on. For this purpose, identical goods are included in pools. In the year LIFO is adopted, the inventory as of the beginning of the year is restated at cost and is referred to as the *base inventory*. Unit costs of the base inventory are used to price out quantities in future years.

**Increments and Decrements.** In applying LIFO, volume increases in specific items on LIFO are called *increments*. Volume decreases are called *decrements*. An increment is valued using current costs, as discussed previously.

Increments are added to the base inventory. Decrements, which are sometimes referred to as *impairments*, reduce increments in inverse order. For example, if a decrement were to occur in 1981, the cost entered for a 1980 increment would flow to cost sales to the extent eliminated by the decrement. A greater decrement would serve to also reduce increments in 1979, 1978, and so on. A severe reduction in volume of goods could serve to wipe out all the increments in prior years and could ultimately affect the base inventories, resulting in a significant increase in income for financial and tax reporting purposes.

**Drawbacks.** Experience has shown that the specific identification method is likely, in the long run, to produce unwanted impairment and the consequent loss of LIFO benefits. It is not uncommon for the quantity of goods in one pool to increase considerably (requiring valuation at current prices for the increase) while quantities in another pool correspondingly decrease. Both events contribute to higher reported income, although the true LIFO cost investment in total inventory may not have changed. Impairments in volume can result from the unavailability of specific goods at any price because of strikes, natural disasters, and excessive demand. The specific identification method is also affected by radical changes in product mix and substitutions in basic raw materials. From the standpoint of achieving the desired objectives under LIFO, most businesses prefer a dollar value method.

### Dollar Value Methods

A dollar value method tends to mitigate the effect of substantial changes in product mix. A broader range of goods may be included in a dollar value pool than in a specific-goods pool. In the latter case, volume changes are measured in terms of units of a commodity, and accordingly, the pooled items must be substantially *identical*. Under dollar value, the test for grouping items into pools is *similarity*—similarity as to types of raw material, processing operations applied, interchangeability, or use (see earlier discussion under definition of pools).

The five steps below should be followed in applying a dollar value method (essentially, the mechanics are the same regardless of what method is followed):

1. *Assign a base-year unit value to all items in the base inventory.* Generally, the base-year unit value will be the same as the unit cost used for individual methods under the previous inventory valuation method (i.e., FIFO), except for adjustments required for market write-downs.

2. *Extend all items in the ending inventory at base prices.*

3. *Compute the increment or decrement at base prices.* This determination results from comparing the current year's ending and beginning inventories priced at base prices. If the ending inventory at base prices exceeds beginning inventory at base prices, the excess constitutes an increment representing a quantity or volume increase expressed in terms of base dollars. If a decrement occurs, the beginning inventory will exceed the ending inventory at base prices.

4. *Convert the increment at base prices to current cost levels.* The ratio of inventory at current cost to the inventory at base prices is determined and then applied to the increment at base prices. The pricing of current-year inventory at current and base costs is usually referred to as *double extension* or *double pricing.*

5. *Either add the priced-out increment to beginning-year LIFO inventory or apply the decrement against prior-year increments and, if necessary, the base inventory.*

For purposes of determining the index to price out the current-year increment discussed above, the IRS regulations contemplate that the total inventory will be double-extended. That is, each item in the ending inventory will be priced at current and base costs. If a company can justify that this procedure is not practical because of technological changes, changes in product mix, significant number of different inventory items and other factors, other methods may be used—the index and link-chain methods described below are acceptable alternatives. A company using the retail method of valuing inventories may use the retail dollar value LIFO method to value inventories at LIFO. The remainder of this section discusses briefly the mechanics followed in applying the dollar value methods.

**Full Double-Extension Method.** In the following illustration of the application of the double-extension method, assume the following facts:

1. Base inventory and current-year inventory (year three) for XYZ Company are:

| Inventory Item | Quantity | Unit Cost Base | Unit Cost Current | Total Cost Base | Total Cost Current |
|---|---|---|---|---|---|
| A | 500 | $ 150 | $ 190 | $ 75,000 | $ 95,000 |
| B | 200 | 300 | 360 | 60,000 | 72,000 |
| C | 100 | 50 | 66 | 5,000 | 6,600 |
| D | 20 | 200 | 250 | 4,000 | 5,000 |
| E | 100 | 230 | 290 | 23,000 | 29,000 |
| F | 10 | 2,500 | 3,100 | 25,000 | 31,000 |
| G | 50 | 400 | 480 | 20,000 | 24,000 |
| H | 60 | 300 | 300 | 18,000 | 18,000 |
| | | | | $230,000 | $280,600 |

2. XYZ Company uses latest costing in valuing increments and has elected a single pool for purposes of applying the dollar value method.
3. A summary of inventory valued at LIFO at the end of year two is presented below:

| | At Base Prices | Index | LIFO Cost |
|---|---|---|---|
| Base inventory | $175,000 | 1.00 | $175,000 |
| Year one increment | 25,000 | 1.06 | 26,500 |
| Year two increment | 20,000 | 1.14 | 22,800 |
| Inventory at LIFO | $220,000 | | $224,300 |

A calculation of LIFO inventory at the end of year three for XYZ Company using the double-extension method would be approached as follows:

1. *Assign a base-year unit value to all items in the base inventory.* (This was done in year one when LIFO was adopted.)
2. *Extend ending inventory in year three at base prices.* (See above.) Ending inventory at base prices is $230,000.
3. *Compute the increment or decrement at base prices.* Ending inventory at base prices in year two is $220,000. Therefore, an increment at base prices of $10,000 occurred in year three.
4. *Convert increment at base prices to current cost levels.* A latest-cost index of 1.22 is computed by dividing ending inventory at current costs ($280,600) by ending

inventory at base costs ($230,000). The priced-out year three increment is $12,200 ($10,000 @ $1.22).

5. *Add priced-out increment to beginning-year LIFO inventory.* LIFO inventory at the end of year three is $236,500, calculated as follows:

|  | At Base Prices | Index | LIFO Cost |
|---|---|---|---|
| Base inventory | $175,000 | 1.00 | $175,000 |
| Year one increment | 25,000 | 1.06 | 26,500 |
| Year two increment | 20,000 | 1.14 | 22,800 |
| Year three increment | 10,000 | 1.22 | 12,200 |
| Inventory at LIFO | $230,000 |  | $236,500 |

It should be noted that XYZ Company has elected to use a single pool. If more than one pool is formed, a similar calculation would apply to each pool. It should be noted also that only eight items are included in this example. Obviously, businesses having an inventory comprising a large number of individual items face a formidable problem in using the double-extension dollar value method. Alternatively, the index or the link-chain methods described below may prove more practical for companies with large and varied inventories. Many companies use a computer to price the inventory at both current and base costs for the double-extension method in order to substantially reduce the clerical effort.

**Index Method.** The index method is essentially the same as the full double-extension method except that a representative *sample* of the items in a pool is double-extended in lieu of all items in the pool. Company management should seek technical advice in determining the best way to develop a representative sample in the particular circumstances.

In the following illustration of the index method, assume the same facts as in the XYZ Company example above. Assume further that the inventory is not made up of eight items with a total current cost of $280,600, but rather consists of some 20,000 different low-cost items. Finally, assume that through the use of a sound statistical method consistent with prior years, an index of 1.19 is calculated for year three. At the end of the year, quantities on hand of items selected for purposes of calculating the index were extended at both base- and current-year costs, and the total base and current costs for all items in the sample were aggregated for use in the 1.19 index calculation.

Given the above facts, the calculation of LIFO inventory at the end of year three for XYZ Company using the index method would be approached as follows:

1. *Assign a base-year unit value to all items in the base inventory.* (This was done in year one when LIFO was adopted.)

2. *Extend ending inventory in year three at base prices.* (See discussion above.) The index method is used, and the sample selected for purposes of computing an

index resulted in a calculation of 1.19. Under the index method, the index calculated using the representative sample is used to discount total year-end inventory at current cost to base cost. Ending inventory at base prices is $235,600, which is calculated as follows:

| | |
|---|---|
| Year-end inventory at current cost | $280,600  (a) |
| Index of base cost to current cost | 1.19  (b) |
| Year-end inventory at base cost | |
|    (a) ÷ (b) | $235,600 |

3. *Compute the increment or decrement at base prices.* The year-end inventory at base cost determined using the calculated index is compared to the prior year-end inventory to calculate the increment or decrement. This calculation results in an increment of $15,600 ($235,600 less $220,000).

4. *Convert increment at base prices to current cost levels.* The current increment at base prices at $15,600 is priced out using the 1.19 latest-cost index. The priced-out year three increment is $18,560.

5. *Add priced-out increment to beginning-year LIFO inventory.* LIFO inventory at the end of year three is $242,860, calculated as follows:

| | At Base Prices | Index | LIFO Cost |
|---|---|---|---|
| Base inventory | $175,000 | 1.00 | $175,000 |
| Year one increment | 25,000 | 1.06 | 26,500 |
| Year two increment | 20,000 | 1.14 | 22,800 |
| Year three increment | 15,600 | 1.19 | 18,560 |
| Inventory at LIFO | $235,600 | | $242,860 |

Generally speaking, the index is always derived from internal information; however, pursuant to special permission from the IRS (Rev. Proc. 72-21), department stores and certain specialty stores using the retail method may use indices published by the Bureau of Labor Statistics (BLS) to perform the LIFO calculations.

**Link-Chain Method.** Some companies may find even the indexing method burdensome because of rapid changes in technology and product mix, which may result in a complete change in inventory mix over a relatively short period of time. In this environment, a company using a double-extension or index method will be required to develop a new base cost for new items entering the LIFO pool. The link-chain method overcomes this problem by requiring only a double pricing of year-end inventory at end-of-year costs and beginning-of-year costs to develop an annual inflationary index. The annual inflationary index determined for the current year is "chained" to the indices determined in prior years by multiplying the annual inflationary index for the current year against the cumulative inflationary index determined as of the close of the preceding year. Usually, a sampling technique is used in applying the link-chain method. Some companies, however, double price all or a substantial portion of the inventory.

Under the link-chain method, the theory of dollar value is the same as with the double-extension and indexing methods—only the mechanics are different. In this illustration of the application of the link-chain method, assume the following facts:

1. Inflationary indices for ABC Company are:

|  | Annual Ratio | Cumulative Ratio |
|---|---|---|
| Base, January 1, year one | 1.00 | 1.00 |
| Year one increment | 1.08 | 1.08 |
| Year two increment | 1.06 | 1.14 |
| Year three increment | 1.07 | 1.22 |

2. In year four, year-end inventory priced at end-of-year and beginning-of-year unit costs are $2,800,000 and $2,500,000, respectively.

3. ABC Company uses latest costing in valuing increments.

4. A summary of inventory valued at LIFO at the end of year three is presented below:

|  | At Base Prices | Index | LIFO Cost |
|---|---|---|---|
| Base inventory | $1,750,000 | 1.00 | $1,750,000 |
| Year one increment | 150,000 | 1.08 | 162,000 |
| Year two increment | 50,000 | 1.14 | 57,000 |
| Year three increment | 100,000 | 1.22 | 122,000 |
| Inventory at LIFO | $2,050,000 | | $2,091,000 |

Calculation of LIFO inventory at the end of year four for ABC Company using the link-chain method would be approached as follows:

1. *Assign a base-year unit value to all items in the base inventory.* This was done in year one when LIFO was adopted; however, under the link-chain method, these base unit costs will only serve as documentation for the initial base inventory. The base unit costs have no relevance to subsequent years' computations.

2. *Extend ending inventory in year four at base prices.* This step is achieved in three steps under link-chain:

   a. Ending inventory is priced at the end-of-year and beginning-of-year unit costs. An index of 1.12 results from double pricing the year-end inventory in this manner ($2,800,000 ÷ $2,500,000);

   b. The annual inflationary index is "chained" to the prior year-end cumulative index, resulting in a cumulative index at the end of year four of 1.37 (1.22 ×

1.12). The 1.37 cumulative index represents the inflation from the base period through the end of year four; and

c. The 1.37 index is used to discount year-end inventory of $2,800,000 to base prices in the same manner as the index calculated under the index method is used:

| | |
|---|---|
| Year-end inventory at current cost | $2,800,000 (a) |
| Cumulative index through year four | 1.37 (b) |
| Year-end inventory at base cost (a) ÷ (b) (approximate) | $2,050,000 |

3. *Compute the increment or decrement at base prices.* There is no increment or decrement in year four, because year-end inventory at base prices and beginning-year inventory at base prices are both $2,050,000.

Ending-year LIFO inventory is the same as beginning-year LIFO inventory, because there is no increment or decrement during year four. No further calculations are required.

When a company adopts the link-chain procedure, it must demonstrate to the IRS that the use of either an index method or a double-extension method would be impractical or unsuitable because of the nature of the LIFO pool.

**Retail Method.** A company using the retail method of valuing inventories may elect to use the LIFO retail method of inventory costing. Discussion here of the LIFO retail method will be brief and assumes that the reader understands the mechanics of the retail method.

A key consideration in the LIFO retail method is the calculation of the cost complement. Under both FIFO and LIFO, the calculation of the cost complement considers mark-ups, additional mark-ups, and mark-up cancellations. However, the LIFO method also considers mark-downs (net of mark-down cancellations) in computing the cost complement, whereas the FIFO method, using lower-of-cost-or-market pricing, does not. An illustration showing the mechanics of the retail LIFO method and the use of the FIFO and LIFO cost complements is presented below:

| | Base Inventory | Year 1 | Year 2 | Year 3 |
|---|---|---|---|---|
| (a) BLS LIFO index | 180.1 | 198.1 | 270.2 | 234.1 |
| (b) Converted to terms of base year (180.1 = 100.0) | 100.0 | 110.0 | 150.0 | 130.0 |
| (c) Physical inventory at retail | $12,000 | $15,400 | $22,500 | $16,900 |
| (d) Physical inventory at base-year retail prices [(c) ÷(b)] | $12,000 | $14,000 | $15,000 | $13,000 |

| | Base Inventory | Year 1 | Year 2 | Year 3 |
|---|---|---|---|---|
| (e) Buildup of LIFO layers at retail (applicable index noted parenthetically)— | | | | |
| (1) Base year (100.0) | $12,000 | $12,000 | $12,000 | $12,000 |
| (2) Year one (110.0) | — | 2,200 | 2,200 | 1,100 |
| (3) Year two (150.0) | — | — | 1,500 | — |
| (4) Year three (130.0) | — | — | — | — |
| (5) Total LIFO inventory at retail | $12,000 | $14,200 | $15,700 | $13,100 |
| (f) Cost complement— | | | | |
| (1) FIFO | .65 | .65 | .64 | .66 |
| (2) LIFO | .70 | .72 | .66 | .70 |
| (g) LIFO layers at cost— | | | | |
| (1) Base year [(e)(1) × .70] | $ 8,400 | $ 8,400 | $ 8,400 | $ 8,400 |
| (2) Year one [(e)(2) × .72] | — | 1,584 | 1,584 | 792 |
| (3) Year two [(e)(3) × .66] | — | — | 990 | — |
| (4) Total LIFO inventory at cost | 8,400 | 9,984 | 10,974 | 9,192 |
| (h) FIFO inventory [(c) ×(f)(1)] | 7,800 | 10,010 | 14,400 | 11,154 |
| (i) Cumulative LIFO reserve [(h) − (g)(4)] | $ (600) | $ 26 | $ 3,426 | $ 1,962 |

Note that in the above illustration, the buildup of LIFO layers at retail results from calculation of increments and decrements using the physical inventory at base-year retail prices. For example, in year one the inventory at base-year retail is $14,000, resulting in a $2,000 increment at base-year retail. The increment is priced using the year one index of 1.10, giving a priced-out increment of $2,200. The LIFO inventory at retail is converted to cost using the LIFO cost complement. LIFO inventory at cost is then compared to FIFO inventory calculated using the FIFO cost complement. The difference between FIFO inventory at cost and LIFO inventory at cost is the cumulative LIFO reserve. Note that in the first year, the use of LIFO has resulted in $600 additional income.

In applying the retail LIFO method, there are special factors to consider in connection with restoring mark-downs to opening inventories in the initial year of converting to LIFO. A retailer should seek professional advice when converting to LIFO to ensure that this area is dealt with appropriately.

## COMPLIANCE WITH FULL ABSORPTION REGULATIONS

When a company adopts the LIFO method, it must comply with the full absorption costing regulations of the IRS. Under these regulations, all direct and indirect costs are applied to goods produced during the year. (Under the full absorption regulations, indirect production costs include all costs other than direct production costs that are incidental to the manufacturing process.)

The IRS regulations segregate indirect production costs into three categories:

- Costs that must be included in inventory;
- Costs that may be excluded from inventory at the option of the taxpayer; and
- Costs that are includable in or excludable from inventory depending on treatment in the financial statements.

Changes in any one category constitute a change in method of accounting. Such a change requires permission from the IRS and has potential ramifications for financial reporting.

Figure 3.1 provides examples of indirect production costs in each of the three categories defined by the IRS regulations. One brief comment is in order regarding the third category of costs. The key to these costs is whether or not they are included in inventory for financial reporting purposes. If excluded from inventory for financial reporting purposes, such exclusions must be consistent with generally accepted accounting principles.

If a company elects to adopt LIFO and has not followed full absorption costing in prior years, the company will need to change to full absorption costing to be consistent with the provisions of I.R.C. § 481. Any income effect derived from the adoption of full absorption costing will serve to reduce the benefits of LIFO in the initial year of adoption.

## FINANCIAL REPORTING

### Allowable Financial Disclosures

Over the years, the IRS has imposed stringent limitations on companies reporting any earnings data other than earnings determined under the LIFO method. Accordingly, many companies avoided any disclosures other than those disclosures specifically sanctioned by IRS rulings and regulations, because failure to meet these conformity requirements meant that the violating company had to live with the possibility that the IRS might terminate the LIFO election upon examination.

In January 1981 the IRS issued amended regulations applicable to the financial statement conformity requirements related to the use of the LIFO method. These amended regulations allow supplementary and explanatory disclosures not pre-

| Category I | Category II | Category III |
|---|---|---|
| *Includable In Overhead By All Taxpayers (To Extent Related to Production)* | *May Be Excluded From Overhead* | *Treatment Dependent On Financial Reporting, Provided Latter Not Inconsistent With GAAP (To Extent Related to Production)* |
| Repair expenses<br>Maintenance<br>Utilities<br>Rent<br>Indirect labor and production supervisory wages, including—<br>—Basic compensation<br>—Overtime pay<br>—Vacation and holiday pay<br>—Sick leave pay<br>—Shift differential<br>—Payroll taxes<br>—Contributions to S.U.B. plan<br>Indirect materials and supplies<br>Tools and equipment not capitalized<br>Quality control and inspection<br>(also items of a similar nature) | Marketing expenses<br>Advertising expenses<br>Selling expenses<br>Other distribution expenses<br>Interest<br>Research and experimental expenses, including engineering and product development<br>Casualty and theft losses<br>Excess of percentage depletion over cost<br>Excess of tax depreciation over book<br>Income taxes<br>Past service cost of pension contributions<br>General and administrative, overall activities<br>Officers' salaries, overall activities<br>(also items of a similar nature) | Taxes, property and other local and state<br>Depreciation and depletion (in total)<br>Employee benefits<br>Current service costs, pension and profit sharing<br>Workmen's compensation expenses<br>Wage continuation<br>Nonqualified pension, profit sharing, stock bonus (to extent taxable to employee)<br>Life and health insurance premiums<br>Safety, medical treatment<br>Cafeteria<br>Recreational facilities<br>Membership dues<br>Costs attributable to strikes, rework labor, scrap and spoilage<br>Factory administrative expenses<br>Officers' salaries (production)<br>Insurance costs<br>(also items dissimilar to Categories I or II) |

FIGURE 3.1 EXAMPLES OF TYPES OF INDIRECT PRODUCTION COSTS UNDER RULES FOR FULL ABSORPTION OF OVERHEAD IN INVENTORIES

viously allowed by the IRS regulations, and provide additional guidance as to what specifically violates IRS conformity requirements.

The amended regulations allow companies to use other inventory methods and disclosures made as a supplement to or as explanation of the LIFO method, provided these additional disclosures are made in the *same* report. Some of the more significant points addressed by the regulations are summarized below:

1. The income statement included in the company's financial statements *must* be presented on a LIFO basis. No information of any kind (pertaining to inventory methods other than LIFO), *including parenthetical disclosures,* may be included on the income statement.

2. The balance sheet may include disclosures of inventory on other than a LIFO method. For example, it is now permissible to parenthetically disclose inventories on a FIFO basis.

3. Internal management reports need not conform to the LIFO method; however, the company should document that these reports are issued for internal purposes only to company personnel solely in their capacity as employees of the company.

4. Appendices and supplementary footnotes to the financial statements are not required to meet IRS conformity requirements, as long as this information is clearly identified as a supplement to or explanation of the primary presentation of LIFO appearing on the face of the income statement *and* the company's income statement is in the *same* report. Again, it is important to understand that this information may *not* appear on the face of the income statement.

5. Disclosures on other than a LIFO basis will be permitted in *other* reports, including news releases, president's letters to shareholders, reports to creditors, financial highlights, company summary of operations, and other publicity material. Again, the disclosure must be clearly identified as information supplementing or explaining the taxpayer's income statement presentation on a LIFO basis *and* the additional supplementary or explanatory information being disclosed must also be disclosed in the *same* report using the LIFO method. In other words, if a company wishes to disclose certain information on a FIFO basis, it must also disclose the same information on a LIFO basis.

6. The proposed regulations do not allow the preparation on other than a LIFO basis of income statements covering a twelve-month period other than the taxable year. This restriction includes interim reports that are combined to reflect a twelve-month period.

An additional complication is that the Treasury Department has urged Congress to repeal the LIFO conformity rule. If adopted, such a law would wipe out all of the IRS regulations relating to financial statement conformity.

Although the IRS has liberalized the conformity rules, questions arise from the standpoint of generally accepted accounting principles. Does it make any sense for a company to adopt LIFO on the premise that the LIFO method is preferable for reporting income in periods of changing prices and then also disclose what earnings would be under another method of inventory valuation? At the time of this writing, the SEC, while having issued no bulletins addressing this issue, has in practice required some companies to change their FIFO-related disclosures in instances the Commission believed the supplementary information provided was misleading.

## Specifically Required Disclosures

Because the SEC (and possibly even the FASB) may restrict companies from disclosing information other than what has been specifically required or allowed by either the SEC's or the FASB's pronouncements, it is helpful to outline the disclosure requirements under current generally accepted accounting principles. Appendix 3-1 provides examples of disclosures that are specifically required by various AICPA and SEC pronouncements. The appendix also indicates the IRS procedures and rulings that specifically permit the indicated disclosures. Until the release of the proposed regulations discussed earlier, the IRS had only approved those disclosures that were specifically required as outlined in Appendix 3-1. Now, as discussed earlier, it allows additional disclosures under certain circumstances.

## Acceptable Footnote Disclosures

Let's now review examples of acceptable footnote disclosures without regard to the additional explanatory and supplementary disclosures that may be included in accordance with the proposed IRS regulations. In the initial year of the adoption of LIFO, an example of acceptable footnote disclosure would be as follows (assuming a calendar year of 1979 for reporting purposes):

As of January 1, 1979, the company adopted the last-in, first-out (LIFO) method of determining inventory costs. The company had previously used the first-in, first-out (FIFO) method. The new method is considered to be preferable because it more closely matches current costs with current revenues in periods of price level changes: under the LIFO method, current costs are charged to cost of sales for the year. This change in method of accounting for inventories has the effect of reducing net income for the year 1979 by $_____, or $_____ per share below that which would have been reported using the company's previous inventory pricing method. For this type of accounting change, there is no cumulative effect on retained earnings as of December 31, 1978.

Had the FIFO method of inventory costing been used by the company, inventories would have been $_____ higher than reported at December 31, 1979.

In years subsequent to the year LIFO is adopted, an acceptable footnote disclosure such as the following would be used (assuming the calendar year 1980 for reporting purposes as well as a partial liquidation of the 1979 LIFO increment resulting in a material impact on 1980 cost of sales and net income):

Inventories are priced using the last-in, first-out (LIFO) method of determining inventory costs. Had the first-in, first-out (FIFO) method of inventory costing been used by the company, inventories would have been $_____ and $_____

higher than reported at December 31, 1980 and 1979, respectively. During 1980, the company achieved significant reductions in inventory levels. Since LIFO inventory quantities are carried at lower costs prevailing in prior years as compared with the cost of 1980 purchases, the liquidation of these quantities resulted in a reduction of cost of sales of approximately $_____ and an increase in net income of $_____, or $_____ per share.

As can be seen in Appendix 3-1, the disclosures pertaining to FIFO in the above footnote examples are specifically required in accordance with generally accepted accounting principles.

The principle of required disclosures is just as applicable to financial disclosure in the chief executive officer's letters to shareholders, financial highlights, summary of operations, and other sections of the company's annual report as it is to the basic financial statements. It applies to press releases and other publicity material as well.

### Financial Reporting and Market Valuation Reserves

A key consideration in financial reporting is the application of the lower-of-cost-or-market principle. As stated earlier, for tax purposes LIFO is essentially a cost method. The IRS's Rev. Rul. 77-50 discusses whether the specific cost restorations required for tax purposes (because LIFO inventories must be valued at cost) also apply to financial reporting to ensure compliance with the LIFO conformity requirements. In that ruling, the IRS concludes that a company may value LIFO inventories for financial reporting purposes at the lower of LIFO cost or market. It should be noted that Rev. Rul. 77-50 is cast in the form of a specific situation. (For example, general market reserves or excess stock reserves do not qualify under the ruling.) Application of the ruling is complex, and experienced tax advice should be sought when an attempt is made to do so.

### Impact of LIFO Liquidations

An example of financial disclosure relating to liquidations of LIFO inventory is provided above. In the following illustration of how the effects of liquidations are calculated, assume the following facts:

1. ABC Company's LIFO inventory at end of year two is:

|  | At Base Prices | Index | LIFO Cost |
|---|---|---|---|
| Base inventory | $100,000 | 1.00 | $100,000 |
| Year one increment | 40,000 | 1.10 | 44,000 |
| Year two increment | 20,000 | 1.20 | 24,000 |
|  | $160,000 |  | $168,000 |

2. ABC Company's index for year three is 1.25. Current cost is determined using average costing.

3. A $30,000 decrement at base prices occurred in year three.

To determine the impact on cost of sales arising from the liquidation in LIFO inventories, the following calculation is presented:

| | | |
|---|---|---|
| Liquidation at base prices | $30,000 | (*a*) |
| LIFO index | 1.25 | (*b*) |
| Inventory liquidation at current cost | | |
| (*a*) × (*b*) | 37,500 | |
| Inventory liquidation at LIFO cost: | | |
| Liquidation of year two increment | | |
| ($20,000 × 1.20) | (24,000) | |
| Partial liquidation of year one increment | | |
| ($10,000 × 1.10) | (11,000) | |
| Gain from liquidation included | | |
| in cost of sales | $ 2,500 | |

If current cost were defined as *earliest* or *latest* cost, the IRS, under Revenue Ruling 76-7, would require the use of earliest or latest cost, respectively, in calculating the liquidation impact. There may be alternative approaches, however, that theoretically make more sense. For example, *average costs* would be representative of the costs that would have been incurred had the liquidated stock been replenished during the year. It would be assumed that in most cases replacement stock would be acquired throughout the year rather than at the beginning or the end of the year.

Disclosure is required in the financial statements if material impacts on earnings result from a liquidation of LIFO inventory. The principle underlying LIFO is that LIFO matches current costs with current revenues. This principle is violated when reductions of inventories result in liquidation of LIFO layers. Therefore, disclosure of significant impact on income is required.

## Interim Reporting

Application of LIFO on an interim basis is difficult. A company can either perform a full LIFO calculation on an interim basis, or estimate year-end inventory cost and levels and spread the estimated annual provision on the basis of volume or cost of sales.

**Effect of Fluctuations.** When the LIFO inventory is calculated each quarter and the calculated LIFO inventory is used to compute the profit for that quarter, significant fluctuations in profit can result if there are inventory fluctuations. The results can be so peculiar that there is no way to explain income variations by quarter other than to say "That's the way it figures." If the quarterly method is used and inventory levels are lower during an interim period, some disclosure would be appropriate if it is anticipated that the reduced inventory will not be replenished by year-end. If replenishment of inventory is anticipated by year-end, an offsetting charge to earnings would be appropriate.

**Annual Estimates.** The annual method, in which year-end costs and levels are estimated, obviously involves the hazards of forecasting. To address these hazards, the following procedures would be helpful:

- Reliable techniques that accurately account for inventories on an interim FIFO basis;
- A satisfactory system that determines LIFO adjustments; and
- A good budget review and update system that permits the company to continually reevaluate the projected LIFO charge for the year.

When the annual method is used, interim reports should include a footnote that discloses the estimates inherent in interim reporting under the LIFO method. If inaccurate estimates in earlier quarters result in the need for significant adjustments in the fourth quarter, disclosure should be considered.

**Use of FIFO Earnings.** The statutory requirements for LIFO reporting relate only to annual reports. Therefore, quarterly or other reports on a non-LIFO basis that cover less than a year would not violate tax rules. Rev. Rul. 78-49 allows a company having LIFO inventory to disclose income on a FIFO basis in the interim financial statements issued for the first three quarters of the year. However, the company *cannot* disclose FIFO earnings for the fourth quarter, because the four quarterly interim financial statements combined would reflect operating results on a non-LIFO basis for the entire year.

## CONCLUSION

What does a company face when it considers LIFO? Nothing less than a formidable body of regulatory rules and economic factors that have an important bearing on the LIFO decision. The decision to elect LIFO, as well as the choice of LIFO elections, must be based on known facts as well as on expectations. Each election must be carefully considered and evaluated in the light of the company's operations and circumstances.

There is a compelling case for the use of LIFO despite its rigorous requirements and restrictions. In the current economic environment of capital shortages and high-cost financing, and in the expectation of future cost increases, management should avail itself of all means possible to conserve cash—something LIFO will do.

## SUGGESTED READING

Jannis, D. Paul, Poedtke, Carl H. Jr., and Ziegler, Ronald R. *Managing and Accounting for Inventories: Control, Income Recognition, and Tax Strategy.* New York: John Wiley and Sons, 1980.

"LIFO: Inflation Accounting and the IRS." *SEC Accounting Report*, Vol. 5 (May, 1979).

*LIFO Method of Inventory Valuation.* Internal Revenue Training Manual, No. 3127-01. Washington, D.C.: June, 1976.

## APPENDIX 3-1. EXAMPLES OF SPECIFICALLY REQUIRED DISCLOSURES UNDER THE LIFO METHOD OF INVENTORY VALUATION

| *Disclosures* | *Required By* | *Permitted by IRS By (e)* |
|---|---|---|
| I. In the Initial Year of Election, Disclosure Allowable to LIFO Only | | |
| A. Disclose effect of the change to LIFO on the results of operations of the period of change (including per share data). | APB Opinion No. 20 | Rev. Proc. 73-37, 1973-2 C.B. 501 Rev. Proc. 75-10, 1975-1 C.B. 651 |
| B. Disclose reason for the change to LIFO, including an explanation as to why LIFO constitutes an improvement in financial reporting. | APB Opinion No. 20 | Rev. Proc. 75-10, 1975-1 C.B. 651 |
| C. Disclose reason for omitting (i) accounting for the cumulative effect of the change in accounting principle as of the beginning of the year of change, and (ii) disclosure of pro forma amounts. | APB Opinion No. 20 | Rev. Proc. 75-10, 1975-1 C.B. 651 |
| D. Disclosures required for annual financial statements are also required for purposes of interim quarterly reporting. | APB Opinion No. 28 as amended by SFAS No. 3 | Rev. Proc. 75-10, 1975-1 C.B. 651 |
| E. Disclosures in the year of changes must be repeated anytime the financial statements for that year are subsequently reported. | Regulation S-X, Rule 3.09 | Rev. Proc. 75-10, 1975-1 C.B. 651 |
| F. Disclose effect of change to LIFO on reported net income, if effect is material in management analysis section of annual report. | Accounting Series Release No. 159 of the SEC | Rev. Proc. 75-10, 1975-1 C.B. 651 (*a*) |

| Disclosures | Required By | Permitted By IRS By (e) |
|---|---|---|
| II. Disclosures Allowable in All Years Where LIFO is Used | | |
| A. Disclose inventories priced under the LIFO costing method either on the face of the balance sheet or in a footnote to the financial statements. | ARB No. 43, Chapter 4 | N/A(b) |
| B. If material, disclose the excess of replacement or current costs over reported LIFO inventory either parenthetically on the balance sheet or in a footnote to the financial statements. In this connection "current costs" is defined as FIFO or average cost which results in a figure approximating current cost levels. | Regulation S-X, Rule 5-02-6(B), and Accounting Series Release No. 141 of the SEC | Rev. Rule 73-66, 1973-1 C.B. 218 Rev. Rule 75-50, 1975-1 C.B. 152 |
| C. If material, disclose the amount of income realized as a result of any liquidation of LIFO inventories either parenthetically on the face of the income statement or in a footnote to the financial statements. | Staff Accounting Bulletin No. 1 of the SEC (c) | Rev. Proc. 76-7, 1976-7 IRB 25 |
| D. Disclose operating profit by product or segment of business in a footnote to or commentary on the financial statements. | Accounting Series Release No. 159 of the SEC | Rev. Proc. 76-3, 1976-7 IRB 17 (Extension of Rev. Proc. 75-10) (a) |
| E. Disclose impact of material year-end LIFO cost estimates used in interim financial statements that subsequently prove to be erroneous. | APB Opinion No. 28 | Rev. Rul. 76-76-475, 1976 |
| F. Disclose replacement cost inventory and cost of sales data. | Accounting Series Release No. 190 of the SEC | Rev. Proc. 77-7, 1977, as extended by Rev. Proc. 77-46 and 78-39 (applies only to years ending before December 25, 1979) (a) |
| G. LIFO inventory should be valued at the lower of LIFO cost or market. | ARB No. 43, Chapter 4 | Rev. Rul. 77-50, 1977(d) |

| Disclosures | Required By | Permitted By IRS By (e) |
|---|---|---|
| H. Disclose differences between LIFO inventory for financial reporting and tax reporting purposes resulting from accounting for a business combination in accordance with generally accepted accounting principles. | APB Opinion No. 16 | Rev. Proc. 72-29 |

(a) Rev. Proc. 75-10, 1975-1 C.B. 651 gives clearance for this disclosure only to those taxpayers subject to SEC regulations. This limitation also applies to Rev. Proc. 77-7.

(b) As this disclosure pertains to the use of LIFO, no permission from the IRS is required.

(c) While the SEC has pointed out that staff accounting bulletins are not official releases of the Commission, the bulletins nevertheless carry substantial weight in determining accounting practices and necessary disclosures.

(d) Rev. Rul. 77-50 only applies in certain situations for financial reporting purposes. It does not apply to determining LIFO inventories for tax purposes.

(e) In July, 1979, the IRS proposed regulations that allow disclosure of earnings and other information on other than a LIFO basis as supplementary and explanatory information. Reference is made to the text for a discussion of these proposed regulations.

Although not specifically required by generally accepted accounting principles or the SEC, Rev. Rul. 78-49 allows a company having LIFO inventories to disclose income on a FIFO basis in interim financial statements issued for the *first three* quarters of the year. However, the company *cannot* disclose FIFO earnings for the fourth quarter because the four quarterly interim financial statements can be combined to reflect operating results on a FIFO basis for the entire year.

# 4

# Lease Capitalization Accounting

*Martin Benis*

## BACKGROUND

Although the lease of property for a stated term of years traces its development to the reign of William the Conqueror, it wasn't until after World War II that accounting for leases became a problem. Prior to this, a lease was considered to be executory in nature, conveying to the lessee the right to use the leased property for a specified period of time. Therefore, each year the lessee recorded an expense equal to the required annual payments to the lessor.

After World War II, the nature of the lease changed significantly, and it was difficult to distinguish between a lease of property and an installment purchase of property. Business enterprises began to lease property not previously subject to lease agreements—offices, factories, and construction and transportation equipment. Manufacturers entered into long-term lease agreements for products designed to the specifications of lessees. Lease terms increased so that many leases were for the economic life of the underlying property. In this new environment, the accounting profession attempted to establish standards by which a lease could be distinguished from a purchase.

In November 1976 the Financial Accounting Standards Board (FASB) adopted Statement of Financial Accounting Standards (SFAS) No. 13, *Accounting for Leases,* thereby apparently resolving a most difficult and controversial issue that had confronted the accounting profession for thirty years. The statement introduces symmetry of treatment of leases by the lessor and lessee and provides overall guidance for reporting of leases. However, since its adoption, this statement has been amended seven times and interpreted five times, and has been issued as a consolidated statement, *SFAS No. 13 as Amended and Interpreted Through May 1980.*

## SFAS 13, ACCOUNTING FOR LEASES

### Scope of Statement

SFAS 13 establishes standards of financial accounting and reporting for leases by both lessees and lessors. It defines a lease as "an agreement conveying the right to use property, plant or equipment (land and/or depreciable assets) usually for a stated period of time" (par. 1).

This definition excludes contracts exclusively for services; however, agreements that convey the right to use property are leases even if the lessor must perform substantial services in connection with the property. Specifically excluded from the definition of a lease are agreements concerning the rights to explore for or exploit natural resources and agreements licensing items such as films, plays, manuscripts, patents, and copyrights.

This statement applies to regulated enterprises in accordance with the provisions of the Addendum to APB Opinion No. 2, *Accounting for the Investment Credit.* It supersedes APB Opinion Nos. 5, 7, 27, and 31, as well as APB Opinion No. 18, paragraph 15, which pertains to related-party leases.

## Effective Dates

Although all lease transactions and lease revision agreements entered into on or after January 1, 1977, are covered by this statement immediately, leases entered into prior to this date are not covered until calendar or fiscal years beginning after December 31, 1980. Earlier application of this statement, including retroactive application to all leases no matter when executed, is encouraged but not required.

Although the FASB requires retroactive application of SFAS 13 for financial statements for calendar or fiscal years beginning after December 31, 1980, the SEC required earlier retroactive application of the statement. In ASR No. 225, issued August 31, 1977, the Commission concluded that financial statements filed with it for fiscal years ending after December 24, 1978, should reflect retroactive application of the accounting requirements of SFAS 13 unless such application caused a violation or probable future violation by 1980 of a restrictive clause in an existing loan indenture or other agreement. In such a situation, the registrant must describe the potential violation and its impact on the financial statements.

If financial statements for earlier periods are presented after retroactive application is adopted, they shall be restated to conform to SFAS 13 as follows:

- Restatements shall include the effects of leases that were in existence during the periods covered, even if those leases are no longer in existence.
- Balance sheets presented as of December 31, 1976 and thereafter, and income statements presented for periods beginning after December 31, 1976, must be restated to conform to SFAS 13.
- If balance sheets dated prior to December 31, 1976, and income statements for periods beginning before December 31, 1976, are presented, they should be restated for as many consecutive periods immediately preceding December 31, 1976, as is practicable.
- If restatement of financial statements for all prior periods presented is not practicable, the cumulative effect of retroactive application on the retained earnings at the beginning of the earliest period restated should be included in determining net income of that period. The reason for not restating prior periods presented must be disclosed. If all periods presented are restated for all leases in effect during those periods, the opening adjustment should be included in retained earnings for the earliest period presented.

## DEFINITION OF TERMS

The controller must understand certain definitions contained in SFAS 13 in order to apply the statement.

### Inception of the Lease

The *inception of the lease* is the date the lease agreement is signed, even if the property covered by the lease has not been constructed or has not been acquired by the lessor. However, if a written commitment specifically stating all principal provisions of the transaction and signed by all interested parties is executed prior to the date of the lease agreement, this date shall be considered to be the inception of the lease. The inception of the lease is the date on which the *classification* of a lease is determined.

### Bargain Purchase Option

A *bargain purchase option* is one that allows the lessee, at his option, to purchase the leased property for a price that, at the inception of the lease, appears to virtually assure transfer of the property to the lessee at the date the option becomes exercisable.

There are no rules for determining if the option price is a bargain; judgment must be used. At inception of the lease, the controller should:

- Estimate what the fair value and the economic life of the leased property will be when the option becomes exercisable. (This should be based on current prices; the effect of future inflation on the fair value of the property should be ignored.)
- Estimate if there will be an increase in the fair value of the leased property after the option date.
- Compare the total rentals paid over the lease term with the option price.

If the controller then finds that any of the following conditions exist, it is reasonable to assume that the purchase option is a bargain and will be exercised:

- The option price is less than the estimated fair value of the leased property.
- The option price is small in relation to the estimated economic life of the leased property at the option date.
- The option price equals the fair value of the leased property at the date of exercise; however, it is possible to reasonably predict subsequent increases in the fair value (ignoring future inflation).
- The option price is small in relation to the total payments made prior to its exercise.

In making his determination, the controller should consult with dealers and appraisers of the leased property as well as with his independent auditor.

## Bargain Renewal Option

*A bargain renewal option* is one that gives the lessee the option to renew the lease for a rental that, at the inception of the lease, appears to virtually assure such renewal at the date the option becomes exercisable. There are no rules for determining if a renewal option is a bargain. One indication, however, could be a rental during the renewal period significantly less than that paid during the initial lease term.

## Lease Term

The *lease term* is the fixed noncancelable term plus all periods:

- Covered by bargain renewal options;
- For which failure to renew the lease imposes a penalty sufficient to make renewal reasonably assured;
- Covered by ordinary renewal options during which a guarantee by the lessee of the lessor's debt related to the leased property is expected to be in effect;
- Covered by ordinary renewal options preceding the date at which a bargain purchase option is exercisable; and
- For which renewals or extensions of the lease are at the lessor's option.

In no case shall the lease term extend beyond the date a bargain purchase option becomes exercisable.

**Cancelability.** A cancelable lease is considered to be noncancelable if cancellation is determined by one of the following:

- Occurrence of a remote contingency;
- Permission of the lessor;
- The lessee entering into a new lease with the same lessor; or
- Payment by the lessee of a cancellation penalty sufficient to make continuation of the lease reasonably assured.

**Determining Lease Terms.** The following example illustrates the computation of a lease term. These assumptions are made:

- It is a five-year noncancelable lease.
- There are 13 ordinary renewal options of one year each.
- The lessee guaranteed the lessor's 15-year bank loan obtained to acquire the leased property.
- There is a termination penalty assuring lessee renewal for three years beyond the expiration of the loan guarantee.
- There is an option allowing the lessor to extend the lease for two years beyond the last renewal option exercised by the lessee.

The lease term is computed as follows:

| | |
|---|---|
| Noncancelable term | 5 years |
| Lease guarantee | 10 years |
| Termination penalty | 3 years |
| Lessor option | 2 years |
| Lease term | 20 years |

## Fair Value of the Leased Property

In a lease transaction, the fair value of the leased property must be determined by the lessee's controller at the inception of the lease. *Fair value* is the selling price the lessor may obtain in a contemporaneous sale of the property to an unrelated purchaser. If the lessor is a manufacturer or dealer, the fair value of the property at the inception of the lease will be the normal selling price less volume or trade discounts. If the lessor is not a manufacturer or dealer, the fair value of the property at the inception of the lease will ordinarily be its cost less volume or trade discounts. Whether or not the lessor is a manufacturer or dealer, fair value of the leased property is always determined in light of market conditions prevailing at the inception of the lease. Therefore, it could be greater or less than cost or less than normal selling price.

In many lease situations, the lessee knows the fair value of the leased property because of his negotiations with the lessor. When this is not so, the controller must estimate the fair value. He may do this in one of the following ways:

- Direct contact with the manufacturer;
- Review of catalogues, dealer price lists, and other sales literature;
- Comparison with the sales price of similar property; or
- Appraisal.

## Estimated Economic Life of the Leased Property

SFAS 13 defines the *estimated economic life of the leased property* as "the estimated remaining period during which the property is expected to be economically usable by one or more users, with normal repairs and maintenance, for the purpose for which it was intended at inception of the lease, without limitation by the lease term" (par. 5(g)). The estimated economic life is similar to the life used for depreciation purposes and is determined by considering similar factors. (See Chapter 5 for a discussion of depreciation factors.)

## Estimated Residual Value of the Leased Property

*Estimated residual* value is the estimated fair value of the leased property at the end of the lease term. It is based on an estimate of the market at the lease expiration date and is similar to salvage value of depreciable assets. (See Chapter 5.)

## Unguaranteed Residual Value

The *unguaranteed residual* value is that value of the leased property not guaranteed by the lessee, a third party related to the lessee, or a third party unrelated to the lessor. The guarantee of a residual value prior to the end of the lease is a termination penalty for purposes of determining the lease term.

## Minimum Lease Payments

The determination of the minimum lease payments is critical both to the lessor and to the lessee, for it is the present value of this amount at the inception of the lease that determines whether a capital lease exists.

From the standpoint of the *lessee,* minimum lease payments include the minimum rentals required over the lease term (exclusive of contingent rentals and executory costs), plus the payment required under a bargain purchase option. A guarantee by the lessee of the lessor's debt is excluded from the computation of minimum lease payments. If there is no bargain purchase option, the minimum lease payments include the following:

- The minimum rentals over the lease term;
- The amount of any guarantee of the residual value of the property at the expiration of the lease term by the lessee or a third party related to the lessee (a lease provision requiring the lessee to make up a residual value deficiency attributable to damage, extraordinary wear and tear, or excessive usage is not a lessee guarantee of the residual value for the purpose of determining minimum lease payments);
- The amount the lessee may be required to pay the lessor for purchase of the leased property at termination of the lease; and
- The amount of the payment the lessee must make for failure to renew or extend the lease at the expiration of the lease term. (If the failure to renew was considered in determining the lease term, and if the lease term was extended because of this provision, this payment is not included in the minimum lease payments.)

The following example illustrates the lessee's determination of the minimum lease payments. These assumptions are made:

- The leased property is machinery.
- The initial lease term is five years, during which time cancellation is prohibited.
- The rental is $3,000 a month.
- The renewal options are five one-year periods at the same terms as above.
- There is a penalty clause that states that failure to renew during the renewal period results in a penalty payment of 40 percent of the undepreciated cost of the machinery.
- The lessee guarantees $10,000 of the residual value at the end of the lease term.

Because the termination penalty is severe enough to reasonably assure lease renewal, the lease term is considered to be ten years, and the minimum lease payments are as follows:

|                          |          |
|--------------------------|----------|
| $3,000 × 120 months      | $360,000 |
| Lessee guarantee         | 10,000   |
| Minimum lease payments   | $370,000 |

If at the end of eight years the lessee has the option to purchase the machinery for $20,000 and this is considered to be a bargain purchase option, the minimum lease payments are as follows:

|                          |          |
|--------------------------|----------|
| $3,000 × 96 months       | $288,000 |
| Bargain purchase option  | 20,000   |
| Minimum lease payments   | $308,000 |

From the standpoint of the *lessor,* minimum lease payments include the payments the lessee is obligated to make or can be required to make as described above plus any guarantee of the residual value or of rental payments beyond the lease term by a third party unrelated to either the lessee or the lessor, provided such third party is financially capable of fulfilling the guarantee.

## Contingent Rentals

*Contingent rentals* are increases or decreases in lease payments resulting from changes occurring subsequent to the inception of the lease in factors on which lease payments are based. These factors include, among others, prime interest rate, sales volume, real estate taxes, and either the consumer price index or the wholesale price index. Contingent rentals are not included in the computation of minimum lease payments.

When a lease agreement is entered into prior to construction of the leased property and the lease contains a provision to escalate minimum lease payments for increases in construction or acquisition costs of the leased property, such increases are not contingent rentals.

## Interest Rates

The interest rate is important, since this is the rate used to determine the present value of the minimum lease payments. The lower this rate, the higher the present value of the minimum lease payments. The two rates of importance are the *interest rate implicit in the lease*—the lessor's rate—and the *lessee's incremental borrowing rate.*

**Rate Implicit in the Lease.** The interest rate implicit in the lease is the rate that, when applied to the minimum lease payments, exclusive of executory costs, plus the unguaranteed residual value at the beginning of the lease term, discounts such amounts to a sum equal to the fair value of the leased property, less any investment tax credits retained by the lessor, at inception of the lease.

The controller can determine the interest rate implicit in the lease either by trial and error or by using a computer program. The following illustration is a simplified way to determine the implicit rate.

These assumptions are made:

- The leased property is machinery.
- The fair value is $111,111.
- The unguaranteed residual value is $3,200.
- The investment tax credit retained by lessor is 10 percent, or $11,111.
- The lease term is ten years.
- The rental is $15,000 per year, payable in advance.

The interest rate implicit in the lease is determined through the following calculations:

|  | *Annual Rate* | |
|---|---|---|
|  | *10½%* | *11%* |
| Present value of: | | |
| Minimum lease payments | | |
| $15,000 × 6.65 | $ 99,750 | |
| $15,000 × 6.54 | | $ 98,100 |
| Unguaranteed residual value | | |
| at end of tenth year | | |
| $3,200 × .37 | 1,184 | |
| $3,200 × .35 | | 1,120 |
| Present value of minimum lease | | |
| payments and unguaranteed residual | | |
| value | $100,934 | $ 99,220 |
| | | |
| Fair value of property | $111,111 | |
| Less investment tax credit retained | | |
| by lessor | 11,111 | |
| Net value | $100,000 | |

Since the fair value of the property less the investment tax credit ($100,000) falls between $100,934 and $99,220, the interest rate is between 10.5 and 11 percent. Through a process of trial and error, an implicit rate of 10.75 percent is determined. This is proved as follows:

Present value of:
    Minimum lease payments
        $15,000 × 6.59                               $ 98,850
    Unguaranteed residual value at the
    end of the tenth year
        $3,200 × .36                                    1,152
Present value of minimum lease
    payments and unguaranteed
    residual value                                  $100,002

If the controller has difficulty determining the implicit interest rate, he should seek the aid of his auditors, who may have a computer program for determining the rate or will know of service companies that have such programs available for a fee.

**Lessee's Incremental Borrowing Rate.** The lessee's incremental rate is the rate that, at the inception of the lease, the lessee would have incurred to borrow, over a period similar to the lease term, the funds necessary to purchase the leased asset. The controller may obtain an incremental borrowing rate from the following sources, among others:

- Vendor's price quotations;
- Debt incurred for purchases of similar property that will be repaid over a period equal to the lease term;
- Opinions of either commercial or investment bankers; and
- Market prices of lessee's publicly traded debt.

If the rates obtained vary, the controller will have to make a judgment as to which rate to use. If the lessee company does not wish to capitalize the lease, it should use the highest rate, since this will result in the lowest present value of the minimum lease payments.

## CRITERIA FOR CLASSIFYING LEASES

### Classification of Leases by Lessees

The controller must classify leases at their inception date as either *capital leases* or *operating leases*. A capital lease transfers substantially all benefits and risks of ownership of the leased property. A lease not classified as a capital lease is an operating lease. In order to be classified as a capital lease, a lease must, at inception, meet any *one* of the following criteria:

1. Ownership of the property is transferred to the lessee by the end of the lease term.
2. The lease contains a bargain purchase option.

3. The lease term is at least 75 percent of the economic life of the leased property, unless the lease term begins within the last 25 percent of the total estimated economic life of the leased property. Thus, if an asset, when new, had an estimated economic life of 20 years, it would not meet this criterion after its 15th year.

4. The present value of the minimum lease payments, exclusive of executory costs, at inception of the lease is at least 90 percent of the fair value of the leased property to the lessor less any related investment tax credit retained by the lessor. (Executory costs are the normal costs of operating and maintaining an asset. They include insurance, property taxes, and maintenance and repair services.) This criterion is also subject to the 25 percent constraint noted in (3) above. The controller should compute the present value of the minimum lease payments using his incremental borrowing rate, unless he can determine the rate implicit in the lease and such rate is less than the incremental borrowing rate.

Note that the first two criteria pertain to ownership and use, whereas the last two pertain only to use. This distinction is important when computing depreciation and determining the classification of land subject to a lease.

**The Transfer of Ownership Criteria.** A lease may explicitly state that at the conclusion of the lease term the property will belong to the lessee. In this situation, it is not difficult to determine if the first criterion has been met.

The determination of whether a purchase option is a bargain is a difficult one. This problem has already been discussed in a previous section. If the lease meets either of the first two criteria, the controller will account for it as a purchase of the property.

**The Transfer of Use Criteria.** The third and fourth criteria transfer the right to use the property to the lessee, since at the end of the lease term the leased property reverts to the lessor. In applying the 75 percent criterion, the estimated *economic life* of the property must be determined. Some of the factors to be considered in estimating the economic life are:

- Anticipated technological developments;
- Anticipated maintenance and repair policy; and
- Anticipated pattern and circumstances of use.

Determining the present value of the minimum lease payments, exclusive of executory costs, requires an estimation of the lease term if bargain purchase or bargain renewal options are included in the lease. In addition, the following estimates must be made:

- The lessee's incremental borrowing rate;
- The interest rate implicit in the lease;
- The fair value of the leased property at inception of the lease; and
- Executory costs and profit thereon.

If executory costs are not known, they must be estimated. The controller should estimate executory costs by:

1. Consulting his insurance broker for insurance costs;
2. Reviewing existing maintenance contracts on similar property;
3. Obtaining tax rates from local taxing authorities; and
4. Reviewing his experience with similar assets.

## Classification of Leases by Lessors

A lessor's controller must classify leases at the inception of the lease as one of the following:

- *Sales-type leases.* These leases give a manufacturer's or a dealer's profit or loss to the lessor and are normally used when manufacturers or dealers market their products through leasing.
- *Direct financing leases.* These leases do not contain a manufacturer's or dealer's profit or loss; they merely contain an interest factor for the lessor's use of his money.
- *Leveraged leases.* These leases are defined and explained in a subsequent section.
- *Operating leases.* These are leases not classified as sales-type, direct financing, or leveraged leases.

If at the inception of the lease it meets one of the four criteria for classification as a capital lease by the lessee, the controller must classifiy it as a sales-type or direct financing lease if it also meets *both* of the following criteria:

1. Collectibility of the minimum lease payments is reasonably predictable; and
2. No important uncertainties surround the amount of unreimbursable costs yet to be incurred by the lessor under the lease.

In order for a lessor's controller to classify a lease as a sales-type or direct financing lease when the lessee has classified it as a capital lease, he must resolve certain uncertainties surrounding a normal sale.

**The Resolution of Uncertainties.** The first uncertainty to be resolved by the controller pertains to the collectibility of the minimum lease payments. In order for a lease to be classified as a sales-type or direct financing lease, collection of these payments need not be assured; they must only be predictable. This means that classification as a sales-type or direct financing lease is not precluded if a reasonable estimate can be made of uncollectible rents.

The fact that the lessor must still incur costs subsequent to inception of the lease does not preclude classification as a sales-type or direct financing lease if these subsequent costs can be reasonably estimated. Important uncertainties would include a lessor guarantee protecting the lessee from property obsolescence or a performance guarantee more extensive than usual.

If property covered by the lease is yet to be constructed or has not been acquired by the lessor at inception of the lease, cost uncertainties do not include costs necessary to complete construction or to acquire the leased asset. The determination of cost uncertainties is made on the date construction is completed or the property is acquired by the lessor.

## ACCOUNTING AND REPORTING

### Procedures by Lessees

A lease classified as a capital lease by the lessee is recorded at inception as an asset and a liability at an amount equal to the present value of the minimum lease payments during the lease term, exclusive of that portion of the payments representing executory costs. If the present value of the minimum lease payments, exclusive of executory costs, exceeds the fair value of the leased property at the inception of the lease, the amount to be recorded as an asset and a liability shall be the fair value. Under these circumstances, the interest used to determine the present value must be increased.

**Amortization of Asset Recorded Under a Capital Lease.** With the exceptions noted in the section dealing with leases involving land, assets recorded under capital leases shall be amortized as follows:

1. If the lease meets either of the first two criteria for a capital lease—that is, the transfer of ownership criteria—the asset is amortized in a manner consistent with the lessee's normal depreciation policy or method over the estimated economic life of the leased asset.
2. If the lease meets the third or fourth criteria for a capital lease—that is, the transfer of the right to use criteria—the asset is amortized in a manner consistent with the lessee's normal depreciation policy over the term of the lease.

**Allocation of Lease Payments.** During the lease term, each minimum lease payment is allocated between interest expense and a reduction of the liability so as to produce a constant periodic rate of interest. The effective interest method, as described below, should be used in recording the minimum lease payments. Contingent rentals are charged to rent expense in the period incurred.

**Termination of Capital Lease Prior to Expiration.** If a capital lease is terminated prior to the expiration of the lease term, the account balances of the asset and the liability must be removed. A gain or a loss on termination is recognized to the extent of any difference in these account balances.

**Accounting for Operating Leases.** Under an operating lease, the controller reports the lease payments as rental expense on a straight-line basis. However, if another systematic and rational basis is more representative of the time pattern in which use benefit is derived from the leased property, this basis should be used.

The following example illustrates how a lessee accounts for an operating lease. These assumptions are made:

- The leased property is office space.
- The rent is $1,000 a month.
- The lease is an operating lease.
- The lease term is five years, with no rent for the first six months.
- The monthly charge to rent expense is $900.

The monthly rent expense was determined as follows:

Total rent to be paid: 54 months × $1,000 = $54,000
$54,000 ÷ 60 months = $900

Thus, during the first six months of the lease, the controller will accrue $900 a month rent. For the seventh and subsequent months, cash will be reduced by $1,000, rent expense will be charged for $900, and the $100 difference will reduce the accrual of the first six months.

### Accounting for Capital Leases

The following example illustrates how a controller accounts for a capital lease. These assumptions are made:

- The leased property is machinery.
- The fair value of leased property at the inception of the lease is $230,000.
- The residual value guaranteed by the lessee at the end of the lease is $1,000.
- The lease period is five years.
- The estimated economic life of the machinery is seven years.
- The lease terms are an annual rental of $55,000, which includes $5,000 for insurance and maintenance, payable on the first day of each year (at the end of lease term, machinery reverts to lessor).
- The lessee's incremental borrowing rate is 10 percent.

The following computations were made to determine present value at the inception of the lease:

| | |
|---|---|
| Present value of an annuity in advance of $50,000 ($55,000 — $5,000) for five years at 10 percent a year: $50,000 × 4.17 | $ 208,500 |
| Present value of $1,000 (residual guarantee) at the end of five years at 10 percent a year: $1,000 × .620 | 620 |
| Present value of minimum lease payments | $ 209,120 |

The above lease does not meet the first two criteria—the transfer of ownership criteria—for classification as a capital lease. It does not meet the third criterion—lease term equal to at least 75 percent of the estimated economic life of the leased property. However, it does meet the fourth criterion inasmuch as the present value of the minimum lease payments—$209,120—exceeds 90 percent of the fair value of the leased property—90 percent × $230,000 = $207,000—at the inception of the lease. Therefore, at the inception of the lease, the controller will make the following journal entries:

|  | Dr. | Cr. |
|---|---|---|
| Capitalized lease—machinery | $209,120 | |
|     Obligation under capital lease | | $209,120 |
| To record lease transaction at inception of lease. | | |
| | | |
| Obligation under capital lease | $ 50,000 | |
| Insurance and maintenance | 5,000 | |
|     Cash | | $ 55,000 |
| To record first year's rent payable at inception of lease. | | |

At inception of the lease, the controller should develop an amortization table similar to the one illustrated below:

| Beginning of Year | Total Payment | Interest | Principal | Loan Obligation at End of Year |
|---|---|---|---|---|
| 1 | $50,000 | $ -0- | $50,000 | $159,120 |
| 2 | 50,000 | 15,912 | 34,088 | 125,032 |
| 3 | 50,000 | 12,503 | 37,497 | 87,535 |
| 4 | 50,000 | 8,754 | 41,246 | 46,289 |
| 5 | 50,000 | 4,711 | 45,289 | 1,000 |

Interest for the fifth year is computed as follows:

| | | |
|---|---|---|
| Lease obligation at the end of the fourth year | | $ 46,289 |
| Payment on the first day of the fifth year | $ 50,000 | |
| Less interest at 10 percent | 4,629 | |
| Balance applied to principal | | 45,371 |
| Lease obligation after payment | | $ 918 |
| Interest at 10 percent adjusted for rounding | | $ 82 |
| Interest included in $50,000 payment | | 4,629 |
| Total interest | | $ 4,711 |

At the end of the first year, the controller must make the following entries:

|  | Dr. | Cr. |
|---|---|---|
| Interest expense | $15,912 | |
|     Obligation under capital lease | | $15,912 |
| To record interest expense for year one payable on first day of year two. | | |
| | | |
| Amortization—capital lease | 41,824 | |
|     Accumulated amortization— capital lease | | 41,824 |
| To record amortization of asset under capital lease over the lease term of five years. | | |

In this illustration, amortization was computed on the total present value of the minimum lease payments, or $209,120. The assumption is that there is no residual value for the asset at the expiration of the lease. Thus, at the end of the fifth year the leased asset will have a book value of zero; however, the obligation under capital lease will have a balance of $1,000. This balance represents the guaranteed residual value of the leased asset, which the lessee must pay to the lessor if the asset has no value at that date. (It it has value, the $1,000 would be reduced, possibly to zero.) If the residual value is zero, the final entry will be as follows (if the residual value is $1,000 or more, the credit would be to amortization expense):

|  | Dr. | Cr. |
|---|---|---|
| Obligation under capital lease | $ 1,000 | |
|     Cash | | $ 1,000 |
| To pay to the lessor the guaranteed residual value of the leased asset. | | |

**Disclosure Requirements for Operating Leases.** For operating leases having an initial or remaining noncancelable lease term in excess of one year, the following disclosures are required in the notes to financial statements:

1. Future minimum rental payments required as of the date of the latest balance sheet, in the aggregate and for each of the five succeeding fiscal years; and
2. Total future minimum rentals to be received under noncancelable subleases as of the date of the latest balance sheet presented.

For all operating leases, the following disclosures are required in the notes to financial statements of the lessee:

1. Rental expense for each period for which an income statement is presented;
2. Minimum rentals and contingent rentals incurred and sublease rentals earned; and
3. A general description of the leasing arrangements, including but not limited to
   a. The basis on which contingent rentals are determined;

   b. The existence and the terms of renewal or purchase options and escalation clauses; and

   c. Restrictions imposed by lease agreements.

**Disclosure Requirements for Capital Leases.** For all capital leases, the following information must be disclosed either in the lessee's financial statements or in the notes to financial statements:

1. The gross amount of assets reported under capital leases as of the date of each balance sheet presented; these assets should be reported by major classes according to nature or function;

2. Future minimum lease payments as of the date of the latest balance sheet presented, in the aggregate and for each of the five succeeding fiscal years; from the total lease payments, separate deductions should be taken for executory costs and interest, thus reducing the minimum lease payments to their present value after executory costs;

3. The total of the minimum sublease rentals to be received in the future under noncancelable subleases as of the date of the latest balance sheet presented;

4. Total contingent rentals incurred for each period for which an income statement is presented;

5. A general description of the leasing arrangements including, but not limited to

   a. The basis on which contingent rentals are determined;

   b. The existence and the terms of renewal or purchase options and escalation clauses; and

   c. Restrictions imposed by lease agreements.

Figure 4.1 is an example of a financial statement footnote on leases. The capitalized leases and the related obligations may be (1) disclosed separately on the face of the balance sheet or (2) combined with property, plant, and equipment and long-term debt provided the required disclosures are shown in the footnotes. Figure 4.2 illustrates a note disclosure of required lease information. The related debt structure was shown on the face of the balance sheet.

## Procedures by Lessors

Lessors classify leases as either sales-type leases, direct financing leases, operating leases, or leveraged leases. Each lease requires its own unique accounting and reporting.

**Accounting for Sales-Type Leases.** A sales-type lease is accounted for by the controller at the inception of the lease in the following manner:

1. The minimum lease payments, exclusive of executory costs, plus the unguaranteed residual value of the asset accruing to the benefit of the lessor is recorded as the gross investments in the lease. (No residual value is assumed to accrue to the

**Debt Structure**

At December 31, 1979 and 1978 debt consisted of:

| | 1979 | 1978 |
|---|---|---|
| Notes payable to banks: | | |
| Domestic | $ 5,500,000 | $ 8,300,000 |
| Foreign | 3,370,000 | 2,183,000 |
| Total | $ 8,870,000 | $10,483,000 |

Long-term debt
11⅛ % senior notes due December 30, 1990 payable in quarterly installments of $162,500 beginning March 30, 1981 — $ 6,500,000 $ 6,500,000

Term notes payable to banks, due June 30, 1988, variable interest rates based on prime (16% and 12½ % at December 31, 1979 and 1978 respectively), payable in quarterly installments of $375,000 beginning September 30, 1980 — 12,000,000 8,000,000

Term notes payable to banks, variable interest rates based on prime (19% at December 31, 1979 and 9% to 14¾ % at December 31, 1978), payable in varying installments through May 15, 1982 — 803,000 1,342,000

**Leases**

The company leases certain property, plant and equipment. Rent expense during the years ended December 31, 1979 and 1978 was $2,134,000 and $1,758,000, respectively.

Annual future minimum lease payments as of December 31, 1979 are as follows:

| Year Ending December 31 | Operating Leases | Capital Leases |
|---|---|---|
| 1980 | $1,018,000 | $ 279,000 |
| 1981 | 842,000 | 260,000 |
| 1982 | 614,000 | 224,000 |
| 1983 | 492,000 | 198,000 |
| 1984 | 411,000 | 152,000 |
| 1985-1989 | 1,468,000 | 655,000 |
| 1990-1992 | 122,000 | 292,000 |
| Total minimum lease payments | $4,967,000 | $2,060,000 |
| Less interest and executory costs | | 853,000 |
| Present value of minimum lease payments | | $1,207,000 |

| | | |
|---|---|---|
| 9% and 6¼% mortgages payable in varying installments through January 1, 1993 | 983,000 | 1,309,000 |
| 8% notes payable | — | 660,000 |
| 7½% subordinated notes payable quarterly with final payment of $324,000 on July 1, 1980 | 405,000 | 567,000 |
| Foreign note payable, variable interest rate based on either the Interbank or Euromarket rate (9% and 5¼% at December 31, 1979 and 1978 respectively) due November 15, 1982 | 5,799,000 | 5,510,000 |
| Capitalized lease obligations payable through March 1992 | 1,207,000 | 1,337,000 |
| Long-term debt | 27,697,000 | 25,225,000 |
| Less current portion | 1,646,000 | 1,641,000 |
| Due after one year | $26,051,000 | $23,584,000 |

Certain of the leases also require the company to pay property taxes and insurance and are subject to escalation.

The following is an analysis of capital leases included in property, plant and equipment at December 31:

| | 1979 | 1978 |
|---|---|---|
| Buildings and improvements | $1,028,000 | $1,028,000 |
| Machinery and equipment | 562,000 | 830,000 |
| | 1,590,000 | 1,858,000 |
| Less accumulated amortization | 649,000 | 749,000 |
| Net capital leases | $ 941,000 | $1,109,000 |

FIGURE 4.1  CAPITALIZED LEASES AND RELATED OBLIGATIONS

## LEASES

Fuqua and its subsidiaries are lessees of freight terminals, theatres, manufacturing facilities, and other properties under numerous noncancelable leases.

Capitalized lease property, which is included in property, plant and equipment is as follows (in thousands):

|  | December 31, | |
|  | 1979 | 1978 |
| --- | --- | --- |
| Land | $ 435 | $ 435 |
| Buildings and improvements | 21,200 | 22,244 |
| Terminals and improvements— Interstate Motor Freight | 13,546 | 14,026 |
| Machinery and equipment | 13,657 | 11,153 |
| Less: allowances for depreciation | (18,096) | (15,529) |
|  | $ 30,742 | $ 32,329 |

Future minimum payments for the capital leases and non-cancelable operating leases with initial or remaining terms of one year or more are summarized as follows (in thousands):

| Year Ending December 31, | Total Commitments | Operating Leases | Capital Leases |
| --- | --- | --- | --- |
| 1980 | $ 15,403 | $ 9,569 | $ 5,834 |
| 1981 | 12,960 | 7,536 | 5,424 |
| 1982 | 11,424 | 6,341 | 5,083 |
| 1983 | 9,907 | 5,369 | 4,538 |
| 1984 | 8,557 | 4,470 | 4,087 |
| Thereafter | 76,528 | 30,262 | 46,266 |
| Total minimum lease payments | $134,779 | $63,547 | $71,232 |
| Executory cost | | | (78) |
| Amounts representing interest | | | (31,743) |
| Present value of net minimum lease payments | | | $39,411 |

Rental expense for all operating leases was $14,182,000 and $11,818,000 for the years ended December 31, 1979 and 1978, respectively.

Certain noncancelable leases have renewal options for up to 10 years. Related real estate taxes, insurance and maintenance expenses are obligations of Fuqua. Certain leases have escalation clauses which provide for increases in annual rentals in certain circumstances.

FIGURE 4.2 LEASE DISCLOSURE FOOTNOTE

benefit of the lessor if the lease either transfers ownership of the asset to the lessee or contains a bargain purchase option.)

2. The difference between the gross investment in the lease and the sum of the present value of its two components—minimum lease payments, exclusive of executory costs, and unguaranteed residual value—is recorded as unearned income.

   a. The present value is determined by using the interest rate implicit in the lease.

   b. The present value as determined is considered to be the net investment in the lease.

3. The unearned income is amortized to income over the life of the lease in a manner that will produce a constant periodic rate of return on the net investment in the lease.

4. In a classified balance sheet, the net investment in the lease is reported as current and noncurrent assets as appropriate.

5. Contingent rentals are credited to income as they are earned.

6. The present value of the minimum lease payments only, exclusive of executory costs, is recorded as the sales price of the leased asset.

7. The cost or carrying amount of the leased property less the present value of the unguaranteed residual value is charged against income in the period in which the lease transaction occurs.

8. Initial direct costs of the lessor are deducted from income in the period in which the lease transaction occurs. Initial direct costs are those costs directly associated with negotiating and consummating completed lease transactions. They include the following:

   a. Commissions, legal fees, costs of credit investigations, and costs of preparing and processing documents for new leases acquired.

   b. That portion of salespersons' compensation (other than commissions) and the compensation of other employees applicable to time spent negotiating and consummating completed lease transactions.

If a sales-type lease is terminated prior to the expiration of the lease term, the net investment (gross investment minus unamortized unearned interest) is removed from the accounts; the leased asset is reinstated at the lower of its original cost, present fair value, or present carrying amount; and the net adjustment is charged to income.

The following example illustrates how a lessor's controller accounts for a sales-type lease. These assumptions are made:

- The leased property is machinery.
- The normal selling price is $209,120.
- The costs to manufacture are $100,000.
- The commissions and other costs incurred in obtaining the lease are $5,000.
- The unguaranteed residual value of the machinery is $1,000.
- The lease period is five years.
- The estimated economic life of the machinery is seven years.
- The lease terms are an annual rental of $55,000, which includes $5,000 for insur-

ance and maintenance, payable on the first day of each year (at the end of lease term, machinery reverts to lessor).

- The rate implicit in the lease is 10 percent.
- The collectibility of lease payments is reasonably predictable, and no additional costs have to be incurred.

The lessor's gross investment is computed as follows:

| | |
|---|---|
| Minimum lease payments, net of executory costs—$50,000 × 5 years | $250,000 |
| Unguaranteed residual value of lease property at end of lease term | 1,000 |
| Gross investment in leased asset | $251,000 |

The initial present value of the gross investment is computed as follows:

| | |
|---|---|
| Present value of an annuity in advance of $50,000 for 5 years at 10 percent a year: $50,000 × 4.17 | $208,500 |
| Present value of $1,000 at the end of 5 years at 10 percent a year: $1,000 × .620 | 620 |
| Present value of gross investment | $209,120 |

The journal entries at the inception of the lease are as follows:

| | Dr. | Cr. |
|---|---|---|
| Gross investment in leased asset | $251,000 | |
| Cost of sales ($100,000 minus present value of unguaranteed residual, $620) | 99,380 | |
| Sales (present value of minimum lease payments net of executory costs) | | $208,500 |
| Property held for lease (cost to manufacture machinery) | | 100,000 |
| Unearned interest income (gross investment, $251,000 minus net investment, $209,120) | | 41,880 |
| | | |
| Selling expenses | 5,000 | |
| Cash | | 5,000 |
| | | |
| Cash | 55,000 | |
| Gross investment in leased asset | | 50,000 |
| Insurance and maintenance | | 5,000 |
| To record receipt of first year's rent. | | |

The following table shows the computation of the amortization of the annual lease payments:

| Year | Present Value of Net Investment at Beginning of Year | Annual Payments | Amortization of Unearned Interest Income | Reduction of Net Investment | Present Value of Net Investment at End of Year |
|------|------|------|------|------|------|
| 1 | $209,120 | $ 50,000 | $15,912 | $ 34,088 | $175,032 |
| 2 | 175,032 | 50,000 | 12,503 | 37,497 | 137,535 |
| 3 | 137,535 | 50,000 | 8,754 | 41,246 | 96,289 |
| 4 | 96,289 | 50,000 | 4,629 | 45,371 | 50,918 |
| 5 | 50,000 | 50,000 | 82[1] | 49,918 | 1,000 |
| TOTALS | | $250,000 | $41,880 | $208,120 | |

The present value of the net investment at the end of the fifth year—$1,000—represents the unguaranteed estimated residual value.

At the end of the first year, the following journal entry must be made:

| | Dr. | Cr. |
|---|---|---|
| Unearned interest income | $15,912 | |
| Interest income | | $15,912 |

To record interest income, which was determined as follows:

| | |
|---|---|
| Initial present value | $209,120 |
| Initial payment | 50,000 |
| Balance on which interest at 10 percent is computed | $159,120 |

**Accounting for Direct Financing Leases.** A direct financing lease is generally accounted for at the inception of the lease in the same manner as a sales-type lease except that a sale is not recorded. However, unearned income equal to the amount of initial direct costs charged against income is recognized as income. The remaining unearned income is amortized to income over the lease term so as to produce a constant periodic rate of return on the net investment in the lease.

The following example illustrates how a controller accounts for a direct financing lease. These assumptions are made:

- The leased property is machinery.
- The cost (and fair value) of the leased property is $209,120.

---

[1] Difference due to rounding.

- Commissions and other costs incurred in obtaining the lease are $5,000.
- The unguaranteed residual value of the machinery is $1,000.
- The lease period is five years.
- The estimated economic life of the machinery is seven years.
- The lease terms are an annual rental of $55,000, which includes $5,000 for insurance and maintenance, payable on the first day of each year (at the end of the lease term, machinery reverts to lessor).
- The collectibility of lease payments is reasonably predictable, and no additional costs have to be incurred.

The lessor's gross investment is computed as follows:

| | |
|---|---|
| Minimum lease payments, net of executory costs: | |
| $50,000 × 5 years | $250,000 |
| Unguaranteed residual value of leased property at end of lease term | 1,000 |
| Gross investment in leased asset | $251,000 |

The initial net investment in the lease is the cost of the leased property, $209,120, and the unearned income at inception of the lease is $41,880 ($251,000-$209,120). The journal entries at inception of the lease are as follows:

| | Dr. | Cr. |
|---|---|---|
| Gross investment in leased asset | $251,000 | |
| Property held for lease | | $209,120 |
| Unearned interest income | | 41,880 |
| | | |
| Selling expenses | 5,000 | |
| Cash | | 5,000 |
| | | |
| Unearned interest income | 5,000 | |
| Interest income | | 5,000 |
| To recognize unearned income (to the extent of the initial direct costs) as income. | | |
| | | |
| Cash | 55,000 | |
| Gross investment in leased asset | | 50,000 |
| Insurance and maintenance | | 5,000 |
| To record receipt of first year's rent. | | |

At the inception of the lease, the controller should develop a lease amortization table as follows:

| | | |
|---|---|---|
| Initial net investment | $ 209,120 |
| Initial direct costs | 5,000 |
| Net investment as adjusted | $ 214,120 |

| Year | Annual Rental Payment | Interest Income | Reduction of Net Investment | Net Investment at End of Year |
|---|---|---|---|---|
| 1 | $ 50,000 | $ 14,098 | $ 35,902 | $ 178,218 |
| 2 | 50,000 | 11,014 | 38,986 | 139,232 |
| 3 | 50,000 | 7,665 | 42,335 | 96,897 |
| 4 | 50,000 | 4,028 | 45,972 | 50,925 |
| 5 | 50,000 | 75[2] | 49,925 | 1,000 |
| Totals | $250,000 | $ 36,880 | $213,120 | |

The net investment at the end of the fifth year represents the unguaranteed estimated residual value.

In order to amortize the unearned income so as to produce a constant periodic rate of return on the net investment as adjusted for the initial direct costs, the rate of 8.59 percent was used. This rate can only be determined by trial and error or by using a computer program. (If the controller has difficulty determining this rate, he should seek the aid of his auditors, who generally will have a computer program for determining the rate or know where to obtain one.)

Interest for the first year is computed as follows:

| | |
|---|---|
| Net investment as adjusted | $ 214,120 |
| Rental payment | 50,000 |
| Balance | $ 164,120 |
| 8.59% of $164,120 | $ 14,098 |

**Accounting for Operating Leases.** From the standpoint of the lessor, all leases that do not meet at least one of the criteria for capital leases and both of the criteria for sales-type or direct financing leases are operating leases. A controller should account for an operating lease as follows:

1. The cost of the leased property should be included with or near property, plant, and equipment in the balance sheet.
2. The property should be depreciated using the lessor's normal depreciation policy.
3. Rental income should be reported on a straight-line basis unless another systematic and rational basis is more representative of the time pattern in which use benefit

---

[2] Difference due to rounding.

from the leased property is diminished, in which case that basis should be used. (This requirement is similar to the requirement for reporting operating leases by the lessee.)

4. Material initial direct costs are deferred and allocated over the lease term in proportion to the recognition of rental income.

**Disclosure Requirements for Operating Leases.**  When leasing (exclusive of leveraged leasing [see below]) is a significant part of the lessor's business activities, the controller is responsible for including the following information with respect to operating leases in the lessor's financial statements or the notes thereto:

1. The cost of property on lease, or held for leasing, by major classes of property according to nature or function and the related amount of accumulated depreciation as of the date of the latest balance sheet presented;

2. Minimum future rentals on noncancelable leases as of the latest balance sheet presented, in the aggregate and for each of the five succeeding years;

3. Total contingent rentals included in income for each period for which an income statement is presented; and

4. A general description of leasing arrangements.

**Disclosure Requirements for Sales-Type and Direct Financing Leases.**  When leasing (exclusive of leveraged leasing [see below]) is a significant part of the lessor's business, the controller is responsible for disclosing the following information with respect to sales-type and direct financing leases in the lessor's financial statements or the notes thereto:

1. The components of the net investment as of the date of each balance sheet, presented as follows:
   a. Future minimum rentals, net of executory costs,
   b. Unguaranteed residual values, and
   c. Unearned interest income;

2. Future minimum lease payments to be received for each of the five succeeding fiscal years as of the date of the latest balance sheet presented;

3. Total contingent rentals included in income for each period for which an income statement is presented;

4. For direct financing leases only, the amount of unearned interest income included in income to offset initial direct costs charged against income for each period for which an income statement is presented; and

5. A general description of leasing arrangements.

Figure 4.3 is an example of the required disclosures by a lessor in the notes to its financial statements.

**Accounting for Leveraged Leases.**  A leveraged lease is a lease transaction involving three parties—the lessors (or owner-participants), the lenders (or loan participants), and the lessee. Leveraged leases are used primarily to provide financing of large capital equipment projects with economic lives of ten to twenty-five years. It essentially involves a trade-off between rental payments and tax benefits and residual values. From the standpoint of the lessee, a leveraged lease is accounted for and reported as any other capital lease described previously in this chapter.

A leveraged lease is a unique type of lease that is set up with the advice and counsel of accountants, attorneys, tax specialists, and financial advisers. When the lessor is involved in such a lease, the controller should consult immediately with his independent auditor.

## LEASES INVOLVING REAL ESTATE

From the standpoint of the lessee, leases involving land, land and building, or part of a building, present problems not normally found in leases involving other property.

### Leases Involving Land Only

A lease solely involving land is accounted for as a capital lease by the lessee only if the lease transfers ownership or contains a bargain purchase option; otherwise, it is accounted for as an operating lease. Thus, the classification of a lease for land only is not determined by using either the 75-percent or the 90-percent rule.

If the lease is a capital lease, as defined above, and the collectibility and cost uncertainty tests are also met, the lessor must account for the lease as a sales-type or direct financing lease, whichever is appropriate. If the capital lease does not meet the additional two tests or if the lease is an operating lease for the lessee, the controller must report the lease as an operating lease.

### Leases Involving Land and Building

A lease involving land and building is accounted for according to which criterion for classification it meets. Under certain circumstances in a lease for land and building, it is possible to amortize land costs.

**Transfer of Ownership or Bargain Purchase Option.** If a lease involves both land and building and transfers ownership or contains a bargain purchase option, the land and building are separately capitalized by the lessee, and the building is amortized in a manner consistent with the lessee's normal depreciation policy for owned assets. The present value of the minimum lease payments is allocated between the land and building in proportion to their fair values at inception of the lease. Fair values may be determined by:

- Recent sales in the area of similar land or a similar building;

## Note 3.  DESCRIPTION OF EQUIPMENT LEASE TRANSACTIONS

The Company's equipment lease transactions involve the leasing, management and
   financing of principally railroad equipment, IBM/3000 and 370 series computer systems and computer related peripheral equipment. Lease terms are
   generally for periods of from 2 to 15½ years.

The Company's equipment lease transactions generally involve the purchase of
   equipment for committed leases and the arrangement of non-recourse loans to
   provide for the payment of the purchase price of the equipment, or the acquisition of equipment subject to existing leases and prior financing. The
   equipment lease transactions are consummated by the sale of title to the
   equipment to a third party generally pursuant to arrangements for the leaseback of the equipment to the Company. A substantial portion of the revenue
   which the Company earns from equipment lease transactions is in the form of
   the future rental proceeds to be derived from the re-lease of the equipment
   (residual value) during the leaseback period and will not be received until
   future periods. In the case of equipment lease underwriting transactions, the
   Company includes in revenues the present value of the estimated future proceeds. (See Notes 4, 6, 7 and 11 for additional information regarding equipment lease transactions.)

## Note 4.  NET INVESTMENT IN LEASE RECEIVABLES AND RESIDUAL VALUES

The following lists the components of the net investment in lease receivables and
   residual values at December 31, 1978 and 1977 (000 omitted):

|  | 1978 | | | 1977 | | |
| --- | --- | --- | --- | --- | --- | --- |
|  | Finance leases | Lease under-writing trans-actions | Total | Finance leases | Lease under-writing trans-actions | Total |
| Minimum lease receivables (no executory costs) | $13,317 | $ — | $13,317 | $25,719 | $ — | $25,719 |
| Estimated residual value of leased equipment (original equipment cost to the Company of $180,834 as of December 31, 1978 and $136,709 as of December 31, 1977) .............. | 2,691 | 32,940 | 35,631 | 5,292 | 20,174 | 25,466 |
| Less unearned income .............. | ( 1,276) | (14,893) | (16,169) | ( 4,976) | ( 9,870) | (14,846) |
|  | $14,732 | $18,047 | 32,779 | $26,035 | $10,304 | 36,339 |
| Less provision for losses .............. |  |  | ( 2,866) |  |  | ( 3,107) |
| Net investment in lease receivables and residual values .............. |  |  | $29,913 |  |  | $33,232 |

Finance lease receivables at December 31, 1978 mature as follows (000 omitted):

| | |
| --- | --- |
| 1979 ......................................................................... | $ 6,812 |
| 1980 ......................................................................... | 2,171 |
| 1981 ......................................................................... | 1,689 |
| 1982 ......................................................................... | 1,092 |
| 1983 ......................................................................... | 713 |
| 1984 and thereafter ................................................ | 840 |
| | $13,317 |

FIGURE 4.3   NOTES TO THE FINANCIAL STATEMENTS
SHOWING REQUIRED LESSOR DISCLOSURES FOR
SALES-TYPE AND DIRECT FINANCING LEASES

The estimated residual value maturities and the portion of such value recorded as revenue from lease underwriting transactions at December 31, 1978 are as follows (000 omitted):

|  | Estimated residual value maturities | Portion recorded as revenue through December 31, 1978 |
|---|---|---|
| 1979 | $   726 | $   668 |
| 1980 | 1,320 | 1,903 |
| 1981 | 1,973 | 1,471 |
| 1982 | 2,851 | 1,914 |
| 1983 | 4,428 | 2,675 |
| 1984 | 6,521 | 3,547 |
| 1985 | 7,444 | 3,645 |
| 1986 and thereafter | 7,677 | 3,034 |
|  | $32,940 | $18,047 |

The above schedule of maturities does not assume that secondary and tertiary leases could be used as collateral for future borrowings. Such borrowings would accelerate cash proceeds from the residual values.

## Note 6.  EQUIPMENT HELD UNDER OPERATING LEASES

At December 31, 1978 and 1977, equipment on operating leases consisted of the following (000 omitted):

|  | 1978 | 1977 |
|---|---|---|
| Equipment cost (data processing equipment) | $35,378 | $14,245 |
| Accumulated depreciation | (3,323) | (298) |
| Net book value | $32,055 | $13,947 |

In connection with certain operating lease transactions, the Company has sold title to the underlying equipment (subject to existing leases and indebtedness) to third parties receiving cash payments and retaining a substantial portion of the estimated residual value of the leased equipment. The proceeds received from the third party, deferred fee income, which is included in accounts payable and other liabilities, are amortized to income over the useful life of the equipment. Fee income deferred in connection with operating lease transactions was $3,545,000 in 1978 and $2,203,000 in 1977.

The following is a schedule of aggregate future noncancellable rentals on operating leases at December 31, 1978 (000 omitted):

| 1979 | $ 7,411 |
|---|---|
| 1980 | 6,085 |
| 1981 | 2,176 |
| 1982 | 639 |
| 1983 | 89 |
|  | $16,400 |

The Company's estimates of rental proceeds to be derived upon the re-lease of equipment in excess of amounts required to meet scheduled payments of related indebtedness are as follows (000 omitted):

| 1979 | $   164 |
|---|---|
| 1980 | 408 |
| 1981 | 869 |
| 1982 | 1,348 |
| 1983 | 3,197 |
| 1984 | 3,283 |
| 1985 | 2,667 |
| 1986 and thereafter | 2,579 |
|  | $14,515 |

- Recent tax assessments, which may not provide fair value but which do indicate proportions for land and building; and
- Appraisal.

If the lease is separately capitalized and the collectibility and cost uncertainty tests are also met, the lessor's controller should account for the transaction as the lease of a single unit. It is either a sales-type lease or a direct financing lease, whichever is appropriate.

**Application of Third and Fourth Criteria When Land Is Less Than 25 Percent of the Value.** If a lease does not transfer ownership or contain a bargain purchase option, and if the fair value of the land is less than 25 percent of the total fair value of the land and building at inception of the lease, the lessee and the lessor must consider the land and building as a single unit for purposes of applying the 75-percent test and the 90-percent test. For purposes of applying the 75-percent test, the estimated economic life of the building is considered to be the estimated economic life of the unit.

If either the 75-percent test or the 90-percent test is met, the lessee must capitalize the land and building as a single unit and amortize it over the term of the lease. In this situation, both land and buildings will be amortized.

If either the 75-percent test or the 90-percent test is met and the collectibility and cost uncertainty tests are also met, the lessor must account for the lease as either a sales-type or direct financing lease, as appropriate.

**Application of Third and Fourth Criteria When Land Is 25 Percent or More of the Value.** If the lease does not transfer ownership or contain a bargain purchase option, and if the fair value of the land is 25 percent or more of the total fair value of the leased property at inception of the lease, both the lessee and the lessor must consider the land and building separately for purposes of applying the 75-percent and the 90-percent tests. The minimum lease payments, net of executory costs, are separated by both the lessee and the lessor by determining the fair value of the land and applying the lessee's incremental borrowing rate to it to determine the amount of rent applicable to the land element. The balance is attributed to the building element.

If the building element of the lease meets the 75-percent or 90-percent test, the lessee must classify this element as a capital lease and amortize it over the term of the lease. The land element of the lease is accounted for separately as an operating lease.

If the building element of the lease meets either the 90-percent test or the 75-percent test and the collectibility and cost uncertainty tests are also met, the lessor's controller must classify this element as a sales-type lease or a direct financing lease, as appropriate. The land element of the lease is accounted for as an operating lease.

**Special Rule for Lessor.** In the situations specified above pertaining to the lessor, the controller may not classify the lease as a sales-type lease unless the lease terms meet the conditions necessary for full and immediate profit recognition as specified in the AICPA industry accounting guide, *Accounting for Profit Recognition on Sales of Real Estate*. These conditions relate to the adequacy of the buyer's initial and continuing investment in the property acquired and the seller's continued investment in the property sold. Depending on the nature of the property, the guide specifies initial payments by the buyer of from 5 percent to 25 percent of the sales value of the property. This requirement essentially eliminates the sales-type lease classification from leases of land and land and building. When this requirement is not met, the lessor must account for the lease as an operating lease. A controller engaged in a lease transaction involving land or land and building should consult the AICPA industry accounting guide requirements and his independent auditor.

### Lease Involving Part of a Building

In situations in which the leased property is part of a building—for example, office space—and its cost and fair value are objectively determinable, both the lessee and the lessor must classify and account for the lease in the same manner as a lease involving both land and building.

If the fair value of the leased property is objectively determinable, the lessee must classify and account for the lease in the same manner as a lease involving land and building. If the fair value of the leased property is not objectively determinable, the controller should capitalize the lease only if the lease term is equal to 75 percent or more of the estimated economic life of the building in which the leased premises are located. Therefore, a lessee will be required to capitalize a lease for office space if the lease term is at least 75 percent of the remaining economic life of the building and the lease was not entered into during the last 25 percent of the economic life of the building.

If either the cost or the fair value of the leased property is not objectively determinable, the controller should account for the lease as an operating lease.

### Accounting for Sale-Leaseback Transactions

Except in circumstances noted below, a sale and leaseback are considered one transaction in which the terms of the sale and the terms of the lease are inseparable. Seller-lessees must clarify leases arising from these transactions as capital leases or operating leases based on the criteria for these classifications. Gain or loss on the sale must be deferred and amortized in proportion to the amortization of the leased asset if a capital lease, or in proportion to rental payments over the lease term if an operating lease. However, a loss must be recognized immediately up to the amount of the difference between the carrying value of the property and its fair value at the time of the transaction.

The following example illustrates the accounting by the seller-lessee in a sale-leaseback transaction. These assumptions are made:

• The book value of the property is $50,000.

- The fair value of the property is $45,000.
- The sale price is $40,000.
- Of the $10,000 loss ($50,000 minus $40,000), the seller-lessee will immediately recognize $5,000 and defer and amortize the other $5,000 over the life of the lease.

The seller-lessee journal entry at inception of the lease is as follows:

|  | Dr. | Cr. |
|---|---|---|
| Cash | $40,000 | |
| Loss on Sale of Property | 5,000 | |
| Deferred Loss on Sale of Property | 5,000 | |
| Property | | $50,000 |

If the property had been sold for $60,000, the $10,000 gain would have been deferred and amortized over the life of the lease.

The purchaser-lessor must record the transaction as a purchase and a direct financing lease if the appropriate lessor criteria are met; otherwise, it must record the transaction as a purchase and an operating lease.

**Lessee Exceptions to the General Rule.** If the seller-lessee relinquishes the right to substantially all the remaining use of the property sold, retaining only a minor portion, the sale and leaseback must be accounted for as separate transactions, and gain or loss on the sale will be recognized immediately. A *minor portion* is defined as one in which the present value of the leaseback payments is 10 percent or less of the fair value of the asset sold.

If the seller-lessee retains more than a minor part but less than substantially all of the use of the property through the leaseback and realizes a profit on the sale in excess of the present value of the minimum lease payments for an operating lease, or the recorded amount of the asset for a capital lease, that excess must be recognized as income at the date of the sale.

## RELATED-PARTY TRANSACTIONS

SFAS 13 defines related parties as follows:

- A parent company and its subsidiaries;
- An owner company and its joint ventures and partnerships; or
- An investor and its investees.

For purposes of this statement, in order for the parties to be considered related, the parent company, the owner company, or the investor must have the ability to exercise significant influence over operating and financial policies of the related party. Significant influence is indicated in the following situations:

- Representation on the board of directors;
- Participation in policy-making processes,
- Material intercompany transactions;
- Interchange of managerial personnel;
- Technological dependency;
- Stock ownership of 20 percent or more;
- Guarantees of indebtedness;
- Extensions of credit; and
- Two or more entities under common ownership.

### Classification of and Accounting for Leases Between Related Parties

In the separate financial statements of related parties, leases between the parties are classified in the same manner as similar leases between unrelated parties. The criteria used to determine lease classification are the same for leases between related parties as they are for leases between unrelated parties. However, in lease transactions in which the lease terms have been significantly affected by the related-party situation, classification of and accounting for the lease should be determined by the controller based on its economic substance, not its legal form.

The nature and extent of leasing transactions between related parties must be disclosed in the notes to financial statements.

**Intercompany Profits and Losses.** In consolidated financial statements or in financial statements of an investor reporting its investment in an investee under the equity method, intercompany profits and losses from leasing transactions must be eliminated.

**Leasing Subsidiaries.** A subsidiary whose principal business activity is leasing property to its parent or other affiliated companies must be consolidated with its parent. The equity method of accounting for this type of subsidiary is not adequate for the fair presentation of financial position, results of operations, and changes in financial position.

## SUGGESTED READING

Alderman, J. Kenneth, and Alderman, C. Wayne. "Accounting for Leases." *Journal of Accountancy*, Vol. 147 (June, 1979).

Baker, C. Richard. "Leasing and the Setting of Accounting Standards: Mapping the Labyrinth." *Journal of Accounting, Auditing and Finance*, Vol. 3, No. 3 (Spring, 1980).

Deming, John R. "Analysis of FASB No. 13." *Financial Executive*, Vol. 46 (March, 1978), pp. 46-51.

Financial Accounting Standards Board. *Accounting for Leases*. Statement of Financial Accounting Standards No. 13 as amended and interpreted through May, 1980 (incorporating Statements 13, 17, 22, 23, 26, 27, 28, and 29 and Interpretations 19, 21, 23, 24, 26, and 27). Stamford, Conn.: 1980.

Meigs, Walter B., Msoich, A. N., and Johnson, Charles E. "Accounting for Leases," *Intermediate Accounting*. 4th ed. New York: 1978.

# 5

# Depreciation Methods

*Max Block and Richard R. Rosen*

## INTRODUCTION

Depreciation as an accounting concept has not been difficult for accountants to grasp. The difficulties arise partly because other professionals, such as engineers or economists, have a different definition of depreciation, and partly because certain complex methods of depreciation have come into use. The official definition used by the American Institute of CPAs in its *Professional Standards of Accounting* is "the allocation of the depreciable amount of an asset over its estimated useful life. Depreciation for the accounting period is charged to income directly or indirectly." To an economist, depreciation is a decrease in market value; to an engineer, depreciation is a decrease in physical efficiency or the deterioration of capital equipment or a building. The controller uses the accounting concept of depreciation, which is a process of allocation of cost, not valuation or physical evaluation.

### Management Considerations

The nature of the depreciation provision affects management in various ways. If depreciation is a substantial portion of product or service cost, it affects pricing, it affects operating results, it becomes part of the matrix for operational decisions, and it affects the amount of income taxes that the firm must pay. The depreciation factor also has significant impact on the financial statements issued to credit grantors and other third parties. Since audited statements prepared for the third-party users must adhere to generally accepted accounting principles, the choice of a depreciation method must conform to the accepted standards.

### The Cash-Flow Myth

There is a persistent but erroneous myth, believed by some investment analysts, investors, and even many businessmen, that depreciation contributes to cash flow. Controllers should avoid this trap when they review depreciation methods with management. Cash flow is derived only from revenues, borrowings, and equity investments. The confusion arises because most statements that measure or project cash flow start with a figure for net earnings to which is added the periodic depreciation charge. This type of presentation perpetuates the myth that depreciation increases cash flow. Depreciation is a charge to earnings that did not require a cash outlay in the current period. A reduction in prepaid expenses or an increase in accrued expenses are also charges to earnings not requiring a cash outlay, yet no one thinks of these items as sources of cash.

Controllers should advise management that increasing or decreasing depreciation will have no effect on cash flow, except to the extent that it affects income taxes for a profitable company.

## DEPRECIABLE ASSETS AND COST BASIS

### Depreciable Assets

Depreciable assets should meet these tests:

- They should have a limited useful economic life of more than one year; and
- They should be held for use in the production or supply of goods and services for sale or rental to others or for administrative purposes.

Examples of common depreciable assets are buildings, machinery, office equipment, autos and trucks, and leasehold improvements. (Although a building is a prototypical depreciable asset, a building purchased for definite later demolition should not be depreciated. It is a part of land cost.)

Other types of depreciable assets are leased property (capitalized), inactive and standby equipment, emergency facilities, large tools and parts, returnable containers, and equipment used for rental purposes. Such items require special consideration because of their unique nature and use.

Land, having an indefinite life, is not a depreciable asset. However, land improvements, though added to land cost, may be depreciable (e.g., a fence or irrigation installation). In a unique situation in which land in time will be unusable and abandoned, a periodic cost write-off would be justifiable.

### Use of the Cost Basis

Accounting standards prescribe the cost basis method of accounting for external reporting purposes, but this method is not necessarily applicable for management purposes or for internal cost accounting and reporting purposes.

It is a simple matter to determine the cost of a new typewriter. But the cost of a new plant or warehouse for depreciation purposes sometimes cannot readily be established, particularly if the company is doing some or all of the construction. Even if the building is built by an independent contractor on a lump-sum basis, management must make sure that the asset's depreciable basis includes taxes prior to completion, legal fees, architect's fee, surveys, and other items directly related to the cost of the building.

Incremental costs and all expenses necessary to put an asset in place, ready for use, should be added to the cost. To illustrate, suppose a company purchases a ten-ton punch press. The price of the press is set, but there will probably be large additional costs for haulage, construction of a concrete foundation, setting up of the machine, electrical wiring, pollution controls, noise abatement and safety installations, and other such items. The time cost of company personnel used is not capitalized, as a rule. If considerable time is spent in work that might otherwise be contracted out, an exception might be made.

Firms should adhere to the policy that asset cost should be kept as "lean" as possible. Expenditures should not be capitalized unless they are necessary, material, and clearly related to the production or purchase of a depreciable asset.

Capitalization used as an expedient measure to reduce current expense and increase current income for external financial reporting purposes may boomerang in the future.

An exception to the cost basis arises when a company undergoes a quasi reorganization or reorganizes under a bankruptcy law. Also, when a company's total assets are purchased for a lump-sum price, the price must be allocated by the buyer among the various assets acquired. A new cost based on appraisal or relative values is an accepted procedure for such transactions.

If the owner of a business contributes personally owned property in exchange for shares of stock, the property should be independently appraised to set an objective cost for accounting purposes. However, for income tax calculations, other considerations apply.

### Fully Depreciated Assets in Use

There are two major schools of thought on how to deal with fully depreciated assets that are still in use. One takes the simple approach that the assets and the related reserves should be written off and no further depreciation charge be made, unless they are part of a group and covered by a composite useful life and rate. The other school prefers that both the assets and the reserves be retained, because the balance sheet thus discloses the total cost of the assets in use and a record of their existence is maintained.

Some controllers go even further. They continue the depreciation as long as the asset is used, to more correctly state manufacturing costs. To avoid an income distortion, they credit a depreciation variance or adjustment account for the excess depreciation. Internal cost records simply continue to apply the existing depreciation charge.

### Standby and Idle Equipment

Standby equipment should be treated as equipment in use. The treatment of idle equipment, on the other hand, depends on why it is not being used. If it is scheduled for disposal or is being held for a trade-in, its cost should be written off or reduced to realizable value. If it is idle because of a business lag, it should be treated as if it were in use.

## DEPRECIATION POLICIES

Depreciation policies should be formalized through management decisions and should be reviewed periodically and revised when necessary. Revisions should be made only when conditions change or estimates must be corrected, not just for management's convenience. However, consistency does not imply inflexibility.

A company may change its depreciation policy (i.e., from the straight-line method to an accelerated method or vice versa) if the new method more correctly reflects the company's operations. When a change is made in accounting policy, all the criteria used to determine the need for the new policy should be documented and reviewed with the company's outside accountants, who must agree that the new policy is preferable in the circumstances. If the accountants do not agree, they may qualify their opinion on the company's financial statements.

## Adoption of Standards

Policy sets rules, but problems arise in their application. Specifying in advance the size and type of expenditures that should be expensed and the salvage values that may be ignored substantially reduces day-to-day decisions. In complex situations, management should confer with outside sources such as suppliers, appraisers, engineers, and trade associations regarding estimated useful lives. The firm's outside accountants should also be consulted.

The following standards will guide controllers in developing a workable depreciation policy:

- It should meet the tests of objectivity, usefulness, and ease of record keeping.
- It should make possible a systematic and rational allocation of the asset cost.
- It should be applied consistently from period to period, except for changes that are clearly warranted.
- It should produce reliable data for product and service costs and for internal and external company financial statements.
- It should match expense and related revenue, insofar as such determination is feasible.
- It should be useful to management in its decision making.

In a business climate in which income tax considerations play a dominant role, tax minimization is another standard that influences depreciation policy. However, tax considerations should not distort financial planning. The depreciation methods that yield the most favorable results for income tax return purposes may not necessarily coincide with good management policy and need not be used for financial statements.

Applying standards of reasonableness to depreciation decisions is not a simple matter. With the exception of the asset's original acquisition cost, the criteria used may represent estimates, opinions, viewpoints, and even speculations. Thus judgment must always be applied. On the one hand, management must be willing to make necessary policy revisions as needed. But it is equally true that management should not change its depreciation policy, including the various methods used, except for valid reasons, such as material changes in operating conditions, technological developments, or changes in manufacturing processes.

### Determining the Depreciation Provision

**Initial Considerations.** A number of considerations enter into the determination of the ultimate depreciation provision. Ordinarily, they are:

- What is the depreciable asset?
- What is its useful economic life?
- What is the total cost of the asset, taking into account expenditures for moving and installing the asset?
- Will there be a material salvage value when the asset is replaced or sold? If so, how much, as presently estimated?
- What policy should be adopted for small items—should they be expensed or capitalized? What are the standards?
- What allowance should be made for normal obsolescence?
- Does the company have a replacement policy? (For example, a rental-car dealer may replace cars at a fixed age.)
- Is interest on investment in property to be added to the cost for depreciation purposes? (See SFAS 34.)
- Is depreciation to be coordinated with maintenance, and if so, how?
- Will depreciation be higher in early years of asset use?
- Will depreciation policy differ for income tax purposes and financial reporting purposes?

**Subsequent Considerations.** In the course of business operations, many factors can affect the basic depreciation assumptions and necessitate changes in the computations or methods. Some events can usually be foreseen, and policy should be established to deal with them. Controllers should be alert to the following events and must determine their impact on the depreciation provision:

- A premature replacement or disposition;
- A significant change in remaining useful life;
- A significant change in salvage value;
- Extensive repairs and alterations;
- Equipment transferred to idle or standby status;
- Inadequate maintenance or inexpert and careless handling of machinery and property;
- A speedup or slowdown in production rates; and
- New products and processes.

Controllers should revise depreciation methods or computations only after careful consideration and a review with the outside accountants of all factors necessitating a change.

**Excessive or Inadequate Depreciation.** There may be visible evidence that depreciation policy is unreasonable or inadequate. For example, if the accumulated depreciation is very high in relation to the cost, it may indicate either excessive rates or deferred modernization. On the other hand, if the accumulation is low in relation to the cost and the expired life of the asset, it may signal an inadequate depreciation provision. Large profits and losses on the sale of used equipment may also indicate faults in the depreciation policy. Such excesses merit investigation.

**Depreciation as a Cost Element.** In the case of capital-intensive companies, depreciation is usually (1) a cost of production or service or (2) administrative and marketing overhead. It becomes directly part of product cost when absorption accounting is used, and part of overhead when variable or direct costing is used. However, cost accounting should serve management in decision making (e.g., pricing policies) and in supervision of operations. It need not conform to generally accepted accounting principles. The cost system should be tailored to meet the unique requirements of the product, processing, and other operating aspects that will best serve management.

## Determining Rates

When management selects a depreciation method, it must examine a multiplicity of sometimes contradictory factors and considerations. The discussion that follows includes only the most obvious factors.

**Useful Life.** The depreciation rate must bear a significant relationship to the useful economic service period and the estimated realizable salvage value of the asset at the end of its life term. (An exception will be noted later.)

**Obsolescence.** Obsolescence affects almost all assets, especially those subject to the vagaries of changing style (e.g., automobiles) and those for which continuing research and development create new and more efficient models. *Normal* obsolescence can usually be taken into account in determining an asset's useful life. *Abnormal* obsolescence, when it occurs, may require management to reduce the net asset balance to its realizable value in further production or through a sale.

**Tax Implications.** Accelerated depreciation techniques, applicable only to time-based methods, are almost always tax motivated. Judgments about acceleration cannot be made without knowledge of the income tax status of the taxpayer. (Some managements use acceleration techniques in an attempt to cope with inflation and escalating replacement costs. This approach is discussed later in the chapter.)

## Depreciation Methods

There are two major categories of depreciation methods:

- Depreciation as a function of time; and
- Depreciation as a function of use or depletion.

**Time Method.** Depreciation based on an estimated useful economic life, regardless of how intensively the asset is used, is the concept underlying the time depreciation method. (All buildings, for example, are depreciated over time.) Time methods are subdivided into *straight-line* and *accelerated* methods.

**Use or Depletion Method.** The use or depletion method is applicable to natural resources (coal, oil, minerals, etc.) and certain types of equipment (such as aircraft) whose economic life is more related to use than to elapsed time. The cost of an asset is expensed over its estimated units of production, hours of use, or some similar use factor. Estimating the total expected units of production or other use factor is more difficult than estimating useful economic life.

## SELECTING DEPRECIATION METHODS

The selection of the most appropriate method—the one that may yield the most useful financial information—requires an understanding of the available alternatives and the effect of each on the firm's income. Often a company may use several methods if the nature of its assets and their use warrant it. Thus, it may be entirely proper for a company to use the straight-line method, an accelerated method, and a units-produced method for different classes of assets and operations in computing its periodic depreciation.

There are five generally accepted techniques of depreciation: straight-line, declining-balance, sum-of-the-years'-digits, units-of-production or hours-of-service, and annuity or sinking fund methods. (The last method is seldom used and is not discussed here.)

Depreciation may be applied to individual assets, a machine for example, or to a production line of machines as a group. Other such unit-group relationships exist. The various techniques here cited, with some exceptions, are applicable to either units or groups of assets.

### Straight-Line Method

The straight-line method is the method most commonly used, because of its relative simplicity. The cost of an asset, less estimated salvage value, if any, is expensed in equal amounts over the estimated life of the asset. A simple example illustrates the straight-line method. Suppose a truck costs $30,000 and has a useful economic life of four years. Its salvage value is $3,000. The annual depreciation provision is $6,750 (one fourth of $27,000).

A criticism of the straight-line method is that depreciation of certain assets may occur at a faster rate in the early years of use rather than evenly throughout the asset's life. From a value viewpoint, this is often true, especially in the case of products that are subject to frequent style changes, such as the automobile. However, from a cost allocation viewpoint, if an asset is to be used equally throughout its life, the straight-line method would be appropriate.

When it is known that an asset depreciates more in the early years than in later years, a modified straight-line method incorporating an acceleration feature may be used. Some authorities recommend this rule of thumb:

- Write off one half of the cost in the first third of the asset life; or
- Write off two thirds of the cost in the first half of its life.

Thus, in the case of a truck for which one half of the cost is to be written off over the first third of its six-year life (two years), the following depreciation would be charged:

| | | |
|---|---|---|
| Total to be written off | | $27,000 |
| In each of the first two years | $6,750 | |
| Total for the two years | | 13,500 |
| In each of the next four years | 3,375 | |
| Total for the four years | | 13,500 |
| Total depreciation | | $27,000 |

## Accelerated Depreciation Methods

The objective of the tax privilege of allowing a deduction (where not otherwise warranted) for depreciation at a rate faster than the straight-line method is to help industry build working capital and productivity, and thereby enable it to cope with inflation and higher replacement costs. It must be borne in mind, however, that the company using these methods is, in effect, deferring lower depreciation deductions and higher income taxes to future years.

Accelerated depreciation methods have a clear advantage over the straight-line method for tax purposes. Tax payments may be postponed for a considerable period, and working capital increased because of the larger deductions in the early years. However, care must be taken that the methods used conform to the Internal Revenue Code and related regulations.

When different methods are used for tax purposes and financial accounting, a dual accounting system must be created for income tax purposes that requires extra time and effort for the exercise of adequate controls. Moreover, account must be kept of the disparity between the book tax expense and the tax paid. The difference is recorded in a deferred income tax account, a noncurrent liability under normal circumstances.

Accelerated depreciation takes the form of declining-balance methods and the sum-of-the-years'-digits method. Declining-balance methods can vary from 125 to 200 percent of the straight-line percentage. The most popular method is the 200 percent or double-declining-balance method, which is the maximum allowed for tax purposes. This is the method that will be discussed, but the principle applies to any lower percentage method.

**Double-Declining-Balance Method.** For tax purposes, only new assets having a life of three years or more and new residential rental property are eligible. Other types of new real estate are generally eligible to use 150 percent declining-balance depreciation. (See I.R.C. § 167(b).) Note that a declining-balance method always leaves an undepreciated balance; it cannot reach zero. The balance might possibly be regarded as the salvage value (if reasonable), particularly if the asset is not a substantial item.

The Internal Revenue Code permits a shift from the declining-balance method to the straight-line method when the depreciation deduction is reduced to an amount that is less than it would be under the straight-line method. If the salvage value is zero and the asset life is an odd number (nine, eleven), the year of change will be half the life plus one and a half years; if the asset life is an even number, the year of change will be half the life plus two. If the asset has a salvage value, the year of change will be a later year.

The following table demonstrates the results of using the double-declining-balance method without the shift to the straight-line method for an asset that cost $5,000 and has an estimated life of ten years, a double rate of twenty percent, and no salvage value:

| Year | Cost Balance | Annual Depreciation |
|------|------|------|
| 1 | $5,000 | $1,000 |
| 2 | 4,000 | 800 |
| 3 | 3,200 | 640 |
| 4-10 | | 2,024 |
| 10 | 536 | |

The balance of $536 could either be considered salvage value or written off as additional depreciation in the tenth year.

In a shift to the straight-line method for an asset that cost $2,000 and has an estimated life of ten years and a rate of twenty percent, the accounting is as follows (this also illustrates the formula for computing the year of change—10 ÷ 2 = 5 + 2 = 7, the year to switch to straight-line):

| Year | Cost Balance | Annual Depreciation |
|------|------|------|
| 1 | $2,000 | $400 |
| 2 | 1,600 | 320 |
| 3 | 1,280 | 256 |
| 4 | 1,024 | 205 |
| 5 | 819 | 164 |
| 6 | 655 | 131 |
| 7 (switch to straight-line) | 524 | 131 |
| 8 | 393 | 131 |
| 9 | 262 | 131 |
| 10 | 131 | 131 |
| | Total depreciation | $2,000 |

Salvage value is not considered in computing depreciation under the declining-balance method, but the asset should not be depreciated below a reasonable salvage value.

**Sum-of-the-Years'-Digits Method.** This method accelerates the depreciation deduction in the early years of an asset's life by using a fraction, the numerator of which is the remaining life of the asset at the beginning of the year, the denominator the sum of the life in years. The formula for the sum of the years for an asset with a life of $n$ years is $n(1 + n) \div 2$. For an asset with a five-year life the formula would be $n = \dfrac{5 (1 + 5)}{2}$, or 15.

The following example illustrates how the sum-of-the-years'-digits method works (the asset cost $5,000 and has a life of five years and a salvage value of $500):

| Year | Rate[1] | Annual Depreciation |
|------|---------|---------------------|
| 1 | 5/15 | $1,500 |
| 2 | 4/15 | $1,200 |
| 3 | 3/15 | $ 900 |
| 4 | 2/15 | $ 600 |
| 5 | 1/15 | $ 300 |
| 15 | Total depreciation | $4,500 |

The sum-of-the-years'-digits method can be used for income tax purposes on the same basis and for the same types of assets as the double-declining-balance method (see above).

The two accelerated depreciation methods are popular because of their tax advantages, but they are not widely used for financial reporting or internal management reports.

## Comparison of Primary Methods

Now that we have examined the operation of the three primary depreciation methods, it should be helpful to compare the annual and cumulative depreciation under the straight-line, double-declining-balance, and sum-of-the-years'-digits methods for the same asset, an asset whose newly acquired asset cost was $100,000 and that has an estimated life of ten years and zero salvage value.

---

[1] The fractions represent the remaining life.

| Year | Straight-line 10% | | 200%-declining-balance 20% | | Sum-of-the-years'-digits | |
|------|-------------------|----------|----------------------------|----------|--------------------------|----------|
| | Annual charge | Cumulative | Annual charge | Cumulative | Annual charge | Cumulative |
| 1 | $10,000 | $ 10,000 | $20,000 | $ 20,000 | $18,182 | $ 18,182 |
| 2 | 10,000 | 20,000 | 16,000 | 36,000 | 16,364 | 34,546 |
| 3 | 10,000 | 30,000 | 12,800 | 48,800 | 14,545 | 49,091 |
| 4 | 10,000 | 40,000 | 10,240 | 59,040 | 12,727 | 61,818 |
| 5 | 10,000 | 50,000 | 8,192 | 67,232 | 10,909 | 72,727 |
| 6 | 10,000 | 60,000 | 6,554 | 73,786 | 9,091 | 81,818 |
| 7 | 10,000 | 70,000 | 6,554 | 80,340 | 7,273 | 89,091 |
| 8 | 10,000 | 80,000 | 6,554 | 86,894 | 5,455 | 94,546 |
| 9 | 10,000 | 90,000 | 6,553 | 93,447 | 3,636 | 98,182 |
| 10 | 10,000 | 100,000 | 6,553 | 100,000 | 1,818 | 100,000 |

The double-declining-balance method was switched to straight-line in the seventh year in order to depreciate the entire cost in the ten years. If this had not been done, there would have been a balance of $10,738 remaining at the end of the period.

## Production and Service Methods

In certain industries there is a direct relationship between usage and physical wear. The useful lives of the assets, therefore, can be estimated within reasonable limits in units of output, hours of service, or mileage.

To fix the periodic depreciation charge, it is necessary to first estimate the total asset life in terms of units that can be produced, hours of use, or mileage. The total units, hours, or mileage for the period are then applied to the total life, and the percentage so derived is applied to the depreciable cost to determine the annual expense. Another way to apply this method is to divide the total estimated units into the total asset cost to get a unit cost. The units, hours, or mileage for the period are then multiplied by the unit cost to arrive at the depreciation for the period. However, it is not always practical to compute plant or equipment life in terms of units produced or hours of service.

The units-produced method is used in the extractive industries, such as coal, oil and gas, gravel and sand pits. The hours-of-use or mileage method is suitable for the transportation industry, e.g., heavy trucks.

It may be useful in certain circumstances to use a combination of units-produced and straight-line methods. In this way, part of the cost is written off over the useful life, the balance on a units-produced basis. This method could be used in a mining operation, where the mechanical equipment is written off on a straight-line basis (but within the mine life period) and the coal deposits (depletion) are written off on a tons-extracted basis.

## GROUP DEPRECIATION

This method consolidates the depreciation of many units into one determination. It is possible to treat all of a factory's installations as one unit. This offers a considerable accounting economy. However, the determination of useful life and salvage can be challenging, and unit replacement and retirement problems can also be perplexing.

Some items, such as small parts, dies, tools, and molds, logically fit into groups, particularly if the items are numerous and are not very costly.

### Categories of Group Assets

Group assets fall into these categories:

- A homogeneous group of assets purchased within a year (e.g., a battery of ten printing presses purchased in one year);
- A homogeneous group of assets whenever purchased;
- All assets purchased within a year (a *vintage group*); and
- All assets (total plant, geographical division, etc.).

Groups also are characterized as *open end,* in which additions are permitted, and *closed end,* in which they are not.

When nonhomogeneous assets are treated as a group, the term *composite rate* is substituted for *group rate.* Composite depreciation is used for a total plant, for all the varied equipment in a plant or department, or for any other desired, practical grouping of nonhomogeneous items.

The determination of the periodic provision for homogeneous units is essentially similar to that for a single unit as previously described. Management must establish the depreciable cost base, salvage value, useful life, and normal obsolescence factor and from this information determine the periodic depreciation charge. A group account should be maintained for the asset and for the accumulated depreciation.

The following illustration demonstrates the depreciation determination for a group of 50 items whose components have a varying life. The cost of the items was $600,000, and they have a salvage value of $30,000, leaving a depreciable cost of $570,000. The useful life of the items is as follows:

| Subgroups | Useful Life | Total Service Years |
|-----------|-------------|---------------------|
| 20 items | 3 years | 60 |
| 20 items | 4 years | 80 |
| 10 items | 5 years | 50 |
| | | 190 |

The total of 190 service years gives a depreciation per service year of $3,000. On an annual basis the depreciation provision would be computed as follows:

| Year | Items in Use (Service Years) | Depreciation |
|------|------------------------------|--------------|
| 1 | 50 | $150,000 |
| 2 | 50 | 150,000 |
| 3 | 50 | 150,000 |
| 4 | 30 | 90,000 |
| 5 | 10 | 30,000 |
|   | 190 | $570,000 |

## Retirement of a Group Unit

The treatment of the retirement of a group unit depends on whether the retirement is *normal*, that is, close to group estimated life, or *abnormal*. Gain or loss on normal retirements is generally not recognized; instead, the asset balance is charged against the group accumulated depreciation, and realized salvage is credited to that account. For abnormal retirements, the group rate should be recalculated. Gain or loss may be recorded for significant early retirements.

## Composite Depreciation

A composite group of assets may be dissimilar in form but must be related in function. Thus, every piece of equipment in a shoe plant, however varied, serves the same function—to help make, pack, ship, and account for shoes. A single depreciation rate, however complex its determination, could be established for the total entity. As an alternative, segments of the plant could be treated as groups, the building, the machinery, the office equipment, for example.

Assets may also be grouped geographically for depreciation purposes. A company having several scattered factories or other facilities could deal with each separately. Rates at each location may vary because of local conditions.

If assets having dissimilar lives are combined in a group, it may be difficult to apply salvage values. Here is one way to handle it:

| Cost or Other Basis | Estimated Useful Life | Annual Depreciation Before 10% Salvage |
|---------------------|-----------------------|-----------------------------------------|
| $10,000 | 15 years | $ 667 |
| 10,000 | 5 years | 2,000 |
| $20,000 |  | $2,667 |

$$\text{Rate} = \frac{\$\,2,667}{20,000} = \qquad 13.33\%$$

| | |
|---|---|
| Less 10% salvage value | 1.33 |
| Annual adjusted rate after salvage | 12.00% |
| Annual depreciation | $2,400 (12% of $20,000) |

Note that the composite life is seven and a half years, with or without a salvage value reduction.

Retirement accounting for a varied group unit would be similar to that for the uniform group described earlier.

### Composite Versus Segment Depreciation of a Building

Depreciation of a factory or service building is of special interest, because it may be determined on a total or partial composite basis. On the total composite basis, the structure is given a useful life (salvage is rarely applied) and so depreciated. On a partial composite basis, component parts of a structure—roof, elevators, other mechanical equipment, heating plant—can be depreciated over a much shorter life basis, with the remainder treated as a composite.

Determining component costs may be no problem when a building is constructed. However, if purchased at a lump-sum price, the amount must be allocated over all segments of the building. Since the Internal Revenue Service views such allocations intently, independent expert assistance should be utilized to achieve a reasonably sound, supportable basis for the allocation.

### Cautions About Group and Composite Depreciation

Large errors can result when significant changes occur in the mix of items in a group, when replacement costs of components change sharply, or when errors have been made in estimating the useful life of components. Abnormal gains or losses on retirement of units may be an indication of unrealistic depreciation. Revisions in the composite depreciation rate should be made promptly when they are required, to minimize distortions.

The size of a group, particularly a homogeneous one, affects the accuracy of its average estimated useful life. A large group absorbs differences with less impact than a small one.

## SALVAGE VALUE

Salvage value is the estimated sum that will be recovered upon the disposition of an asset. Materiality of amount is the guide for determining whether it is to be used. For example, a firm's depreciation policy may rule out the use of salvage value of ten percent or less of cost. This might reduce the firm's accounting burden considerably. Most firms ignore all salvage value except for very large assets or assets that are frequently traded in before the end of their useful lives.

### Estimating Salvage Value

The recovery value should be estimated when an asset is acquired, though such an estimate involves a long-range forecast. Thus the depreciable cost of the asset can be determined, and periodic depreciation established. In the case of equipment that is usually traded in (e.g., autos, trucks), previous experience can guide management in determining recovery values. In other instances, suppliers, other users of the equipment, and second-hand-equipment dealers can be called on for advice. Management should consider the effect of inflation on salvage values as used-equipment prices escalate.

### Estimated Disposal Costs

Disposal costs should reduce the salvage realization. When heavy, stationary equipment is involved, for example, disposal costs may offset all or a substantial part of the salvage value. If the asset is in poor condition or is totally obsolete, there may be a disposal cost rather than a salvage value.

### IRS Provisions

The Internal Revenue Code requires that the depreciation rate allow for salvage value. However, Section 167(f) provides that salvage value up to ten percent of the cost of the asset may be ignored in computing annual depreciation.

## USEFUL ECONOMIC SERVICE LIFE

The concept of useful economic service life is vital in the depreciation formula, regardless of the method used; it affects both units and groups. This concept should not be confused with possible physical life, which is usually longer.

Useful life means useful *economic* life; allowance is therefore required for normal obsolescence. Assets that are consumed on one job (as is the case with some heavy equipment on a long-term construction project) would have a life limited by the job term or their own usefulness, whichever is shorter. Useful life, where material, should be reviewed every three to five years or at any other interval deemed appropriate. It should be reviewed more frequently when technological conditions are changing rapidly and markedly. For example, when a new generation of computers is announced, the economic life of computers in use may be drastically reduced.

### Maintenance Policy

Maintenance policy has a definite effect on useful life. Preventive maintenance, timely repairs, timely replacement of worn parts, frequent greasing and lubricating, careful handling of equipment—all these factors serve to increase economic life. Poor maintenance or an inconsistent policy will shorten the service life.

A company's experience will help set future useful life. In the absence of sufficient experience, the opinions of suppliers, trade associations, peer companies, and independent experts can be solicited.

## Obsolescence

The period of useful life can change drastically if abnormal obsolescence occurs. In that event, some accounting action should be taken. If the asset is to be retired, the amortized cost should be written off against the accumulated depreciation and the residue expensed. If the asset's term of use is significantly reduced, the depreciation rate should be increased to write off the asset over its remaining economic life. No retroactive adjustment should be made.

In the case of the obsolescence of a group component, no adjustment should be made unless the unit is so large as to materially affect the group's useful life. In that event, no loss or gain should be recognized, but the depreciation rate should be increased to cover the remaining life. This adjustment may not be retroactive.

## IRS Criteria

In the determination of the useful life of assets, controllers may find it helpful to consider the information in the IRS class life asset depreciation range. If sufficiently important, court decisions involving useful-life determination for specific assets might also be considered.

## Variations in Useful-Life Estimates

Although outside sources may be helpful in the useful life estimates of specific assets, the same type of asset may have a markedly different life in one company than in another. Variations may occur for any one or more of several reasons: the need for or lack of the most up-to-date equipment, regular overuse of equipment, inadequate time provisions for necessary repairs, climatic variations, employee efficiency, and others.

Useful life is a concern in dealing with tools, dies, and molds. Since such items have an uncertain life (from very short to very long) because of breakage, losses, and obsolescence, the inventory method is practical. Thus, depreciation is not used; instead the cost of the items consumed is charged to expense. The inventory method is also useful for spare parts.

# OTHER DEPRECIATION CONSIDERATIONS

## Depreciation Timing of Acquisitions and Disposals

If asset additions occur frequently throughout the year, the depreciation accounting could be burdensome in the year of acquisition because of the partial period. This problem can be overcome by use of one of the methods listed below (disposals are treated in similar fashion):

- Charge a half-year's depreciation on all acquisitions during the year. This basis presumes that the excess charges and the omissions will reasonably offset each other. This method can be used with the sum-of-the-years'-digits and declining-balance methods as well as with the straight-line method.
- Charge a full year's depreciation on assets acquired in the first six months and none for those acquired in the second six months. Disposals would be handled in reverse, with no depreciation charge for assets disposed of during the first half of the year and a full year's depreciation for second-half disposals.

## Real Estate Construction

When a building is constructed by the owner, the commencement of depreciation may be the date of completion or the date use starts. However, depreciation of a major component (e.g., a roof) may be considered to start when the component is completed. Materiality, as well as the method to be used to depreciate the building, should be taken into account in any such consideration.

## Additions to Existing Assets

An addition can increase the original asset cost but not necessarily its useful life. For example, a three-color litho press can be converted into a four-color press by the addition of another roller, a rather expensive item. This will permit a company to run a four-color job more economically or at least more rapidly than before. Given that the original cost in 1974 was $60,000, that the press has a useful life of 20 years and a salvage value of $8,000, and that the fourth roller was added on December 31, 1978, at a cost of $24,000, with a salvage value of $4,000, depreciation would be increased as follows:

|          |              |                     | End of Period | |
| -------- | ------------ | ------------------- | --- | --- |
| Year     | Depreciation |                     | Net Cost | Depreciable Balance |
| 1974-1978 | $13,000     | 5/20 of $52,000     | $47,000 | $39,000 |
| 1979     | 3,933        | 1/15 of  59,000[2]  | 67,067  | 55,067 |
| 1980     | 3,933        | 1/15 of  59,000     | 63,134  | 51,134 |
| 1981-1993 | 51,134      | 13/15 of  59,000    | $12,000[3] | –0– |
|          | $72,000      |                     |         |     |

Note that it is also possible to depreciate the original press and the addition separately.

---

[2] Depreciable asset balance, December 31, 1978, of $39,000 ($52,000 less $13,000) plus depreciable amount of addition, $20,000.

[3] Salvage value of the equipment ($8,000 + $4,000).

## Decision to Capitalize or Expense

Judgmental problems arise in determining whether all or part of certain expenditures should be capitalized or immediately charged to expense. Common items about which this decision must be made are extraordinary repairs, improvements (to increase efficiency, capacity, speed, and quality, and to reduce cost and upkeep), and replacement of a part or an entire unit. Some improvements and partial replacements may include an element of expense and, in part, a reduction of accumulated depreciation. Generally, an improvement that increases the economic value or life of the asset should be capitalized.

In borderline cases, a policy of reasonable conservatism is recommended. Though useful life may be increased, conservative policy suggests using the original life basis of the asset if a substantial portion remains, unless circumstances clearly call for an extension of the useful life period.

## Replacements

When a machine or other asset becomes so inefficient or inadequate (too slow, too costly to run and maintain, of poor quality), management must decide whether to renew it or replace it. This is a make-or-buy question, and it can be answered only after careful evaluation of the facts. A guide to accounting policy and depreciation is the general rule that expenditures that do not benefit future operations should not be capitalized.

From a depreciation viewpoint, the purchase of a new machine as a replacement presents no unique problem. It is a new asset and its depreciation will be in accord with established policy. The treatment of the replaced machine depends on its disposition. If it is regarded as standby equipment, it should be depreciated as in the past or, as a conservative measure, written down to salvage value and treated as a fully depreciated asset. If it will be sold, it should obviously be written down to realizable value (or written off if the salvage value is minimal).

## Extensive Overhauls

When an item is renewed rather than replaced, the nature of the overhaul becomes important. The renewed item may be like the old in all respects, or it may be significantly improved. Management has these options:

- If there will be no significant change, it may treat the expenditure as a repair expense; or
- If the renewal is very extensive, affecting remaining useful life, it may charge the expenditure to the reserve for depreciation and depreciate the net asset cost over the extended useful life.

## IRS Criteria

The IRS generally accepts the standard accounting criteria for determining whether a repair or overhaul should be capitalized or expensed. If the expenditure appreciably prolongs the life of an asset, materially increases its value, or adapts it to a different use, it should be capitalized.

If a taxpayer uses the asset depreciation range (ADR) system, it has the option of electing the percentage repair allowance rule, which is designed to reduce the repair capital-expenditure question to a mechanical computation. Under this rule, all repair-type expenditures are treated as currently deductible repairs to the extent they do not exceed the repair allowance provided for each class of assets. For example, if an asset class has an allowance of 3.5 percent and $100,000 of ADR assets, the first $3,500 of repairs are deductible currently, and any excess expenditures are capitalized as property improvements.

## Capitalized Leased Property

Property under a long-term lease that is tantamount to ownership should be recorded in the books as if owned, and depreciated accordingly. (See Chapter 4 for an explanation of SFAS 13, *Accounting for Leases*, and for the lease terms that necessitate capitalization.) The cost basis is established at the amount of the present value of the lease payments, disregarding renewal periods (with certain exceptions). This valuation is consistent with the cost basis concept. To illustrate, total lease payments of $1 million might result in a discounted depreciable cost of $600,000. The difference of $400,000 would be charged to income as periodic interest over the life of the lease. This is equivalent to the accounting for the installment purchase of an asset.

## Subsidized Plants

Governments anxious to attract industry into their territory offer financial inducements to companies. One inducement provides financing by a bond issue to construct a plant for the company. The plant is leased to the company for a long term at a rental sufficient to service the bonds to maturity. At the end of the term the building reverts to the occupant. The property should be accounted for and depreciated similarly to capitalized leased property discussed in the preceding paragraph.

# COPING WITH INFLATION

Many businesses are affected by continuing high rates of inflation, because costs tend to advance faster than prices and cannot always be passed on to consumers. However, companies with substantial amounts of fixed assets and/or inventories are particularly affected, because these assets are charged to operations at historical cost rather than at current cost, resulting in an inflation gain that requires the payment of higher income taxes. In 1979 economists claimed that fully one third of the earnings that companies reported for 1978 were gains created by inflation. Whether or not this estimate is accurate, the consensus is that in an inflationary era the use of historical cost as a basis for depreciation and inventory costs will overstate profits. The current solution to the inventory problem is to switch from the first-in, first-out method to the last-in, first-out method. (This method is explained in Chapter 3.) Unfortunately, there is no generally accepted method for coping with the depreciation problem. Some of the suggested methods are current cost depreciation, constant dollar depreciation, or some version of very rapid depreciation.

## Current Cost Depreciation

The FASB's SFAS 33, *Financial Reporting and Changing Prices*, requires the largest public corporations ($1 billion of assets or $125 million of inventory and gross fixed assets) to report inflation-adjusted income, plus other data, on a *current cost basis* and on a *historical cost/constant dollar basis*. Although the statement does not currently apply to smaller companies, the problem of inflation affects the reported earnings of all companies. Many companies not subject to the statement are voluntarily reporting to management and third parties in accordance with SFAS 33.

The FASB defines the current cost of property, plant, and equipment as

the current cost of acquiring the same service potential (indicated by operating costs and physical output capacity) as embodied by the asset owned; the sources of information used to measure current cost should reflect whatever method of acquisition would currently be appropriate in the circumstances of the enterprise.

**Measurement Methods.** The statement recommends three methods for measuring the current cost of a used asset:

- "By measuring the current cost of a new asset that has the same service potential as the used asset had when it was new (the current cost of the asset as if it were new) and deducting an allowance for depreciation";
- "By measuring the current cost of a used asset of the same age and in the same condition as the asset owned";
- "By measuring the current cost of a new asset with a different service potential and adjusting that cost for the value of the differences in service potential due to differences in life, output capacity, nature of service, and operating costs."

The FASB's current cost concept focuses on the cost of a similar asset, whereas the SEC's replacement cost concept is primarily concerned with the cost of a similar productive capacity. The results of the two concepts should be reasonably similar.

**Depreciation Expense.** The depreciation methods, estimates of useful lives, and salvage values of assets should be the same for purposes of current cost and historical cost depreciation calculations. This allows users to compare the effect of inflation on the result of operations applicable to depreciation expense. However, SFAS 33 requires that straight line depreciation be used.

## Constant Dollar Depreciation

As noted above, one of the requirements of SFAS 33 is a presentation of income from continuing operations on a historical cost/constant dollar basis. The FASB defines constant dollar accounting as

a method of reporting financial statement elements in dollars each of which has the same (i.e. constant) general purchasing power. This method of accounting is often described as accounting in units of general purchasing power or as accounting in units of current purchasing power.

In order to present financial data in constant dollars, it is necessary to convert historical costs through the use of a consistent index. The index selected by the FASB is the *Consumer Price Index for All Urban Consumers* (CPI), published monthly by the Bureau of Labor Statistics of the U.S. Department of Labor.

**Measurement Method.** SFAS 33 requires that property, plant, and equipment (at year-end) and depreciation expense at historical cost/constant dollar amounts be computed by multiplying the components of the historical cost dollar measurements by the average level of the CPI for the current fiscal year and dividing by the level of the index at the date of acquisition. This computation can be illustrated assuming the following facts: an item of equipment was acquired in 1973 at a cost of $50,000 and is being depreciated over ten years on a straight-line basis with no salvage value; for the fiscal year 1980 the average CPI was 220.9; and for 1973, the year of acquisition, the average CPI was 133.1. The historical cost/constant dollar amount is computed as follows:

$$\$50,000 \times \frac{220.9}{133.1} = \$82,983.$$

The depreciation expense for the year is $8,298, and the accumulated depreciation at year-end is $66,386 (80% of $82,983).

If comprehensive financial statements are presented on a historical cost/constant dollar basis, the level of the index at the end of the year should be used, and if a five-year summary of financial data is presented, it is acceptable to restate all items in base-year dollars or in current-year dollars. The current CPI base year (index = 100) is 1967.

**Pro and Con.** The advocates of the historical cost/constant dollar method cite as its advantages the ease of computation as compared to the current cost or replacement cost methods, and the relative objectivity gained by the use of an index prepared by the U.S. Department of Labor.

The critics of the method (who are generally those who favor the current cost method) point out that a general price index may not be applicable to the specific cost factors affecting a company or an industry. Current cost, despite its faults, will more closely measure the effects of inflation on a company's earnings and financial position. For the time being, the FASB has hedged its position by requiring companies to present inflation-adjusted financial data under both methods.

## Capital Cost Recovery System

As noted above, the use of historical cost depreciation during an inflationary period results in an inadequate charge to current earnings. To correct this undercharging of depreciation, various methods have been proposed for adjusting historical cost to record the effect of inflation (as discussed above). At the same time, businessmen have argued that because depreciation is understated, they are overpaying taxes and not retaining sufficient profits to replace their productive assets at current costs.

To aid businesses and also to reflect an inflation-adjusted charge for depreciation, a Capital Cost Recovery Act (CCRA) has been proposed for tax purposes. The CCRA would depart drastically from traditional concepts. It would permit recovery of the capital costs of most types of assets over periods of time unrelated to their actual useful lives. Other countries, including England and Canada, have successfully used similar methods for several years.

**Tax Benefits.** By permitting the recovery of fixed asset investment over a shorter time, the system enables a company to realize greater tax benefits in earlier years. This would presumably generate increased cash flow, which could be used to reinvest in new productive assets or to further modernize facilities. Some economists have estimated that the CCRA would provide a depreciation expense equivalent to the historical cost/constant dollar method at the rate of inflation in effect in 1979. However, capital cost recovery would not change with inflation, and like all accelerated depreciation methods, it provides a much lower depreciation charge toward the end of an asset's life. Capital cost recovery cannot be considered an inflation accounting method, but it would help businesses during an inflationary period by reducing the effects of inflation on taxes paid.

**The Basic System.** The CCRA would classify assets into three groups. Class I assets would generally include buildings and structural components and would be eligible for a ten-year recovery period. Class II assets, primarily machinery and equipment, would be recovered over a five-year period. Class III would apply to such short-lived assets as automobiles and light-duty trucks; they would use a three-year recovery period.

To determine the cost recovery allowance (depreciation) in any given year, the capital cost recovery system would apply the appropriate percentage to the amount of asset cost in each class. The system would use accelerated depreciation principles and the so-called half-year convention. Salvage value would be ignored.

**CCRA Allowances.** The following table shows a proposal for recovery percentages that would be allowable each year for the three classes of assets (the system could be adjusted to any series of percentages):

| Ownership Year | Class of Asset | | |
|---|---|---|---|
| | I | II | III |
| 1 | 10% | 20% | 33% |
| 2 | 18 | 32 | 45 |
| 3 | 16 | 24 | 22 |
| 4 | 14 | 16 | |
| 5 | 12 | 8 | |
| 6 | 10 | | |
| 7 | 8 | | |
| 8 | 6 | | |
| 9 | 4 | | |
| 10 | 2 | | |
| | 100% | 100% | 100% |

**Variable Deductions.** As proposed, the capital cost recovery system would allow a taxpayer to choose to deduct all or a portion of the cost recovery allowance for any given year. Any unused portion of the allowance could be carried forward and deducted in future years. This would permit flexibility for companies with losses or with widely fluctuating income.

## Conclusions and Observations

At present, the only consensus that can be noted in any discussion of the effects of inflation on financial reporting is that there is a problem and that historical cost accounting is inadequate. Various groups have their own preferred solution, but as yet none of the proposed methods for inflation-adjusted depreciation have met with general approval. This is also true in other countries where high inflation has affected the usefulness of traditional financial reporting.

There is little agreement on a method of inflation-adjusted accounting because both accountants and users are uncomfortable with the gap between the objective standards of historical cost accounting and the subjective standards of the inflation models. Although the constant dollar method is the least subjective in application, it raises serious objections with regard to the index being used. How relevant is the CPI (influenced heavily by food and clothing) to a paper manufacturer, for example?

**Does a Solution Exist?** Experimentation with the FASB methods may in time provide an acceptable method for measuring the effects of inflation on corporate earnings. The question arises whether there is some reasonably simple method that would bridge the gap and give users an acceptable indication of inflation-adjusted corporate earnings.

In 1979 the AICPA published the results of an experiment in which twenty-three major public companies recast their financial statements under four different approaches of inflation accounting methods. The participants then ranked each of the methods in terms of overall usefulness, relevance, measurability, reliability, and comparability. The method that received the highest ranking was the one that used historical cost financial statements incorporating inventories based on last-in, first-out (LIFO) costs and depreciation based on current cost of depreciable assets.

This popular method may be subject to some of the same criticisms as those recommended by the FASB, but it is reasonably easy to implement, and it does provide a measure of income that eliminates the major effects of inflation. This method, or one similar, will be required in the near future to help management, lenders, and creditors distinguish between real earnings and the illusions of inflationary earnings.

## SUGGESTED READING

Bierman, Harold, Crichfield, Timothy, and Dyckman, Thomas R. "Depreciation Policy and Decision Making." Ross Institute of Accounting Research, Proceedings . . . on Topical Research in Accounting, pp. 49-88. New York: 1979.

Coughlan, Joseph D., and Strand, William K. *Depreciation: Accounting, Taxes and Business Decisions.* New York: Ronald Press, 1969.

Feinschreiber, Robert. *Tax Depreciation Under the Class Life ADR System.* New York: AMACOM, 1975.

# 6

# Cost Accounting Methods

*Arthur J. Schomer*

## COST ACCOUNTING SYSTEMS

Cost accounting systems provide a powerful management tool for planning and controlling operations, product pricing, and similar decisions. If the cost system of a particular company is to meet these objectives effectively, the controller must carefully design and construct the system with these specific objectives in mind. He must also ensure that the collection and processing of appropriate production and inventory data is comprehensive, accurate, and timely (within practical limits), so that the system will be capable of producing meaningful information and meeting management needs. Too often a controller charges ahead with the mechanics of building a cost accounting system without carefully defining its goals or evaluating the complexities and alternative means of collecting and analyzing production data.

A cost accounting system is complex to design, install, and operate because it reflects the intricacies of the production operation. Because of the complexities and dynamics of the production function, the system will never function perfectly, but it must function in a controlled, responsive, and reasonably accurate manner to justify the investment required for its development and operation. This requires not only an initial investment of time and effort but also a commitment to keep the system functioning properly and in tune with a dynamic production environment.

## Types of Systems

Cost accounting systems can be characterized in several ways.

**Job Cost Versus Process Cost.** The distinction between *job cost* and *process cost* systems is based on the nature of the manufacturing operation to which the cost system will apply. Job costing is appropriate for companies producing custom products to order. Since each product is different and is produced in response to the customer's specifications, the actual cost of producing each order or job lot must be captured and reported. Identification of the cost of each job lot permits identification of the profitability of each order. It also permits evaluation of cost performance by comparison with the cost estimate on which the customer price quotation was based and provides a valuable tool in evaluating the quality of the cost estimating procedure itself.

Process costing, on the other hand, is appropriate to the manufacturing environment in which a standard line of products is offered for sale (i.e., mass production for stock in the expectation of customer orders). The primary emphasis is on the cost and efficiency of the process in each department, cost center, and operation over a period of time, rather than on each of the multitude of products and lots that may flow through the operation and cost center. That is not to say that the individual product is ignored. To the extent practical in the given situation, actual cost data should be captured by product in the detailed cost records, but the accumulation and reporting of costs should follow the process rather than the product.

Some companies have both job shop and mass production environments existing within the same plant. In such cases, a mixture of job and process costing techniques should be applied as appropriate to the individual phases of production.

**Actual Cost Versus Standard Cost.** Job or process cost systems can each be structured to accumulate actual costs only or, alternatively, to accumulate and record both *actual costs* incurred and *standard cost* allowances for the actual level and mix of production. In a standard cost system the emphasis is on the variances, which are the differences between the actual and the standard costs. A standard cost system is primarily a management control device, with variances highlighted and reported to management by cost element and by area of responsibility. Standard cost data is also useful in developing profitability reporting by business segment, in making pricing decisions, and in facilitating the development of a profit plan. If the standard cost system is properly structured, it can also provide valuable data for management decision analysis, which is discussed in more detail later in this chapter.

**Absorption Versus Direct Costing.** A given cost system can also be characterized as either an absorption costing or a direct costing system. The basic structural distinction between these two systems lies in the definition of factory costs capitalized through inventory. *Absorption costing,* which is required under generally accepted accounting principles (GAAP), includes all factory costs—direct material, direct labor, and factory overhead—in the costing of work in process and the finished goods inventory. *Direct costing* (also known as variable or marginal costing) capitalizes only variable manufacturing costs—direct material, direct labor, and variable factory overhead—through inventory. Under direct costing, fixed manufacturing overhead costs are expensed directly on the income statement in the period incurred. *Variable costs* are those costs that are expected to rise or fall proportionally with fluctuations in the level of production. *Fixed costs* are expected to remain more or less constant in the short run, since they represent the cost of operating capacity. A direct costing system is managerially oriented; the classification of costs according to cost behavior patterns (i.e., variable versus fixed) provides a tool for profit planning and for use of the profit plan as a control device. Direct costing also provides the foundation for cost/volume/profit analysis and incremental cost analysis for decision-making purposes.

### Systems Characteristics

This section describes the structure of each type of cost system discussed above. Methods of accumulating and processing the data required to operate a cost system are described later in this chapter.

**Actual Job Cost System.** An actual job cost system is structured to accumulate actual costs by job lot as incurred. The costs are recorded on a job cost sheet (Figure 6.1) by cost element and stage of production. Labor distribution records and material requisitions provide the source data for direct job charges. Overhead is applied on the basis of direct labor hours or dollars expended on the job or some other production measure appropriate to the particular manufacturing operation (e.g., machine hours). When the job is complete, the costs are totalled and divided by the actual quantity produced to determine the actual manufacturing cost per unit. This unit cost is used to cost finished goods inventory and to determine cost of goods sold. At the end of each month, total costs recorded on the cost sheets for uncompleted jobs represent work-in-process.

Typical journal entries for a job cost system include:

1. To record raw material used:
   *Dr.* Work-in-Process
   *Cr.* Raw Materials Inventory

**STAR FURNITURE MANUFACTURING COMPANY**

MANUFACTURED FOR: Harold's Department Store          ORDER NO. 110

PRODUCT: #105—Platform rockers

SPECIFICATIONS: Attached drawings and blueprints

QUANTITY ORDERED: 500

DATE ORDERED: 9/22/—                           DATE WANTED: 12/10/—

DATE STARTED: 11/21/—                     DATE COMPLETED: 12/5/—

**DIRECT MATERIALS**

| Date | Department | Req. No. | Description or Stores No. | Quantity | Cost Per Unit | Total |
|------|-----------|----------|--------------------------|----------|---------------|-------|
| 11/12 | Cutting | 2947 | support lumber oak and pine | 500 pieces oak 10 ft. | 1.80 | $ 900.00 |
| | | | | 250 pieces pine 8 ft. | .50 | 125.00 |
| 11/15 | Assembly | 3080 | glue, pegs, and screws | 500 standard | .20 | 100.00 |
| 11/27 | Upholstery | 3407 | upholstery cloth | 3,000 yds. | 1.00 | 3,000.00 |
| | | | Total Materials Cost | | | $4,125.00 |

**DIRECT LABOR**

| Date | Department | Time Rept. Nos. | Description of Labor or Process | Hours | Rate | Cost |
|------|-----------|-----------------|--------------------------------|-------|------|------|
| 11/12–14 | Cutting | 867–901 | power saw cutting | 120 | 2.75 | $ 330.00 |
| 11/14 | Planing | 1125–1130 | planing | 50 | 2.50 | 125.00 |
| 11/15–21 | Assembly | 1360–1397 | assembling frames | 200 | 2.25 | 450.00 |
| 11/25–27 | Upholstery | 1480–1505 | padding and upholstery | 250 | 3.00 | 750.00 |
| | | | Total Labor Cost | | | $1,655.00 |

**APPLIED FACTORY OVERHEAD**

| Date | Department | Basis of Application | Hours | Rate | Cost |
|------|-----------|----------------------|-------|------|------|
| 11/15 | Cutting | $2 per direct labor hour | 120 | 2.00 | $ 240.00 |
| 11/15 | Planing | $3 per direct labor hour | 50 | 3.00 | 150.00 |
| 11/22 | Assembly | $1 per direct labor hour | 200 | 1.00 | 200.00 |
| 11/29 | Upholstery | 100% of direct labor cost | — | — | 750.00 |
| | | Total Factory Overhead Applied | | | $1,340.00 |

**SUMMARY ON JOB NO. 110**

Materials . . . . . . . . . . $4,125.00       Selling Price . . . . . . . . . . . . . . . $10,850.00

Direct Labor . . . . . . . 1,655.00       Factory Cost . . . . . . . . $7,120.00

Factory Overhead . . . 1,340.00       Marketing Expenses . . 1,206.00

     Total Factory Cost $7,120.00      Adm. Expenses . . . . . . 905.00

                                           Cost to Make and Sell . . . . . . 9,231.00

                                           Profit . . . . . . . . . . . . . . . . . . . . $ 1,619.00

FIGURE 6.1 JOB ORDER COST SHEET—DEPARTMENTALIZED OPERATION

2. To record the factory payroll:
   *Dr.* Work-in-Process (for direct labor)
   *Dr.* Manufacturing Overhead Control
       (for indirect labor)
   *Cr.* Accrued Payroll
3. To record overhead expenses:
   *Dr.* Manufacturing Overhead Control
   *Cr.* Accounts Payable, Accumulated Depreciation, etc.
4. To record overhead applied to production:
   *Dr.* Work-in-Process
   *Cr.* Manufacturing Overhead Applied
5. To record finished production:
   *Dr.* Finished Goods Inventory
   *Cr.* Work-in-Process
6. To record cost of sales:
   *Dr.* Cost of Goods Sold
   *Cr.* Finished Goods Inventory

If job lots are shipped immediately upon completion of production, it is appropriate to bypass the finished goods inventory account and charge completed production directly to cost of goods sold. The manufacturing overhead control and/or the work-in-process accounts may be set up by department. These departmental control accounts are useful in isolating out-of-control conditions to a particular department. Departmental work-in-process data may help management evaluate levels of inventory investment and potential departmental bottlenecks. Departmental overhead data can be used to develop departmental overhead rates and to analyze and report on overhead costs by department.

The manufacturing overhead control account(s) should be supported by detailed expense accounts in a subsidiary ledger. It is also valuable from a managerial information and analysis standpoint to separate the overhead control and detailed records into fixed and variable expenses. Thus, a company's general ledger might have two overhead control accounts—fixed and variable—per department.

**Actual Process Cost System.** The classic actual process cost system relates to a continuous processing environment for the manufacture of one product. Under this system, costs are accumulated monthly by cost element for each department. Since costs are accumulated by process rather than by job, total departmental costs must be related to total departmental production for the month to develop a product unit cost for the department. This unit cost is needed to price the month-end departmental (work-in-process) inventory and to determine the cost of goods completed and transferred out of the department.

Unlike the job costing approach, in which unit cost is determined only when a job lot is completely manufactured, monthly product costing under process costing involves partial work effort on incomplete units. Therefore, an *equivalent produc-*

*tion* count must be obtained. Equivalent production represents a restatement of partially completed units into equivalent work effort expressed in terms of completed units. For example:

|                          | Units  | Material  | Labor & Overhead |
|--------------------------|--------|-----------|------------------|
| *Assume:*                |        |           |                  |
| Beginning WIP            | 2,000  | $   270   | $    625         |
| Started this month       | 28,000 | $16,650   | $41,000          |
| Completed and transferred| 27,000 |           |                  |
| Ending WIP               | 3,000  | 40% complete | 25% complete  |

| *Equivalent Production:*   | Material | Labor & Overhead |
|----------------------------|----------|------------------|
| Completed                  | 27,000   | 27,000           |
| Ending WIP—3,000 @ 40%  =  | 1,200    |                  |
| —3,000 @ 25%  =            |          | 750              |
| Total equivalent units     | 28,200   | 27,750           |

*Cost/Equivalent Unit:*
$16,920 ($270 + $16,650) ÷ 28,200 = $ .60
$41,625 ($625 + $41,000) ÷ 27,750 = $1.50

*Valuation of:*
  Ending WIP:
    Material—1,200 equivalent units @ $.60                = $    720
    Labor & Overhead—750 equivalent units @ $1.50  =          1,125
                                                              $ 1,845

  Completed and Transferred:
    27,000 equivalent units @ $2.10 ($.60 + $1.50)   = $56,700

As goods are transferred from one production department to another, the transfer costs (calculated as illustrated above) are recorded as an additional cost element in the next department and are treated separately in the equivalent-production and cost-per-unit calculations.

In a multiproduct manufacturing situation, application of an actual cost system requires that costs be accumulated separately for each product produced in each department. This burdensome effort can be avoided by using a standard process cost system.

As with job costing, the variable and fixed overhead costs can be identified and accumulated separately in each department. The required journal entries for an actual process cost system are basically the same as those previously illustrated for job costing, except that costs and work-in-process accounts *must* be maintained by department. As goods move from one department to another, the preceding department's work-in-process inventory is credited and the subsequent department's work-in-process inventory is charged with the transfer cost (determined as illustrated above). This transfer cost is cumulative for *all* preceding departments, not just for the immediately preceding department. Also, if spoilage or other loss of units occurs *after* the first manufacturing step, the transfer cost "element" *per unit* must be adjusted by: (1) multiplying the quantity of lost units by the per-unit "transferred in" cost, and (2) dividing the resulting dollar amount by the number of good units yielded in the process step in which the loss occurred.

**Standard Cost System.** Since most mass production factory environments involve discrete production activities (i.e., departments or cost centers) with staging of partially completed materials or parts between departments, and since many products may be processed simultaneously through the plant, most firms have adopted a standard process cost system. This system records standard cost allowances throughout the flow of costs into work-in-process, finished goods, and cost of sales. As the standard cost allowances are recorded, actual costs incurred are closed out and the resulting variances are recorded on the books of account. As a result, the general ledger accounts serve as controls over the accuracy of the multitude of cost and inventory records and reports generated under a standard cost system. Variances are recorded by cost element and area of supervisory responsibility and thus provide a means of evaluating performance and identifying reasons for problem situations.

*Standard job cost system.* Under a standard *job cost* system, the standard costs for a particular job lot ideally will be the cost estimate data developed initially to cost the job and to quote a price to a customer. In some companies this system is not practical because the sales price quote is often based on preliminary, "rough" cost data. In such cases, the standard cost factors for the job lot will be developed in detail *after* the order is accepted. Often, a job shop factory can build up a given job cost standard based on a reference file of standard operations and raw material standards and yields.

*Standard process cost system.* Under a standard *process cost* system, industrial engineers develop a standard bill of materials (Figure 6.2) for each new product as the product is put into the line. Labor operations and time required per operation are also defined for the new product (Figure 6.3) based on appropriate engineering studies, with allowances for machine downtime, employee rest time, and so on. The objective is to establish realistic standards of performance under acceptable operating conditions and efficiency requirements. When industrial engineering support is not available, knowledgeable factory supervisory and staff personnel should develop the standards.

*Overhead budgets and rates.* Standard overhead rates are established on the basis of periodic overhead budgets. Separate overhead budgets should generally be established for each factory department or cost center, because types and levels of cost incurrence patterns differ from department to department. Furthermore, the appro-

| Product | | | Unit | Prepared By | | Date | |
|---|---|---|---|---|---|---|---|
| Material/Part number | Description | | Quantity | Unit | Price | Cost | |
| | | | | | | | |
| | | | | | | | |
| | | | | | | | |
| | | | | | | | |
| | | | | | | | |
| | | | | | | | |
| | | | | | | | |
| | | | | | | | |
| | Total Standard Material Cost | | | | | | |

FIGURE 6.2   STANDARD BILL OF MATERIALS

priate basis for measuring production activity may vary from one department to another. That is, it may be appropriate to establish a standard overhead rate per labor hour in one department (e.g., assembly) and a standard rate per machine hour in another (e.g., metal stamping). Departmental budgeting also allows the controller to evaluate actual overhead spending levels by comparing actual costs with budget allowances based on each department's level and mix of production for a given month.

A breakdown of the overhead budget and standard overhead rates between fixed and variable cost components adds a valuable dimension to the standard cost system. Standard overhead factors categorized by cost behavior patterns form the basis for overhead control reporting based on actual production levels and provide expected cost behavior data for decision analysis. Figure 6.4 is an example of a departmental overhead budget. (See Chapter 12 for a detailed discussion of budgeting.)

*Updating standards.* Once developed, the standards must be periodically updated to reflect current operating conditions in a dynamic operating environment. However, continuous random updating of individual product standards can damage the effectiveness of the standard cost system by hampering meaningful analysis of variances from standard cost. Furthermore, every time product standard cost factors are changed, inventories must be revalued at the latest standards. To avoid an uncontrolled situation with "floating" standards, a regular schedule for updating should be established with at least annual review and revision. Many companies also review current standards quarterly or semiannually for possible updating.

## OPERATIONS LIST

| Stock number | | Description | Date prepared | By | |
|---|---|---|---|---|---|
| Dept. no. | Oper. no. | Operation description | Machine requirements | Stand. hours | Set-up hours |
| | | | | | |
| | | | | | |
| | | | | | |
| | | | | | |
| | | | | | |
| | | | | | |
| | | | | | |
| | | | | | |
| | | | | | |
| | | | | | |
| | | | | | |
| | | | | | |

FIGURE 6.3 OPERATIONS LIST

| Per Month | Per D. L. Hour | Total Budget |
|---|---|---|
| Budgeted Production Level—in Direct Labor Hours | | 10,000 |
| Budgeted Manufacturing Overhead | | |
| Variable Costs: | | |
| Indirect Labor—Material Handling | $ .15 | $ 1,500 |
| Overtime Premium | .05 | 500 |
| Shift Premium | .10 | 1,000 |
| Fringe Benefits | .67 | 6,700 |
| Factory Supplies | .20 | 2,000 |
| Power | .30 | 3,000 |
| Total Variable Costs | 1.47 | 14,700 |
| | | |
| Fixed Costs: | | |
| Supervision | | 2,000 |
| Indirect Labor—Mechanics | | 2,500 |
| Fringe Benefits | | 800 |
| Heat and Light | | 1,000 |
| Depreciation | | 5,000 |
| Rent | | 2,000 |
| Total Fixed Costs | 1.33 | 13,300 |
| Total Monthly Budgeted Overhead | $2.80 | $28,000 |

FIGURE 6.4 VARIABLE BUDGET MANUFACTURING OVERHEAD—STAMP AND PRESS DEPARTMENT

*Calculating departmental cost allowances.* Standard costs are recorded or charged for the number of acceptable units of product manufactured in each department. A common misconception about standard costing is that standard cost allowances are calculated *only* for units completely manufactured and placed in finished stock. On the contrary, standard cost allowances are determined at *each* stage of production by multiplying the quantity of each product processed at that stage by the predetermined unit standard cost factors for material, labor, and overhead for that stage of processing. Figure 6.5 illustrates the buildup of standard cost allowances for the production of one department.

Figure 6.6 depicts the flow of cost data in the operation of a standard cost system. It shows the recording and flow of actual and standard costs and the resulting variances. The variances depicted by solid-line boxes on the chart are basic to most cost systems. The broken-line variances are optional, depending on the nature of the manufacturing process and the needs and desires of management. In some manufacturing situations, additional or modified types of variances are appropriate.

All of the accounts carried at standard cost as depicted on the flowchart (i.e., all inventory accounts and cost of goods sold) function as control accounts and should

Month of _____

Dept. _____

| Production | | Standard Unit Cost | | | Standard Cost Allowed | | |
|---|---|---|---|---|---|---|---|
| Product No. | Quantity Produced | Material | Labor | Overhead | Material | Labor | Overhead |
| | | | | | | | |
| | | | | | | | |
| | | | | | | | |
| | | | | | | | |
| | | | | | | | |
| | | | | | | | |
| | | | | | | | |
| | | | | | | | |

Total Standard Cost Allowed

FIGURE 6.5  STANDARD COST ALLOWED

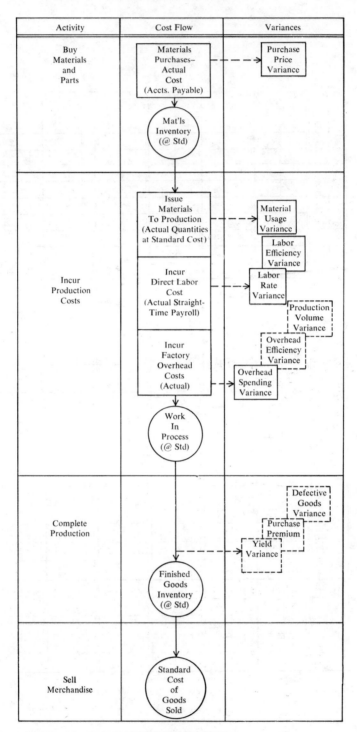

**FIGURE 6.6 STANDARD COST SYSTEM**

be supported by detailed product quantity listings extended at the appropriate unit standard costs.

The following are representative journal entry requirements related to this flow of cost data (variances are indicated as debit or credit, depending on whether unfavorable or favorable):

1. To record the purchase of raw materials:
   *Dr.* Raw Materials Inventory (at standard)
   *Dr./Cr.* Material Purchase Price Variance
   *Cr.* Accounts Payable

2. To record raw materials used in production:
   *Dr.* Work-in-Process (at standard)
   *Dr./Cr.* Materials Usage Variance
   *Cr.* Raw Materials Inventory (actual usage at standard cost)

3. To charge direct labor cost to process:
   *Dr.* Work-in-Process (at standard)
   *Dr./Cr.* Labor Rate Variance
   *Dr./Cr.* Labor Efficiency Variance
   *Cr.* Direct Labor Cost Applied (actual cost)

4. To apply overhead cost to production:
   *Dr.* Work-in-Process (at standard)
   *Dr./Cr.* Overhead Spending Variance
   *Dr./Cr.* Overhead Efficiency Variance
   *Dr./Cr.* Overhead Production Volume Variance
   *Cr.* Manufacturing Overhead Applied (actual cost)

5. To record finished production:
   *Dr.* Finished Goods Inventory (at standard)
   *Cr.* Work-in-Process (at standard)

6. To record cost of sales:
   *Dr.* Cost of Goods Sold (at standard)
   *Cr.* Finished Goods Inventory (at standard)

The work-in-process inventory should be segmented into separate accounts by department or, alternatively, by broad stages of production. This segmentation helps isolate possible accounting errors within particular production segments and enables management to determine the location and nature of any significant build-ups in inventory. In similar fashion, variance accounts should be detailed by department or cost center in order to identify the source and nature of significant non-standard conditions and to assign responsibility for manufacturing performance.

*Materials purchase price variance.* The materials purchase price variance represents the difference between the actual and standard unit purchase prices multiplied by the actual quantity of material purchased. It is calculated separately for each purchase of each type of raw material or part used in manufacturing. For example, assume the following transactions:

|  | Material A | Material B |
|---|---|---|
| Purchases—quantity | 10,000 lbs. | 3,000 ft. |
| —cost | $11,000 | $1,200 |
| Actual price/unit | $1.10/lb. | $0.40/ft. |
| Standard price/unit | $1.00/lb. | $0.45/ft. |

The purchase price variance would be calculated as follows:

$$\text{Material A: } 10{,}000 \text{ lbs.} \times (\$1.10 - \$1.00) = \$1{,}000.00$$

$$\text{Material B: } \phantom{0}3{,}000 \text{ ft.} \times (0.40 - 0.45) \phantom{00} = \phantom{0}(150.00)$$

$$\text{Net unfavorable variance} \phantom{0000000000} \$\phantom{0}850.00$$

The journal entry to record the purchase is:

| | | |
|---|---|---|
| *Dr.* Materials Inventory | 11,350.00[1] | |
| *Dr.* Material Purchase Price Variance | 850.00 | |
| *Cr.* Accounts Payable | | 12,200.00 |

The purchase variance should be recorded as each invoice is entered into the accounts payable system. A monthly report should be issued by item, categorized by type of material and/or associated product line (Figure 6.7).

Because the purchase price variance is an outgrowth of the purchase function (as illustrated in Figure 6.6), it is an exception to the general rule that standard costs are allowed and variances determined at the time of production.

*Material usage variance.* The materials usage variance identifies the efficiency of use of materials in each production step by comparing actual quantities of materials issued and used in production with the quantities that should have been used for actual production output (i.e., standard allowed). The difference between actual and standard materials quantities for each item is extended at the respective standard unit purchase price. To continue our example:

| | |
|---|---|
| Material used—A | 8,400 lbs. |
| —B | 1,600 ft. |
| Units produced | 500 |

Standard material quantities/unit:

| | |
|---|---|
| Material A | 16 lbs./unit |
| Material B | 3.5 ft./unit |

---

[1] Material A: 10,000 lbs. @ $1.00 = $10,000.00
Material B:  3,000 ft.  @ $0.45 =   1,350.00
                                           $11,350.00

Month Ended _____

Product Line _____

| Material | | Current Month | | | Year to Date | | |
|---|---|---|---|---|---|---|---|
| Item | Code | Actual Cost | Standard Cost | Favorable (Unfavorable) | Actual Cost | Favorable (Unfavorable) | |
| | | | | | | | |
| | | | | | | | |
| | | | | | | | |
| | | | | | | | |
| | | | | | | | |
| | | | | | | | |
| | | | | | | | |
| | | | | | | | |
| | | | | | | | |
| | | | | | | | |
| | | | | | | | |
| | | | | | | | |
| | | | | | | | |
| | | | | | | | |
| Totals | | | | | | | |

FIGURE 6.7  PURCHASE PRICE VARIANCE REPORT

The material usage variance would be calculated as follows:
Material A: (8,400 lbs. - 8,000 lbs.[2]) × $1.00 = $400.00
Material B: (1,600 ft. - 1,750 ft.[3])   × $ .45 =   (67.50)

Net unfavorable variance:                          $332.50

The entry to charge the standard material cost to work-in-process inventory and to record the variance is as follows:

Dr. Work-in-Process                          8,787.50[4]
Dr. Materials Usage Variance                    332.50
Cr. Materials Inventory                                     9,120.00[5]

Material usage reports are issued weekly or monthly (or, in some cases, daily), showing usage and variances by responsibility area (e.g., department), as illustrated in Figure 6.8.

*Direct labor variances.* The *labor rate variance represents* the effect of deviation of actual hourly pay rates from standard (anticipated) rates for direct labor effort expended. Assume the following data for the same production department illustrated in the discussion of the materials usage variance:

| | |
|---|---|
| Actual direct labor hours | 2,200 |
| Actual direct labor payroll | $11,220 |
| Actual hourly rate ($11,220 ÷ 2,200 hours) | $5.10 |
| Units produced | 500 |
| Standard hours/unit | 4 |
| Standard rate/hour | $5.00 |

The labor rate variance is calculated by multiplying the actual payroll hours for direct labor by the difference between the actual and standard hourly pay rates. In our illustration:

$$2,200 \text{ hours} \times (\$5.10 - 5.00) = \$220$$
unfavorable labor rate variance

The *labor usage (efficiency) variance* is calculated by multiplying the *standard* hourly rate (to eliminate any rate variance effect) by the difference between the

---

[2] 500 units × 16 lbs./unit

[3] 500 units × 3.5 ft./unit

[4] Material A: 8,000 lbs. @ $1.00 = $8,000.00
 Material B: 1,750 ft.   @ $0.45 =    787.50
                                   $8,787.50

[5] Material A: 8,400 lbs. @ $1.00 = $8,400.00
 Material B: 1,600 ft.   @ $0.45 =    720.00
                                   $9,120.00

Month Ended _____

Department _____

| Material | | Current Month | | | Year to Date | |
| --- | --- | --- | --- | --- | --- | --- |
| Item | Code | Material Used (@ Std Price) | Standard Material Cost Allowed | Favorable (Unfavorable) | Material Used (@ Std Price) | Favorable (Unfavorable) |
| | | | | | | |
| Totals | | | | | | |

FIGURE 6.8  MATERIAL USAGE REPORT

actual direct labor hours incurred and the number of hours that should have been expended to achieve the actual quantity produced (i.e., the standard labor hours allowed). To continue the illustration:

$$\$5.00 \times (2{,}200 \text{ hours} - 2{,}000 \text{ hours}[6]) = \$1{,}000$$
$$\text{unfavorable labor efficiency variance}$$

The entry required to charge the standard direct labor cost to work-in-process inventory is as follows:

| | | |
|---|---:|---:|
| *Dr.* Work-in-Process | 10,000[7] | |
| *Dr.* Labor Rate Variance | 220 | |
| *Dr.* Labor Efficiency Variance | 1,000 | |
| *Cr.* Direct Labor Cost Applied | | 11,220 |

If separate standard labor factors (hours and/or rates) are established for several operations within a department, several calculations of the type illustrated above must be made. The results of the calculations are summarized into one entry for the department.

Typically, labor performance reports like the one illustrated in Figure 6.9 are issued weekly to departmental supervisors. A summary report (Figure 6.10) is prepared for senior management personnel. Some companies use daily labor performance reports to identify problems that require immediate action.

*Overhead variances.* Since overhead or indirect factory costs represent an amalgam of many types of expenses not directly traceable to specific production lots, management needs a different approach to analyze variances between actual and expected (standard) overhead cost levels. As noted earlier, a breakdown of overhead into its fixed and variable components is a prerequisite to meaningful overhead analysis. Assume the following as a continuation of our illustration:

| | |
|---|---:|
| Actual overhead cost—variable | $14,900 |
| —fixed | $ 7,400 |
| Units produced | 500 |
| Standard capacity units | 600 |
| Direct labor hours—actual | 2,200 |
| —standard | 2,000 |
| Budgeted overhead cost—variable | $16,800 |
| —fixed | $ 7,200 |
| Standard overhead cost | |
| per direct labor hours—variable | $7.00 |
| —fixed | $3.00 |
| Standard overhead cost/unit[8]—variable | $28.00 |
| —fixed | $12.00 |

---

[6] 500 units $\times$ 4 hrs./unit.

[7] 2,000 hrs. @ $5.00.

[8] Standard cost/hr. $\times$ 4 hrs./unit.

Week Ended _____

Dept. _____

| Operation | Actual Labor Cost | | | | Standard Direct Labor Cost Earned | Variances | | | | | |
|---|---|---|---|---|---|---|---|---|---|---|---|
| | Total Payroll | Over-Time Premium | Down Time | Straight Time Direct Labor | | Week | | Month To Date | | Year To Date | |
| | | | | | | Rate | Efficiency | Rate | Efficiency | Rate | Efficiency |
| | | | | | | | | | | | |
| | | | | | | | | | | | |
| | | | | | | | | | | | |
| Total Dept. | | | | | | | | | | | |

FIGURE 6.9  LABOR PERFORMANCE REPORT—DEPARTMENTAL

There are numerous alternative methods used to analyze overhead variance analysis. The most common methods are illustrated below.

The *three-variance approach* consists of spending, efficiency, and production volume variances. The *spending variance* is the difference between total actual overhead costs (usually by department) and a budget allowance based on the *actual* production effort (input). For the department in our illustration:

| | | |
|---|---|---:|
| Actual overhead—variable | | $14,900 |
| —fixed | | 7,400 |
| —total | | 22,300 |
| Adjusted budget—variable: 2,200 actual | | |
| | labor hours × $7.00 | 15,400 |
| | —fixed (as originally budgeted) | 7,200 |
| | —total | 22,600 |
| Overhead spending variance | | |
| | —favorable | $ (300) |

The *overhead efficiency* variance, which is similar to the labor efficiency variance, is calculated by multiplying the standard *variable* overhead rate by the difference between actual and standard direct labor hours:

$$\$7.00 \times (2,200 \text{ hours}—2,000 \text{ hours}) = \$1,400$$
unfavorable overhead efficiency variance

The *production volume variance* reflects the portion of budgeted *fixed* overhead under- or over-absorbed into inventory because of the difference between standard and actual production levels. This difference in production units is multiplied by the standard fixed overhead cost per unit:

$$\$12.00 \times (600 \text{ units}—500 \text{ units}) = \$1,200$$
unfavorable production volume variance

The journal entry needed to record the overhead variances for the department and to charge standard overhead cost to work-in-process inventory is:

| | | |
|---|---:|---:|
| *Dr.* Work-in-Process | 20,000[9] | |
| *Dr.* Overhead Efficiency Variance | 1,400 | |
| *Dr.* Overhead Production Volume Variance | 1,200 | |
| *Cr.* Overhead Spending Variance | | 300 |
| *Cr.* Manufacturing Overhead Applied | | 22,300 |

---

[9] 500 units @ ($28.00 + $12.00).

Week Ended _____

Plant _____

| Department | Actual Labor Cost | | | | Standard Direct Labor Cost Earned | Variances | | | | | |
|---|---|---|---|---|---|---|---|---|---|---|---|
| | Total Payroll | Over-Time Premium | Down Time | Straight Time Direct Labor | | Week | | Month To Date | | Year To Date | |
| | | | | | | Rate | Effi-ciency | Rate | Effi-ciency | Rate | Effi-ciency |
| | | | | | | | | | | | |
| | | | | | | | | | | | |
| | | | | | | | | | | | |
| Total Plant | | | | | | | | | | | |

FIGURE 6.10   LABOR PERFORMANCE REPORT—SUMMARY

Many companies use a *two-variance approach* to overhead analysis. This approach combines the spending and efficiency variances into one "budget variance" (often referred to as the spending variance) and is appropriate if the level of overhead spending is not deemed to be significantly affected by the relative efficiency or inefficiency of the manufacturing effort. Under this approach, the budget (spending) variance is calculated by comparing total actual overhead cost with a budget allowance based on the *standard* production effort required to achieve the actual output. In our example, a budget based on *standard* direct labor hours allowed:

| | |
|---|---:|
| Actual overhead—variable | $14,900 |
| —fixed | 7,400 |
| —total | 22,300 |
| Adjusted budget—variable: 2,000 standard | |
| labor hours × $7.00 | 14,000 |
| —fixed (as originally budgeted) | 7,200 |
| | 21,200 |
| Overhead budget (spending) variance | |
| —unfavorable | $ 1,100 |

The journal entry for the two-variance approach would be:

| | | |
|---|---:|---:|
| *Dr.* Work-in-Process | 20,000 | |
| *Dr.* Overhead Budget (Spending) Variance | 1,100 | |
| *Dr.* Overhead Production Volume Variance | 1,200 | |
| *Cr.* Manufacturing Overhead Applied | | 22,300 |

This discussion of overhead variances has assumed operation of an absorption cost system. The overhead variances generated with a direct cost system are illustrated later in this chapter.

*Estimated* overhead rates are often used in an *actual* cost system in order to facilitate timely recording and processing of cost data and to avoid seasonal and other fluctuations in overhead rates during the year. When estimated overhead rates are used, a similar type of variance analysis to that discussed above can be employed. In such a situation, two variances are possible:

(1) A spending variance based on a budget allowance keyed to *actual* direct labor hours, and
(2) A production volume variance (as calculated above).

A monthly departmental overhead performance report is illustrated in Figure 6.11. To prepare this report the standard variable overhead rate must be established by cost element for calculation of the budget allowances based on actual production.

| | Total Cost | | | | ¢ Per lb. | | |
| --- | --- | --- | --- | --- | --- | --- | --- |
| | Actual | Budget | Spending Variance | Efficiency Variance | Actual | Spending Var. | Efficiency Var. |
| Pounds Processed | | | | | | | |
| Direct Labor Hours | | | | | | | |
| Variable Overhead: | | | | | | | |
| | | | | | | | |
| | | | | | | | |
| | | | | | | | |
| | | | | | | | |
| | | | | | | | |
| | | | | | | | |
| | | | | | | | |
| | | | | | | | |
| Total Variable Overhead | | | | | | | |
| Fixed Overhead: | | | | | | | |
| | | | | | | | |
| | | | | | | | |
| | | | | | | | |
| | | | | | | | |
| | | | | | | | |
| Total Fixed Overhead | | | | | | | |
| Total Overhead | | | | | | | |

_____ Cost Center

_____ Weeks Ended _____

FIGURE 6.11  MONTHLY COST REPORT

*Other variances.* Production circumstances and characteristics unique to a particular manufacturing environment may require additional variance determinations. It is not possible to discuss all such permutations within a general discussion of this type. However, certain additional variances that are required with some frequency are discussed herein.

At times the entries and variance calculations explained above are based on the quantity of units being processed through the plant as distinct from the final yield of good useable product. In such a situation a *yield variance* determination is required. Assume the following, within the context of our running illustration (for this purpose, assume that we have a one-department plant *or* that the yield variance is being calculated for each department):

| | |
|---|---|
| Expected (standard) yield | 95% |
| Actual yield—good product | 450 units |
| —spoiled product | 50 units |

Under these circumstances, the *total* standard cost allowance per unit of good product is:

| | |
|---|---|
| Material A: 16 lbs. @ $1.00 | $16.000 |
| Material B: 3.5 ft. @ $.45 | 1.575 |
| Direct labor: 4 hrs. @ $5.00 | 20.000 |
| Overhead—variable | 28.000 |
| —fixed | 12.000 |
| Total standard cost/unit (good *or* spoiled) | 77.575 |
| Allowance for spoiled goods[10]: ($77.575 × (100% − 95%)) ÷ 95% | 4.083 |
| Total standard cost/good unit | $81.658 |

Based on this data, the yield variance (actual vs. standard rate of spoiled goods) is:

| | |
|---|---|
| Actual spoilage: 50 units @ $77.575 standard cost | $3,878.75 |
| Standard spoilage allowance: 450 good units @ $4.083 | 1,837.35 |
| Unfavorable yield variance | $2,041.40 |

The journal entry to record the variance is:

| | | |
|---|---|---|
| *Dr.* Finished Goods Inventory | $36,746.10[11] | |
| *Dr.* Yield Variance | 2,041.40 | |
| *Cr.* Work-in-Process | | $38,787.50[12] |

---

[10] Assuming no cost recovery.
[11] 450 @ $81.658.
[12] 500 @ $77.575.

Some manufacturing processes necessarily include production of a certain amount of defective, or second quality, goods that are saleable at a reduced price. Accounting for defective goods is very similar to the technique for spoiled goods accounting. The major distinction is that the expected sales value (net of costs of disposal) should be used to reduce both the standard cost allowance for the defective goods and the actual loss for the calculation of the defective goods variance. For purposes of our illustration, assume that the data presented above for spoiled goods applies, except that the expected net sales value of the defective merchandise is $50 per unit. The standard allowance for defective goods would read:

$$(($77.575 - $50.00) \times (100\% - 95\%)) \div 95\% = $1.451$$

The defective goods variance would be calculated as follows:

| | |
|---|---:|
| Actual defective goods loss: | |
| 50 units @ ($77.575 − $50.00) | $1,378.75 |
| Standard defective goods loss allowance: | |
| 450 good units @ $1.451 | 652.95 |
| Unfavorable defective goods variance | $ 725.80 |

The journal entry to record the situation would be:

| | | |
|---|---:|---:|
| *Dr.* Finished Goods Inventory—1st Quality | 35,561.70[13] | |
| *Dr.* Finished Goods Inventory—2nd's | 2,500.00[14] | |
| *Dr.* Defective Goods Variance | 725.80 | |
| *Cr.* Work-in-Process | | 38,787.50[15] |

If the expected sales value equals or exceeds the standard manufacturing cost, there is no loss, and no cost accounting entries or calculations are required.

Another operating condition often encountered involves companies that both manufacture and purchase merchandise for sale. If a company sometimes buys in finished form an item that it normally manufactures, it almost invariably results in a purchase price higher than the standard manufacturing cost for the item. This premium should be charged to a variance account as a nonstandard condition.

Some companies find the need to establish certain "variances" that represent differences between two or more sets of standards (rather than differences between actual and standard costs). As noted earlier, it is not practical to update the cost accounting standards every time engineering standards are changed for a particular product or operation. Usually, this methods change is reflected in the operating variances until the company's next periodic comprehensive update of the cost account-

---

[13] 450 @ ($77.575 + $1.451).
[14]  50 @ $50.
[15] 500 @ $77.575.

ing standards. However, it is possible to measure actual costs against the *updated* operating standards in order to make performance reports more meaningful to the factory supervisors. If this is done, a "shadow" set of "*standard-to-standard*" variances must be recorded, accounting for the differences between the cost accounting standards and the current operating standards.

Companies with multiplant operations often produce a given product in more than one plant location. Each plant will develop its own standard cost of manufacturing that product. Since the product will presumably be commingled in inventory regardless of where it is produced, *one* standard valuation for the product must be selected to value inventory and cost of sales. This standard can be the cost associated with the primary production location, or it can be a weighted average of the standard costs of all plants manufacturing the product. The weighting would be based on the projected production mix by location. As the product is manufactured and placed into finished stock, the individual plant work-in-process account must be relieved at that plant's standard cost. Finished goods inventory is charged at the selected inventory standard. The difference between the two standards represents a production location variance.

*Disposition of variance.* For internal reporting purposes, the variances are usually closed directly to cost of sales each month. For external reporting purposes, good accounting practice requires that any significant variances be allocated among inventories and cost of sales as an adjustment to the previously recorded standard costs, unless a variance represents an abnormal condition that should not be capitalized through inventory.

**Direct Cost System.** As previously noted, a direct cost system values inventories at variable manufacturing costs only and expenses fixed manufacturing costs as costs of capacity. Emphasis is placed on cost behavior and its impact (actual or potential) on profitability. This is accomplished by focusing on the profit contribution generated by various products and operating segments of the business. The technique is particularly well suited for managerial decision analysis, as is illustrated later in this chapter.

*Comparing direct and absorption costs.* By including only variable manufacturing costs in inventory, direct costing avoids the irrational swings in profitability that can result from significant changes in the level of inventory and the correspondent changes in the level of fixed (period) costs deferred through inventory. This is illustrated graphically and in financial statement form in Figures 6.12 and 6.13.

Figure 6.12 demonstrates that the amount of each quarter's period, or fixed, costs included in inventory fluctuates with the level of the inventory. Thus, in the first two quarters period cost deferred in inventory *increased* by $800,000 as a direct consequence of production exceeding sales during that period. In other words, $800,000 of the period costs incurred during the first six months was capitalized as a result of excess production, with a corresponding increase in net income. In the third quarter sales exceeded production, with the result that $1,500,000 of period costs pre-

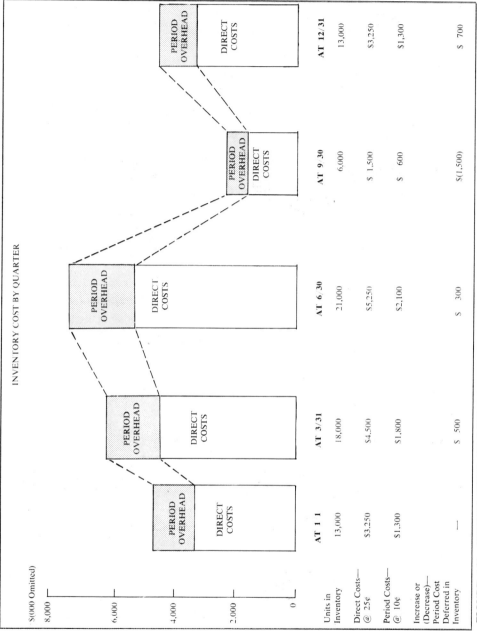

FIGURE 6.12 ILLUSTRATION OF INVENTORY VALUATION METHODS

viously deferred through inventory is now written off against income in addition to the period manufacturing overhead cost incurred in the third quarter. The fourth quarter again demonstrates the effect of an inventory build-up.

The impact of these inventory fluctuations on the income statement under absorption costing techniques is illustrated in Figure 6.13. This exhibit contrasts absorption and direct costing income statements; it demonstrates that the quarterly pattern of net income follows the quarterly pattern of sales more logically under direct costing than under absorption costing. Under direct costing, each quarter is charged with its own period manufacturing overhead costs of $1,500,000 (no more, no less) because of the valuation of inventory at variable manufacturing costs and the flow-through of period costs to the income statement.

Figure 6.13 also illustrates the difference in financial statement format under absorption versus direct costing. The gross margin under direct costing represents the profit contribution generated by sales after deducting all variable costs. This profit contribution is volume-related and is the amount available to cover period manufacturing costs and other fixed operating expenses and, hopefully, to generate net income.

*Direct cost income statement.* Figure 6.14 further illustrates a direct costing income statement by operating segment of the company. The operating segments reported on (in this case, divisions) should be selected on the basis of the company's operating and marketing structure. Segments reported on might include manufacturing divisions, product lines, geographical regions, types of customers, and so on. The following features of Figure 6.14 should be noted carefully:

- *All* variable costs (manufacturing, selling, etc.) should be deducted from sales to identify the profit contribution from each division's sales.
- Any period costs (manufacturing or otherwise) that are *specifically* and *wholly* attributable to the support of an individual operating segment should be charged to that segment. Examples include (a) machinery and/or plant facilities devoted exclusively to a manufacturing division's product line, and (b) advertising costs devoted exclusively to a product line or brand operating segment being reported on.
- All *general company* period (fixed) expenses are charged *only* to the total company and *are not* allocated to the segments, since to do so would necessarily involve arbitrary allocation decisions that would serve only to obscure the profitability analysis of an individual segment.

*For internal use only.* Direct costing is not acceptable for external reporting purposes under generally accepted accounting principles or for income tax reporting, because it does not provide for "full" costing of inventory. This should not preclude its use as a valuable management tool, since it is a simple matter to adjust inventory valuation and income reporting to full costing. Exhibit 6.15 shows one method of making such an adjustment, by allocating period manufacturing costs to inventory on the basis of direct labor dollars. The exhibit also shows the necessary journal entry to record the adjustment. This entry adjusts both inventory valuation and net income; the amount of the adjustment should be reported at the bottom of the direct costing income statement as a "reconciliation" with absorption costing net income.

| COMPARATIVE INCOME STATEMENTS | | | | | |
|---|---|---|---|---|---|
| | Q U A R T E R | | | | Total |
| | 1 | 2 | 3 | 4 | Year |
| **Absorption Costing** | | | | | |
| Sales | $ 6,000 | $ 8,000 | $12,500 | $ 3,500 | $30,000 |
| Cost of Goods Sold: | | | | | |
| Beginning Inventory | 4,550 | 6,300 | 7,350 | 2,100 | 4,550 |
| Manufacturing Costs | 5,750 | 6,250 | 4,000 | 5,000 | 21,000 |
| | 10,300 | 12,550 | 11,350 | 7,100 | 25,550 |
| Ending Inventory | 6,300 | 7,350 | 2,100 | 4,550 | 4,550 |
| | 4,000 | 5,200 | 9,250 | 2,550 | 21,000 |
| Gross Profit | 2,000 | 2,800 | 3,250 | 950 | 9,000 |
| Other Operating Exp. | 1,000 | 1,000 | 1,000 | 1,000 | 4,000 |
| Net Income (A) | $ 1,000 | $ 1,800 | $ 2,250 | $ ( 50) | $ 5,000 |
| **Direct Costing** | | | | | |
| Sales | $ 6,000 | $ 8,000 | $12,500 | $ 3,500 | $30,000 |
| Cost of Goods Sold: | | | | | |
| Beginning Inventory | 3,250 | 4,500 | 5,250 | 1,500 | 3,250 |
| Direct Costs | 4,250 | 4,750 | 2,500 | 3,500 | 15,000 |
| | 7,500 | 9,250 | 7,750 | 5,000 | 18,250 |
| Ending Inventory | 4,500 | 5,250 | 1,500 | 3,250 | 3,250 |
| | 3,000 | 4,000 | 6,250 | 1,750 | 15,000 |
| Gross Margin | 3,000 | 4,000 | 6,250 | 1,750 | 15,000 |
| Period Overhead | 1,500 | 1,500 | 1,500 | 1,500 | 6,000 |
| Other Operating Exp. | 1,000 | 1,000 | 1,000 | 1,000 | 4,000 |
| Net Income (B) | $ 500 | $ 1,500 | $ 3,750 | $ (750) | $ 5,000 |
| Difference (A−B) | $ 500 | $ 300 | $(1,500) | $ 700 | — |
| **Units** | | | | | |
| Beginning Inventory | 13,000 | 18,000 | 21,000 | 6,000 | 13,000 |
| Produced | 17,000 | 19,000 | 10,000 | 14,000 | 60,000 |
| Available | 30,000 | 37,000 | 31,000 | 20,000 | 73,000 |
| Sold | 12,000 | 16,000 | 25,000 | 7,000 | 60,000 |
| Ending Inventory | 18,000 | 21,000 | 6,000 | 13,000 | 13,000 |

FIGURE 6.13  ABSORPTION COSTING VERSUS DIRECT COSTING

*Direct standard cost system.* A *direct standard* cost system is a powerful management tool, since it integrates the features of both techniques into one system. The features of standard costing discussed earlier in the chapter apply equally to absorption or direct costing except for overhead variance analysis and accounting. Since only variable costs are included in standard costs under direct costing, the overhead variances include only variable costs. The overhead variances illustrated earlier under a standard cost system would be modified as follows:

*Two-variance approach:*

| | |
|---|---|
| Actual variable overhead | $14,900 |
| Adjusted budget: 2,200 actual labor hours | |
| ×  $7.00 | 15,400 |
| Favorable overhead spending variance | $ (500) |

THE PROFITABLE COMPANY
INCOME STATEMENT
BY DIVISION

| | Total Company | Division X | Division Y |
|---|---|---|---|
| Net Sales | $900,000 | $750,000 | $150,000 |
| Variable Costs | | | |
|   Variable Cost of Sales | 462,000 | 417,000 | 45,000 |
|   Variable Selling Expenses | 90,000 | 67,500 | 22,500 |
|     Total Variable Costs | 552,000 | 484,500 | 67,500 |
| Marginal Contribution | 348,000 | 265,500 | 82,500 |
|   % of Net Sales | 38.7% | 35.4% | 55.0% |
| Period Manufacturing Costs | 97,500 | 40,500 | 57,000 |
| Divisional Contribution | $250,500 | $225,000 | $ 25,500 |
|   % of Net Sales | 27.8% | 30.0% | 17.0% |
| Other Period Expenses | | | |
|   Manufacturing Overhead | 51,000 | | |
|   Selling Expense | 76,500 | | |
|   General and Administrative Expenses | 57,000 | | |
|     Total Other Period Expenses | 184,500 | | |
| Net Operating Income | 66,000 | | |
| Other Income and Expense | 4,500 | | |
| Net Income before Taxes | 70,500 | | |
| Provision for Income Taxes | 35,500 | | |
| Net Income | $35,000 | | |

FIGURE 6.14   DIRECT COST INCOME STATEMENT

$7.00 × (2,200 actual hours − 2,000 standard hours) = $1,400
unfavorable overhead efficiency variance.

Note that the efficiency variance is identical with that calculated under absorption costing, since under both systems only variable costs are used in the calculation.

*One-variance approach:*

| | |
|---|---|
| Actual variable overhead | $14,900 |
| Adjusted budget: 2,000 standard labor hours × $7.00 | 14,000 |
| Unfavorable overhead budget (spending) variance | $   900 |

Note that the overhead production volume variance disappears under direct costing, since it represents merely an under- or over-absorption of fixed costs into inventory. With direct costing, fixed costs are not absorbed into inventory at all. The other distinction is the disappearance of the fixed cost portion of the spending variance. This variance regarding fixed costs can still be reported to management as an operating budget variance outside the structure of the formal cost system.

It should also be noted that the yield and defective goods variances would be calculated *excluding* fixed costs from the computations.

## Implementing the Cost System

The development and implementation of an effective cost system requires considerable planning, structuring, and commitment over an extended period of time. The project tends to have definite stages that should be thoroughly understood and anticipated. With some variations in individual cases, these stages are:

| | (1) Standard Direct Labor Dollars | (2) Actual Period Costs | | |
|---|---|---|---|---|
| Opening Inventory | $ 50,000 | $ 5,000 | | |
| Add:   Current Period | 250,000 | 45,000 | | |
| Total Available | 300,000 | 50,000 | = | 16.7% |
| Deduct:   Cost of Sales | 200,000 | 33,000 | @ | 16.7% |
| Ending Inventory | $100,000 | $17,000 | | |

JOURNAL ENTRY

| | | |
|---|---|---|
| *Dr.* Period Cost Deferred in Inventory | 12,000 | |
| *Cr.* Adjustment for Change in Level of Period Costs Deferred in Inventory | | 12,000 |

FIGURE 6.15  INVENTORY ADJUSTMENT

1. Staffing the project;
2. Deciding on the fundamental characteristics and objectives of the system;
3. Determining appropriate data collection and data processing techniques;
4. Having management review and approve the system structure and objectives;
5. Developing the detailed system specifications;
6. Collecting and organizing the initial data;
7. Setting up the files; and
8. Performing the trial run.

Since most modern cost systems installed currently employ direct costing and stand-ard cost techniques to some extent, implementation of a direct standard process cost system is assumed throughout this section. For the most part, however, this discus-sion applies with equal validity to cost system implementation in general.

**Staffing the Project.** The staffing structure can be either formal or informal, de-pending on the company environment. If the company style is structured, a working committee is appointed and a format of meetings and progress reporting is estab-lished. In either case, it is important to the success of the project that the implemen-tation team include not only accounting and systems personnel but representatives of the various user functions as well. A typical team composition might include representatives from the manufacturing, purchasing, marketing, industrial engineer-ing, accounting, and systems departments. Some functional representatives might participate only in those stages or aspects of the project that directly involve their function and responsibilities.

This working team or committee should report to a management committee that is responsible for overall guidance, direction, and control of all aspects of the imple-mentation of the cost system. It is essential that management involvement and sup-port be active and sustained throughout the project. Otherwise, lagging interest and resistance to change may become severe obstacles to a successful conclusion of the project.

**Deciding on Systems Characteristics and Objectives.** The systems objectives must be clearly defined at the outset. If not, the company runs the severe risk that the mechanics of the system will be developed without a clear perspective of what those mechanics may or may not achieve for the company. The work team must talk with the future users of the system (presumably represented *on* the team) to determine their needs. The objectives of the system regarding cost control, decision analysis, profit planning, profitability reporting, pricing analysis, and inventory costing should be clearly defined and documented.

The next step is to develop preliminary output report formats to be produced by the system in response to the user requirements. These formats should be reviewed with the user departments and modified as necessary on the basis of the reviews. Only then is the company ready to consider data collection and processing require-ments to *meet* those objectives.

**Determining Data Collection Processing Techniques.** Detailed information must be accumulated concerning materials used, labor effort expended, and production and flow of product through the plant. The data needed to meet the system objectives must be collected accurately and processed promptly. The choices regarding the methods of data collection and the degree of detail to be collected and processed will depend to a considerable extent upon the cost-benefit ratios involved. That is, the benefit to be gained from collecting each type of data must be weighed against the cost of that data collection effort.

*Identifying materials consumption.* Materials consumed in production can be identified on the basis of requisitions of materials from stock. The requisition (Figure 6.16) should identify the type and quantity of material issued and the product and department for which the material was issued. If an actual cost system is involved, the requisition must also be priced, usually on a FIFO (first in, first out) or moving average cost basis. An inventory record maintained at the storeroom can be used to cost the requisition as the material is used. Alternatively, the factory office can cost the requisition.

An effective requisitioning system requires physical control over the materials storeroom in order to get a complete accounting for materials consumed. This often becomes difficult or impractical in a multi-shift operation. An alternative technique is reporting of materials as used in production, often on the same form used to record each stage of production. However, this is basically an uncontrolled method of reporting relying on factory rather than clerical employees.

Another common alternative is the *explosion of material consumption* based on the actual quantity of production in the department using the particular item(s) of material. The explosion technique is simply a multiplication of the number of units of each product manufactured by the standard quantities of each type of raw material per unit of product. This technique depends upon frequent physical inventory counts, perhaps on a cycle basis, to identify material usage variances. Under these circumstances, it may not be possible to identify the particular departments or products responsible for the variances.

Some companies bypass the record-keeping requirement entirely for materials by taking complete monthly physical inventory counts. Combinations of these various methods of accounting for materials may be used for different material items, depending on cost significance and difficulty of obtaining the data.

*Labor distribution and payment reports.* Each direct labor employee prepares a labor distribution report (Figure 6.17) showing the time spent and operation performed on each production lot. This report is separate from time and attendance for payroll purposes. The hours noted on the distribution report are extended at the employee's actual straight-time hourly rate; the employees' hours and time charges are summarized by operation, cost center, and department. Each employee's total hours as reported on the labor distribution report should be reconciled to the payroll records to maintain control over the accuracy of the cost accounting records. Most companies summarize and record labor costs in this manner on a weekly basis. Any

**STORES REQUISITION**

PAGE NO. _____ OF _____

Requested By:
Department
Job No.

| Part No. | Description | No. Required | Stores Code No. | Deliv. To | Price | Per Unit | Total Amount | Completed By | When Issued | Authorization |
|---|---|---|---|---|---|---|---|---|---|---|
| | | | | | | | | | | |
| | | | | | | | | | | |
| | | | | | | | | | | |
| | | | | | | | | | | |
| | | | | | | | | | | |
| | | | | | | | | | | |
| | | | | | | | | | | |
| | | | | | | | | | | |

When Required — When Issued

Comments — Total This Form

Total Brought Forward

Total Amount of Material

FIGURE 6.16  GROUP-STORES REQUISITION

time spent by direct labor employees on indirect labor activities (e.g., maintenance) should be included on the distribution report and charged to the appropriate overhead accounts. In similar fashion, idle time (because of machine downtime, etc.) and overtime premium pay should be recorded as overhead costs.

A company with an incentive pay system accumulates incentive piece-work pay or incentive hours earned and records the cost in a manner similar to that described above for hourly workers. Any make-up or guaranteed pay supplements to such incentive pay are charged to overhead. In this type of situation there is no need for a labor efficiency variance. If incentive pay is earned on an "hours" rather than on a "piece-work pay" basis, it will still be necessary to calculate a labor rate variance.

Some companies find it appropriate to have the factory foreman report on labor effort expended on a crew basis, with or without identification of individual employees involved. Although this usually simplifies the reporting effort, it also usually reduces reporting accuracy.

*Production data.* Production data can be obtained from whatever type of production order records is used in the particular plant to control and report on the manufacturing process (Figure 6.18). The production data must be summarized by stage *and* product with whatever frequency is required by the reporting cycle, since this production data is needed to calculate standard cost allowances and determine variances. For example, if a company needs daily labor reporting, then it needs daily production data on which to base the daily standard hours and/or dollar allowances.

*Overhead data.* Accumulation of overhead cost data usually presents the least difficulty. The prime requirement is an appropriate chart of accounts so that manufacturing overhead costs will be accumulated by cost element, department, and cost behavior category (i.e., variable or fixed).

*Use of data processing facilities.* The preceding discussion indicates that a voluminous amount of reporting and recordkeeping is required in order to operate a cost accounting system. Two problems generally arise because of this condition:

1. Difficulty in obtaining complete and accurate data about the production activity; and
2. The extensive effort of recording and analyzing the data and developing the detailed cost reports.

Many companies have utilized data processing facilities in order to cope with both of these problems. Several companies manufacture equipment specifically designed to collect data in the factory. The typical configuration consists of a central processing unit (CPU) located either in the factory or in the office, terminals at appropriate work stations throughout the factory, a tape drive, and a printer. The factory employees use the terminals to enter into the system such data as time and attendance, labor distribution, units produced, and units transferred to the next operation

| EMPLOYEE NO. | ACCOUNT | EMPLOYEE NAME | SHIFT | YR. / MO. / DAY | WEEK | DIVISION | UNIT | T/K | DEPARTMENT |
|---|---|---|---|---|---|---|---|---|---|

| PART NUMBER | SPECIAL | EXPENSE FUNCTION | MJO | WORK ORDER | WORK CENTER | OPER. | QUANTITY | UNIT STANDARD | HOURS WORKED | CLOCK TIMES |
|---|---|---|---|---|---|---|---|---|---|---|
| | | | | | | | | | | STOP<br>START |
| | | | | | | | | | | STOP<br>START |
| | | | | | | | | | | STOP<br>START |
| | | | | | | | | | | STOP<br>START |
| | | | | | | | | | | STOP<br>START |

AUTHORIZED SIGNATURE ____________________ **DAILY JOB CARD**

**FIGURE 6.17 DAILY JOB CARD**

| Production Tag | Amount Scheduled | Amount Finished | Rate | | |
|---|---|---|---|---|---|
| Machine No. _____ Operator No. _____ | | | | Out | In |
| Operation & No. | | | | Out | In |
| Labor Code No. | | | | Out | In |
| Helpers' Code Nos. _____ | | | | | |
| Signature | | | | | |

FIGURE 6.18  PRODUCTION TICKET

or department. This data is printed out and recorded on magnetic tape. At the end of the day, the tape is transferred to the company's main computer facility for further processing and preparation of management reports.

**Management Review and Approval.** After the work team has established the objectives and defined the data collection and processing requirements and methods, the team should document this proposed system structure for presentation to the management committee. This presentation should include the expected one-time implementation costs (including cost of computer hardware and software required) and an estimate of the ongoing costs of operating the system.

Modifications to the system structure are common at this stage in response to management's appraisal of both the nature and the cost of the system. The work team is now in a position to develop the *detailed* system specifications.

**Developing the Detailed Specifications.** This step involves simply the detailed documentation of the nature and method of data collection, the method and steps required to process the data, and the procedures for generation and analysis of the appropriate management reports. If the system is computer-based, the specifications will include the layout of each of the computer files. All appropriate forms should also be designed at this time.

**The Initial Data Requirements.** The basic data files (manual or computerized) must be established before any processing of data can be accomplished. With a standard cost system, the primary effort involves development and documentation of the specifications for the manufacture of each product. The detailed product and operational standards must then be established on the basis of the specifications, so that standard cost allowances can be calculated as production data is gathered and processed through the system. The standard cost data must include:

- Material quantities and prices by operation and department (including an acceptable waste allowance);
- Labor time to perform each operation on each product;
- Departmental labor rates;
- Departmental variable and fixed overhead rates by cost element; and
- Spoilage or defective cost allowances by product (and, perhaps, by stage of operations).

See Figure 6.19 for a typical standard cost sheet format.

*Departmental overhead rates.* Development of the departmental overhead rates requires establishment of overhead budgets upon which to base the rates. For a direct cost system, only the variable overhead costs will become part of the product standards. The rates should be based on production activity bases appropriate to each department's operation (e.g., direct labor hours, machine hours).

Style No. _____  Date _____

Description _____  Prepared By _____

Materials

| Item | Description | Basic Yards | Waste % | Total Yards | Price/Yd. | Cost/Dozen |
|------|-------------|-------------|---------|-------------|-----------|------------|
|      |             |             |         |             |           |            |

Total Material Cost Per Dozen _____

Direct Labor and Variable Overhead

| | Direct Labor | | | Variable Overhead | | |
| Operation | Labor Time | Hourly Rate | Labor Cost | % of Direct Labor | Overheard Cost | Total |
|-----------|------------|-------------|------------|-------------------|----------------|-------|
|           |            |             |            |                   |                |       |

Total Cost Per Dozen

Total Processing Cost _____

Allowance for Loss on Seconds - _____% 2nds × $_____ Loss/Dz. _____

Total Variable Inventory Cost _____

Fixed Plant Overhead - $_____ D.L. Cost × _____% _____

Total Inventory Cost _____

FIGURE 6.19  PRODUCT COST SHEET

*Inventory records.* Inventory files must be established and maintained for raw material, work-in-process and finished goods. These inventories should be valued at standard cost as a starting point for operation of the cost system. This implies the need to establish the product standards by stage of operation, so that work-in-process inventory may be properly valued. Once the inventory starting points are established, it is imperative that the company be prepared to continue the maintenance of these perpetual records, so that the initial effort of establishing the inventories will have continuing value in the operation of the cost system. The journal entries described earlier in this chapter establish control accounts on the general ledger for all categories of inventory. During the operation of the cost system, the control accounts are used to verify the accuracy of the monthly valuation of all detailed inventories at standard cost. This procedure also serves to verify the accuracy of the data flowing through the cost system upon which the monthly journal entries (and, thus, the control accounts) are based.

**The Trial Run.** Once the data files are established, it is possible (and necessary) to begin processing actual data through the system, using the forms and procedures that comprise the detailed system specifications. This can be done in phases or on a comprehensive basis for a trial period. The phases might consist of separate implementation of collection and processing of:

- Production data;
- Labor distribution data;
- Material usage records; and
- Departmental overhead accounting.

Another "phasing-in" approach is complete implementation of any or all of the above data flows on a department-by-department basis.

The primary purpose of this initial trial run is not to collect accurate, useful cost information. Rather, it is to test the accuracy, reliability, and practicality of the cost system procedures. The results of this trial run should be carefully reviewed and evaluated to define possible bottlenecks and unexpected complications in the operation of the system and to uncover factory operating conditions not anticipated in the original system design.

Invariably, it will be necessary to modify the cost system on the basis of this trial run and evaluation. After modification, the system should again be tested thoroughly. This time the work team is interested in both the accuracy and practicality of the system and the reliability and meaningfulness of the data generated by operation of the system.

This process of testing, review, evaluation, and modification should be repeated as many times as necessary until the team is satisfied that the company has a working system.

This does not mean that the system development work is finished. In a sense, this effort is never finished. In the typical case, it requires at least two years of operation of the system until management is completely satisfied with the established standards and the meaningfulness of the cost reports. In a broader context, a cost system is continually evolving, partly as a consequence of growing company sophistication in the use of such a system and partly because a factory operation is dynamic and the cost system must likewise be dynamic if it is to be a permanently useful management tool.

**Pitfalls in Implementation.** There are innumerable varieties of problems and pitfalls that may be encountered in as complex a project as implementation of a cost system. This section summarizes the types of situations that may be encountered. If management is adequately prepared, problems of this type appear less formidable to cope with and to resolve.

*Resistance to change.* Since installation of a cost system involves extensive change, it is likely to meet with extensive resistance from the factory workers and supervisors. The extensive demand upon them for disciplined processing and collection of factory operating data will be met only if the factory personnel understand the reason for the system and the benefits that will accrue therefrom for them and for the company. The success of the project depends on the work team demonstrating to the factory supervisors that the operation of the cost system will provide them with information to help them meet their responsibilities. During the trial run, management should pay careful attention to the extent and nature of the demands made upon the factory personnel by operation of the system, and it should make every effort to keep those demands within practical limits without degrading the quality of the system. At the same time, corporate management must demonstrate continuing involvement and support, so that factory management will understand the importance that the company places on the objectives of the cost system.

*Effect of substitutions.* Many companies find it necessary at times to substitute materials other than those originally specified for the manufacture of certain products. Unless the factory reporting system is structured to identify those substitutions (i.e., to identify the materials *actually* used), the cost reports and variance calculations and the perpetual inventory records will be inaccurate.

In similar fashion, it is essential to capture information regarding substitution of finished product in the fulfillment of customer orders. Otherwise the standard cost of sales will be calculated incorrectly and the finished goods perpetual inventory records will be inaccurate.

*Material losses.* It is important to capture appropriate information regarding the production stage at which material losses occur. Otherwise, responsibility performance reporting will not be achievable and appropriate corrective action will not be possible.

*Rework and idle time costs.* Failure to isolate rework labor cost from normal direct labor results in excessive build-up of unfavorable labor variances and an inability to identify the reasons for those variances. Failure to identify idle time of the direct labor force has similar consequences. The rework and idle time costs should be charged to variable overhead.

*Coding errors.* A cost accounting system places a heavy demand for coding of direct and indirect costs incurred (both labor and expenses). This almost invariably results initially in a high incidence of coding errors. A continuing emphasis on clerical and factory staff training is necessary to overcome this system start-up problem.

*Undue emphasis on product costing.* A common danger in both the design and implementation of a cost system is the placing of undue (or, at times, exclusive) emphasis on the product costing objective of cost accounting. Usually, the objectives of cost control and performance reporting deserve the primary emphasis in order to maximize the management usefulness of the system, as opposed to the "pure accounting" objectives.

## DECISION ANALYSIS

The proper analysis of data relevant to a decision confronting management is one of the most important functions a financial executive can perform. The financial executive's ability to analyze data effectively is greatly enhanced by the operation of an effective cost system. A cost system utilizing both direct costing and standard costing techniques provides a valuable and comprehensive data base for this purpose.

As discussed earlier in this chapter, direct costing emphasizes cost behavior patterns (variable vs. fixed) in response to changing activity levels (e.g., production and sales volume). It also emphasizes profit contribution (sales minus variable costs), which is fundamental to many aspects of analysis for management decision-making.

The availability of standard cost data facilitates the definition of expected cost patterns. Since decision analysis is a forward-looking technique, such a data base is invaluable. Standard costs represent, by definition, the costs that management expects to incur at desired levels of operating efficiency. Of course, if, in a given situation, management expects to incur variances from standard costs, those expected variances should be part of the projected cost data utilized in the analytical process.

### Cost-Volume-Profit Analysis

The interrelationship of costs and volume, and the resulting impact on profitability, is at the heart of much of decision analysis. This interrelationship can best be understood by means of *breakeven analysis*. Breakeven analysis utilizes projected revenue and expense patterns to define the level of sales at which revenues and expenses are expected to equal each other; that is, the breakeven point. More importantly, though, this technique also defines the expected impact on profit, or loss, as the sales level moves above or below the breakeven point. There are two approaches to breakeven point determination: mathematical formula and charting. The *breakeven formula* approach emphasizes *only* the breakeven sales level, while a *breakeven chart* depicts the expected cost-volume-profit relationship over a range of activity levels.

**The Breakeven Formula.** The formula approach can be used to define the breakeven point either in sales dollars or in units. The sales dollar version of the formula is as follows:

$$\text{Breakeven Sales \$} = \frac{\text{Total Fixed Costs}}{\text{Profit Contribution as a} \atop \text{\% of Sales}}$$

To illustrate:

Assume:

| | |
|---|---|
| Budgeted fixed costs | $200,000 |
| Selling price per unit | 10.00 |
| Standard variable costs per unit | 6.00 |

The profit contribution (also known as marginal contribution) is:

| | | |
|---|---|---|
| Selling price | $10.00 | 100% |
| Variable cost | 6.00 | 60 |
| Profit contribution | $ 4.00 | 40% |

Therefore, breakeven sales are:

$$\frac{\$200,000}{40\%} = \$500,000$$

In other words, $500,000 sales @ 40% contribution = $200,000 of profit contribution, which is just sufficient to cover fixed costs of $200,000.

The breakeven sales *units* can be determined by use of the following formula:

$$\text{Breakeven Units} = \frac{\text{Total Fixed Costs}}{\text{Profit Contributions per Unit}}$$

Continuing our example, breakeven units are:

$$\frac{\$200,000}{\$4.00} = 50,000 \text{ units}$$

Thus, 50,000 units at $4 profit contribution per unit = $200,000 total contribution, which is just sufficient to cover fixed costs of $200,000.

Either version of the formula can be modified to define the sales volume needed to achieve a target income level (pretax), by adding the target income dollars to the expected fixed costs. In our example, assuming that management wants to know the sales level needed to achieve $40,000 of pretax income, the calculations would be:

$$\frac{\$200,000 \ + \ \$40,000}{40\%} \ = \ \$600,000$$

or

$$\frac{\$200,000 \ + \ \$40,000}{\$4.00} \ = \ 60,000 \ \text{units}$$

In this case, the target sales dollars ($600,000) exceed breakeven sales dollars ($500,000) by $100,000. Since the breakeven sales level will, by definition, yield just enough profit contribution to cover fixed costs, the additional sales volume of $100,000, at 40 percent contribution rate, will generate $40,000 of pretax income. Similarily, 10,000 units above breakeven (60,000 – 50,000) at $4.00 contribution per unit equals $40,000.

To summarize:

$600,000 sales* @ 40% profit contribution = $240,000
Fixed cost                                               200,000
Target income                                    $ 40,000

*60,000 units @ $10 selling price

**The Breakeven Chart.** The charting approach to breakeven analysis provides a more comprehensive picture of the inherent cost-volume-profit relationships. Figure 6.20 illustrates the breakeven chart of a company's profit plan. (The same technique can be utilized with historical data.) The vertical axis of the breakeven chart represents volume (usually expressed in sales dollars). The horizontal axis (in dollars) is used to plot and read the various relationships depicted in the chart. The first line drawn is the sales line; it is plotted by reading *both* axes as sales dollars. Next, the variable cost line is drawn, starting at "O," since by definition such costs rise or fall proportionately with volume, and plotting any additional variable cost points by multiplying the expected variable cost percentage by a given sales level. The difference between the sales and variable cost lines represents the marginal contribution (also known as profit contribution) at any given level of sales.

Period, or fixed, costs are plotted as a *constant* addition to variable costs at all levels of sale; this yields the total cost line. The breakeven sales point is simply that point at which the sales line crosses the total cost line. Stated another way, it is the sales volume level that provides just enough marginal contribution to equal the period costs.

The sales level inherent in the company's profit plan can then be identified as

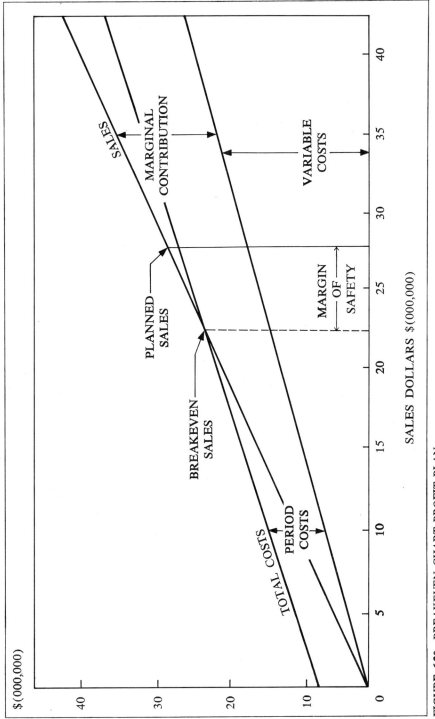

FIGURE 6.20 BREAKEVEN CHART PROFIT PLAN

depicted on Figure 6.20. The difference between planned and breakeven sales is referred to as the margin of safety, since it represents the portion of planned sales that management can fail to achieve without operating at a loss. More importantly, perhaps, the chart depicts graphically the profit potential at each sales level above breakeven, and, conversely, the potential loss at any sales level below breakeven. In other words, it highlights the cost-volume-profit interrelationship.

**Constraints of Breakeven Analysis.** Breakeven calculations or charts are effective only so long as the underlying assumptions remain valid. Specifically, the following assumptions must remain static:

- Sales prices;
- Product sales mix, and the resultant impact on a composite (weighted average) profit contribution rate;
- Variable cost rate (i.e., spending and efficiency patterns); and
- Level of period (fixed) cost.

If any of these assumptions change, the analysis must be redone. Furthermore, the relationships depicted on a breakeven chart can be expected to be valid only within a "relevant" range of activity. That is, sales volume below or above a normal range of activity is likely to drastically alter the relationships underlying the chart. At very low volumes, operating efficiency might suffer (raising the variable cost percentage), any deferrable fixed costs will be put off in the interest of corporate survival, advertising costs may be increased, and management may offer significant price reductions to generate sales volume. At very high volumes, inefficiencies might develop, and operating capacity may have to be increased to meet the production and sales demand.

**Interpretation of Breakeven Charts.** Figure 6.21 presents the breakeven charts depicting the cost-volume-profit relationships of two companies in the same industry. Note that the planned sales and expected operating profit are identical for both companies. However, one company has a low level of fixed cost (and a corresponding high ratio of variable costs to sales). This company's operations are labor-intensive, with relatively little factory automation. In contrast, the other company has high fixed costs because it is highly automated; it has a low rate of variable costs because of the degree of automation.

If the respective managements of each of these companies were unaware of their companies' underlying cost behavior patterns, they might be expected to react identically to marketplace conditions during the year. Examination of the implications of the two charts will reveal that very different responses may well be in order.

For example, the low-fixed-cost company has very little incentive to lower prices in order to attract additional sales volume, since operating profit increases at a very low rate on higher volume. The high-fixed-cost company has significant profit potential from increased volume and may benefit substantially from price reductions (and other forms of sales promotion).

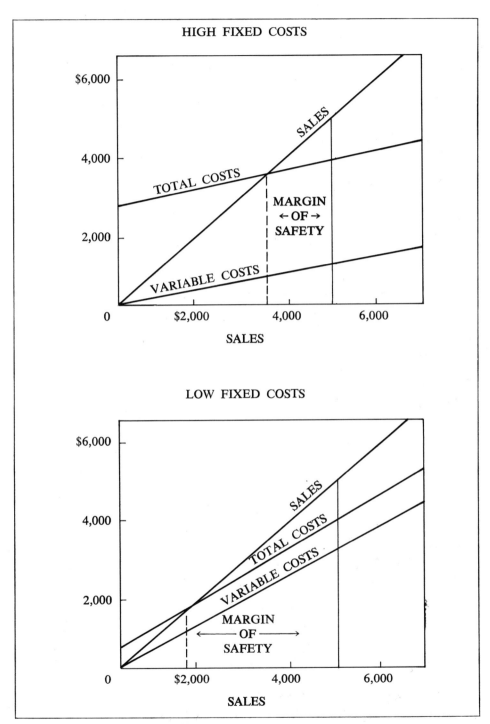

FIGURE 6.21 BREAKEVEN CHARTS

Conversely, the low-fixed-cost company has a considerable margin of safety against falling sales. Since most of its costs are variable, it can lose a considerable amount of volume before reaching the breakeven point. The high-fixed-cost company has a strong incentive to maintain its planned sales level, since the fixed costs will remain substantially at the same level as volume drops, thus providing only a small margin of safety.

Other uses of the breakeven technique will be illustrated in some of the examples presented in the following section.

### Incremental Cost Analysis

Incremental cost (and revenue) analysis is simply the analysis of changes that can be expected to occur as a result of a particular course of action. The ability to define expected incremental (i.e., relevant) costs is greatly enhanced by the existence of a properly constructed and smoothly operating cost system, and an understanding of the company's cost-volume-profit relationships. Without these foundations, the data needed to perform the types of analyses illustrated below may simply not be available with any degree of reliability.

A discussion of some of the more significant types of incremental cost analysis follows.

---

PRELIMINARY PROFIT PLAN

| | |
|---|---:|
| Net Sales | $2,000,000 |
| Variable Cost | 1,360,000 |
| Marginal Contribution | 640,000 |
| % of Net Sales | 32% |
| Fixed Cost | 440,000 |
| Net Profit Before Taxes | $  200,000 |

PRICING DECISION

Decrease in Price:
$2,000,000 @ (5%) =                                                  ($  100,000)

Increase in Volume:
$1,900,000 (at reduced prices)
@ 25% = $475,000 additional sales
@ 28.42% * contribution (after price reduction) =                    135,000

Projected Profit Improvement                                         $    35,000

*($640,000−$100,000) ÷ ($2,000,000−$100,000) = 28.42%

BREAKEVEN VOLUME INCREASE
$100,000 (price reduction effect) ÷ 28.42% = $351,865

---

FIGURE 6.22   PROFIT PLANNING ILLUSTRATION—PRICING LEVEL

**Profit Planning Decisions.** The development of a corporate profit plan involves establishing management policies that are designed to attain the profit goals set forth in the plan. This distinguishes a true profit plan from a budget based largely on prior results and wishful thinking. After a preliminary profit plan has been developed for the coming year, management should evaluate that plan to determine whether the profit targets contained therein need to and can be improved. Figures 6.22 and 6.23 provide examples of the type of decision analysis applicable to this process.

---

PRELIMINARY PROFIT PLAN

| | TOTAL COMPANY | PRODUCT A | PRODUCT B |
|---|---|---|---|
| Net Sales | $1,000,000 | $800,000 | $200,000 |
| Variable Cost | 700,000 | 600,000 | 100,000 |
| Marginal Contribution | 300,000 | 200,000 | 100,000 |
| % of Net Sales | 30% | 25% | 50% |
| Fixed Cost | 270,000 | | |
| Net Profit Before Taxes | $    30,000 | | |

PRODUCT MIX CHARGE

| | |
|---|---|
| Decrease in Product A Sales: | |
| (100,000) @ 25%  = | ($ 25,000) |
| Increase in Product B Sales: | |
| $70,000 @ 50%  = | 35,000 |
| Projected Profit Improvement | $ 10,000 |

BREAKEVEN ANALYSIS

| | |
|---|---|
| $25,000 (contribution loss on Product A) | |
| ÷ 50% (Product B contribution rate)  = | |
| Product B sales increase required to break even, or | $ 50,000 |

ADDITIONAL ADVERTISING CAMPAIGN

| | |
|---|---|
| Cost of Additional Advertising for Product A | ($ 30,000) |
| Expected Volume Increase: | |
| $800,000 @ 25%  = $200,000 additional sales | |
| @ 25% contribution  = | 50,000 |
| Projected Profit Improvement | $20,000 |
| Breakeven Volume Increase | |
| $30,000 Advertising Cost ÷ 25% Contribution Rate  = | $120,000 |

FIGURE 6.23   PROFIT PLANNING ILLUSTRATIONS—PRODUCT MIX AND SALES PROMOTIONS

*Pricing level.* Figure 6.22 illustrates the means of evaluating the trade-off between selling price and sales volume. In the illustration, management is considering a 5 percent reduction in selling prices (from the level inherent in the preliminary profit plan). Management believes this price decrease will generate a 25 percent increase in volume. The reduction in prices will cause a dollar-for-dollar decrease in profit, since operating costs are not affected by the price at which a product is sold (with the possible exception of sales commission paid on dollars of sale). In the case illustrated in the figure, a 5 percent reduction in selling prices will reduce profits by $100,000. Since the additional sales volume will take place at the lower prices, the expected marginal contribution on the additional sales will be less than the 32 percent rate contained in the original profit plan. As shown in Exhibit 6.22, the post–price reduction contribution rate of 28.42 percent applied to the anticipated additional sales volume of $475,000 will yield $135,000 in additional profit, assuming that no increase in fixed cost is necessary to provide the capacity to handle the additional business. If a company's operating capacity is not sufficient to handle projected increases in volume, then the incremental fixed costs of providing that capacity must be considered as well. In our illustration, it appears that the price reduction is worthwhile, since it is expected to improve pretax profit by $35,000. However, there is the risk that the 5 percent price reduction will yield *less than* the anticipated 25 percent increase in volume. In order to help evaluate the degree of risk involved, it is possible to calculate the *minimum* level of volume increase needed to offset the impact of lower prices (i.e., to "break even" on the decision). This is accomplished by dividing the revenue loss of $100,000 from lower prices by 28.42 percent, the marginal contribution rate expected at the lower price level. This tells us that additional sales of $351,865 at 28.42 percent will yield the $100,000 of incremental contribution needed to offset the price reduction impact. Management can now evaluate the degree of risk it believes is involved in achieving at least this breakeven increment in sales volume.

*Product mix.* In Figure 6.23, management is contemplating shifting some of its sales effort from Product A to Product B. This appears desirable because Product B has a higher marginal contribution rate than does Product A (50% vs. 25%). However, it is expected that a reduction of $100,000 in sales of A will be replaced with only $70,000 of incremental sales of B. As shown in Figure 6.23, the higher rate of contribution on B makes this change in product mix appear worthwhile. Again, the degree of risk must be evaluated. The reduction in sales of A will cause a $25,000 loss in profit ($100,000 @ 25%). Dividing this $25,000 loss by the 50 percent contribution rate for B tells us that the company will need at least $50,000 of sales of B to cover the product A contribution loss ($50,000 @ 50% = $25,000).

*Sales promotion.* Figure 6.23 evaluates the expected impact on profits of attaining additional sales by expanding funds on a particular advertising program (in addition to whatever advertising budget is already included in the preliminary profit plan). As shown in the figure, management expects that the new advertising campaign for Product A, which will cost $30,000, will result in additional sales of

$200,000. At the projected contribution rate of 25 percent for A, the additional advertising expenditure appears worthwhile ($200,000 @ 25% = $50,000). Once again, it is possible and worthwhile to determine the minimum sales increase needed to cover at least the incremental $30,000 advertising commitment. This is accomplished by dividing the advertising cost ($30,000) by A's marginal contribution rate (25%). The company must achieve incremental revenue of $120,000 to "break even" on the expenditure ($120,000 @ 25% = $30,000). In other words, it must achieve at least 60 percent of its expected sales increase ($120,000 ÷ $200,000) or its profits will be reduced.

**Marginal Pricing Decisions.** Management is often faced with the decisions to accept or reject a specific order. Usually this type of decision involves a lower than customary price for the product or products that the customer is offering to buy. Figure 6.24 presents the data associated with a typical "special order" situation. It is assumed that, before consideration of the special order, the company expects to sell 50,000 units at a selling price of $8.00 per unit. As indicated in the figure, this is projected to yield a pretax profit of $50,000. The customer has offered to buy an additional 30,000 units at $6.00 per unit. This compares unfavorably with the cost of $7.00 per unit at the current level of operations. It also compares unfavorably with the *average* unit cost of $6.25 projected for the higher volume level of 80,000 units. However, neither of these *average* cost factors is relevant to this decision. Simply stated, the question is: will the *incremental* revenue ($180,000) exceed the *incremental* cost expected to be incurred ($150,000) to attain that revenue? In this illustration, the special order will yield an incremental profit ($30,000) and presumably should be accepted.

It should be noted once again that the ability to project the impact on costs as presented in the figure depends largely on the availability of reliable cost data, including an understanding of the cost behavior patterns of the company.

In a given situation, it may be that the company has sufficient idle capacity to fill the special order. If so, the incremental overhead costs will represent variable costs only. If capacity is not sufficient, management must project the increase in fixed costs that will be necessary to provide the required capacity. Also, the specific conditions of the order under consideration must be considered. Will a sales commission be paid on the order? Will the company or the customer pay shipping costs? Are there any other specific out-of-pocket costs (e.g., sales aids or advertising allowances) that the company must incur to obtain the order? If such costs are relevant, they must be included in the total of projected incremental costs.

Other critical factors that management must consider with respect to a marginal pricing decision are not always easily quantifiable. Nevertheless, they may be the determining factors in deciding whether or not to accept the order. Among these factors are the following:

- Will the customer expect the same low price on future orders, when the company may not have the idle capacity available? If so, the cost of providing that capacity may make the business undesirable.
- Will customers represented by the *base* volume (the 50,000 units, in our example)

expect to receive the favorable $6.00 selling price (as opposed to $8.00 at present)? If so, the company profits may disappear, since the *average* cost ($6.25) for all 80,000 units is more than the $6.00 selling price. The *total* sales of a company must, of course, cover *all* operating costs, both variable and fixed.

**Make Versus Buy.** A common problem facing many companies involves a decision to manufacture or purchase either a component used in the company's manufacturing process or a finished product itself. The relevant costs for the manufacturing alternative are those additional costs that will be incurred if the item is produced in-house. If the company has sufficient available capacity, only variable costs are relevant. Otherwise, the fixed costs related to the additional capacity required should be considered as well.

As with marginal pricing decisions, the *full* cost per unit for *all* production is not relevant, since much or all of the fixed cost incurred will not be affected by the deci-

|  | Current Volume | | Projected Volume | | Incremental Volume | |
|---|---|---|---|---|---|---|
|  | Total Cost | Per Unit | Total Cost | Per Unit | Total Cost | Per Unit |
| Units | 50,000 |  | 80,000 |  | 30,000 |  |
| Costs: |  |  |  |  |  |  |
|   Direct Material | $ 75,000 | $1.50 | $120,000 | $1.50 | $ 45,000 | $1.50 |
|   Direct labor | 75,000 | 1.50 | 120,000 | 1.50 | 45,000 | 1.50 |
|   Overhead | 200,000 | 4.00 | 260,000 | 3.25 | 60,000 | 2.00 |
|     Total Cost | $350,000 | $7.00 | $500,000 | $6.25 | $150,000 | $5.00 |

| Sales Price: | |
|---|---|
|   Current | $8.00 |
|   Special Order | $6.00 |

| Current Volume: | |
|---|---|
|   Sales (50,000 units @ $8.00) | $400,000 |
|   Total Cost (above) | 350,000 |
|   Expected Profit | 50,000 |

| Incremental Volume: | |
|---|---|
|   Sales (30,000 @ $6.00) | $180,000 |
|   Incremental Costs (above) | 150,000 |
|   Incremental Profit | 30,000 |
|   Total Expected Profit | $ 80,000 |

FIGURE 6.24   MARGINAL PRICING ILLUSTRATION

sion to manufacture the part. To illustrate, if it is estimated that in-house production of a particular item will require $3.00 material cost and $2.50 direct labor cost per unit, and if the company's standard factory overhead rate is 200 percent of direct labor, then the *full* cost of manufacturing one unit will be:

| | |
|---|---|
| Materials | $ 3.00 |
| Direct labor | 2.50 |
| Overhead ($2.50 @ 200%) | 5.00 |
| Total cost | $10.50 |

If the same item can be purchased for $8.00, the company might logically decide to "save" $2.50 per unit ($10.50 – $8.00) by purchasing the item.

However, if we assume that sufficient productive capacity exists to produce the item (e.g., without adding equipment, space, supervision, etc.) then only the *variable* overhead costs are relevant to the decision. If we further assume that the company's 200 percent standard factory overhead rate comprises a 60 percent *variable* overhead rate and a 140 percent *fixed* overhead rate, then the proper cost analysis would be:

| | |
|---|---|
| Materials | $3.00 |
| Direct labor | 2.50 |
| Variable overhead ($2.50 @ 60%) | 1.50 |
| Total relevant cost | $7.00 |

On a *relevant* cost basis, the "manufacture" option now appears attractive ($7.00 cost to manufacture vs. $8.00 outside purchase price).

As with most incremental, or relevant, cost analysis, the direct financial analysis as presented above may not tell the whole story. For instance, other considerations in a "make versus buy" decision might include:

- Is there another *more attractive* use for the available productive capacity?
- What is the expected *quality* of the product if manufactured, compared to acquisition from the outside vendor?
- How *reliable* is the outside source in terms of delivery commitments?

Nevertheless, without the availability of a reliable incremental cost analysis, management will be missing a vital component in its ability to make an informed, rational decision.

**Other Incremental Decision Analysis.** The analytical approach inherent in the examples presented above applies equally well to many other situations confronting management. For example:

- For a multiplant company, determining the plant at which to produce a particular product;

- Whether to expand into a new product line (or to abandon an existing line);
- Whether to expand into a new territory;
- Whether to market existing products to a new class of customers; or
- Whether to close a particular plant, or store, or warehouse.

In all of these cases, the requirement is simply to determine the manner in which revenues and/or costs are expected to be affected by each decision alternative. The ability to make such a determination depends upon the availability of sound cost data and an understanding of the company's cost-volume-profit relationships.

## SUGGESTED READING

Anderson, Henry R., and Raiborn, Mitchell H. *Basic Cost Accounting Concepts.* Boston: Houghton, Mifflin Co., 1977.

Bierman, Harold, Jr., and Dyckman, Thomas R. *Managerial Cost Accounting.* 2nd ed. New York: Macmillan Publishing Co., Inc., 1976.

Corcoran, A. Wayne. *Costs: Accounting, Analysis, and Control.* New York: John Wiley & Sons, 1978.

Davidson, Sidney, and Weil, Roman L. *Handbook of Cost Accounting.* New York: McGraw Hill Book Company, 1978.

Dopuch, Nicholas, Birnberg, Jacob G., and Demski, Jack. *Cost Accounting: Accounting Data for Management's Decisions.* New York: Harcourt Brace Jovanovich, Inc., 1974.

# 7

# Distribution Cost Accounting

*Richard Lancioni*

## INTRODUCTION

The period from World War II to the early 1970s produced remarkable technological advances in materials handling, transportation, and information processing. Governmental, industrial, and commercial organizations have reorganized to improve management of logistics activities and to take advantage of the new logistics technology. But as the population stabilizes and markets level out, organizational managers face new questions about the logistical systems under their control. What effects will pressures for new products and product individuality have on the logistical system? How can the logistical system respond to the congestion within many cities and the dispersion and growth of suburban markets? And, finally, can the new technology continue to provide logistics managers with the means to deal with these problems?

## New Bases for Decision Making

It appears that these questions will be answered not by a wave of new logistics technology but by major institutional changes that reorganize functions and facilities within individual organizations and among cooperating organizations. Within the area of physical distribution, there has been a change in emphasis from decision making based upon superficial cost analyses to decision making based more on intensive cost and profit analyses and interorganizational cooperation.

The new emphasis on solving logistical problems by institutional changes has come about for the following reasons:

- There are physical constraints on various methods of transportation and materials handling. Existing physical facilities, such as highways, tunnels, bridges, and underpasses set limits on the size and weight of carriers. Public attitudes do not encourage the construction of roadways and bridges that would permit the manufacture or use of substantially larger carriers.
- Public resistance to change has been heightened by ecological and environmental concerns.
- As facilities and carriers are made larger, economies of scale reach the point of diminishing returns.
- In some cases, new transportation technology has created pdoblems that have been solved only by cooperation between institutions (i.e., by causing a more efficient flow of freight).
- There is a more positive attitude and interest in cooperation among businessmen and government officials. For example, some difficult distribution problems—such as congested city centers—have been partially solved by coordination of inbound freight movements and consolidated distribution centers.
- There is a new concern for coordinated transportation management because retailers and wholesalers have tried to limit their speculative risk by keeping inventories of any one item to a minimum, or by investing commensurate amounts of money in inventory for a broader line of products, while still demanding fast product delivery.

Firms are beginning to see that the economic benefits brought about by institutional rather than technological change can be substantial. Great cost savings can be achieved by coordinating transportation, warehousing, materials handling, inventory control, order processing, and procurement activities. By shifting functions, where possible, to other parts of the distribution channel they can be integrated into other activities.

This new view of logistics, combined with recent efforts to make the physical distribution area as efficient and effective as possible, have highlighted certain problems. First, financial reporting systems as presently constituted do not provide the analyses necessary to make sound decisions or to implement effective controls in distribution management. Financial planners have overlooked the individual costs associated with transportation, materials handling, warehousing, and order processing. Second, costs generated by other groups within the organization (such as the marketing group), are often charged against the physical distribution department.

## THE CONTROLLER'S ROLE

Many firms are solving the problem of providing accurate and meaningful cost data for distribution by assigning the controller (or a member of his staff) to the physical distribution function. If the controller ensures that all costs incurred after goods have been made available for sale are accurately documented and reported, management can make realistic and accurate decisions about its distribution operations.

### Organizational Responsibilities

The following definition of distribution cost analysis outlines the scope of the controller's responsibility in this area:

The assembling of the various items of distribution cost into meaningful classifications and their comparision in this form with alternative expenditures and with related sales volumes and gross margins . . . the determination of the cost of performing specific marketing activities and . . . the determination of costs and profits for various segments of the business such as products or product groups, customer classes, or units of sales—and a study of these findings in the light of possible alternatives.[1]

Simply stated, the long-term objective of the controller in charge of physical distribution must be to make a meaningful contribution to the firm's profit picture. The short-run objectives are the efficient and effective collecting, recording, and reporting of current cost data connected with the physical distribution segment of the business.

The controller, in his staff function, acts as a liaison between the distribution operation and the corporate finance group. He is responsible for the preparation of financial analyses, assists in the establishment of economic policies, and justifies or criticizes the expenditures of the distribution department. He also directs the preparation of budgets and financial forecasts for the distribution group and is involved in determining depreciation rates for the appropriate capitalized items. The controller's responsibilities may also include the preparation of government cost reports applying to his operation, participation in distribution accounting audits, and advice to top management regarding insurance coverage to protect against property losses and potential liabilities.

### Relationship of Distribution Cost to Manufacturing and Marketing Decisions

There is a definite relationship between the cost of distribution and decisions made in the manufacturing and marketing area. Distribution costs are all the costs incurred after the goods have been made available for sale. Manufacturing and marketing decisions can directly increase or decrease distribution costs.

---

[1] Marketing for Executives Series No. 2. "The Values and Uses of Distribution Cost Analysis," *American Marketing Association Committee on Distribution Cost and Efficiency.*

**The Effect of Manufacturing Decisions.** Distribution costs can be affected, both directly and indirectly, by management decisions that may change manufacturing production flows, product standards, or materials. An example of a direct correlation between a manufacturing choice and distribution cost is the effect of an increase in production to achieve optimum operation of the plant. While this decision may reduce manufacturing costs it will increase storage, handling, and carrying costs of the excess inventory. An indirect cost could result from the marketing department's efforts to move the increased inventory. And this might cause higher than normal bad debts or higher discounts.

The controller must alert management to the relationship between manufacturing decisions and distribution costs. Contemplated changes must be evaluated from an overall cost basis—not just in relation to manufacturing costs.

**The Effect of Marketing Decisions.** The tremendous pressure exerted on the marketing department distribution costs is described by one analyst in the following way:

> . . . Marketing requirements establish the servicing limits within which the system must work. Marketing tactics impose locks on physical distribution which substantially affect its costs. Marketing management, therefore, has and must accept responsibility for the decisions and operating cost of physical distribution systems.[2]

As marketing decisions on product line content, sales tactics, and channels of distribution are made, the physical distribution department must be prepared to assist marketing in reaching its predetermined objectives. For example, if the marketing group decides to change the size of the product box and offer a new size for a new consumer segment, the distribution group may have to alter its warehouse configuration or require that new pallets be purchased to handle the new size. Both actions may not seem especially critical, but they can have a significant impact on distribution costs. In short, the distribution function must adjust to the company's changing marketing strategy.

It is important that the costs related to marketing decisions be properly identified. Marketing decisions will affect the cost of order processing, inventory control, transportation, and warehousing. If the marketing group requires that a special package be used or that special offers be made to customers, the cost of distribution may increase.

**Utilizing Distribution Channels.** In some firms, organization and direction of the sales and marketing activities are based on the company's distribution channels. Separate divisions of the sales organization might be responsible for directing sales to jobbers and the larger industrial customers. In these situations, the cost of the sales activity is directly related to individual channels of distribution. Costs must be

---

[2] J.F. Magee, *Physical Distribution Systems* (New York: McGraw-Hill, 1967), p. 34.

correctly allocated to assign proper responsibility for the costs as they are incurred. Changes in direct selling expenses (salaries, commissions, training, insurance, tax payments, supplies, work that is spoiled because of salesman error, etc.), advertising and promotional allowances, transportation and warehousing, and credit and collection expenses are all sales related and must be assigned to the proper distribution channel.

**Delivery Terms.** The costs associated with product delivery are a function of the terms of delivery. Although these costs are repetitive in nature they are not easily standardized. Special techniques, such as time studies, may be needed in order to keep accurate track of delivery expense. The physical distribution controller should be kept informed of changes in delivery terms or methods and, whenever possible, his advice should be solicited.

**Tradeoffs.** Tradeoffs occur when marketing and manufacturing decisions are made that give the sales department the best possible support, and at the same time meet the cost and efficiency objectives of the physical distribution function. Some tradeoffs frequently encountered in distribution decision making are grouped into the following areas:

*Materials Handling*

- Customer requirements; and
- Product characteristics.

*Transportation*

- Rail cost; and
- Truck cost.

*Utilization or Packaging*

- Manual handling systems;
- Labor costs; and
- Costs of alternative packaging materials.

*Storage*

- Public versus private warehousing;
- Break bulk costs; and
- Location.

*Inventory*

- Quantity requirements;
- Production requirements;

- Marketing requirements;
- Order cycle time; and
- Warehousing requirements.

*Purchasing*

- Vendor reliability;
- Costs of raw materials; and
- Degree of standardization.

An effective trade-off of these elements will achieve the most cost efficient results for the company.

## TRADITIONAL DISTRIBUTION COST ACCOUNTING AND CONTROL APPROACHES

In the past, it has been difficult to obtain a comprehensive accounting of distribution costs because of a lack of accurate information. Some costs are located in manufacturing or marketing rather than in the distribution function where they belong. Others are just not available in the detail required for a proper analysis. As a control approach, the traditional practice has been to keep distribution costs to a minimum, without considering the interrelationship of distribution with other organizational functions. This traditional position or distribution cost control developed because the distribution function was not viewed as a separate operation or department in its own right, but was considered as an extension of marketing or manufacturing.

In his book, *The Analysis and Control of Distribution Costs*, J. Heckert states that:

> Just as accounting and production executives have joined forces in developing methods of production cost control, so must the accounting and marketing executives work jointly in the control of distribution costs.[3]

### Classifying Distribution Costs

In Heckert's view, distribution costs include all costs except the cost of the goods purchased or produced. He classifies these costs as follows:

1. Direct selling expense—all direct expense of salesmen, sales offices, sales, supervisors, and services connected to the selling effort;
2. Advertising and sales promotional expense—all advertising, sales promotion, pub-

---

[3] J. Heckert, *The Analysis and Control of Distribution Costs* (New York: Ronald Press Co., 1940) p. 5.

licity, educational, and market development activity, as well as other associated expenses;

3. Transportation expense—all transportation charges on outbound goods, returned sales, and local deliveries, maintenance and operation of outbound transportation facilities, and the distribution share of traffic service expense;

4. Warehousing and handling expense—the total expense of warehousing, storing, and handling finished goods beyond the point of production;

5. Credit and collection expense—all the expense of maintaining a credit and collection department, expense of accounts receivable records, collection expense, and loss from bad debts.

6. Financial expense—the cost of carrying accounts receivable and finished inventories, the cost of fixed and working capital for distribution activities, and cash discounts allowed on sales;

7. General distribution expense—the expense of distribution accounting and market research, the distribution share of general administration expenses, and all other expenses related to distribution activities not included above.[4]

Using Heckert's cost classification it is obvious that it would be difficult to obtain accurate data regarding the distribution function. Distribution costs are often included within other cost centers, thus making it difficult to determine the impact of distribution operations on the particular firm.

### Isolation of the Distribution Function

Distribution costs may be analyzed on the basis of the functional operations performed, the manner in which the distribution function is carried out, or by the nature of the various cost items associated with the distribution effort. Important in any distribution cost analysis is the need to separate the distribution operational functions from others performed in the company.

The operating statement chart shown in Figure 7.1 illustrates the traditional methods of controlling direct departmental costs by matching budgeted, or standard costs, against actual cost on a periodic basis. The cost of the distribution function does not appear. This cost has been absorbed somewhere within the other cost centers; it is thus impossible to determine the true value of services provided by the distribution function to the profit before taxes figure. Figure 7.2 demonstrates that even when costs specific to one or more product lines are shown separately, it is impossible to measure the contribution made and the cost generated by the distribution function.

## LATEST ADVANCES IN DISTRIBUTION COSTING

The new concepts of integrated logistical systems, total cost analysis, and the use of computers have enabled distribution controllers to make major advances in pinpointing, collecting, and analyzing distribution costs. These improvements manifest

---

[4] *Ibid.*

| Details | Actual | Budget | Variance favorable or (un-favorable) | Responsibility of Name | Title |
|---|---|---|---|---|---|
| Sales | $3,100,000 | $3,400,000 | | | |
| Cost of sales (at std.) | 1,922,000 | 2,040,000 | | | |
| MARGINAL INCOME (at std.) | $1,178,000 | $1,360,000 | (182,000) | J. Smith | V.P. of Sales |
| Variations from standard | | | | | |
| On purchasing materials | 5,000 | — | 5,000 | T. Brown | V.P. of Pur. |
| On processing materials | (28,950) | — | ( 28,950) | W. Lowe | V.P. of Mfg. |
| MARGINAL INCOME (Actual) | $1,154,050 | $1,360,000 | (205,950) | | |
| Period expenses: | | | | | |
| Manufacturing | $ 185,400 | $ 182,000 | ( 3,400) | W. Lowe | V.P. of Mfg. |
| Personnel | 125,400 | 124,500 | ( 900) | C. Downs | V.P. of Per. |
| Accounting | 89,100 | 84,000 | ( 5,100) | B. Brown | Controller |
| Marketing | 90,175 | 82,000 | ( 8,175) | J. Smith | Mgr. of Mkt. |
| Purchasing | 67,800 | 62,900 | ( 4,900) | T. Brown | V.P. of Pur. |
| Plant engineering | 38,225 | 40,500 | 2,275 | R. Roy | Dir. of Eng. |
| Legal | 43,290 | 38,750 | ( 4,540) | A. Wiley | Secretary |
| Treasury | 35,410 | 37,200 | 1,790 | W. Cash | Treasurer |
| Public relations | 25,200 | 26,800 | 1,600 | D. Cole | Dir. of P.R. |
| Research & Development | 21,850 | 18,300 | ( 3,550) | A. Mack | V.P. of Res. |
| Total period costs | $ 721,850 | $ 696,950 | ( 24,900) | | |
| PROFIT BEFORE TAXES | $ 432,200 | $ 663,050 | (230,850) | | |

*Source:* "Current Application of Direct Costing," National Association of Accountants, Research Report no. 37, January, 1971.

FIGURE 7.1  OPERATING STATEMENT SHOWING PERIOD EXPENSES BY FUNCTIONAL RESPONSIBILITIES

| | Total | | No. 1 | | No. 2 | | No. 3 | |
|---|---|---|---|---|---|---|---|---|
| | Amount | Pct. | Amount | Pct. | Amount | Pct. | Amount | Pct. |
| Net Sales | $600,000 | 100.0 | $300,000 | 100.0 | $200,000 | 100.0 | $100,000 | 100.0 |
| Direct costs | | | | | | | | |
| *Manufacturing* | | | | | | | | |
| Direct materials | $150,000 | 25.0 | $ 75,000 | 25.0 | $ 55,000 | 27.5 | $ 20,000 | 20.0 |
| Direct labor | 90,000 | 15.0 | 30,000 | 10.0 | 30,000 | 15.0 | 30,000 | 30.0 |
| Direct overhead | 60,000 | 10.0 | 30,000 | 10.0 | 20,000 | 10.0 | 10,000 | 10.0 |
| *Selling* | | | | | | | | |
| Freight out | 12,000 | 2.0 | 9,000 | 3.0 | 3,000 | 1.5 | — | |
| Salesmen's commissions | 24,000 | 4.0 | 12,000 | 4.0 | 8,000 | 4.0 | 4,000 | 4.0 |
| Total direct costs | $336,000 | 56.0 | $156,000 | 52.0 | $116,000 | 58.0 | $ 64,000 | 64.0 |
| Marginal income | $264,000 | 44.0 | $144,000 | 48.0 | $ 84,000 | 42.0 | $ 36,000 | 36.0 |
| *Period costs specific to product lines* | | | | | | | | |
| Depreciation | $ 40,000 | | $ 20,000 | | $10,000 | | $ 10,000 | |
| Property taxes & insurance | 20,000 | | 10,000 | | 2,000 | | 8,000 | |
| Advertising | 24,000 | | 20,000 | | — | | 4,000 | |
| Total | $ 84,000 | | $ 50,000 | | $ 12,000 | | $ 22,000 | |
| Margin after specific period costs | $180,000 | 30.0 | $ 94,000 | 31.3 | $ 72,000 | 36.0 | $ 14,000 | 14.0 |
| *Allocated general period costs* | | | | | | | | |
| Manufacturing | $ 40,000 | | $ 20,000 | | $ 13,320 | | $ 6,680 | |
| Selling | 30,000 | | 15,000 | | 10,000 | | 5,000 | |
| Administrative | 30,000 | | 15,000 | | 10,000 | | 5,000 | |
| Research & development | 20,000 | | 10,000 | | 6,666 | | 3,334 | |
| Total | $120,000 | | $ 60,000 | | $ 39,986 | | $ 20,014 | |
| Profit (loss) before taxes | $ 60,000 | 10.0 | $ 34,000 | 10.3 | $ 32,014 | 16.5 | $ 6,014 | ( 6.0) |

*Source:* "Current Application of Direct Costing," National Association of Accountants, Research Report no. 37, January, 1961.

FIGURE 7.2 PRODUCT LINE INCOME STATEMENT

themselves in improved freight accounting methods, customer service, warehouse evaluation, techniques for calculating inventory carrying costs, improved logistical reporting systems for top management, and in the analysis of distribution operations.

## Use of Computers For Freight Control

Since freight costs may account for more than fifty percent of all distribution costs, many firms have adopted computerized freight control systems.

**Data Collection.** Computers are used to store information pertaining to tens of thousands of routes and various modes of transportation. Simulation models are then used to analyze the cost and service charges when transportation methods and route changes are instituted. Freight information may be entered on an accrual basis and matched with actual freight. The system is capable of reporting customer profitability—broken down by amount sold, costs of goods sold, freight, and net after freight. The computerized freight control system may also be used to audit freight bills, or the system may provide customer data with a functioning sale-or-der-billing computer system. Shipping data may be collected for all products shipped from the plant, plant warehouses, field sales warehouses, and terminals. In-transit data on fleet location may also be collected. Freight cost information is also generated by the computer for each shipment. Figure 7.3 shows the source and type of data collected as part of the data base. Figure 7.4 depicts the output documents generated.

**Establishing Standards.** In a computerized freight control system a set of standards may be used for the significant repetitive moves of products to customers. The standards indicate the least expensive and most practical method of moving the goods in question to their destination. The freight costs may be divided into those associated with moving goods from the plant to a warehouse, and the costs associated with moving the goods a greater distance, from the warehouse to the customer.

Standards that utilize historical data on freight movements may also be developed. The computer can then compare all movements for all products shipped to customer destinations. The program can be set to select the appropriate standard for a particular product customer destination. The information in the freight standard may be categorized by complete identification of a particular movement, freight cost computations, illustration of movement pattern, size of the freight expense, and miscellaneous information.

Once freight standards are established, actual freight expenses can be compared. Deviations from the standard are shown on an *exception report;* both the standard and exception are compared. The exception report not only highlights deviations from standard but also shows the incremental costs associated with the exception. Basic documentation on the movement is also provided so that the cause of the variance may be determined.

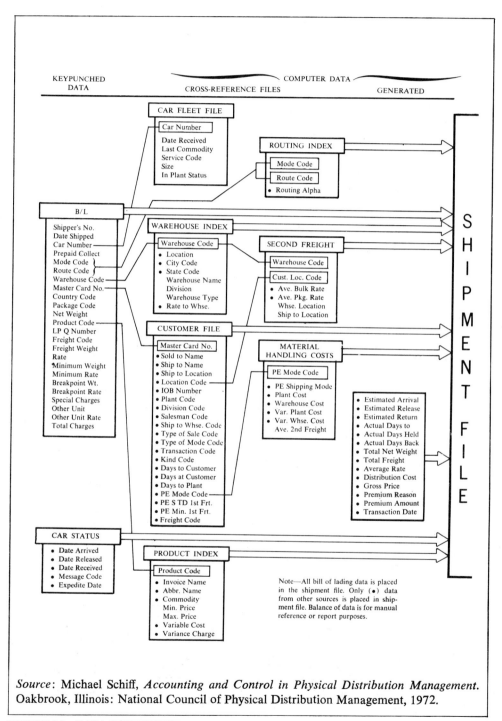

Source: Michael Schiff, *Accounting and Control in Physical Distribution Management.* Oakbrook, Illinois: National Council of Physical Distribution Management, 1972.

FIGURE 7.3  DATA COLLECTION

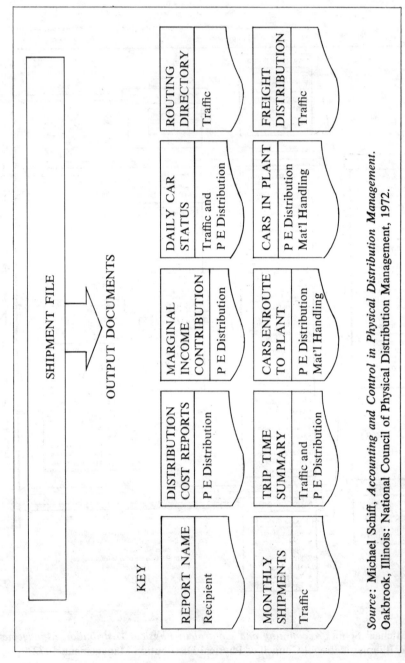

*Source:* Michael Schiff, *Accounting and Control in Physical Distribution Management.* Oakbrook, Illinois: National Council of Physical Distribution Management, 1972.

FIGURE 7.4   COMPUTERIZED FREIGHT CONTROL OUTPUT DOCUMENTS GENERATED

### Summary Reports

Distribution cost control has also benefited from the development of distribution operations summary reports. The reports are used in firms with well-defined systems of account classifications. The summary report reviews the major areas of distribution expense, such as freight, storage, receiving, packaging, shipping, distribution operations, and staff expense. In the area of freight accounting, for example, the summary report's section on tonnage and cost analysis provides important information concerning freight movements. The detailed tonnage and cost report shows individual products, customers and their locations, supply points, methods of shipment, quantities by type of shipment, total quantities, total costs, and unit costs. Effective control and peak operating performance depend upon the proper recording of freight operating information in a systematic manner.

### Coding Freight Weights and Costs

Another development that has aided traffic cost analyses is the adoption of the *two data fields* concept of coding both freight weights and freight costs. Figure 7.5 illustrates the use of this code method of freight expense recording.

The use of computers to aid in the recording of freight expenses and the controlling of freight systems permits access to accurate cost data as well as the selection of optimum modes of shipments for various quantities of goods.

### Improvements in Customer Service Controls

Computers have also permitted improved controls in the area of customer service. In an effort to improve inventory turnover, some firms have reduced the number of warehouses and field stocking locations for specific products or have reduced production levels below demand levels (thereby lowering inventory). Some have done both. Increases in wages and prices have reduced the number of alternatives available for cost control in the customer service area. The measurement of the customer service function is taken quite seriously, and through the use of computers it can be done on a real time basis so that adjustments in the distribution system can be made when necessary.

### Highlighting Specific Areas

It is now possible for distribution controllers to develop a series of summaries to highlight specific areas for study and action. For example, in the area of transportation, these summaries list the total number of transportation units delayed due to equipment shortages, transportation units shipped on time, and the number of orders calling for custom packing or special transportation. These summaries permit distribution controllers and managers to define the geographical distribution of transportation equipment by type, identify how long a delay due to transportation equipment shortages may last, the number of pool shipments, the number of stopover shipments, and the daily demand for transportation equipment.

| Type of Movement | Sub-Account or Cost Center | Character Of Expense | Main Account and Item Code | 1 | 2 |
|---|---|---|---|---|---|
| Freight on purchases of raw materials, intermediates and or finished product. | Type of Purchase: Raw Material Intermediate Finished Product Freight Packages Additives or     Trace Elements Import Duties Other Charges | Freight Type: Rail Truck Ship Barge (See Character of expense Code 551 through 579) | 21 Code to Designate Vendor's (Supplier's) Name and Location | Product Code | Number of Packages Tank Cars, Tank Trucks |
| Freight costs associated with inter-plant or intra-plant movements. | Cost Centers 500 through 749 | Freight Type: Codes 551 through 579 | 25 Receiving Location | Product Code | Number of Packages T/C, T/T |
| Freight associated with sale of product shipped to customer from plant or from intermediate storage in warehouse or terminal. | Cost Centers to Designate Product line or Freight—General | Freight Type: Codes 551 through 579 | 31 Shipping Point | Product Code | Number of Packages T/C, T/T |
| Freight on movements of finished products from plant to intermediate storage in warehouses or terminals. | Cost Centers to Designate Product line or Freight—General | Freight Type: Codes 551 through 579 | 31 Receiving Location | Product Code | Number of Packages T/C, T/T |
| Movement in Company Operated equipment of finished products from plant to intermediate storage in warehouses or terminals. | Cost Centers to Designate Company Operated transportation equipment by product line or General | All Codes 100 through 749 | 31 Equipment Serial or Identifying Number | Location Equipment Assigned to | Number of Deliveries in Month |
| Movement in Company Operated equipment with sale of product shipped to customer from plant or from intermediate storage in warehouse or terminal. | Cost Centers to Designate Company operated transportation equipment by product line or General | All Codes 100 through 749 | 31 Equipment Serial or Identifying Number | Location Equipment Assigned to | Number of Deliveries in month |

> *—Mode of shipment gives further identity to freight type—Segregates rail into tank car, package car, hopper car or flat car.
> **—Type of payment designated of freight is for seller's account, equalized with competitive point, etc.

FIGURE 7.5  TWO DATA FIELDS CONCEPT OF FREIGHT CLASSIFICATION

| Other Statistical Data | | | | | | | Quantity & Value Data | | |
| 3 | 4 | 5 | 6 | 7 | 8 | 9 | 1 | 2 | 3 |
|---|---|---|---|---|---|---|---|---|---|
| Type of Package | Receiving Location | Purchase Order Number | Receiving Date | Mode of Shipment* | Vendor Type (Affiliate, Outsider, Petroleum Products) | | Quantity Billed | Quantity Received | Value as Billed |
| Type of Package | Shipping Location | Shipping Order Number | Shipping Date | Mode of Shipment* | | | Quantity Shipped | Quantity Received | Value |
| Type of Package | Customer Code Designation of Name & Location | Sales Order Number | Shipping Date | Mode of Shipment* | Type of Payment** | Sales Invoice Number | | Quantity Invoiced | Value |
| Type of Package | Shipping Location (Supplier) | Shipping Order Number | Shipping Date | Mode of Shipment* | | | Quantity Shipped | Quantity Shipped | Bslur |
| Number of hours operated | | | Month and year of operation | | | | Quantity Shipped in Month | Number of miles operated in Month | Cost |
| Number of hours operated | | | Month and year of operation | | | | Quantity Shipped in Month | Number of miles operated in Month | Cost |

Source: Michael Schiff, *Accounting and Control in Physical Distribution Management*. Oakbrook, Illinois: National Council of Physical Distribution Management, 1972.

### Controlling Warehousing Costs

There have also been some interesting advances in controlling warehousing costs. These techniques usually begin with a well-defined account classification that captures all the cost associated with warehouse operation and enables the distribution controller to track the costs incurred at each facility as the product input varies. New methods of warehousing control enable the firm to make decisions regarding the closing down or starting up of a new warehouse, the total capacity required at each location for a specific product, and the advantages or disadvantages of leasing space in a public storage facility versus building the firm's own warehouse.

### Direct Order Entry Systems

Another development affecting distribution cost control is the installation within firms of direct order entry systems. These *single base inventory recording systems* have enabled distribution managers to control their inventory levels more effectively. Data regarding both the quantity and dollar value of the items coming into or going out of inventory are keypunched on a daily basis and fed into a central computer; the warehouse location of all items is also tracked. The distribution controller can keep track, on a daily basis, of items held in inventory, as well as their location and rate of turnover. The system enables the manager to classify the inventory into high value pilferable, high volume, medium volume, and low volume merchandise. Direct order entry systems work best when customers have terminals at their own locations. They can place orders directly into the firm's computer and quickly check the availability of the item.

If the controller can quickly determine what inventory is stored at which location and how often the various items will be shipped to what customers, he can regulate the amount of inventory held. Inventory carrying costs can be reduced and the money that would otherwise be tied up can be invested elsewhere for higher returns.

### Management Information Systems

With the computer as the basis for management information systems, distribution controllers can now get specific information regarding optimal distribution patterns, potential rate reduction areas, and the best location for new storage depots. This information is important in the strategic planning and budgeting activities of many companies.

### The Distribution Audit

The distribution audit has become an important element in distribution in the five years. It is basically a periodic audit of the distribution operation, and it takes into account its ability to respond to changes in product line composition, changes in marketing policies, and alterations in manufacturing techniques. The audit points

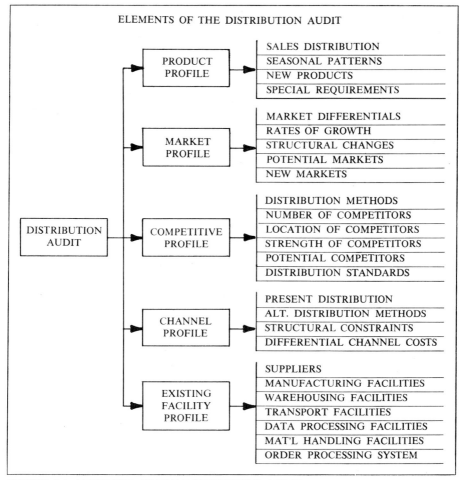

FIGURE 7.6   ELEMENTS OF THE DISTRIBUTION AUDIT

out areas of difficulty and signals management as to where and under what circumstances a change is needed. Figure 7.6 lists the elements contained in a typical distribution audit.

## SUGGESTED READING

Grabner, John, ed., "Distribution System Costing," *Proceedings of the Fourth Annual James R. Riley Symposium*, Columbus, Ohio: Ohio State University, 1972.

Heskett, J., "Sweeping Changes in Distribution." *Harvard Business Review*, (March-April, 1973), pp. 123-32.

Kashman, R. and Stolle, John, "The Total Cost Approach to Distribution." *Business Horizons*, (Winter, 1965), pp. 33-46.

Lancioni, Richard A., "The Decision Process in Physical Distribution Management." *Journal of Business Logistics*, 1978.

Lalonde, Bernard J. and Zinszer, Paul, *Customer Service—Measurement and Performance.* Chicago, Ill.: National Council of Physical Distribution, 1976.

Longman, Donald R. *Distribution Cost Analysis.* Assael, Henry, ed. New York: Arno Press, 1978.

Magee, J.F., *Physical Distribution Systems.* New York: McGraw-Hill, 1967.

Schiff, Dr. Michael, *Accounting and Control in Physical Distribution Management.* Chicago, Ill.: National Council of P.D. Management, 1972.

# 8

# Management Reports

*Donald E. Mitchell*

## PREPARING AN EFFECTIVE REPORT

Effective control of a business operation requires that management have access to pertinent information. An efficient controller's department produces timely, pertinent, and readable management reports. These reports provide management with the information needed to prepare the company's business plan and assess the company's potential to achieve the plan's objective, to make judgments about alternative courses of action, and to find solutions for the unforeseen problems that always occur.

### Important Elements

**Usefulness.** Useful information is information that has been evaluated, that is, information that has been measured and compared. Comparisons should be made with the management plan or standards or with prior periods. The information in the report must be self-explanatory; if it is not, simple interpretations should be added. Finally, the controller should direct the report format toward the needs of the reader rather than reflect the viewpoint of the accountant.

**Timeliness.** Careful thought should be given to when and how often the report should be issued, but once the schedule and frequency are established, the timetable must be met. Ancient history may be interesting to read, but it has absolutely no value in managing a business. *"Flash" reports* (early estimates of results) are excellent substitutes for completed reports when exact details are not yet available.

**Simplicity.** Good reports are almost always brief. They must compete with other material for the reader's time. Clarity rather than length should be emphasized. Technical accounting language should be avoided, and complicated financial statements should be omitted. The "telephone-book" report, which may take many hours to prepare, is usually the first report that gets filed to be read when the reader has more time.

**Accuracy.** The need for accuracy in accounting reports is a self-evident principle. Yet, the need for dependable information cannot be overemphasized. Errors in a report reduce the report's credibility and, more importantly, decrease confidence in the department that produced it.

**Clarity of Purpose.** The report's aim must be well thought out and defined before the form can be set and the content decided. Since each report should identify an area of responsibility for the recipient, the level of detail in the information presented should be related inversely to the level of control exercised by the reader. The inventory supervisor may need to see the actual activity breakdown for the period by stock number, whereas the materials manager may wish to know only the total dollars or units actually received during the period compared to the planned receipts.

**Identification of Responsibility.** In reporting actual expenses compared to those budgeted, for example, the reports should be prepared in pyramid form. The total controllable expenses of the lowest subordinated areas should represent one item in the summary of expenses of the next higher area of responsibility. In this way, a discussion or review of performance can be coordinated at any level without losing sight of the specific area or department responsible for the expense. At the same time, higher levels of management can see totals at a glance without being encumbered by a mass of detail.

When reports are properly integrated and responsibility is clearly identified, it generally indicates a well-organized company. The reports should reflect the vertical flow of information and clearly define the company's objectives and its plans to achieve those objectives. If the reporting flow is good, the company's plans and objectives are then clearly understood by all levels of management.

The information must flow vertically in both directions. On the one hand, the policies and objectives set by the various levels of management should flow downward to the line managers. On the other hand, the specific plans and actual performance data should flow upward from the operating managers to top corporate management. As plans are altered and objectives are changed, the vertical flow of management reports must move swiftly, conveying the changes and the resultant impact on the attainment of the original goals.

## Other Considerations

The following procedures are standard in some types of reports but vary in importance depending on the report being prepared:

- Adoption of a standard format enables management to move quickly to a line or column to identify a specific element, thus facilitating comparisons.
- Exception reports call management's attention to exceptional performance or to favorable or unfavorable deviations from anticipated conditions. They save management time and effort that might otherwise be spent on meaningless statistical information.
- Evaluation of the report's cost in terms of its benefit to management ensures that the reports are worthwhile.
- Periodic reviews of report distribution and use avoid the issuance of reports that have ceased to serve any useful purpose. Too often, a report is issued to identify a certain problem long after the problem has been resolved.

## TYPES OF REPORTS

All reports issued by the controller's department should be prepared for the primary purpose of assisting management in operating the business. However, the form and content of the reports vary. Generally, reports can be broken down into four distinct categories.

### Control Reports

The control report is the basic type of report issued by the controller's office. The control report measures actual performance in comparison to a management plan, an objective standard, prior periods, or general industry performance. Control reports can be issued daily, weekly, or monthly. Each report points out the deviation from the particular standard being used, to enable prompt corrective action to be taken if needed. Examples of this type of report would be:

- A weekly report on incoming orders by product or by territory compared to the plan;
- A weekly report on product yield by grade compared to the management plan;
- Monthly cost center expense statements compared to the flexible budget;

- A monthly statement of inventory levels by plant compared to the plan; and
- A monthly product-line income statement compared to the plan and last year's actual results.

## Information Reports

These reports trace the results of a certain activity over a period of time. The information is used to indicate a pattern, trend, or change in composition. This type of report can be issued in several forms, but graphs or charts are typically used. However, the report can be expressed in ratios or merely as a series of statistical data in units or dollars. Some typical information reports include:

- Growth of market share by product;
- Change in demographic trend by year; and
- Ratio of labor cost to total cost by product and by year.

## Analytical Reports

Reports that include an analysis of the report's findings have become increasingly important. Many companies now have professionals on the controller's staff whose prime responsibility is analyzing the performance of a particular division, plant, product line, or function. With the increased amount of data now available and the many economic variables to consider today, it is useful to have the comments of an expert who is completely familiar with the input and output information.

Analytical reports are usually brief and are distributed to the top operating and corporate members of management. Some examples of this type of report would be:

- Analysis of changes or variances in product mix, margins, cost, or profit;
- Analysis of company or division profit performance compared to the plan or prior period;
- Analysis of changes in financial condition; and
- Analysis of impact of inflation on income and assets of company.

## Forecast Reports

The forecast report has gained popularity in recent years because of the rapidly changing economy and the upgrading of computer technology. The report can result from straightforward internal forecasting of, say, sales and costs that project the future performance of the company over the next year or several years. However, with the additional flexibility and the increased speed provided by computers, forecast reports can be produced under several different assumptions concerning economic growth, market growth, inflation rates, and so on. These "what if" projections are a valuable tool that management uses to assess the degree of risk associated with its current decisions under several different sets of future economic conditions.

## FREQUENCY OF REPORTS

The frequency with which reports should be issued is related to management's ability to react to the information received. A deviation from plan, budget, or schedule may be favorable or unfavorable. Should a deviation occur, management is expected to react quickly to correct a problem or take advantage of a favorable situation. It is of little value for a production manager to wait a month to learn from a control report that the yield in a particular production department has deteriorated badly. Therefore, most production reports are usually issued daily and are followed by weekly and monthly summary reports.

How often the report is issued is also related to the level of management that receives it. The higher in the hierarchy of management the recipient is, and the less concerned he is with day-to-day operations, the less frequently he needs to receive most types of reports. He wants to know quickly, of course, when there is a significant problem, but top management will generally receive only monthly or quarterly summary reports.

The overriding determinant in deciding how frequently a report should be issued is the degree of impact on the company if a problem in that area develops. Those areas in which deviations can cause serious problems if they are not detected early must be monitored more frequently than others. Once a particular problem is resolved or under control, the area needs less constant supervision and reduced reporting.

## FORMS OF REPORTS

The form of the report is often as important as its content. The information contained in the report is usually the key factor to consider when deciding on the proper form. Some examples of different forms are:

1. *Statistical data forms.* Reports that provide a great deal of statistical data, such as a sales report by product line and by salesmen reflecting actual versus planned figures for the current month and year to date, are generally produced by a computer. Whenever possible, the computer printout should be used; statistical reports should not be retyped. The varying print type available on most computers, along with the ability to reproduce the printout at standard sizes, permits the distribution of reports that are readable and acceptable at most corporate levels.

2. *Narrative analytical forms.* The financial analysis report, written in narrative form, should have a standard, consistent format. The report should be brief and should summarize the conclusion of the analysis in the first paragraph. The language should be simple, and the schedules, if included, should be kept simple and have clear headings. Too many schedules should not be included in this type of report, as they may tend to confuse the reader rather than help him.

3. *Graphic forms.* Certain types of reports are best produced in graphic form. Reports that indicate a trend over a period of time or compare the company's per-

formance with the industry are examples of such reporting. Graphs or charts should be kept simple and uncluttered. Different colors enhance the effect and readability of a graph and should be used when possible. The size of the graph and its scale are important. Scales that indicate sharp changes in trend when, in fact, the movement is not unusual or significant in its effect should not be used.

All reports, regardless of form, should indicate who issued the report and the date it was issued. Any revisions in form or content should also be noted, along with the date of the revision.

One note of caution in this age of fast and easy form reproduction: how a report looks is frequently the prime factor in determining whether the report gets read or is quickly discarded. Often reports that are issued frequently to many recipients are reproduced from a master form that is continuously being updated. Each copy should be examined before distribution to make sure it is legible. A poorly produced copy does just as much damage to the credibility of a report as an inaccuracy does.

## DISTRIBUTION OF REPORTS TO MANAGEMENT LEVELS

The basic considerations for report preparation discussed above constitute the general rules and guidelines that apply to reports from the controller's office to all members of management. Specific references to a typical company's financial reporting system may prove helpful in applying these basic principles to the reports made to different executive levels.

Figure 8.1 outlines the organizational structure of a typical manufacturing company, ABC Corporation, a fully integrated company that has combined decentralized profit center responsibility with centralized financial controls. The profit centers are called divisions; each has direct responsibility for the manufacture and sale of its product line.

The ABC Corporation is headed by the president of the company, who has several staff assistants reporting to him at the chief executive office level. In addition, there is a corporate staff level consisting primarily of the functional financial management, with the corporate secretary (legal counsel) and manager of human resources also having corporate responsibility in their functional areas.

The company manufactures and distributes industrial, commercial, and retail products. Figure 8.1 indicates that the corporation has three major manufacturing divisions (Divisions A, B, and C) engaged in each of these distinct market areas. In general, each division is completely responsible for the development, production, marketing, and distribution of its products. Figures 8.2 through 8.15 illustrate ABC Corporation's financial reporting system. The division reports and the explanatory comments in the text concentrate on Division B, the industrial division that specializes in the manufacture of steel products. Similar reports and comments would be prepared for the other divisions.

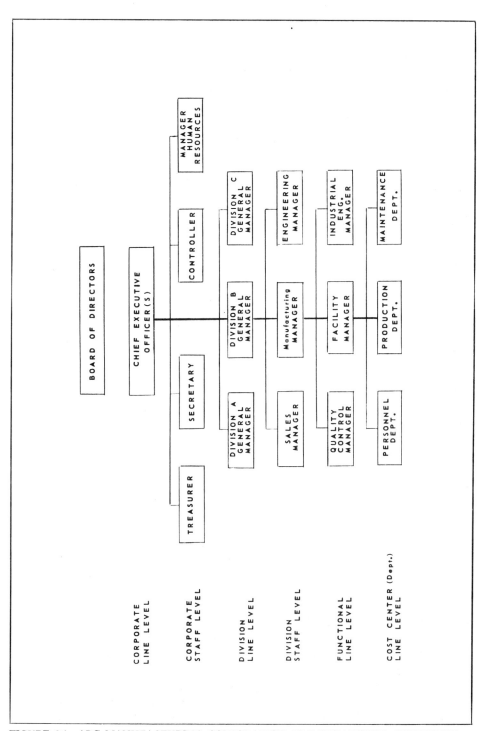

FIGURE 8.1  ABC MANUFACTURING CORPORATION ORGANIZATIONAL STRUCTURE

### Reports to Corporate Line Management

Reports to top operating management are usually in summary form. The monthly financial reports, for example, will be a group of reports, usually in a book format, that summarize the results for all the operations as to bookings, sales, income, cash flow, and certain key balance sheet items.

Other than the financial reports that are issued monthly in a set format, most top management reports will be on an exception basis. There is no need to burden corporate management with reports that merely state that everything is proceeding according to plan. As a result, reports to top operating management tend to be less standardized. Rather, special forms are designed to highlight a certain problem area or a potential profit opportunity. The frequency with which reports are made to top management also varies. Most reports will be monthly, but "flash" reports may be issued weekly depending on the significance of the variations in results.

The financial highlights report of the ABC Corporation (Figure 8.2) is the first report that would be prepared for top management's review. This report summarizes the sales and income for the month, showing the performance of each division compared to plan as well as the consolidated results. Other statistical data, such as gross margin and income percentages, financial ratios, and earnings per share figures, are also shown. (Only public companies compute earnings per share.)

A more detailed statement of income, showing the month- and year-to-date comparisons to the plan and the previous year-to-date, is illustrated in Figure 8.3. This consolidated statement identifies any significant movement in the various income and expense statements that may indicate some loss of management control. Another top-level consolidated statement is a statement of changes in cash position (Figure 8.4), which highlights the cash provided or consumed by operations and other transactions. It also shows the movement in the total amount of short- and long-term debt borrowings that reflects corporate treasury decisions.

### Reports to Corporate Staff Management

The corporate staff management is defined as corporate executives whose responsibility is confined to a certain area, such as the treasury function, the legal function, or the marketing or personnel functions. Their primary responsibility is to monitor changes or variances in their particular functional area. Executives in these areas receive reports that are similar in substance to those distributed to corporate line management, but each receives more data in his specialty area than that sent to other staff management. For example, in the area of cash management, the staff specialist may need to see a report that shows the cash balance at month-end by each bank used by the company. Other staff members would need to know only the total cash balance at the end of the month.

Reports to corporate staff management identify trends so that attention can be focused quickly on potential problem areas. A corporate marketing manager, for example, would want reports that indicate a change in market growth or that identify changes in size, strength, or market share of competitors. He would then coor-

| | ABC Corporation | | Division A | | Division B | | Division C | |
|---|---|---|---|---|---|---|---|---|
| | Actual | Profit Plan | Actual | Profit Plan | Actual | Profit Plan | Actual | Profit Plan |
| Net sales | $79,900 | $74,700 | $25,600 | $24,000 | $39,900 | $38,200 | $14,400 | $12,500 |
| Gross margin | 30,900 | 29,200 | 8,400 | 8,400 | 16,000 | 15,500 | 6,500 | 5,300 |
| Period costs | 16,100 | 15,900 | 5,900 | 6,000 | 7,100 | 7,000 | 3,000 | 2,900 |
| Income before taxes | 14,800 | 13,300 | 2,500 | 2,400 | 8,900 | 8,500 | 3,400 | 2,400 |
| NET INCOME* | 7,500 | 6,800 | 1,300 | 1,200 | 4,500 | 4,400 | 1,700 | 1,200 |
| Percent of sales: | | | | | | | | |
| Gross margin | 38.7% | 39.1% | 32.8% | 35.0% | 40.1% | 40.6% | 45.1% | 47.4% |
| Period costs | 20.2 | 21.3 | 23.0 | 25.0 | 17.8 | 18.3 | 21.5 | 23.2 |
| NET INCOME* | 9.4 | 9.1 | 5.1 | 5.0 | 11.3 | 11.5 | 11.8 | 9.0 |
| Statistical data: | | | | | | | | |
| Month's sales in receivables | | | 1.31 | 1.30 | 1.40 | 1.30 | 3.71 | 3.50 |
| Inventory turnover | | | 3.48 | 3.80 | 3.84 | 3.75 | 6.24 | 6.00 |
| Earnings per share: | | | | | | | | |
| Primary | $ .68 | $ .61 | | | | | | |
| Fully diluted | .60 | .54 | | | | | | |
| Book value per share | 36.11 | | | | | | | |
| Current ratio | 1.73 | | | | | | | |
| Annual return on shareholders' equity | 19.05 | | | | | | | |
| Debt to net tangible assets | 22.18 | | | | | | | |

* Before preferred dividends.

FIGURE 8.2　ABC CORPORATION FINANCIAL HIGHLIGHTS, AS AT AND FOR THE MONTH ENDED JUNE 30, 19X8 (DOLLARS IN THOUSANDS)

|  | Month Ended June 30, 19X8 | | | | Six Months Ended June 30 | | | | | |
|  | Actual | | Profit Plan | | 19X8 Actual | | 19X8 Profit Plan | | 19X7 Actual | |
|  | Amount | Pct. to Sales | Amount | Pct. to Sales | Amount | Pct. to Sales | Amount | Pct. to Sales | Amount | Pct. to Sales |
|---|---|---|---|---|---|---|---|---|---|---|
| Net sales—external | $79,900 | 100.0% | $74,700 | 100.0% | $468,500 | 100.0% | $450,000 | 100.0% | $403,800 | 100.0% |
| Cost of sales | 49,000 | 61.3 | 45,500 | 60.9 | 295,200 | 63.0 | 292,500 | 65.0 | 266,500 | 66.0 |
| Gross margin | 30,900 | 38.7 | 29,200 | 39.1 | 173,300 | 37.0 | 157,500 | 35.0 | 137,300 | 34.0 |
| Period costs: | | | | | | | | | | |
| Manufacturing overhead | 8,800 | 11.0 | 9,000 | 12.0 | 52,000 | 11.1 | 51,000 | 11.3 | 48,000 | 11.9 |
| Provision for major maintenance | 1,600 | 2.0 | 1,600 | 2.1 | 9,500 | 2.0 | 9,500 | 2.1 | 8,100 | 2.0 |
| Depreciation | 1,200 | 1.5 | 1,200 | 1.7 | 6,900 | 1.5 | 6,800 | 1.6 | 6,700 | 1.7 |
|  | 11,600 | 14.5 | 11,800 | 15.8 | 68,400 | 14.6 | 67,300 | 15.0 | 62,800 | 15.6 |
| Selling expense | 1,800 | 2.3 | 1,600 | 2.1 | 10,500 | 2.3 | 10,800 | 2.4 | 9,700 | 2.4 |
| Administrative expense | 2,400 | 3.0 | 2,200 | 2.9 | 11,800 | 2.5 | 11,400 | 2.5 | 10,200 | 2.5 |
| Interest expense | 300 | .4 | 300 | .5 | 2,000 | .4 | 2,500 | .5 | 2,000 | .5 |
|  | 16,100 | 20.2 | 15,900 | 21.3 | 92,700 | 19.8 | 92,000 | 20.4 | 84,700 | 21.0 |
| Income before taxes | 14,800 | 18.5 | 13,300 | 17.8 | 80,600 | 17.2 | 65,500 | 14.6 | 52,600 | 13.0 |
| Provision for income taxes | 7,300 | 9.1 | 6,500 | 8.7 | 41,900 | 8.9 | 34,100 | 7.6 | 27,400 | 6.8 |
| Net income | 7,500 | 9.4% | 6,800 | 9.1% | 38,700 | 8.3% | 31,400 | 7.0% | 25,200 | 6.2% |
| Dividends on preferred stock | 100 | | 100 | | 600 | | 600 | | 600 | |
| Net income available to common shareholders | $ 7,400 | | $ 6,700 | | $ 38,100 | | $ 30,800 | | $ 24,600 | |
| Earnings per share of comon stock: | | | | | | | | | | |
| Primary | $ .68 | | $ .61 | | $ 3.50 | | $ 2.83 | | $ 2.34 | |
| Fully diluted | .60 | | .54 | | 3.10 | | 2.50 | | 2.03 | |
| Average number of common shares: (000) | | | | | | | | | | |
| Outstanding and common share equivalents | 10,900 | | | | | | | | 10,500 | |
| Assuming conversion of Ser. A & Ser. B Pfd. | 12,300 | | | | | | | | 12,100 | |

FIGURE 8.3  ABC CORPORATION STATEMENT OF INCOME, MONTH AND SIX MONTHS ENDED JUNE 30, 19X8 (DOLLARS IN THOUSANDS)

dinate this information with the operating management of the group or with the divisions that could be affected by such a change.

For example, the treasurer of the ABC Corporation, in addition to the consolidated statement of changes in cash position (Figure 8.4), receives a cash-flow statement showing the details of cash movement for each of the major divisions (Figure 8.5). This statement reveals that, although the cash flow overall is positive and fairly close to planned performance, Division B is beginning to show a deviation in its inventory buildup ($8 million more than planned) that could indicate a potential problem.

Other ABC corporate staff reports include an order backlog report (Figure 8.6) and various graphic reports, by division, such as an inventory trend report (Figure 8.7), and a gross margin report (Figure 8.8). These types of reports are distributed to the various corporate line and staff managers, but the corporate controller analyzes each of these reports in detail. The graph of Division B's inventory (Figure 8.7) would also warn the controller that a control deficiency might be developing.

### Reports to Division Management

Division management is discussed here in terms of the management of distinct profit centers. Each division has a separate reporting structure and generates most of its management reports internally.

The corporate controller is concerned that all divisions have a similar report structure and in some cases is responsible for the coordination of the design and issuance of all reports of the division controllers. In any event, he must be aware of how the emphasis of corporate and divisional reports differ.

Division reports to management will be more product-line and facility oriented than other corporate reports. They should display the actual cost and profit data in much greater detail as well as give more specific variance analyses. This emphasis and detail are required because the responsibility for performance is more direct at the division level than at the corporate level.

The corporate controller must issue reports (based on information provided by the division) from his office to each division concerning its performance during a specific period. These reports serve an important purpose and should be as objective and as brief as possible. They tell division management how corporate management views its performance against stated goals or objectives. Frequently, the causes for deviation from the plan are seen quite differently at the division and corporate level, and major communication problems may develop. Performance reports coming from both vantage points permit the differences in opinion to surface quickly and then be reconciled.

To ensure this two-way flow of management information, the corporate controller should make sure that each division regularly receives all pertinent reports. Any management report that is critical of a division's performance should be forwarded to the division management. If the criticisms are valid, the division can act promptly to counter the criticisms, and the corporate control function is enhanced.

| | Month Ended June 30, 19X8 | | Six Months Ended June 30, | | |
| | Actual | Profit Plan | 19X8 Actual | Profit Plan | 19X7 Actual |
|---|---|---|---|---|---|
| **From operations** | | | | | |
| Cash provided: | | | | | |
| Net income | $ 7,500 | $ 6,800 | $38,700 | $31,400 | $25,200 |
| Depreciation | 1,200 | 1,200 | 6,900 | 6,800 | 6,700 |
| Subtotal | 8,700 | 8,000 | 45,600 | 38,200 | 31,900 |
| Cash consumed: | | | | | |
| Capital expenditures | 2,000 | 3,500 | 18,800 | 21,000 | 17,500 |
| Accounts receivable increase (decrease) | 8,900 | 2,700 | 22,700 | 15,600 | 12,200 |
| Inventory increase (decrease) | (500) | (1,000) | 10,500 | 7,100 | 8,100 |
| Accounts payable (increase) decrease | (800) | 1,500 | (2,900) | 1,500 | (2,500) |
| Operating reserves (increase) decrease | (600) | (500) | (10,200) | (10,200) | (8,000) |
| Other | (1,600) | 100 | (3,300) | (4,300) | 100 |
| | 7,400 | 6,300 | 35,600 | 30,700 | 27,400 |
| Cash provided (consumed) | 1,300 | 1,700 | 10,000 | 7,500 | 4,500 |
| **Other transactions** | | | | | |
| Proceeds from borrowing: | | | | | |
| Long-term proceeds | 1,200 | — | 1,200 | — | — |
| Long-term payments | (2,000) | (1,000) | (5,200) | (4,000) | (3,000) |
| Short-term (payments) | — | — | (4,200) | (1,100) | (2,800) |
| Proceeds from sale of stock | — | — | — | — | — |
| Deferred income taxes | 300 | 200 | 1,000 | 1,000 | 800 |
| Cash dividends | (700) | (700) | (2,800) | (2,800) | (2,600) |
| Income tax payments below provision | 1,800 | 1,300 | 4,000 | 3,000 | 2,400 |
| Cash provided (consumed) | 600 | (200) | (6,000) | (3,900) | (5,200) |
| Cash increase (decrease) | 1,900 | 1,500 | 4,000 | 3,600 | (700) |
| Cash and equivalents: | | | | | |
| Beginning of period | 3,500 | 4,000 | 1,400 | 1,400 | 5,200 |
| End of period | $ 5,400 | $ 5,500 | $ 5,400 | $ 5,000 | $ 4,500 |

FIGURE 8.4   ABC CORPORATION CONSOLIDATED STATEMENT OF CHANGES IN CASH POSITION, MONTH AND SIX MONTHS ENDED JUNE 30, 19X8 (DOLLARS IN THOUSANDS)

| | Total Divisions | | Division A | | Division B | | Division C | |
|---|---|---|---|---|---|---|---|---|
| | Actual | Profit Plan | Actual | Profit Plan | Actual | Profit Plan | Actual | Profit Plan |
| Cash provided: | | | | | | | | |
| Net income | $38,700 | $31,400 | $ 7,800 | $ 7,200 | $21,200 | $17,500 | $ 9,700 | $ 6,700 |
| Depreciation | 6,700 | 6,600 | 1,000 | 1,200 | 4,800 | 4,400 | 900 | 1,000 |
| From operations | 45,400 | 38,000 | 8,800 | 8,400 | 26,000 | 21,900 | 10,600 | 7,700 |
| Cash consumed: | | | | | | | | |
| Capital expenditures | 18,800 | 21,000 | 4,600 | 5,000 | 10,200 | 12,000 | 4,000 | 4,000 |
| Accts. receivable increase (decrease) | 22,700 | 15,600 | 5,800 | 4,200 | 7,200 | 5,000 | 9,700 | 6,400 |
| Inventory increase (decrease) | 10,500 | 7,100 | (8,000) | (6,000) | 20,000 | 12,000 | (1,500) | 1,100 |
| Accts. payable (increase) decrease | (2,900) | 1,500 | 400 | 200 | (3,500) | 1,000 | 200 | 300 |
| Operating reserves (increase) decrease | (10,200) | (10,200) | (2,000) | (2,000) | (5,200) | (5,200) | (3,000) | (3,000) |
| Other | (1,300) | (2,300) | (400) | (400) | (900) | (1,500) | — | (400) |
| Subtotal | 37,600 | 32,700 | 400 | 1,000 | 27,800 | 23,300 | 9,400 | 8,400 |
| Cash provided or (consumed) | $ 7,800 | $ 5,300 | $ 8,400 | $ 7,400 | $(1,800) | $(1,400) | $ 1,200 | $ (700) |

FIGURE 8.5   ABC CORPORATION STATEMENT OF CASH FLOW—DIVISIONS ONLY, SIX MONTHS ENDED JUNE 30, 19X8 (DOLLARS IN THOUSANDS)

|                     | Consolidated | Division A | Division B | Division C |
|---------------------|-------------:|-----------:|-----------:|-----------:|
| Receipts:           |              |            |            |            |
| Current month       | $ 82,300     | $ 28,000   | $ 37,100   | $ 17,200   |
| Prior month         | 77,400       | 24,800     | 34,800     | 17,800     |
| Year-to-date        | 498,200      | 159,500    | 248,600    | 90,100     |
|                     |              |            |            |            |
| Shipments:          |              |            |            |            |
| Current month       | 79,900       | 25,600     | 39,900     | 14,400     |
| Prior month         | 75,000       | 22,400     | 37,600     | 15,000     |
| Year-to-date        | 468,500      | 150,000    | 233,800    | 84,700     |
|                     |              |            |            |            |
| Ending balance:     |              |            |            |            |
| Current month       | 239,700      | 76,800     | 119,700    | 43,200     |
| Prior month         | 237,300      | 71,700     | 120,300    | 45,300     |
| At 12-21-X7         | 210,000      | 67,300     | 104,900    | 37,800     |

FIGURE 8.6   ABC CORPORATION ORDER BACKLOG, JUNE 30, 19X8
(DOLLARS IN THOUSANDS)

However, if the division management finds out about the criticisms secondhand, it may react defensively, and the episode may seriously affect future communications between the corporate controller and the division.

The ABC Corporation division management reports cover both the divisional line and staff level illustrated in the organizational structure in Figure 8.1. The primary report is usually the division income statement (Figure 8.9), which shows the division's performance for the month and year-to-date compared to its profit plan. The division income statement, with its detailed information, clearly highlights any variances.

Division B is using a direct cost system that identifies separately the direct manufacturing cost variances and the manufacturing period costs. Figure 8.9 indicates that, although the manufacturing gross margin (35 percent) is good on a year-to-date basis, the standard margin improvement has been eroded by the manufacturing variances, particularly by melting and conversion costs.

The improvement in the standard gross margin would be reviewed by the sales department at the divisional staff level. A product profit-contribution report similar to Figure 8.10 would be prepared to identify the standard profit contribution by product. The report indicates that product lines C and D generate the most profit margin dollars, yet the increase in margin apparently did not come from price increases. The product-line profit report shows that the unit selling price of product D was right on target, while the other product lines reflect relatively small increases over their target prices. A better mix of product, that is, selling more of the more profitable items, appears to be the main reason for the standard margin improvement.

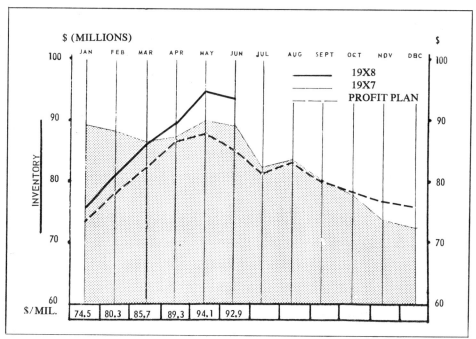

FIGURE 8.7 ABC CORPORATION DIVISION B INVENTORY TREND REPORT

| | JAN | FEB | MAR | APR | MAY | JUN | JUL | AUG | SEPT | OCT | NOV | DEC |
|---|---|---|---|---|---|---|---|---|---|---|---|---|
| $/MIL. | 74.5 | 80.3 | 85.7 | 89.3 | 94.1 | 92.9 | | | | | | |

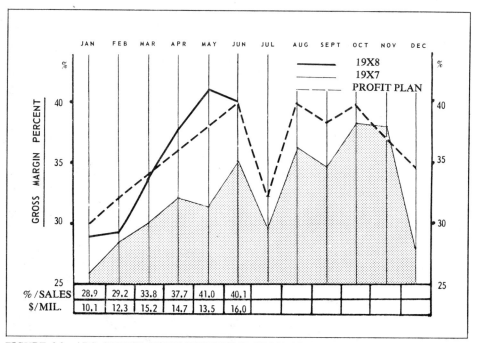

FIGURE 8.8 ABC CORPORATION DIVISION B GROSS MARGIN REPORT

| | JAN | FEB | MAR | APR | MAY | JUN | JUL | AUG | SEPT | OCT | NOV | DEC |
|---|---|---|---|---|---|---|---|---|---|---|---|---|
| %/SALES | 28.9 | 29.2 | 33.8 | 37.7 | 41.0 | 40.1 | | | | | | |
| $/MIL. | 10.1 | 12.3 | 15.2 | 14.7 | 13.5 | 16.0 | | | | | | |

| | Month Ended June 30, 19X8 | | | | | Six Months Ended June 30, 19X8 | | | | |
|---|---|---|---|---|---|---|---|---|---|---|
| | Actual | Pct. to Sales | Profit Plan | Pct. to Sales | Variance | Actual | Pct. to Sales | Profit Plan Annual | Pct. to Sales | Variance |
| Net sales | $39,900 | 100.0% | $38,200 | 100.0% | $ 1,700 | $233,800 | 100.0% | $224,800 | 100.0% | $ 9,000 |
| Cost of sales: | | | | | | | | | | |
| Direct standard costs | 24,700 | 62.0 | 23,300 | 61.0 | 1,400 | 142,600 | 61.0 | 143,900 | 64.0 | (1,300) |
| Direct cost variances (favorable): | | | | | | | | | | |
| Purchase price | (400) | (1.0) | (1,000) | (2.5) | 600 | (800) | (.3) | (1,100) | (.5) | 300 |
| Melting variance | 200 | .5 | 200 | .5 | – | 4,000 | 1.7 | 2,250 | 1.0 | 1,750 |
| Abnormal scrap loss | 200 | .5 | 100 | .2 | 100 | 1,800 | .8 | 1,100 | .5 | 700 |
| Conversion cost variance | (900) | (2.3) | 100 | .2 | (1,000) | 3,600 | 1.5 | 2,250 | 1.0 | 1,350 |
| Other | 100 | .2 | – | – | 100 | 800 | .3 | – | – | 800 |
| | (800) | (2.1) | (600) | (1.6) | (200) | 9,400 | 4.0 | 4,500 | 2.0 | 4,900 |
| Total cost of sales | 23,900 | 59.9 | 22,700 | 59.4 | 1,200 | 152,000 | 65.0 | 148,400 | 66.0 | 3,600 |
| Gross margin | 16,000 | 40.1 | 15,500 | 40.6 | 500 | 81,800 | 35.0 | 76,400 | 34.0 | 5,400 |
| Period costs: (Mfg.) | | | | | | | | | | |
| Manufacturing overhead | 4,200 | 10.5 | 4,000 | 10.5 | 200 | 25,200 | 10.6 | 24,800 | 11.0 | 400 |
| Period cost in inventory | (400) | (1.0) | – | – | (400) | (5,200) | (2.2) | (1,200) | (.5) | (4,000) |
| Depreciation | 800 | 2.0 | 700 | 1.8 | 100 | 4,800 | 2.1 | 4,400 | 2.0 | 400 |
| Provision for maintenance | 200 | .5 | 200 | .5 | – | 1,200 | .6 | 1,200 | .5 | – |
| | 4,800 | 12.0 | 4,900 | 12.8 | (100) | 26,000 | 11.1 | 29,200 | 13.0 | (3,200) |
| Net margin | 11,200 | 28.1 | 10,600 | 27.8 | 600 | 55,800 | 23.9 | 47,200 | 21.0 | 8,600 |
| Selling, G&A expenses | 2,300 | 5.8 | 2,100 | 5.5 | 200 | 13,800 | 5.9 | 13,500 | 6.0 | 300 |
| Income before tax | $ 8,900 | 22.3% | $ 8,500 | 22.3% | $ 400 | $ 42,000 | 18.0% | $ 33,700 | 15.0% | $ 8,300 |

FIGURE 8.9   ABC CORPORATION DIVISION B STATEMENT OF INCOME, JUNE 30, 19X8 (DOLLARS IN THOUSANDS)

| Product | Weight #'s | Invoice amount | Standard direct cost | Standard Profit Contribution | | Average selling price # | Target selling price # |
| --- | --- | --- | --- | --- | --- | --- | --- |
| | | | | Amount | Percent | | |
| Product A | 958,000 | $ 4,198,914 | $ 3,010,614 | $ 1,188,300 | 28.3% | $ 4.383 | $ 4.200 |
| Product B | 5,538,000 | 39,602,238 | 27,602,838 | 11,999,400 | 30.3 | 7.151 | 7.000 |
| Product C | 4,480,000 | 46,453,120 | 27,541,820 | 18,906,300 | 40.7 | 10.369 | 10.200 |
| Product D | 11,500,000 | 143,534,078 | 84,441,078 | 59,093,000 | 41.2 | 12.481 | 12.481 |
| | 22,176,000 | $233,788,350 | $142,601,350 | $ 91,187,000 | 39.0% | $10.542 | $10.000 |

FIGURE 8.10 ABC CORPORATION DIVISION B PRODUCT PROFIT CONTRIBUTION AT STANDARD DIRECT COST FOR THE SIX MONTHS ENDED JUNE 30, 19X8

A report on sales by markets illustrates this point (Figure 8.11). In recent years, many companies have been establishing a series of planning units, usually based on markets or industries, called strategic business units (SBUs), which can be structured at the division, facility, or cost center level. SBU strategic plans concentrate on growth and on ways to increase market share, exploit market areas, and/or offset competitors' product advantage. Figure 8.11 identifies the aerospace market as a strategic area for Division B. As can be seen, products C and D exceeded the SBU's original forecast by 12 and 6 percent, respectively, in terms of units sold. The increase in dollar sales in those product lines was slightly higher, indicating that the unit prices were higher than forecast. (Figure 8.10 indicated that products C and D had good profit margins, so the improved standard gross margin referred to earlier was due in part to the better sales mix of the aerospace market area.)

The division staff would also receive periodic performance reports, such as engineering project status reports and departmental spending reports. Figure 8.12 shows a typical selling expense report.

### Reports to Functional Management

Reports to cost center management are always generated by the operating division rather than by the corporate controller. However, the controller may be involved in the design and layout of the various reports and should be familiar with them. Ultimately, cost control rests on the personal responsibility of the cost center manager. These reports reflect this responsibility by emphasizing current performance. The closer the manager is to the action, the more timely the reporting system must be. He will need daily and weekly reports of actual performance along with monthly summary reports.

The report should concentrate on the areas over which the manager can exercise some degree of control. It may measure performance in terms of manpower, units of production and/or materials, or dollars. Most of the reports at this level will identify variances (exceptions) from a standard cost or budget for the period.

Finally, the timing of the issuance of each report to cost center management is critical. Cutoff times for data used as input to the report must be specific and must be adhered to if the report is to be issued on time. Decisions at this level in the

| Product | Actual | | Forecast | | % Change (±) | |
|---|---|---|---|---|---|---|
| | #<br>(000) | $<br>(000) | #<br>(000) | $<br>(000) | # | $ |
| Product B | 1,108 | 7,756 | 1,090 | 7,630 | + 1.7 | + 1.7 |
| Product C | 1,030 | 10,661 | 920 | 9,380 | + 12.0 | + 13.7 |
| Product D | 2,875 | 35,940 | 2,710 | 33,820 | + 6.1 | + 6.3 |
| Total | | $54,357 | | $50,830 | | + 6.8 |

FIGURE 8.11   ABC CORPORATION DIVISION B (AEROSPACE MARKET AREA) PRODUCT SALES REPORT FOR THE SIX MONTHS ENDED JUNE 30, 19X8

| | Current Month | | | Year-to-Date | | |
|---|---|---|---|---|---|---|
| | Actual | Budget | Variance | Actual | Budget | Variance |
| Employment costs: | | | | | | |
| Salaries | $ 85,674 | $ 78,056 | $ 7,618 | $ 503,844 | $ 458,334 | $ 45,510 |
| Vacation | 3,014 | 2,690 | 324 | 22,179 | 20,190 | 1,989 |
| Group insurance | 7,642 | 6,931 | 711 | 45,488 | 41,222 | 4,266 |
| Compensation insurance | 61 | 45 | 16 | 2,099 | 1,968 | 131 |
| Unemployment insurance tax | 1,465 | 1,300 | 165 | 8,050 | 7,060 | 990 |
| F.I.C.A. | 5,338 | 4,865 | 473 | 30,750 | 27,912 | 2,838 |
| Profit sharing | 869 | 782 | 87 | 4,711 | 4,327 | 384 |
| Pension cost—gross | 11,472 | 10,100 | 1,372 | 68,817 | 60,600 | 8,217 |
| Cost of living | 4,400 | 3,860 | 540 | 21,349 | 18,698 | 2,651 |
| | 119,935 | 108,629 | 11,306 | 707,287 | 640,311 | 66,976 |
| Expenses: | | | | | | |
| Commissions on sales | 159,538 | 135,982 | 23,556 | 1,317,193 | 1,211,849 | 105,344 |
| Advertising | 4,000 | 4,000 | — | 25,000 | 25,000 | — |
| Travel and entertainment | 17,848 | 17,606 | 242 | 106,914 | 104,425 | 2,489 |
| Stationery and supplies | 2,106 | 2,106 | — | 10,792 | 8,900 | 1,892 |
| Telephone | 8,863 | 6,930 | 1,933 | 58,624 | 48,326 | 10,298 |
| General office expense | 1,583 | 1,083 | 500 | 8,651 | 5,941 | 2,710 |
| Equipment rentals | 689 | 623 | 66 | 3,999 | 3,599 | 400 |
| Dues and subscriptions | 5,036 | 4,961 | 75 | 12,876 | 12,801 | 75 |
| Interdivision services billed | (862) | (862) | — | (7,588) | (7,588) | — |
| Lease expense | 2,598 | 2,598 | — | 15,696 | 15,696 | — |
| Miscellaneous | 254 | — | 254 | 2,241 | — | 2,241 |
| | 201,653 | 175,027 | 26,626 | 1,554,398 | 1,428,949 | 125,449 |
| | 321,588 | 283,656 | 37,932 | 2,261,685 | 2,069,260 | 192,425 |
| Allocation of division aircraft expense | 1,235 | 1,235 | — | 12,959 | 12,959 | — |
| | $322,823 | $284,891 | $37,932 | $2,274,644 | $2,082,219 | $192,425 |

FIGURE 8.12  ABC CORPORATION DIVISION B SELLING EXPENSE, MONTH AND SIX MONTHS ENDED JUNE 30, 19X8

management process must be made daily, and the information on which the decision is made must be fresh and up-to-date. Unnecessary costs are incurred when decisions are delayed because the information is not available.

The reports issued to the ABC Corporation's functional and cost center managers would be more detailed than the division reports and would identify performance variances from the standard or plan in still greater detail. In Division B, the variances within the melting operation for the six months were fairly significant and would be examined closely by division management. A report that the manufacturing manager and each facility manager (such as the manager of the melt shop facility) would receive is a variance on conversion cost report (Figure 8.13). This report shows that the melt shop and primary operations (B) had the biggest variances from standard, with the melt shop contributing $2.1 million of the $3.6 million conversion cost variance during the first six months.

The facility manager of the melt shop would look to the various production departments or cost center reports to help identify the source of the specific variances. A machine utilization report (Figure 8.14) would be useful in this regard. The report indicates that most of the melt shop furnace operations were only 80 percent efficient and that furnace #4 was reduced to an efficiency of only 73.8 percent for the six-month period. This low efficiency would affect both the direct labor performance to standard and the variable expense absorption. A department budget variance report (Figure 8.15) would give the detail expense variance from standard for the furnace #4 cost center.

## MEASURING THE SUCCESS OF REPORTING SYSTEMS

The financial reporting system illustrated here is a typical one, but the system, as well as the reports, must be tailored to fit the particular management style and need. The success of any reporting system established by the corporate controller is measured by the way the reports are used and by the way they assist managers at all levels to operate the business effectively. There are several ingredients that are always present in any good management reporting system:

1. *The interrelation of reports.* The various levels of reports must relate to each other logically. The summarized totals of the details contained in one level of reports become the detail of the next-higher level.

2. *The use of the exception concept.* The items or areas that vary significantly from profit plan or forecast must be highlighted in the management report. These exception items should be the first to be analyzed, so that the situation can be corrected or exploited depending on whether the variance was favorable or unfavorable.

3. *The adaptability of reports.* Every effort should be made to construct reports that can be used for all divisions or groups within the company. An income statement or an inventory report should be adaptable with only slight modification for all lines of business. It is important, particularly at the corporate management level, that the report format be consistent for each division or profit center. Different formats only confuse the reader.

Unfavorable (Favorable)

| Department | Direct Labor | | | Variable Expense | | |
|---|---|---|---|---|---|---|
| | Actual | Standard | Variance | Actual | Standard | Variance |
| Melt Shop | $ 2,800 | $ 1,900 | $ 900 | $ 6,900 | $ 5,700 | $ 1,200 |
| Primary Operations—A | 850 | 950 | (100) | 3,130 | 2,850 | 280 |
| Primary Operations—B | 1,350 | 800 | 550 | 3,050 | 2,400 | 650 |
| Secondary Operations | 1,700 | 1,800 | (100) | 5,150 | 5,400 | (250) |
| Finishing Operations | 1,800 | 1,500 | 300 | 4,570 | 4,600 | (30) |
| Inspection | 200 | 150 | 50 | 600 | 450 | 150 |
| Conversion Cost of Production | $ 8,700 | $ 7,100 | $ 1,600 | $23,400 | $21,400 | $ 2,000 |
| Total (Direct Labor & Variable Expense) | | | | | | $ 3,600 |

FIGURE 8.13 ABC CORPORATION DIVISION B, VARIANCE ON CONVERSION COST FOR THE SIX MONTHS ENDED JUNE 30, 19X8 (DOLLARS IN THOUSANDS)

| Area | Capacity hours | Scheduled hours | Delay Hours (Actual) | | | | | Operating hours | Hours earned | Cap. % | Eff. % | Delays % |
|---|---|---|---|---|---|---|---|---|---|---|---|---|
| | | | Set up | Mech. | Elec. | Other | Total | | | | | |
| Melt Shop: | | | | | | | | | | | | |
| Furnace #1 | 1,440 | 1,008 | | 61.55 | 13.75 | 182.10 | 257.40 | 1,152 | 949.02 | 80.0 | 82.4 | 22.3 |
| #2 | 1,440 | 1,008 | | 25.58 | 10.66 | 226.43 | 262.67 | 1,152 | 942.84 | 80.0 | 81.8 | 22.8 |
| #3 | 384 | 240 | | 2.91 | 6.25 | 38.47 | 47.63 | 240 | 218.10 | 62.5 | 90.9 | 19.9 |
| #4 | 1,440 | 1,008 | | 20.00 | 19.75 | 197.75 | 237.50 | 1,152 | 850.70 | 80.0 | 73.8 | 20.6 |
| #5 | 1,056 | 768 | | 52.17 | 11.17 | 159.78 | 223.12 | 912 | 750.60 | 86.4 | 87.3 | 24.5 |
| Total | 5,760 | 4,032 | | 162.21 | 61.58 | 804.53 | 1,028.32 | 4,608 | 3,711.26 | 80.0 | 80.5 | 22.3 |
| Primary A | 1,440 | 557 | 20.1 | 17.1 | 9.1 | 32.7 | 79.00 | 554.4 | 570.04 | 38.5 | 102.82 | 14.2 |
| Primary B | 1,440 | 768 | 22.1 | 42.9 | 11.7 | 20.3 | 97.00 | 520.6 | 430.64 | 36.2 | 82.72 | 18.6 |
| Secondary | 1,440 | 816 | 112.55 | 33.5 | 5.85 | 88.65 | 240.55 | 864.0 | 901.93 | 60.0 | 104.39 | 27.8 |
| Finishing | 1,440 | 768 | 213.0 | 62.3 | 42.3 | 81.2 | 398.80 | 823.1 | 664.7 | 57.2 | 80.76 | 48.5 |

FIGURE 8.14 ABC CORPORATION DIVISION B MACHINE UTILIZATION REPORT, SIX MONTHS ENDED JUNE 30, 19X8

| | Department: Electric Furnace #4 | | | | Period Ending: 6/30/X8 | |
| | Current Month | | | | Year-to-date | |
| Description | Actual | Budget | Variance | Actual | Budget | Variance |
|---|---|---|---|---|---|---|
| Operating labor: | | | | | | |
| Direct labor | $110,220 | $ 72,830 | $ 37,390 | $ 661,200 | $ 437,000 | $ 224,200 |
| Indirect labor | 21,280 | 16,420 | 4,860 | 127,810 | 98,470 | 29,430 |
| Total Operating labor | 131,500 | 89,250 | 42,250 | 789,010 | 535,470 | 253,540 |
| Direct expense: | | | | | | |
| Electric power | 127,300 | 102,622 | 24,678 | 763,500 | 615,720 | 147,780 |
| Electrodes | 43,275 | 34,900 | 8,375 | 259,650 | 209,390 | 50,260 |
| Oxygen | 7,230 | 5,830 | 1,400 | 43,380 | 34,980 | 8,400 |
| Repairs and maintenance | 24,250 | 19,558 | 4,692 | 145,520 | 117,350 | 28,170 |
| Lubricants, tools and supplies | 4,605 | 3,710 | 895 | 27,630 | 22,280 | 5,350 |
| Fluxes | 6,370 | 5,130 | 1,240 | 38,200 | 30,800 | 7,400 |
| Refractories | 7,060 | 5,700 | 1,360 | 42,360 | 34,190 | 8,170 |
| Miscellaneous | 1,940 | 1,600 | 340 | 11,920 | 9,610 | 2,310 |
| Total Direct expense | 222,030 | 179,050 | 42,980 | 1,332,160 | 1,074,320 | 257,840 |
| Service expense: | | | | | | |
| Auxiliary electric power | 7,615 | 6,140 | 1,475 | 45,690 | 36,850 | 8,840 |
| Water | 3,225 | 2,600 | 625 | 19,340 | 15,600 | 3,740 |
| Diesel cranes | 4,520 | 3,650 | 870 | 27,140 | 21,890 | 5,250 |
| Yard switching | 9,655 | 7,790 | 1,865 | 57,930 | 46,720 | 11,210 |
| Chemical laboratory | 3,780 | 3,050 | 730 | 22,680 | 18,290 | 4,390 |
| Metallurgical laboratory | 3,355 | 2,690 | 665 | 20,100 | 16,200 | 3,900 |
| Total Service expense | 32,150 | 25,920 | 6,230 | 192,880 | 155,550 | 37,330 |
| General expense: | | | | | | |
| General works expense | 1,180 | 950 | 230 | 7,050 | 5,690 | 1,360 |
| Employee fringe benefits | 14,830 | 11,960 | 2,870 | 89,000 | 71,770 | 17,230 |
| Total General expense | 16,010 | 12,910 | 3,100 | 96,050 | 77,460 | 18,590 |
| Total Variable expense | $401,690 | $307,130 | $ 94,560 | $2,410,100 | $1,842,800 | $ 567,300 |

FIGURE 8.15  ABC CORPORATION DIVISION B VARIABLE EXPENSE SUMMARY

4. *The flexibility of the reporting system.* Although certain reports, such as the income statement, will always be required, the importance of other reports will vary. There must be enough flexibility in the reporting system to alter data accumulation procedures quickly in response to changes in the company's control emphasis. If, for example, interest costs increase dramatically, the cash management will then become a critical management area, and the reporting function must be adjusted to focus more attention on it. Dynamic changes in business conditions mandate a reporting system that is responsive to a company's ever-changing needs.

There may be other ingredients just as important to the success of a management reporting system in a particular company. However, if the basic reporting system is established properly, the controller will recognize specific needs and respond in an effective fashion to provide the required information. The ability to react promptly to any reporting requirement is the final measure of a successful reporting system.

## SUGGESTED READING

Cohen, Jerome B., and Robbins, Sidney M. *The Financial Manager: Basic Aspects of Financial Administration.* New York: Harper & Row, 1966.

McFarland, Walter B. *Concepts for Management Accounting.* New York: National Association of Accountants, 1966.

Osborne, George S. *Management by Objectives.* New York: Pitman Publishing Corp., 1965.

Peat, Marwick, Mitchell & Co. *Responsibility Reporting,* ed. K. S. Axelson. New York: 1961.

# 9

# Stockholder Reports

*Charles Gibson*

## INTRODUCTION

The annual report to stockholders is a powerful communications tool used for purposes other than just the reporting of financial data. It is effective in marketing, public relations, promoting management policies, boosting employee morale, and influencing investor attitudes. (See Chapter 45.)

In recent years, however, the annual report has become increasingly important as a document of basic financial disclosure, as its contents are increasingly affected by SEC and FASB requirements and regulations. The controller plays a key role in ensuring that the financial reports fairly present the company's financial position and the results of its operations.

## Basic Financial Statements

In the annual report, the controller must include the company's basic financial statements: its balance sheet, its income statement, and a statement of changes in financial position. Appropriate explanatory notes must also be included. Companies that meet specified size requirements must also include supplementary information that report inflation data, required by FASB Statement No. 33, *Financial Reporting and Changing Prices*. (The inflation data and size requirements are described later in this chapter.)

## Integration of Annual Report With Form 10–K

In 1980, the SEC adopted several rules intended to make a company's annual report to shareholders its basic disclosure document by making it the principal resource for Form 10–K. Under this plan, the annual report requirements have been expanded in some respects—such as calling for three years' income statements instead of the usual two years'. Its intention is to require a more meaningful analysis of the registrant's business and financial condition in order to capture, at least in summary form, some of the detailed business description formerly required in Form 10–K and in most other registration statements. The former management's discussion and analysis of the summary of earnings has been replaced by a discussion and analysis of the issuer's financial statements, liquidity, and capital resources.

The shareholders' annual report may be incorporated by reference into Form 10–K, or the information may be repeated in the 10–K. This procedure assures that the annual shareholders' report will contain information which the Commission believes should be given maximum public exposure. The principal matters covered by the proposed changes are reviewed in Chapter 10.

## Reporting Requirements for SEC and GAAP

Under the SEC's current rules, which integrate the shareholders' annual report with Form 10–K (and other SEC filings), there are only minor differences between the SEC requirements for financial statements and what are *generally accepted accounting principles* (GAAP). Nevertheless, companies that are subject to the periodic reporting requirements of the SEC must submit financial statements prepared in conformity with the Commission's regulations, as well as with the rules and interpretations of its staff.

In general, the present differences between GAAP and Regulation S-X (which covers the form and content of SEC financial statements) are not very substantial. The SEC requires more information on segment reporting, certain supplementary information from gas and oil producers not required by GAAP, additional information for pension plans and stock options, and Regulation S-X requires various supplementary schedules. The SEC has professed its intention of bringing its requirements into conformity with GAAP, except in areas where the Commission believes investors require certain information not mandated under GAAP. (See Chapter 10.)

**What is GAAP?** When we speak of generally accepted accounting principles we mean accounting rules issued by a standard-setting body and accepted by the accounting profession. In accounting situations where no standards have been issued, GAAP means rules that have developed over time and are "generally accepted." (See Chapter 2.)

A controller preparing financial statements for public use is expected to use GAAP in the preparation of these statements. The auditor's opinion is specifically directed to whether or not the financial statements consistently conform to GAAP. If a company issues financial statements that include one or more items not acceptable under GAAP, or fails to disclose information required by GAAP, the auditor will issue a qualified opinion if the matter is material to the financial statements. Theoretically, if the matter is sufficiently serious the auditor could issue an adverse opinion. However, auditors rarely issue an adverse opinion; it is only used as a threat to force the controller to conform his statements to GAAP.

**Big GAAP Versus Little GAAP.** As accounting principles became more complex and disclosure requirements more extensive, many smaller companies and their outside accountants complained about the cost and burden of compliance. Finally, in 1978, the Financial Accounting Standards Board (FASB), the present official standard-setting body, issued Statement No. 21, suspending the requirements to show segment information and earnings per share for nonpublic enterprises. While there have been no additional suspensions of GAAP requirements for smaller and nonpublic companies, the requirement for inflation-adjusted financial disclosures was specifically applicable only for large public companies. The FASB has stated its intention of considering the problems of smaller businesses when it prepares future accounting standards.

## ANNUAL REPORT PREPARATION

In most public companies, the preparation of the shareholders' annual report is a major undertaking for the controller and his entire staff. An efficient controller will begin preparations before the year-end by: reviewing the prior year's financial statements to determine if any changes in classification are necessary; determining the effect on the financial statements of any recent pronouncements by the FASB or the SEC; and reviewing developments within the company that would affect the format of the statements or that would require additional footnotes. Having made such determinations, the controller should have his staff prepare a layout for the annual report, insert the required comparative prior year figures, and include the footnotes that will continue unchanged from the prior year, leaving room for current year amounts and new footnotes.

### Structuring the Report

While the financial statements included in the shareholders' annual report are pre-pared in accordance with GAAP, the requirements for financial disclosures are determined under SEC rules, primarily Rule 14A, covering annual proxy state-ments. For example, GAAP only requires a balance sheet as of the current year-end date and an income statement and statement of changes in financial position for the year then ended. The SEC rules now require comparative balance sheets for two years and income statements and statements of changes in financial position for three years. In addition, the SEC rules require a detailed description of the busi-ness, information regarding officers and directors, and other related data not required by GAAP. The nonfinancial sections of the shareholders' annual report are discussed in Chapter 45.

While most of the financial statement requirements are familiar to the controller, there are some that may be difficult to prepare. These problem areas are comprised of *segment reporting, earnings per share computations,* and *inflation accounting,* and are discussed in the remainder of the chapter.

### Segment Reporting

In 1969 the Securities and Exchange Commission issued requirements for seg-ment reporting in registration statements. Segment reporting requirements were later extended to cover annual reports filed on Form 10–K and annual reports to security holders of public companies. In 1976, the Financial Accounting Standards Board issued Statement No. 14, mandating financial reporting for segments of a business enterprise. The Board concluded that information related to an enterprise's industry segments, foreign operations, export sales, and major customers would be useful in understanding the financial statements of the firm. As noted above, the requirement has been suspended for nonpublic enterprises.

**FASB No. 14 Requirements.** FASB No. 14 directs that a disaggregation of consolidated financial information be reported in the form of business segments. In general, this amounts to breaking down the income statement and the balance sheet into related industry divisions.

Segment reporting is not required for unconsolidated subsidiaries and investment in 50 percent or less owned investees. However, both the industries and the geo-graphic areas of operation must be disclosed for all equity method investees.

Special disclosure requirements pertain to equity method investees whose opera-tions are vertically integrated with those of a reportable segment of the firm. These reportable segments must disclose the equity in the net income and net assets of these unconsolidated investees.

*Reportable segments.* A segment is termed a reportable segment if it satisfies at least one of the following tests of paragraph 15 of FASB No. 14:

1. Its revenue (including sales to unaffiliated customers as well as intersegment sales or transfers) is 10 percent or more of the combined revenue (sales to unaffiliated customers and intersegment sales or transfers) of all of the enterprise's industry segments.
2. The absolute amount of its operating profit or operating loss is 10 percent or more of the greater, in absolute amount, of:
   a. The combined operating profit of all industry segments that did not incur an operating loss, or
   b. The combined operating loss of all industry segments that did incur an operating loss.
3. Its identifiable assets are 10 percent or more of the combined identifiable assets of all industry segments.

In applying the 10 percent tests, interperiod comparability must be considered. Thus, an industry segment that does not meet the 10 percent test may be reported if it has been significant in the past and is expected to be significant in the future. A segment may also meet the 10 percent tests but not be reported if it is not considered to be representative of current or future operations.

An additional test is known as the 75 percent test. The 75 percent test directs that combined revenue from sales to unaffiliated customers of reportable segments must constitute at least 75 percent of consolidated net sales as shown on the income statement. If the firm's industry segments do not satisfy the 75 percent test, additional segments must be identified as reportable segments until the 75 percent test is met.

When determining the industry segments, each firm must consider its own characteristics. The FASB stipulates that the nature of the product, the nature of the production process, and the company's marketing and marketing methods are characteristics that should be considered. The FASB also points out that broad categories such as manufacturing and retailing are not indicative of an industry segment.

*Information to be disclosed.* Disclosure should be made of the type of product and service from which the revenue of the segment was derived as well as the relevant accounting policies followed.

The firm should report the following for each industry segment reported:[1]

1. Revenue (show intercorporate transfers separately);
2. Profitability (operating profit)—in addition to presenting operating profit the firm may present some other measure of profitability, such as gross margin. In these cases it is necessary to reconcile and describe the difference between operating profit and the other measure of profitability;
3. Identifiable assets; and
4. Related disclosures—
   a. Aggregate amount of depreciation, depletion, and amortization expense for each reportable segment;

---

[1] Details of the required disclosure are specified in paragraphs 23-27 of FASB No. 14.

b. Amount of each reportable segment's capital expenditures;

c. Equity in the net income from, and investments in, the net assets of unconsolidated subsidiaries and other equity method investees whose operations are vertically integrated with the operations of that segment; and

d. Effect of a change in an accounting principle on the operating profit of reportable segments during the period in which the change is made.

*Foreign operations.* Information about foreign and domestic operations must be presented if either of the following conditions is met:[2]

- Revenue generated by the enterprise's foreign operations from sales unaffiliated customers is 10 percent or more of consolidated revenue as reported in the enterprise's income statement.
- Identifiable assets of the enterprise's foreign operations are 10 percent or more of consolidated total assets as reported in the enterprise's balance sheet.

When foreign operations are conducted in more than one geographic area, the information about these foreign operations should be presented separately for each *significant foreign geographic area.* (A significant foreign geographic area is one that has revenue from sales to unaffiliated customers or identifiable assets that are 10 percent or more of the related consolidated amounts.) Foreign geographic areas not meeting this criteria should be presented in the aggregate.

If the test for disclosure of foreign operations is met, the following disclosure requirements apply:[3]

- Revenue, with sales to unaffiliated customers and sales or transfers between geographic areas shown separately;
- Operating profit or loss, or net income, or some other measure of profitability between operating profit or loss and net income; and
- Identifiable assets.

*Export sales.* Domestic operations include sales to unaffiliated customers within the home country and sales to customers in foreign countries. When the export sales to unaffiliated customers are 10 percent or more of the total revenue from sales to unaffiliated customers, the amount must be reported separately, in the aggregate as well as by geographic areas.

*Major customers.* When 10 percent or more of a firm's revenue comes from sales to a single customer, this fact, along with the amount, should be disclosed. To

---

[2] FASB No. 14, paragraph 32.
[3] FASB No. 14, paragraph 35.

determine this, a group of customers under common control are regarded as one customer.

Domestic government agencies and foreign governments are considered in the aggregate for this 10 percent test. Disclosure of the name or names of major customers is not required by Statement No. 14, but is required for SEC reporting.

*Restatement of previously reported segment information.* Paragraph 40 of FASB No. 14 directs that previously reported segment information must be restated if any of the following conditions exist:

- Financial statements as a whole are restated.
- Groupings or products and services in the industry segments are changed.
- Groupings of foreign operations in the geographic areas are changed.

**Financial Reporting for Segments of a Business Enterprise.** FASB Statement No. 18, issued in 1977, removed the segment reporting requirements for interim financial statements. However, if a firm elects to report segment information in interim financial statements, this segment information must be consistent with the requirements of FASB No. 14.

*Nonpublic enterprises.* A corporation previously considered nonpublic is no longer considered as such when its financial statements are issued in preparation for a sale of securities to the public.

### Earnings Per Share

**Background of Computation Rules.** Earnings per share (EPS) is usually considered the most important profitability measure. The concept of earnings per share is fairly simple: how much was earned or lost per share of common stock?

For many years, EPS was computed by dividing net earnings (after removing preferred dividends) by the outstanding shares of common stock. During the 1960s this method of computing EPS came under attack as too simplistic. The Accounting Principles Board decided that the earnings per share computation should consider the potential *dilution* of securities and that the computation should follow formal guidelines. (Dilution occurs when a company has outstanding securities or rights that would reduce EPS through an issuance of common stock. Examples are convertible bonds, convertible preferred stock, stock rights, warrants, and options.)

APB Opinion No. 9, issued in 1968, set guidelines—that were widely criticized—for the computation of earnings per share. The following year, the guidelines were revised and are now contained in APB Opinion No. 15.

**Earnings Per Share Requirements.** A company is often required to present several EPS figures on the face of the income statement. The EPS computation is required for income from continuing operations when the corporation has discontinued operations on the face of the income statement. When the corporation has extraordinary items and/or the cumulative effects of an accounting change, earnings per share should then be presented for income before these factors are taken into consideration. EPS should also be presented for net income.

In addition to the required earnings per share figures, a corporation may elect to present additional EPS figures on the face of the income statement, for instance, earnings per share for an extraordinary item. This earnings per share figure is not required, but most corporations elect to present it when an extraordinary item is present.

*Primary and diluted EPS.* Depending on the capital structure, earnings per share may have to be shown in a dual presentation of primary EPS and fully diluted EPS. When the capital structure would cause an aggregate three percent or greater dilution from primary earnings per share, then a dual presentation is required under Opinion No. 15.

The three percent dilution test is computed by comparing EPS computed without considering any dilution factors and EPS computed on a fully diluted basis. The fully diluted basis considers the maximum potential dilution. Many misinterpret the three percent test and believe it to be a comparison between primary earnings per share and fully diluted earnings per share. Actually, it is possible that a corporation could be required to present a dual earnings per share presentation, in which the primary and the fully diluted earnings per share would be the same. This could result because the primary earnings per share computation may include the same dilutive common stock equivalent securities that are included in the fully diluted earnings per share (such as stock rights and options). The SEC does not accept the three percent test. For SEC filings, a dual presentation is required if there is any dilution in EPS.

**Weighted Average Number of Shares.** The weighted average of shares outstanding during the period should be used as the basis for computing EPS. For example, assume that a corporation had two million common shares outstanding on January 1, acquired 300,000 treasury shares on July 1, and issued 500,000 shares on October 1. The weighted average computed for the year ending December 31 would be as follows:

$$
\begin{array}{ll}
\text{January-June} & \\
\quad 2,000,000 \times 6/12 \;=\; & 1,000,000 \\
\text{July-September} & \\
\quad 1,700,000 \times 3/12 \;=\; & 425,000 \\
\text{October-December} & \\
\quad 2,200,000 \times 3/12 \;=\; & \underline{\quad 550,000 \quad} \\
& 1,975,000 \text{ shares}
\end{array}
$$

**Retroactive Recognition to Stock Dividends and Stock Splits.** Retroactive adjustments must be made in order to compute the EPS in terms of the new number of shares outstanding after a stock dividend or stock split. Note that this is not a weighted average computation.

Using the weighted average example above, the following computation illustrates the effect of stock dividends and stock splits. Assume that on December 1 there was a two for one stock split. The weighted average computed for the year ending December 31 would be as follows:

$$
\begin{array}{lllll}
\text{January-June} \\
\quad 2,000,000 \times 6/12 & = & 1,000,000 \times 2 & = & 2,000,000 \\
\text{July-September} \\
\quad 1,700,000 \times 3/12 & = & 425,000 \times 2 & = & 850,000 \\
\text{October-December} \\
\quad 2,200,000 \times 3/12 & = & 550,000 \times 2 & = & \underline{1,100,000} \\
& & & & 3,950,000
\end{array}
$$

Earnings per share should be reduced by one-half.

**Claims of Senior Securities.** Earnings per share is a concept that applies to common stock. Therefore, dividends on senior securities should be deducted from net income before computing EPS, as in the following example:

*Assumptions:*

| | |
|---|---|
| $1,000,000 | Net Income |
| 200,000 | Common Shares Outstanding (No Change During Year) |
| 500,000 | 6% Preferred Stock |

*Computation of Earnings per Share:*

| | |
|---|---|
| $1,000,000 | Net Income |
| 30,000 | Preferred Dividend |
| 970,000 | Adjusted Net Income for Common |
| 200,000 | Divide by Common Shares |
| $4.85 | Earnings per Share |

**Pooling Versus Purchase.** In a *pooling of interests*, operations are combined for all periods presented. Two or more companies are combined by uniting their ownership interest. Therefore, a weighted average computation that reflects the total of the weighted average outstanding of the combining companies should be used. This weighted average for EPS should be adjusted to the equivalent shares of the surviving company for all periods presented.

Assume that on July 1, 1980, Companies X and Y merge in what is considered to be a pooling of interests, and the resulting company reports on a calendar-year basis.

|  | Company X | Company Y |
|---|---|---|
| Net income January 1 to June 30 | $200,000 | $100,000 |
| Outstanding shares of common stock on July 1, 1980 | 20,000 | 40,000 |
| Shares of Company X issued to Company Y stockholders | | 30,000 |
| Net income of combined company July 1 through December 31, 1980 $400,000 | | |

*Computation:*

Net income: $200,000 + $100,000 + $400,000 = $700,000

Average shares outstanding during year

| Company X stock used in the merger | 20,000 shares |
|---|---|
| Company X stock used in the merger | 30,000 shares |
| | 50,000 shares |

Net income per share: $\left(\dfrac{\$700,000}{50,000 \text{ shares}}\right)$ $\underline{\$14.00}$

In a purchase, one company is acquired by another. The reported income of the acquiring corporation includes the income of the acquired company from the date of acquisition. The weighted average shares for earnings per share should reflect the new shares only from the date of purchase.

Using the same assumptions, the following example is computed to illustrate a purchase:

*Computation:*

Net income: $200,000 + $400,000  =  $600,000

Average shares outstanding during year:

| January-June | 20,000 × ½ = 10,000 |
|---|---|
| July-December | 50,000 × ½ = 25,000 |
| | 35,000 shares |

Net income per share: $\left(\dfrac{\$600,000}{35,000 \text{ shares}}\right)$ $\underline{\$17.14}$

**Primary Earnings Per Share.** *Primary earnings per share* refers to the amount of earnings attributed to each share of common stock and common stock equivalents outstanding during the period.

*Common stock equivalents.* A *common stock equivalent* is a security that gives its holder the right to acquire shares of common stock. Typical common stock equivalents are convertible bonds, convertible preferred stock, stock options, stock warrants, stock purchase contracts, participating securities, and contingent shares.

Common stock equivalents should not be included in the computation if their inclusion results in either higher earnings per share or in a decrease of a loss per share. These common stock equivalents are referred to as "anti-dilutive." Each common stock equivalent should be considered separately for the anti-dilution criteria.

Convertible bonds, or convertible preferred stocks, must meet a test if they are to be considered as common stock equivalents: the cash yield to the purchaser at the time of issuance must be less than 66⅔ percent of the then current bank prime interest rate. The 66⅔ percent test is subjective; it determines whether or not the conversion feature had a significant influence on the market price of the security. Once such securities meet the test as common stock equivalents, they retain that designation as long as they are outstanding—no matter what changes occur in the prime interest rate. Conversely, securities that do not meet this test at issuance can never become common stock equivalents.

*Treasury stock method.* Stock options, stock warrants, and stock purchase contracts are always considered as common stock equivalents. In computing the common stock equivalents, the *treasury stock method* is generally used. One exception occurs when the funds must be used toward the retirement of debt; another exception is stipulated for convertible securities that require cash payments upon conversion. This makes them equivalent to a warrant. In these cases, the *if converted* method should be used. If there are any excess proceeds they should be applied to the purchase of common stock under the treasury stock method.

The following example illustrates the treasury stock method of computing earnings per share for stock options, stock warrants, and stock purchase contracts:

|  | *Normal Treasury Stock Method* |
|---|---|
| Net income for the year | $ 6,000,000 |
| Common shares outstanding (no change during year) | 4,000,000 |
| Options outstanding to purchase equivalent shares | 500,000 |
| Exercise price per share | 20 |
| Average market price per share | 25 |
| Application of assumed proceeds $20 × 500,000 = $10,000,000 | |
| Toward repurchase of common shares | 10,000,000 |
| Shares repurchased $10,000,000 ÷ $25 | 400,000 |
| Shares issued | 500,000 |
| Incremental shares | 100,000 |
| Adjustment of shares outstanding: | |
| Actual outstanding | 4,000,000 |
| Net incremental shares | 100,000 |
| Adjusted shares outstanding | 4,100,000 |
| Primary earnings per share | $1.46 |
| Earnings per share before considering options $6,000,000/4,000,000 | $1.50 |

Earnings per share is computed as if the options and warrants were exercised at the beginning of the period or at the time of issuance, if later. To prevent an anti-dilutive quarter from offsetting a dilutive quarter, the determination of the average market price is made separately each quarter. The weighted average for the year-to-date earnings per share computation is calculated by adding the incremental shares determined on a quarterly basis and then dividing by the number of quarters.

It is not necessary to assume that a stock option would be exercised until the market price of the common stock has been in excess of the exercise price for sub-stantially all of three consecutive months, including the last month of the period to which earnings per share relate. This practice is recommended in order to eliminate short-term swings that could distort earnings per share in the market price of the common stock.

**Fully Diluted Earnings Per Share.** *Fully diluted EPS* is the designation for the per share earnings, after having considered all possible dilutions. Unlike primary earnings per share, there is no common stock equivalent test for measuring the effect of convertible bonds or convertible preferred stock.

Presumed conversions that result in an increase in EPS (or decrease of a loss per share) would not be used. This is the same anti-dilution rule that applied to pri-mary earnings per share.

The same basic computations that apply to primary earnings per share also apply to fully diluted earnings per share. Some assumptions used in the computations differ in order to reflect the maximum potential dilution.

When computations are made under the treasury stock method, the market price at the close of the period reported upon should be used instead of the average price, if such market price is higher than the average price.

**Additional Disclosures.** The financial statements should include a description of the rights and privileges of the various securities outstanding. The bases upon which primary and fully diluted earnings per share were calculated should also be explained.

**Supplementary Earnings Per Share.** Conversions to common stock made during a period are included in the computation of the weighted average shares outstanding from the conversion date. However, if conversions during the period would have affected primary earnings per share had they taken place at the beginning of the period, or if similar conversions occur after the close of the period but before com-pletion of the financial report, it becomes necessary to show what primary earnings per share would have been if such conversions had taken place at the beginning of the period. This supplementary EPS data should preferably be presented in a note rather than on the face of the income statement.

## Inflation Accounting

**Background.** There are two basic approaches to preparing financial statements that reflect the influence of inflation. They are usually referred to as the *constant dollar approach* and the *current cost approach*.

*The constant dollar approach.* The constant dollar approach utilizes the conventional statements and principles that were used to prepare them. Appropriate indexes representing the general inflation factor are then applied to the conventional statements. The result is financial statements that represent whether or not the purchasing power of the entity has been maintained.

If, for example, land had been purchased for $10,000 when the price index was 110, and the current end of the period price index is 165, the land would be presented on this year's price-level statement at $15,000 (165/110 × $10,000), or the prior year cost may be reduced to $6667 (110/165 × $10,000). The $15,000 amount may or may not be realistic in terms of the current value of the land.

*Current cost approach.* Current cost accounting could indicate current buying price or the current cost of equivalent operating or productive capability. In the land example, the current value may differ from either the historical cost or the historical cost adjusted for a general price index. The current cost of the land in the above illustration may be $20,000, or some other amount.

In 1976 the SEC issued Accounting Series Release No. 190 (ASR No. 190), requiring certain replacement cost accounting on a supplemental basis. ASR No. 190 required replacement cost data to be disclosed on a supplemental basis for inventories, cost of goods sold, productive capacity and depreciation, depletion, and amortization. This data had to be disclosed in the annual Form 10–K report and was to be included in the annual report. (If the data is not included in the annual report, a footnote in the report should indicate that this information is available in the Form 10–K report.) ASR No. 190 applied to public enterprises with inventories and gross property plant and equipment in excess of $100 million. This requirement has been dropped in favor of the disclosures required by FASB Statement No. 33.

**FASB Statement No. 33.** In September 1979, the FASB issued Statement No. 33, "Financial Reporting and Changing Prices." The Statement requires public enterprises with inventories and gross property, plant, and equipment in excess of $125 million, or with total assets in excess of $1 billion to report certain inflation data to the conventional statements on a supplemental basis.

The Statement does not require computation of current cost information that relates to income-producing real estate properties. This exception does not apply to the constant-dollar disclosures. The Statement also does not require interim financial reports of a business enterprise to report the supplemental inflation data. FASB No. 33 does require the disclosure of both current-year supplementary information and five-year summary supplementary information.

*Current year supplementary information.* The following supplementary information is required for current fiscal years:

1. Income from continuing operations (income after applicable income taxes, less the results of discontinued operations, extraordinary items, and the cumulative effect of accounting changes)—

    a. Adjusted for historical cost/constant dollar; and

    b. On a current-cost basis;

2. Purchasing power gain or loss on net monetary items;

3. Increases or decreases in the current cost amounts of inventory and property, plant and equipment both before and after eliminating the effects of general inflation; and

4. Explanatory notes.

The constant-dollar information must be expressed in dollars having a purchasing power equal to that represented by the average level of the Consumer Price Index for All Urban Consumers (CPI-U) over the current fiscal year.

*Five-year supplementary information.* Supplementary information is required for a five-year summary as follows:

1. Historical cost information adjusted for general inflation—
    a. Net sales and other operating revenues;
    b. Income from continuing operations;
    c. Income per common share from continuing operations; and
    d. Net assets at fiscal year-end.

2. Current-cost information—
    a. Income from continuing operations;
    b. Income per common share from continuing operations;
    c. Net assets at fiscal year-end; and
    d. Increases or decreases in the current cost amounts of inventory and property, plant and equipment, net of inflation.

3. Other information—
    a. Purchasing power gain or loss on net monetary items;
    b. Cash dividends declared per common share;
    c. Market price per common share at fiscal year-end;
    d. Average level of the Consumer Price index for All Urban Consumers (or the year-end CPI-U if that was used in computing income from continuing operations); and
    e. Explanatory notes.

One option under FASB No. 33 is to present the five-year supplementary information in dollars, with a purchasing power equal to either dollars of the base period used by the Bureau of Labor Statistics for the CPI-U, or that represented by the average level of the CPI-U during the current fiscal year.

The other key option is to present a comprehensive restatement instead of the piecemeal approach of FASB No. 33. It is not likely that many firms will select comprehensive restatement because of the additional work required. Firms wishing to consider a comprehensive restatement should review APB Statement No. 3 "Financial Statements Restated for General Price-Level Changes" and the FASB Exposure Draft "Financial Reporting in Units of General Purchasing Power." The inflation data required by FASB No. 33 may be disclosed in formats similar to those illustrated in Figures 9.1a and 9.1b.

Footnotes should be included to give the reader of the statements an understanding of the data upon which the supplemental information was based. The footnotes should include a comment disclosing that certain effects of inflation were computed for the company's inventory and property, plant and equipment as required by Statement of Financial Accounting Standards No. 33, *Financial Reporting and Changing Prices*, as well as a description of the adjustments related to the income statement accounts of cost of goods sold and depreciation expense.

Inflation Company
Supplementary Financial Data Adjusted for the Effects
of Changing Prices
For the Year Ended December 31, 1980
(In 000s of Dollars)

| | *As Reported in the Primary Statements* | *Adjusted for General Inflation* | *Adjusted for Changes in Specific Prices (Current Cost)* |
|---|---|---|---|
| Net sales | $90,000 | $90,000 | $90,000 |
| Cost of goods sold | 45,000 | 46,500 | 48,000 |
| Depreciation and amortization | 4,000 | 4,800 | 16,000 |
| Other operating expenses | 6,000 | 6,000 | 6,000 |
| Interest expense | 3,200 | 3,200 | 3,200 |
| Provision for income taxes | 4,000 | 4,000 | 4,000 |
| | $62,200 | $64,500 | $77,200 |
| Income from continuing operations | $27,800 | $25,500 | $22,800 |
| Purchasing power loss on net monetary assets held during the year | | $550 | $550 |
| Increase in specific prices (current cost) of inventories and property, plant, and equipment held during the year | | | $12,300 |
| Effect of increase in general price level | | | 10,850 |
| Excess of increase in specific prices over increase in the general price level | | | $ 1,450 |
| Current cost of inventory | | | $18,000 |
| Current cost of property, plant and equipment, net of accumulated depreciation | | | $30,000 |

FIGURE 9.1a  FORMAT FOR DISCLOSING INFLATION DATA

## QUARTERLY REPORTS

Some firms publish quarterly financial statements because stockholders seek detailed and informative interim reports. Other firms, such as those registered with the New York Stock Exchange, are required to publish interim financial reports. The SEC requires reporting firms to file Form 10–Q, a quarterly comparative financial statement, within forty-five days after the end of each quarter.

Inflation Company
Supplementary Five-Year Comparison of Selected
Financial Data Adjusted for the
Effects of Changing Prices
(Average 1980 Dollars, in 000s Except Per Share Data)

| | Years Ended December 31 | | | | |
| --- | --- | --- | --- | --- | --- |
| | 1976 | 1977 | 1978 | 1979 | 1980 |
| Historical cost information adjusted for general inflation | | | | | |
| Net sales | $85,000 | $99,000 | $98,000 | $95,000 | $90,000 |
| Income from continuing operations | * | * | * | 24,000 | 25,500 |
| Income from continuing operations per common share | * | * | * | 1.40 | 1.60 |
| Purchasing power loss on net monetary assets held during the year | * | * | * | 450 | 550 |
| Net assets at year end | * | * | * | 36,100 | 39,280 |
| Current cost information | | | | | |
| Income from continuing operations | * | * | * | 21,000 | 22,800 |
| Income from continuing operations per common share | * | * | * | 1.25 | 1.40 |
| Excess of increase in specific prices over increase in the general price level | * | * | * | 1,600 | 1,450 |
| Net assets at year end | * | * | * | 38,000 | 42,100 |
| Other information | | | | | |
| Cash dividends declared per common share | .90 | .73 | .75 | .85 | 1.00 |
| Market price per common share at year end | 15.50 | 16.00 | 15.00 | 14.00 | 12.00 |
| Average Consumer Price Index | 170 | 180 | 189 | 205 | 220 |

*Disclosure is not required for years ended before December 25, 1979.

FIGURE 9.1b  FORMAT FOR DISCLOSING INFLATION DATA

## APB Opinion No. 28

In 1973 the Accounting Principles Board issued APB Opinion No. 28, *Interim Financial Reporting*, to standardize generally accepted accounting principles relating to interim reports. Prior to its issuance, many firms held different views as to the objectives as well as the format and content of interim reports.

The Opinion sees each interim period as an integral part of the annual report. Therefore, revenues and expenses for the annual reporting period need to be allocated on a reasonable basis to each interim period. For example, if a major repair is incurred during a period, the expense should be charged over all of the periods.

Paragraph 30 of APB No. 28 requires that at least the following data be reported:

- Sales or gross revenues, provision for income taxes, extraordinary items (including related income tax effects), cumulative effect of a change in accounting principles or practices, and net income;
- Primary and fully diluted earnings per share data for each period presented;
- Seasonal revenue, costs, or expenses;
- Significant changes in estimates or provisions for income taxes;
- Disposal of a segment of a business and extraordinary, unusual, or infrequently occurring items;
- Contingent items;
- Changes in accounting principles or estimates; and
- Significant changes in financial position.

This information should be reported for the current quarter. In addition, data for the current year-to-date or the last twelve months to date should be furnished, together with comparable data for the preceding year, in addition to events material to the proper understanding of the interim report.

The current SEC rules for preparation of the quarterly report, Form 10–Q, as well as proposed changes in the requirements for the form are reviewed in Chapter 10.

## SUGGESTED READING

American Institute of Certified Public Accountants, *Accounting Trends and Techniques: Thirty-Fourth Annual Cumulative Survey of the Accounting Aspects of the Annual Reports of 600 Industrial and Commercial Corporations.* . . . George Dick and Richard Rikert, eds., 34th ed. New York: 1980.

Arthur Andersen and Company, *Management Guide to Better Financial Reporting: Ideas for Strengthening Reports to Shareholders and the Financial Analyst's Perspective on Financial Reporting Practices.* Duff and Phelps, Inc., 1976.

Crane, Allan, "Modern Annual Report—More Information, Faster," in James Don

Edwards, ed., *Modern Accountant's Handbook*. Homewood, Ill.: Dow Jones-Irwin, 1976.

Goff, Harrison H., "Annual Reports: They Don't Have To Be Dull." *Public Relations Journal*, Vol. 33 (September, 1977), pp. 28-34.

Reyes, Eugenio R., "Effective Financial Reporting—to Investors and Management." *Industrial Accountant*, Vol. 16 (April-June, 1977), pp. 31-41.

Romans, Donald B., "Drafting a Meaningful Annual Report." *Financial Executive*, Vol. 47 (June, 1979), pp. 26-30.

# 10

# SEC Reporting Requirements

*David P. Boxer*

## INTRODUCTION

Perhaps of greatest significance and challenge to the controller of a public reporting corporation is the continuing obligation of the company, under the Securities Exchange Act of 1934 ('34 Act), to file periodic reports and proxy material with its shareholders and the Securities and Exchange Commission. This requirement places great responsibility and time demands on the controller's office; the complex nature and constant change in SEC reporting requirements mandate careful study and a need to keep current with these requirements. Although the primary responsibility for the filing of these reports rests with the reporting company, the corporate preparer should consult and work closely with its independent auditor (in connection with the financial statements) and counsel (in connection with the nonfinancial portions of the filing).

## Criteria for Required Reporting

Companies become subject to the periodic reporting requirements of the '34 Act under the following circumstances:

- Companies whose securities are listed on a national securities exchange (e.g. NYSE and AMEX) must register these securities under Section 12(b) of the '34 Act, thereby becoming subject to that Act's reporting responsibilities.

- An unlisted company with total assets of more than $1 million and a class of equity securities held by more than 500 persons at any fiscal year end must register under the '34 Act, pursuant to Section 12(g). When the number of equity shareholders falls below 300, Section 12(g) companies may cease reporting if they notify the SEC to that effect.

- A company that has registered its securities for sale to the public under the Securities Act of 1933 ('33 Act) must periodically file reports with the SEC under Section 15(d) of the '34 Act, at least for the balance of the year in which the registration became effective. The reporting company's obligation to file with the SEC will continue until such time as the number of holders of the securities registered under the '33 Act falls below 300 at the beginning of a fiscal year, and it notifes the Commission to that effect.

In addition to the above circumstances, a company may voluntarily register under the '34 Act (Section 12(g)). Registration of securities under the '34 Act is usually accomplished by using Form 10.

Companies subject to responsibilities under the '34 Act must file reports with the SEC annually, quarterly, or on an ad hoc basis if specified reportable events occur. These are generally filed on Forms 10-K, 10-Q, and 8-K, respectively. Many public companies with '34 Act periodic reporting responsibilities must also conform to the proxy rules (Section 14 of the '34 Act) when soliciting proxies from their shareholders. If the proxy is being solicited for an annual meeting at which directors are to be elected, an annual report must be furnished to the company's shareholders. The following sections of this chapter discuss the form and content of each of these filings; emphasis is given to the financial statement requirements because that section of the report should be of most interest to the corporate controller.

## FORM 10-K—THE ANNUAL REPORT

Form 10–K is the principal annual report form used by commercial and industrial companies required to file annual reports with the SEC in connection with the periodic reporting requirements under the Securities Exchange Act of 1934. In the interest of providing continuing disclosure of material facts concerning the company, the report requires both financial and nonfinancial information about the registrant's activities during the year. As a result of recent changes in the SEC rules and regulations, the required financial statements and supplementary financial data in the Form 10-K and most registration forms may be incorporated by reference from the annual report to shareholders.

### General Rules and Instructions

The Form 10–K must be filed within 90 days of the registrant's fiscal year-end; required schedules may be filed by amendment on Form 8 within 120 days of the fiscal year-end. The requirements as to number of copies to be filed, signatures, style, kind and size of paper, and so on, are the same as those for other filings under the '34 Act and are set forth in the General Rules and Regulations under such Act (see Figure 10.1). There is a $250 filing fee.

If a registrant is unable to file the form (or any periodic report) when due, it is required to file with the SEC no later than one day after the due date, a notification on Form 12b–25 that identifies the late report or portion thereof and the reasons for not filing on time. Any report filed with missing information must prominently disclose on the cover the portions omitted. There is also a procedure for a 15-day automatic extension for hardship situations.

Of the eight copies required to be filed with the SEC, three copies must include all exhibits required by the form filed. In addition, one complete copy must be filed with each stock exchange on which any of the securities (debt or equity) of the registrant is registered. One of the complete copies filed with the SEC and the copy filed with each stock exchange must be signed manually by the registrant's principal executive officer or officers, its principal financial officer, its controller or principal accounting officer, and by at least a majority of the board of directors.

### Form and Content

Like other reports filed with the SEC, Form 10–K is not a blank to be filled in (unlike a tax return), but is intended for use as a guide in the preparation of the report. However, the cover page should be reproduced in accordance with the format specified in the form.

As is the case in most SEC filings, the report is comprised of both financial and nonfinancial (textual) information. In addition to the requirements set forth in the form itself, a preparer of the report should be aware of the following, which will

---

### GENERAL INSTRUCTIONS (EXCERPT) FOR PREPARING
### FORMS 8-K, 10-Q, AND 10-K (Rule 12b-12)

(a) Statements and reports shall be filed on good quality, unglazed, white paper approximately 8½ × 11 inches or approximately 8½ × 13 inches in size, insofar as practicable. However, tables, charts, maps, and financial statements may be on larger paper if folded to that size.

(b) The statement or report and, insofar as practicable, all papers and documents filed as a part thereof, shall be printed, lithographed, mimeographed, or typewritten. However, the statement or report or any portion thereof may be prepared by any similar process that, in the opinion of the Commission, produces copies suitable for a permanent record. Irrespective of the process used, all copies of any such material shall be clear, easily readable, and suitable for repeated photocopying. Debits in credit categories and credits in debit categories shall be designated so as to be clearly distinguishable as such on photocopies.

(c) The body of all printed statements and reports and all notes to financial statements and other tabular data included therein shall be in Roman type at least as large and as legible as 10-point modern type. However, to the extent necessary for convenient presentation, financial statements and other tabular data, including tabular data in notes, may be in Roman type at least as large and as legible as 8-point modern type. All such type shall be leaded at least two points.

(d) Statements and reports shall be in the English language. If any exhibit or other paper or document filed with a statement or report is in a foreign language, it shall be accompanied by a translation into the English language.

---

FIGURE 10.1   GENERAL INSTRUCTIONS FOR PREPARING FORMS

provide guidance in the preparation of both the financial and textual portions of the Form 10–K:

- General Rules and Regulations under the Securities Exchange Act of 1934 (e.g., Rule 12b—Applications and Reports, and Rule 13a—Reports of Issuers of Listed Securities);
- Guides for Preparation and Filing of Reports;
- Regulation S-K;
- Regulation S-X;
- Accounting Series Releases; and
- Staff Accounting Bulletins.

Inasmuch as the securities regulations are complex, an enlightened corporate controller with responsibility for the filing of his company's Form 10-K should understand that preparation of the form requires the cooperation of corporate officers, the registrant's attorneys, and independent accountants.

| Item | Title |
|------|-------|
| | **Part I** |
| 1 | Business |
| 2 | Properties |
| 3 | Legal Proceedings |
| 4 | Security Ownership of Certain Beneficial Owners and Management |
| | **Part II** |
| 5 | Market for the Registrant's Common Stock and Related Security Holder Matters |
| 6 | Selected Financial Data |
| 7 | Management's Discussion and Analysis of Financial Condition and Results of Operations |
| 8 | Financial Statements and Supplementary Data |
| | **Part III** |
| 9 | Directors and Executive Officers of the Registrant |
| 10 | Management Remuneration and Transactions |
| | **Part IV** |
| 11 | Exhibits, Financial Statement Schedules and Reports on Form 8-K |

FIGURE 10.2  OUTLINE OF FORM 10-K

**Form 10-K Outline.** The 1980 revisions to Form 10-K increased its parts from two to four, but reduced the total items from fifteen to eleven. Figure 10.2 is an outline of the new Form 10–K.

The nonfinancial textual information is generally the responsibility of the corporate secretary and either the in-house or outside counsel. The controller's responsibility, in addition to preparing the financial statements and related schedules, is to prepare or review financial information required for other sections of the 10-K. The review of the form follows the item sequence to the extent that any financial information is required. Items requiring only textual data are not covered in this discussion.

**Item 1—Business.** The information for this item is covered in Item 1 of Regulation S–K (the regulation is discussed later in this chapter). The controller is concerned principally with part (b) of this item. Part (b) calls for financial information about industry segments for each of the last three fiscal years. The required information is similar to the industry segment information required in financial statements under GAAP (SFAS No. 14), and the information may be cross referenced from Item 1 to the financial statements, or vice versa. The Regulation S–K requirements are somewhat broader than the GAAP requirements. If the financial statement data is cross referenced to Form 10–K, it must therefore be in accordance with Regulation S–K requirements, or supplementary data must be included in the 10–K. The main difference between GAAP and S–K is the latter's requirement (part c) for disclosing product sales within segments for any products (or services) that account for 10 percent or more of consolidated revenue in either of the last three years, or 15 percent or more of consolidated revenue if total revenue did not exceed $50 million during the last three fiscal years.

**Item 6—Selected Financial Data.** The 1980 amendments to Form 10-K deleted the five year summary of operations and substituted a requirement for certain financial data as defined in Item 10 of Regulation S–K. Item 10 of S–K calls for a comparative summary of selected consolidated financial data for each of the last five fiscal years. If applicable, the following items are required in the summary:

- Net sales or operating revenues;
- Income (loss) from continuing operations;
- Income (loss) from continuing operations per common share;
- Total assets;
- Total long-term obligations and redeemable preferred stock (including leases); and
- Cash dividends declared per common share.

Registrants required to provide five-year summary information in accordance with SFAS 33 (inflation adjusted financial data) may present such information under this item.

**Item 7—Management's Discussion and Analysis of Financial Condition and Results of Operations.** The information required for this item was substantially increased in the 1980 Form 10–K revisions. The requirements are now contained in Item 11 of Regulation S–K. The discussion must, at the minimum, provide information on the following areas:

- *Liquidity.* Identification of any known trends or other factors likely to materially increase or decrease liquidity. Identification and description of internal and external sources of liquidity such as expected sales of assets or lines of credit.
- *Capital resources.* Description of material commitments for capital expenditures as of the latest year-end, the general purpose of such commitments, and the anticipated source of funds required.
- *Results of operations.* Description of any unusual or infrequent events, transactions, or economic changes that materially affected income from continuing operations. In addition, information is required regarding any known trends or uncertainties that have had or will have a material effect on sales or income from continuing operations; the impact of inflation and changing prices on sales and on income from continuing operations; the extent to which material increases in sales are attributable to price increases, volume increases, or new products; and any other significant changes in sales, costs, or income from continuing operations. A discussion of the impact of inflation and changing prices is required even if the registrant is not required to comply with SFAS No. 33.

The management's discussion must cover the last three fiscal years on a comparative basis. The instructions for Item 11 of Regulation S-K contain guidance for preparing the management's discussion and should be carefully reviewed.

**Item 8—Financial Statements and Supplementary Data.** The consolidated financial statements of the registrant and its subsidiaries included in its annual report to shareholders may be incorporated by reference into the Form 10-K. Proxy rule 14a-3(b) requires the following financial statements for the shareholders' annual report:

- Audited balance sheets as of the end of the two most recent fiscal years; and
- Audited statements of income and changes in financial position for each of the three most recent fiscal years.
- Audited statement of changes in shareholders' equity for each of the three most recent fiscal years.

The financial statements must be prepared in accordance with Regulation S–X. Separate financial statements of the parent, unconsolidated subsidiaries, 50 percent owned companies and any other special financial statements that may be required by Regulation S–X (but are not required by Rule 14a–3(b) in the annual shareholders' report), may be filed as "Financial Statement Schedules" under Item 11 of the 10–K.

Registrants who become obligated to file a Form 10–K due to registration on Form S-18 (a short form for registrations of securities not exceeding $5 million) are allowed to use financial statements that do not comply with Regulation S–X in their first Form 10–K after the registration, and are allowed certain other exemptions for the second year.

*Supplementary financial information.* Item 8 of Form 10–K and Rule 14a–3(b) both require supplementary financial information specified by Item 12 of Regulation S–K. This item requires selected quarterly financial data for each of the two most recent fiscal years, as follows:

- Net sales;
- Gross profit;
- Income before extraordinary items and cumulative effect of a change in accounting;
- Income per share (based on the previous amount); and
- Net income.

The quarterly information is only required of registrants meeting certain tests detailed in Item 12. Basically, companies will meet the tests if:

- They are registered on a national securities exchange or their shares are quoted on the National Association of Securities Dealers Automated Quotation System (NASDAQ); and

- They have had net income after taxes but before extraordinary items and the cumulative effect of a change in accounting of at least $250,000 for each of the last three fiscal years; or
- They had total assets of at least $200 million at the last fiscal year-end.

There are also specific tests relating to number of shareholders, number of shares held by unrelated shareholders, and the market value of the outstanding shares.

If the quarterly data presented varies from the amounts previously reported on Form 10–Q for any quarter, the difference must be reconciled and explained. Any unusual transaction that occurred in any quarter should also be described.

Item 12 also requires, under certain circumstances, that transactions related to a disagreement with a former accountant (included in a Form 8–K filing during the past two fiscal years) be described and explained. (Form 8–K is reviewed later in this chapter.)

**Item 10—Management Remuneration and Transactions.** The required information is described in Item 4 of Regulation S–K, which calls for listing the remuneration of each of the five most highly compensated executive officers or directors who earn in excess of $50,000 per annum, as well as all officers and directors as a group. The remuneration data must be shown in a table with the following captions:

- A. Name of individual or number of persons in group;
- B. Capacities in which served;
- C–1. Salaries, fees, directors' fees, commissions, and bonuses;
- C–2. Securities or property, insurance benefits or reimbursement, personal benefits; and
- D. Aggregate of contingent forms of remuneration (including pensions and similar contingent benefits).

The SEC has amended Item 4 since it was first issued in 1978, and at the end of 1980 there were additional proposals for the revision of management remuneration data awaiting final approval. Most of the revisions relate to the column in which information is to be placed, or allow or require certain information to be shown in a note to the table or as a separate disclosure.

**Item 11—Exhibits, Financial Statement Schedules, and Reports on Form 8–K.** This item requires a listing of all financial statements, schedules, and exhibits filed as part of the report. Certain financial statements not required in the shareholders' annual report are included in this item (see Item 8 above).

*Financial statement schedules.* The financial statement schedules required of commercial and industrial companies (Rule 5–04 and Article 12) are listed below. Schedules I, VII, XI, XII, and XIII are filed as of the date of the latest balance sheet. All other schedules are filed for the periods for which an income statement is required (three years).

The following schedules are to be filed:

- Schedule I. Marketable securities—other investments. Filing of this schedule is required if either the short-term or long-term securities, on either a cost or market value basis, equal at least 10 percent of total assets, or both types of securities (using cost or market value) aggregate 15 percent or more of total assets.

- Schedule II. Amounts receivable from related parties and underwriters, promotors, and employees other than related parties. Only amounts receivable in excess of $100,000, or 1 percent of total assets, whichever is less, should be reported. The schedule must include amounts owed at any time during the last three fiscal years. Items arising in the ordinary course of business, such as purchases or expense advances, need not be listed.

- Schedule III. Investments in, equity in earnings of, and dividends received from related parties. This schedule is required only if the investment exceeds 5 percent of total assets.

- Schedule IV. Indebtedness of and to related parties—not current. If the related amounts due from or to the related parties are less than 5 percent of total assets, the schedule may be omitted.

- Schedule V. Property, plant, and equipment. This schedule also has a 5 percent of assets minimum requirement. Assets must be listed by class, with all additions and deductions during the periods.

- Schedule VI. Accumulated depreciation, depletion, and amortization of property, plant, and equipment. This schedule may be omitted if Schedule V is omitted.

- Schedule VII. Guarantees of securities of other issuers. Details are required of any such guarantees.

- Schedule VIII. Valuation and qualifying accounts. This schedule requires details for other valuation accounts, such as allowance for bad debts.

- Schedule IX. Short-term borrowings. An analysis of all short-term borrowings is required for the last three fiscal years. Alternatively, the information may be included in Management's Discussion and Analysis (see Item 7 of Form 10–K above).

- Schedule X. Supplementary income statement information. A schedule must list the amounts of the following expenses for each income statement filed, to the extent that each item exceeds 1 percent of total sales and revenues:

  – Maintenance and repairs;

  – Depreciation and amortization of intangible assets, preoperating costs, and similar deferrals (by category);

  – Taxes, other than payroll and income taxes (state separately any category of tax that exceeds 1 percent of sales);

  – Royalties; and

  – Advertising costs.

  This schedule may be omitted if the information is included in a note or in the income statement.

- Schedule XI. Real estate and accumulated depreciation. Companies in the real estate business must file this schedule.
- Schedule XII. Mortgage loans on real estate. This schedule is also required for real estate companies.
- Schedule XIII. Other investments. This schedule requires a description of any investment not required in any other schedule and that exceeds 5 percent of total assets on the latest balance sheet.

The Schedules are required to be filed in support of each set of financial statements filed. Accordingly, if separate parent company financial statements are required to be filed, then applicable Schedules are to be filed in support of both consolidated and company financial statements. If the financial statements included in the filing are audited, then the Schedules must also be audited.

*Reports on Form 8–K.* A statement is required as to whether any reports on Form 8–K (discussed later in the chapter) have been filed during the last quarter of the latest fiscal year, listing the items reported, any financial statements filed, and the date of the report.

*Exhibits.* The requirements for exhibits are covered in Item 7 of Regulation S–K.

## ANNUAL REPORT TO SHAREHOLDERS

Companies subject to the SEC's proxy rules are required to send an annual report to their shareholders in connection with proxy solicitations for election of directors. The 1980 revisions of the various security rules and regulations integrated the requirements of the shareholders' annual report with the financial statement requirements and certain other requirements of the Form 10–K and as previously discussed, allowed the annual report to be incorporated by reference in the Form 10–K.

The financial statement requirements for the shareholders' annual report (Rule 14a–3(b)) are explained under Item 8 of Form 10–K (discussed above). In addition, the report must include the following information, most of which is also required in Form 10–K:

- The supplementary financial information specified in Item 12 of Regulation S–K;
- The selected financial data described in Item 10 of Regulation S–K;
- Management's Discussion and Analysis in accordance with the provisions of Item 11 of Regulation S–K; and
- The market price of the company's common stock and related security holder matters in accordance with the provisions of Item 9 of Regulation S–K.

Regulation S–K Items 10, 11, and 12 were explained under the review of Form 10–K. The information required by Item 9 of S–K is not new, but has been transferred from the proxy rules as well as other places. If the annual report is not incorporated into Form 10–K, it must contain an undertaking to furnish a copy of Form 10–K to any shareholder who requests one.

In addition to the required financial statements, the shareholders' annual report may contain any other information, graphs, pictures, and so on, that management wishes to provide to the shareholders (see Chapters 9 and 45). The SEC encourages the use of graphics to make the report more understandable to a reader, as long as the information is consistent with the required data.

Seven copies of the shareholders' annual report must be mailed to the Commission solely for its information. If the report has been incorporated by reference in Form 10–K, then the required information is considered as "filed" with the SEC and thus subject to the securities laws.

## SEC DISCLOSURE GUIDES

In addition to the specific guidance and instructions found in the various periodic reporting forms required to be filed under the Securities Exchange Act of 1934, there are a number of general, but comprehensive, disclosure regulations and guides whose requirements must be adhered to in the preparation of the periodic reports. Principal among these are Regulations S–X and S–K; also needed are Accounting Series Releases (ASRs) and Staff Accounting Bulletins (SABs). The preparer of reports to be filed with the SEC must have a working knowledge of each.

### Regulation S–X

Regulation S–X is the principal accounting regulation of the SEC. With Regulation S–K and the Accounting Series Releases it states the requirements applicable to the form and content of the financial statements (both audited and unaudited) required to be filed under most of the various Securities Acts, including the 1934 Act. The Regulation also sets forth requirements of the accountants' reports and the qualifications (e.g. independence) of the accountants issuing the reports included in filings with the SEC. The 1980 amendments to the Securities Acts standardized the financial statement requirements of the shareholders' annual report with the Form 10–K and most other registration forms. Financial statements and other financial information are now interchangeable among the various reporting and registration forms. Care should be taken to use the most current version of the Regulation when working with S–X, since it is continuously being amended by additions, changes, and deletions.

**Format.** The Regulation is divided into a series of twelve Articles which are in turn subdivided into Rules principally relating to specific required disclosures. Figure 10.3 lists the Articles that comprise S–X. As the table indicates, the first four articles contain rules of general application. The next six articles prescribe the

| | |
|---|---|
| Article 1. | Application of Regulation S–X |
| Article 2. | Qualifications and Reports of Accountants |
| Article 3. | General Instructions as to Financial Statements |
| Article 3A. | Consolidated and Combined Financial Statements |
| Article 4. | Rules of General Application |
| Article 5. | Commercial and Industrial Companies |
| Article 5A. | Companies in the Development Stage |
| Article 6. | Management Investment Companies |
| Article 6A. | Unit Investment Trusts |
| Article 6B. | Face-Amount Certificate Investment Companies |
| Article 6C. | Employee Stock Purchase, Savings and Similar Plans |
| Article 7. | Insurance Companies other than Life Insurance Companies |
| Article 7A. | Life Insurance Companies |
| Article 8. | Committees Issuing Certificates of Deposit |
| Article 9. | Bank Holding Companies and Banks |
| Article 10. | Natural Persons |
| Article 11. | Content of Statements of other Stockholders' Equity |
| Article 11A. | Statement of Source and Application of Funds |
| Article 12. | Form and Content of Schedules |

FIGURE 10.3  REGULATION S–X CONTENTS

form and content of financial statements for various types of companies. The last two articles deal with the form and content of statements of shareholders' equity, source and application of funds, and the supplemental S–X schedules. Generally, most commercial and industrial companies need address themselves only to Articles 1 through 5, and 11, 11A, and 12; Articles 5A through 10 relate to specific types of businesses (e.g., Article 7A—Life Insurance Companies) for which the general disclosures and financial statement presentations would not be appropriate. The form and content of the statements of stockholders' equity, and source and application of funds specified in S–X Articles 11 and 11A are substantially the same as those that would be prepared in accordance with generally accepted accounting principles.

**Specific Disclosure Requirements.** The bulk of the specific disclosure requirements for commercial and industrial companies is to be found in Articles 4 and 5. These disclosures include those required by generally accepted accounting principles (GAAP) as well as some additional "compliance" items required to satisfy the increased disclosure requirements of the SEC. The Commission has attempted to conform S–X to GAAP, but there are still a few disclosure requirements in S–X that exceed the requirements of GAAP. Examples of such disclosures include:

- Allowance for doubtful accounts and notes receivable and the related provision;
- Aggregate maturities of long-term debt for five years;
- Redeemable preferred stock;

- Interest rates and other details of short-term borrowings;
- Oil and gas reserves;
- Disagreements with accountants;
- Excess of replacement or current cost over the stated LIFO value of inventories; and
- Disclosures relating to restrictions on retained earnings, compensating balances, and income tax expense in excess of that required by GAAP.

The SEC has deleted from S–X all disclosure requirements that duplicated GAAP, so it should not be used as a disclosure checklist but as guidance in determining what information is required in excess of GAAP requirements. Certain of the information may be included in a schedule or in a supplementary financial data section.

**Proposed Instructions as to Interim Financial Statements.** In September, 1980, the SEC issued a new Article 3 of Regulation S–X, "General Instructions as to Financial Statements," specifying the financial statements to be included in disclosure documents prepared in accordance with S–X. Article 3 provides that whenever interim financial statements are required, they must be at least as current as the statements filed in the most recent Form 10–Q and may be presented in the same condensed format. At the same time, the Commission proposed a new Article 10, "Interim Financial Statements," which would contain the instructions for such statements in all disclosure documents. The present Article 10, "Natural Persons," would be moved to Article 3. The discussion of Form 10–Q later in the chapter covers this proposal in more detail.[1]

## Regulation S–K

This Regulation reflects the SEC's decision to establish uniform guidelines for disclosures in the various registration and reporting forms to be filed with the SEC under the '33 and '34 Acts. It includes guidelines and instructions for disclosures common to more than one SEC filing form. In a sense, it is similar to Regulation S–X, the uniform standard for accounting disclosures. Prior to the promulgation of S–K under ASR 236 (1977), the items in the various forms replaced by S–K contained instructions and guidelines for the completion of the items, which varied (although generally not significantly) from form to form. A preparer of an SEC filing is now referred to an item in S–K for guidance in completing the item. By the end of 1980, the Regulation included uniform rules relating to twelve items. Table 10.4 lists the items comprising Regulations S–K. The SEC intends to expand S–K to incorporate other uniform disclosure instructions.

## Accounting Series Releases

In 1937, in the interest of furthering the development of uniform standards and practice relating to major accounting and auditing issues, the SEC began to issue opinions relating to such matters. These opinions are set forth in the almost 300

---

[1] The new Article 10 and the revised Form 10–Q were adopted in February 1981, essentially as proposed.

| | |
|---|---|
| Item 1. | Description of Business |
| Item 2. | Description of Property |
| Item 3. | Directors and Executive Officers |
| Item 4. | Management Remuneration |
| Item 5. | Legal Proceedings |
| Item 6. | Security Ownership of Certain Beneficial Owners and Management |
| Item 7. | Exhibits |
| Item 8. | Open |
| Item 9. | Market Price of the Registrant's Common Stock and Related Security Holder Matters |
| Item 10. | Selected Financial Data |
| Item 11. | Management's Discussion and Analysis of Financial Condition and Results of Operations |
| Item 12. | Supplementary Financial Information |

FIGURE 10.4    REGULATION S–K CONTENTS

Accounting Series Releases issued since the program was initiated (actually considerably fewer ASRs remain in effect since many are outdated and have been rescinded). A number of ASRs are actually opinions of the Chief Accountant of the SEC. In many instances, an ASR initiates a new accounting disclosure (ASR 148 [1973]—Compensating Balances and Short-Term Borrowing Arrangements, and ASR 190 [1976]—Replacement Cost Data) or changes an existing requirement by amending Regulation S–X (ASR 280 [1980] General Revision of Regulation S–X). In addition to addressing issues on accounting, reporting, and auditing, the ASRs also relate to matters concerning independence of accountants (ASR 126 [1972]—Guidelines and Examples, and ASR 251 [1978]—Interpretations and Guidelines Relating to Accountants' Litigation and Independence) and disciplinary actions against accountants (many ASRs are issued in connection with Rule 2(e) proceedings). The ASRs also always include any amendments to the various SEC filing forms for which financial statements are needed (ASR 279 [1980]—Amendments to Annual Report Form [10–K], Related Forms, Rules, Regulations and Guides).

A careful reading of the ASRs is important when preparing financial statements to be included in SEC filings—especially those that relate to specific Regulation S–X disclosures. A particular ASR will often include background information and guidance in the preparation of the specific S–X disclosure promulgated by the ASR. For example, ASR 148 amended S–X to include disclosures of compensating balance arrangements. This ASR, in addition to identifying the required disclosure, also provided guidance regarding the background of the issue, definition of terms, forms of disclosure, and measurement problems encountered in determining the amount of compensating balances.

### Staff Accounting Bulletins

In 1975 the SEC published ASR 180, which announced a new series of administrative interpretations and practices utilized by the Commission's staff (Division of Corporation Finance and Office of the Chief Accountant of the SEC) in reviewing financial statements. These Staff Accounting Bulletins (SABs) are intended to broaden on a more timely basis the dissemination of new or revised informal staff interpretations and practices. The SEC hopes that the increased availability of these previously unpublished interpretations will reduce repetitive comments and inquiries and thereby save the SEC staff, registrants, and their professional advisors both time and money in the registration and reporting process.

Unlike Regulation S–X and the ASRs, the SABs are not official accounting rules or interpretations of the Commission; they also do not bear the Commission's official approval. However, since the SEC staff will use these positions in reviewing a registrant's filings (both under the 1933 and 1934 Acts) it is advisable, in order to save time and money in avoiding comments by the SEC staff, to follow the guidelines and interpretations found in the SABs.

The Bulletins are comprised of a series of statements of surrounding facts, questions, and the staff's interpretations of each item. The following is a simple example of a Staff interpretation to be found in the SABs (Topic 10–H).

"H. LIFO LIQUIDATIONS

Facts: Registrant on a LIFO basis of accounting liquidates a substantial portion of its LIFO inventory and as a result includes a material amount of income in its income statement which would not have been recorded had the inventory liquidation not taken place.

Question: Is disclosure required of the amount of income as a result of the inventory liquidation?

Interpretative Response: Yes. Such disclosure would be required in order to make the financial statements not misleading. Disclosure may be made either in a footnote or parenthetically on the face of the income statement."

The first SAB was a lengthy and comprehensive compilation of the many interpretations that existed at the time the series was instituted. From 1975 through mid-1980, 38 Bulletins have been issued.[2] Figure 10.5 lists the broad topics covered by the SABs.

## FORM 10-Q—THE QUARTERLY REPORT

Form 10–Q is to be used by registrants required to file quarterly reports with the SEC in connection with the periodic reporting requirements under the Securities Exchange Act of 1934. Since the initial adoption of the Form in 1970, the information required to be included has been significantly expanded. Accordingly, the

---

[2] In February 1981, the SEC issued SAB No. 40 that revised and updated the prior 39 bulletins.

Topic 1.  Financial Statements
Topic 2.  Business Combinations
Topic 3.  Senior Securities
Topic 4.  Equity Accounts
Topic 5.  Miscellaneous Accounting
Topic 6.  Interpretations of Accounting Series Releases
Topic 7.  Real Estate Companies
Topic 8.  Retail Companies
Topic 9.  Finance Companies
Topic 10. Miscellaneous Disclosure

FIGURE 10.5  STAFF ACCOUNTING BULLETINS—TOPICS

report has grown from one containing only highly condensed information to one that is a comprehensive multi-page report about matters affecting the registrant occurring during the quarter reported upon. It includes conventional (although condensed) financial statements and other information. Added insights to the preparation of the Form can be obtained by reading the instructions to the Form, Accounting Series Releases 177 (1975) and 206 (1977) and Topic 6H(2) of the Staff Accounting Bulletins.

### General Rules and Instructions

The Form must be filed within forty-five days after the end of each of the first three fiscal quarters of each fiscal year; no report need be filed for the fourth quarter. The requirements as to number of copies to be filed, signatures, style, kind and size of paper, and so on, are the same as those for other filings under the '34 Act and are set forth in the General Rules and Regulations under such Act (see Figure 10.1). There is no filing fee for the quarterly report.

At least one of the eight copies filed with the SEC and one of the copies filed with each exchange on which any class of securities of the registrant is listed and registered must be signed manually. The report is to be signed on the registrant's behalf by a duly authorized officer of the registrant and by the principal financial officer or chief accounting officer of the registrant (e.g., treasurer and controller, respectively). If the principal financial officer or chief accounting officer is also duly authorized to sign on behalf of the registrant, one signature will be accepted if both titles are indicated below the signature.

Similar to other reports filed with the SEC, the Form is not a blank to be filled in, but is for use as a guide in the preparation of the Report. However, the cover page should be reproduced in accordance with the format specified in the Form.

If, at the time of filing the Report, the registrant intends to file in the near future a registration statement under the '33 Act on Form S–7 or short form S–16, the transmittal letter accompanying the Report should advise the SEC of such intention.

### Part I—Financial Information

As is the case in most SEC filings, the Report is comprised of both financial and nonfinancial (textual) information. Part I, Financial Information, provides for financial statements, footnotes, management's analysis of the quarterly income statements, and exhibits.

**Financial Statements Required.** The financial statements may be, and normally are, unaudited. The following financial statements for the indicated periods are to be included:

- *Income statements.* For the current quarter and year-to-date for the current year, and for the corresponding periods of the preceding year. These statements may also be presented for the cumulative twelve month period ended during the most recent quarter and for the corresponding period of the preceding year in lieu of the year-to-date statements.
- *Balance sheets.* As of the end of the current quarter and as of the comparable quarter of the preceding year.
- *Statements of changes in financial position.* For the current year-to-date and for the corresponding period of the preceding year.

By way of illustration, and assuming a calendar year company, the following financial statements would be included in the registrant's third quarter 10–Q report:

| | |
|---|---|
| Income Statements | 3 months September 30, 19X9 |
| | 3 months September 30, 19X8 |
| | 9 months September 30, 19X9 |
| | 9 months September 30, 19X8 |
| Balance Sheet | As of September 30, 19X9 |
| | As of September 30, 19X8 |
| Statements of Changes in Financial Position | 9 months September 30, 19X9 |
| | 9 months September 30, 19X8 |

Unconsolidated parent company financial statements or data are not required in Form 10–Q, and Rule 3A–02(e) of Regulation S–X, which relates to requirements for separate financial information of certain consolidated subsidiaries of diverse financial companies is not required to be followed. However, if separate financial statements of unconsolidated subsidiaries and investees were required in the registrant's annual report on Form 10–K, summarized income statement information of these companies should be disclosed in a footnote, unless these entities would not be required to file quarterly reports if they were registrants.

**Basis of Financial Statement Preparation.** The Form provides that although the financial statement "presentation and related disclosures" may be unaudited and on a somewhat condensed basis (see below), the statements should be prepared in accordance with the standards of accounting set forth in Opinion No. 28 of the Accounting Principles Board (Interim Financial Reporting). That Opinion establishes guidelines for the preparation of interim financial statements and the application of accounting principles to such statements; the computational guidelines in that Opinion should be adhered to regardless of the extent of optional disclosure condensation opted for by the registrant.

It is not intended that the Form 10–Q financial statements include all disclosures necessary to comply with generally accepted accounting principles. Accordingly, certain disclosures (e.g. pension and depreciation expense) necessarily included, if applicable, in financial statements intended to comply with generally accepted accounting principles, are not required for inclusion in Form 10–Q financial statements.

*Optional condensation.* Although the financial statements must generally follow the form of presentation specified in Regulation S–X, there are provisions in the Form which permit the financial statements to be condensed. Many of the disclosures generally required to comply with Regulation S–X may be omitted; there are no Regulation S–X schedules required. Balance sheets and income statements must only include major S–X captions—these are the numbered captions included in the applicable sections of the Regulation; subcaption disclosures are not required. As an example: If a balance sheet were prepared for inclusion in a Form 10–K (which requires full compliance with S–X disclosure requirements), S–X Rule 5.02.20 (a numbered caption) would require separate disclosure of Other Current Liabilities; instructions to the caption require that the caption be further analyzed to disclose accruals that exceed 5 percent of total current liabilities such as those relating to payrolls, taxes, and interest expense. The Form 10–Q balance sheet need only include the broad disclosure relating to Other Current Liabiities. Some further condensation is allowed if complex materiality tests are met. An exception to the numbered caption rule relates to disclosure of the components of inventory—separate disclosure is required for components of the balance sheet inventory amount (i.e.—raw materials, work in process, and finished goods).

The statement of changes in financial position may be abbreviated by beginning with a single figure of funds provided from operations. Other sources and applications of funds must be presented separately only when they exceed 10 percent of the average of funds provided by operations for the most recent three years.

Apparently, it is not intended that the Form 10–Q financial statements be supplemented by customary and often voluminous footnotes. As mentioned above, full compliance with the disclosure requirements of Regulation S–X and generally accepted accounting principles is not required. The Form specifies that footnotes detailing a summary of accounting principles and practices as well as other general notes to financial statements are not required. Caution is in order, however—the instructions to the Form specify that " . . . disclosures must be adequate to make the information presented not misleading." The instructions do not elaborate further, and a Registrant must use judgment in determining which additional disclosures must be included. It may be assumed that normal recurring disclosures, such as those detailing principles of consolidation and terms of long term debt and lease and stock option arrangements, need not be repeated in the quarterly report since those disclosures would generally be required in the registrant's annual report.

*"Updating" concept.* The financial statements and other disclosures in the Form 10–Q should be viewed as an updating of that information included in the annual report. Adopting this concept, those significant events modifying previously reported conditions should be considered for disclosure in Form 10–Q. Examples include significant changes in the arrangements specified above and the institution of new, or changes in the status of existing, litigation or other contingent obligations.

**Specific Required Disclosures.** In addition to the general standards of disclosure discussed above, the instructions to the Form require certain specific disclosures.

*Business combinations.* Where a business combination accounted for as a pooling of interests occurs during the quarter covered by the report, the financial statements for all included periods must reflect the pooling combination as if it had occurred during the earliest period presented. Also required is supplemental disclosure of the separate results of the combined businesses for periods prior to the combination. If the business combination occurs during any period covered by the report and is accounted for as a purchase, condensed pro forma operating results are to be included; these should reflect the results of operations as though the companies had combined at the beginning of the period. Such condensed pro forma information should include as a minimum revenue, income before extraordinary items and cumulative effect of accounting changes, income per share, and net income.

*Discontinued operations.* If a significant portion of the registrant's business has been disposed of during any period covered by the report, disclosure must be made of the effect on revenues and net income, both in total and per share for all periods covered by the report.

*Per share amounts.* If applicable, earnings and dividends per share for each period must be shown on the face of the income statement; the basis of computing such amounts and the number of shares used in the computation should also be disclosed. Unless the basis of computation of per share amounts is very simple (e.g., based on weighted average number of shares outstanding) or is clearly set forth in the footnotes, an exhibit detailing the computation must be included as part of the report.

*Accounting changes.* The SEC has expanded on the disclosures relating to changes in accounting required by generally accepted accounting principles. In addition to those disclosures, the registrant is required to state the date of the change and the reasons for making the change. A letter from the registrant's independent accountants must be filed as an exhibit to the first Form 10–Q filed subsequent to the date of the accounting change, indicating whether or not the change is to an alternative principle which in his judgment is preferable under the circumstances; the accountants' letter is not required if the change is made in response to a standard adopted by the FASB.

*Statement as to necessary adjustments.* The instructions specifically require a statement to be made to the effect that ". . . all adjustments which are, in the opinion of management, necessary to a fair statement of the results for the interim periods" have been reflected in the preparation of the financial statements. The type of adjustment the SEC is referring to is, for example, quarterly accruals for anticipated year-end adjustments (e.g. accruals for bonus and profit sharing arrangements), which should be assigned to the quarter so that the quarter bears a reasonable portion of the anticipated annual amount.

*Prior period adjustments.* Material retroactive prior period adjustments are to be disclosed, including the effect on net income, total and per share, and on the balance of retained earnings.

**Management's Analysis of Quarterly Income Statements.** As is the case in most SEC filings which include profit and loss information, Form 10–Q contains a requirement for management's narrative analysis of that data. The format and guidelines for the preparation of the analysis is similar to that to be included in a Form 10–K report. (See the section on Form 10–K above.) However, until Form 10–Q is revised (as proposed), there exist substantial differences in the requirements for the management's discussion between Form 10–K and Form 10–Q. Explanations for material changes in the amount of revenue and expense items for the following periods are to be included: the most recent quarter compared to the quarter immediately preceding it, the most recent quarter compared to the corresponding quarter in the preceding year, and the current year to date compared to the same period in the preceding year. The comparison of the most recent quarter and the quarter preceding it is required even though the prior quarter is not included in the 10–Q report.

**Part II—Other Information**

Part II of the Form includes the items listed below that call for disclosure of textual information. Items that are inapplicable or that call for a negative response may be omitted. A copy of the Form should be referred to for detailed instructions relating to the responses to the items in Part II. To the extent that responses to certain items lend themselves to legal interpretations, the preparer should consult legal counsel.

**Part II Items.** The following items, to the extent applicable, are required in Part II of Form 10–Q.

1. Legal proceedings;
2. Changes in securities;
3. Changes in security for registered securities;
4. Defaults upon senior securities;
5. Increase in amount outstanding of securities or indebtedness;
6. Decrease in amount outstanding of securities or indebtedness;
7. Submission of matters to a vote of security holders;
8. Other materially important events;
9. Exhibits and reports on Form 8–K:
    a. List of exhibits;
    b. Reports on Form 8–K. State whether any reports on Form 8–K have been filed during the quarter, listing the items reported, any financial statements filed, and the dates of any such reports.

### Proposed Revisions of Form 10–Q[3]

At the end of 1980, the SEC had open a proposed revision of Form 10–Q and related rules and regulations. The proposed revision is designed to accomplish the following:

- Encourage and facilitate the integration of formally filed quarterly reports with informal quarterly reports furnished to shareholders;
- Make certain the disclosure requirements for interim periods are consistent with the disclosure requirements for annual periods;
- Centralize a uniform set of instructions for interim financial statements in Regulation S–X; and
- Simplify present rules and reduce the reporting burdens of most registrants.

**The Specific Proposals Reviewed.** Under the proposals, the structure of the Form 10–Q would remain unchanged. However, the information called for by Part I—Financial Information, could be incorporated by reference from an informal quarterly report to shareholders.

*New S–X Article.* The proposals include a new Article 10 of Regulation S–X which would contain a uniform set of instructions for interim financial statements in all SEC filings under the 1933 and 1934 Acts. The proposed Article 10 instructions are substantially similar to the present financial statement requirements reviewed above.

*Footnote disclosure clarified.* The Commission proposes to revise the instruction regarding footnote disclosure to make clear that only certain disclosures are

---

[3] See footnote 1.

required.  Generally, only significant events or changes that have occurred since the end of the most recent fiscal year would require a note to the interim financial statements.

*Management's discussion and analysis.*  The proposal would call for the Management's Discussion to follow the requirements of Item 11(b) of Regulation S–K (also a proposal).  It is intended that the proposed 10–Q discussion would serve as an update to the discussion in the annual report and would need to address only material changes.  The current requirement to discuss the immediately preceding quarter is proposed to be deleted.

**Modifications to Part II.**  Items 3, 5, and 6 of the present form are proposed to be deleted.  They relate to changes in outstanding securities, and the Commission believes that the information is otherwise generally available.  Another proposed change would delete the instruction requesting issuers to advise the staff of their intention to file a registration statement on Form S–7 or S–16 because experience has proven that the instruction is not useful.

*Other matters.*  Other proposals would extend the "safe harbor rule" (exemption from liability) to projections (included in Part I of Form 10–Q), and revise the requirements when a registrant refers to an accountant's review of the interim financial statements.


# FORM 8-K—THE CURRENT REPORT

The third major report required to be filed by companies subject to the periodic reporting requirements under the Securities Exchange Act of 1934 is Form 8–K. Form 8–K should be considered an ad hoc filing to the extent that it is only required to be filed if one of the six events identified in the Form occurs. Actually, only five specific reportable events are identified in the Form; Item 5, Other Materially Important Events, is a loosely constructed general item calling for the reporting of events " . . . not otherwise called for by this form, which the registrant deems of material importance to security holders." Since the need to file a report under such Item lends itself to a good deal of interpretation, legal counsel should be consulted for guidance as to whether an event should be reported under Item 5.

## Format

Form 8–K includes the following items:

1. Changes in control of registrant;
2. Acquisition or disposition of assets;
3. Bankruptcy or receivership;

4. Changes in registrant's certifying accountant;
5. Other materially important events;
6. Resignation of registrant's directors; and
7. Financial statements and exhibits.

Most of the events specified in the Form are required to be reported on Form 8–K within fifteen days of the occurrence of the event. If an event is reported under Item 5, the Form 8–K is due within ten days of the end of the month in which the event occurred (e.g., if an event which is being reported under Item 5 occurred on January 15, the Form 8–K would be due on February 10).

As is the case in Forms 10–K and 10–Q, the Form is a guide, not a form to be filled in except that all the information set forth in the model cover sheet in the Form should be furnished. Three complete copies of the report and five additional copies that need not include exhibits must be filed with the Commission. The report must be signed by a duly authorized officer of the corporation.

## Financial Statement Requirements

Controllers and accountants generally become involved in filings of Form 8–K only if a business combination or change in certifying accountants is reported. There are no financial statement requirements for Form 8–K other than in response to Item 2, Acquisition or Disposition of Assets. If the registrant acquires a significant amount of assets, financial statements for the acquired business are generally required. An acquisition as used in the Form is a broad term and would include a merger, purchase, consolidation, exchange, succession, or possible other acquisition. An acquisition or disposition of assets is significant if:

- The registrant's equity in the net book value of the assets or the amount paid or received for such assets exceeded 10 percent of the total assets of the registrant;
- The business acquired or disposed of would be considered a "significant subsidiary" (Regulation S–X provides standards for the determination of a significant subsidiary by establishing a series of 10 percent tests relating to the registrant's investments in, and advances to or proportionate share of, the total assets of the tested acquisition, and the registrant's proportionate share of the total sales and revenues and equity in pretax income of the tested acquisition); and
- It involved the acquisition of a business that would meet the test of a significant subsidiary and would be required to be accounted for by the equity method.

If the acquisition is determined to be significant, the following financial statements of the acquired business, specified in the Form, are required:

1. A balance sheet ". . . as of a date reasonably close to the date of acquisition." If that balance sheet is not audited, an additional audited balance sheet as of the close of the acquired business's preceding fiscal year is required to be filed.

2. Income statement and statement of changes in financial position for each of the last full three fiscal years and for the period, if any, between the close of the latest fiscal year and the date of the latest balance sheet filed.

## SUGGESTED READING

*Securities Regulation and Law Report.* Washington, D.C.: Bureau of National Affairs (A weekly reporting service).

*Touche Ross Analysis of the SEC's Integrated Disclosure System.* Chicago: Commerce Clearing House, Inc., 1980.

*Touche Ross Guide to Filing the 1980 10-K Under the SEC's Integrated Disclosure System.* Chicago: Commerce Clearing House, Inc., 1980.

Weinstein, Stanley, Schechtman, Daniel, and Walker, Michael, *SEC Compliance— Financial Reporting and Forms.* Englewood Cliffs, New Jersey: Prentice-Hall (a monthly reporting service).

Wendell, Paul J. *SEC Accounting Report.* Boston: Warren, Gorham & Lamont, Inc. (a monthly newsletter).

# 11

# EDP for Accounting and Reporting

*Alan D. Yohalem*

*David E. Finkler*

# INTRODUCTION

In any business environment, one of a controller's most important responsibilities is to provide senior management with timely, accurate, and meaningful financial information upon which to base prudent business decisions. The controller often determines the manner in which this data is accumulated, controlled, and then reported.

## Historical Perspective

Information processing, in one form or another, has taken place as long as commercial trade has been conducted. Methods utilized to accumulate business data prior to the advent of industrialization would seem primitive today. However, these methods, as well as manual accounting processes used later, accomplished the same essential purpose as today's sophisticated systems: the summarization, classification, and reporting of financial transactions.

Significant breakthroughs in computer technology during the mid-1950s created an environment of increased interest in data processing applications in the business community. Data processing provided business with a rapid and controlled system of accounting for financial events and transactions. The earliest, or first generation computers, were extremely large, and their costs were prohibitive to all but the biggest and most profitable companies. But during the past twenty years, further technological innovation, particularly in microcircuitry, has brought the size of many computers down to desk top proportions, and the cost is now within the reach of most business entities.

## The Controller's Role in an EDP Environment

Because the nature of electronic data processing is highly technical, many business organizations have excluded it from the controller's direct sphere of responsibility. Similarly, because many controllers do not feel comfortable within an EDP environment, they have shied away from their responsibilities in this critical area. Not only is this attitude shortsighted, but it can have potentially disastrous results for a company neglecting to adequately plan, control, and administer its computer installation. The controller of yesterday would never have relinquished his responsibility for the integrity of manually prepared information. The controller of today, therefore, should be equally interested in ascertaining that essential financial data has been properly accumulated, adequately controlled and summarized, and finally, reported to management on a timely basis and in a meaningful format.

**Planning and Designing.** In converting from manual to computerized systems, the controller should be directly involved in the planning and design stages. During these phases of the plan, his expertise in defining user requirements, setting priorities, providing for the integration of systems, and selecting the computer environment will be invaluable to management. Mistakes made during the planning and design stages will have the most widespread effect on future operations and will be the most difficult and costly to correct.

**Implementation.** The project, or team leader, is the key person in controlling the implementation stage. The project leader is responsible for defining objectives, assigning tasks, and setting realistic time schedules during the implementation of the system. The controller may wish either to assume this role himself or to retain an independent consultant. The controller also takes an active role in establishing criteria for testing the system, running parallel systems, and final acceptance of the financial accounting and reporting systems.

**Administration.** Depending upon the organizational structure of a company, and the particular personal strengths and weaknesses of its senior financial management, the controller may have direct administrative responsibility for all EDP operations. In situations where EDP falls outside the controller's direct jurisdiction, he must ascertain that the operating relationships between the accounting and administrative functions under his control and the data processing group have been clearly defined and closely monitored. The controller's responsibility for the accuracy, timeliness, and format of reported financial information is not minimized by a lack of direct control over EDP operations.

**Technical Specialists.** In many areas, the complexities of modern business necessitate specialized expertise. Tax experts interpret the tax laws and guide corporate tax planning. Specialists in SEC compliance assist the controller in formulating accounting and reporting policies. Similarly, a technically competent EDP director must assist the controller in managing the total information system.

### Criteria for Converting to Data Processing

It is rare that a controller will have the foresight, initiative—or equally as important—the time, to objectively evaluate his administrative operations and information processing requirements to determine whether a conversion of manual systems to data processing would be both feasible and cost justifiable. The ability to judge the most appropriate time for such a transaction can result in substantial cost savings. Regardless of how the possibility of an EDP conversion is introduced, the burden of decision-making responsibility should ultimately rest with the controller.

The controller should be aware of certain signs or warnings that indicate potential information processing problems, and should be encouraged to consider computerization as a viable alternative.

Some reasons for introducing computerization could include:

- Increasing volume of transactions of a similar nature (i.e., billing, payroll, disbursements);
- Paperwork bottlenecks created by an increase in volume coupled with insufficient labor resources;
- Delays in processing "turn around" time and in timely reporting of financial data;
- Increasingly higher costs of processing information manually;
- Increased frequency of errors due to the higher volume and inadequacy of existing accounting controls;
- Management dissatisfaction with the form and/or content of operating reports; and
- Changes in the scope and/or direction of the business that require more innovative and resourceful approaches to information processing.

Once the controller has ascertained that any or all of these conditions are of significant magnitude and impact, he should obtain authorization to conduct a feasibility study. This will determine whether converting existing manual systems to EDP can be cost justified.

### The Feasibility Study

Studying the practical and economic feasibility of converting from manual to computerized systems is essential to determine whether additional resources (labor, as well as funds) should be allocated to the project. The controller should ascertain that the study is conducted in a manner that produces complete and meaningful recommendations in terms of predetermined objectives. He must not shorten the process by permitting vague or ill-defined goals or by utilizing incomplete data.

A feasibility study essentially is a fact-finding mission that analyzes pertinent data and provides recommended alternatives to a specific problem. The study could be internally conducted with the controller or his designee acting as the project leader, or could be assigned to an independent consultant. In either case, the objectives should be clearly defined and the responsibilities of all parties (particularly where an independent consultant is involved), clearly delineated.

**Accumulation of Data.** The fact-finding phase of the study is designed to accumulate all pertinent historical as well as projected information. In a review of order processing and billing procedures, for example, the following data should be developed:

- Number of customers;
- Average number of transactions per month;
- Average line items per transaction;
- Number of items in inventory;
- Number of sales representatives;
- Number of order takers and billing clerks necessary to process the monthly volume; and
- Total labor cost of the order processing and billing operations, including overtime and fringe benefits as well as direct wages.

**Forecasts.** Each of the above categories should include both current data and a projection of future levels. Forecasts should be for a minimum of three years, perhaps at annual or biannual intervals, and should consider anticipated growth trends, diversification of operations or product lines, and an assumed annual rate of inflation. The controller should always remember that since computer installations generally take more than one year from inception to completion, realistic forecasting is essential.

**Cost Estimates.** Similarly, preliminary information relating to the costs of carrying out these functions in a computerized environment should be gathered. Without conducting a full-scale survey of alternative equipment and systems, the project leader can provide a range for both hardware and software investment, as well as for annual maintenance expenditures. Because of the computer's other anticipated uses, it may be necessary to allocate only a portion of the computer's amortized or rental cost to the process being studied. During a feasibility study, the controller must remember that highly subjective determinations have been made. A meaningful guideline for cost comparisons can be obtained from a service bureau with an applicable package program.

**Labor Requirements.** In addition to equipment costs, the study should forecast the manpower requirements necessitated by computerization and translate them into labor costs. Among the new positions often created by the introduction of EDP are input operators (either key punch or CRT), batch control clerks, programmers, systems analysts, maintenance crews, and certain supervisory and managerial personnel. Once again, certain assumptions must be made as to which functions will be staffed internally and which will utilize independent consultants. Data processing supplies, printing of input and report forms, electricity and climate control requirements, and insurance involve other costs that should be anticipated.

The feasibility study must also address itself to the following labor costs, associated with designing and implementing the system:

- Defining the applications required, the long-range integration plan, and the priorities for development;
- Gathering broad user requirements and specifications;
- Reviewing, evaluating, and selecting the computer environment;

- Designing the system and the file and report layout;
- Programming;
- Providing for quality control, testing, and implementation (including the necessity for running parallel systems during conversion).

**Written Report.** After the controller determines that the feasibility study has been thoroughly prepared, that its assumptions are valid, that its data appears complete and reasonable, and that the conclusions and recommendations are consistent with its findings, he should require a written report to document clearly the study's findings and conclusions. Based upon his evaluation of the study, the controller must submit his recommendations to senior management. Assuming that a conversion to EDP has been justified, recommended, and approved, the controller must now prepare for the next stage in the computerization process . . . the development of a long-range plan.

## DEVELOPING A LONG-RANGE SYSTEMS PLAN

### The Financial Systems Plan

A company's decision to convert its manual systems to data processing often involves significant commitment in both dollars and management time. Even computer installations on a small scale generally require a significant allocation of resources relative to the company's size. Commitments of this nature should not be made without an initial feasibility study (as discussed in the previous section) and the development of a comprehensive long-range financial systems plan.

**Basic Elements.** A well-defined systems plan should include the following components:

- Analysis of current operations;
- Definition of systems objectives;
- Selection of applications and priorities;
- Systems integration;
- Systems design;
- Systems specifications;
- Programming;
- Implementation and evaluation; and
- Management and administration.

**The Controller's Input.** The controller's role is particularly important in the analysis through the design phases, as well as during implementation and evaluation. Depending upon a company's organizational structure, the controller may have ongoing responsibility for the administration of data processing operations.

The systems specifications and programming phases of the plan require greater technical expertise, and should therefore be assigned to systems analysts and programmers. The controller, however, should also be involved with the development and approval of the systems plan itself.

### Analysis of Current Operations

A basic principle of navigation (expressed rather simply) states that "in order to determine where you are going and how to get there, it helps to know where you are." This analogy is particularly valid in planning for a computer installation and systems conversion. Full and comprehensive knowledge of a company's current operations is essential in order to have effective planning for the future. A systems review and analysis, conducted on a professional level, can be an effective means of evaluating current systems and procedures.

**The Systems Review.** A systems review involves a study of the current methods of operation, an indication of major strengths and weaknesses, and includes recommendations for improvement. The review should be conducted by a technically oriented person, one with in-depth knowledge of accounting systems and internal controls, as well as strong analytical ability and communicative skills. A full systems review should include the following elements:

- General background material;
- Organizational chart;
- Job descriptions;
- Flow chart of procedures; and
- Specimen copies of forms and documents.

Systems reviews may be directed at a company's entire administrative operations or limited to a specific function (i.e., billing) or group of interrelated functions (i.e., order entry, billing, inventory control, and accounts receivable). To avoid costly and unproductive effort, the scope of the systems review should be clearly defined at the outset.

**Verification of Data.** Information for a systems review is generally gathered by interview, although certain documentation, such as organizational charts and job descriptions, may be available to the analyst. In utilizing these documents, however, the analyst must be able to distinguish between fact and fiction. This means ascertaining that they accurately reflect the current, rather than an ideal, situation. Similarly, the analyst must verify, through observation and investigation, the information obtained through interviews.

**Documentation.** The systems review must be fully documented. This point cannot be overemphasized. A complete file of notes, flow charts, specimen forms, job descriptions, and so on should be maintained as support and back-up material for the final report. This information will prove invaluable during subsequent phases of the development of computer based systems.

### Statement of Objectives

A basic component of any systems project is a statement or definition of objectives. The controller should play a vital role in determining and defining the objectives of the systems plan.

**Structuring the Statement.** A statement of objectives should be developed in a pyramid sequence that builds from the broadest and most general goals up to the most specific and detailed requirements. Figure 11.1 illustrates how the pyramid places the greater volume of detail at the lowest level.

*Broad purpose.* The broad purpose of the project should be defined in general terms, such as profit maximization, increased control or efficiency, more timely collection, and so on. It should indicate the benefits that management anticipates as a result of the systems conversion.

*Specific objectives.* The specific objectives represent the distinct results that the system is designed to achieve within the framework of the broad purpose. If, for

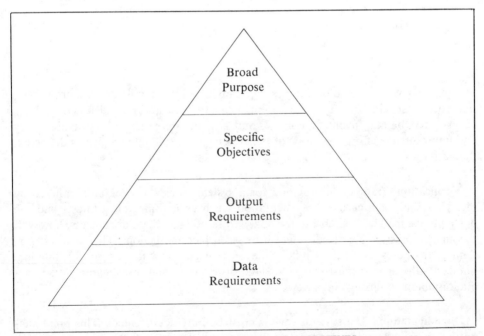

FIGURE 11.1   STRUCTURE OF THE STATEMENT OF OBJECTIVES

example, the broad purpose of developing a computer based accounts receivable system is to generate more timely collection of cash, a specific objective might be the production of a monthly report of aged balances due from customers.

*Output requirements.* Moving backward through the cycle of objectives, the next step is to define the output requirements that will enable the system to accomplish these specific objectives. This output generally consists of data, sequenced and summarized in a meaningful manner, and reported in a format acceptable to the final user. The monthly aging of accounts receivable, for example, could be in customer number sequence and could indicate balances due for periods of 30, 60, 90, and 120 days.

*Data requirements.* The data requirements of a system necessarily involve the highest level of detail. Included could be systems files for customer name, address, and credit limits as well as transaction files for invoices, and cash receipts updating the customer master file. In order to produce the output contained in the monthly aging of receivables, all transactions affecting accounts receivable during the month must be entered, processed, and updated in the master files.

**Effective Controls.** The development of effective internal controls, both within and external to the computer environment, should be a further objective of the systems project. These controls insure the integrity of the data throughout the system, provide documentation and proper audit trails, and reduce the possibility of computer fraud. The essential elements of effective internal control within a computer based system are similar in many respects to the traditional controls in manual systems. Among the more important of these would be:

- Well-defined segregation of duties;
- Adequate procedures for processing transactions;
- Use of prenumbered documents and forms;
- Suitable back-up facilities;
- Adequate physical security over assets and records; and
- Independent verification and review.

### Integration of Applications

The functions to be converted to an EDP environment are generally referred to as *applications*. In many cases, they will have been determined well in advance of any formal planning process. The strategic systems plan, however, represents a disciplined approach to identifying these applications, establishing objectives and priorities, and integrating related applications and systems within the plan.

**Applying Criteria.** The criteria for converting manual systems to data processing have been described previously. These criteria should be applied to each function to determine whether it would benefit from a systems conversion. The feasibility study and long-range systems plan should include all functions that appear to meet these criteria.

**Related Functions.** In selecting the applications for conversion, consideration should be given to the interrelationships among systems within the broad financial and accounting spectrum. Certain functions may be so clearly related and interdependent that their integration within the systems plan is both desirable and justifiable. Examples of this integration process would include customer related functions (order entry, billing, inventory control, and accounts receivable) and vendor related functions (purchasing, accounts payable, and cash disbursements). The general ledger function is an application that can be either integrated with or omitted from all other financial functions without affecting other applications. Figure 11.2 illustrates these relationships.

If computerization of order entry and billing functions has been justified, the integration of accounts receivable into the systems plan would appear to be warranted. Although accounts receivable might not satisfy all criteria if evaluated on its own, a common data base is required by each of the three systems (customer master file data), and there should be a logical flow of data between systems.

**Data Base.** The concept of a common data base that can be utilized by a collection of interrelated programs is fundamental to the integration of functions within a computer based financial system. As noted above, the data base containing a customer file (name, address, credit terms, unpaid invoices) can be utilized by the order entry, billing, and accounts receivable programs, separate but interrelated applications.

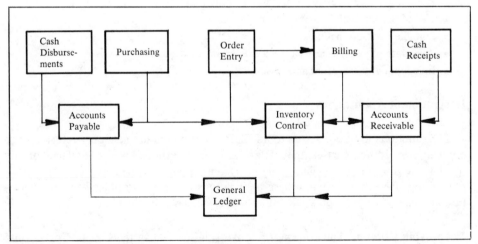

FIGURE 11.2  INTEGRATION OF FINANCIAL SYSTEMS

**Nonintegrated Systems.** In independent, or nonintegrated systems, separate input is required for each program. For example, the processing of an order received from a customer would require each of the separate steps noted below:

- Order received from customer;
- *Input* into order processing program;
- Credit verified/stock availability verified;
- Sales confirmation produced/inventory requisition produced;
- *Input* into billing program;
- Invoice produced;
- *Input* into accounts receivable program;
- Update of customer file;
- *Input* into perpetual inventory program; and
- Update of inventory.

A total of four separate input operations, all involving similar information, is required to complete the processing cycle for this transaction. It should be evident that the maintenance of individual programs is an inefficient and costly means of processing data.

**Benefits of Systems Integration.** Had the customer order noted above been entered into a totally integrated system, the processing cycle would be significantly different. The following steps illustrate this clearly:

- Order taken by salesman;
- Input into an integrated order processing program
  (Note: This function could be accomplished by the salesman at the point of sale through telecommunications equipment available today.);
- Credit verified/stock availability verified;
- Sales confirmation produced/inventory requisition produced;
- Invoice produced;
- Customer file updated; and
- Inventory updated.

The integrated system has, through a single input, verified credit and stock availability, produced all necessary documents, and updated master files as appropriate. The cost savings of such a system can be substantial, but would, of course, have to be measured against the increased time and cost requirements of designing, developing, and implementing a totally integrated system.

### Determination of Priorities

Once the financial application for conversion to data processing has been selected, the sequence and time schedule for that conversion must be determined. In setting priorities for conversion to a long-range integrated systems plan, the controller should give primary consideration to operational and business factors. Only after this has been done should systems design and development factors be considered.

**Sound Business Judgment.** The controller is in a unique position to evaluate objectively the operational and business considerations. He should appraise inherent weaknesses in the systems and procedures, problems in workflow and information processing, and the current financial condition of the company. Each of these factors will influence the recommendation of priorities and conversion sequence.

In the integration of order entry, inventory, billing, and accounts receivable systems, for example, there may be compelling reasons for preferring the earliest possible conversion of accounts receivable. Customer accounts may be erroneously stated, detail ledgers might not reconcile to control totals, and the collection process might have slowed considerably because of inaccurate and untimely information. From a purely "sound business" viewpoint, it would make sense to put the greatest initial effort into developing the receivable application. On the other hand, a critical backlog in recording and processing customer orders, resulting from increased volume and inadequate personnel, might dictate that the order entry function be given first priority for conversion.

**Design Considerations.** In discussions of systems design and development logistics, the controller should seek the advice of more technically oriented staff, or consultants who would have detailed knowledge of the mechanics of converting manual systems to EDP. They would be better able to recommend the most logical and cost effective sequence of developing and integrating systems. In the integrated system discussed above, design considerations might dictate priority for the inventory control system. It has the highest level of detail, and its data base (product codes and descriptions) must be established prior to the development of either an order entry or billing system. Both of the latter systems require input from the inventory data base to process information and produce documents.

The controller must analyze and evaluate all of the priority considerations, many of which will conflict. He must understand all of the "trade-offs" involved, particularly with regard to short- versus long-range objectives as well as the cost benefit consideration. He must clearly delineate and document his recommendations and must ultimately incorporate them into the financial systems plan.

## SELECTING THE COMPUTER ENVIRONMENT

As the long-range integrated system plan is being developed and the objectives and user requirements are defined, the controller must address himself to the single most important decision in a conversion to data processing: the selection of the computer environment.

In selecting the most appropriate computer environment for his company, the controller should be aware of the alternatives available. These options have two basic components: (1) hardware, and (2) software. *Hardware* refers to the equipment necessary to process transactions and includes input devices, memory and storage capacity, central processing, and output devices. *Software* refers to the programs and applications developed to achieve the company's information processing objectives.

## Hardware Options

In selecting the computer hardware environment the controller has the following basic options:

- In-house facility;
- Service bureau; and
- Time share.

**In-House Facility.** If the controller decides to set up an in-house facility, all equipment will be purchased or leased and located on the company's premises. The company, therefore, must assume total responsibility for operation and maintenance of the equipment and for providing adequate backup facilities. All processing is done by an internal staff, and the work flow must be scheduled and controlled by an operations supervisor. The company may select from a vast array of computer manufacturers with models ranging from desk size microcomputers (generally with limited applications) to mainframe computer systems. This decision will depend, to a great extent, on the program and application requirements of the system. Criteria for selecting the most appropriate hardware for an in-house facility will be discussed in greater detail in a subsequent section.

**Service Bureau.** An alternative to the substantial investment needed for an in-house facility is to have all transactions processed by an independent service bureau. A service bureau generally has on-site equipment with backup capacity and has developed specific applications available to its customers. Service bureaus usually charge customers on the basis of a cost per transaction processed; this includes file maintenance.

Processing can be done entirely by the service bureau, with the company providing documents controlled by batch for input, or the company can input at its own location through a key punch or terminal (CRT) device and a communications line directly to the bureau's central processing unit. Similarly, output in the form of computer reports or documents can be produced at the service bureau and delivered to the company by means of a high speed printer. A service bureau will generally offer a predesigned program that, to some extent, can generally be modified to accommodate a customer's specific needs.

**Time Share.** Another option available to a company hesitant to make the investment in an in-house facility is to share processing time with an organization having excess computer capacity. The user company is responsible for its own pro-grams and applications and must provide its own input and output capability. It communicates directly with the time share company's central processor through a telephone line known as a *modem*. The user company generally pays only for actual processing time, used at a predetermined hourly rate.

**Summary of Hardware Selection Criteria.** In selecting the most appropriate hard-ware environment, the controller should develop a series of criteria based upon planned systems requirements, and he must gauge how effectively each option can satisfy them. Figure 11.3 lists some advantages and disadvantages of each type of computer environment.

### Software Package or Custom-Designed Programs

In selecting the most appropriate computer hardware environment, the controller must consider investment and operating cost factors, as well as the "trade-offs" in the relative advantages and disadvantages of each alternative. Similarly, the control-ler must determine whether the software requirements of the system can be satisfied by predeveloped program "packages" for specific applications, or will be met only

|  | *Advantages* | *Disadvantages* |
|---|---|---|
| In-House Facility | • Total control over operations<br>• Flexibility in applications<br>• Capacity for new applications<br>• Easy access to data | • Major investment in hardware<br>• Larger staff requirements<br>• Must provide backup capability<br>• Must provide for maintenance<br>• Special physical requirements |
| Service Bureau | • Cost based on usage<br>• Predeveloped programs<br>• Minimal staff requirements<br>• No, or small, investment in hardware<br>• No maintenance cost | • Lost of control over documents<br>• Limited access to data<br>• Slow turn-around time<br>• Limited applications<br>• Limited growth capacity |
| Time Share | • Cost based on usage<br>• Flexibility in applications<br>• Minimal staff requirements<br>• Small investment in hardware<br>• No maintenance cost | • Limited control over data<br>• Limited access time<br>• Down time in communications |

FIGURE 11.3   HARDWARE COMPARISONS

through a full scale systems development and customized programming effort. The controller must attempt to anticipate the company's position and systems requirements in the years ahead. He should not hesitate to utilize technical expertise in approaching the problem of software selection.

**Cost Benefits.** The lower initial cost of a software package is the best reason for selecting it. These packages have been developed by specialized systems and programming firms known as *software houses,* or by service bureaus who offer the package through their transaction processing program. Software packages, therefore, may be purchased, rented, or used as part of a service bureau arrangement. Where a company's operations and systems are for the most part standard (by industry guidelines), a software package can meet substantially all of the company's requirements. However, where major modifications to the package are required, the cost justification becomes more marginal. A program package, nevertheless, is an excellent starting point for the controller when he reviews his software requirements and develops basic cost guidelines.

**Flexibility.** The major limitation of most software packages is their lack of flexibility. Through the use of certain computer languages (i.e., English and Basic) many software packages now permit the user to develop and implement minor program modifications. Major changes, however, will often result in significant reprogramming effort and cost. Similarly, software packages may be programmed in languages incompatible with a future conversion to an in-house facility. The eventual cost of reprogramming or of purchasing or licensing the software package must be factored into the controller's evaluation of the software environment.

## Selecting the Most Appropriate Hardware

If the organization has evaluated its basic hardware requirements and determined that an in-house facility is its best option, it must make an intensive effort to determine which piece of equipment best satisfies its needs.

**A Wide Range of Options.** There are many lines of computer equipment that will fulfill the immediate needs of a company and also allow gradual growth without major conversions. However, there are also those that can't effectively do the job. Many vendors, especially of mini and micro business computers, concentrated in one business area or another in order to penetrate a specific market. Therefore, some offer accounting oriented systems, others offer manufacturing oriented systems, and so on. Many machines are best suited to centralized processing in a batch environment while others are better utilized in a dispersed or distributed operation. The array of hardware, associated software, and services and contractual terms can be dazzling. The organization about to enter a data processing environment may find it desirable, during the selection process, to seek the technical expertise of qualified consultants.

**Getting Started.** An effective method to sort out those systems and capabilities best suited to a company's needs is to call upon a number of vendors to review the company's requirements and present the equipment, software, and services that they believe to be appropriate. This presentation provides a basic education and familiarity with computer terminology and capability, as well as giving the vendors' orientation. In some cases, it quickly becomes obvious that particular vendors cannot adequately satisfy a company's needs. In other cases, the controller must carefully evaluate the marketing claims and sales promises of each vendor.

**The Request for Proposal.** After this basic education phase, the real effort of selection begins with the development and submission to vendors of a formal *Request For Proposal* (RFP). This document specifies the user's needs and objectives and asks the vendors to respond with a proposal for a system that will satisfy these needs. The RFP serves two very important functions:

- It forces the vendors to respond to specific criteria in a predetermined format, enabling the decision maker to easily compare alternative features and costs.
- It forces each vendor to take a competitive position and to offer the most cost effective systems and services.

The RFP should include the following information:

- Brief statement of purpose.
- Brief history of the company and its industry. This background offers insight into the company's problems and objectives, particularly if the vendor has served other clients in the same industry.
- Deadline for submitting responses. Setting a firm but reasonable deadline results in timely responses.
- Statement of confidentiality. Vendors generally treat this information concerning an organization and its plans with discretion, but this statement should be included for protection.
- Requirements. The specific requirements should be detailed in a comprehensive manner, and should include all identifiable aspects of the anticipated environment:
  - Application systems;
  - Work load, current and future;
  - Performance, instant turnaround, etc.;
  - Mode of operation, interactive, batch, combination;
  - Communications;
  - Security features;
  - Training requirements; and
  - Conversion assistance.

**Guidelines for Response.** If the vendors are required to respond in a standard and predetermined manner, the controller will save an enormous amount of time. The RFP should set forth specific lists of sections (and the order in which they must be addressed) describing the vendors' capability and services. These sections should adequately reflect the user organization's needs and should include information on hardware, software, performance, support (in terms of conversion, training, application, and development, as required), maintenance, and cost. The vendor should be encouraged to provide any additional information it deems appropriate and helpful, but only after responding specifically to the RFP guidelines.

**Validation of Proposal.** The vendor must be advised that efforts will be made to verify that the claims and statements made are accurate. In addition, the vendor should be prepared to provide guarantees of performance.

**Evaluating the Responses.** Vendors will want to present their proposals formally in most cases. The controller may then wish to meet with the vendors so they can clarify their responses in particular areas or can alter their responses if they weren't specific enough.

If the RFP has been constructed properly, the evaluation of responses should go quickly. The most convenient method to use in comparing the proposals is to construct a chart, listing the company's requirements and specifications in the left column and assigning a weighted value to each vendor's responses in the adjacent columns. Assuming that its responses can be validated, the controller should then select the vendor with the highest total.

**Validation of Responses.** Considerable effort can be spent on validation. The quickest method is to compile a list of organizations that have engaged the vendor to install similar equipment and then inquire about the vendor's performance. An alternative is for the company to construct a series of comprehensive benchmarks. This would require development of programs simulating the expected environment and workload. The vendor(s) would be expected to run tests under controlled conditions and then present the results.

The latter approach provides a sound basis for selection, one that will adequately meet both current and future requirements.

**Contract Negotiations.** At this point, the controller should open contract negotiations with the vendor. Once again, it pays to specify in detail the expectations of performance, the guarantees by the vendor, and the remedies if performance is not met. The controller and the purchasing and legal staffs should work closely together to assure a comprehensive agreement that will protect the company and satisfy its hardware requirements.

### Physical Installation Requirements

The physical installation of equipment requires detailed consideration and forethought. The vendor has a decided interest in seeing that the installation and operation run smoothly and should provide assistance in the preparation and planning.

**Use of a Checklist.** The vendor should provide a checklist indicating all specific physical requirements. The following is a brief sampling of the items generally included:

- Floor space requirements;
- Electrical specifications;
- Climate control requirements;
- Security provisions—access to the computer;
- Fire prevention and extinguishers;
- Tape and disk storage; and
- Storage for supplies—paper, etc.

**Renovation Requirements.** Many smaller computers and small business systems require minimum environmental control because the equipment is being manufactured for use in a standard office area. However, larger systems may require extensive renovation or construction to accommodate needed features. During the computer selection process, the vendor should be required to submit the physical and environmental specifications so that they can be considered in the evaluation of the equipment.

## CONTROLLING THE DEVELOPMENT PROCESS

### Development and Implementation Phases

Once the system plan is approved and the computer selection is in the final stages, the project team should direct its attention to the development and implementation of the system.

**Structuring an Outline.** An outline of the stages of development and implementation should be structured as follows:

- Systems design:
  - Functional specification,
  - Technical or detail specifications;
- Programming;
- System testing;
- User training;
- Parallel running;
- Conversion;
- Implementation;
- Operation;
- Post installation audits; and
- On-going maintenance.

**Software Selection.** If a preprogrammed system is being purchased, a similar outlining process is undertaken, substituting software selection for programming activities. Software selection requires much the same effort as the hardware selection described earlier. While the package to be purchased may be attractive because it performs most of the required functions, it might still require modification to handle unique specifications. Although the vendor may agree to make the changes, programming, nevertheless, may become an important activity.

## Staffing the Project

As stated previously, a project team should be assigned and given formal responsibility for the design and development of the various application systems.

**User Representation.** In many organizations, the project team is viewed as a technical group comprised only of personnel with EDP skills. This viewpoint can result in significant development problems. A technically superior system, although maximizing the computer resources, may not adequately meet the processing requirements of the user department. An important, if not critical, member of the team must be a user representative. A knowledgeable member of the controller's staff, who is thoroughly familiar with the company's operations, should be assigned to the project and made directly responsible for defining requirements and acting as liaison between the user and the technical group. He must be able accurately to translate needs into a workable product. In large organizations, or in cases where the impact of the new system will be considerable, this user representative often is relieved of all other duties and is assigned to participate in the computerization effort on a full-time basis.

**Project Team Members.** The size and makeup of the project team depends on a number of factors:

- Scope of the project;
- Time available for development; and
- Whether the system is being purchased or custom built.

In addition to the user representative(s), a technical (EDP) or systems oriented individual must also be assigned. If the scope of the project is small, these two may comprise the entire project team throughout its installation and implementation. If the system is complex, other specialized personnel may be required as the project moves from phase to phase. The team might then include systems analysts, programmers, equipment optimization analysts, communications analysts, key entry or key punch operators, machine operators, specialized consultants, and additional user personnel for conversion and implementation. In instances where equipment is being installed, a vendor representative should also be included. Many vendors provide this assistance under the contractual arrangements for equipment installation.

### Gathering User Requirements

In the development of the long-range integrated system plan, specific emphasis was placed on the statement of objectives. Throughout the planning and development stages of an EDP conversion, these objectives must be restated into detailed and specific user requirements. Soliciting and obtaining this data is an important function of the project team.

**Motivating Company Personnel.** A major, yet often overlooked problem associated with converting manual systems to data processing is the effect of such a change on the company's employees, particularly those directly involved in the functions selected for conversion. There is anxiety about job security, concern over changes in responsibility, and a general negative feeling about the entire process. An important part of management's responsibility in assuring the success of a computer project is to convince employees that the change will have a positive effect upon their operations.

It is equally important to motivate supervisory and management level personnel to work within the framework of a new system. These key employees should be encouraged to help determine the broad objectives of the system and to define their requirements as end users of the data. Most supervisory employees will react positively to this approach. In addition, their active participation provides the systems' development team with an in-depth knowledge of current systems and procedures as well as a clearer indication of the major problems. For this approach to be effective, however, supervisors or managers must objectively evaluate their operations and define their informational needs.

**Establishing and Ranking Priorities.** After the supervisors are briefly introduced to the concept of computerization and the applications selected for conversion, they should then be asked to provide the systems analysts with a *wish list* of items that would enable them to function more effectively. These generally should be related to information and controls, although physical considerations (such as more office space and greater filing capacity), are also meaningful objectives. In its purest form, the wish list should be compiled with no regard for cost considerations.

Using the list as a starting point, the analyst then requests that each supervisor rank each "wish" in terms of priority. The following three categories are useful in the ranking process:

- Items that are essential and without which the supervisor cannot properly function;
- Items that the supervisor feels are important in improving his department's productivity or efficiency; and
- Items that would be beneficial, but are not essential to maintain effective operations.

A wish list ranked by priorities enables the systems analyst to obtain a broad perspective of the data and control requirements of particular departments or subsections. This information is then consolidated, and the broad elements of systems design and specification begin to take form.

**Continuing Involvement.** Supervisors and managers must be continually involved in the systems planning and development stages. Each supervisor should have additional input into developing the data base, report layout, and internal controls of the system as it relates to his function. His direct involvement is also required in both the implementation and evaluation stages.

The controller should play a major role in coordinating these activities, motivating his subordinates and key operating employees, and making certain that an effective working relationship is established and maintained between the supervisory personnel and the project team. In addition, his input will be of particular value in reviewing and editing consolidated wish lists, as well as in evaluating cost considerations for each application.

## Developing Project Control Techniques

The larger the project, the more planning, coordination, control, and monitoring required. The key to an effective project control system is the development of a work breakdown structure, accompanied by techniques for monitoring the scheduled activities.

**The Work Breakdown.** A work breakdown divides the project into reasonably manageable, monitorable, and timely tasks or activities. Activities with too large a scope span such a long period of time that it is difficult to gauge progress or take timely corrective action when it has been determined that problems exist. Alternately, if the scope of activities is too small, the project team will be unnecessarily burdened with administrative tasks—scheduling, collecting, reporting, and justifying variations from the plan. Management should assign resources (manhours) and develop a schedule for each activity. Examples of activities that might apply to the development of an order entry system are noted in Figure 11.4.

**Monitoring the Schedule.** A time collection mechanism should be organized so that work performed on each activity can be compared to the original budget and schedule. As the work progresses, it will become apparent which phases or groups of activities are having problems, and where significant deviations from the plan occur, corrective action must be taken. Corrective action might include the employment of additional staff, the freeing of user personnel from normal duties to give greater attention to the project, rescheduling, or providing greater motivation to the team.

Problems arise because system design and development is a complicated and poorly understood process. Original budgets and schedules represent informed estimates and guidelines set up to measure progress. Although most projects progress as planned, some targets are unfortunately not met. But before management jumps

| Phase | Activity No. | Activity | Man-Hours | Schedule |
|-------|--------------|----------|-----------|----------|
| System Design | SD 12 | Define Customer Data Base | 100 | 3/6—4/10 |
|  | SD 42 | Develop Specifications For History Data Base Update | 80 | 5/7—5/25 |
| Programming | P 19 | Program Update Audit Report | 60 | 6/3—6/12 |
|  | P 26 | Program Order Status Report | 10 | 6/15—6/18 |
| System Testing | ST 14 | Test System Modules | 40 | 8/12—8/30 |
| Parallel Run | PR 6 | Parallel Customer Order Cycle For October | 80 | 11/2—11/16 |

FIGURE 11.4   WORK BREAKDOWN OF ORDER ENTRY SYSTEM

to conclusions and prescribes corrective action, it must obtain a clear picture of the causes for the problems and delays.

**PERT and CPM Techniques.** On very large projects with a considerable number of activities to be coordinated, sophisticated tools for scheduling are available. *PERT* (Program Evaluation and Review Techniques) and *CPM* (Critical Path Method) are similar network scheduling systems that aid the user in developing, changing, and monitoring schedules. Both are often used on computer systems. For each activity, the user enters the start date, the expected duration and the required predecessor and successor activities. The computer system then produces a network and schedule of activities. CPM's principal advantage is that it indicates the *critical path* and points up those activities that interrelate to form a path through the network that allows for the least slack or allowable slippage time. A delay of any of the activities along the critical path delays the entire project. A pictorial representation of CPM is shown in Figure 11.5.

**Gantt Charts.** For most small to medium projects, a simpler planning tool, such as a Gantt or bar chart, can be quite effective. (See Figure 11.6.) A Gantt chart lists the activities in the left hand column. The schedule bar for each activity is then overlaid on a time grid.

Typically, each bar is color coded or shaded to indicate scheduled progress versus actual progress. A quick glance at the chart indicates the progress of the project against plan.

**Review Meetings.** Formal review meetings of the project team and the controller should be included in the plan and should be scheduled on a regular basis. Reviews of progress, problems, specifications, future planning, and so on, should take place at these sessions. The controller thereby verifies or audits the project

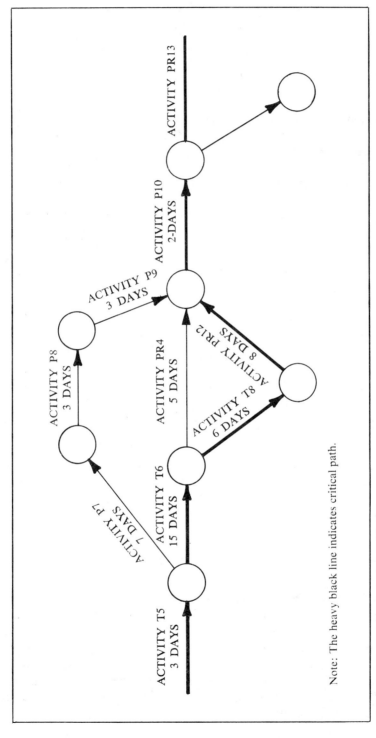

Note: The heavy black line indicates critical path.

FIGURE 11.5 CRITICAL PATH METHOD

| | | | | | | | | |
|---|---|---|---|---|---|---|---|---|
| *BAR SCHEDULE* | | | | | | | | |
| | | | | Time Now Line | | | | |
| Activity | No. | 10/1 | 11/1 | 12/1 | 1/1 | 2/1 | 3/1 | 4/1 |
| Design Audit Report | DR12 | | | | | | | |
| Design Customer Update | DC6 | | | | | | | |
| Program Order Entry Update | P15 | | | | | | | |
| Program Audit Report | P22 | | | | | | | |
| Test Billing Interface | T17 | | | | | | | |
| Design Inventory Update | D12 | | | | | | | |
| | | | | | | | | |
| Schedule | | | | | | | | |
| Actual | | | | | | | | |

FIGURE 11.6  GANTT CHART

control mechanism, shows his continuing personal interest in the project, and has an opportunity to take immediate corrective action to clear troublesome bottlenecks.

# DEVELOPMENT AND IMPLEMENTATION

### Re-Emphasis on User Participation

As stressed in previous sections, user involvement is critical to the success of the project during the design and programming stages. The continuous participation and cooperation of the key members of the controller's staff with the project team are also equally important during the systems development and implementation phases. The controller and his staff should view this involvement as a normal and necessary element in the overall effort.

## Systems Design

Systems design, one of the most important phases of the development process, requires two distinct levels of effort.

**Basic Systems Design.** The *basic systems design* should provide an overall feel for the operation of the system, its flow of data, and its interface points with users. This phase also sets the criteria for mode of operation (interactive or batch), documents the audit criteria, the security features, and the interfaces with other integrated systems. The controller must be completely satisfied that all operational aspects have been defined and that the system will work adequately within his environment.

**Detail Systems Design.** The *detail systems design* describes the system in technical language and provides the documentation required by the programmers. Detailed flow charts, coding schemes, file descriptions, and programming logic should be included. This phase requires less personal attention from the controller, but he should refer a considerable amount of the responsibility for details to the next line management, such as the accounts payable or general ledger supervisors.

## Programming

If proper attention has been paid to the systems design, much less interaction is required during the programming phase. If the design is sound and comprehensive, and care has been taken to hire qualified programming personnel, this phase can proceed quickly and productively.

## System Testing

System modules will typically be tested by the systems designers and programmers to assure that the system meets the criteria expressed in the design documents. Final design and programming adjustments are usually required before the user again becomes heavily involved.

## Reconciling Different Systems

Exactly as the name implies, *parallel running* is the process of running the new system in a simulated operational state, while at the same time operating the existing system. The results are compared at the end of each cycle of processing (daily, weekly, monthly). Parallel running attempts to assure all participants that the new system performs as specified and that placing it in operation will not damage the organization. If the new system is being developed with enhanced or different features, a significant amount of reconciliation might be required to satisfy the controller that the new system is performing as planned.

Considerable effort may be expended by the controller's staff during parallel running. Temporary clerical personnel are often required to help carry the burden. The staff must run two systems, simultaneously inputting, auditing, reviewing results, and reconciling differences. After a sufficient number of parallel cycles prove the sound operation of the new system, the critical decision to go live must be made.

### Final Conversion

If all activities have progressed as planned, the parallel running will be concluded at an appropriate point, and the system can be placed in operation with minimum additional effort. Generally, the most effective procedure is to continue operating the new system and pack up the old one. However, significant thought should be given to the optimum time to convert.

There will be advantages and disadvantages to nearly all times selected for conversion. The controller's functions, including closing the books, clearing the files, and starting the new year clean, are geared to the fiscal year. This would seem an ideal time to convert to a new system since many files and/or systems would not have to be tied back to existing or ongoing file balances. However, the controller's department usually is at its busiest then with year-end closing activities. On the other hand, converting at a mid-year point could require a massive effort to recode all transactions and/or file all records in order to bring the system up to date.

Once again, the controller must consider all of the business and operational factors relative to the conversion. His selection of a conversion date should reflect the cost of continuing parallel systems and possible interruptions of critical business activities as well as the fiscal year considerations noted above.

## BUILDING AND MANAGING THE EDP ORGANIZATION

Until the mid- to late-1960s the EDP organization reported to the finance division (usually the controller) because most of the systems were accounting oriented. As the EDP function grew, many other areas of the corporation (manufacturing, engineering, marketing, sales, etc.) demanded its services. The technical complexity of running such a department required the services of specialized managerial talent. Questions of priority of development and processing began to be of concern to the company. As a result, the EDP function became increasingly independent of the controller's direct supervision.

### Distributed Data Processing

Another change in the approach to structuring an EDP organization is currently taking place. With computers becoming more powerful and less expensive, *distributed data processing* attempts to provide computer resources as close as possible to the source and use of the information. Instead of the controller's department coding input forms that are then sent to a central keypunch area, processed by the computer, and returned in the form of a computer report, the information is being entered directly in the user area via an intelligent input/output device in direct communication with a central processor. The data is processed, edited, and audited, and reports or brief specific answers are delivered immediately. As with any organization, size will be a factor in determining the hierarchy and reporting relationships. An example of a classical functional EDP organization is shown in Figure 11.7.

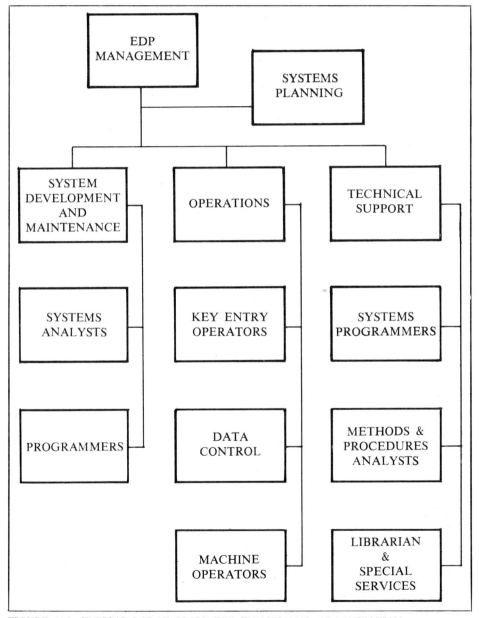

FIGURE 11.7  TYPICAL LARGE SCALE EDP FUNCTIONAL ORGANIZATION

This department could report directly to the controller or could function as an independent service group. In small to medium companies where EDP is integrated with the controller's department, the same functional skills will still be required, but they will typically be handled by existing personnel. The key-entry, operations, and control tasks can be performed by existing clerical personnel. For instance, the accounts payable clerk would formerly have coded, batched input, and reviewed error audit reports; now that employee can enter transactions directly into a visual screen (*CRT*) and check errors and controls immediately. In addition, upon instructions from authorized management, the clerk can directly release from the CRT designated transactions for payment.

Depending on the amount of new development work or the ongoing maintenance of existing systems, one or more technical employees (such as programmers or analysts) will be required. If such work is required only periodically, the firm should engage consultants rather than use full-time support staff.

### Maintaining Adequate Controls

As with any function in the controller's department, strict internal controls must also be maintained here. Because a great deal of processing is done within the EDP system, the controller's staff cannot visually review every detail of the processing of a transaction.

**Incorporating Controls During Design Phase.** The specific automated and external controls required will be dictated by the nature of the system as well as by the organizational constraints. They should, however, be instituted during an early stage in order to become an integrated part of the system. It is often desirable to have the company's outside auditor review the controls before they are finalized and incorporated in the design. This will minimize objections, problems, and changes after the system is in operation.

Controls can consist of transaction counts, dollar balances of key fields on the files, hash totals, check digits, automated reconciliations on various key reports, and so on. Those responsible for the system's operation should be required to enter the control figures from the reports in a control ledger; they should then be compared to manually generated figures to show that the system is in balance at any given time.

**Separation of Duties.** An equally important and complementary procedure which provides a series of checks and balances through separation of duties should be established. For example, the programmer should not enter the transaction data, produce or sign the checks, or reconcile the bank statements. As an effective control measure, the separation of duties is as critical in an automated environment as it is in a manual operation.

### Physical Security

Another important aspect of sound systems operation is early provision for the security of the equipment and data. The main computer equipment should be placed in a secure location to prevent damage due to vandalism and/or malicious causes. Adequate steps must also be taken to assure protection from fire and water damage. In anticipation of physical damage (which would prevent the system from operating), an arrangement should be made for a compatible backup computer. Other local companies with similar equipment usually welcome mutual backup agreements.

In addition to security for the computer, provisions must be made for the programs, data, and documentation. A suitable off-premises site for storage of the latest version of the programs and documentation should be found. The data files, constantly changing, should be copied periodically and also stored off premises. Careful analysis of the systems operation and processing cycles generally reveals where appropriate backups should be taken. Many systems require daily backups, others weekly, but the frequency chosen must take into account the cost and effort required to reconstruct and place the system back into timely operation.

### Data Security

It may be desirable to restrict access to certain data in order to maintain the privacy of confidential files. For example, only the payroll department should have access to salary history files. One technique to insure this level of security is to provide for a set of programs strategically placed in the system to code the data with a key given only to the proper operating department. Special procedures would be required to process the data and produce reports in coherent form. Anyone else who obtains access to the files would see only garbled, unintelligible data. Another method restricts access to the affected files by requiring the use of a special password. Each method has advantages and disadvantages, and technical assistance must be consulted to assure their proper application.

## SUMMARY

The introduction of EDP should be viewed as an advanced tool to aid and supplement the company's operations by providing:

- Efficient processing of large volumes of data, thus reducing the clerical burden;
- Ability to accumulate large volumes of data and provide sophisticated and manageable analysis of information in a timely manner; and
- Selective reporting of key management information.

The start-up and operation of the EDP function requires considerable planning and monitoring in order to obtain the desired results. The personal and continuing attention of the controller and his staff is required to assure proper development and operation of the financial systems. This function should be accepted as a natural and integral part of the operation of the department. If sound objectives are set and a realistic time frame established, the significant potential of EDP can be realized.

## SUGGESTED READING

Biggs, Charles, Birksand, Evan, and Atkins, William, *Managing the Systems Development Process*. Englewood Cliffs, New Jersey: Prentice-Hall Inc., 1980.

Brandon, Dick, and Segelstein, Sidney, *Data Processing Contracts*. New York: Van Nostrand Reinhold, 1976.

Cohen, Jules A., and McKinney, Katherine Scott, *How To Computerize Your Small Business*. Englewood Cliffs, New Jersey: Prentice-Hall Inc., 1980.

Data Pro 70—Data Pro Research Corporation (annual publication with periodic update).

Eckhouse, Richard H. Jr., and Morrison, L. Robert, *Minicomputer Systems: Organization, Programming and Application*. Englewood Cliffs, New Jersey: Prentice-Hall Inc., 1979.

ICP Interface—International Computer Programs, Inc. (quarterly publication).

Kinderlehrer, Robert, *Handbook for Data Center Management*. Wellsley Hills, Mass.: QED Information Sciences Inc., 1980.

Lines, M. Vardell, *Minicomputer Systems*. Englewood Cliffs, New Jersey: Winthrop Publishing Co., 1980.

Sanders, Norman, *A Manager's Guide to Profitable Computers*. New York: AMACOM, 1979.

# Part III

# Management Decision Functions

Part III

# 12

# Preparation and Use of Budgets

*James W. Pattillo*

# INTRODUCTION

Budgets are a quantitative expression of management's short-range and long-range goals, and they help management establish its most profitable course of action. Numerous decisions need to be made as to the policies to follow and the methods to use, including products and services, markets, production methods, customer identification, prices, distribution methods, credit terms, the number and pay level of employees, and reporting procedures. If this planning process is intelligently conceived and effectively administered, the budget then becomes a creative tool for accomplishing management's goals.

# THE CONTROLLER'S ROLE

The controller's role in budgeting begins early in the management process. The company's broad objectives for both long-range and short-range planning may be set by higher management authority, but the controller should be heavily involved in the firm's detailed planning, to assure that these broad goals are attained.

Since the controller is responsible for the financial information system used by management to control its operations and safeguard its resources, he should also take the lead in developing the annual budget—the numerical expression of management's plan for achieving the firm's objectives for the subsequent year. This short-range quantified business plan should include measuring and reporting techniques that act as an early warning system. The system alerts those directly responsible to take corrective action, as well as those who ultimately must keep the firm on the charted course.

## Definition of a Budget

The meanings of the terms *forecast* and *budget* should not be confused. They are different in content and intent.

A *forecast* is a quantitative report that attempts to predict the outcome of a series of events, with little or no effort made to control the results of those events. Further, there is not necessarily an intention to take corrective actions if the forecast does not reflect the desired position. Forecasts are often produced on a "what if" basis for alternative conditions. (See Chapter 13.)

A *budget*, on the other hand, is a plan that calls for a series of actions to produce certain outcomes, with controls incorporated into the execution of the actions that maximize the chances of achieving the desired position.

A budget should also be differentiated from a profit plan. The two terms are used loosely and often interchangeably. *Budget* often connotes a detailed schedule used for controlling expenditures. Control, rather than the planning that preceded the preparation of the budget, is the main focus. Furthermore, the word *budget* often makes one think of the activities of an individual department, rather than those of the whole organization. Finally, a budget often denotes annual planning rather than planning over a longer period.

On the other hand, a *profit plan* connotes an emphasis on planning as well as control, on revenues as well as expenses, on broad functions as well as individual departments, and on the long term as well as the short term. Although profit plan best describes the concept embodied in this chapter, budget is used here because it is more common, traditional, and familiar.

### Components of a Major Budget System

Effective budgeting, like the management process of which it is a part, has three basic functions: planning, execution, and control. The type and level of operations must be planned in advance, the planned operations must be implemented, and the operations must be continually monitored to ensure that deviations from the plan are properly identified, analyzed, and corrected.

Within a well-managed organization, subunits are assigned specific authorities and responsibilities for certain activities. Each separate subunit is interrelated to the others, and is often called a *responsibility center*. Depending on its specific objective, the nature of its activities, and the resources assigned to it, the responsibility center may be a cost center, profit center, investment center, department, division, plant, district, or function. With this organizational structure acting as a framework, budgets are planned and implemented, control is achieved, and the firm's broad goals are attained.

**Universal Principles.** The types of organization—manufacturing or sales or service, profit or not-for-profit—is immaterial. The principles of management in general, and of budgeting in particular, are broad enough to cover all types of organizations. The reference here to firms, therefore, should be interpreted broadly to cover all types.

Firms with a responsibility center structure may operate successfully without a budget. However, if one probes, one would probably find that the essential ingredients of good budgeting are present but are not formalized into a separate system. This may work satisfactorily, particularly in firms that are dominated by strong top executives or that are in such a favorable market position that profit is achieved regardless of the lack of planning and control. But these instances are unusual. Typically, competition forces a degree of organization, a system of planning and control, on virtually all but the smallest firms. The components of a typical budget system are illustrated in the flowchart in Figure 12.1.

**Budget Inputs.** The inputs to the budget process are management's overall goals, strategies, long- and short-range objectives and plans, and the market forecast. The sales budget is prepared and becomes the basis for the production plan and budget. Its requirements are then translated into budgets for purchases, direct labor, factory overhead, and inventory.

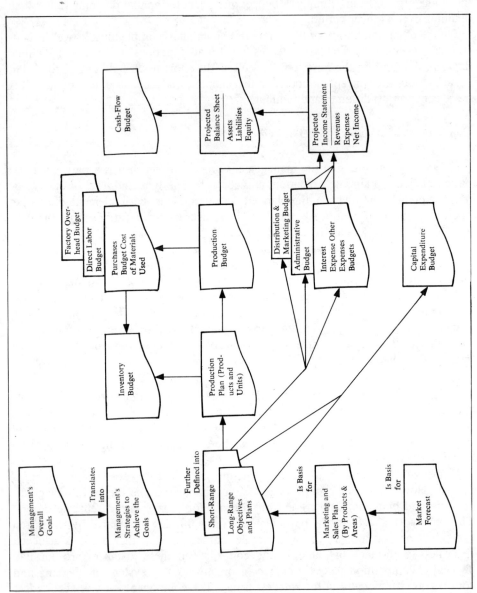

FIGURE 12.1   COMPONENTS OF THE BUDGET

The long- and short-range plans are also the basis for budgets that cover capital expenditures, distribution and market costs, administrative costs, interest, and other expenses.

The cash inflows and outflows indicated by the projected revenues and operational and capital expenditures are translated into a cash-flow budget. The resulting figures are then reflected in the projected balance sheet and income statement.

### Establishing Budget Objectives

The objectives of the budgeting system must obviously correlate with and reflect management's perspective—its attitudes, directions, and objectives. This perspective is embodied in the goals it sets, the long-range plans it makes, and the policies and procedures it establishes.

Management may have both short- and long-range objectives in such areas as sales growth, cost containment, factory productivity, return on assets employed, cash flows, personnel evaluation and development, and product research. The objectives for each of these areas need to be quantified for both the long term and the short term.

The controller's role in the organization is to establish an atmosphere conducive to budgeting—to planning and controlling the activities. His first task is to set the specific objectives of the budgeting system:

- To engage in only those activities designed to attain the firm's goals;
- To identify undesirable deviations from the plan and analyze them;
- To make the necessary corrections on a timely basis; and
- To produce the results called for by the plan.

### Communicating Budget Objectives

The controller must communicate the objectives of the budgeting system to the organization's operating units through the policies, procedures, and forms established to implement the budgeting system. But communication involves more than mechanical implementation. It includes transmitting, to all concerned, management's emphasis on attaining the established goals through effective planning and control of operations.

### Organizing the Budget Department

The specific organization of a firm's budget staff depends on the size of the firm, the nature of its organization, its separation into functional areas, its degree of centralization, the type of products or services it offers, and the inclinations and personalities of management. However, the following general discussion applies to all but the smallest firms.

**Line and Staff Responsibilities.** Like any successfully administered program, the budgeting function must be supported by proper organization. Authorities and responsibilities must be set; the interrelationships between functions must be defined and established. It is particularly important to delineate line and staff functions in the budgeting process.

*Line executives* are responsible for providing information on which to base decisions, implementing the decisions made, and exercising control over the results. The whole budget must be viewed as a tool and technique for helping managers carry out their responsibilities for planning and resource allocation. By participating in the budgeting process, they become committed to the program the budget portrays.

*Staff personnel*, likewise, have related responsibilities. For the budgeting staff, these responsibilities are to design the system, oversee and coordinate the system's operation, provide technical assistance, provide analyses, and prepare and distribute performance reports.

**Overall Responsibility.** Overall staff responsibility for the budget system should rest with the chief financial officer, that is, the vice-president of finance or the controller, whose position commands attention, respect, and authority throughout the firm. In large organizations, a budget director or department head may have primary responsibility for the budget and report to the chief financial executive. In this case, the budget director has a staff function. The chief financial executive, in turn, has line authority over that department's operations but has a staff relationship to all other functions.

The trend toward having the budget responsibility placed at the highest organizational levels reflects management's awareness that the budget function must be broadly based throughout the firm's operating areas. A recent phenomenon is the establishment of budget committees both at the operating management level and within the board of directors. Properly administered, these committees can coordinate and reconcile the diverse points of view within the firm.

## PLANNING, PREPARING, AND IMPLEMENTING THE BUDGET PROGRAM

The budget process comprises three phases: planning, preparation, and implementation. In carrying out these functions the budget department would normally be responsible for:

- Advising line management and the board of directors, and their committees, on all aspects of the budget process and program;
- Formulating the technical requirements and policies for each component of the budget program;
- Organizing budget procedures, including designing the forms, schedules, reports, and the budget manual;

- Providing overall technical supervision of the budget program;
- Furnishing preliminary data to top management as a basis for preliminary policy decisions and evaluation of alternatives;
- Translating preliminary policy decisions into forecasts of their effects on future operations;
- Distributing planning assumptions and operating guidelines;
- Organizing, coordinating, and conducting information and training sessions related to preparing and/or implementing the budget;
- Receiving tentative plans and projections from operating management, coordinating them, and transmitting them to appropriate executives for review and revision;
- Reproducing and distributing the components of the budget according to management's directives;
- Providing performance reports classified by responsibilities or other relevant factors, variance reports, and other statistical analyses;
- Monitoring the budget's implementation and the overall control system; and
- Presenting suggested revisions to the adopted budget when changed conditions warrant.

## Procedures for the Budget Process

Budget process procedures are fairly easy to state, but are harder to carry out. Planning, implementing, and controlling the budget involve working with and through personnel, designing forms and paper flows, predicting future events, and making reasonably accurate projections based on these predictions.

**Budget Planning.** Successful budget planning has many benefits. It:

- Forces formulation of goals and strategies;
- Encourages management to participate in the budgeting process and strengthens management's commitment to its proper implementation;
- Develops coordination and cooperation between budget units and programs;
- Encourages a more effective and efficient use of material, labor, facilities, and capital;
- Encourages the development of a sound organizational structure with clear lines of authority and descriptions of positions;
- Encourages the development of an accounting system that generates current accurate data; and
- Forces management to determine its capital requirements and consider optimum means for obtaining the capital.

The planning phase includes preparatory work to provide the framework of the budget. Typically it would be done in the third quarter of the year preceding the next budgeted fiscal year. Pertinent data should be accumulated about the current economy and predictions made about its direction the following year. These predictions provide a basis for considering the company's objectives and its strategies for achieving them. A critique of the current year's budgeting experience would provide additional information for revising or formulating budget process procedures.

**Budget Preparation.** After the long-range plans are established and the short-range plans developed, the staff initiates the budget preparation phase. All managers who authorize expenditures receive the year's planning parameters and other instructions from the president or budget committee. The market or sales forecast and the marketing plan by products and areas form the second most important input to the long- and short-range objectives and plans. Each manager then prepares an operating plan. Figure 12.1 illustrates the sequence of events in the budgeting process.

*Production budget.* The sales plans are basic to the production plan, which is formulated in units of output of specific types of products. The standard cost determinations also may be made at that time. The production plan provides manufacturing management with quantity requirements and usage schedules.

The production budget is the result of the compilation of these requirements and their translation to dollar amounts. It serves as the basis for preparing a purchasing budget and for making price and quantity commitments. Integrated into the production budget may be a direct labor budget, a production overhead budget, and an inventory budget.

*Other budgets.* Long- and short-range objectives and plans are also the bases for projecting budgets for capital expenditures, distribution and marketing, administrative expenses, interest expense, and other expenses.

The controller and/or budget director are deeply involved in preparing the operating budget. Although the extent and type of involvement depends on the firm, the controller generally assigns the dollar values to the operating and financial plans submitted by the line managers. The budget forms, typically in responsibility report format, are then issued to the line managers.

*Preparation steps.* Two steps are involved in translating the plans into the budgeted responsibility reports. First, the controller sets up budget forms that correspond to the chart of accounts, so he can determine the accounting effect of the budget plans on each department. Second, he takes cost and price projections and incorporates them into the budgeted figures.

The individual departmental budgets are then consolidated into a budgeted operating statement (income statement), a position statement (balance sheet), and a funds-flow projection (statement of changes in financial position). These statements are compiled in the same format as the historical financial statements. The degree of detail presented will depend on the requirements of the individual managers or on established policy. The statements may be on a monthly, quarterly, or semiannual basis for the short term, and yearly for the next five years. The funds-flow projections should be on a monthly basis to facilitate cash management control.

Next, these budget summaries and projected financial statements are presented to top management personnel for review, together with the comments and recommendations of the controller or budget director. If the initial effort is found to be unsatisfactory because desired goals or dollar profits or return on investments are not met or the planning assumptions have changed, revisions are made either by top management or through specific directives to the line and staff managers submitting the original budgets.

After the revisions are made, the departmental budgets are resubmitted. The compilation and review process is then repeated until, ultimately, a satisfactory operating budget is approved.

**Coordinating Responsibilities.** The controller and/or budget director have a vital role in coordinating the various phases of budget preparation and implementation. Among their various responsibilities are:

- Compiling the facts on which the planning assumptions are made;
- Determining and monitoring the forms design and paperwork flows;
- Issuing instructions to the various department heads;
- Assisting the departments in preparing the initial operating plans and the budgets, or actually preparing the budgets after discussions with the department heads;
- Consolidating the operating budgets of the various departments and compiling them into the management summaries and financial statements;
- Revising unsatisfactory budgets;
- Distributing the approved budget to the departments; and
- Monitoring the department's actual performance compared with that budgeted, and preparing periodic reports on the variances (see discussion below).

The controller and budget director are staff personnel in the budget process and do not have direct decision-making responsibilities. Operating plans and operating decisions must be made only by operating managers. Therefore, the controller is only responsible for obtaining the proper approvals at each step of the process and for distributing the budget once final approval is given by executive management.

**Postcompletion Procedures.** Periodic reports comparing actual performance with budgeted performance are essential for effective management control. The controller is responsible for designing these variance reports to provide timely danger signals.

Analyses of the variances should be more than just a recitation of the quantity and dollar differences. The line managers should be queried to determine the reasons for the variances, and such reasons should be verified with the company records.

When variances occur, operating decisions must be made. Line managers may decide to change the operating plan to achieve the results anticipated in the budget, or the budget may be modified to reflect changed conditions and more realistic objectives. In the latter case, operating deviations may be approved, and the resulting variances would be acceptable.

Some operations and expenditures, such as plant expansion, sales promotion, or benefit plans, are subject to precise control. On the other hand, some operations or expenditures may be affected by external factors such as market conditions, consumer demand, or the level of economic activity. If changes occur in external conditions beyond management's control, the budget program must be promptly revised or other corrective measures taken.

### Supervising the Budget Program

In supervising the budget program, the controller has four major responsibilities: streamlining the system, promoting uniformity, coordinating responsibilities, and coordinating information flow.

**Streamlining the System.** The budget preparation system is tedious and time-consuming for all the managers involved, no matter how efficiently it is designed. Improper design makes any system more unpleasant and unproductive. The controller should be especially aware of opportunities to streamline the system to make the budget preparation as easy as possible.

**Promoting Uniformity.** Part of the streamlining process is to design a high degree of uniformity of methods into the system—the fewer variations in preparation methods and forms the better. The controller should try to promote communication and understanding through standardization of methods.

**Coordinating Responsibilities.** The budget responsibilities within management include determining programs and methods to carry out directives regarding specific goals and strategies, accumulating relevant operating data, preparing and/or reviewing the tentative budget, making changes as directed, and operating according to the approved budget.

**Coordinating Information Flow.** The controller expedites the accumulation of relevant data, their revision and recasting, and their output in various formats, and coordinates this information flow from and back to operating management.

### Design and Use of Models

Companies may now automate the mechanical part of planning and budgeting. Budgets may be integrated into the accounting information system, and variance reports may be prepared more easily and frequently.

Budgeting steps that require alternative assumptions or decisions may be programmed so that "what if" modeling is an easy application. Simulating different conditions and methods of operations is a great help in exploring the alternatives available in the planning and budgeting process. (See Chapter 13 for a discussion of the use of models and simulation in forecasting.)

## BUDGET PREPARATION

### Budget Periods

The budget year may be made to coincide with the financial fiscal year. This budget period is the logical choice unless other considerations override. One of these considerations might be a long production period, as is true for some construction and distilling operations; the budget period might then appropriately be longer than a year.

Budget periods may also be allocated within the year. For example, expenditures for programs or activities may be budgeted by months or quarters or semiannual periods. This is especially appropriate when cash management considerations are involved.

The nature of the firm's operations is another factor that determines the budget periods appropriate for a particular firm. If the firm's operations are easily separated into discernible projects, these can be categorized by time segments to facilitate the budgeting process. If the firm engages in seasonal operations, such as clothing manufacturing, a seasonal budget period would be more meaningful. For companies that engage in small day-to-day transactions, the annual budget period works best.

It may be to the firm's advantage to also budget for extended time periods. For example, in addition to next year's budget, the budget department may prepare budgets for the next four or five years and for the tenth and fifteenth year. The yearly budgets would be "rolled forward." This means that as the current year is completed and a new budget year begins, the current budget is adopted, the next three years' budgets are updated for recent developments, and a new fifth year budget is added. The tenth and fifteenth year projections are also revised accordingly. The advantage of such long-term budgeting is to develop a strategic plan for the corporation and integrate each year's budget into the long-term concept. It also allows management to determine if the firm is moving in the direction dictated by the long-term strategic plan.

### Choosing a Budget

Just as management determines the timing of its budget periods, it must consider whether to prepare a fixed (static) or variable (flexible) budget.

**Fixed Budgets.** Firms often start with a *fixed budget*, because it is the simplest to construct. The firm assumes a certain level of operations—by production units, sales, service, or some other relevant measure of volume. The level of revenues and costs that are expected at that level then constitute the budget.

A fixed budget is an adequate tool if the firm can reasonably predict sales volume, if the actual sales approximate the budgeted level, and if the comparisons are meaningful. Variances can be calculated and explained.

On the other hand, a fixed budget is an ineffective planning and control tool if actual volume differs materially from that budgeted. The variances may be caused partly by factors outside management control. The larger the variance, the less meaningful the budget is. It becomes merely a benchmark for determining a difference.

Variances become difficult to explain because of the existence of the fixed cost and the nature of its behavior. Fixed costs do not vary proportionately with volume, but, typically, they are not completely "fixed" either. They can be set at any level, depending on management's decision, or they may change when volume goes from one level to another. For example, if management decides to increase volume to a higher "relevant range," more capacity (buildings, machinery, insurance, electricity) may be needed, and a higher level of fixed costs is reached. As long as actual volume stays within a range that does not change the level of present fixed costs, the analysis of the variances should be meaningful.

**Variable Budgets.** Variable budgets (also called flexible budgets, sliding scale budgets, and formula budgets) are based on the premise that a budget can be derived for whatever volume level is attained. Therefore, the comparison between actual and budgeted operations is more meaningful.

The process of deriving a budget based on any volume level is facilitated by separating costs into fixed and variable categories. Each variable cost can be further converted into a factor that relates the cost to a measure of volume. A formula can then be derived that indicates the relationship of each fixed and variable cost to the output (or volume measure) of the department. Each departmental formula includes a constant factor (the fixed cost) and a variable rate (the variable expense). Costs that have both fixed and variable elements are called semivariable costs; they are separated into their elements and predicted accordingly. (There are several methods for separating the semivariable costs into their fixed and variable elements and for determining the correlation between the variable element and the volume measure. These are explained in introductory cost accounting textbooks and will not be discussed here.)

Calculating the flexible budget formula for each department facilitates preparing performance reports when actual production (or volume) is known. A budget formula for an assembly department might be:

Budget total = fixed costs + (variable cost rate × volume measure).

Assume the standard fixed and variable costs comprise the following:

| *Fixed Costs Per Month* | | *Variable Costs Per Unit Produced* | |
|---|---|---|---|
| Set Up | $ 500 | Direct Material | $20.00 |
| Maintenance | 1,000 | Direct Labor | 15.00 ($5 × 3 labor hours) |
| Property Taxes | 300 | Indirect Labor | 3.00 ($6 × .5 machine hours) |
| Research | 3,400 | Rework | .75 (.25 × 3 labor hours) |
| Training | 4,100 | Depreciation | 1.25 (2.50 × .5 machine hours) |
| | | Supplies | 2.00 (4.00 × .5 machine hours) |
| Total | $9,300 | Total | $42.00 |

Applying the above equation, the budget total equals $9,300 + ($42 × production volume). The relevant range of production for the assembly department is between 4,000 and 8,000 units this month. Therefore, at 5,000 units expected production, the budgeted amount is $219,300 [$9,300 + ($42 × 5,000)].

The formula is valid as long as actual production is within the normal, or relevant, range, as discussed above. However, production levels outside this range may require different fixed costs, and variable costs will assume different levels. The original budget formula becomes invalid, and a new one must be calculated.

The fixed and variable budget costs are not forecasts of these costs. They reflect management's expected standards (i.e., a goal to be achieved). By measuring actual results against these standards, the controller can focus on significant variances and inform management why its expectations were not achieved. This procedure allows management to correct problem areas or to revise its goals.

## Sales Forecasts and Budgets

Without a reasonably accurate sales forecast, planning and budgeting is questionable at best and probably useless. The sales forecast may be considered to have three elements: current products sold to current customers, current products sold to new customers, and new products sold to current and potential customers.

The factors below must be considered in forecasting sales.

**Analysis of Past Performance.** A business's past performance is related to two factors: the effects on operations of external business conditions and of internal managerial policies and procedures. Analysis requires general background about economic conditions, as well as detailed information about products, customers, salesmen, and returns.

**Determining "Soft Spots."** Analyzing the purchase, storage, and movement of materials, the hire and use of labor, and the purchase and use of facilities and support items will help pinpoint the factors that can be improved next year. The controller's monitoring of ongoing operations should uncover opportunities for improvements in efficiency and effectiveness. Additional once-a-year, after-the-fact analyses may uncover other avenues for changes. Outside consultants also contribute an objective perspective to the productive process.

**Methods of Sales Forecasting.** Four methods may be used to estimate the three elements of the sales forecast.

*Statistical forecasting.* The most common method, statistical forecasting, involves projecting historical trends for various factors: economic indicators, specific markets, products and product groups, and other relevant factors. The techniques used to determine the trends include correlation analysis and exponential smoothing.

*Market research study.* Various types of market research studies examine factors that are not reflected in historical data, or that have changed substantially from that reflected in the data available. (Changes resulting from technological, legislative, and fashion industry developments are examples of changes that affect data.) These studies rely on published information from various sources, surveys of suppliers or consumers, and contacts within the distribution system. Special types of statistical techniques are used by market researchers to project trends.

*Market simulation.* This method is complex, requires a computer, and involves determining the interactions of several components to the model constructed to simulate the market in which the company operates.

*Management's forecast.* Reports supplied by the sales organization to management show short- and long-run needs of each salesman's individual customers. The customer profiles may be summarized at the local, district, or headquarters level. Likewise, all customers may be queried, or a representative sample may be the basis for a statistical projection.

**Timing.** The order in which elements are brought together to produce the forecast is important. First, management must establish the basic assumptions to be used in developing the forecast. These include assumptions about overall economic trends, product changes, distribution changes, and contemplated marketing actions. For all or selected changes, market research studies or market simulations must be made. Individual customer's needs must be surveyed, and the data collected and analyzed. The basic assumptions may then be refined, and the statistical projections made. These steps must be taken well in advance of the other budgeting efforts, since the sales forecast and sales plan/budget usually serve as the basis for other budget computations.

**Marketing Plan.** After the sales forecast is established, a realistic marketing plan should be developed that shows unit and dollar sales for products and product groups by relevant time period. It may also describe the assumptions, related sales policies, and supporting promotion programs. The controller and/or budget director should assist the marketing staff by supplying or helping to compile the statistics and financial data and analyses necessary to develop the plan. These analyses may include a comparison with the prior-year historical figures and an explanation of the increases and decreases.

The marketing plan includes an assumption about the promotion support that is necessary to achieve the proposed sales level. Depending on the type of company and its products, the expenses are grouped by expenditures (such as types of media) or by program (which may be related to products or product groups).

**Sales Staff Expenses.** The costs of the sales and sales-related administrative teams and the expenses they incur in carrying out the sales plan must also be estimated and included in the budget. Some companies use a *factored sales value* plan to control sales force costs. This plan recognizes that different factors affect field sales performance, such as customer density and size, product popularity and profitability, and economic conditions.

### Production Planning and Budgeting

Management uses the sales budget as the basis for setting inventory levels and planning production. Establishing policy that balances the desirability of a stable production schedule with minimal inventory levels against that of adequate inventory to ensure meeting customer demands is an important responsibility of production management.

**Inventory Levels.** Establishing an inventory policy involves determining the minimum and maximum levels, in units and/or dollars, of each item of inventory at specified points in time.

The minimum level is established by observing the quantities used or sold, the lead time required, and the pattern of replacement of a particular unit or product. Several factors must be considered:

- The longer the production period, the more inventory must be on hand to fill unexpected increases in demand.
- The less stable the demand for the product, the greater the minimum inventory levels that must be maintained.
- The less stable the raw material source, the greater the minimum inventory that must be on hand in order to ensure against shortages.
- The less stable the price of the products, the more management may be willing to increase inventory levels to hedge against possible price increases.

The maximum level is established after considering the following factors:

- Available storage facilities may limit the quantity kept on hand.
- The inventory may be susceptible to spoilage or obsolescence.

- Inventory maintenance requires expenditures for handling, storage, insurance, financing, and protection.
- Inventory levels are affected by seasonal variations in sales and the desirability of stabilizing production levels.

Management then determines the optimum range of inventory levels, subject only to changes in economic conditions or in the manufacturing processes.

**Production Budget.** The production plan presents the balance and the trade-offs that must be made between sales, inventory, and production. The controller is involved in such policy decisions as the delivery-time objective and related restrictions, the inventory levels that must be maintained to accommodate the delivery-time objective, the costs of carrying inventory, and the acceptable fluctuations in employment levels.

Once approved, the production plan becomes the basis for projecting and budgeting the raw material, direct labor, overhead, equipment, and other capital requirements.

*Direct materials budget.* The first element of the production budget is the requirement for direct materials. Determining raw materials requirements may be simple or complex, depending on what products the firm produces and the degree of mechanization in its plant. The products may require raw materials, fabricated parts, and/or subassemblies; each of these have different use rates and inventory requirements.

Once the individual requirements for each finished unit have been determined, total requirements for each type of raw material or part must be calculated as the basis for the purchase allocations. Purchase requirements are derived from the amounts required for production less beginning inventory plus ending inventory. Procedures established by management then determine when and how much to buy.

*Direct labor budget.* The second element of the production budget is the amount of *direct* labor required for fabricating the products. All other manufacturing-related labor cost is classified as *indirect* and is budgeted with other manufacturing overhead costs. The direct labor budget is a projection of personnel requirements for meeting the production plan, in hours and dollars. It is used to prepare the cash-flow budget, to project overtime requirements, and to stabilize production. The budget can be estimated from piece rates, hourly rates, or total cost. It is simple to calculate hours times average wage rate if this method applies to the particular situation; otherwise, a ratio of direct labor cost to the measure of productive activity or standard costs may be used. If labor requirements are directly related to equipment usage, the labor cost can be determined from production and crew schedules for operating the facilities.

*Indirect manufacturing costs budget.* This third element of the production budget includes all manufacturing costs other than direct materials and direct labor.

Some of the more typical costs are factory supplies, indirect labor, taxes, insurance, and depreciation.

Constructing the indirect manufacturing costs budget involves preparing a budget for each expense for each department. This may be done on a fixed or variable budget basis, as explained earlier. When variable budgets are used, the figures are based on the planned level of activity, and the calculations may be prepared independently. If a fixed budget is used, the amounts cannot be estimated until the budgeted level of activity is set.

## Flexible Expense Budgets

Flexible budgeting, briefly introduced earlier in this chapter, is discussed here in the context of indirect manufacturing costs. However, flexible budgeting is applicable to all types of costs. In flexible budgeting, fixed and variable costs are separated, and the specific expenses are calculated as the fixed cost plus the sum of the variable cost rate times the activity measure. Some costs, such as direct materials and direct labor, are usually entirely variable. Others, such as certain types of taxes, insurance, administrative salaries, and nonmanufacturing depreciation, are usually entirely fixed. In general, expenses are a mixture of fixed and variable costs: They are considered fixed up to a certain activity level, and then variable in relation to the measure of activity.

**Establishing Budget Allowances.** Budget allowances should be based on past experience and expected future conditions. Expenses for each production and service department should be separated into their fixed and variable components, and a variable expense rate determined. Variable budgets for a service department and a production department are illustrated in Figures 12.2 and 12.3, respectively. Note that activity measures for producing departments may be units of output, direct labor hours, direct machine hours, direct labor dollars, or units of raw material used. For service departments, the rate is usually directly applicable to the type of service rendered: repair hours for the maintenance department; kilowatt hours supplied for the power department; net purchase dollars for the purchasing department; and number of employees for general factory administration.

## Nonmanufacturing Overhead Costs Budgets

Nonmanufacturing departments incur many of the same costs as manufacturing production and service departments. Many of the costs have both fixed and variable elements. Others are entirely fixed, and a few may vary in proportion with production or other activity measure.

The word *overhead* is often used to indicate the indirect manufacturing costs included in the manufacturing budget. Sometimes it is used to indicate nonmanufacturing costs, such as general administrative, treasury, accounting, selling, and other operating costs. Either connotation is acceptable if its meaning is clearly established.

| | Service Departments | | | | | |
|---|---|---|---|---|---|---|
| | General and Administrative | | Power | | Maintenance and Repair | |
| *Direct Departmental Costs* | *Fixed per Month* | *Variable per 100 DLH\** | *Fixed per Month* | *Variable per KWHR\*\** | *Fixed per Month* | *Variable per Repair Hour* |
| Wages | $ 1,500 | | $4,500 | | $6,300 | |
| Supervisory salaries | 12,000 | | 1,700 | | 1,500 | |
| Supplies | 100 | | 30 | | 140 | $.65 |
| Fuel | | | | $6.50 | | |
| Maintenance | 100 | | 250 | .30 | 250 | |
| Utilities purchased | | | 1,000 | | | |
| Telephone | 350 | | 70 | | 50 | |
| Travel & entertainment | 250 | $.50 | | | | |
| Taxes | 200 | | 100 | | 50 | |
| Insurance | 100 | | 200 | | 50 | |
| Depreciation (time basis) | 300 | | 800 | | 200 | |
| Total | $14,900 | $.50 | $8,650 | $6.80 | $8,540 | $.65 |

\*Direct Labor Hours.
\*\*Kilowatt Hour.

FIGURE 12.2  A VARIABLE BUDGET FOR A SERVICE DEPARTMENT'S INDIRECT MANUFACTURING COSTS

**Classifying Costs.** Fixed, variable, and semivariable costs may be further classified into *committed* and *discretionary* costs. These classifications are useful because costs differ in accordance with the management decisions that produce them.

For planning and control purposes, fixed costs may be viewed as either committed or discretionary. Generally, fixed costs are not affected by daily and monthly routine management decisions. However, top-management long-range decisions will be concerned with the fixed costs that will be incurred.

Committed fixed costs are those related to the use of plant and equipment and to administration. Property taxes, insurance, rent, depreciation, and management salaries are examples. The firm's long-range operations, dictated by the long-range sales forecast, determine the level of these committed costs. They can be reduced, but their reduction in some cases may jeopardize the firm's ability to meet long-run goals. Decisions of this nature are often reflected in the capital expenditures budget.

Discretionary fixed costs are also called *managed costs* or *programmed costs*. They result from decisions directly reflecting top-management policies, which are usually made at the beginning of the budget period, and include such costs as consulting fees, advertising, research and development, and training fees. Discretionary

| Direct Departmental Costs | Production Departments | | | | | |
|---|---|---|---|---|---|---|
| | *1.* | | *2.* | | *3.* | |
| | *Fixed per Month* | *Variable per 100 Depr. DLH\** | *Fixed per Month* | *Variable per 100 Depr. DLH\** | *Fixed per Month* | *Variable per 100 Depr. DLH\** |
| Supervisory salaries | $4,900 | | $11,000 | | $3,600 | |
| Indirect labor | 3,500 | $14.50 | | $3.50 | | $ 8.70 |
| Maintenance parts | 400 | 3.00 | 100 | 1.00 | 300 | 2.50 |
| Supplies used | 500 | 6.00 | 200 | 2.50 | 250 | 3.00 |
| Taxes | 250 | | 100 | | 500 | |
| Insurance | 200 | | 300 | | 400 | |
| Depreciation (output basis) | | 4.50 | | 2.00 | | 8.00 |
| Total | $9,750 | $28.00 | $11,700 | $9,00 | $5,050 | $22.20 |

\* Direct Labor Hours.

FIGURE 12.3 A VARIABLE BUDGET FOR A PRODUCTION DEPARTMENT'S INDIRECT MANUFACTURING COSTS

costs have no relation to volume of activities, and can often be reduced in the short run without jeopardizing the firm's ability to meet long-term goals. However, reducing or eliminating these expenses over a long period would affect the firm's operations.

### Zero-Base Budgeting

Traditional budgeting methods have not been useful in relating manufacturing overhead and nonmanufacturing support costs to production results in meaningful terms, and therefore planning and controlling discretionary costs has been difficult. A new budgeting technique called *zero-base budgeting* brings these costs under control. It is a program budgeting approach but it is applicable to manufacturing and service firms as well as to governmental operations that are typically structured around identifiable separate programs.

As indicated earlier in this chapter, traditional budgeting methods generally take the approach that the manufacturing activities budget will be based on the sales forecast and that the nonmanufacturing support costs and capital expenditures will be based on the availability of funds and the relative urgency of meeting specific long-range and short-range objectives. Typically, to allow for the support costs in both the manufacturing and nonmanufacturing areas, a percentage is added on to the previous year's budgeted (or estimated current actual) amount to represent the increase in input costs as a result of inflation or new activities. Rarely are the activities of the budgeted year investigated to determine if they met the objectives set initially, or if they were efficient and effective, or if they should be continued in the next budget year. Once an item is in the budget, its presence and magnitude thereafter are rarely seriously questioned. The costs are assumed to be related to acceptable activities, and no specific decision is necessary to continue to include them.

**Methodology.** *Zero-base* budgeting differs in several ways from traditional budgeting. Zero-base budgeting is program oriented. The firm's activities are divided into functions, as in an organization chart. Then the function's goals are examined as the basis for determining what specific programs are necessary to accomplish them. The programs are further subdivided into specific activities, and these are cost-justified by matching identified benefits with identified costs necessary to achieve them. The term *zero-base* comes from the process of building "up from zero" the benefits and costs associated with each program proposed to be funded.

The decision to fund each activity is based on the degree of desirability of the activity, that is, how it is expected to contribute to achieving the firm's goals. The final step in the process is the allocation of resources to each activity on the basis of its ranking on the scale of desirability.

**Decision Units.** Zero-base budgeting is goal oriented. The sequence of strategies, programs, and organizational structure, and the resulting organizational interrelationships established determines the formation of *decision units*. A decision unit is that activity or group of activities for which a single manager has the responsibility for successful performance and, generally, also has control over related expenditures.

Although this definition roughly corresponds to that of a box on a traditional organization chart, the decision unit may be identified in different ways in different areas and under different managers. For example, a decision unit may be a traditional cost center, or it may be a collection of cost centers. It may be a group of people, such as a sales team, or a project, such as one in research and development. It may be a capital project, an expenditure (e.g., advertising campaign expenses or professional consulting fees), or a service center (e.g., a computer installation). It may even be an entire function, such as the jurisdiction of the financial vice-president. Any or all of these may be considered decision units within the organizational structure.

Each decision unit is responsible for a set of activities that are related in that they all work toward a common goal. If, for example, the controller's office is considered a decision unit, the types of activities involved are departmental clerical duties, administration of the various subunits, budget preparation, general accounting, internal and external reporting, and so on. All these activities are concerned with the financial management of the firm. Each activity may be subdivided to identify the specific tasks required to complete the activity. Defining the separate activities and tasks is a key element of zero-base budgeting, for it is within that structure that the decision is made to fund or not fund the activity, based on its merits relative to other activities competing for a limited amount of money.

Another distinguishing feature of a decision unit is that its separate activities may be carried on at various effort levels. The activity's effort level is largely determined by the amount of money allocated to the materials and personnel, and support costs needed to accomplish it. For example, a minimum feasible personnel and support level for the controller's departmental administration may be the controller, a secretary, and related equipment and space. Higher levels of effort would be to add a second secretary, then an assistant controller. Each activity analyzed and possibly funded at increasingly higher levels of effort means that specific operational objectives must be attained at incrementally higher cost levels.

**Decision Packages.** A decision package is a document or form that describes the level of effort required to meet a decision unit's objectives. A decision unit will typically have two or more decision packages representing the levels of effort associated with each activity of the decision unit. For example, the controller's office described above included several separate activities within its jurisdiction. A decision package series—a group of decision packages—would describe each of these activities. For example, the three levels of effort for the controller's department administrative activity represents a decision package series.

Decision packages may be formulated in two ways, depending on the nature of the activities. *Incremental packages*, described above, identify the sequential levels of effort and funding that may be expended on a specific function. If, for example, there are four packages in a series and three of four are funded, then the minimum level (one) is approved and funded along with incremental levels two and three. *Alternative packages* define mutually exclusive means of performing the same function. The alternatives are evaluated, and the best one chosen. The competing packages are discarded or preserved for further review should conditions change.

The mutually exclusive alternative packages (such as those involving capital expenditure projects) generally are further defined into incremental levels of effort in excess of the basic effort. Frequently the initial step is to define the activity or project, then analyze it in terms of feasible alternative ways to accomplish the objectives, and finally break down the more attractive of the feasible approaches into incremental levels of effort—that is, incremental packages.

*Content.* The content of the decision packages must be relevant and meaningful to the managers preparing them as well as those reviewing them. The decision packages must reflect a detailed analysis of each separate effort level of the activity performed. The detailed analysis should include the following basic information:

- Objectives of the activity in general and of the specific effort level being described in the decision package in particular;
- Methods of achieving the objectives—the actions to be taken, and the procedures to be followed in carrying out the actions;

- Benefits to be derived from the specific effort level of the activity, preferably in quantitative measures of performance;
- Consequences of not funding the effort level of the activity (this is important information in considering the trade-offs);
- Costs to be incurred at the effort level described in the decision package, and the number of people required; and
- Alternative (mutually exclusive) approaches that have been considered and rejected in favor of the one described, or a summary of the other incremental decision packages in the series.

*Form.* The decision package's form is simple. Space is needed for replies to the six items above and for identifying information, such as the department, function/activity, and responsible personnel. Decision packages are preferably printed on one side of a single sheet. The reverse side may show the buildup of costs shown in summary on the front. Using separate sheets facilitates shuffling the forms for review and marking purposes. On the other hand, the process of identifying and describing discrete activities and varying levels of efforts (both current and proposed) may produce excessive paperwork. Write-ups should be informative but as succinct as possible.

Generally each manager having the responsibility for carrying out certain activities develops the decision packages for those activities. They are then reviewed by his supervisors and successively higher levels of management. Considerable effort should be expended to develop a standardized format and standardized content categories to systematically and effectively communicate the analyses and recommendations.

**Ranking Decision Packages.** The focus on benefits—achieving the organization's goals—dictates that limited resources be allocated on the basis of projected results. All decision package series at the outset are equal in priority, but individual packages in a series, because of their sequencing, are listed in priority order. The manager of each organizational unit first ranks in priority order those decision packages that he is submitting for review. The next review is done by these managers' superior, who collects all decision packages from the decision units under his jurisdiction and then ranks them. His recommendation, reflected in the rank order, is then passed up to the next management level, where all decision packages entering at that level are reranked. When the process reaches top management, the funding decision is made.

The simple ranking form lists in rank order the titles (or other departmental identifiers) of the decision packages. It may also indicate certain summary information taken from the decision packages, such as the dollar amounts and the number of personnel involved.

Shortcuts have been designed to save time in ranking a high volume of decision making. Since the high-priority decision packages are almost always funded, they may not need to be specifically ranked. Likewise, since the low-priority packages are not likely to be funded, they may also not need to be specifically ranked. If high-

and low-priority packages are not ranked, more time can be spent ranking the middle group in which the funding cutoff normally will occur. There are other shortcut methods, but because of space limitations they cannot be explored here. However, Suggested Reading lists books on zero-base budgeting that explain these methods in detail.

**Allocation of Resources.** Top management reviews the ranked decision packages presented from lower levels and may require a final consolidation before it decides the funding levels. After the final rankings are produced, management determines the resource allocations. To meet the overall objectives of the organization and to consider the trade-offs necessary in making its evaluation, top management may review all the packages, review the marginal funding packages, or rely on summary analyses.

The activities subject to the zero-base budgeting procedures are placed by management into two categories: those funded and those not funded. The funded activities are combined with the production figures and the other non-zero-base-budgeted items (e.g., capital expenditures, possibly) to produce the total expenditures target.

The list of remaining activities represents a rank-ordered set of activities that may be funded if resources become available. Conversely, the ranking of the accepted packages provides a framework for eliminating programs if resources should become restricted or if other plans go awry.

After the funding decision is made, the decision packages are reshuffled according to organization chart groupings, and the budget (consisting of the approved and funded decision packages) for each decision unit is prepared and communicated to the appropriate managers.

**Managing the Zero-Base Budgeting Process.** Managing the process involves implementing the funding decisions, controlling the approved activities, and evaluating the results of the activities.

Executive management must be both committed and involved in the implementation of zero-base budgeting. Top management must devise the implementation strategy, operational objectives, and policy and procedure guidelines. It must organize and coordinate the actions to be accomplished, assign personnel to carry out those actions, direct the personnel toward the stated goals, and motivate them to achieve those goals. It must also design the paper flow that documents these activities.

Some of the implementation policies for zero-base budgeting that management must consider include:

- At what pace should the system be implemented? Should all functions be implemented at one time? Sequentially? Or should a pilot be instituted first and then spread to other functions?
- How should a decision unit be defined? Where within the organization should the decision units be located, and how are they to be related to one another?
- Who should be responsible for developing the decision packages?

- How should the decision packages be reviewed and ranked?
- What implementation timetable should be followed? (The time required will depend on several factors: organization size, nature of its operations, management's familiarity with the concept and its procedures, extent of personnel training, volume of decision packages, procedures for review and ranking, and management's attitudes and support.)
- What costs should be reflected in the decision packages?
- How should personnel movements and reductions be handled?
- How should revisions in the approved budget be handled?
- Should outside consultants be engaged to install the system?

*Selling zero-base budgeting.* Zero-base budgeting must be sold to individual managers on the basis of the benefits that both they and the organization will derive. In other words, it must be sold to managers as both an operational concept and as an effective tool for meeting their responsibilities. The following major strengths of zero-base budgeting should be emphasized:

- Good planning and the establishment of goals are required to set up the decision units and their activities.
- Zero-base budgeting makes management systematically review and evaluate activities and rank them in order of importance.
- Zero-base budgeting makes management evaluate the results of implementing (funding) the approved activities.
- Management has more control over operations, because it must monitor more closely the ongoing activities and their results.
- There is improved communication among managers within the functions and throughout the organization's management levels.

**A Flexible Tool.** Zero-base budgeting is a flexible tool that is adaptable to varying environmental and operational circumstances. The system provides a base of analyzed and ranked activities to which managers can quickly orient themselves. It also provides a set of procedures by which those activities are documented and that can be relied on to produce new or modified decision packages. Most importantly, the system indicates the positive and negative consequences of the various activities, so that management can make the proper trade-offs in reallocating resources whenever that becomes desirable. The flexibility that zero-base budgeting promotes is one of its major benefits.

## BALANCE SHEET BUDGETING

Up to this point this discussion has emphasized operations—the revenues and expenses that ultimately make up a projected income statement. The controller is also concerned with the cash inflows and cash outflows that are associated with those revenues and expenses.

The balance sheet reports the level of net resources available to support a given level of operations. While present operations may be adequate to generate the necessary cash, any expansion of activities requires increased amounts of net resources. The expansion will likely be in both operating capital and in capital expenditures, so the increased level of net resources must correspondingly be in both short-term and long-term resources.

Balance sheet budgeting establishes standards of performance for the firm, is a basis for control over actions, and forecasts the firm's future position. It provides the basis for improving management's general understanding of the business and for questioning the soundness of specific operating decisions.

### Planning Short-Term Funding Requirements

Short-term funding, like sales and production, must be planned. Controllers must be aware of the importance of planning for sufficient cash to finance operations and of having a good working capital turnover. Planning the short-term funding requirements is a conscious effort and process; it does not simply occur as a result of normal operations.

**Working Capital Budget.** In order to exert budgetary control over working capital, cash inflows and outflows, and capital expenditures, management must prepare budgets for these areas, as well as periodically monitor the results. It may accomplish the monitoring through relating the level of investment to operations or to an activity base. *Turnover* is a term used to describe one commonly used monitoring device whereby, for example, sales divided by average working capital provides a working capital turnover rate.

The working capital budget consists of projected amounts for the components of working capital—current assets and current liabilities. Since the two elements are the products of separate cycles and are not subject to the same operational planning requirements, they must be considered separately.

In preparing the working capital budget, management must take into account the relationships discussed earlier between the sales forecast, production and inventory levels, materials and labor purchases, and overhead items. All these must be considered in terms of the timing and the amounts of the expenditures as well as the desired levels of each item at interim dates and at the year-end balance sheet date.

Accounts receivable and cash balances, determined in part by the volume of credit sales and credit/collection policies, and in turn related to sales and marketing policies, must also be scheduled out on an interim and year-end basis.

**Cash Budget.** The schedules of two cycles (sales → receivables → cash inflows, and expenditures → payables → cash outflows) represent the cash sources and expenditures from the firm's operations. The two together form the basis for a cash budget and need to be supplemented for budget purposes only by the nonoperating sources of cash—borrowings, capital stock issuances, and purchases or sales of plant or equipment items.

Distinguishing between a firm's three types of cash holdings (working balance, accommodation balance, and excess balance) is useful for planning and control over cash flows. *Working cash* is the amount the firm needs for day-to-day operations. *Accommodations cash* is the amount it requires to support services rendered by financial institutions to the firm (such as a compensating balance required to support a loan). The remainder represents *excess cash*, which management should keep to a minimum in order to earn the highest return possible.

Cash management is closely tied to cash budgeting. This responsibility of the controller or financial manager assumes special importance after the initial cash budget is prepared and approved. (See Chapter 23 for a full discussion of cash management principles and techniques.)

### Planning Long-Term Funding Requirements

The capital budget is very important for purposes of planning and control. Management must determine the amounts it wishes to invest in productive capacity, but its decision must be based on a workable balance between funds availability, the extent of capacity it plans to provide, the customer demands it expects for existing and new products and services, and the types of investments it plans to make in order to maximize the return on its investment.

Because capital expenditures typically involve large commitments of funds, their impact on the firm extends over a relatively long period. Capital expenditures are preferably viewed as separate projects having unique time dimensions that can be fit into the next year's budgeted expenditures, a longer-range profit plan (say, five years) if one is produced, and a longer-range capital addition plan (say, another ten years), as appropriate.

**Project Planning.** The firm's long-range goals serve as the basic guidelines for future progress and position. The long-range goals are transformed into plans and projects, including capital expenditure projects. These plans, of course, must be coordinated with the firm's short- and long-range cash availability and financing plans.

The capital budget normally includes both major and minor projects. *Major projects* are those in which large amounts of funds are committed for long periods. They frequently involve construction extending beyond a year. *Minor projects* require less planning and involve less extensive time periods and smaller expenditures, such as tools and small machines and small renovations and improvements that are essential to day-to-day operations. Minor projects may be included in a blanket rather than an itemized appropriation.

Project planning includes a scheduling of the fund outlays required for each project in each of the future years. The budget also includes the amounts already committed to each project, the amounts to be authorized in the budget year, and the unexpended balance of the total appropriation.

Project planning also involves preparing proposals for capital addition projects recommended by individual managers. (Obviously, proposals for major expenditures should come from top management.) Specific procedures should ensure that top management properly analyzes and evaluates each proposal.

A proposal normally should include:

- A project description;
- The reasons for the proposal/recommendation (the project's advantages);
- The possible disadvantages of the project;
- An evaluation of the return on the investment;
- The financing requirements and timing; and
- Other relevant data.

If the proposal merits additional study, it may be referred to a specific department —the controller or plant engineer or others—as appropriate. If the verdict is favorable, it is then included in the capital budget for further consideration by top management.

When the project is approved, control is maintained by collecting data on costs, work progress, and cumulative expenditures relative to those budgeted. The records established for each project should specify costs by responsibility and type. A status report form may be used to periodically report the project's status to top management.

After the project is completed, its results should be studied regularly and compared with those projected in the original or revised proposal.

**Capital Budget Manual.** As a firm grows larger and proposals for capital investments increase accordingly, there is a greater need to control and coordinate these requests. A capital budget manual details the procedures for requesting capital projects, for evaluating alternative proposals, and for implementing and controlling the approved expenditures.

A firm should design a capital budget manual to fit its specific needs. The manual may include sections on objectives, procedures for administration of the capital budgeting process, definitions of types of capital projects, classification of capital expenditures by project types, evaluation procedures, budget preparation by functions, preparation of project status reports, and postaudit evaluation procedures and reports. Specialized books and courses on budgeting and capital budgeting give further details of manual design as well as helpful illustrations.

**Resource Allocation.** The discussion above on project planning presumes that the resource allocation decision has been a favorable one. However, the requests for funds typically exceed the funding available or feasible. As previously noted, management has many investment alternatives continuously proposed, from which priorities must be established and choices made. The funding decision is even more critical when projects are long-term and involve large dollar commitments. Therefore, management must use systematic and reliable approaches to evaluate the proposals. (See Chapter 34 for a detailed review of methods for evaluating capital projects.)

## SUGGESTED READING

Anderson, Donald N. "Ingredients for Successful Zero-Based Budgeting Implementation." *Managerial Planning*, Vol. 27 (March/April, 1979).

Austin, L. Allan. *Zero-Base Budgeting: Organizational Impact and Effects.* New York: AMACOM, 1977.

Chandra, Gyan. *Budgeting for Profit.* Ed. by Gyan Chandra and Surendra Singhvi. Oxford, Oh.: Planning Executives Institute, 1975.

Cheek, Logan M. *Zero-Base Budgeting Comes of Age: What it is and What it Takes to Make it Work.* New York: AMACOM, 1977.

Dillon, Ray D. *Zero-Base Budgeting for Health Care Institutions.* Germantown, Md.: Aspen Systems Corporation, 1979.

Dudick, Thomas S. *Cost Controls for Industry.* 2nd ed. Englewood Cliffs, N.J.: Prentice-Hall, 1976.

Lin, W. Thomas. "Corporate Planning and Budgeting: An Integrated Approach." *Managerial Planning*, Vol. 27 (March/April, 1979).

Matthews, Lawrence M. *Practical Operating Budgeting.* New York: McGraw-Hill, 1977.

Pattillo, James W. *Zero-Base Budgeting: A Planning, Resource Allocation and Control Tool.* New York: National Association of Accountants, 1977.

Pyhrr, Peter A. *Zero-Base Budgeting.* New York: John Wiley and Sons, 1973.

Welsch, Glenn A. *Budgeting Profit Planning and Control.* 4th ed. Englewood Cliffs, N.J.: Prentice-Hall, 1976.

# 13

# Preparation and Use of Forecasts

*G. Edward Powell*

## INTRODUCTION

Good planning is clearly an integral factor in the success of any endeavor or enterprise. Planning is essentially a decision-making process to determine a course of action that will result in the most advantageous consequences to the enterprise making the decisions. The critical element in planning and related decisions is the likelihood that expectations will in fact materialize. Success in realizing such expectations obviously depends heavily on the ability to reasonably predict or forecast what consequences will result from a given decision or set of decisions over a specific time period.

In other words, if one accepts the premise that planning is an essential ingredient to business success, it then follows that the ability to reasonably predict or forecast the future impact of present decisions is an equally essential ingredient. Empirically, there is almost universal acceptance of the need for complete and timely planning by the business community. Likewise, the science or art of forecasting has become a generally accepted business technique.

## THEORY AND APPLICATION OF BUSINESS FORECASTS

There are few business enterprises that cannot benefit from business planning. Obviously, a growing business in a dynamic, expanding market must have a plan and a projected course of action, and clearly defined alternate plans and options as well. Such plans not only enhance a company's growth and profitability, but ensure its survival in the competitive marketplace.

### Dealing With the Business Environment

Even the mature or static business runs serious risks if it cannot or will not deal with the regulatory, economic, and competitive pressures applied by its own unique business environment.

The diverse environmental factors working for or against the success of a business have to be identified, measured, understood, and dealt with. The marketplace will not tolerate poor planning, bad decisions, and faulty forecasting. In extreme cases, poor planning and inaccurate forecasting result in the firm's inability to compete, and ultimately in its failure.

### Reasons for Business Failure

There are literally thousands of business failures reported annually by the U.S. Chamber of Commerce. There are many reasons for business failure, not the least of which are undercapitalization, poor financial controls, weak management, and a dearth of business planning. Endemic to the smaller or new business is the lack of financial skills, particularly those that reveal where the business stands and where it is going. Unfortunately, these deficiencies also occur in larger, well-known business enterprises.

### A Change in the Controller's Role

The emergence of the corporate takeover and the "go-go" company, along with the rapid economic expansion of the sixties, resulted in a curious, although in retrospect logical, phenomenon. The focal point within the most aggressive enterprises changed from the boardroom to the financial manager and the controllership function. The corporate battles and corporate successes in the financial arena were principally fought and won by those with the ability to assess the present and prospective financial strengths of a given enterprise. The controller's access to and ability to generate and use financial information resulted in a fundamental change in the controller's role in corporate decisions, actions, and plans.

The pervasiveness of governmental regulation and the insidious effects of inflation on the economy in the 1970s have thrust more responsibility on the corporate controllership function. Financial control in the most fundamental sense is the number one corporate imperative today. Effective financial control is essential not only for the success of today's business and financial activities, but also of those of tomorrow, next month, next year, and the next five years. It is in this context that the controller's function becomes so important.

## CONTEMPORARY FORECASTING TECHNIQUES

There are a bewildering variety of forecasting methodologies, approaches, and techniques. The typical corporate controller must understand most of the common approaches in order to select those appropriate to his business. In selecting a specific method or combination of methods that best suits the facts and circumstances of a given business enterprise, one must consider these important criteria:

- Practicality from the standpoint of available data;
- Usefulness in terms of reliable results; and
- Cost-effectiveness.

Although these criteria are easily stated, determining whether a given method reasonably meets such criteria requires a study of its application and use as well as assessments of the results.

For purposes of this discussion, the forecasting methods most commonly used are grouped under two approaches, the statistical approach and the estimate approach.

### Statistical Approach Methods

Most short-term business forecasts and budgets are based largely on the presumption that the future will follow the pattern of the past. Compiling historical financial and operating statistics and projecting trends and amounts derived therefrom to future periods is clearly an approach to forecasting that is practical, useful, and cost-effective. Useful and reliable projections can be developed from simple extrapolations of limited data. For example, percentage changes in sales or production volumes for two or three years can provide the basis for projecting similar information one or two years into the future. Results can be made even more useful by employing simple modeling techniques or regression analysis, which tends to produce more accurate trend information.

Some of the more common statistical forecasting methods are discussed below.

**Time-Series Analysis.** Several different methods are included in this category. The most common are *exponential-smoothing* methods and *moving-average* methods. The general approach is to identify a pattern representing a combination of trend, seasonal, and cyclical factors based on historical data for that variable. That pattern is then smoothed to eliminate the effect of random fluctuations and extrapolated into the future to provide a forecast.

**Regression Analysis.** Regression analysis is a statistical technique that fits the specified model to the historical data available. This technique assumes that the variable to be forecast (the dependent variable) can be predicted on the basis of the value of one or more independent variables. For example, if company sales is the variable to be forecast, it may be dependent on time, the economy, or sales of major customer industries. One of the major attractions of this method is that as independent variables take on new values, the dependent variable also changes. This type of forecast goes beyond simple time-series extrapolations and is based on a causal relationship with statistical validity, that is, the relationship is not due to chance.

**Index Numbers.** Index numbers are most commonly used to provide a basis for anticipating short-term fluctuations caused by seasonal or cyclical patterns. For example, seasonal indices are often projected in order to determine how a company's sales might be distributed by month of the year. Such indices can be determined by simply looking at the ratio of sales for a given month to annual sales for each of the past several years. The most common use of index numbers is that made by the federal government for seasonal adjustments of variables describing unemployment and general economic activity. The index of industrial production, which predicts a general trend for the aggregate level of output of the industrial sector, is another example. In preparing their own forecasts, many companies use index numbers obtained from a government agency.

**Econometric Models.** This approach to forecasting uses a system of simultaneous regression equations that take into account the interaction between various segments of the economy and/or areas of corporate activity. Often, companies use the results of national or regional econometric models as a major portion of a corporate econometric model. Although such models are helpful in forecasting, their major use tends to be in answering "what-if" questions. These models allow management to investigate the impact of various changes in the environment and in major segments of the company's business on the performance and sales of the company.

**Box-Jenkins Method.** This technique is a highly sophisticated approach to time-series forecasting. It seeks to identify patterns in the historical values of a time series and then to extrapolate those patterns into the future. It has the advantage of being able to handle a wide range of time-series patterns and to provide statistics indicating the level of accuracy that can be expected in a given situation. However, it is extremely complex and somewhat difficult to understand.

**Comparison With Other Companies.** This approach to forecasting considers the decisions and experience of other companies. For example, a vendor of home appliances might forecast its prospective sales on the basis of the total number of housing starts in its sales territory. Another variation considers the forecasts of other businesses of similar size in the same industry.

The statistical approach has a number of disadvantages. On the one hand, the historical trends on which the forecasts are based may not be fully understood. Also, it may be impossible to predict future changes and events that have no historical precedence.

### Estimate Approach Methods

The estimate approach to forecasting is almost totally subjective. It presumes that the forecaster's experience, knowledge of the business, judgment, and intuition are sufficient bases for developing meaningful and reliable forecasts. This approach is practical in that hard statistical information is not necessarily required, and cost-effective in that a limited number of persons contribute a limited amount of time. Its reliability, however, depends primarily on the intuition and predictive skills of the forecaster. His previous success in subjective forecasting may or may not be indicative of his future success.

Three forecasting methods under the estimate approach are discussed below.

**Jury of Executive Opinion.** This method consists of combining and averaging top executives' views concerning the item to be forecast. Generally, the company brings together executives from areas such as sales, production, finance, purchasing, and staff operations in order to get the benefit of broad experience and opinion. Often staff groups supply background information to the members of the executive group. Management may prefer this approach, because forecasts can be provided easily and quickly without elaborate statistics and because a range of management viewpoints can be considered. Also, this method requires the assembling of less data than mathematical techniques. (In the smaller organization, participation in this jury may be limited to the top two or three members of management.)

**Sales Force Composite.** The sales force composite approach to forecasting involves obtaining the views of salespersons, sales management, or both on the outlook for individual products and/or total sales. In this "bottom-up" approach, individual salespersons estimate sales for their subdivisions of the company, and these estimates are then combined to get an aggregate forecast of sales. Like the jury of executive opinion, this approach is not statistical, but rather integrates judgmental factors and experience in situations where historical data may not be available or applicable. However, it has the disadvantage of being susceptible to the biases of those who are most influential in the sales group.

**Customer Expectations.** Like the preceding methods, this technique combines managerial judgments in arriving at forecasts. However, rather than using judgments from those strictly within the company, this method uses customers' expectations of their needs and requirements as the basis for forecasting. This information is often obtained through selected surveys administered by a corporate staff group or may be gathered from selected customers by the sales force. While it has the advantage of recognizing changes in customer expectations fairly promptly, this technique is difficult to use in markets where customers are numerous or not easily identified. Much of the forecasting done by market research groups is based on variations of the customer expectation approach.

The principal disadvantage of the techniques that employ estimates is that these forecasts cannot be verified or assessed objectively. Further, because of the inherent subjectivity of the forecast, bias and specious reasoning can go undetected, with potentially disastrous results.

### Modeling

Modeling is a technique whereby elements of both the statistical and estimate approaches are used to construct a discrete business and economic model of a specific product, cost center, operating unit, corporation, or industry, or a model of an entire national economy. The objective is to construct a model, based essentially on historical activities and relationships between variables modified for predetermined future environmental influences, that enables management to forecast future activities with some degree of precision. Once the parameters and trends of a model have been established, it is assumed that the forecaster can predict the behavior of the model under any given set of circumstances. In short, it enables the forecaster and business planner to obtain answers to "what-if" questions.

Modeling can be very practical, reliable, and cost-effective, depending, of course, on the complexity and sophistication of the model. By employing features of both the statistical and estimate approaches, modeling can eliminate or at least ameliorate the deficiencies of both.

With the advent of the computer, the use of modeling techniques increased. The computer permits rapid preparation of future projections based on historical trends and statistical relationships. Such purely mathematical projections can then be adjusted by expected changes in conditions, input of different assumptions, and otherwise modified for that subtle but important consideration, the intuition of the planner. Computer modeling techniques allow projections and forecasts to be generated quickly and cheaply using an almost infinite variety of factors.

The mathematical capabilities of computers also permit more sophisticated and complex modeling techniques to be employed. The two most common techniques that have evolved are macroeconomic models and microeconomic models.

**Macroeconomic Models.** In this technique, a model is made of the economy as a whole, and a projection is then made of the subject business's share. This technique is more likely to be used by a very large business enterprise and is not suited for smaller businesses or those in fragmented industries. Macroeconomic modeling with many different theories and techniques has been attempted by economic forecasters in government, business, and academia. (The term *econometrics* was coined to describe the highly sophisticated and complex macroeconomic modeling that evolved.)

**Microeconomic Models.** The microeconomic approach starts with an economic model of a business and an analysis of how its particular production and sales activities relate to the economy as a whole. A projection can then be made of the enterprise's operations based on the projected direction of the economy.

## SELECTING A FORECASTING METHOD

The specific methodology or approach that is best for a given business depends on a number of factors, the two most important being: (1) the effectiveness of the method in providing useable projections from available data, and (2) the cost of the approach.

The smaller business will probably find that forecasts of up to two or three years can be developed fairly easily by using a combination of the statistical and estimate approaches. Forecasts using these two methods can be done manually by persons with minimal statistical skills. The results are as reliable as the data on which the projections are based and the interplay of the various assumptions employed. A manually produced projection is frequently the least expensive, as long as the assumptions used are fairly straightforward and the data base is not overly complex.

Larger companies, on the other hand, may find computer modeling techniques to be both the most effective and the least costly. Many computer modeling techniques are readily available at a modest cost and can be used to prepare forecasts using historical data, known changes in business operations, and intuitive conjecture. Programs can be purchased for use on in-house computers, but it is generally more cost-effective to rent or buy a terminal that can interface by telephone with a modeling package on a timesharing computer. The costs for initial licensing, computer time, and rental of terminals and printers are very reasonable.

Modeling programs adaptable to the most well-known and popular equipment are available from a wide variety of equipment manufacturers and software houses. Costs vary depending on the vendor and the sophistication of the packages.

Other factors that should be considered in the selection of a forecasting method include: (1) the frequency with which forecasts must be updated, (2) the turnaround required for an updated forecast, (3) the complexity of the business and of the data base on which a forecast will be based, (4) the capability of personnel involved in the forecasting process, and (5) the manner in which the forecast will be employed. These factors, as well as others that could be considered, are individually and collectively important in the selection of a forecasting method. However, the business seeking a good forecasting capability should also look to more subjective factors. For example, some believe that forecasting is more an *art* than a science. That is, the various underlying subjective skills and capabilities may be as important or perhaps more important than the scientific techniques employed to make forecasts. Consistently reliable forecasts with a high degree of accuracy are achieved by some forecasters who possess a happy combination of knowledge and facts about the business and the industry in which it operates, and intuitive talent. The presumption must be that a skilled forecaster can achieve meaningful results regardless of the methodology employed.

Others would take the position that forecasting is a scientific process of the highest order. The accuracy of the predicted impact area of a returning lunar vehicle is a familiar example of a non-business forecasting problem solved by the application of scientific and engineering resources.

## COMMON TYPES OF BUSINESS FORECASTS

In theory, forecasting can be employed to develop an infinite variety of information. In practice, the typical business is interested in forecasting only a few key aspects of business activities. Because of the interrelationship of an enterprise's activities, the formal forecasting of key operating data will generally provide a sound basis for estimating minor activities and needs.

The most common forecasts deal with sales, net income, capital requirements, and cash flow. Even these key items are interrelated. Net income is to a large extent a function of sales levels. Cash flow is largely a function of net income and capital requirements. Capital requirements are directly related to the level of sales activity.

### Sales Forecasting

Most business forecasts start with the estimation of future revenue based on the quantity or number of units expected to be sold times the price of those units. With few exceptions, sales forecasting is the root of collateral forecasting activities. Once sales projections have been developed, the levels of related business activities can be projected. For example, cost of sales, margins, and operating expenses are typically a function of sales. Future sales levels can also indicate time parameters in which production or sales capacity will have to be increased, which in turn provide time and amount parameters for additional debt or equity financing if related projected cash flow is not sufficient to maintain adequate working capital levels and provide capital funds.

### Integrated Planning

Well-managed companies typically integrate their financial planning so that cash requirements, inventory levels, sales, employment levels, plant and equipment expansion plans, etc., are all considered. Financial forecasting should be likewise integrated.

## A Case Study

A case study illustrating these common types of business forecasts and their relationship is presented in Appendix 13–1. This case study demonstrates how historical operating results can be input into a remote terminal for generation of forecast sales, cost, operating expense, net income, and cash-flow information by a garden-variety timesharing computer-modeling program. The forecast information is then modified for the described assumptions representing expected departures from historical operations. The case study also demonstrates how to achieve a combination of statistical and estimate forecasting.

Among other things, this case study demonstrates several fundamental prerequisites to meaningful and reliable forecasts:

- *Homogeneous base.* A reliable, reasonably homogeneous base of historical data is critical. Without this data base, any regression analysis on which projections are based may be faulty, biased, and ultimately useless.
- *Clearly defined assumptions.* Conjectural or intuitive fine tuning of the forecast must be based on well-thought-out assumptions. These assumptions must be expressed in writing in clearly defined terms. One of the advantages of modeling techniques is the ability to measure changes in assumptions within the parameters of the model. Consequently, assumptions must be clearly understood if the results are to be understood.
- *Short time periods.* The reliability of a forecast is generally inversely proportional to the length of the time period being forecasted. That is, the shorter the forecasted period, generally the more reliable the forecasted data. The longer the time period, the more likely the possibility that forecasted results are significantly affected by assumption bias, standard deviation of statistical projections, and the occurrence of unexpected events. Simple modeling techniques tend to lose reliability rapidly beyond a two-year time frame.

## ORGANIZING AND IMPLEMENTING A CORPORATE FORECASTING FUNCTION

As the corporate managerial decision process becomes more complex and formalized, the controller is being called on to provide an ever-wider variety of information, both historical and projected, and must use sophisticated techniques to analyze this information for forecasting purposes. If the controller is to assume responsibility for the quality of information provided to management to be used in its decision making and budgeting, it is in his best interest to create the organization, the information-gathering process, the interpretative capability, and the personnel to do the job properly.

There is no single theory or formula for the controller to use in organizing his department or in enhancing the effectiveness of his company's planning and forecasting ability. If he is to make logical decisions, he must base them on his assessment of the needs and structure of his organization.

## Assigning Responsibility

Whether a business is large or small or has an extensive or limited need for business forecasts, there has to be one person designated as the coordinator, translator, or interface between the preparers and users. In all but the largest companies, this interface tends to be the controller or the chief financial officer.

Management is typically conditioned to looking to the chief financial officer for both historical and projected financial information. Because of his experience and background, the chief financial officer is typically most qualified to translate forecasts, particularly highly technical ones, into language that management can easily comprehend.

By the same token, the preparers of forecasts are accustomed to turn to the chief financial officer to obtain understandable current and historical financial information. The chief financial officer is able to translate the needs and desires of users into language the preparers can understand.

When, for whatever reasons, the controller or chief financial officer delegates this interface position to a subordinate, it is wise to designate a person fairly high up in the financial organization. The position demands a high profile as well as the exercise of reasonable authority in order to deal effectively with members of management.

Other organizational choices depend on the importance placed on the forecasting function within the individual firm. The specific people assigned to forecasting, the number of persons allocated, and the budget allotted to the forecasting function are largely a matter of corporate need.

## Improving Communications

Probably the greatest obstacle to a company's efforts to develop useful forecasts is the lack of meaningful communication between the preparers and the users of such forecasts. Unless the preparer understands the needs and desires of the user, the forecast preparer's finished product may be largely wasted. By the same token, unless the user understands the benefits and limitations of a forecast, he runs the risk of making potentially dangerous decisions.

Communication problems arise between the user and preparer of forecasts because of their different training and expectations. For example, the user faced with making real decisions about production or marketing may find a 10 percent error in forecasting unacceptable. By the same token, such an error may be clearly within the statistical deviation that the preparer would expect. These differences in perception may reflect basic differences in the criteria each group uses to evaluate the usefulness of forecasting. While improved communication may be important in improving forecasting, an understanding of the differences in criteria would require cross-training. In other words, an overlapping of the skills utilized by the user and the preparer would result in more effective communication.

Many larger companies promote overlapping skills and communication within their ranks by decentralizing the preparation function. Preparers are positioned both physically and functionally adjacent to the users. With close physical proximity, communication is fostered to the point where the user becomes familiar with the benefits and limitations of forecasting and the forecaster is more apt to empathize with the user's need for reliable information on which to base his business decisions.

## Specifying Required Skills

The levels of skill and experience of the forecasting specialists should be commensurate with the degree of reliability that is expected from the forecasted information. Some companies find it advantageous to employ persons with specific experience in the forecasting techniques required in their industry. Other companies prefer to train their own specialists in forecasting methods by exposing them to courses now available in graduate schools of business. This approach is feasible in those corporate environments in which a complete and reliable forecasting capability can be created over a moderate period of time. Most companies, however, run a greater risk if they use "homegrown" forecasting specialists. Clearly, an experienced forecaster will be better prepared to make an effective contribution in a shorter time, add new dimensions to the forecasts, adapt his forecasts to different situations, identify new forecasting opportunities, and select appropriate methods for new problems.

## Evolutionary Approach

The typical corporation should approach the creation of a forecasting capability as it would any new aspect to its business—by stages. Careful planning for each stage greatly enhances the likelihood of successfully developing reliable forecasting capabilities. As experience is obtained and the value of the forecasting activities is measured, questions of staff size and skill levels can be better addressed. The forecasting activities that tend to be centralized in newly formed forecasting groups often later evolve into more decentralized forms that better serve the users of forecasted information.

The evolutionary approach also improves communication between the forecasting specialist and the users of forecast data. As the forecaster's skills typically improve with experience and maturity, so does the user's ability to utilize the forecast. It is sometimes painful and difficult for old-line management, accustomed to an environment where "gut feelings," hunches, and experience are the foundation for business planning, to move to one where reliance is placed instead on scientific approaches and results; this transition can be eased if it is done gradually.

## Establishing an Information Flow

Finally, the controller, as a member of the management team, must establish procedures to measure the effectiveness and the reliability of forecasted data. This is accomplished by establishing circular patterns of information flow. Historical data that flows from the controller to the forecaster is used by the forecaster to prepare his forecasts. The forecasts based on this information are later evaluated by management by comparing actual to previously projected information. Forecasters and management can then work together to correct deficiencies and pinpoint trouble areas.

## Supplying Direction

The controller must also supply direction in terms of at least initially identifying the forecasted information required. For example, marketing and production information are typically the key forecasts desired by management. After that, management may require data on cash flow, capital requirements, manpower requirements, *ad infinitum*, to the point of sophisticated general economic projections. A written plan presented to the forecasters at the outset of their assignment helps them to supply the information needed.

# PUBLIC REPORTING OF EARNINGS FORECAST

The corporate controller's responsibility for financial reporting has traditionally been divided between internal reporting for management purposes and external reporting for investors and other interested outside parties. Until fairly recently, this division did not apply to business forecasting. Traditionally, corporate forecasting has been used only by internal decision-makers; little, if any, forecasted financial information was ever published. However, significant changes in regard to public-forecasting may be in the offing.

In November 1978, the Securities and Exchange Commission published Guides 62 and 5, *Disclosure of Projections of Future Economic Performance for Companies*. The commission pointed out that the guides are not rules and their publication does not signify the commission's official approval. Rather, they represent practices followed by the commission's Division of Corporation Finance in administering the disclosure requirements of federal securities laws.

By the same token, the SEC release stated that the Division of Corporation Finance encourages the disclosure in registration statements of management's projections of future economic performance that have a reasonable basis and are presented in an appropriate format. A synopsis of the guidelines articulated in Guides 62 and 5 is given below. (The SEC has proposed relocating these guidelines to Regulation S-K.)

## A Reasonable Basis for Projections

Management should have the option to present in commission filings its good-faith assessment of a registrant firm's future economic performance. However, management must have a reasonable basis for such assessments. Although a history of operations or experience in making projections may provide a basis for management's assessment, the fact that a company has neither history nor experience in this area should not preclude its ability to formulate projections having a reasonable basis.

An independent review of management's projections may furnish additional support for having a reasonable basis for a projection. If a report of such a review is included in the registration statement, disclosure should be made of the qualifications of the reviewer, the extent of the review, the relationship between the reviewer and the registrant, etc. The reviewer would be deemed an "expert," and his appropriate consent must be filed with the registration statement.

**Format for Projections**

The guides concluded that projections for revenue, net income, and earnings per share would be presented, but placed no restriction on the presentation of additional projected information. Such projected information must be disclosed in a fashion that is not misleading to the reader. There was no specific requirement as to the period to be covered by a projection; management has complete discretion in this area. If management is reluctant to disclose specific projected amounts, it is then permissible to disclose ranges. Additionally, the guides allow disclosure of different forecasted amounts based on different assumptions.

**Safe Harbor Provisions**

In June 1979, the Securities and Exchange Commission established safe harbor rules for published projections. In general terms, the commission stated that reasonably based and adequately presented projections should not subject issuers to liability under the federal securities laws solely because the projected results did not materialize. An advisory committee to the commission recommended that the safe harbor provisions be applied to all management projection information, whether or not it is set forth in a filing with the commission; but the rules adopted are only applicable to information filed with the commission.

While the commission's attitude toward publication of a financial forecast is quite clear, there appears to have been no immediate response from publicly held companies in terms of publishing such information. For example, *Accounting Trends and Techniques,* published annually by the American Institute of Certified Public Accountants, discloses no instances of financial forecasts being published in annual reports to shareholders.

**Examination by Independent Accountants**

In 1980, the AICPA published a guide on procedures that should be applied in reviews of financial forecasts. The guide refers to the Management Advisory Service Executive Committee of the AICPA forecast standards published in 1975. Although the guide does not specifically so state, it implies that any published forecast should be compiled in accordance with those standards.

The guide also enumerates the accountant's responsibilities in examining financial forecasts and describes examination procedures that should be undertaken. In substance, the accountant is required to assess and/or test the methodology and assumptions on which the forecast is based. He is to perform such work in sufficient depth to enable him to report whether the financial forecast was prepared using assumptions that form a reasonable basis for management's forecast and was presented in conformity with applicable guidelines established by the AICPA.

The jury is still out as to whether a significant number of businesses will publish financial forecasts and, if they do, whether or not they will call on their independent accountant to review and report on them. The whole picture could change dramatically, of course, if the SEC requires that financial forecasts be included in filings with the commissions.

## SUGGESTED READING

Chang, Davis L. S., and Liao, Shu S. *Measuring and Disclosing Forecast Reliability.* The Journal of Accountancy, May 1977, p. 76.

Claycombe, W. W., and Sullivan, William G. *Current Forecasting Techniques.* Journal of Systems Management, September 1978, p. 18.

*International Business and Forecasting.* The Columbia Journal of World Business. Winter 1976.

*Review of a Financial Forecast*, Exposure Draft—November 1979, American Institute of Certified Public Accountants.

Securities and Exchange Commission Releases 33-5362, 33-5581, 33-5699 and 33-5992.

Warren, C. *Timesharing Systems.* Popular Electronics, June 1980, p. 39.

Whittle, Jeremy, *Problems of Corporate Forecasting.* Accountancy, April 1978, p. 105.

## APPENDIX 13–1   CASE STUDY OF AJAX CORPORATION

The financial aspects of the case study company, Ajax Corporation, have been kept as simple as possible. The transaction amounts presented are modest and are presented in thousands of dollars. Ajax Corporation is a stable, family-owned business. The manufacturer and marketer of a single high-quality household utensil, it has been run at a satisfactory profit since its inception in 1950. Recently Ajax's bank inquired about the company's forecasted requirements for external financing during the next five years.

The bank had been concerned about the recent large increase in the company's current liabilities, and requested that Ajax take action to maintain the minimum current ratio of 1.5, as specified in the existing loan agreement. The bank's inquiry included a specific request for the company's estimates of net income and working capital requirements during the five-year period.

As a result of this inquiry, the controller met with the other members of management to consider known or expected changes in the business for the next five years. The following assumptions are developed as to expected changes in the firm's operations:

1. *Sales volume* and *sales price* will both increase by 5 percent compound over the next four years. This will be achieved by product improvements (item 3), and a more aggressive advertising campaign (item 5).

2. *Labor costs* will increase because of increased wages under union contract agreements and additional overtime expenses brought about by the increase in sales. However, economies resulting from the expansion to the factory (item 16) and the new plant and equipment program (item 17) should limit the increase in labor costs to 10 percent compound.

3. *Material costs* will increase because of higher raw material costs and because the product improvement program (item 1) will require more expensive, better-quality materials. The new plant and equipment (item 17) should reduce scrap costs, bringing the net effect to 15 percent compound.

4. *Overhead*, which is to some extent fixed, will not increase as much as other direct costs. However, more supervision on overtime rates for the foremen will be required initially (item 2) and higher depreciation charges subsequently are expected to increase overhead at an annual compound rate of 5 percent.

5. *Selling costs* will increase by $20,000 in year one as a result of publicizing the new product improvement program (item 1) and thereafter by $10,000 as a result of higher delivery expenses including truck depreciation (item 18).

6. *G & A costs* will increase at 5 percent per annum. This item is affected by the general inflation. Also, the new sales campaign (item 1) will generate more billing and clerical paper work, which in turn will require one additional clerk in year one and year two at a salary of $7,500 per year.

7. *Other costs* will stay the same if management acts to control these costs at this level. In particular, audit fees will be watched closely.

8. *Interest costs* on the existing loan will decline as the loan is repaid at a rate of $20,000 per annum. The annual rate was fixed at 10 percent, so a change in interest rates does not affect the cost.

   However, additional borrowing for short- and long-term debt would be made at an annual rate of 9 and 10 percent respectively.

9. *Taxes* for forecasting purposes have been calculated at an average rate of 50 percent. No allowance has been made for the amount of investment tax credit, because management is uncertain about future governmental taxation policies.

10. *Dividend* payments of $10,000 per annum should be maintained and, if possible, increased. Only dire extremity would force a reevaluation of the dividend policy.

11. *Cash balance* should be increased from the current level of $50,000 to $70,000 to provide a sufficient cushion to meet payroll and other working expenses. A larger balance will enable management to spend less time monitoring cash requirements.

12. *Receivables* will stay in the present proportion to sales.

13. *Raw materials inventory* should stay at the present overall ratio to sales, because increased prices of certain materials (item 3) will be counterbalanced by better management control of other large items.

14. *Finished goods inventory* value will rise because of the improved quality and higher prices of materials (item 3) and larger production runs of the smaller products. However, the reliability and greater production capacity of the new plant (item 17) will allow a decrease in the number of units of high-volume prod-

ucts kept on hand. The net effect will be to increase inventory from 12.5 percent of sales to 15 percent.

15. *Land* was purchased in 1950 for $20,000. A current valuation would be close to $200,000. However, the owners of the business consider the land value to be their "retirement fund" and are very reluctant to sell or mortgage it.

16. *Building expansion* at a cost of $75,000 is required now, but planning procedures will delay the work until year two.

17. *Plant and equipment* is, on the whole, modern and efficient, except for a few 20-year-old machine tools. The new plant will be bought from a large industrial company that currently has a financing subsidiary but that charges 3 percent over prime when the machinery is purchased. Management considers this to be an expensive source of financing. The required cost of the equipment is: year one—$20,000, year two—$40,000, and year three—$15,000.

18. *Trucks* will be required for the extra activities and increased sales. Management prefers to buy rather than lease, since the effective interest rates on manufacturers' truck-leasing arrangements are about 4 percent over prime.

19. *Depreciation* has been averaging about 10 percent of the gross asset cost for the last five years. Management does not expect this percentage to change for the forecasted period.

20. *Accounts payable* have not been settled promptly, because cash flow has been affected by a fall in profit margins from between 25 and 30 percent to about 20 percent. (In large measure, this occurred because the energy crisis increased material costs, and these increases were not fully passed on to customers in price increases.) However, three major suppliers have warned that they will cut off further supplies if they are not paid promptly. Management now considers that it must reduce payables to at most 20 percent of sales, and would prefer to reduce them to the historical level of between 10 and 15 percent of sales.

21. *Short-term debt* is the borrowing that can be incurred on a short-term basis without causing the current ratio to go above 1.5. It is not the current portion of long-term debt.

22. *Taxes and accruals* are not expected to change.

23. A *loan* of $100,000 is being repaid at the rate of $20,000 per annum. Additional long-term borrowing is also included here.

24. *Capital* will not change.

25. *Retained earnings* will increase in line with net income after paying the annual dividend of $10,000.

Using actual historical financial data from the preceding year, the assumptions set out above, and a timesharing computer-modeling program made available by the company's CPA, the controller produced the financial forecast presented in Figures 13.1, 13.2, and 13.3.

A quick review of these projections indicated to the controller that the assumptions used in the forecast would not result in the desired income or cash flow. After considering the options available, the following changes were made to the assumptions:

1. *Prices and volume.* If prices were raised 10 percent a year rather than 5 percent, actual volume would remain unchanged throughout the five-year period. That is, sales would increase, but deliveries would not. In addition, the static volume would reduce overtime and keep labor costs to an approximate 8 percent increase each year rather than 10 percent.

2. *Material costs.* It was decided to retain existing suppliers rather than go to higher-priced materials. Scrap would increase, however, and material costs were projected to increase at 10 percent per year rather than 15 percent. Finally, overhead could be kept to a 3 percent increase per year rather than 5 percent, because of the anticipated flat volume and reduced overtime.

3. *Selling expenses.* Selling expenses would not increase as originally planned in the first year, because the advertising campaign on the high-quality products would be dropped. Instead, advertising would increase only $10,000 in the first year and 8 percent for each following year. The lower expected volume would not require hiring additional administrative people, resulting in a projected 8 percent increase per year.

| | Actual Last Year | Projected - Year 1 | 2 | 3 | 4 | 5 |
|---|---|---|---|---|---|---|
| Net sales | $1,000 | $1,102 | $1,215 | $1,339 | $1,477 | $1,628 |
| Labor | 300 | 330 | 363 | 399 | 439 | 483 |
| Material | 400 | 460 | 529 | 608 | 700 | 805 |
| Overhead | 100 | 105 | 110 | 116 | 122 | 128 |
| Total cost of sales | 800 | 895 | 1,002 | 1,123 | 1,261 | 1,416 |
| Operating margin | 200 | 207 | 213 | 216 | 216 | 212 |
| Selling expenses | 50 | 70 | 60 | 60 | 60 | 60 |
| Administrative expenses | 50 | 60 | 71 | 75 | 79 | 83 |
| Other expenses | 40 | 40 | 40 | 40 | 40 | 40 |
| | 140 | 170 | 171 | 175 | 179 | 183 |
| Operating income | 60 | 37 | 42 | 41 | 37 | 29 |
| Interest expense | 10 | 15 | 26 | 33 | 36 | 37 |
| Earnings (loss) before income tax | 50 | 22 | 16 | 8 | 1 | (12) |
| Income taxes | 25 | 11 | 8 | 4 | – | (6) |
| Net income | 25 | 11 | 8 | 4 | 1 | (6) |
| Common dividends | 10 | 10 | 10 | 10 | 10 | 10 |
| Increase (decrease) in retained earnings | $ 15 | $ 1 | ($ 2) | ($ 6) | ($ 9) | ($ 16) |

FIGURE 13.1  AJAX CORPORATION PROJECTED STATEMENT OF INCOME (AMOUNTS IN THOUSANDS)

4. *Raw material and finished goods.* Raw materials and finished goods could be better controlled as a result of lower projected costs, resulting in a 6.5 percent and 12.5 percent increase, respectively, each year.
5. *Acquisitions and expansion.* The planned fixed asset acquisitions and plant expansion were retained to give the most conservative picture, even though these plans could be postponed.

The forecast was run again with the results set out in Figures 13.4, 13.5, and 13.6. The results of the amended forecast were much more favorable in terms of meeting bank requirements. The projections display incoming cash flow essentially

| Assets | Actual Last Year | Projected - Year 1 | 2 | 3 | 4 | 5 |
|---|---|---|---|---|---|---|
| Cash | $ 50 | $ 70 | $ 70 | $ 70 | $ 70 | $ 70 |
| Receivables | 150 | 165 | 182 | 201 | 222 | 244 |
| Raw materials | 75 | 83 | 91 | 100 | 111 | 122 |
| Finished goods | 125 | 165 | 182 | 201 | 222 | 244 |
| Current assets | 400 | 483 | 525 | 572 | 625 | 680 |
| Land | 20 | 20 | 20 | 20 | 20 | 20 |
| Buildings | 50 | 50 | 125 | 125 | 125 | 125 |
| Plant and equipment | 70 | 90 | 130 | 145 | 145 | 145 |
| Trucks | 10 | 10 | 10 | 20 | 30 | 30 |
| Accumulated Depreciation | (50) | (67) | (96) | (127) | (159) | (183) |
| | 80 | 83 | 169 | 163 | 141 | 117 |
| | $500 | $586 | $714 | $755 | $786 | $817 |
| Liabilities and Equity | | | | | | |
| Accounts payable | $250 | $220 | $243 | $268 | $295 | $326 |
| Short-term debt | 0 | 27 | 32 | 38 | 46 | 52 |
| Accruals | 75 | 75 | 75 | 75 | 75 | 75 |
| Current liabilities | 325 | 322 | 350 | 381 | 416 | 453 |
| Loan | 100 | 188 | 290 | 306 | 311 | 321 |
| Total liabilities | 425 | 510 | 640 | 687 | 727 | 774 |
| Capital | 25 | 25 | 25 | 25 | 25 | 25 |
| Retained earnings | 50 | 51 | 49 | 43 | 34 | 18 |
| Total equity | 75 | 76 | 74 | 68 | 59 | 43 |
| | $500 | $586 | $714 | $755 | $786 | $817 |

FIGURE 13.2 AJAX CORPORATION PROJECTED BALANCE SHEET (AMOUNTS IN THOUSANDS)

on a worst-case basis, because of the retention of the planned $170,000 fixed asset expansion program. If actual results of operations were to track the projection reasonably closely, management could consider retaining certain of its original plans concerning product upgrading, advertising, and higher volumes of business.

This problem or one similar to it can be completed either using computer-modeling techniques or manually, with identical results. Obviously, a refinement of the projection through changes of additional assumptions is significantly easier, quicker, and consequently less costly when computer-modeling techniques are used.

| | Projected - Year | | | | |
|---|---|---|---|---|---|
| | 1 | 2 | 3 | 4 | 5 |
| Sources of funds | | | | | |
| Net income (loss) | $ 11 | $ 8 | $ 4 | $ 1 | $(6) |
| Depreciation | 17 | 29 | 31 | 32 | 24 |
| Loan | 88 | 102 | 16 | 5 | 10 |
| Total sources | 116 | 139 | 51 | 38 | 28 |
| | | | | | |
| Uses of funds | | | | | |
| Common dividends | 10 | 10 | 10 | 10 | 10 |
| Fixed assets | 20 | 115 | 25 | 10 | – |
| Total uses | 30 | 125 | 35 | 20 | 10 |
| | | | | | |
| Net change in working capital | $ 86 | $ 14 | $16 | $18 | $18 |
| | | | | | |
| Change in working capital | | | | | |
| Cash | $ 20 | – | – | – | – |
| Receivables | 15 | $ 17 | $19 | $21 | $22 |
| Inventory | 48 | 25 | 28 | 32 | 33 |
| Less current liabilities | 3 | (28) | (31) | (35) | (37) |
| Net change in working capital | $ 86 | $ 14 | $16 | $18 | $18 |

FIGURE 13.3   AJAX CORPORATION SUMMARY STATEMENT OF CHANGES IN FINANCIAL POSITION (AMOUNTS IN THOUSANDS)

|  | Actual Last Year | Projected - Year | | | | |
|---|---|---|---|---|---|---|
|  |  | 1 | 2 | 3 | 4 | 5 |
| Net sales | $1,000 | $1,100 | $1,210 | $1,331 | $1,464 | $1,610 |
| Labor | 300 | 324 | 350 | 378 | 408 | 441 |
| Material | 400 | 440 | 484 | 532 | 586 | 644 |
| Overhead | 100 | 103 | 106 | 109 | 113 | 116 |
| Total cost of sales | 800 | 867 | 940 | 1,019 | 1,107 | 1,201 |
| Operating margin | 200 | 233 | 270 | 312 | 357 | 409 |
| Selling expenses | 50 | 60 | 65 | 70 | 75 | 82 |
| Administrative expenses | 50 | 54 | 58 | 63 | 68 | 73 |
| Other expenses | 40 | 40 | 40 | 40 | 40 | 40 |
|  | 140 | 154 | 163 | 173 | 183 | 195 |
| Operating income | 60 | 79 | 107 | 139 | 174 | 214 |
| Interest expense | 10 | 13 | 19 | 21 | 15 | 6 |
| Earnings (loss) before income tax | 50 | 66 | 88 | 118 | 159 | 208 |
| Income taxes | 25 | 33 | 44 | 59 | 79 | 104 |
| Net income | 25 | 33 | 44 | 59 | 80 | 104 |
| Common dividends | 10 | 10 | 10 | 10 | 10 | 10 |
| Increase (decrease) in retained earnings | $ 15 | $ 23 | $ 34 | $ 49 | $ 70 | $ 94 |

FIGURE 13.4   AJAX CORPORATION PROJECTED STATEMENT OF INCOME (AMOUNTS IN THOUSANDS)

| Assets | Actual Last Year | Projected - Year | | | | |
|---|---|---|---|---|---|---|
| | | 1 | 2 | 3 | 4 | 5 |
| Cash | $ 50 | $ 70 | $ 70 | $ 70 | $ 70 | $ 70 |
| Receivables | 150 | 165 | 182 | 200 | 220 | 242 |
| Raw materials | 75 | 72 | 79 | 87 | 95 | 105 |
| Finished goods | 125 | 138 | 151 | 166 | 183 | 201 |
| Current assets | 400 | 445 | 482 | 523 | 568 | 618 |
| Land | 20 | 20 | 20 | 20 | 20 | 20 |
| Buildings | 50 | 50 | 125 | 125 | 125 | 125 |
| Plant and equipment | 70 | 90 | 130 | 145 | 145 | 145 |
| Trucks | 10 | 10 | 10 | 20 | 30 | 30 |
| Accumulated depreciation | (50) | (67) | (96) | (127) | (159) | (183) |
| | 80 | 83 | 169 | 163 | 141 | 117 |
| | $500 | $548 | $671 | $706 | $729 | $755 |
| **Liabilities and Equity** | | | | | | |
| Accounts payable | $250 | $220 | $242 | $266 | $293 | $322 |
| Short-term debt | – | – | – | – | – | – |
| Accruals | 75 | 75 | 75 | 75 | 75 | 75 |
| Current liabilities | 325 | 295 | 317 | 341 | 368 | 397 |
| Loan | 100 | 155 | 222 | 184 | 110 | 13 |
| Total liabilities | 425 | 450 | 539 | 525 | 478 | 410 |
| Capital | 25 | 25 | 25 | 25 | 25 | 25 |
| Retained earnings | 50 | 73 | 107 | 156 | 226 | 320 |
| Total equity | 75 | 98 | 132 | 181 | 251 | 345 |
| | $500 | $548 | $671 | $706 | $729 | $755 |

FIGURE 13.5  AJAX CORPORATION PROJECTED BALANCE SHEET
(AMOUNTS IN THOUSANDS)

| | Projected - Year | | | | |
|---|---|---|---|---|---|
| | 1 | 2 | 3 | 4 | 5 |
| Sources of funds | | | | | |
| Net income | $ 33 | $ 44 | $ 59 | $ 80 | $104 |
| Depreciation | 17 | 29 | 31 | 32 | 24 |
| Loan | 55 | 67 | – | – | – |
| Total sources | 105 | 140 | 90 | 112 | 128 |
| Uses of funds | | | | | |
| Loan | – | – | 38 | 74 | 97 |
| Common dividends | 10 | 10 | 10 | 10 | 10 |
| Fixed assets | 20 | 115 | 25 | 10 | – |
| Total uses | 30 | 125 | 73 | 94 | 107 |
| Net change in working capital | $ 75 | $ 15 | $ 17 | $ 18 | $ 21 |
| Change in working capital | | | | | |
| Cash | $ 20 | – | – | – | – |
| Receivables | 15 | $ 17 | $ 18 | $ 20 | $ 22 |
| Inventory | 10 | 20 | 23 | 25 | 28 |
| Less current liabilities | 30 | (22) | (24) | (27) | (29) |
| Net change in working capital | $ 75 | $ 15 | $ 17 | $ 18 | $ 21 |

FIGURE 13.6  AJAX CORPORATION SUMMARY STATEMENT OF CHANGES IN FINANCIAL POSITION (AMOUNTS IN THOUSANDS)

# 14

# Inventory Management

*Robert A. Bonsack*

## INTRODUCTION

Inventory, a single line item on the balance sheet, is in reality the summation of a very complex array of raw materials, component parts, subassemblies, work-in-process, and finished products disbursed throughout the plants and warehouses of a company, or in transit between them. Inventory control involves the decision process whereby these diverse segments of inventory are planned, controlled, manipulated, expedited, and managed. These processes are all complex.

This chapter highlights major issues and presents some useful and effective management concepts to permit the controller, in conjunction with management, to make informed and thoughtful decisions about specific inventory planning and control techniques best suited to the needs of the company.

## THE SIGNIFICANCE OF INVENTORY MANAGEMENT

There are as many points of view regarding inventory as there are departments in a company. The paragraphs below identify two basic approaches to inventory—operating and financial.

### Financial Significance of Inventory

Inventory is as much a capital investment as a machine or a building and should be analyzed and managed as such. Inventory policy must strike a balance between operating savings and the costs and capital requirements associated with larger stocks.

The pressure for capital and the growth of the return on investment concept as a measure of business performance has made management increasingly conscious of the importance of inventories as cost elements. Trends toward heavy fixed investments to reduce direct labor costs as well as the growing pressure from labor for employment stability have combined to force more careful inventory planning.

The "action" questions of: how much inventory? when? and where? are best answered by stepping back and asking rather different questions. Why do we have inventories? What affects the inventory balances we maintain? How do these effects take place?

Controllers now have a wide range of techniques for analyzing the place of inventories in a business organization and for designing production and inventory control systems responsive to management policies in the areas of investment, customer service, employment, and cost reduction.

The problems of planning, scheduling, and controlling production in the face of uncertain market conditions and outside demands and limitations, plus maintenance of reasonable levels of all types of inventories, is almost universal in business. The objective of sound production planning, scheduling, and control of inventories is either to minimize friction in these internal-external relationships, or to adapt them to the company's advantage.

The following financial risks associated with an increasing inventory investment can be significant:

- Illiquidity. Inventory can absorb cash resources (in the absence of adequate funding) to the point of bankruptcy.
- Risk of loss through major price declines in a commodities stock, either raw materials or the firm's own finished goods.
- Risk of inventory obsolescence. This risk can affect raw materials and work in process as well as finished stocks. (A good example is found in what happened to mechanical calculators and vacuum tubes.)

The commitment of substantial funds to inventories involves considerable business risk. Many of these risks have been obscured in a period of generally rising prices. The inventory investment of many firms is large enough, in relation to sales and normal profit margins, to contain very substantial loss potential. Many examples of company failures can be traced to the mismanagement of inventories.

#### Operational Significance of Inventory

Inventories serve basically to decouple successive operations in the process of making a product. For example, inventories make it possible to make a product at a distance from customers, or from raw material supplies, or to do two operations at a distance from one another (even if from only across the plant or room).

Inventories make it unnecessary to gear production directly to consumption, or alternatively, to force consumption to adapt to the necessities of production. Inventories free one stage from the next in the production-distribution process, thus permitting each to operate more economically.

The essential question is: At what point does the decoupling function of inventory stop earning enough advantage to justify the investment required? This is what inventory planning and management is all about.

**Functions of Inventory.** Inventories facilitate organization in that the more such inventories are carried between stages, the less coordination effort is required to keep the process running smoothly. Conversely, if inventories are being used efficiently, they may be reduced further only by increasing the clerical and expediting efforts of scheduling and planning.

*Lot-size inventories.* Lot-size inventories are maintained wherever the user makes or purchases materials in larger lots than are needed for his immediate purposes. They may be accumulated or held for the following reasons:

- To take advantage of price discounts for bulk purchases;
- To economize on shipping costs;
- To hold down clerical costs; and
- To reduce costly set ups of machinery.

*Fluctuation stocks.* Inventories may be held to cushion the shocks arising from unpredictable demand fluctuations:

- To ensure the ability to meet customer or warehouse demands;
- To ensure flexibility in stocks of subassemblies in the face of sudden changes in the mix of orders;
- To balance out the load when new orders cause an unexpected demand on individual departments that is out of balance with long run requirements.

A firm need not maintain fluctuation stocks if it can make its customers wait until it can produce. Maintenance of fluctuation stocks is the price paid for promptly serving its customers' needs.

*Anticipation stocks.* This type of inventory is needed under the following conditions, where goods are consumed on a predictable but changing pattern through the year:

- Seasonal changes in demand for a product (toys, for example); and
- Steady consumption but seasonally fluctuating rates of production (canneries and agricultural products, for example).

Some of these changes can be absorbed by building and depleting inventories rather than by changing production rates; attendant fluctuations in employment and additional capital capacity requirements will result. As more of these basic types of inventory are carried, less coordination and planning are needed, less clerical effort is required to handle orders and production, and greater economies can be achieved in manufacturing.

Unfortunately, these gains are not achieved in proportion to the size of the inventory. As inventories increase, even if balanced, the benefits do not increase as rapidly. On the other hand, warehouse, obsolescence, and capital costs associated with maintaining inventories rise at a faster rate than the inventories themselves.

**Business Characteristics.** Both sales and production characteristics affect the design of an inventory system. The sales factors to consider are:

- The size and frequency of orders. More orders for smaller lots can be supported with less inventory; forecasts are better and more reliable.
- Uniformity or predictability of sales. Whether level or seasonal, if sales follow predictable paths they require less inventory.
- Service policy or allowable delay in filling orders.
- Distribution pattern. The more complex, the larger the inventory required.
- The accuracy, frequency, and detail of sales forecasts.

The production characteristics to be considered include:

- The form of production organization. Job shop organizations require more inventory than production line types to maintain flexibility.

- The number of manufacturing stages. With a large number of stages, the inventory control system should take advantage of the manufacturing process by keeping inventory at the proper level for the critical stages.
- The degree of specialization of the product at specific stages. Economies may be gained by keeping stocks in a semi-finished state.
- Physically required processing times at each stage. The time needed before a replenishment order becomes effective affects optimum inventory levels.
- Production flexibility. Inventory planning must take advantage of the flexibility that does exist. Inflexible facilities result in larger inventories.
- Capacity of production and warehousing. Capacity sets limits on flexibility to plan inventories (e.g., frozen food storage is very expensive).
- The nature of the process. The size of batches may be fixed or flexible.
- Quality requirements. Shelf life or obsolescence risks set upper limits to any inventory plan.

## WHO REALLY CONTROLS INVENTORY?

In a recent survey of a large inventory management group, less than one third of the group felt they had direct responsibility or accountability for the financial aspects of inventories. They were concerned principally with quantity and dealt with availability and physical control.

When the question, "Who is responsible?" is asked, the answers often run something like this: "Obviously, the inventory control manager," or upon a little more reflection, "The inventory control manager and the controller." Then someone might add: "Well, marketing has responsibility for finished goods," and upon further thought, "Well, the president really calls the shots." The following paragraphs suggest criteria to help clarify the accountability question.

### Criteria For Accountability

Direct responsibility or accountability for inventory management differs with various aspects of a company's profile.

**Annual Sales.** The larger a company, the typically lower in the organization and the more splintered is the accountability for inventories. The inventory control department itself often resides in multiple locations with somewhat differing responsibilities. In a large organization with multiple locations and diverse product lines, the inventory problem is quite complex. By contrast, in a very small company it is not uncommon to find its president personally involved in most major inventory decisions while day-to-day operations are supervised by the controller.

**Multiple Locations.** Obviously, the greater the number of factory or warehouse locations, the more complex the control and the greater the likelihood for splintered responsibility. Marketing, or the distribution cost accountant, often has responsibility for warehousing and distribution centers in this type of environment. (See Chapter 7.) If the company is involved in foreign operations and is importing products or parts from foreign suppliers or subsidiaries, an entirely new discipline is added to the inventory control problem.

**Type of Industry.** Accountability, with inventory makeup and complexity, varies from industry to industry. An aircraft manufacturer may have millions of part numbers on file, whereas an aluminum smelter may have less than one hundred. One company may have mostly work-in-process while another has largely finished goods or raw material. Companies manufacturing custom products generally have no finished goods. And organizations that require large stocks of spare parts inventory require yet additional controls.

**Organization Structure.** Differences in organizational philosophy will affect accountability. Under a *materials manager* concept, all inventory related activity is controlled by this one position. Under other more common concepts, the various inventory related functions (purchasing, distribution, or warehousing) may report to marketing, manufacturing, or sales. In a small company, the organization and inventory accountability are not usually well defined.

**Management Style.** An organization typically reflects the style of top management. Depending on the background of the chief executive, whether in marketing, manufacturing, finance, or engineering, the emphasis on and interest in clear accountability for inventories may vary widely.

### Establishing Inventory Accountability

Establishing inventory accountability can be as complex as the inventory problem itself. Several factors that influence a company's decisions and procedures are discussed below. Several are left as open questions which must be answered in terms of the company's unique environment.

**Computerized Systems.** A computerized system (which generates all the inventory control reports) is sometimes "held responsible" for inventory control. A poorly designed system can, in fact, cause as well as hide problems. Sometimes the computer system will cover up real accountability. In this environment, does the MIS director then take on some of the responsibility for inventory control? Consider the situation where the perpetual inventory records are not integrated with the accounting records. Who is then responsible for the inventory dollars?

**Material Requirements Planning.** The implementation of a sophisticated inventory management system such as one based on material requirements planning (M.R.P.) concepts should help clarify accountability. It will not be helpful, however, if important interfaces—with accounting or marketing—are overlooked. In fact, in that circumstance, accountability becomes even more clouded.

**Cycle Counting.** If cycle counting is used to adjust inventory records, who establishes the cycle count criteria and who authorizes the adjustments? Are adjustments made to material control records also reflected on the accounting records? The question of integration of systems again arises. If the accounting and inventory control systems are not integrated, it will show up as a result of cycle count activity.

Cycle counting also brings to mind the interests of, and involvement in, inventory management of the outside public accounting firm. Well designed and properly managed cycle counts can greatly assist the auditing function and may, in fact, help reduce audit fees by reducing the effort required for an annual physical inventory. The controller should review and coordinate cycle count procedures with the firm's public accountant.

**Sales Forecasts.** Who prepares sales forecasts? The answer to this question is often a function of how detailed a forecast is required. Under an elaborate M.R.P. system, where the forecast must be detailed enough to drive a planning system and must be in units (not dollars), the sales and marketing people must be heavily involved. Inventory control analysts often assist by analyzing and providing the sales people with historical data.

In a less demanding systems environment, the accounting and inventory control people under the supervision of the controller may prepare the forecast very informally and on an as-needed basis. To provide a new forecast, usage data is extrapolated and factored up by a fixed percentage. Very little, if any, consideration is given to changes in product line, changing markets, product obsolescence, and the like.

**Inventory Reporting.** What is the principal source of internal inventory control reports? The department that prepares and publishes inventory control reports and maintains the records or source data from which those reports are developed is often assumed to have the accountability for inventories. However, the computer factor mentioned above often clouds the issue.

The list of inventory reports may be long. A key question to ask is how and by whom are those reports used? What action is taken based on the reported information? Accountability should be reflected by the report structure and distribution.

How do the details of the dollarized inventory reports correlate with the management responsible for those dollars? Is the reported information segregated by location, by product, or by inventory segment? All too often a less than adequate accounting system will not provide detail by responsible area on inventory dollars. Again, during the financial audit, some brainstorming by the controller and the company's CPA firm can result in positive action to improve systems, controls, and organizational weaknesses related to inventory management.

**Inventory Decisions.** Insight concerning the individuals who make inventory decisions within the firm should help management define responsibility and accountability. Figure 14.1 presents a list of the types of decisions required to manage inventories and also provides an opportunity to assign authority for each responsibility.

**Inventory Investment Levels.** Inventory levels in many companies are planned and monitored only in gross terms—not by product, location, or segment. Furthermore, the planning may be done using historical ratios or percentages which no longer apply. The level of inventory investment should flow from a well thought-out business plan, a sales forecast, and a master production plan for the coming year. If the controller is responsible for developing the inventory numbers for the business plan or budget, he should get his source data from the inventory control manager.

**Inventory Standards.** Whoever has the responsibility for establishing standard material cost has a significant influence on inventory investment. In many companies, the purchasing department establishes unit prices based on the previous year's experience and estimated future price changes. One major weakness of this approach (although unrelated to the accountability issue) appears if the purchasing

| Who has authority to: | Con-troller | I.C. Mgr. | Purch. Mgr. | Sales Mgr. | Other |
|---|---|---|---|---|---|
| Add purchased items to inventory | | | | | |
| Add manufactured items to inventory | | | | | |
| Reduce overall inventory levels | | | | | |
| Declare items obsolete | | | | | |
| Dispose of obsolete items | | | | | |
| Declare items slow moving | | | | | |
| Establish R.O.P.'s | | | | | |
| Establish safety stocks | | | | | |
| Establish the budgeted level of: | | | | | |
|    – raw material | | | | | |
|    – work-in-process | | | | | |
|    – finished goods | | | | | |
| Make cycle count adjustments | | | | | |
| Call for a physical stock count | | | | | |
| Establish a new warehouse location | | | | | |
| Revise the design of the I.C. system | | | | | |
| Take corrective action if actual investment exceeds plan | | | | | |

FIGURE 14.1   INVENTORY RESPONSIBILITIES

department's performance is to be measured by comparing actual prices paid to standard cost. In this instance, it has set its own standard. This responsibility for inventory should perhaps rest with the controller, using data provided by purchasing. Again, this is an area of extreme interest to the firm's outside accountant, who should be consulted for ideas.

### Assigning Primary Responsibility

The number of issues raised above confirms that the answer to the basic question of who really controls inventory is not a simple one. The inventory control manager in large firms, and the controller in smaller firms, should carry full and primary responsibility for planning and management of inventories. They should thereby be held accountable for financial performance within the limits prescribed by the formal business plan.

## INVENTORY CLASSIFICATION

In order to permit proper control over inventory throughout the manufacturing process, and to facilitate the accountability for inventories discussed earlier in the chapter, inventory must be divided into manageable segments. Inventories should be classified for both accounting and operational reasons so that methods for planning and control can be properly aligned with, or correlated to, the unique characteristics of each class.

### Accounting Classification

The basic accounting classifications used are raw material, work-in-process, and finished goods. Inventories are often classified further according to the unique characteristics of the company and its product.

**Raw Materials.** Raw material refers to those items purchased that are to be further processed or fabricated, or to material in or almost in its natural or original state. Raw materials are often separated into: (1) basic raw materials such as bar stock, steel sheet, liquid, or bulk commodities, and (2) purchased component parts such as hardware, small mechanical and electrical devices, and the like.

**Work-in-Process.** Work-in-process refers to those materials released to production. Labor and overhead have already been added to transform the material into finished products, but they are not yet completed. Work-in-process is sometimes divided into stages of completion. Subassemblies can be manufactured in quantity and stored for use in future assembly orders. These "staged" subassemblies can be accounted for and controlled as a subset of work-in-process.

**Finished Goods.** Finished goods are those items completed and available for sale to a customer. Finished goods may be subdivided into finished assembled products and spare parts, or may be segregated by product line. Companies with multiple locations or with finished product at several distribution points (warehouses) will further segregate finished goods by location. Classification of inventory to location is done by proper coding of inventory records, files, and transactions.

It is not uncommon, particularly in companies with large distribution networks or products susceptible to high fluctuation in sales demand, to assign the accountability for finished goods investment and turnover to the marketing or sales department. Separate classification of finished goods within the accounting system facilitates reporting of inventory performance and provides marketing management with needed control information.

## Control Classification

**Stratification Analysis.** The philosophy of management by exception should be extended to inventories. *Selective inventory control* or *A B C control* is an exception method. A basic premise of this approach assumes that good control for one part may be poor control for another. There is little business sense in spending the same effort and dollars to control a low cost item, such as a nut or bolt, as spending to control a relatively high priced item, such as an electric motor.

Figure 14.2 illustrates a typical stratification of an assembled product manufacturer's inventory. A very small percentage of items (Class A), perhaps 10 to 15 percent of the total items in inventory, account for 65 percent of the dollar investment. Conversely, most of the items in the inventory are relatively low in value and account for only 10 to 15 percent of the total dollar investment.

The message is clear. The control system should be designed to concentrate planning and control emphasis on high value items. This does not imply that low value items need not be planned and controlled. It is obviously unacceptable to run out of any inventory item with any value if it shuts down a production operation or prevents a sale. The essential point is that tight planning and control of high value items, characterized by frequent status reviews and short intervals between purchases, results in lower average inventory dollars without risk of stock out. Conversely, because many items are of low value, a firm can afford to buy less frequently in larger quantities without significantly raising investment. Planning and control are less expensive.

**Numbering and Defining Classes.** The number of classifications identified in the stratification process need not be limited to three. It is not unusual to find six or eight classes more appropriate to fit a particular inventory. Spare parts are often set out as a separate group. For better control, raw materials and purchased components can be separated. In several industries, precious metals clearly stand out as a unique classification. Analysis of the company's inventory profile will dictate the number and definition of classes.

### Degrees of Control

Inventory is divided into classes so that different degrees of techniques of control can be applied to each class of like items. Like items are those with relatively the same dollar usage, unit value, and other similar characteristics. The degree of control can be varied by: (1) changing the frequency of ordering, (2) varying the quantity of protective stock, and (3) using either physical or perpetual record control. Figure 14.3 illustrates some general rules related to classes of inventory. These, of course, should be modified to fit the specific needs and classification of a company's inventory and system (manual or computerized) used for control.

As the data in Figure 14.3 implies, the use of an MRP system for inventory planning and control requires different ordering and control rules than a traditional recorder point (ROP) and economic order quantity (EOQ) techniques.

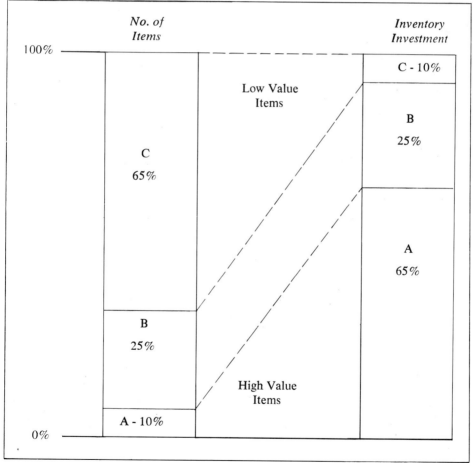

FIGURE 14.2  INVENTORY STRATIFICATION

| Control Feature \ Class | A<br>High dollar usage | B<br>Medium dollar usage | C<br>Low dollar usage |
|---|---|---|---|
| ORDERING | As required under MRP system or one month supply twelve times per year (or more frequently if justified). Delivery related to demand, and bulk are key factors. | Two or three month's supply. Turnover target of four to six times per year. May also order as required under MRP system but more consolidated than A items. | Six or twelve months supply. Turnover of one to two times acceptable. |
| PROTECTIVE STOCK | Little or none. High value makes stocking impractical. Protection is in frequent review, delivery, and expediting, or frequent replanning under MRP. | Moderate amount based on variability of lead time. One or two week supply not uncommon. Under MRP, no protective stock may be planned. | Two to four week's protective stock. |
| TYPE OF CONTROL SYSTEM | Perpetual records. Daily or real-time updating and analysis of records. If under MRP, regular regeneration or net change runs. | Perpetual records. | Physical control techniques. Reorder when physically segregated safety stock is used. No perpetual records or transaction control. |

FIGURE 14.3　DEGREE OF INVENTORY CONTROL

# INVENTORY PLANNING

The systems used for inventory planning and inventory control are generally designed and implemented as a single system. For ease of discussion, the planning and control functions are separated here, based on the following definition of scope:

- Inventory planning. The process whereby requirements for raw materials, components, and assemblies are determined, and the appropriate purchases or factory work orders are suggested. Two basic methods will be employed: (1) conversion of end product demand forecasts into requirements for dependent demand items (material requirements planning—MRP), and (2) forecasting demand for independent demand items (materials and components), using historical data and the application of reorder point (ROP) techniques.
- Inventory control. The records management and physical control of raw materials, components, and finished goods from receipt to shipment to customers.

An inventory planning and control system should support the following objectives of inventory control:

- Maintain inventory investment at the lowest point consistent with sales and financial goals;
- Assure material availability to maintain level and efficient production adequate to meet customer demand;
- Disclose slow moving, defective, or obsolete items;
- Prevent loss by waste, damage, or pilferage;
- Assure physical inventory is properly reflected in accounting and operating records;
- Highlight over-under stocked conditions; and
- Provide accurate data needed to support short and long term inventory planning.

The ability to meet these objectives requires a planning process based on the proper combination of strategic decisions coupled with planning and control techniques.

## Strategic Decisions

Inventory strategy is the product of a long list of considerations affecting the operation of the company, with its particular products, in the marketplace. Strategic planning requires an awareness of the interrelationships of factors internal and external to the company, those a company can control and those it cannot. Consider the complexity implied in the simple block diagram of a production system shown in Figure 14.4. Changes in any of the information flowing through these interrelated systems require action to adjust plans and schedules. Clear strategies and related policies will make the corrective action more active than reactive.

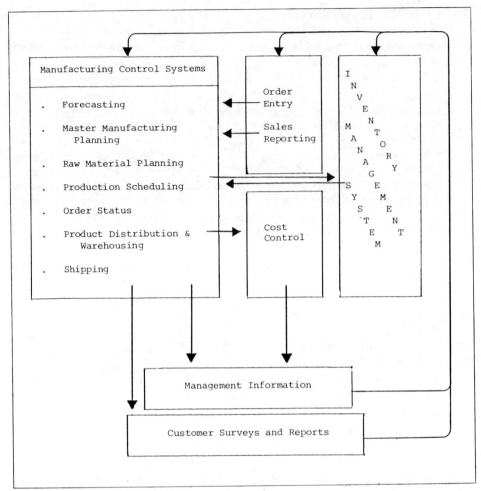

FIGURE 14.4   A PRODUCTION SYSTEM

**Customer Service.** The level of customer service is a major consideration when developing inventory strategy. Of major importance is an awareness of the cost of a high level of customer service. Figure 14.5 illustrates the dramatic rise in required inventory investment as service level exceeds 90 percent. Customer service can be measured in several ways. It is usually expressed as the percentage of time required to fill a customer's order upon demand (or within normal lead times). To perform at 100 percent is virtually impossible; to perform close to 100 percent is financially impractical. A level high enough to meet or beat competition and at the same time be consistent with financial limits or goals should be the target of a company's strategic planning.

**Depth of Market.** Consider the number of inventory stages between the factory

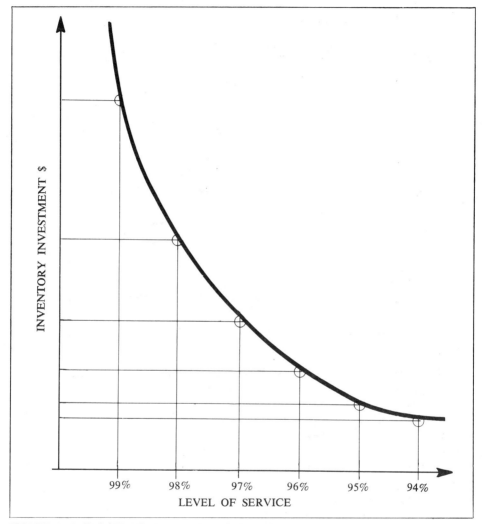

FIGURE 14.5   RELATIONSHIP BETWEEN INVENTORY LEVEL AND
   CUSTOMER SERVICE

and the marketplace—factory inventory, inventory-in-transit, distributor inventory wholesaler inventory, and retail inventory. Figure 14.6 illustrates the impact over time of a 5 percent reduction in retail sales. Unless the system can react quickly to the 5 percent change, within a short period factory inventories will increase by 87 percent, and the factory may have to be shut down for some period of time—at least until excess inventories are consumed. The extent to which a company has a multiplant organization or a large multiwarehouse distribution network dictates the degree to which fluctuations in demand at the consumer level will affect its inventory planning.

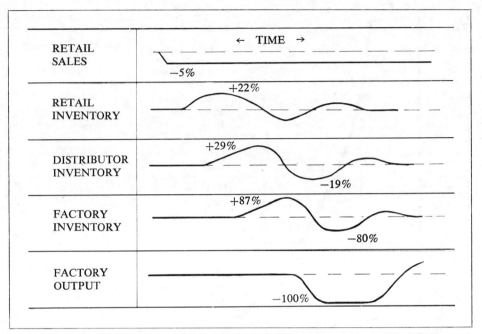

FIGURE 14.6    EFFECT OF SALES VOLUME ON INVENTORIES AND PRODUCTION

**Product Life.** Two examples of the extremes in product life might be baking soda, produced and packaged in essentially the same manner for decades, and a woman's high fashion dress, with perhaps a ninety-day life cycle. Consider the different strategies involved in planning raw material purchases for these two products. When dealing with high technology or fashion products, it is essential to define the life cycle of the product and then build that life cycle profile into the planning and control techniques. Figure 14.7 illustrates the two-year life cycle of a semiconductor product. Four phases are defined: introduction, growth, maturity, and obsolescence. Material ordering and production decisions must be made with full awareness of the company's position on the life cycle curve.

**Make-to-Order or Make-to-Stock.** A major part of the customer service strategy is whether or not a given item should be produced and held in finished goods (make-to-stock) or produced only when a customer order is received. The trade-offs are important to evaluate.

"To-order" production results in:

- Lower inventory investment;
- Longer customer lead times;
- Reduced exposure to obsolescence;
- More exposure to random demand fluctuations; and
- Lower utilization of plant resources.

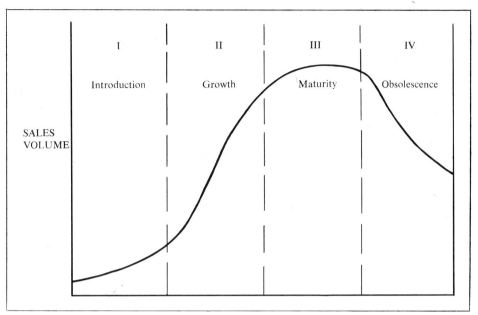

FIGURE 14.7   PRODUCT LIFE CYCLE PHASES

"To-stock" production results in:

- Higher inventory investment;
- Shorter lead time;
- Increased exposure to obsolescence;
- Level production volume, since inventory serves as a buffer to demand fluctuations; and
- Higher resource utilization.

These decisions will vary between product lines and for selected products within each line.

### Master Manufacturing Planning

Prerequisites to successful planning and control of inventories are formal, rigorous demand forecasting and master manufacturing planning techniques. Forecasting is discussed in depth in Chapter 13, and several references are available in the Suggested Reading.

Master manufacturing planning is the process of deciding on the resources required for future operations and then allocating these resources to produce the desired product, in the required amounts, at the least total cost. Master manufacturing planning, therefore, involves setting the levels of manufacturing operations for the future. Arriving at a final production plan requires that manufacturing management make a number of important decisions. These decisions will focus on the economic consequences and alternative allocations of resources needed to meet future requirements. This would include, for example, a determination of the number of lines or machines required for each future time period and the number of shifts that the lines will operate during each time period. Once the plan has been established, the framework has been fixed within which detailed scheduling and production and inventory control activities must operate.

The master manufacturing planning subsystem performs a transitional function by converting sales projections into production and material plans and schedules. The sales forecast is a company's best guess of future demand (shipments) by time period. To operate efficiently, a factory must produce at a fairly uniform rate. It cannot readily adjust output or capacity to large forecast fluctuations. Therefore, master manufacturing planning flattens the peaks and valleys in the forecast and permits production facilities to operate on a uniform efficient basis throughout the year.

Several data elements necessary for the conversion of a sales forecast to a master manufacturing plan include:

- Inventory availability;
- Plant capacity, output rates;
- Capacity flexibility;
- Distribution locations; and
- Planned changes in capacity—new machine tools, plant shutdowns, planned overtime.

The first consideration, determining whether inventory is currently available to satisfy some of the early demand, should be a routine capability of the inventory management system. The gross forecasted amounts for each commodity should be reduced to a net figure by time period before preparing the master schedule.

One way to look at capacity constraints is to consider the limitations on inventory or the inventory capacity of the operation. One side of this question is physical; it includes warehouse space availability. The other side is financial. Management must determine the maximum levels of investment in inventory, by location, by product line, and by classification. Its policies should reflect the various cost tradeoffs such as set up costs, cost of money, insurance, space, and so on.

### Inventory Planning Techniques

**Developing a Profile.** The first step toward development of a system tailored to a particular company's need is to develop a profile of the inventory. Different systems, design concepts, and features may be necessary to properly manage the various segments of the inventory.

Consider the generalized flow diagram shown in Figure 14.8. Raw materials and components are supplied to a manufacturing process that produces both finished products and certain spares items. Each segment of the diagram represents a portion of the total inventory, and each has unique characteristics that require different methods for planning and control. Furthermore, within each of these major segments, subdivisions with still different characteristics that require special systems considerations might be found. The systems designer should challenge each segment of the inventory to test its significance or materiality (from a control or financial viewpoint).

*Demand relationships.* A basic question should be raised about each inventory segment. Is the demand for any particular item (raw materials, spares, or finished product) related to, dependent upon, or correlated with the demand for any other item? All inventory systems fall into one of two major categories: those based on *dependent demand relationships*, and those based on *independent demand relationships*. The architecture of the inventory system will be determined largely by the nature of the relationships within each inventory segment.

Finished goods relationships are easily defined. Demand for any given finished product is generally independent of demand for other products. Forecasting and marketing information systems provide the data required to predict demand at the finished goods level. This is an example of an independent demand relationship. Obviously, there may be some dependence within product groups or families in which historical usage characteristics are valuable to predict item demand. In these cases, however, the group demand is considered as independent.

By contrast, demand for a given raw material item or component part may be totally dependent upon sales of (demand for) the finished product in which it is used. If so, a dependent demand relationship exists. If, however, a given raw mate-

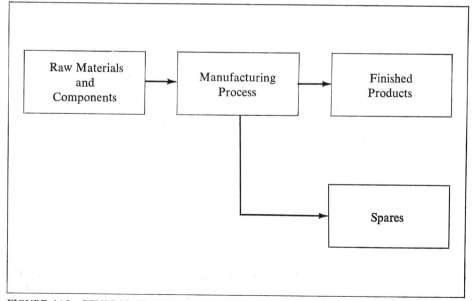

FIGURE 14.8  GENERAL FLOW OF PRODUCTION

rial item is common to numerous end products sold, it should be considered as an independent demand item. Spare items may fall into either dependent or independent categories and must be studied to determine which category best fits. During early years of end product life, demand for spares is dependent on end item sales. As time goes by, this correlation will decrease, and demand will tend to become independent of end product sales (which may in fact cease).

Independent demand systems have been the most traditional in industry and are based on the techniques of economic ordering quantity rules (EOQ) and order point action criteria. Various approaches are used for safety stock determination. To predict annual usage rates, various forecasting techniques can be used at all levels of raw material and subassembly. As the name implies, each item in such systems is treated independently. Generically, independent demand systems are referred to as *reorder point* (ROP) *systems*.

**Material Requirements Planning.** Dependent demand systems have been developed during the past decade and are known as *material requirements planning* (MRP) systems. Due to some overselling on the part of the profession and the computer community, MRP has become synonymous with inventory management in some quarters, and is looked upon as a panacea for manufacturing management.

MRP is actually nothing more than a new tool to be included in the inventory management kit. Experience has shown that it is not universally applicable or appropriate. Many firms have been disappointed by the performance of MRP because they failed to recognize that good systems analysis and sound judgment are still required to structure an inventory management system for a particular company.

MRP is designed around the concept of independent demand relationships that exist between low level components, raw materials and subassemblies, and their respective top level finished products. MRP is primarily applicable to an assembled product manufacturer. A typical bill of materials for Product A might consist of two subassemblies, B and C, and parts W, X, Y, and Z. Two parts Z are required in one subassembly C and thereby in each end product A. The demand for and usage of Z is dependent on the demand for and sales of A. However, should Z be used in several other end products, this dependency relationship diminishes; usage of Z may be independent of sales of A or any other single end product. For common usage parts having independent demand relationships, historical usage data may be more practical to forecast future demand plan requirements.

*The MRP process.* An MRP system is a set of logically linked procedures, decision rules, and records that translates the master production schedule into time-phased net requirements and planned coverage for each component inventory item needed to meet the schedule. During the planned coverage process, such a system allocates existing on-hand quantities to item gross requirements and reevaluates the timing of open orders relative to net requirements. To cover net requirements, the system calculates the level-by-level gross-to-net requirements and offsets component requirements by the manufacturing lead time required to meet the master production schedule. It then establishes a schedule of planned orders for each item and signals the need for rescheduling orders to realign coverage with net requirements. The minimum data requirements for operating MRP are:

- An end item master schedule (based on forecast, backlog);
- Product structure files; and
- Item master files (including availability data).

The MRP process consists of these basic steps:

- Determine gross item requirements by time period for end products, options, and service parts.
- Calculate net requirements by subtracting available inventory (e.g., on hand plus on order minus safety stock minus allocated quantities to released orders).
- Determine the order or lot size (fixed order quantity, economic order quantity, fixed period requirements, parts period balancing, etc.).
- Explode the quantity of planned orders through the bill of materials to determine lower level requirements.
- Offset lower level requirements by the production lead time needed to manufacture and assemble the order by the due date.

This description of MRP is vastly oversimplified; such a system is not easily designed and installed. Significant computer power is required, and the software is the most complex of any business data processing application. The relatively few successful installations of MRP attest to this.

**Choosing the Appropriate System.** Both the MRP and ROP systems have their place in inventory management systems. The system design decisions must be related to at least three primary factors:

1. The complexity of the product structure;
2. The degree to which parts are common to many end products; and
3. The nature of the manufacturing process and the business as a whole.

Generally speaking, MRP should be applied to the more complex assembled products with multilevel bills of materials. It is equally applicable to process industries in which the product has complex formulations or recipes with multilevel structuring. If, however, many parts or materials are common in either of these cases, statistically based independent demand systems may work. Both techniques may be quite appropriate within the same company. The system chosen should be related to the nature and usage characteristics of the parts involved.

With respect to the distribution or warehousing business, MRP is generally not appropriate. Such businesses have no assembly operations, no bills of materials, and therefore no dependent demand relationships within the product structure.

**Complexity of Decision-Making.** The payoff in good inventory systems results from the decision rules used to determine when to reorder, how much to order, how to predict shortages and excesses, and how to achieve desired service levels. A few words regarding the complexity of these issues is appropriate. Figure 14.9 is a classic "sawtooth" diagram used to depict inventory item activity. The quantity shown on the x-axis is the available inventory; it consists of on hand plus on order commitments. The slope of the line represents usage or demand rate. The reorder point quantity is that point along the demand line at which ordering action is to take place. The amount ordered (order quantity) is intended to bring stock levels back up to some acceptable level or maximum. The amount below the horizontal line is safety stock—that amount of inventory required to absorb unplanned fluctuations in demand rate. The time period between reorder and recipt of replenishment stock is the lead time.

Figure 14.9 gives the impression of a very orderly sequence of events and actions that manage stock levels and activity. The truth of the matter is portrayed in Figure 14.10. There are several variables simultaneously at work that must be recognized in designing a system to cope with reality. Lead time will vary from order to order. Demand rates will vary or will actually be a step function rather than a linear function. Order quantities can be varied due to availability or price break advantages. For an effective reorder point-based system, frequent monitoring is required to adjust for changing conditions of these variables. Design and testing using live company data are required to determine the best combination of tools for the circumstances. Space does not permit full development of the specifics of the several techniques available for inventory decision rules on when and how much to order or how much safety stock to maintain. Several of the reference texts shown in the Suggested Reading cover these topics in detail.

**The Computer's Role.** The computer is a powerful tool that can be used to assist the planning process. With the advent of inexpensive minicomputers, substantial

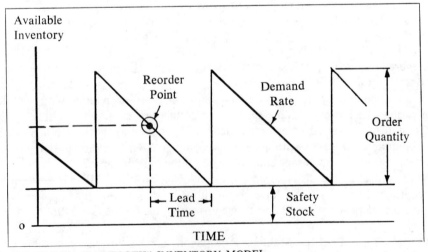

FIGURE 14.9 "SAWTOOTH" INVENTORY MODEL

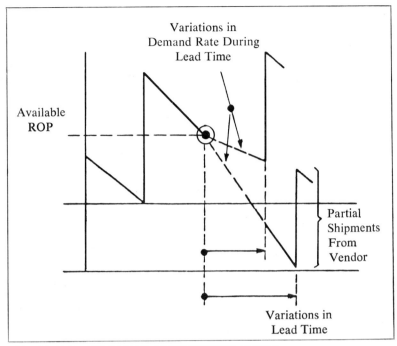

FIGURE 14.10   VARIABLES IN INVENTORY MODEL

computing power is now available at a very reasonable cost. In the past decade, major advances have been made in application software; this power is now available to most small manufacturers. High quality MRP software is within reach of most companies with sales of over $5 million annually.

In certain environments, however, the computer is not essential. In stable or make-to-order environments with relatively few product variables, it is not uncommon to do the forecasting and master planning work manually. Inputs to the MRP system are keypunched from manually prepared worksheets or reports.

The computer is valuable in that it can simulate the effect of various situations on the inventory status of a company. Alternative strategies can be developed for varying demand patterns. This "what if" capability is a powerful planning tool.

## INVENTORY CONTROL

In the discussion of inventory planning, the functional area of inventory control was defined as "records management and physical control of raw materials, components, and finished goods. . . ." The physical control side of this division deals with control of materials while they are in the plant or warehouse. The records management side is much broader in scope and is one of the most critical and complex segments of a sound inventory management system.

Inventory control can be divided into three sections:

- Physical controls;
- Record accuracy; and
- Inventory shrinkage control.

## Physical Controls

Good management of material movement starts with a well-organized and disciplined stockroom and warehouse. Storage facilities should be secured with locks, and access should be limited to personnel who have reason to be there. Without such security, movement of materials without proper documentation in or out will sometimes occur. This major source of shrinkage will be discussed more fully later in this chapter.

**Warehousing Practices.** Management can take several approaches toward organizing a storage facility. Selecting the best system for its products can result in reduced handling and storage cost, less damage to products, and less shrinkage and obsolescence.

*Organization techniques.* Arranging products in sequence by part number is a common approach. This is the easiest way to locate a part. However, unless the firm has stable usage and replenishment levels, the sequential organization is generally the most inefficient use of space. Space must be provided to accommodate the maximum amount of each item to be stored. A portion of that space will generally be vacant. Should space run out in the primary location, a remote location will have to be selected, thereby destroying the integrity of the sequential system and mandating extra record-keeping. This approach will work adequately if a disciplined, computerized locator system is available to control the overflow quantities.

*Random storage,* as the name suggests, is the opposite of the sequential approach. It results in the most effective use of space, since the next available and closest spot is selected for whatever material is at hand. This system requires a computerized locator system and a look-up capability by part number.

*Important considerations.* The following important procedures should be part of storage facility design and layout:

- Locate fastest moving parts near the front of the storage area to minimize picking time.
- Store materials in product line or assembly groupings.
- Use cubic space by storing as high as possible.
- Standardize container size and characteristics. Often, significant efficiencies can be achieved by working closely with vendors to design their packaging to make it compatible with the firm's storage system.
- Code parts that require special handling.

The practice of placing components and materials required for a specific assembly in a common container in the stockroom prior to release to the production floor is called *kitting*. If used judiciously, this practice can be an important aid to efficient production; if misused, the financial and operational consequences are significant. If kits are picked more than a week before scheduled release, a significant amount of inventory is taken out of available stock. Replenishment action is thereby triggered, and inventory investment skyrockets.

If kits are left in the stockroom for any period of time, stockroom personnel will tend to "borrow" parts from these kits to fill other demands for those parts. Although they fully intend to replace the borrowed parts, they forget or lose track of what they have done. This results in inventory records that are inaccurate, production that cannot proceed once the kit is issued, and planning work done to schedule the plant that has been wasted. Inventory is up, production performance down, and customer service misses target.

**Importance of Physical Security.** A locked storeroom not only prevents pilferage but permits the data base to be accurately informed as to material movement and status. Stockroom personnel cannot be held accountable unless they have authority to carry out their jobs. Perpetual inventory records are the basis of many critical decisions, so the prime responsibility of the storeroom is to ensure record accuracy, not to issue and put away parts. To achieve accuracy, there must be some way to measure it. It should be possible to state that a set of inventory records is, for example, 95, 98.2, or 98.8 percent accurate based on a sample or series of samples of cycle counts versus record balances. *Cycle counting,* as described below, is the only effective way to verify the condition of the inventory records and thereby measure their accuracy.

Bonus programs help to ensure the security of the stockroom and the validity of the data. The cycle counts are often performed by independent personnel, and a bonus is paid to storekeepers if record accuracy is maintained above 95 percent, for example. Personnel in a bonus program usually make it extremely difficult to effect a physical movement without a corresponding transaction—which is what perpetual inventory records are all about.

**Physical Inventory Versus Cycle Counting.** Inventory records serve two main purposes: they state the correct value of a significant segment of a firm's assets, and they provide information for production control decisions. Thus, both financial and physical control needs must be fulfilled by an inventory system. Because top management is often more concerned with periodic reporting of the asset valuation, emphasis is usually on the dollar value of inventory. The results of a physical inventory are, therefore, anxiously awaited so that dollar adjustments and write-offs can be made. One corporation with $25 million in inventory was very pleased when the physical inventory showed a net variation of only $40,000 (.16 percent) from the book value. It was later disclosed that this included compensating errors between two of the manufacturing units of almost $1 million. Financial control is impossible without disciplined systems which guarantee a reasonable inventory accuracy.

*Physical inventory drawbacks.* Inaccurate inventory data wastes the time of managers and employees; moreover, it wastes the physical assets, computer programs, and systems dedicated to inventory control. The cost of taking physical inventories, the agonizing reconciliation process, the lost production and lost sales if operations are halted for the physical count, prompt management to take inventory as infrequently as possible. The annual physical inventory is often described as the single most disruptive and expensive event of the year, annual fiscal Russian roulette, and a once-a-year chance to foul up more inventory records than have been fouled up during the entire year.

*Benefits of cycle counting.* Cycle counting is an alternative to the annual physical inventory. While cycle counting requires more frequent adjustment of the inventory records to keep them current—thereby avoiding the end-of-the-month or -year crunch—its primary purpose is to identify causes of transaction errors. All the time spent in adjusting incorrect balances is wasted if errors recur day after day and the causes remain unidentified and uncorrected. Cycle counting is thus not just an alternative to the annual physical inventory. If it were, auditors would still insist on a physical check for preparation of financial statements.

Cycle counting is a program to: (1) identify causes of errors, (2) assist in preventing them from recurring, (3) measure the inventory accuracy, and (4) assist in the maintenance of the highest possible level of accuracy. In addition, cycle counting detects discrepancies, determines the performance of stockroom personnel, validates the inventory for financial reporting, and maintains the level of accuracy required for MRP systems and purchasing and production control decisions.

The specific benefits of cycle counting and the valid inventory data resulting from it are listed below:

- No annual physical;
- No annual shutdown of manufacturing, shipping, or receiving;
- No year-end write-offs and few surprises;
- Less work-in-process inventory;
- Few shortages;
- Less obsolete inventory;
- Lower safety stocks;
- Accurate stock status reports;
- Flexible auditing (frequency can depend on item activity);
- Flexible accuracy standards depending on the time (ABC);
- Valid MRP output reports;
- Valid reorder and expediting notices;
- Fewer experienced stockroom specialists needed; and
- Improved vendor and shop relationships.

An excellent article on cycle counting by John G. Carlson is cited in the Suggested Reading.

## Record Accuracy

The success of a manufacturing control system depends on management's commitment to inventory record accuracy. Accuracy of inventory records determines the effectiveness of a reorder point system or a material requirements planning (MRP) system. Of the three major elements of an MRP system—the master schedule, bills of material, and inventory status—none has as much opportunity to cause errors as the inventory status, because of the frequency of transactions involved.

Data input is the key for maintaining the validity of perpetual inventory records. On-line editing permits detection of most errors as they occur. Check digit routines, hash totals, range checks, and other tests of reasonableness, together with user-oriented feedback and exception information, can prevent input errors. User-controlled data input also contributes significantly to the accuracy of data. The user is more aware of the consequences of incorrect data and assumes more responsibility for the integrity of inventory balances, the reports, and the decisions based on them. User-oriented, interactive approaches have contributed markedly to both self-discipline and organizational discipline in creating legible, accurate, and complete source documents, as well as more understandable, effective, and valid reports.

**Engineering and Product Data Control.** Information that describes the product and the manufacturing processes is created, organized, and maintained within the scope of the engineering and product data control system. This information is used throughout the organization and is the base for several systems: inventory planning and control, production order release and scheduling, shop floor control, cost and performance reporting, purchasing, and the like. Deficiencies in either the accuracy or the completeness of this information will affect most other functional areas.

Engineering and product data control deals with the following files, records, and subsystems:

- Item master file;
- Product structure file (bill of material);
- Where-used file;
- Routing file;
- Work center file;
- Part numbering system;
- Engineering change control system; and
- Drawing control system.

The principal responsibility for these files and systems lies with product and manufacturing engineering groups; however, certain records and data must be provided by other departments. A more complete discussion of these responsibilities appears later in this section.

**Problems and Shortcomings.** Perhaps the most significant shortcoming of most systems is the lack of consistency and control over the assignment of part numbers. Several common problems represent major bottlenecks to the successful operation of all other manufacturing control systems:

- Part numbers are assigned inconsistently as to number of digits used and significance of grouped digits. This is most probably an outgrowth of new product lines, added over the years as new businesses were acquired. System changes were not well controlled.

- Sales branches assign new numbers to parts that bear no relationship to engineering part number and that vary from branch to branch.

- Raw materials have no part numbers.

- Parts purchased incomplete (lacking final manufacturing operations) carry the same part number as the finished parts.

- Certain part numbers are related to a particular customer even though they may be used on multiple customers' products.

- International part numbers are different from domestic part numbers.

Within the engineering department, the numbering system usually functions adequately. The changes developed over the years, however, have had dramatic impact on systems areas outside engineering.

In some companies, bills of material are an integral part of assembly and piece part drawings. Many of these drawings contain the name of a particular customer for whom the product was initially designed, even though the product has subsequently been sold to other customers. This is an inflexible system and makes change control and bill of material maintenance cumbersome and costly. As a result, bill of material data is often inaccurate or out of date. This is, of course, a difficult situation regarding both material planning and cost control, since the interpretation of material and production needs requires the exercise of a high degree of judgment at lower levels in the organization.

Some companies develop special products for a particular customer. These often involve only minor modifications to products previously engineered and produced for another customer. If information on where a particular part is used is not readily available, the engineer has difficulty determining if a product similar to the one requested already exists in the system or cannot determine to what extent a contemplated design change will impact other products or parts.

**Major Design Considerations.** The following summarizes what are considered the major design considerations:

- Item Master File. The item master file contains many records used to describe the product and its characteristics. The responsibility for maintaining this data will vary, based on the nature of the information. This responsibility must be clearly defined and is illustrated in Figure 14.11.

- A major data element in the item master file is where-used information. Access to this data is essential to the engineering group as part of their design of custom products and modification of existing components. It is also critical to maintaining the integrity of product cost data. Consideration may be given to maintaining where-used data on a separate file.

- Product Structure. The development and maintenance of the Product Structure File is principally the responsibility of the design engineering department. Inputs may also be provided by inventory control (issue methods, units of measure) and methods engineering (routing operation used-on) if those elements are a part of this file. The major outputs that must be considered in the design of this file and the system for its maintenance and use include cost implosions, indented bills of material, parts lists, picking lists, and bill of material explosions used for material planning and component scheduling.

- Routing File. The routing file should contain a description of the manufacturing process for each manufactured item, in terms of both sequence and location of operations performed and detailed descriptions of the operation. Alternative routings should also be included. Scheduling and loading and detail cost summarization are dependent on the availability of a ranking with attendant current lead times and cost elements.

- Part Numbering System. A single uniform part numbering system should be developed and utilized in all operations. The structure of the part number should be standardized as to length and significance of certain digits. The use of significant digits should be kept to a minimum so as not to restrict the flexibility of the system.

| Record or data element | Responsibility of |
| --- | --- |
| Product description | Product engineering |
| Ordering factors | Inventory control/purchasing |
| Purchase lead time | Purchasing |
| Manufacturing lead time | Production control |
| Inventory status | Computer processing* |
| Requirements summary | Computer processing |
| Stock status | Inventory control/computer processing |
| Engineering specifications | Product engineering |
| Cost (standard and actual) | Cost/computer processing |
| Price | Marketing/cost/computer processing |
| Order status | Computer processing |
| Production planning factors | Production control |
| Where used | Product engineering |

* Indicates that these records are created and maintained through processing transactions within the system, and that the results are to be automatically recorded in these records.

FIGURE 14.11 RESPONSIBILITY FOR MAINTAINING MASTER FILE DATA

To the extent that certain digits have significant meaning, the risk of running out of numbers is increased.

- Engineering Change Control. The principal concern in the area of engineering change control is that: (1) the impact of a change is recoded and evaluated before it is implemented, and (2) that when implemented, all affected product and cost records are properly adjusted. The change process should include the following actions:

  - When a design change is contemplated, determine what other products are affected by the change;
  - Based on form-fit-function criteria, determine whether change can be made to all products;
  - Determine impact on inventory based on current available balance and estimate resultant obsolescence cost; and
  - If change is to be implemented, determine the effectivity of the change. This may be based on specified data, immediate, at inventory run-out point, or at the convenience of purchasing or manufacturing.

  Engineering or product data changes can result from changes other than in product design. A manufacturing method may change which affects cost. Essentially, the same checklist for change control must be completed.

- Drawing Control. The bill of material should not be an integral part of the product drawing. The bills of material should be maintained and produced by computer. There is no advantage to integrating them on the drawing, and there are significant disadvantages involving substantial cost if they are integrated. The most obvious advantage is in changes to the bill of material that can be made without the need to revise all affected drawings.

**Bill of Material System Design Checklist.** A sound BOM system has been defined as a system that ". . . provides for the appropriate organization of all data defining the product in one central (computer-based) filing system with necessary supporting manual files stressing minimal redundancy, and for the retrieval and reporting of multiple, diverse user requirements."

The following design criteria should be considered when undertaking the BOM data base design task. The system should:

- Facilitate new product definition and introduction;
- Be useful for product standardization and group technology purposes;
- Lend itself to forecasting of optional or variable product features (for the sake of MRP);
- Permit the master schedule to include the fewest possible end items;
- Allow easy identification of obsolete and low interchangeability items;
- Enhance the possibilities of economic change to the product to be carried out;
- Permit easy order entry in terms of model and feature numbers and be able to translate the entry data into BOM numbers for MRP;
- Allow efficient maintenance and storage for users, programming personnel, and computers;
- Provide the basis for cost control;

- Be usable for purposes of final assembly scheduling;
- Allow planning of subassembly and component part priorities; and
- Provide means for easy recognition of errors and timely corrective action.

### Inventory Shrinkage Control

Inventory shrinkage signals a weakness in inventory controls or a breakdown in the inventory accounting system. Determining the cause of inventory shrinkage and defining remedial actions is a formidable task and can require substantial resources. Appendix 14-1 is a questionnaire that assists in structuring an investigation and plotting the results of the study. This questionnaire provides a logical approach to identifying the causes of an inventory shrinkage problem and will be useful to those wishing to undertake a review of their inventory control system. The questionnaire is broad in nature and is designed to serve a number of industry environments. This broad scope precludes a finite quantification of reasonable or acceptable shrinkage within a given environment.

## INVENTORY PERFORMANCE MEASUREMENTS

An effective management system requires a "closed loop." Reporting of performance against prescribed goals and objectives closes the loop and permits continuous fine tuning or refinement not only of the daily decisions made regarding operations, but also of the system itself.

### Inventory Policies and Goals

A principal objective of an inventory management system is to provide both a method and the data by which to measure performance with respect to inventories. Performance measurement requires a "standard" or "yardstick" as a basis for measurement, and this requirement translates into the need for inventory policies and specific, quantifiable goals.

Inventory policy statements should emanate from executive management and should provide the guidelines for operating managers responsible for planning, procurement, distribution, and maintenance of inventories at all levels and at all locations. These policies should be formally documented and reviewed annually to determine if refinement or additions are necessary. Inventory policies should address the following tasks:

- Identify the classes of inventory for which inventory should be maintained (make-to-stock versus make-to-order);
- Define the level of investment desired, for each class, expressed in number of months' supply;

- Define the classes and levels of inventory to be maintained at branch warehouses and the criteria for performance measurement at each;
- Define the levels of service to be provided from inventory, relating both to material and components required by the production organization (stock-out performance) and to finished products required by the customer (customer service);
- Define the general methodology related to the valuation of inventory and the treatment of variances from standard;
- Define obsolescence criteria and control strategy;
- Define guidelines for control and disposition of obsolete and slow-moving inventory;
- Define the classes of inventory, including the accounting and physical separations of:
  - Raw material,
  - Component parts,
  - Work-in-process,
  - Finished goods,
  - Branch inventories by location,
  - Classifications related to value or customer (A, B, C, etc.); and
- Define organizational accountability for each segment of the inventory so there is no question as to who is responsible for meeting inventory performance goals.

The specific goals related to these policies often require a significant amount of analysis for quantifying. If inventory accounting data is not segmented and available in the level of detail required, it may take six to eighteen months to refine performance measurement yardsticks. Each manager should be responsible for setting his own targets, and the executive committee will have to judge the reasonableness of the initial figures.

Performance measurement should be based on *on-hand inventory*, not *available inventory* (net of allocations or reservations). The objective is to measure and control inventory investment (the asset), and as long as inventory is in a plant or warehouse and owned by the company, it is an asset. The on-hand balance is a better measure of investment than available balance. To exclude reserved stock still physically on the premises is to limit management's ability to control the inventory asset.

## Inventory Ratios

Ratios are one of the most commonly used management control tools for goal setting, trend monitoring, and performance measurement. They are easy to compute; they graph nicely; and they represent a common language among divisions, groups, and departments. Ratios put large and small groups on a common basis; the fact that ratios are nonaccounting-oriented rids them of the bookkeeper's stigma.

On the other hand, ratios are frequently misused because they are misunderstood. Because they appear conceptually simple, the reader does not concern himself with the elements that make up the ratio. Yet, management can learn a great deal through understanding the elements and their characteristics, and by using the ratios to draw operating conclusions.

This section illustrates how a simple ratio such as inventory turnover can be calculated in no less than eight different ways, using essentially the same financial data.

**Inventory Turnover, a Basic Ratio.** To the warehouse manager, *inventory turnover* is an expression of how many times per year a warehouseful of inventory is physically moved in and out. Mathematically, it is expressed as a ratio between sales (at cost) and average inventory investment. Both are correct and both have their place. The accepted formula is:

$$\frac{\text{Cost of Sales}}{\text{Average Inventory}} = \text{Inventory Turnover or "Turns"}$$

Why use *cost of sales* instead of *sales*? Sales for a given number of units of product over a period of time varies depending on discount practices, commissions, returns and allowances, and so on. The standard cost of those same products, however, does not vary. Sales volume, for purposes of expressing how much product flowed through the warehouse, is therefore best expressed in terms of the standard cost of those products sold. This volume of sales activity can then be compared to the value of inventory, also expressed at standard cost value, normally found in the warehouse. The formula, more completely stated, is:

$$\frac{\text{Annual Cost of Sales (at Standard)}}{\text{Average Inventory Cost (at Standard)}}$$

Other factors are occasionally used to compute the turnover rates appearing in business publications and technical papers. *Sales* can be expressed as gross sales, net sales, sales at standard cost, or sales at actual cost. Industrywide studies, such as those published by Dun & Bradstreet, usually use net sales because that is the only sales figure available on published financial statements. Cost of sales at standard is not generally shown on these statements.

**Why Ratios Are Erratic.** The simplified illustration that follows will set the stage for further discussion of inventory ratios:

### Different Cost Figures

| | |
|---|---|
| Gross sales | $120 |
| Net sales | $100 |
| Actual cost of sales | $ 85 |
| Standard cost of sales @ 80% of sales: | |
| Using $100 | $ 80 |
| Using $120 | $ 96 |
| Average inventory | $ 20 |

Some companies do not compute standard cost of sales, and turnover is computed using actual cost figures. From the above, the computation would be:

$$\frac{\$85}{\$20} = 4.25 \text{ turns}$$

If cost of sales is computed as a percent of sales, it is possible from the above to compute two additional turnover figures, using $80 and $96 as cost of sales figures:

$$\frac{\$80}{\$20} = 4.00 \text{ turns}$$

$$\frac{\$96}{\$20} = 4.80 \text{ turns}$$

The other element of the formula, *average inventory*, can be just as difficult a number to agree upon. Generally, an annual average is used. If the year being analyzed has been completed, inventory could be computed by taking the average of the beginning and ending inventory levels for the year or by averaging the monthly averages throughout the year. It could also be an average of month-end figures. Or it could simply be the year-end balance, assuming it typified the year. If midyear and month-end or year-to-date figures are being annualized, even more erratic numbers can be calculated.

*Different Inventory Figures*

| | |
|---|---|
| Beginning inventory | $18 |
| Ending inventory | $20 |
| Annual average based on actual monthly average balances | $22 |

Selection of beginning, ending, or average inventory will yield three different ratios, as shown below:

$$\frac{\$80}{\$18} = 4.4 \text{ turns}$$

$$\frac{\$80}{\$20} = 4.0 \text{ turns}$$

$$\frac{\$80}{\$22} = 3.6 \text{ turns}$$

These examples merely suggest the numerous ways to express the elements of the inventory turnover ratio. Further exploration should prove interesting and should provide some insight as to how best to present and use these ratios.

**Playing by Various Rules.** With respect to inventory ratios, the following hypothetical financial data illustrate the "bookkeeping games people can play."

*Case A—inventory responsibility.* Overall ratios are as dangerous as averages. They hide a great deal that may be significant. Often, responsibility for the various segments of inventory—raw material, work-in-process, and finished goods—is divided organizationally, and an inventory turnover ratio that combines all three is of questionable value. No one is accountable for total performance; management action cannot therefore be properly directed. The ratio analysis and performance reporting must be structured according to at least two criteria: (1) inventory accountability (organization), and (2) availability of data from the accounting system.

The second criterion reflects the fact that not all companies account for inventories in the same manner. Companies with high throughput rates or low work-in-process often recognize only raw material and finished goods. Nonmanufacturing companies have only finished goods. Notice how turn rates vary when dealing with selected segments of the inventory:

$$\text{Overall turn: } \frac{\$80}{\$20} = \qquad\qquad 4.0$$

$$\text{Finished goods turn: } \frac{\$80}{\$\,7} = \qquad\qquad 11.4$$

Raw material turn:

$$\frac{\$80 \times (\% \text{ of Material in Product})}{\$10}$$

$$\text{Turn: } \frac{\$80 \times 50\%}{\$10} = \qquad\qquad 4.0$$

In some companies, marketing is accountable for finished goods inventory. Note the significant difference in the turnover rates illustrated above. In this case, if management decided that raw material performance should be improved sharply, say, to 100 percent, note how the impact of such an adjustment is softened when combined into the total turnover computation.

| | |
|---|---|
| Reduced raw material to | $ 5 |
| Work-in-process | 3 |
| Finished goods | 7 |
| Adjusted total | $15 |

$$\text{Turn: } \frac{\$80}{\$15} = 5.33\text{—only 30\% higher than above}$$

This comparision suggests a rule for clarity and consistency: pinpoint inventory responsibility and structure the ratio analysis and reporting accordingly.

*Case B—bookkeeping method.* The financial reporting practices and methodol-ogy, in addition to basic segmentation illustrated above, will cause changes in the turn numbers. Consider a situation in which the accounting department, for the sake of simplicity in reporting to management, has decided to summarize certain inventory account details, such as supplies and reserves for obsolescence, before computing operating ratios or before preparing management-level operating state-ments. The total inventory remains consistent with "the books," but the makeup is distorted, as shown below.

|                  | *Was* | *Is*       |
|------------------|-------|------------|
| Raw material     | $10   | $ 9        |
| Work-in-process  | 3     | 3    } = 22 |
| Finished goods   | 7     | 10         |
| Supplies         | —     | 1          |
| Reserves         | —     | (3)        |
|                  | $20   | $20        |

It appears that $1 of the $10 raw material is actually manufacturing supplies and that $3 is a reserve for obsolescence against finished goods. On this basis, one could argue that real inventory value is $22 and that turnover is 3.64, not 4.0.

$$\text{Turn: } \frac{\$80}{\$22} = 3.64$$

The method of cost accounting can also change cost of sales. Direct costing, where only the variable portion of product cost is included in cost of sales, yields a lower figure than absorption costing, where all factory-related costs (both fixed and variable) are included in cost of sales.

|                       |      |
|-----------------------|------|
| Direct material       | $40  |
| Direct labor          | 20   |
| Total direct cost     | $60  |

|                         |      |
|-------------------------|------|
| Fixed manufacturing cost | 20  |
| Total cost of sales     | $80  |

$$\text{Turn: } \frac{\$60}{\$20} = 3.0, \text{ not } 4.0$$

If only direct cost of sales were used to compute turnover, a sharp change in the ratio would result. A further refinement of direct costing often used is inclusion of the variable portion of factory overhead costs in cost of sales. If this were the case, the ratio would fall somewhere between 3.0 and 4.0.

With regard to accounting treatment, management must also be aware of inventory revaluation (cost standard adjustments and physical adjustments) which can influence turn statistics. The accounting method, as it relates to cost accounting data versus general ledger (balance sheet) data, can distort ratio reporting.

*Case C—product lines.* If significant product line differences exist, or company management is product line oriented, additional stratification may be necessary and desirable. One difficulty with this is that a significant portion of raw materials is common to more than one product line. Computation of turns by product line for raw material may be impractical, or at best, arbitrary, because portions of the total raw material inventory would have to be assigned or allocated to product line categories on a basis that is itself arbitrary.

A practical solution to this dilemma is to control raw material as a total and to monitor finished goods by product line. Work-in-process should be handled on the ease of segregation by product line. In the example below, it is handled as raw material and is not segregated.

|  | *Total* | *Product A* | *Product B* |
|---|---|---|---|
| Raw material | $10 | — | — |
| Work-in-process | 3 | — | — |
| Finished goods | 7 | 4 | 3 |
|  | $20 | | |

To compute turns, cost of sales must also be broken down by product line. Product line management should set turnover goals based on the characteristics of the markets served. Response time, service levels, and standard products versus specials are some considerations. Note how the computation of turnover by product line can dramatically change the finished goods turnover ratio from a composite of 11.4, shown in Case A, to the figures below.

| Cost of sales: Product line A | $30 |
|---|---|
| Product line B | 50 |
|  | $80 |

$$\text{Finished goods turn (A)} = \frac{\$30}{\$ 4} = 7.5$$

$$\text{Finished goods turn (B)} = \frac{\$50}{\$ 3} = 16.5$$

If ratios are thus product oriented, line management must understand the differences between product lines and how raw materials and work-in-process are handled.

*Case D—multiple locations.* Closely related to the example above, as it pertains to finished goods inventory management, is the situation that can arise in a multiwarehouse environment. Warehouse managers usually have inventory responsibility, and it is important to set attainable and realistic goals for turn at each location. Assure that the cost of sales used in the turn computation relates properly to the goods moving through the subject warehouse. If a significant portion of the merchandise sold is drop-shipped from the factory and never appears as part of the warehouse inventory, the turn figures computed for that warehouse may be misleading. A comparable warehouse with the same cost of sales base but no drop-shipment activity will have a much higher inventory and will appear to be doing a poorer job. Plant warehouse location and distribution strategy can have a significant impact on apparent turnover performance. Across-the-board turn goals are dangerous. Proper use of ratios for field warehouse management will require analysis of the distribution strategy related to each.

*Case E—annualized data.* Perhaps the most dramatic distortions of turnover data occur when midyear cost data is annualized to provide a basis for comparison to average inventory. Monthly and fiscal year time intervals are really quite arbitrary and are primarily for the convenience of the outside accountants. They should not be permitted to distort the data.

If monthly data is annualized, the following may have had an effect on those figures: seasonality, a four-week or five-week month, 18 to 25 work days per month, holidays, demand fluctuations, and strikes. Computing an annualized cost of sales using any one month's cost of sales figures can result in distortions of turnover rates of several hundred percent. Instead, when computing an annual cost of sales figure, use one of the following:

- Year-end (full year actual) total;
- Rolling average of at least six months; or
- Year-to-date cumulative average, annualized (at least three months—ignore fiscal year).

**Managing Through Ratios.** Let us summarize the conclusions that have been drawn. Several steps may be necessary to improve the usefulness and accuracy of inventory ratios. Depending on how "tuned in" management has been to this subject over the years, a fair amount of education may be necessary.

In order to be able to use ratios to manage inventories, sound and acceptable ratios must be developed. Consider the following approach:

- Profile the inventory and define each manageable segment: natural inventory groupings, product lines, warehouse locations, organization accountability.
- Interview key managers about how they use ratios and about other data they might find helpful. To make this meaningful, some education may be required in this area.
- Develop a recommendation to incorporate changes that appear significant, accompanied by a plan for their implementation. This may include training sessions at various levels in the sales, warehousing, and general management areas.

Managing better by using ratios is a function of several considerations. Is the controller creative and operations oriented? Is he empathetic to line management needs? Is inventory accountability clearly stated and understood? Is it clear enough that inventory performance is tied to personal income? Is line management capable of understanding and using ratio data effectively in its day-to-day decision making?

## Reporting Considerations

The following major objectives should guide the development of operating and financial reporting and control systems:

- The system should provide appropriate inventory and operating costs in a reporting scheme to help management control operating results:
  - By responsible manager or cost center,
  - By cost type—material, labor, and overhead,
  - By product line,
  - By salesman or territory,
  - By job,
  - By marketing channel,
  - Compared with standard costs, and
  - Compared with planned costs.
- The system should provide for the development of special cost analyses needed for operating decisions, such as:
  - Standard gross margins by product to be used in marketing strategy,
  - Cost center/machine cost profiles for improved estimating and pricing,
  - Fixed and variable cost profiles for incremental cost analysis, and
  - Scrap and yield loss cost information.
- The system should provide for transactions and costs required to properly record profit and loss performance and inventory valuation.
- The system should be fully integrated (common source data and processing linkage) with the appropriate operating and financial systems.
- All information provided by the system must be timely and accurate.

The major factors to consider in defining the cost and inventory control reporting systems are the following:

- Cost profile. Using recent financial data, develop the overall manufacturing cost mix:

| Item | % |
|---|---|
| Direct materials | ? |
| Direct labor | ? |
| Manufacturing overhead | ? |
| Total manufacturing costs | 100.0% |

  The control system must reflect the significance of each cost element.
- Number of products. How many major product lines are there? Is there a large variety of configurations and sizes within each line? How many active part numbers are there?
- Product complexity. Product complexity may vary by product line. What is the number of component parts per product?
- Manufacturing process. How many manufacturing steps are there and how many related inventory control points?
- Lot sizes. Order sizes may vary from small quantities of less than ten to large orders of over 100,000 units. This requires a manufacturing operation geared both to small-run, job-shop type work as well as continuous production high-volume work, accompanied by an inventory system to support each.
- Manufacturing cycle time. What is the lead time from initial stock requisitioning to shipment?
- Cost of data collection versus value of data collected. The amount of control gained over operations is the major decision factor in this design consideration.

## SUGGESTED READING

*APICS Dictionary of Production and Inventory Control Terms*, Washington, D.C.: American Production and Inventory Control Society (APICS), 1980.

*Bibliography of Articles and Books, Production and Inventory Control and Regulated Topics, 1974-1978*, 6th ed. Washington, D.C.: APICS, 1979.

Bonsack, Robert A., "Computerized Manufacturing Planning and Control Systems." New York: Auerback Publishers, Inc., 1975.

Carlson, John G., and Gilman, Richard, "Inventory Decision Systems: Cycle Counting." *Journal of Purchasing and Materials Management* (Winter, 1978).

Donovan, Michael R., and King, Stephen, "Are You Ready for M.R.P.?" *Management Review* (October, 1977).

*National Conference Proceedings*, (annual publication of APICS), Washington, D.C.

*Production and Inventory Management* (a quarterly journal of the American Production and Inventory Control Society), Washington, D.C.

## APPENDIX 14-1  INVENTORY SHRINKAGE ANALYSIS QUESTIONNAIRE

REPORTING UNIT _____

DATE COMPLETED _____

COMPLETED BY _____

The general checklist provides a list of possible causes for shrinkage. Using this approach to determine causes of shrinkage may be the most expedient type of survey to "narrow in" on the most likely causes. By its very nature, a general checklist does not result in a uniform response. The disadvantages may be mitigated to some extent if example control procedures or reports are provided for each possible cause.

| Inventory Category | Possible Causes | Responses | | |
|---|---|---|---|---|
| | | Not Applicable | Possible Problem | Reference Procedure and Comments |
| Raw Material | • Incorrect raw material standards on bills of material which identify material other than the material actually used. | | | |
| | • Failure to consider the effects of raw material tolerances when applying standard costs. For example, the standard weight of a given part blanked from a certain gauge of steel coil may be less than the actual part weighs, resulting in fewer pieces actually produced than was theoretically planned and priced into inventory. | | | |
| | • Failure to allow for kerf loss when sawing material—again, resulting in fewer pieces produced than planned. | | | |
| | • Inaccurate or forgotten drop-off allowances placing more material dollars into inventory than the worth of parts actually produced. | | | |
| | • Unreported substitutions of gauge or grade of material resulting in consumption of more expensive material than standards called for. | | | |
| | • The unit of purchase (feet) differs with unit of use (piece) and cost standards are not consistent with the physical usage. | | | |

REPORTING UNIT _____

DATE COMPLETED _____

COMPLETED BY _____

| Inventory Category | Possible Causes | *Responses* | | |
|---|---|---|---|---|
| | | *Not Applicable* | *Possible Problem* | *Reference Procedure and Comments* |
| Raw Material (cont'd) | • Bills of material are in error in not reflecting amount of raw material actually used. | | | |
| Purchased Parts | • Identifical parts have different part numbers because they are purchased from different vendors and at differing prices. Actual part usage is virtually impossible to control and match to its specific cost control. | | | |
| | • Informal or unreported parts substitutions at time of sub- or final assembly where more expensive parts are consumed than standards allow. | | | |
| | • Unattended or uncontrolled stores allowing access by parts users who make no record of parts withdrawn. | | | |
| | • Changing part numbers and possibly cost records based on engineering drawing revision number. Existing parts in inventory will look exactly like the new parts produced under the new number if only tolerances or word spellings were changed on the drawings. | | | |
| | • Items received but lack of quantity verification results in short shipments being booked at inflated value. | | | |
| Work-In-Process | • Inflated production counts by incentive workers builds work-in-process labor that will never be relieved from work-in-process inventory until a physical inventory reveals the error. | | | |

REPORTING UNIT _____

DATE COMPLETED _____

COMPLETED BY _____

| Inventory Category | Possible Causes | Responses | | |
|---|---|---|---|---|
| | | Not Applicable | Possible Problem | Reference Procedure and Comments |
| Work-In-Process (cont'd) | • Unreported scrap will also remain in inventory until realized by a physical/book discrepancy. | | | |
| | • Mishandling of repair work allowing production (labor and piece count) to be counted twice for the same item. | | | |
| | • Bill of material usage errors where bills call for one amount of an item to be used, but more of the item is actually required. | | | |
| | • Slow processing of quality failures allowing cannibalism to occur to the item set aside awaiting disposition. | | | |
| | • Inconsistent processing of either labor or material variances or both, allowing more dollar build up into inventory than will be relieved by standards. | | | |
| | • Varying overhead and labor rates for like operations producing like parts in two or more locations, where variances from standards are not recognized. | | | |
| | • Use of out-dated bills that inaccurately reflect the components required to make the product. | | | |
| | • Mishandling specially negotiated contracts such that labor reported does not reflect work performed. This often happens with paint lines or fixed speed conveyors where a constant production rate is reported, but, due to missing hooks or conveyor elements, actual production is less. | | | |

REPORTING UNIT _____

DATE COMPLETED _____

COMPLETED BY _____

| | | Responses | | |
|---|---|---|---|---|
| Inventory Category | Possible Causes | Not Applicable | Possible Problem | Reference Procedure and Comments |
| Work-In-Process (cont'd) | • Strikes or similar disruptions result in supervisory personnel doing direct labor at much higher than average labor cost. Failure to recognize the variance will inflate inventory value. | | | |
| | • Recording labor into inventory at actual and relieving at standard. | | | |
| Finished Goods | • Open storage of finished goods which, aside from the risk of outright theft, can be cannibalized by service personnel for needed spare parts. | | | |
| | • Failure to report quality rejections returned for repairs prior to shipment, leaving the books with the impression that the units are in finished goods inventory. | | | |
| | • Mishandling warranty returns and items to be rebuilt by reporting them into inventories where there may be attempts to ultimately relieve them at a standard that differs from the amount entered into inventory. | | | |
| | • Occasionally, minor manufacturing modifications may change finished goods model numbers, and, if the correct inventory transactions are not recorded, errors will occur when shipments are made. | | | |
| | • Products shipped but not billed. | | | |
| Accounting and Systems | • Material received in at standard cost and relieved at actual cost— or, vice versa. | | | |
| | • Incorrect physical inventory counts. | | | |
| | • Accounts payable fraud using a dummy purchase order and receiver. | | | |

REPORTING UNIT _____

DATE COMPLETED _____

COMPLETED BY _____

| Inventory Category | Possible Causes | Responses | | |
|---|---|---|---|---|
| | | Not Applicable | Possible Problem | Reference Procedure and Comments |
| Accounting and Systems (cont'd) | • One person control of order desk where cash sales can occur without supporting paperwork. | | | |
| | • One copy move tickets allowing transfer of parts from one location to another without verification of the transaction. | | | |
| | • Too few reporting and control stations allowing too many opportunities for "disappearance." | | | |
| | • Not allowing computerized on-hand balances to go negative, which would naturally happen if issues were entered into the computer before receipts. | | | |

# 15

# Pricing Decisions

*Edward M. Bixler*

## THE CONTROLLER'S ROLE

### Establishing a Pricing Policy

The controller must work with management to establish a framework within which managers can make pricing decisions on individual projects or products. The pricing policy may be more or less formalized, depending on the needs of the business unit; however, at a minimum it should include return-on-investment standards, should relate to the unit's marketing and competitive philosophies, and should provide for a comparison of the actual results to the planned results of the pricing action. In addition, management should establish an authority hierarchy that delegates pricing authority in a manner that is appropriate for the business unit and the products.

The controller's leadership role in developing pricing policy is particularly important in the following areas:

- Establishing return-on-investment objectives for both new and existing products;

**15-1**

- Developing measurement methods and criteria to be used in assessing the impact and results of pricing actions;
- Establishing a pricing authority hierarchy; and
- Ensuring that the pricing policy is consistent with the unit's business plan, so that the individual pricing actions contribute to the accomplishment of the firm's business objectives.

The other principal functions involved in the development of a pricing policy are marketing, sales, and general management. The marketing and sales functions provide product and market intelligence, and general management determines that overall pricing policy is formulated within the framework of the total business needs.

### Integrating Forecasts Into Summary Reports

The controller's leadership role in measuring the results of specific actions can be particularly critical in assessing the impact on the business unit of new-product and pricing decisions. Without this type of leadership, management often gives way to the temptation to attend to new needs or problem areas without assessing the results of prior decisions. As a result, the effects of new decisions cannot be projected accurately, and management often may not implement the early corrective action that is needed to prevent lost sales or added costs.

The controller generally has the data available to ensure proper measurement of both the unit's overall operating performance and the major components that contribute to that operating performance. In addition, he is capable of comparing the various aspects of the unit's performance with historical and planned performance. One of the most effective ways of communicating this information to the other members of the management team is through well-conceived summary reports that compare actual performance in key areas to the planned or forecast results. These reports enable him to identify deviations from the plan or forecast quickly, establish criteria for assessing the validity of projections, and measure managerial performance. These summary reports should provide management with a clear understanding of the forecast as well as of how actual results to date compare with that forecast. The comparison of actual results to date should generally be presented in a way that points out the current trends of the business.

The plan or forecast must fully integrate the marketing and production plans with the operating budget if it is to be used effectively. Through the reporting process, the controller can assess the dynamics of the business relative to the various elements of the company and should use this information to provide full integration of marketing and production forecasts, whether they be for a business period, a new-product venture, a pricing action, or the implementation of other business decisions.

### Analyzing Alternative Return-on-Investment Objectives

In the final analysis, the controller must measure a business's performance by its return on investment. He must view this return as the ultimate measure of ongoing or short-term performance in the case of a mature business, or over the long run in the case of a growth business. The development of appropriate overall and project or product return-on-investment goals against which the business will measure its performance should be based on the strategic role of the business or on the goals the business has set for itself in terms of the markets it wishes to serve, its product portfolio, its market penetration, and its growth objectives.

A business in a growth environment or a business that suddenly finds itself confronted with the need to protect aggressively its market share may decide to introduce new products or major marketing programs that individually may not provide an acceptable return on investment but in the context of the total business are critical in meeting its objectives. Although these situations may arise, they stand in contrast to a careful management analysis of incremental return on investment when the introduction of a new product or the implementation of a major marketing, manufacturing, or other business program is under consideration.

## RETURN ON INVESTMENT

### Factors to Be Considered

The two components of return on investment of an activity are demonstrated in the following equation:

$$\frac{\text{Net Income}}{\text{Sales}} \times \frac{\text{Sales}}{\text{Investment}} = \text{Return on Investment (ROI)}$$

$$\frac{\text{Net Income}}{\cancel{\text{Sales}}} \times \frac{\cancel{\text{Sales}}}{\text{Investment}} = \text{ROI}$$

$$\frac{\text{Net Income}}{\text{Investment}} = \text{ROI}$$

The return on investment, therefore, is the combined function of the rate of return on sales ( $\frac{\text{Net Income}}{\text{Sales}}$ ) and the investment turnover ( $\frac{\text{Sales}}{\text{Investment}}$ ). Some products or business ventures may show very high or favorable rates of return on sales when compared to the existing business or products; however, they may require an extensive investment that "turns" or is cycled very slowly. On the other hand, some products carry very low rates of return on sales (such as most supermarket food items) but "turn" or are cycled many times in a very short period.

Using the above formula, we can see the effect on return on investment of differing rates of return on sales and turnover rates:

*High Return on Sales/Low Cycle Time:*

$$\frac{\text{Net Income}}{\text{Sales}} = \frac{25}{100} \times \frac{\text{Sales}}{\text{Investment}} = \frac{100}{200} = \text{ROI}$$

$$\frac{25}{100} \times \frac{100}{200} = \frac{25}{200} = 12.5\% \text{ ROI}$$

*Low Return on Sales/High Cycle Time:*

$$\frac{\text{Net Income}}{\text{Sales}} = \frac{5}{100} \times \frac{\text{Sales}}{\text{Investment}} = \frac{100}{25} = \text{ROI}$$

$$\frac{5}{100} \times \frac{100}{25} = \frac{5}{25} = 20\% \text{ ROI}$$

Using the components of return-on-investment analysis, the controller can determine the price/volume combination of a product that will maximize the return on investment of that product. The analysis requires an estimate of

- The cost of capacity;
- The quantities that would be sold at a given price;
- Direct product costs; and
- The utilization of working capital for given levels of sales.

The following is a simple analysis of optimum pricing in terms of return on investment. (It ignores the cost of money, which may be significant.) It includes the following assumptions:

| | |
|---|---|
| Capacity | 800 units |
| Cost of capacity | $1,600.00 |
| Product cost | $.50 per unit |

*Working capital utilization:*

| | |
|---|---|
| Accounts receivable | 14 percent of sales |
| Inventory | 17 percent of cost of sales |

*Price/Volume Combinations:*

| Unit Price | Volume |
|:---:|:---:|
| 1.00 | 800 |
| 1.10 | 700 |
| 1.20 | 600 |
| 1.30 | 475 |

The calculations for the four price/volume combinations follow:

1. $1.00 × 800 = $800
   0.50 × 800 = $400
   $400

   Investment                          = $1,600
   Accounts receivable (800 × 0.14) =    112
   Inventory (400 × 0.17)           =     68
                                      $1,780

   Return on sales       = 50%

   Turnover = $\dfrac{800}{1780}$ = 44.9%

   ROI = 0.50 × 0.449 = 22.45%

2. $1.10 × 700 = $770
   0.50 × 700 =  350
   $420

   Investment              $1,600.00
   Accounts receivable
      (770 × 0.14)           107.80
   Inventory
      (350 × 0.17)            59.50
                          $1,767.30

   Return on sales       = 54.5%
   Turnover = $\dfrac{770}{1767.3}$ = 43.6%
   ROI = .545 × .436 = 23.8%

3. $1.20 × 600 = $720
   0.50 × 600 =  300
   $420

   Investment              $1,600.00
   Accounts receivable
      (720 × 0.14)           100.80
   Inventory
      (300 × 0.17)            51.00
                          $1,751.80

   Return on sales       = 58.3%
   Turnover = $\dfrac{720}{1751.8}$ = 41.1%
   ROI = .583 × .411 = 24%

4. $1.30 × 475 = $617.50
   .50 × 475 =   237.50
   ─────────────────────
                $380.00

| | |
|---|---|
| Investment | $1,600.00 |
| Accounts receivable | |
| (617.50 × 0.14) | 86.50 |
| Inventory | |
| (237.50 × 0.17) | 40.40 |
| | $1,726.90 |

Return on sales     = 61.5%

$$\text{Turnover} = \frac{617.5}{1726.9} = 35.8\%$$

ROI = .615 × .358  = 22%

The above analysis indicates the best price for return on investment would be $1.20 per unit. Although this price does not maximize either the return on sales or the asset turnover, it does provide the best combination of the return-on-investment components. Of course, marketing or competitive factors may result in pricing that is above or below that providing the maximum return on investment, but in such cases pricing would be based on a rational analysis of these external factors, and management would be aware of the decision's impact on profitability.

In order to assess the true impact of the new or incremental product on the business, management should restrict its analysis to the incremental revenue, cost, and investment resulting from the business decision. This incremental analysis should confine itself to the discounted cash flow (DCF) impact of the project on the business, in order to take into account the cost of money and timing of the cash inflows and outflows. For example, assume an existing plant is being used at 60 percent capacity. Management has an opportunity to add a product that will use an additional amount of that capacity. Assume also, to keep the example simple, that the new product will use existing sales and distribution channels without increasing these costs and that the cash outlay (investment) is limited to the inventories necessary to support the product. Finally, assume that all other costs associated with this new product are variable costs of manufacturing and handling, but that the marketing environment is such that the firm's normal markups (or return-on-sales objectives) will not prevail. The incremental return on this investment, even in the case of a low rate of return on sales, could well add substantially to the overall return on investment of the business.[1]

───────────────

[1] In the situation described above, the controller's understanding of the dynamics of the business and his awareness of the proper method of measuring return on investment of new product opportunities could well have a significant impact on the unit's pricing policies or actions. If only the rate of return on sales or a markup percentage were taken into consideration in determining the viability of a new product, the overall profitability or return on investment might not be maximized.

### Fallibility of Past Experience

Historic rates of return for a business are often the yardsticks against which new products or ventures are measured. In today's dynamic business environment this approach may not be in the best interest of the business. In order to set realistic return-on-investment objectives or *hurdle rates* for new products or ventures, the controller must give the competitive environment a great deal of consideration. The return on investment being generated by competitors, short- and long-term industry capacity situations, and the unit's strategic role or charter should have a great deal more bearing on the development of return-on-investment hurdle rates than the historical rate of return.

The controller has access to a considerable amount of data from different sources (e.g., Federal Trade Commission product-line statistics, public company financial statements, and trade sources) to help him calculate or estimate the rates of return being generated by competitors, often on a product-line basis. In addition, there are various sources and means of estimating industry capacity and capacity utilization. The controller who uses this data to understand the competitive environment better can contribute to the formulation of enlightened target rates of return for use in determining the unit's pricing policy. In addition, he may find that this data is valuable to the marketing department in its formulation of marketing strategies and tactics.

### Integrating Return on Investment With Overall Financial Objectives

The ultimate long-term objective of the business unit is maximizing return on investment. The approach to achieving this objective normally involves a myriad of business needs, strategies, and judgments that often take on an importance to a business unit that obscures the return-on-investment objective. This statement is not intended to imply that issues other than return on investment are not important, even vital, to the business unit, but rather to emphasize that return-on-investment objectives must be integrated with the key unit objectives, particularly the unit's financial objectives. This need is perhaps more important in the area of new products and new-product pricing decisions than in any other single area. When management considers new products and makes decisions regarding their introduction into the unit's product line, it is often tempted to look at return on investment as the only financial criterion, without fully assessing the impact on other financial objectives.

Within a framework of fully integrated financial objectives, the controller can develop new-product or new-adventure criteria that are consistent and easily understood and that contribute to the achievement of long-term return-on-investment goals. The development of an integrated financial objective profile should include consideration of the risk, the level and timing of capital investment, the liquidity of the product, the relationship of the project to other aspects of the business, and the growth potential of the product.

The components of return on investment, return on sales, and investment turnover represent a logical starting point for the development of a sound framework of integrated financial objectives. As a general rule, decisions regarding return on sales (i.e., pricing, market penetration, costs) have greater short-term flexibility, whereas decisions regarding the level of investment in a project often require a longer time to become effective. For this reason, when management establishes return-on-investment hurdle rates, it should view separately the components of return on investment and establish standards for each. The unit's cash position in all likelihood will be a key factor in developing the specific return-on-sales and turnover objectives. A tight cash position could well make a project with a lower return on investment and a shorter time cycle much more attractive than a project with a higher return on investment that tied up the unit's cash resources for a long time or for a period in which other cash demands are high.

### Pricing in an Inflationary Economy

An inflationary environment presents a different set of financial considerations for all business decisions. Traditional measures of financial performance become of limited or questionable value. The income statement and balance sheet are subject to severe distortions if based on historical cost data that are not adjusted for inflation. These distortions have been discussed somewhat in recent years by various disciplines and groups; not until the Securities and Exchange Commission issued Accounting Series Release (ASR) 190 and the Financial Accounting Standards Board (FASB) released Statement on Financial Accounting Standards No. 33, however, was the impact of inflation on traditional financial measures recognized by the business community in general.

A *Business Week* article ("The Profit Illusion," March 19, 1979) demonstrated that based on several financial measures (effective taxation rates, dividend pay-out rates, and changes in retained earnings), 1978 appeared to be a generally healthy business year. However, when these measures were adjusted for inflation, they indicated a tax rate of 52.5 percent of income compared to a reported tax rate of 41.6 percent, a dividend rate of 65 percent on after-tax earnings compared to a reported dividend rate of 42 percent, and reduction of retained earnings from $69 billion as reported to actual retained earnings of $27 billion.

High rates of inflation contribute to inadequate cost recognition, which results in recognition of illusory profits. In order to properly assess the true return on investment of new products or other business ventures, or to compare various enterprises of the business over time, financial results must be adjusted for inflation.

**Anticipating Pressures on Costs.** Developing pricing decisions in an era of high inflation requires that management project increases in the cost of the material and labor components of the product and in the cost of the money invested in the product. The controller must either develop a forecast on a constant dollar basis, or provide for the effects of inflation on each of the components of production. Because of the difficulty of such forecasting, an approach to dealing with inflation used by most managements is to adjust sales prices as a reaction to increases in costs. The trouble with this method is that sales prices lag behind costs to the detriment of corporate profits. The controller must convince management that in budgeting for product prices, it is imperative to anticipate inflationary pressures on costs. It is the controller's responsibility to be cognizant of the effects of inflation on the various components of the business and to provide the best available information for project analyses and pricing decisions.

**Adjusting Financial Data.** For external reporting purposes, SFAS 33 provides methods of adjusting historical accounting data to recognize inflation. These methods attempt to identify the impact of inflation on most aspects of the business—inventory profits, holding gains, monetary gains (losses), real volume changes, etc. While it is not practical in most situations to adjust financial data in accordance with SFAS 33 for ongoing internal use, financial analyses prepared for decision-making purposes must be adjusted for inflation to provide management with pertinent decision-making data. While in many institutions adequate management data on the impact of inflation can be developed by adjusting historical and forecast-information for current and projected inventory costs and depreciation on a replacement cost basis, the controller must have a good understanding of both the business and the art of inflation accounting in order to ensure that management needs are properly met in this volatile area.

## EVALUATION TECHNIQUES

### Evaluating Alternative Assumptions

An evaluation of alternative assumptions for pricing decisions frequently involves analysis of the impact of production, product mix, and working capital changes. Financial data reported in the traditional financial reports is generally not adequate for this analysis. In analyzing production costs for purposes of pricing decisions, the controller should consider only the *incremental* production costs or *incremental changes* in production costs of each of the alternatives. Fixed costs already spent or committed independent of a new-product venture are "sunk" costs, or costs that are unaffected by the decision under analysis, and therefore should not be considered as relevant in the analysis. The costs of existing plant capacity, manufacturing or operating staff, leases, depreciation, etc., are costs that are generally not affected by the addition of a new product, and while they represent costs that must be absorbed or carried by the business, only the true incremental costs are included in the decision analysis.

The full range of incremental costs of each alternative, however, must be considered. In the production area one must consider all relevant variable costs of production, such as direct labor and material, as well as such incremental indirect costs as utilities, maintenance, and supplies. In addition, changes in support costs (such as supervision or other staffing, sales and marketing, and lease or other building expenses) and the effect of income and property taxes should be included in the analysis in order to assess the full incremental impact of the product on the company's profitability.

As a general rule, a product or project decision will affect working capital accounts receivable as well as inventories and accounts payable. No financial analysis would be complete without fully recognizing the incremental cost of funds invested in net working capital for each of the alternatives.

### Analytical Summary Reports

After the basic financial analysis of the alternatives is completed, additional information and analyses can aid management in determining the risks and likelihood of success associated with a product or pricing decision.

**Sensitivity Analysis.** As a general rule, management must determine the sensitivity, or range of feasible results, of a particular decision, as well as the impact of variations in one or more of the key assumptions. A sensitivity analysis incorporating the range and probabilities of each of the various assumptions is required in order to establish the estimated high, low, and probable results of a decision. A sensitivity analysis often requires subjective assessments by a number of knowledgeable individuals as to the likelihood, in terms of probabilities, of a range of key assumptions. The controller must determine that the data are stated in a fashion that is consistent with the requirements of the analysis.

**Expected Value Calculations.** Once a set of assumptions and their probability ranges are established, the next step is the development of a range of likely outcomes or results and their likelihood of occurrence. If the number of variables being considered and/or the number of sets of assumptions regarding their probability of occurrence is small, expected value analysis calculations can be used to develop the set of likely outcomes.

For example, assume a pricing decision in which the price and quantity sold are dependent variables, and there is a defined quantity at each price level and a defined probability of achievement of that sales combination:

| Unit Price | Quantity | Probability |
|:---:|:---:|:---:|
| 1.50 | 1000 | .30 |
| 1.50 | 1500 | .60 |
| 1.50 | 2000 | .10 |

Assume further that the unit profit contribution at a sales price of $1.50 is $0.60. The expected value of sales (in terms of profit) at a sales price of $1.50 is:

| Unit Profit Contribution | | Units Sold | | Probability | |
|:---:|:---:|:---:|:---:|:---:|:---:|
| 0.6 | × | 1000 | × | .3 = | $180.00 |
| 0.6 | × | 1500 | × | .6 = | 540.00 |
| 0.6 | × | 2000 | × | .1 = | 120.00 |
| | | | Expected profit at the $1.50 unit price = | | $840.00 |

A unit price of $1.75, but with fewer quantities, can then be analyzed as an alternative:

| Unit Price | Quantity | Probability |
|---|---|---|
| 1.75 | 750 | .30 |
| 1.75 | 1200 | .60 |
| 1.75 | 1600 | .10 |

With no change in unit costs, the unit profit contribution would be $0.85, and the expected value would be:

| Unit Profit Contribution | | Units Sold | | Probability | |
|---|---|---|---|---|---|
| 0.85 | × | 750 | × | .30 = | $191.25 |
| 0.85 | × | 1200 | × | .60 = | 612.00 |
| 0.85 | × | 1600 | × | .10 = | 136.00 |
| | | | Expected profit at the $1.75 unit price = | | $939.25 |

When the expected profit at the $1.50 unit price is compared to the expected profit at the $1.75 unit price, the lower volume notwithstanding, the higher unit price would be the recommended figure.

**Monte Carlo Simulation.** The expected value calculation technique obviously can handle only a limited number of variables or sets of assumptions regarding the probability of occurrence before the calculations become excessive. Analysis involving several variables or a large number of sets of probabilities (which may tend to decrease bias and improve the level of accuracy) can readily be handled through Monte Carlo simulation techniques, which often require computer processing. Essentially, the Monte Carlo approach involves determining probability distributions and assigning Monte Carlo numbers to each class of probability distributions in proportion to the probability of the class. The Monte Carlo numbers are then selected at random, and the results tabulated until a sufficiently large number of trials to estimate the likely outcome have been simulated.

Assume, for example, that the objective of the analysis is to assess the profit contribution on sales of a new product line with variables that include unit price, mix of products within the line, and sales in units. The sales force, sales manager, and market analyst (all of whom must understand the product and market) have provided their assessments of high, expected, and low values and their probabilities of occurrence for unit prices; sales in units at each pricing level; and product mix. A computer programmed in Monte Carlo simulation can quickly calculate the feasible price, volume range and product mix and will provide the most likely outcome at a predetermined level of confidence (i.e., at a confidence level of 75 percent, sales will be $X$ units at unit price $Y$ for each of the products within the line), as well as that same set of data at the high and low ends (again at predetermined confidence levels) of the feasible range of outcomes.

The Monte Carlo approach also offers an estimate of the frequency distribution; this information is particularly useful when alternative projects are compared.

## MANAGEMENT REPORTS

Once a pricing decision is made or a new venture is decided and implemented, the controller takes on added responsibilities as he begins to measure the success (or failure) of the decision or project. By carefully preparing a management reporting structure that focuses management attention on the key indicators of the trends of the venture, the controller provides one of the most important elements of management control. (See Chapter 8 for a detailed discussion of management reports.)

Perhaps the single most important management report is the actual-versus-budget report; it is particularly significant in measuring the effect of a pricing action. In order to report useful data, the budget must be developed in adequate detail prior to the implementation of the pricing action, and all parties concerned must accept it as the standard against which performance will be measured.

### Variance Analysis

The actual-versus-budget report forms the basis for variance analysis, and should identify the significant factors that contribute to differences between actual and planned results. The key to an effective variance analysis is to summarize the important variance factors in an easy-to-read format that is readily understood by the management team.

A meaningful approach to variance analysis, particularly in a new-product or new-market venture, is to compare the actual profit contribution statement to the budget or planned profit contribution statement and to recap the results in terms of the profit contribution of each of the variance areas. An example is illustrated in Figure 15.1.

The variance analysis should focus on those aspects of the variances on which action can be taken. The analysis then becomes a useful guide to implementing corrective action in a timely fashion.

### Return-on-Investment Analysis

As discussed earlier in the chapter, return-on-investment analysis (focusing on the two aspects of return on investment, return on sales and turnover) calls attention to the profitability of the product in terms of both *profit margin* and *asset utilization*. Return-on-investment analysis should compare actual data to a predetermined budget or plan, as well as point out trends in each area. If the product or venture life cycle is relatively long, a return-on-investment analysis stated in constant dollars provides a much more effective basis for measurement of trends and relative performance.

There are any number of ways to present return-on-investment analysis data. A sample format might be:

|        | Return on Sales | | Asset Turnover | | ROI |
|--------|-----------------|---|---------------|---|------|
| Actual | 18%             | × | 1.82          | = | 32.8% |
| Plan   | 18.5%           | × | 1.75          | = | 32.4% |

The above analysis points out that more effective use of working capital or a higher utilization of plant capacity, partially offset by lower profitability, resulted in a better return on investment than planned. Further analysis to determine more specific causal factors, that is, the actual variance from plan in terms of working capital or other assets used, provides a clear understanding of the variances in actual return-on-investment performance compared to plan.

The controller should make every effort to measure performance against external as well as internal standards. Clearly the best way to do this is to compare company performance to industry standards. This tends to give a measure of the firm's competitive performance and keeps its attention sharply focused on the competitive strengths or weaknesses its product enjoys in the marketplace.

| | *Actual* | *Planned* | *Variance* |
|---|---|---|---|
| Sales—Units | 130 | 150 | (20) |
| Sales—Dollars | 120 | 150 | (30) |
| Variable Cost of Product (Standard) | 78 | 90 | 12 |
| Variances Standard Cost | 12 | 0 | (12) |
| Profit Contribution | 30 | 60 | (30) |
| Fixed Expenses | 8 | 9 | 1 |
| Product Profit | 22 | 51 | (29) |

VARIANCE ANALYSIS

| | |
|---|---|
| Profit Variance Due to Volume | (8) |
|     Quantity difference at original price × profit contribution rate | |
|     (20 units × \$1/unit × .4 = \$20 × .4 = \$8) | |
| Profit Variance Due to Pricing | (10) |
|     Actual quantity at original unit price less actual quantity | |
|     at actual unit price | |
|     ([130 × \$1/unit] − [130 × \$.92/unit] = \$10) | |
| Profit Variance Due to Cost Changes | |
|     Standard cost at actual volume less actual cost at actual volume | |
| Labor Use | (6) |
| Labor Rate | (4) |
| Material Use | 2 |
| Material Rate | (4) |
| Profit Variance Due to Fixed Expenses | 1 |
|     Budget fixed cost less actual fixed cost | |
| Product Profit Variance | (29) |

FIGURE 15.1   PRODUCT PROFIT REPORT

## SUGGESTED READING

Bierman, Harold Jr., Bonini, Charles P., and Hausman, Warren H. *Quantitative Analysis for Business Decisions.* Homewood, Ill.: Richard D. Irvin, 1977.

Davidson, Sidney, Stickney, Clyde P., and Weil, Romal L. *Inflation Accounting, A Guide for the Accountant and the Financial Analyst.* New York: McGraw-Hill, 1976.

Diedick, Thomas J. *Cost Controls for Industry.* Englewood Cliffs, N.J.: Prentice-Hall, 1976.

Lere, John C. *Pricing Techniques for the Financial Executive.* New York: John Wiley & Sons, Inc., 1974.

Miller, David W., and Starr, Martin K. *Executive Decisions and Operations Research.* Englewood Cliffs, N.J.: Prentice-Hall, 1969.

Oxenfeldt, Alfred R. *Pricing Strategies.* New York: American Management Assn., Inc., 1975.

# 16

# Monitoring Techniques

*Arthur D. Perrone*

## ROLE OF THE CONTROLLER

### Management Systems Development

Monitoring of results and proper interpretation of information is possible only after an environment has been created that allows management to properly exercise its judgments and decisions. The management environment considers the company's business philosophy, objectives, strategies for accomplishing those objectives, organizational structure, and management systems. The management systems bring together all of the interrelated processes and information by which management:

- Formulates objectives, strategies, and plans;
- Initiates, monitors, and controls activities; and
- Evaluates results and compensates performance.

Monitoring is only as valuable as the information being evaluated. Management systems must therefore be effective and must facilitate the interpretation of performance. Monitoring then becomes an important role. The controller's responsibility is to develop functional management systems that facilitate proper interpretation of information.

**Business Plans/Budgets.** Business planning is an important first step in the management system. Management must relate the ongoing roles and responsibilities of operating units, functions, and individuals to the company's business philosophy and objectives, changing needs and opportunities, and ultimately translate them into effective programs of action.

In capital intensive businesses, planning should extend far enough into the future to properly reflect the expected impact of major capital expenditures on revenue, income, return on investment, and financing arrangements. When planning for long periods of time (five years or more), proper consideration must be given to the effect inflation will have on future costs and revenues. Most companies will utilize a three- or five-year period for profit planning. (See Chapter 12 for a detailed discussion of the preparation and uses of budgets.)

**Reporting.** Many business failures are attributed to one of two things: either failure to plan or deviation from plan. Like most truisms, this is somewhat misleading; a plan alone cannot guarantee success, and some deviation from plan will always occur. In the latter case, business failures are generally due not to deviations from plan, but rather to management's failure to recognize deviations in time to react with appropriate action.

Ideally, management should constantly monitor performance against plans and adjust plans as often as necessary to fit the current situation. Business plans are usually prepared at fixed times, and performance against plan is measured and reported at discrete time intervals. The time span between performance reports depends both on the character of the activity reported and on the degree of control required. Thus, product sales might appropriately be reported to unit management on a weekly basis and to corporate management on a monthly basis; or both levels of management might be satisfied with an estimate of market penetration on a quarterly basis. (See Figure 16.1 for a schematic of a planning and reporting system.)

At least two important corollaries may be drawn from the reporting concept outlined above. First, the nature and timing of performance reports should be tailored to fit the information needs of those reporting and monitoring at each management level. (This requirement generally results in greater selectivity and quantitative reduction of information as it is transmitted upward.) Secondly, all reports should relate directly to a plan. Conversely, plans are not meaningful benchmarks unless they are periodically matched against actual performance. (See Chapter 8.)

**Forecasting.** Business plans are normally fixed for a period (usually a year), and reports are then compared against plan on a monthly basis. In this case, a mechanism should be built into the management system to reflect short-term changing conditions. Monthly or quarterly forecasts should be prepared for a twelve-

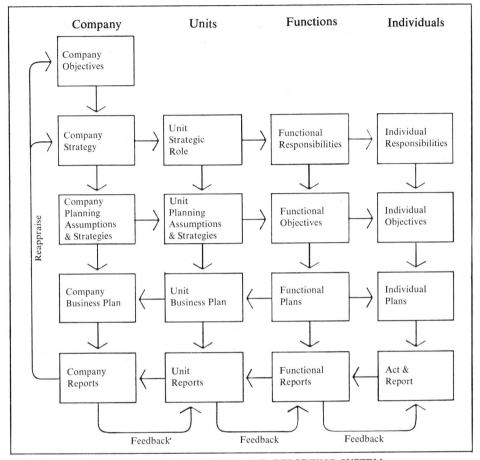

FIGURE 16.1 SCHEMATIC OF A PLANNING AND REPORTING SYSTEM

month period, with periodic revisions during the year. Forecasting allows management to evaluate changing conditions; decisions to respond to the new environment can then be made.

When requesting new forecasts, explanations of significant changes from original planning assumptions should be indicated. This will provide management with a better understanding of the forecast, as well as with a basis for evaluating its credibility.

The kind of information included in the forecast is again dependent upon the level of control required. Normally, only major financial data should be included—items far more significant than the detail included in the financial plan. The income statement, balance sheet, cash flow, capital expenditures, and return on investment are the typical variables and schedules that should be forecasted.

Because business plans are normally prepared several months before the plan period begins, and since the plan will cover a one- to five-year period, certain variations will occur. Forecasting, on the other hand, is current each month, and many of the variables and uncertainties that may exist in the plan are reduced. The ability of management to properly plan and forecast is directly related to its understanding of the business and its ability to manage and control events. Comparison of actual results to plan as well as to current forecasts provides a good indication of the competency of the management. (See Chapter 13 for a detailed discussion of forecasting methods and techniques.)

### Value of Monitoring

Monitoring provides management with a tool for evaluating its performance against plan or objectives. It directs management's attention to the critical areas of profitability, assists in establishing management's priorities, and should be an early indication of an opportunity or problem. Further investigation and inquiry can result in a reallocation of resources or a change in management priorities. Determining the importance and timeliness of the information monitored (and how it is interpreted and utilized in the management process) is a key responsibility of the controller and a key element in the success of a business.

The controller should direct the development of a monitoring system and the techniques that control, review, and evaluate the critical performance segments of the business. He must be sure that management understands the monitoring system, is properly interpreting its results, and is prepared to take action when necessary. Many companies suffer from information paralysis—they accumulate too much information and do too little in response.

### Important Monitoring Areas

Management must first determine the critical areas affecting profitability. It must pinpoint the risks of gain or loss and the areas that generate significant revenues or expenditures. The selection of critical information varies according to type of business and related risks.

Some important areas that affect revenues and that should be considered for monitoring are:

- Orders,
- Backlog,
- Shipments,
- Projects (i.e., projects bid/lost/won, etc.),
- Distributors' inventory levels,
- High or low margin products,
- Key customer accounts, and
- Sales by salesman/territory/etc.

The following key areas of cost control should be monitored:

- Manufacturing cost (raw materials cost, waste/usage/rejection/rework, productivity, slow moving and obsolete inventory);
- Salaries (head counts); and
- Travel cost.

The controller must monitor the investment (working capital and fixed investment) required to support operations. The cost of capital will continue to remain high, and continued emphasis must be placed on effective cash management, maintenance of minimum inventory balances, and aggressive credit collection efforts.

## MONITORING TECHNIQUES

### Reporting

**Objectives.** The most widely used monitoring technique is a system that reports comparative actual results. Results alone normally do not indicate good or bad performance unless a comparison is being made. Comparison to plan, prior year, or industry averages are indicators as to how well the plan has performed.

A reporting system is most useful if it provides *advance* indication of deviation from plan and triggers responsive action at the *lowest appropriate action level*. Failure to respond promptly and properly affects performance against plan at the next management level, and the responsibility for action is thereby moved upward. Therefore, reporting should be generated at the lowest level necessary to create any active response and distributed to those levels having responsibility or accountability for that response. The form of the reporting may vary at each level.

**Monitoring Income.** The income statement, or a modification thereof, concisely reports the results of a number of business functions or segments. The income statement provides a good summary of activities if the major segments of consolidated activities are listed separately and the contribution of each major function is clearly indicated.

Figure 16.2 is an example of how the income statement can be analyzed. An alternative presentation would show the actual, plan, and prior year figures rather than the variances. Comparisons to plan, forecast, or prior year are helpful in evaluating performance and spotting trends.

*Revenue.* If management wants to obtain an early indication of plan deviations, it must monitor not just the final revenue amount, but also those activities generating the revenue. For example, if sales revenue is based on shipments, then order activity and backlog by major product line would be useful items to monitor and would be reported at the lowest action level—possibly a sales region. Figure 16.3 illustrates how the key elements for controlling revenue can be shown on a single report. This format can be consolidated (in all regions) and reported to the next level of management.

| (000) | Current Month Variance from | | | Year to Date Variance from | | |
|---|---|---|---|---|---|---|
| | Actual | Plan | Prior Year | Actual | Plan | Prior Year |
| Gross Sales | ___ | ___ | ___ | ___ | ___ | ___ |
| Less Discount | ___ | ___ | ___ | ___ | ___ | ___ |
| Net Sales | | | | | | |
|   Domestic | | | | | | |
|   Export | | | | | | |
|   Foreign Subsidiaries | ___ | ___ | ___ | ___ | ___ | ___ |
| | ___ | ___ | ___ | ___ | ___ | ___ |
| Variable Costs | | | | | | |
|   Material | | | | | | |
|   Labor | | | | | | |
|   Overhead | | | | | | |
|   Transportation | ___ | ___ | ___ | ___ | ___ | ___ |
| | ___ | ___ | ___ | ___ | ___ | ___ |
| Profit Contribution — | ___ | ___ | ___ | ___ | ___ | ___ |
|     — % | ___ | ___ | ___ | ___ | ___ | ___ |
| | ___ | ___ | ___ | ___ | ___ | ___ |
| Fixed Costs — Manufacturing | ___ | ___ | ___ | ___ | ___ | ___ |
| Gross Profit — | ___ | ___ | ___ | ___ | ___ | ___ |
|    — % | ___ | ___ | ___ | ___ | ___ | ___ |
| Operating Expenses | | | | | | |
|   Selling | | | | | | |
|   R&D | | | | | | |
|   Administration | | | | | | |
|   Interest | ___ | ___ | ___ | ___ | ___ | ___ |
|     Total — | ___ | ___ | ___ | ___ | ___ | ___ |
|     — % | ___ | ___ | ___ | ___ | ___ | ___ |
| Operating Contribution | ___ | ___ | ___ | ___ | ___ | ___ |
| Other Income (Expense) | | | | | | |
|   Royalties | | | | | | |
|   Technical Service Fees | | | | | | |
|   Other | ___ | ___ | ___ | ___ | ___ | ___ |
| Income Before Joint Venture | | | | | | |
|   Operations | ___ | ___ | ___ | ___ | ___ | ___ |
| Income Taxes | ___ | ___ | ___ | ___ | ___ | ___ |
| Net Income Before Joint | | | | | | |
|   Venture Operations | ___ | ___ | ___ | ___ | ___ | ___ |
| Equity in J-V Operation | | | | | | |
|   Company X | | | | | | |
|   Company Y | ___ | ___ | ___ | ___ | ___ | ___ |
| Net Income — | ═══ | ═══ | ═══ | ═══ | ═══ | ═══ |
|    — % | ═══ | ═══ | ═══ | ═══ | ═══ | ═══ |

FIGURE 16.2  STATEMENT OF INCOME VARIANCES

SALES REGION XYZ

| (000) Month of | SALES | | | | PROFIT CONTRIBUTION | | | | ORDERS | | | | BACKLOG MONTH END | | | | INVENTORY OF MONTH END | | | |
|---|---|---|---|---|---|---|---|---|---|---|---|---|---|---|---|---|---|---|---|---|
| | Actual | Plan | Var. Plan | Var. Last Year | Actual | Plan | Var. Plan | Var. Last Year | Actual | Plan | Var. Plan | Var. Last Year | Actual | Plan | Var. Plan | Var. Last Year | Actual | Plan | Var. Plan | Var. Last Year |
| Product A | | | | | | | | | | | | | | | | | | | | |
| Product B | | | | | | | | | | | | | | | | | | | | |
| Product C | | | | | | | | | | | | | | | | | | | | |
| All Other | | | | | | | | | | | | | | | | | | | | |
| *Year to Date* | | | | | | | | | | | | | | | | | | | | |
| Product A | | | | | | | | | | | | | | | | | | | | |
| Product B | | | | | | | | | | | | | | | | | | | | |
| Product C | | | | | | | | | | | | | | | | | | | | |
| All Other | | | | | | | | | | | | | | | | | | | | |

FIGURE 16.3  ELEMENTS OF REVENUE CONTROL

*Costs/Expenses.* Costs normally should be monitored at the lowest level of control. Analysis and identification of what initiates the cost and what will affect its change is an important starting point. Once the cost affecting factor has been determined, assumptions regarding that factor should then be made, and cost budgets can be prepared. Listed below are some cost affecting factors:

- Purchases (units of production, inventory levels);
- Materials cost (units of production/unit purchase cost);
- Labor (labor hours/rate per hour);
- Variable overhead (labor hours/dollars);
- Depreciation (units of production, capital expenditures); and
- Operating costs (number of employees).

From a reporting standpoint, controlling cost consists of reporting both the actual and planned costs as well as the cost affecting factors. Some examples appear in Figure 16.4.

| | Month Unit Cost | | Year to Date Unit Cost | |
|---|---|---|---|---|
| | *Actual* | *Var. Std.* | *Actual* | *Var. Std.* |
| Material | | | | |
| Labor | | | | |
| Overhead | | | | |
| | ___ | ___ | ___ | ___ |
| | ___ | ___ | ___ | ___ |
| Purchase Cost | ___ | ___ | ___ | ___ |

| | Month | | | Year to Date | | |
|---|---|---|---|---|---|---|
| | *Actual* | *Var. Plan* | *Var. Last Year* | *Actual* | *Var. Plan* | *Var. Last Year* |
| Purchase (Qty.) | | | | | | |
| Inventory—Raw | | | | | | |
| Units Produced | | | | | | |
| Units Per Hour | | | | | | |
| Scrap Qty. | | | | | | |
| Rework Qty. | | | | | | |
| Labor Hours | | | | | | |
| Overtime Hours | | | | | | |
| Lost Time Hours | | | | | | |
| Maintenance & Repair—Hours | | | | | | |
| $ | ___ | ___ | ___ | ___ | ___ | ___ |

FIGURE 16.4  COST REPORT

UNIT XYZ

PERIOD BEGINNING *March 1, 198X*

MONTHS

| Description | 1 | 2 | 3 | 4 | 5 | 6 | 7 | 8 | 9 | 10 | 11 | 12 |
|---|---|---|---|---|---|---|---|---|---|---|---|---|
| Receipts | | | | | | | | | | | | |
| Payments — Hourly Payroll | | | | | | | | | | | | |
| Salary Payroll | | | | | | | | | | | | |
| Accounts Payable* | | | | | | | | | | | | |
| Total | | | | | | | | | | | | |
| Net Cash Change | | | | | | | | | | | | |

*All payments are processed through Accounts Payable

FIGURE 16.5a  TWELVE-MONTH CASH FORECAST

### Monitoring the Balance Sheet.

*Cash flow.* Monitoring of cash on a daily, weekly, and monthly basis is necessary in order to use funds effectively, to keep bank borrowings to a minimum, and to permit short-term investments of temporary cash surpluses. Reporting locations will normally follow financial reporting lines or can be broken down by cash generating or spending responsibility areas within the profit centers.

*Twelve-month cash forecast.* The starting point in monitoring cash flow is a simplified twelve-month forecast which should be updated each month. (See Figure 16.5a.)

*Weekly cash forecast.* The first month of the twelve-month forecast should be broken down by weeks, as shown in Figure 16.5b. This forecast should be updated each week and should be rolled forward one week.

*Daily analysis and investment.* The final step analyzes daily receipts and disbursements by bank account. On the basis of this analysis, and in conjunction with the weekly forecast, decisions on future borrowings or investments should be made. (See Chapter 23 for a detailed review of cash management.)

Much has been said recently about the value to management of the statement of funds or changes in working capital, but it has not become the most important financial statement—perhaps because it is too difficult for the non-accountant to understand. An expanded cash flow statement that shows cash generated from internal sources and segregates discretionary spending items, along with cash generated from external sources, may be more useful and more germane to cash management problems. (Figure 16.6 illustrates this format.) When appropriate, a column reflecting plan numbers may be added to this schedule.

| | *WEEK ENDING* | | | |
| --- | --- | --- | --- | --- |
| *Description* | 3/7 | 3/14 | 3/21 | 3/28 |
| Receipts | | | | |
| Payments — <br>   Hourly Payroll | | | | |
|   Salary Payroll | | | | |
|   Accounts Payable | | | | |
|   Total | | | | |
| Net Cash Change | | | | |

FIGURE 16.5b   WEEKLY CASH FORECAST

*Working capital other than cash.* The management of working capital has always been an important business requirement, but with the ever-increasing cost of money, special attention is required to use efficiently the components of working capital. For most companies, the major current assets, excluding cash, are trade accounts receivable and inventories, while the major current liability is trade accounts payable.

To control these items and report them properly, management must analyze the most important factors and must establish appropriate objectives. Once these objectives are converted into company policies and procedures, the reporting and monitoring forms can be established. What are the major considerations in a company's

| | Month | Year To Date | YTD Last Year |
|---|---|---|---|
| Net Income | | | |
| Non-Cash Items Included in Net Income | | | |
| Depreciation | | | |
| Equity in Earnings of Jointly Owned Companies | | | |
| Deferred Taxes | | | |
| Other | | | |
| Cash Flow From Operations | | | |
| Working Capital — Source (Use)* | | | |
| Other Sources (Uses) of Cash | | | |
| Additions to Plant and Equipment | | | |
| Dividends | | | |
| Investments | | | |
| Cash Flow From Internal Sources | | | |
| External Sources (Uses) of Cash | | | |
| Sale of Stock | | | |
| Short-Term Debt | | | |
| Long-Term Debt | | | |
| Net Increase (Decrease) in Cash | | | |

*Excluding Cash and Short-Term Debt

FIGURE 16.6 CASH FLOW STATEMENT

reporting system? A comparative view of the composition of the balance sheet items is needed in order to determine these. Figure 16.7 illustrates a format of this kind that can, of course, be broken down by regions, profit center, and so on.

*Capital expenditures.* Management must first identify the system being used to approve the expenditure of funds. The system indicates how project expenditures are controlled (normally by a project number) and the level where reporting control should begin.

Monthly forecasts of the costs to complete the approved projects in process or the forecasted costs of future projects are required from the project manager (or from whomever is responsible for the expenditure of funds). A consolidation of these projects by cost center or profit center into a total company report would appear on a chart similar to that shown in Figure 16.8.

Line managers are sometimes overly optimistic in estimating costs and about their ability to complete a project within the approved costs. Reviews, on a regular basis, of cost-to-complete estimates are strongly recommended.

Another problem often arises when management cannot spend the approved monies within the forecasted time frame. In order to obtain insight into the reason-

| | Current Month | Plan | Prior Month | Prior Year |
|---|---|---|---|---|
| Trade Accounts Receivables | | | | |
| — Amount (Total) | \$____ | \$____ | \$____ | \$____ |
| — Average Collection Period | ___Days | ___Days | ___Days | ___Days |
| — Percent of Receivables to Sales | ___% | ___% | ___% | ___% |
| — Past Due over 60 days | | | | |
|     Amount | \$____ | \$____ | \$____ | \$____ |
|     Percent to Total | ___% | ___% | ___% | ___% |
| | | | | |
| Inventories | | | | |
| — Raw Material | \$____ | \$____ | \$____ | \$____ |
| — Work in Process | ____ | ____ | ____ | ____ |
| — Finished Goods | ____ | ____ | ____ | ____ |
| — Supplies | ____ | ____ | ____ | ____ |
|     Total | \$____ | \$____ | \$____ | \$____ |
| — Percent Raw Material to Sales | ___% | ___% | ___% | ___% |
| — Percent Total Inventory to Sales | ___% | ___% | ___% | ___% |
| — Slow Moving | | | | |
|     Amount | \$____ | \$____ | \$____ | \$____ |
|     Percent to Total | ___% | ___% | ___% | ___% |
| | | | | |
| Working Capital | | | | |
|     Amount | \$____ | \$____ | \$____ | \$____ |
|     Percent to Sales | ___% | ___% | ___% | ___% |

FIGURE 16.7   BALANCE SHEET ITEMS

| Unit | Expenditures Requiring Approval | | | | Expenditures Not Requiring Approval | | | | Total YTD Spent | Total YTD Spent, Forecast, and Contemplated | Total Plan | (Over) Under from Plan |
|---|---|---|---|---|---|---|---|---|---|---|---|---|
| | Completed & Spent | In Process Spent | Forecast | Contemplated | Completed & Spent | In Process Spent | Forecast | Contemplated | | | | |
| X | 1,000 | 100 | 150 | 300 | 300 | 100 | 100 | 150 | 1,500 | 2,200 | 2,000 | (200) |
| Y | | | | | | | | | | | | |
| Z | | | | | | | | | | | | |

FIGURE 16.8  REPORT OF COMPANY EXPENDITURE OF FUNDS (THOUSANDS)

ableness of the estimates, it is useful to compare the funds actually disbursed to date against the total funds forecasted to be spent on both approved and contemplated projects.

**Monitoring Issues/Activities.** At some point during the planning period each opportunity or the avoidance of a potential problem. Examples of these *critical* accomplishment of its plan or to its overall profitable performance. It could be an opportunity or the avoidance of a potential problem. Examples of these *critical issues* are:

- A labor negotiation;
- An introduction of a new product key to the sales growth;
- Building of a plant required for additional capacity; and
- A major reorganization.

By identifying critical issues within each operating unit, the controller can focus and direct management's attention toward developing appropriate programs and plans. These issues are more easily monitored if reported in narrative form. Each month, functional reports by the unit managers or division heads should include an update on how the unit is managing its critical issues.

*Functional reports.* Each functional manager in areas such as marketing, manufacturing, sales, technical (R&D), and accounting should develop workable objectives and plans each year, subject to approval as part of the overall plan. These objectives should identify what must be accomplished in each functional area to support the unit in accomplishing its plan, or what involvement is required in the program to resolve the unit's critical issue. The monthly operating manager's report should describe progress in accomplishing functional objectives, explain variances from plan, and outline actions to be taken to correct or avoid such variances. These reports should be distributed to the unit manager and to corporate staff managers with corresponding functional responsibilities. The reports give the corporate staff members concerned a broad view of activities in their areas of responsibility and expertise. In turn, staff managers are expected to comment on the reports they receive and to offer appropriate advice and assistance to their counterparts in the operating units.

## Ratios

Another way to monitor performance is through the use of ratios. If ratios are to be used effectively, it is important that management fully understand what they represent. Ratios are extremely helpful in highlighting a trend in performance and in providing an additional vehicle for interpreting operating results. In general, a ratio by itself is not significant, but should be compared to plan (how well the firm is doing versus estimated performance), to the previous year (any improvement, trends, etc.), and to industry averages (competition).

In several of the following presentations, the ratios that reflect operating conditions have been calculated by using the monthly average for the last three months as the numerator, and sales for the last three months annualized as the denominator. This is done in lieu of only using twelve-month annual figures. Normally, figures representing a three-month period will reflect a significant trend earlier and more dramatically than twelve-month figures. Using a three-month average has advantages over using a one-month annualized number because the dramatic effect of a one-month major change is diluted and may not be representative of a trend. In addition to using a three-month ratio calculation, which reflects current trends, rolling twelve-month calculations should also be used to show actual trends without any cyclical influence.

The following ratios do not represent all types in current use, but are considered significant from the standpoint of monitoring performance.

**Monitoring Income (Operating Performance and Productivity of Capital Employed).**

*Gross profit to sales.* Gross profit is the difference between selling price (sales) and the actual cost of goods sold. This ratio indicates how well the company is maintaining and improving its markup on costs incurred in manufacturing the product. This ratio is especially important during inflationary periods because of the tendency to pass on cost increases in the form of price changes. This practice lowers the gross profit percentage because the company is not achieving its primary business objective—making a markup on the cost increases it has incurred. Any lowering of the ratio should be analyzed in terms of cost/price changes or product mix changes.

*Operating expenses to sales.* This ratio measures the efficiency of managing operating expenses in relationship to changing sales volumes. The ratio is generally compared to that of prior periods or industry averages. With continuing inflationary cost increases, management of these costs is imperative to a profitable operation. The ratio should decrease with an increasing sales volume if costs are being properly managed. Any increase in the ratio should be analyzed and promptly brought to the attention of management.

*Operating profit to sales.* This ratio is an important test of management's overall performance. It should be compared to industry averages, prior periods, and the budget.

*After-tax return on average stockholders' equity.* This ratio is a significant test of management's performance and determines what return has been earned on the shareholders' investment. The ratio is expressed as follows:

$$\frac{\text{After-Tax Earnings}}{\substack{\text{Average Equity} \\ \text{(Beginning} + \text{Ending Equity} \div 2)}}$$

Industry averages, as well as historical data and management's objectives (budget), are a good basis for comparison. A drop in this ratio may be caused by many factors—unexpected expenses, higher than normal production costs, a poor product mix, or even inventory losses. The reasons for a low ratio must be documented by the controller and presented to management for corrective action.

*After-tax return on average stockholders' equity plus average long-term debt.* The following ratio measures the earning power of the business, based upon the total investment in the business.

$$\frac{\text{After-Tax Earnings}}{\text{Average Equity} + \text{Average Long-Term Debt}}$$

Many analysts consider it to be the real test of management performance because it is based upon the total investment made in the business by both the shareholders and the long-term creditors. The controller should alert management to a drop in the ratio or an unfavorable variance from plan.

*Number of times interest expense is covered.* This ratio determines the relationship of interest expense to pretax income and is expressed as follows:

$$\frac{\text{Pretax Income} + \text{Interest Expense}}{\text{Interest Expense}}$$

This ratio is used by long-term creditors to check the safety of their interest payments. The higher the ratio, the safer the interest coverage. Two to one is a minimum satisfactory ratio. Loan covenants will often provide for certain interest coverage to be maintained.

*Return on parent's investment in a division or subsidiary.* What should be considered in determining a division's or subsidiary unit's operating income? Should corporate interest costs apply? Should an allocation of corporate overhead be made? Should long-term research and development be charged to an operating unit?

How should a subsidiary investment be calculated? Total assets? Net worth? Should a portion of corporate long-term debt be allocated?

Whatever determination works for a specific company will depend upon a number of factors, but regardless of the method chosen, a return on a subsidiary unit's investment should be established and reported on during each reporting period. Generally, the ratio is computed on the basis of total assets and pretax income, including corporate interest charges or credits. Corporate overhead is usually excluded from the computation.

This ratio should be a key performance criterion and should be tied directly into management incentive bonus calculations.

*Unit's investment turnover.* Calculating investment turnover is helpful for comparison purposes in analyzing the investment required to support the unit's sales levels. The ratio is expressed as follows:

$$\frac{\text{Annualized Sales}}{\text{Average Monthly Investment in Unit}}$$

*Number of times fixed cost is covered by profit contribution.* Profit contribution is defined here as sales less variable cost.

$$\frac{\text{Profit Contribution}}{\text{Fixed Cost}}$$

This is another way to look at breakeven. A ratio of one is a breakeven. Anything less than two indicates a situation highly sensitive to any change in either variable costs, fixed costs, or sales volume and should be watched closely.

*Productivity.* No concept has received more attention during the latter part of the 1970s than productivity, and it will continue to be a "hot" issue in the 1980s.

Defining and measuring productivity involves a review of the specific business and its product lines. In general terms, productivity compares output to input, or, the change in the product obtained for the resources expended. The resources expended could be material, labor, power, facilities, or any combination of these. Therefore, a change in productivity is any alteration in the output-input relationship. If dollars are used as a unit of measure, the effect of changing prices (inflation) must be removed by using a price index.

There are several general ratios that can be used to measure productivity. A productivity ratio for any one period is not significant. Significance is only derived from comparing the ratio for similar producing units, industries, or sectors *over time* (rate of change), or in comparing *levels of productivity* (actual change).

Attempts should be made to measure both output and input in physical volumes, thereby eliminating the effect of price changes. The controller should be familiar with the following commonly used productivity ratios:

$$\frac{\text{Output (Physical Goods or Services Quantified)}}{\text{Input (Direct Labor Hours or Machine Hours)}}$$

The above ratio measures the number of direct labor or machine hours for each unit (goods or services) produced. If the company has developed standards for each product or service, the ratio would be compared to standard for significant variance as well as to the reference points mentioned above.

$$\frac{\text{Net Sales}}{\text{Number of Employees}}$$

The net sales to employees ratio measures the average sales dollars produced per employee. This ratio is frequently used by service organizations as a basic measure of productivity.

$$\frac{\text{Net Sales}}{\text{Direct Labor Dollars}}$$

This ratio measures productivity of the labor force. A reduction in the ratios from prior periods, industry averages, or a company standard would require the controller to investigate the reasons for the variance and report to management for corrective action. Where the reasons for the drop in productivity can be localized, the controller should review the reasons for the drop with the production supervisor and request his suggestions for improvement. This information should be included in the report to management.

### Monitoring Accounts Receivable.

*Average collection period.* The average collection period, or the number of days the average sales remains outstanding, should be compared to the business's terms of sale, plan, last year, and industry average, as follows:

$$\frac{\text{Average Monthly Trade Receivable (last three months)}}{\text{Average Sales Per Day}^1 \text{ (last three months)}}$$

If certain receivables are tied up in litigation or long-term customer claim problems, these items should be eliminated from the numerator.

*Percent of trade receivables to sales.* The following ratio indicates the percentage of sales invested in trade receivables. Comparison to plan and prior year is important in order to evaluate the performance of the credit department.

$$\frac{\text{Average Monthly Trade Receivables (last three months)}}{\text{Net Sales (last three months annualized)}}$$

This ratio is used to supplement the average collection period computation, which is the more common ratio.

*Receivables Turnover.* The following ratio is another way to evaluate the efficiency of the credit department in keeping receivables low in relation to sales.

$$\frac{\text{Net Sales (last three months annualized)}}{\text{Average Monthly Trade Receivables (last three months)}}$$

---

[1] $\dfrac{\text{Net Sales for Last Three Months}}{\text{Number of Selling Days (last three months)}}$

*Past due (over sixty days) trade receivable percent.* The following ratio gives a quick look at the percentage of total receivables more than sixty days past due.

$$\frac{\text{Trade Receivables More Than 60 Days Past Due}}{\text{Total Trade Receivables}}$$

A system for reviewing these accounts on a regular basis should be established. Any increase in the percentage over prior periods or over the previous year should be investigated. Complete aging of trade receivables should be prepared on a periodic basis and a list of past due accounts with comments as to collectibility should be prepared for management review.

**Monitoring Inventories.**

*Percent of total inventory to sales.* Inventories represent one of the more important and more difficult assets to control (see Chapter 14). The following ratio indicates the percentage of sales invested in inventory. Comparison to plan, last year, and industry averages will indicate relative performance.

$$\frac{\text{Average Monthly Inventory (last three months)}}{\text{Net Sales (last three months annualized)}}$$

How reasonable the inventory total is in relationship to sales depends upon the company's inventory management system, which must consider some of the following variables: market response needs, distribution channels, facility and equipment capacities, and raw material availability—to name just a few. Inventory levels as a percentage of sales should then be set for the most practical, manageable level of customer service by product line. The ratio calculation should then be made for each major product line and compared to the inventory goals or objectives for that product line. Analysis by distribution centers is also useful.

*Inventory turnover.* The following ratio indicates management's efficiency in keeping inventory low in relation to cost of sales.

$$\frac{\text{Cost of Sales (last three months annualized)}}{\text{Average Inventory (last three months)}}$$

The higher the ratio the better the grade management receives on meeting its inventory management goal. In times of tight credit and high interest rates it may be worthwhile to forego some marginal sales in order to improve inventory turnover.

*Percent of raw material to sales.* It is helpful to analyze periodically the inventory investment in raw material. The following ratio provides another diagnostic review of the inventory composition and can be compared to plan and prior year.

$$\frac{\text{Average Monthly Raw Material Inventory (last three months)}}{\text{Net Sales (last three months annualized)}}$$

Unfavorable trends may require a review of purchasing policies as they relate to the total inventory management program.

*Percent of slow moving/obsolete inventory to total inventories.* Once the controller has determined that the inventory quantity is reasonable—both in total and by product line segment—he still needs a diagnostic review of the composition of inventory quality in terms of its saleability. Identification, on a regular basis, of slow moving and obsolete inventory is important to alert management to a program of disposition. Special marketing programs (reduced price), exchange of product (settlement of customer claim), recycling of product, or total scrapping are some of the available options. The cost of carrying inventory in terms of warehousing, handling, administration, and financing is currently high and is a prime factor toward encouraging identification and disposition of these items.

$$\frac{\text{Identified Slow-Moving or Obsolete Inventory Dollars}}{\text{Total Inventory}}$$

More specific product line comparison (i.e., slow-moving Item A to total Item A inventory, obsolete Item B to total Item B inventory) is always more desirable.

Comparison to the prior year and the industry's norm is helpful, but the objective should always be zero (no slow-moving or obsolete inventory).

*Number of months of supply.* The following ratio evaluates the current level of inventory in comparison with future sales forecasts.

$$\frac{\text{Current Month's Inventory}}{\text{Forecasted Monthly Cost of Sales}}$$

Unlike most traditional methods of evaluating inventory that calculate historical results, this increasingly popular ratio clearly indicates the adequacy of the current inventory level.

**Working Capital Analysis.** *Working capital* (the net of current assets minus current liabilities) is an important liquidity factor that successful businesses manage well. If the need for working capital is reduced, more money can be applied to expansion and growth of the business, without increasing long-term debt and interest expense.

*Quick asset ratio.* The following ratio indicates the ability of the business to satisfy the immediate demands of creditors. A minimum ratio of one to one is desirable. It is useful to compare results with industry averages.

$$\frac{\text{Cash, Receivables, and Marketable Securities}}{\text{Current Liabilities}}$$

*Current ratio.* The following ratio provides an index of the liquidity of the business, or the margin of safety for short-term creditors. A minimum of two to one is desirable, but is no longer considered essential in an era of tight credit.

$$\frac{\text{Current Assets}}{\text{Current Liabilities}}$$

Many loan covenants will indicate the current ratio the company must maintain. Comparison to industry averages is particularly relevant for this ratio because of the peculiar credit needs of certain businesses, as well as seasonal peaks and lows.

*Percent of current liabilities to sales.* The ratios discussed above affect receivables and inventories, normally the two largest elements of current assets. But how well are current liabilities managed? In fact, what is meant by *managing current liabilities?* Purchases (trade creditors) are normally the biggest items in current liabilities. How well have the prices, terms, and conditions of purchases been negotiated? Have cash flow and creditor terms been maximized to the fullest? Ratios provide some insight into these areas.

The following ratio indicates to what extent trade creditors are being used to finance sales. The higher the ratio, the more trade credit is supporting sales. The danger of a high ratio lies in the fact that any interruption in trade credit will force the company to seek other lines of credit, possibly under unfavorable circumstances.

$$\frac{\text{Average Monthly Current Trade Liabilities (last three months)}}{\text{Sales (last three months annualized)}}$$

The controller should warn management about depending too heavily on trade credit and should request permission to negotiate bank lines of credit as a backup in case trade terms or credit are reduced.

*Current liabilities to working capital.* The following ratio indicates the extent to which current operations are financed by short-term creditors:

$$\frac{\text{Average Monthly Current Liabilities (last three months)}}{\text{Average Working Capital (last three months)}}$$

*Percent of working capital to sales.* The following ratio reflects the combined result of management's efforts in receivables, inventory, and trade payables. A comparison with management's goals, plan, prior year, and industry average should be made.

$$\frac{\text{Average Monthly Working Capital (last three months)}}{\text{Sales (last three months annualized)}}$$

**Fixed Assets.**

*Fixed asset turnover.* The following ratio measures the sales dollars generated per dollar invested in fixed assets.

$$\frac{\text{Annual Sales (last three months annualized)}}{\text{Monthly Average Fixed Assets (last three months)}}$$

Caution must be taken because the dollars involved are from different periods. The ratio could reflect excess plant investment or recent plant expansion.

*Depreciation/Capital expenditure ratio.* The following ratio was a former guideline that used depreciation as a minimum level for replacement of assets.

$$\frac{\text{Annual Depreciation}}{\text{Annual Capital Expenditures}}$$

Inflation conditions have reduced the importance of this ratio. Firms that still use this ratio now substitute replacement cost depreciation for historical cost depreciation.

**Capital Analysis.** The following ratios indicate the sources of the capital employed in the business. Comparison should be made to industry averages or to the company's own financing philosophy.

*Stockholders' equity to total assets.* This ratio measures the relationship of the owners' equity to the total assets employed, and the extent to which the business is financed by its owners.

$$\frac{\text{Stockholders' Equity}}{\text{Total Assets}}$$

The lower the ratio, the more the business is leveraged and the more vulnerable to a credit crunch. The results of this ratio are supplemented by some of the following ratios.

*Long-term debt to total capital.* This ratio indicates the percentage of total capital that the long-term creditors have provided. As a rule of thumb, the long-term debt should not exceed 50 percent of the total.

$$\frac{\text{Total Long-Term Debt}}{\text{Total Capital (including long-term debt)}}$$

*Long-term debt to stockholders' equity.* Another way to analyze the relative size of the long-term debt is to use the following ratio, which compares the owners' investment in the company with that of the long-term creditors.

$$\frac{\text{Total Long-Term Debt}}{\text{Stockholders' Equity}}$$

The higher the ratio, the greater the leverage or use of borrowed funds. A ratio greater than one to one is an indication that the company is too heavily in debt. However, comparison should be made to industry averages and the company's prior history.

*Dividend payout ratio.* The following relationship shows how much income is going to the stockholders instead of being returned to the business to meet operating requirements.

$$\frac{\text{Dividends Paid (Accrued)}}{\text{Net Income}}$$

There is no level of comparison for this ratio because some stockholders are seeking income and want a high payout while others are interested in capital gains and would approve of more earnings being reinvested in the business.

## Graphs

The discussion of monitoring techniques thus far has centered on the reporting and the use of ratios that represent results at a particular time or for a particular period. However, it is sometimes difficult to grasp the trend line. This year's gross margin percentage may be an improvement over last year's and significantly better than plan or industry averages, but management may overlook the fact that over the last several months a deterioration has actually begun.

A graphic presentation of key information allows management to see the complete picture with the trend that has developed. Not only does it aid in obtaining a better interpretation of what has happened, but it also gives insight into evaluating the credibility of future plans and forecasts.

Most businesses have their particular cyclical or seasonal variations. In order to eliminate cyclical variations and obtain a true trend, use of a rolling twelve-month average in presenting the data is useful. Short-term cycles and trends can be reflected by using a three-month annualized number. Presentation of both numbers on a graph provides a better understanding of the business trend. These graphs can be used in several ways.

**Annual Financial Graphs.** Many companies are using graphs more frequently in annual reports. They are very effective in presenting data that covers several years. It's interesting that graphs are used more frequently for outside reporting when operating results have improved. Figures 16.9 and 16.10 are examples of the type of information depicted on annual graphs.

**Operating Graphs.** Monthly graphs of key operating data are useful in monitoring variances and in detecting trends. Another way to present financial data is to give a charting system to management each month.

A rolling twelve-month average eliminates cyclical variances, and when used in conjunction with a three-month annualized number is more responsive to short-term changes or deviations from plan. Some examples follow:

*Gross profit percentage.* Figure 16.11 shows year-to-date actual compared to year-to-date plan and the rolling twelve-month average. This data was charted because the business incurs major month-to-month variations, and it was felt that a year-to-date number better reflected the actual business trend. Charting of monthly

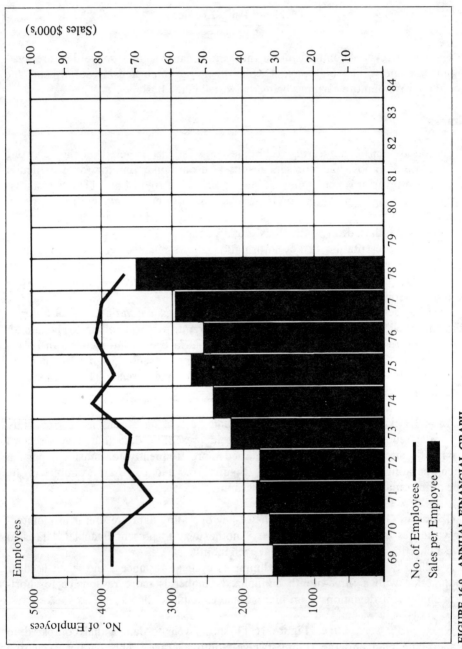

**FIGURE 16.9    ANNUAL FINANCIAL GRAPH**

percentages against plan and last year could be useful for some businesses. Note that the operation had an especially poor start, but was able to improve and ended the year slightly under plan but ahead of 1978.

*Capital expenditures.* In Figure 16.12 the plan amount for the total year ($7.0 million) was charted. Each month, the forecasted expenditures for the year were charted against the year-to-date actual. Note the rush to spend during the last two months of the year and how the forecast in August still did not realistically project expenditures for the year. This same information can be charted for different business segments as shown in Figure 16.13.

*Inventories—percent of sales.* Figure 16.14, while initially appearing difficult, is really easy to understand. The plan is for average monthly inventory for 1979 to be 16.2 percent of sales. The twelve-month rolling average shows the improvement from 1978 of 18.2 percent (see December) to 15.8 percent in 1979. The monthly plan and actual are using three-month annualized numbers and show the cyclical nature of the business and how well the unit performed during those periods (i.e., above plan earlier in year and below plan most of the last nine months).

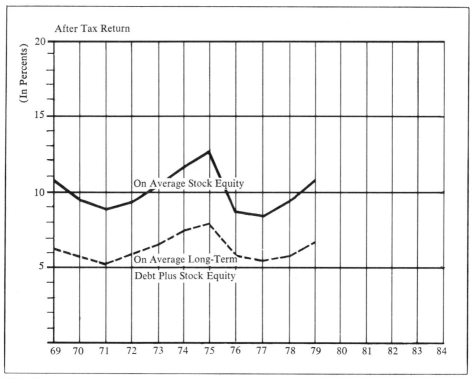

FIGURE 16.10   ANNUAL FINANCIAL GRAPH—RETURN ON INVESTMENT

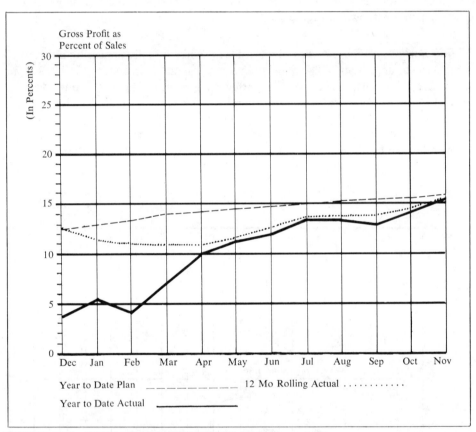

FIGURE 16.11   GROSS PROFIT PERCENTAGE GRAPH

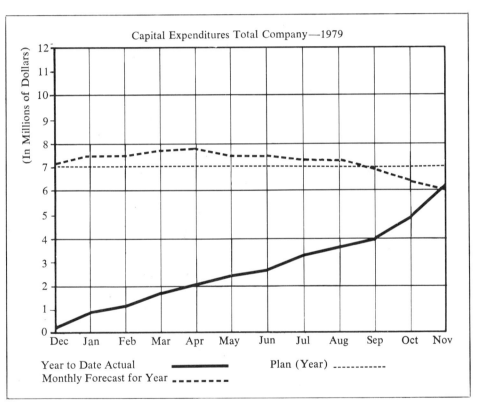

FIGURE 16.12  CAPITAL EXPENDITURES GRAPH

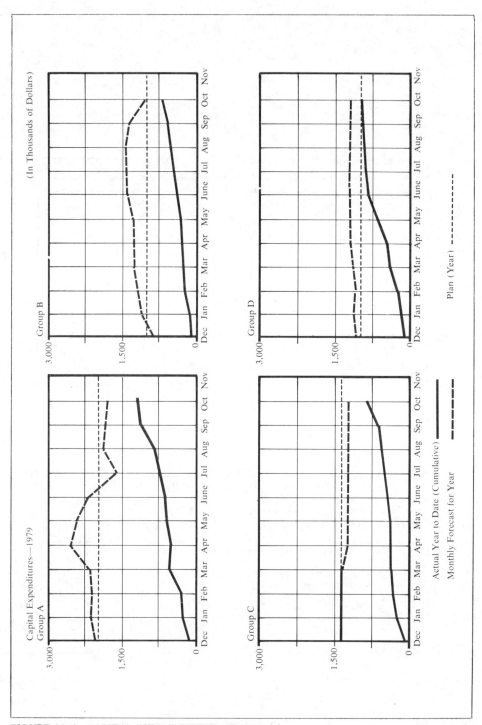

FIGURE 16.13   CAPITAL EXPENDITURES GRAPH

**Other Uses of Graphs.** Graphs can be used in ways other than just for monitoring the financial/operational results of a business. They are very helpful in tracking the trend of a business over a long period of time or to see if the business is related to any outside indices which will affect its sales. For example, sales and orders may be compared to outside market indicators such as housing permits or construction permits to see what effect they have on the sales of a business.

## REVIEW MEETINGS

There is no better way to understand, interpret, and evaluate the results of a business on an ongoing basis than to have direct contact and discussion with the people who are making it happen. Scheduled meetings could include the following:

- Monthly/quarterly—operating performance review, actual versus plan;

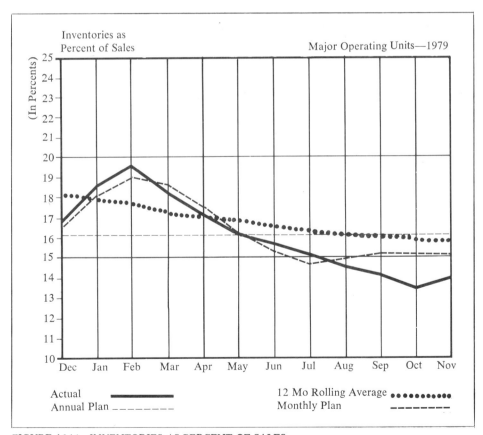

FIGURE 16.14  INVENTORIES AS PERCENT OF SALES

- Planning assumptions and strategies meeting; and
- Plan presentation and acceptance meeting.

Meetings like these provide corporate management with opportunities to meet with unit operating management as a group. Open and candid discussions provide an environment not only for better interpretation of performance but also provide a chance to clarify policies and strategies.

## SUGGESTED READING

Coleman, Almand R., "Restructuring the Statement of Changes in Financial Position." *Financial Executive*, (January, 1979), pp. 34-42.

Copeland, Ronald M. and Dascher, Paul E., *Managerial Accounting.* New York: Chichester, Brisbane, Toronto: John Wiley & Sons, 1978.

Davis, Hiram S., *Productivity Accounting*, Reprinted. Philadelphia: University of Pennsylvania, The Wharton School, 1978.

Kendrick, John W., *Understanding Productivity.* Baltimore: Johns Hopkins Press, 1977.

*Management Philosophy.* Monterey Park, California: Ameron, Inc., August, 1978.

# Part IV

## Internal Control Functions

# 17

# Internal Control Systems

*Frederick L. Neumann*

## NATURE OF INTERNAL CONTROL

The growth and increased complexity of business has fostered an awareness of the need for improved methods of internal control. The rapid proliferation of computers and electronic data communication facilities has provided new opportunities for errors and irregularities, and these opportunities demand a new variety of controls. One contribution of the computer is its ability to rapidly prepare and disseminate reports. Time allowed for decisions is becoming shorter, and more factors must be considered. New controls are needed to ensure the reliability of the information these reports contain.

The scope of the term *internal control* can be gleaned from the AICPA definition formulated in 1948:

> Internal control comprises the plan of organization and all of the coordinate methods and measures adopted within a business to safeguard its assets, check the accuracy and reliability of its accounting data, promote operational efficiency, and encourage adherence to prescribed managerial policies.[1]

The publication in which this definition appeared acknowledged that it was very broad. Subsequently, the definition was divided into *administrative control* and *accounting control*. The two types are not mutually exclusive, since certain procedures and records may serve as both types of control. Management is interested in, and internal auditors remain responsible for, the entire range of control.

### Accounting Control

Accounting control is of primary interest to the external auditor. It comprises:

> [t]he plan of organization and the procedures and records that are concerned with the safeguarding of assets and the reliability of financial records and consequently are designed to provide reasonable assurance that:
> a. Transactions are executed in accordance with management's general or specific authorization.
> b. Transactions are recorded as necessary (1) to permit preparation of financial

---

[1] Committee on Auditing Procedure, *Internal Control* (New York: American Institute of Certified Public Accountants, 1949), p. 6.

statements in conformity with generally accepted accounting principles or any other criteria applicable to such statements and (2) to maintain accountability for assets.

c. Access to assets is permitted only in accordance with management's authorization.

d. The recorded accountability for assets is compared with the existing assets at reasonable intervals and appropriate action is taken with respect to any differences.[2]

This definition has been widely publicized, since it is the one included, virtually verbatim, in the Foreign Corrupt Practices Act (see Chapter 18).

### Administrative Control

According to the current definition, administrative control "includes but is not limited to the plan of organization and the procedures and records that are concerned with the decision processes leading to management's authorization of transactions."[3] The AICPA points out that such authorization is a management function that precedes the establishment of accounting control of transactions.[4]

## AN EXPLANATION OF CONTROL

### Control by Accountability

Control, in a general sense, encompasses the entire effort made to conform results to plans. Control becomes an important part of any activity when the delegation of authority and the assignment of responsibility to subordinates call for some accountability for that stewardship. Accountability requires that the responsible individual or unit provide some evidence that the assigned task was accomplished and submit a report comparing the outcome to the plan. This concept of control through accountability focuses on the major reason for management's introduction of controls. Managers are unable to perform or even personally oversee much of what is accomplished in an organization, yet they need some assurance that their desires have been carried out.

In summary, control is a major management responsibility. It is a mandated surrogate for a manager's effective personal performance.

---

[2] *Codification of Auditing Standards and Procedures*, Auditing Standards Board, Statement on Auditing Standards No. 1 (New York: American Institute of Certified Public Accountants, 1973), p. 20.

[3] *Ibid.*

[4] *Ibid.*

## Reasons For Controls

There are a number of supporting reasons controls are used:

- Plans may lack clarity or be poorly communicated. Controls can reduce the possible losses from potential misunderstanding.
- The objectives of individuals selected to carry out the tasks may be different from the objectives of those who planned them. Controls can help keep the two in agreement.
- Circumstances may change during delays in implementing plans. Controls can help keep activity on target nevertheless.

In general, through anticipation, measurement, and adjustment, controls help organizations realize their planned objectives.

## Control As Part of the Accounting Process

Control has traditionally been regarded as an integral part of the planning and implementation process. It consists of the following steps:

1. Formulation of plans and the appropriate organizational patterns to carry them out. Plans provide a predetermined blueprint for performance.
2. Creation of plan objectives and relevant standards of performance. The standards provide the basis for evaluating performance and may be either quantitative or qualitative.
3. Establishment of controls and the communication thereof to those involved in implementing the plans. Controls attempt to keep performance within acceptable limits and point out instances when this is not the case.
4. Measurement of performance. This measurement, denominated in the same units as the appropriate predetermined standards, is necessary to determine progress and to perform the next step.
5. Comparison of measured performance to relevant standards. The purpose of this comparison is to ascertain the extent to which performance is conforming to plan.
6. Analysis of causes of deviation. Management must determine the causes of significant actual and potential deviations in order to take the next step.
7. Corrective action. Such action is the goal of the control process and may be accomplished by changing the plans or altering the activity.

It is important to recognize the entire scope of the control process and the significance of each step, from planning through corrective action. Promulgation of controls cannot reasonably take place without relevant standards, which are developed from plan objectives. Implementation of controls is not complete without suitable corrective action against potential and actual deviations or variances.

## Characteristics of Controls

Effective controls must meet the standards discussed below.

**Timeliness.** Controls should detect, in a cost-effective manner, potential or actual deviations from plans early enough to limit costly exposures. Ideally, problems should be anticipated and prevented. But if this is not possible, problems should be promptly discovered and dealt with when they do occur.

**Economy.** Individual controls and systems of control, taken together, should provide "reasonable assurance" of achieving intended results at a minimum of cost and undesirable consequences. As in any economically defined decision, the costs should not outweigh the benefits expected to be achieved. Management is therefore responsible for considering the economy and efficiency of controls as well as their effectiveness. These concerns may be evident not only in the selection of controls but also in their application on a test or sampling basis.

One of the questions often asked is, how much control is enough? In concept, at least, the economic law of diminishing returns should govern. That is, controls should be increased as long as the marginal benefit they provide is greater than their incremental cost.

**Accountability.** Controls should be available to those responsible for carrying out the plan and should help achieve effective performance and detect deficiencies.

**Placement.** Controls should be located at those points and occur during those periods where they will be most cost-effective. Possible control points include those: (1) prior to a particularly expensive portion of a project; (2) prior to the stage after which reversal of activity would be difficult; (3) between two significant phases; (4) where measurement is convenient; (5) at which it may be easy (or possible) to take corrective action; and (6) after completion of a complex task or an error-prone activity.

**Flexibility.** Since alterations in plans and procedures are certain to occur, controls that can tolerate such modifications without themselves requiring adjustment are preferred.

**Standard Implementation.** Standard responses can be prepared in advance and readily implemented if the problem addressed is clearly indicated.

**Measurability.** Controls that allow objective quantification in the same denomination as the established standards permit direct evaluation without translation. Simple, specific, and relevant measures for both controls and standards greatly facilitate comparisons and evaluations.

**Appropriateness.** Controls should be consistent with their purpose and setting. They should fit the nature and structure of the plan, mesh with the personnel and organization to which they are applied, and be responsive to the needs of the individuals responsible for the activity.

For purposes of efficiency, controls are often designed to work on an exception basis, reporting only significant deviations.

### Classification of Controls

**Type of Impact.** Controls may be considered direct or indirect, depending on their relationship to the actual flow of activity and on how they affect problems. Direct controls are preferred, other things being equal, because they immediately impact the problem.

**Purpose.** Controls are commonly considered preventive, detective, or corrective, based on whether they take effect before or after the problem occurs or are part of the ameliorative effort. Mair, Wood, and Davis point out that *preventive controls*, which are commonly built-in, are often less expensive than the others but are usually less effective as well.[5] Authorization and some record-keeping procedures are examples. *Detective controls* do not reduce the frequency of problems but rather signal their occurrence. Detective controls are essential to ascertain whether preventive controls are effective and whether corrective controls are needed. Generally, detective controls are more expensive than preventive controls, but the latter may not be available. *Corrective controls* are intended to ensure the removal or reduction of problems without creating any new ones. Corrective controls are often the most expensive of all and the most difficult to implement.

**Levels of Control.** Control may also be examined at two levels.

*Organizational controls.* Some controls apply to the operation of the entire organization or a substantial portion thereof. Evaluations based on accounting measures are examples of such controls.

*Operational controls.* Controls at the operating level deal with individual activities and transactions. The consequences of deviations at this level are usually less severe but demand a more prompt response. The quality of organizational controls may influence the effectiveness of controls at the operating level.

**General and Application Controls.** General and application controls, often discussed in connection with an EDP environment are comparable to organizational and operational controls. *General controls* relate to all EDP activities and comprise:

---

[5] W. Mair, D. Wood, and K. Davis, *Computer Control and Audit* (Altamonte Springs, Fla.: The Institute of Internal Auditors, 1977), p. 36.

- A plan of organization and operation of all EDP activity;
- The procedures for documenting, receiving, testing, and approving systems or programs and changes thereto;
- Controls built into equipment by manufacturers;
- Controls over access to equipment and data files; and
- Other data and procedural controls affecting overall EDP operations.[6]

*Application controls* relate to specific accounting tasks performed by EDP and are usually categorized as *input, processing,* and *output controls.*

**Timing of Controls.** Controls are sometimes categorized as to their timing. *Ex ante controls* act in anticipation, warning of potential problems before they occur. They are preventive. Cash-flow forecasts used to plan investment and borrowing needs are an example. *Real-time controls* (such as quality control techniques) are detective controls and permit a corrective response while the activity is still in process. They act to limit exposure. *Ex post controls* provide information about how well objectives were met after the processing has been completed. The major contribution of ex post controls is as a basis for rewards or sanctions and as a possible source of information for future planning. Most accounting information is of this type.

### Problems With Controls

Controls are a mixed blessing. Although they keep an activity on course, they do so at a price. Controls and their implementation involve both monetary and human costs. Systems can be overcontrolled. Redundant or unimportant checks intended to provide additional assurance may in reality produce increased confusion, frustration, and decreased effectiveness. Furthermore, controls may not be cost-beneficial and may protect against problems the costs of which do not approach the cost of the controls themselves. Some controls may also shift attention from areas where control is needed and deserved.

**Confusion of Means and Ends.** If controls receive such emphasis that they are viewed as ends rather than means, concern will be with satisfying the controls rather than accomplishing the objectives. Operational controls may work to the detriment of organizational controls if an appropriate sense of relative importance is not preserved. Controls may also engender rigidity and inflexibility, both in fact and in attitude. Controls must be kept in proper perspective if they are to satisfactorily fulfill their role.

---

[6] *The Effects of EDP on the Auditor's Study and Evaluation of Internal Control,* Auditing Standards Board Statement on Auditing Standards No. 3 (New York: American Institute of Certified Public Accountants, 1974), p. 3.

**Obsolescence.** Controls can become obsolete and may no longer relate to current management objectives. Controls may even become counterproductive and hinder those activities. The purpose of controls must be kept constantly in mind. When those purposes are no longer appropriate, or other controls can meet them in a more cost-effective manner, existing controls should be modified or removed.

**Redundancy.** Overlapping controls provide expanded protection and back-up assurance against various problems and their related exposures. Nevertheless, controls are costly and must be evaluated in terms of the benefits they provide.

**Nonresponsiveness.** Effective controls may not be useful ones for several reasons. A control's signal may be insufficient to identify the problem or irrelevant in terms of the needed response. Alternatively, it may be accompanied by so much detail that it delays any response. If reporting mechanisms fail to match organizational needs, information may go to individuals who are not in a position to respond. An appropriate, timely response is a key objective of a control.

**The Human Element.** Controls have been known to frustrate creative and imaginative responses. Individual initiative, a very valuable resource, may be destroyed by inappropriate controls. Attitudes toward control and the organization may suffer if controls are not thoughtfully implemented. If the staff does not understand controls and had no role in their design or imposition, staff members may resist attempts to interfere with their activity and resent any added effort required on their part that detracts from an activity's main purpose. To the extent that controls become a basis for personnel rewards and sanctions, they take on further importance in the eyes of those affected. In the design and execution of controls, the human element and the effect on the persons involved must always be considered.

## INTERNAL CONTROL ENVIRONMENT

The term *internal control environment* describes the factors that impinge on a system of internal controls by affecting the general atmosphere in which they are implemented. These factors can have a significant positive or negative impact on the selection and performance of internal controls. Furthermore, a strong control environment tends to reduce the likelihood of irregularities. Among those factors that affect the control environment are:

- The organization plan;
- Management support;
- Personnel and personnel policies;
- Internal auditing; and
- Procedures and practices.

### Organization Plan

The size and type of business, geographical dispersion, management philosophy, and other factors may all influence an organization's structure and the nature and form of its controls. Moreover, a change in one or more of these factors often necessitates some alteration of the organizational structure. Nevertheless, there are some general observations that can be made about how an organization plan is constructed and implemented that have wide applicability.

**Elements of Good Planning.** Sound organizational principles reflect both good management practice and appropriate control considerations. How well an organization plan serves its function may be judged by how effectively it provides a framework for performing and controlling prescribed activities. A sound organization should avoid gaps in responsibility, overlapping functions, duplication of effort, unreasonable spans of control, and working at cross-purposes.

*Simplicity and flexibility.* Simplicity makes the plan easier to understand, and flexibility permits it to deal more swiftly with a wider variety of conditions, both anticipated and unanticipated. Excessive detail in specifying functions and responsibilities may be stifling. Yet, the structure of an organization should be logically designed and well enough defined to take advantage of work specialization.

*Clear lines of authority and responsibility.* Authority is the grant of power to carry out a mandate; responsibility comes with accountability for results. To be effective and fair, the assignment of responsibility should provide a commensurate delegation of authority to accomplish it. Responsibility and authority need to be clearly established at appropriate levels, with no gaps or overlaps in assignments. It is important to know not only what is planned but also who is responsible for carrying out the plan, who is to act if it breaks down, and what power they have at their disposal. Subordinates need to know who can make decisions that affect their behavior. Open communication between superior and subordinate should make this clear. The delegation and circumscription of authority over specific activities should be structured to facilitate effective review and evaluation.

**Lines of Communication.** The plan should set forth in unambiguous terms the defined authority for each staff member and how that authority relates to the roles of others. Putting all members' responsibilities and the accompanying delegation of authority in writing and making such information readily available to all parties affected will help to avoid misunderstandings. Up-to-date organization charts, position descriptions, and procedures manuals are ways this may be achieved. Clear, explicit descriptions of personnel responsibilities will help operating employees learn their duties and those of others, and facilitate review by those who monitor controls.

**Areas of Responsibility.** There are several parties who should play specific roles in a plan of organization for control.

*Board of directors and audit committee.* The board of directors and its audit committee must perform certain authorizations, and they should approve others. They should vote on specific large outlays and budgets. In discharging their fiduciary responsibility, directors need to understand internal control and, in general, how it works. Specifically, they should be concerned that the system of control is responsive to company needs. They should review and approve basic control policies and their dissemination. The board or its audit committee may review the system with management and the auditors. They may oversee compliance by requiring periodic tests of, and reports on, the functioning of the system. They may suggest changes or revisions as needed and see that appropriate action is taken regarding possible violations of policy.

*Senior management.* Senior management is primarily responsible for guiding the business and providing the internal control environment. It also has responsibility for the overall design of the internal control system. It sets the tone and disseminates policy. It is responsible for the implementation of internal control, as well as for its continual monitoring. In this role, it identifies exposures and establishes the factors used in evaluating their significance and determining cost-benefit relationships. Senior management should see that the system is documented and that any significant weaknesses are corrected. It should initiate any required changes in policy. Close relations and excellent communication between senior management and the members of the board are required to achieve a successful system of internal control.

*Financial management.* The controller and his staff are involved with the establishment and continual supervision of major portions of the control environment. They must establish the appropriate control objectives, design the control procedures, and supervise their implementation. They are responsible for the design of the financial planning and reporting systems as well as for all related communication.

## Management Support

Continual support of controls by management is essential, not only to achieve compliance with the controls but also to establish a proper employee attitude toward them. The absence of active management support may lead to erratic performance of some controls or their neglect altogether. Opposition by management may make some controls inoperative, because employees may fear management reprisals if they comply with the controls. Management's attitude at every level—from the board of directors down through the first-line supervisors—should be clearly supportive of internal control. It should encourage the installation of appropriate controls and foster compliance by providing suitable reinforcement of desired behavior.

Management's attitudes can be manifested directly or indirectly. They may be explicitly enunciated in policy statements such as codes of conduct, or indirectly communicated through responses to reports. It may be helpful to formalize positive management attitudes by putting such policies and procedures in writing.

**Continual Monitoring.** Continual monitoring by management is necessary to prevent neglect and deterioration of a system. Systems are prone to breakdowns, or even manipulation, if not given adequate supervision. The monitoring system must itself be monitored if it is to be effective over a sustained period. Prompt detection of weaknesses is essential to preserve a system's integrity. Constant surveillance is necessary to ensure not only that controls are implemented but also that employees remain alert and effective.

Management must see that:

- Prescribed policies are being interpreted properly and are being carried out;
- Changes in operating conditions have not made procedures cumbersome, obsolete, or inadequate;
- Effective corrective measures are taken promptly when breakdowns in the system appear; and
- Proposed changes are carefully screened to be sure they are an improvement and will not cause any problems for the system.[7]

Monitoring may take the form of direct observation, analysis of budget variances, reports, audits or similar examinations, or authorization of changes. Whatever the form of monitoring adopted, there should be documentation of its implementation and of its results. Standard procedures for updating documentation should be a regular part of system changes. (One of those procedures would be prompt notification of any change to all personnel concerned.)

Personal observation and review are valuable forms of monitoring, particularly if employees are inexperienced and transactions are sensitive. It may be the only formal means of validating controls when documentation is absent.

## Personnel and Personnel Policies

There is perhaps no clearer means of detecting management's attitude and its policy toward controls than by examining how it staffs its operations. In a well-run business, management hires capable and trustworthy people, gives them appropriate and well-defined authority and responsibility, and monitors their performance. People implement a system and can cause it to succeed or fail, based on how well they perform. The person responsible for controls is usually in the best position to assess their adequacy and ensure their effectiveness.

**Errors and Irregularities.** There can be no perfect system of control—that is, a system in which no causes of exposure exist. People, like machines, can fail.

---

[7] Committee on Auditing Procedure, p. 18.

Employees may misunderstand instructions, make honest mistakes of judgment, or err through carelessness caused by fatigue or distraction. They may intentionally circumvent controls by colluding with others or, if they are in positions of management, simply by overriding the controls. Controls are designed primarily to prevent and detect problems caused by single individuals acting in isolation.

**Effective Staffing Procedures.** Hiring practices, personnel evaluation policies, and training programs all may influence the effectiveness of internal controls involving staff participation, but do not guarantee its achievement. Careful selection of employees and, when appropriate, investigation of their backgrounds, as well as adequate recognition of their efforts, can all help to build an honest, highly motivated work force as well as to reduce employee turnover. It is still wise to require fidelity bonds for positions of trust. Although their preventive attributes are questionable, their corrective benefits are clear.

Effective training not only improves performance but also impresses employees with the importance of implementing and abiding by procedures and controls. In addition, training meetings can inform employees of developments and changes in the organization. Instruction alone cannot assure compliance. Employee performance at every level must be recognized, reviewed, and evaluated. Sufficient resources to enable the performance of assigned tasks are one form of adequate recognition given employees. Appropriate remuneration and timely advancement are others. Corrective steps, when warranted, should be promptly taken.

## Internal Auditing

**Auditors' Duties.** Management, and therefore the internal auditor, has a broader internal control focus than the external auditor has. External auditors are immediately concerned only with the reliability of the financial statements; internal auditors have a wider scope. They do perform financial examinations, but they are interested not only in controls to safeguard assets and ensure the integrity of financial records but also in promoting operational efficiency and encouraging adherence to prescribed managerial policies and corporate objectives. Internal auditors provide information about the adequacy and effectiveness of an organization's system of internal control and the quality of performance in carrying out assigned responsibilities. They evaluate operational efficiency in operational audits and consider adherence to management policies in compliance examinations. They also provide analyses, appraisals, recommendations, counsel, and information concerning activities reviewed.

Internal auditing then is a supracontrol, determining whether results are efficiently obtained and whether controls are operating effectively. It serves as an organizational control at the highest level as well as a link between management planning and operating performance.

**A Written Charter.** A written charter should define the internal auditor's purpose, authority, and responsibility—as well as his position within the organization. The charter should also define the scope of internal audit activities and authorize access to records, personnel, and physical properties pertinent to audit performance. This charter should be approved by management and by the board of directors, with whom the auditor should have direct and regular communciation.

**Preserving Independence.** To accomplish their responsibilities, internal auditors (although they are an integral part of the organization) must be so positioned in the organizational structure that they can perform their work in a free and objective manner. This has been interpreted to mean being responsible to an individual in the organization with "sufficient authority to promote independence and to insure broad audit coverage, adequate consideration of audit reports, and appropriate action on audit recommendations."[8]

Internal auditors should endeavor to maintain their objectivity by carefully avoiding conflicts of interest. Internal auditors should not be assigned operating responsibilities, but if they are, they should not audit those activities. In any event, it is a good idea to rotate staff assignments.

To produce reliable reports, the internal audit department must be free of any influence from the departments about which it reports. Neither its scope nor its programs nor its reports should be arbitrarily circumscribed by auditees. The actions of internal auditors, in turn, should fully justify the support of management.

The internal audit staff should be large enough to accomplish its tasks. Members should be competent and objective. The training and experience of staff and supervisors is important and should be continually attended to. There should be sufficient supervision to guide staff personnel and to review their work.

## General Procedures and Practices

There are extensive procedures and practices related to effective control. Some characteristics are quite general and are widely applicable. Consider, for example, the following guides to improve operational efficiency and control in two areas common to all firms: communication media and management information systems.

**Communication Media.** Communication media (including documents, forms, and other records) should be:

- *Unobtrusive.* They should be programmed to accomplish their purpose in a manner that facilitates the performance of the related activity without interference.
- *Simple.* They should be sufficiently straightforward to permit easy understanding and prompt processing, with a minimum of error or cost. For example, a line for proper authorization should be prominently displayed.
- *Comprehensive.* They should be designed to serve multiple uses to keep the number of forms to a minimum.

---

[8] *Standards for the Professional Practice of Internal Auditing* (Altamonte Springs, Fla.: The Institute of Internal Auditors, 1978), pp. 100-101.

- *Control-oriented*. They should be constructed to reinforce adherence to control procedures and to encourage correct preparation. For example, spaces should be conveniently provided to indicate performance of various clerical checks.
- *Effective*. They should be adequate to provide reasonable assurance that all assets are controlled and all transactions recorded.

**Management Information Systems.** Management information systems (including budgets, cost accounting systems, and operating analyses) should be:

- *Adequate*. Information should be in proper form and in sufficient detail to meet the needs of the decision model being used.
- *Accurate*. Information should be appropriate for the designated use. If it is an accounting report, generally accepted accounting principles will govern.
- *Timely*. Enough time should be provided to permit ample consideration of the information before a decision is required. This will vary with the significance of the item and the nature of the decisions based on it.
- *Complete*. Within reason, information should answer all the decision maker's questions. Comparative data (including nonfinancial data) and analytical comments should be considered.

## SYSTEMS AND THE FLOW OF TRANSACTIONS

Increasingly, organizations are being looked at as systems composed of mechanical, economic, and human parts. A systems orientation permits an orderly and organized approach to widely varying elements. The hallmark of a system is a structure or arrangement of interdependent parts or subsystems that interact to achieve a specific enterprise objective and are monitored to ensure that the desired results are obtained. The effect of this interaction is often greater than the sum of the effects of the individual parts—a phenomenon called *synergism*.

When an organization is viewed as a system, it is itself part of a supersystem, the economy, and is in turn composed of marketing, production, financial, and information subsystems, among others.

An advantage of using a systems orientation in viewing an activity is the emphasis it gives to identifying critical variables and important constraints, their interaction with each other, and the effect of external forces on the system that may influence, modify, or change it.

### Information Subsystem

One of the more important subsystems of an organization is that of information. Sometimes referred to as MIS, or *management information system*, this organizational subsystem is an integrated process whose elements accept data from internal and external sources and transform them into useful and timely information for the common purpose of facilitating decision making by management. It therefore includes accounting information as one of its own subsystems. Accounting in turn, comprises subsystems for revenues, expenses, inventories, and others.

Systems orientation has become the predominant influence in control evaluation. Rather than emphasizing functions or accounts, the approach to controls has shifted to the complete span of activity involved in processing a transaction.

### Transaction Analysis

Transactions include exchanges of assets or services with parties outside the business entity and transfers of assets or services for use within it. They thus encompass any activity involving accountable resources.

**Transactions and Record Keeping.** The basic relationships between transactions and record keeping are diagramed in Figure 17.1. Initiation is placed outside the external auditors' definition of internal accounting control. Internal auditors look to authorization as the point of first concern because it is not until this point that a transaction affecting resources is actually set in motion. In regard to segregation of duties, however, the person who initiates a transaction should not be ignored.

**Authorization.** Authorization that signifies management's intentions with regard to the disposition of assets for some specific purpose or under some specific conditions should be present in some form for all transactions. As a preventive control, it screens a proposed transaction. It also provides standards for evaluation of performance. Sometimes it is general, in that it applies across the board, in blanket fashion, to all transactions that are of a given type or that meet a given set of conditions. *General authorizations* are predicated on established policy. General price lists and inventory reorder formulas are examples of such authorizations. *Specific authorizations* are required for transactions for which management has not granted general authority. They are given for individual transactions involving specific parties and conditions. A purchase of major equipment usually warrants specific authorization by the board of directors. Whatever the type of authorization to be used, management must see that knowledge of it is communicated, and available, to employees who need it. Authorizations should be issued only by competent and

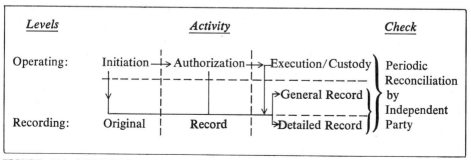

FIGURE 17.1   RELATION OF TRANSACTIONS TO RECORD KEEPING

knowledgeable individuals who are acting within the scope of their authority and have no further involvement in the transaction.

**Execution.** For purposes of control, it is often helpful to analyze the execution of an activity or cycle in smaller segments or steps. A sales transaction, for example, would involve an order entry segment and a picking, packaging, and shipping component. This, in turn, should initiate a billing step and a collection of that billing or its eventual write-off.

Execution embraces whatever series of steps is necessary to carry out the exchange or transfer of assets or services encompassed by the authorization. The term "approval" is often applied to the review process that determines whether the execution has complied with the standards established by the authorization.

Execution may or may not result in the disposal of an asset or the rendering of a service. If it does, a related transaction is usually triggered for the receipt of an asset as part of an exchange (unless a total loss has been incurred). If it does not, custody and custody records must be provided until the next transaction involving the resources occurs.

**Custody of Assets.** Assets should be afforded such physical safeguards as their nature, value, and risk of loss or abuse warrant. Physical safeguards involve environmental protection as well as actual segregation. Physical, direct access (or indirect access through documentary directives) should be limited to those individuals designated by management and by the specified procedures. The nature of the assets, their value, and their susceptibility to manipulation or loss through errors or irregularities may influence who and how many have access. It should be remembered that books and records are valuable assets, too. Access limitations should not, however, unduly stifle business operations.

**The Recording Responsibility.** A dual purpose has been enunciated for the recording responsibility: (1) to permit preparation of financial statements in conformity with generally accepted accounting principles or any other criterion applicable to such statements and (2) to maintain accountability for assets.

*Preparation of statements.* Statement preparation comprises all the appropriate bookkeeping procedures necessary to permit the preparation of financial statements by summarizing the results of transactions. It assumes transactions will be clearly described and recorded at the correct amounts, in the proper period, and in the appropriate accounts. It encompasses a chart of accounts, a complete set of books, and all functions and procedures necessary to keep them. No false entries should be allowed, and valid entries should be recorded in the proper period. This aspect of control is particularly critical because it affects management's ability to make decisions and monitor performance.

*Accountability for assets.* This aspect of the recording responsibility requires that individual responsibility be assigned to resources from the moment a transaction is set in motion until it is completed. It involves the maintenance of custodial records and all procedures necessary to keep them current.

Accountability also makes possible periodic comparisons and reconciliations between the physical assets and the records. Comparisons may also be made between records of the same information kept by different individuals, such as control accounts and detailed subsidiary balances. The frequency of the comparisons and who makes them vary depending on the nature of the asset involved, its value, and the cost of the comparison. Appropriate action is then possible with regard to any variances between records and assets or between records and other records that result from unrecorded or improperly recorded transactions. Agreement of accounts and records, however, is no assurance of correct recording, since both could be in error. Such a comparison at reasonable intervals (with regard to asset materiality and susceptibility to loss) is an integral part of internal accounting control. Physical counts of inventory, and their reconciliation to perpetual records, are but one example of this activity. Bank reconciliations are another.

The accounting responsibility requires adjustments in records for changes in assets, their value, or ownership. Accountability also calls for notification of changes in custody. As a consequence, the recording function must be promptly apprised of any events or activities that affect assets.

**Segregation of Recording Responsibility.** Control is enhanced if the authorization function and the recording function are performed by individuals not responsible for assets in a custodial or executive role. The insertion of separate authorization and approval procedures into the implementation of a transaction provides cross-checks on performance and limits the opportunity for defalcations. The independence of the recording responsibility is required to sustain the integrity of the accountability function. Accountability and periodic reconciliation help to indicate the effectiveness of other controls.

*Avoiding cover-ups.* For an irregularity to pass unnoticed, an individual, besides having access to assets, must have the ability to conceal his actions involving these assets. Since some access to assets is required to operate a business, the elimination of opportunities to conceal actions involving them is the focus of most accounting controls in this area. *Access* to assets encompasses not only physical contact with assets but also the ability to influence their disposition. The opportunity to have a check sent to a certain destination is just as effective an access to cash as if one held custody of the cash to begin with. *Concealment* is necessary to prevent the accountability function from disclosing differences. Concealment may be accomplished in many ways if free access to records is attained.

*Eliminating deliberate distortions.* Deliberate distortions of records may occur if those responsible for the execution of transactions also record them. The calculation of bonuses based on accounting figures is an example of an area in which such distortions might arise if such functions were combined. Such misrepresentations can badly mislead management as well as engender some loss.

*Reduction in errors.* Independence of the recording function may substantially reduce errors. Mistakes, for whatever reason, may be overlooked by the asset custodian but should be caught by an independent record keeper. Errors resulting from lack of knowledge or understanding, for example, may go unnoticed if the asset custodian also maintains the records.

*Check on other controls.* A separate recording function also checks adherence to other controls. Independent personnel are more apt to detect such problems as the omission of proper authorizations or the absence of prenumbered documents. Procedures to prevent and detect errors and irregularities should be performed by those not in a position to perpetrate them.

*More reliable accounting reports.* Accounting reports act as a significant control in themselves and may provide information to management for possible control modifications. Reports indicate the success or failure of planned activity and point out areas where deviations have occurred. When they are properly prepared, accounting reports can indicate adjustments that would be appropriate to the process or to future plans. The actual as well as the perceived reliability of such reports may be directly related to the independence of the recording function.

**General Checks and Balances.** To prevent undetected errors and irregularities, no one individual should have complete control of a transaction. Consideration should be given to the work of one employee possibly serving as a check on that of another. To be effective, checking and balancing procedures need to be performed by different persons. In many cases, such subdivision of a function adds strength to an activity without duplicating effort or substantially increasing its cost. Requiring one clerk to keep the subsidiary ledger and another to maintain the general ledger is an example of such subdividing. Rotation of duties and mandatory vacations during which others perform one's duties are other means by which such checks can be introduced into a system. The opportunities for separation of duties within an EDP system are somewhat different but just as critical to internal control. Instead of frequent cross-checking, emphasis is on control over improper programming and the modification of data for any reason.

Sheer economics may force small businesses to skimp on segregating duties. In such circumstances, other forms of control, such as careful management supervision and review, should be considered.

# EVALUATION OF CONTROL SYSTEMS

There are two approaches to evaluating internal control today. Both assume that an organization's activity is analyzed by classes of related transactions. This grouping of transactions may be by function, department, or cycle or on some other basis and may vary from organization to organization in terms of type and number of transaction classes.

One approach suggests that a cycle first be examined for the types of errors and irregularities (causes) which could occur. Next, control procedures should be determined to avoid the kinds of errors and irregularities identified in that examination. These desired controls are then compared to the existing system and its operation to reveal any weaknesses that would result from either the omission of such controls or from the commission of unauthorized acts.

The alternative approach adopts a positive view and identifies certain broad control objectives. It then examines a system to see how well existing system attributes and procedures contribute to meeting these objectives.

The first step in either approach is to group all related transactions into meaningful subsystems. The first approach then asks what could go wrong and tries to discover if the subsystem is reasonably defended. The second approach, however, states what should be happening under controlled conditions and seeks, as well, to find out if it is likely to be accomplished. In both approaches, controls should be tested to determine not only whether they exist but also whether they are functioning as expected. The success of both approaches depends on the ability to identify appropriate errors or irregularities (or conversely, appropriate objectives) and then to evaluate correctly the effectiveness of existing controls in those terms. Omissions, oversights, or faulty evaluations in either approach could permit undetected weaknesses.

Subsystem evaluations should be based on reasonable assurance criteria and thus should take into consideration the relationship of costs and benefits. Such evaluations must also be considered in the broader context of the internal control environment. Surrounding conditions may influence the effectiveness of individual controls.

Specific control problems may come to light from various sources. Reports on examinations by both internal and external auditors may disclose them. Unexplained variances in operating reports may provide a clue. Changes in operations may reveal or create shortcomings.

## Sample Subsystems and Their Functions

For purposes of illustration, sample functions commonly found within four subsystems of a manufacturing business are identified in Figures 17.2-17.5. These functions (or others) can then be examined for potential errors or irregularities that might occur during their performance. Alternatively, specific control objectives may be formulated for each. For example, take the first sample function under the revenue subsystem—receiving and accepting requests for goods and services. A typical error in this function might be accepting an order that management policies would have rejected. Or an irregularity might occur through creation of a fictitious order. A control objective might be to establish an advance-approval requirement for

---

- Receiving and accepting requests for goods and services
- Approving credit terms and delivery arrangements
- Providing goods and services
- Billing promptly and for correct amounts
- Receiving and collecting cash
- Advertising and promotion efforts
- Accounting for shipments, revenues, accounts receivable, freight and delivery costs, commissions, warranties, sales taxes and other deductions, returns, allowances, discounts and cash receipts, uncollectible accounts, and other related entries

---

FIGURE 17.2  SAMPLE FUNCTIONS IN A REVENUE SUBSYSTEM

orders from parties either not on the approved customer list or seeking special terms.

It must be remembered that control systems, although often established for these common, routine transactions, may also need to be set up for more critical purposes —to include unusual or nonrecurring transactions involving larger amounts of money and key personnel.  Management often is involved directly in such transactions, either through authorization, execution, or close monitoring.

---

Purchasing:
- Requisitioning goods and services
- Selecting vendor, method, and terms of acquisition
- Placing purchase order
- Receiving and accepting goods and services ordered, including appropriate inspections and counts
- Accounting for accounts payable, including freight and commission expense, purchase returns, prepaid expenses, and related entries

Payroll:
- Hiring and terminating employees
- Setting, adjusting, and administering compensation and other forms of benefits
- Recording attendance and performance
- Accounting for labor costs, payroll taxes and other deductions, employee benefits and related liabilities, and other related entries

Disbursements:
- Preparing and subsequent canceling of vouchers and supporting documentation
- Preparing, signing, and disposing of checks
- Accounting for allowances, discounts, and cash payments

---

FIGURE 17.3  SAMPLE FUNCTIONS IN AN EXPENDITURE SUBSYSTEM

Production:
- Determining goods to produce or services to render
- Maintaining inventories
- Scheduling productive activity
- Disposing of materials and services
- Accounting for costs accumulated in transforming goods and providing services
- Adjusting inventories for physical and value changes

Plant and equipment:
- Determining facilities and machinery required
- Selecting vendors and methods and terms of acquisition
- Letting contracts and arranging for trade-ins or retirements
- Supervising construction or installation
- Protecting and preserving plant and equipment
- Accounting for assets and related liabilities, and their depreciation, repair, maintenance, and disposal with attendant gain or loss

FIGURE 17.4  SAMPLE FUNCTIONS IN A TRANSFORMATION SUBSYSTEM

Obtaining capital:
- Sale of capital stock and bonds
- Computation and payment of dividends and interest
- Redemption or conversion of securities
- Purchase of treasury stock and bonds
- Loans, leases and other forms of credit and related expenses
- Calculation and payment of interest and principal
- Compliance with provisions of equity instruments
- Accounting for various liabilities related to debt and debt management, premium and discount, and interest expense
- Capital stock and dividend lease transactions

Investing capital:
- Selection of securities
- Purchase of securities
- Physical protection of securities
- Maintenance of securities and revenue therefrom
- Arrangements for advances to and from related companies
- Accounting for current and long-term securities, revenue earned, cash received, changes in value of securities, and gain or loss on disposal

FIGURE 17.5  SAMPLE FUNCTIONS IN A FINANCIAL SUBSYSTEM

### The Financial Statement Cycle

The information provided by transactions is necessary for financial statement preparation, but it alone is not sufficient. As a consequence, a fifth subsystem, the financial statement cycle, is required. Sample functions in the financial statement cycle include:

- Determining accounting policies, principles, and practices;
- Preparing and documenting write-offs, estimates and other adjustments;
- Making such entries and posting them as required to complete the preparation of external financial reports;
- Accumulating necessary information for required and desired disclosures; and
- Preparing financial statements in accordance with generally accepted accounting principles or other stated basis.

The objectives often provided in illustrations of subsystems are of necessity formulated in broad, general, ambiguous terms. A specific organization would undoubtedly tailor them to its own circumstances and supplement them with more detailed questions or objectives. Nevertheless, the objectives are usually sufficiently articulated to be independent of the media utilized. Thus, they apply to EDP systems as well as to manual ones.

## ASSESSMENT AND DOCUMENTATION

The Foreign Corrupt Practices Act of 1977 made internal accounting control the legal concern of all registrants under the 1934 Securities Exchange Act. Relative to the 1977 Act, the SEC stated in ASR 242 that "it is important that issuers subject to the new requirements review their accounting procedures, systems of internal accounting controls and business practices in order that they may take any actions necessary to comply with the requirements contained in the Act."[9] (See Chapter 18 for a detailed discussion of these requirements.) The commission, however, does not describe in this ASR what such a review should consist of nor state what would be sufficiently material to warrant taking action to comply with the requirements of the Act. The professional accounting literature, because of its orientation toward an examination of the financial statements in accordance with generally accepted auditing standards, is not much more helpful.

### Preliminary Survey

In order to respond to the requirements of the Act, managements should undertake a review of their individual internal accounting control systems.

---

[9] Securities and Exchange Commission, *Accounting Series Releases and Staff Accounting Bulletins as of July 6, 1978* (Chicago: Commerce Clearing House, Inc., 1978) p. 3633.

**Limiting Objectives.** An early step would be to define the objectives of such a review. Although management has broader control concerns, the Act's requirements as to accounting provisions are limited to the maintenance of accurate records and adequate systems of internal accounting control. The review will, of necessity, cover some of the broader areas such as efficiency and compliance and should thoroughly consider relevant elements of the internal control environment. Nevertheless, in the interests of time, it may have to focus on the areas cited in the Act.

**Considering the Environment.** Before undertaking such a survey, a company needs to consider its internal control environment. Any of the groupings suggested in the evaluation section may be used to organize the survey. However, significant operating components should be identified to organize the effort, and control objectives then established for each component. Documentation appears an important concern, so consideration should be given to whether policies and procedures in the internal control environment should be formalized in writing and appropriately disseminated to all interested parties.

**Establishing Priorities.** Although the survey should cover all areas, it might be best to emphasize those with the greatest potential for exposure (risk). These may not necessarily be the most significant operations nor the ones with the greatest volume of transactions. Special consideration should also be given to areas in which control appears weak (as indicated by reports of internal and external auditors), to unexplained or unusual variances in operating analyses; and to known recent changes in organizational structure, products, personnel, or recording systems. Management, however, has the final say, and their priorities, however determined, must govern.

It is important that responsibility for such reviews be clearly fixed. Such a survey might be performed by internal auditors, external auditors, or operating personnel under their guidance and review. Common approaches include reading existing documentation, including narrative descriptions, flowcharts, and procedures manuals; interviewing appropriate personnel; obtaining responses to questionnaires; and observing the activity in question.

## Detailed Study

The purpose of the preliminary survey is to gain an understanding of the system and identify the internal control procedures that are, or should be, in effect. A more detailed analysis of individual control systems should then be undertaken. General objectives used in the preliminary survey would need to be made more specific for this level of review.

**Independent Review.** To save time, more attention should probably be paid to the areas of greatest exposure in terms of the nature of the activity, the absence of appropriate control, or the likelihood of a breakdown. The order in which the analyses are performed, the effort devoted to each, and the frequency of examination might well be influenced by these considerations. Even within individual areas, emphasis may vary, depending on the importance of certain controls. The relative importance of specific control objectives to identified exposures provides a valuable clue to the significance of the nature and location of specific controls.

A reviewer must consider the entire system before deciding whether a specific control objective is met. A systems analyst often designs a group of controls that, acting in concert, provides reasonable assurance regarding a potential exposure. A specific control may be more reliable in response to a particular control objective, but a combination of lesser controls may be selected because the combination is more efficient—that is, it gives the same service at less cost or greater service at the same cost—or because the controls fulfill control objectives that the individual control did not.

If all areas cannot be reviewed in a timely fashion, senior management may request representation letters from operating management concerning the reliability of information, adequacy of controls, and compliance with statutes, regulations, and corporate policies and procedures, including the code of conduct. Eventually, however, every area should be examined, tested, and evaluated by independent parties such as the internal or external auditors.

**Corrective Action.** Corrective action may be called for as the result of a review. Control procedures may be found missing, inoperative, or useless. New controls may need to be designed and implemented; old controls may need to be improved; or some exposures may not be considered worth controlling under cost/benefit analysis.

**The Cost Benefit Issue.** An effective approach to corrective action is to identify the controls that would correct the weaknesses in question and to evaluate their respective costs and benefits.

*Measuring costs.* Costs of proposed controls may be both direct and indirect. *Direct costs* involve increased investments required in material, machinery, and manpower. *Indirect costs* may be more difficult to quantify but must be considered. Damage to employee morale and customer service or convenience can be very expensive.

*Measuring benefits.* Benefits of controls may be more difficult to measure. *Direct benefits* result primarily from reduced costs or reduced losses because of more efficient use of resources or more reliable information. They are relatively easy to determine. Statistical samples may be used to estimate error rates and indicate probable losses. Infrequent and unusual possibilities, such as fires or defalcations, may be best dealt with on a "worst case" basis. Successively narrower bracketing of possible amounts may help determine a reasonable estimate of potential loss.

Indirect or *intangible benefits* are more difficult to estimate. It may be difficult to assign dollar amounts to increased customer satisfaction, to an enhanced corporate image of social responsibility, to strengthened employee respect, or to management confidence—but some quantification is desirable.

The bottom line in evaluating or comparing controls is the *net benefit* or, when controls have similar net benefits, the lowest cost. This approach is appropriate not only in selecting new controls but also in assessing existing ones. Overcontrol can be just as real a problem as undercontrol and can result in comparable losses from waste and employee frustration. Changed circumstances or changes in the system or the people who operate it may affect the net benefit of controls.

## Importance of Documentation

**Documenting the System.** Whatever approach is taken to evaluating internal controls, both the considerations and their quantifications should be carefully documented. Decisions not obvious from the supporting data should be explained in detail. Any decision to let a cause remain uncontrolled should be supported by cost justification or comparable analyses.

Good documentation is the place to begin the analysis of a system and provides the basis for any reports on such a system. It makes it easier to spot gaps in the control system or excessive or useless controls. If up-to-date flowcharts, narrative descriptions, and procedures manuals do not exist, efforts should be made to prepare them as resources permit and conditions warrant.

Proper documentation of the internal control system not only facilitates assessment but also provides substantial future benefits. A well-documented system helps to sensitize new employees to the importance of controls and serves as a model for the documentation of other systems.

It may be a further help to management and the audit committee to summarize characteristics of the internal control environment, system objectives, and related control procedures in a single document. Relevant corporate policies, internal memorandums, and even pertinent minutes may be included in such a compendium.

**Documentation at the Operating Level.** At the operating level, documentation should be more detailed. Specific duties of key personnel (and the ways in which they are appropriately segregated) may be spelled out, together with specific steps for carrying out individual control procedures.

The more detailed analysis, in addition to gathering more specific information, may involve tests of existing controls to determine whether transactions are being processed as expected and whether control procedures are functioning as planned. In preliminary surveys, it may be sufficient to follow two or three transactions from start to finish—*a walk-through*. In more detailed analyses, more comprehensive and more thorough tests of specific objectives may be required. The focus should be on those controls most likely to fulfill key objectives. Such compliance tests are necessary to validate the effectiveness of the system.

**Documentation of Evaluation Surveys.** Careful documentation of both the preliminary survey and the detailed analysis is imperative and appears an important concern of the SEC. Documentation is desirable to provide evidence that appropriate reviews and tests were planned and executed and that the results were properly considered. The following material should be included:

- Minutes or memorandums of board of directors' considerations and audit or other committees' deliberations;
- Pertinent correspondence or memorandums of discussions with internal and external auditors or with legal counsel;
- Efforts to inform personnel of management's attitude, as well as policies issued to carry it out;
- Programs and working papers;
- Copies of system documentation such as questionnaires, narrative descriptions, flow-charts, procedures manuals, and memorandums of interviews and observations;
- Reports of the external auditors or other outside consultants;
- Consideration given, and action taken at every level, to findings from all sources; and
- Follow-ups on compliance.

## SPECIAL PROBLEMS

### Small Companies

Neither the Foreign Corrupt Practices Act nor SEC comments on the Act's implementation to date have taken special cognizance of smaller registrants, although a greater possible burden is acknowledged. This leaves smaller companies with no alternative under the Act but to conduct evaluations of their internal accounting control similar to those made by their larger counterparts.

In conducting such reviews and assessments, it becomes apparent that the range of control options is usually narrower. The volume of activity for some companies is not sufficient to create exposures that would justify some controls commonly found in larger entities. Separation of duties is an example of a practice that may not be economically feasible for a smaller company.

Alternative controls may be possible, however. Greater participation by management in transaction activity is one. The board of directors may choose to authorize a wider range of items and more closely review others. A corporate audit committee of the board, composed solely of outside directors, might participate in this as well as expand its expected oversight of controls. Increased management supervision may be another possibility. In any event, these problems, their consideration, and their resolution should all be clearly documented.

Documentation, too, may be a greater burden for a smaller company, but it is a key to the successful implementation of any system of controls. There are many benefits to be gained from careful attention to internal control and its documentation.

## International Companies

The foreign operations of some companies may suffer from the same difficulties described here for small companies. The more pertinent question, however, is the role American laws and practices have in foreign countries. The legal issue remains to be resolved. The best course of action, in the meantime, is probably to treat them the same as any domestic division. Failure of controls to prevent or detect illegal activity by a foreign subsidiary, even if it is not directly subject to the law, may make the U.S. parent subject to severe penalties.

## SUGGESTED READING

American Accounting Association. *A Statement of Basic Auditing Concepts.* Committee on Basic Auditing Concepts, Studies on Accounting Research No. 6. Sarasota, Fla., 1973.

AICPA. *Codification of Auditing Standards and Procedures.* Auditing Standards Board, Statement on Auditing Standards No. 1. New York, 1973.

————.*The Effect of EDP on the Auditor's Study and Evaluation of Internal Control.* Auditing Standards Board, Statement on Auditing Standards No. 3. New York, 1974.

————. *Report of the Special Advisory Committee on Internal Control.* New York, 1979.

Connor, Joseph E. and DeVos, Burnell H., Jr. *Guide to Accounting Controls.* Boston: Warren, Gorham & Lamont, Inc., 1979.

Institute of Internal Auditors. *Standards for the Professional Practice of Internal Auditing.* Altamonte Springs, Fla., 1978.

Mair, W., Wood, D., and Davis, K. *Computer Control and Audit.* Altamonte Springs, Fla.: Institute of Internal Auditors, 1977.

Securities and Exchange Commission. *Accounting Series Releases and Staff Accounting Bulletins as of July 6, 1978.* Chicago: Commerce Clearing House, 1978.

# 18

# Foreign Corrupt Practices Act Requirements

*David N. Ricchiute*

## INTRODUCTION

On December 19, 1977, President Carter signed into law the Foreign Corrupt Practices Act (FCPA) of 1977. The Act amends the Securities Exchange Act of 1934 to: (1) make it *unlawful* for either Securities and Exchange Commission (SEC) registrants or domestic nonregistrants to *influence* foreign governments or officials through payments or gifts and (2) require that SEC registrants comply with certain *internal accounting control and record-keeping requirements.* As a result of the FCPA, a system of internal accounting control for SEC registrants is no longer a matter of technical proficiency; it is a matter of law.[1]

The title of the Act suggests that its provisions apply only to companies engaging in bribes or questionable payments to foreign officials. However, because of the language contained within two of its sections, Accounting Standards and Foreign Corrupt Practices by Issuers, the Act applies to all domestic and foreign companies subject to the Securities Exchange·Act of 1934, even those companies with no international operations.

## THE CONTROLLER'S ROLE

The FCPA mandates specific requirements about a company's accounting control and record-keeping functions. The corporate controller is the member of the corporate management team with primary responsibility for a company's accounting controls and record keeping. Because of his education and experience, the controller is qualified to monitor accounting-related danger signals and organize a responsible management task force to supervise FCPA compliance efforts. Thus, many companies look to the controller for guidance in complying with the specific accounting-related provisions of the Act.

### Danger Signals

The existence of one or more danger signals may suggest that a company's accounting control and record-keeping functions are not fully capable of preventing foreign corrupt practices. Figure 18.1 lists several such danger signals, all of which are discussed below.[2]

---

- Unclear lines of authority

- Frequent adjustments to interim or annual financial statements

- General or unclear explanations for significant unexpected fluctuations of account balances

- Overemphasis on audit function, both internal and external

---

FIGURE 18.1   DANGER SIGNALS: CLUES TO POTENTIAL PROBLEMS

---

[1] The author acknowledges the thoughtful title of an article appearing in the *Journal of Accountancy,* which first brought this point to bear. See J. Michael Cook and Thomas P. Kelly, "Internal Accounting Control: A Matter of Law," *Journal of Accountancy,* January, 1979, pp. 56-64.

[2] The danger signals discussed in this section and listed in Figure 18.1 are adapted from Craig D. Choate, "Assessing and Managing Accounting Controls: It's a 1979 Job for Top Management," *Price Waterhouse Review,* Vol. 24, No. 1 (1979), pp. 4-8.

**Unclear Lines of Authority.** The lines of authority (i.e., who reports to whom) within a company are dictated by the formal organization chart. However, the lines of authority may not be as clear as the organization chart suggests. For example, many people in authority may in fact be powerless. When power differs from authority, the formal organization chart is less meaningful. Power vested in only one or a small number of individuals can be counterproductive to monitoring foreign corrupt practices and achieving strong internal accounting control.

**Frequent Adjustments to Financial Statements.** If frequent adjustments must be made in interim or annual financial statements, the accounting system may not be properly handling transactions and events recorded during the period. For example, many companies record *accounting adjustments* or *unreconcilable differences* when the physical inventory does not agree with perpetual records or the accounts payable trial balance does not agree with the general ledger balance at the end of the period. Often such accounting adjustments or unreconcilable differences result from harmless errors or incorrect account postings and are too small to justify the time required to resolve them. However, frequent or large adjustments should be investigated; both inventory and accounts payable are closely tied to cash disbursements, and cash disbursements may be related to foreign payments.

**General or Unclear Explanations for Fluctuations.** A normal and recurring financial statement review procedure of corporate controllers and auditors alike is to compare the dollar balances of balance sheet and income statement accounts with balances from comparable prior periods. The purpose of the comparison is to determine whether individual account balances have fluctuated or have remained relatively constant. There should be a sound reason or series of reasons for the balance in trade accounts receivable at year-end, for example, to be twice what it was at the end of the prior year; for example, there may have been loosening of credit terms, increased sales volume, slow collections at year-end and/or a new product sales line. Additional investigation would be warranted in the event of general or unclear explanations by management for significant unexpected fluctuations of account balances. Account balances do not change by magic; they change as a result of transactions and events that should be authorized or approved by management.

**Overemphasis of Audit Function.** The early debate with corporate boardrooms and the financial press about foreign corrupt payments suggested that primary responsibility for complying with the FCPA in general, and for detecting material questionable or illegal payments in particular, rests with a company's internal and external auditors. This preconceived yet highly inaccurate notion is understandable, since auditors are frequently expected to serve an oversight function within large organizations. Clearly, auditors should be engaged actively within corporate management's overall plan to comply with the Act; however, overemphasis of either the internal or external audit responsibility is foolhardy. Penalties for violations of the FCPA can be imposed on the company, a company officer, a director, or the stockholders; auditors are not liable.

## Corporate Task Forces

Every economic transaction and event affecting a company has some legal, financial, and audit implications. For example, a credit sale of finished-goods inventory to a bona fide trade customer has legal implications because of antitrust legislation, financial implications because of anticipated subsequent cash collections, and audit implications because income must be recorded only in the period earned. In short, economic transactions and events affect several departments within a company simultaneously—the legal department, several financial departments (e.g., controller, treasurer), and the internal audit department. Therefore, just as these departments work collectively toward common corporate goals, they can and should work collectively toward organizing a multidepartment committee to cope with FCPA requirements, such as a corporate task force on foreign corrupt practices.

**Composition.** Ideally, the corporate task force should include the controller, the treasurer, and representatives from the legal and internal audit departments. To communicate the importance of the task force and to combat the tendency on the part of some segments of corporate management to regard it as routine, the group should wherever possible include senior executives from the various departments represented. As a recent article relating accounting controls to the FCPA pointed out, "[the] greater the stature of the task force, the clearer the message will be within the organization that assessing and managing accounting controls is a priority matter for top management."[3]

**Objectives.** The objectives of the task force should be fourfold:

1. It should become thoroughly familiar with the provisions of the Act as a basis for determining whether the company needs to change current policy to comply with the Act.
2. It should institute a continuing oversight role as a basis for determining whether the company is complying with the Act.
3. It should keep abreast of all current or proposed SEC pronouncements related to the Act as a basis for planning and discharging its oversight role.
4. It should coordinate the activities of all corporate functions related to the Act (e.g., the internal audit function and the external auditors' review of internal controls typically conducted during the interim phase of an annual opinion audit).

Only in rare cases will the "ostrich" approach satisfactorily discharge a company's compliance responsibility under the Act. More often, a coordinated, multidepartmental task force will prove more successful.

---

[3] Choate, p. 5.

## PERTINENT PROVISIONS OF THE ACT

The FCPA contains three sections relevant to the corporate controller:

- Foreign Corrupt Practices by Domestic Companies;
- Foreign Corrupt Practices by Issuers; and
- Accounting Standards.

The foreign corrupt practices sections comprise the unlawful-influence provisions of the Act. In general, these sections are relatively clear and deal with the prohibition of bribes and questionable conduct. On the other hand, the accounting standards section, which identifies the internal accounting control and record-keeping provisions of the Act, is somewhat more difficult to interpret. Accordingly, the compliance guidelines outlined later in this chapter emphasize the accounting standards section of the Act.

### Unlawful Influence

The unlawful-influence provisions of the Act make it illegal for any domestic company—publicly held or privately owned—or its officers, directors, employees, agents, or stockholders, to arrange payments or gifts to foreign governments, officials, political parties, or political candidates for purposes of obtaining or retaining business by:

- Influencing any official act or decision; or
- Inducing the recipient to use his or her influence over any official act or decision.

Thus, the unlawful-influence provisions apply to domestic concerns and prohibit bribes intended to influence foreign acts or decisions. The Act does not mention foreign subsidiaries of U.S. domestic companies. However, as indicated in the following excerpt, the House of Representatives conference report on the FCPA does suggest that indirect foreign corrupt payments or offers by foreign subsidiaries are outlawed:

> . . . [the] conferees recognized the inherent jurisdictional, enforcement, and diplomatic difficulties raised by the inclusion of foreign subsidiaries of U.S. companies in the direct prohibitions of the bill. However, the conferees intend to make clear that any issuer or domestic concern which engages in bribery of foreign officials indirectly through any other person or entity would itself be liable under the bill.[4]

---

[4] House of Representatives, *Conference Report No. 95-831*, December 6, 1977. It is not altogether clear that this quote also applies to nonregistrant subsidiaries of SEC-registered subsidiaries. This point is developed further in a later section of this chapter.

It is important to note that the Act prohibits *payments to influence official acts or decisions*; the Act does not prohibit "grease" or "facilitating" payments made to ministerial or clerical government employees for the purpose of, for example, expediting government service. Examples of grease or facilitating payments include:

- Payments to secure police protection and required permits or licenses; and
- Payments to speed the processing of shipments through customs.

A company convicted of making a foreign bribe—whether willful or not—can be fined up to $1 million. A company officer, director, or stockholder can be fined up to $10,000 and/or imprisoned up to five years, although foreign bribes by these parties must be willful. Fines imposed on individuals may not be paid by a company.

## Internal Accounting Control and Record Keeping

The internal accounting control and record-keeping provisions of the Act require that publicly held domestic companies:

1. Make and keep books, records, and accounts that, in reasonable detail, accurately and fairly reflect the transactions and dispositions of the assets of the company; and
2. Devise and maintain a system of internal accounting control sufficient to provide reasonable assurances that:
   a. Transactions are executed in accordance with management's general and specific authorization;
   b. Transactions are recorded as necessary: (1) to permit preparation of financial statements in conformity with generally accepted accounting principles or any other criteria applicable to such statements, and (2) to maintain accountability for assets;
   c. Access to assets is permitted only in accordance with management's general and specific authorization; and
   d. The recorded accountability for assets is compared with the existing assets at reasonable intervals and appropriate action is taken with respect to any differences.

In general, the intent of the record-keeping provision is to enable preparation of accurate and fairly stated external financial reports; the intent of the internal accounting control provisions is to signal questionable or illegal payments.

The language of the internal accounting control provisions is taken almost verbatim from the definition of accounting control contained in Section 320.28 of the AICPA's Statement on Auditing Standards (SAS) No. 1, *Codification of Auditing Standards and Procedures*, originally issued in 1973. This observation is particularly interesting because in adopting the definition of accounting control, Congress specifically ignored administrative control, a definition of which appears in Section 320.27 of SAS 1. Thus, the FCPA pertains to a company's accounting controls (i.e., controls relating to the safeguarding of assets and reliability of financial records), not to a company's administrative controls (i.e., controls relating to decision processes leading to management's authorization of transactions). The Act purposely avoids administrative controls, because Congress intended to outlaw only those acts that circumvent the safeguarding of assets and reliability of financial records (i.e., accounting controls); Congress did not intend to outlaw poor decision processes. If it had, management decisions to purchase subsidiaries that prove unprofitable or equipment that proves unproductive would have been illegal under the Act.

A company violating the internal accounting control or record-keeping provisions of the Act can be fined up to $10,000. A company officer, director, or stockholder can be fined up to $10,000 and/or imprisoned up to five years. Again, fines imposed on individuals may not be paid by a company.

## SOME UNANSWERED QUESTIONS

The FCPA may well represent the single most significant corporate-governance legislation enacted within the past several decades. Nevertheless, alarmingly few specific authoritative compliance guidelines have been published by agencies of the federal government.

This section discusses some of the unanswered questions resulting from the Act in general and from the lack of authoritative compliance guidelines in particular. The purpose is not to provide definitive answers; to date there are none. Rather, the purpose is to highlight specific compliance questions left unanswered by the Act and provide corporate controllers with a *reasonable course of action* for each question.

### Distinguishing Accounting and Administrative Controls

The earlier discussion relating to the internal accounting control and record-keeping provisions of the Act implicitly assumes that accounting controls are always distinguishable from administrative controls. However, that assumption is clearly unrealistic: many controls fall within the scope of both accounting controls and administrative controls. For example, product-line cost-of-sales records may be used to monitor the reasonableness of the volume of materials requisitions (i.e., an accounting control) and to determine unit selling prices (i.e., an administrative control). Thus, how should controls that bear both accounting and administrative characteristics be interpreted for purposes of complying with the Act? The most conservative, and therefore safest, course of action would be to interpret all questionable controls as accounting controls.

A related problem stems from the Act's definition of internal accounting control, which was adopted from SAS 1. Since the Act uses language from SAS 1, the implication is that other related sections of SAS 1 can be used to interpret the meaning of accounting controls under the FCPA. However, how can management or corporate controllers, both unintended audiences of SAS 1, be expected to interpret this document, which is unrelated to and predates the FCPA? Assuming a corporate controller is not familiar with SAS 1, the safest course of action would be to consult with a company's independent auditor.

### Nonregistrant Subsidiaries

Although it is clear that the Act applies to SEC registrants, it is not clear whether the Act applies to nonregistrant subsidiaries of SEC-registrant companies. A more difficult question arises when a SEC registrant's minority interest in a nonregistrant subsidiary is accounted for under the equity method of accounting for unconsolidated subsidiaries.[5] The equity method signals a problem because its application presupposes that an investor (parent) company has the ability to exercise significant influence over an investee (subsidiary) company, even though only a minority interest is owned. Because the equity method presupposes this ability to exercise influence, the safest course of action would be to assume that the Act applies to nonregistrant subsidiaries. Otherwise, it would be necessary to argue that significant influence does not extend to a subsidiary's illegal acts.

### Unrealistic Expectations

There is some justifiable concern that the publicity surrounding the sensitive payments uncovered as a result of the Watergate investigations may lead unknowing third parties to place unrealistic expectations on a system of internal accounting control. For example, there is a danger that increased emphasis on internal accounting control systems may suggest to external parties that the system can prevent all foreign corrupt payments. Clearly, no system of internal accounting control can unequivocally prevent all possible circumvention. There is also a danger that the courts may not consider the explicit cost of any newly installed accounting control and thus not recognize that some controls may be foregone because their costs exceed their anticipated benefits. Because resources are limited, no system of internal accounting control can be designed without regard to this cost-benefit relationship. In short, controls are not always worth the cost.

## RELATED SEC PRONOUNCEMENTS

Since enactment of the FCPA, the SEC has proposed or finalized authoritative pronouncements that do not provide compliance guidelines but do draw attention to

---

[5] See Accounting Principles Board Opinion No. 18, *The Equity Method of Accounting for Investments in Common Stock,* (New York: AICPA, March, 1971).

the Act or impose additional reporting requirements upon SEC registrants. This section reviews the following SEC pronouncements or proposals, all of which resulted from or relate to the FCPA:

- Accounting Series Release (ASR) No. 242, *Notification of Enactment of the FCPA;*
- Release No. 34-15570, *Falsification of Records and Representations to Auditors;* and
- Release No. 34-15572, *Public Reporting on Internal Accounting Control.*

## ASR 242

Unlike most SEC Accounting Series Releases, ASR 242 does not represent the SEC's official position regarding specific accounting practices. Rather, it merely draws attention to the Act by recapping the Act's internal accounting control requirements and applicability and highlighting the SEC's enforcement responsibilities.

The release underscores the Act's requirements regarding the maintenance of internal accounting controls; however, it imposes no new obligations about disclosing material questionable and illegal activities. Instead, the release reaffirms the reporting requirements of the Securities Act of 1933 and the Securities Exchange Act of 1934 to disclose all material information necessary to prevent other disclosures from clouding the impact of such activities. In keeping with traditional SEC policy, the Commission will not provide registrants with interpretative advice on how the Act applies to specific situations.

## Release No. 34-15570

SEC Release No. 34-15570, effective March 23, 1979, prohibits both the falsification of books and records and the omission of statements (or the making of misleading statements) to accountants.

The rule relating to falsification of accounting records provides:

No persons shall, directly or indirectly, falsify or cause to be falsified, any book, record or account subject to Section 13(b)(2)(A) of the Securities Exchange Act.

The FCPA is included within Section 13(b) of the Securities Exchange Act of 1934.

In turn, the rule relating to representations to auditors provides:

No director or officer of an issuer shall, directly or indirectly,
(a) make or cause to be made a materially false or misleading statement, or
(b) omit to state, or cause another person to omit to state, any material fact neces-

sary in order to make statements made, in the light of the circumstances under which such statements were made, not misleading to an accountant in connection with (1) any audit or examination of the financial statements of the issuer required to be made pursuant to this subpart or (2) the preparation or filing of any document or report required to be filed with the Commission pursuant to this subpart or otherwise.

**Lack of Scienter Provision.** Because the FCPA is not limited to intentional acts (i.e., with scienter), neither of the rules in Release No. 34-15570 include a scienter provision. Some critics believe that communication between company management and auditors could thus be impeded, in that management may fear unintentional violations of the release. However, the SEC believes that a scienter provision is unwarranted, since an individual could negligently, though unintentionally, falsify a transaction. In short, the SEC believes that negligence should be *actionable* (i.e., subject to adjudication) regardless of intent.

**Extent of Coverage.** Both written or oral statements are covered under the representations-to-auditors rule; representations to internal auditors are also covered. The falsification-of-records rule covers not only journals and ledgers but also correspondence, memorandums, tapes, papers, and other documents, whether expressed in ordinary or machine language.

Although the representations-to-auditors rule includes a materiality standard, the falsification-of-records rule does not. The SEC believed that a materiality standard for the falsification-of-records rule would result in an unintended loophole by providing room for "harmless falsifications." In the SEC's view, creating a class of harmless falsifications would be counterproductive to the objectives of the FCPA.

## Release No. 34-15572

In 1979, the SEC, in Release 34-15572, proposed a requirement for a management report designed to reinforce the internal accounting control provisions of the FCPA.

The proposed rule would have required that management provide a report on the company's internal accounting controls, including an opinion that these controls were satisfactory and in compliance with the provisions of the FCPA. This management report would have been included in the annual report to shareholders and the Form 10-K filed with the SEC.

After substantial criticism by corporations and their representatives, the SEC agreed in 1980 to drop the proposal. The Commission, however, urged management to provide voluntarily a report on internal accounting control. The Commission has promised to review its proposal if substantial voluntary compliance is not evident in the next few years.

## COMPLYING WITH THE ACT

Despite anticipated additional pronouncements related to the FCPA, the corporate controller's most significant task is to demonstrate compliance with the Act's internal accounting control and record-keeping provisions.

Because of the Act's somewhat broad language and the relatively small number of cases to date involving compliance violations, it may be quite some time before the questions what is a questionable payment and what is an illegal payment can be resolved. In fact, it may not be irresponsible to argue that they may never be resolved. Thus, the emphasis in this section is on compliance *guidelines,* not on foolproof compliance procedures.

### Cost Versus Benefit

Simply stated, the cost-benefit relationship means that the cost of a particular internal accounting control should not exceed the anticipated benefits of instituting the control. Cost-versus-benefit considerations have long been integral to the design and implementation of internal accounting control systems. However, measuring costs and benefits does present rather difficult practical problems, especially since internal accounting control is now a matter of law.

These practical problems are highlighted in the AICPA's *Codification of Statements on Auditing Standards*, which underscores the importance of the cost-benefit relationship by describing it as "the primary conceptual criterion that should be considered in designing a system of accounting control. . . ."[6] However, the *Codification* also states that "precise measurement of costs and benefits usually is not possible; accordingly, any evaluation of the cost-benefit relationship requires estimates and judgments by management."[7]

These statements give a reasonably accurate portrayal of the dilemma confronting corporate controllers. On the bright side, however, Congress is apparently aware of the dilemma. For example, the *Report of the Senate Banking, Housing and Urban Affairs Committee* states:

> While management should observe every reasonable prudence in satisfying the objectives called for (in the internal accounting control and record-keeping provisions of the Act), the committee recognizes that management must necessarily estimate and evaluate the cost/benefit relationships of the steps to be taken in fulfillment of its responsibilities. . . . The size of the business, diversity of operations, degree of centralization of financial and operating management, amount of contact by top management with day-to-day operations, and numerous other circumstances are factors which management must consider in establishing and maintaining an internal accounting controls system.[8]

---

[6] *Codification of Statements on Auditing Standards* (New York: AICPA, 1979), par. 320.32.
[7] *Ibid.*
[8] United States Senate, *Report No. 95-114,* May 2, 1977.

Still, management may well become much more conservative when evaluating the results of a cost-benefit analysis. That is, management may elect to adopt a control even though the costs outweigh the benefits. Given the particularly harsh potential penalties to companies and individuals alike for violations of the FCPA, this course of action may be understandable, even if uncalled for by the Act.

## Compliance Guidelines

Figure 18.2 lists a series of suggested guidelines for monitoring compliance with the internal accounting control and record-keeping provisions of the Act. Of course, the list is by no means exhaustive; however, it does address issues relevant to the FCPA. The following discussion deals with how corporate controllers can implement each guideline.

**Assessing the Existing System of Internal Accounting Control.**[9] An adequate and effective system of internal accounting control can represent a company's best defense against violations of the FCPA. However, before a system can be deemed adequate and effective, it must be reviewed to determine whether the system is capable of detecting material questionable and illegal payments.

The *transaction cycle approach* is a particularly effective means of reviewing the adequacy and effectiveness of a system of internal accounting control. Unlike the traditional approach to reviewing accounting controls, the cycle approach emphasizes controls over particular transaction cycles within a company rather than controls over particular balance sheet accounts. For example, consider the journal entries typically required for a credit sale (assuming a periodic inventory system) and for subsequent cash collection:

|                                   | *Dr.*   | *Cr.*   |
| --------------------------------- | ------- | ------- |
| Accounts receivable               | $xxxx   |         |
| Sales                             |         | $xxxx   |
| To record sales on account        |         |         |
| Cash                              | $xxxx   |         |
| Accounts receivable               |         | $xxxx   |
| To record collection of sales on account |  |         |

The traditional approach examines controls over each of the three accounts represented within the above entries, accounts receivable, sales, and cash. In contrast, the transaction cycle approach examines controls over the two cycles represented by the recorded transactions, the revenue cycle (sales entry) and the collection cycle (cash collection entry).

---

[9] The reader is referred to Chapters 17, 19, and 20, which deal more fully with internal control and the internal audit function.

- Review the existing system of internal accounting control to determine its adequacy for detecting material questionable and illegal payments

- Promote optimal segregation of functional employee responsibilities

- Establish a code of conduct for all responsible management personnel

- Promote communication between auditors (both internal and external) and the audit committee, if one exists

- Establish a means for responding to all internal accounting control weaknesses noted in the external auditor's internal control review memorandum

FIGURE 18.2   INTERNAL ACCOUNTING CONTROL COMPLIANCE GUIDELINES

The logic underlying the transaction cycle approach is that balance sheet and income statement accounts are merely location devices and are not necessarily informative about the business cycles that lead to the ultimate dollar balance in an account. In the above entries the ultimate dollar balance in accounts receivable is actually the result of transactions affecting both the revenue cycle and the collection cycle. Therefore, it is more meaningful to review the controls underlying a transaction cycle than those underlying a particular balance sheet or income statement account.

Most companies maintain at least four cycles:

1. The collection cycle;
2. The revenue cycle;
3. The payment cycle; and
4. The cost/expense cycle.

Figure 18.3 depicts the interrelationship among internal accounting control, the four representative transaction cycles, and representative accounts that serve as components of the transaction cycles. Of course, the transaction cycles and accounts will vary from company to company. Figure 18.4 represents an overview of how the transaction cycles and accounts in Figure 18.3 can be used in a review of the existing system of internal accounting control.

*Identification.* Initially, all of a company's balance sheet and income statement accounts should be reviewed and classified into representative transaction cycles. This can be accomplished by identifying the normal debits and normal credits to each balance sheet and income statement account. Cash, which is normally debited for cash collections and credited for cash payments, is a simple example and demonstrates how one account can be a member of two separate transaction cycles, i.e., the collection cycle and the payment cycle.

*Flowcharting.* Each transaction cycle should then be flowcharted as a framework for isolating the critical control points within the cycle. Because the flowchart is important as a record of critical control points, it should be confirmed by tracing at least one representative transaction through each cycle.

*Review of accounting controls.* Next, existing controls, as determined from the flowchart, should be reviewed for their adequacy to detect questionable and illegal payments. This stage of the review process is conceptual and essentially asks two questions. Are individual existing controls adequate? Are particular controls missing?

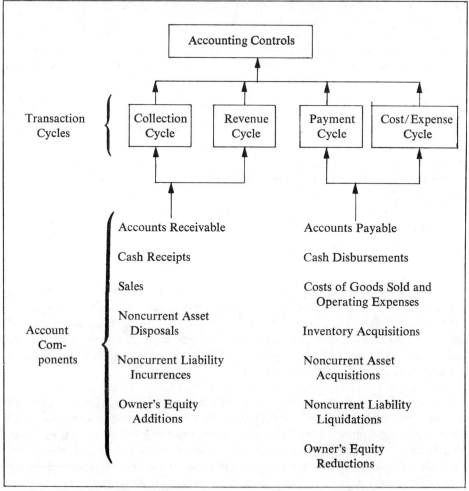

FIGURE 18.3 ILLUSTRATION OF THE TRANSACTION CYCLE CONCEPT
ADAPTED FROM: David N. Ricchiute, "Foreign Corrupt Practices: A New Responsibility for Internal Auditors" (*Internal Auditor*, December, 1978), Fig. 1, p. 63.

1. Identify the transaction cycles associated with a company's normal recurring transactions

2. Flowchart each transaction cycle, noting the existing critical accounting controls within each cycle

3. Assess the adequacy of existing accounting controls (i.e., Are existing controls adequate, are particular controls missing?)

4. Perform compliance tests (i.e., test representative documents) for each existing critical accounting control

5. Document weaknesses and suggest improvements

FIGURE 18.4  OVERVIEW OF THE TRANSACTION CYCLE APPROACH

*Compliance tests.* Finally, compliance tests should be performed for each critical accounting control to determine if the control is functioning properly and to isolate weaknesses in the system. Steps should be taken to correct any such weaknesses if the cost of required controls does not exceed anticipated benefits.

Suggesting the transaction cycle approach to reviews of the adequacy and effectiveness of internal accounting controls under the FCPA is not without precedent. In 1979, the AICPA's Special Advisory Committee on Internal Accounting Control issued a final report, which although recognizing the effectiveness of alternative review approaches, strongly supports the transaction cycle approach. The committee states that its report should be useful to management in considering whether a company complies with the internal accounting control provisions of the Act.

**Division of Duties.** The most significant characteristic of an adequate and effective system of internal accounting control is the segregation of functional employee responsibilities, or *division of duties.* In general, this means that no one employee should have so much responsibility that the company's system of checks and balances—accounting controls—cannot prevent that individual from diverting company assets. More specifically, division of duties means that no one employee should have responsibility over more than one of the following functions:

- Authorizing a transaction, e.g., authorizing a cash payment;
- Recording a transaction, e.g., preparing a journal entry to record a cash payment; and
- Maintaining custody over assets involved in a transaction, e.g., preparing a check for a cash payment.

Segregating functional responsibilities is particularly critical to preventing foreign corrupt payments. For example, any employee who had responsibility over all three of the functions above could: (1) authorize an illegal payment to a foreign official,

(2) record the transaction erroneously (e.g., debit advertising expense), and (3) divert funds by drawing the check payable to a nonexistent third party. The check would be mailed to the foreign official, who would endorse it in the name of the nonexistent third party.

A checklist similar to the sample in Figure 18.5 is a convenient way to determine whether functional employee responsibilities are adequately segregated within a company. Figure 18.5 relates to several approval and payment responsibilities typically associated with the payment cycle (i.e., cash disbursements). A separate checklist should be prepared for each major series of responsibilities associated with a transaction cycle.

The names of employees with approval and payment responsibilities are listed across the top of the checklist. Below each employee's name, a checkmark is made for each of an employee's responsibilities. For example, if Marc David, a company employee, is responsible for controlling blank checks, approving supporting documentation, and signing checks, a checkmark would be made beneath his name in the blocks associated with these responsibilities. When completed, the checklist

| *Responsibility Relative to the Approval and Payment of Cash Disbursements* | *Employee Names* | | | |
|---|---|---|---|---|
| • Controls blank (unused) checks | ☐ | ☐ | ☐ | ☐ |
| • Approves supporting documentation (e.g., purchase order, receiving report and invoice) for payment | ☐ | ☐ | ☐ | ☐ |
| • Prepares adding machine tape of total daily cash disbursements | ☐ | ☐ | ☐ | ☐ |
| • Prepares checks | ☐ | ☐ | ☐ | ☐ |
| • Signs checks | ☐ | ☐ | ☐ | ☐ |
| • Cancels (e.g., perforates) supporting documentation | ☐ | ☐ | ☐ | ☐ |
| • Mails checks | ☐ | ☐ | ☐ | ☐ |
| • Controls supporting documentation | ☐ | ☐ | ☐ | ☐ |

FIGURE 18.5 SAMPLE CHECKLIST FOR REVIEWING FUNCTIONAL EMPLOYEE RESPONSIBILITIES

would immediately draw attention to Marc David, who obviously has responsibility over authoritative and custodial functions. Corrective action should then be taken by reassigning some of David's duties.

Promoting optimal segregation of functional responsibilities reduces the risk of any one individual's diverting assets for improper purposes. Nevertheless, optimal division of duties is ineffective if two or more employees act in collusion. Unfortunately, no system of internal accounting control can prevent collusion.

**Corporate Codes of Conduct.** In several recent instances of material questionable payments, relatively high-ranking corporate officials implied they were not aware that a particular payment was against company policy. Monitoring compliance with the FCPA requires a corporate plan that clearly describes company policy; however, to be effective, corporate policy must be communicated to all responsible management personnel. No responsible employee should be unaware that a particular payment or act violates company policy.

Since enactment of the FCPA, many companies have either developed corporate codes of conduct or amended existing codes to guide management in both domestic and foreign business activities. The scope and content of corporate codes vary widely in practice; therefore, it is not feasible to attempt to develop a model code of conduct. In light of the FCPA, however, a code of conduct should include company policy related to the following:

- The intent and dollar amount of political contributions;
- Gifts and entertainment;
- The definition of bribes and questionable payments;
- Conflicts of interest;
- Confidentiality of financial and accounting information; and
- Compliance with domestic laws, rules, and regulations.

As a further guide to developing a corporate code of conduct, a condensed actual code of conduct follows:[10]

1. The use of any funds or other assets of, or the providing of any services by, the company or any subsidiary for any purpose that is unlawful under the laws of the U.S., any state thereof or any jurisdiction (foreign or domestic) is strictly prohibited.

2. No undisclosed or unrecorded funds or assets of the company or any subsidiary shall be established for any purpose.

3. No false or artificial entries shall be made in any books or records of the company or any subsidiary for any reason, and no employees shall engage in any arrangement that results in such prohibited act.

---

[10] Adapted from Ernst & Whinney, *Foreign Corrupt Practices Act of 1977: An Overview of the Law and its Implications* (1978), pp. 9-10.

4. No payment on behalf of the company or any subsidiary shall be approved or made with the intention or understanding that a part or all of such payment is to be used for any purpose other than that described by the document supporting the payment.

5. Any employee having information or knowledge of any unrecorded fund or asset or any prohibited act shall promptly report such matter to the controller of the company.

6. All managers shall be responsible for the enforcement of and compliance with this policy, including necessary distribution to ensure employee's knowledge and compliance.

7. Appropriate employees will periodically be required to certify compliance with this policy.

As a periodic reminder of and reference to a company's code of conduct, appropriate members of management should be requested to complete a year-end questionnaire on improper payments. The purpose of the questionnaire is to solicit information regarding the knowledge of company-wide political contributions, non-political payments, and general information related to improper payments. A sample questionnaire appears in Appendix 18–1.

**Communication Between Auditors and the Audit Committee.** Audit committees are composed of outside directors who report to the board of directors and are responsible, among other functions, for overseeing the external auditor's engagement and monitoring the internal auditor's activities. However, because such committees came into vogue only within the past several years,[11] their role regarding foreign corrupt practices has been somewhat underestimated.

Much like auditors, audit committees should be viewed as independent representatives of a company's outside interests (e.g., shareholders), not as internal representatives of management. Clearly, the specific functions of internal auditors, external auditors, and the audit committee differ; nevertheless, they can and should serve an important checks-and-balances or oversight role. Cooperation and communication among these three groups can be essential toward promoting compliance with the FCPA. In short, their respective roles regarding the FCPA should be defined and coordinated by the corporate task force on foreign corrupt practices so as to minimize duplication of effort and optimize effectiveness.

The internal and external auditors and the audit committee should meet at regularly scheduled intervals to discuss their objectives, coordinate their efforts, and monitor compliance with the FCPA in conjunction with the task force on foreign corrupt practices. Their meetings should be adequately documented (e.g., minutes), and the results communicated to the board of directors. (See Chapter 44 for a full discussion of the role of the audit committee.)

---

11 Although encouraged since 1939, audit committees were not mandated until June 30, 1978, when the New York Stock Exchange required them of all listed domestic companies.

**External Auditors' Internal Control Memorandum.** In compliance with the standards of their profession, all external auditors evaluate the reliability of a company's system of internal control as a basis for determining the nature, extent, and timing of detailed substantive audit testing. The auditors are required to communicate to management any material weaknesses in internal accounting control that come to their attention. The external auditors typically prepare for management a detailed internal control memorandum or management letter listing all significant control weaknesses.[12] In response to this memorandum or letter, management should institute a formal means for assuring that all weaknesses are corrected or, at a minimum, for demonstrating why the weakness should not be corrected (e.g., cost versus benefit).

An external auditor's evaluation of internal control typically represents the most exhaustive continuing annual review of a company's system. The resulting memorandum often represents management's most informative feedback about the adequacy of internal accounting controls and, therefore, about potential compliance violations under the FCPA. The internal control memorandum or management letter should not be overlooked; it is the only continuing outside review of accounting controls available to management.

## SUMMARY

This chapter has reviewed the FCPA, a landmark congressional act originating in part from investigations conducted by the Office of the Watergate Special Prosecutor. The Act includes three relevant sections—Foreign Corrupt Practices by Domestic Companies, Foreign Corrupt Practices by Issuers, and Accounting Standards—which prohibit bribes intended to influence foreign acts or decisions and impose internal accounting control and record-keeping requirements. Two related SEC pronouncements notify registrants of the FCPA and mandate rules related to the falsification of records and representations to auditors.

Certain danger signals, such as unclear lines of authority within a company and frequent adjustments to interim or annual financial statements, may suggest that a company is prone to foreign corrupt practices. Companies should be aware of these signals and, for purposes of adhering to the Act's provisions, consider establishing a corporate task force on foreign corrupt practices.

Complying with the Act's provisions can present some difficulties, because relatively few cases of violations have been resolved to date. Nevertheless, some compliance guidelines can be followed, such as reviewing the adequacy of the existing internal accounting control system, promoting optimal segregation of employee responsibilities, and establishing a code of conduct for all responsible management personnel.

---

[12] Note that the practice of issuing management letters is neither mandatory nor related to the FCPA; some but not all public accounting firms have been issuing such letters for years.

The FCPA may represent the most significant corporate-governance legislation since the Securities Act of 1933 and the Securities Exchange Act of 1934. However, despite its importance, the Act merely codifies concepts and practices that already existed when the Act's provisions were legislated. Thus, a company that previously followed good practice and now adopts a responsible plan to assure continued compliance with the Act need not overreact to its rather harsh penalties. The key, however, is *continued compliance;* an accounting control that is effective today may not necessarily be effective tomorrow.

## SUGGESTED READING

Baruch, Hurd. "The Foreign Corrupt Practices Act." *Harvard Business Review*, January-February, 1979, pp. 32-50.

Benjamin, James J., Dascher, Paul E., and Morgan, Robert G. "How Corporate Controllers View the Foreign Corrupt Practices Act." *Management Accounting*, June, 1979, pp. 43-45, 49.

Chira, Robert. "Deception of Auditors and False Records." *Journal of Accountancy*, July, 1979, pp. 61-72.

Cook, J. Michael, and Kelly, Thomas P. "Internal Control: A Matter of Law." *Journal of Accountancy*, January, 1979, pp. 56-64.

Fisher, Marguerite H. "Internal Control: Guidelines for Management Action." *Journal of Accounting, Auditing and Finance*, Summer, 1978.

Horn, Stephen A. "How to Cope with the Corrupt Practices Act." *Tax Executive*, January, 1979, pp. 154-163.

Marsh, Hugh L. "The Foreign Corrupt Practices Act: A Corporate Plan for Compliance." *Internal Auditor*, April, 1979, pp. 72-76.

Martin, Albert S. Jr., and Johnson, Kenneth P. "Assessing Internal Accounting Control: A Workable Approach." *Financial Executive*, May, 1978, pp. 24-32.

McKee, Thomas E. "Auditing Under the Foreign Corrupt Practices Act." *CPA Journal*, August, 1979, pp. 31-35.

Pomeranz, Felix. "A Corporate Response to the Foreign Corrupt Practices Act." *Journal of Accounting, Auditing and Finance*, Fall, 1978, pp. 70-75.

Ricchiute, David N. "Foreign Corrupt Practices: A New Responsibility for Internal Auditors." *Internal Auditor*, December, 1978, pp. 58-64.

# APPENDIX 18-1   QUESTIONNAIRE ON IMPROPER PAYMENTS

*Yes   No*

[ ]  Background Information

1.  Please list all divisions, subsidiaries, or other operating entities of the company with which you are involved, and briefly describe your responsibilities.

.......................................................................................................................
.......................................................................................................................
.......................................................................................................................

2.  In your position, do you attend meetings of the board of directors

    (a)  On a regular basis?                                       [ ]  [ ]
    (b)  Infrequently?                                             [ ]  [ ]

3.  Do you receive a copy of any minutes prepared at such meetings?  [ ]  [ ]
4.  Are you familiar with the content of the corporate code of conduct, issued on October 10, 19xx?                            [ ]  [ ]

[ ]  Political Contributions

1.  Do you know of any program, meeting, or discussion concerning utilization of the company's assets in an attempt to influence

    (a)  Legislation proposed or pending at any governmental level?  [ ]  [ ]
    (b)  The enforcement of existing statutes?                 [ ]  [ ]
    (c)  The attitudes or discharge of their lawful responsibilities by an agent or representative of any governmental authority?  [ ]  [ ]

2.  Are you aware of any instance where corporate funds or other property were paid to or otherwise donated, loaned, or made available to any political party, candidate, or election committee?  [ ]  [ ]
3.  Do you know of any instance where any payments were made by the company to an officer, director, or employee for the purpose of his making a contribution to or being reimbursed for a contribution made to any political party, candidate, or election committee?  [ ]  [ ]
4.  Did you make or authorize any payments of the nature contemplated by questions 1 through 3, either with or without the approval or knowledge of any other individual within the company?  [ ]  [ ]
5.  Have you been granted a leave of absence to work for the nomination or election of an individual to public office?  [ ]  [ ]

[ ]  Payments Other Than Those of a Political Nature

1.  During the last twelve months, did you seek to affect the decisions of others by offering to pay monies, goods, or services in return for some special consideration?  [ ]  [ ]

|  | *Yes* | *No* |
|---|---|---|

2. Do you know of any disbursements which were made by the company to or through foreign bank accounts such as a numbered Swiss account?  [ ]  [ ]

3. Have you or any other employee received payments from the company, such as a bonus, with the understanding that the full amount received was not to be retained?  [ ]  [ ]

4. Do you know of any associations, circumstances, or payments which, if revealed, would cause embarrassment to the company?  [ ]  [ ]

[ ] General

1. Are you aware of any corporate bank account whose existence was not reflected in the company's books and records?  [ ]  [ ]

2. Do you know of any instance where the company or an individual acting on behalf of the company maintained a bank account in a name other than the corporate name?  [ ]  [ ]

3. Do you know of any instance where a transaction may not have been properly recorded on the company's books, or where transactions were not recorded at all?  [ ]  [ ]

4. Do you know of or suspect instances where supporting documents were altered or falsified to disguise the true purpose of a transaction?  [ ]  [ ]

5. To the best of your knowledge, have there been any instances where the company's internal control procedures were circumvented or where transactions were handled in what seemed to be an extraordinary or unusual manner?  [ ]  [ ]

6. Do you know of any present or former officer, director, or employee who might have knowledge concerning any of the areas contemplated by this questionnaire?  [ ]  [ ]

7. Have you been in contact with any law enforcement or regulatory agency, voluntarily or otherwise, in respect of investigations concerning the company or any of its subdivisions?  [ ]  [ ]

8. Are there any improvements in control procedures or systems which you would recommend? If so, please elaborate.  [ ]  [ ]

STATEMENT:

To the best of my knowledge and belief, the information provided in respect of each of the foregoing questions is correct and complete.

....................................................................................

....................................................
(Date)

# 19

# Internal Auditing—Organization and Planning

*Felix Pomeranz*

# THE CONCEPT OF SERVICE TO MANAGEMENT

## Definition

In the language of the Institute of Internal Auditors, "internal auditing is an independent appraisal activity within an organization for the review of operations as a service to management. It is a managerial control which functions by measuring and evaluating the effectiveness of other controls."[1]

Internal auditing is expected to enhance profitability. Consequently, the tenor of internal auditors' reports is constructive. To the extent possible, findings are accompanied by explanations and recommendations for improvements. Internal auditors frequently work closely with an internal consulting or systems group to expedite corrective action. Indeed, internal auditors have increasingly become responsible for seeing that their findings are evaluated by management and that corrective action is taken.

---

[1] "Statement of Responsibilities of the Internal Auditor," *The Internal Auditor*, 28 (September/October, 1971), p. 12.

### The Modern Versus the Traditional Concept

Traditionally, internal auditing departments have evaluated compliance with company policies and practices. In a modern internal auditing organization, that aspect has been broadened to include responsibility for recommending the development of policies when none exist or their improvement when deficiencies exist. Traditionally, protection of assets from fraud and thievery has been emphasized; the modern approach incorporates protection from waste and dissipation. Traditionally, internal auditors have functioned in tandem with independent accountants; this role can lead to the performance by internal auditors of numerous chores considered burdensome or time-consuming by the independent accountants. The modern concept uses internal auditors to engage in professional work, subject to independent accountants' evaluation.

Traditionally, internal auditors have emphasized reviews of *internal accounting controls*. The newer *operational control* reviews (sometimes called operational audits or management audits) focus on profitability improvement. In an industrial environment, all controls should support management's objectives. Accordingly, there is little incentive to classify controls based on arbitrary types. Understandably, the integrated review is gaining favor.

Essentially then, the traditional internal auditor engages primarily in activities akin to those of independent public accountants. Since such work supports the expression of an opinion on financial statements, management should evaluate whether this circumscribed activity should constitute the total mission of its internal auditors. The modern concept involves the evaluation of all controls that exist—or should exist—in the management information system, and the presentation of comments and suggestions relative to their functioning. Operational control reviews are absorbing an increasing share of internal audit efforts. In the United States fully half these resources are devoted to reviews of operational controls. In Europe, the percentage is higher.

### Special Projects

Regardless of the nature of its basic charge, an internal audit staff may also be required to engage in special projects. For example, internal auditors may examine expense reports and corporate perquisites. They may monitor the submission of conflicts-of-interest statements by key employees. They may be assigned responsibilities pertaining to documentation of systems when this documentation is necessary to comply with the Foreign Corrupt Practices Act of 1977. (See Chapter 18.)

Other variations in responsibilities do not seem as professional as the foregoing activities. For example, some persons referred to as internal auditors may engage in processing functions such as original bank reconciliations or voucher approvals. Such production activities can consume much of an internal auditor's time, leaving little opportunity to exercise his professional judgment. Ultimately, performance of extensive administrative and clerical activities can impair the independence of internal auditors.

## CREATING AN INTERNAL AUDIT DEPARTMENT

### Determining the Need

At a certain point in a company's growth, it becomes advantageous to create an internal audit department. It is impossible to set a magic number in terms of revenues or employees that signals the arrival of that moment.

Some matters that should be considered in assessing a need for internal auditors are:

- The complexity of operations;
- The extent of clerical processing and the probability of errors;
- The number, nature, and extent of potential causes of losses that are subject to control by the system; and
- Requirements of regulatory agencies.

While the addition of an internal audit staff is being considered, independent auditors may be asked to accomplish internal audit functions on a *pro tem* basis. Some companies assign these internal audit tasks to an independent accounting firm other than that which regularly audits the accounts and achieve considerable success, possibly because of an element of rivalry between competing firms. Another temporary measure involves the assumption of certain internal audit responsibilities by a corporate systems group.

### The Charter

The organization of an internal audit function differs with the operating philosophy of each company, the nature and complexity of the business, its size, and the risks to which it is subject. Frequently, the creation of a charter setting forth the responsibilities of the internal audit department is a logical first step.

The charter should make clear that members of the department are to enjoy free access to all units of the organization. It should protect the department's independence, which is of cardinal importance with respect to internal auditors. Independence does not mean that an internal auditor should not sympathize with the objectives and goals of his employer. It does mean, however, that he should be free from conflict of interest; that he should conduct examinations without mental reservation; and that he should comment on all deficiencies, regardless of the positions of those on whom this may reflect. Figure 19.1 is an example of a typical charter for an internal audit function.

**Responsibilities.** The responsibilities of the internal audit department should be tailored to each concern's requirements. Typical responsibilities include:

- Developing a comprehensive long-term audit program;
- Setting policies for the audit activity;

---

The Internal Audit Function Has These Objectives:

1. Establish policies for the audit activity.
2. Develop and execute a comprehensive long-range audit program.
3. Examine management's stewardship at all levels for effectiveness and compliance with company policies and procedures.
4. Recommend improvement in management controls to safeguard assets, promote corporate growth, and increase profits.
5. Review functional operations to evaluate internal and management controls and accomplishment of objectives.
6. Issue audit reports on the results of reviews including appropriate recommendations for improvement.
7. Appraise the effectiveness of the actions to be taken to correct deficiencies until satisfactorily resolved.
8. Conduct special examinations at the request of management, external auditors, and the company's vendors.
9. Investigate all discovered defalcations to determine cause and extent of loss and to recommend appropriate action.
10. Assist chief financial officer in coordinating work of the public accountants and audit committee.

To accomplish these internal audit objectives, the department is authorized to have full, free, and unrestricted access to all company functions, records, property, and personnel.

---

FIGURE 19.1  TYPICAL CHARTER FOR AN INTERNAL AUDIT FUNCTION

- Conducting financial audits;
- Recommending improvements in control to strengthen protection over assets, promote corporate growth, and increase profitability;
- Examining management's stewardship at all levels for compliance with company policies and procedures;
- Reviewing operations covering all controls;
- Monitoring the effectiveness of actions taken to correct deficiencies and seeing that "open" findings are appropriately resolved;
- Conducting special examinations of sensitive areas;
- Investigating fraud to discover the *modus operandi*, the extent of loss, and systems slippages or other deficiencies that warrant redress;
- Assisting the audit committee as needed; and
- Coordinating the work of the internal auditors with that of the independent public accountants.

In large companies some corporate staff executives, such as those directing purchases, production, and marketing, may have individual staffs to monitor compliance with company policies and procedures. When such specialized *ad hoc* staffs exist, the chief internal auditor should plan for reasonable coordination of review activities (1) to ensure that all audits—whether labeled such or not—follow professional standards and (2) to reduce the possibility of duplication and, more significantly, the possibility of an activity's not being reviewed at all.

**The Financial/Operational Dichotomy.** Some companies have created two auditing groups, to engage in financial and operational auditing, respectively. This dual approach incorporates prima facie inefficiencies. Jurisdictional difficulties are likely to arise, since information systems do not distinguish between internal accounting and operational controls. Further, the dual approach requires both groups to understand the system, and involves a risk of duplicated audit documentation.

## Lines of Authority and Responsibility

The trend for having internal auditors report to higher levels of management is on the upswing. A 1975 survey by the Institute of Internal Auditors indicated that no less than 54 percent of chief internal auditors reported to a vice president or higher; 11 percent reported to the president or chief executive; 7 percent reported to the chairman of the board; and 19 percent reported to the controller.

**Reporting to the Company President.** A reporting line to the president of the company may have drawbacks. Some presidents do not attach sufficient importance to internal auditing to give it enough attention. On the other hand, some presidents may use audit data to chastise executives who are in disfavor. Thus, a line to the president may cause apprehension on the part of some auditees, who may then become defensive. (However, regardless of the merits of presidential involvement, regulatory bodies have mandated specific reporting lines for internal auditors in certain regulated industries, e.g., banking.)

**Reporting to a Financial Officer.** At first glance the reporting line to a financial officer seems compromised on the grounds that such an officer thereby would be placed in the position of reviewing systems designed under his direction. However, on further reflection it appears that the internal audit activity does need a congenial home base. Other staff members who report to the financial officer have educational and experience backgrounds similar to internal auditors; the association of internal auditors with these people speeds transmission of ideas. In any event, the position level and function to which the internal auditor reports are less significant than the professional and intellectual attributes of the officer concerned and that officer's appreciation of the significance of the internal auditor's role. The officer should also wield substantial influence in the overall organization. This factor becomes important when clout is needed to ensure that internal audit findings, irrespective of locus, are evaluated and corrective actions taken.

**Housekeeping Versus Technical Direction.** If the internal auditor reports to a financial officer, that executive will provide certain "housekeeping" services. For instance, he will approve the budget of the internal audit staff, grant preliminary approval of the audit schedule, authorize tables of organization, and approve personnel actions. Most financial officers will assume only limited responsibility for technical aspects of reviews and technical contents of reports. If a financial officer releases audit reports over his own signature, that action can be viewed as denoting support. However, he should have no power to emasculate or suppress findings. Stated differently, his role should be administrative rather than technical.

**The Chief Internal Auditor's Responsibility to the Board of Directors.** Audit committees are now required for companies listed on the New York Stock Exchange. (See Chapter 10.) The Securities and Exchange Commission has emphasized the need for audit committees to take an active part in directing and controlling the internal audit program. (In a company that is not publicly held and not subject to other legal mandates decreeing audit committees, the entire board of directors could serve as an audit committee of the whole, or the function might be assigned to another board committee.) The interaction of the chief internal auditor with the board transcends reporting arrangements. The board committee, especially its chairman, and the chief auditor must each feel comfortable with the other. Aside from committee meetings set aside to consider the internal audit program, informal two-way communication should be established to transmit matters of mutual interest.

**The Board's Need for Internal Auditors.** The duties imposed on directors—and the legal risks of serving as a director—have grown in recent years. Yet, few directors have been provided with trained staffs to carry out their burgeoning role in corporate governance. The internal audit staff can fill this vacuum and provide the directors with objective and documented input. The audit staff can offer some assurance to the directors that corporate policies are being implemented. Again, the overriding consideration is the need for the chief internal auditor and the chairman of the audit committee to establish a working relationship.

**Internal/Independent Auditor Relationships.** The work of the internal and independent auditors requires close coordination. That coordination is typified by joint setting of an annual audit schedule for submission to the audit committee. Many view the mere anticipation of an audit, with its deterrent effect on improper acts, as a significant psychological benefit. Thus, both internal and independent auditors should be deployed to achieve appropriate aggregate coverage, with some element of surprise incorporated whenever possible within scheduling constraints.

In Statement on Auditing Standards No. 9 the public accounting profession set ground rules for relying on the work of internal auditors. Even prior to this recognition of the relationship in the professional liturgy, some independent accounting firms developed training programs designed to familiarize internal auditors with that firm's audit approach and techniques. Using the independent auditor as a trainer can speed the activation of a new internal audit group and, conceivably, enhance productivity of an existing group. However, the typical independent auditor is likely to contribute most effectively to the *financial* audit capabilities of internal auditors.

With respect to operational auditing, even if independent auditors have provided the initial impetus for such activities, the growing sophistication of internal auditors is likely to quickly overtake that of the erstwhile teachers.

**Internal Auditors and Systems Personnel.** If, as is common, the internal audit group conducts financial as well as operational audits, the internal audit staff should be placed at an organizational level that adds impact to findings and recommendations. In addition, the internal auditors should be closely associated with the systems or internal consulting group, so that they can have a continuing impact on systems modifications. And, the internal auditors should review controls being built into new systems while such systems are still in a preoperational phase. Coordination of auditing and systems personnel fosters efficiency by eliminating redundant fact finding and invites cross-pollination of ideas. Further, the systems group's plans and programs often offer clues to matters requiring correction. By reporting deficiencies and highlighting the need for attention by systems personnel, the chief internal auditor can influence the allocation of scarce resources. Also, the chief internal auditor should obtain the assistance of systems people as reviewers of technically complex reports, or as members of audit teams when technical functions are examined.

### Departmental Organization

As already pointed out, the departmental mission influences organization. Three approaches may be useful: centralization, decentralization, and a hybrid of the two.

**Centralization.** Centralization has these advantages:

1. The internal audit staff will be independent of local management, and audit objectivity will be fostered;
2. The auditors will be likely to enjoy the support of corporate management and corporate staff groups;
3. The audit staff will have relative flexibility in responding to demands for its services; and
4. The internal auditors will be in an excellent position to coordinate with the independent auditors.

However, centralization also has disadvantages. Local management may consider the internal auditors as agents of the head office, or, as a control rather than as a service. Accordingly, they may resist review or show lack of receptivity to suggestions. This can lead to "adversary" proceedings likely to vitiate many of the benefits of internal auditing.

**Decentralization.** The advantages of the decentralized approach are the obverse of the disadvantages of the centralized approach:

1. When internal auditors maintain ties with local management, sympathetic consideration of comments and recommendations will be promoted;
2. Internal auditors resident in a particular location are likely to specialize in the industries or functions involved, thereby improving audit productivity;
3. Assuming that the internal auditors develop a record of contributing to local profits, they will be given special cooperation; and
4. When auditors are stationed in local areas, travel expenses are likely to be reduced (although geographic dispersal of auditors—properly controlled and subject to rotation of individuals—should reduce expenses regardless of organizational approach).

A disadvantage of decentralization is that the internal auditors could come to identify with local management. Impairment of objectivity is likely to pose risks, especially when reasonable personnel rotation has not been implemented. Moreover, in a highly decentralized organization it could become difficult to establish audit standards, standardize audit approaches and philosophies, and perform quality control reviews.

**The Hybrid Arrangement.** Here the chief internal auditor has under his immediate direction a small group of experienced and well-trained auditors. Major operating units have their own staff of internal auditors reporting to the respective managements. Such auditors maintain a dotted-line relationship to the chief internal auditor. Rotation assures that each auditor maintains independence. Quality control reviews by the headquarters staff add assurances of independence and quality.

The hybrid arrangement combines features of the centralized and decentralized structures. The headquarters group, operating in proximity to corporate management, performs the following functions:

1. Evaluates and communicates pertinent findings to all entities, thus serving as a catalyst for the dissemination of cost reduction and revenue improvement ideas;
2. Monitors responses by operating units to findings and recommendations and checks progress of agreed-on corrective actions;
3. Sees that all units observe professional standards;
4. Conducts research into advanced auditing techniques to enable the company to improve audit productivity;
5. Coordinates with the independent public accountants; and
6. Coordinates with the corporate systems group to ensure that audit findings are considered in new systems development and in modifications to existing systems.

The hybrid arrangement facilitates introduction of a new management technique that has come into vogue in engineering organizations. This technique is referred to as *matrix management*. Under this system a corporate staff group consists of members offering various professional skills. Work proceeds on a project basis. The staffing of each project mirrors the staff in microcosm, since different specialists are assigned to different projects. Their service on projects may be part-time or of limited duration. The project staff reports to the project manager as well as to the specialist at the corporate level. This system, which is directly transferable to the hybrid audit organization, helps to "stretch" talent in short supply.

The disadvantage of the hybrid arrangement arises because field auditors wear two organizational hats. They have responsibilities to the managements of the operating units as well as to the chief internal auditor at headquarters. They perform dual control and service functions. This potential problem of conflicting loyalties can, however, be overcome by judicious training of the auditors and by effective coordination of auditing activities throughout the organization.

## ACTIVATING AN INTERNAL AUDIT FUNCTION

### Personnel Considerations

Personnel hired as internal auditors should be intelligent, creative, and imaginative. Such people are likely to want to influence their own careers, and they will probably derive satisfaction from seeing their own ideas implemented. Therefore, they should be permitted to participate in setting their own goals and targets and in evaluating their own performance. A climate that emphasizes productivity should be maintained, in which professionals can grow through challenge.

**Personal Integrity.** Internal auditors should run a tight ship. Sensitive responsibilities may be entrusted to them. For example, they are often charged with reviewing the expenses of others. Thus, an internal auditor should be like Caesar's wife—beyond suspicion.

**Participative Management.** Assuming the selection of individuals with appropriate intellectual qualifications, a participative managerial approach should set departmental direction over the near and long terms. Dictatorial management is unlikely to succeed in a professional environment. The participative approach should be pervasive, including determination of the audit schedule, its execution, and the evaluation of results. As a prerequisite, there should be effective channels of communications running from top to bottom and, conversely, from bottom to top.

Budget development lends itself to participative management procedure. If staff members assigned to an engagement do not participate in budgeting, they will have only a limited incentive to comply with it. The chief internal auditor should issue instructions outlining the ground rules for budget development. He should critically review preliminary budgets submitted to him. He should not be concerned solely with efforts to cut expenses, but should try to concentrate the audit effort on areas in which audit risk can be minimized and/or areas that contribute to the firm's profitability.

After challenge by the chief internal auditor, budget developers should revise and resubmit data. After the revised budget has been rereviewed and approved, it becomes the *modus vivendi* for an engagement. Changes to budgets should not be effected without written approval from the chief internal audit officer; in a large audit organization it may be desirable to install a system under which changes are controlled, perhaps by numbered authorizations.

**Job Title.** The title of the chief internal auditor, like his reporting line, often represents a "red herring," rather than an issue of substance. A chief internal auditor's title is less important than his imagination, integrity, ethics, and courage. Further, to some degree, the chief internal auditor needs the attributes of a salesman—he needs to sell his services and those of his group to operating executives. The selling effort should be grounded in solid contributions to profitability improvement.

**Job Description.** The chief internal auditor should be given a job description specifying his primary duties, the basis on which his performance will be measured, and his reporting relationships. A job description is also useful for internal and external recruiting for the position. (However, a successful applicant should be allowed the privilege of modifying the job description.) A job description helps communication between the executive hiring the chief internal auditor and the appointee. Reasonable job tenure results only if the behavioral characteristics of the directing executive are cohesive with the behavioral characteristics of the person recruited. Further, a job description is often the basis for preparing manpower specifications used for setting compensation. The description also guides the chief internal auditor in his selection of individual goals, which is important to performance evaluation. A representative job description is provided as Appendix 19-1.

## Workload Determination

The department's philosophy influences workload. Financial audits are usually less time-consuming than operational audits. If an internal audit department that has been performing only financial audits expands into operational areas, additional audit time will be required, especially until personnel perfect their operational review skills.

**Two Approaches: Entity and Functional.** The entity approach involves a review of an entire organizational entity. The scope of the review may combine financial and operational elements. In the functional approach, an individual activity, say marketing, is reviewed; the review may involve one entity only, or it may be extended "across the board." The functional approach usually is biased toward operational reviews. The choice of approach is affected by availability of staff, as well as by requirements of the auditees. Opportunities exist for combining both approaches.

**Optimal Staff Size.** In determining the optimal size of the internal audit staff, consideration should be given not only to the immediate workload, but also to the prospective workload for the next few years, since it takes anywhere from six months to two years to bring internal auditors to full effectiveness.

There is no hard and fast rule regarding preferred size of an internal audit department. Some have suggested an average standard of one internal auditor per 1,000 employees; that ratio seems low. The "right" ratio depends on the control philosophy of the company and the objectives of the internal audit department.

**Audit Frequency and Its Scheduling Implications.** Management should participate in determining audit frequency and scope and in seeing that all concerned understand that scope. These determinations may be expressed in assumptions, such as:

- Financial audits only are to be performed;
- The independent auditors will visit one third of the entities, the internal auditors a second third, the remaining third will not be visited;
- Annual visits are to be made to all entities that are material relative to the financial statements, or have a history of accounting adjustments, or have systems that are in a debugging phase, or have experienced executive turnover; or
- Requests for audits by operating management are to be given priority.

Once management has provided direction, a list of entities to be served should be created. Priorities should be indicated on the list; sequence of performance should be influenced by materiality considerations, the desirability of achieving surprise, and known need.

## Operational Auditing

A proven financial auditing program is fundamental. If such a program is operative, the independent accountant can rely on it, thereby reducing the extent of his own coverage and often achieving a favorable cost trade-off. Also, the audit approaches used are similar whether the department's emphasis is on financial auditing or has been extended into operating areas. Consequently, excellence in the familiar preserve of the financial audit represents a prerequisite training toward operational reviews.

**Selling the Operational Audit.** Operational audits are best sold on a building block basis; each operational audit should sell itself as well as the next such audit. Some axioms emerge:

- In establishing the audit schedule, the chief internal auditor must aim first at adequate financial audit coverage;
- When he initiates an operational audit program, he should devote a token percentage, perhaps 10 percent, of overall effort to the new practice area;
- He should increase operational audit time as success becomes apparent and as demand by operating personnel grows.

## Engagement Considerations

**Staffing.** Under a typical staffing arrangement, a large engagement will be supervised on site by an in-charge auditor, usually a person with three to five years experience. An in-charge auditor normally supervises up to five persons in the field. Usually, the in-charge auditor reports to an audit manager. Managers may be assigned on the basis of entity, geography, or type of business. (In addition to audit managers with line jurisdiction, the manager title may be held by functional specialists concerned with such techniques as statistical sampling, other quantitative auditing techniques, and EDP auditing.)

**Scope and Budget.** Individual engagement budgets should be premised on rank, hours, and required skills. In most cases, the engagement budget is heavily influenced by the steps involved in verifying account balances. Time estimates may be developed by referring to prior-period actual time expenditure. The writer would generally opt for a zero-base budgeting approach, with a fresh look taken at each examination. In any event, historical time data must be examined critically, with consideration given to the latest information concerning control effectiveness, materiality, and risk. After a time estimate has been made for accounts, an overall estimate may be made of time needed to review internal accounting and/or operational controls. As an average standard, an internal accounting control review is likely to consume 20 to 30 percent of total audit time, or roughly half the time required for account balance tests. (The term *internal control review* includes interviewing the persons who maintain the system, flowcharting, compliance testing, and evaluating internal control conditions.) However, a 50 percent increase in control review time would result from an operational review.

**The Scheduling Process.** A list of staff members eligible for assignment should be prepared, showing rank and available hours. Engagement budgets, sequenced for priorities, should be measured against manpower. Care should be taken not to exhaust available resources. Time should be allowed for training, professional development, and experimentation with emerging audit technology. For instance, if an internal audit department is about to initiate its first EDP auditing engagement, a reasonable number of hours should be set aside for learning. Also, time should be allowed to cover expected growth in activities (and in the size of the enterprise), plus special assignments such as fraud investigations, evaluations of mergers and acquisitions, and special tasks assigned by the audit committee.

Given unslackening expansion in governmental requirements, a 10 percent cushion for contingencies would seem minimal. However, that cushion should not be viewed as free time. Standby work should be budgeted to keep personnel gainfully employed if special work fails to materialize. Some examples of work that should be done but that commonly carries relatively low priorities are visits to sales offices, petty cash counts, and examinations of expense reports. In short, the standby allowance can be linked to endeavors that should be performed on time but will not result in cataclysmic penalties if postponed.

# DIRECTION OF AN ENGAGEMENT

## Audit Approach

Each audit is unitary in that an audit cannot be divided into self-contained components. However, an analytical approach can be used for discussion purposes. The framework used by the writer's firm for many years involves:

- Obtaining an understanding of the business and system;
- Recording that understanding;
- Performing transaction reviews to see that the recording is correct;
- Testing controls to see whether the auditor can rely on their functioning;
- Testing account balances, together with completing other audit procedures; and
- Reporting results in financial statements and management letters.

**The Behavioral Aspects of Interviewing.** Obtaining the understanding required for an audit involves an analysis of the industry, the business, and the system. Interviewing is the most effective technique for understanding the system and involves a knowledge of the behavioral characteristics of the interviewees. Careful preparation and programming are necessary. Yet the interviewee must be at ease; accordingly, the interview should be conducted in an informal atmosphere. The interviewer must modify questions based on the input he obtains—the relationship calls for a high order of interpersonal skills. Therefore, internal auditors should be trained in investigatory interviewing, with emphasis on interpreting interviewee reactions.

**Flowcharting.** Usually, documentation of a system is efficiently achieved by use of flowcharts. Although simplified systems have been devised for audit use, standard flowcharting methodology is recommended for an industrial environment. Further, the standard approach enhances the value of flowcharting as a communications device. Training in the use of the standard system is available.

Flowcharting should start with recognition of the need for a transaction and should terminate in the recording of that transaction in the accounts. The flowcharts should cover all operations, including the creation and processing of documents. Activities not involved in transaction processing—for example, control activities such as the taking of inventories—may be documented in narrative form.

**Questionnaires.** Questionnaires should not become a "crutch" or an end in themselves. They serve as a reminder of control concerns and offer some assurance that the auditor has considered all significant matters. Many serviceable internal control checklists and questionnaires are available; one such list was published recently by the Special Advisory Committee on Internal Control of the AICPA. Other questionnaires, covering both internal accounting and operational controls, are available through the Institute of Internal Auditors.

**Evaluation of Controls.** The practices of a particular auditee should be evaluated by comparing them to practices considered preferred, that is, found successful.[2] When such practices have been established by a professional organization or by corporate policy, the auditor will find it relatively simple to audit for conformance. The questionnaires mentioned previously may be useful as indicators of preferred practices relating to internal accounting controls. The auditee should be acquainted with the content of the questionnaires to ensure some agreement on criteria. The description of preferred practices should be sufficiently broad to facilitate their adaptation to diverse environments. Only in this way can practices become supportive of a particular auditee's control objectives.

**Departures From Preferred Practices.** Departures from preferred practices must be evaluated in monetary, or at least, in quantified, terms. When a preferred practice is not in effect, the significance of the deficiency should be measured in terms of the operational effect. The selection of pertinent effects may be made from a predetermined list of possible consequences. The impact of the consequence is then measured in monetary terms. It is a truism that although noncompliance with preferred practices may be obvious, many managements will do nothing until the impact of the delinquency is converted to dollar amounts.

**Immediate Correction of Deficiencies.** When a control deficiency is noted, the auditor should consider its effect on the nature, timing, and extent of audit procedures designed to substantiate individual account balances, as well as its effect on profitability. However, rather than expand the audit program, it may be preferable to seek an immediate change to the system. Such a change helps to realize benefits early and should be attractive to auditees.

### Programming Considerations

When audit programs are developed, there is a somewhat different emphasis with respect to new audits than to repeat audits.

**New Audits.** In the case of a newly audited activity, a preliminary program should be prepared. The core of such a program consists of procedures designed to accomplish specific audit objectives. An auditor senior to the program drafter should review the initial draft and arrange for any necessary changes. The program should then be applied in the field. After this initial use of the program, its effectiveness and efficiency should be evaluated. When a satisfactory operational program has evolved, its future use involves (1) updating it in the light of changes in internal control or regulatory requirements, and (2) updating it to achieve greater effectiveness and efficiency based on emerging technological developments.

---

[2] A list of suggested preferred operating practices may be found in Pomeranz, Felix, et. al., *Auditing in the Public Sector* (Boston: Warren, Gorham & Lamont, 1976).

**Audit Procedures.** Steps in an audit program are directed toward *evaluation of internal control* or *substantiation of account balances*. In addition, an auditor may consider other audit procedures to determine whether relationships between accounts, and account trends, are consistent and reasonable.

*Evaluation of internal control.* The auditor's evaluation of internal control enables him to decide on the nature, timing, and extent of his audit program for substantive tests. Normally, when an internal control is considered present, support for that belief should be entered in the auditor's working papers. The auditor must then decide whether to rely on it for his purposes, that is, for restricting his substantive tests. If he determines to do so, he must perform compliance tests in reasonable depth, following appropriate criteria for selection of documents to be examined. These tests are intended to establish whether a control is in place and functioning as planned. If the control is malfunctioning, the auditor changes his recorded understanding, and refrains from restricting substantive tests.

When a control is absent, the auditor must evaluate the effect of its absence on the timing, nature, and extent of his substantive tests. His thought process relative to a "no" answer involves his determination of whether material error could arise, and, if so, whether the existing audit program adequately addresses the risk. If it does not, the auditor revises that program.

All control deficiencies should be conveyed to management. Management should then (1) reach agreement as to accuracy of the finding, (2) consider whether correction is cost-effective in the light of professional and regulatory standards, and (3) set up a program to take the least expensive corrective action. If such action can be taken immediately after the auditor's discovery, it may be possible to avoid having the auditor do additional work as a result of the deficiency.

*Substantiation of balances.* Lists of substantive procedures can be found in auditing texts. Some of the steps are almost always accomplished near the balance sheet or reporting date; others can be performed at any time. Some procedures need to be completed *in toto* at all times; the extent of others is variable. And certain procedures will be accomplished only if there is an extraordinary pattern of deficiencies; examples of such procedures include the preparation of a "proof of cash" for a period following the review period, the confirmation of accounts payable, and confirmation of written-off accounts receivable.

*Evaluation of operational controls.* Programming to determine the existence of operational controls resembles programming to establish the existence of internal accounting controls. The operational review tends to involve fewer documents. Again, when a control is absent, an attempt is made to quantify, or express in dollar terms, the effect upon profitability. Shortcuts are used to the extent possible. Appendix 19-2 illustrates a control question and suggests actions to be taken by the auditors when the control is absent. The tests to be applied to each step are whether it accomplishes the audit objectives and whether it provides optimal value for effort expended.

## Enhancing Audit Productivity

The shortage of audit resources may be alleviated by improved productivity. The productivity issue has been raised by the United States General Accounting Office; in the absence of concerted remedial efforts, it could become a significant national problem in its own right. Increasing audit productivity is a challenging problem. The chief internal auditor must resist the temptation to establish "law-and-order" rules over professional endeavors. He must strike a happy balance between allowing auditors free rein to exercise judgment and circumscribing their efforts through compliance routines such as check lists and sign-offs.

**Standard Audit Programs.** If an organization consists of entities that are similar in terms of systems and controls, opportunities may exist for systematizing audits. For example, assume that a company operates a number of carton plants, and that production equipment, organization, and product lines of the plants are similar. Assume too that a rigorous approach exists toward management control, as exemplified in standard policies, procedures, control techniques, and instructions. Given a standardized system and a standard approach to control, it should be possible to develop a standard audit program, although minor tailoring of the program may still be necessary to meet individual plant exigencies. On the other hand, suppose a conglomerate is engaged in unrelated businesses, the company has a decentralized approach to management, and a variety of systems is in effect. In such a company, it would be necessary to develop customized audit objectives, together with procedures to accomplish those objectives. However, to the extent possible, standard audit programs should be used to enhance productivity.

**Value Analysis in an Audit Environment.** Value analysis consists of weighing the cost of an article or a procedure against the benefits to be received. The application of this technique to auditing means that each procedure should be examined to determine its effectiveness, that is, whether it advances the achievement of the audit objective. Some thought should also be given to whether the objective can be accomplished at lower cost. If the internal audit staff is large, it may be worthwhile to appoint a value analysis committee to ferret out productivity improvement opportunities. Typically, the committee's work would be directed initially toward reviewing the more significant expenditures of audit effort.

**The Interdisciplinary Task Force.** Task forces may help to overcome staffing constraints. Further, task forces composed of individuals representing various professional disciplines may promote quality. In most instances—depending on the nature of the engagement—the task force leader will be an accounting and auditing generalist. Task force personnel may include representatives of other disciplines as needed: EDP auditing, industrial engineering, statistics, actuarial mathematics, civil engineering, and others. The professional background of an individual member matters less than his imagination, ingenuity, and creativity. It may be easier to teach a nonauditor the rudiments of auditing than to imbue a trained auditor with the basics of other disciplines.

An example of the use of nonauditors by a task force may be of interest. An auditor was responsible for ascertaining informational needs for managing a group of carton plants; he was to furnish input to the design of a model carton plant system. Since marketing concerns are vital in the folding box business, two carton salesmen, college educated and with good track records but with no prior experience in auditing or systems analysis, were assigned to the task force. The men were trained intensively in interviewing techniques, flowcharting, and evaluating informational needs. Because of their background in selling the product, in assisting in the construction of price quotations, and in customer service, they made many contributions. The redesigned system incorporated numerous tactical features to support an aggressive salesman in a competitive marketplace.

**Overview Audit Procedures.** Historically, financial analysis has tended to be static. Hence, its value for identifying out-of-line conditions has been limited. However, newer dynamic financial analysis approaches based on simulation and "what if" games can focus the audit effort by revealing trends that merit audit investigation. Multiple regression (by highlighting inconsistent relationships among accounts), decision theory (by helping to identify unnecessary work that does not affect conclusions), and statistical sampling all enhance audit productivity. A basic factor in applying those techniques is an understanding, by both auditors and auditees, of their advantages as well as their limitations and disadvantages. It is important to remember, moreover, that it may be dangerous for a chief internal auditor to turn his staff into second-rate statisticians or mathematicians. All but the most routine mathematical and statistical applications should be supported and controlled by professionals trained in those disciplines.

**Systems Tests Versus Account Balance Tests.** Current AICPA rules entitle an auditor to restrict the extent of substantive testing by relying on the functioning of controls. The auditor must test controls to satisfy himself as to the propriety of such reliance. Accordingly, a cost trade-off exists in deciding whether to test controls and restrict substantive tests, or not test controls and therefore not restrict substantive tests. Given current rules, which permit cost-benefit tests, an unrestricted computer-supported substantive test approach is likely to be more efficient in most cases than restricted substantive tests with control testing. (The Foreign Corrupt Practices Act of 1977, and the initiatives of the Commission on Auditors' Responsibilities and the Securities and Exchange Commission, may lead to extensions of tests of internal control.)

**The Cybernetics Approach.** Opportunities for enhancing audit productivity exist in the creative use of operating information to confirm financial information. In many organizations, separate fact gathering takes place for financial and operating purposes. Information processing often maintains the gulf between the financial and operating information. It may be possible for the auditor to "price out" certain operating information. If so, he can compare the results to the financial information —both data sets should be pretty much the same. If they are not, the auditor should investigate the reasons for the divergence.

## SELECTING AND TRAINING PERSONNEL

### Staff Selection

Staff selection vitally affects the success of an internal audit program. Interaction between the field auditors and the operating personnel of the auditee establishes the tenor of the audit program. Operating personnel will be influenced in their attitudes toward the department, if not toward an entire company, by their reactions to individual auditors. Accordingly, the standards of staff selection, and the extent to which they are achieved, bear on success.

**A Business Orientation.** An internal auditor should be equipped by outlook and training with an analytical mind and the detached attitude of the professional fact finder. As an insider, he should be familiar with the organization's personnel, problems, and needs. If his skills are firmly rooted in the financial audit, and if expansion into operational areas is appropriately planned and programmed, he should quickly be able to use the available records effectively. He will maintain an overview of the entire business; this perspective should give him insight into management's problems and their resolution. In general, the qualities desired in an internal auditor do not differ significantly from those of most supervisors or executives. Each successful candidate should possess the capacity to view his employer's business as his own, so he will spot avenues for profit improvement.

**Communicating Ability.** If business orientation is an initial requisite, communicating ability, both in speech and in writing, ranks a close second. Communication means *understanding*—understanding the corporate directives an auditor must implement, the instructions of the in-charge auditor that govern the objectives and scope of the engagement, and the behavioral aspects that may be reflected in the actions of auditee personnel. Further, the auditor should be able to *transmit* that understanding to the persons of different estates with whom he will work—he should be able to address company presidents with respect but without appearing servile, he should be able to converse with unskilled workers without being condescending. His oral and written remarks should generally be in the recipient's language.

**Job Descriptions.** Prior to recruiting, job descriptions should be developed for each internal audit classification. The descriptions should take into account corporate goals and, especially, the internal audit department's charter. Each job description should indicate responsibilities, expected accomplishments, and relationships.

Formal manpower specifications should be developed to guide recruiters. Experienced internal auditors should participate in the recruiting effort—if necessary, side by side with representatives of the personnel department. Applicants should be given a feeling for the atmosphere of the department. The qualifications and behavior of potential employees should be supportive of the personality, ideals, and even idiosyncracies of supervisory audit personnel.

**Understanding the Corporate Philosophy.** Before he starts to recruit associates, the chief internal auditor should understand the ground rules affecting his own department. For example, if the company is decentralized and authority has been delegated to local managers, internal auditors must have the selling ability to secure acceptance of findings and recommendations.

**Career Potential.** Applicants should be considered from the standpoint of their suitability for advancement to managerial positions within the company. A record of successful placements helps to attract talent. For this reason, a career development program that considers the needs of the employee as well as of the employer and that provides for consistent and orderly professional and personal development is desirable. In effect, such a program should allow each individual to advance to the level he is capable of achieving.

**Educational Background.** It is impossible to prescribe the specific educational background that would identify an applicant as a potential success in internal auditing. A liberal arts background, perhaps with exposure to economics and/or graduate work in accountancy, may be desirable. Some companies have found that persons with undergraduate degrees in industrial engineering seem to take to internal auditing naturally. The personal attributes of the individual outweigh specific preparation. Psychological aptitude tests, especially if constructed for the unique requirements of a particular company and internal audit department, can be valuable in identifying potential successes and potential failures.

**Senior Auditor Positions.** Of the two sources that should be considered, the first is individuals elsewhere in the company who may be interested in an internal audit career. Identification of such individuals presumes compilation and maintenance by the personnel department of an inventory of employee backgrounds, aptitudes, and interests. The success of midcareer transfers to internal auditing would be enhanced if a systematic career development program exists within the company.

A second source of senior auditor personnel is national public accounting firms. Recruiters are cautioned to explore candidates' reasons for leaving. The chief internal auditor should consider the extent to which the training given an individual by his public accounting firm is transferable to the work the candidate will be expected to accomplish in the internal audit department. Transferability will be fostered if the employee has been trained in a systems approach to auditing that transcends internal accounting controls and extends to operational controls, and has acquired a sense of professional pride and integrity.

**The Critical Interview.** The most expert interviewers force an applicant to "carry the ball." This technique involves posing a hypothetical question, listening to the applicant's response, and assessing that response. For instance, the applicant's answer to a simple question such as, How would you go about determining what caused an inventory shortage? could reveal whether the applicant has an appreciation of the bookkeeping quirks that frequently afflict cost accounting systems.

## Developing Staff Potential

**Initial Orientation.** In the initial orientation, a fledgling auditor should be given the opportunity to review company goals, policies, procedures, and operating instructions. He should be introduced to key corporate personnel and made to feel accepted. He should also be briefed on problems, especially human relationships, that may affect his assignments.

He may be asked to review significant audit reports. This aspect of his orientation should be structured. The new auditor should be asked to describe what he learned from each report, what he liked and why, what he disliked and why, and how he would improve the next audit if he were to run the engagement. It is apparent that sufficient time must be devoted to this introductory phase by the chief internal auditor (or his designee) to realize full benefits.

**On-the-Job Training.** On-the-job training should be conducted by an experienced in-charge auditor, whose task is to guide the fledgling through the sensitive phases of an engagement. The trainer's participation should be active. He should ask the trainee, subject to the trainer's critical inputs, to participate in planning, executing, and evaluating audit tasks. For example, in preparing the new auditor for his first interview, the trainer should provide background on the value of the interview procedure and on sensitive matters. It may be worthwhile to train the new auditor in the behavioral aspects of interviews, most typically through role playing. The new recruit should prepare the interview questions, subject to review by the trainer, and conduct the interview in the trainer's presence. Subsequent to the interview, the trainer should apprise the trainee of any matters he should have observed but did not (especially in terms of interpreting interviewee responses), as well as commend him for any points he did cover that indicated particular perception.

**The Need for Skilled Trainers.** Some individuals have an innate knack for training, others do not. The chief internal auditor must identify those with special empathy for training and use that aptitude. In any event, controls must be instituted —through engagement time records, evaluations by trainer and trainee, and trainee debriefings—to ensure that needed on-the-job training actually takes place.

**Self-Development.** Internal auditors should be encouraged to participate in activities that lead to self-improvement and development as well as in their strictly professional duties. Superior audit reports should be circulated to the staff to stimulate performance. Subscriptions to professional journals, the establishment of an in-house library, and special training courses all can be valuable. Individuals should be encouraged to prepare for—and pass—the examination for Certified Internal Auditor (CIA). That encouragement should take the form of time off to study, together with monetary and promotional incentives.

In encouraging utilization of available training courses, the chief internal auditor should understand the department's training needs as well as the nature of the material being offered. Useful material is written in a manner that integrates the teaching situation, the instructor, and the student. The objectives of the material in question are important; some material merely conveys information, some is concerned with concepts, and some teaches "how to." Audit procedures may be taught through a blend of techniques involving lectures, discussions, and audio-visual materials. The preparation of how-to-learn-by-doing materials is difficult and time-consuming; conceivably, the requisite knowledge can be conveyed in most cost-effective fashion on the job, rather than in a classroom setting.

**Professional Guidelines.** The AICPA and the Institute of Internal Auditors have published extensive materials that may be useful.[3]

## EVALUATING AN INTERNAL AUDIT DEPARTMENT

### Winning Acceptance

In order to gain operating support, the internal audit staff should be organized to permit quick responses to changing requirements. All auditors should have an in-depth understanding of the business and an awareness of significant changes in the business environment. This is especially important for auditors in contact with line personnel. The auditors' expertise should reflect itself in the ability to communicate with operating personnel in *their* language and on *their* terms.

**Covering Departmental Expenses.** Savings signaled by internal auditors should offset a significant portion of departmental expenses. The best chance for having these savings recognized is to report findings so they can be readily understood by operating people.

*Simple corrective action.* Savings can be easily estimated when corrective action is relatively uncomplicated; for example, by eliminating a redundant purchase order copy, measurable savings can be realized in stationery, as well as in postage, handling, and filing.

---

[3] See *Statement of Responsibilities, Code of Ethics,* and *Summary of General and Specific Standards,* all published by the Institute of Internal Auditors.

*Savings in time and effort.* Often, time expended by other corporate staff groups can be reduced when internal auditors assume additional responsibilities; for example, if availability of internal audit documentation reduces similar efforts by, say, the corporate systems group, a legitimate audit contribution can be perceived.

**The Role of the Humble Auditor.** Studies by the United States General Accounting Office have shown that the major retrogressive factors impacting auditing involve (1) insufficient resources and (2) inadequate training. The second problem has already been discussed. The right to resources must be earned. The only way an auditor can earn his keep is to signal potential revenue improvements and cost reductions. Often the auditor can do little more than identify matters for investigation. The implementation of the steps to realize paybacks from improvements is the province of others. Thus, an internal auditor should not try to take all the credit for savings. Savings attributions must be shared if internal auditors are to gain the acceptance necessary to conduct a cost-effective program.

The wise internal auditor does not try to "manage" or trespass on managerial prerogatives. There is a thin line between an auditor's evaluation of controls built into a system and an evaluation of the personnel who administer those controls. Evaluation of controls should be based on objective principles (that is, preferred practices), which have been discussed elsewhere in this chapter. An auditor had best avoid the direct evaluation of personnel, since it requires subjective judgment; moreover, he is not likely to have the information necessary to make an informed comprehensive judgment.

### Measuring Achievement

**Progress Reporting.** Time records, in sufficient detail, are needed to assess progress against the schedule. In essence, two types of records should be maintained, and exception-type reports prepared therefrom: (1) a man record and (2) a job record. The man record should indicate the engagements an individual has been assigned to, hours expended, and, in condensed form, duties performed. The job record should show, for each engagement and each major program step, budget, actual hours incurred by employee category, and an indication of special problems. (Among other things, job records should facilitate comparisons of estimated percentages of completion to actual percentages of completion; such records could show the original budget, actual time expended to date, and time required to complete. This type of report aids early problem recognition.)

**Monitoring Information.** Periodically, an internal audit department should provide the following summary-type information to its administrative and board monitors:

- Updated organization chart;
- Significant education, experience, and skills;
- Progress of recruiting;

- State of professional development and staff retention;
- Long-range plans;
- A comparison of performance and schedule;
- Summarization of findings and actions taken on them;
- Open matters; and if desired,
- Copies of technically significant reports, preferably in "executive summary" form.

## Appraisal Authorities

**The Independent Auditor's Evaluation.** Independent auditors will seek to determine the extent of reliance they may place on the work of the internal audit department. Because of its pervasive importance, they should review the work of the internal audit department relatively early in the audit engagement. The professional standards of the independent auditor relative to this evaluation are set forth in Statement on Auditing Standards No. 9, *The Effect of an Internal Audit Function on the Scope of the Internal Auditor's Examination.*

**Evaluation by the Chief Internal Auditor.** The chief internal auditor should concern himself with four areas: organization and independence, professional skills, audit performance, and reporting practices. He may find it useful to employ a questionnaire in this task. Such a questionnaire appears in *Auditing in the Public Sector,* referred to previously. Audit reports and management letters should be emphasized in his evaluation, because these are the means by which the auditor communicates findings, observations, conclusions, and recommendations.

**Audit Debriefing.** When the audit is complete, the engagement team should conduct a self-critique. Such a review supplements the customary supervisory review of the working papers and report draft prior to report issuance. The self-review assesses performance relative to the plan. Its purpose is to provide input to improve future performance, and to contribute to future planning.

**Review by Supervisory Officer.** A quick feel for the effectiveness of an internal audit department may be obtained by applying a preestablished set of minimal criteria (see Appendix 19-3). Further, an evaluation should be made of the extent to which operating managements have backed the conclusions and recommendations of the internal auditors. Lack of support results in the continuation of inefficient operating practices; also, vitiated auditing efforts are very costly. Again, audit reports and management letters are to be emphasized in reviews; evaluation criteria should include logic, dollarization, and motivation.

**Evaluation by the Board of Directors.** Directors should focus on the breadth of responsibilities assigned to the department, audit scope, schedule attainment, communications and reports, and credentials of personnel in the internal audit group.

## AUDITING'S DYNAMIC FUTURE

Change in auditing has become pervasive and has affected the following areas:

1. The subject matter of auditing. Audits are shifting to operational areas and are becoming prospective rather than retrospective.
2. Recipients of audit reports. Audit committees are now *de rigueur*, regulatory authorities are thinking of extending the responsibilities of internal audit departments, and an employee constituency is emerging.
3. Auditors. Multidisciplinary task forces are being set up.
4. Audit technology. EDP auditing, quantitative auditing techniques, systems development, and life cycle audits pose challenges and offer opportunities.

### Growth and Professional Stature

Internal auditing is heading toward professional maturity. Courses, conferences, and publications are devoted to the subject. The CIA title has become established and is being protected by increasingly rigorous entrance requirements. College majors are available in the subject; the New York-based New School of Social Research has pioneered a two-year master's degree in management auditing; the curriculum transcends the financial auditing aspect.

### EDP

The use of distributed systems involving input/output at terminals remote from the computer is spreading. In small organizations, proliferating minicomputers have introduced new internal control exposures. Although new control techniques are emerging to redeem some situations, it is difficult to cope with fundamental difficulties. For example, dealing with a small number of employees provides limited opportunity for achieving separation of duties. Consequently, systems design may take greater advantage of organizational alignment—the output of one department could become input to the next, subject to verification at entry.

In addition to recognizing control deficiencies, the auditor must utilize EDP to reduce audit costs and to preserve the psychological benefits inherent in surprise auditing. (The General Accounting Office of the United States, which has been in the forefront of auditing development for some years, has just issued a new guide setting EDP auditing standards for government auditors.)

### International Progress

In some industrial nations, internal auditors perform sophisticated functions beyond the techniques of independent auditors. For example, German industry is a leader in applying social measurement to employee compensation and benefits; the internal auditors have been in the forefront of the new approaches. In some less developed countries, government auditors have been moving into new areas. For example, operational auditing is practiced effectively in nations such as Algeria and Saudi Arabia; program effectiveness audits are being introduced.

### New Frontiers

**Program Effectiveness.** Evaluation of program effectiveness involves determining whether programs have been achieved and whether they have been achieved in the most cost-effective manner. The approach has possibilities for acceptance beyond government, especially by not-for-profit entities. Advertising programs, research, personnel development, and other relatively self-contained endeavors would seem to represent prime candidates for the evaluation of program effectiveness in an industrial company.

**The Preemptive Audit.** In a preemptive audit the auditor endeavors to control costs or enhance revenues before the fact. Such audits focus on planning and budgeting, on systems in a design stage, and on pro forma contracts before they have been let. Consideration is given to addressing exposures from risk and to seeing that appropriate controls have been introduced. Findings are conveyed immediately, with a view to timely corrective action. Although the preemptive concept is emerging in regulated industries, it would appear to have usefulness in the not-for-profit sector and for industry generally.

## SUMMARY

The continued growth of the internal audit profession seems assured in both large and small enterprises, although in the smaller enterprise the financial officer may at times have to act as a part-time internal auditor. Growth in internal auditing is likely to be paced only by the vision exercised by its practitioners. It may be apt to close with a quotation from a senior partner in a national public accounting firm. When asked by a young man what he should do to obtain challenging work and monetary reward he replied: "Buy internal auditing."

## SUGGESTED READING

American Institute of Certified Public Accountants (AICPA). "The Effect of an Internal Audit Function on the Scope of the Independent Auditor's Examination." Auditing Standards Executive Committee, Statement on Auditing Standards No. 9. New York: 1975.

Brink, Victor Z., Cashin, James A., and Witt, Herbert. *Modern Internal Auditing—An Operational Approach*. 3rd ed. New York: Ronald Press, 1973.

Pomeranz, Felix. "Auditing by Perception." Reports to Management. New York: Coopers & Lybrand, 1974.

Pomeranz, Felix, et al. *Auditing in the Public Sector.* Boston: Warren, Gorham & Lamont, 1976.

Robertson, Jack C., and Alderman, C. Wayne. "Comparative Auditing Standards." *Journal of Accounting, Auditing and Finance,* Vol. 4, No. 2 (Winter, 1981).

Sawyer, Lawrence B. *The Practice of Modern Internal Auditing.* Orlando, Fla.: Institute of Internal Auditors, 1973.

Sawyer, Lawrence B. *Manager and the Modern Internal Auditor.* New York: AMACOM 1979.

# APPENDIX 19-1   A SUGGESTED JOB DESCRIPTION FOR A GENERAL AUDITOR

## Objective

1. To preserve the assets and financial health of the corporation and to improve profits through regular audits that determine and report on the extent of compliance by components of the corporation with its authorized policies and practices.

2. To contribute to the maintenance of effective policies and practices through the expression of opinions and comments in formal audit reports based on audit examinations. Such comments may be directed toward the strengthening of existing policies and practices or toward the establishment of policies and practices in areas where there are none and a need exists.

## Function

The General Auditor is responsible for conducting regular audits of all components of the corporation's operations and for communicating the results of such examinations to appropriate division and corporate management levels through the medium of formally issued audit reports.

## Responsibilities

Within the limits of authorized corporation policies, procedures, programs, and budgets, he is responsible for the duties set forth below:[4]

1. Develops modern auditing techniques and programs for use in conducting audits of all components of the corporation's operations, with primary emphasis given to an assessment of the extent to which overall procedures and systems of the various components effectively support authorized policies and practices.

---

[4] Matters of primary importance have been marked with an asterisk.

*2. Schedules reviews and assessments to be made of the adequacy of both financial controls and the underlying operational controls.

3. Plans, programs, and through periodic field visits, continually administers the scope, technical aspects, and duration of field audits.

4. Assures the review of audit findings with management responsible for operations of the functions examined; supervises the presentation of findings in final audit reports and assists in interpreting and evaluating the significance and impact of audit findings on management's objectives; assists in the development of appropriate comments and recommendations for inclusion in final audit reports; promptly issues final audit reports to the president of the corporation and to responsible division management and appropriate staff executives.

*5. Reviews and evaluates formal letter-replies to audit reports to ascertain the adequacy of indicated remedial action.

*6. Prepares a final report for the president and chief financial officer of the corporation consisting of a digest of the audit findings and of action taken or to be taken, supplemented by a copy of the formal audit report.

*7. Provides members of the audit committee of the board of directors with internal audit schedules, data, and explanations necessary to the performance of their function.

8. Makes available to the independent public accountants audit working papers, copies of audit reports, and pertinent management replies thereto as a means of aiding them in determining the scope of their examination.

9. Informs the independent public accountants of the internal audit schedule, past and projected, to avoid unnecessary duplication of effort with respect to the audits of particular units.

*10. Obtains and maintains an audit staff capable of accomplishing the internal audit function.

11. Develops a system of cost and schedule control over audit projects.

## Authority

Executes the general responsibilities common to all executive and supervisory positions.

## Relationships

He will observe and conduct the following relationships:

1. *The Chief Financial Officer*
   He is accountable to this executive for proper interpretation and fulfillment of his function, his specific and general responsibilities and related authority, and his relationships.

2. *Audit Committee of The Board of Directors*
   He will be responsible for providing the audit committee of the board of directors with internal audit data necessary to the performance of their function.

3. *Corporate Officers and Divisional Management-Level Personnel*
   He will conduct such relationships with corporate officers and divisional management-level personnel as will engender the maximum cooperation in the performance of his function.
4. *Independent Public Accountants*
   He will conduct such relationships with the independent public accountants as the chief financial officer may direct.
5. *Professional and Management Associations*
   He will conduct such relationships with institutions in these and related categories as are necessary to the accomplishment of his function.
6. *Field Audit Staff*
   He will exercise professional and technical supervision over the activities of the field audit staffs, with particular emphasis on the coordination of audit activities throughout the corporation, maintenance of appropriate auditing standards and techniques, training and professional development of field auditors, and dissemination of audit results throughout the corporation.

## APPENDIX 19-2   SAMPLE CONTROL QUESTION

### Question

Are agreements to purchase (purchase orders), and changes to such agreements, *in writing* and signed?

### Significance

If written purchase orders are not used for significant purchases, the company is deprived of a record of his contract. Vendors may interpret the terms of the transaction to their own advantage. Thus, the firm incurs risks in the acquisition of articles in excessive quantities, of unsuitable quality, and on unfavorable terms. These conditions invite slow movement and valuation problems.

### Audit Steps

| | *Extent* | *Timing* |
|---|---|---|
| 1. Compare prices used to value the inventory to market prices as reflected on recent invoices from vendors. | Variable | Optional |
| 2. Calculate the age of the inventory, preferably in terms of the number of months' supply on hand of selected articles: | Variable | Optional |
| a. Interview manager with respect to sales probability of slow-moving articles; | | |
| b. Examine documentary support for disposal assertions; | | |

c. Compare this year's allowance for obsolescence to prior years' experience, bearing in
mind the aggregate investment in purchased
inventories, the inventory turnover, and the
results of the current aging in relation to
prior periods;

d. Prepare any entries necessary to increase
the allowance or to write down the inventory.

## Dollarization Steps

1. Excessive inventories:

a. Determine whether the company has reports indicating the relationship of quantities on hand to usage, for example, "number of months' supply on hand." If
so, summarize this information in the next step.

b. Develop the following summary by reference to available reports or by a sampling of inventory records. Consider taking a sample sufficiently broad to permit
the results to be projected over the entire inventory.

- Dollar value of stock that has shown no movement at
all during the review period ........................................... $_____

- Dollar value of stock for which there is a year's supply,
or more, on hand ........................................... _____

- Dollar value of stock for which there is less than a year's
supply but more than a six-month supply ........................................... _____

- Dollar value of stock with a six-month supply or less

      Total value tested ........................................... $_____

Computation of months' supply may be made by the following formula:

$$\text{Inventory} \div \frac{\text{Annual Usage}}{12} = \text{Number of Months' Supply}$$

This data can be obtained by summarizing usage in the inventory records or by
taking the opening inventory plus receipts and adjustments and subtracting returns and the ending inventory. If it is difficult to obtain annual usage, shorter-
term usage may be employed, provided that such period usage does not fluctuate
nor is it distorted by factors such as seasonality.

c. Calculate the dollar effect of slow-moving inventories by multiplying the first
two categories of stock by a rate representing variable annual carrying cost—
say 10-15 percent.

2. Noncompetitive buying:

a. Identify a significant number of commodities that the client purchases from
more than one vendor.

b. Prepare a schedule showing:

- Commodity description

- Current annual or period usage
- Vendors
- Quantities bought, dates, unit prices, total dollars
- Difference between the unit price charged by the lowest-priced qualified vendor, or the lowest obtainable quantity price per a qualified vendor's catalog, and the actual prices paid
- Potential savings (quantities extended by price difference).
(Caution: Be sure that (1) prices are adjusted for freight and (2) all vendors are qualified from the standpoint of delivery and quality.)

c. Review your schedule with management.

Name _____ , Title _____
Reaction of Auditee:

_____
_____
_____
_____
_____
_____
_____
_____
_____
_____

# APPENDIX 19-3   CHECKLIST OF INTERNAL AUDIT PROCEDURES

### Overseeing the Internal Audit Function: A Checklist for Executives and Directors

The internal audit function is assuming ever-increasing importance as corporations expand and their accounting systems become more complex. Pressures, moreover, continue to mount on executives and boards of directors, requiring them to maintain the utmost vigilance over all aspects of their companies' operations, including audit procedures. Equally important, a properly functioning internal audit system can help pinpoint areas of potential revenue improvement and cost reduction. As a basic guide, directors and executives may wish to use the following as a minimum checklist of internal audit procedures:

### Organization

☐ The board of directors' audit committee should participate in approving the audit schedule, guiding the work of the internal audit staff in a broad sense, and overseeing the coordination of internal and external audit operations.

☐ The manager in charge of the internal audit function should report to an upper echelon executive who can ensure that deficiencies are considered promptly and that corrective action is monitored.

☐ The internal audit schedule should be established annually, in consultation with the company's external auditors.

## Qualifications

☐ Appointments to the internal audit staff should be on the basis of capacity to advance to higher positions.

☐ Internal auditors, like their external counterparts, should engage in continuous training and self-improvement.

☐ Internal auditors should be in a position to maintain independence in matters they review.

## Performance Guides

☐ Internal auditors should not be overly burdened with routine tasks.

☐ Internal auditors should have full access to all areas of the company that their work requires.

☐ The internal audit schedule should provide for coverage of all physical facilities within a reasonable time cycle.

☐ Internal auditors should submit periodic reports, which permit management to evaluate progress in terms of the established schedule.

☐ Internal auditors should observe generally accepted auditing standards as incorporated in the Statements on Auditing Procedures issued by the American Institute of CPAs.

☐ The team's work should be guided by written programs.

☐ Audit programs should be responsive to changing control conditions.

☐ The audit staff's workpapers should include comprehensive documentation of all tests, stating what was examined, procedure followed, and results.

☐ All audit programs should be signed off to indicate completion of steps.

☐ The results of each examination should be expressed in a written report oriented towards management and suitable for follow-up.

☐ The follow-up should include a mechanism to ensure that all control deficiencies signaled by the internal audit are corrected as soon as possible.

☐ The internal audit staff should review operational and administrative controls on a cyclical basis, with special attention to areas of potential revenue improvement and cost reduction.

# 20

# Performing the Internal Audit

*Charles J. Catèr Jr.*

## INTRODUCTION

The internal audit is a major control function performed by the internal auditor and his staff to appraise the company's operations objectively and independently. The detailed review and examination of financial transactions and operational procedures supply reliable information for managerial decisions affecting all levels of business activity. The internal audit techniques described in this chapter cover accepted principles in general use, but they may require modification to meet each company's particular needs.

Beyond the basic considerations of organization and planning, four general considerations determine what internal auditing accomplishes and how internal audits are performed:

1. Company expectations;
2. The types of audits to be performed;
3. The approach of the internal auditor; and
4. The method of reporting audit results.

Top management's position on the first factor, and the methods it uses to communicate that position to the internal audit group and all levels of company management, determine the direction and effectiveness of internal auditing.

## Company Internal Audit Expectations

Each company sets the stage for performing an internal audit by first answering the question, What does the company expect to accomplish from internal auditing? To help management find out *if its policies are being followed* and *if they are appropriate* is a concise, general, and all-inclusive way of stating the objective. However, an expanded formal written policy statement published as an integral part of the company organization plan is more effective. Such a policy statement gives the internal audit group general direction and establishes its charter for all to see. Figure 20.1 is an example of how this might be written.

Adoption of a policy statement such as this is merely a first step. Top management's attitude toward internal auditing determines its successful implementation. The internal audit is a successful tool in firms where it is respected as a means of assuring better performance. When management considers it a necessary but unpalatable control to satisfy business standards, it will be less effective. The controller's role in top management is to fortify the internal auditing function and contribute to higher audit performance by addressing internal auditing and its accomplishments positively when the opportunity to do so arises.

Figure 20.2 is an example of an internal corporate communication that demonstrates management's support for the internal auditing function.

## Types of Internal Audits

The audit group must understand the types of internal audits and the corporate objectives and the circumstances that would require each type. This simplifies planning and prevents important omissions and oversights in the areas delegated to internal auditing in the corporate policy statement. Some of the common types of internal audits are discussed below.

**Protective Audit.** The protective audit indicates whether company assets are adequately protected and controlled. It examines such functions as protection of

| OBJECTIVE | The objective of this policy is to state the corporate audit policy and set forth certain guidelines and responsibilities with respect thereto. |
|---|---|
| POLICY STATEMENT | It is the policy of the corporation to establish and support the audit department for the purpose of assisting management in the effective discharge of its responsibilities for the control of corporate assets. This basic function of inspection, evaluation, and reporting is the constant responsibility of the audit department. |
| GUIDELINES | The following principal objectives are set forth as a guide to auditing practices: |

- Determine the adequacy of the system of internal control.
- Investigate the compliance with company policies and procedures and suggest policy or its modification where required.
- Verify the existence of company assets and assure that proper safeguards are maintained to protect them from losses of all kinds.
- Audit the reliability and operation of the accounting and reporting system.
- Identify opportunities for improved operational performance (in terms of both economy and efficiency) by appraising functional effectiveness against corporate and industry standards.
- Participate in the planning and definition of the scope of the financial audit to be undertaken by the corporation's public accountants. Submit these plans for review by division and corporate financial management and consider their suggestion as to audit emphasis.
- Coordinate its audit efforts with those of the corporation's public accountants.
- Submit annual audit plans to the president and the audit committee for review and suggested changes in scope, if any, prior to the July audit committee meeting.
- As directed by corporate management, participate in the planning of the audit coverage of potential acquisitions with the company's outside accountants and other members of the corporate staff. Follow up on acquisition audit work to assure the proper accomplishment of the audit objective.

FIGURE 20.1   A CORPORATE INTERNAL AUDIT POLICY

company funds by a cash teller or the security and control exercised over the physical assets of the company. These audits involve a review of systems controls and compliance procedures and are usually relatively simple to perform.

**Compliance Audit.** A compliance audit determines whether or not a specific standard is adequately controlled and whether it meets government regulations and laws. The audit is designed primarily to forestall unfavorable government investigations and/or the imposition of penalties. Examples of areas in which compliance audits are essential are pension plans, safety plans, and administration of employee equal-opportunity and antidiscrimination laws.

**Financial Audit.** The financial audit concentrates on the effectiveness of financial management and the accuracy of the financial records of the company. Although the external auditors are charged with validating the accuracy of financial statements and determining whether a company's financial reports are prepared in accordance with generally accepted financial principles, the internal audit group can make a significant contribution in the financial area by auditing more extensively the underly-

---

TO: All managers and supervisory personnel.

It is my desire that all managers in the company look upon the internal audit program as:

- An opportunity to improve the overall efficiency and effectiveness of their operation by an independent review and appraisal of the administrative controls in their major areas of responsibility.
- An opportunity to have qualified personnel review their controls in the same manner that they would conduct the review if sufficient time were available. Our internal audit goal is to identify profit improvement opportunities, cost-saving opportunities, and/or potential problem areas in conjunction with our regular field audit work.
- An opportunity to benefit from and participate in a company-wide exchange of ideas concerning good methods and techniques observed by the audit staff at other locations.

Thank you for your continued cooperation with this important management control program.

Yours very truly,

B. R. McRobin
Chairman of the Board

---

FIGURE 20.2  EXAMPLE OF AN INTERNAL CORPORATE COMMUNICATION

ing transactions that affect the financial statements and records of the company. (A financial audit may also be a compliance or operations audit.)

**Operations Audit.** An operations audit reviews the effectiveness, efficiency, and economy of segments of company operations, and includes financial, production, marketing, and staff service functions. The audit determines if an operation is properly controlled, if it is accomplishing the expected results, and if results can be improved. For example, an operations audit that covers control of a large product inventory would review all phases of the inventory. Are inventory categories overstocked or understocked? Are inventory records accurate? Are the shipping and receiving operations handled for maximum profit?

**Follow-Up Audit.** A follow-up audit determines whether unsatisfactory conditions previously reported in an internal audit have been corrected. The audit is generally made from one to three years after the original audit, is limited in scope, and normally reviews only the problem areas originally exposed.

**Electronic Data Processing (EDP) Audit.** An EDP audit can be a segmented part of any of the previously described audits or a separate audit of a phase of the company's EDP operations. A separate schedule for specific audits of computer operations is recommended to ensure that this important aspect of company operations is not absorbed within other types of audits and receives sufficient attention.

## Internal Auditing Systems and Procedures

Whether the internal audit group is small or large, the internal audit procedures must be clearly documented in advance. Although the small internal audit group may find this a tedious task initially, it should not be difficult to keep the auditing instructions current once the job is completed. The systems and procedures should be outlined in sufficient detail for a new auditor to read them and perform the audit with very little additional instruction. If management is to obtain well-documented audits and useful reports from the audit group, it must provide in writing specific instructions in the following areas:

- Preaudit contacts;
- Performing field work;
- The annual audit plan;
- Working papers;
- Statistical sampling;
- Writing the audit report;
- Electronic data processing (EDP) auditing;
- Follow-up on findings; and
- Administering the internal audit office.

### Approach of the Internal Auditor

While good auditors are best known for writing ability, inquisitiveness, thoroughness, and professionalism, a good auditor must also understand and appreciate human nature. If the internal auditor is sensitive to and respects the personal feelings of auditees, he will be accepted as a partner in a close working relationship that promotes mutual exploration of the subject by the auditor and the auditee towards viable, profitable solutions and the ultimate acceptance of the recommendations. In the absence of a healthy environment, the free flow of information between auditor and auditee is impeded.

Good personal relationships between auditors and auditees are valuable audit tools. An auditor will gain respect and promote his credibility by keeping the managers and employees informed of his audit objectives. He should begin by making preaudit contacts informing the target unit of the planned audit and requesting time for interviews and access to the auditee's records. He should name the individuals he wishes to interview and indicate the types of information he requires.

The internal auditor should maintain a close working relationship with the outside independent auditor. Such a relationship should improve the efficiency of both groups by reducing overlapping audits, keeping the outside auditor informed of new company operations, and informing the internal auditor of new audit techniques and accounting rules.

## THE INTERNAL AUDIT PLAN

The internal audit plan defines the areas within the company that are to be audited during a specified time period, and then catalogues them in a listing of objectives. The completed plan becomes the stated goal of the audit group. Often, the opinion of company managers is sought in determining the subjects that should be covered in internal audits. Also, individual internal auditors can make valuable contributions to plan preparation. The areas for study are usually classified to determine which are likely to be the most productive and how much time is needed to give each the concentrated attention it requires. This facilitates the assigning of manpower to each of the planned audits.

### Short- and Long-Term Programs

A short-term master program usually covers a one-year period. A long-term program covering three to five years further defines what the internal audit group plans to accomplish. Of course, the plan must be flexible enough to be adapted to changing priorities and conditions, but should provide the framework that enables the internal audit group to produce at its maximum capacity.

**Budget**

In preparing the audit plan, particular attention should be given to the internal auditing department's budget. The amount of money that can be spent on each audit should be coordinated between both the long- and short-term plans. The plan should also be examined in conjunction with the budget to determine if additional funds may be required.

Once the audit plan is formalized, each internal auditor should be furnished an individual plan to guide him in performing audits. The individual plan should include the following basic information:

- Audit subject;
- Type of audit (protective, financial, operations);
- Dates and location of working papers of prior audits on subject;
- Recommended time of year to be performed (i.e., quarter, month of year); and
- Estimated days required to perform audit.

## THE INTERNAL AUDIT PROGRAM

The audit program describes the procedures the individual auditor will follow to perform an audit. A well-thought-out and documented program saves considerable audit time, because it results in logical audit procedures and helps provide an accurate estimate of how audit time will be utilized.

Drawing up the audit program is a vital first step in preparing an audit. The use of a printed form for internal audit programs is recommended. The simple audit program format shown in Figure 20.3 illustrates the principles described.

In some companies, the audit program is prepared by the manager of the audit group or by a staff group organized to prepare all audit programs; in others, the individual auditor has primary responsibility for its preparation. When the individual auditor assigned to the audit does not personally prepare the program, he should review it to ensure that it fits his specific objectives.

Often a brief survey of the operation to be audited is conducted prior to program preparation to familiarize the auditor with the objectives to be achieved, the organizational procedures and control methods used, and the problems that will be encountered.

The completed program should be submitted to the audit manager for review shortly after the audit is started, and should be included as part of the working papers.

| AUDIT TITLE Payroll Processing | AUDIT NO. 36 |
|---|---|

**AUDIT OBJECTIVE**

To determine whether the controls exercised over preparation of payrolls are sufficient to provide accurate payments to employees and accurately maintained records of payroll deductions.

| STEPS TO ACHIEVE OBJECTIVE | CROSS REFERENCE |
|---|:---:|
| Analysis of preparation of weekly time reports to determine if the correct number of hours worked are reported by individual employees | A |
| Review of controls used by top-level managers to verify that the correct number of hours worked are reported to the payroll department | B |
| Review of procedures used in the payroll office to determine whether payrolls are controlled in preparation and distribution | C |
| Analysis of input to and output of the computer to determine if programs are computing pay and deductions in accordance with company contracts or agreements | D |

**INITIAL TIME ESTIMATE-DAYS**

| Preparation | Auditing | | Reporting | Total |
|---|---|---|---|---|
| | In office | In field | | |
| 3 | 2 | 9 | 2 | 16 |

DATE RELEASED TO MANAGEMENT 9-1-80   AUDITOR'S INITIALS

FIGURE 20.3  INTERNAL AUDIT PROGRAM

## INTERNAL AUDIT TECHNIQUES

The basic techniques used in performing an internal audit will be discussed in three subsections: procedures undertaken prior to field work, during field work, and after field work is completed. Working papers, which are utilized throughout the audit, will be discussed later in the chapter.

**Prior to Field Work**

Before the auditor goes to the field to gather audit data, he must thoroughly familiarize himself with the operation. In addition to preparing the audit program discussed above, he must undertake the following steps.

**Preaudit Meetings and Contacts.** The auditor should review the proposed audit with the company managers whose operations will be audited or who have input into that area. It is important that the auditor see and understand these operations through the eyes of those who deal most closely with them.

In one contact method, a short letter or memo announces the audit to the affected levels of management after verbal contacts with the corporate staff have previously determined that the audit is necessary and timely. In the letter or memo, the opinions of executives and staff should be solicited. Care should be taken to contact each executive who might be affected by the audit and to handle all replies promptly, preferably in person. Figure 20.4 is a sample memo announcing an internal audit.

Audits that must be a surprise to be effective, of course, cannot be announced in writing. However, a planning meeting to discuss this type of audit with auditees at a date well in advance of the anticipated audit date can provide valuable data for audit planning.

**Preaudit Research.** Extra time taken for research often results in considerable time savings during field work. Company systems, organizational structure, job instructions, and procedures for particular audits should be carefully studied. Previous audits of the subject area should be analyzed, and applicable federal and state government regulations carefully reviewed. Also, similar audits in related

---

TO: Mr. J. C. Thompson
    Production Manager

    cc: Mr. C. F. Hawkins
        Purchasing Manager

FROM: J. J. Burns
      Manager, Internal Auditing

SUBJECT: *Internal Audit of Tubular Performance Measurement Plan*

We plan to review the controls exercised over the Tubular Performance Measurement Plan at the Decatur Plant. In developing our audit plans, contacts will be made with members of your staff so that we may consider coverage of those aspects of the plan they deem significant. Leroy Alexander (601-942-7686) of the Operations Internal Auditing group will be responsible for this audit.

If you have some concerns about this subject, or believe some aspect of the work needs particular attention during the audit, please call Leroy or me (601-942-7680).

---

FIGURE 20.4  SAMPLE MEMO ANNOUNCING AN AUDIT

industries can provide valuable insights, providing such data is available. The independent auditors are often a good source of related audit materials.

Prior to audits of technical subjects, it is often helpful to have a manager at a nonaudit site "walk through" with the auditor the areas in which the functions are physically performed. During the walk-through, many control problems can be resolved. A walk-through will also help the auditor prepare a flowchart of the area or function being audited to crystalize the procedures used and to identify the control points to be audited.

A survey of steps to be accomplished during the audit will also help determine time requirements, sample sizes, and expected error levels.

**Sampling Plan.** Scientific *sampling for attributes* can be used to help provide yes or no answers in testing controls. Also, sampling for variables or dollar estimation can be used in auditing controls with variable values. *Judgment sampling* may be undertaken when scientific statistical sampling is not possible.

Sampling during auditing can be difficult. Without proper techniques, incorrect conclusions are drawn about data collected. To guard against faulty sampling conclusions, a sampling plan prepared in writing by someone experienced in the technique, prior to beginning the audit, is essential. It should contain at least the following information:

- Universe location, description, and size;
- Period and/or volume to be reviewed;
- Sample size;
- Sample-selection method (i.e., random, systematic, judgment);
- Definition of errors and establishment of error level; and
- Desired reliability range.

For additional help, numerous texts on sampling and statistical sampling tables are available.

### Field Work

Field work is probably the most interesting part of performing an internal audit. During this phase, the auditor's research, sampling techniques, interview skills, audit procedures, and perceptiveness are used to determine what is taking place during a company operation and whether or not the operation is adequately controlled and recorded. During field work, the auditor collects all the data he will need to properly document his audit findings.

**Documentation.** One area that must not be overlooked during field work is careful documentation. One cannot arrive at a significant conclusion about a condition without the recorded factual data to substantiate that conclusion. The auditor cannot rely on his memory or plan to come back later to get needed data.

**Recommendations.** The products of an audit are recommendations to improve operations or remove weaknesses in controls. A brief discussion of the auditor's findings is appreciated by auditees and leads to further two-way communication. When conclusions cannot be made during the visit, the auditees should be informed of the conclusions before the audit report is published. In addition, the auditor should review with them any recommendations that will appear in the report. Auditees' acceptance of recommendations or their ideas for improved operations can be extremely valuable.

**Specific Field Work Techniques.** The audit techniques discussed below should be understood by all internal auditors.

*Compliance testing.* Compliance testing is performed to provide reasonable assurance that accounting control procedures are being applied as prescribed. A study of internal accounting controls should first identify the control procedures, the performance level at which the controls are applied, and the proper method of applying. each control procedure. When these criteria are identified, tests can then be performed to ascertain that the standards are being followed and are operating satisfactorily. What constitutes a "reasonable" degree of assurance is a matter of auditing judgment, depending in large part on the extent of the tests and the results obtained.

Statistical sampling may be a practical way to perform compliance testing if there is a limited sample size and a statistical basis for evaluating the results.

*Variance analysis.* Variance analysis is a proven technique used during field work to compare the results obtained from one operation with those from the same operation at another location or with overall company performance. (See Chapter 16 for a full discussion of this and other analysis techniques.) The analysis may also be based on deviations from anticipated company performance levels.

In performing variance analysis, it is important to ensure that abnormal results investigated are significant and that extenuating circumstances are considered.

*Interviews.* A useful interview requires careful planning. Open questions generally produce the most helpful answers. How do you make sure the necessary supplies are on hand when needed? is an example. It is preferable to take few notes during the interview in order not to intimidate the interviewee, but to record what was said soon afterwards. All information obtained through interviews must be corroborated by hard audit evidence.

*Direct observation.* A visit to actually see what is taking place or the physical condition of an item is an effective and frequently used audit technique. Whenever possible, a photograph of the condition encountered should be taken and included in the working papers.

*Confirmation.* In some audits, confirmation by third parties is an accepted verification technique. This is particularly effective in auditing accounts receivable and accounts payable. When using confirmations, it is important to reconcile all differences and to follow up significant unanswered confirmations.

**EDP Auditing.** The impact of EDP on business operations and record keeping mandates that EDP auditing (auditing what the computer is doing) be incorporated into the systems and procedures of the internal audit group. EDP is also used as a technique in performing audits. Following is a review of both aspects of EDP auditing. (See Chapter 11 for a more complete discussion of EDP policies and techniques.)

*General EDP auditing.* An auditor should be trained to perform general EDP auditing as part of his field work for audit subjects that include some form of computer-generated records. The auditor reviews general controls such as hardware controls, procedure controls, and access to equipment and data files. He should also review specific input and output controls. Input controls should be examined to verify that:

- All input is intact;
- Key entry data is accurate;
- All input is received by the computer; and
- Necessary time schedules for submission of input are followed.

Output controls should be audited to verify that:

- Data generated is complete;
- Data generated is accurate;
- Records substantiate the sending of output data to the appropriate distribution point; and
- Processed data is released in accordance with prescribed time schedules.

*Specific EDP auditing.* In specific EDP auditing, the auditor functions much as a computer systems analyst. He will have acquired a working acquaintanceship with EDP equipment and techniques, and will evaluate the EDP controls on the basis of his program analysis and the EDP design rather than from analysis of input and output. The auditor asks the question, Does this system have adequate controls? and he must answer the question through analysis of program controls and procedures. Many companies assign an EDP auditor to serve on the audit team if new programs or systems are involved. In this assignment, the auditor evaluates controls as the planning and design take place, and makes recommendations to the analysts. Because of the special nature of the EDP audit, whenever practical, an EDP audit group should be established within the internal audit organization.

*Control analysis.* This technique involves using the computer to audit controls that do not necessarily test the EDP process itself. Many companies have designed *audit analysis programs* that can be used by auditors to extract specific data from *data processing center* (DPC) files and summarize the information in a manner suitable to the audit. Also, financial data collected by the auditor can be entered into the computer and analyzed using existing programs or specially designed audit programs. Large samples can easily be processed whenever the DPC has available computer time.

### Post-Field Work

During this phase of audit performance, field work is tied together and the audit report is prepared. All the analytical skills of the auditor are used to prepare an intelligent presentation of what he has examined and analyzed. The following elements are part of the post-field work process.

**Summarizing Collected Data.** In summarizing, the auditor should look for significant relationships. For example, when the auditor is determining if supplies are properly protected, the relationship between the number of locations reviewed, the number of locations where supplies were found unlocked, and the value of supplies at each location would be significant. Variables that distort results must be carefully considered and documented when summarizing data. Of course, any summary of data should be cross-referenced to the working papers and basic documents from which it was obtained.

**Evaluating Data.** The evaluations and conclusions reached should be related to specific summarized data. For example, when ten of forty inspected items are found in an unsatisfactory condition, a logical conclusion would be that 25 percent of the overall group may be in an unsatisfactory condition. Conclusions related to statistics are far more meaningful than general unsubstantiated statements. Auditors are often tempted to overstate or magnify an audit finding. When they exaggerate, they lose their credibility with the auditees and their substantiated recommendations may not be accepted.

**Working Paper Review.** When data has been summarized and conclusions reached, the auditor reviews the working papers to be certain that all the data necessary to support the conclusions is logically and completely filed and that all the working papers are properly cross-referenced and complete. A detailed discussion of working paper preparation and review is included later in this chapter.

**Follow-Up on Unresolved Items.** For many reasons, some items remain unresolved at the time an audit is complete. Delaying completion of the audit until they are resolved may be impractical. However, the auditor must take steps to be sure the unresolved items are not overlookel. Often, an unresolved item can be added to the scope of a similar or parallel audit that is being or will soon be performed. Or, if the item is a significant one, it may be possible to handle it as a separate audit. A schedule of unresolved items and their final disposition should be filed with the working papers.

## Postaudit Review Meeting

The postaudit meeting is the key link between effective field work and a good written report. It is held prior to issuing the formal audit report to give the auditee a preview of the audit findings and an opportunity to contribute to the solution of the problems.

The discussion format at the meeting should be the same or similar to that of the written audit report. Therefore, a draft copy of the written report should be completed prior to the meeting.

Although the top levels of management are already aware of the audit results, the executive manager is formally informed at the meeting. (Formal meetings are normally not held when all phases of the internal audit are satisfactory.) The executive manager or managers affected by the audit should be encouraged to bring staff members to the meeting to contribute to the findings or help in developing a program of corrective action. The auditors' supervisor should attend the meeting as well. The supervisor can help evaluate the findings and keep the meeting moving. Following the meeting, the supervisor and auditor can together evaluate the auditees' comments and arrive at meaningful conclusions.

The following key reminders are important to bear in mind when holding a postaudit review meeting:

1. *Hold the meeting within two weeks following completion of field work.* Waiting longer will cause a loss of immediacy and impact.
2. *Conduct the meeting on neutral ground.* In a more relaxed atmosphere, the auditee will not be surrounded by the pressures of the normal job environment. Care should be taken in arranging seating to avoid the appearance that the auditors are on one side and auditees are on the opposing side.
3. *Restrict the meeting to one hour or less.* The time of executive managers is extremely valuable. A manager will be more willing to attend postaudit meetings when he knows they are short and efficiently handled.
4. *Encourage auditee participation.* Auditees should be asked to share their feelings about the audit findings and procedures. Open questions, such as Can you suggest another way to take inventory? will encourage discussions that can be extremely valuable. The auditor should never give the impression that the audit's conclusions are firm and cannot be changed. Frequently, points brought up by auditees at the postaudit meeting significantly improve the audit and make its recommendations more acceptable to the managers concerned.
5. *Obtain comments of auditees.* The written report should include auditee comments and recommendations. If these suggestions require further investigation, the report should indicate the corrective action that is being studied.
6. *Use visual aids.* Visual aids highlight findings, impact, and remedies, and show

that the internal auditor is well prepared for the meeting. They capture attention and can be used as memory joggers during the presentation. Types of visual aids that may be used are flipcharts (which need not be professionally prepared), easel posters, 35 mm slides, view-graphs and typed handouts.

## Working Papers

Internal audit working papers provide evidence of audit work performed and conclusions reached. Working papers accomplish the following purposes:

1. *They support findings.* Working papers supply the evidence needed to describe the conditions encountered during the audit, both satisfactory and unsatisfactory.
2. *They are a reference file.* They record the information obtained through interviews, reviewing practices, analyzing systems, and processing and examining transactions.
3. *They are an organizational technique for writing the audit report.* Well-structured working papers make it easier to organize the data gathered during an audit for the written internal audit report.
4. *They are a tool for supervisory review.* The supervisor uses the working papers to review audit progress and to substantiate the auditor's conclusions. All working papers should be organized in a standard format to facilitate preparation and review.
5. *They provide background for future audits.* Professionally prepared working papers make follow-up audits easier to plan and more economical to execute.

One of the most effective ways to help individual auditors is to provide them with a standard set of working paper forms. As the audit progresses, these forms enable them to prepare, assemble, and logically file data necessary for the audit. Along with the forms, well-documented procedures should be available to explain how the forms are to be used; these procedures should include such things as a standard numbering system, cross-referencing, sizing pages, binding, filing and retention, labeling, and the initialing of the working papers by the preparer and the audit manager reviewer.

In designing working paper forms, a company should tailor them to fit the company's particular needs. Some examples of working paper forms that have been successfully used are presented in Appendix 20-1.

Two additional forms to consider are:

1. *Audit Contact List Form,* which is a convenient place for the auditor to list the name, location, telephone number, and title of persons contacted during the audit; and
2. *Reference Form,* which serves as a convenient list of reference material used during the audit. Both material filed with the working papers and material used but not retained should be listed on the form. (The internal audit group's responsibilities for retaining reference data should be spelled out clearly.)

## INTERNAL AUDIT REPORTS

The internal audit report formally conveys the results of the audit to top management. It explains the impact of findings on the company's operations, revenues, and so on, and offers practical remedies for the problems disclosed. If the auditor's concepts are concise and clear, the thoughts orderly, and a distinction is established between significant and insignifiant comments, the audit report is effective and useful, and helps top management take appropriate corrective action.

### Audit Report Formats

There are several types of recognized audit report formats or styles, and the company's preferences should be documnted among the audit group procdures. Some of the commonly used report formats are:

1. *Formal narrative.* A formal narrative report describes in prose what was audited, how the audit was accomplished, and what was found during the audit. It is probably the most popular type of report.

2. *Summary outline.* This report covers the essentials of the audit subject in outline form. Its principal advantage is that it can be read rapidly. However, unless extreme care is taken, the reader will not completely understand what is being reported. Many audit groups prepare both a formal narrative report and a summary outline report. The summary report can be used to provide a rapid reference file of the results.

3. *Management summary.* This brief report is written in narrative form and describes only the basic significant conditions encountered during an audit and the auditors' conclusions and/or recommendations. Management summaries are not normally prepared for conditions that are judged fully satisfactory. Management summaries can be used to give top management an overview of a subject audited. Figure 20.5 illustrates this type of report.

4. *Annual report.* The annual report presents the audit group's work for the year in the form of an overview of its accomplishments. Management summaries are included to describe the significant audits, together with a description of the corrective action taken. Audits that do not disclose significant findings are usually only listed. Other work accomplished by the internal audit group that relates to other internal auditing functions can also be described in the annual report.

5. *Audit report content outline.* A specific content outline for audit reports should be developed by the audit group. This will ensure that audit reports are uniform and include all necessary data. Figure 20.6 is a sample audit report content outline.

### Writing the Audit Report

Each audit report should be the best product of the entire audit group. Prior to its release, several auditors should review it for style and clarity. The audit supervisor should also thoroughly review and edit the report.

In many companies there are prescribed rules to ensure consistency in style and expression. For example, it may be preferred that all numbers be expressed in arabic numerals, or that certain names or terms be capitalized or italicized. A style manual with clear and simple guidelines should be developed by the internal audit group.

## Attachments

Material needed in a report can often be included as an attachment to avoid details and elaboration in the text. It should be possible to understand a good attachment without referring to the text of the report. In some situations, an exhibit

---

### MANAGEMENT SUMMARY

GROUP LIFE INSURANCE PROGRAM

An audit made in 1977 disclosed that Group Life Insurance Enrollment and Beneficiary Designation forms submitted to the Comptrollers Department were inaccurately prepared, and insurance records of inactive employees were not accurate, resulting in an overpayment of insurance premiums to EXTRA of over $85,000.

In response to the 1977 audit, the Comptrollers Department indicated appropriate steps had been taken to correct the insurance records of inactive employees. Also, they indicated a claim would be made with EXTRA in January, 1978, to recover $85,000 in premium overpayments. In addition, Personnel advised each department of the problems experienced with the preparation of Group Life Insurance forms and stressed the need for accuracy. To determine if the corrective action taken following the 1977 audit is effective and if overall controls over the Group Life Insurance Program are adequate, the insurance records of 201 employees were analyzed, and the January, 1978 adjustment made to recover premium overpayments was examined. Also, 217 Group Life Enrollment and Beneficiary Designation forms were checked for accuracy and completeness.

SIGNIFICANT FINDINGS

Beneficiary Designation forms submitted to the Comptrollers Department are now reasonably accurate. However, records for employees on leave of absence are still inaccurate, resulting in an additional estimated overpayment to EXTRA of $107,000.

SUGGESTED REMEDIES

During the postaudit review meeting, representatives of the Comptrollers Department indicated plans to correct insurance records for inactive employees and to request a credit from EXTRA for overpayment of insurance premiums. Also, a new print-out of leave-of-absence data will be used to assist in the accurate computations of premiums for inactive employees.

---

FIGURE 20.5 SAMPLE MANAGEMENT SUMMARY AUDIT REPORT

reinforces facts stated in a report. For example, a copy of an incorrectly prepared time report card will reinforce a finding that the company is losing money due to this type of inaccuracy.

## Distribution of Reports

The systems and procedures of the internal audit group should specify how reports are to be distributed. Audit reports are generally sent to company executives whose operations were involved or will be affected by the audit, executives whose action is needed or desired, and executives who requested the audit. Copies of the report may also be transmitted to those who would find the audit of particular interest but do not have direct involvement.

The transmittal letter should request that the managers involved submit a report on the corrective action they plan to take as a result of an audit. Replies to audit

---

I. Introduction
   A. Importance of subject
   B. General information about subject
   C. Summary of results of prior audits of subject

II. Scope
   A. Reason for performing the audit
   B. Work done to evaluate the subject being audited:
      1. Number of transactions reviewed
      2. Number of locations visited
      3. Number of auditees interviewed and connection with audit
   C. Identification of auditor

III. Findings
   A. Good points found during audit (audit reports without unsatisfactory findings go no further)
   B.* Statement of unsatisfactory finding and explanation of finding:
      1. What should be happening
      2. What is happening
      3. What is the effect of unsatisfactory condition
      4. What can be done to correct unsatisfactory condition
         a. Must be practical and simple
         b. Must consider cost-benefit trade-off
      5. What auditees say about condition found.

IV. Summary
   A. Brief statement of work done to perform audit
   B. Statement of each unsatisfactory finding
   C. Statement of what can be done to correct each unsatisfactory condition

*Repeated for each unsatisfactory audit finding

---

FIGURE 20.6   SAMPLE AUDIT REPORT CONTENT OUTLINE

reports enable the internal audit group to measure the effectiveness of internal audits. Frequently, the company's outside auditors will use company internal audit reports and the replies to the audits to monitor overall company operations, particularly those of a financial nature or those that deal with government regulations.

## SUGGESTED READING

AICPA. *An Auditor's Approach To Statistical Sampling.* Vols. 1-3. New York, 1974.

————. *Computer Assisted Audit Techniques.* New York, 1979.

Brink, Victor Z., Cashin, James A., and Witt, Herbert. *Modern Internal Auditing.* 3rd ed. New York: Ronald Press, 1973.

Cashin, James A. *Handbook for Auditors.* Altamonte Springs, Fla.: Institute of Internal Auditors, 1971.

Cook, John W., and Winkle, Gary W. *Auditing: Philosophy and Technique.* Boston: Houghton Mifflin, 1976.

Institute of Internal Auditors. *Auditing Computer Centers.* Altamonte Springs, Fla., 1974.

————. *Standards for the Professional Practice of Internal Auditing.* Altamonte Springs, Fla., 1978.

Macchiaverna, Paul. *Internal Auditing.* New York: The Conference Board, 1978.

Roberts, Donald. *Statistical Auditing.* New York: AICPA, 1978.

Sawyer, Lawrence B. *Modern Internal Auditing. What's It All About?* Altamonte Springs, Fla.: Institute of Internal Auditors, 1974.

————. *The Manager and the Modern Internal Auditor.* New York: ONACON, 1979.

————. *The Practice of Modern Internal Auditing.* Altamonte Springs, Fla.: Institute of Internal Auditors, 1973.

Stettler, Howard. *Auditing Principles.* Englewood Cliffs, N.J.: Prentice-Hall, 1977.

## APPENDIX 20-1   SAMPLE WORKING PAPERS

### Cover Sheet

This form serves as the cover to a complete set of working papers forms. It is used to remind internal auditors of some of the key things to be done in assembling working papers. The legend of tick marks is helpful, saves time in looking them up, and reminds auditors to use tick marks in identifying data.

---

**SUMMARY OF WORKING PAPER ASSEMBLY STEPS**

PRIOR TO FIELD WORK:          Set up Working Paper Binder, Forms and Tabs. Secure and Review Reference Material and Prior Audits. Plan Audit and Develop Time Budget. Make Contacts of Informed People.

DURING FIELD WORK:          Document and File Supporting Data as Developed. Adhere to Audit Plan, Modifying Where Situation Demands Change.

WHEN AUDIT RELEASED:          File Reports, Final Meeting Notes and Flip Charts; Complete Cross-Referencing and Submit Working Papers for Approval.

---

**LEGEND OF COMMON WORKING PAPER TICK MARKS**

T    Footed or crossfooted

⋀    Traced to another account, general ledger, trial balance, etc., and agreed to balance

¢    Calculated

√    Examined voucher for approval

-⊖-    Observed a process (Specify process)

√    Confirmed

λ    Errors or exceptions worthy of noting

Δ    Reconciled to _____(Specify what the item was reconciled to)

★    Examined supporting documents

*INCLUDE EXPLANATION OF THESE AND ANY OTHER TICK MARKS USED IN WORKING PAPERS.*

## Working Papers Index

This form allows space to list essential information that identifies the audit. It also gives the main segments of the working papers. The steps to achieve objectives beginning at Tab I are the major phases of the audit. The auditor writes in an abbreviation of the step on this form, and at the appropriate tab reference the details of the audit step are recorded.

AUDIT TITLE: _____ _____

AUDITOR: _____ DATE ISSUED: _____

AUDIT NO. _____ M-255A: _____ (        ) (        ) ____

| ITEM | | TAB |
|---|---|---|
| REPORTS | TRANSMITTAL LETTER, AUDIT REPORT, DIGEST AND REPLIES | A |
| PLANS | AUDIT OBJECTIVE, STEPS TO ACHIEVE OBJECTIVES, EXECUTIVE CONTACT LETTER AND PRE-AUDIT MEETINGS/CONTACTS | B |
| FLOWCHARTS | FLOW CHARTS AND SAMPLING PLAN | C |
| REFERENCES | COMPANY PRACTICES, DEPARTMENTAL PRACTICES | D |
| PRIOR AUDITS | REPORTS AND REPLIES | E |
| FINAL MEETING | RECORD AND FLIP CHARTS | F |
| TIME | ESTIMATED AND CHARGED | G |
| ADMINISTRATIVE | AUDIT CONTROL SHEET, YELLOW COPY TRANSMITTAL LETTER AND UNMARKED COPY OF AUDIT REPORT, ETC. | H |
| STEPS TO ACHIEVE OBJECTIVES | | |
| | | I |
| | | J |
| | | K |
| | | L |
| | | M |
| | | N |
| | | O |
| | | P |
| | | Q |
| | | R |
| | | S |
| | | T |
| | | U |
| | | V |
| | | W |
| | | X |
| | | Y |
| | | Z |

## Final Audit Review Meeting Record

The details of the post-audit review meeting are listed on this form. Space is provided for identifying information about the meeting, personnel who attended, and significant details that occurred. The block at the bottom of the form reminds the auditor to describe what the auditees said about audit recommendations.

LOCATION _____

DATE _____ START/STOP TIME _____

| PERSONNEL | TITLE – FUNCTION | DEPARTMENT |
|-----------|------------------|------------|
|           |                  |            |
|           |                  |            |
|           |                  |            |
|           |                  |            |
|           |                  |            |
|           |                  |            |

RECORD OF DISCUSSION

INCLUDE COMMENTS ABOUT SUGGESTED REMEDIES.

## Standards for Working Papers Review

Working papers should be reviewed by an internal auditing manager before they are filed. This form standardizes the review and provides a means of recording the results. The block at the bottom of the form identifies entries to be made on the form by the manager.

AUDIT TITLE _____　AUDIT NO. _____

| SECTION | STANDARDS | * |
|---|---|---|
| **REPORTS** | Reported findings sufficiently cross-referenced to adequate supportive documentation. | |
| A | Evidence scope carried out. | |
| | Other items # : | |
| **PLANS** | Functional audit plan with steps included. | |
| B | Pre-audit planning documented. | |
| | Omissions of audit plan steps explained. | |
| G | Estimated and charged audit time adequately documented. | |
| | Other items # : | |
| **GENERAL** | Flow chart included. | |
| C | Sample documentation informative. | |
| D | Reference material retained serves constructive purpose. | |
| E | Prior audit reports and replies included. | |
| | Prior audit deficiencies investigated. | |
| F | Post audit meeting notes documented. | |
| H | Administrative data complete. | |
| | Other items # : | |
| **FIELD WORK** | Each section summarized adequately as to what done and findings. | |
| | Summaries cross-referenced to appropriate supportive material. | |
| | Auditor's conclusions shown. | |
| I-Z | Work done identified as to purpose and nature. | |
| | Other items # : | |

REVIEWED BY _____　DATE APPROVED _____

> * OK=STANDARD MET; NA=STANDARD NOT APPLICABLE.
> # PER M—255A, PART 101, SECTION 7—ADDENDUM, APPENDIX B.

## Steps to Achieve Objective

This form is prepared as a summary to each major step of the audit plan. It corresponds with I to Z on the working papers index form. Behind this form are filed all the data necessary to substantiate a major step of the audit, along with the auditor's conclusions. The block at the bottom reminds the auditor of key points to accomplish.

| SUMMARY OF WHAT DONE AND FINDINGS FOR THIS SECTION | Ref. |
|---|---|
| | |
| | |
| | |
| | |
| | |
| | |
| | |
| | |
| | |
| | |
| | |
| | |
| | |
| | |
| | |
| | |
| | |
| | |
| | |
| | |
| | |
| | |
| | |
| | |

EXPLAIN PRINCIPAL CONDITIONS FOUND IN CONCRETE TERMS, NOT "SATISFACTORY" OR "UNSATISFACTORY".
OMISSIONS OF AUDIT PLAN STEPS ARE TO BE EXPLAINED.
CROSS-REFERENCE SUPPORTING DOCUMENTS INCLUDING THOSE FILED UNDER OTHER TABS.

## Worksheet

This form is designed for the auditor's use in documenting work performed during the audit. It divides the information collected into three logical areas: why it was done, what was done, and what was concluded.

PURPOSE OF THIS WORK:

WORK DONE:

WHAT AUDITOR CONCLUDED:

# Part V

## Treasury Functions

# 21

# Sources of Funds

*Harold B. Shapiro*

## TYPES OF FINANCING

Every business, regardless of its size, must obtain funds during the course of its business cycle for the proper management and expansion of its operations. The appropriate sources and the timing and duration of periods of heavy funds use vary in different types of businesses and with the equity position of specific firms.

The various types of financing can be divided into the following broad categories:

1. *Short-term credit* is generally used to obtain current assets for the business. Thus, short-term credit is used to finance short-term working capital needs of one year or less. If the financial need continues for more than one year, the short-term credit should be replaced by a more permanent source of funds.

2. *Intermediate-term loans* are sources of funds for current assets as well as for long-term or fixed assets. Intermediate-term loans are sought when funds are needed for a period of one to five years.

3. *Long-term debt* is used to finance fixed assets or long-term business needs. Long-term debt has a term of at least five years and matures any time thereafter as agreed on by the parties.

4. *Equity* has no specific term. It reflects the shareholders' at-risk investment in the business and should be used to meet the company's permanent financial needs.

## SELECTING THE PROPER SOURCE OF FUNDS

A business enterprise's needs, as well as its relative financial strength, determine the fund sources it selects, the terms of the debt it prefers, the cost of the funds, and the restrictions that the lender places on the company's activities as conditions of the loan. Before management seeks funds, it should perform the following tasks:

1. *Define its financing needs.* Management must analyze the firm's operation to determine its present financial status and projections for its future. The business must determine if it needs (a) permanent capital that does not have to be repaid; (b) long-term funds to finance the purchase of fixed assets (which will enhance earnings, which in turn will be used to repay the borrowings); or (c) short-term working capital to carry inventory or receivables, which in turn will be used to repay the debt. In addition, management must analyze the effect of equity financing, long-term borrowings, and short-term borrowings on the company's balance sheet.

2. *Define how the debt will be repaid.* Whenever funds are borrowed, the business must accurately project how these funds are to be repaid. Utilizing improper sources of funds can mean disaster to the business. For example, if the business needs permanent equity funds but obtains short-term funds, it may not be able to repay the funds or renegotiate additional funds at maturity. On the other hand, if the business needs short-term funds but borrows funds on a long-term basis, the business will be faced with needless expense and repayment problems. Thus, the business must carefully analyze its ability to meet the predetermined repayment terms of its borrowings.

3. *Analyze lender restrictions.* Whenever funds are borrowed, the lender places certain restrictions on the corporation, such as repayment terms, ratios, dividends, and so on. Each business, prior to entering into the loan agreement, must evaluate these restrictions and the effect they will have on the business's future operations, and determine if it will be able to operate within the constraints. If the restrictions are too onerous, the firm must either negotiate more acceptable terms or look for alternate sources of funds.

## SHORT-TERM CREDIT

Short-term credit (funds generally borrowed for a period of one year or less) can be obtained from various sources, depending on the firm's size and credit standing and its financial strength. Since short-term credit is used to finance current financial needs, the company must be able to demonstrate that it can repay the loan from operations.

A firm generally requires short-term credit to carry inventory or receivables. Thus, it will repay these short-term loans by reducing the inventories or receivables, or from earnings.

### Bank Credit

Bank credit, a traditional source of short-term funds, can take various forms:

1. *Line of credit* is an agreement that fixes the maximum amount of credit that the bank will extend to the business. The company pays interest only on the funds actually borrowed. The line of credit remains available for its term, provided that the firm's financial circumstances have not changed when the funds are required and the firm otherwise remains an acceptable credit risk. In addition, banks often stipulate as a condition of the credit agreement that the business repay all outstanding loans for a limited period of thirty or sixty consecutive days during each twelve-month period. The ability to clean up loan balances assures the bank of the financial soundness of the business. Although the line of credit indicates the amount of funds that the bank is willing to make available at the time of the agreement, the business has no guarantee that the funds will actually be available when they are required. In order to be guaranteed the availability of funds, a company must obtain a revolving credit agreement.
2. *Revolving credit agreement* is a standby agreement between the bank and the company for a guaranteed line of credit. The revolving credit agreement is a formal agreement guaranteeing the company a certain maximum amount of credit if given conditions agreed on in advance are met. For this guaranteed availability of funds, the business will not only pay interest for monies actually borrowed but also a commission or commitment fee to the bank for the total amount of money available to the business. Under a revolving credit agreement, the business can borrow and repay funds as its needs arise. An example of a revolving credit agreement is presented in Appendix 21-1.

3. *Demand note* is a short-term loan agreement between a business and a bank, evidenced by a note. The note usually has a specific due date. However, it permits the bank to call for immediate payment at any time, and it also permits the business to repay the note at its discretion.

## Commercial Paper

*Commercial paper* is a form of business borrowing whereby the firm sells its notes to a bank or brokerage house, which in turn resells these notes to outside parties. The commercial paper note has a specific repayment date. A corporation will utilize commercial paper loans in preference to bank borrowings whenever possible, because the effective cost of such borrowing is usually lower than bank rates. A company selling commercial paper must have a high credit rating. In addition, the bank or brokerage house selling the commercial paper generally requires that the firm have unused standby lines of credit in excess of the amount of commercial paper sold to support and guarantee the repayment of the notes.

## Finance Company Borrowing

Finance company borrowing (also known as *factoring*) is a form of credit used by companies that do not have access to standard bank loans. It is also used to supplement bank borrowings during periods when the firm requires larger amounts of funds to support seasonal operations. Companies that borrow from a finance company must pay high rates of interest (interest rates charged by a finance company usually range from 4 to 6 percent higher than the *prime rate* of interest—the rate charged by banks to their best customers). In addition, finance companies only extend credit that is fully secured by receivables and inventories. When lending against receivables, the finance company requires specific sales invoices as collateral and must approve the customers to whom advances are to be made. The finance company usually extends credit equal to 70 to 80 percent of a given invoice amount. When the company collects the receivable, it must turn over the entire proceeds to the finance company. The finance company then returns to the firm the difference between the proceeds and the factored percentage. In some arrangements, the customer is instructed to make payment directly to the factor. When the finance company lends against inventories, it generally advances up to 50 percent of inventory values. Under this type of arrangement, the company must agree to maintain minimum inventory amounts to support the advances.

In order to make the interest rate more attractive, the finance company often agrees to participate with the company in a bank loan. Thus, the company would pay a blended rate depending on the participation percentage. For example, if the bank and finance company agree to participate in the loan on a 50-50 basis, the bank charging 2 percent over prime and the finance company 6 percent over prime, the company would pay a blended rate of 4 percent over prime. The finance company assumes the responsibility for monitoring the collateral and evaluating the credit risk.

Since the finance company is receiving a high rate of interest and is fully secured for its risk, it usually does not insist on the mandatory repayment schedule that banks generally require.

### Other Types of Short-Term Credit

Business enterprises that need short-term funds also have access to (1) *letters of credit;* (2) *bankers' acceptances;* (3) *field warehousing;* and (4) *trust certificates,* all of which are used in conjunction with other financing methods.

**Letter of Credit.** The letter of credit is traditionally used in the export and import of merchandise but can be used in some domestic transactions as well. It is a document issued by a bank, at the request of a customer, that guarantees the honoring of drafts or other demands for payment if certain specified conditions in the letter of credit are met. (For example, the letter of credit may require proof that a given quantity of merchandise has been delivered to a specified place.) Letters of credit are often required in offshore transactions, because the seller wants to be sure of collecting on its invoice after delivery and does not know the credit standing of the purchaser. Letters of credit are instruments by which a bank substitutes its own credit for that of the business firm, and thus constitute a form of borrowing. The bank must consider whether the company requesting the letter of credit is a good risk and has the financial ability to pay the required amount when the specified documents are presented for payment.

The obvious advantage of a letter of credit is that the business need not use its own assets or pay interest on borrowed funds for an advance payment the seller might otherwise require. Its only cost is a relatively small annual fee paid to the issuer. However, to obtain this type of credit, the company generally must have a high credit rating or provide acceptable collateral.

**Banker's Acceptance.** The banker's acceptance is more commonly used in international transactions but may be utilized in domestic trade as well. It is a note given by a business to a creditor for the purchase of merchandise, with payment of the note "accepted," or guaranteed, by the firm's bank. The bank's acceptance of the note guarantees payment for the merchandise at a specified future date. The vendor can either hold the note until maturity, at which time it is presented to the maker's bank for payment, or he can take the acceptance to his own bank, discount the instrument, and receive immediate funds. The bank charges a small percentage for the use of its name and credit, as well as the specified rate of interest on the note.

**Field Warehousing.** Field warehousing is used in certain types of financing agreements in which the lender requires assurance that the borrower will maintain minimum inventory levels to support a loan. In order for the lender to be assured that inventory levels are maintained, he will require that the business deposit the merchandise in a bonded and licensed warehouse. Since it is usually impossible to move the inventory to a warehouse for storage, an outside field warehousing organization establishes a bona fide warehouse on the premises of the borrowing business establishment and receives a fee for its services in supervising and operating the storage space for the pledged goods. The field warehousing company segregates the facility by fencing off a segment of the borrower's warehouse, and leases the area from the borrower. In addition, the warehousing company hires one or more of the borrower's employees to guard against improper removal of inventory from the segregated area and to account for all material moving in or out. Thus, through the use of a field warehouse, the lender can be assured that the pledged quantity of inventory is maintained on the premises at all times. If inventory shortages should occur, the lender would hold the warehousing company responsible.

**Trust Certificate or Holding Certificate.** A trust certificate or holding certificate is used when a company makes a loan secured by inventory that it does not have in its possession. For example, company X purchases a quantity of goods from company Y, and tells company Y to hold the merchandise for future delivery. In order for company X to borrow against the material, it must obtain a trust or holding certificate from company Y, which then is presented to company X's bank as evidence of the inventory that will be used to secure the loan.

## INTERMEDIATE-TERM LOANS

Intermediate-term loans generally run for a period ranging from more than one year to approximately five years. An intermediate-term loan can best be characterized as a *hybrid*, having the characteristics of both short-term and long-term loans. Regardless of the source of the intermediate-term loan, the lender would normally look to the earnings ability of the business over the period of the loan as the prime source of funds to repay the borrowing.

The intermediate-term loan is used by companies of different sizes for different reasons. Moderate-sized companies will use intermediate-term debt financing because they usually do not have access to the public markets. Large public corporations often find intermediate-term loans more flexible, and perhaps more liberal, than the financing they can obtain on the open market. Finally, the revolving credit agreement provides companies, regardless of size, with interim loans that may, at a later date, be refinanced with long-term loans from public financing or other sources.

Intermediate term loans can be obtained from various sources, depending on the size, the type of business, and the credit worthiness of the borrower.

**Insurance Companies**

Insurance companies are traditionally considered a major source of long-term funds for businesses, and are important lenders in the bond and mortgage markets. However, insurance companies also are important lenders to the intermediate funds market. Insurance companies usually enter the intermediate funds market when short-term interest rates are higher than long-term interest rates, or when quantities of funds must be kept relatively liquid to meet specific future long-term investment commitments.

Insurance companies also participate with banks in joint financial term loan agreements when the loan period called for is longer than that permitted to lending banks. Such an arrangement usually requires that annual repayment installments be applied against the bank's portion of the loan until that portion is repaid. Thus, the bank holds an intermediate-term loan, and the insurance company holds the long-term portion of the loan.

Loans obtained by a business directly from insurance companies generally must be secured. However, larger companies in sound financial condition may be able to borrow funds on an unsecured basis.

**Commercial Paper**

Commercial paper is a prime source of short-term funds for the most creditworthy corporations. However, commercial paper can also be sold for terms that make them intermediate-term credits. The buyers are usually institutions such as insurance companies or pension funds that wish to invest funds for one to five years with a fair rate of return, in order to meet their relatively short-term cash timing requirements. Dealing in commercial paper enables these institutions to resell the notes whenever their money needs so require.

**Conversion of a Revolving Credit Loan**

Under some revolving credit arrangements, the corporation can convert the agreement into a term loan repayable over a period of three to five or more years, provided the corporation meets certain predetermined conditions, such as a specified level of earnings or maintenance of certain operating ratios. This enables the firm to use the funds it needs during the interim period, to terminate or reduce the credit in accordance with its needs, and to convert into a term loan only the amount required for future use. The option to convert, if predetermined conditions are met, rests with the company, which thus has access to a firm source of funds when money market conditions may be less favorable.

**Bank Credit**

Banks provide the most traditional form of loans for periods of three to five years. These intermediate-term bank loans have specific maturities and usually require formal loan agreements, which is not always true for short-term borrowings.

The bank expects the loan to be repaid out of earnings or cash flow from operations rather than from the normal liquidation of current assets. Revolving credit agreements, discussed under short-term credit options, are another form of bank credit. They can be held for periods longer than one year, and thus provide the business with a formal commitment of funds for an intermediate term, subject to the company's maintenance of specified levels of financial health.

Banks also provide corporations with *bridge financing*, which is particularly useful for construction needs. Under this type of arrangement, the bank provides short-term financing between the termination of one loan and the commencement of another (i.e., between the maturity of a construction loan and the negotiation of permanent financing). The corporation normally obtains a commitment for permanent financing before it applies for bridge financing.

Banks traditionally require secured loans. Unsecured loans are usually made only to high-quality companies. Banks usually insist on collateral such as stocks or bonds, or on property security, which may include real estate, machinery, and inventory. Banks particularly prefer that intermediate- and long-term loans be secured, because such loans have an increased risk factor.

## LONG-TERM DEBT

Long-term debt is used to finance the long-term working capital needs of the business as well as to finance its fixed assets. Firms also use long-term financing to retire ownership shares they do not wish to retain in their capital structure or to provide necessary funds to effect a merger or acquire the assets of another business organization.

The primary sources of long-term funds are organizations such as insurance companies, bank trust funds, pension funds, and investment companies. Although each of these organizations may invest in short-term loans as a temporary measure when short-term investments are more profitable, these institutions generally invest their funds in long-term investments. Many individuals also invest funds in long-term securities.

Long-term debt can take many forms, depending on the need, the size, and the status (public or private) of the business.

### Mortgages

Mortgage loans are loans made on real estate (land and buildings) in which a mortgage is given to secure payment of principal and interest. Mortgage funds are obtained both to acquire new facilities as well as to obtain long-term funds by pledging existing facilities as collateral. A mortgage may be described as a conveyance or transfer of title to property, given by the *mortgagor* (debtor) to a *mortgagee* (creditor) as security for the payment of the debt and subject to cancellation on payment of the debt according to the mortgage terms. If the borrowing business fails to meet the obligations of the loan contract, the mortgage may be foreclosed, that is, the property may be seized through appropriate legal channels and sold to satisfy the indebtedness.

Savings associations and banks, insurance companies, pension funds, and similar financial institutions are the main sources of business mortgage funds. Commercial banks may make mortgage loans if long-term interest rates are favorable.

## Debentures

Unlike mortgages, which are secured by specific collateral, *debenture bonds* are certificates of debt issued by a corporation that are secured by the general credit and strength of the corporation. Since there is no specific pledge of collateral, the debenture holders are considered general creditors of the corporation and have a general claim on all its unpledged assets.

The bond *indenture*, or debenture agreement, defines how the debenture holder is classified in case the corporation is liquidated. The bond indenture also specifies the terms under which the debentures are issued. The issuing corporation appoints an independent trustee (normally a bank or trust company) to see that the terms of the debenture agreement are followed, as well as to look after the interests of the debenture holders in case of default. The following items are generally contained in the indenture:

1. The rate of interest that will be paid as long as the debentures are outstanding, as well as when the interest will be paid; normally, the rate will be constant during the life of the debentures;
2. A definition of events that may lead to default, the grace period during which an event of default can be cured, and the procedure the trustee will follow if an event of default is not cured;
3. The operating ratios, if any, that the corporation must maintain, as well as any restrictions on the payment of dividends or repurchase of capital shares;
4. The term of the debentures;
5. A provision that allows the corporation to retire the debentures prior to maturity by "calling" the bonds for payment (If the corporation does so, it usually must pay a premium above the principal amounts of the debentures. The indenture will usually specify a reduced premium as the debentures approach maturity);
6. A provision preventing the corporation from retiring the debentures for a period of years after they are issued; this provision is usually included when interest rates are high;
7. A specification of how the debentures are to be retired and of some method of reducing the liability of the corporation each year (The sinking fund is the most common method of reducing the size of the debt before maturity. It calls for annual deposits with the trustee of a certain sum of money, or its equivalent in principal amounts of debentures, sufficient to retire a specified percentage of the debentures annually); and

8. An amendment procedure. This generally involves obtaining the approval of a specified percentage of the holders of all debentures currently outstanding (usually two-thirds).

### Debentures in Publicly Held Corporations

Debentures, like equity securities, are sold for publicly held corporations by underwriters either through private placements or underwritten issues. The terms, interest rate, and restrictions of these issues are negotiated with the underwriter. Three general classifications of debentures are discussed here.

**Straight Debt Debentures.** The debenture agreement usually specifies that the debentures are *pari passu* with all other senior debt that is currently outstanding or will be issued in the future. The indenture also provides that the debentures will be *pari passu* with any subsequent senior issues of securities or securities of a similar class. The straight debt debenture gives the corporation a long-term guarantee of a fixed interest rate.

**Convertible Debentures.** The holders of the debentures, at their option, may convert the debentures into common shares of the corporation at a fixed number of shares for each debenture. Accordingly, the corporation, especially during periods of high interest rates, is able to sell such debentures at a rate of interest below the then-prevailing rate. The differential in interest rate is compensated for by the value placed on the ability to convert the debentures into shares of the company. Marginal companies often must offer the conversion option to induce investors to purchase debentures.

Convertible debentures offer advantages to both the investor and the issuing corporation. The investor is able to get capital appreciation on the common stock of the corporation if its value should rise above the conversion level, while he receives a fixed rate of return. In addition, the investor has the option of converting his debentures or waiting to redeem them. On the other hand, the conversion feature allows the corporation to sell a security at a lower interest rate than it could otherwise obtain. If the corporation does well and its shares appreciate in value, the conversion of the debentures will convert corporation debt into permanent equity.

Convertible debenture agreements, like those of straight debentures, specify the ranking of the debentures in case the corporation must be liquidated. However, convertible debentures usually are not ranked with senior securities.

**Subordinated Debentures.** Subordinated debentures have claims to interest and principal that are subordinated to all other long-term credit claims of the corporation, both secured and unsecured. The subordinated debenture, because of its junior position in liquidation, has almost the same characteristics as preferred stock. However, corporations issue subordinated debentures rather than equity securities because debt interest is fully deductible as a business expense, whereas dividends on preferred stock are paid from after-tax income; therefore, the corporation has a lower after-tax cost. However, since the subordinated debentures are still considered debt, the corporation must pay interest and principal when due, whereas the payment of preferred dividends is discretionary.

Subordinated debentures usually yield a higher rate of interest than straight debenture debt, because the investor takes a greater risk. However, to make these issues more attractive to the investor, as well as to hold down the effective interest cost, the subordinated debenture is sold together with some other feature. This feature could take the form of a conversion provision, as was previously discussed, or an offer of *detachable warrants*. These warrants are an option to buy other securities, usually common stocks, at a given price for a specified period.

Examples of restrictive covenants contained in various indentures are shown in Appendix 21-2.

### SBIC Loans

Loans from Small Business Investment Companies are a relatively new form of private venture capital funds, which are regulated by the federal government. An SBIC is licensed by the Small Business Administration (SBA) to provide both money and management services to small businesses. The SBA may, in turn, provide an SBIC with financing for its operating capital needs. SBIC loans are meant to provide equity funds to small businesses, which may not have access to funds from other sources.

An SBIC loan can be a combination of subordinated convertible debt and equity. An SBIC, by law, can only make long-term loans, running for a period of not less than five years or more than twenty years, with the right of prepayment.

Although SBIC loans are a good source of funds for new companies, an SBIC prefers to invest in companies with an operating history. Current profitability is not a criterion for an SBIC loan. In order to qualify for an SBIC loan, a company must meet the SBA definition of a small business, that is, it must have assets not in excess of $5 million, a net worth of not more than $2.5 million, and an average net income over the previous years of not more than $250,000. Furthermore, an SBIC cannot invest more than 20 percent of its assets in any one company, nor own more than 50 percent of the equity in a company in which it invests.

### Venture Capital

Venture capital is a source of capital funds for the business enterprise in the process of organization or in the initial stages of expansion. In contrast to the SBIC, venture capital companies are private companies and are not controlled by the government. Firms seeking venture capital funds can be characterized as those that cannot at the outset obtain risk capital from other sources and need more capital to obtain additional funds from conventional sources.

Venture capital loans are high-risk investments, usually made by subsidiaries of banks or other financial institutions or corporations. Their primary function is to provide venture capital not otherwise available to new businesses that display growth and superior return potential.

Funds provided by a venture capital organization are generally equity funds or subordinated funds that can be converted to equity capital, or a combination of loan and equity funds. The venture capital organization will often require a substantial percentage of the equity of the corporation in which it invests in order to be compensated for the risk it is taking. When the business has achieved some success, the venture capital company will generally dispose of its equity investment at a substantial profit through a public offering.

### Lease-Purchase Financing

This type of financing plays a significant role as a source of funds for the business enterprise. It has two major uses. In one use, the business needs to acquire personal property, but instead of expending working capital funds for the property, it arranges to lease the property for a period of years. After the lease period is over, the lessee acquires an option to purchase the property for a minimal amount, say a dollar. This type of arrangement does not require the immediate outlay of working capital funds; however, the interest rate charged is generally higher than that of other types of bank financing. Lease-purchase financing should not generally reduce the normal credit lines of the corporation.

One aspect of lease-purchase financing that must be considered is the effect of applying the rules of SFAS 13, *Accounting for Leases*. If there is a bargain purchase at the end of the lease, or the lease covers 75 percent of the economic life of the property, or the present value of the lease payments equals at least 90 percent of the value of the property, the asset and the related obligation must then be shown on the balance sheet as if the property had been purchased on a payout basis. This capitalization of the lease agreement may affect other credit agreement restrictions and will reduce working capital to the extent of the next year's installments. (See Chapter 4 for a complete explanation and discussion of current lease accounting rules.)

The *sale-leaseback* is a variation of the lease-purchase arrangement. Here the property owned by a business is sold and leased back from the company to which it was sold. This type of arrangement has several advantages to the corporation, in addition to the cash that is generated. Any gain on the sale will be taxed at the lower capital gain rates, and the lease payments will be deductible from ordinary income and will usually exceed the prior depreciation deduction. The cash can be used to retire existing debt if it is not needed for working capital. However, the property would probably have to be capitalized at the present value of the lease payments and the related obligation recorded for balance sheet purposes in accordance with SFAS 13 (see discussion above). A sale-leaseback is advantageous when there are capital losses that can offset the gain. Otherwise, the same result can be achieved by refinancing the property.

Under the sale-leaseback arrangement, the effective cost of funds may be higher than under a refinancing of the property. The total cost must take into account specific tax savings and the benefits of using an alternative source of financing.

### Municipal Bonds

This type of financing is usually available only in areas of high unemployment, depressed areas, or in smaller communities of the United States. A given taxing authority issues a revenue bond, the proceeds of which will be used to either build or purchase a plant site. The business enterprise arranges to lease the facility from the taxing district. The rental payments are fixed to equal the principal and interest payments that the governmental body is required to make. The agreement with the taxing authority provides that after the bond is retired, the facility will be turned over to the corporation, or the rent reduced to an amount equal to the local property taxes on the plant.

The effective cost of the *municipal revenue bond* issued is cheaper than that obtainable by the corporation, because the interest received by the holders of the bond is tax-free for federal and most home state taxes. Therefore, the bonds can be issued with a lower coupon rate than the corporation would be required to pay for a debenture issue or for a mortgage. (See the previous discussion relating to the requirement to capitalize such a lease and record the related obligation in accordance with SFAS 13.)

## EQUITY

In addition to the temporary funds that a business requires for its operations, it needs permanent or *equity funds* to carry out sound financial planning. The distinction between borrowed funds and equity funds is that borrowed funds must be repaid either from earnings or the sale of assets whereas equity funds are retained permanently in the business. It is for this reason that lenders will ascertain if an adequate equity investment has been made by the stockholders before entrusting their own funds to the corporation's use.

There are similarities between certain debt instruments and equity holdings. However, lenders have certain privileges not possessed by the holders of equity capital in a corporation. The holders of debt instruments have priority over stockholders up to the limit of their claim against the corporation if the company is liquidated. Lenders may force the business to abide by the terms of the contract under which the funds were obtained, even though it may mean the company's reorganization or dissolution. The company must make the periodic interest and principal payments due to lenders; the equity holder is not assured of receiving dividends.

Equity funds can be divided into two classifications: common and preferred stock.

### Common Stock

The holders of common stock have complete claim to the profits and assets of the business after the holders of all other classes of debt and equity instruments have received their stipulated returns. Common stockholders enjoy the benefits of business success and have an indirect voice in management because they elect the board of directors. But the holders of common stock suffer the brunt of business failure. When financial difficulty results in the firm's liquidation, preferred stockholders must, as a rule, be paid in full before common stockholders may participate in the liquidation proceeds.

**Privately Held Corporations.** In discussing funds obtained from the sale of common shares, a distinction must be made between the privately and publicly held corporation. Equity funds in the privately held corporation are obtained from the business founder, friends and associates of the founder, and those willing to risk funds in the operation. There is generally a limit, in most states, to the number of individuals to whom a company can sell its shares without registering such shares with either a state regulatory agency for intrastate sales or the Securities and Exchange Commission for interstate securities sales. Individuals are generally reluctant to purchase common shares in a private corporation because of the difficulty in selling the shares and the lack of a known purchase and selling price. The ownership of the private closely held corporation also must consider the problem of retaining its control if additional common shares are sold to outside individuals. It is primarily for these reasons that the private corporation will generally obtain additional funds through borrowing rather than through the sale of common shares.

**Publicly Held Corporations.** The publicly held corporation, or the privately held corporation that anticipates becoming a publicly held corporation, can raise additional funds through the sale of shares to the public. Such sale is generally handled by an underwriter, who provides the market for sale and distribution. Some of the factors evaluated by the underwriter in determining the market price of the shares to be sold by a private company going public are:

- The book value per share;
- The current earnings per share and the EPS trend over the past five years;
- The past earnings history of the corporation;
- The projected earnings ability of the corporation;
- Characteristics of the industry;
- The past dividend history of the company and a projection of its ability to pay dividends in the future; and
- The number of shares to be sold and the relationship of this amount to the company's total equity.

The decision to sell shares must take into account the possibly negative effects of the sale on management control. However, companies should weigh the three main advantages of equity sales versus alternate methods of raising funds: (1) equity funds do not have to be repaid as borrowed funds do; (2) dividends paid to shareholders depend on earnings and the corporation's need for funds, whereas interest and principal payments on debt are mandatory whether or not the corporation has funds available; and (3) raising equity funds through the sale of shares makes it easier to obtain borrowed funds.

When considering the advantages and disadvantages of equity funds compared to borrowed funds, the tax effects should not be overlooked. Whereas interest paid on borrowed funds is deductible for tax purposes, dividends paid on common and preferred stock are not.

### Preferred Stock

Preferred stock is an equity security similar to common stock, except that preferred shares:

- Have preference over common shares in case the corporation is liquidated;
- Receive a limited, but guaranteed, dividend before any distribution to common shares; and
- Accept a limitation on the amount of dividends as a fair exchange for the priority they have on the earnings of the company.

The sale of preferred stock has certain advantages over common stock. Whereas the sale of common shares dilutes the ownership of the management, the preferred shareholder generally does not participate in the control of the corporation or the election of directors.

There are many variations in the types of preferred stock that can be negotiated at the time of sale to make the sale more attractive. A summary of some of the variations (any or all of which may be a part of a preferred issue) follows:

1. *Cumulative preferred stock* requires that before common stock dividends may be paid, preferred dividends must be paid not only for the dividend period in question but also for all previous periods in which no preferred dividends were paid.

2. *Participating preferred stock* refers to equity that is entitled to some residual participation in the profits of a corporation after the basic dividend amount specified in the preferred stock certificate has been received. That is, a specified dividend is paid to the preferred stockholder, after which the common stockholder receives a comparable amount per share, followed by an equal share-for-share participation between preferred stockholders and common stockholders in any residual distribution.

3. *Preferred stock may be callable* by the corporation, in which case the corporation may retire the preferred stock at its option, usually at some premium over par value.

4. *Preferred stock may carry a conversion clause* that makes it possible to convert the preferred stock into common stock of the corporation at the stockholder's option.

The private corporation finds the sale of preferred shares somewhat more attractive than that of common shares, because the former entails less risk and guarantees a return to the investor. Like common stock, preferred stock can be sold by the public corporation through the use of an underwriter. The various provisions of the preferred stock, including the rate of return, must be negotiated with the underwriter, who is interested in being able to offer a stock that is attractive in the marketplace. If he believes the stock is going to be hard to sell, he may not wish to underwrite the issue.

## WARRANTS

Warrants are options to buy other securities, usually common stock, at a stated price for a specific period. Warrants usually are not sold directly by the corporation, except as a form of compensation to underwriters, finders, and so on. Rather, they are sold in conjunction with securities that might not be readily marketable on their own investment merits without the speculative appeal of unattached warrants or, in the case of bonds, could not be sold at a reasonable interest rate. Warrants may be either *detachable* (the investor may resell it separately from the security with which it was issued) or *nondetachable*.

Since warrants represent a right to purchase common shares, the exercise of these warrants represents a source of funds to the corporation. However, corporations cannot rely on warrants as a source of funds, since other factors, such as the price of the securities in question, are beyond the control of management and thus are not predictable.

## INVESTMENT BANKERS AS A SOURCE OF FINANCING

Unlike the standard sources of debt financing, such as banks, insurance companies, pension funds, and similar institutions, investment bankers normally deal only with publicly held companies.

Investment bankers (sometimes called *underwriters*) act on behalf of the corporation to sell debt or equity securities either to the general public or in a private placement. Investment bankers are essentially middlemen who bring together the corporation and a buyer or buyers. What they offer, for a fee, is their knowledge of the marketplace—the terms or price that makes a security currently saleable—as well as their ability to line up buyers.

### Security Sales Methods

**The Private Placement.** In a private placement, the corporation sells its securities to private individuals or institutions, either directly or through an investment banker. Under this arrangement, the underwriter, serving only as an agent and assuming no risk, receives a fee based on the services rendered. A private placement has the advantage of eliminating the complexities of a registration with the Securities and Exchange Commission. Securities purchased in a private placement are not registered, and the institutions or individuals purchasing the securities must generally hold them until their maturity or until the securities are included in a registration statement filed with the SEC.

**Public Offering.** This term describes a sale of securities to the general public. In order to sell securities on an interstate basis, they must be registered with the SEC in accordance with the Securities Act of 1933. The requirements of a public offering and the different types of registration forms available to a business enterprise are described in Chapter 22.

### The Underwriting Process

Before the underwriting process can begin, the company must select an underwriter who will manage the issue. The company should enter into a *letter of intent* with the underwriter. The letter usually indicates the approximate number of shares to be sold, the compensation of the underwriter, and whether he will commit to a firm purchase of the shares or only a "best efforts."

Under *a firm-purchase commitment*, the investment banker purchases all the securities at the market price, less a discount. Under the *best-efforts method,* as the name implies, the underwriter markets the securities and pays only for those sold, less his discount or fee. Usually, if a specified minimum number of shares are not sold, the underwriting is rescinded. In both types of transactions, the investment banker also receives a sum to cover his expenses and legal fees. In many cases, the banker also receives (or purchases for a nominal sum) warrants, which are usually good for five years, to purchase the company's common stock at the current market price or below. The investment banker's fee or discount and his expenses, warrants, or other types of compensation are all negotiable. A strong company with an easily marketable security may find it pays to shop for a lower fee, but smaller companies may find that a lower fee may only buy an inferior effort.

Management of companies selling securities for the first time often misunderstand one point regarding a firm-offer agreement—the deal is not really firm until the night before the actual sale to the public. As noted earlier, the letter of intent commits the underwriter to marketing the securities on either a firm-offer or best-efforts basis and states the appropriate size of the offering in shares or face value of bonds. Thereafter, all the work of preparing the registration statement, underwriting agreement, and other legal documents goes forward without any agreement on the specific price at which the securities will be sold, other than an understanding on a price range. The actual price is negotiated (after the markets close) on the evening before the public sale. If the company is not happy with the price suggested by the investment banker, it can try to persuade him to do better or decide to abort the offering. The underwriter also has the right to abort the deal at any time before the sale for a variety of reasons having to do with market conditions and unfavorable changes in the company's earnings or financial condition. Many a public offering has been killed or postponed at the last minute. This is a risk that management must be prepared to take before undertaking a public offering.

Appendix 21-3 is a time schedule that indicates not only the order of steps necessary to satisfy the requirements of the 1933 Securities Act, but also the usual allocation of the required work between the corporation, the various legal counsel, and the accountants.

## Cost Factors

A cursory review of the fees charged by investment bankers would indicate that the cost of a private placement is cheaper than a public offering. However, there are other factors to be considered that make it difficult to compare the overall cost of each type of transaction. The following factors should be considered in making a decision:

- A public offering involves a higher underwriting fee, much higher expenses, higher legal and accounting fees, and a substantial investment of time by the controller and other executives. The underwriting fee for a public offering can range from 6 to 12 percent, depending on the size of the offering, whether the company is already public, the marketability of the securities, and other factors. The fee for a private placement can range from 3 to 10 percent, again depending on various factors.
- A public offering will generally bring a higher price for stock or a lower interest rate for debt than a private placement.
- A private placement will usually include restrictive covenants for a debt issue, which may be onerous to management.
- A private purchaser will often demand warrants or some other equity "kicker" with a debt issue.
- A private purchaser will often require security for its debt, which may interfere with the company's other credit arrangements.
- If the private placement involves stock (only available to a public company), the purchaser may reserve the right to require a public offering (at its own expense) within a specified time period. It may also retain the right to participate in any subsequent public offering by the company (*piggyback rights*). Such rights may make it difficult for the company to have a public offering at a later date.
- If the company is not already public, a public offering may subject the company to the periodic reporting requirements of the SEC, which are quite expensive. (See Chapter 10.)

Some of these factors cannot be quantified into a dollar cost, but very often the nonmonetary factors, such as restrictive covenants or public offering rights, may be as significant as the initial cost of the offering. When management has a choice as to a private placement or a public offering, the controller should prepare a list of pro and con considerations for each type of transaction, so management can make an informed decision.

## NEGOTIATING THE DEBT AGREEMENT

The process of negotiating the debt agreement involves many factors; some restrictions are required by all creditors, whereas others are negotiable. Before entering into a debt agreement, the corporation must analyze its financial structure and its projected status (both balance sheet and operations) during the periods that the loan will be outstanding, in order to determine if it will be able to operate within the agreement's restrictive covenants. The corporation and the financial institution should have a mutual understanding of the terminology contained in the agreement prior to its execution, in order to avoid disputes involving interpretation of the agreement at a later date.

### Compensating Balances

Most credit agreements with banks require that the corporation maintain a specified minimum balance (*compensating balance*) in a non-interest-earning account with the bank. Compensating balances can be calculated on the basis of either collected or uncollected balances, and the requirement can vary from a fixed minimum amount to a percentage of either the amount of the loan outstanding or the amount that can be borrowed from the bank (the commitment). If the compensating balance requirement exceeds the customer's normal balances with the bank, the requirement will raise the effective cost of borrowing. If the corporation fails to meet the required compensating balance requirements, it must pay a deficiency charge, which has the effect of raising the interest rate of the loan. The amount of the compensating balance, the method of calculating it, and the rate of any deficiency charge are all negotiable. The compensating balance terms should be negotiated as part of the interest rate.

### Restrictive Covenants

All credit agreements have restrictions that the corporation must follow. If the corporation does not meet these requirements, a default is created that must be cured within an agreed period of time, or the company must repay the loan on the lender's demand. Restrictive covenants are most often contained in long-term credit agreements and provide a means by which the financial institution can monitor the performance of the corporation and enforce compliance with the loan terms. The restrictive covenants are also designed to ensure that funds will be available to repay the borrowed funds when payment is due. The examples below are typical restrictive covenants in credit agreements.

**Dividends.** A clause in the agreement may limit the amount of dividends that a corporation can pay. The typical dividend restriction may provide that:

- Dividends can be paid only from accumulated earnings after a given date;

- Cumulative dividends paid cannot exceed an agreed-on percentage of accumulated earnings from a given date; or
- Dividends paid cannot exceed a given amount plus an agreed-on percentage of accumulated earnings from a given date.

Such a clause is designed to prevent the corporation from paying excessive dividends or from paying dividends if losses have been incurred. Additionally, most credit agreements will combine a provision restricting the repurchase of common stock with the dividend repayment provision.

**Operating Ratios.** In order to monitor the performance of a corporation, most credit agreements will specify minimum operating ratios that the corporation must maintain. Examples of the typical ratios contained in credit agreements are:

- Minimum working capital requirement in dollars;
- Ratio of current assets to current liabilities or working capital ratios;
- Ratio of debt (either total liabilities or borrowed funds) to net worth; and
- Ratio of debt to net worth, as above, except that subordinated debt is included with net worth.

**Inventory and Receivable Levels.** Those credit agreements that base loan amounts on inventory or accounts receivable will contain a clause that requires that the inventory level or current accounts receivable outstanding be maintained at a given level. The clause generally states that the loan outstanding will not exceed a predetermined level of inventory or accounts receivable outstanding.

**Ability to Incur Additional Debt.** Credit agreements generally contain a clause stating that the corporation cannot incur additional debt (borrowed funds) until the loan has been repaid. Or the agreement may permit the corporation to incur additional debt provided the debt incurred is subordinated to funds loaned under the credit agreement and the subordinated debt so incurred has a later maturity. It is also possible to negotiate for a limited amount of new debt for a specific purpose such as the purchase of fixed assets.

**Capital Expenditures.** Credit agreements will generally place a restriction on the amount of funds that can be reinvested in fixed assets. This amount can be a percentage of depreciation, a percentage of earnings, a fixed amount, or a combination of these factors.

**Earnings Requirement.** Many revolving credit agreements with banks have a clause stating that if a given predetermined earnings level is maintained over the term of the revolving credit agreement, the revolving credit agreement, at maturity, will be converted to a term loan.

**Clearing Up Balances on Short-Term Revolving Loans.** Most short-term revolving credit agreements provide that the corporation must completely repay its borrowings under the agreement for a period of either 30 or 60 consecutive days during each 12-month period. Lenders thus insist that the corporation demonstrate to them its ability to repay the funds borrowed. What usually happens is that the company uses an alternate lender to supply the loan for the repayment period.

Restrictive covenants in credit agreements vary widely. The important thing to remember is that normal fluctuations in earnings, working capital, and so on, may affect the acceptability of the proposed restrictions. If the corporation cannot operate under the restrictions contained in the agreement, it must negotiate a set of workable restrictions with the financial institution. Furthermore, it should insist that a provision be included in the credit agreement that allows the parties to agree to modify the restrictions during the life of the agreement. It is usually not difficult to obtain a *waiver of a default* from the lender if the company is not in financial difficulties.

It is important to remember that creditors do not want to be surprised with adverse news. If a default appears likely, the firm should discuss its position with the lender in advance and keep him informed. The debtor can usually work out some modification in the agreement so as to eliminate a default. On the other hand, if the lender believes that the company is hiding information or doesn't know enough about its business to anticipate adverse financial down-turns, it will not hesitate to call the loan when a default occurs.

### Costs of Financing

When a corporation has alternate sources of funds, the total cost of a loan over its life is probably the most significant factor in the decision as to which source to use. Since interest rates change rapidly as the demand for funds and the available supply varies and the Federal Reserve Board increases or decreases interest rates, the controller must consider the interest costs of alternative sources of credit.

**Short-Term Rates.** These rates are most directly affected by the state of the money market. If short-term funds are needed, there are only a few things that can be done to keep interest costs to a minimum:

1. Commercial paper should be sold whenever possible, because the rates on such borrowing are usually below the bank prime rate. Unfortunately for most companies, commercial paper is only marketable by the largest corporations.
2. On bank loans, an attempt should be made to negotiate compensating balances and commitment fees. Credit should be sought for uncollected funds in computing the average compensating balance.
3. When a finance company (factor) is used for credit, banks should be urged to participate in the arrangement, because they will usually charge a lower rate on their outstanding loan.

**Long-Term Rates.** These rates do not increase or decrease as rapidly as short-term rates, and they are more affected by a company's credit rating. Some suggestions for reducing interest rates are:

1. On a public offering of debentures, the rate can be lowered by making the debentures convertible or attaching warrants to purchase common stock.
2. Insurance company loans can be negotiated at a lower interest rate if the lender is given warrants or some other equity interest as an additional form of compensation.
3. Some long-term or intermediate-term bank loans can have an interest rate that varies with the prime rate. However, this variable rate should only be negotiated if the rates are expected to drop during the loan period. Such an arrangement should always have a maximum and minimum interest rate so the corporation can compute its maximum interest exposure during the term of the loan.

**Indirect Costs.** The direct cost, or percentage rate, is usually obvious. However, the indirect costs should also be considered and compared when a corporation weighs alternate sources of funds. Examples of indirect costs are:

- The cost of recording fees and title insurance when mortgage funds are sought;
- The cost incurred in connection with a public underwriting (legal, accounting, printing, and underwriter's discount) for both debt and equity funds;
- Additional clerical costs incurred in preparing reports, as in processing pledged receivables;
- Additional outside accounting costs if special reports are required;
- Commitment fees on unused revolving lines of credit; and
- The interest cost of maintaining compensating balances.

A company should not normally make short-term loans for long-term needs. Sometimes, however, it pays to borrow short-term if interest rates are expected to drop sharply within a year and a long-term loan or a debenture issue can then be negotiated at lower interest rates. On the other hand, it sometimes makes sense to make a long-term borrowing before the funds are needed if the loan is made at a low rate when interest rates are climbing, or if a credit crunch is on the way.

## SUGGESTED READING

Hayes, Rick Stephen. *Business Loans—A Guide to Money Sources and How to Approach Them Successfully.* Boston: Cohners Books International, 1977.

Hemingway, G. S. *An Introduction to Business Finance.* London: William Heinemann, 1976.

Loffel, Egon W. *Financing Your Business.* New York: David McKay Company, 1977.

Markstein, David L. *Money Raising and Planning for the Small Business.* Chicago: Henry Regnery Company, 1974.

Rausch, Edward N. *Financial Management For Small Business.* New York: AMACOM, 1979.

## APPENDIX 21-1   REVOLVING CREDIT AGREEMENT

THIS AGREEMENT, entered into as of this 1st day of February, 1980, by and between XYZ Manufacturing Company, a Delaware corporation (herein sometimes called "Company"), and Third National Bank of Anywhere, a national banking association (herein sometimes called "Bank"), superseding the existing Revolving Credit Agreement between the parties dated January 26, 1977.

WITNESSETH:

### Section 1.   Amount and Terms of Loan

1.1 Bank agrees, on the terms of this agreement, to lend and relend to Company such amounts as Company may request from time to time from the date hereof until December 31, 1982, provided the aggregate unpaid principal amount borrowed by Company hereunder shall not exceed at any time the amount of Two Million Dollars ($2,000,000.00).

1.2 Each disbursement shall be in an amount of at least $50,000.00 or multiples thereof.

1.3 Each disbursement shall be evidenced by a promissory note in the usual form of Bank's 90-day demand note, and shall be payable 90 days after the date thereof, but in no event after December 31, 1982.

1.4 The notes hereunder shall accrue interest on the unpaid balance at a rate per annum which shall be equal to the prime rate of Bank on 90-day commercial loans to large national companies (which rate shall fluctuate as and when said prime rate shall change) payable on the first day of each month to maturity, commencing August 1, 1979, and after maturity with interest at a rate per annum of Two Percent (2%) above said prime rate whether due by reason of acceleration of maturity or demand. The interest accruing under each such note shall be computed on the basis of an actual day, 360-day year.

1.5 Company may at any time or from time to time repay in whole or in part the principal outstanding hereunder, provided (i) that interest is current on said notes; and (ii) prepayment shall be without premium or penalty, unless made from or in anticipation of borrowing from any bank or lending institution other than Bank, in which event Company shall pay a premium in the amount of One Percent (1%) of the principal prepaid.

1.6 Company shall pay to Bank a commitment fee at the rate of One-Fourth of One Percent (1/4 of 1%) per annum on the daily average of the undisbursed portion of Bank's commitment hereunder, which fee shall accrue from the date hereof, and shall be payable monthly on the first day of each month commencing August 1, 1979. The commitment fee shall be computed on the basis of an actual day, 360-day year.

### Section 2.   Representations and Warranties

Company represents and warrants that (i) it is a corporation duly incorporated, validly existing and in good standing under the laws of the State of Delaware and is duly qualified as a foreign corporation to do business and is in good standing in every jurisdiction in which the ownership of property or the nature of its business made such qualification necessary; (ii) that it has full corporate power and authority to execute this agreement and that the execution and delivery hereof by its officers have been duly authorized; (iii) that it has full corporate power and authority to execute notes and borrow hereunder, and that the execution and delivery of notes hereunder has been duly authorized; (iv) the execution and delivery of this agreement and the notes hereunder will not violate any Articles of Incorporation or By-Laws of Company; (v) there are no suits or administrative proceedings pending or, to the knowledge of Company, threatened against or affecting the Company which might have a material adverse effect upon the financial condition or business of Company; and (vi) that no part of the proceeds of any loan hereunder will be used to purchase or carry margin stock (within the meaning of Regulation U of the Board of Governors of the Federal Reserve System) or to extend credit to others for the purpose of purchasing or carrying any such margin stock.

### Section 3. Particular Covenants

3.1 Company covenants and agrees that so long as any amount borrowed hereunder shall remain outstanding and unpaid, it shall

A. Provide to Bank, within 120 days after the close of each fiscal year a financial statement on a consolidated basis, in a form and detail satisfactory to Bank, certified to by a certified public accountant and prepared in the course of an audit contracted in accordance with generally accepted auditing standards consistently applied, and, within 45 days after the close of each of the other fiscal quarters, a financial statement on a consolidated basis prepared and certified to by an officer of the Company.

B. Furnish to Bank such other financial and operating information, and permit representatives of Bank to examine its books and records, all as may be reasonably requested by Bank from time to time.

C. Carry insurance of the kinds and in the amounts satisfactory to Bank and in accordance with general policies and the types of business and operation of similar companies in the area in which Company is located, on all of its buildings, machinery, equipment and other property.

D. On a consolidated basis, maintain: (i) minimum working capital of $1,000,000.00, and (ii) minimum tangible net worth of $1,500,000.00, each to be determined in accordance with generally accepted accounting principles consistently applied. Said minimum levels of working capital and tangible net worth shall be increased for a 12-month period effective each December 31 during the term hereof by an amount equal to 25% of the net profit of the Company, after taxes and deduction of extraordinary items, as reported in the audited year-end consolidated financial statement of the Company as of the immediately preceding July 31.

E. Maintain a ratio of total debt to tangible net worth of not more than 3:1 (tangible net worth being defined herein as tangible assets minus liabilities, it being understood that tangible assets include, but are not limited to, all of the categories of assets included on the audited financial statements of Company as of December 31, 1979).

F. Pay and discharge all taxes, assessments and governmental charges and levies imposed upon it or upon its income or profits or any property belonging to it, prior to the date on which penalties attach; provided payment thereof shall not be required so long as the same is being contested in good faith and by proper proceedings, if it shall maintain such reserves, if any, in respect thereto as shall be deemed adequate by Bank.

G. Cause to be done all things necessary to preserve and maintain its corporate existence, and authority to do business in the State of Missouri and in every jurisdiction in which the ownership of property or the nature of the Company's business makes such qualification necessary.

H. Keep and maintain adequate books and records of the operations of Company on a consolidated basis and permit the examination of the same by Bank, or any agent or officer or employee thereof, at such time as shall be requested.

I. Comply with all state and federal statutes applicable to the operation of Company's business and further to comply with all rules and regulations of any governmental or quasigovernmental party which may affect the operation of Company's business.

J. Notify Bank immediately of any change or proposed change of the firm of independent public accountants used by Company as of the date of this agreement, and of the reasons for such change or proposed change.

K. If Company has a pension and/or profit sharing plan, comply with Employee Retirement Income Security Act of 1974, as amended.

3.2 Company covenants and agrees that so long as any amount borrowed hereunder shall remain outstanding and unpaid, it will not without prior written consent of Bank:

A. Create or incur or allow to remain outstanding any indebtedness except (i) to Bank; (ii) to trade creditors in the ordinary course of business; (iii) other indebtedness permitted hereunder or consented to by Bank; or (iv) other indebtedness which shall be subordinated in form and substance satisfactory to Bank to all indebtedness of Company to Bank.

For purposes of this Agreement, the term "trade creditors" as used herein shall be deemed to include those finance company clients and other clients of the Company to whom the Company may at various times become indebted for customer list rental fees, merchandise sale proceeds and refunds in the ordinary course of its traditional business.

B. Mortgage, pledge or otherwise encumber, or permit any lien to be placed upon or against, any assets now owned or hereafter acquired, except (i) liens for taxes, assessments or governmental charges or levies not yet due or asserted, or which are being contested in good faith and by proper proceedings; (ii) liens of creditors, warehousemen, mechanics, suppliers and materialmen incurred in the ordinary course of business for sums not yet due, or being contested in good faith and by proper proceedings; (iii) liens incurred in the ordinary course of business in connection with workmen's compensation, unemployment insurance, social security obligations, and obligations under similar social legislation; (iv) purchase money mortgages incurred in connection with the acquisition of property and equipment as permitted hereby, and other liens, charges and encumbrances incidental to the conduct of Company's business or the ownership of its property and assets not incurred in connection with the borrowing of money or the obtaining of advances or credit, and which do not in the aggregate materially detract from the value of its property or assets or materially impair the use thereof in the operation of its business; (v) any judgment lien, unless the judgment which it secures shall not, within 60 days' written notice thereof, have been discharged or execution thereof stayed pending appeal, or shall not have been discharged within 60 days after the expiration of any such stay; provided, however, that except as permitted by exception (iv) above, Company shall not mortgage, pledge or otherwise encumber or permit any lien to be placed upon or against any of its accounts receivable or inventory.

C. Merge into or consolidate with any other entity; provided, however, a subsidiary of Company may be merged into Company.

D. Sell, lease, transfer or otherwise dispose of any property or assets except in the ordinary course of business, or except for full value, provided, however, Company shall give written notice to Bank prior to any sale for full value in excess of $50,000.00.

E. Declare or pay any cash dividends on any common or preferred stock in excess of ten cents per share outstanding per fiscal quarter; provided, however, that the maximum dividend payable in any given calendar year shall not exceed $41,640.00.

F. Acquire, redeem, or retire any of its outstanding shares of stock between the Company and its shareholders.

G. Make loans or advances to, or guarantee the debts of, any other person, firm or corporation except in the normal course of business and except with respect to its subsidiaries.

H. On a consolidated basis, make expenditures for fixed assets in any one fiscal year in excess of $150,000.00.

## Section 4. Events of Default

If any one of the following events of default shall occur and shall not have been remedied within the time provided:

A. Default shall be made in the payment when due of any principal or interest under the notes issued hereunder, and such default shall remain unremedied for a period of 10 days after receipt by Company of written notice thereof from Bank; or

B. Breach or nonperformance of any of the covenants or agreements set out in part 3.1 above, and such breach or nonperformance shall continue for a period of 10 days after Bank shall have demanded performance thereof; or

C. Breach of nonperformance of any of the covenants or agreements set out in part 3.2 above, and such default shall continue for a period of 10 days after receipt by Company of written notice thereof from Bank; or

D. The present shareholders of Company shall sell, agree to sell, transfer or agree to transfer control of Company, unless such sale or transfer is to a present shareholder and, if Bank is notified of such transaction, if such default continues for a period of 10 days after receipt by Company of written notice thereof from Bank; or

E. Company shall become insolvent in either the equity or bankruptcy definition of the term;

THEN and in any such event Bank's obligation to make further disbursements hereunder shall terminate, and the holder of the notes issued hereunder may at its option declare the principal of and accrued interest thereon to be immediately due and payable, whereupon the balance of the principal of said notes then unpaid and the accrued interest thereon shall forthwith become due and payable without presentment, demand, protest or notice of any kind.

## Section 5. Miscellaneous

5.1 No failure on the part of the Bank to exercise, and no delay in exercising, any right hereunder shall operate as a waiver thereof nor shall any single or partial exercise by

Bank of any right hereunder preclude any other or further exercise thereof or the exercise of any other right of Bank.

5.2 This Agreement can be modified or amended only by written agreement signed by the parties hereto.

5.3 This Agreement, and any notes issued hereunder, shall be governed by the laws of the State of Missouri.

5.4 The Company covenants that if default be made in any payment of principal of or premium or interest on the Bank obligation, it will pay to the holder hereof, to the extent permitted under applicable law, such further amount to cover the reasonable costs and expenses of collection, including reasonable compensation of the attorneys and counsel of the holder thereof for all services rendered in that connection.

5.5 Company may from time to time, on at least 5 days' prior written notice to Bank, permanently reduce the unused portion of the aggregate amount of Bank's commitment to lend under this Agreement. Any such reduction shall be in an amount of at least Fifty Thousand Dollars ($50,000.00) or multiples thereof. Further, Company may at any time on at least 5 days' prior written notice to Bank, terminate in full Bank's commitment to lend under this Agreement, upon the payment in full of all of the outstanding and unpaid notes and other liabilities of Company under this Agreement.

5.6 This Agreement shall be binding upon the Company, its successors and assigns, and shall inure to the benefit of Bank and its successors and assigns.

IN WITNESS WHEREOF, the parties hereto have executed this agreement the day and year first above written.

XYZ MANUFACTURING COMPANY

ATTEST:

_____
President

_____
Secretary

THIRD NATIONAL BANK

ATTEST:

_____
Vice President

_____
Assistant Secretary

# APPENDIX 21-2    EXAMPLES OF INDENTURE COVENANTS

**Limitation on Senior Funded Debt and Funded Debt.** The Company will not, and will not permit any Consolidated Subsidiary, to incur Funded Debt (other than the Debentures) unless, after giving effect thereto, Consolidated Tangible Net Assets shall not be less than 200 percent of Senior Funded Debt or 175 percent of Funded Debt. However, Funded Debt may be renewed or refunded so long as the total Funded Debt is not increased thereby.

**Limitation on Liens.** The Company will not, and will not permit any Consolidated Subsidiary, to incur or suffer to exist any lien upon any properties, or acquire any property subject to lien, except (a) existing liens as of the date of the Indenture; (b) Purchase Money Mortgages and Capitalized Lease Obligations securing Indebtedness otherwise permitted; (c) liens imposed by law in the ordinary course of business and certain other liens incident to accounts receivable financing; (d) liens between and among the Company and Consolidated Subsidiaries; (e) liens existing on property when it is acquired provided that the Indebtedness secured by these liens would be permitted Indebtedness under the Indenture (for the purpose of this clause); (f) the designation of an Unconsolidated Subsidiary as a Consolidated Subsidiary shall be deemed to constitute an acquisition as of the date of designation; and (g) liens (in addition to liens permitted by other clauses hereof) securing Indebtedness of the Company if the Debentures are secured equally and ratably with any other Indebtedness thereby secured.

**Limitation on Dividends and Other Payment Restrictions Affecting Consolidated Subsidiaries.** The Company will not, and will not permit any Consolidated Subsidiary, to create or otherwise cause to exist or become effective any encumbrance or restriction on the ability of any Consolidated Subsidiary to (a) pay dividends or make any other distribution on its capital stock owned by, or pay any Indebtedness owed to, the Company or any other Consolidated Subsidiary; (b) make loans or advances to the Company or any other Consolidated Subsidiary; or (c) transfer any of its properties or assets to the Company or any other Consolidated Subsidiary. The foregoing limitation shall not prohibit any such encumbrance or restriction existing (1) by reason of the Indenture; (2) by reason of any otherwise permitted mortgage, pledge, lien, encumbrance or security interest of, upon or in the properties subject to such encumbrance or restriction; (3) at the date of the Indenture or on the date a Person is acquired by the Company or any Consolidated Subsidiary which encumbrance or restriction is not applicable to any Person or the properties or assets of any Person other than the Person or its subsidiaries, or the property or assets of the Person or its subsidiaries, so acquired (for the purpose of this clause (3) the designation of an Unconsolidated Subsidiary as a Consolidated Subsidiary and/or the formation of a new Consolidated Subsidiary shall be deemed to constitute an acquisition as of the date of designation); (4) at the date of the Indenture in connection with Indebtedness of the Company and any renewal, extension or refunding of such Indebtedness so long as the principal amount thereof is not increased thereby; or (5) on the properties or assets of a Consolidated Subsidiary in connection with Indebtedness of such Consolidated Subsidiary maturing on demand or within one year from the date of the creation thereof, except that any such encumbrance or restriction shall be permitted to exist only so long as neither the Company nor any Consolidated Subsidiary is guaranteeing such Indebtedness.

**Limitation on Dividends and Stock Purchases.** The Company will not pay dividends or make distributions on its capital stock (other than in shares or stock rights) and the Company will not, and will not permit any Consolidated Subsidiary to, purchase the stock of the Company, if the sum of (a) the amount expended for any such purpose; (b) all other amounts expended for such purposes subsequent to October 1, 1979 through the date of the instant expenditure; and (c) the aggregate amount of certain investments and contingent liabilities (see clause (f) "Limitation on Investments" and clause (b) under "Limitations on Guarantees and Other Contingent Liabilities") outstanding at the end of such period would exceed the sum of (i) 75% of Consolidated Net Income accrued subsequent to October 1, 1979, (ii) the net proceeds received by the Company after October 1, 1979 from the sale of its capital stock, other than to a Subsidiary, for cash, or upon certain conversions and (iii) $4,000,000. In addition, transactions between and among the Company and its Consolidated Subsidiaries and certain stock redemptions upon conversions or exchanges or in settlement of disputes are permitted.

**Limitation on Dispositions of and by Consolidated Subsidiaries.** The Company will not, and will not permit any Consolidated Subsidiary to, dispose of any capital stock or options therefor that would result in any Consolidated Subsidiary ceasing to be a Consolidated Subsidiary, unless such stock is sold for fair value (as determined by the Board of Directors) and, after giving effect to such sale, the aggregate amount of investments by the company and its Consolidated Subsidiaries in, and contingent liabilities of the company and its Consolidated Subsidiaries with respect to, all other Persons shall not exceed the amount available for dividends and stock purchases as described under "Limitation on Dividends and Stock Purchases."

**Limitation on Investments.** The Company will not, and will not permit any Consolidated Subsidiary to, purchase or otherwise acquire securities of any other Person or make investments (other than in the ordinary course of business) in any other Person, except (a) readily marketable "AA" or better rated short-term governmental securities; (b) obligations of, or guaranteed by, the United States of America or any agency thereof; (c) investment quality short-term commercial paper; (d) short-term certificates of deposit of substantial domestic commercial banks; (e) investments between and among the Company and its Consolidated Subsidiaries or any Person which simultaneously therewith becomes a Consolidated Subsidiary; (f) investments in other Persons to the extent of the amounts available for dividends and stock purchases as described under "Limitations on Dividends and Stock Purchases" (for the purpose of this clause (f), any investment in a Person outstanding when such Person shall cease to be a Consolidated Subsidiary shall be deemed to be made at such time); and (g) investments in other Persons by any Subsidiary in which a third party has a joint ownership interest and by any Consolidated Subsidiary only to the extent of the amounts that would have been available for dividends and stock purchased if such amounts had first been paid as dividends to the Company.

**Limitation on Guarantees and Other Contingent Liabilities.** The Company will not, and will not permit any Consolidated Subsidiary to guarantee, endorse (other than for collection or deposit in the ordinary course of business), or become liable on any Indebtedness or other liability of any other Person (all of the foregoing being herein called "contingent liabilities"), except (a) contingent liabilities of the Company or any Consolidated Subsidiary with respect to Indebtedness of the Company or any Consolidated Subsidiary; (b) contingent liabilities of the Company or any Consolidated Subsidiary with respect to any other Person to the extent such contingent liabilities relate to investments referred to in clauses (f) and (g) under "Limitation on Investments" (for the purpose of this clause (b), any contingent liability with respect to a Person outstanding when such Person shall cease to be a Consolidated Subsidiary shall be deemed to be made at such time); and (c) certain letters of credit and contingent liabilities arising in the ordinary course of business.

**Limitations on Sales and Leasebacks.** The Company will not, and will not permit any Consolidated Subsidiary to, dispose of any property owned by it on October 1, 1979, in a transaction whereby the Company or any Subsidiary shall leaseback such property, unless the Company (and it covenants that it will) within 120 days thereafter applies the greater of (a) the net sales proceeds or (b) the fair value of such property to the redemption (other than as a mandatory Sinking Fund payment) of the Debentures in accordance with the terms of the Indenture.

**Limitation on Mergers.** The Company will not, and will not permit any Consolidated Subsidiary to, merge with any other Person or dispose of any property, except that so long as the Company would continue to be in compliance with the Indenture, (a) the Company may merge with any other corporation, if the company shall be the survivor; (b) the Company may merge into, or sell its property to, any other corporation, if the surviving corporation is a domestic corporation and assumes, by supplemental indenture, all obligations of the Company under the Indenture; (c) subject to certain limited exceptions, Consolidated Subsidiaries may merge with or dispose of their property to other Consolidated Subsidiaries; and (d) the Company or any Consolidated Subsidiary may dispose of any property for fair value if the Company (and it covenants that it will) within 120 days thereafter applies the net proceeds therefrom to the redemption (other than as a mandatory Sinking Fund payment) of the Debentures in accordance with the terms of the Indenture, provided however that the Company may retain such proceeds except to the extent the net book value of such property and all other property disposed of during the preceding 12 months exceeds 10% of Consolidated Tangible Net Assets. Sales of assets in the ordinary course of business (including any sale of accounts receivable by the Company and its Consolidated Subsidiaries) and sales and leasebacks shall now be deemed to be dispositions of assets for the foregoing purpose.

**Maintenance of Working Capital.** The Company will not permit Consolidated Current Assets less Consolidated Current Liabilities to be at any time less than 125 percent of Funded Debt.

**Reports to Debentureholders.** The Company will provide debentureholders with its quarterly and annual reports to shareholders and will disclose in its quarterly reports filed pursuant to the Securities Exchange Act of 1934 and its annual reports to shareholders the amount available for dividends and other payments, the amount of additional permitted Senior Funded Debt and Funded Debt and the ratio of Consolidated Current Liabilities to Funded Debt.

## APPENDIX 21-3   TIME SCHEDULE FOR A PUBLIC OFFERING

1981

| | | |
|---|---|---|
| May 6 | Preliminary meeting at XYZ Company —all parties. | |
| May 7 | Begin drafting of S-1 Registration Statement including prospectus | (XY) |
| May 12 | Completion of time schedule and allocation of duties—submitted to all parties | (CLC) |

| | | |
|---|---|---|
| May 16 | First draft of underwriting section of prospectus and underwriting agreements | (ULC) |
| May 18 | Prepare form of questionnaire for officers and directors | (CLC) |
| May 22 | First draft of prospectus received from company | |
| May 26 | Company sends letter to stockholders regarding their sale of shares | (XY) |
| May 31 | Fiscal year ends | |
| June 9 | Mail questionnaire to officers and directors | (XY) |
| June 15 | Financials for fiscal 1978 through 1980 to be submitted | (IA) |
| June 18 | Last day for stockholders to commit for participation in sale | |
| June 20 | Meeting to review draft of Form S-1 | (XY, U, ULC, IA, CLC) |
| June 23 | First draft of S-1 sent to printer | |
| July 15 | Audited financials for fiscal 1981 to be submitted (IA)—send financials to printer (CLC) | |
| July 16 | Meeting to review proofs S-1 | (XY, U, ULC, IA, CLC) |
| July 17 | Revised proofs of S-1 sent to printer | (CLC) |
| July 21 | File S-1 with SEC | (CLC) |
| July 22 | Chairman of the board sends letter to employees regarding their purchase of shares | (XY) |
| July 24 | Blue Sky filings | (ULC) |
| Aug. 14 | Last day for employees to indicate intent to purchase shares | |
| Sept. 10 | Due-diligence meeting at XYZ, Inc. at 4:15 P.M. | |
| Sept. 11 | Meeting to discuss comments and changes necessary—call SEC for clarifications | (XY, U, ULC, IA, CLC) |
| Sept. 12 | Revised proof of amendment sent to printer | (CLC) |
| Sept. 15 | Changes cleared with SEC | |
| Sept. 16 | Responsible amendment filed with SEC if necessary | (CLC) |
| Sept. 16 | Meeting at XYZ, Inc. at 4:15 P.M. to set price of stock | (XY, U) |
| Sept. 16 | Auditors provide underwriter with comfort letter | (IA) |
| Sept. 17 | File price amendment with SEC at 9:00 A.M.—underwriters sign agreement among underwriters at XYZ, Inc. at 9:30 A.M.—underwriters and company sign underwriting agreement at company's office at 10:00 A.M. | (CLC) |

Sept. 17   Registration statement effective—stock is sold to public

Sept. 24   Closing and payment for shares at company's office

XY     Company controller
U      Underwriter
ULC    Underwriter's legal counsel
CLC    Corporate legal counsel
IA     Independent auditor

# 22

# Public Offering Requirements

*Maureen Conners Kessler*

## INTRODUCTION

The Securities Act of 1933,[1] (Securities Act) generally requires that before securities may be offered for sale to the public, a registration statement must be filed with the Securities and Exchange Commission (SEC or the Commission) disclosing

---

[1] 15 U.S.C. §§ 77a-77aa, as amended.

prescribed categories of information.[2] Before the actual sale of securities can begin, the registration statement must be declared effective by the SEC.

This chapter provides an overview of the registration process and the controller's role in that process. In addition, it examines the applicability and content of specific registration forms. Finally, it discusses various aspects of the small offering.

## THE REGISTRATION PROCESS

### Underwriting

Once a company decides to publicly offer its securities, it usually chooses an underwriting firm to distribute the securities to the public. The company and the underwriter may then execute a *letter of intent* (which is actually an "agreement to agree") setting forth their understanding concerning the terms and conditions of the proposed public offering.[3] At a later stage in the offering process, the underwriter normally assembles a group, or *syndicate,* of other underwriters to help distribute the securities. Throughout the registration process, the principal underwriter acts as the representative of the other underwriters in conducting necessary transactions with the issuer.

The principal underwriter and its counsel work closely with the issuer to determine the terms of the offering and the content of the registration statement. The underwriter is concerned not only with the success of the offering, but also with the potential liability that may be imposed in the event of a violation of the anti-fraud or other provisions of the Securities Act or of the Securities Exchange Act of 1934 (the Exchange Act).[4]

### Stages in the Registration Process

After the selection of the principal underwriter and the commencement of preliminary negotiations, the registration process is formally underway. The process can generally be viewed in five stages:

1. Planning, information gathering, and drafting;
2. Filing the registration statement;

---

[2] Congress exempted certain securities as well as certain transactions from the registration requirements in Sections 3(a) and 4, respectively, of the Securities Act.

[3] The actual contract between the company and the underwriter (the Underwriting Agreement) and the document setting forth the rights and obligations of the underwriters among themselves (the Agreement Among Underwriters) are not signed until a short time before the registration statement becomes effective.

[4] 15 U.S.C. §§ 78a-78jj, as amended. See Sections 11, 12, and 17 of the Securities Act and Section 10(b) of the Exchange Act.

3. Filing pre-effective amendments to the registration statement;
4. Declaration of the effectiveness of the registration statement by the SEC; and
5. Filing posteffective amendments to the registration statement.

The initial stage of the registration process is normally the most time-consuming. Its successful culmination requires thorough organization and a clear division of labor with respect to the tasks to be performed. In most instances, issuer's counsel assumes the primary planning responsibility for the public offering. This function involves scheduling a timetable for the registration process and delegating information-gathering duties to the various parties involved and coordinating their efforts. In addition, issuer's counsel usually does the initial drafting of the nonfinancial sections of the registration statement with appropriate assistance from, and review by, the underwriter's counsel and others. At this time, the controller normally prepares the required financial statements and related data for later audit or review by the independent auditors.

After the initial stage of the process is completed, the registration statement is filed at the SEC offices in Washington, D.C., together with the registration fee prescribed by Section 6(b) of the Securities Act. Section 8(a) of the Act provides that a registration statement will become effective 20 days after the statement is filed, or 20 days after any amendment is filed. In practice, the registration statement is generally not declared effective until sometime after the nominal 20-day waiting period has elapsed.

The waiting period enables dealers and investors to become acquainted with the information contained in the registration statement and to make an informed decision regarding the merits of the securities offered through an examination of the preliminary, or *red herring,* prospectus.[5] During the waiting period, offers to sell the securities are permitted, but no sales of the securities may be consummated until after the registration statement is declared effective by the SEC.

### Examination and Effectiveness of the Registration Statement

Registration statements filed with the SEC are examined by its Division of Corporation Finance for compliance with the SEC's standards of adequate disclosure. The SEC has no authority to evaluate the merits of the securities to be offered or the fairness of the terms of the distribution.[6]

---

[5] The term *red herring* refers to the legend printed in red ink that must appear on the cover page of a preliminary prospectus informing the reader that although a registration statement relating to the securities has been filed with the SEC, it has not yet become effective and that the information contained therein is subject to completion or amendment.

[6] This differs from the authority granted state securities administrators who, under certain circumstances, may refuse registration if the terms of a particular offering are not deemed just or equitable.

After the Division completes its review, it sends a *letter of comment* to the registrant setting forth the perceived deficiencies. Such deficiencies may be cured by appropriate explanation to the SEC staff or by the filing of one or more amendments to the registration statement.

If the SEC has no further comments, the Underwriting Agreement and the Agreement Among Underwriters are then signed, and an amendment setting the price of the securities to be sold is filed with the SEC. A request for the acceleration of the effectiveness of the registration statement must be filed with the Commission at or before the time the pricing amendment is filed in order to avoid a mandatory additional 20-day waiting period. After the SEC declares that the registration statement is effective, a closing takes place, at which the company and the underwriters exchange documents, and the sale of the securities to the underwriters is completed.

In certain cases, it may be necessary to file one or more posteffective amendments in accordance with certain undertakings contained in the registration statement, to update information, or to report material events affecting the company. As a final stage in the registration process, companies having their first public offering must periodically file reports of sale with the SEC on Form SR. Such reports must initially be filed three months after the effective date of the registration statement, and on a semiannual basis thereafter until the completion or termination of the offering.

### Periodic Reports Under the Exchange Act

The controller and other members of management should be aware that every issuer filing a registration statement is required to file certain of the periodic reports prescribed by Section 13 of the Exchange Act. Principally, these are quarterly reports on Form 10-Q and annual reports on Form 10-K. This obligation may be suspended (pursuant to Section 15(d) of the Exchange Act) if the company has less than 300 shareholders. (The obligation is reinstated if the company has 300 or more shareholders at the beginning of any fiscal year.) In addition, an issuer may be required to register its securities pursuant to Section 12(g) of the Exchange Act (such registration is not related to the sale of securities) if it meets the asset and shareholder requirements of that section, that is, total assets in excess of $1 million and a class of equity securities held of record by 500 or more persons. Issuers of securities registered pursuant to Section 12(g) must also file the reports prescribed by Section 13.[7] In light of such periodic reporting requirements, the controller may wish to consult the independent auditor, counsel, and other financial officers of the company to establish an internal procedure of financial record keeping that will be compatible with future SEC reporting requirements.

---

[7] Companies required to file such periodic reports are henceforth referred to as reporting companies.

## THE CONTROLLER'S ROLE IN THE REGISTRATION PROCESS

The controller's normal responsibilities require that he be familiar with the details of all facets of his company's operations. Thus, in addition to his information-gathering and drafting duties, the controller often functions as an adviser to counsel, management, and the independent auditors during the registration process.

### Working With Counsel

In most instances, the controller works closely with the company's counsel throughout the registration process. As previously noted, such counsel often assumes the primary administrative responsibilities connected with the registration process in addition to acting as a legal consultant. However, counsel should not substitute his judgment of matters arising during registration for that of management. This discussion assumes that counsel is actively working with members of management who are fully aware of their responsibilities under the federal securities laws.

The controller can assist counsel and management in the following areas:

- Selecting independent auditors (if the company has not previously retained them);
- Structuring a realistic time schedule for the registration process;
- Providing advice on the company's financial disclosure requirements and the materiality of information drawn from the company's records;
- Advising counsel and others as to any differences in the financial disclosure required pursuant to SEC requirements and that required pursuant to generally accepted accounting principles;
- Reviewing drafts of the registration statement prepared by counsel and others;
- Making arrangements, if necessary, for a prefiling conference with the staff of the SEC in connection with unusual or problematic financial disclosure matters;
- Preparing an analysis of historical events and trends and other information to be used in developing financial projections; and
- Establishing post registration procedures to facilitate compliance with the periodic reporting requirements of the Exchange Act.

If the controller is not competent in one or more of these areas, the independent auditors may be used in an advisory capacity without affecting their independence on the audit.

### Assisting the Independent Auditors

Independent auditors must examine the financial statements and notes included in a registration statement. The controller's primary function in assisting the independent auditors involves marshalling the necessary data and preparing the required financial statements so as to expedite the auditors' review. The controller can also assist the auditors by clearly presenting additional explanatory information, not necessarily reflected in the company's records, that may have a bearing on the auditors' examination of, and opinion on, the company's financial statements. The controller can effectively expedite the independent auditors' examination by disclosing any unusual or extraordinary matters that affect or may affect the company and its business. The controller can also act as a conduit in facilitating the verification procedures that must be undertaken by the auditors. In this regard, the controller can assist the auditors by arranging easy access to company records as well as communication channels with various members of management.

## Gathering Information

The information-gathering stage of the registration process involves two steps. The first step calls for an examination of the documents that specify the matters to be disclosed in a registration statement filed pursuant to the Securities Act. Using such documents as a guide, the second step of the process involves an investigation of the issuer's affairs to ascertain its unique disclosure obligations.

The controller will generally be called on to help compile and present the financial data that is to be included in the registration statement. The controller may also be asked to draft needed narrative items, such as management's discussion and analysis of the financial statements. The controller's responsibilities may also include compiling nonfinancial information. However, this responsibility varies with the size of the issuer as well as with the controller's overall role in his company's internal affairs.

**General Sources of Information.** The data that the controller and others must compile depends in part on the requirements of the particular form of registration statement that the issuer will use in connection with the public offering. (See Registration Forms.) After examining the appropriate registration form and the relevant provisions of the Securities Act (particularly Sections 5, 6, 7, and 8 and Schedule A), it is advisable to refer to Regulation C, which contains the rules governing the preparation of registration statements and the registration process generally.[8] The SEC has interpreted various disclosure requirements in a series of releases (Accounting Series Releases)[9] which should be consulted in determining disclosure obligations.

After these materials have been examined, any previous registration statement filed by the issuer, together with any periodic reports filed by the issuer pursuant to

---

[8] Regulation C consists of Rules 400 through 494, which have been promulgated by the SEC pursuant to the Securities Act. Regulation C is found in Commerce Clearing House, Inc.'s *Federal Securities Law Reporter* (hereinafter CCH), Vol. 2, beginning at ¶ 5798.

[9] The Accounting Series Releases are found in 6 CCH beginning at ¶ 62351.

the Exchange Act, should be thoroughly analyzed. An examination of recent registration statements filed by registrants in the same or similar industries can also be helpful in connection with information gathering and drafting. The *SEC News Digest* and certain other publications, such as the *New York Law Journal*, indicate which issuers have recently filed registration statements and the particular registration form used. Volume 6 of CCH also contains a list of recently filed registration statements. A copy of any registration statement may be obtained from the SEC in Washington, D.C., at a specified fee per page. A prospectus may sometimes be obtained from the issuer of the securities or from a local investment banking firm or broker.

**Sources of Financial Information.** Since the controller is mainly responsible for the presentation of the financial data to be included in the registration statement, certain specific steps will be particularly useful to him.

*Assembling information.* The following suggested plan of action will help the controller assemble the needed information:

1. The controller should carefully examine the items of the registration form that require the disclosure of financial data, as well as any instructions as to financial statements contained in such form. The controller should also examine the proposed Underwriting Agreement for specific requirements concerning the financial statements. For planning purposes, the controller should consult Regulation S-X regarding the updating of financial statements that may become outdated as a result of delays in the registration process.

2. He should also analyze the relevant items of Regulation S-K, which sets forth certain of the substantive disclosure requirements that apply to the majority of registration statements filed with the SEC.

3. If he has not already done so, the controller should familiarize himself with the requirements of Regulation S-X, which governs the form and content of the financial statements and supporting schedules to be filed as part of the registration statement.

4. The controller should also examine the Accounting Series Releases promulgated by the SEC. These releases set forth the view of the Commission with respect to interpretations of Regulation S-X and general matters of accounting policy.

5. He might also examine the Staff Accounting Bulletins. Although the statements in these bulletins are not rules or interpretations of the Commission, they represent interpretations and practices followed by its staff in reviewing financial statements.

6. The controller should also examine pronouncements of the Financial Accounting Standards Board, its predecessors, and the American Institute of Certified Public Accountants for guidance in determining generally accepted accounting principles.

*Examining data.* Having assembled his basic tools, the controller should examine the relevant financial records and other material documents of the company for use in preparing the required financial statements and in anticipation of the audit to be made by the independent accountant.

*Keeping current.* The controller should keep abreast of accounting developments during the registration process to avoid delays caused by noncompliance with recent pronouncements. The independent accountants can usually provide help in this area. It may then be helpful to update counsel and others regarding various financial disclosure requirements. Although counsel may be reluctant to admit any deficiencies in this area, a tactful refresher course may expedite the registration process and aid counsel in future communications with the auditors, management, and if necessary, the staff of the SEC.

*Coordinating efforts.* The controller should frequently confer with counsel, other financial officers (including financial officers of subsidiaries), and the independent auditors to coordinate their efforts in presenting financial information in the registration statement. The controller is in a unique position to act as an effective liaison between these parties during the registration process, particularly if a disagreement should arise with respect to a material disclosure or presentation issue. Since the financial statements are the statements of management and not those of the auditors, the controller should not unquestioningly defer to the auditor's judgment in case of such controversy. Early conferences with management and counsel will usually resolve such problems satisfactorily.

*Related activities.* In addition to the examination conducted by the controller and the independent auditors, counsel and other appropriate parties should undertake (1) an examination of the registrant's basic corporate documents, minutes, stock ledgers, material agreements, and employee plans; (2) the circulation and evaluation of questionnaires for management and five-percent beneficial owners; (3) personal interviews with members of management and other persons responsible for different aspects of the issuer's business; (4) communications with other persons having knowledge of the issuer's affairs; and (5) physical inspections of inventory, property, and so on.

## FORM S-1 REGISTRATION STATEMENT

When the above investigation is completed, the drafting of the registration statement begins. The format and substantive content of a registration statement filed on Form S-1 is discussed below.

### Use of Form S-1

Form S-1 is the form most often used to register the securities of commercial and industrial companies. General Instruction A to Form S-1 provides that the form be used for the registration of securities of all issuers for which no other form is authorized or prescribed. However, the form is not used for securities of foreign governments or their political subdivisions.

The purposes of other frequently used registration forms are summarized under Registration Forms.

### Format of Form S-1

Form S-1 consists of (1) the facing page; (2) the cross-reference sheet; (3) the prospectus containing the information specified in Part I of Form S-1; (4) the information called for by Part II of Form S-1; (5) the necessary undertakings; (6) the required signatures; (7) the consents of experts named in the registration statement; and (8) the exhibits called for by the form.

**The Facing Page.** The facing page of the registration statement must set forth the information required by the official text of the form, including the name and address of the registrant and its agent for service, the approximate date the proposed sale is to begin, and a chart showing the calculation of the registration fee.

**The Cross-Reference Sheet.** Pursuant to Rule 404(c), the cross-reference sheet must show the location in the prospectus of each item of information required by Part I of the form. If any such item does not apply or calls for a negative answer, the cross-reference sheet must so indicate.

**The Prospectus.** The prospectus is the major component of the registration statement. It presents in narrative form the relevant information called for by the twenty separate items contained in Part I of the form. The final prospectus is usually printed on smaller paper than the rest of the registration statement and is the document that is separately printed and furnished to each purchaser at or before the time of delivery of the securities. Regulation C and the Guides set forth specified information that must be presented on the cover page of the prospectus, on the inside cover page, and in other prominent places in the prospectus. Pursuant to Rule 421(a), the substantive disclosure contained in the prospectus need not follow the order of the items of the form. However, it must not be presented in a manner that obscures any required information. The prospectus must contain a table of contents as well as the summary of the contents of the prospectus as required by Guide 59.

**Part II.** Part II of the registration statement (Items 21 through 30) is presented in an item and answer format. Part II requires disclosure concerning marketing arrangements, expenses associated with the issuance and distribution of the securities being registered,[10] relationships between the registrant and experts named in the statement, information regarding sales to special parties and sales of unregis-

---

[10] The controller may wish to examine the listing of such expenses in other registrant's statements (Item 22) at an early stage in the registration process to help him estimate the cost of the public offering. Expenses such as registration fees, printing costs, and legal, accounting, and engineering fees must be separately itemized.

tered securities, subsidiaries of the registrant, franchises and concessions, indemnification of officers and directors, and the treatment of proceeds from the sale of stock being registered, and a listing of the financial statements and exhibits filed as a part of the registration statement.

**Undertakings.** Certain undertakings on the part of the registrant follow Part II. All registrants must agree to file periodic reports in accordance with Section 15(d) of the Exchange Act. Other undertakings set forth in Form S-1 and elsewhere must only be included in the registration statement if applicable.

**Required Signatures and Consents.** The registration statement must be signed by the registrant, a majority of the registrant's board of directors, and specified officers of the registrant, including the controller or principal accounting officer. The controller should consult with counsel regarding the civil liabilities, specified in Section 11 of the Securities Act, that may be incurred by each signer of the registration statement if any part of it is found to be false or misleading. Consents of experts named in the registration statement (including independent accountants, engineers, and appraisers) must also be included.

**Exhibits.** The applicable exhibits specified in Form S-1 must be filed as a part of the registration statement. Necessary exhibits include copies of the underwriting agreements, basic corporate documents, an opinion of counsel as to the legality of the securities being registered, and certain material contracts. All exhibits filed are available for public inspection.

## Substantive Disclosure

The prospectus contains the information considered most significant to the investing public. The five major categories of information that must be disclosed in the prospectus, together with the item numbers of Form S-1 requiring such disclosure, are:

1. Information concerning the registrant and its business (Items 5, 6, 7, 8, 9, 10, 11, 12, and 20);
2. Information concerning management, security ownership, and certain transactions (Items 16, 17, and 18);
3. Information concerning the offering (Items 1, 2, 3, and 4);
4. Information concerning the securities being registered (Items 13, 14, and 15); and
5. Specified financial statements (Item 19).

Items 9, 10, 12, 16, 17, and 18 of Form S-1 incorporate by reference the disclosure requirements of Regulation S-K. As previously noted, Regulation S-K is an integrated disclosure regulation relating to various areas of information (including description of business, description of property, directors and executive officers, management remuneration, legal proceedings, and security ownership), some or all of which must be included in certain reports and registration statements filed with the SEC. The Regulation states the requirements applicable to the non-financial statement portions of such documents.

Appendix 22-1 is a checklist of the substantive disclosure that must be contained in the prospectus filed as a part of the Form S-1 registration statement.[11] In addition, Rule 408 requires the disclosure of such further information as may be necessary to ensure that the information included in the registration statement is not misleading. Although inclusion of such material is not always specified in this checklist, Form S-1 often requires disclosure of information with respect to parties other than the registrant, including its parents, subsidiaries, and predecessors. Certain terms used in the checklist, such as *parent, control, promoter,* and *voting securities* are defined in Rule 405.

### Financial Statement Requirements for Form S-1

**Required Statements.** The Instructions as to Financial Statements contained in Regulation S-X specify the balance sheets, statements of income, and changes in financial position that must be filed as a part of the registration statement. These instructions also specify certain entities for which such statements must be filed, certain historical financial data that must be set forth, and the conditions under which the registrant must file individual financial statements, consolidated financial statements, or both.

Regulation S-X, together with the Accounting Series Releases, governs the form and content of the financial statements and specifies the schedules to be filed in their support. In addition, Regulation S-X prescribes the statements of retained earnings and other stockholders' equity that must be filed. All financial statements specified in the instructions must be included in the prospectus. However, Item 19 of Form S-1 provides that nearly all the supporting schedules, as well as specified historical financial data, may be filed in Part II of the registration statement.

The financial statements that must be filed as a part of the Form S-1 registration statement include:

1. Audited balance sheets as of the end of each of the two most recent fiscal years. If the filing is made within ninety days of the end of the registrant's fiscal year and audited financial statements for the most recent fiscal year are not available, special rules apply (Regulation S-X, 3-01);

2. Audited statements of income and changes in financial position for each of the three fiscal years preceding the date of the most recent balance sheet being filed and for the interim period, if any, between the end of the most recent of such fiscal years and the date of the most recent balance sheet being filed; and

3. Statements of other stockholders' equity (additional paid-in capital, other additional capital, and retained earnings) and changes in stockholders' equity for the same periods as required for the statements specified in 2 above.

---

[11] The checklist does not include the financial statement requirements of Form S-1. These are discussed elsewhere in this chapter.

'Any interim balance sheet required and the related interim statements of income and changes in financial position need not be audited and need not be presented in greater detail than is required by instructions to Form 10-Q. The interim statements, other than the balance sheet, must be presented on a comparative basis with the corresponding period of the previous fiscal year.

The report and opinion of the independent accountants concerning the audit of the financial statements must also be included in the prospectus and must comply with the requirements of Article II of Regulation S-X.

**Requirements of Regulation S-X.** Regulation S-X is a uniform set of accounting requirements that applies to the majority of registration statements and other reports filed under the federal securities laws. As previously noted, Regulation S-X sets forth the requirements of the form and content of required financial statements; it does not prescribe the statements that must be filed as part of a particular form. The SEC has recently made extensive revisions of the regulation to delete inappropriate requirements and requirements already covered by generally accepted accounting principles.

## TIME SCHEDULE FOR A PUBLIC OFFERING

Several factors must be taken into account in developing an appropriate time schedule for the registration process. A very important factor is the date on which the required financial statements will be available. The financial officers of the company, together with the independent auditors, are in the best position to judge (1) in the case of an initial public offering, whether financial information concerning the company has been maintained in such a manner that financial statements may be prepared in accordance with SEC requirements and generally accepted accounting principles, and (2) the length of time required to complete the preparation of the financial statements and their examination by the independent auditor.

Before a time schedule can be established, the general condition of the issuer's records and other internal matters must also be considered. Counsel and others should conduct a preliminary examination in the early stages of the registration process in order to determine (1) categories of information that might present troublesome disclosure questions; (2) the need for future action in connection with the public offering, such as shareholder approval, charter amendments, or consents of creditors or government agencies; and (3) the need for "housecleaning" procedures with respect to prior corporate action, such as board of directors' or shareholder ratification of certain transactions, or the payment of delinquent taxes.

The sample time schedule in Figure 22.1 sets forth the basic steps in the registration process and may be used, with appropriate modifications, to schedule the filing of a registration statement.[12]

---

12 See Chapter 21 for a more detailed time schedule.

| | |
|---|---|
| January 3 | Preliminary meeting of working group. Delegation of information-gathering and drafting duties. |
| January 5— January 7 | Preparation and distribution of questionnaires for management and 5 percent beneficial owners. |
| | Commence preparation of required financial statements. |
| February 1 | Commence preparation of blue sky survey.* |
| | Review returned questionnaires. |
| February 15— February 25 | First draft of registration statement prepared and submitted to printer. |
| February 27— March 5 | Review and revision of first draft of registration statement. |
| March 8 | Audited financial statements available. |
| March 11 | Submission of complete registration statement to printer. |
| March 12— March 15 | Meeting to review new proof of registration statement. Printing in final form. |
| March 15 | Board of directors' meeting. |
| March 18 | Registration statement filed with the SEC in Washington, D.C. Blue sky filings. |
| April 15— April 30 | Comments received from the SEC. |
| April 15— April 20** | Preparation and printing of first amendment to registration statement. |
| April 21** | Filing of first amendment to registration statement. |
| April 25** | Signing of Underwriting Agreement and Agreement Among Underwriters. |
| | Filing of pricing amendment together with request for acceleration. |
| | Registration statement declared effective. |
| May 2** | Closing. |

\* Blue sky laws are state laws governing the offer and sale of securities. Such laws usually require registration of those dealing in securities, or registration of the security itself, or both, absent an applicable exemption. Counsel for the underwriter traditionally prepares the blue sky survey.

\** Such dating assumes that comments were received from the SEC on April 15. Appropriate modifications will be required if the comments were received at a later date.

FIGURE 22.1  SAMPLE TIME SCHEDULE FOR A PUBLIC OFFERING

## REGISTRATION FORMS

### Primary Uses

The registration form used by an issuer for a particular offering depends primarily on the nature of the issuer as well as on the purpose of the offering. As previously noted, Form S-1 is the form most frequently used by industrial and commercial companies registering securities. Other frequently used registration forms are summarized below:

- *Form S-2* is used to register shares of stock of commercial or industrial corporations that are in the developmental stage.
- *Form S-7* is used to register the securities of reporting companies that meet certain conditions. (See discussion below.)
- *Form S-8* is used for the registration of securities offered in connection with certain employee benefit and stock option plans.
- *Form S-10* is used for the registration of oil or gas interests or rights.
- *Form S-11* is used for the registration of securities of certain real estate companies.
- *Form S-14* is used for the registration of securities issued in certain business combination transactions, such as mergers, consolidations, or reclassifications, and for the reoffering of securities acquired in such transactions.
- *Form S-15* is used for the same type of transactions as Form S-14 except for reofferings of securities. It is a short form.
- *Form S-16* is used to register the securities of issuers that are eligible to use Form S-7 provided the securities are offered in connection with specified transactions. (See discussion below.)
- *Form S-18* is used to register the securities of nonreporting companies that are to be sold for cash for an aggregate offering price not to exceed $5 million.

### Short-Form Registration Statements

Forms S-7 and S-16 are short-form registration statements available for the registration of securities under the Securities Act.[13] Since the short-form registration statements are simpler than Form S-1, the time and expense of preparing the statements are considerably reduced. In addition, the short-form statements are usually examined and declared effective more quickly by the SEC staff.

Form S-7 may be used by issuers meeting certain conditions, as well as by selling shareholders of such issuers, regardless of the security offered or the nature of the offering. Form S-16 may be used to register the securities of companies eligible to

---

[13] Another short-form registration statement, Form S-18, is discussed later in this chapter. The new short-form registration statement Form S-15 is not covered because it is used only for business combinations.

use Form S-7, provided the securities are offered in certain specified transactions. In addition, Form S-16 may be used to register the securities of certain management investment companies. Both forms allow the registrant to omit some of the detailed information required in a Form S-1 or to incorporate by reference certain information previously filed with the SEC.

The following conditions must be satisfied before a registrant may use Form S-7:

1. The registrant must be a domestic corporation subject to, and in compliance with, certain reporting requirements of the Exchange Act for a 36-month period (with timely filing of all reports during the preceding 12 months), and if subject only to the requirements of Section 15(d), the registrant must have sent an annual report to its security holders within the preceding year.

2. The registrant and its subsidiaries must not have defaulted in the payment of certain obligations during the preceding 36 months.

3. The registrant must have had consolidated net income before extraordinary items of at least $250,000 for three of the last four fiscal years, including the most recent fiscal year.

Form S-7 may also be used to register the securities of a majority-owned subsidiary that are guaranteed by the parent as to principal and interest if the parent meets the conditions set forth above, even though the subsidiary issuer may not.

Form S-16 may be used for the registration of securities in the following transactions if the issuer is eligible to use Form S-7 at the time the registration statement is filed:

1. The offering of debt or equity securities for cash by or on behalf of the issuer if certain conditions concerning the market value of the voting stock of the issuer or its parent are met;

2. The registration of securities to be offered upon the conversion of outstanding convertible securities or upon the exercise of outstanding transferable warrants if (a) no commissions are paid for soliciting the conversion or exercise or (b) certain conditions concerning the market value of the voting stock of the issuer or its parent are met;

3. The registration of securities to be offered upon the exercise of outstanding rights that were granted on a pro rata basis to security holders;

4. The registration of securities to be offered to the issuer's existing security holders pursuant to a dividend or interest reinvestment plan that meets certain conditions; and

5. Transactions involving secondary offerings (i.e., for the account of a person other than the issuer) if securities of the same class are registered on a national securities exchange or are quoted on the automated quotation system of a national securities association.

In addition, Form S-16 may be used to register the securities of certain closed-end management investment companies in specified transactions.

## SMALL ISSUES AND THE SECURITIES ACT

The SEC has the power (under Section 3(b) of the Securities Act) to exempt certain small public offerings from the registration provisions of Section 5 if the Commission finds (1) that registration is not necessary in the public interest and (2) that the aggregate amount of the offering does not exceed $5 million. In accordance with this authority, the SEC has adopted various exemptions, the most significant of which are Regulation A, Rule 240, and Rule 242.

The Commission has also adopted a new simplified registration form, Form S-18, now available for the registration of the securities of nonreporting issuers, to further help small businesses obtain needed capital.

### Regulation A

Regulation A, a collection of Rules 251 through 264, permits qualified issuers, as described in Rule 252, to obtain up to $1.5 million in any one year from a public offering of its securities without registration, provided specified conditions are met. Among other things, a notification on Form 1-A and an offering circular must be filed with the Commission at least ten days prior to the initial offering or sale of the securities. The offering circular is a document similar to a prospectus that supplies basic information about the issuer and the securities to be offered. The requirements governing the delivery of the offering circular to purchasers and prospective purchasers are set forth in Rule 256. No offering circular is required in connection with certain offerings of securities if the aggregate offering price is less than $100,000 and the conditions of Rule 257 are satisfied.

Regulation A has recently been amended to provide for the distribution of a preliminary offering circular as soon as Form 1-A is filed with the commission. Rule 256(i) limits such distribution to certain offerings that are to be sold through underwriters who are registered as broker-dealers under the Exchange Act. In other cases, no securities may be offered for sale under Regulation A until ten days after the filing of the notification.

A balance sheet, as well as statements of income, source and application of funds, and other stockholders' equity, must be included in the offering circular. These statements need not be audited unless the issuer is otherwise required to file audited statements with the Commission. In such a case, audited financial statements for the issuer's latest fiscal year are required. The financial statements must be prepared in accordance with generally accepted accounting principles, but compliance with Regulation S-X is not required with respect to unaudited statements. Reports of sale must be filed with the Commission in accordance with Rule 260.

### Rule 240

Rule 240 exempts from registration limited offers and sales of securities by small, closely held issuers. The following conditions must be satisfied in order to obtain this exemption:

1. The securities may not be offered or sold by any means of general advertising or general solicitation.
2. No commission or similar remuneration may be paid for the solicitation of prospective buyers or in connection with sales of securities.
3. The aggregate sales price of all sales of securities of the issuer and its affiliates made in reliance on the rule or otherwise without registration under the Securities Act within the preceding twelve months may not exceed $100,000.
4. Both immediately before and after any transaction made in reliance on the rule, securities issued by the issuer and its affiliates may not be beneficially owned by more than 100 persons.
5. The issuer must exercise reasonable care to assure that the purchasers are acquiring the securities for their own account.
6. With a certain exception for an initial offering under Rule 240, a notice of sale must be filed with the Commission within ten days after the close of the first month in which a sale in reliance on the rule is made.

Rule 240 exempts only the transactions in which the securities are offered or sold by the issuer, not the securities themselves. Thus, securities acquired in a transaction effected in reliance on the rule are unregistered securities and cannot be resold without registration under the Securities Act or under a specified exemption.

## Rule 242

In response to criticisms concerning Rule 240's limited availability to and use by small issuers, the Commission has approved Rule 242, which is designed "to help certain corporate issuers raise limited amounts of capital from the public by providing objective requirements which are less burdensome than those found in other exemptions from registration under different sections of the Act."[14]

Rule 242 permits qualified issuers, such as domestic or Canadian corporate issuers that are not (1) investment companies, (2) engaged in oil, gas, or mining operations, or (3) majority-owned subsidiaries of nonqualified issuers to offer and sell up to $2 million per issue of their securities in any six-month period to an unlimited number of accredited persons and to thirty-five other purchasers. In computing the $2 million ceiling, the proceeds, from all securities sold pursuant to any Section 3(b) exemption during the preceding six-month period would be included. The term *accredited person* includes certain institutions (e.g. banks and insurance companies) and persons purchasing $100,000 or more of the securities. Paragraph (f) of the rule gives the requirements for furnishing information to purchasers during the transaction. The rule does not specify the information that must be supplied by the issuer if only accredited persons are purchasers. If the purchasers include non-accredited purchasers, information must be provided similar to that required for a Form S-18 prospectus. Paragraph (d) of the rule prevents the offer or sale of

---

[14] Securities Act Release No. 33-6121, 1 CCH ¶ 2358F (September 11, 1979).

securities by means of general advertisement or solicitation. In addition, the issuer is required to file notices of sale with the Commission according to paragraph (h) of the rule.

Securities acquired pursuant to the proposed rule cannot be resold without registration under the Securities Act or an applicable exemption. As in the case of a Rule 240 exemption, the issuer is required to exercise reasonable care to assure that the purchasers are acquiring the securities for their own account.

## Form S-18 Registration Statement

Form S-18 is a simplified form of registration statement that is available to nonreporting companies seeking to raise no more than $5 million in capital. A synopsis of the availability of the form as well as the substantive content of a Form S-18 registration statement follows:

1. *Use of the form.* Form S-18 may be used to register the securities of domestic or Canadian corporate issuers that are not reporting companies, provided the securities are sold for cash by the issuer or for the account of security holders.

2. *Exclusions.* Corporations offering limited partnership interests; investment companies; corporations engaged in certain oil, gas, or mining operations; certain insurance companies; and majority-owned subsidiaries of an issuer if the parent does not meet the qualifications for use of the form may not use the form.

3. *Limitation of amount.* Aggregate offering price may not be more than $5 million. Up to $1.5 million of this amount may be used for sales by security holders. In computing the $5 million ceiling, the offering price of all securities of the issuer and certain predecessors sold within the preceding year (a) in violation of Section 5 of the Securities Act or (b) pursuant to a Form S-18 registration statement must be included.

4. *Format.* Generally, the format is the same as Form S-1. The rules contained in Regulation C, as well as the disclosure requirements of the Guides, are applicable to Form S-18 filings.

5. *Disclosure.* Form S-18 calls for less extensive narrative disclosure than Form S-1; however, the items included in Form S-18 are generally consistent with the corresponding items in Form S-1. Unlike Form S-1, Form S-18 does not specifically incorporate by reference the disclosure requirements of Regulation S-K.

6. *Financial statements.* Form S-18 requires (a) a consolidated balance sheet as of a date within 90 days prior to the date of filing the registration statement (it need not be audited if an audited balance sheet as of a date within one year is also filed) and (b) consolidated statements of income, changes in financial position, and other stockholders' equity for the two fiscal years preceding the date of the most recent balance sheet being filed. Such statements must be audited to the date of the most recent audited balance sheet being filed. Statements for interim periods may also be required in accordance with Item 15 of the form. Appropriate financial statements are also required with respect to certain acquisitions. It is important that Form S-18 financial statements be prepared only in accordance with generally accepted accounting principles. Regulation S-X is inapplicable to such statements

except to the extent that it relates to the report of the independent accountants. Thus, since much supplementary financial information and the supporting schedules may be omitted, the time and expense of preparing the statements are considerably reduced.

## SUGGESTED READING

Bloomenthal, Harold S. *Securities and Federal Corporate Law*. Rev. ed. New York: Clark Boardman Company, Ltd., 1978.

Castruccio, Louis M., and Hentrich, John J. "Developments in Federal Securities Regulation—1978." *Business Lawyer*, Vol. 34 (April, 1979), p. 1159.

Jennings, Richard W., and Marsh, Harold. *Securities Regulation, Cases and Materials*. 4th ed. New York: Foundation Press, 1977.

Robinson, Gerald J., and Eppler, Klaus. *Going Public*. Rev. ed. New York: Clark Boardman Company, Ltd., 1978.

Sargent, James C. "The Federal Securities Laws and Small Business." *Business Lawyer*, Vol. 33 (January, 1978), p. 901.

Soderquist, Larry D. "Due Diligence Examinations." *Practical Lawyer*, Vol. 24 (March 1, 1978), p. 33.

Weinstein, Stanley, Schechtman, Daniel, and Walker, Michael. *SEC Compliance—Financial Reporting and Forms*. Englewood Cliffs, N.J.: Prentice-Hall, 1977.

## APPENDIX 22-1 CHECKLIST OF SUBSTANTIVE DISCLOSURE REQUIRED IN FORM S-1

I. INFORMATION CONCERNING THE REGISTRANT AND ITS BUSINESS
   1. *General Information*
      - Organization of registrant
      - Information concerning any parents of registrant and the basis of control
      - Information concerning transactions with promoters (if registrant was organized within past five years)
   2. *Five-Year Description of Business* (Regulation S-K—Item 1)
      - Information relating to the business of registrant generally
      - Plan of operations for approximately one year (for certain new registrants)
      - Financial information relating to industry segments, including revenues, operating profit or loss, and identifiable assets attributable to each segment

- Narrative description of the business by industry segment (includes discussion of ten separate items for each reportable segment if material to an understanding of the business taken as a whole)
- Special disclosure requirements concerning research and development expenditures, significant customers, effects of compliance with environmental regulations, and number of persons employed
- Financial information relating to foreign and domestic operations and export sales (by geographic area)

3. *Selected Financial Data* (Regulation S–K—Item 10) (for each of the last five fiscal years)
   - Net sales or operating revenues
   - Income (loss) from continuing operations
   - Income (loss) from continuing operations per common share
   - Total assets
   - Long-term obligations and redeemable preferred stock (including capital leases and preferred stock defined in ASR 268)
   - Cash dividends declared per common share
   - Five-year summary information in accordance with SFAS No. 33.

4. *Capitalization*
   - Information concerning the capital structure of registrant and certain subsidiaries set forth in tabular form
   - Information includes title of each class of securities, amounts authorized, amounts outstanding, and amounts to be outstanding on completion of the offering

5. *Description of Property* (Regulation S-K—Item 2)
   - Includes statement of location and general character of material properties and the industry segments using them
   - Additional information required with respect to oil and gas operations and extractive enterprises

6. *Material Pending Legal Proceedings* (Regulation S-K—Item 3)
   - Description required if registrant or its subsidiaries are parties or if their property is the subject of the proceedings

- No description required if routine
  litigation incidental to the business
  or if damages claimed do not exceed
  ten percent of consolidated current assets
- Description required with respect to
  proceedings known to be contemplated
  by governmental authorities
- Special disclosure requirements for
  bankruptcy, receivership, proceedings
  involving certain parties, and proceedings involving environmental law
  violations

7. *Miscellaneous Information*
   - Certain funds, trusts, or accounts for assets
     of employee benefit plans required to dis-
     close brokerage placement policies

II. INFORMATION CONCERNING MANAGEMENT, SECURITY OWNERSHIP,
    AND CERTAIN TRANSACTIONS

1. *Background of Management and Nominees* (Regulation S-K—Item 20)
   - Name, age, position, term of office,
     arrangements made concerning position,
     and five-year business history
   - Family relationships with other mem-
     bers of management
   - Other directorships of directors and
     nominees in certain companies
   - Involvement in specified legal proceed-
     ings during past five years

2. *Remuneration of Specified Officers and Directors* (Regulation S-K—Item 21)
   - Disclosure required for five most highly
     compensated (if remuneration exceeds
     $50,000) and for all officers and direc-
     tors as a group
   - Cash remuneration, cash-equivalent forms
     of remuneration (including "perquisites"),
     and contingent forms of remuneration
     separately set forth in tabular form[15]
   - Description of proposed remuneration
     to be made under existing plans or
     arrangements
   - Directors' fees and other such ar-
     rangements

---

[15] See Regulation S-K, Item 4; Securities Act Release No. 33-5856, 2 CCH ¶ 23,019 (August 18, 1977); Securities Act Release No. 33-5904, 2 CCH ¶ 23,019A (February 6, 1978); and Securities Act Release No. 33-6027, 2 CCH ¶ 23,019B (February 22, 1979).

- Information as to stock options
  granted, exercised, or held unexercised

3. *Security Ownership* (Regulation S-K—Item 31)
   - Specified disclosure required concerning selling shareholders and beneficial owners or voting trustees of more than 5 percent of any class of registrant's voting securities
   - Security ownership of management
   - Arrangements that may result in a change in control of registrant

4. *Certain Transactions*
   - Disclosure required concerning indebtedness of certain insiders to registrant or its subsidiaries
   - Description of material interests of certain insiders, significant shareholders, and certain family members of the foregoing in transactions with the registrant, its subsidiaries, or certain pension or similar plans

III. INFORMATION CONCERNING THE OFFERING
   - Table setting forth distribution spread, i.e., price to the public, payments to underwriters, and proceeds to registrant
   - Disclosure required concerning the manner in which the securities are to be offered
   - Information concerning underwriters and dealers involved in the offering.
   - Disclosure of principal uses of proceeds of the offering
   - Appropriate disclosure required if securities are offered otherwise than for cash

IV. INFORMATION CONCERNING THE SECURITIES BEING REGISTERED
   - Separate items in Form S-1 specify the information to be furnished if (a) capital stock is being registered (Item 13); (b) long-term debt is being registered (Item 14); or (c) other securities are being registered (Item 15)
   - Information required concerning trading markets, market prices, and registrant's dividend policy

# 23

# Cash Management

*Leslie N. Masonson*

## INTRODUCTION

Cash management has become a subject of increasing importance to the small-to-medium-sized corporation. Although cash management has traditionally been the responsibility of the treasurer, its responsibility within the corporation now varies with the company's historical development, the industry norm, and the company size. In the small-to-medium-sized company, these functions are often handled by the controller. In all cases, the methods and techniques used to manage cash are similar, although the level of sophistication varies greatly on a company-to-company basis.

In the last decade the cyclical nature of the economy has been more pronounced compared to previous times. This has resulted in prolonged periods of tight money, increased rates of inflation, high short-term interest rates, and increased borrowing costs. To meet this ever-changing environment and counteract these influences, it is essential that the controller use the most appropriate techniques to maximize his most precious resource—cash. This chapter reviews those cash management techniques that can be applied by the controller to accelerate collection of receivables, control disbursements, concentrate cash, and measure the effectiveness of his present system.

Evidence of increased awareness of cash management is illustrated by the declining long-term trend in corporate liquidity over the past three decades. Corporations are utilizing cash more efficiently for many day-to-day and long-term functions, resulting in less cash being shown on the corporate balance sheet. Corporate liquidity measured by demand deposits and currency as a percentage of total financial assets of nonfinancial businesses declined from 29 percent in 1946 to 7.8 percent in 1978.[1] There are still a few innovative large companies (over $1 billion in sales) that are so cash-rich that they are constantly on the lookout for ways to invest productively, such as mergers, acquisitions, and open market purchase of their own stock. On the other hand, the middle-market companies with sales of $5 million to $100 million, not being so fortunate, must use every resource available to run their treasury operations efficiently at minimal cost.

Cash management techniques have been refined and expanded at an ever-increasing pace during the past decade. Emphasis has shifted from the basic collection and disbursement mechanics to the electronic capture of transactional information and the initiation of funds movements through terminals in the controller's office. The degree of cash management sophistication needed by a particular company depends on a number of factors, including the daily magnitude of the cash flow, staff allocations, the existing system's efficiency and internal cost, projected future needs (expanding sales, new acquisitions), corporate objectives, and short-term investment policies. Therefore, an ongoing evaluation by the controller of his existing cash management system is vitally important if he is to continue to maximize his cash flows.

## COLLECTION ACCELERATION

The controller can improve accounts receivable cash flow by designing a system that shortens the processing cycle that occurs from the date a customer orders goods

---

[1] Board of Governors of the Federal Reserve System, Flow of Funds Section.

to the date the invoice is generated and mailed to the date the customer's funds become available for use in the corporate bank account.

### Invoice Preparation

The first step in this process is the preparation and mailing of customer invoices. When this step is delayed, the entire processing stream is slowed. From the cash management standpoint, time lost is money lost. For example, collecting $1 million in receivables one day earlier is equivalent to earning $278 daily (assuming overnight money at a per annum rate of 10 percent). The long-term benefits of redesigning and automating the invoice preparation function will in most cases far exceed the initial cost of setting up the system.

**Advantages of Centralization.** Depending on the corporation's industry and organizational structure, the invoicing function is either centralized or decentralized. The ideal situation is to centralize this function, if practical, so that it receives attention from the corporate perspective. In a centralized system, invoices for all the company's divisions are prepared and mailed from corporate headquarters. Each division independently forwards its invoice detail directly to headquarters for processing by a specific cutoff date.

**Use of Automation.** Through specially designed packages available from software vendors, many corporations have automated their invoicing system by using separate minicomputers or by tying such computers directly into their company's mainframe computer system. The importance of computers should not be overlooked when efforts are made to reduce the clerical burden and improve the quality, efficiency, and timeliness of this important function. Reports obtainable from such a system would normally include a monthly or weekly aging of receivables and account status, as well as provide statements and invoices. In addition, up-to-date management information reports for the controller, such as a trend analysis of receivable aging, can be generated as a by-product.

The benefits of automating the receivable invoicing function include:

- Timely invoice mailing;
- Up-to-date reports on open items and delinquent accounts;
- Reduced customer inquiry lookup time; and
- Minimized clerical costs.

### Lock Box Processing

The *lock box system* was one of the first collection techniques used to accelerate receivables, and was developed by an RCA executive in 1947. His recommendation to use a post office box (lock box) to collect large dollar remittances was then pursued and refined by two banks. The objective of a lock box is to minimize mail and processing time so that checks are converted into available funds more rapidly.

*Funds availability,* in banking terminology, refers to the length of time before deposited funds become usable by the corporation. Presently, funds are available the same day (*immediately available funds*) or in one or two days, depending on where the check is drawn and the assigned availability schedule of the depositor's bank. A bank's availability schedule indicates the number (0, 1, or 2) of days applied to each check deposited. For example, a check drawn on a Chicago money center bank deposited in a New York City money center bank by that bank's cutoff time is available in one day, whereas if it were drawn on a Cicero, Illinois, bank it would be available in two days.

Another term to understand is *collectibility,* which is the time required for a check to be presented, examined, and accepted by the drawee bank or returned to the sending bank for any number of reasons (lack of endorsement, missing signature, forgery). Collectibility normally ranges from two to five days, depending on the geographical location and travel time to the drawee bank. As far as money management is concerned, availability is the more important factor, since available funds are transferable and investable today.

Lock box operations tend to be labor intensive and volume- and pressure-oriented. The corporation, through an authorization letter to the postmaster, permits a designated bank to extract mail from the corporation's box around the clock. The bank is able to process these remittances for entry into the check-processing stream much earlier than if they were directed to company headquarters. In essence, the bank is able to speed the conversion of funds into available funds in the corporate demand deposit accounts as well as handle the processing details for the corporation. Companies with a large volume of receipts for small dollars (*retail lock box*) or with a small number of checks for large dollars (*wholesale lock box*) could potentially benefit from this collection technique.

**Types of Lock Box Plans.** Lock box plans vary in complexity as well as cost. The three most common variants are the *photocopy, envelope,* and *report plans.* Each of these plans has numerous options within it.

*Photocopy plan.* The most common type of lock box arrangement is the photocopy plan. Under this plan the bank is instructed by a signed agreement with the corporation to deposit the remittances in the corporate account, photocopy the front of each check, and send it with the invoice and the envelope to the corporation by express mail, courier, or regular mail. On receipt, the corporation updates its accounts receivable file. A typical cost nationally for supplying this service is approximately $.25 an item, with a $30 flat charge per month. (These charges are in addition to the regular deposit account charges, deposit notification, and transfer costs.)

*Envelope plan.* A less costly alternative is the envelope plan. Here the bank records the check amount directly on the envelope without producing a photocopy and forwards the envelopes to the company. This service costs approximately $.20 per item, with a flat charge similar to that of the photocopy plan.

*Report plan.* The report plan is a more expensive plan in which typewritten or computer reports are generated based on the corporation's information requirements. The report usually includes customer name, address, check number, invoice number, postmark date, and dollar amount. The costs of this plan vary with the services provided.

*Optional services.* Some corporations require additional information to that supplied by the standard reports. The complexity of the optional services determines the cost of each plan. For example, some of the more commonly requested options are check number sequencing, photocopy of back of check, extra tape listing, additional photocopy, alphabetizing checks, check sorting by city or state or invoice number, time stamping, and substitute invoice preparation.

**Selecting a Lock Box Bank.** In essence, a controller can usually customize his lock box plan to meet his company's specific requirements at a cost lower than that of performing this activity at corporate headquarters. In determining the cost benefit of performing this function internally versus having the bank do the processing, it can be assumed that internal costs would normally include staff salaries and benefits, equipment purchase or rental, rent, courier service to bank, and supplies. Moreover, using a credit line bank that permits compensating balances to cover both credit and deposit services simultaneously should not be overlooked.

Most large banks have separate operating departments that specialize in handling lock box deposits. They have the equipment, personnel, and expertise to move thousands of checks per hour through the various processing steps, including preparing them for entry into their check-processing department for crediting to the corporate account. Banks expect this service to expand and have been researching methods and equipment that will improve their clerical productivity and at the same time maintain high-quality standards. Controllers should keep abreast of the automation efforts of the banking industry, since future innovations will affect their future costs and service quality.

In selecting a lock box bank, cost is just one factor a controller should consider. Other major considerations are:

- Present bank relationships, credit requirements, and compensating balance requirements;
- Bank's operational reputation in the industry;
- Professional staff (years experience, turnover ratio);
- Up-to-date processing methods and equipment (Optical Character Recognition readers, minicomputers, video capture);
- Quality-control checkpoints (low error rates);
- Competitive availability schedules;
- Extensive direct-send schedules (checks sent via courier to the drawee banks for more rapid availability);
- Timely problem resolution;
- Frequent post office pickups;

- Weekend processing;
- Unique zip code (a post office box solely for lock box mail); and
- Customer references (a recent list of dissatisfied customers as well).

To compare the lock box capabilities of various banks, most corporations send candidate banks a detailed questionnaire (Appendix 23-1) covering all the above items. After evaluating the banks on the basis of the questionnaire, the next step would be to personally visit the top-ranking banks, if possible. A tour of their lock box, check-processing, and computer departments during prime hours should provide adequate opportunity to view the bank's capabilities under time constraints. The viewpoint of an operations or systems-oriented person from the company is helpful in assessing the bank's operational systems. Direct and pointed questioning concerning the bank's lock box processing will elicit useful information regarding the bank's capabilities. (The methodology for selecting optimal lock box locations is reviewed later under Accounts Receivable Study.)

**Benefits of Lock Box Operation.** Benefits obtainable from a lock box network usually include:

- Reduction in mail-processing time;
- Increased and earlier availability of funds;
- Lower cost (staff expense) of processing mail; and
- More productive use of internal clerical time.

## Data Transmission

Banks began using data transmission because of the corporate requirement that lock box processing not slow the capture of accounts receivable data. Basically, the bank key-enters lock box data (invoice and account number and dollar amount) on magnetic tape or a computer disc pack for scheduled electronic tape (data) transmission via telephone lines directly to the corporation's tape unit.

Data transmission is used by companies that have developed an automated accounts receivable updating system. After the tape transmission is received, the data is applied automatically against the accounts receivable file to record the changes from that day's activity. In addition to the invoice number(s) and dollar amount(s), some corporations also capture the customer's checking account number and his bank's transit-routing number from the magnetic ink characters on the bottom of the check. By incorporating this additional data, a corporation is able to improve its matching against open items. However, this might require expanded computer memory and frequent updating when a customer changes his drawee banks.

**In-House Versus Outside Vendors.** The controller can build an automated accounts receivable system in-house with assistance from his systems staff, or he can purchase a software package from outside vendors. In the latter case, the controller should carefully review the capabilities of the package to assure that the product meets all his operational and accounting requirements. Since most packages are not flexible, and could require major modifications, the assistance of an in-house systems analyst and computer specialist in selecting the right package is beneficial. Again, the use of a cost-benefit analysis to determine whether the system should be developed in-house or outside is an important step in this decision-making process. (See Chapter 11.)

**Benefits.** The benefits of data transmission coupled with an automated accounts receivable system are:

- Rapid application of receipts to the accounts receivable file;
- Minimum in-house clerical activity;
- Fewer customer complaints; and
- Automatic handling of matching receipts to open items.

### Deposit Reporting

In order to manage corporate funds efficiently, the controller should monitor the daily dollar amount of deposits from all receiving locations, including lock box banks, regional offices, stores, and plants. To meet this informational need, large money center banks, regional banks, and third-party vendors (National Data Corporation, RAAM Information Services, Automatic Data Processing, Interactive Data, and General Electric, among others) have developed *deposit-reporting systems*. In some cases, corporations have developed an in-house capability to perform this function.

The purpose of this system is to consolidate daily the deposit activity of all corporate entities for reporting to the controller early the next morning. The typical scenario is for each corporate location to call a toll-free number at the close of business and report the dollar amount of deposits at the local bank. The caller identifies himself by giving a user ID number, the location code, and the dollar amount of the deposit. In turn, the operator gives the caller a verification number (some vendors incorporate the dollar value of the deposit in this number for quality-control purposes). After that day's call-in deadline has passed, any reported information is consolidated with the following business day's totals. A typical report is shown in Figure 23.1.

Many corporations have this deposit detail electronically transmitted to one or more of their concentration banks, where DTCs (depository transfer checks drawn on each local bank in the exact amount of the reported deposit at that individual bank) are prepared automatically and deposited. (This low-cost method of funds consolidation works very well, especially if there are many reporting locations with low dollar deposits. A more detailed explanation of the DTC is explained later in this chapter under Funds Concentration and Control.)

ACME MANUFACTURING CO.

DAILY DEPOSITS TO BANK OF UNITED STATES FOR JANUARY 22, 1980

| | UNIT NO. | DEPOSITS VER. REPORTED | NMBR | DATE | TIME | OP ID | XMIT TIME |
|---|---|---|---|---|---|---|---|
| **NORTHEAST REGION** | | | | | | | |
| BOSTON MA | 1010 | 1,234.56 | 1721 | 01/22 | 1519 | AB | 19 |
| HARTFORD CT | 1020 | 12,456.21 | 2928 | 01/22 | 1750 | CD | 19 |
| NEW YORK NY | 1030 | 3,265.26 | 3431 | 01/22 | 1103 | GH | 12 |
| NEW YORK NY | 1030 | 4,208.49 | 1602 | 01/22 | 1103 | GH | 12 |
| NEWARK NJ | 1040 | 18,462.01 | 0188 | 01/22 | 1652 | IJ | 19 |
| TRENTON NJ | 1050 | 2,468.02 | 0921 | 01/22 | 1255 | KL | 15 |
| SUB-TOTAL | | $42,094.55 | | | | | |
| **MID-ATLANTIC REGION** | | | | | | | |
| DOVER DE | 2044 | 22,345.66 | 3328 | 01/22 | 0935 | GH | 12 |
| WASHINGTON DC | 2142 | 118,096.12 | 8684 | 01/22 | 0925 | LK | 12 |
| TOWSON MD | 2145 | 1,096.18 | 0772 | 01/22 | 1010 | KL | 12 |
| ROANOKE VA | 2160 | *10,009.50* | 0848 | 01/22 | 1515 | DR | ** |
| CHANGED TO | 2160 | 10,900.50 | 1828 | 01/22 | 1516 | DR | 19 |
| CHARLESTOWN VW | 2205 | 3,285.12 | 3165 | 01/22 | 0905 | DW | 12 |
| SUB-TOTAL | | $155,723.58 | | | | | |
| **SOUTHERN REGION** | | | | | | | |
| RALEIGH NC | 3150 | 111,305.29 | 2064 | 01/22 | 1033 | KH | 12 |
| COLUMBUS SC | 3160 | 14,702.09 | 3182 | 01/22 | 1528 | LM | 19 |
| ATLANTA GA | 3205 | 1,382.06 | 1788 | 01/22 | 1425 | GR | 15 |
| JACKSONVILLE FL | 3306 | 3,123.09 | 1694 | 01/22 | 1058 | SR | 12 |
| MIAMI FL | 3310 | 19,382.06 | 0105 | 01/22 | 1652 | KP | 19 |
| MONTGOMERY AL | 3500 | 29,353.09 | 1680 | 01/22 | 1212 | JR | 15 |
| SUB-TOTAL | | $179,247.68 | | | | | |
| **NORTH CENTRAL REGION** | | | | | | | |
| INDIANAPOLIS IN | 4200 | 16,879.43 | 3112 | 01/22 | 1030 | AR | 12 |
| CINCINNATI OH | 4225 | 19,802.65 | 7503 | 01/22 | 1150 | SD | 12 |
| LEXINGTON KY | 4250 | 20,888.06 | 8905 | 01/22 | 0830 | ER | 12 |
| SUB-TOTAL | | $57,570.14 | | | | | |

| | UNIT NO. | DEPOSITS VER. REPORTED | NMBR | DATE | TIME | OP ID | XMIT TIME |
|---|---|---|---|---|---|---|---|
| **NORTH CENTRAL REGION CON'D** | | | | | | | |
| CHICAGO IL | 4300 | 105,689.63 | 1032 | 01/21 | 0905 | WE | 12 |
| SPRINGFIELD IL | 4310 | 29,038.65 | 4362 | 01/22 | 1002 | DF | 12 |
| DUBUQUE IA | 4400 | 9,023.02 | 6390 | 01/22 | 0831 | RF | 12 |
| LINCOLN NB | 4500 | 28,623.39 | 6390 | 01/22 | 1120 | EW | 12 |
| SUB-TOTAL | | $229,944.83 | | | | | |
| **SOUTH CENTRAL REGION** | | | | | | | |
| BATON ROUGE LA | 5016 | 16,289.58 | 8260 | 01/21 | 1920 | JK | 09 |
| NEW ORLEANS LA | 5257 | 19,386.50 | 0199 | 01/22 | 1650 | LM | 19 |
| LITTLE ROCK AR | 5300 | 29,832.65 | 1682 | 01/22 | 1339 | OP | 15 |
| NASHVILLE TN | 5310 | 69,838.42 | 1012 | 01/22 | 1733 | RS | 19 |
| JACKSON MS | 5402 | 14,263.39 | 5383 | 01/22 | 0930 | ST | 12 |
| NORMAN OK | 5501 | 17,129.65 | 1387 | 01/22 | 1658 | AR | 19 |
| SUB-TOTAL | | $166,740.19 | | | | | |
| **LOCK BOX BANKS** | | | | | | | |
| FIRST OF CHICAGO | 9901 | 28,695.20 | 8765 | 01/22 | 1250 | AB | 12 |
| CHEMICAL BANK | 0201 | 16,893.58 | 1044 | 01/22 | 1733 | AR | 19 |
| FIRST OF ST. PAUL | 0502 | 17,129.63 | 4422 | 01/22 | 0930 | ST | 12 |
| BANK OF U.S. | 0106 | 14,838.65 | 1082 | 01/22 | 1610 | RS | 19 |
| SUB-TOTAL | | $77,557.06 | | | | | |

Source: Printed with permission RAAM Information Systems.

FIGURE 23.1 TYPICAL DEPOSIT REPORT

## Preauthorized Transactions

The use of *preauthorized debit transactions* is another method by which the controller can speed the dollar flow from receivables into the corporate account. In certain industries, the repetitive fixed payment can be adapted to automatic debiting of the customer's account on a periodic basis either through a preauthorized check or an electronic debit to his checking account. This technique is practical for such industries as insurance (life and medical), banking and finance companies (mortgage and car payments), utilities (budget plan and telephone charges), and cable television companies (fixed monthly payments). In simplified terms, the customer agrees in writing to permit the company to debit his account on a specified recurring date either with a check drawn against it or an electronic debit. The company notifies the appropriate bank to accept such transactions with the usual proviso that the company is responsible for any check or electronic presentment problems.

**Benefits.** The controller's benefits from using preauthorized transactions are:

- Reduction of mail and processing float;
- Elimination of invoice preparation and postage cost; and
- Accurate information on the amount of funds collected.

The consumer eliminates check preparation and postage charges but gives up control of the timing of his payment. To make preauthorized transactions more attractive to customers, some corporations decrease the payment amount if this arrangement is used.

## Automated Clearing House

As electronic funds transfer systems develop larger and larger user bases, the volume of preauthorized electronic transactions such as the applications mentioned earlier will increase substantially. The automated clearing house (ACH) is basically a computerized network for processing electronic debits and credits between banks for its customers through the Federal Reserve system. Paper checks are not used in this application; instead, payment information is recorded on magnetic tape and electronically transmitted from the originating financial institution to its local ACH to the receiving bank's ACH to the receiving financial institution. The ACH network, which consists of thirty-two interconnected regional ACHs in forty-eight states, is currently used by the U.S. government for social security and civil service retirement payments, by consumers for payment of mortgage loans and insurance payments, and by many companies for such uses as direct deposit of payroll across the country to employees. Presently, about 10,360 banks and 2,700 thrift institutions are ACH members, and 10,400 companies originate items through them.[2]

---

[2] National Automated Clearinghouse Association, *Sure Pay Update* (August, 1980).

The controller could consider using the ACH for issuing payroll to widely dispersed employees, paying dividends to shareholders, and arranging preauthorized electronic bill payments to his company if there are many recurrent payments. Of course, the controller should not overlook the fact that he is losing potential float earnings by using this technique for dividends or payroll. However, as commercial banks continually increase their check-processing charges, the time will come when the ACH per-item cost and the float earnings loss will be equal to or less than these check charges. At that point the ACH volume will expand significantly.

## PAYABLE CONTROL

Just as speeding collections is a recognized cash management tool, so is the control of disbursements. The controller should be aware of the most common methods of handling bill payments from the cash management viewpoint.

### Timing and Control

Essentially, although payments should be made as late as possible, cash discounts should be considered when the funds cannot be used more productively for other purposes. For instance, paying a $10,000 invoice with 2/10 net 30 terms within 10 days results in an actual payment of $9,800. Even investing $10,000 in a short-term money market instrument for 30 days with an average annual yield of 10 percent would only accrue $83.33 in interest. Thus, taking the discount is the preferable financial alternative in this instance, since the annual interest equivalent is 36 percent (360 days earlier/20 days = 18 × 2 percent = 36 percent).

Payments normally should not be mailed out earlier than necessary, since the disbursement account funding would be needed at an earlier date. It is a common practice for companies to mail the majority of their large payments on Wednesday through Friday to benefit by the weekend delay in mail and processing float. Studies of mail receipt time have indicated that the heaviest collection day is Monday, with Tuesday a close second.

### Disbursement Accounts and Funding Techniques

The disbursement function is handled through corporate checking accounts at selected banks. The number and type of separate accounts usually opened for trade payables, payroll, and dividends depend on whether the corporate structure is decentralized or centralized. Disbursement accounts are often set up in local banks to serve local payroll distribution. In a centralized environment, trade payable disbursement accounts are usually located in major money center or regional banks.

Corporations with a centralized and automated accounts payable system have an option to draw disbursement checks on banks in various cities. For example, West Coast vendors can be paid with checks drawn on East Coast banks and vice versa.

Usually banks located outside Federal Reserve cities are used in order to maximize the float. Through the use of a Troy check printer (a device that applies the drawee bank's transit-routing symbol and the corporation's account number in magnetic ink on the blank check), a corporation can program its computer to print drawee bank data on a check-by-check basis based on the vendor location, and thereby lengthen the presentment time of the check. Thus, the corporation is increasing float earnings without additional cost other than the Troy printer. Some companies use preprinted checks on separate print runs to accomplish the same result. Of course, the corporation must consider the reaction of the recipients (vendors), as well as its own disbursement philosophy, before implementing a cross-country disbursing system. (See Remote Disbursing for a more detailed discussion of this technique.)

**Zero Balance Accounts.** It is the controller's responsibility to determine the most feasible method of funding disbursement accounts on a daily basis. Some controllers prefer to disburse funds from and deposit funds into the same account, thus maintaining a fluctuating balance that is difficult to forecast. One popular disbursement account variation is the zero balance account (ZBA). From the controller's standpoint, it minimizes control of many disbursement accounts and keeps minimum balances in those accounts.

For example, a ZBA is opened at one bank for each division of a ten-division company. Each day the checks to be charged to each division's account are totaled. A corresponding credit equal to the exact amount of the debits is automatically transferred from the corporation's master concentration account at that bank into each ZBA that evening. Thus, at the opening of business on the next day the ledger balance in each account is zero. This is a *true ZBA* as compared to one in which a bank prepares manual entries the next morning to zero out the account. The ZBA technique pinpoints the exact dollar outflows for each division. At the same time it minimizes the division's idle funds to zero. In addition, each division can continue to handle its disbursements independently of corporate headquarters. Wire transfers or depository transfer checks are alternative funding mechanisms that can usually be used when the master concentration account is located in a different bank than the ZBAs.

*Funding by wire transfer.* When the concentration account does not reside in the same bank as the ZBA, a daily wire transfer from another bank is made to cover the funding requirement (Figure 23.2). The amount of the transfer can be based on historical disbursement check-clearing patterns. Of course, it is prudent to draw up an automatic overdraft line of credit in case the deposit account is inadvertently overdrawn on any particular day. The wire transfer technique, based on a forecast, is not the controller's most reliable funding method, but it can be used when a stable check-clearing pattern exists and the daily dollar value of the disbursements is relatively constant.

*Controlled disbursing.* A more refined method of funding disbursements or a

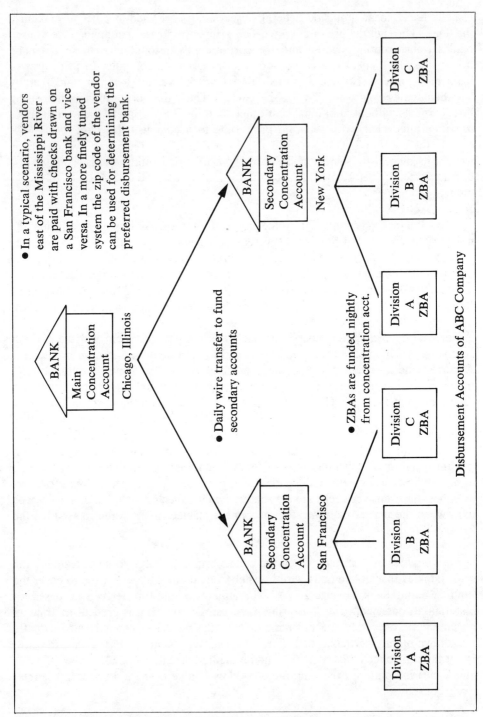

FIGURE 23.2   CROSS-COUNTRY DISBURSEMENT SYSTEM

daily basis via wire transfer is to set up *controlled disbursement accounts* with selected banks that receive only a limited number of early-morning check deliveries from their local Federal Reserve bank or branch and are willing to supply the dollar value of checks to be charged to the company account that evening. The controller can call this bank before noon and obtain the dollar amount required to fund the account by wire transfer that afternoon.

*Funding by depository transfer check.* A less popular funding alternative is to deposit daily a DTC (drawn on another bank) in the regional deposit account to cover the disbursements. Since the DTC does not represent immediately available funds on the day of deposit, the ledger balance in the account will increase, but the available balance will not. Assuming the DTC becomes available funds the next day, the bank must be compensated for the corporation's use of its available funds for one day. In most cases, the bank charges for this usage through the float calculation on the corporation's monthly account analysis statement or through the corporation's use of an overdraft line of credit. Corporations may find that banks do not choose to offer DTC funding, because it not only increases clerical requirements but raises the possibility of potential loss and unnecessary risk exposure if the corporation becomes illiquid and does not have adequate funds in the bank on which the DTC is drawn.

**Payable-Through Drafts.** The payable-through draft is another disbursing method. This check-like instrument is drawn by a corporate nonbank payor on itself and is payable through a specified bank as indicated on its face. A check and a payable-through draft are very similar in appearance. Most people are not concerned with the technical differences, as long as they receive payment when they cash them.

Basically, the bank that the draft is payable through is only needed for presentation. It verifies neither the signature nor the endorsement, nor does it debit the corporate account the evening the draft is processed through the bank. The bank sends the checks early the next morning to the corporation for approval or return by late that afternoon and only then debits its account. Therefore, the corporation using this type of instrument delays payment to its processing bank by at least one day. The bank will charge the corporation for its one-day loss of use of funds by debiting its checking account with the previous day's date (back-valuing), charging at least one day's interest expense, or charging for a float day on the corporation's account analysis statement.

*Benefits to corporations.* Corporations continue to use payable-through drafts, as evidenced by the increased dollar volume and number of drafts being issued. A 1978 survey by Greenwich Research Associates, an independent consulting firm, indicated that 44 percent of the middle-market companies use payable-through drafts.[3]

---

[3] Payment Systems, Inc., *PSI Payment Systems Newsletter,* Vol. 11, No. 8 (September, 1979), p. 3.

The most common corporate uses for these instruments are settling insurance claims by field agents, paying accounts payable, paying employees at geographically diverse locations, reimbursing salesmen for travel expenses, paying for freight, and paying dividends to shareholders. Generally, one of the main advantages of this instrument is that the corporation retains the final word as to its acceptability, since it is drawn on itself. For example, the firm can check the validity of an insurance claim settlement by the field agent before agreeing to have its account debited.

Although banks are not particularly interested in offering payable-through drafts to their customers because of potential float loss, settlement and presentation time constraints, return item losses, and extra handling costs, some corporations request this instrument because with it they can monitor their cash flows more precisely, fund the account on a delayed basis, and retain final word on the document's acceptability.

In summary, this instrument offers corporations a method to monitor closely, on an item-by-item basis, the validity of each payment. Additionally, many corporations seem to be interested solely in extending the float. In either case, each bank in its compensation and pricing schedule usually prices the product to take into account the float loss and exception processing. If a corporation is solely interested in float extension, remote disbursing could be used instead.

**Remote Disbursing.** Inefficiencies in the transportation and processing of checks by the Federal Reserve banks have brought about the practice of remote disbursing. In this process, corporations write checks on banks located in geographically distant locations to pay local vendors. For example, a corporation paying its vendors located in Philadelphia with checks drawn on a Boise, Idaho bank is probably trying to gain the extra float earnings inherent in the check-clearing system by engaging in remote disbursing (unless it has corporate offices or business in Boise.)

Before using this method, a corporation should be aware of its implications. First, the vendor depositing such a check is usually denied the use of available funds for at least one day longer than if the check were drawn locally. A corporation may tarnish its public image or antagonize vendors by using such a practice solely to gain a few extra dollars. In turn, the vendors may retaliate by changing the credit terms, thereby negating any benefit to the corporation. Moreover, this method to increase float earnings by delaying final payment by two or three days has recently been scrutinized by federal authorities. The Federal Reserve Board concluded that this practice abuses the check collection system, increases Federal Reserve check float, delays funds availability to recipients, and increases the risk exposure of financial institutions. It has requested that banks cooperate in eliminating its use.

Management should carefully review its corporate philosophy on remote disbursement to determine the cost versus benefits, tangible and intangible, of using this technique, especially in light of the Federal Reserve's continued monitoring of this activity. In a landmark case, a court required a well-known New York-based brokerage firm to pay damages to its customers for paying them with checks drawn on a California bank. (The 1978 Greenwich Research Survey concluded that only 2 percent of the middle-market companies use this practice compared to 35 percent of the largest 500 industrials.[4])

## FUNDS CONCENTRATION AND CONTROL

The controller who wants better control over cash flow can consolidate funds into a master concentration bank account via electronic funds transfer systems or through the use of depository transfer checks.

A master concentration account is usually opened with a company's primary bank. Excess funds from the company's other bank accounts are transferred into the concentration account on a predetermined schedule, such as daily or weekly. The controller can then wire funds to other banks with funds shortfalls, invest excess funds in overnight or other short-term instruments, pay down credit lines, or build his compensating balance levels in the concentration account to satisfy target balance requirements. Figure 23.2 illustrates a master concentration account funding two regional concentration accounts in New York and California to cover disbursement activities.

### Wire Transfer Systems

**Fedwire.** One of the most popular and fastest growing methods of funds transfer is the Fedwire (Federal Reserve Communications System). Member banks in the twelve Federal Reserve Districts use the Fedwire to send and receive federal funds transfers for their corporate and banking clients via an electronic message switching system. Banks are entitled to use this service without charge as a benefit of their Federal Reserve membership. (Transfers below $1,000, however, are charged to the banks at the rate of $1.50 each. This cost is supposed to discourage the use of this service for small dollar amounts.) However, beginning in January 1981, member banks are being charged for this service according to the Monetary Control Act of 1980.

A Fedwire is an electronic transfer of available funds between any two of the 550 or so on-line Federal Reserve member banks for their customers. A net settlement occurs each night between the banks through their accounts at the local Federal Reserve banks. To initiate a Fedwire, a corporation issues an authorization to its banks via phone, facsimile transmission, letter, or telex, indicating the following information:

- Receiving bank's name and location;
- Dollar amount of transaction;

---

[4] *Ibid.*

- Beneficiary's name and account number (if known) at receiving bank; and
- Text information referencing the payment.

The sending bank will transmit the message the same day to the receiving bank, as long as the message is received before the sender's internal cutoff time. (A bank not on-line must route the message through one of its correspondent banks.) Moreover, these funds can be resent by the recipient that same day for other purposes, assuming he instructs his bank to notify him upon receipt. In New York, for example, the Fedwire deadline is 3:00 P.M. EST for transfers outside the Second Federal Reserve District (New York, Northern New Jersey, and Fairfield County, Connecticut) and 4:00 P.M. EST for transfers between banks within the district. In California, a Fedwire must be sent to New York by noon PST, because of the time zone variations. Additionally, the controller should be aware that the on-line member bank's internal deadline to customers is usually fifteen minutes to one hour earlier than the Fedwire deadline, to allow time for processing.

**Bank Wire II.** An alternative system to Fedwire is Bank Wire II. This is a privately owned network of 190 banks directly connected via an electronic network. The major distinction between these two competing services is that BW II transmits transactional information, whereas Fedwire is actually transferring funds. In a typical message using BW II, bank A instructs bank B to debit its account at bank B and credit ABC Company on its books for X dollars.

The controller usually need not be concerned with which transfer method a bank uses to move its money. Under most circumstances, either method accomplishes the same objective at the same cost, which is currently between $2.50 to $5.50 per wire. However, if he expects to use the funds for a particular cash transaction that day at the receiving location, he should specify the use of Fedwire. Using Fedwire will assure a rapid transaction without any internal bookkeeping complications at the receiving bank, because the funds are considered cash on receipt.

**CHIPS.** Large corporations, as well as smaller companies that deal with international customers and vendors, must arrange for payment efficiently and cheaply. One system that serves this need is the New York Clearing House's Interbank Payments System (CHIPS), which when initiated in April 1970 was one of the first commercial banking systems to use electronic technology to transfer payment instructions between New York banks. Although initial payments via CHIPS were made for international customers of banks that were New York Clearing House members, the network was eventually also used for transfers between accounts within the same bank, as well as for the more frequent transfers between its member banks (and their correspondents). Unlike the Fedwire system, in which transactions are immediately funds, CHIPS payments are available the next day. As long as the controller's bank is a member of the CHIPS system or is a correspondent of a member, he can arrange for payments. Normally, the member bank will determine whether the recipient bank has a correspondent relationship with one of the other members before effecting payment.

**S.W.I.F.T.** Through the use of a relatively new international bank-to-bank telecommunications system called S.W.I.F.T., those corporate controllers responsible for transferring funds internationally and obtaining banking data from overseas are now able to accomplish these objectives in a more timely and reliable fashion. The Society for World Wide Interbank Financial Telecommunications (S.W.I.F.T.) was established under Belgian law in May 1973 by 240 of the largest banks in Europe and North America for the purpose of providing a private nonprofit cooperative telecommunications network for the routing of confidential and proprietary international financial messages between member banks. U.S. banks were connected to the system in September 1977, and Far East banks were added in 1980. Presently, nearly 750 banks in 26 countries, including 85 U.S. banks, are connected to the system.

S.W.I.F.T. has proved to be reliable and less costly and more convenient and timely than cable, telex, or mail. A telex between the United States and Europe, for instance, costs approximately $3.25, compared to $.49 for the typical S.W.I.F.T. message. Three days is usually the minimum traveling time for airmail to reach Europe, whereas a S.W.I.F.T. message can be sent in ten minutes.

Categories of information transferred over S.W.I.F.T. include customer transfers, bank transfers, foreign exchange data, and special messages such as confirmation of debits and credits and bank statements. Again, as with CHIPS, the bank receiving its customer's instructions for an international transfer will determine the quickest and most efficient method of making the payment.

### Depository Transfer Checks

Under many circumstances, the controller can utilize a less costly method of cash concentration than the wire transfer systems. A depository transfer check (DTC) is a nonnegotiable, unsigned instrument (under some circumstances, it can be signed or have an official signature) drawn payable to a company and used to move funds. (See Figure 23.3.) Depository transfer checks are used most often by companies who have geographically diverse depositing banks and wish to consolidate these funds on a daily or weekly basis at the lowest cost. About 22 percent of the middle-market companies use this technique.[5]

In a typical transaction, each local company entity's branch manager deposits the daily receipts in his local bank and phones the deposit amount, branch location, and his unique identification code to a toll-free number of a third-party vendor's deposit-reporting service. The individual reports are consolidated and sent via data transmission to the company's concentration banks that evening on a preset time schedule. The receiving bank prepares a DTC automatically for each location's deposit amount drawn on each local bank. The DTCs are then deposited into the corporation's concentration account and become available funds in one to two days. Thus, for about $.20 to $.45 per DTC, plus $.40 per item for deposit reporting, funds are concentrated rapidly from numerous outlying locations.

---

[5] *Ibid.*

DEPOSITORY TRANSFER CHECK

011-4444
―――――
8888

Pay to the
order of   Bank of the United States

for credit to:   ABC Company
Concentration Acct #6-4375-48

Third First Bank

Tulsa, Oklahoma

Date: April 21, 1980
Serial no. 12345678

No official signature required

⑈⑆0 2800032 5⑈:   1 1 2ⁱⁱ⁎30  1931ⁱⁱ⁎     3 1 4 8

FIGURE 23.3  DEPOSITORY TRANSFER CHECK

Each day the concentration bank forwards a report that lists by location the dollar value of the DTCs issued, the total for all locations, and those locations that did not report. The third-party vendor will also forward a separate report to the client as shown previously in Figure 23.1. These two reports can be easily compared for discrepancies. This type of system not only moves the corporate funds to one central location but provides the controller with daily or weekly deposit data to use in cash forecasting or detecting dollar-volume trend changes at specific locations.

A controller may prefer a manual system to the bank-initiated depository transfer check system reviewed above. In a manual system, each branch office prepares a DTC drawn on its local bank for that day's deposit and mails it to the concentration bank for credit to the corporate account. The manual approach is less costly to administer, but does not offer as much control as the bank's system. Also, the float loss incurred by the manual system in mailing DTCs to the concentration bank tends to build up balances in the local banks.

**Concentration Via the ACH**

Corporate concentration of cash via the ACH has recently begun to replace use of the paper-based DTC. When this technique is used, a third-party vendor collects the deposit information and in the late afternoon forwards a magnetic tape to the concentration bank, which then sends it to the local ACH for transmission through the regional ACHs to the drawee banks. Settlement occurs the next day on all transactions.

The principal advantage of using ACH is the reduced cost of an ACH item (approximately $.05 versus $.30 for an individual DTC transaction). One negative aspect of using the ACH is the potential loss of float earnings to the corporation. When using DTCs, it is possible that some checks will not be presented to the drawee bank on schedule because of paper log jams or transportation problems in the Federal Reserve clearing system. In this instance, the corporation experiences unanticipated but usable funds at the drawee bank. This is not the case when it uses the ACH, since the date of the debit entry is known with certainty. The controller should perform a cost-benefit analysis to determine the actual benefits to the corporation of using the ACH application to concentrate funds.

### Balance Reporting

**Background and Purpose.** The geographic expansion of corporate operations and banking relationships necessitates consolidated daily balance information that is accurate and timely. To fill this control function, the controller can now use automated balance reporting systems developed by banks and third-party vendors. From this system, a corporate controller can extract in one report the previous day's balance in each of his bank accounts by 9:00 A.M. the next morning via a touch-tone phone, computer terminal, or CRT display in his office. The corporation specifies to each of its banks the balance information and format they are to call in or send via magnetic tape or data terminal each morning to a toll-free number for consolidation. Typical information reported is ledger and collected balance, one- and two-day available funds, and total dollar value of debits and credits. A sample daily balance report is shown in Figure 23.4.

With this information the controller is able to determine his previous day's cash position more precisely than if he were to use cash forecasting techniques. Funds can now be allocated according to his banking needs in any part of the country. For example, excess balances in one bank can be wired to another bank to increase the required compensating balance (*target balance*) for the month or to cover a large disbursement coming due.

**Enhancements.** Controllers may select from many optional balance-reporting features when they wish to improve their daily tracking of cash. Some of the more useful features are dealt with below.

*Target balance calculation.* On a daily basis, the average available balance position at each bank is calculated for the current month and compared to the agreed-to target (compensating balance) level. The controller can take appropriate action to increase the balance levels in deficient accounts by wiring in funds or investing excess balances in overnight or short-term instruments.

*Terminal-initiated wire transfers.* Controllers with terminals located on their premises can prepare and send preformatted repetitive wire transfers to their banks. The corporation supplies the bank with a *line sheet* indicating the checking account number to be debited; the receiving bank's name, address, and transit/routing field (if known); and the reference information for the individual transfers. Each of these individual transactions is numbered consecutively and placed on a sheet of paper (line sheet). Each day an authorized person from the corporation, via the ter-

REPORT FOR APRIL 21, 1980, 8:15 A.M. EST

| Bank/Account | Gross Balance | Available Balance | Total Credits | Total Debits |
|---|---|---|---|---|
| ABC Bank | | | | |
| Acct. 137-456-8 | $680,000 | $579,500 | $48,675 | $93,743 |
| Manhattan National Bank | | | | |
| Acct. 53-7348-29 | $ 78,563 | $ 63,416 | $15,144 | $ 3,712 |
| Acct. 23-4843-52 | 143,541 | 103,478 | 35,019 | 16,848 |
| Acct. 17-4737-01 | 55,047 | 53,742 | 14,719 | 18,444 |
| Totals | $277,151 | $220,636 | $64,882 | $39,004 |
| San Francisco First Bank | | | | |
| Acct. 141-765-3 | $754,653 | $723,817 | $47,823 | $33,797 |
| Acct. 141-747-7 | 48,134 | 36,689 | 13,673 | 18,498 |
| Acct. 138-632-9 | 185,437 | 142,439 | 6,847 | 58,542 |
| Totals | $988,224 | $902,945 | $68,343 | $110,837 |
| Grand Totals | $1,945,375 | $1,703,081 | $181,900 | $243,584 |

BANK/ACCOUNTS NOT REPORTING:

| Bank | Account |
|---|---|
| Southern Trust Co. | 758356-1 |
| Chicago Second N/B | 463835-2 |

FIGURE 23.4 DAILY BALANCE REPORT FROM ABC BANK

minal, types in his appropriate password and user identification with the line numbers and dollar amounts of that day's transfers. The receiving bank transcribes the dollar amount on the appropriate line and then executes the transaction. This technique minimizes security problems, since the initiator cannot change the destination or the account number of the receiving party. This data is controlled at a higher management level in the company.

As electronic communications have become more sophisticated and system security has improved, corporations are now sending nonrepetitive wire transfers with the same ease. To minimize any fraudulent transactions, the corporate controller must ensure that different authorized personnel enter and verify outgoing funds transfers. As a further security step, a more senior person should verify certain unusually large dollar transactions. This authorization hierarchy can be set forth in a written agreement with the bank when the system is established.

*Detailed debit and credit reporting.* Under this option, the entire unedited text of all incoming and outgoing wire transfers for the previous day is displayed on the terminal. This is a useful feature for verifying the transaction detail to ensure that the sending bank executed a specific outgoing transaction properly, for determining whether an expected transfer has arrived, and for double-checking the dollar amounts of important transactions.

A few banks offer on-line real-time balance reporting as well as debit/credit information. Under this system the corporate controller, through a terminal or CRT, can access the details of all incoming and outgoing wires during the day up to that moment. Although corporations with less than a billion dollars in sales would probably not be able to justify this system in terms of cost, some smaller companies with large dollar transactions might benefit from this reporting system.

*Money market and foreign exchange rate quotations.* This service enables the controller to get previous day's rates in the early morning. Updates in mid-morning provide him with the latest quotations. Because conditions in the financial markets change so rapidly, the usefulness of this service is questionable. To obtain up-to-the-minute rates for a particular investment, the controller would have to call the bank directly, thus minimizing the effectiveness of this service.

In summary, balance-reporting systems offer the controller consolidated, timely, and accurate information on his corporation's entire prior-day's balance in one concise report early the next morning.

Depending on the features added and the volume of transactions, the monthly operating cost of these systems varies from $50 to $1000, not including the cost of the terminal rental.

## CASH MANAGEMENT CONSULTING SERVICES

Increased emphasis on cash management in recent years has spawned the development by banks, third-party vendors, and financial consultants of computer models to analyze corporate receivable and disbursement patterns. Most models are based on linear programming techniques that maximize or minimize equations with certain constraints. The controller should understand the methodology and assumptions, and discuss the external and internal cost before engaging in a study.

A number of banks now provide their client base with in-depth cash management reviews of the client company's cash flows. These studies are being handled more and more by professional fee-based bank consultants, who visit the client, provide a systems-oriented workflow of the incoming and outgoing cash flows, analyze the client's bank relationship needs, costs, and future direction, review bank compensation policies, and determine the efficiency of the existing receivable and payable systems.

For small-to-medium-sized companies, an accounts receivable or payable analysis is usually one of the first steps in quantifying the efficiency of their cash flows after a corporate systems audit has been performed.

**Accounts Receivable Study**

Many small-to-medium-sized companies are experiencing rapid growth in their accounts receivable volume and dollar value. When lock box networks are used to maximize and improve funds availability, these boxes must be placed properly to obtain the quickest funds capture. Banks (among others) have developed computer models to analyze a company's receivables flow and evaluate each potential lock box location with regard to minimizing mail, processing, and check-availability float while taking into account the operating lock box costs. Usually, one to two month's receivables are used for the analysis. However, to avoid biased results, the months should be carefully chosen so that they represent a typical accounting period in the company's normal operating cycle. In a comprehensive analysis, the information extracted from each receivable check and envelope includes:

- Sending and receiving zip codes,
- Mailing and receiving dates,
- Dollar amount,
- Drawee bank, and
- Customer name.

The corporation's opportunity cost of capital with the projected lock box charges should be used in the analysis to evaluate the float earnings in hard dollars. Most models use mail times between major cities compiled by Phoenix-Hecht (an independent company that surveys mail times between major cities three times a year) and the availability schedules from the twelve Federal Reserve Districts banks, or from individual banks, or from a composite of individual banks from particular cities.

Study results usually indicate the mail, processing, and check-availability float of the existing, alternative, and optimal systems with varying numbers of lock box locations. A cost-benefit analysis that evaluates the savings potential for each of these alternatives is included.

Examples of two useful reports from such a study are illustrated in Figures 23.5 and 23.6. Figure 23.5 clearly shows that the more lock box locations in the system the higher the cash flow over the existing system. However, as Figure 23.6 indicates, the incremental benefit of adding lock boxes decelerates rapidly after a three-box system.

A controller can expect the following benefits from an accounts receivable analysis:

- Quantifying the present system's mail, processing, and check-availability float;
- Increasing cash flow by improving the efficiency of the present collection system to an optimal or near-optimal solution;
- Reducing the in-house clerical expense of monitoring the system;

| | Time (Days) | | | Gain Over Existing System (Days) | Cash Flow Improvement Over Existing System ($) | Annual (Dollars) | | |
|---|---|---|---|---|---|---|---|---|
| | Mail | Avail. | Total | | | Cash Flow at 15% Opport. Cost | Cost of Lock Box Operation | Net Benefit |
| Existing System | | | | | | | | |
| New York City, San Francisco | 2.57 | 1.43 | 4.00 | — | — | — | $10,650 | — |
| Optimal System Alternatives | | | | | | | | |
| One Box | | | | | | | | |
| Chicago | 3.05 | 1.05 | 4.10 | (.10) | (50,000) | (7,500) | 10,130 | (17,630) |
| Two Boxes | | | | | | | | |
| New York City, St. Louis | 2.08 | 1.04 | 3.12 | 0.88 | 440,000 | 66,000 | 10,650 | 55,350 |
| Three Boxes | | | | | | | | |
| New York City, Chicago, San Francisco | 1.55 | 1.02 | 2.57 | 1.43 | 715,000 | 107,250 | 13,320 | 93,930 |
| Four Boxes | | | | | | | | |
| New York City, Chicago, Atlanta, San Francisco | 1.40 | .99 | 2.39 | 1.61 | 805,000 | 120,750 | 15,990 | 104,760 |
| Five Boxes | | | | | | | | |
| New York City, Chicago, Atlanta, San Francisco, Dallas | 1.15 | .97 | 2.12 | 1.88 | 940,000 | 141,000 | 18,660 | 122,340 |
| Six Boxes | | | | | | | | |
| New York City, San Francisco, Atlanta, Dallas, Chicago, St. Louis | 1.11 | .97 | 2.08 | 1.92 | 960,000 | 144,000 | 21,330 | 122,670 |

FIGURE 23.5  COST-BENEFIT ANALYSIS OF ALTERNATIVE LOCK BOX SYSTEMS

- Minimizing total system cost of operating the lock box network; and
- Obtaining a zip code directory indicating the city to which each customer's remittances should be sent.

## Accounts Payable Analysis

From a mathematical standpoint, an accounts payable study attempts to maximize the check-clearing float for the benefit of the issuing corporation. The usual intent of such a study is to investigate the ways to lengthen the check-clearing float in order to slow the funding of the disbursement account.

Because of the recent Federal Reserve position on remote disbursing discussed earlier, the continued offering of this type of study may in time diminish. However, corporations are still interested in determining how the float in their existing system compares to alternative and optimal systems. To perform an accounts payable analysis, a typical month's paid checks and bank statements are reviewed with the following information extracted:

- Check issue and paid date,
- Deposit date,
- Dollar amount, and
- Drawee bank.

This information is keypunched and run on a computer model to obtain the analysis. Typical reports indicate the existing system's mail and check-clearing time as well as that for alternative systems. The opportunity cost and disbursement account costs are taken into account in determining the overall economic impact on the corporation.

A controller should address certain considerations before selecting a disbursement location. First, he should consider the corporate philosophy regarding remote disbursing, in light of its potential negative vendor feedback and damaging effect on the corporate image. Second, the addition of a new bank relationship requires added expenses and additional control for corporate headquarters. A corporation may prefer to use a bank in its present network, which was probably established for other reasons, such as obtaining loans. Other important factors to consider in selecting a disbursement bank are whether it can perform the required services such as account reconcilement and balance reporting, whether it offers same-day funding (controlled disbursement), and whether it will accept fees in lieu of compensating balances.

Controllers often overlook the effect direct-sends to the disbursement bank can have on the potential benefits indicated in the study results. Most large banks have extensive transportation and courier networks to their large correspondent banks to speed the flow of large dollar checks drawn on those banks and other banks in that region, thus clearing these checks one day earlier than the Federal Reserve clearing system and gaining availability one day earlier. Checks sent directly to a disbursement bank will tend to reduce the gains that are indicated in a study (if only Fed

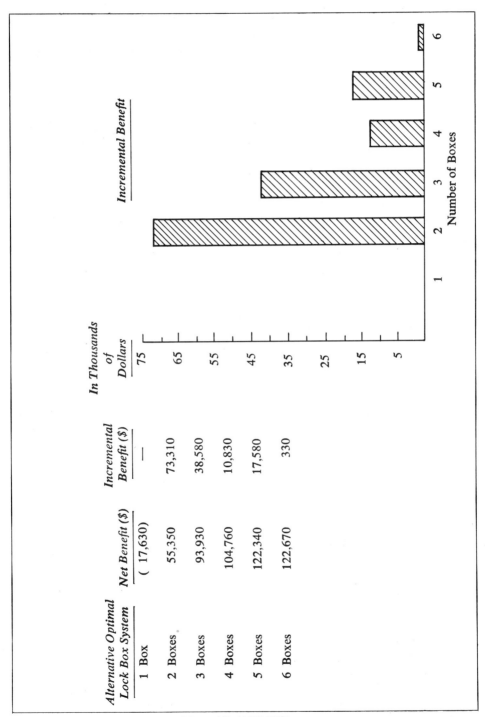

| Alternative Optimal Lock Box System | Net Benefit ($) | Incremental Benefit ($) |
| --- | --- | --- |
| 1 Box | ( 17,630) | — |
| 2 Boxes | 55,350 | 73,310 |
| 3 Boxes | 93,930 | 38,580 |
| 4 Boxes | 104,760 | 10,830 |
| 5 Boxes | 122,340 | 17,580 |
| 6 Boxes | 122,670 | 330 |

FIGURE 23.6 INCREMENTAL LOCK BOX ANALYSIS

availabilities were used in the analysis), since the check is arriving one to two days earlier than by conventional clearing systems. Thus, it is important for the controller to obtain a list from the disbursement bank indicating those banks that have a direct-send program with that bank.

The expected benefits from an accounts payable analysis are similar to those delineated for the accounts receivable analysis. A one- or two-network disbursement location is usually sufficient from the standpoint of minimizing the manpower required to monitor the system, reducing the cost, and extending the clearing float.

### Selecting a Consultant

Choosing a bank or consulting firm to perform a cash management study is a very important step that should be addressed when the need for a study is first determined. Most likely, the controller's credit-line banks would be interested in performing this service. However, proposals from nonline banks or other interested consultants should also be obtained for comparative purposes. Factors a controller should review in evaluating a consulting proposal normally include:

- The firm's or bank's reputation in the consulting field;
- The expertise of the consultants; the controller should obtain a short biography that gives their professional background;
- The degree of flexibility in producing reports and addressing results to the corporation's specific needs;
- The methodology of the approach;
- The computer model's logic, capabilities, and options;
- A sample study of the same type and depth of the study the corporation is considering;
- Who prepares the study—an individual or team of consultants, junior or senior members—and who presents final results;
- The cost—fee based, compensating balances, or no charge;
- The completion time requirements;
- The need for implementation assistance after completion;
- The references furnished; the controller should contact all references for their opinions, ask about any perceived weaknesses, and determine if results were implemented; and
- The objectivity of the results. For example, the controller should consider whether banks performing a study for no charge will produce completely objective, unbiased results or whether their solution will perhaps present their city as one of the recommended locations.

If the controller does not believe that his experience enables him to select the most qualified professional consultant, he should contact his counterpart at other companies in his industry group for recommendations. In large metropolitan areas, the controller could join one of the growing cash management practitioners associations to broaden his general understanding of the area as well as to obtain expert guidance in seeking professional advice.

## Study Costs

Regional and money center banks, along with a few well-known accounting firms, provide most cash management consulting services. Fee-based studies range from $1,000 to $50,000 and possibly higher, depending on the study's complexity, the number of consultant hours expended, travel expenses, required computer time, and data entry costs. The quality, approach, and professionalism differ greatly from bank to bank and from firm to firm. In some cases, a cautious controller will corroborate results by selecting two independent consultants to study the same data. This option usually doubles the cost of a study.

A few banks perform studies without charge in the hopes of obtaining future cash management service or credit business. Other banks double count the balances used to pay for credit and deposit services and thus effectively absorb the cost of performing a study. Since these banks often have a strong banking relationship with the corporation, this service tends to solidify the relationship. Since cost is only one factor, no matter what method of payment is used, the controller should weigh all the factors before choosing a bank to work with. Above all, he must be sure that the study is professionally and objectively performed by skilled consultants.

# BANK COMPENSATION

## Pricing Options

A corporation pays a bank for its services by a compensating balance or a direct fee or a combination of the two. The former method is the most prevalent, since balance requirements are used to support a credit-line extension. For example, a credit line of $2 million would typically require a 10 percent balance for the initiation of the line plus an additional 10 percent of any credit-line usage. In this case, using $500,000 of the line would necessitate keeping $250,000 in compensating balances (10 percent of $2 million + 10 percent of $500,000). Any other bank services would require additional balances, unless a bank permits double counting of balances. Here, the $250,000 would support utilization of the line as well as any bank services up to that balance equivalent.

A less common alternative is the payment of a monthly fee for services. This practice is growing steadily, because corporations are becoming aware that they can invest these balances in higher-income-producing instruments (or reduce borrowings) rather than receive the value from a bank's earnings allowance (usually equivalent to a short-term treasury bill rate adjusted for reserve requirements) and come out ahead.

Some corporations prefer a combination of fees and compensating balances. When monthly activity charges are greater than the balance required to support services, the difference can be billed to the corporation as a monthly fee. Using this arrangement, the corporation does not have to tie up large balances that could be used more productively elsewhere.

## Account Analysis

The controller can determine his banking expenses by requesting a monthly account analysis from each bank. This report (Figure 23.7) summarizes the activity performed by the bank for a particular month, with its associated per-item costs and the balances required to cover these expenses. The components of an account analysis are:

- Net available balance,
- Reserve requirement,
- Services provided, and
- Activity expense.

---

ACCOUNT NO. 1256-7350          XYZ CORPORATION

ACCOUNT ANALYSIS STATEMENT FOR MONTH ENDING APRIL, 1980

| | | |
|---|---|---|
| Average ledger balance | $1,000,000 | |
| Less average float | − 200,000 | |
| Average available balance | 800,000 | |
| Less R.R. @ 10%* | − 80,000 | |
| Net available balance | $720,000 | |
| @ 6% earnings allowance | | $3,600 |

---

MONTHLY ACTIVITY—APRIL 1980

| Service | Quantity | Unit Price | Amount |
|---|---|---|---|
| Account maintenance | 1 | 2.50 | $  2.50 |
| Lock box activity | 300 | .10 | 30.00 |
| Account reconcilement | 5,000 | .03 | 150.00 |
| Checks paid | 5,000 | .12 | 600.00 |
| Wire transfers | 10 | 5.00 | 50.00 |
| Total service charges | | | $832.50 |
| Balance required to support activity | | | $185,000.00 |
| Balances available to support other services | | | $535,000.00 |

*Used for ease of illustration instead of actual requirement.

FIGURE 23.7   MONTHLY ACCOUNT ANALYSIS OF ABC NATIONAL BANK

The net available balance is calculated by subtracting the average check float (dollar value of unavailable funds) from the average ledger balance and adjusting for the bank's reserve requirement.[6]

The earnings allowance is used to convert the net available balance into a fee-based equivalent for comparison to the cost of services. Usually the preceding three-month treasury bill rate or the average of the weekly treasury bill auction rate is used as the earnings allowance.

In our example, the balances are equivalent to $3,600 in fees to support activity expenses. For April 1980, the total service charge expense is $832.50, which is more than adequately covered by the balances. To convert these activity expenses to an equivalent balance, the following formula is used:

$$\text{Balance Required} = \frac{\text{Cost of services} \times 12 \text{ months}}{(1 - \text{Reserve requirement}) \times \text{Earnings allowance}}$$

$$= \frac{832.50 \times 12}{(1 - .10) \times .06} = \$185,000$$

Therefore, the balance available to support other services is $535,000 ($720,000-$185,000). Assuming that there is no credit-line-balance requirement nor other intangible services with this bank, the controller should attempt to maintain only the required balance ($185,000) in this account. Any excess balances are being wasted, since they are not providing any earnings for the corporation.

## Bank Cost Comparison

In selecting a bank to perform services (excluding credit requirements), the controller is usually interested in finding one that provides the highest-quality service at the lowest cost. In doing so, one must analyze three components: monthly service charges, reserve requirement, and earnings allowance. These variables can be compared by using the formula shown above, as in the following example:

---

[6] This requirement is promulgated by the Federal Reserve Act and applies to all member banks of the Federal Reserve system. The table below indicates the requirement for various size deposit bases:

| Bank's Net Demand Deposits | Bank's Reserve Requirement |
|---|---|
| $  0 -    2 million | 7.00% |
| 2 -   10 million | 9.50% |
| 10 - 100 million | 11.75% |
| 100 - 400 million | 12.75% |
| Over    400 million | 16.25% |

| Bank Costs | Bank A | Bank B | Bank C |
|---|---|---|---|
| Monthly service charges | $200 | $250 | $250 |
| Reserve requirement | 16% | 12% | None |
| Earnings allowance | 9.0% | 8.5% | 7.5% |

*Solution*

Bank A    Balance Required $= \dfrac{200 \times 12}{.84 \times .09} = $ $31,746    Lowest Cost

Bank B    Balance Required $= \dfrac{250 \times 12}{.88 \times .085} = $ $40,107    Highest Cost

Bank C    Balance Required $= \dfrac{250 \times 12}{1 \times .075} = $ $40,000

In this example, Bank A has the lowest cost. Although this bank has the highest reserve requirement, it has the highest earnings allowance and lowest service charges. (In comparing service charges among banks, one should be aware that they are only comparable in common geographic areas by size of banking institution.)

By comparing the variables that comprise the cost equation, the controller can ascertain, at least on an equivalent-cost basis, the true cost of service at candidate banks. He can determine the quality of services in much the same way as he would select a lock box bank or a consulting bank—that is, via a questionnaire, reference checks, and personal meetings.

## SUMMARY

This chapter reviewed for the controller the contemporary techniques in cash management. By carefully selecting those cash maximization tools that fit his individual situations, the controller should be able to improve his existing system. Keeping abreast of the latest developments in cash management, including the evolutionary changes in electronic funds transfer, will enable the controller to maintain a system that contributes maximally to the bottom-line profits of his company.

## SUGGESTED READING

Beehler, Paul J. *Contemporary Cash Management: Principles, Practices, Perspectives.* New York: John Wiley and Sons, 1978.

"Cash Management: The Art of Wringing More Profit From Corporate Funds." *Business Week*, March 13, 1978, pp. 62-68.

*CHIPS.* New York: New York Clearing House Association, June, 1976.

DeSalvo, Alfred. "Cash Management Converts Dollars into Working Assets." *Harvard Business Review,* May-June, 1972.

*Electronic Banking.* New York: Price Waterhouse & Co., 1978.

"Fed Policy Draft Calls Remote Disbursal An Abuse of Checking, Asks Elimination." *American Banker,* January 22, 1979.

Fisher, David I. *Cash Management in the Moderate-Sized Company.* The Conference Board, Report 559. New York: 1972.

Gitmann, Lawrence J., et al. "An Assessment of Corporate Cash Management Practices." *Financial Management,* Spring, 1979, pp. 32-41.

Hoel, Arline. "A Primer on Federal Reserve Float." Federal Reserve Bank of New York, *Monthly Review,* October, 1975, pp. 245-253.

Hunt, Alfred L. *Corporate Cash Management: Including Electronic Funds Transfer.* New York: American Management Association, 1978.

Keitler, Jeffrey. "Big Banks Build Management Services To Help Firms Track International Funds." *American Banker,* June 30, 1978.

Lordan, James F. "Cash Management: The Corporate-Bank Relationship." *The Magazine of Bank Administration,* January, 1975, pp. 14-19.

Lordan, James F. *The Banking Side of Corporate Cash Management.* New York: Financial Publishing Company, 1973.

"Making Millions by Stretching the Float." *Business Week,* November 23, 1974, pp. 89-90.

Rose, Sanford. "Checkless Banking is Bound to Come." *Fortune,* June, 1977.

———. "More Bang For the Buck: The Magic of Electronic Banking." *Fortune,* May, 1977.

"Treasurer's Try to Fine Tune the Float." *Business Week,* May 17, 1976, pp. 5-6.

## APPENDIX 23-1   TYPICAL LOCK BOX QUESTIONNAIRE

1. Indicate your monthly lock box item and dollar volume, as well as the number of retail and wholesale customer accounts that are processed.

2. What are the working hours of your lock box department daily and on weekends?

3. What are the daily and weekend mail pickup schedules from your post office box(es)? Cumulatively indicate the volume and percent of mail picked up beginning at 12 midnight through the last pickup of that day.

4. Describe in detail the methodology of processing remittances and the organizational structure of the lock box area.

5. What types of lock box plans do you offer? What are the associated costs of all the options of these plans?

6. What quality control procedures are used to assure high quality standards? Describe your methodology and measurement techniques. Indicate whether the measurements are posted in the working areas.

7. Are very large remittances (over $100,000) identified and processed more rapidly to assure maximum availability to your customers?

8. What are the internal cut-off times to assure same-day posting?

9. What is the earliest time and by what method can deposit information be forwarded to the corporate client? What is the earliest time that hard copy material can be picked up or mailed each day?

10. Do you have a unique zip code that applies only to lock box mail? What is the average time it takes for mail to be delivered to the bank from the post office(s).

11. Is availability determined individually check-by-check?

12. Indicate your direct send network cities and attach your present availability schedule.

13. Describe your data transmission capabilities and equipment compatibility in detail. Indicate your price schedule.

14. Supply a current price list of all deposit services as well as the earnings allowance for the past twelve months including your present reserve requirement.

15. Can you supply deposit and balance information to third-party vendors? What type of medium (phone, tape-to-tape) do you use? What are your associated charges?

16. Indicate ten large volume retail and wholesale customers that can be used for reference purposes.

17. Describe the type of equipment by vendor that is presently used for lock box processing. Do you plan to obtain more technologically advanced equipment within the next eighteen months?

# 24

# Credit Management

*William H. Bryan*

# WHY CREDIT MANAGEMENT?

Credit management, the management of business funds invested in accounts receivable, is one of the more important of the controller's numerous responsibilities —and one for which there is often little advance preparation. This chapter discusses the ingredients the controller works with in managing credit, and the policies and objectives that determine effective procedures.

### Credit Defined

Credit is defined as the delivery today of goods, monies, or services in exchange for a promise to pay at a future date. In making a *credit decision*, management must determine if the promise to pay will be kept; it usually is. *Collection* efforts are necessary in those relatively few cases where it is not.

### The Importance of Credit

Credit has made possible the explosive growth in the world's economy. In this country, business activity is based, to a large degree, on the use of credit.

Almost all of the goods and services that make up our multi-trillion dollar gross national product are moved from manufacturer to wholesaler to retailer on credit, on the basis of a simple promise to pay. The introduction of bank credit cards also enables a substantial portion of retail sales to consumers to be transacted on credit. It would not be physically possible to use coins or currency in the amounts our economy requires. The sheer weight and bulk of cash transactions makes them impractical. The existence of credit, with the introduction of electronic funds transfers, may make even the check obsolete, and what is a check if not a scrap of paper promising to pay?

### Accounts Receivable

**The Investment in Trading Assets.** When plans are made to start a new business, provisions must be made for the necessary initial financing. If the business plans to own its plant facilities, it must purchase land, construct a plant building, and acquire machinery and equipment. These costs are carefully calculated, and the source of funds is projected. Some of the money will come from the owner's investment, and the remainder will be financed by mortgage. In this way, all of the funds required for the construction of the new plant are provided.

Too often, management does not plan as carefully to obtain the working capital needed to operate the business on a day-to-day basis. Yet the new plant is of no use until it produces goods, sells them to customers, collects payment for them, and buys more raw materials for manufacture in order to repeat the cycle, thus earning the owners a return on their investment.

In most businesses, accounts receivable comprise a substantial part of the capital invested; they are often the largest single asset on the balance sheet. Amounts due from customers are an essential part of the capital investment and should earn a portion of the required return for the owners, just as the plant itself should.

If accounts receivable are *not* controlled, if credit management is *not* efficient, excess funds are invested in amounts due from customers. These excess funds have no more chance of earning a return on investment than unused equipment, or cash carried in a non-interest bearing bank account, or excess inventory.

**Accounts Receivable Records.** Open customer billings are recorded in two different ways. The *Open Invoice File*, the simpler system of the two, lists by date the unpaid invoices due from each customer. As invoices are mailed to the customer, an extra copy is retained and filed in the customer's *Open Invoice Folder*. This open invoice is removed when payment is received and is then filed in a *Paid Invoice File*.

A somewhat more sophisticated record is maintained in the *Accounts Receivable Ledger*. This ledger book has a page for each customer. In the first column, the date, number, and amount of each invoice is entered. In a second column, the date and amount of each payment received is entered, and the invoices in the first column that are now paid are checked off. A third column is provided for the entry of a balance due after each entry in the first two columns.

Computerization of accounts receivable records is based primarily on the open invoice method. Early computer applications used punched cards for each open invoice, and mechanically pulled them from the open invoice file when the invoices were paid. More advanced data processing techniques are now in use, but all involve the creation of the open item and its subsequent erasure upon payment. Part payments, credits, and adjustments cause problems for computer programs, but the problems are solvable. (See Chapter 11.)

**Aging of Accounts Receivable.** One of the ways in which a company can evaluate its collection performance is by aging accounts receivable. Basically, this involves distributing outstanding accounts by time periods and classifying them as follows: current, overdue—less than 30 days, 30–60 days, 60–90 days, and over 90 days. These reports are generally prepared monthly (see Figure 24.1). The aging of a single customer's unpaid accounts receivable is done by adding unpaid invoices for each month of issue and then totaling the months for a final total of the amount due. Thus:

| Customer | Total | Current | 30–60 | 60–90 | Over 90 |
|---|---|---|---|---|---|
| ABC Co. | $25,000.00 | $20,000.00 | $2,000.00 | $1,500.00 | $1,500.00 |

A combined aging of the accounts receivable of all customers is provided by totalling the open accounts of each and then breaking down the total by month of invoice date. Thus:

```
Advance Petrochemical Corporation
              Division

                              Period _____

                              Month of _____

                              Fiscal Yr. _____
```

| Account Name | Total Balance | Current | Over 30 | Over 60 | Over 90 | Comments |
|---|---|---|---|---|---|---|
|  |  |  |  |  |  |  |
|  |  |  |  |  |  |  |
|  |  |  |  |  |  |  |
|  |  |  |  |  |  |  |

FIGURE 24.1   ACCOUNTS RECEIVABLE AGING REPORT

*Accounts Receivable Aging at December 31, 19—.*

| Total | Current | 30–60 | 60–90 | Over 90 |
|---|---|---|---|---|
| $100,000.00 | $90,000.00 | $5,000.00 | $3,000.00 | $2,000.00 |

An accounts receivable aging for a company, a plant, a division, or a product line will usually show each customer separately, with a horizontal listing of open account by month, and then a total for the entire unit of operation at the bottom of the page.

**Measuring the Condition of Accounts Receivable.** In addition to developing a file of customers who require special attention in the form of some collection activity, aging accounts provides a receivable condition report and data for evaluating credit operations.

*Percentage current and past due.* Probably the most commonly used method of measuring accounts receivable liquidity is to determine the percentage of unpaid accounts dated within the current month, and those that fall within each of the preceding months. If selling terms are 30 days, and if 90 percent of open accounts receivable at the close of a given month represent unpaid invoices dated that month, then the accounts are in good condition. If no more than 3 percent date from 90 or more days before, then the past due situation is not serious. On the other hand, if only 60 percent of the open accounts are current, and 20 percent date from more than 90 days before, a serious accounts receivable situation exists.

Figure 24.2 shows a monthly analysis of receivables. It allows the controller, credit manager, and sales manager to monitor sales and collections. By preparing the report on a cumulative basis, the trend of collections can be easily followed and collection procedures concentrated where necessary.

*Collection period—days' sales outstanding—DSO.* A companion and more sophisticated method of measuring the condition of accounts receivable relates the dollar amount of unpaid accounts to sales volume. This ratio is based on the theory that any firm would be happy to have accounts receivable increase by 50 percent in the face of a doubling in dollar sales, but would consider it a serious matter if accounts receivable tripled in the same situation.

The following formula is used for computing the *Collection Period* or the *Number of Days' Sales Outstanding*:

$$\text{Collection Period or Days' Sales Outstanding (DSO)} =$$

$$\frac{\text{Accounts Receivable}}{\text{Average Daily Sales}}$$

$$\text{Average Daily Sales} =$$

$$\frac{\text{Credit Sales for Period}}{\text{No. of Days in Period}}$$

This commonly used method of evaluating the investment in accounts receivable is a simple calculation dividing accounts receivable dollars by the number of dollars in an average day's credit sales. (The formula uses a thirty day month even though there are not thirty selling days in a month.) Credit managers speak regularly of DSO figures and compare their own DSO with DSO figures for their industry.

Credit Research Foundation, the research arm of the National Association of Credit Management, publishes quarterly DSO figures for industry generally, and also breaks them down by lines of business. To even out sharp month-to-month fluctuations, Credit Research Foundations uses a formula that totals credit sales for the previous three months, divides this total by ninety, and then divides this daily credit sales average into the total of accounts receivable for the previous three months.

This method of measuring accounts receivable will work well in most situations. It is not helpful when a business is characterized by sharp month-to-month sales fluctuations and the payment of customer accounts over an extended period of time. In such a rare instance, a more meaningful method of measurement uses the percentage of each month's bills unpaid at the close of the succeeding months. For example, of January's total billings, 70 percent may be unpaid at the end of January, 25 percent at the close of February, 15 percent in March, and 5 percent in April. February's bills are followed through in the same way as are succeeding months'.

(000)

| Month Ended 198___ | Monthly Sales | = Days Sales/Rec | Total Accts Rec | Aging 30-60 PD Amount | % | 61 + PD Amount | % | Collections 30-60 PD Amount | % | 61 + PD Amount | % |
|---|---|---|---|---|---|---|---|---|---|---|---|
| JAN | 600 | 60 | 1255 | 377 | 30 | 276 | 22 | 164 | 45 | 78 | 26 |
| FEB | 612 | 62 | 1290 | 413 | 32 | 322 | 25 | 162 | 43 | 77 | 28 |
| MAR | 724 | 66 | 1315 | 433 | 33 | 355 | 27 | 186 | 45 | 64 | 20 |
| APRIL | 580 | 65 | 1306 | 430 | 33 | 300 | 23 | 173 | 40 | 96 | 27 |
| MAY | 620 | 69 | 1359 | 571 | 42 | 353 | 26 | 180 | 42 | 90 | 30 |
| JUNE | 640 | 60 | 1260 | 378 | 30 | 252 | 20 | 268 | 47 | 88 | 25 |
| JULY | 652 | 62 | 1269 | 393 | 31 | 288 | 21 | 170 | 45 | 66 | 26 |
| AUG | 612 | 65 | 1348 | 513 | 38 | 365 | 27 | 157 | 40 | 84 | 29 |
| SEPT | 601 | 65 | 1355 | 542 | 40 | 406 | 30 | 195 | 38 | 110 | 30 |
| OCT | 576 | 67 | 1392 | 515 | 37 | 390 | 28 | 222 | 41 | 110 | 27 |
| NOV | 587 | 64 | 1332 | 466 | 35 | 333 | 25 | 221 | 43 | 97 | 25 |
| DEC | 567 | 60 | 1256 | 364 | 29 | 314 | 25 | 233 | 50 | 67 | 20 |
| | | | | | | | | | | | |
| 198— | | | | | | | | | | | |
| JAN | 615 | 59 | 1230 | 332 | 27 | 246 | 20 | 190 | 52 | 72 | 23 |
| FEB | | | | | | | | | | | |
| MAR | | | | | | | | | | | |
| APRIL | | | | | | | | | | | |
| MAY | | | | | | | | | | | |
| JUNE | | | | | | | | | | | |
| JULY | | | | | | | | | | | |
| AUG | | | | | | | | | | | |
| SEPT | | | | | | | | | | | |
| OCT | | | | | | | | | | | |
| NOV | | | | | | | | | | | |
| DEC | | | | | | | | | | | |
| | | | | | | | | | | | |
| | | | | | | | | | | | |

FIGURE 24.2  MONTHLY ANALYSIS OF RECEIVABLES

*Current month unpaid—CMU.* Another significant measure of the condition of accounts receivable, particularly where a cash discount is offered for payment in ten days, is the percentage of each month's credit sales still unpaid at the end of the month. This ties in closely with Days' Sales Outstanding because each three percent of the current month's sales unpaid will obviously add one day's sales to DSO. It is possible to have 100 percent of accounts receivable current, and despite an attractive cash discount offer, have none of the current month yet paid. CMU or Current Month Unpaid will spotlight two conditions for correction:

- A delay in getting invoices out to customers; and
- Inefficient policing of cash discount violations.

Either will add unnecessarily to the firm's investment in accounts receivable.
The following formula is used to derive Current Month Unpaid (CMU):

$$CMU = \frac{\text{Accounts Receivable Within 30 Days}}{\text{Month's Credit Sales}}$$

The controller must not view figures measuring the condition of accounts receivable as dry statistics. Percentage Current, Days' Sales Outstanding, and Current Month Unpaid all represent dollars—cold, hard cash. One day's variation in DSO or a 3 percent variation in CMU equals one day's sales. For a business with annual sales of $2 million, each day's sales represents $5,500. If DSO is reduced by even one day, the sum of $5,500 is available for profitable use—perhaps to buy a much needed piece of equipment—or to reduce the total sum the firm must borrow at the current high interest rates. (See Chapter 16 for other commonly used accounts receivable ratios.)

# CREDIT POLICIES, OBJECTIVES, AND PROCEDURES

The distinction between policies and procedures is not always clearly understood. *Policy* is an overall statement of principle, a philosophy of management, a projection of broad objectives. *Procedures*, on the other hand, detail how the job is to be done and prescribe a course of action in terms of the steps that must be followed.

### Relationship to Corporate Policy

Since both credit management policies and credit management procedures must be based on the overall corporate policies, the latter must be clearly defined and understood by the personnel who make credit decisions.

The controller responsible for the management of credit is expected to make credit management policies coincide with corporate policies and objectives. The failure to adopt credit policies that contribute to the accomplishment of corporate objectives results in conflict with other segments of the business, particularly sales.

In most businesses—particularly smaller ones—the controller will search in vain for any clear, concise policy statement, written or oral, that deals with corporate goals in the areas of marketing and sales. But policy can be read between the lines of official pronouncements, management messages at company meetings, specific problem discussions, or in casual conversations. Only if corporate policy and management philosophy are clearly recognized will the controller or his credit manager be able intelligently to formulate—or adjust—credit policy and procedure.

### Credit Management Policy

Credit policy must tie in with corporate policy concerning the use of available funds and must incorporate courses of action to be followed in dealing with situations that involve creditworthiness, terms of sale, collections, and write-offs. A "loose" credit policy makes no sense in the face of an overall company approach favoring the use of available dollars for plant and equipment rather than obtaining new business by extending favorable financial terms to customers. The reverse is also true; too often, persons responsible for credit try to enforce a tight credit policy while the company as a whole pursues sales growth at any cost.

Credit policy need not necessarily be written (although it helps), but it must be clearly formulated, enunciated, and understood by all who share responsibility for credit decisions.

Here is an example of a credit policy followed by a company that does not choose to finance customers beyond regular terms:

> It is a financial policy of our company to selectively employ available capital in ways that will best serve our customers' interests as well as our own. We feel we do this best by using our money for the purchase of needed plant and equipment to provide more efficient production and better service, rather than using it to finance customer accounts receivable beyond regular terms.

The following example illustrates a different credit policy. This business intends to pursue sales growth by using its funds to help financially ailing customers. It offers special terms and is willing to accept slow payment:

> It is the company's intention to build its business aggressively by every available means. This includes the use of capital funds to finance customers with future potential or market position who may be in need of financial help. This may be accomplished by extending special selling terms or accepting, on a controlled basis, payment beyond the regular terms of sale.

If such credit policies are clearly understood, company personnel can follow appropriate procedures and can respond in an informed and decisive manner to recurring situations and questions concerning special terms.

## Credit Management Objectives

Broadly speaking, the credit management function should manage the extension of credit and the collection of accounts receivable in a way that contributes to the attainment of corporate goals. These goals vary from company to company, and in the same company, from one occasion to the next. Credit management objectives must accommodate themselves to these differences.

An important point that is often misunderstood is the fact that the best credit management is not the one that has no losses. Every successful enterprise takes well-calculated risks. A sound credit policy accomplishes the following:

- Keeps slow collections and credit losses at a minimum and, at the same time,
- Contributes to the sales effort by helping to maximize *profitable* sales.

**Line or Staff Responsibilities.** Some credit departments—even in large, multi-plant corporations—approve each individual extension of credit, either through the establishment of prearranged credit limits or through individual order approval. These favor a high degree of centralized control in the credit management function even when they have a generally decentralized management environment.

In other organizations—particularly those embracing decentralized profit responsibility—credit management, along with other management functions, is decentralized in each plant. In this case, the role of the corporate credit management function is to act as advisor and consultant—while still exercising a measure of control.

For the controller in the relatively small concern, the centralized versus decentralized question may not be relevant. But if there is more than one plant or division or profit-centered product line, the question may, indeed, need to be considered.

There are those with credit management responsibility who assume that they must be given authority over the work assigned to them and are frustrated by being "overruled" by a superior at times. However, in every business, the president or owner has final responsibility for the success or failure of the enterprise, and in critical situations must make the final judgments. The credit person's responsibility is to make the best, most persuasive case for the position he or she thinks is right. Following this, he must implement, effectively and with good grace, the decision that has been made.

**The Salesperson's Role.** The sales representative's role in the credit and collection process varies widely from company to company. In some, sales representatives participate in the credit decisions and are responsible for collecting past due items. Other organizations make a conscious effort to exclude their sales representatives from the credit and collection function, feeling that such participation might mar cordial sales relationships or detract from the representatives' primary job of getting orders.

Whether or not it makes sense for salespersons to be involved in the credit-collection procedure depends primarily on the following factors:

- The way in which the business operates: what it sells, the number of customers, the size of the territory, and the nature of customer contact; and
- How the company looks upon its sales force: Are they company representatives in all aspects of the customer relationship or are they merely order takers?

In situations where sales representatives call frequently on a limited number of customers and maintain close relationships with them, they can effectively participate in the credit and collection function. In addition to the preparation of prospect lists, they should also be given all the information the credit department can furnish, not only about each prospect's credit standing, but about anything else that will help with the contact. Salespeople can contribute to the credit appraisal; even a chronically empty employee parking lot should raise questions and suggest an update of the prospect's financial situation.

Many professional salespeople want to be the point of contact when a customer account is delinquent. They not only fear that a contact from the office, if not handled properly, will harm the relationship, but they take pride in their total responsibility for all phases of the customer relationship—including payment. Functioning on the theory that the salesperson and the purchasing agent were the representatives of their respective companies in the negotiation of the sales contract, salespeople prefer to approach their counterparts, the purchasing agents, when an account is past due and a contract commitment has been broken, rather than have the contact be between the credit department and the customer's accounts payable department.

This approach is often successful. The purchasing agent knows his future negotiating position will be weak if his company has not honored its payment commitment. It is his job, then, to contact his own accounts payable department to see that the situation is corrected. This is no less than the purchasing agent would expect of the sales representative if the product ordered were not delivered as specified.

## Credit Procedures

Some organizations are highly structured and outline each operation in detail in a procedure manual. Others fear this process inhibits creativity and innovation and prefer a looser structure, in which the steps to be taken in performing each task are only generally prescribed. Once again, the controller's approach to credit procedures should be compatible with the overall corporate environment.

The following is an example of a credit procedure:

*Credit Approval at Order Entry*
Upon receipt of an order, the order entry clerk will check it against the Credit Approved File for credit approval. If the customer name appears in the Approved Credit File, the order entry clerk will initial the "Credit OK" square on the order form and pass it through. If the customer does not appear in the Credit Approved File, then the order will be passed to the Controller for credit approval.

Procedures are useful because they ensure that proper steps are followed in maintaining needed controls and accomplishing a job. They are also helpful in training new personnel. If credit procedures are formulated, however, they must be updated promptly whenever changes in operation occur.

### Managing Accounts Receivable

**Terms of Sale.** Accounts receivable result from the extension of credit providing for the delivery today of goods in exchange for a promise to pay at a future date. Terms of sale specify what that future date is to be.

Selling terms are agreed upon during sales negotiations and become a part of the sales/purchase contract. The payment commitment to which the buyer agrees must be as clearly understood by both parties as the delivery commitments undertaken by the seller. The salesperson should make this understanding clear, and making him aware of his role in achieving such an understanding is a first step in good credit management.

*Net terms.* Terms of sale specify when a bill is due for payment: in 10 days, or 30, or 60 from the date of the invoice, which should also be the date of the shipment. Payment at or before the due date is *prompt* under the terms of sale. In expressing terms, *EOM* means end of month and 10th prox. means the tenth of the following month.

*Cash discount.* To encourage immediate payment *before* the due date, the firm may offer a discount to be deducted from the face amount of the invoice if payment is made more quickly, usually within 10 days. Commonly encountered selling terms call for payment in 30 days with a one or two percent discount allowed for payment within ten days. The discount is expressed as 1–10–30 or 2–10–30 or 8–10–60, according to the terms offered.

**Effect of Terms of Sale on Receivables.** Terms of sale are a management decision and affect the amount of money tied up in accounts receivable. If the company specifies selling terms of Net 30 days or Net 60 days and offers no cash discount, DSO will surely run beyond the net terms of 30 or 60 days. Where terms are net, well-controlled DSO will exceed the due date by about 10 days—including mail time and the normal run of unavoidable past dues.

Terms of sale may be of long standing and may have been dictated by competition and industry practice. They should still be reexamined periodically in the light of changing conditions. Changing interest rates, for example, may suggest that the firm should shorten the terms, and institute or eliminate a cash discount.

## THE CREDIT DECISION

### The Three C's of Credit

The credit decision is based on the following questions: Will the promise to pay made by the buyer when credit is extended be honored? Will the order be paid for, and will it be paid for within the terms of the sale?

This determination involves an appraisal of the three C's of Credit—Character, Capacity, and Capital. Some credit managers will add other C's, such as Conditions and Coverage (insurance), but Character, Capacity, and Capital are basic.

**Character.** Businesses generally give prime importance to the appraisal of character. This quality makes individuals determined, in good times or bad, to meet commitments and pay just debts. If unexpected difficulties arise, there may be a delay in payment, but the person with character will honor obligations. Without the presence of "character," the situation is difficult from the beginning; it's hard to do business with someone who doesn't *want* to do the right thing.

**Capacity.** The ability to pay debts is important, too. An indication of capacity is found in the past record. Has there been past experience in the line? Is this a first business venture and, if so, does the past record of employment give an indication of the skills needed for the new venture? Do previous business failures cast a shadow over present chances for success? A checkered business career may indicate a lack of stability.

**Capital.** This asset must also be considered, but is possibly not as important as the others. Financial statements, if available, give information as to the capital available to the customer. Is it sufficient to carry on business in an orderly manner? Are operations being conducted at a profit? Are earnings kept in the business to finance sales growth? Are trading assets—inventory and accounts receivable—turning rapidly enough to allow for the prompt retirement of obligations?

## Financial Analysis

The controller managing credit is already well acquainted with financial analysis. But preparing and understanding—to say nothing of interpreting and analyzing—financial figures in relation to the credit decision, particularly in a marginal situation, requires a different perspective. Financial analysis tells a lot about Capital, but it also gives insight into a customer's Character and Capacity. The person possessing these traits is not likely to embark upon an ill-advised enterprise.

*Internal financial analysis* relates various items on single balance sheet and profit and loss statement, one to another, in percentage terms. It then compares these ratio percentages against median percentages for the subject's line of business. *Comparative financial analysis* follows trends in these ratios from one year to the next to determine in what direction the business is headed. (See Chapter 16.)

**The Marginal Risk Credit Decision.** When an investigation finds all three C's—Character, Capacity, and Capital—to be first-rate, the credit decision is easy. When one or more is uncertain and large dollar amounts are involved, the risk is then marginal. The marginal risk calls for more exhaustive investigation and consideration than the clearly defined case.

The marginal risk must be considered within the framework of corporate and credit policy. Do these policies allow for the taking of marginal credit risks? If so, then those responsible for credit management must balance the degree of risk and the probability of money tie-up against the benefits of making the sale.

The following *positive* factors might tip the scales in a marginal situation:

- This account has an unusually high profit margin.
- This account falls within a new plan/distribution area/sales territory whose growth the firm would like to encourage.
- This transaction features a new product, and the prospective customer controls important distribution.
- This account is a new company that, while weak at the start, has growth potential.
- This account is a longtime loyal customer whose prospects are likely to improve.

Negative aspects must also be taken into consideration. A major damaging aspect would be the fact that the potential business shows little chance for profit.

To summarize, the crucial question that must be answered in the affirmative before the marginal risk is taken is: Will an affirmative decision in this case contribute to overall corporate objectives?

## IMPLEMENTING THE CREDIT DECISION

### Credit Checking the Prospect List

The best time to make and implement the credit decision is before the customer's first order is received—even before any serious attempt to make the sale. This is particularly true in business situations with a long lead time and considerable expense between the first call on the prospect and the consummation of the sale. It is embarrassing and wasteful to expend time and money upon a prospect who, based upon a later credit investigation, is deemed unacceptable as a customer. The controller should, therefore, emphasize the importance of early credit checking to sales manager and salesperson alike.

### Approving Each Order for Credit

Once a prospect has become a customer, each order must be approved for credit before the goods go into production or are shipped. The means employed vary according to the type of business.

In some lines of business each order is for one or more custom made products that require close adherence to specifications and very careful costing. In this situation, the controller should approve each order for credit as he checks it for other important features, such as correct pricing, standard quantities, and arithmetic accuracy.

In most businesses, however, orders are relatively small, frequent, repetitious, and are received from the same customers. Given this situation, orders must be approved for credit by the controller *on an exceptions basis* and in an automatic fashion. If not, the controller will be bogged down in unnecessary paper work, and a stack of orders will await his personal attention, thus causing possibly harmful delays.

### Automatic Credit Approval at Order Entry

The fact that the controller does not personally scan every individual order need not mean that each order fails to receive approval for credit. In most businesses, 95 percent of all orders can be checked for credit at the *Order Entry Desk* and only the exception passed to the controller for attention. This involves the preparation of an *Approved Credit List* of customers who may be approved for credit without review or limitation. Order Entry, locating the customer's name on the Credit Approved List (or file), immediately initials the order to indicate credit approval. Orders from customers not in the file (or on the list) are passed to the controller for consideration.

For his own reference, the controller may wish to set up a Credit Control card file on all active customers and prospects. A green card might signify a "no limit" account, a yellow card might carry a dollar limit within which the account should be maintained, while a red card would signify those few customers and prospects to whom credit is *not* to be extended. Names on the green cards would make up the Approved Credit List for the automatic approval of orders at Order Entry.

The Credit Control file is no better than the decisions it reflects. It should be reviewed at least annually in the light of payment experience and outside information. Changes, as necessary, must be made promptly, and the sales manager and sales representatives must be immediately informed.

It is difficult to overemphasize the importance of a procedure (written or unwritten) that provides for the automatic approval of orders on an exceptions basis. In most situations, the controller should not see more than 5 or 10 percent of orders received and will thus be free to devote the time and attention to those few that need it.

### Sources of Information

**The Importance of Facts.** Every credit decision involves choosing the most attractive (and sometimes the least *unattractive*) from among all available alternatives. Since making these choices requires the weighing of information, part of the job of managing credit is investigative.

The controller must foster and maintain relationships with reliable sources of information and must know how to approach these sources. However, no time should be spent on unnecessary investigation. A first grade credit rating or one's own payment experience may be sufficient for the relatively small order. On the other hand, it is well worth spending time and money investigating the marginal risk —the risk involving large sums of money where the decision may mean success or failure to the credit grantor.

The controller, acting as credit manager, should also establish relationships with others having similar responsibilities in their firms. The fostering of such relationships is one of the many benefits to be derived from participation in the activities of a local credit management association affiliated with the National Association of Credit Management. Such contacts can be particularly helpful when they are formed through a local or national industry credit group.

Name of
Company _____ Date _____

Street Address _____

City _____ State _____ Zip Code _____

BANK REFERENCE _____

Street Address _____

City _____ State _____ Zip Code _____

TRADE REFERENCES

1. Name _____

   Street Address _____

   City _____ State _____ Zip Code _____

2. Name _____

   Street Address _____

   City _____ State _____ Zip Code _____

3. Name _____

   Street Address _____

   City _____ State _____ Zip Code _____

Anticipated Amount of First Order _____

Anticipated Monthly Requirements _____

Frequency and Amount of Shipments _____

Comments _____

Attach Copy of Latest Financial Statements.

FIGURE 24.3  CUSTOMER'S CREDIT APPLICATION

**Direct Sources.** These sources are in a position to supply information from firsthand experience. Some of this information can be obtained through references supplied by the prospective customer on a routine credit application. (See Figure 24.3 for a standard application form.) Direct investigation involves verbal and/or written contacts with these and other sources.

*The subject.* It may be feasible for the controller to start by interviewing the subject of the investigation, but only when the expected results will justify the expenditure of time by both parties. During the interview, the approach should be forthright. If financial figures are needed, they should be requested beforehand, and a discussion of finances should logically follow. The subject may want to refer to others in a position to add information: his banker, accountant, or other suppliers.

*The banker.* The prospective customer's banker can be an invaluable source, and the customer often gives his bank as a credit reference. Figure 24.4 is an example of a follow-up to such a referral. When the customer does not authorize his bank to release other than routine data, it is unreasonable to expect the banker to enter into a discussion with an unknown firm and reveal confidential information about a customer. It is often best to use an indirect connection to the customer's bank, through the inquirer's own bank. Once a relationship of confidence has been established, information flows more readily. The inquirer should first explain the nature of the problem that prompts the inquiry—the amount of the order, payment terms, and its own past payment experience.

---

Date _____

Central City Bank
Anytown, U.S.A.

Gentlemen:

    (Customer Name, Street Address, City, and Zip Code)
The _____, has referred your bank to us as reference.

They are requesting open account credit on our regular 30-day terms and will probably require up to $ _____ .

We would appreciate comments on your banking experience with them, and any other information which would be useful to help us make a credit decision.

A stamped, self-addressed envelope is enclosed for your convenience.

Thank you for your cooperation.

                                Sincerely,

                                COMPANY

                                Name
                                Title

---

FIGURE 24.4   CREDIT INFORMATION REQUEST—CUSTOMER'S BANK

What can be learned varies from bank to bank and also depends on the relationship the bank has with *its* customer. Generally, the following can be learned: the relationship in general terms, size of balances, how long the account has been opened, and if it has been handled satisfactorily. The banker may also indicate, in general terms, the size and frequency of the prospect's loans and whether they are unsecured, guaranteed by a third party, or secured by collateral. Under some circumstances, the banker may even express an opinion as to the ability of management.

*Another supplier.* The prospective client's supplier is a third source of firsthand information. If a supplier is given as a reference by the subject of the investigation, a standard credit inquiry can be sent. A typical form is shown in Figure 24.5. Payment information in a routine case can also be obtained from a credit reporting agency. Specific person-to-person inquiries should be confined to the marginal cases.

In such marginal cases, the inquirer should carefully identify himself and the reason for the inquiry. He should ask concise questions and terminate the interview as soon as he acquires the needed information.

The supplier as a source is in a position to furnish information about the relationship established with the subject of the inquiry: how long the relationship has existed, how large the account has been in the recent past, whether or not payments have been received within terms, and, if not, how many days beyond the due date.

**Indirect Sources.** As indicated earlier, firsthand information may be valuable, but it may not be practical to pursue these sources when, for a minimal charge, the same facts can be supplied by others.

*Credit Interchange and NACIS.* Under the auspices of local affiliated associations and the National Association of Credit Management, in cooperation with TRW, Inc., Credit Interchange and the National Credit Information Service (NACIS) provide secondhand information obtained from suppliers concerning their payment experience with customers, as well as from banks concerning their relationships. A number of agencies in the consumer credit reporting area also provide payment experience on individuals.

*Credit reporting agencies.* In the commercial credit field, Dun & Bradstreet is the general credit reporting agency. Other agencies cover specialized fields, such as textiles, clothing, furniture, produce, and soft drink bottlers. Most of these agencies, like Dun & Bradstreet, write credit reports that are condensed into credit ratings.

Dun & Bradstreet ratings, with those of the specialized agencies, can and should be used to pass on run-of-the-mill credit applications. The rating is broken down into two parts: one indicates financial strength and the other indicates credit stability. Dun & Bradstreet ratings range from 5 A1, $50 million of capital and first grade, to H H4, less than $5,000 and fair. In most cases the credit rating alone will suffice. Figure 24.6 is an example of a form that can be used to request credit ratings and/or reports.

Date _____

Name _____

Street Address _____

City and State _____

To _____

_____

_____

In order that we may consider opening a credit account with the above, we ask you in confidence to give us the following information:

√    Check Manner
       of Payment

☐ Discounts

☐ Prompt and Satisfactory

☐ Prompt to ........ days slow

☐ Pays on account

☐ Asks for more time

☐ Slow but collectible

☐ Slow and unsatisfactory

☐ Accepts C. O. D.'s promptly

☐ Settles by trade acceptance

☐ Notes paid at maturity

☐ Account secured

☐ Collected by attorney

☐ In hands of attorney

Sold from _____ To _____

Terms _____

Largest amount owing recently      $_____

Total amount now owing      $_____

Amount past due .......................... $_____

Recent trend
toward            ☐ Promptness      ☐ Slowness

Makes unjust claims (State them) _____

_____

_____

Credit refused (State cause) _____

_____

_____

_____

⟶ If you have had no experience within a year. please check and return. ☐

Stamped addressed envelope is enclosed for your reply.

We will be pleased to reciprocate in giving you any information we have regarding credits.
Yours truly,

_____

_____

_____

FIGURE 24.5   STANDARD CREDIT INQUIRY

```
                                              (Division)
To: _____ From _____

Subject: _____ Date: _____

Company _____

Street Address _____

City _____ State _____ Zip Code _____

Rating _____ Date Established _____

_____  Rating
_____  If "Fair," Order Report
_____  If Not Rated, Order Report
_____  If Not Listed, Order Report
_____  Order Report
```

FIGURE 24.6  REQUEST FOR D&B RATING AND/OR REPORT

*Retail credit bureaus.* In the consumer credit field, retail credit bureaus bring together information concerning an individual's paying habits, the extent of credit buying, and the ability to handle the payment of accounts promptly. Most metropolitan credit bureaus are linked by computer to form large national consumer credit reporting services. These services are computerized and offer immediate access to millions of individual files. For instance, Trans Union Systems Corporation in Chicago, which claims files in the 70 millions, answers 110,000 inquiries each day, 60 percent of them instantaneously processed through the use of terminals.

*Newspapers, periodicals, record information.* Magazines, business periodicals, and the daily press are valuable indirect sources for providing information. The investment manuals, *Moody's* and *Standard & Poors*, are readily available sources of information on listed companies.

Court House, Secretary of State, and other filings are sometimes necessary ingredients in the credit investigation. The filing of a tax lien indicates that the debtor is in extreme financial difficulty, and that the general creditor's asset protection is removed; the filing of several supplier suits for payment is another indication of the customer's financial straits. *Daily Record* publications are available in most cities.

**Internal Sources.** The controller managing credit should not overlook sources of information under the company's own roof. In-house business associates will be able to make valuable contributions to the credit decision.

*The sales representative.* Some firms require the salesperson to obtain credit information on every new or prospective customer in the form of a credit application form. Other businesses consider this procedure an unnecessary deterrent to the closing of the sale, particularly in the case of a large national concern of unquestioned credit standing.

Companies that decide to involve salespeople in the credit decision find that their constant contact and close relationship with the customer put them in a position to evaluate the following:

- *Management.* They can judge the customer's management attitude and capability.
- *Plant and Equipment.* Visiting many businesses in the same line, they can evaluate plant efficiency, the attitude of plant personnel, and in the case of a retailer, the attractiveness of the store layout.
- *Location.* They can form an opinion of the economic desirability of the location and its competitive advantages or disadvantages.
- *Conditions.* Selling to other companies in the same industry and area, they can evaluate conditions as they affect the customer or prospect.

Salespeople can also be on the alert for changes and, as required, can obtain trade references and financial statements.

*Company records.* Accounts receivable records reveal past payment experience and how large the account has been. This information is helpful when the controller considers extending credit to a former customer or considers expanding credit to an existing customer.

*Sales analyses and cost estimates.* Sales analyses provide facts concerning volume and profitability, an integral part of any intelligent credit decision. Cost estimates inform the credit manager of projected profitability that, too, must be a part of the decision.

*Line management.* Everyone from the president/owner of the business down to the shift foreman in the plant can contribute facts that enter into the credit decision. How does the job run on the equipment? Is there costly preparation that may destroy profitability? Are there delivery problems, and will trucks be tied up unreasonably at the customer's dock? Such considerations may seem unrelated to the credit decision, but the balanced judgment must weigh all known risks against profit potential.

The controller and his staff should gather all pertinent facts on a potential customer, but should cease promptly once they have learned enough to make the credit decision. It is wasteful to go further just to "build a file," and unnecessary time, effort, and expense should be avoided.

## COLLECTING THE DELINQUENT ACCOUNT

There are those who look upon collection as an unpleasant duty to be avoided or put off if possible. This is the wrong attitude for approaching the job. Following up on a past due account is not "begging for money;" it is merely asking that the customer fulfill his promise to pay for the delivery of specified goods or services. Once the supplier has delivered as ordered, the customer is committed to payment.

## Sales Follow-Up

Company policy determines whether or not the salesperson is the first point of collection follow-up. If so, the action must be instituted by specific procedures. The controller may point out a specific delinquency that needs attention. Or the procedure can take the form of a regularly furnished aging of the customer accounts handled by each sales representative on the basis of which the controller automatically takes action. In this case, when payments are received the sales representative must also be given timely information.

## Credit Department Follow-Up

**Mail Approach.** Some firms favor a succession of collection letters at regular intervals and in ascending urgency. The first communication is sent promptly as the account becomes past due—perhaps on the 35th day from invoice date in the case of 30 day terms. It should be routine in tone and something like the following:

> May we call your attention to our Invoice No. 2345 for $1,234.56 dated April 25, 19__, which was due for payment May 24.
> We would appreciate your payment of this item, which is now past due.
> Thank you very much.

A second letter to be mailed on the 45th day might read:

> Please once again let us call your attention to our Invoice No. 2345 for $1,234.56 dated April 25, 19__ and now considerably past due.
> May we ask that you let us have immediate payment.

A third and final letter to be mailed 60 days from invoice date would be more forceful and would indicate the possibility of further action in the absence of payment:

> We have received no response to our previous letters of _____ and _____ calling your attention to our unpaid and seriously past due Invoice No. 2345 dated April 25, 19__ in the amount of $1,234.56.
> We hope that you will let us have payment immediately. If we do not receive your check by _____, we will have no choice but to take other action.

**Phone Approach.** Follow-up by telephone uses the same pattern. Three successive contacts at regular intervals are made in ascending order of urgency. The first calls attention to the unpaid item and suggests that it might have been overlooked. The second is more forceful, and the third raises the possibility that the firm will take further action if it does not receive payment.

If the credit manager, or the person designated to make the calls, has no particular person to contact, he would direct the phone inquiry to the Accounts Payable Department. If possible, the call should be directed to someone of authority in the customer's organization.

**Importance of a Tickler.** The necessity for strictly adhered-to follow-up cannot be overemphasized. Consistent follow-ups are essential, not only in connection with the regular succession of follow-up contacts by phone or mail, but, more importantly, in cases when a promise of payment has been made. When Mr. Jones promises to mail a check on Monday, he must be called on Tuesday if the check has not been received. Failure to follow up encourages future broken promises.

It is foolish to rely on memory for such a tickler; some mechanical means is a must for the controller managing credit. Many find that a daily calendar serves the purpose.

### Working With the Problem Account

Many different problem situations are encountered when handling individual accounts for which payment cannot be obtained in a normal manner.

**Payment Double-Up.** Sometimes an account will build up to the point where the customer is unable to pay without being given some extra time. The credit grantor may then believe that it makes sense to work with the customer. One way to work down a past due account under these circumstances is to continue deliveries, provided payment is made for each new delivery. An additional amount is added to apply against the old balance. An objection to this method is that it discourages new orders because of the extra payment requirement and therefore works against both additional business and old account reduction. This is particularly true when the customer can easily turn to another supplier.

**Promissory Notes to Close Out an Account.** Another method of reducing a past due account is to take interest bearing notes for the full amount of the old account. Installment payments that are in line with the customer's ability to pay can be scheduled until the old balance is paid in full. In the meantime, new deliveries can be made if principal and interest note payments are up to date.

**Voluntary Standby Agreement.** A creditor or group of creditors may agree to postpone the collection of an account until a temporary difficulty is resolved. This makes sense only if the creditor believes the debtor is doing something to resolve the temporary problem.

**Out-of-Court Arrangements.** The controller, acting as credit manager, will encounter situations in which a customer, in financial difficulty and unable to pay bills as they fall due, calls a number of creditors together and, in order to avoid bankruptcy, makes an out-of-court settlement offer. This may be a compromise offer to pay less than 100 cents on the dollar, a stretch-out of payment over an extended period of time, or both. In out-of-court situations, each creditor is free to accept or reject the offered proposal. If an individual creditor does not accept the proposed plan, then that creditor is not bound by its provisions and is free, having rejected the plan offered, to negotiate independently with the debtor or pursue collection independently. In other words, in an out-of-court settlement, each creditor is on his own and is not bound by the majority. However, the settlement offer is usually contingent upon acceptance by a substantial majority of the creditors in both number and amount.

**Creditors' Committees.** In out-of-court cases, creditors' committees are sometimes formed to oversee the operation of the settlement plan, including an overview of operations. Such committees usually consist of six or eight creditors who have a major interest. Participation in creditors' committees can involve considerable time, attention, and often frustration. Membership on such a committee makes sense *if* the creditor's financial involvement is substantial *and* if the plan for rehabilitation agreed to by debtor and creditors appears to have a reasonable chance of success.

**Collection Agencies.** When all the above efforts have failed to produce results, the controller may want to place the delinquent account with an outside collection agency. Such an agency can often collect when the client has been unable to do so. The agency may be operated as an independent business or it may be an adjunct of a local chapter of the National Association of Credit Management. The collection fee, a percentage *of the amount collected,* varies according to the amount of the claim (the usual range is 10 to 25 percent).

The controller should select the collection agency that subscribes to the principles of the American Bar Association but does not offer legal services as such. If its services include a forwarding service, the attorneys to whom accounts are forwarded should abide by the rules suggested by the Commercial Law League of America, or by their local bar association.

### Working With a Bankrupt Customer

Bankruptcy is a legal proceeding conducted in a court of law. The controller, acting as credit manager, will do well to consult legal counsel in such matters, but some background in the nature of bankruptcy and the proper procedures to follow when a customer files a bankruptcy petition will be helpful.

The purpose of bankruptcy legislation is two-fold:

- As a creditor's remedy it marshalls all of the assets of the debtor and provides equal distribution to all creditors.

- As a debtor's remedy it provides the debtor with a fresh start in economic life by discharging past debts.

The *Bankruptcy Reform Act of 1978*, effective October 1, 1979, was passed by Congress as the first completely new bankruptcy legislation in the United States, replacing the Bankruptcy Act of 1898.

**Voluntary and Involuntary Bankruptcy.** A *voluntary* case is begun when the debtor files a voluntary petition in bankruptcy, which then constitutes "an order for relief." An *involuntary* petition in bankruptcy may be filed by three or more creditors with unsecured claims totalling at least $5,000, or, if there are fewer than a total of 12 creditors, one or more creditors having claims of at least $5,000 may file.

**Liquidation.** Chapter 7 of the Bankruptcy Reform Act provides the framework for an ordinary liquidation proceeding. This is sometimes called a "straight bankruptcy," and provides for the appointment of a trustee, the appointment of a creditors' committee, the collection, liquidation, and distribution of the assets of the debtor on a pro-rata basis, and the discharge of the debtor from bankruptcy.

**Reorganization.** Chapter 11 of the new code provides for reorganization of the debtor firm in order to promote its rehabilitation and its continued viability. The filing of a Chapter 11 case, either voluntarily or involuntarily, operates as an automatic stay of legal action, which might threaten the continued existence of the business.

The new code authorizes the trustee appointed by the court—and this may include the debtor-in-possession—to continue operation of the business. If, in ordinary business operations, the trustee or debtor-in-possession requires additional supplies, these may be obtained in the form of unsecured credit, which debt, as a part of the cost of administration, then has priority over any pre-Chapter 11 debts.

**Plan of Arrangement.** The debtor, in a Chapter 11 proceeding, has the exclusive right to file a plan of reorganization for 120 days after the filing of the bankruptcy petition. Thereafter, any party at interest, including the debtor, the trustee, a creditors' committee, or a creditor, may file a plan. The plan must: designate classes of claims and classes of interest; provide the same treatment for each claim or interest of a particular class; and provide adequate means for the plan's execution.

After notice and upon disclosure of the plan details to all those affected, the court holds a hearing on confirmation of the plan, conditioned upon acceptance by each class of creditors and by the shareholders. Two-thirds of the amount of claims and more than half of the number of each class of creditors must accept the plan; two-thirds in amount, regardless of number, is required for the shareholders. At least one class of claimants must accept the plan, but if one class does not accept, the plan may still be confirmed if the court finds that the class is treated fairly by the plan.

Once a plan of reorganization has been confirmed by the court, it then goes into effect, and all creditors, whether or not they voted to accept individually, are bound by its provisions.

**Creditors' Committees.** Chapter 7 of the Bankruptcy Code concerns *liquidation* proceedings. It provides that the creditors should meet within a reasonable time after the filing. At this meeting, the creditors may elect a creditors' committee of not less than three, nor more than eleven creditors. This committee may consult with the trustee concerning his administration of the estate, make recommendations concerning the performance of duties, and bring to the court's attention any question affecting the administration of the estate.

Creditors' committees in *reorganization* are appointed by the court as quickly as possible after the filing of the petition. The creditors' committee in a bankruptcy reorganization will ordinarily consist of the seven largest unsecured creditors willing to serve. The court may appoint a creditors' committee organized prior to the bankruptcy filing if that committee was fairly chosen and fairly represents the different claims in the proceeding. A creditors' committee in a reorganization case will have considerable input in the administration of the estate and may select attorneys, accountants, or other agents who are usually paid compensation by the debtor. If the controller is appointed to the creditors' committee, he should accept the appointment in order to have a voice in the formulation of the plan of reorganization.

**Filing of Claim.** When a bankruptcy has been filed in court, all creditors are notified. The notification is accompanied by a Proof of Claim form used in filing the creditor's claim in court. It is essential that each creditor file this form by the final date specified; otherwise, the claim may not be allowed.

The Bankruptcy Reform Act includes a provision for a creditor to set off a mutual debt owed by the creditor to the debtor if the debt being offset arose before the commencement of the bankruptcy proceedings. In this event, the payable being offset against the receivable should be subtracted to arrive at the amount of the claim being filed.

**Grounds for Filing Involuntary Petition and Penalties if Controverted.** Grounds for the filing of an involuntary bankruptcy petition are:

- The debtor is generally not paying its debts as they become due; or
- Within 120 days before the filing of the involuntary petition a custodian other than a trustee, receiver, or agent appointed to take charge of enforcing a lien on *substantially less than all of the property of the debtor*, was appointed or took possession of the property.

If an involuntary bankruptcy petition is successfully controverted by the debtor, the court may award a judgment against the petitioning creditors for all costs and reasonable attorneys' fees. Also, if a trustee took possession after the filing of the involuntary petition, the court may award damages resulting from the taking of possession by the trustee, which damages may include those sustained by the loss of business. If the court determines the involuntary petition to have been filed in bad faith, the court may also award punitive damages.

A *Bankruptcy Reform Act Manual* has been published by the Commercial Law League of America and is included in the list of suggested readings that accompanies this chapter. Once again, it is recommended to the controller managing credit that such a manual and/or legal counsel be consulted in collection cases involving bankruptcy proceedings.

### The Uncollectable Account

There comes a time when the controller, acting as credit manager, determines that an account receivable appearing on the books is no longer collectable and must be written off as a bad debt. Bad debts as a percentage of annual sales range between .05 percent or less in certain lines of manufacturing to 1 percent in retail trade.

**Bad Debt Write-Off.** Some concerns follow a policy of quick bad debt write-off. The account is written off almost as quickly as doubt of collectability occurs. Then, if the account is later collected, there is a *bad debt recovery*. Other concerns follow the opposite practice of waiting until an account offers virtually no hope of collection before writing it off. This action might be taken in the case of a judgment having been returned uncollectable, a no-distribution-to-unsecured creditors bankruptcy closing, or an absconding, in which the debtor has disappeared and cannot be found.

From the standpoint of the Internal Revenue Service and the outside auditors, the important thing is for the write-off policy to be consistent from one year to the next. The IRS frowns on a firm inconsistently using bad debt write-offs to influence profits.

**Allowance for Doubtful Accounts.** When an uncollectable account receivable is written off, it must be charged against something. This can be either a direct charge against operations or a charge against an allowance set up to provide for doubtful accounts. If the charge is against the allowance, then the allowance may, in turn, need to be replenished, and the replenishment becomes a current operating charge.

The allowance for doubtful accounts should relate to write-off experience, but it need not be confined within write-off experience of the recent past. Current receivables should be analyzed and an adequate allowance developed. Conservative practice often has the allowance for doubtful accounts in the neighborhood of 3 to 5 percent of gross accounts receivable. If accounts receivable average one month's sales, a reserve of 3 percent of accounts receivable translates into about one quarter of one percent of sales.

## THE COMPUTER AND CREDIT MANAGEMENT

The development of minicomputers has lowered the cost of data processing and made its application practical to businesses of medium and even smaller size. A number of companies now offer *applications software* packages that perform most of the functions required in the management of accounts receivable.

Applications software packages can: maintain accounts receivable records, adding new invoices and applying payments immediately; automatically approve orders; answer requests for payment information; assist with collection activities; help control unauthorized customer deductions and adjustments; and prepare management reports on accounts receivable condition.

The controller managing credit should become familiar with the possibilities of data processing for accounts receivable management. (See Chapter 11.)

## EVALUATING THE CREDIT MANAGEMENT FUNCTION

The controller's management of the accounts receivable investment—credit and collection—is evaluated in the light of its contribution to overall business objectives. Reports to management might include the following:

- *Accounts Receivable Aging.* The total of accounts receivable broken down by those current, 30–60 days old, 60–90, and over 90.
- *DSO Report.* A report of Days' Sales Outstanding with month-to-month and year-to-year comparisons.
- *Bad Debt Reporting.* A listing of accounts written off, with the reason, a total of all bad debts, and their percentage to sales.

Given terms of 30 days, accounts receivable will usually run 80 to 85 percent current, with 3 to 5 percent over 90 days old. DSO should be no more than 10 days beyond due date under net selling terms. The inclusion of a cash discount will reduce DSO below the net due date to something like 25 or 27 days. Bad debt write-offs should be within an acceptable range for the industry and prior company history.

Basic to credit management is its contribution to *profitable* sales. An effective performance starts with constructive aid in the preparation of the prospect list, continues with a significant contribution to the sales training process, and culminates in the exercise of tact and diplomacy—along with firmness—in the collection effort.

## SUGGESTED READING

*Bankruptcy Reform Act Manual.* Chicago: Commercial Law League of America, 1979.

Barzman, Sol. *Everyday Credit Checking: A Practical Guide.* New York: The National Association of Credit Management, 1980.

————. *The Collection Program: A Practical Guide.* New York: The Service Corporation of the National Association of Credit Management, 1979.

Bryan, William H. *New Horizons in Credit Management.* New York: The Service Corporation of the National Association of Credit Management, 1977.

Cole, Robert H. *Consumer and Commercial Credit Management.* Homewood, Illinois: Richard C. Irwin, Inc., 1979.

*Collier Bankruptcy Manual,* 3rd ed. New York: Matthew Bender, 1979.

*Credit Manual of Commercial Laws.* New York: National Association of Credit Management, 1980.

Redding, Harold T. and Knight, Guyon H., III. *Credit and Collections.* New York: Thomas Y. Crowell Company, 1974.

# 25

# Investment of Surplus Funds

*Robert Ford*

## THE CONTROLLER'S ROLE

### Sources and Uses of Surplus Funds

There are two main sources of surplus funds within a corporation:

- Transaction balances. The cash necessary to meet day-to-day business expenses does not coincide exactly with receipts. The daily mismatch of receipts and disbursements, when the former is greater, gives rise to surplus funds.
- Precautionary balances. These balances, held as a buffer against unforeseen events, are surplus in nature until an event occurs that requires their use.

**25-1**

Although economists identify the transaction and precautionary motives (along with speculative) as reasons for holding cash, these funds may be in cash, or near-cash assets, (i.e., marketable securities).

There are a wide variety of uses for long-term surplus funds other than holding cash or short-term marketable securities. Included among these are the retirement of debt, acquisition of outstanding stock, new business acquisition, and so on. The controller must be in a position to adequately evaluate the options and to make recommendations consistent with management philosophy, objectives, and guidelines.

## Planning and Control

The controller has a key role in determining what funds will be available for investment and the period for which those funds will be available. This planning of cash resources must be done on both a long-term and short-term basis.

**Long-Term Planning.** On a long-term (or intermediate) basis, the controller can project financing needs, investable funds and the options available for these by use of such a tool as the *statement of sources and uses of funds*. While helpful in planning an investment strategy for surplus funds, this analysis does not provide sufficient detail for determining the future amount of funds available for short-term investment, or the duration of their availability.

**Short-Term Planning.** It is necessary to develop a month-by-month projection of funds available or funds required. The first phase of this projection is the forecasting of cash receipts on a monthly basis. Figure 25.1 illustrates a cash receipts schedule for a six-month period. Using sales projections and historical data on accounts receivable collections, it is possible to forecast receipts over a short-term period. The same is true of disbursements. As illustrated in Figure 25.2, a six-month projection can be made which includes all significant cash disbursements for that period. The resulting balance projections in Figure 25.3 indicate that surplus funds will be available in April, May, and June, while financing must be secured during the two preceding months.

|  | Jan. | Feb. | Mar. | Apr. | May | June |
|---|---|---|---|---|---|---|
| Cash Sales | 34 | 40 | 25 | 50 | 62 | 70 |
| A/R Collections | 312 | 260 | 320 | 460 | 510 | 440 |
| Investment Interest | 6 | 4 | 8 | 5 | 5 | 6 |
| Rents & Royalties | 10 | 12 | 12 | 12 | 10 | 16 |
| Total Receipts | 362 | 316 | 365 | 527 | 587 | 532 |

FIGURE 25.1   FORECAST OF MONTHLY CASH RECEIPTS (IN THOUSANDS OF DOLLARS)

The balance projections may be made on a monthly basis, as shown, or they may be done weekly, or even daily. As the time period for the projection becomes shorter, it becomes necessary to draw a distinction among *company ledger balances*, *bank ledger balances* and *bank available balances*. The example of a check received in payment illustrates this distinction. When the check is received in the company's office, cash is debited, accounts receivable is credited, and the company has recorded an increase of cash on its books. When the check is deposited and the bank posts the item to the company's account, the bank ledger balance is increased. Based on the mechanics of check clearing, when the check has been "collected," the company's account will show an increase in its available bank balance. It is this available balance that comprises surplus funds for investment.

## MANAGEMENT GUIDELINES

Every portfolio manager is limited, to some extent, in his choice of investments. Sometimes, he is simply limited by the choice of investment instruments available at a particular time, or by the funds available over a certain time period. More often, however, senior management of the company has imposed certain investment guidelines under which he must operate. These guidelines are often a formal statement of the company's investment objectives and usually establish constraints in three areas.

### The Investment Instrument

Many companies have guidelines limiting the short-term portfolio to the instruments of specific issuers. For example, one major industrial company limits its portfolio to U.S. Government issued or U.S. Government guaranteed securities. There may also be limits placed on the proportion of any one instrument in the portfolio,

| | Jan. | Feb. | Mar. | Apr. | May | June |
|---|---|---|---|---|---|---|
| Accounts Payable | 260 | 210 | 220 | 300 | 325 | 320 |
| Payroll | 95 | 100 | 100 | 115 | 120 | 118 |
| Taxes | 35 | | | 35 | | |
| Capital Expenditures | | | 15 | | 100 | |
| Dividends | | | | | | 75 |
| Miscellaneous | 20 | 25 | 25 | 25 | 25 | 25 |
| Total Disbursements | 410 | 335 | 360 | 475 | 570 | 538 |

FIGURE 25.2   FORECAST OF MONTHLY DISBURSEMENTS (IN THOUSANDS OF DOLLARS)

or dollar limits set on a particular type of investment. Typically, this is done for reasons of diversification. Limits may range to a high of 100 percent on Treasury issues, while 20 to 30 percent may be the maximum on commercial paper or bankers' acceptances.

## Specific Groups or Names

This type of guideline attempts to restrict exposure to credit risk by limiting the portfolio to a select group of creditworthy issuers, or by necessitating diversification into more than one issuer's securities. The portfolio manager is often restricted to commercial paper that is rated highest by the rating services, or to the certificates of deposits issued by the ten largest banks. These limits are sometimes expressed in dollar amounts, such as "no more than $1 million of CDs of any one bank." Occasionally, the limits will be much narrower, as in "only CDs of banks with which we have a major borrowing relationship."

## Maturity Limits

There are often limits to the maturity of investments, particularly in a *passively managed* portfolio. A passively managed portfolio is one in which the majority of the instruments are held to maturity unless the firm's liquidity dictates otherwise. In such cases, management guidelines might restrict the portfolio manager to investments of no longer than ninety days, or to an average maturity of thirty days. It is less common in an actively managed portfolio, where the manager might routinely go out five or ten years on a Treasury Note and in times of falling rates sell it in three months for a gain.

The manager of the investment portfolio should have a set of guidelines defining the parameters under which he may operate, but it is just as important that the manager inform senior management of the consequences of such restrictions. He must explain the risk/reward trade-offs inherent in each of their expected long-term effects on the portfolio's return on investment.

|  | Jan. | Feb. | Mar. | Apr. | May | June |
|---|---|---|---|---|---|---|
| Total Receipts | 362 | 316 | 365 | 527 | 587 | 532 |
| Total Disbursements | 410 | 335 | 360 | 475 | 570 | 538 |
| Net Cash Flow | (48) | (19) | 5 | 52 | 17 | (6) |
| Beginning Cash | 50 | 2 | (17) | (12) | 40 | 57 |
| Ending Cash | 2 | (17) | (12) | 40 | 57 | 51 |

FIGURE 25.3   NET CASH FLOW AND BALANCE PROJECTIONS (IN THOUSANDS OF DOLLARS)

## INVESTMENT CRITERIA

Acting within the guidelines that senior management has prescribed, the portfolio manager must set certain criteria as to how much risk he is willing to assume in order to achieve a given yield for the portfolio. On a particular day, the portfolio manager might find money market instruments[1] yielding from 7 to 14 percent. To properly evaluate these securities, he must assess the types of risk involved to achieve the higher yields. As a general rule, the greater the risk, the higher the yield one should expect. The portfolio manager is attempting to find the proper mix of safety, liquidity, and yield. In making this investment decision, the areas for concern are *credit risk* and *market risk*. For foreign instruments, there is also the question of sovereign risk.

### Credit Risk

Simply stated, credit risk is the possibility that the issuer of a security may default on his obligation, and the firm will not receive full principal at maturity. In broad terms, this risk is defined by the type of instrument and the guarantees behind it. For example, in the tax exempt market, what is referred to as General Obligation Bonds (GOs) are secured by the full faith and credit of the issuer. As a class, they carry more credit risk than a U.S. Treasury Bond, which is guaranteed by the U.S. Government. In more specific terms, the credit risk can be defined within the same type of instrument. The credit risk of a particular GO can be approximated by the ratings issued by services such as Moody's and Standard & Poor's.

**The Rating Services.** Ratings provided by outside services enable the portfolio manager to better evaluate the credit risk of certain money market securities. The most useful are the ratings of Moody's and Standard & Poor's for municipal bonds; those two, plus Fitch, are used to rate commercial paper.

Moody's Investors Service rates both municipal bonds and notes as well as commercial paper. The ratings for municipals range from Aaa for best-quality grade through C for the lowest-rated grade. Additionally, the highest-quality bonds carry the additional designation "1." Higher-rated bonds in the "high-quality grade" would be designated Aa-1. Moody's also rates short-term notes in four grades, MIG1, the highest, through MIG4, the lowest. Commercial paper is rated by Moody's as P-1, P-2, P-3, with P-1 being the highest rating.

The Standard & Poor's ratings for municipal bonds are very similar to Moody's. The criteria used for rating are also similar. Standard & Poor's rates commercial paper issuers into four broad categories, A through D. The highest rating, A, is further subdivided into A-1, A-2, and A-3. The fact that there are fewer categories for commercial paper ratings is due to the nature of the inherent credit risk. The

---

[1] As referred to in this chapter, the money market is the short-term (under one year) market for low-risk, highly liquid debt securities.

issuers of commercial paper are unlikely to default due to insolvency. The major concern is one of liquidity. As the paper matures, does the issuer have sufficient access to the cash necessary to refund it?

**Other Credit Criteria.** The instruments that do not need to be analyzed for credit risk are Treasury Securities. With these securities, the exposure to credit risk is nonexistent, short of the fall of the government. In that case, most investors would have more worries than just the loss of an investment in Treasuries.

Other instruments, such as certificates of deposit, do expose the investor to credit risk. As a result, the risk must be measured in terms of the creditworthiness of the issuing bank. Some investors in CDs limit themselves to the banks with which they have lending or depository relationships. Others delve into the financial statements published by banks and digest the minutely detailed information issued by firms that track banks, such as Keefe, Bruyette and Woods, or Sheshunoff and Company.

The same might be said for the risk inherent in bankers' acceptances. Although the BA is a primary obligation of the bank that "accepted" it, it is a contingent obligation of the drawer. The resulting credit risk is minimal, and since the Federal Reserve in 1913 permitted banks to accept time drafts, giving rise to a bankers' acceptance market, no investor has ever lost a dollar of principal.

The amount of credit risk that the investor is willing to assume in order to raise his yield is dependent upon the importance he places on safety.

## Market Risk

The volatility of interest rates gives rise to a measure of market (or price) risk in money market instruments. When rates move up, the price of money market obligations falls until it reaches a level that offers a return consistent with the new level of rates. It is important to note that the longer the current maturity of a money-market security, the more volatile the price. Also, for securities that bear a stated interest rate (or coupon),[2] the lower the coupon, the greater the relative change in price when interest levels change.

The amount of market risk that an investor is willing to take is in direct relation to liquidity as one of his primary criteria. If he must sell when rates are rising, there is a possibility that he will not recover his entire principal. If rates are falling, he may wish to hold a particular security to produce a gain, but cannot because of his liquidity requirements. In this case, he incurs the opportunity cost of the foregone earnings.

Since the yields on money market instruments are not quoted on a comparable basis, a restatement needs to be made and a common yield applied. This is referred to as the *equivalent bond yield*.

---

[2] Instruments such as Treasury notes and bonds, municipal securities, and bank certificates of deposit carry a fixed rate of interest paid on their face values. The return is the interest paid. Other instruments, such as Treasury bills, bankers' acceptances, and commercial paper are traded on a discount basis. They are sold for a price below their face value. The difference between the two is the return to the investor.

**Equivalent Bond Yield.** The method of comparing the yields of discount and coupon securities restates the yield of a discount security on an equivalent bond basis. The calculations for converting discount basis yield to equivalent bond yield is quite complicated, but the quote sheets of dealers restate the yield of T-Bills on an equivalent bond basis.[3]

**Equivalent Taxable Yield.** The yield comparison of a tax exempt security with a taxable security must be made so that the income received from each is considered on an after-tax basis. For example, if a corporation has a 46 percent marginal tax rate, the equivalent taxable yield of a municipal security offered at 8 percent would be 14.81 percent. The equivalent taxable yield of a tax exempt security can be found by the following calculation:

$$\text{Equivalent Taxable Yield} = \frac{\text{Nominal Yield} \times 1}{(1 - \text{Marginal tax rate})}$$

$$= .08 \times \frac{1}{(1-.46)} = 14.81\%$$

The interest on municipal securities is not taxable by the Federal Government and, in most cases, is not taxable by the states in which they are issued. Federal income tax applies to all securities except tax exempts, but there are various types of Federal agency securities discussed below that do not incur a state tax liability.

## Price Information

The two major sources of obtaining price quotations on money market instruments are commercial banks and investment dealers. The geographic dispersion of the participants in the money market makes the market dependent on continuous communication. Although the center of activity is in New York, a price quotation is never more than a telephone call away. The primary sources are the "money center" banks,[4] the two dozen or so government securities dealers, and a slightly smaller number of dealers in commercial paper and bankers' acceptances.

The typical corporate transaction takes place after information has been gathered that indicates what funds have been collected and disbursed the prior day, and how much money is available for investment that day. Combining that information with an updated short-term forecast, the decision on how much to invest, and for

---

[3] This is true for securities with a current maturity greater than six months. For current maturities of less than six months, $Y = \dfrac{365 \times d}{360 - (d \times t)}$, where Y is the equivalent bond yield, d is the discount rate, and t is the current maturity. For example, for a 3 month bill purchased at 9% discount, equivalent bond yield is $Y = \dfrac{365 \times .09}{360 - (.09 \times 91)} = 9.34\%$.

[4] Although traditionally confined to the large banks in New York and Chicago, this definition has been expanded to include major banks in other financial centers such as San Francisco and Houston.

how long a period, can be made. This transaction is commonly completed by 11 A.M., New York time. Two or three telephone calls to banks and dealers should give the portfolio manager a good "feel" for the market that day, in addition to some price quotes.

## MONEY MARKET INVESTMENTS

There is almost a limitless supply of short-term investment opportunities available in the market on any given day. There are also various ways in which to group them for purposes of discussion. Investment vehicles, categorized by length of original maturity, are described below. As stated earlier, the longer the maturity, the greater the market risk.

### Day-to-Day, No Market Risk

**Corporate Savings Accounts.** These savings accounts are a relatively new vehicle for short-term investments of corporations, having been authorized by the Federal Reserve in 1975. They are a safe, convenient, and relatively simple means of investing small amounts of excess cash. They are limited, however, to $150,000 at commercial banks and pay the regular passbook savings rate. The current maximums on these are 5 percent at commercial banks and 5¼ percent at thrift institutions such as savings and loan associations and mutual savings banks. An additional drawback to these accounts is their inability to automatically cover checks presented for payment, even in an account at the same bank. Also, the service charges that some banks levy after a certain number of transfers further reduce the already low rate of return.

### Money Market Funds

Since the introduction of money market funds in 1972, they have become a popular vehicle in which to invest excess cash for many small and medium sized companies. A money market fund, by definition, is a mutual fund that invests in short-term money market instruments. Presently, there are over eighty of these funds with investment strategies that range from 100 percent investment in Treasury issues (Merrill Lynch Government Fund) to almost total investment in the certificates of deposit of foreign branches of U.S. banks (Reserve Fund).

**Required Information.** Certain information should be obtained before making a decision concerning investment in a money market fund. In most cases, this information can be found in the prospectus issued by each fund.[5]

---

[5] A list of over eighty funds, including addresses and telephone numbers, can be obtained from Donoghue's Money Fund Report, PO Box 411, Holliston, MA 01746, or Wiesenberger Financial Services, 210 South Street, Boston, MA 02111.

Key information required is:

- Are the allowable money fund investments consistent with corporate policy?
- What is the minimum investment level and the amount of subsequent investment?
- Can checks be written to redeem fund holdings?
- Is there a telephone redemption option?

**Investment Methods.** When these questions have been answered satisfactorily, it is a simple matter to begin investing in money market funds. The two typical methods of deposit are by check and by wire transfer. Wire transfer is by far the most efficient and cost effective. Even if the firm's bank levies a service charge for the wire, the cost is more than offset by the extra interest earned by earlier investment. Typically, the fund will not credit funds deposited into an account by check until two or three days after the check is received. That doesn't include the time lost while the check is in the mail. With a wire transfer, however, funds received prior to the close of business will have interest credited the next day. Even two days of interest on $100,000 is worth $66 at 12 percent, thus more than justifying the cost of the wire.

**Redemption Features.** Two of the key redemption features of money funds are telephone withdrawal and check writing privileges. With the former, any or all of the firm's investment can be withdrawn and credited to its bank account on the same business day. In using the check redemption feature, funds continue to earn interest until the check "clears." Essentially, the firm gains the benefit of the "float," a benefit which can be substantial. Typically, a check may take two or three days to clear, earning daily interest each day.

Rates available on money market funds can be obtained by calling the various funds. A weekly list of current rates of most money market funds is published in the Wall Street Journal (on Monday) and other newspapers.

## Short-Term, Limited Market Risk

The area of short-term instruments attracts most of the activity in corporate funds management and investment of surplus cash. The most popular short-term investment vehicles for corporations have been:

- Treasury Bills,
- Bankers' Acceptances,
- Certificates of Deposit,
- Commercial Paper,
- Repurchase Agreements, and
- Federal Agency Securities.

**Treasury Bills.** Treasury bills are the most widely-held liquid investment. On December 17, 1979, investors held $172.2 billion in outstanding bills, made up of

39 separate issues. Maturities ranged from one to 351 days. The high demand for T-Bills is derived chiefly from their extreme liquidity. There is little risk of loss in converting them to cash. There is a depth and breadth to the highly organized secondary market[6] that insures this easy convertibility.

T-Bills are auctioned by the Treasury each week for maturities of ninety-one days and six months. Bills of one year maturity are auctioned every four weeks. Treasury Bills can be purchased at auction, either competitively or noncompetitively, or through a dealer.

Treasury bills are issued at a discount. For example, if one wishes to make a competitive bid, the bid is expressed on the basis of 100, with three decimals, 98.381, for example. That bid represents a yield of 6.405 percent on a 91 day bill. Noncompetitive bids are accepted at the average price of accepted competitive bids. The most common source for purchasing T-Bills is through a dealer in government securities. However, most banks will handle the purchase for a small service charge.

All Treasury bills are in book-entry form, that is, no physical certificate is issued, but a record is carried on the Federal Reserve's computer file.

The income from T-Bills is subject to all Federal taxes, but not to state or local taxes. The difference between the purchase price and the sale price is treated as ordinary income (or loss), not as a capital gain (or loss).

The rates on ninety-day bills are usually very close to the Federal Funds rate, the rate at which banks borrow excess reserves. Figure 25.4 depicts that relationship.

**Bankers' Acceptance.** Bankers' acceptances (BAs) are one of the least understood and, therefore, least utilized short-term investment instruments. A typical bankers' acceptance is created through foreign trade transactions, such as the import into the U.S. of manufactured goods or commodities.

Although an acceptance can be created in connection with U.S. exports, trade between two other countries or the warehousing of commodities, an example of a U.S. import transaction should suffice to explain the creation of a bankers' acceptance.

Assume that a U.S. retailer wishes to purchase Italian shoes and finance them on an acceptance basis. He instructs his U.S. bank to issue an irrevocable letter of credit in favor of the Italian exporter. Under the terms of this letter of credit, the exporter draws a time draft on the U.S. bank and negotiates it for immediate payment with his local bank. The Italian bank then sends it to the importer's bank, which stamps the draft "accepted." An acceptance has been created, and it becomes an irrevocable primary obligation of the accepting bank. This newly created acceptance is either returned to the Italian bank—which would hold it to maturity as an investment—or it is kept by the U.S. bank, which can then hold it or sell it to an investor. Eventually, the importer must supply funds at maturity to his bank to cover the acceptance. Even if he does not, the bank is still liable for making payment.

---

[6] The secondary market refers to the resale of securities after they are initially issued by the Treasury.

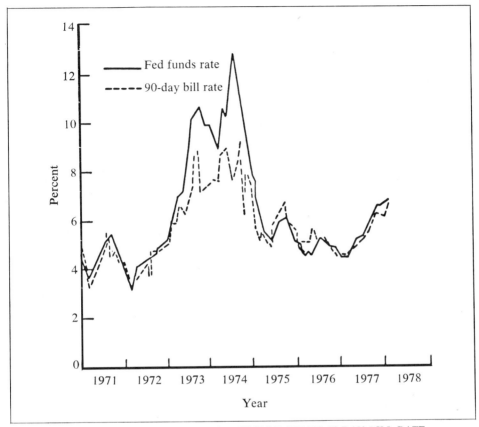

FIGURE 25.4 COMPARISON OF FEDERAL FUNDS RATE TO 90-DAY BILL RATE

The eventual holder of the BA, whether the exporter's bank, the importer's bank, an acceptance dealer, or an investor who purchased it, is the financer of the foreign trade transaction.

The holder of a bankers' acceptance incurs minimal risk. A bankers' acceptance is an irrevocable primary obligation of the accepting bank, a contingent obligation of the drawer, an obligation of any endorser, and usually has an underlying goods transaction. Since the National City Bank of New York accepted the first draft in 1914, no investor in BAs has ever suffered a loss of principal.

BAs are traded on a discount basis and the yield basis used is the same as that for Treasury Bills. Although BAs are created in various denominations, the market trades in round lots of $100,000, and typically $500,000.

The rates on BAs track very closely to the T-Bill rate, usually within 15 to 25 basis points. The spread tends to widen when money is tight. See Figure 25.5 for an illustration of this.

**Certificates of Deposit.** In its most basic form, a negotiable certificate of deposit (CD) is a marketplace receipt for funds deposited in a bank for a specified period

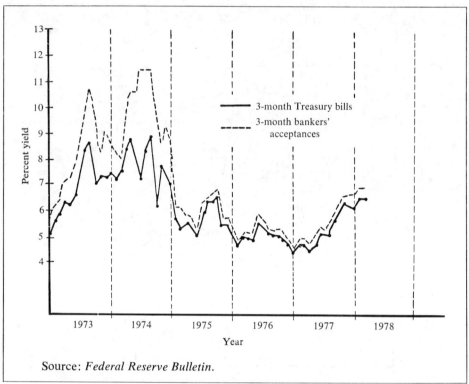

Source: *Federal Reserve Bulletin.*

FIGURE 25.5  COMPARISON OF TREASURY BILL RATES TO BANKER'S ACCEPTANCES
RATES

at a specified rate of interest. CDs are issued for maturities of 30 days or more.
They are interest-bearing, and the interest is quoted in actual days on a 360 day
basis.

Most of the CDs issued by U.S. banks are in the 30-90 day range. Because
CDs do have some credit risk attached, large investors track the credit worthiness
of the issuing banks. Money center banks such as Morgan Guaranty, Manufacturers
Hanover, and Chase can get by with lower rates than many regionals, due to the
active secondary market in their paper and the resulting liquidity. As investors
began to realize that some major regional banks might be better credit risks than
their New York counterparts, the spread began to narrow.

External forces also have a bearing on the rates. When New York City was on
the verge of bankruptcy, the major New York banks were paying higher rates than
the top Chicago banks. But, as the crisis passed, the situation reversed itself.

A recent phenomenon has been the variable rate CD issued for one year or less,
in which the rate is adjusted at intervals, either monthly or quarterly, and usually
includes a fixed premium over the composite average for major bank CDs. The
primary reason for the higher rate is the longer maturity of these variable rate certificates.

Certain foreign banks issue CDs through their U.S. branches. They often have to pay a premium due to unfamiliarity with their name, or through lack of perception on the investor's part that Barclays or Commerzbank is a major world bank.

Domestic CDs trade at rates higher than T-Bills because they are less liquid and because the investor perceives them as bearing a greater, albeit small, credit risk. As shown in Figure 25.6, CD rates consistently exceed T-Bill rates, and the spread widens considerably in periods of tight money.

**Eurodollar CDs.** Eurodollar CDs are dollar-denominated negotiable instruments evidencing a time deposit with a foreign commercial bank or a foreign branch of a U.S. bank. Although there are some CDs issued outside London, London is the heart of the Euro CD market. Like its domestic counterparts, Euro CDs are quoted as interest-bearing instruments, calculated in actual days on a 360 day basis.

CDs traded on the secondary market are deliverable in London, and payment is made two days forward in New York in Clearing House Funds.

The rates in Eurodollar CDs track very closely with their U.S. counterparts. The Euro CD has a generally higher rate due to relatively lower liquidity and because investors perceive a measure of sovereign risk.[7]

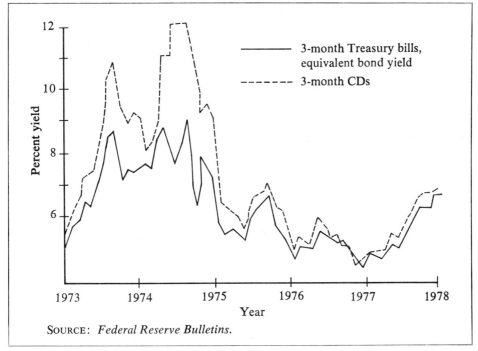

FIGURE 25.6  COMPARISON OF TREASURY BILL RATES TO CD RATES

---

[7] Sovereign risk arises when the investor's funds are in a country (other than his own) whose political or economic stability can be influenced by various factors.

If you look at the CD market both domestically and in London, it is possible to tier the issues relative to the rates they must pay. The top twenty-five U.S. banks issuing CDs in the U.S. are first. Next are the top five or six banks issuing in London, followed by major foreign banks in New York, and finally these same banks in London.

**Commercial Paper.** Commercial paper is an unsecured promissory note issued by a company for a fixed amount and maturing on a fixed date. There are two broad classes of commercial paper, *dealer placed* and *direct placed*. Most of the direct placed paper is that of finance companies such as GMAC, Ford Credit, and Household Finance. They typically represent about 70 percent of all outstanding paper.

The initial maturity of commercial paper may not exceed 270 days to maintain exemption from SEC registration and the requirement to publish a prospectus. In practice, there is little paper issued over thirty days.

Traditionally, commercial paper was issued at a discount, but it is becoming more common for it to be issued in interest-bearing form. In the latter case, rates are still quoted on a discount basis.

The secondary market for commercial paper is extremely thin. Most dealers, however, are willing to buy back the paper sold to an investor for a spread of ⅛ or so over the going market rate for similar quality and maturity. Most major direct issuers will also buy back their paper (referred to as pre-payment) if the investor needs immediate liquidity.

Commercial paper yields are slightly higher than T-Bills of comparable maturity. There is a small, but real, credit risk inherent in commercial paper in the event the issuer undergoes bankruptcy. All issuers of commercial paper establish backup lines of credit with their banks for the amount of outstanding paper.

**Repurchase Agreements (Repos).** In simplest terms, (from the investor's perspective) a repurchase agreement is the simultaneous purchase and contract to sell a security. In effect, it is a secured loan with the underlying security serving as collateral.

The investor buys a security, for example, $1 million of U.S. Treasury Notes at 8 percent, due August 15, 1986. The seller, typically a securities dealer or bank, will simultaneously confirm a repurchase of the securities in ten days. A rate is agreed upon, say 9 percent. If the pricing is "flat," the purchase price and the sale price will both be $1 million. The investor will receive simple interest based on a 360 day year basis. In this case:

$$\text{Interest} = \text{Principal Amount} \times \text{Rate} \times \frac{(\text{\# of days})}{360}$$

$$= \$1,000,000 \times 0.09 \times \frac{10}{360}$$

$$= \$2500$$

Alternatively, the repurchase price might have been set at $1,002,500, yielding the same 9 percent.

Repos can be arranged for any time period, but there is a great deal of activity in the overnight and weekend repo market. As cash management practices became more sophisticated, portfolio managers needed an outlet for surplus funds on a day to day basis. The repo market provided this outlet.

Most of the repos done are primarily in governments and agencies, but some are done in BAs and CDs. The investor incurs a degree of market risk in a repo if interest rates rise, and the borrower is adversely affected if rates fall. Assuming that the investment were exactly equal to the market value of the securities, the repo would represent a 100 percent collateralized loan. But, if rates went up and the repurchase were not affected (for example, by bankruptcy), the collateral would be less than the amount of the investment. One means of protecting against this is to have the repoed securities priced below their market value. This margin might be as low as ¼ of a point on shorter maturity transactions or as high as 2 points on a six month repo.

Overnight repos tend to trade just below the Federal Funds rate, the rate at which commercial banks buy and sell funds among themselves.

As many investors have noted, the key to dealing safely in the repo market is to know whom you are dealing with.

**Federal Agency Securities.** The market for Federal agency securities encompasses a wide variety of issues with varying maturities. In general, they are not direct obligations of the Treasury, but many are guaranteed by the Treasury or by rights to borrow from the Treasury. A few are backed by the full faith and credit of the United States. Figure 25.7 lists the major Agency Securities.

The secondary market for Federal Agencies is made by recognized dealers. The spreads in agency securities are wider than in governments, which makes them less liquid. Their credit risk is a function of the type and degree of backing from the United States Government.

## ADDITIONAL INFORMATION

Information on the investment of surplus funds can be obtained from the institutional sales departments of major securities dealers such as Salomon Brothers, A.G. Becker, and Merrill Lynch. Commercial banks are also prime sources of information and advice regarding the money market.

Many of these institutions publish helpful digests to put into perspective the economic climate and its effect on money markets. Among these are:

| Agency | Security | Minimum denomination ($) | Bearer (B) and/or registered (R)″ | Original maturity |
|--------|----------|--------------------------|-----------------------------------|-------------------|
| Federal Home Loan Bank† | Bonds | 10,000‡ | B | 1–20 years |
| Federal Land Bank† | Bonds | 1,000 | B, R§ | 2–15 years |
| Federal Intermediate Credit Bank† | Debentures | 5,000 | B | 9 months–4½ years |
| Bank for Cooperatives† | Debentures | 5,000 | B | 6 months–5 years |
| Federal National Mortgage Association | Debentures | 10,000 | B | 2–25 years |
| Government National Mortgage Association* | Participation certificates | 5,000–10,000 | B, R | 10–20 years |
| Government National Mortgage Association* | Pass-through securities | 25,000 | R | 12-year expected life |
| Federal Home Loan Mortgage Corporation | Guaranteed mortgage certificates | 100,000 | R | 10-year expected life |
| Federal Home Loan Mortgage Corporation | Mortgage participation certificates | 100,000 | R | 12-year expected life |
| Federal Farm Credit Administration† | Bonds Notes | 1,000–5,000 | B, R | 1–10 years |

\* Backed by the full faith and credit of the U.S. government.
† Interest income exempted from state and local taxation.
‡ Smaller denominations available on some issues.
§ Bearer only on bonds with an original maturity of less than 5 years.
″ These agencies are moving, except on pass-throughs, to book-entry securities.

FIGURE 25.7  MAJOR FEDERAL AGENCY SECURITIES

| Publication | Source |
|-------------|--------|
| Financial Digest | Manufacturers Hanover Trust |
| Monthly Economic Bulletin | Manufacturers Hanover Trust |
| Weekly Money Market Bulletin | Morgan Guaranty Trust |
| Economic Week | Citibank |
| Weekly Economic Package | Chemical Bank |

Monthly Economic Indicators
Weekly Government Securities
  Bulletin

Chemical Bank
Merrill Lynch Government
  Securities

## SUGGESTED READING

Stigum, Marcia. *The Money Market: Myth Reality and Practice.* Homewood, Illinois: Dow Jones–Irwin, 1978.

*Handbook for Securities of the U.S. Government and Federal Agencies.* Boston: First Boston Corp., 1978.

"Cash Management: A Look at Money Market Funds." *Association Management*, Vol. 31. (November, 1979), pp. 35–7.

# Part VI

# Personnel Functions

# 26

# Staffing and Supervision

*Richard J. Melucci*

## INTRODUCTION

The success of a business depends on the integrity and competence of those who run it and have the primary responsibility for its financial resources, production, and marketing. These human resources must be carefully organized into a cohesive and well-defined corporate environment, one that permits and encourages the successful execution of managerial functions.

The controller's concern with an effective organization is central and primary—it provides the structure within which he measures, evaluates, coordinates, advises, and controls. Because the controller is both an adviser on top policy concerns, as well as the administrator of the financial department, he should perform the following functions in the areas of staffing and supervision:

- Supervise the assembling of a capable department staff, monitor its performance, and evaluate its effectiveness;
- Advise top management on the allocation of authority and responsibility throughout the organization;
- Review all proposed major organizational changes; and
- Reassess the organizational structure as the company develops and its needs change.

## THE ORGANIZATIONAL PLAN

Management's primary goal is to achieve optimum employee productivity by assembling a capable work force and motivating it to work conscientiously, and by utilizing new and efficient methods and equipment. Accomplishing this goal requires top level strategic planning by tailoring accepted organizational principles to individual company needs and by developing and maintaining a workable organizational structure.

### Major Principles of Sound Organizational Planning

The major principles of organizational planning coincide with those of effective administration. These principles include:

- An effective division of labor;
- The proper relationship of authority to responsibility;
- Unity of command—a subordinate should report to only one superior;
- A balance between centralized and decentralized control; and
- Assumption by management of responsibility for planning, organizing, staffing, directing, coordinating, and controlling resources.

### Patterns of Organization

A company structure can be designed on general organizational principles, but must be tailored to meet individual company needs.

**Division of Labor.** In every organization, work must be apportioned, arranged, and combined to maximize overall economic performance.

*Departmentalization.* In most companies, responsibility and authority are separated into individual units, or departments. Departmentalization can be based on the function each unit performs, the product it makes or the projects it performs, its customers, or its location. A company that departmentalizes on the basis of more than one of these distinctions is called a *hybrid* organization. (See Figure 26.1)

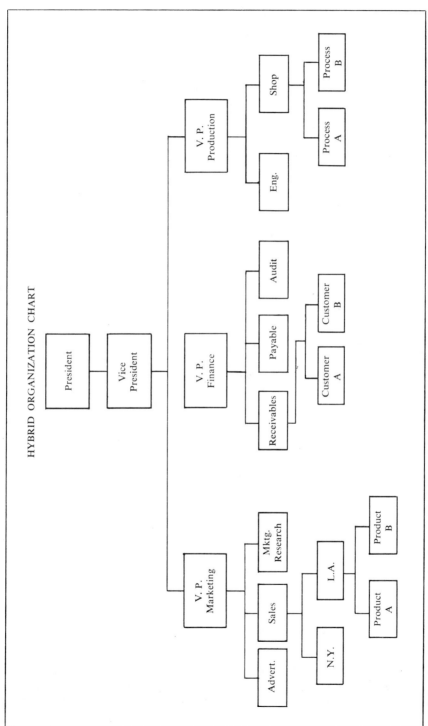

FIGURE 26.1  DEPARTMENTATION BY FUNCTION, PRODUCT, PROCESS, CUSTOMER, AND LOCATION

*Matrix organization.* A matrix organization contains the normal functional departments, but also has product or project managers with horizontal authority; they coordinate and integrate activities within each department. These managers borrow staff from the functional departments and form committees, as needed, under the combined direction of the supervisor of the functional unit and the project manager. The committee operates as long as the project requires it, and is then disbanded. The matrix system is used when a project must have special access to resources in order to accomplish specific goals. It is also useful for projects that must be accomplished under time constraints and have immediate but temporary staffing requirements.

*Span of control.* The span of control concept relates to the number of employees reporting to one supervisor. In companies with a *narrow span,* only a few employees report to one supervisor; in companies with a *broad span,* each supervisor is responsible for many employees. A broad span of control is usually found in companies that perform a standard service or manufacture a standard product; they are organized *horizontally,* with few levels. Those that perform a custom service or manufacture a custom product require complex technical know-how and are usually organized *vertically,* with many levels and a narrow span of control.

*Line, staff, and functional relationships.* The distinction between line and staff is most clearly delineated in manufacturing organizations. *Line* executives are those groups and individuals directly involved in accomplishing the company's purpose—the creation and sale of a product. Staff comprises auxiliary support and services and coordinates, advises, and controls the line personnel. In a typical company, the marketing and purchasing functions are staff responsibilities, as is the personnel department, concerned with organization and structure as they affect company personnel.

There are many approaches to the line and staff concept but it is important to distinguish between line personnel and *line authority.* Every supervisor has line authority and responsibility in that he must execute, direct, and control the actions of his subordinates in a formal reporting relationship. (See discussion below.) Staff responsibility and authority is peripheral, is less sweeping and direct, and encompasses investigation, recommendations, and informal advice.

**Relationship of Authority to Responsibility.** Authority in any organization originates at the top level of the firm. Parts of it are passed downward or delegated through prescribed channels or paths to the subordinates responsible for specific actions or functions. Figure 26.2 illustrates one way in which authority relationships may be established within a production division of a single plant.

The authority to act, on the other hand, arises from the acceptance by the subordinate of the responsibility to perform. Acceptance and sharing of responsibility is the very essence of the reporting relationship. Figure 26.3 illustrates the components of authority and how these components are tied to responsibility.

However, it is important to remember that while a company's formal structure may represent management intention, and lines of authority and responsibility may be clearly defined, there are many factors that modify this structure. The formal lines of authority might follow the formal structure, but functional authority could also be horizontal and not follow the structural lines. Communications, on a day-to-day basis, may bypass the formal structure. Even decision-making frequently takes a different form.

Organization cannot be static because it involves functions as well as individuals. When control is vested in individuals, it is subject to their capabilities, interests, and, above all, their temperaments. And the center of political power may not coincide with the seat of authoritative power.

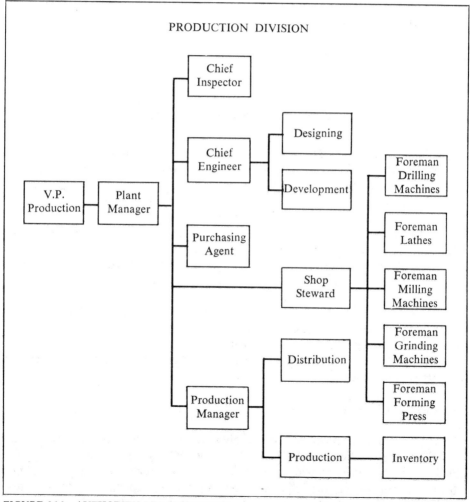

FIGURE 26.2  AUTHORITY RELATIONSHIPS

---

**Authority and Responsibility Must Be Coequal**

*Authority Is:*

*Right*—The legal right to perform the delegated function according to the given job description.

*Power*—The capacity to make oneself obeyed.

*Ability*—Personal skill.

*Capacity*—The needed resources to do the job.

    Labor
    Capital
    Equipment
    Materials
    Space
    Energy
    Data
    Time

*Responsibility Is:*

*Duty*—To use one's ability to do the job using the right and power given by the job description.

*Accountability Is:*

The liability for the proper use and control of the Resources given.

---

FIGURE 26.3  COMPONENTS OF AUTHORITY AND RESPONSIBILITY

**Centralization Versus Decentralization in Decision Making.** Centralization, or central direction, refers to a management system in which most major decisions are made at a central point, headquarters, or at the upper levels of the hierarchy. In a decentralized system, decisions are made wherever the action occurs, either at multiple points or at lower levels of the organizational structure.

The distinction between centralization and decentralization involves two areas: operation and decision making. For example, if each department did its own buying in the absence of a central purchasing department, the purchasing function would be decentralized. When all buying is done through a purchasing department, the function is, of course, centralized. However, when the operating function is decentralized, but a central body retains the final decision over such key questions as quantities to be purchased, or pricing, then the decision-making function is centralized:

In general, decentralization in decision making is more prevalent in vertically integrated organizations whose technology is characterized by a high volume and sophisticated controls.

## Organization Charting

A department's organization chart evolves as its functions are outlined. Figure 26.4 shows the positions needed to staff the controller's department. This type of chart should be accompanied by a "functional" organization chart (see Figure 26.5) that lists in detail the functions performed by the department and the activities that should be completed by the supervisor of each area. A detailed job descrip-

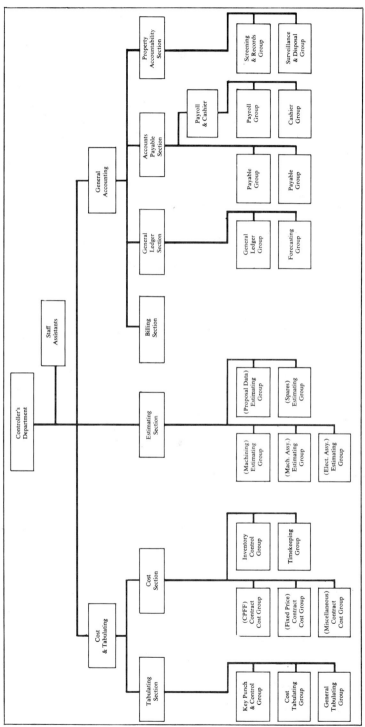

FIGURE 26.4   POSITIONS NEEDED TO STAFF THE CONTROLLER'S DEPARTMENT

### Billing Section

Responsibilities:

1. Prepare sales invoices, promptly billing the customer for materials shipped or other costs.

2. Maintain collections of outstanding accounts on a current basis, monitoring receipts, forwarding statements or notices to delinquent accounts.

3. Review shipments, determining contract accountability and applicability, entering appropriate unit prices and initiating billing of all firm priced items as negotiated.

4. Maintain accounts receivable ledgers reflecting open unpaid balances, receipts and preparation of other standard monthly journal entries affecting billings, sales, etc.

5. Prepare monthly cash forecasts for receipts and disbursements and long range forecasts as required; monitoring each, accounting for variances.

6. Prepare reports on loan progress and inventory, status of funds, unreimbursed expenditures and other special assignments as directed by the assistant division controller.

7. Prepare daily and weekly cash reports for management review.

8. Maintain schedules of obligated funds against major contracts.

9. Review and refer all forms of disallowed billing, received from the contracting officer, to the assistant division controller for resolution with contracts.

### General Ledger Section

Responsibilities:

1. Maintain general books of accounts, and other subsidiary financial ledgers.

2. Schedule, expedite and prepare required financial statements and special reports as required, reviewing each for unusual changes or fluctuations; monitoring input and insuring timely completion.

3. Prepare sales and profit forecasts; revising monthly and comparing forecasts to actual performance.

4. Interpret financial requirements and in conjunction with cost section recommend action on reserves, inventory write-offs, overruns and disallowed contract costs; compute insurable values; verify account classifications of purchase requisitions, travel authorizations, non-contractual and other documents.

5. Coordinate the resolution of policy and accounting problems arising from the preparation of financial statements, or affecting books and/or forecasts.

6. Review travellers' expense reports for compliance; arranging for reimbursements as required; maintaining subsidiary ledgers of outstanding travel advances.

7. Review disallowed overhead expense, analyzing each; advising negotiators of all opportunities for reimbursement.

8. Summarize and analyze accumulated accounting and forecast data; preparing periodically reports and forecasts such as, but not limited to: master authorization, capital overtime and government funding reports and forecasts of expenditures, labor rates, overhead rates and manpower, and charting as required.

9. Using cost and other actual performance information, prepare the operating control report and direct labor performance report; analyzing and interpreting as necessary, directing management's attention to any critical variations.

10. Maintain records of forecasts and performance data necessary to prepare control reports.

**FIGURE 26.5  FUNCTIONS AND ACTIVITIES OF SUPERVISORS**

### Accounts Payable Section

Responsibilities:

1. Verify and pay vendor invoices which conform to purchase orders, and are substantiated by receiving records or by obtaining other certification as necessary.

2. Issue checks on a timely basis to take full advantage of discount rates.

3. Initiate correcting debit or credit memoranda relative to vendor vouchers as required; maintaining adequate supporting records for legal presentation of claims for collection; and corresponding with vendors in connection with their accounts.

4. Maintain vendor invoice and voucher records and other data as required to support and verify payments.

5. Prepare and forward standard journal entries and accruals of division's outstanding liabilities to the general ledger section.

6. Review accuracy and completeness of the monthly purchase commitment report.

7. Prepare weekly and bi-weekly payrolls; arranging for cash and check disbursements as required and imprinting facsimile check signatures; verify payment with tabulated registers, cash receipt statements and reconciling each to ensure correct payroll distribution.

8. Control payroll deductions of withholding taxes, union dues, and other deductions specifically authorized by employees, or as required by state and federal laws; prepare payroll census, tax disbursement, workmen's compensation and state and other statistical reports as required.

9. Prepare and maintain records of deductions, rate changes and terminations or other change of status adjustments to employees pay, provide daily cash receipt and disbursement data as required.

10. Control U.S. savings bonds sales, sales remittance, mailing bonds to employees and refunding balances of terminated bond accounts.

11. Arrange for payment of stock or cash awards to employees for approved suggestions.

12. Process all insurance claims for material damage or loss with insurance carrier, with the assistance of affected departments, as required.

13. Record the receipt and disbursement of all cash transactions; process bank deposits, mail checks, perforate vouchers and prepare petty cash reimbursement vouchers.

### Property Accountability Section

Responsibilities:

1. Continuously monitor all property records, recording accumulated cost data on accountability records; planning, scheduling and conducting or maintaining surveillance of all inventories.

2. Prepare adjustment vouchers necessary to reconcile inventory counts and accountability records.

3. Review requisitions, production orders for the disposal of capital equipment or government owned equipment; to determine property class and for the assignment and control of property identification numbers.

4. Prepare property records upon receipt of receiving or work completion documentation; tagging and identifying items immediately.

5. Process requests for property transfer obtaining approvals as required for government owned property supplied subcontractors or vendors, verifying lists with accountability and/or custodial records.

6. Initiate forms for disposition of government property; directing inventories and segregation of all residual material upon contract completion and/or termination; arranging final disposition of surplus.

7. Schedule and conduct a bailed property survey inventory; preparing and submitting bailment survey and status of funds reports, as required, to the government property administrator.

8. Monitor record retention schedules to assure that only current records are maintained in active areas; and administer record archives services.

tion for each position completes the organizational planning for the department (see Figure 26.6). A periodic audit of these charts assures reasonable conformance with current conditions.


## MANPOWER PLANNING

Keeping a department properly staffed involves more than the recruitment and placement of qualified people. Management must ensure that appropriate personnel are available to meet the organization's changing manpower needs.

In most firms, manpower planning starts with forecasting (see Chapter 13) and drawing up production schedules. From these schedules, future staffing requirements can be determined, and plans can be developed to meet them. Generally, information concerning future schedules can be found in the *Master Schedule* or in the *Long Range Sales Forecast*.

### Master Schedules

A typical master schedule shows the known workload in terms of the products or jobs scheduled for completion during the stated time periods. (See Figure 26.7.) The jobs shown can be based on sales forecasts or can be jobs that are already contracted.

**Long- and Short-Range Plans.** A *long-range plan* that indicates each department's authority to produce according to that schedule is then issued. The long-range plan should show all assignments for the plan's time period. Incorporated in it is an initial *short-range plan* that authorizes immediate action and is backed up by a detailed budget. (See Figure 26.8.)

### Preparing a Monthly Work Plan

All departments of the organization identify their monthly objectives and determine how they are to be met. The results of this monthly work plan are incorporated into the comprehensive budget, which includes a detailed schedule of departmental manpower needs.

**The Gantt Loading Chart.** The Gantt Loading Chart is an efficient way to record the planned monthly manpower requirements. It is a graphic depiction of both the work planned and the work accomplished over a period of time. Each department schedules the jobs to be completed during any month along the time period line. The number of people needed for each job is shown in terms of hours of work required. This figure is then converted to labor hours and the types of manpower required. A separate manpower loading chart is drawn up, and decisions can be made concerning types of labor required, overtime needs, and so on. (See Figure 26.9.)

POSITION DESCRIPTION

HEAD—COST SECTION

DEPARTMENT: CONTROLLER

I.  *Organizational Relationships*
    Responsible to: Assistant Division Controller
    Responsible for: Cost Section

II.  *Occupational Summary*
    Directs the operation of the Cost Accounting Section and decides on action
    to be taken by subordinates in matters pertaining to the proper operation of
    the respective groups.

III.  *Responsibilities*
    Responsible for scheduling and assignment of work, estimating requirements
    for materials and personnel, planning administrative procedures for the sec-
    tion, and planning improvements in methods and procedures.
    Recommends the selection of personnel for the positions of supervisors and
    selects personnel for other subordinate positions in his section.
    Directs, through his subordinate staff, the coordination of their work with
    other organizational elements of the company.
    Guides group supervisors in the administration of activity of the groups, and
    guides company-wide policies as they affect the cost accounting section.
    Assumes responsibility in executing special assignments for coordination of
    various matters as well as the solution of problems involving interdepart-
    mental and intradivisional relationships.
    Prepares and submits special verbal and written reports to the assistant con-
    troller and keeps him informed concerning the overall operation of the cost
    accounting section.
    Maintains necessary records for the purpose of reviewing the activity of the
    cost accounting section.
    Analyzes reports directed to his attention by the assistant controller and
    initiates action indicated thereby within his delegated responsibility and
    authority.

IV.  *Contacts*
    To expedite the solution of any problems affecting the department, maintains
    continuous contact with other sections in the controller's department.
    Contacts government agencies regarding problems directly concerning the
    Cost Accounting Section. Makes numerous contacts with other departments
    concerning various problems that arise.

    *Authority*
    Has authority to request and receive information relative to his section from
    all personnel in the company.
    Makes administrative decisions in accordance with functions outlined in
    Section III.
    To assure an efficient and adequate operation, recommends adjustment of
    clerical support within the section.

VI.  *Qualifications*
    Bachelor's degree in accounting, or the equivalent in experience or self-
    education.
    Five or more years of applicable progressive experience in administrative
    functions; at least two in a position of general supervisory capacity with
    responsibility for performance.

FIGURE 26.6  POSITION DESCRIPTION

| PRODUCT | J F M A M J J A S O N D J F M A M J J A S O N D J F |
|---------|------------------------------------------------------|
| A | ○————————————□ |
| B | ○————————————□ |
| C | ○——□   ○——□   ○————□ |
| D | ○————————————□ |
| E | ○————————□   ○————————————□ |
| F | ○————————————□ |
| G | ○————————————□ |
| H | ○————————————————————□ |
| I | ○——□   ○————□   ○————————□ |
| J | ○————————————□ |
| K | ○————————————————□ |

### TYPICAL MASTER SCHEDULE

A master schedule illustrates on one chart all of the existing and planned jobs for the entire company. The work is then broken down by specific departments to pinpoint individual departmental responsibility. This departmental master schedule is then compared to the short range plan and the budget before work is actually begun.

○—required starting time
□—expected and required completion time

FIGURE 26.7   TYPICAL MASTER SCHEDULE

The Gantt chart's major advantage is that it is easy to make, and is especially valuable for short-range jobs having no more than several dozen activities. However, the Gantt Chart has many disadvantages: its inadequacy for large programs, its reliance on the one estimate of most likely time, and its poor visualization of time periods, critical items, and program relationships.

**Using PERT To Focus On Potential Bottlenecks.** PERT is an alternate system that uses what is called a *time-event network*. A network is composed of a series of activities, events, and paths required to complete a particular job. An *activity* is an operation required to accomplish a particular goal and, as such, takes time. An *event* is the starting or completion of an activity, and as such does not take time. A path includes at least one event and one activity. The network not only identifies all the activities and events, but also establishes a relationship among them.

A network is constructed on the basis of a careful evaluation of the job that has to be done. Attention is then focused on the time factor. At this point, the PERT differs greatly from the Gantt chart. PERT does not rely simply on the most likely time. It arrives at the *expected time* by using the formula shown in Figure 26.10. These time estimates are obtained from the past records of each network. The earliest times recorded are termed *Optimistic,* the times clustered around the mean are considered *Most Likely,* and the latest time is considered *Pessimistic.* Using these values in the formula, a weighted average, the *Expected Time,* is calculated. The Expected Time is placed just below the activity line; in each case, to the end of the network. Adding all the expected times along the paths to the end event will give the existence of the longest path in time. This is termed the *Critical Path.* The

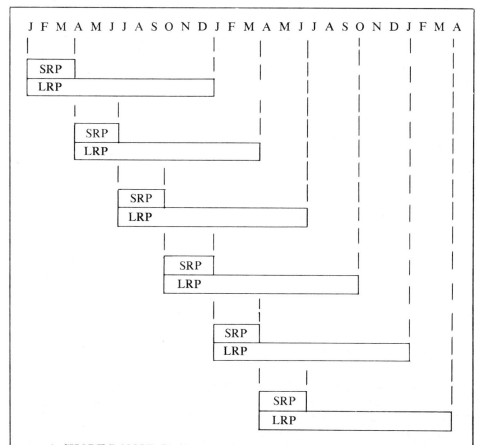

A SHORT-RANGE PLAN—LONG-RANGE PLAN RELATIONSHIP

The SRP (short-range plan) is a fully authorized plan with a corresponding budget. Upon authorization, all departments affected by this plan are given the go ahead to begin the outlined operations. The SRP is an integral part of the LRP (long-range plan). As the LRP progresses in the course of the period, the SRP is brought along into the next quarter period.

FIGURE 26.8  SHORT-RANGE/LONG-RANGE PLAN RELATIONSHIP

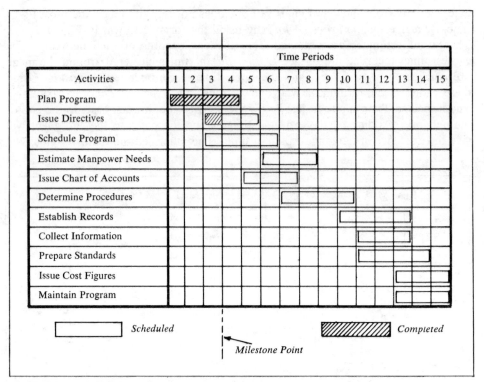

FIGURE 26.9   A TYPICAL SCHEDULED PROGRAM USING THE GANTT CHART

final component to be considered is *Slack,* the difference in time between the Critical Path and each other path. (See Figure 26.11.) The noncritical paths can be delayed up to the total slack time without affecting the project. However, any delay in the critical path will directly delay the project.

### Allowing For Peak Work Periods

A certain degree of flexibility must be built into effective manpower planning, particularly for job assignments on the operating level. When additional staff is required, a company can use several methods to prepare for peak periods of work. These include subcontracting work to vendors, placing the workforce on overtime, and hiring "temporaries" from agencies. These methods of adding to the workforce avoid the problems that would otherwise arise if the permanent work force had to be reduced as the peak period wanes. The use of temporary help is especially expedient because the discontinuance of temporary help has little effect on the morale of the permanent employees.

Problems of changing manpower needs are also reduced if the company's make-buy decisions are geared to peak period planning. As the peak period wanes,

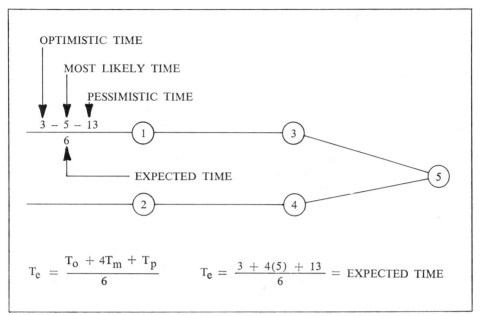

FIGURE 26.10   TIME-EVENT NETWORK

increasing in-house production should be considered; as the peak period increases, additional purchases may be made. However, any decision to buy large quantities of a product normally produced in-house will affect morale. Employees will generally view this buy decision as a means of reducing their overtime, and thus their income.

## PRODUCTIVITY MEASUREMENT AND CONTROL

Measurement of productivity is concerned with the results that producing organizations or any of their components achieve. Since productivity is generally defined as the relationship between output and input, it is concerned with eliminating waste and reducing costs per unit of output.

The following four factors can lead to successful business operations: productive work; a smooth, balanced flow of human resources, materials, and paperwork; simple methods; and employee motivation. Separate tools measure each one of these four factors. Productive work or "performance" can be measured and controlled by time study and work sampling; a smooth flow of manpower, materials, and paperwork by the use of flow process charting; simple methods by a system of method analysis; and better employee motivation by the use of employee evaluation techniques and analyses. (See Figure 26.12.)

## Performance Standards

The concept of *performance standards* must be separated from the frequently used term, "standards of performance." The latter is directly related to the accomplishment of the specific duties of a job description. In this discussion, performance standards relate to the precise time needed to perform any specific job. These specific times are then categorized into acceptable standards for each job. Just as there is no universal method for determining specific time standards for all jobs, there is also no specific performance standard for any specific job. In general, performance standards of companies engaged in standardized work will differ from those of companies engaged in custom operations.

The need for performance standards, whether in a hospital, a manufacturing plant, or in the controller's office, is becoming increasingly apparent. Every segment of industry affected by inflation is compelled to improve productivity in each sector.

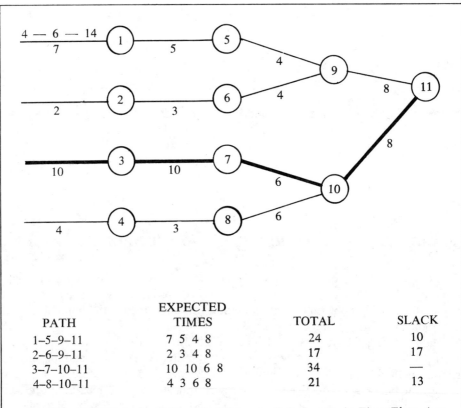

| PATH | EXPECTED TIMES | TOTAL | SLACK |
|------|----------------|-------|-------|
| 1–5–9–11 | 7 5 4 8 | 24 | 10 |
| 2–6–9–11 | 2 3 4 8 | 17 | 17 |
| 3–7–10–11 | 10 10 6 8 | 34 | — |
| 4–8–10–11 | 4 3 6 8 | 21 | 13 |

*Path 3–7–10–11 is the Critical Path Because It Is Longer in Time Than Any Other Path.*

FIGURE 26.11  CRITICAL AND SLACK PATHS

The value of performance standards far outweighs their cost. They are used to determine:

- Labor requirements for manpower loading;
- Calculation of anticipated actual hours needed;
- Conversion of estimated hours to direct labor dollars;
- Direct labor control and forecasting;
- Determining overtime requirements;
- Forecasting overhead rates; and
- Comparison with rates of vendors and competitors.

## Performance Measurement Techniques

Performance measurement techniques are well established. Work measurement, for example, evaluates activities performed within a manufacturing or processing facility. It may also apply to work of a semi-skilled or clerical nature, and work that is susceptible to visual or quantitative analysis.

**Time Study.** A record of the time required to perform various components of a task can be expensive, but is most useful in developing an accurate time standard for many repetitive activities.

The object of a time study is to find out how much time it should take to do a job,

| WORK FACTOR | TOOL |
| --- | --- |
| Productive Work | *Time Study*—The use of a stop watch for continuous observation of continuous operations (standard manufacturing). *Work Sampling*—The use of a stop watch for intermittent observations of intermittent operations (custom manufacturing). |
| Smooth Balanced Flow of Manpower, Materials, and Paper Work | *Flow Process Charting—Work Process Charting—Assembly Flow Diagrams—Procedural Flow Charts.* |
| Simple Methods | *Methods Improvement*—A cost reduction technique—that includes *Value Analysis.* |
| Personal Interest of Employees | *Employee Evaluation Reports — Job Analysis—Attitude Surveys.* |

FIGURE 26.12  RELATIONSHIP OF WORK FACTORS TO MEASUREMENT TOOLS

not how much time it does take. It is easy to find out how much time it does take; simply divide the amount of hours worked by the amount of units made. However, to find out how much time it *should* take requires accurate observations and careful attention to elements (logically sequenced subtasks), as well as allowances for employee fatigue and personal needs.

The procedure is as follows:

1. Obtain a series of at least ten observations, using a stop watch (see example below), and chart on a sheet similar to that depicted in Figure 26.13.
2. Add these times together and divide by ten (obtain the mean).
3. Multiply the mean by the speed rate (given), and get the *base time*.
4. Obtain the fatigue allowance by using the formula: fatigue equals the last observation time less the first time divided by the last time, times 100. Add the fatigue allowance to the personal allowance (given) and the machine care allowance. Multiply these allowances by the base time, add them all to the base time, and get the *normal time*.
5. With the *lot size** and the *set up time* given,** obtain the unit set up time. Add that to the normal time and get the *standard time*.
6. Divide the *performance ratio**** into the standard time and get the *estimating (or pricing) standard*. Add the overhead cost to the estimating standard (the overhead is given as a percent of direct time), multiply by the hourly rate (given), then add commission and profit to obtain the selling price for one lot size.

An example of this procedure follows:

| *Observations* | *Mean* | | *Speed Rate* | | *Base Time* |
|---|---|---|---|---|---|
| .30 .30 .31 .31 .32 .32 .33 .33 .34 .35 | .321 | × | 1.05 | = | .33705 |

The Speed Rate was given as 1.05.

$$\text{Fatigue} = \frac{.35-.30}{.35} \ (100) = 14.28\%$$

Machine Care given as     10.
Personal Allowance given as     8.

Total allowances of 32.28 percent, multiplied by .33705 (base time) equals .10879. Add the base time and the allowance time and get .44584. This is the normal time. With a set up time of 12.00 hours and a lot size of 100 units, the set up time per unit is .12. Add this to the normal time and get .44584 + .12 =

---

* Lot size equals the number of units before requiring a new set up.
** Set up time equals the amount of time necessary for preparation of a machine or work station before a run can begin.
*** The actual productive time worked during a day (excluding wasted time) divided by the full available time.
*Note:* Percentages for speed rate, machine care, personal allowance, and performance ratio are obtained as a result of studying many jobs in the same department.

.56584. This is the standard time. With a performance ratio of .55 the estimating standard will be $.55 \times \dfrac{.56584}{X}$, then $.55x = .56584$.

$$X = .55 \;/\; .56584 = 1.0288$$

1.0288 is the estimating standard time. Add the overhead of 200 percent (for this example) and get the *total estimating time* of 3.0864 times the hourly rate (given here as $5.00 per hour), and get $15.432. A commission of 20 percent and a profit of 20 percent gives the selling price for one of a lot size of 100 units. Thus $15.43 + .20x + .20x = X$, and $15.43 = .60x$, and $X = 60 \sqrt{1543.} = \$25.72$ for one unit of a lot size of 100.

**Work Sampling.** Work sampling is most valuable in the area of white collar activities; it is a convenient method to obtain meaningful information by observing and translating the activities of many individuals.

| ELE·NO· | DESCRIPTION OF ELEMENT | NUMBER OF OBSERVATIONS | | | | | | | | | |
|---|---|---|---|---|---|---|---|---|---|---|---|
| | | 1 | 2 | 3 | 4 | 5 | 6 | 7 | 8 | 9 | 10 |

TIME STUDY OBSERVATION SHEET

FIGURE 26.13   TIME STUDY OBSERVATION SHEET

*On or off form.* The on or off form is often used to evaluate a request for additional capital equipment. When the finance department receives a request for additional capital equipment, say a new machine, the controller may request a work sampling study to ascertain if the additional machine is needed. Operations of existing machines will then be observed for periods of use and idleness. After a suitably large number of observations are taken at random intervals, the ratio  of the number of "offs" to the total number of observations taken will approximate the degree of the machine's use. Care must be taken to ensure that the observations are made during a normal work period.

*Ratio of delays form.* This type of work sampling is more extensive because it can be used to observe many elements at the same time. This technique consists of random but frequent spot checking of many activities and the recording of the activities at the moment of observation. (Figure 26.14 depicts a form that is frequently used for this purpose.) From the work sampling obtained, the time spent on each type of operation, in relation to the total time available, is determined.

*Motion study.* This method of work measurement uses film to record a continuous operation. One type, *micromotion study*, can reduce the costs of very fast, very repetitive activities by analyzing the fine motions made. *Memomotion* study attempts to reduce costs of intermittent operations by using a time-delayed camera to record activities.

## Smoothing Work Flow

The pattern of work flow is basic to job simplification and efficiency. *Flow process charting* is a basic tool in critically examining the task to be performed and challenging every detail—from the legitimacy of its purpose to the validity of each step taken toward its completion. It can make a valuable contribution to revamping a department's flow process or procedures, or can help in redesigning a department's layout. It can do a great deal to simplify existing methods, thus saving both time and money. The process is described in Figure 26.15 and charted in Figure 26.16.

## The Personal Factor

Staffing various types of jobs, from clerks to assembly line workers to executives, involves the following varied activities: identification of the supply sources; recruiting; establishing screening standards; testing; interviewing; hiring; orientating; placing people in specific jobs; promoting; counseling; and most important, evaluating job performance.

**Employee Evaluation Reports.** The standards used to evaluate employee performance are contained in the job description. Most job descriptions identify the

| WORK SAMPLING SHEET | | | | | | | | | | | | | | | | |
|---|---|---|---|---|---|---|---|---|---|---|---|---|---|---|---|---|
| Location | | | | | | | | Dept. No. | | | File No. | | | | | |
| Observer | | | | | | | | Category | | | | | | Date | | |
| Task(s) | | | | | | | | | | | | | | | | |

| Time of Observation | | 1 | 2 | 3 | 4 | 5 | 6 | 7 | 8 | 9 | 10 | 11 | 12 | 13 | 14 | 15 | Number of Observation |
|---|---|---|---|---|---|---|---|---|---|---|---|---|---|---|---|---|---|
| | | | | | | | | | | | | | | | | | |
| Total | | | | | | | | | | | | | | | | | |
| Percent | | | | | | | | | | | | | | | | | 100.00 |

FIGURE 26.14   WORK SAMPLING SHEET

job, outline the work to be performed, specify both the requirements for those who seek to fill the job, as well as the kind of behavior expected, and the goals that should be attained. (See Figure 26.17.)

The evaluation report must assess relative job worth by measuring the performance of job duties against some sort of standard. Any really complete evaluation report must be based on the *critical incident* concept, in which both satisfactory and unsatisfactory activities are carefully documented. This kind of evaluation report includes the following factors that must be considered in devising any review system:

- *Validity.* The conclusions reached through the use of the evaluation must be an accurate account of the employee's performance.
- *Standardization.* The same criteria should be used for all members of the job category.
- *Reliability.* The results of an evaluation should be comparable, even when the evaluation is done by different people.
- *Bias.* Bias becomes a factor when the evaluator allows his personal opinions of the employee to affect his judgment of the review.

## REPORTS TO MANAGEMENT

Reports on the management of human resources should answer questions concerning productivity, manpower requirements, flexibility in handling personnel and equipment, employee turnover, and so on. The following reports are helpful to management in determining personnel policy:

*Employee Productivity*
- Department work distribution summary (Figure 26.18);
- Overtime reports;
- Shift differential reports;
- Manufacturing variance reports;
- Idle time reports; and
- Personnel performance review report.

*Employee Turnover Reports*
- Monthly analysis of turnover (Figure 26.19);
- Temporary employee cost report;
- Personnel forecast report;
- Employee replacement cost report; and
- Summary of separations by reasons (Figure 26.20).

*Employee Absenteeism Reports*
- Monthly analysis of absenteeism (Figure 26.21); and
- Employee leave report—sick leave, jury duty, military.

*Purpose:*

The purpose of the flow process chart, or work process chart, is to emphasize distance and lapsed time. This chart clearly shows the route of the object being followed, from the beginning to the end of the cycle.

The flow process chart is a graphic representation of the sequence of events in any process or procedure; it includes the information necessary for analysis, such as time required and distance moved.

*Details of Making Out the Flow Process Chart:*

1. State the activity being studied:
   Be sure you are really breaking down the job you intend to break down.
2. Choose the subject to follow:
   Stick with it. Pick a person, material, or paper form, depending upon which goes through the entire process you are studying. Once you have chosen a subject, don't change. Each detail must be pertinent to that subject.
3. Pick a starting and ending point:
   This is to be sure you cover the ground you want to cover, but no more.
4. Write a brief description of each detail:
   Step by step, no matter how short or temporary, every operation, every move, every storage, every inspection must be indicated. To list every detail, make the chart on the job as you see it.
5. Apply the symbols:
   The description determines the symbol. Draw a connecting line between each of the proper symbols.
6. The symbols used on a flow process chart are:
   $\bigcirc$ = Operation: When something is being changed or created use a large circle to show that an action or "operation" is taking place (typing a letter or picking up an object).
   = Transportation: When something is moved from one place to another, use an arrow to show "transportation" (a letter carried to another desk).
   D = Delay: When the object is interrupted or delayed in its flow—an interference—use the large letter "D" (a letter in an "outgoing" box).
   = Storage: When an object is kept and protected against unauthorized removal, show by an inverted triangle (goods in warehouse or stockroom).
   $\square$ = Inspection: When something is checked or verified but not changed, use a square to denote an "inspection" (proofreading a letter, checking a requisition).

*Enter Distance:*

Enter distance in feet every time a transportation occurs.
Enter delay in time every time a delay occurs.

*Summarize:*

Add up all the facts and put them in a summary book. This summary should indicate the total number of operations, transportations, delays, storages, inspections, the distance traveled, and the time lapsed.

Be careful not to confuse the object being followed when making up a chart on either a person or product. This is perhaps one of the most common faults in "process charting." If a man is carrying an object, puts it down and goes to look for a truck, and we are following the man, we do not show a delay symbol. The object may be delayed, but the man is not. We continue to follow the man in whatever he does. Watch this point carefully.

FIGURE 26.15  DESCRIPTION OF FLOW PROCESS CHARTING

## FLOW PROCESS CHART

DETAILS OF ☐ PRESENT ☐ PROPOSED METHOD

| SUMMARY | PRESENT | | PROPOSED | | DIFFERENCE | | JOB |
|---|---|---|---|---|---|---|---|
| | NO. | TIME | NO. | TIME | NO. | TIME | |
| ○ OPERATIONS | | | | | | | |
| ⇨ TRANSPORTATIONS | | | | | | | |
| ☐ INSPECTIONS | | | | | | | CHART BEGINS AT |
| D DELAYS | | | | | | | |
| ▽ STORAGES | | | | | | | CHARTED BY |
| DISTANCE TRAVELLED | FT. | | FT. | | FT. | | |

FIGURE 26.16  FLOW PROCESS CHART

PERFORMANCE EVALUATION
STAFF PERSONNEL

Name: _____     Position: _____

Office: _____     Department: _____

_____     Evaluation Date: _____

Supervisor: _____     Evaluation By: _____

| Importance of the Function | | | | Section I — JOB FUNCTIONS | Performance | | | |
|---|---|---|---|---|---|---|---|---|
| Essential to Job | Important to Job | Marginally Related to Job | Unrelated to Job | | Exceeds Job Requirements | Regularly Meets Job Requirements | Occasionally Does Not Meet Job Requirements | Does Not Meet Job Requirements |

The purpose of the section is to determine how effectively the employee is performing the functions of his or her position.

*Instructions*: First, note how important each listed function is to the job by placing an "x" in the appropriate space in the IMPORTANCE columns at the left. Then, rate the employee's performance of each job-related function by placing an "x" in the appropriate space in the PERFORMANCE columns on the right.

*Note: Space for adding functions not listed here will be found at the end of this section.*

| | | | | Function | | | | |
|---|---|---|---|---|---|---|---|---|
| | | | | Takes and transcribes dictation | | | | |
| | | | | Transcribes mechanical dictation | | | | |
| | | | | Types drafts | | | | |
| | | | | Types draft where some editing or arranging is required | | | | |
| | | | | Types tables and standard forms | | | | |
| | | | | Proofreads and corrects grammar, spelling, and punctuation | | | | |
| | | | | Proofreads for content errors or omissions which distort meaning | | | | |
| | | | | Prepares and types bank letters and tabulations | | | | |
| | | | | Composes simple letters and memos on routine matters | | | | |
| | | | | Places and answers telephone calls, takes and relays messages | | | | |
| | | | | Places and receives telephone calls to provide information and instructions and follows up on inquiries, e.g., security transactions, cash transfers, fails, incorrect items | | | | |
| | | | | Traces sources of information on above and rectifies discrepancies | | | | |
| | | | | Answers simple questions and furnishes information to save principal's time | | | | |
| | | | | Updates appraisals, research or other statistical records | | | | |
| | | | | Checks account cash balances, bond maturities, etc. | | | | |
| | | | | Checks records for completeness and accuracy and obtains correct or missing data | | | | |
| | | | | Compiles information from a variety of sources | | | | |
| | | | | Performs arithmetic computations | | | | |
| | | | | Prepares charts and exhibits | | | | |
| | | | | Prepares reports in accordance with established procedures | | | | |
| | | | | Clips articles, routes and files | | | | |
| | | | | Maintains files | | | | |
| | | | | Assembles data from files | | | | |
| | | | | Opens and sorts mail | | | | |
| | | | | Operates office machines: (Please circle appropriate equipment) typewriter, Wordstream typewriter, transcriber, adding machine, calculator, Xerox copier, Telex, Telecopier | | | | |
| | | | | Makes travel arrangements and reservations | | | | |
| | | | | Greets visitors and directs them to proper locations | | | | |
| | | | | Schedules meetings and maintains related records | | | | |

FIGURE 26.17   PERFORMANCE EVALUATION OF STAFF PERSONNEL

| Organizational Unit | | | DEPARTMENT WORK DISTRIBUTION SUMMARY  Page__ of__ SECTION | | | | | | | |
|---|---|---|---|---|---|---|---|---|---|
| Period Covered | Date: | | Name: | | Name: | | Name: | | Name: | |
| Charted By: | Approved By: | | Position: | | Position: | | Position: | | Position: | |
| Activity No. | ACTIVITY | Av. Hrs. per Mo. | TASKS | Av. Hrs. per Mo. | TASKS | Av. Hrs. per Mo. | TASKS | Av. Hrs. per Mo. | TASKS | Av. Hrs. per Mo. |
| | | | | | | | | | | |
| | | | | | | | | | | |
| | | | | | | | | | | |
| | | | | | | | | | | |
| | | | | | | | | | | |
| | | | | | | | | | | |
| | | | | | | | | | | |
| | | | | | | | | | | |
| | | | | | | | | | | |
| | | | | | | | | | | |
| | | | | | | | | | | |
| | | | | | | | | | | |
| | | | | | | | | | | |
| | | | | | | | | | | |

FIGURE 26.18  DEPARTMENT WORK DISTRIBUTION SUMMARY

## MONTHLY ANALYSIS OF TURNOVER

Period covered: From: ............................... To: ...............................

| | Male | Female | Total |
|---|---|---|---|
| All employees as of fifteenth of month | | | |
| Accessions during calendar month | | | |
| Separations during period | | | |
| Separation rate | | | |
| Transfers: | | | |
|     To other establishments of the firm | | | |
|     From other establishments of the firm | | | |
| Resignations | | | |
| Discharges | | | |
| Layoffs | | | |
| Military separations | | | |
| Miscellaneous separations | | | |
|     Total separations | | | |

*Analysis of Resignations*

| | | Male | Female | Total |
|---|---|---|---|---|
| *Shifts* | No. 1 | | | |
| | No. 2 | | | |
| | No. 3 | | | |
| *Departments* | No. 1 | | | |
| | No. 2 | | | |
| | No. 3 | | | |
| | No. 4 | | | |
| | No. 5 | | | |
| *Occupations* | *Code* | | | |
| *Reasons* | Wages | | | |
| | Supervision | | | |
| | Working conditions | | | |
| | Fatigue | | | |
| | Home responsibilities | | | |
| *Service* | Under three months | | | |
| | Three to six months | | | |
| | Over six months | | | |
| *Age groups* | Under 25 | | | |
| | 25 to 34 | | | |
| | 35 to 44 | | | |
| | 45 to 54 | | | |
| | 55 to 64 | | | |
| | 65 and over | | | |
| *Dependents* | Single (no dependents) | | | |
| | Married (no dependents) | | | |
| | Workers with dependents | | | |

FIGURE 26.19    MONTHLY ANALYSIS OF TURNOVER

## SUMMARY OF SEPARATIONS BY REASON

|  | 19.... | 19.... | 19.... |
|---|---|---|---|
| *Action of the Company* | | | |
| Irregular attendance | | | |
| Poor conduct | | | |
| Neglect of duty | | | |
| Not adapted for work | | | |
| Work unsatisfactory | | | |
| Total | | | |
| *Action of employee* | | | |
| Another position | | | |
| Did not like work | | | |
| Needed at home | | | |
| Health | | | |
| School | | | |
| Failed to return from LOA | | | |
| Failed to report to work | | | |
| Left city | | | |
| Pregnancy | | | |
| Marriage | | | |
| Enter military service | | | |
| Retirement | | | |
| Personality problems | | | |
| Death | | | |
| Other—unaccounted for | | | |
| Too far to travel | | | |
| More money | | | |
| Completed exchange visitor program | | | |
| Total | | | |
| Grand Total | | | |

Courtesy of Hospital Authority of Gwinnett County, Ga.

FIGURE 26.20   SUMMARY OF SEPARATIONS BY REASON

## MONTHLY ANALYSIS OF ABSENTEEISM

**Period covered: From:** . . . . . . . . . . . . . . **To:** . . . . . . . . . . . . . .

| | | Male | Female | Total |
|---|---|---|---|---|
| | Number of man-days lost through absence | | | |
| | Number of workdays during month | | | |
| | Average number of employees on payroll during month | | | |
| | Rate of absenteeism | | | |
| *Shifts* | Production employees—all shifts | | | |
| | First shift | | | |
| | Second shift | | | |
| | Third shift | | | |
| *Departments* | (1) | | | |
| | (2) | | | |
| | (3) | | | |
| | (4) | | | |
| | (5) | | | |
| *Occupations* | *Code* | | | |

| | | Male | Female | Total |
|---|---|---|---|---|
| *Reasons* | Illness on the job (covered by workmen's compensation) | | | |
| | Illness (nonoccupational) | | | |
| | Child care | | | |
| | Accident on the job (covered by workmen's compensation) | | | |
| | Accident (nonoccupational) | | | |
| | Tardiness | | | |
| | Other | | | |
| *Service* | Under three months | | | |
| | Three to six months | | | |
| | Over six months | | | |
| *Age groups* | Under 25 | | | |
| | 25 to 34 | | | |
| | 35 to 44 | | | |
| | 45 to 54 | | | |
| | 55 to 64 | | | |
| | 65 and over | | | |
| *Dependents* | Single | | | |
| | Married | | | |
| | Dependent children | | | |
| | Other dependents | | | |

FIGURE 26.21   MONTHLY ANALYSIS OF ABSENTEEISM

## SUGGESTED READING

Niebel, Benjamin W., *Motion and Time Study*. Homewood, Illinois: Richard D. Irwin, Inc., 1976.

Davis, Louis E., and Taylor, James C., *Design of Jobs*. Santa Monica, California: Goodyear Publishing Company, Inc., 1979.

Henderson, Richard I., *Compensation Management*. Reston, Virginia: Reston Publishing Company, Inc., 1979.

Glueck, William F., *Foundations of Personnel*. Dallas, Texas: Business Publications, Inc., 1979.

Tosi, Henry L., *Theories of Organization*. Chicago, Illinois: St. Clair Press, 1978.

Levin, Richard I., and Kirkpatrick, Charles A., *Quantitative Approaches To Management*. New York: McGraw-Hill Book Company, 1978.

# 27

# ERISA Reporting Requirements

*James R. Ratliff*

## INTRODUCTION

After the end of World War II the United States saw a rapid increase in the number and size of pension plans (prior to the enactment of ERISA). These plans have a significant impact on the economy of the country as a whole (they now hold over $400 billion in assets), as well as on the sponsors and participants involved in them. Because of their preferential tax treatment, the effect upon the revenue of the Federal Government has been substantial.

However, Federal laws such as the Internal Revenue Code (IRC), with their scope of available remedies and disclosure requirements, were considered inadequate by most representatives of labor and many employee benefit professionals. There was no single law that regulated private pension plans, monitored their actuarial soundness, and prevented serious abuses. Congressional hearings in the early 1970s disclosed that participants in many plans were not receiving anticipated benefits after long years of service because their plans did not happen to provide for vested benefits. Many pension plans were found to be unstable because they lacked adequate funds to meet their benefit obligations. Other plans were terminated because of inadequate assets needed to meet vested obligations.

With the enactment of the Employee Retirement Income Security Act of 1974 (ERISA), a new era began of federal control over employee benefits. Its primary purpose is to protect the interests of workers and their beneficiaries who participate in employee benefit plans. ERISA seeks to attain that objective by requiring financial reporting to government agencies and disclosure to participants and beneficiaries, by establishing standards of conduct for plan fiduciaries, and by providing appropriate remedies, sanctions, and access to the Federal courts. Another objective of ERISA is to improve the soundness of employee benefit plans by requiring that plans:

- Vest the accrued benefits of employees with significant periods of service;
- Meet minimum standards of funding; and
- With respect to defined benefit pension plans, subscribe to plan termination insurance through the Pension Benefit Guaranty Corporation (PBGC).

ERISA was designed to replace all provisions of the Welfare and Pension Plans Disclosure Act of 1958, based on implementation in various phases through 1984. ERISA amended certain sections of the Internal Revenue Code and generally preempted state laws that related to employee benefit plans.

This chapter is intended to familiarize the controller with some of ERISA's more important provisions and with the types of pension benefit plans most subject to federal regulations and control. But this summary is not intended to serve as a substitute for the advice of legal counsel.

## TYPES OF PLANS COVERED BY ERISA[1]

ERISA generally applies to employee benefit plans qualified under the IRC, or established or maintained by plan sponsors engaged in interstate commerce or in any industry or activity affecting interstate commerce. This chapter describes pension benefit plans in detail because employer and employee financial stakes in these plans are most extensive; operational abuses appear to have been pervasive. It must be noted however, that welfare benefit plans are also subject to ERISA reporting and disclosure requirements, and those who operate and administer such plans are limited and governed by the provisions of that Act.

### Pension Benefit Plans

A plan is called a "pension benefit plan" under ERISA if it provides retirement income to employees or results in a deferral of income by employees for periods extending to or beyond the termination of covered employment. Pension benefit plans are divided into two distinct categories, and there are a number of types of plans in each category. The two categories are *defined benefit plans* and *defined contribution plans*. (See Chapters 28 and 29 for discussion of tax qualified pension plans and management of other employee benefit programs.)

The distinguishing feature of the defined benefit plan is that it promises a specific result. Under such a plan, an employee knows that, upon attainment of a specific age and/or the completion of a specific period of service or plan participation, he will be entitled to a fixed and determinable benefit, calculable from a formula under the plan.

In the defined contribution category, no promise is made as to result. Instead, the employer essentially tells the employee that money will be put aside from time to time (perhaps annually, pursuant to a formula) and that the employee will be entitled to a benefit at a later date, based on what the employer has contributed, what the employee has contributed (in some plans), and what the investment performance of the investment vehicle has been during the period between the contribution of funds and the withdrawal of funds. In short, defined benefit plans "guarantee" outcome, while defined contribution plans focus upon the input of funds with the benefit resulting as a function of that input.

Defined benefit plans may be grouped into four major subcategories. These are:

- The flat benefit plan;
- The fixed benefit plan;
- The unit benefit plan; and
- The variable benefit plan.

---

[1] This section is comprised of material written by Robert A. Bildersee for the Institute For Paralegal Training and is included here with their permission.

In addition, there is a peculiar hybrid variety of plan called the *target* or *assumed benefit* plan which resembles both a defined benefit plan and a defined contribution plan.

Defined contribution plans may be grouped into four major subcategories as well. These are:

- The profit-sharing plan;
- The money purchase pension plan;
- The thrift or savings plan; and
- The stock bonus plan.

There are also a number of minor subcategories, such as salary reduction plans and employee stock ownership plans (called ESOPs or ESOTs, and, if intended to meet the requirements of the Tax Reduction Act of 1975, called TRASOPs). As noted above, the target or assumed benefit plan is partially a defined benefit plan and partially a defined contribution plan.

The largest plans (multiemployer, collectively bargained plans) tend to be defined benefit plans, but the number of benefit plans has decreased markedly since the passage of ERISA in 1974. While the rate of installation of new defined contribution plans has also declined since the passage of ERISA, the vast majority of newly established plans are of the defined contribution variety. Such plans are considered easier to understand and operate by most small employers and may involve a lesser degree of financial commitment and administrative cost.

**Defined Benefit Plans.** A defined benefit plan is characterized or classified by the manner in which benefits are calculated. The major classifications are identified below, and the manner in which benefits are calculated in each is briefly described. Some plans have compound benefit calculation formulas; they thus exhibit the characteristics of several different types of plans.

*Flat benefit plan.* The flat benefit plan is the simplest type of defined benefit plan. The benefit under a flat benefit plan depends on *neither* the participant's compensation history nor the length of his or her service (as long as the plan's minimum service requirement is met). Every employee who satisfied the plan's minimum service requirement for benefit eligibility gets the same benefit. For example, a plan providing a monthly income for life of $120 to any person retiring at or after age 65 with 20 or more years of service would be a flat benefit plan. An employee whose average compensation over his career was $20,000, and who worked 32 years for the employer, would get the same benefit as the employee who never earned more than $10,000 and only worked 21 years. Under a flat benefit plan, the lower-paid employee's benefit is a larger percentage of his compensation than the percentage benefit paid to the higher-paid employee. In each case, the benefit is the same in dollar terms, but in the case of the lower-paid employee, the ratio of the benefit to his career average compensation before retirement is more favorable than is the ratio for the higher-paid employee.

*Fixed benefit plan.* The fixed benefit plan provides a retirement benefit expressed as a function of compensation. The normal retirement benefit is usually stated as a percentage of compensation. Any plan participant will receive the benefit calculated under the plan's formula upon retirement at normal retirement date. Compensation for plan purposes may be computed in several ways. A plan providing all participants retiring with 20 or more years of service with a benefit equal to 30 percent of "compensation" (as defined in the plan) is a fixed benefit plan. Length of service does not matter in the benefit computation as long as the participant has satisfied the plan's minimum for benefit eligibility. Thus, two employees having "compensation" for plan purposes of $30,000 per year would receive an annual pension benefit under a 30 percent plan of $9,000, even if one employee worked 22 years before retiring and the other worked 35 years.

*Unit benefit plan.* The unit benefit plan generates a benefit which is a function of time (either years of service or years of plan participation) in every case. The benefit formula may or may not also include a factor for compensation. If the benefit formula, is, for example, $10 per month for every year of service completed prior to retirement by the employee, the benefit is based on service alone. All employees who retire after completing 25 years of service under the plan in the example would receive a monthly pension of $250, regardless of their respective rates of compensation during their active careers. As with the flat benefit plans, lower-paid employees get relatively larger pension benefits than do higher-paid employees when comparing the pension benefits with career compensation levels. However, the employer may provide a unit benefit plan which rewards employees on the basis of *both* time and compensation levels achieved. In such a plan, the benefit formula is a function of both time and pay levels. For example, the plan could provide a benefit of one percent of compensation (as defined in the plan), multiplied by years of service or participation completed. Two employees with identical service records would then get benefits that differed on the basis of their respective compensation levels.

*Variable benefit plan.* The variable benefit plan includes a basic pension formula as is found in any of the three types of plans described above. An adjustment factor is, however, added to the benefit computation. After the basic benefit is determined, it is multiplied by a factor that reflects some variable external indicator, such as "cost of living." An example of such a plan would be one that included a flat benefit of $100 per month or everyone, but provided that the benefit would be adjusted annually to reflect changes in the national Consumer Price Index. If the factor to be applied in the example is the change in the Consumer Price Index from 1967 (under the current CPI, 1967 = 100), and if the CPI at December, 1979 is 230.7, then the monthly benefit payable to retirees in 1980 would be $230.70. Of course, there are other indicators that may be used instead of the CPI.

Among the more popular indicators are the Dow Jones Industrial Average, the New York Stock Exchange common stock averages, the minimum wage rate, the Social Security taxable wage base, and the investment performance of a specific fund of reference (which might be the plan's own trust fund).

*Target or assumed benefit plan.* The target plan contains a benefit formula as does any defined benefit plan. Contributions are made by the employer in such a fashion that, if every actuarial assumption were absolutely correct, the contributions would provide precisely the targeted, or assumed, benefit. The target plan thus looks like a defined benefit plan when it comes to funding. However, once the money is in the plan, it begins to resemble a defined contribution plan because a separate account is set up for each and every participant. The employer contribution, made in accordance with the actuary's calculations for each employee, is invested in an account for the participant for whom the contribution was made. The benefit that the participant will receive will be whatever his or her account balance provides when benefit commencement occurs. Unlike all defined benefit plans, and just like all defined contribution plans, the target plan does not promise a result. It focuses instead on input, and the result in whatever the input plus the investment performance together yield. The ultimate benefit received by the participant may be more or it may be less than the targeted benefit. It would be the greatest of coincidences if the target benefit and the actual benefit were exactly the same.

Defined benefit plans all have one thing in common. The amount that must be contributed by the employer during the working careers of the participants is determined actuarily. (See Chapter 28 for a discussion of the various actuarial factors and their effect on annual pension costs.)

**Defined Contribution Plans.** All defined contribution plans have two things in common:

- No specific benefit is promised in dollar terms.
- The amount of the benefit to be received by each participant is a function of the contributions made during his or her working career, and the investment performance of the fund between the time that contributions are made and benefits are paid.

If investment performance is unfavorable, the value of a participant's retirement benefit may actually decline during his or her working career and may ultimately be even less than the total of the contributions made by the employer for his or her benefit. On the other hand, in defined benefit plans there is a stated ceiling on the benefit receivable (the formula benefit is both a minimum and a maximum). In a defined contribution plan, there is no ceiling on the benefit that a participant may obtain, if investment performance has been good.

*Profit-sharing plans.* The profit-sharing plan is probably the most popular of all the defined contribution plans. Under such a plan, the employer makes contributions out of profits from time to time. Profits must exist in order for the employer to contribute (although "profits" need not mean taxable net income as long as the definition is a reasonable one). If the profit-sharing plan is a *discretionary plan*, the employer decides each year how much (if anything) it will contribute. Even though there are profits out of which contributions may be made, the employer is not obligated to make a contribution in any given year (so long as contributions are substantial and recurrent over a reasonable period). If the plan is a *formula plan*, the employer is then obligated to make the contributions called for by the formula under the plan. For example, the plan could provide that the employer will contribute the lesser of 15 percent of the compensation of the plan participants or 10 percent of the net income of the company for each fiscal year. The formulas used vary infinitely, but they all have one thing in common. They are tied in some way to the earnings of the company. If there are no earnings from which a contribution can be made, then no contribution is made under the formula. Once the employer money has been put into the plan in a given year, the money is allocated among individual accounts established for each participant. In most plans, the allocation is made on the basis of relative current compensation. If employee A earns twice as much as employee B, A's share of the company contribution will be twice B's share. In making this statement, we are disregarding certain refinements that may be added to these plans. The benefit that the participant ultimately receives will depend on:

- How much the employer contributed (and his share of those contributions);
- The investment performance of the trust fund; and
- The timing of his departure.

Under a profit-sharing plan, amounts forfeited by employees who do not stay in the plan long enough to be entitled to their full account balances (that is, those who leave before they are "fully vested") are usually reallocated among the accounts of the remaining employees in the plan on the same basis as new employer contributions would be allocated, or on the basis of their interest in the plan assets.

*Money purchase plan.* A money purchase pension plan is somewhat like a profit-sharing plan in that:

- Employer contributions are made annually;
- The amounts contributed are allocated among the accounts of the individual participants; and
- The size of the benefit depends on contributions, investment experience, and timing of departure.

In all money purchase pension plans, however, the employer is obligated to contribute pursuant to a formula in the plan each year, even if the employer has no profit out of which to make the contribution. For example, under a typical money purchase pension plan, the employer might be obliged to contribute an amount equal to 10 percent of the compensation of the participants. The contribution must be made without regard for the success of the employer; failure to make the contribution called for in the plan results in a funding deficiency punishable by government imposition of excise taxes. The contribution formula in a money purchase pension plan is almost always related to employee compensation, and is never related to profit levels. In money purchase pension plans, amounts forfeited by employees leaving prematurely are always applied to reduce the next employer contribution that will become due.

*Stock bonus plan.* A stock bonus plan operates like a profit-sharing plan in that the amount the employer contributes each year may be discretionary. However, unlike a profit-sharing plan, there need not be any profits in order for the employer to contribute. In other words, a contribution can be made in a loss year when there are neither current earnings nor earnings accumulated from prior years. Employer contributions to stock bonus plans are made either in cash or in stock of the employer sponsoring the plan (or of a parent or subsidiary corporation of the employer). If the contribution is made in cash, the trustees operating the plan's trust fund (the assets under an employee benefit plan are held either in the form of an insurance or annuity contract or in a trust fund) use the cash to make purchases of employer stock in the open market. Distributions from stock bonus plans are made in the stock of the plan sponsor (or its parent or subsidiary) and not in cash (except for fractional shares). Since stock has no value to employees unless they have a way to dispose of it, stock bonus plans are generally limited to companies whose shares are traded in the public marketplace. In theory, stock bonus plans are incentives to productivity among employees because the value of the stock they will receive is supposed to reflect the profitability of the company, which in turn is supposed to reflect the efforts of the employees.

*Employee stock ownership plans.* Employee stock ownership plans may be money purchase pension plans or combination money purchase pension plans and stock bonus plans. In any event, substantially all of the money contributed by the employer is invested in stock of the plan sponsor. These plans have been granted special status under ERISA, and have thus found popularity in recent years. They are useful as corporate funding devices, especially when used to improve the cash flow of closely held corporations, or to obtain loans indirectly from financial institutions through an employee benefit trust. (These plans are discussed further in Chapter 28.) The important thing to note here is that employees obtain distributions in employer stock; these plans are thus a mutant strain of money purchase and stock bonus plans, having been granted special exemptions and privileges under ERISA.

*Thrift plans.* Thrift (or savings) plans are defined contribution plans in which the employee *must* contribute in order to share in the employer's contribution. The employer's contribution will be allocated among employees each year, at least in part on the basis of the amount contributed by each employee. If the employer is obligated to make contributions without regard to the profitability of the company, the plan is a thrift plan of the money purchase type. Such a plan might provide, for example, that the company will contribute to the account of each participant fifty cents for each dollar contributed by the participant. Even in a loss year, the company must make its contribution if the participants made theirs. A thrift plan can also be of the profit-sharing type. The employer's obligation to contribute is conditioned upon there being profits out of which such a contribution can be made. If the thrift plan is a formula plan of the profit-sharing type, the employer must make the contributions called for by the formula as long as there exist profits out of which to make the contributions. For example, the plan might call for the employer to contribute an amount equal to the lesser of 25 percent of the amount contributed by the participants in a given year, or 50 percent of the company's profit for the same year. Employer contributions would then be proportionally allocated among the accounts of the participants, according to the amount contributed by each. Finally, the thrift plan could be of the discretionary profit-sharing type. Contributions by the employer to such a plan can only be made out of profits, but the employer is under no obligation to contribute in any particular year, even a good year. Instead, each year the employer will decide how much money, if any, is to be contributed by the company, and the amount that the company contributes will then be allocated among the accounts of the participants on the basis of their respective contributions.

*Salary reduction plans.* Salary reduction plans are arrangements between employers and employees in which the employee agrees to accept a reduction in compensation (or to forego a raise) in order to have the amount of the reduction (or foregone raise) contributed by the employer to a defined contribution plan on the employee's account. Under the law prior to December 7, 1972, amounts contributed to a plan under such an arrangement were considered to be employer contributions. The tax consequence was favorable in that the corporation received a tax deduction for the amount contributed, and the employee was excused from recognizing the contribution as income for tax purposes until such time as he received the benefits from the plan. On December 7, 1972, the Internal Revenue Service reversed its view of the contributions, declaring them to be employee contributions. As a result, the employer was still allowed a deduction for the contributions (because they were treated as compensation paid to the employee, an ordinary and necessary business expense), but the employee was deemed to be immediately taxable on the full amount. Congress, uncertain of how to react to the new IRS position, provided a "safe harbor" in ERISA for plans in existence on or before June 26, 1974, declaring that contributions to such plans should be considered employer contributions until studies were completed to determine whether or not salary reduction plans were to survive. To date, studies are incomplete, and old plans (pre-June 26, 1974) are "grandfathered" (protected from the application of new IRS policy). However, new plans are not so protected, and are therefore risky. As a practical matter, it is unlikely that a firm would establish a salary reduction plan until the direction in which the law is moving is made clear. However, a number of old ones still exist and must be rewritten to conform to ERISA.

## EMPLOYEE PARTICIPATION

Under ERISA, an employee who has completed a year of service is eligible to participate in an employee benefit plan. An exception to this rule permits a plan to exclude from participation any employee who has not yet reached the age of twenty-five. The waiting period may thus be longer than one year for employees who are hired prior to age twenty-four. A second exception permits a plan that provides participants with immediate 100 percent vesting of accrued benefits to wait for a period of up to three years.

In the case of a defined benefit pension plan, the plan may exclude from participation any individual who is hired and commences work within five years of the normal retirement age. This provision was written into the law so as not to discourage employers from employing older workers.

ERISA defines a year of service as one thousand hours of work during a twelve-month period. A participant has one year of service if he works one thousand hours during the initial twelve months following his employment. If he is twenty-five years of age, has met the thousand hour requirement, and is participating in a plan that does not require a two or three year working period for participation, he must be permitted to participate in the plan on the earlier of: (1) the beginning of the first plan year after the anniversary date of his employment, or (2) six months after the anniversary date of his employment. If the employee does not work one thousand hours during the initial twelve months of his employment, he may be required to start once again to accumulate the required thousand hours in a new twelve-month period. The controller should set up a system to monitor the work records of new employees and alert the plan administrators as to when an employee becomes eligible to participate in the plan.

## EMPLOYEE VESTING

Vested benefits are those retirement benefits to which the employee is entitled, whether or not he continues in the service of the employer organization. Accrued benefits derived from an employee's contributions to a pension benefit plan are non-forfeitable. The rules concerning vesting therefore relate to the employer's contributions.

### Requirements

The vesting requirements of the Act apply to tax-qualified pension, profit-sharing, and stock bonus plans, as well as to employee pension plans in or affecting interstate commerce. The Act provides three alternative minimum vesting schedules:

- The five-to-fifteen year rule;
- The ten year rule; and
- The rule of 45.

The controller should review with management the cost implications of each method before a decision is finalized.

**Five-to-Fifteen Year Rule.** This is a graded standard for the vesting of accrued benefits. It requires that the employee must have at least 25 percent vesting by the end of the fifth year of service, at least 5 percent each year thereafter for five years, and 10 percent each year after that; the employee's accrued benefit would be 100 percent vested after fifteen years of service. The schedule is as follows:

*Schedule 1*

| Years of Covered Service | Nonforfeitable Percentage |
|:---:|:---:|
| 5 | 25 |
| 6 | 30 |
| 7 | 35 |
| 8 | 40 |
| 9 | 45 |
| 10 | 50 |
| 11 | 60 |
| 12 | 70 |
| 13 | 80 |
| 14 | 90 |
| 15 | 100 |

**Ten Year Rule.** This rule provides for 100 percent vesting of accrued benefits after ten years of service, with no vesting required before the end of the ten-year period.

**Rule of 45.** Under the Rule of 45 an employee with five years or more of service must be at least 50 percent vested in the accrued benefits from the employer's contributions when the sum of his age and years of service total 45. Each year thereafter, the employee's vested percentage increases in accordance with the following schedule.

*Schedule 2*

| If years of service equal or exceed | and sum of age and service equals or exceeds | then the nonforfeitable percentage is |
|:---:|:---:|:---:|
| 5 | 45 | 50 |
| 6 | 47 | 60 |
| 7 | 49 | 70 |
| 8 | 51 | 80 |
| 9 | 53 | 90 |
| 10 | 55 | 100 |

Under this rule, the minimum vested benefit after 10 years of service must be at least 50 percent with an additional 10 percent vested for each additional year of service.

### Special Instances

**Class-Year Plans.** A special minimum vesting schedule applies to certain defined contribution plans referred to as *class-year plans*. These plans must provide 100 percent vesting of benefits derived from employer contributions within five years after the end of the plan year for which any contribution was made.

**Mandatory Rapid Vesting.** In some instances, the IRS may require more stringent vesting standards, particularly if it believes the vesting schedule of a plan tends to favor highly compensated employees or officials of a company (IRC § 411 (d)). In those instances, the IRS may require more rapid vesting; for example, 40 percent vesting after four years of service, 5 percent vesting for each of the next two years, and 10 percent vesting for each of the next five years; resulting in 100 percent vesting after eleven years of service (Rev. Proc. 75–49 and 76–1).

### Temporary and Seasonal Service

With respect to his position in the vesting schedule, an employee who works at least one thousand hours during the year is considered to have worked for the year. He may, however, accrue benefits at a slower rate. If a full-time employee normally works fifteen hundred hours, and a seasonal employee works only one thousand hours, the seasonal employee may accrue only two thirds of a year's benefits.

### Rules for Accrual of Benefits

The Act includes three alternative rules for accruing benefits for defined benefit pension plans; these are included to prevent *backloading* in benefits accruals. Backloading occurs when benefits are accrued at a faster rate in the latter years of an employee's participation, than the rate applied in the earlier years. An example would be a plan that provides for the accrual of benefits at one percent of compensation prior to the age of fifty-five and 2 percent of compensation after age fifty-five. On the other hand, the Act does not forbid *frontloading*. The Act requires benefit accruals to meet one of the following three alternative tests:

- The 133⅓ percent rule;
- The 3 percent rule; and
- The fractional portion rule.

**133⅓ Percent Rule.** Under this alternative, the accrual rate for any given year cannot be more than 133⅓ percent of any other year on either a dollar or percentage rate. The plan must provide for a full accrued retirement benefit at normal retirement age.

For example, Plan A may provide a monthly pension benefit equal to 2 percent of the employee's average compensation for the five highest years, multiplied by the years of participation before the age of sixty-five. To avoid violating the 133⅓ percent rule, to backload its accruals the company would be limited to an approximately 1.8 percent accrual in the early years and a 2.4 percent accrual in the later years.

**3 Percent Rule.** Under the 3 percent rule, the minimum rate of accrual for any year before the end of 33⅓ years of participation is 3 percent of the maximum benefits to which the participant would be entitled if he began participation in the plan at the earliest possible entry age and participated continuously until either the earlier of normal retirement age or age sixty-five.

For example, Plan B may provide for a flat amount pension payable at a normal retirement age of 65. Mr. Smith became a participant in the plan at age 25 and participates continuously until he reaches the retirement age of 65. His pension after 40 years of service would be $150 per month or $1,800 per year. This pension benefit under the 3 percent rule would accrue at the minimum rate of $54 per year for 33⅓ years ($1,800 × 3%). No accrual would be necessary after 33⅓ years. The accrued benefit at the end of any year must be equal to at least $54 times the number of years of participation to the end of the plan year.

This rule may also be followed if the pension benefit is based on an individual's compensation. In this case, the maximum benefit would be based on the average compensation for the employee's most highly compensated continuous period of not more than ten years.

**Fractional Portion Rule.** This rule requires an employee's accrued pension benefits at any given date to be an allocable portion of the benefits he would be entitled to at his normal retirement age. The minimum benefit to be accrued is determined in the following manner:

Annual benefits due the employee on separation are equal to the annual benefits beginning at normal retirement age (to which he would have been entitled), multiplied by the years of the employee's active participation over the total years the employee would have participated if he continued until normal retirement age.

As an example, Plan C provides for pension benefits based on 2 percent of the average annual compensation of the employee's highest five years of participation, multiplied by the number of years of participation. Mr. Johnson began participation in the plan at age 25. Normal retirement age is 65 and Mr. Johnson's average annual compensation for the highest 5 years of participation is $40,000. Mr. Johnson has been a participant in the plan for 20 years. The accrual of benefits to the 20 years of participation must be at least $16,000 and is determined as follows:

$$2\% \times 40 = 80\% \times \$40,000 = \$32,000$$
$$\$32,000 \times \frac{20}{40} = \$16,000$$

### Disclosure of Employee Benefits

Sufficient records must be maintained to determine an employee's benefits. ERISA Section 105 requires that the plan administrator, on request, must furnish to participants and beneficiaries under the Plan the latest information available about their total benefits accrued and the nonforfeitable benefits, if any, that have accrued, or the earliest date on which benefits will become nonforfeitable.

## FUNDING

ERISA changed the rules for funding defined benefit pension plans. Formerly, employers' contributions to a qualified pension plan had to be sufficient to fund normal pension costs plus interest on the unfunded accrued pension liabilities (past service costs).

### Minimum Funding Requirements

For most defined benefit plans, the sponsor's annual contribution to the plan must be sufficient to cover the normal cost for the period, annual interest on unfunded amounts, amortization of past service liability, increases or decreases in past service liability resulting from plan amendments, and experience gains or losses and actuarial gains or losses from changes in actuarial assumptions. The controller should have an actuary compute amortization on a level payment basis, including interest and principal needed to comply with the minimum funding requirement.

Assuming that a plan does not have an accumulated funding deficiency from prior years, the contribution will be sufficient to satisfy the minimum funding standard if it accomplishes all of the following:

- It pays the normal cost for current services incurred, with respect to the plan year for which the contribution is made;
- It is sufficient to amortize the past service cost (including principal and interest) on a level payment basis over a period not to exceed forty years in the case of any multiemployer plan or of any single employer plan in existence on January 1, 1974, or over a period not to exceed thirty years in the case of any single employer plan coming into existence after January 1, 1974;
- It is sufficient to amortize separately, with respect to each plan year, the net increase (if any) in unfunded past service liabilities arising from plan amendments adopted in such year over a period not to exceed forty years in the case of a multiemployer plan and not to exceed thirty years in the case of a single employer plan;
- It is sufficient to amortize over a period not to exceed thirty years any net loss resulting from changes in actuarial assumptions used with respect to the plan;
- It is sufficient to amortize over a period not to exceed twenty years in the case of a multiemployer plan or fifteen years in the case of a single employer plan any net experience gain or loss suffered by the plan; and

- It is sufficient to amortize on an equal annual installment basis over a period of fifteen years each waived funding deficiency that may have occurred.

It is the controller's responsibility to make these calculations or have them made (or at least reviewed) by an actuary. Defined benefit pension plans require that an enrolled actuary prepare for inclusion in the report an actuarial statement at least every third year.

### Funding Standard Account

ERISA requires plans subject to the minimum funding standards to maintain an account called the *funding standard account* (FSA). This account is a memorandum account maintained for tax qualification purposes and is not included in the plan's financial statements. Defined benefit pension plans are required to maintain an FSA. Certain defined contribution plans (money-purchase and target-benefit plans) must maintain FSAs, but on a more limited basis.

The controller should charge the funding standard account each year with normal costs for the year-end and with the minimum amortization payment required for initial past service cost, increased plan liabilities, experience losses (in investments), and waived contributions for each year. Offset against these charges each plan year are credits for the employer's contribution for the year, the amortization of any cost decreases due to plan amendments, experience gains, and any waived contributions.

A funding standard account must also be maintained in the case of a money purchase (defined contribution) plan to the extent that the employer is charged each year for the amount that must be contributed under the plan formula, and is credited with the amount actually paid.

The Secretary of the Treasury may waive all or part of the minimum funding requirements for a plan year in which the minimum funding standard cannot be met without imposing substantial business hardship on the employer(s). That waiver is only issued if failure to do so would be adverse to the participants' interests.

In the absence of a waiver, and if the employer does not make sufficient contributions (either under a defined benefit plan or a money purchase plan) to meet the minimum funding requirements, the IRS will directly impose a nondeductible excise tax on the employer, equal to 5 percent of the accumulated deficiency at the end of the year. If an employer fails to correct an accumulated funding deficiency within ninety days after the date of mailing of notice of such deficiency under Section 6212 of the IRC (which ninety-day period is subject to extension by any period in which a deficiency cannot be assessed under Section 6213(a) and by any other period the Internal Revenue Service determines is reasonable and necessary to permit a reduction of the accumulated funding deficiency to "zero"), there is imposed upon the employer a further excise tax equal to 100 percent of the accumulated funding deficiency to the extent the deficiency is not corrected.

Before issuing a deficiency notice, the Internal Revenue Service is to notify the Department of Labor so it will have an opportunity to require the employer to correct the deficiency and to comment on the prospective imposition of the tax.

**Operation of a Funding Standard Account**

The operation of a funding standard account is illustrated in the following example.

In 1979, the Able Corporation established a defined benefit pension plan for its employees. When the plan was established, a past service liability of $1.5 million existed to provide for benefits attributable to employees' service prior to the adoption of the plan. Normal cost for current service is $100,000. The interest rate used to determine the plan cost is 7 percent. In the first year, the Able Corporation contributes $220,880. All amounts are credited and charged to the accounts at the beginning of the year. The plan's funding standard account for 1979 would be as follows:

|  |  |
|---|---|
| *Credits:* | |
| Able Corporation's contribution | $220,880 |
| *Charges:* | |
| Normal cost | $100,000 |
| Amortization of past service cost | 120,880* |
| Total | $220,880 |

\* Required annual payment over 30 years at 7%.

In 1980, the Able Corporation amended the plan to improve employee benefits. The past service liability was increased by $200,000. This increase was to be amortized over a 30-year period, beginning in 1980. This change also increased the plan's normal cost to $120,000. The plan had a net actuarial gain of $8,000 over 1979, to be amortized over a 15-year period. All amounts other than interest are charged and credited to the accounts at the beginning of the year. The Able Corporation contributed $261,180 in 1980. The plan funding accounts for 1980 would be as follows:

|  |  |
|---|---|
| *Credits:* | |
| Able Corporation contribution | $261,180 |
| Amortization of $8,000 actuarial gain over | |
| 15 years (at 7%) | 878 |
| Total | $262,058 |
| *Charges:* | |
| Normal cost | $120,000 |
| Amortization (initial past service cost) | 118,146 |
| Amortization of $200,000 additional past service cost from amendment plus | |
| 7% interest over 30 years | 16,117 |
|  | $254,263 |
| *Positive Balance* | $   7,795 |
| *Interest on balance* (at 7%) | 545 |
| Net Balance (credit for future years) | $   8,340 |

## PLAN FIDUCIARIES

ERISA establishes standards for plan investments and transactions and imposes restrictions and responsibilities on plan fiduciaries.

### Definition of a Fiduciary

ERISA defines a fiduciary in very broad terms. Under the law, a person is considered a fiduciary if he: (1) exercises any discretionary authority or discretionary control over the management of a plan or over the management or disposition of the assets of the plan; (2) renders investment advice (direct or indirect) to the plan for a fee or other compensation or has the authority or responsibility to do so; or (3) has any discretionary authority or discretionary responsibility in the administration of the plan.

### Fiduciary Responsibilities

A fiduciary's responsibilities include managing plan assets solely in the interest of participants and beneficiaries (with the care a prudent man would exercise) and diversifying investments in order to minimize the risk of large losses unless it is clearly not prudent to do so. Most plans are required to have no more than 10 percent of the fair market value of the plan assets invested in a combination of "qualifying employer securities" and "qualifying employer real property."

### Prohibited Transactions

**Transactions With Parties-in-Interest.** A plan fiduciary is prohibited from engaging in certain specific transactions with a *party-in-interest*. ERISA defines a party-in-interest as any fiduciary or employee of the plan, any person who provides services to the plan, an employer whose employees are covered by the plan, an employee association whose members are covered by the plan, a person who owns 50 percent or more of such an employer or employee association, or relatives of one of the persons described above.

The following transactions between the plan and a party-in-interest are prohibited:

- The sale, exchange, or leasing of property;
- A loan or other extension of credit;
- The furnishing of goods, services, or facilities, except as allowed under the Act;
- A transfer of plan assets to a party-in-interest for the use or benefit of a party-in-interest; and
- An acquisition for the plan of any employer securities or real property, except to the extent allowed.

ERISA also prohibits defined benefit plans and new money purchase plans from acquiring any employer securities if, immediately after such acquisition, the aggregate fair market value of the employer's securities and employer real property held by the plan exceeds 10 percent of the fair market value of the assets of the plan.

Despite these carefully spelled out prohibitions, ERISA permits certain types of transactions between the plan and a party-in-interest. Under certain circumstances, a party-in-interest may make a loan to an employee stock ownership plan; if required by the plan, plan assets may be invested in savings accounts, etc., at banks and other financial institutions acting as a plan trustee, and banks or brokerage firms are permitted under certain circumstances to perform "multiple services" for the plan.

**Other Prohibited Activities.** A fiduciary is also prohibited from: (1) dealing with the assets of the plan in his own interests or for his own account; (2) receiving consideration for his own account from any party dealing with the plan, in connection with the transactions involving the plan's assets; and/or (3) acting in any transactions involving a plan on behalf of a party whose interests are adverse to that of the plan, its participants, or beneficiaries.

ERISA Section 408 allows specific exceptions to these rules, and the Secretaries of Labor and the Treasury have granted special exemptions from the prohibited-transaction rules. For example, ERISA specifies that a fiduciary may receive reasonable compensation from a plan for his services (unless he is a full-time employee of the sponsoring employer or employee organization), reasonable benefits as a plan participant, and reimbursement for expenses. Other exceptions are described in ERISA and other regulations and rulings. The controller should obtain advice of legal counsel when investigating a possible prohibited transaction or other breach of fiduciary duties.

## REPORTING REQUIREMENTS

ERISA significantly increased the reporting and disclosure requirements for pension benefit and welfare benefit plans. Various reports must be prepared and filed with the IRS, and others must be furnished to plan participants and beneficiaries, the Department of Labor, and the Pension Benefit Guaranty Corporation. The plan administrator is required to file with the Department of Labor an initial plan description and summary of the description, supplemented by amended descriptions. Most plans must file an annual report that includes financial statements and schedules, an actuarial statement (for defined benefit pension plans) certified by an enrolled actuary, and other information with the IRS, which in turn provides a copy to the Department of Labor.

### Annual Report/Return—Series 5500 Forms

The report of most significance to the controller is the annual report. For plans with 100 or more participants, the annual report (Form 5500) must contain, with certain exceptions, financial statements, separate schedules, notes required for a full and fair presentation, and an independent public accountant's report. Plans with fewer than 100 participants at the beginning of the plan year must file Form 5500-C. A Keogh plan with fewer than 100 participants must file Form 5500-K.

**Who Must File.** All administrators of plans covered by ERISA must file annual reports with the IRS. These reports must be filed for all plans whether they are tax qualified or not, including plans that have ceased to accrue and plans to which contributions have been discontinued. If the controller is not directly responsible for filing the reports, he should be sure that they have been timely filed.

**Exemptions.** Welfare benefit plans with fewer than 100 participants at the beginning of the plan year are exempt from filing the annual return/report if: (1) benefits are paid as needed strictly from the general assets of an employer or employee organization sponsoring the plan; or (2) benefits are provided exclusively from insurance contracts or policies issued by an insurance company or similar organizations authorized to do business in any state. In the latter case, the premiums must be paid from the general assets of the employer or employee organizations sponsoring the plan, or paid partly from a sponsoring organization and partly from contributions by its employees or members.

Certain other types of pension benefit plans and welfare benefit plans are excluded from the filing requirements. These include: (1) unfunded pension benefit plans and unfunded or insured welfare plans maintained by the employer to provide benefits to a select group of management or highly compensated employees (these plans must meet certain requirements set forth by Department of Labor regulations); (2) plans maintained solely to comply with Workers' Compensation, Unemployment Compensation, or Disability Insurance Laws; (3) unfunded excess benefit plans; and (4) welfare benefit plans maintained outside the United States for persons who substantially are all nonresident aliens.

Government pension plans and church pension plans not having elected coverage under ERISA are not required to file reports with the Department of Labor. However, they *must file Form 5500* with the **IRS**.

*Limited exemption.* Some plans covering 100 or more participants have been granted a limited exemption from some types of reporting. This limited exemption exempts unfunded welfare plans, fully insured welfare plans, combined unfunded and fully insured welfare plans, and fully insured pension plans from filing financial statements, schedules, and the accountant's report. This limited exclusion does not eliminate the necessity for the administrator to file an annual report or Schedules A and B if applicable.

**Where and When to File.** The series 5500 reports must be filed with the IRS and must be filed within seven months after the plan's year end. (For example, a plan with a December 31st year end must file with the IRS not later than July 31st of the following year.) An extension of this due date of up to two and a half months may be obtained by filing Form 5558 with the IRS. The controller should mark his calendar to make sure that the 5500 form, or an extension form, is filed prior to the due date.

Plan administrators are subject to a penalty of $10 a day, up to a maximum of $5,000, for failing to file timely returns with the IRS unless reasonable cause for delinquency is shown. There are no specific monetary penalties for a late filing with the Department of Labor. However, ERISA provides for criminal and civil actions for violation of the DOL regulations.

### Audit Requirements

ERISA requires that independent auditors audit the financial statements of pension and welfare plans (which are generally prepared by the corporate controller), and that they submit a report of the results of their examination. Department of Labor regulations generally do not require the accountant's opinion to encompass information pertaining both to custodial accounts and discretionary trust accounts that are certified by certain financial institutions such as banks and insurance companies. However, this proviso does not eliminate the need for an auditor; an independent audit must be made of other transactions and information included in the financial statements of the plan.

Department of Labor regulations waive the auditor's report requirement for employee pension and welfare benefit plans with fewer than 100 participants. Further, the regulations do not require an auditors' report from certain pension plans funded through allocated insurance contracts, where the benefit payments are guaranteed by the insurance company.

### Financial Statement Requirements

Department of Labor Regulations Section 2520.103–1 permits plans with 100 or more participants to file a standard annual report, or simplified report, under an alternative method.

There are at least *five* major differences between ERISA requirements and the alternative method.

- The alternative method does not require that financial statements be prepared in accordance with generally accepted accounting principles.
- The alternative method permits the financial statements to be prepared on a cash basis, accrual basis, or a modified cash basis.
- The alternative method requires the financial statements to be given in a comparative form, whereas the statutory method does not have this requirement. (The statutory method does, however, require a comparative schedule of assets and liabilities.)
- The alternative method requires all assets and liabilities in the financial statements to be stated at their current value. Although this is not a statutory requirement,

ERISA does require that they be stated on the assets and liabilities schedule on a current value basis.

- The statutory method requires that the schedules include a statement of cash receipts and disbursements. The alternative method does not require this schedule.

As a practical matter, the controller should follow the alternative method of reporting. Plans that follow the statutory method generally do not wish to report their assets and liabilities at their current value in the primary financial statements.

**Statements Required.** Financial statements required under both methods are, for pension plans, a statement of assets and liabilities and a statement of changes in net assets available for plan benefits. For health and welfare plans, a statement of assets and liabilities, a statement of changes in fund balance, and a statement of changes in financial position are required. The defined benefit pension plan financial statements required by FASB Statement No. 35 are acceptable to the DOL.

Footnotes to the financial statements that should be "considered" under ERISA but "shall be included" under the alternative method are the following:

- A description of the plan including any significant changes in the plan made during the period and the impact of such changes on benefits;
- The funding of the plan, including policy with respect to prior service cost and any changes in such policy during the year;
- A description of any significant changes in plan benefits made during the period;
- A description of material lease commitments, other commitments, and contingent liabilities;
- A description of agreements and transactions with persons known to be parties-in-interest;
- A general description of priorities upon termination of the plan;
- Information concerning whether or not a tax ruling or determination letter has been obtained; and
- Any other information required for a fair presentation.

In addition, the alternative method requires a footnote giving a description of accounting principles and practices and, if applicable, variances from generally accepted accounting principles. While this requirement is not specified under the statutory method, it would be necessary under GAAP, even though it is not set forth as a separate item in the statutes.

**Schedules.** Both the statutory method and the alternative method require certain schedules, usually prepared by the controller, to be attached to the financial statements. The statutory method requires two schedules not required by the alternative method: comparative statements on assets and liabilities at current value and statements of cash and disbursements. Both methods require five other schedules:

- A schedule of assets held for investments;
- A schedule of each transaction involving a person known to be a party-in-interest;

- A schedule of all loans or fixed income obligations that were in default at the close of the plan fiscal year and were classified during the year as uncollectible;
- A list of all leases that were in default or were classified during the year as uncollectible; and
- A schedule of transactions, or a related series of transactions involving an amount in excess of 3 percent of the current value of plan assets (at the beginning of the plan year).

### Form and Contents of Returns and Schedules

**Schedule of Assets Held for Investment.** This schedule requires a detailed listing of assets held for investment purposes at the end of the year. It should include:

- The identity of the issuer, borrower, lessor, or similar party;
- A description of investments, including the trading date, rate of interest, collateral, and par or maturity value;
- Cost; and
- Current value.

In addition, information should be given on certain assets acquired and disposed of within the plan year.

Certain investments, however, need not be included in this schedule in accordance with the Department of Labor Regulations Section 2520.103–11. These are specified assets that are not held at the end of the plan year. They include:

- Debt obligations of the United States or any agency of the United States;
- Interest issued by a company registered under the Investment Company Act of 1940;
- Bank certificates of deposit with a maturity of not more than one year;
- Commercial paper with maturity of not more than nine months if it is ranked in the highest rating category by at least two nationally recognized statistical rating services and is issued by a company required to file reports with the Securities and Exchange Commission under Section 13 of the Securities and Exchange Act of 1934;
- Participation in a bank common or collective trust;
- Participation in an insurance company pooled separate account; and
- Securities purchased from a person registered as a broker-dealer under the Securities Exchange Act of 1934 and listed on a national securities exchange or quoted on NASDAQ.

**Schedule of Party-in-Interest Transactions.** Except in cases where the transaction was a party-in-interest and is exempt under an administrative exemption granted by the Department of Labor under Section 408(a) of the Act or a statutory exemption under Part 4 of Title I, a schedule of each transaction involving a known party-in-interest must be prepared. This schedule must include:

- Identity of the party involved;
- Relationship to the plan, the employer, or other party-of-interest;
- Description of transactions, including maturity date, rate of interest, collateral, par or maturity value;
- Purchase price;
- Selling price;
- Leased rental;
- Expense incurred in connection with transaction;
- Cost of assets;
- Current value of assets; and
- Net gain or loss on each transaction.

**Schedule of Obligations in Default.** A schedule is required of all loans or fixed income obligations that were in default at the end of the plan's fiscal year or that were classified during the year as uncollectible. This schedule, prepared by the controller, must include:

- Identity and address of the borrower;
- The original amount of the loan;
- The amount of both principal and interest received during the year;
- The unpaid balance at the end of the year;
- A detailed description of loans, including the date the loan was made, maturity date, interest rate, type and value of any collateral, any renegotiations of the loan and the terms of renegotiation, and any other material items;
- The principal and interest amount overdue. The schedule should also note any of the items due from individuals identified as parties-of-interest; and
- An explanation of steps that have been taken or will be taken to collect the overdue amount.

**Schedule of Leases in Default.** The controller must also prepare a schedule of any leases in default as of the end of the plan year or classified as uncollectible during the year. This schedule should include the following information relating to the lease transaction:

- The identity of the lessor or lessee and his relationship to the plan, employer, employee organization, or any other party-in-interest;
- The type of property leased and a description of that property, including the location and date it was purchased;
- Terms relating to the rent, taxes, insurance, repairs, expenses, renewal options, and date the property was leased;
- The original cost of the property, its current value at the time the lease was entered into, the gross rental receipts during the year, the expenses paid during the plan year, the net receipts, and the accrual in arrears; and
- The steps taken to collect the amount due or otherwise to remedy the default.

**Schedule of Reportable Transactions.** Reportable transactions consist of the following four separate categories of transactions:

- A single transaction in excess of 3 percent of the current value of the plan assets;
- A series of transactions with or in conjunction with the same person involving property other than securities which amount in the aggregate to more than 3 percent of the current value of the plan assets;
- A series of transactions with respect to securities of the same issue which amount in the aggregate to more than 3 percent of the current value of the plan assets; and
- Any transaction with respect to securities with or in conjunction with a person if a prior or subsequent single transaction with that same person was a reportable transaction.

Transactions in the fourth category involving a bank, insurance company, broker-dealer registered under the Securities Exchange Act of 1934, or investment company registered under the Investment Company Act of 1940 do not include (1) debt obligations of the United States or any United States agency with maturity of not more than one year; (2) debt obligations of the United States or any United States agency with the maturity of more than one year if purchased or sold under a repurchase agreement with the term of ninety-one days; (3) interest issued by a company registered under the Investment Company Act of 1940; (4) bank certificates of deposit with the maturity of not more than one year; (5) commercial paper with the maturity of not more than nine months if it is ranked in the highest rating category for commercial paper by at least two nationally recognized statistical rating services; (6) participants in a bank common or collective trust; or (7) participants in an insurance company pooled separate account. Further, for the purpose of the fourth category only, a transaction shall not be considered "with or in conjunction with the person" if: (1) the person is a broker-dealer registered under the Securities Exchange Act of 1934; (2) the transaction involves the purchase or sale of securities listed on a national securities exchange or quoted on NASDAQ; and (3) the broker-dealer does not purchase or sell securities involved in the transaction for his own account or the account of an affiliated person.

The schedule must contain both the identity of the parties and a description of the assets involved, including interest rates and maturity in the case of a loan. It must also include, where appropriate, the purchase price, selling price, lease rental, expenses incurred with the transaction, cost of the asset, current value of the asset on the transaction date, and the net gain or loss.

The controller should complete the 3-percent figure by comparing the current value of the transaction at the transaction date with the current value of the plan assets at the beginning of the plan year.

**Schedule A—Insurance Information.** The controller should attach Schedule A to Forms 5500, 5500–C, and 5500–K where benefits are provided by insurance companies or similar organizations.

**Schedule B—Actuarial Information.** ERISA requires all pension plans that must file an annual report to engage an enrolled actuary. This actuary, in addition to supplying information necessary on Forms 5500, 5500–C, and 5500–K, is responsible for the preparation of Schedule B.

**Schedule SSA—Annual Registration Statement.** The Internal Revenue Code requires a plan administrator to file a report giving information on participants of pension plans with deferred vested benefits who have separated from a sponsoring organization and who did not receive pension benefits under the plan prior to the due date of Form SSA. This information is forwarded to the Social Security Administration where it is maintained. When the individual applies for social security he will be notified by the Social Security Administration of these deferred vested benefits. The information required on such a schedule must include the name of the participant, his Social Security number, the nature and form of benefit, and the amount of vested benefit. Regulations also require that the plan administrator give this information to the individuals involved.

### Rules for Pooled Separate Accounts and Collective Trusts

Many employee benefit plans invest in funds sponsored by banks and insurance companies. If these investments are in common or collective trusts of a bank or an insurance company's pooled separate account, the Department of Labor regulations do not require that the plan include in its annual report the statement of assets and liabilities of such trusts if the bank or interest carrier files a statement of assets and liabilities directly with the Department of Labor. In such a case, the bank, in addition to filing with the Department of Labor, must give the plan a copy of the annual statement of assets and liabilities of any common or collective trusts or pooled separate accounts in which any plan assets are held. The plan then must include in its annual report a certificate that the plan has received the statement from the bank or insurance carrier.

## DISCLOSURES TO PARTICIPANTS

In addition to filing reports with the Federal Government, the plan is required to make certain information available to the participants. The controller should alert the plan administrator to this requirement.

### Summary of Annual Reports

Generally, plans which file annual reports with the Department of Labor must also distribute summary annual reports to the participants. The content of the summary annual reports depends upon whether the company is using the statutory or alternative method of reporting. If the alternative method is being used, the summary report must include: (1) a statement of assets and liabilities, presented at current value; (2) separate or combined statements of income and expense and changes in net assets; (3) notes to the financial statements; and (4) a notice that the complete annual report is available upon request for a reasonable charge and is available for examination at the plan's administrative offices as well as at other specified locations.

Plans electing to report on the statutory basis must include in the summary annual report the information specified in Section 104(b)(3) of ERISA: a comparative schedule of assets and liabilities at current value; a schedule of receipts and disbursements; and any other material necessary to summarize the annual report.

The summary annual report of plans required to file Form 5500 and that elect the alternative method of reporting must include a copy of the appropriate form, including required schedules, and a notice to the participant that a complete annual report may be obtained (for a reasonable charge) on request.

The summary annual report must be distributed to participants and beneficiaries within nine months after the plan's year-end.

## Summary Plan Description

Section 104(b) requires that a summary plan description be published and distributed to each participant and each beneficiary receiving benefits under the plan within ninety days after he becomes a participant or, in the case of a beneficiary, within ninety days after he first receives benefits.

The summary plan description must contain the following information: (1) the name and type of administration of the plan; (2) the name and address of the person designated as agent for service of legal process; (3) the name and address of the administrator, or names, titles, and addresses of any trustee or trustees if they are different than the administrator; (4) a description of the relevant portions of any collective bargaining agreement; (5) the plan's requirement respecting eligibility for participation and benefits; (6) a description of the vesting requirements of the plan; (7) the circumstances which may result in disqualification, ineligibility, or denial or loss of benefits; (8) the date and end of the plan year and whether the records of the plan are kept on a calendar or fiscal year basis; and (9) the process to be followed in presenting claims for benefits under the plan and any remedies for redress of claims that are denied.

Every fifth year, the administrator must furnish each participant and each beneficiary receiving benefits under the plan with an updated summary plan description that integrates all plan amendments made within the five-year period. If any modifications are made to the plan, a summary description of such modifications or change must be furnished to participants and beneficiaries not later than 210 days after the end of the plan year in which the modification was made. This information should be reviewed by corporate counsel before distribution to plan participants to ensure that it complies with applicable regulations.

# FASB STATEMENT NO. 35

The Financial Accounting Standards Board Statement No. 35, "Accounting and Reporting by Defined Benefit Pension Plans," sets generally accepted accounting principles for defined benefit pension plans. Plans reporting on a statutory basis are expected to follow this statement because the Act requires plans to report in accordance with generally accepted accounting principles. FASB No. 35 rules are effective for plan years beginning after December 15, 1980.

## Financial Statements

The statement requires all defined benefit plans to issue the following annual financial statements:

- A statement that includes information regarding the net assets available for benefits as of the end of the plan year (balance sheet);
- A statement that includes information regarding the changes during the year in net assets available for benefits (revenue and expenditures);
- Information regarding the actuarial present value of accumulated plan benefits as of a benefit valuation date that is either the beginning or the end of the plan year; and
- Information regarding the effects of certain factors affecting year-to-year changes in the actuarial present value of accumulated plan benefits.

**Net Assets Available for Benefits.** The statement requires plans to use the accrual basis of accounting. Plan investments, whether in debt securities, equity securities, real estate, or any other assets, should be presented in the financial statements at their fair value at the reporting date. However, the operating assets (fixed assets) of the plan must be presented at their historical cost, less accumulated depreciation or amortization.

If the plan is financed either partially or fully through contracts with insurance companies, the rules require that the recognition of the contracts and their measurement as plan assets should be the same as that reported under ERISA reporting requirements.

**Changes in Net Assets Available for Benefits.** The minimum disclosure of changes in net assets available for benefits include:

- The net appreciation or depreciation in the fair value of each significant class of investments;
- Investment income;
- Contributions from employers segregated between cash and non-cash contributions;
- Contributions from participants, including those transmitted by the sponsor;
- Contributions from other identified sources;

- Benefits paid to participants;
- Payments to insurance companies to purchase contracts that are excluded from plan assets; and
- Administrative expenses.

**Actuarial Present Value of Accumulated Plan Benefits.** Set forth in some detail are rules for measuring accumulated plan benefits and the significant assumptions concerning future experience, such as the treatment of expected rates of inflation and expected rates of return.

For presentation purposes, the actuarial present value of accumulated plan benefits must be segmented into at least three categories: (1) vested benefits of participants currently receiving payments; (2) other vested benefits; and (3) nonvested benefits.

Significant effects of certain factors affecting the changes in the present value of accumulated plan benefits must be disclosed. This disclosure can be made either in the form of a statement that accounts for such changes between two benefit valuation dates or elsewhere in the financial statements.

Changes in the actuarial present value of accumulated benefits shall include such factors as: (1) plan amendments; (2) changes in the nature of the plan; and (3) changes in actuarial assumptions.

**Additional Required Disclosures.** The financial statements should disclose the plan's accounting policies and should include a description of the methods and significant assumptions used to determine: (1) the fair value of the investments; and (2) the actuarial present value of accumulated plan benefits. Any significant changes of method or assumptions between benefit valuation dates must be described.

Statement No. 35 also lists the following disclosures in the financial statements required, where applicable. Many of these disclosures are also required by ERISA:

- A brief general description of the plan agreement including vesting and benefit provisions;
- A description of significant plan amendments and whether they became effective after the benefit valuation date;
- A brief general description of: (a) the priority order of participants' claims to the assets of the plan upon plan termination, and (b) benefits guaranteed by the Pension Benefit Guaranty Corporation;
- The funding policy and any changes in the funding policy during the plan year;
- Policy regarding the purchase of contracts with insurance companies that are excluded from plan assets;
- Federal income tax status of the plan;
- Identification of individual investments that represent 5 percent or more of the net assets available for benefits;
- Significant real estate or other transactions in which the plan may be involved with the sponsor, employer, or employee organizations; and

- Unusual or significant events or transactions occurring after the latest benefit valuation date but before the issuance of the financial statements that might significantly affect the usefulness of the statements in an assessment of the plan's present and future ability to pay benefits.

ERISA rules and regulations are continually being revised and interpreted. The controller who has the responsibility for preparing the annual plan financial statements and filing the required 5500 forms with IRS should either subscribe to a reporting service that will keep him up-to-date on proposed and adopted changes, or should confer with corporate counsel and the outside accountants on current rule changes.

## SUGGESTED READING

Allan, Everett T., Melone, Joseph J., and Rosenbloom, Jerry S., *Pension Planning: Pensions, Profit Sharing, and Other Deferred Compensation Plans*, 3rd ed. Homewood, Illinois: Richard D. Irwin, Inc., 1976.

Bildersee, Robert, *Pension Regulation Manual*, Vol. 1. Boston: Warren, Gorham & Lamont, Inc., 1979.

Gilbert, Geoffrey M., Lachowicz, Gregory J. and Zid, James F. *Accounting and Auditing for Employee Benefit Plans*. Boston: Warren, Gorham & Lamont, Inc., 1978.

Mamorsky, Jeffrey D., *Pension and Profit Sharing Plans: A Basic Guide*. New York: Executive Enterprises, Inc., 1977.

McGill, Dan M., and Grubbs, Donald S., Jr., *Fundamentals of Private Pensions*, 4th ed. (Published for Pension Research Council) Homewood, Illinois: Richard D. Irwin, Inc., 1979.

*Pension Reform Update 1978*. (Tax Law and Estate Planning Course Handbook Series 1978–79, Vol. 128) New York: Practicing Law Institute, 1978.

# 28

# Tax Qualified Retirement Plans

*Vincent C. Hennessy*

## INTRODUCTION

Since the end of World War II, the private retirement system has undergone a metamorphosis; it has gone from a relatively minor financial intermediary to one of the principal financial institutions in the United States. During this period, retirement costs of private industry have risen to over $30 billion annually. At the same time, the assets controlled by noninsured private retirement programs have multiplied more than twenty times to over $250 billion.

### Increased Public Attention

This rapid ascendency within the hierarchy of financial institutions has brought with it increasing attention from the financial community, government regulators, and corporate management. Since the mid-1970s, a considerable amount of attention has been focused by the financial press on the impact of pension costs on corporate profitability and the burden of pension obligations on the financial strength of American corporations. It is now common to see articles or studies exposing the unfunded liabilities and increasing annual costs of corporate retirement plans. Almost invariably, it will ominously be noted that untold billions of dollars owed to pension plans appear nowhere on the corporate balance sheets and that the annual outlay for pensions is increasing both in absolute amount and as a percent of total labor costs. The existence of these "hidden obligations" as well as increasing annual costs has led some to observe that the financial well-being of many corporations may be imperiled.

The increasing awareness and concern over corporate pension costs and unfunded liabilities has been prompted by two recent developments.

**Expansion of Corporate Pension Obligations.** The first development has been the rapid growth of pension costs and liabilities of major corporations. This was due to an unparalleled expansion of corporate pension obligations during the 1970s, both in terms of absolute dollars and as a percentage of corporate net worth. This off-balance sheet liability probably now exceeds $50 billion for all American corporations.

**ERISA.** The second and probably most important stimulus has been the Employee Retirement Income Security Act of 1974 (ERISA). Among other things, this legislation established a Federal corporation to insure workers against loss of certain benefits if a pension plan terminated for any reason. It also included a requirement that corporations comply with minimum annual funding standards. Prior to enactment of ERISA most pension plans contained provisions limiting employees' benefit claims in the event of a plan termination; other plan provisions generally provided, in effect, that the annual funding of pension costs was entirely at the discretion of the employer. These provisions effectively limited the employer's liability to assets that had previously been set aside in a pension trust. ERISA, however, established the Pensions Benefit Guaranty Corporation (PBGC) to administer terminated plans and empowered it to impose a lien on corporate assets for certain unfunded pension liabilities. (See Chapter 27.)

ERISA is an extremely complex piece of legislation; the regulatory and judicial interpretations of it thus far are incomplete and ambiguous. This has contributed substantially to the difficulties facing management in evaluating the probable future impact of retirement plans on corporate cash flows and obligations. In addition, the wide range of funding options and the diversity of pension plan provisions often frustrate corporate managers trying to make comparisons with other companies of pension costs and obligations.

## Management's Information Needs

Corporate managers have often approached questions of pension costs and liabilities as so much mumbo-jumbo better left to accountants and actuaries. Several recent developments, however, have forcefully brought home the importance for corporate executives of having a full understanding of what pension numbers really mean as well as the importance of assessing the probable future financial effects of retirement plans. The corporate controller is in a particularly effective position to assist senior management in developing an understanding of pension numbers. But it is first necessary to develop an appreciation of just when and how management will have to deal with pension numbers.

Obviously, pension costs are an important element in developing both short- and long-range financial plans as well as in formulating corporate strategy to deal with external economic factors. Beyond this, an understanding of pension numbers is necessary to deal with a variety of problems and opportunities:

- Establishing or changing pension plans. An understanding of the financial implications of pension plan provisions and available alternatives is essential to making decisions that are consistent with overall corporate strategy.
- Answering questions from stockholders and financial analysts. These groups have increasingly pressed corporate management for clear explanations of pension costs and liabilities.
- Negotiating with organized labor. Pension costs are obviously a significant aspect of any labor agreement and can often have an unexpected impact on total labor costs.
- Evaluating mergers and acquisitions. The future impact of pension plans is not revealed in traditional financial reports. Special analysis is usually required when a merger prospect has a pension plan for its employees.

All of this raises several difficult questions for corporate executives, accountants, and financial analysts. What is the nature of these "pension obligations"? Should certain pension liabilities be recognized on corporate balance sheets? How can these pension obligations be meaningfully measured? Will future pension costs impose an intolerable burden on corporate cash flows? These and other questions about pension accounting are complex and require careful consideration. But one thing becomes clear—the answers to these questions require an appreciation both of pension accounting rules and of the operation of the alternative funding methods.

# GENERALLY ACCEPTED ACCOUNTING

### Historical Perspective

Accounting Principles Board Opinion No. 8, "Accounting for the Cost of Pension Plans," is the authoritative pronouncement of corporations' financial reporting of pension costs and liabilities. The Opinion was developed during a period of almost total flexibility in both the funding and accounting for pension costs. As an effort to bring some order to that situation, it represented a compromise between those who would have preferred to establish a single, uniform method of accounting for pension costs and those who favored allowing the fullest possible flexibility. The Opinion is primarily concerned with the measurement and reporting of pension costs; little attention is given to corporate liabilities for pension claims. The objective of the APB was to assure that pension costs would be recognized in a rational and systematic manner in the periods after a plan was adopted or amended, generally over the years between when employees are hired and when they retire.

Opinion No. 8 was issued in 1966, its objective and provisions in apparent harmony with the environment that then existed. Corporations typically included provisions in their pension plans specifying that they could not be compelled to make contributions to the plan or to pay beneficiaries' claims, except to the extent that assets were available in the pension fund. As a matter of law, pension plans were little more than memoranda of intention as far as any unfunded pension claims were concerned.

The corporation was free to do as it pleased. The termination of the Studebaker pension plan made this dramatically, and for many participants, painfully, clear.

### General Considerations

As a compromise solution, Opinion No. 8 contains very few dictates. It provides guidelines within which the determination of pension costs is considered to be acceptable. Within this rather permissive framework there are several pervasive considerations to be kept in mind.

**Consistency.** Although a substantial amount of latitude is permitted in selecting a set of accounting practices, a basic precept of Opinion No. 8 is that, once adopted, these methods and techniques will be applied in a consistent manner. This adds some degree of predictability to the pension numbers.

**Use of Actuarial Techniques and Expertise.** Opinion No. 8 relies heavily on actuarial methods and techniques to determine annual pension costs. The APB indicated that pension costs should generally be based on a study by an actuary, giving effect to the provisions set forth in Opinion No. 8.

**Accounting Distinguished From Funding.** Although the determination of pension costs for financial reporting is similar in many respects to the procedures used in determining periodic funding of pension plans, Opinion No. 8 is concerned solely with the financial reporting of pension costs. Most companies, however, use the same amounts for accounting and funding purposes.

### Nature and Scope of Pension Cost

Opinion No. 8 recognized a diversity of view as to the nature of pension cost. The competing views are generally divided as to whether they view pension costs as relating to benefits identifiable with the existing employee group or as identifiable with the continuing employee group as a whole. The APB expressed a preference for the former school of thought, but indicated that the preference was not held by all members. Accordingly, it acknowledged that the requirements of the Opinion were a compromise to accommodate both views. Thus, the APB did not intend the Opinion to establish a unitary system of accounting for pension costs. Rather, the Board explicitly recognized that "accounting for pension cost is in a transitional stage" and that narrowing the range of acceptable practices was the best that could be attained.

Within the limitations imposed by the lack of a definition of pension costs, Opinion No. 8 established a comprehensive set of guidelines for accounting for pension costs. They are applicable to any "arrangement whereby a company undertakes to provide its retired employees with benefits that can be determined or estimated in advance from provisions of a document or . . . the company's practice." Specifically included are written and unwritten plans, defined contribution plans, and defined benefit plans, whether they take the form of insured plans, trusteed plans, or unfunded plans.

### Basic Accounting Methods

The major premise of the Opinion maintains that the cost of pension benefits should be *accrued* on a systematic and rational basis. The minor premise maintains that such accrual is best accomplished by use of actuarial cost methods. From this base, the Opinion specifies the parameters within which the various aspects of accounting for pension costs are to be handled.

**Actuarial Methods.** Any rational and systematic method is an acceptable basis for pension cost accounting. The exception is terminal funding, which does not relate pension costs to the period of employee active service.

**Actuarial Gains and Losses.** If the routine application of the actuarial method does not accomplish a spreading or averaging of actuarial gains and losses, they are to be spread over a 10–20 year period, or averaged, or (if net gains) offset against any past service costs. Gains and losses arising from a single occurrence not directly related to operation of the pension fund and not arising in the ordinary course of the employer's business (such as a plant closing) are to be currently recognized. Figure 28.1 illustrates the alternative methods of recognizing actuarial gains and losses.

- Spreading (over 10 years on a straight-line basis)

| *Actuarial Gain/(Loss)* | | *Gains/(Losses) Spread Over Years* | | | | |
|---|---|---|---|---|---|---|
| *Year Incurred* | *Amount* | *1980* | *1981* | *1982* | *1983* | *1984* |
| 1980 | $1000 | $100 | $100 | $100 | $100 | $100 |
| 1981 | (500) | | (50) | (50) | (50) | (50) |
| 1982 | 1500 | | | 150 | 150 | 150 |
| 1983 | (2000) | | | | (200) | (200) |
| 1984 | 1000 | | | | | 100 |
| Decrease/(Increase) in annual pension expense | | $100 | $ 50 | $200 | –0– | $100 |

- Averaging (over 5 years)

| *Actuarial Gain/(Loss)* | | *Cumulative Gain/(Loss) for Five Years Ending* | | | | |
|---|---|---|---|---|---|---|
| *Year Incurred* | *Amount* | *1980* | *1981* | *1982* | *1983* | *1984* |
| 1976 | $ 500 | | | | | |
| 1977 | 1500 | | | | | |
| 1978 | 2000 | $4000 | | | | |
| 1979 | (1000) | | $3000 | | | |
| 1980 | 1000 | | | $3000 | | |
| 1981 | (500) | | | | ($1000) | |
| 1982 | 1500 | | | | | $1000 |
| 1983 | (2000) | | | | | |
| 1984 | 1000 | | | | | |
| | | ÷5 | ÷5 | ÷5 | ÷5 | ÷5 |
| Decrease/(Increase) in annual pension expense | | $ 800 | $ 600 | $ 600 | ($200) | $ 200 |

- Applying Net Actuarial Gains to Reduce Prior Service Cost

| | *Unamortized Prior Service Cost* | *Remaining Amortization Period* | *Prior Service Cost Charged to Pension Expense* |
|---|---|---|---|
| Amount before application of actuarial gain | $20,000 | 15 years | $1,333 |
| Actuarial gain | ( 1,000) | | (66) |
| Amount after recognition of actuarial gain | 19,000 | | 1,267 |

*Note:* This alternative is seldom applied in practice. Although the Opinion refers to net actuarial gains applied to reduce amortization of prior service cost, or the interest equivalent thereon, it seems reasonable that both actuarial gains and losses could be applied to reduce or increase prior service costs respectively.

FIGURE 28.1  ALTERNATIVE METHODS FOR RECOGNIZING ACTUARIAL GAINS AND LOSSES

**Unrealized Gains and Losses.** For equity securities (and debt securities not intended to be held to maturity), unrealized gains and losses are to be recognized on any rational and systematic basis (without giving undue weight to short-term market fluctuations), either by adjusting the actuarial assumptions or by treating them as actuarial gains and losses.

**Effect of Funding.** If amounts funded differ from annual pension expense, the interest equivalent on such difference should be reflected in the annual pension provision.

The basic accounting devised by the APB to carry out its compromise solution is actually quite simple. In essence, the annual pension expense is the amount determined by consistent application of any one of several acceptable actuarial cost methods; the principal constraint is that the amount of pension expense so determined must fall within defined minimum and maximum limits.

The application of these minimum and maximum limits often makes pension cost accounting appear maddeningly complex. But the definitions of the minimum and maximum are not unduly intricate. (See Figure 28.2.) The difficulty is due in large part to the fact that the definitions refer to elements of costs calculated by actuarial cost methods: normal cost, prior service cost, and past service cost. The various actuarial cost methods often calculate distinctively different amounts for each of these elements of cost. Figure 28.3 illustrates these differences for the five actuarial cost methods referred to in Opinion No. 8.

### Current Developments in Pension Cost Accounting

The FASB has issued two statements affecting future accounting and reporting for pension costs. One (SFAS No. 35) establishes accounting standards for financial statements prepared by certain pension plans themselves, and the other (SFAS No. 36) expands the disclosure requirements for corporate sponsors of pension plans. The disclosure requirements are discussed in the next section and outlined in Appendix 28–1.

Corporation retirement costs have increased rapidly in recent years. In addition to pension plans, these costs include new post-retirement benefits, such as supplementary pension benefits, continuation of group life insurance, and medical benefits. The costs of these benefits can be estimated just as actuaries estimate the cost of future pension benefits. The new disclosure standard therefore requires disclosure of these post-retirement benefits, the accounting policies employed, and the annual expense charged to income.

**Defined Benefit Plan Accounting.** The accounting methods required in SFAS No. 35 "Accounting and Reporting by Defined Benefit Pension Plans" differ from those presently followed by the vast majority of corporations in accounting for such pension costs. The most important difference is that in completing the actuarial present value of accumulated plan benefits—that is, future payments attributable to service rendered to date—no allowance is made for future increases in compensa-

*Limits of Annual Provision for Pension Costs*

| Element of Pension Cost | Minimum | Maximum |
|---|---|---|
| 1. Normal cost | Included in full | Included in full |
| 2. Prior service cost (includes past service cost arriving at adoption of pension plan and increases in prior service cost due to plan amendments) | Interest on unfunded portion | 10% of initial amounts (until fully amortized) |
| 3. Vested benefits | Provision required under certain circumstances (note) | Not applicable |
| 4. Interest equivalents on any difference between prior years' accounting provisions and amounts funded | Included (or deducted) | Included (or deducted) |
| 5. Provision for actuarial gains or losses | Included in full | Included in full |
| 6. Provision for unrealized investment appreciation or depreciation | Included in full | Included in full |
| 7. Employer contributions, if any | Subtracted | Subtracted |

*Note:* Provision for vested benefits is required in the minimum test if unfunded vested benefits at the end of the year are greater than 95% of unfunded vested benefits from the prior year. In that case, the provision for vested benefits is the lesser of (a) the amount necessary to reduce year end unfunded vested benefits to 95% of the comparable amount at the beginning of the year, or (b) amortization of unfunded prior service costs over 40 years, including interest equivalents.

FIGURE 28.2  COMPONENTS OF PENSION COSTS USED IN CALCULATING MINIMUM AND MAXIMUM PROVISIONS

tion, other than certain automatic cost-of-living adjustments. This is a divergence in calculating pension costs from the bases presently followed by most corporations. The amount of accumulated plan benefits (and the excess, if any, of plan benefits over plan assets) will tend to be smaller (under SFAS No. 35) than the amount of past or prior service cost (and any unfunded costs) that normally reflects an assumption about future salary increases.

The recognition and valuation of insurance contracts posed many problems the FASB was unwilling to resolve. It thus chose to require that insurance contracts be valued in the same way as reports filed with the Department of Labor under ERISA. Contracts may, therefore, be presented at other than their fair value; the valuing of insurance contracts will be largely left to the discretion of the insurance companies. See Chapter 27 for a fuller discussion of the accounting standards for defined benefit pension plans in SFAS No. 35.

**Disclosures.** SFAS No. 36, "Disclosure of Pension Information," effective for fiscal years beginning after December 15, 1979 includes an illustrative example of pension plan disclosure covering the items specified in Appendix 28-1. That illustration will probably become more or less boilerplate for most companies' pension footnote, as was its predecessor in Opinion No. 8. (See Appendix 28-2.) In 1980 when this chapter was written, however, no actual use of Statement No. 36 disclosures was available. In recent years, a number of companies have been including information not specifically required by either the FASB or the SEC in their financial statements. These disclosures include the kind of information filed with the Department of Labor for the vast majority of plans subject to ERISA reporting requirements, such as the actuarial cost methods, assumptions, and summary information about the financial resources and obligations of the pension plan. The disclosures made by Monsanto are frequently cited by financial analysts as the kind of information required to understand and compare various companies' pension costs and obligations. Appendix 28-3 illustrates the disclosures included by Monsanto in its 1978 financial statements.

**Future Requirements.** Statement No. 36 is merely an interim step in the FASB's plan to reevaluate the entire subject of accounting for pension costs. A task force of financial analysts, actuaries, corporate financial executives and members from public accounting firms are working with the Board and its staff on a study of all issues related to pensions and other post-retirement benefits. A final Statement is not expected before 1982.

## ACTUARIAL COST METHODS

Actuarial cost (or funding) methods are techniques used to estimate the amounts and timing of pension plan contributions. The purpose of these actuarial estimates is threefold:

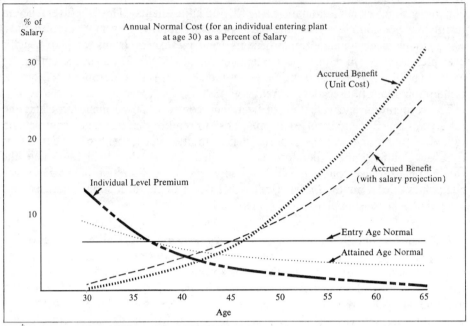

FIGURE 28.3   ACTUARIAL COST METHODS

1. To assist management in evaluating the adequacy of the pension fund (actuarial soundness) and the present and future demands upon company resources;
2. To maximize the range of contributions that will be deductible under the tax laws and, where applicable, retain the qualified status of the pension plan; and
3. To serve as the basis from which the amount of pension plan costs and liabilities is calculated for financial reporting purposes.

The diversity of objectives indicates that one method may not be applicable for all purposes. Thus, to a large degree, the actuarial cost method employed is determined by management's view of the pension plan and its objectives in financial reporting.

Pension plan financing policies, of which actuarial cost methods are an element, are categorized as:

- *Pay as you go.* Under this policy, management does no funding for pensions except to make payments to retired employees.
- *Terminal funding.* Under this policy, contributions that are actuarially estimated to be sufficient to provide the specified retirement benefits are made at the time of an employee's retirement.
- *Advance funding.* Under this policy, contributions are made during the service lives of employees according to any one of several actuarial cost methods.

The amount of pension payments made under a plan is independent of either the financing policy or the actuarial cost method followed. The total cost of a pension plan is equal to the benefits actually paid, plus administrative costs, less investment income of the pension fund, if any. However, this cost can be known with any degree of certainty only after the plan has ceased and the last pensioner is deceased. In the intervening period, an actuarial cost method attempts to alleviate the effects of this uncertainty.

The timing of contributions called for by the various actuarial cost methods has an impact on the aggregate contributions by the company over the life of the plan. Methods that require large contributions in the early years will accumulate a greater fund upon which to earn income. This investment income will reduce the aggregate contribution required of the company. Methods that provide small contributions in the early years of the plan will have an opposite result: smaller investment income in the long run and a larger aggregate company contribution.

### Difficulties in Measuring Benefits

Financial accounting and reporting for pension plans is one of the most complex and challenging subjects currently dealt with by the accounting profession. The present enigma connected with pension accounting stems, in part, from the mystique that envelops actuarial concepts and techniques. But the critical aspect of financial accounting for pension plans centers on the fact that pension plan reporting is inextricably bound up with estimates of future events and conditions.

The simple question provoking such extended debate is, "How can you best measure today the pension benefit an employee has earned but will not receive until retirement?" If a plan granted benefits as a fixed amount, say $1,000 for each year of service, the question might be answered rather easily. The $1,000 benefit for each year of service rendered to date could be discounted for the time value of money from the future retirement date to the present, and further reduced for employees with potentially forfeitable benefits—those that might cease to be employed before their benefits become nonforfeitable. This approach would probably be satisfactory to most accountants and businessmen. The questions of what interest rate should be used in the measurement process would still be unresolved, but that problem is of relatively less significance.

Unfortunately for accountants, most private pension plans do not express the retirement benefits so simply. Most plans specify that the benefit to be paid at retirement also depends upon the level of any employee's compensation, either at retirement or over some portion of his career. In such a plan, it may be difficult to obtain agreement on the proper measure of the benefits earned by a participant during any particular year. Some will argue that the earned benefits can only be measured on the basis of present salary levels; benefits resulting from future salary levels will be earned when, and if, those future levels of compensation are actually realized. Others will contend that the measure of benefits earned today must reflect the benefits that will ultimately be paid, including benefits resulting from future salary levels.

The actuarial profession has produced myriad methods and techniques that are intended to deal with this problem. Actuarial cost methods grew out of the need to determine a rational and systematic plan for setting aside money in a trust fund, money sufficient to pay future retirement benefits. These often conflicting and occasionally contradictory methods resulted from the many possible ways of setting aside money to liquidate an obligation at some future date. Each method reflects a different view as to how money should be budgeted to meet future benefit payments.

### Classifying Cost Methods

In general, actuarial cost methods fall into one of three broad classes, with almost endless variations within each class. The first class accumulates each year the amount that would be necessary, with interest, to satisfy an employee's pension rights if he were not to earn any further benefits prior to retirement. This approach measures benefits based upon present salary levels; the other two classes are based upon an estimate of what the employee's salary will be at retirement. The second class accumulates a level annual amount that, with interest, is expected to equal the employee's pension benefits at retirement. The third class accumulates an amount each year that is a constant percentage of the employee's salary, that, with interest, is expected to equal the employee's pension benefits at retirement. These are three fundamentally different ways of determining the cost of benefits earned by an employee each year. Each method has its own logic, and each satisfies various objectives for financing a pension plan.

**Accrued Benefit Cost Methods.** Under the first class of actuarial cost methods (the so-called accrued benefit cost methods), the annual pension cost for an employee will increase, often quite steeply, over the term of his employment. This is attributable to two factors. First, the costs assumed to be funded each year will have a shorter period of time than the cost of prior years in which to accumulate interest until retirement. Even if the same benefit were accrued each year, the cost to provide that benefit would increase. Second, and most important, is that as an employee's salary increases in a final-pay plan, his benefits increase for that year and all prior years of service. The cost for each year must recognize the increase in benefits for all of those earlier years not previously recognized.

**Projected Benefit Cost Methods.** Pension costs under the last two classes of methods, generally referred to as projected benefit cost methods, are either stable or more moderate in their increase. The second method will, by definition, produce a pension cost for the employee that is the same from year to year. It will be a stable cost if all of the factors affecting future pension benefits, particularly salary levels, are accurately estimated in advance. The third class of methods produces a yearly pension cost that changes in direct proportion to changes in the employee's salary —subject to the constraint that future salary levels must have been accurately estimated.

## ACTUARIAL COST FACTORS

Although a great deal of diversity exists among the various actuarial cost methods, they have at least one element in common: determination of the actuarial present value of benefits payable after retirement. The actuarial present value of benefits payable after retirement is allocated, according to the actuarial cost method in use, to determine the pension expense of a particular year. There are a number of factors to be considered in estimating the actuarial present value of pension benefits. These factors are usually referred to as *actuarial assumptions*.

The actuarial present value of a benefit payable in the future is a function of the amount of the future benefit, the probable occurrence of the events on which the benefit is conditioned, and an interest rate. In essence, an actuary calculates the present value of a defined pension benefit by: (1) adjusting the benefit for the estimated impact of subsequent events (such as terminations, changing salary levels, and marital status); (2) multiplying the adjusted benefit by a mortality factor; and (3) discounting at a stipulated rate or rates of interest. The sum of these individual calculations is the actuarial present value of the benefits of the plan as a whole. Some of the significant factors affecting the actuarial calculations are discussed below.

### Population Decrements

Measurement of the current (or present) value of a future benefit recognizes the probability that some employees will leave the plan population before they are entitled to receive the benefit. The fact that some will not remain in the plan population involves terminations (voluntary and involuntary), death, and disability. The probability that a plan participant will leave due to one of these reasons is interdependent with the other two factors. An actuarial valuation to determine contributions to a defined benefit pension plan and the amount of pension expense must consider all probable future decreases in the plan population.

### Salary Scales

When pension benefits are based on final average or highest average earnings, an actuarial valuation usually projects present salaries to retirement age. A salary scale should reflect the sources of all possible changes in compensation, including inflation and merit increases.

An actuarial valuation may employ several salary scales. For example, different scales may be used for executives whose rate of change in salary levels is likely to vary from that of other employees.

### Retirement Age

The age at which retirement occurs may affect the amount of pension benefits, the period during which contributions are made to the plan, and the number of years that the retirees will receive the pensions. It is necessary, therefore, to estimate the age or ages at which employees will retire.

One approach assumes that retirements occur at the various ages at which employees are eligible to retire. Usually, the largest portions are assumed to occur at normal retirement age. In practice, the actuary often assumes that all employees retire at normal retirement, or at some average retirement age.

### Interest Assumption

The present value of future payments is determined by the rate (or rates) of interest used in the calculation. Due to the extended period between the earning of benefits and their payment, pension plan valuations are very sensitive to the interest rate.

In an actuarial valuation of projected benefits, the estimated effect of inflation must be similarly reflected in both salary scales and interest assumptions. The two inflation adjustments do not, however, offset each other. The salary scale generally applies only to active employees, while the interest assumption affects the valuation of benefits for all participants, including retired employees. Plans that adjust post-retirement benefits by a cost-of-living index are the exception.

An actuarial valuation to determine plan funding will generally use as a discount rate the investment yield expected on plan assets during the period the benefits are deferred. A single rate may be used, or different rates may be used for different periods of time.

## MANAGEMENT'S EVALUATION OF PENSION COSTS AND LIABILITY

In recent years, senior corporate executives have paid an increasing amount of attention to the financial implications of pension plans. That attention has probably often produced increased frustration with the seemingly archaic, needlessly complex explanations of pension numbers. Many a corporate executive has been inundated with facts, figures, and reams of computer printouts in response to simple questions such as, "Why did pension costs go up 12 percent this year?" or "What are pension costs likely to be over the next five years?" The sheer volume of data and the complexity of the mathematics give the aura of exactitude without clarifying the fundamental economics of pension plans.

Management's prime concern with pension numbers, as with virtually every other aspect of business, is centered on what they portend for the future. What is the trend in pension costs? How is the relationship between pensions and other elements of compensation changing? What will the effect be of a plant closing on pension costs and liabilities? In a potential merger, are there hidden pension costs that will adversely affect future earnings? How will pension liabilities affect future pension expenses? What will the impact be of pension plan amendments? These and similar questions require answers that go beyond the mechanics of pension cost accounting and actuarial valuations. They require an integration of the mechanical aspects with the economic factors that will determine future cash flow implications.

### Impact of Pensions on Future Operations

Generally, there are four areas that have to be considered in evaluating the future impact of pensions: funding policy, future economic conditions, potential for plan amendments, and extent of asset accumulation in the plan.

**Funding Policy.** Virtually all pension numbers are, of necessity, estimates. Pension costs and liabilities can be determined with certainty only after a pension plan is terminated. To deal with this inherent uncertainty, companies adopt funding policies that enable them to estimate the amount of monies to be set aside, or budgeted, to pay employees retirement benefits when they become due. The funding policy that a company adopts is the principal determinant (with all other things equal) of both the pattern of pension costs and the pension liabilities that a company will report.

The cornerstone of a company's overall funding policy is the actuarial cost method selected. The annual pension costs developed by the actuary are, however, simply recommendations. The actual amounts funded may differ significantly—particularly in the short term—from the actuarially indicated contributions. A company may annually fund greater or lesser amounts due to factors such as the availability of cash, alternative investment opportunities, and tax considerations. This flexibility is somewhat constrained by the requirements of ERISA, but is still a consideration in pension cost comparisons and projections.

**Future Economic Conditions.** In preparing an actuarial valuation of a pension plan, the actuary must factor estimates of future economic conditions into the valuation assumption. This primarily affects the interest and salary assumptions, but may also affect the employee turnover assumptions. The actuary is primarily concerned, however, with the long-range economic outlook. More often than not, actuaries probably adopt valuation assumptions that reflect their best estimate of the average conditions expected to prevail over the forty or more years considered in a plan valuation. Occasionally, actuaries will use assumptions that vary over time to reflect their best estimate of the economic conditions that will prevail in each time period. If the assumptions are properly selected, the differences in these two approaches should have a relatively slight impact on the annual pension costs and liabilities that are actuarially determined over the duration of the pension plan.

Most economic and business analyses, however, are concerned with much shorter time frames—typically from one to five years. The economic conditions, and their impact on a particular company, may be very different in the short run from those implicit in the actuary's valuation assumptions. The effect of these differences on annual pension costs tends to be ameliorated by the fact that these effects (called *actuarial gains and losses*) are typically spread into the future over five or more years. Nonetheless, future economic conditions remain an important factor in assessing future pension costs and funding requirements.

**Future Plan Amendments.** The starting point for the determination of pension costs and liabilities is the benefits provided for employees under the plan. The typi-

cal actuarial valuation develops an estimate of pension costs and funding requirements based upon the benefits as specified by the plan documents at the time of the
valuation. There is an obvious logic to such an approach: as of the present time,
the only benefits a company is committed to provide for are those that are spelled
out in the pension plan.

Pension plans, however, are not static arrangements. They evolve over time, with
a definite tendency towards liberalizing benefits. In assessing the future impact of a
pension plan, the benefits likely to be provided in the future are therefore most relevant. Before changes in plan provisions are implemented, they are usually considered for an extended period of time. Thus, it is usually possible to get some indication of what future plan amendments are being considered. This, in conjunction
with a review of industry trends, should serve as a basis for postulating the plan
benefits likely to affect future operations.

**Extent of Pension Fund Assets.** Conceptually, the primary reason for a company
to set aside assets in a pension fund is to increase the security of plan participants.
The participants won't have to rely solely on the financial resources of the company
to fulfill pension promises at some future time. Pragmatically, the tax laws have
encouraged advanced funding by allowing an immediate tax deduction to the company, while deferring taxation of both the pension fund and employee earnings until
pensions are paid. Most recently, ERISA has added a statutory mandate for certain
minimum levels of funding.

The mandatory funding requirements of ERISA are often viewed as a constraint
on management's financing decision. That is certainly true in the long run. In the
short run, say one to five years, they still provide substantial flexibility in determining the cash demands a pension plan will make on company liquidity. Most companies have adopted funding policies that provide for greater contributions than the
minimums established by ERISA. If the need arises they are therefore able to avail
themselves of the alternative minimum funding standard incorporated in that statute.
This would permit them to reduce, and in some cases eliminate, contributions to the
pension plan for one or more years.

**Pension Cost Forecasts**

Most pension plans have an actuarial valuation every year or so to determine the
actuarial liabilities and annual pension expense. The valuation is based upon the
present group of employees covered by the plan as well as a set of actuarial assumptions reflecting the anticipated long-range experience of the plan. In developing
annual operating budgets and longer range financial forecasts, it is common for
companies to project pension expense as either a constant percentage of payroll or
as a constant amount per employee. This practice probably stems from the fact that
most actuarial cost methods are designed to provide an annual pension expense for
the current plan population; this will basically continue to be a constant dollar
amount or percent of payroll. Changes in the composition of pension plan membership, whether gradual (as in an expanding company) or sudden (as with plant clos-

ings), can have a significant impact over time on the pattern of pension costs. Because of this and the four factors mentioned earlier, it is often advisable to develop a formal pension cost forecast as part of the annual budget or long range financial forecasts. For smaller companies, it would generally be sufficient to obtain an actuarial valuation every three years, unless the company has had a substantial change in pension plan population or benefits.

In a pension cost forecast, the composition of the plan population is projected on assumptions about the number of employees who will die, terminate, become disabled, and retire in each future year; the number of new employees who will be hired; and the number of retired employees who will die each year. Employee salaries must be projected and the plan assets estimated on future contributions, benefit payments, and investment income. A pension cost forecast is basically a series of annual valuations based on projections of the plan population.

The simplest type of pension forecast is one in which the forecast assumptions and the actuarial assumptions are the same. This, however, is seldom appropriate. If the two assumptions are the same, there will be no projected actuarial gains or losses. If forecast assumptions differ from the actuarial assumptions, then gains or losses will be forecast. The financial effects of forecast actuarial and investment gains and losses are treated just as the annual actuarial valuation.

The forecast assumptions may be either *predetermined* or *probabilistic*. Predetermined assumptions about decrement rates, salary rates, and investment rates for each year of the forecast are similar to the annual actuarial assumptions. The experience rates forecast need not be the same year after year, but they are predetermined nevertheless. For example, the interest rate may be reduced from 10 percent in the first forecast year by one half percentage point over five years, down to 7½ percent. On the other hand, probabilistic forecast assumptions allow the rates to vary randomly within limits (which themselves may be changed over the forecast period). For example, the interest rate may be randomly selected from a normal distribution with an average value of 10 percent and a standard deviation of 7 percent with a lower limit of 4 percent.

A forecast may contain a mixture of deterministic and probabilistic assumptions. In forecasts, probabilistic assumptions are most commonly applied to economic factors (salary and investment rates), while deterministic assumptions are most commonly applied to factors affecting plan population (death, disability, termination, and retirement). A deterministic forecast expresses the future financial aspects of the plan as a single set of expected values while a probabilistic forecast produces an array of the plan's likely future financial aspects.

## EMPLOYEE STOCK OWNERSHIP PLANS

ESOPs, as currently structured, have been in existence for over thirty years, but prior to the mid-1970s they were a rarity in corporate benefit packages. Their current popularity was spurred primarily by two pieces of federal legislation. ERISA, in 1974, exempted them from the limits placed on all other employee benefit plans as to the percentage of assets that could be invested in employer issued securities (or property used by the employer in his business). More importantly, the Tax Reduction Act of 1975 granted employers an additional 1 percent investment tax credit if they contributed a like amount to their ESOP. Thus, the federal government is providing corporations, particularly capital intensive ones, with a virtually cost free employee benefit program.

An ESOP is a defined contribution plan, or in the words of ERISA, an individual account plan. In its simplest form, an ESOP involves periodic (usually annual) contributions by an employer. These are then used to purchase shares of the company's stock. The stock purchased is allocated to the accounts of participating employees based upon a formula contained in the plan document. That allocation is most commonly computed on base compensation. There may also be provisions for voluntary employee contributions. This form of ESOP, now quite prevalent among large publicly held corporations, presents no unique accounting problems and is adequately dealt with by the defined contribution provisions of APB No. 8.

Many companies have begun to employ ESOPs to provide both employee benefits and low cost capital financing for the corporation. In such an arrangement, a number of accounting issues that are not dealt with in authoritative literature may be raised. The Accounting Standards Executive Committee of the American Institute of Certified Public Accountants has issued Statement of Position 76–3, "Accounting Practices For Certain Employee Stock Ownership Plans" that provides guidance in this area. Although provisions of SOP 76–3 are not binding, in practice they do seem to be followed generally. The issues raised and the guidance offered by the SOP can be seen from the operation of an ESOP used as a financing mechanism for the corporation. In a typical example of such an arrangement the following would occur:

1. A company forms a tax qualified ESOP.
2. The ESOP borrows money from a financial institution; the company commits itself to make future contributions to the ESOP sufficient in amount to meet the debt service requirements. The commitment is usually accompanied by a formal guarantee of the loan.
3. The ESOP uses the loan proceeds to buy common stock of the company from present stockholders and/or from the company.
4. The debt is collateralized by the company's stock or other assets to be held by the ESOP.

### Accounting for the Debt

When the ESOP's debt is either guaranteed by the employer or the employer is committed to make future contributions to the ESOP sufficient to cover the debt service requirements, the debt should be recorded as a liability. It should be recorded as a liability by the employer since, in substance, the debt is the employer's debt; the employer has every intention (and is legally obligated) to make the contributions required for repayment of the loan.

SOP 76-3 calls for recording a liability regardless of the purpose used for funds received from the ESOP for the sale of shares of employer stock. The SOP also states that the related interest rate and other relevant terms of the debt should be disclosed in the financial statements.

As to how the offsetting debit to the liability should be handled, the SOP requires that it be charged to shareholders' equity. The rationale holds that no real expansion of equity capital has occurred. Only when the related debt is liquidated can those shares acquired by the ESOP be considered outstanding.

### Measuring Compensation Expense

The SOP recommends that the measure of compensation expense should be the amount the employer contributed or committed to an ESOP in a given year. This treatment is consistent with accounting practice for discretionary contributions to profit sharing plans and other defined contribution pension plans.

The portion of the contribution that in substance represents funding of the interest due on the debt is to be reported as interest expense in the income statement. That portion of contributions representing principal liquidation would be identified and charged to compensation expense.

### Earnings Per Share and Dividends

The potential impact on earnings per share after an ESOP has acquired the employer's stock is a significant concern of management. This issue could not be resolved in the SOP; both majority and minority viewpoints are presented.

The majority view stated that all shares held by an ESOP (whether acquired from the employer or from existing shareholders) should be treated as outstanding shares in the determination of earnings per share. The minority viewpoint stated that shares acquired by an ESOP from the employer should be treated as outstanding only to the extent that they become constructively unencumbered by repayments of debt principal. Consistent with this position, the minority believed that dividends on such shares should be charged to retained earnings only to the extent the shares are constructively unencumbered. Any balance of dividends remaining would be reported as additional compensation expense.

### Investment Tax Credit

The Tax Reduction Act of 1975 allows the taxpayer to elect an 11 percent investment credit (in lieu of the normal 10 percent), provided the taxpayer contributes to an ESOP an amount equivalent in value to the extra 1 percent. The Tax Reform Act of 1976 permits an additional investment credit of up to one half of 1 percent (total to 11½ percent) if the employer and employee each contribute an additional 1 percent to the ESOP. The employer thus has the option of paying an amount to the ESOP that otherwise would have to be paid to the Federal government as income tax. Accordingly, the additional 1½ percent investment tax credit is to be reflected as a reduction of income tax expense in the period that the related contribution is charged to compensation expense, regardless of the employer's normal method of accounting for investment tax credits.

## TAX QUALIFICATION OF PENSION PLANS

The tax advantages provided for qualified pension and profit-sharing plans include the facts that:

- Employer contributions are generally deductible as a business expense.
- Investment income of the plan normally is not taxed until paid out as benefits.
- Employees are not taxed until benefits are distributed or made available to them.
- A lump-sum distribution on termination of employment or after the employee attains age 59½ receives favorable tax treatment.

To obtain these tax benefits, the plan must meet the requirements of the Internal Revenue Code as well as the regulations and rulings issued by the Commissioner of Internal Revenue.

### Coverage Requirements

A qualified plan must be for the exclusive benefit of employees or their beneficiaries. Officers and stockholders may participate in the plan if they are bona fide employees. A plan cannot be structured so that it discriminates in favor of officers, stockholders, or highly compensated employees.

The tax law requires that a plan, if it is to qualify, must meet either of the two following requirements:

1. It must cover 70 percent or more of all employees or, if the plan requires employee contributions and if 70 percent or more of all employees are eligible to participate in the plan, at least 80 percent of those eligible must elect to participate.
2. It will benefit employees that qualify under a classification set up by the employer and accepted by the Internal Revenue Service as not discriminatory in favor of officers, stockholders, or highly compensated employees.

It is permissible to exclude any employees who are covered by a collective bargaining agreement if retirement benefits were the subject of good faith bargaining.

In actual practice, the second of these two requirements is the one most frequently used. Under this provision, it is possible to establish a plan solely for hourly or salaried employees or for those employees who work in certain designated classifications, as long as it does not discriminate in favor of the prohibited group of employees.

## Contribution and Benefit Requirements

Contributions or benefits cannot discriminate in favor of officers, stockholders, or highly compensated employees. A plan will not be considered discriminatory merely because it excludes individuals who earn less than maximum taxable wage for social security purposes. The law does not prohibit the use of a benefit formula which provides a larger percentage of benefit for earnings in excess of the social security taxable wage base than it does for earnings under this amount. However, if the benefit formula is in any way integrated with social security benefits, certain requirements are imposed to prevent discrimination in favor of the prohibited group of employees.

## Other Requirements

- *Must be in writing.* A qualified plan must be in writing and must set forth all the provisions necessary for qualification. This is normally accomplished through a trust agreement, a plan instrument, or both.

- *Communication to employees.* The plan must be communicated to employees. An announcement letter or booklet is frequently used for this purpose.

- *Nondiversion of contributions.* The trust must specifically provide that it is impossible for the employer to divert or recapture contributions before the satisfaction of all plan liabilities.

- *Definitely determinable benefits.* A qualified pension plan must provide definitely determinable benefits. A defined contribution pension plan meets this requirement, since the employer's contribution formula is definite and, for this reason, benefits are considered as being actuarially determinable. Because of this benefit requirement, any amounts forfeited by terminating employees may not be used to increase benefits for the remaining pension plan participants—instead, these forfeitures must be used to reduce future employer contributions. The definitely determinable benefit requirement does not apply to qualified profit-sharing plans.

- *Permanency.* The plan must be a permanent one. While the employer may reserve the right to amend or terminate the plan at any time, the plan is expected to be established on a permanent basis.

- *Inclusion of death benefits.* Death benefits may be included in a qualified plan, but only to the extent that these benefits are "incidental."

- *Vesting.* A plan will not qualify unless it provides for full vesting when an employee attains normal retirement age (or a stated age or some other event in the case of a profit sharing plan), and unless it provides for fully vested rights in all participants upon termination of the plan or permanent discontinuance of plan contributions. The plan must incorporate all of the vesting requirements imposed by ERISA.

- *U.S. trust.* If a trust is used, it must be organized or created in the United States and maintained at all times as a domestic trust.

- *ERISA requirements.* The Code was amended by ERISA to require that qualified plans include a number of different provisions. (See Chapter 27 for a summary of ERISA requirements.)

## SUGGESTED READING

Allen, Everett, Jr., Melone, Joseph J., and Rosenbloom, Jerry S., *Pension Planning.* Homewood, Illinois: Richard D. Irwin, Inc., 1976.

Financial Accounting Standards Board, *Statement of Financial Accounting Standards No. 36.* Connecticut: Financial Accounting Standards Board, 1980.

Financial Accounting Standards Board, *Statement of Financial Accounting Standards No. 35.* Connecticut: Financial Accounting Standards Board, 1980.

Financial Executives Research Foundation, *Financial Aspects of Private Pension Plans.* New York: Financial Executives Research Foundation, 1975.

Hall, William D., and Landsittel, David L., *A New Look at Accounting For Pension Costs.* Pennsylvania: Pension Research Council, Wharton School, University of Pennsylvania, 1977.

McGill, Dan M., *Fundamentals of Private Pensions.* Pennsylvania: Pension Research Council, Wharton School, University of Pennsylvania, 1979.

Pomeranz, Felix, Ramsey, Gordon P., and Steinberg, Richard M., *Pensions: An Accounting and Management Guide.* New York: The Ronald Press Company, 1976.

Reichler, Richard, *Employee Stock Ownership Plans: Problems & Potentials.* New York: The Law Journal Press, 1977.

Sloat, Frederick P., and Burgett, David V., *Fundamental Concepts Underlying Pension Plan Financing and Costs.* New York: Lybrand, Ross Bros. & Montgomery, 1970.

U.S., Congress. House, *Employee Retirement Income Security Act of 1974.* Conf. Rept. 93–1280, 93rd Cong., 2nd sess., 1974.

Winklevoss, Howard E., *Pension Mathematics: With Numerical Illustrations.* Pennsylvania: Pension Research Council, Wharton School, University of Pennsylvania, 1977.

## APPENDIX 28–1 EMPLOYER DISCLOSURES CONCERNING PENSION PLANS

SFAS No. 36—Paragraphs 7 and 8

- A statement that such plans exist, identifying or describing the employee groups covered.
- A statement of the company's accounting and funding policies.
- The provision for pension cost for the period.
- Nature and effect of significant matters affecting comparability for all periods presented, such as changes in accounting methods (actuarial cost method, amortization of past and prior service cost, treatment of actuarial gains and losses, etc.), changes in circumstances (actuarial assumptions, etc.), or adoption or amendment of a plan.
- For defined benefit pension plans, the following data determined in accordance with FASB Statement 35 as of the most recent benefit information date for which the data are available:
  - The actuarial present value of vested accumulated plan benefits,
  - The actuarial present value of nonvested accumulated plan benefits,

- The plans' net assets available for benefits,
- The assumed rates of return used in determining the actuarial present values of vested and nonvested accumulated plan benefits,
- The date of which the benefit information was determined.

The data may be reported in total for all plans, separately for each plan, or in such groupings as are considered most useful. For plans for which the above data determined in accordance with FASB No. 35 are not available, the excess, if any, of the actuarially computed value of vested benefits over the total of the pension fund and any balance sheet pension accruals, less any pension prepayments or deferred charges, is to be disclosed instead. The reasons for the information required by the items above not being provided for those plans is required to be disclosed.

## APPENDIX 28–2   EXAMPLE OF PENSION PLAN DISCLOSURE

The company and its subsidiaries have several pension plans covering substantially all of their employees, including certain employees in foreign countries. The total pension expense for 19X1 and 19X2 was $XXX and $XXX respectively, which includes, as to certain defined benefit plans, amortization of past service cost over XX years. The company makes annual contributions to the plans, equal to the amounts accrued for pension expense. A change during 19X2 in the actuarial cost method used in computing pension cost had the effect of reducing net income for the year by approximately $XXX. A comparison of accumulated plan benefits and plan net assets for the company's domestic defined benefit plans is presented below:

|  | *January 1,* | |
|  | *19X1* | *19X2* |
| --- | --- | --- |
| Actuarial present value of accumulated plan benefits: | | |
| Vested | $XXX | $XXX |
| Nonvested | XXX | XXX |
|  | $XXX | $XXX |
| Net assets available for benefits | $XXX | $XXX |

The weighted average assumed rate of return used in determining the actuarial present value of accumulated plan benefits was X percent for both 19X1 and 19X2. The company's foreign pension plans are not required to report to certain governmental agencies pursuant to ERISA and do not otherwise determine the actuarial value of accumulated benefits or net assets available for benefits as calculated and disclosed above. For those plans, the actuarially computed value of vested benefits, as of December 31, 19X1 and December 31, 19X2 exceeded the total of those plan's pension funds and balance sheet accruals, less pension prepayments and deferred charges, by approximately $XXX and $XXX respectively.

## APPENDIX 28–3    FINANCIAL STATEMENT DISCLOSURE

FINANCIAL REVIEW

(Dollars in millions, except per share)

Pension Plans

Most Company employees are covered by pension plans. This section of the Financial Review sets forth information aimed at assisting in the analysis and understanding of Monsanto's pension expense and pension funding position for 1978 and for 1977.

|  | *1978* | *1977* |
|---|---|---|
| Pension Expense: |  |  |
| Amount ........................................................................ | $ 84.2 | $ 74.6 |
| Per primary share ...................................................... | $ 1.21 | $ 1.06 |
| Percent of wages, salaries and employee benefits ...... | 6.4% | 6.5% |
| Pension Plans' Funding Status Data*: |  |  |
| Present value of accrued benefits ............................ | $739.3 | $688.3 |
| Plans' assets (at market value) ............................... | 711.5 | 621.4 |
| Unfunded present value of accrued benefits ........ | $ 27.8 | $ 66.9 |

\* For the Company's two largest plans in the U.S. only. These two plans accounted for 77.2 percent and 84.7 percent of total 1978 and 1977 pension expense, respectively.

Annual valuations of the Pension Plans are made by an outside firm of actuaries. The "entry age normal" actuarial method is used. The key actuarial assumptions used include an annual average investment return on pension assets of seven percent, an average salary increase (when applicable) of six percent and an average retirement age of 61 years.

The actuarial method and the assumptions used were consistent for 1977 and 1978. They are reviewed regularly by both the Company's outside actuaries and by the Pension and Savings Funds Committee of the Board of Directors. The Company believes that the methods and assumptions used, in the aggregate, are reasonable for the purpose of determining the annual pension funding requirements.

The above table of "Pension Plans' Funding Status Data" covers the two largest domestic Plans and reflects the present value of accrued benefits. "Accrued benefits," which include vested and non-vested pension benefits that have been accrued on the basis of employee service and earnings to date, is a different measure of pension funding than either unfunded prior service costs ($384.1 million as of December 31, 1978), which are required to be disclosed in the Company's Form 10-K by the Securities and Exchange Commission, or the excess of vested benefits over the market value of the Plans' assets ($5.4 million as of December 31, 1978), which is required to be disclosed in the Notes to Financial Statements by existing accounting principles.

In the actuarial valuation process, an actuary calculates the present value of prospective benefits which identifies the amount of funds needed to provide benefits in future years to all employees then covered by a pension plan. There are various actuarial methods to budget the present value of prospective benefits that are to be financed. Some methods do not develop unfunded prior service costs (sometimes referred to as "unfunded actuarial liability"). The actuarial method—"entry age normal"—tends to develop relatively large unfunded prior service costs and is used by the Company because it levels out pension costs as a percent of future payroll.

Unfunded prior service costs can vary significantly as a result of the budgeting method used and can include benefits that have not yet been earned by employees. For this reason, the Company believes that the comparison of the market value of the Plans' assets to (i) the present value of vested benefits (as disclosed in the Notes to Financial Statements) and (ii) the "unfunded present value of accrued benefits" (as reflected in the table above) are more meaningful measures of the Pension Plans' funding status than the identification of unfunded prior service costs. The Company considers "accrued benefits" to be a more comprehensive portrayal of funding status than "vested benefits."

Pension expense in 1978 increased as compared with 1977 due principally to the effect of increased wages and salaries and the effect of improved benefits in the United Kingdom.

# 29

# Employee Health and Welfare Programs

*Hugo J. Standing*

*Martin G. Strieter*

# INTRODUCTION

The costs of employee benefits have skyrocketed in recent years because of new legal requirements, growing sociological pressures for expanded benefit programs, and health care costs that have escalated greater than the overall inflation rate. Today, between 25 and 35 percent of a company's payroll is allocated to employee benefits. As a result, employee benefit costs are now major budget items. Controllers of all companies—large, medium-sized, or small—must play a definite role in developing benefit plans and in analyzing and controlling their costs.

This chapter outlines an approach to employee benefits that gives controllers increased understanding and insight into this important and increasingly costly area.

### Typical Problems of Small and Medium-Sized Companies

Insurance carriers base their premium rates on expected losses and administrative costs. The larger the company, and the more employees on its payroll, the more predictable and accurate are the statistics that carriers use to calculate these rates.

Generally, a company with more than 100 but less than 1,000 employees falls into the medium-sized range. Insurance carriers can allow greater flexibility in dealing with companies that fall toward the top of this range, because they find it easier to predict losses based on statistics gathered over the years and to set rates and judge administrative costs on the basis of these loss predictions.

This means that a firm with fewer than 100 employees is at a distinct disadvantage in the insurance marketplace. Insurance carriers generally will not give smaller firms flexibility and freedom of choice in selecting employee benefit programs.

Because they can't predict losses accurately for companies with few employees, insurance companies group small firms together in order to pool the measurements, and then offer them packages that cover the basic benefit areas. In short, smaller companies with fewer than 100 employees can still offer employee benefits, but they are limited to what is available in pooled employee benefit programs. Management's decisions in this area are thereby greatly reduced.

### The Regulatory Environment

Controllers should regard government regulations as external factors that are beyond management's control but that directly influence the kind, size, and cost of benefit programs for company employees. Government regulations are so complex that very large companies maintain staffs of attorneys, accountants, and consultants to work full time on compliance with these regulations. Smaller companies must also deal with this "paperwork jungle," but often find that it is less expensive to retain outside consultants to do the work than to hire and maintain an internal staff.

Four laws enacted by Congress have had considerable administrative and financial impact on benefit programs:

- Employees Retirement Income Security Act (ERISA);
- Health Maintenance Organization Act (HMOA);
- Age Discrimination in Employment Act (ADEA); and
- Equal Employment Opportunities Act (EEOA).

These laws severely restrict the options open to management, significantly increase exposure to severe penalties, add to the administrative costs of operating employee benefit programs, and directly affect the design of the overall employee benefit program.

**ERISA.** The Employee Retirement Income Security Act of 1974 is unquestionably the most sweeping revision of rules applying to employee benefits ever enacted. Although ERISA primarily affects IRS-qualified retirement plans, it also specifies reporting requirements for other types of employee benefit plans, such as health and welfare plans. (See Chapter 27 for detailed discussion of ERISA provisions and requirements.)

**HMOA.** Under the provisions of the Health Maintenance Organization Act, if a company has 25 or more workers in a given location that is serviced by a health maintenance organization, the HMO may attempt to solicit the employees of that company and remove them from the company-sponsored health plan. The company must allow this challenge if it occurs 180 days prior to the renewal date of the plan or when there is a major change in the plan.

Although one might suspect that this kind of "raiding" might hurt the company's own health plan costs, evidence for the most part suggests the contrary. In many cases the HMO is in a better position to contain health care costs, because it has salaried professionals on its staff. The employer is not required to contribute more for employees enrolled in an HMO plan even though the monthly rates for the HMO plan may be higher than the company sponsored plan.

The major problem faced by companies who have employees enrolled in HMOs is that of administrative costs and paperwork: there may be some effect on payroll deductions, there is a dual reporting responsibility, and the company must forward the money separately to the HMO. The problem is compounded for a multilocation employer who has a centralized headquarters operation. Individual plants with 25 or more employees may be open to different HMO challenges.

**ADEA.** Under the Age Discrimination in Employment Act, a company must include older, higher-risk employees in its benefit program. Before this law was passed, companies could, at their option, terminate or reduce coverages for employees at age 65 or even earlier. The regulation does allow some actuarial adjustments to compensate for the increased cost to the company attendant to the higher age risk.

The ADEA raises some interesting points that have not as yet been answered. For example, suppose an employee several years away from retirement has an accident or becomes ill and is placed on long-term disability. Before ADEA was enacted, when that employee reached normal retirement age, he was generally taken off disability and placed on retirement. At this writing, few experts know how best to coordinate long-term disability benefits with retirement benefits. Some employers have reduced the long-term disability benefits at normal retirement age by integrating disability benefits with the retirement benefits for the disabled employee. This has added to administrative costs and affects the overall benefit program.

**EEOA.** The Equal Employment Opportunities Act is more subtle than the ADEA or the HMOA, and forbids discrimination on the basis of race, religion, or sex. Although discrimination on the basis of race and religion can be dealt with forthrightly, sexual discrimination has unusual implications for employers, particularly in the area of health coverage.

Under the EEOA, employers must now pay extended pregnancy benefits for female employees. Prior to EEOA, health and disability plans usually provided some coverage for pregnancy, but benefits were limited in both time and scope.

Unfortunately for employers, the granting of pregnancy benefits for women does not satisfy compliance requirements under the complex law. In order to avoid *reverse discrimination* there are other as yet unclear requirements for further liberalizing health and disability benefits for all employees. These have led to current uncertainty as to the minimum coverages required for compliance, and significant increases in claims cost are likely to occur.

## PLANNING A BENEFIT PROGRAM

Most company benefit programs have not been systematically planned but have evolved as a result of changing government requirements, corporate acceptance of social responsibility, and the competition in the marketplace. Too often, changes in employee benefit programs have been made on a piecemeal basis, without the conceptual and administrative advantages of a comprehensive approach to protecting employees from major hazards or planning for their major life events. As a result, many companies have duplications and/or gaps in coverage, and spend considerable sums on benefit programs that do not serve the best interest of either the company or its workers.

Early benefit planning concentrated on individual plans or benefits. In planning an overall employee benefit program, the controller should consider benefit coverage that constitutes replacement of a portion of an employee's income in the event of four major events or hazards: *premature death, disability, medical expense,* and *retirement.*

As stated earlier in this chapter, smaller companies have limited choices and must accept group plans offered by insurance carriers. However, firms with more than 100 employees can design benefit programs that meet specific employee needs. Insurance carriers and outside consultants, using statistics compiled over the years, can measure the costs of varying amounts of protection coverage.

### Establishing or Reappraising Corporate Objectives

As a first step in planning or reappraising an employee benefit program, company management should determine its objectives in designing a benefit program for its personnel. Periodic reappraisal of objectives often results in subtle changes in benefit design or funding that can profoundly affect the structure of the program. For example, during the reappraisal process the discussion might center on what steps must be taken to comply with a new set of government regulations and what cost implications compliance will have for the company. Furthermore, a periodic reappraisal enables a company to reevaluate what services, assistance, and guidance it wants and expects from its outside consultant.

**Factors That Affect Objectives.** Each company's objectives are unique and are affected by its corporate personality, its product line, its geographic area, the division of white-collar and blue-collar labor within the company, competitive pressures, and the degree of employee unionization. Most of these factors are self-explanatory.

If a company is in a highly competitive market in which the drive to find and keep key employees is critical to the success of a business, that company should attempt to design a benefit program that will attract and retain key personnel. If there is a monopolistic situation, however, the company might not be motivated to offer as strong a benefit program. However, that would totally depend on the degree of unionization—another factor that companies must contend with.

*Corporate personality* deserves some explanation, because many industry executives consider it one of the most important factors. Corporate personality is, of course, the image a firm has established for itself and that it wishes to maintain. If a firm has a reputation for being bold and aggressive, the company would likely be a pioneer or trail blazer in the area of employee benefits and would design its employee benefit program to match this personality, including innovative benefit program elements not likely to be found in other companies. At the other end of the spectrum, a company might be considered solid but conservative. Such a company would tend to have a good benefit program, but it would not necessarily be innovative. Almost without exception, the corporate personality will have a decided effect on the amount of money a company wishes to spend on its benefit program.

**The Management Team.** Management usually appoints a team of executives to plan or reevaluate the benefit program. In smaller companies the team usually consists of the president, the controller, and the personnel manager. In larger firms the team may be composed of a senior vice president from the financial department, the controller, and a labor relations manager and/or the personnel manager. If an outside consultant has been retained by the company to help guide the firm in planning or restructuring the benefit program, he should also participate in the discussions.

Once the management team has an appreciation of the factors that will influence the choice of corporate objectives, it should begin to draw up a list of those objectives.

**Basic Guidelines for Determining Objectives.** The answers to some basic questions provide the guidelines in defining corporate objectives.

*What are the primary reasons for establishing an employee benefit program?* Management must determine from the outset its chief purposes in designing an employee benefit program. If it plans to use the benefit program as a tool for the recruitment of executive, professional, and other key personnel, then the company must make the program attractive to potential employees on the management level. This is particularly true when the company is in a highly competitive market. If it plans to use the program to retain key personnel and promote good morale, then again it must design the program to meet this objective. Here competitive pressures will be a factor, along with unionization and financial considerations.

*How much money is the company willing to spend on an employee benefit program?* Management must determine how much money it wants to spend to establish or improve an employee benefit program. If it wants a program that is adequate but not innovative, the financial and administrative costs will be relatively moderate. If it wants a highly innovative and progressive program, the costs will reflect this decision. Competition, unionization, and corporate personality will have a decided impact in this area.

*At what level does the company want to replace income?* The management team must determine the level of replacement income it wants to provide employees. Obviously, the replacement level will have an impact on cost, with higher levels of replacement income costing the company more in premium payments. Again, as with the other objectives, management's decision will be based primarily on other key factors—in this case, competitive pressures and degree of unionization. The decision should also take into account employee contributions toward coverage. This is an important element because it affects administrative costs and tax benefits. Some companies do permit employees to contribute to a benefit program or to expand coverage in certain areas. (See the discussion on life insurance later in this chapter.)

Management teams are likely to find that discussions in this area can be subjective and heated. For example, a discussion of life insurance coverage (replacement income for premature death) will center on the obligations of the employer: how many years of replacement income should the employer furnish the survivors? The more coverage provided, the more it will cost the company. Another area that the team will likely debate with vigor involves long-term disability coverage. An employee who is out of work because of an accident or illness has to have some replacement of income. But how much is adequate? And who should pay the costs? Too much coverage may tempt the employee to malinger. Too little replacement income may create severe financial hardships. (Both of these examples will be discussed later in the chapter in the sections dealing with premature death and disability.)

*What are the financial considerations involved in an employee benefit program?* Here the discussion generally focuses on how the program is to be funded, the direction in which claim dollars should flow, tax benefits, employee contributions, and the effect the program will have on profits and growth.

The management team may want to fund the employee benefit program on an *as needed basis,* with cash disbursements being distributed to the insurance carrier to cover claims as they occur. If such a one-time increase in cash flow is not a particular economic advantage, the company would then select an alternate method of funding the benefit program. (The various methods of funding benefit programs will be discussed later in this chapter.)

The direction in which claim dollars will eventually flow depends on the type of company and the composition of the work force. (This area of discussion does not always apply to smaller companies, who have few choices in the kinds of benefit coverage.) If the company's demographics lean toward older workers, the claim flow may be greater in the direction of retirement benefits. If the company employs a younger work force, management would likely lean towards a plan in which more claim dollars flow toward other life events, such as premature death or sickness.

During the discussions on objectives an area of significant concern is whether the company is gaining the maximum tax advantage from the current or planned program. Certain benefit elements, as discussed later under long-term disability coverage, do contain tax advantages for a company and its employees.

In deliberations over company profits and growth, the management team should consider the effect changes in benefit coverage will have on the work force. Key factors in this area of discussion are anticipated future growth, competitive pressures, and expansion of product line.

*How is the company going to administer an employee benefit program?* The range of objectives under the general heading of administration is vast. However, in discussing objectives, management must concentrate on two critical points.

First, should the company hire the necessary personnel to administer the program internally or should it hire an outside consultant or group of consultants to administer the program? One of the important factors in this area of discussion is cost. (A more detailed discussion on outside consultants is presented later in this chapter.) The requirements for internal administration of an employee benefit program vary a great deal depending on the size and location(s) of the company and its plants, the collective bargaining units, and the divisions of the work force. Administration requirements for a single-location employer with 200 workers, for example, will be vastly different from those of an employer with 1,500 workers in six different plant locations.

Second, should the company administer the program from a central location or have individual plant units handle the program? Mobility of the work force, transfers, and union requirements are likely to be included in this area of discussion.

### Management's View of Employee Objectives

When analyzing the objectives of the benefit program, the prudent management team should also take into account the overall composition of the work force. It often helps to try to view the program from an employee's viewpoint.

Benefit coverage varies widely depending on what type of workers are employed. The needs of highly schooled professional employees are totally different from the needs of a work force that is primarily part of an assembly line. White collar (professional) employees are very much concerned with their standard of living, long-term financial security, and career advancement. A company's blue-collar work force is also interested in these factors, but does not emphasize long-term considerations in these areas to the same degree.

The age level of the work force is also significant. In every company, employees will be in different career and/or life stages. The older workers will be chiefly concerned about retirement, whereas younger workers will be more interested in financial security (protecting income) and advancement.

A discussion along these lines will lead the management team into another area of employee concern—unionization and collective bargaining.

### Collective Bargaining and Its Impact on the Benefit Program

**Union Versus Nonunion Employees.** When there are both union and nonunion employees in the same company, there should definitely be a distinction in the structuring of the benefit programs offered to each. Each group perceives its needs differently. If the plans are structured differently the union will be less likely to use the nonunion benefit program as a minimum demand.

Union employees and union management typically look for more *first-dollar* pay benefits. In medical coverage, for example, a union worker would want his policy to pay for a $25 laboratory fee or a $35 chest X ray. The nonunion professional would prefer to pay relatively small medical bills himself and have coverage for catastrophic illness. In other words, the professional employee tends to view benefit coverage as *base-pay protection*. The union worker looks at benefit coverage as a *base-pay supplement*.

**Collective Bargaining Methods.** Methods vary depending on the relationship of the bargaining unit with the company. Management may encounter two types of situations, each with different cost implications.

In the first situation, management and the union bargain the *degree* of the benefit coverage, and the company agrees to purchase and administer the benefit program as the policyholder. This type of collective bargaining gives the company slightly more flexibility (selecting the insurance carrier, claims control, the types of coverage), but it binds the company to pay for the program's escalating costs. When the cost of the coverage rises in an inflationary climate, the company can't go back to the bargaining unit to renegotiate, and it can't lower the benefit coverage. However, if a company has a knowledgeable consultant or an insurance company with resources to project the inflation factor, it should be possible to estimate the parameters of the longer-range costs of the benefits being negotiated.

In the other collective bargaining situation, usually in multiple-employer circumstances, the two groups bargain for a *cents-per-hour contribution.* Union/management trustees then determine what benefits those funds will buy, with the trust acting as the policyholder. The advantage from a management standpoint is that an individual company has limited liability. The trustees are responsible for ensuring that there is enough money in the fund and that it is administered properly. This type of collective bargaining is more prevalent in trades or in situations in which employees frequently work for different employers. The trust office can track the number of hours worked toward eligibility for coverage, which would be impossible for employers to administer separately.

In this latter case, bargaining usually takes place between a union and an association or group of companies in a particular industry. The negotiated agreement is then binding on all companies in that particular industry.

### The Competition

Earlier it was suggested that corporate personality and the degree of competition would be key factors in determining company policy in terms of employee benefit coverage. However, knowledge of competitors' practices can be helpful only if this data is readily available. The controller has several ways to determine this information.

First, he can write to the Department of Labor and request information on a competitor's benefit package. However, while anyone is entitled to receive this material, it may not be current.

Controllers may procure more-up-to-date information through a referral service offered by a trade publication, such as *Employee Benefit Plan Review*, published by Charles D. Spencer and Associates, Inc., Chicago, Illinois.

A third way to find out about a competitor's benefit program is through an industry association or trade group. Also, company executives who attend trade association meetings are usually eager to exchange this kind of information bilaterally.

Another method would be to engage an outside benefit-planning consultant or brokerage firm that has a large enough data base to provide meaningful geographic or industry comparisons.

### Plan Flexibility

The term *plan flexibility* applies to company attitudes toward employee contributions to benefit coverage. Companies should permit employees to contribute to their own plans whenever possible. Participation encourages employee interest in the benefit program and makes the employee more conscious of what the company is providing in the way of insured benefits. In addition, employee contributions make the benefits more substantial in the areas of each employee's particular needs. As indicated later in this chapter, there are special tax consequences on certain types of coverage (such as disability coverage and additional group term life insurance) that act to the employees' advantage if they contribute to the plans.

Companies can also promote flexibility by letting employees choose the types of coverage in which they will participate. The term usually applied to this approach is *cafeteria plan,* whereby employees are allowed to select the areas of coverage they desire.

For example, suppose an employer provides the first $1,000 of cost per employee for benefits. Under a cafeteria plan, employees would be free to select the areas of coverage they want up to the $1,000 limit, and would pay the excess if the cost of their selected coverage exceeds this amount.

There are two serious problems associated with this approach to flexibility. First, it is not appropriate to benefit programs where employees may "select against" plans that cover an event or hazard. If employees were allowed free choice in the selection of life insurance coverage, for example, employees with impaired lives would tend to select the highest amounts available, whereas the healthier workers would select lesser amounts of life insurance. This is referred to as *selecting against the plan* and contradicts all logical rules of insurance underwriting.

Second, and more important to the company than selection against the plan, is the problem of *employer liability.* Controllers should be aware that the company can be held liable by the employee or the employee's dependents in the event of an accident or death. For example, if an event occurs for which the employee did not select insurance, he or his dependents can bring legal action, through an attorney, claiming that the employer did not "explain it properly." In the present legal climate, many employers are reluctant to take the risks involved with this kind of plan.

## INSURED BENEFIT PROGRAMS TO GUARD AGAINST SPECIFIC LIFE EVENTS

Earlier it was suggested that the best method of approaching employee benefit programs was to provide basic coverage for each of an employee's major life events or hazards. To review briefly, the four basic life hazards or situations in which an employee would require income replacement or cost coverage are:

- Premature death,
- Disability,
- Medical expenses, and
- Retirement.

## Premature Death Benefits

Heartless as it may sound, the death of an employee has a monetary impact, especially on those who depend on that particular person for support. An employee's death may also represent a monetary loss to the employer. The measurement may be the extent to which that employee contributes to the success of the business, his reputation, and his business contacts. Although this chapter is concerned only with benefits to the employee, the value to the employer is one that companies should consider for their own indemnification.

**Group Term Life Insurance.** There are various levels of replacement income that a company may provide for its employees, depending on its corporate objectives. At one extreme, a company may feel that it is not obligated to the employee much beyond providing the survivors with burial expense and a relatively small lump-sum payment for "clean-up" expenses. Or, the company could go far beyond that approach by providing some form of income continuance to the employee's survivors. This can be accomplished by providing the employee with an amount of group term life insurance based on a multiple of annual salary or by permitting employees an option to purchase (through payroll deductions) amounts of group term life insurance in addition to what the company is already providing. In either event, the final objective is the same: to help survivors bridge the gap without suffering an immediate major loss in their standard of living.

*Burial and final expense benefits (company-paid).* This is a flat amount of group term life insurance paid for by the employer for each employee in the event of premature death. The funds from this benefit are used for burial and other "clean-up" expenses the employee may have. This benefit can vary in amount from one company to another or can vary from one position to another within a single company. If the company is unionized, a typical flat amount of employer-paid life insurance might range from $5,000 to $10,000 for a factory or assembly-line worker. The amount paid on the death of professionals and executives might be based on a multiple of their annual salary, ranging from one half to twice that amount.

*Income protection for survivors (company- and employee-paid benefit plans).* Replacing an employee's income for the purpose of providing income protection for the survivors is the second method of approaching premature death benefits. Here the group term life insurance provides a flat amount that is related directly to a multiple of one or more times the employee's annual salary. This amount in itself is usually more substantial than the amount of money offered under the first approach.

For the employee-paid options, nonunion employees would typically be allowed to select a benefit of one year's salary, while top-ranking executives of a company may be permitted to opt for additional group term life insurance in multiples of three or more times their annual salary. Middle-level management benefits would fall somewhere in between. This practice is not discriminatory under existing laws if the differential relates to classes pertaining to employment, such as position classifications or salary groups.

From an insurance carrier's point of view, such employee-paid (contributory) plans are acceptable provided enough employees purchase additional amounts of group term life coverage. Insurance companies insist on adequate numbers to prevent selection against the plan. Typically, the insurance company would require that 75 percent of the employees in the eligible classes enroll for the optional coverages before accepting the risk.

*Survivor's Income Benefit.* Before covering other aspects of premature death benefits, it should be pointed out that there is one other type of coverage in this same general area. It is called *survivor's income benefit.* In a typical case, the survivor's income benefit provides for a lump-sum payment related to the employee's annual salary. The employer purchases group term life insurance covering, say one half or all the employee's annual salary, while the employee contributes a set percentage of his or her payroll each pay period. On the death of the employee, the survivor or survivors would receive a continuing percentage of the employee's salary on a monthly basis for a set number of years. For example, the benefit may provide 25 percent of the employee's salary for life or until the spouse is remarried, but for not less than 10 years. Dependent children, too, may be factored into the plan.

**Tax Considerations.** Company contributions toward group term life insurance are tax deductible expenses. But what tax advantages do employees enjoy in this area?

Regardless of who purchases group term life insurance, there are no income tax consequences to the employee if the face amount of the employee's benefit does not exceed $50,000. On group term life insurance in excess of $50,000, some income is taxable, but the tax consequences are still favorable to the employee.

Under Section 79 of the IRS Code, amounts of group term life insurance in excess of $50,000 are imputed as taxable income according to the following table:

| Age | Rate per Month |
|-----|-----|
| Under 30 | $ .08 |
| 30-34 | .10 |
| 35-39 | .14 |
| 40-44 | .23 |
| 45-49 | .40 |
| 50-54 | .68 |
| 55-59 | 1.10 |
| 60 and over | 1.63 |

To calculate the amount of imputed taxable income, find the age of the employee and the corresponding applicable tax rate. The rate is then multiplied by every

$1,000 of insurance in excess of $50,000. From this figure the employee's contribution toward his total group term life insurance is deducted.

For example, suppose an employee, age 27, has a total of $100,000 in group term life insurance. The plan requires that the employee contribute a rate of $.30 each month per each $1,000 of insurance in excess of $50,000. The calculation would be:

| | |
|---|---:|
| Face amount of insurance | $100,000 |
| Less first $50,000 | − 50,000 |
| | $ 50,000 |
| | |
| $.08 × 50 × 12 months = | $ 48 |
| $.30 × 50 = $15 × 12 months = | − 180 |
| Taxable Income | 0 |

There is no tax consequence to the employee, because the imputed income is negative.

Now suppose an employee, age 57, has a total of $200,000 in group term life insurance. The plan requires that he contribute $.30 per month per thousand on *all* his coverage. The calculation would be:

| | |
|---|---:|
| Face amount of insurance | $200,000 |
| Less first $50,000 | − 50,000 |
| | $150,000 |
| | |
| $1.10 × 150 × 12 months = | $ 1,980 |
| $.30 × 200 = $60 × 12 months = | − 720 |
| Taxable Income | $ 1,260 |

As can be seen from the two examples, there is a substantial tax break for employees on amounts of group term life insurance in excess of $50,000. And although an older employee must pay some tax on amounts of group term life insurance in excess of $50,000, he still gets a significant fringe benefit. If an employee had to purchase additional life insurance outside the group plan, it would be at considerably higher rates, representing greater after-tax dollars.

From a purely administrative standpoint, companies that cover employees for amounts of group term life insurance in excess of $50,000 need to report on the employee's W-2 any additional income resulting from the Section 79 formula.

**Accidental Death.** Most group life insurance plans are supplemented by accidental death and dismemberment plans, which cover employees on or off the job. The majority of these plans provide coverage in a matching amount to the group life insurance. Thus, if an employee is accidentally killed while on or off the job, such a policy would typically pay an additional sum equal to the face amount of the group term life insurance.

As an alternative, this coverage can be provided on an employee-pay-all basis under a voluntary accidental death and dismemberment plan, with the employee having the right to select the amount of coverage desired. Under the voluntary plan, dependents can also be covered with little additional cost.

Most companies also have employer-paid travel accident insurance for those employees who travel frequently on company business. Again, a great deal of variety can be built into the design of these plans. For example, 24-hour business coverage covers the accidental death of an employee on a business trip after the business at hand has been conducted. Other plans cover employees only while they are traveling on a common carrier—a bus, train, plane, boat, or taxi. These plans can be expanded to cover all forms of conveyance, such as travel by private automobile while on business.

Because travel is such an important part of today's business, controllers should be aware that rates for such insurance coverage are based on the degree of exposure for the entire company. Therefore, it costs little more to cover all employees than to cover just those who travel frequently, since the risk is based on the degree of company travel.

**Self-Insurance for Death Benefits.** Although certain death benefit elements in an overall program can be funded by self-insurance, controllers of small and medium-sized companies will generally find that it is not economically feasible. A company should have a large number of employees before considering whether to self-fund against death benefits. Just one accidental death could present substantial financial losses. Furthermore, there is some question as to whether or not the IRS would consider claim payments under self-insured life insurance to be life insurance for preferred treatment under current interpretations of the IRS Code. Clarification on this point is supposedly forthcoming.

### Disability Protection

Disability insurance provides a predetermined level of replacement income in the event that disability prevents a worker from earning a paycheck. Disability coverage falls into two categories: short-term and long-term.

**Short-Term Disability.** Short-term disability coverage is not as common in states that require state disability insurance (SDI). There are compulsory disability laws in California, New York, New Jersey, Rhode Island, Hawaii, and Puerto Rico.

Under California law, for example, disabled employees can receive about 60 percent of their weekly salary, up to a maximum of $154 per week[1] (60 percent of a weekly salary of $257). The benefits from California SDI are retroactive to the first day of disability if the disability lasts over seven weeks. The maximum duration of

---

[1] This figure was effective on January 1, 1980.

benefits as of January 1, 1980, is 39 weeks, and maternity is handled as any other illness. Employees contribute 1 percent of their first $11,400 of annual salary to SDI through payroll deductions. (The other states have different rates and payments.)

In states that require compulsory disability insurance, some employers will reimburse higher-paid employees for the difference between what the state provides under SDI and what the employee normally earns. However, this income is taxable income at both the state and federal levels.

In states that do not have compulsory disability insurance laws, companies may provide either a flat lump sum per week to disabled employees or pay a fixed percentage of an employee's weekly income. This is commonly called *salary continuance*.

Some companies self-insure this type of coverage, whereas others pay premiums to insure a specific amount. To the extent that the coverage is paid by the employer, benefits are treated as ordinary income for tax purposes (both state and federal), although the IRS may provide some exclusion of the income for lower-paid employees under certain conditions (see discussion below).

If a company permits its employees to purchase either short-term or long-term disability coverage, when and if benefits become payable, an employee will not have to pay either state or federal income tax on those funds while disabled. To the extent that the company pays for the coverage, the income that the disabled worker receives that is equal to the portion of the premium that is employer-paid is taxable at both the state and federal level.

In any case, short-term disability benefits act as a bridge to cover the insurance gap until long-term disability coverage takes effect.

**Long-Term Disability.** Long-term disability coverage typically begins after the first six months of an employee's disability and can last until the employee reaches the age of seventy or retires. Most long-term disability plans also include rehabilitation clauses, which serve as incentives for employees to return to work.

*Tax considerations.* As with short-term disability coverage, tax considerations play an important role. The tax laws are decidedly in the employee's favor if he or she pays the disability insurance premium, because there is no state or federal income tax on the income replacement. However, the insurance premium on long-term (as on short-term) disability is not tax deductible for the employee.

Most long-term disability plans are designed to cover between 50 and 60 percent of the employee's normal salary when the disability benefits are integrated with other income benefits, up to a fixed maximum. In today's inflationary climate, the benefit may not be adequate if it is taxable income. From the point of view of the employee's maximum benefit, therefore, it is definitely advantageous to have the employees rather than the company pay for disability insurance.

Unfortunately, the trend is in the opposite direction. While employees gain a temporary advantage by a reduction in their weekly payroll deductions if the employer pays the premium, they are hurt financially by taxation on both the state and federal level when these benefits become payable.

The Tax Reform Law of 1976 allows an exclusion of up to $5,200 per year in payments to eligible disabled employees. In order for an employee to be eligible for this exclusion, the disability must be permanent and total and be presumed to last for at least 12 months. The exclusion is reduced dollar for dollar for adjusted gross income (from any source) in excess of $15,000. Thus, if a disabled employee has a total adjusted gross income of $20,200, he is not eligible for any exclusion. Higher-paid employees or those with other taxable income can easily fall into this category.

*Split-level arrangements.* Employers and employees can share the payment of long-term disability premiums. This is best accomplished on a split-level basis to accommodate the lower-paid workers, most if not all of whose benefits are made up of government programs such as workmen's compensation, state disability insurance (if compulsory), and social security disability income. It should be remembered that all employees covered by long-term disability plans are not necessarily eligible for social security disability benefits.

If the employee qualifies for social security or other government disability benefit income, the long-term disability plan pays only the amount above what these programs pay. In other words, the portion of the long-term coverage that addresses itself to the lower levels covered by social security and other government programs is heavily discounted in the rate-making formula.

It is obvious that the amount of money paid in long-term disability premiums in this lower layer (to which government programs are addressed) would be a great deal less than that charged for coverage above these levels. There is therefore ample justification for employees who are at this lower level to pay a lesser amount on that portion of the long-term disability benefit that is offset by these other programs. What is most important is that this split-level arrangement provides for a more equitable sharing of costs for all employees, regardless of pay level.

**Short-Term Sick Pay.** In addition to both short- and long-term disability coverage, most companies also have plans for short-term sick pay or salary continuation for short-term illness. These plans provide full pay for employees who are unable to work because of minor illnesses, such as colds, a variety of viral infections, and minor surgery not requiring hospitalization. The short-term sick pay plan is also used in cases of severe illnesses to cover the time that elapses before other disability plans go into effect.

Most companies have a set number of days or weeks allowed for these kinds of contingencies. Usually the number of days or weeks under a short-term sick pay plan is determined by the employee's years of service to the company.

Controllers should note that short-term sick pay plans can be abused by employees. To discourage abuse, many companies provide a monetary bonus at the end of the year to employees who have not used their entire sick-day entitlement. As with all benefit plans, company policy on short-term sick pay plans should be communicated to employees, so that they are aware of the benefits and limitations.

### Health Benefits

There has been a great evolution in health care benefits for employees in recent years. There are two common methods of providing funds to cover medical expenses incurred by an employee: the *reimbursement plan* and the *prepaid plan.*

**Reimbursement Plan.** The reimbursement plan can be underwritten by insurance companies or can be self-insured. In either case, the medical cost reimbursement goes directly to the employee, who then pays the health care provider (unless the employee assigns the benefit to the provider, in which case the reimbursement would be made directly to the provider). The employee is not restricted as to choice of physician or hospital. Reimbursement plans generally fall into two broad categories.

*Basic medical plan plus major medical.* The first is commonly referred to as *basic medical.* Under this plan, employees are reimbursed fixed amounts for specific charges, such as hospital room or specific kinds of surgery.

To guard against catastrophic medical burdens, a second plan, *major medical* coverage, is provided to supplement the basic plan. It generally pays up to 80 percent of the larger costs, after a deductible charge. In effect, major medical coverage is an umbrella over the basic plan.

In theory, the two plans are intended to be coordinated, but in actual practice they are separate plans. Employees often have difficulty calculating what they must actually pay, because some costs can be fully covered, others only partially covered, and still others not covered at all.

*Straight comprehensive major medical.* In an effort to eliminate the confusion and make it easier to communicate the benefits and limitations to employees, many companies now prefer the other category: a straight comprehensive major medical plan. The employer has greater flexibility in adapting this type of health coverage with respect to the application of deductibles and percentages of reimbursement. For example, the coverage may or may not pay 100 percent of the cost of a hospital room during confinement following certain surgical procedures.

Because of the many different medical procedures and illnesses, the variations under this type of plan are almost limitless. Typically, however, the comprehensive major medical plan pays up to 80 percent of all eligible costs incurred after a deductible charge (although the deductible may not apply to certain types of charges). The deductible charge can vary too, but the employee is usually required to pay the first $50-$150.

**Prepaid Plan.** Under the prepaid plan, the health care provider determines how much will be needed from each covered individual subscriber (employee) to keep the plan in operation. In prepaid plans, the health care provider receives the fees for health care service on a monthly per capita basis, whether or not medical treatment is rendered to the individual. These fees are really capitation fees rather than insurance premiums. Additionally the employee must report to specific doctors or health care facilities.

Health maintenance organizations (HMOs) fall into this category, with Kaiser and Ross-Loos being two of the better known names in the field. Blue Cross and Blue Shield, although not true prepaid plans in the aforementioned sense, are often included in this category and are particularly popular in the Midwest and East, where they work in combination. Membership in Blue Cross is designed to provide greater control over hospital costs, in Blue Shield to give greater control over surgical costs. Blue Cross is essentially hospital-sponsored, while Blue Shield is doctor-sponsored, and both groups have agreements with their individual segments of the medical profession.

**Specialized Health Care Plans.** There are some other trends developing in health care coverage of which the controller should be aware.

Closely associated with medical plans are *dental programs* for employees. Dental plans have experienced tremendous growth in recent years, mainly as a result of employee and union demand. A dental plan can be included with the medical plan, but generally is designed as a separate benefit program because of the different nature of the coverage. Companies are usually required to pay the biggest share of dental coverage premiums, and the programs they offer may differ. One program may be similar to the basic medical program, that is, it may offer set amounts for specific dental treatment. Another plan may be set up on a "reasonable and customary" basis with a deductible, whereby an employee would pay an initial amount, say the first $25 or $50, and the plan would pay a specific percentage of the remaining amount. Plans that encourage regular dental checkups by paying 100 percent of the checkup fee may in the long run reduce major dental expenses.

In recent years union bargaining groups have successfully negotiated *prescription drug benefits* that cover most if not all of the cost of buying pharmaceutical products. Another benefit secured by many unions is *vision care.*

**Tax Considerations for Health Benefits.** Companies must consider tax consequences for employees in the area of health benefits, particularly for the higher-paid company executive.

The IRS Code allows individuals a deduction for out-of-pocket medical expenses in excess of the first 3 percent of gross adjusted income. In addition, a deduction is allowed for 50 percent of an employee's contribution to health insurance premiums up to a maximum deduction of $150. For example, if an employee's gross adjusted income is $20,000, he may deduct for tax purposes only his out-of-pocket medical expenses in excess of $600 (in addition to the 50 percent contribution noted above).

For higher-paid executives, this tax bite can be a heavy burden. In order to provide relief, some companies now have executive medical supplement plans. In effect, this coverage wraps around the formal company medical plan and picks up deductibles and other out-of-pocket medical expenses not covered in the formal plan. For example, if an executive has a gross adjusted income of $50,000, under the IRS Code he cannot deduct out-of-pocket medical expenses except to the extent that they exceed $1,500. Under his executive medical supplement plan, the higher-paid executive can have some of the first-dollar medical expenses picked up, thus reducing his out-of-pocket medical expenses.

Controllers should note that under Section 105 of the Internal Revenue Code there are new rules that apply to executive medical supplement plans. If, for example, the plan is self-insured, those extra medical expenses picked up by the company are then regarded as additional income to the executive and are taxable unless all employees are covered under a nondiscriminatory plan. Currently, benefits received under an insured executive medical supplement plan are not taxable.

**Use of Outside Consultants.** Since there are so many plans and programs in the health care marketplace, an employer should discuss the company's particular needs with an experienced outside consultant/broker. A consultant/broker should first help the company define the employer's needs and then work with the company in developing a program to meet the company's requirements, both in respect to coverage and costs.

This is particularly valuable when the company goes to the insurance marketplace to purchase coverage in the health care area. The consultant/broker should be able to help formulate the company's employee benefit objectives and then draft the specifications in precise terms. It is important to make sure that individual insurance companies are submitting bids on essentially the same plan. Insurance companies have their own programs to sell, and the controller may not have the necessary experience and expertise to determine if the company is getting exactly what it is requesting.

### Retirement

Replacing income for older workers in the event of their retirement is a major feature of all employee benefit plans and can take many forms. Pension plans are covered in detail in Chapters 27 and 28. It should be noted, however, that retirement or pension plans are a major employee benefit and should be integrated properly with the other employee benefits described in this chapter.

## EMPLOYEE BENEFIT ADMINISTRATION

### Staffing and Assigning Responsibilities

A discussion of benefit program administration must focus on who is going to be responsible for managing the work. The corporate controller, along with the rest of the management team, must decide the extent to which the company will utilize internal staff or hire outside experts. Staffing was discussed earlier in some detail in the section dealing with corporate objectives.

Small and medium-sized companies may find it more economical to hire outside consultants/brokers to oversee the complex administrative details associated with a benefit program. Of course, the determining factor in the decision is the complexity of each company's benefit program and the reporting requirements.

However, some administrative tasks must be handled internally, usually by the personnel department. In most companies it retains responsibility for reporting all new personnel, terminations, and salary increases.

### Selecting an Outside Consultant/Broker

Insurance of all kinds, including employee benefit coverage, is becoming more complex. Many companies that traditionally awarded their insurance business on the basis of the lowest bid are now more likely to base their decision on how well the prospective consultant/broker can guide the company's overall insurance strategy, especially the benefit program.

Briefly, here are some of the factors a company should consider when selecting an outside consultant:

- *Company growth.* Has the company outgrown its current consulting service? Has the present service provided specialists to assist the company in its growth and expansion plans?
- *Research and development capabilities.* Can the present consulting service, or those being considered, handle special problems that arise in the shifting sociological and legislative environment?
- *New geographic areas.* In the light of planned new plant locations, is the current consultant/broker service adequate?

The employee benefit management team should request conceptual proposals from a selected number of outside consultants/brokers. These proposals provide management with the opportunity to evaluate the capabilities of the consultant/broker as well as the individual(s) who will be assigned to manage and guide the employee benefit program.

This approach to selecting an outside consultant/broker offers a company two major advantages: it avoids the potentially damaging competitive bidding process that can erode the insurance market if quotations for the same coverage are requested indiscriminately from several brokers; and it gives the company an opportunity to consider the creative suggestions of several outside consultants/brokers. At the same time, the company's management team can hold the selected consultant/broker accountable for the development of the program as well as its ongoing operation.

### Employee Communications

When a company commits itself to a heavy investment in an employee benefit program, it must establish an effective communications program to ensure that its employees fully appreciate and understand what is being provided. Otherwise the company is not getting the expected return on its investment.

There are two basic kinds of employee communications:

- *Required communications.* Under the regulations and rules of ERISA, companies must fully inform employees of their rights and benefits under the benefit program. (See Chapter 27 for detailed information on communications required by ERISA.)
- *Voluntary communications.* Management should provide employees with information that goes beyond the "bare-bones" summary plan descriptions of employee benefits; vehicles for providing this information include employee handbooks and orientations, internal house organs, and audio/visual presentations.

**Summary Plan Description.** This written document communicates in easily understood language all of the benefits offered to employees. Although it should be simple and direct, it can often be made into an effective communications tool.

**Employee Benefit Handbook.** Like the summary plan description, a handbook should be written in language that is easily understood. However, it is usually more elaborate and often contains photographs and line drawings to help illustrate points. Publications of this nature are usually written in sections, with each section detailing the benefits and coverage by hazard or life event category. The handbook may also contain information about other employee benefits and company programs and services, such as vacation policy and educational benefits (described later in this chapter).

**Internal House Organ.** Companies often use a vehicle such as a company newsletter, newspaper, or monthly magazine to explain new elements in a benefits program. They also use this publication to describe case histories, actual events that have taken place in the company. A case history can explain how an anonymous employee was saved from financial disaster because of the employee benefits program provided by the company.

**Audio-Visual Presentations.** A-V presentations are being widely used throughout corporate America, even by small companies. These presentations can be used to introduce new employee benefit programs and are very useful in new-employee orientation sessions.

Some large consulting firms that operate their own communications departments have personnel who design A-V programs. Costs for a typical A-V presentation range between $750 and $1,000 per minute for a slide or film strip show with an audio sound track. Motion pictures cost about $2,000–$4,000 per minute, depending on factors such as the cost of actors and script preparation. While these costs may seem rather high, controllers of multilocation companies should note that duplicate copies of audio-visual material can be produced at very low cost. By making duplicate copies of a single A-V presentation, management is assured of a uniform presentation throughout the company.

**Employee Audit and Survey.** An audit determines how employees perceive the quality of their benefits. When these perceptions have been analyzed by a communications specialist, programs can be changed to either reinforce the current attitudes or to shift employee opinions in a new direction.

Surveys can be made of the entire work force or of a random sample. The larger the firm, the more practical the use of the random sample technique. The survey can be in written form, using questionnaires, or can be conducted orally, using groups or one-on-one situations.

### Budgeting and Cost Controls

As pointed out throughout this discussion of employee benefits, small companies with few employees are at a distinct disadvantage. Nowhere is this more true than with costs.

Because it is so difficult to predict losses for companies with few employees, small companies have to settle for simple, packaged programs. The cost to a small company is the *actual rate charged by the insurance company* for that benefit coverage, that is, the premium cost.

But for a medium-sized or large company, losses are more predictable; the *true cost* of employee benefit coverage is thus determined by the *level of claims* plus *all administrative expenses*. If the premium paid by a company exceeds the rate of claims and the administration expenses, the arrangement with the carrier should require the refund of the excess amount.

When the loss and administration costs exceed the premium, the insurance company usually will raise its premium rates for the following year in order to recoup its losses. In the case of a very small company, where wide fluctuations are expected to occur from year to year and the pooling concept is applied, the insurance carrier should not increase the rates because of a one-year loss unless the loss is experienced on its entire category of small accounts.

Since costs in all but the smallest firms depend on accurate projections of claims and administration costs, management should make sure that its benefit plan consultants are capable of making these judgments.

### Processing Claims

Claims processing (administration and analysis) has a significant effect on plan costs. The job of processing claims should be left to experts, and the prudent company will consider retaining a consultant to monitor, analyze, and oversee the claims operation of the insurance carrier.

One of the first rules in claims processing is that companies should never place total, unaudited confidence in a third-party claims administrator (usually the insurer). Either the company or its consultant should audit the claims administrator on a regular basis. They should also analyze and evaluate the claims to see whether the benefits are flowing in the intended direction and whether refinements should be made in the employee benefits program.

For example, suppose a consultant/broker, in examining the periodic claims reports, discovers that a medium-sized company has excessive claims in the area of hospital confinement. On analysis, he determines that the medical plan is more generous for services requiring hospital confinement than for out-patient services. As a result, employees are being confined to a hospital for diagnosis and treatment rather than being treated as out-patients by a family doctor or by a doctor at a hospital or clinic. Although the present plan costs the company more in claims when the employees are confined to a hospital rather than being treated as out-patients, the employees prefer to be confined in a hospital for a day or so, because the company's medical coverage picks up most if not all of the costs. If the employees were to be treated as out-patients, their out-of-pocket medical costs would be much greater. Therefore the employee copayment requirements in the company's medical program should be adjusted to encourage employees to choose out-patient over in-patient services.

Using a consultant in the claims area gives the company an objective view of the situation, which it might not get by dealing directly with the insurance company. But more importantly, this kind of monitoring enables the company to spot troublesome areas in the benefit program or the methods of claims payment that could lead to unnecessarily increased costs. If a company wants the most effective expenditure of its employee benefit costs, monitoring of claims becomes an essential part of the administration of the overall benefit program.

### Changing Insurance Carriers and Terminating Plans

Insurance carriers should only be changed after a careful study by a professional consultant. The danger of precipitous action is that different provisions and interpretations in carriers' policies may expose employees and management to unnecessary risk. For example, under some life insurance programs, premiums are waived for totally disabled workers. If the company terminates coverage under one carrier without checking the future carrier's policy on these premiums, those employees could be left without coverage, and the company would be exposed to liability.

Another common problem involves employees who may have executed an *absolute assignment* of their ownership in group term life insurance benefits to avoid the proceeds being tied to and taxed as part of their individual estate in the event of death. Such agreements are permitted under the IRS Code, but the agreement could be nullified under "contemplation of death" rules should the company change carriers.

Before a change takes place, a consultant should closely inspect the benefits and provisions of both carriers to make sure there are no coverage gaps. It is wrong to rely on a verbal agreement with the new carrier. Promises that "everything will work out," are often broken, with costly consequences to the company and its employees. Competent consultants are alert to these possibilities, and should be retained, particularly by smaller companies.

**Valid Reasons For Change.** Other than special merger-acquisition situations, there is only one valid justification for changing carriers—*unresponsiveness to the needs of the company and its workers*. If a carrier does not respond to inquiries from the consultant or won't cooperate in important claims, rerate analyses, and audits, that carrier should then be terminated.

Many companies think that it is worthwhile to drop an insurance carrier because the carrier has increased its insurance rates or premiums. For medium-sized and large companies especially, this reason may not be valid, because the true costs of insurance are the incidence of claims and the administrative expenses. If there are excessive claims charges, management should investigate the root causes and take steps to correct them.

**Audit-Bids.** However, from time to time, a company may request its consultant to undertake an *audit-bid*, to see if the current insurance carrier is still competitive with the rest of the industry with respect to its administrative charges and reserve provisions. If the current carrier is within competitive margins, and if a good working relationship exists, the company would find that changing carriers would in the long run be more expensive.

## SPECIAL EMPLOYEE PROGRAMS AND SERVICES

In addition to the insured employee benefit program that guards against major hazards and life events, many companies provide special programs and services to their workers. Some of the more common programs and services include:

- Educational-assistance plans and scholarships;
- Company-subsidized cafeterias;
- Purchase discounts;
- Social and recreational programs;
- Clothing allowances;
- Transportation allowances; and
- Time off with pay.

Most of these special programs and services are set up through the personnel department. Larger companies may have managers for special employee programs and services.

### Educational Programs for Employees

Educational programs for employees typically fall into two categories: a tuition-assistance program, whereby a company pays either partially or totally for costs of continuing education; and a scholarship program, whereby a fixed amount of money is made available to an employee.

Most companies have one major guideline with regard to tuition assistance and scholarships: the courses and degree programs must be related directly to the employee's job or the company's business. However, with the costs of higher education becoming a major financial burden, some companies have extended their educational assistance programs to cover dependents of employees. This then becomes a major employee benefit.

Obviously, companies that decide to establish educational-assistance programs for employees should clearly define the guidelines and communicate them effectively to employees. Educational assistance to employees is presently not taxable to them, but payments for dependents would be income under IRS rules.

### Company-Subsidized Cafeterias and Food Services

For any company, the establishment of a subsidized cafeteria is a major expense. Controllers should note that there is some question as to whether employees view such subsidized operations as a tangible benefit, since they must still pay to eat.

However, if a company believes that food should be available on the premises, an alternative that controllers of small and medium-sized companies should consider is contacting one or more of the numerous food-service firms throughout the U.S. who specialize in setting up cafeterias for companies and institutions and choosing one that provides the best service at the best price. Although the employer may not be providing a subsidized meal, the service firm can very likely provide food at costs substantially lower than employees would normally pay in restaurants.

Free coffee and soft drinks are also regarded by employees as important benefits.

### Purchase Discounts

Department and discount stores are eager to obtain business from employees working at major companies. In an effort to attract business from employees, some stores will provide special discounts. Often such stores will make discount arrangements through the union or with the company's personnel office.

### Social and Recreational Programs

Many companies sponsor specialized recreational and social clubs for employees. It is common to find a company-sponsored ski club or bowling team. Some firms even provide rooms for club meetings during non-working hours. Companies may also provide equipment for clubs and teams—including uniforms.

In addition to company-sponsored clubs and teams, some larger firms provide on-site recreational facilities, such as a swimming pool or gymnasium. Small and medium-sized firms, on the other hand, are often approached by private recreational organizations, who, through the company, offer memberships at discount rates to employees.

Major recreational organizations, such as Six Flags Corporation and Walt Disney, openly solicit companies in various parts of the country to provide special discount coupons and passes to employees who wish to visit these attractions.

### Clothing Allowances

Most companies either furnish uniforms or provide a clothing allowance to employees whose jobs require special clothing and protective equipment. Employees who serve in security-related jobs commonly are afforded this benefit, as are workers who must have protective clothing and equipment for assembly-line work.

### Transportation Allowances

A new trend—transportation benefits for employees—has developed in recent years as a result of the national energy shortage. Some companies are now providing special monetary benefits to those employees who car and/or van pool. Additionally, some companies have made special arrangements with municipally-owned bus companies to subsidize the cost of employee bus passes. While these plans are regarded as employee benefits, controllers should note that substantial public relations benefit can also be derived from such plans. Companies that openly promote these benefits are doing their part to cut down on automobile use—thus saving much-needed fuel.

In addition to subsidized travel, employees are often given subsidized or totally free parking. In major metropolitan areas, parking is a major after-tax expense.

The controller should consult with tax counsel regarding the tax status of any planned employee services or allowances before the company decides to adopt them.

### Time Off With Pay

Many companies reimburse employees who must serve on jury duty. Although fees paid to jurors vary from state to state, the compensation is usually very low. Companies usually pay the employees their full wage or reimburse them for the difference.

Another common benefit allows an employee a half-day off in order to vote in specified elections. Usually this applies only to major general elections, either at the state or federal level.

Some companies also offer one or two "floating holidays" in addition to a set number of nationally recognized holidays and a specified number of vacation days.

Payment for time that is not spent at work also includes pay for meeting other social and civic responsibilities (e.g., funeral leave and military reserve allowance), rest-period pay, and severance pay in the event of termination of employment.

### SUGGESTED READING

Employee Benefit Plan Review Research Reports. Weekly. Chicago: Charles D. Spencer & Associates.

International Foundation of Employee Benefit Plans. *Life, Health and Other Group Benefit Programs.* CEBS Course 5, Vols. 1 & 2. 4th printing. Brookfield, Wis.: 1979.

McCaffery, Robert M. *Managing the Employee Benefits Program.* New York: American Management Association, 1972.

Spencer, Bruce. *Group Benefits in a Changing Society.* Chicago: Charles D. Spencer & Associates, 1978.

# Part VII

## Corporate Development

# 30

# Mergers and Acquisitions— Financial and Planning Considerations

*Robert F. Reilly*

## ACQUISITION OBJECTIVES

Many companies mistakenly believe that the primary objective of an acquisition is to increase the size of the acquiring company (usually in terms of sales dollars). This is not the case. The primary objective of a merger or acquisition is to satisfy a need. For a merger or acquisition to make sense and be successful, both firms involved should have a need (e.g., some corporate weakness, liability, or deficiency) that the other firm can satisfy (e.g., with some corporate strength, asset, or capability). For instance, a cash-heavy consumer product goods firm may have a need: a dynamic new product to bolster the sales of its mature product lines. Another consumer product goods firm may have a different need: capital inflow to fund the line of growth-oriented products that it has developed. These two firms would be well advised to consider the benefits of the merger or acquisition strategy. Although both firms would achieve sales increases, these increases would be the *benefits* derived from satisfying business needs and would not be, in themselves, the acquisition *objective*.

Within this basic acquisition objective, there are many specific objectives—all of which have to do with unsatisfied needs. Appendix 30-1 groups a representative list of objectives into five categories: marketing, human resources, financial, legal, and operational.

## DEVELOPMENT OF A LONG-RANGE STRATEGIC PLAN

Before a firm decides to pursue an acquisition strategy, it must undergo a serious process of self-analysis and self-evaluation. Management must ask itself the following questions:

- What business or businesses are we in? (The answer to this question should be specific and detailed.)
- What corporate strengths and weaknesses do we bring to each business we are in?
- What objectives should be established for the firm's growth (usually in terms of sales, profitability, market share, etc.) within a reasonably predictable and manageable time frame (usually five years)?
- How can the firm's strengths be exploited and weaknesses be eliminated to achieve these objectives?

This last step, in essence, calls for the development of a long-range strategic plan for achieving corporate growth objectives. It should identify how the firm's current resources (its strengths) will be utilized, what resources the firm needs (to compensate for its weaknesses), and how these resources will be acquired.

### Minimum Data Required

After the firm's growth objectives have been specifically articulated, a great deal of information is needed to construct the strategic plan. In the *AMA Management Handbook*, David Rowe suggests that the following data are required, at a minimum, for developing a practical strategic plan: external factors, internal factors, resource analysis, and historical trends.[1]

**External Factors.** Before management can undertake effective strategic planning, it must understand the current state of the business environment and be able to forecast changes in this environment. It must take into account such external factors as:

- *The economy*—trends in the relevant local, national, and international economies, and their effect on the markets the firm serves and the material, labor, and financial resources consumed;
- *Market position*—trends in the market, including new product introductions, old product discontinuances, new competitors in the industry, and changes of relative market share of firms in the industry;
- *Technology*—changes in the technology of the products produced and in the methods of production; and
- *Government policies*—forecasts of the government's fiscal and monetary policies as they relate to the corporate income tax structure, the availability of debt capital, and the interest rate charged for those funds. Likewise, consideration should be given to the costs and other ramifications of compliance with various government agencies and regulations, such as OSHA, ERISA, Federal Trade Commission rulings, and the Justice Department Antitrust Division's activities.

**Internal Factors.** Each operating unit should be encouraged to submit its individual objectives to executive management, along with a preliminary strategic plan for accomplishing those objectives. Management should then evaluate each unit's objectives against: (1) the overall growth objectives of the firm, and (2) the resources (e.g., labor, suppliers, technology, funds) available to the firm. As many of the highly ranked unit objectives as possible should be integrated into the firm's overall strategic plan. A few examples of preliminary unit objectives follow:

- The *research and development* unit expects to develop twenty new products during the next five years. Management must evaluate this objective in terms of the funds it can allocate to R&D and to the other strategic activities of the firm.
- The *marketing* unit may plan to increase the market share of certain products to 35 percent during the next five years. Management should evaluate this objective in terms of: (a) the manpower that can be allocated to the marketing group, (b) the advisability of committing the required manpower and other resources to these certain products, and (c) the possible cannibalistic effect on other company products.
- The *manufacturing* unit may want to introduce a new, more efficient product process. Management should consider this objective in light of: (a) the financial resources available for such a project, and (b) how the product or products produced by the proposed new process fit into the firm's long-term strategic plan.

---

[1] David Rowe, "Long Term Planning," *AMA Management Handbook*, ed. Russell F. Moore (New York: American Management Association, 1970), pp. 153-154.

**Resource Analysis.** All internal resources should be evaluated and reviewed for any trends or expected changes. These internal resources include, but are not limited to, the following:

- *Products*—the current product line and the ramifications of changes in product structure, price, mix, quality, or distribution;
- *Financial structure*—the availability of funds for capital asset addition, new product development, and so on, the firm's debt-to-equity ratio and the various components of the firm's capital structure, and the dividend payout policy;
- *Human resources*—any changes in the quantity, mix, or required skills of the professional, technical, support, or hourly personnel; and
- *Organization*—any expected revision in the organizational form (i.e., proprietorship, partnership, corporation) or structure (e.g., centralized versus decentralized).

**Historical Trends.** Historical trend analysis is useful in determining the financial and quantitative forecasts that will be included in the plan and in judging whether the firm's objectives are reasonable. Historical trends may be grouped as follows:

- *Financial trends*, which include financial ratio analysis of significant balance sheet and income statement accounts. For example, if the firm's average days receivables outstanding has never fallen below forty-five days, management should question the reasonableness of the objective of achieving thirty days receivables outstanding.
- *Marketing trends*, which include annual percentage sales increases by product, market share by product, and so on. If a certain mature product has never achieved greater than a 20 percent market share, management should challenge the reasonableness of a 35 percent market share objective.
- *Operating trends*, which include the historical relationships between the material, labor, and overhead components of the cost of goods sold and the relationships between fixed costs and variable costs.

## The Controller's Role

Controllers are uniquely qualified to coordinate and develop the strategic planning function within the firm. Essentially all the activities of every functional or operating unit within the firm has financial ramifications that are manifested in the controller's area of responsibility. The controller should have a broad understanding of the day-to-day operations and functions of the firm. This understanding makes the controller ideally suited for a key role in strategic planning.

## Establishing Acquisition Criteria

A firm that has decided on an acquisition strategy to satisfy some of its business needs must have a very specific, carefully thought out set of acquisition criteria. Before the firm considers any acquisition candidates, the acquisition criteria should be approved by, and have the complete support of, both its top management and board of directors.

The acquisition candidates that meet the specific acquisition criteria on a preliminary or cursory review will be a very small percentage of the entire population of candidates. This initial weeding out of candidates will save time and effort that would be wasted analyzing unacceptable candidates. Representative acquisition criteria are presented below.

**Meeting Business Needs.** The strategic planning process should have identified the business deficiencies that must be rectified before the firm can achieve its strategic objectives. Only firms that have the particular resource to satisfy the deficiency should be considered.

**Acceptable Price Range.** Management must determine how much it can pay. What is the maximum amount of cash available, lines of credit available, or shares of equity it is willing to exchange (depending on the method of financing proposed) to acquire a new entity? Once the price range is established, all candidates whose probable purchase price exceeds the price range can be eliminated. For example, a $250-million, highly profitable firm may be an ideal acquisition—except to a $100-million firm with a maximum of only $5 million available for an acquisition program.

**Profitability.** No matter how perfect the match of size, price, products, customers, geography, or any other criteria, no acquisition makes sense unless the acquisition earns the buyer an after-tax profit. The two considerations are:

- *Available credits.* The candidate may show a before-tax loss but have significant net operating loss carryforwards, investment tax credits, or other tax credit that can be used by the buyer to show an after-tax profit.
- *Potential turnaround.* If the buyer can contribute the right resources to the candidate (e.g., managerial skills, capital, distribution channels), the acquisition may prove profitable to the buyer, even though the candidate could not earn a profit on its own.

**Return on Investment.** No acquisition makes sense unless it earns the buyer an adequate return on the buyer's investment (the purchase price). The following represent some of the variations in establishing ROI criteria:

- *Current overall ROI of buyer.* No acquisition should be made if the ROI on the acquisition is lower than the overall ROI of the buyer.
- *Weighted average cost of capital.* No acquisition should be made if the acquisition's ROI is less than the buyer's weighted average cost of capital.
- *Opportunity cost.* No acquisition should be made if the ROI generated by the acquisition is less than the return the buyer firm could earn on other investments in the same risk class as the acquisition.
- *Subjectively determined hurdle rate.* Many firms subjectively determine a hurdle

rate—a minimum ROI acceptable for acquisition candidates. The hurdle rate is usually established by the firm's chief executive, perhaps in a conference with the board of directors. The subjectively determined hurdle rate is usually the buyer firm's historical ROI plus a risk premium (an incremental increase in the historical ROI) to compensate the buyer for taking on the new, risky venture of the acquisition.

**Fit of the Acquisition Into Buyer's Current Business.** The fit of the acquisition candidate into the buyer's current business is an extremely important criterion for evaluating candidates. There are numerous examples of acquisitions that proved to be unsuccessful because the acquisition candidate made a product the buyer did not understand, sold its products in a market the buyer was not familiar with, or sold its products to customers the buyer did not know. The failure of so many instant conglomerates in the late 1960s indicates the importance of an acquisition's fit into the buyer's business.

## THE ACQUISITION INVESTIGATION

### The Investigating Team

The skills required by the investigating team are much more important than the number of people on the team or the position titles they hold. If the team is to meet its responsibilities, it must have a detailed working knowledge of corporate law (especially related to mergers and acquisitions), SEC requirements and compliance, federal and state taxation, accounting and auditing, marketing, and industrial engineering. The following skills are needed by the investigation team in these areas:

- *Corporate law*—proper legal structure of the merger, possible antitrust problems, compliance with state blue sky laws, and review of legal matters (e.g., leases, contracts) of acquiree firm;
- *SEC compliance*—timely preparation and filings of all SEC forms related to merger and acquisition disclosure, including proxy statements and tender-offer disclosures;
- *Taxation*—determination of tax status of acquiree firm (including a review for possible deficiencies or assessments with federal, state, and local income, franchise, personal property, and real estate taxes) and structure of the merger (taxable versus nontaxable exchanges) to achieve the tax objectives of all parties;
- *Accounting and auditing*—review of accounting principles used by acquiree and the effect of changes to comply with accounting principles used by buyer, review of accounting and reporting systems, review of prior independent audits (or conducting an internal audit, if required), and determination of proper accounting for acquisition (i.e., purchase versus pooling of interests);[2]

---

[2] The tax and accounting implications of mergers and acquisitions are discussed in Chapter 31.

- *Marketing*—review of product quality, pricing structures, distribution systems, customer service, and methods of salesmen's compensation; and
- *Industrial engineering*—review of production processes (for efficiency), grounds and facilities (for adequacy, general condition), machinery and equipment (for age, general condition), storage and warehousing facilities (for adequacy), and receiving and shipping facilities (for adequacy, plant location, general condition).

This is not to say that there must be at least six persons on the investigating team. It is not at all unlikely that individuals on the team possess two or more of the skills required to conduct the investigation. For instance, the buyer's in-house legal counsel may be an expert on both corporate law and SEC compliance. Likewise, the buyer's controller may be an expert in SEC compliance, taxation, and accounting and auditing.

The investigating team should have a chairman to coordinate its activities and facilitate communication between its members. The controller is the likely candidate for team chairman, because of his experience in coordinating and reporting on financial and other quantifiable data. If the controller does not have the time to serve as team chairman, or to serve on the team at all, the team should keep him apprised of its progress and seek his advice on technical accounting matters.

The team should report to the chief executive officer (CEO). This reporting relationship gives the team the status it needs to ensure full cooperation in the investigation, and it minimizes the danger that the CEO will receive misleading information about its findings. The CEO must make the final decision regarding the acquisition (or at least make the decision to recommend the acquisition to the board of directors).

### Planning the Investigation

Each member of the team should be fully apprised of the buyer's acquisition strategy program and of the specific business needs of the buyer that the acquisition should satisfy. A general analysis of the prospective seller and the seller's industry should also be turned over to the investigating team. The thrust of the investigation should then be geared to developing specific facts about the seller's business and industry that the buyer would not have access to from financial publications and other sources of preliminary analysis.

A schedule of periodic meetings of all members of the investigation team should be established; weekly meetings are usually preferred. Each member of the team should receive a list of the investigation's objectives and information enabling him to understand the scope and procedures of the investigation conducted by every other member. Communications problems arise when, for instance, the tax accountant does not know what information the business lawyer needs to structure the merger as a tax-free reorganization.

Another problem that can be avoided with proper planning is having several members of the team investigate the same areas. To avoid this duplication of effort, members of the team should be assigned to review specific topics and report their findings at the next periodic meeting, emphasizing the other members' information needs.

In summary, the following steps should be taken to coordinate the investigative efforts and to minimize investigative problems:

- A timetable should be established and agreed to by all members of the team.
- The chairman of the team should assign overlapping areas to one member of the team and circulate the assignments so that each member of the team knows what the others are doing.
- All findings should be discussed as openly as possible during the periodic team meetings.

### Using Outside Experts

Outside experts are usually called in on an acquisition if the internal staff does not have the time or expertise to complete the required assignment. Outside experts can generally be grouped in two categories: (1) those who provide services after an agreement in principle regarding the acquisition has been signed, and (2) those who provide services in locating and attracting an acquisition candidate. The first category of experts includes legal counsel, CPAs, and specialized appraisers. The second category consists of finders and brokers.

**Legal Counsel, CPAs, and Specialized Appraisers.** Legal counsel is essential during the activity following the signing of the acquisition agreement in principle and leading to the structuring and signing of the final acquisition contract. In addition to the legal and antitrust investigations, legal counsel should be intimately involved in drafting the acquisition contract itself. The acquisition contract should spell out all the terms of the acquisition (i.e., the obligations of both the buyer and seller) and attempt to indemnify the buyer from any potential and unknown liabilities of the seller.

The buyer may engage independent auditors to determine the proper valuation of the candidate's assets, particularly inventory (if that is a material portion of the seller's assets) and liability accounts. The buyer may also ask the independent auditor to recommend the most favorable accounting treatment for the acquisition from both a statutory reporting and a taxation perspective, or if necessary, to conduct a complete audit of the candidate.

When the acquisition is structured as a purchase for cash or debt securities, the buyer should retain outside specialized appraisers to establish current market values for the acquiree's assets for tax purposes. An independent appraisal also substantiates the value of the candidate's assets and liabilities.

**Finders and Brokers.** Finders and brokers are useful in finding leads and bringing buyers and sellers together to achieve a merger or acquisition. A *finder* is one who finds, interests, introduces, and brings parties together for a transaction that the parties themselves then negotiate and consummate. A *broker* is an agent who has the task of bringing the parties to agreement in accordance with the terms specified by his employer, the principal. A broker is required, therefore, to take some part in the actual negotiation between buyer and seller.

Before either the buyer or seller deals with a finder or broker, the following questions should be specifically answered:

- Is the finder/broker employed by the buyer or seller?
- Who will be responsible for compensating the finder/broker, the buyer, or the seller?
- Under what conditions will the finder/broker expect compensation?
- How will the finder/broker's compensation be determined?

The answers to these four questions should be set down in a written agreement signed by the finder or broker. This written agreement, understood by both parties at the inception of the relationship, will alleviate many problems that may possibly arise. An example of such a written agreement between a broker and a potential buyer is included as Figure 30.1.

The buyer must also ensure that the broker or finder has the authority to represent the seller as a company that is actually on the market.

Although the amount of broker's commissions or finder's fees may vary greatly, the following formula is in fairly standard use for determining the commission or fee:

| *If the amount of consideration paid is:* | | *The commission or fee is:* |
|---|---|---|
| *Over* | *But not over* | |
| $0 | $1 million | 5% of consideration |
| $1 million | $2 million | $50,000 plus 4% of excess over $1 million |
| $2 million | $3 million | $90,000 plus 3% of excess over $2 million |
| $3 million | $4 million | $120,000 plus 2% of excess over $3 million |
| $4 million | $5 million | $140,000 plus 1% of excess over $4 million |

## What the Seller (Acquiree) Should Do

If an acquisition agreement in principle has been signed, the acquiree should make every effort to provide the buyer's investigative team with requested information, designating one employee as a liaison to minimize disruption of the seller's business and provide information on a timely basis. The seller's controller is a likely candidate for the liaison responsibility, because of his intimate knowledge of the seller's accounting management information and records system.

Copies of requested documents should be provided whenever possible. These copies, however, should be clearly stamped "Confidential—property of seller company" and should also be alphanumerically coded and logged in and out. The coding system and log will help identify which documents are outstanding and who has them. If the acquisition is not consummated, the acquiree should request that all confidential items be returned. The seller's liaison should keep close track of these original documents at all times to ensure their return.

November 20, 19—

Mr. Conscientious Broker
Conscientious Brokerage, Inc.
500 Wall Street
New York, New York 10010

Dear Mr. Broker:

Thank you for your letter of November 5, 1979. Your letter indicates that you would look to us for a fee if we proceed with you.

We are interested in adding related businesses to our product lines; however, for our mutual protection we have found it best to have a clear understanding before entering into any fee commitment.

The Finder's Fee will be computed as follows: 5% of the first million dollars or less of the purchase price, plus 4% of the second million dollars of the purchase price, plus 3% of the third million dollars of the purchase price, plus 2% of the fourth million dollars of the purchase price, plus 1% of any portion of the purchase price exceeding $4 million.

No fee will be payable if no purchase is consummated. The fee will be based on the consideration, or the value thereof if not paid in cash, and will be payable at the time such consideration passes to the seller. We will not be responsible for any fee obligation incurred by the seller to you or to anyone performing a broker, finder, or similar function in the transaction.

Since our review may require revealing information to various employees and advisers, we cannot agree to hold confidential any information you may provide us.

If you wish to proceed on this basis, we would appreciate it if you would first acknowledge this understanding by signing and returning the enclosed copy of this letter and then forwarding the information you have concerning the manufacturer of widgets.

Agreed:

_____

Signature

Date: _____

Sincerely,

John J. Jones
Vice President, Finance
Buyer Manufacturing Company

FIGURE 30.1 SAMPLE WRITTEN AGREEMENT BETWEEN BROKER AND BUYER

The acquiree should never appear to be withholding even the most confidential information from the buyer's investigating team. Any hint of a cover-up or of non-cooperation, whether real or perceived, could cause an otherwise ideal merger or acquisition to fall through.

If an agreement in principle has not been signed (as in the case of an unfriendly tender offer), obviously the acquiree should provide as little information as possible to the buyer or his employees or agents. Of course, even if the acquiree is the target of an unfriendly takeover attempt, it is required by law to disclose some information to the potential buyer. For example, in Release No. 5731, the SEC has proposed that a target be required to furnish a shareholder list to the bidder. A few recent cases have indicated that Section 14(e) of the Securities and Exchange Act of 1934 may serve, under certain conditions, as a basis for securing the list for a "proper purpose." Securing a list in order to buy additional shares generally has been deemed a proper purpose. Under various state takeover statutes, a refusal by the target company to permit record stockholders to examine its list to make a bid is a fraudulent practice.

## DETERMINING A FAIR PRICE FOR AN ACQUISITION[3]

There are numerous procedures in common practice for determining the fair price or fair market value of a firm that is being acquired. Basically, the various procedures can be grouped into four categories:

- *Appraised value of assets.* The buyer engages an independent appraiser to put a value on all the assets of the acquired firm. This method is used primarily when the acquisition calls for a sale and purchase of assets rather than a sale and purchase of a going concern. It is also used when it is important to have an appraised value for each individual asset for tax purposes.
- *Value of shares outstanding.* The buyer takes the current per-share market price (plus some premium to entice current shareholders to sell to the acquiring firm) and multiplies it by the number of shares outstanding. The resulting product is the value of the firm's equity to its current shareholders, and theoretically, the value of the firm. This procedure is used frequently in the case of tender offers.
- *P/E multiple times earnings.* This method can be applied to either current-year earnings or to a forecast of future earnings (based on the buyer's best judgment of all the factors that may affect the earnings in the future). The purchase price is obtained by multiplying the current year's (or forecasted) after-tax earnings by a price/earnings multiple factor. The specific price/earnings multiple used can be derived in one of three ways:

---

[3] This explanation, as well as the material covered in Appendix 30-2, is adapted and reprinted from an article by Mr. Reilly entitled "Pricing an Acquisition: A 15 Step Methodology," which originally appeared in *Mergers and Acquisitions*, Vol. 14, No. 2 (Summer 1979), © 1979 Information for Industry, Inc., and appears here with permission.

　　a. If the acquired company is publicly traded, the current P/E of its outstanding stock can be used;

　　b. It can be determined by negotiation between the buyer and the seller of the firm; or

　　c. It can be based on the acquiring firm's minimally acceptable return on investment.

To illustrate, an acquisition candidate earns $40,000 this year after taxes, and the acquiring firm requires a minimum 10 percent return on investment. A 10 percent return on investment (on the purchase price) corresponds to a price/earnings multiple of 10. The price/earnings multiple (10) times the candidate's after-tax earnings ($40,000) results in a purchase price of $400,000.

- *Present value of future cash flows.* This method treats an acquisition just like any other capital budgeting problem in which there is a sizeable initial investment and a stream of cash flows in future years. This approach discounts the acquiree's forecast cash flows at the acquiring company's required hurdle rate for similarly risky capital investments. The resultant present value of cash flows is the maximum the buyer would be willing to pay for the candidate, and the internal rate of return of the acquisition investment will exactly equal the buyer's hurdle rate for similarly risky projects.

## Present Value of Future Cash Flows

This method is discussed at length because it is the most technically correct and challenging of the acquisition pricing techniques. The other methods mentioned above are relatively simplistic and easily applied but are not highly regarded on a technical or theoretical basis.

It must be remembered that the price actually paid by the buyer for the acquisition will be a negotiated price. Therefore, the present-value price is either a reference point to begin negotiations or the maximum amount the buyer would be willing to pay. It is a tool for determining and evaluating the acceptability of the final price from the buyer's perspective.

The following steps explain how to use the present-value-of-future-cash-flows method to determine a fair and theoretically correct price for an acquisition candidate firm:

1. Use the prior five years' financial statements (preferably audited statements) as a minimum (ten years, if available). Adjust the financial data to eliminate the effects of changes in accounting principles, discontinued operations, acquisitions, divestitures, and other abnormal items.

2. Prepare trend percentage statements in two ways:
   a. From year to year, and
   b. From an initial base year.
   If only one method is used, the base-year trend is preferable.

3 Prepare common-size financial statements that show balance sheet accounts as a percentage of total assets and income statement accounts as a percentage of net sales.

4. Analyze the trended and common-size financial statements. Identify and investigate unusual fluctuations or deviations from the trend.

5. Using semilogarithmic graph paper, plot the trended data for sales, net income, and earnings per share for the five-year (or ten-year) period.

6. Connect the points on the graph to develop a trend line.

7. Determine the historical growth rate for net income and net sales for the period used. The formula for determining growth rate is:

$$(1 + g)^t = \frac{e_t}{e_o}$$

where:

$g$ is the growth rate through forecast period $t$ (usually five years),

$e_t$ is the net income (or sales) at the end of the period, and

$e_o$ is the net income (or sales) in the base year.

8. Determine the historical cash flows for the period. Include operating cash flows, changes in balance sheet accounts, and financial cash flows.

9. Prepare a financial ratio analysis on the historical financial data. The following twelve ratios are recommended to analyze four significant areas:

   a. Liquidity:
      • Current ratio, and
      • Quick ratio.
   b. Leverage:
      • Debt to total assets ratio,
      • Times interest earned, and
      • Fixed-charge coverage.
   c. Activity:
      • Inventory turnover,
      • Average collection period,
      • Fixed-asset turnover, and
      • Total assets turnover.
   d. Profitability:
      • Profit margin on sales,
      • Return on total assets, and
      • Return on net worth.

Significant deviations in these ratios should be investigated and explained.

10. Use the logarithmic time-series trend developed in step 6 and extend the trend line to forecast sales and net income for the next five years. Although this is an unsophisticated forecast, it is quick and simple.

11. Using the financial ratios developed in step 9 and the sales and net income forecast generated in step 10, prepare pro forma or forecasted financial statements for the next five years.

12. Use the step 11 pro forma financial statements to prepare forecasted cash-flow statements for the five-year forecast period. Dividends are normally ignored in preparing this forecast.

13. Develop an appropriate discount rate to be used to discount the step 12 forecasted cash flows back to the present (see Chapter 34 for an explanation of how to theoretically compute a discount rate or internal rate of return on new investments).

In practice, most firms arbitrarily set a hurdle rate, frequently based on the firm's historical return on investment (or some other profitability measure), adjusted for higher expected returns in the future and some risk premium for the acquisition. Although the rate used is determined subjectively, there should be careful consideration and some rationale for the risk premium.

14. Discount the cash-flow forecast at the determined discount rate for the five-year forecast period. The formula for discounting the cash flows is:

$$\text{present value of cash flow} = \sum_{1}^{5} \frac{\text{Cash flow in time period } t}{(1.0 + d)^t}$$

where $d$ is the discount rate.

15. Determine the salvage value of the potential acquisition at the end of the five-year forecast period and compute the present value. Add the present value of the salvage to the present value of the forecast period cash flows; this sum is the present value of the acquisition and the maximum amount an acquiring firm would be willing to pay.

A detailed application of this pricing technique is presented in Appendix 30-2.

## INTEGRATING THE ACQUIRED COMPANY

Much has been written in financial literature about the purely quantifiable aspects of mergers and acquisitions. Little has been written about the integration of the two corporate entities after the merger or acquisition. Perhaps one reason for this is that the aftermath of each corporate marriage is unique, depending on the companies and individual people involved. Routine formulas and cookbook guidelines and checklists don't easily apply. With an understanding that each merger or acquisition integration presents a unique set of circumstances and challenges, the following integration topics will be briefly discussed: accounting systems, personnel, and other problems.

### Accounting Systems

As part of the acquisition review, the investigating team should have determined if it would be possible to integrate the candidate's accounting systems into those of the acquiring company. Of course, some modifications in the candidate's accounting systems are almost always necessary. Because of the prodigious variety of generally accepted accounting principles and functional accounting and reporting systems, a perfect match between two firms is extremely rare. However, if it was determined that it would be almost impossible to integrate the candidate's accounting systems (without entirely scrapping and redeveloping current systems), the acquisition should probably not be consummated.

The controller should coordinate the integration of the accounting systems. He should establish a schedule for completing the integration process for each system, and then see to it that the schedule is achieved. The schedule should include the following systems and procedures:

- Standardized accounting calendars (indicating dates of closings, report issuances, etc.);
- Standardized chart of accounts;
- Integration of generally accepted accounting principles (e.g., consolidation principles, inventory valuation, depreciation, and bad debt allowances);
- Procedures for setting and revising standard costs;
- Taxation procedures (including tax accounting principles used, filing of consolidated returns, etc.);
- Payroll procedures;
- Accounts receivable procedures;
- Accounts payable procedures;
- Cash management system (and bank accounts); and
- Budgeting, planning, and forecasting procedures.

The acquiring company's first step is to educate the acquired company as to its systems, procedures, and standards. Only then can it institute a program to revise or redesign current systems for the integration process.

## Personnel

The key to minimizing the personnel problems, unrest, and uncertainty that inevitably develop as a result of a merger or acquisition is complete and honest communication. A well-planned program of communication (directed at the employees of both the acquiring and acquired companies) should be launched immediately upon conclusion of the acquisition.

Such a communications program should have three objectives:

1. Educating each major group of employees (hourly, professional, technical) as to the terms of the merger that affect them (e.g., autonomy of the acquiree; continuation of management; changes in job grades, wage scales, union affiliation, and seniority; and handling of employee benefits);
2. Educating all employees as to the benefits of the merger from the standpoint of both companies (e.g., product fit, distribution fit, management fit); and
3. Demonstrating the genuine concern of the acquiring company's management for the feelings and welfare of the acquired company's employees.

If personnel changes, especially at the executive level, are contemplated, the changes should be made as soon as possible after the acquisition. Slow and drawn out personnel changes generate a feeling of anxiety and resentment among the remaining employees of the acquired firm. Once the series of personnel changes is complete, that fact should be communicated to all employees involved, who can then return to performing their jobs with full concentration without worrying about being "next on the list."

**Other Problems**

Every functional area within the acquired company will probably be affected by the acquisition to one degree or another. The degree of centralization or decentralization will obviously affect such functions as purchasing, advertising, and marketing research. Some duplicate functional groups may have to be eliminated; others may have to be relocated. Again, the best way to handle these problems is to communicate the planned course of action and then carry it out as quickly as possible.

## ESTABLISHING A TIMETABLE

After the buyer and seller have signed an agreement in principle regarding the acquisition, a timetable should be established. The timetable should include the proposed dates of the buyer's investigation of the seller, the negotiation of the purchase price, meetings of the two boards of directors to approve the acquisition, required filings with the SEC and appropriate stock exchanges, request for and receipt of a determination letter from the IRS, and the drafting and signing of the acquisition contract. Adequate time should be set aside for dealing with the administrative agencies or sending notices to stockholders in regard to the meetings.

The illustrative timetable in Appendix 30-3 portrays the acquisition of the assets of a seller whose stock is traded over the counter by a buyer whose stock is traded on the American Stock Exchange (Amex). The acquisition will be paid for with cash and shares of the buyer's stock.

## SEC REQUIREMENTS

Publicly held corporations that are required to report periodically to the SEC must provide certain information regarding mergers, acquisitions, and related activities that affect the company. (See Chapter 10 for a discussion of all periodic reporting requirements.)

The filing requirements for registrants involved in a merger or acquisition, either as buyer or seller, may include:

- Form 8-K—Current Report,
- Form 10-Q—Quarterly Report,
- Form 10-K—Annual Report, and
- Proxy Statement.

## Form 8-K Requirements

Item 2 of Form 8-K requires certain disclosures to be filed with the SEC within fifteen days after a firm acquires or disposes of a *significant* amount of assets other than in the ordinary course of business.[4] The required disclosures are generally the responsibility of corporate counsel. The corporate controller will be asked to prepare or supply the following financial statements of the business being acquired or sold as called for by item 7 of Form 8-K:

- A balance sheet (unaudited) as of a date reasonably close to the date of acquisition and an audited balance sheet as of the end of the preceding fiscal year; and
- Audited statements of income and retained earnings and changes in financial position for the preceding three fiscal years and unaudited statements for the interim period to the date of the unaudited balance sheet.

## Form 10-Q Requirements

Part I of Form 10-Q calls for comparative quarterly and year-to-date financial statements and other financial data. However, certain items in Part II relate to mergers and acquisitions, as follows:

- *Item 2—Changes in securities.* The rights of security holders may be changed by the issuance of a new class of securities.
- *Item 5—Increase in amount outstanding of securities or indebtedness.* Various disclosures are required if the amount of outstanding securities or indebtedness has increased by more than 5 percent. (The SEC has proposed deleting this item from Form 10-Q.)
- *Item 7—Submission of matters to a vote of security holders.* If a vote of security holders was held to approve a merger or acquisition, the date of the meeting and certain other information is required.
- *Item 9—Exhibits and reports on Form 8-K.* A list of the Forms 8-K filed during the quarter, the items reported, and the financial reports and other exhibits included is required.

## Form 10-K Requirements

Reporting companies are required to file an annual report with the SEC on Form 10-K. Since the SEC does not require a Form 10-Q for the fourth quarter of the fiscal year, any information with regard to a merger or acquisition during the fourth quarter would be reported in Form 10-K. In addition, information previously

---

[4] "Significant" is defined as more than ten percent of total consolidated assets and relates to the greater of net book value or the purchase price.

reported in Form 10-Q for the first three quarters would be incorporated by reference.

Additional information regarding mergers or acquisitions that took place during the fiscal year would probably be required under Item 1—Business. The effect of the merger or acquisition on the firm's business, product lines, and industry segments would have to be disclosed. Also, Item 3—Properties, may require certain disclosures of new properties or leases.

**Proxy Statement Requirements**

If a vote of security holders (buyer and/or seller) is required to approve the merger or acquisition, various disclosures must be filed concerning the proposed transaction. The requirements are specified in Regulation 14A of the proxy rules. Of concern to the controller is the requirement to include pro forma information on consolidated earnings, earnings per share, and book value per share for the last five fiscal years (as if the two companies had combined at the beginning of the five-year period).

**Registration Requirements**

If securities that require registration with the SEC are being issued in connection with a merger or acquisition, a registration form must be filed. (See Chapter 22 for a discussion of the contents of a registration statement.) One of the following two registration forms would be used:

1. *Form S-14* is used for the registration of securities issued in certain business combination transactions such as mergers, consolidations, or reclassifications, and for the reoffering of securities acquired in such transactions.
2. *Form S-15* is a short-form registration statement used for the same types of securities registrations as Form S-14 if the acquiring company meets the following conditions:
   a. The acquisition will not increase any of the following items by more than 10 percent on a pro forma consolidated basis:
      - Gross sales and operating revenues,
      - Net income,
      - Total assets, and
      - Total shareholders' equity;
   b. The acquirer meets the requirement for the use of Form S-7;
   c. Neither company engages in significant oil- and gas-related operations; and
   d. Neither company is a registered investment company.

Form S-15 is a new form and requires much less information than Form S-14. However, Form S-15 may not be used for reoffers of securities issued in the business combination.

## SUGGESTED READING

Alberts, William W., and McTaggart, James M. "Short Term Earnings per Share Standard for Evaluating Prospective Acquisitions." *Mergers and Acquisitions*, Vol. 12 (Winter, 1978), pp. 4-16.

Barmash, Isadore. *Welcome to Our Conglomerate—You're Fired!* New York: Delacorte Press, 1971.

Betterly, Delbert A. "Inheriting Risk in Acquisition or Merger." *Financial Executive*, Vol. 46 (September, 1978), pp. 32-35.

Byrd, William M., and Dean, James. "Costs of Investigating Prospective Businesses: Federal Tax Consequences." *Mergers and Acquisitions*, Vol. 12 (Fall, 1977), pp. 28-33.

Dory, John Paul. *The Domestic Diversifying Acquisition Decision*. Ann Arbor, Mich.: UMI Research Press, 1978.

Gravits, David H. "Plan Mergers, Spinoffs, and Transfers Under ERISA." *Financial Executive*, Vol. 46 (May, 1978), pp. 38-42.

Gussow, Don. *The New Merger Game, The Plan and Players*. New York: AMACOM, 1978.

Kohers, Theodor, and Simpson, W. Gary. "Financial Performance: Motive for Corporate Mergers." *University of Michigan Business Review*, Vol. 30 (July, 1978), pp. 11-14.

Korman, Abraham K., Rosenbloom, Arthur H., and Wales, Richard J. "People-Organization Fit in Mergers and Acquisitions." *Personnel*, Vol. 55 (May-June, 1978), pp. 54-61.

Lefkowitz, Burton T. "Preliminary Review for Acquisitions and Mergers." *CPA Journal*, Vol. 48 (September, 1978), pp. 13-16.

Lorsch, Jay Williams, and Allen, Stephen A. III. *Managing Diversity and Interdependence; An Organizational Study of Multidivisional Firms*. Boston: Harvard University Graduate School of Business Administration, Division of Research, 1979.

Lurie, Adolph G. *Business Segments: A Guide for Executives and Accountants*. New York: McGraw Hill, 1979.

McCarthy, George D., and Healy, Robert E. *Valuing a Company; Practices and Procedures*. New York: Ronald Press, 1979.

Seidman, Samuel N. "Mergers and Acquisitions." *Journal of Accounting, Auditing, and Finance*, Vol. 1 (Summer, 1978), pp. 391-396.

Steiner, Peter O. *Mergers: Motives, Effects, Policies.* Ann Arbor, Mich.: University of Michigan Press, 1975.

Winslow, John F. *Conglomerates Unlimited, The Failure of Regulation.* Bloomington, Ind.: Indiana University Press, 1973.

## APPENDIX 30-1  AN ILLUSTRATIVE LIST OF ACQUISITION OBJECTIVES

| *Objective (Need)* | *Strategy (For Satisfaction)* |
|---|---|

**Marketing**

| | |
|---|---|
| 1. Develop more growth-phase products. | 1. Acquire a firm that has developed new products in your industry. |
| 2. Increase number of customers. | 2. Acquire a firm whose current customers will substantially broaden your customer base. |
| 3. Increase market share. | 3. Acquire a firm in the same industry as yourself (but be careful of Robinson-Patman Act and Clayton Act antitrust implications). |
| 4. Increase absolute market size. | 4. Acquire a firm in a different industry than yourself—and in an industry that is larger than yours in absolute terms. |
| 5. Improve distribution channels. | 5. Acquire a firm with a recognized superiority in the distribution channel you are currently using. |
| 6. Change distribution channels. | 6. Acquire a firm in your industry that uses a different distribution method. |
| 7. Complete product line. | 7. Acquire a firm that makes products that complement and complete your product line and that you are currently lacking. |
| 8. Develop a low-end product line:<br>a. to complete your product line,<br>b. to foreclose market entry to others,<br>c. to better serve your customer needs. | 8. Acquire a firm that makes a lower-priced version of your product. |
| 9. Develop a high-end product line:<br>a. to increase overall pricing structure of your product,<br>b. to augment the image of your product line,<br>c. to complete your product line. | 9. Acquire a firm that makes a higher priced version of your product. |
| 10. Develop/improve a customer service operation. | 10. Acquire a firm with an established parts service and repair and customer service network for your products. |

| *Objective (Need)* | *Strategy (For Satisfaction)* |
|---|---|

## Human Resources*

1. Develop the necessary skills and/or experience mix in your executive, technical, or skilled and semi-skilled work force.

2. Develop the necessary age mix in your executive and technical staff (i.e., all of your senior or middle-management executives are nearing retirement age and there are no replacements on your staff).

1. Acquire a firm in your industry whose personnel meet your skill and/or experience-mix requirements.

2. Acquire a firm in your industry whose personnel meet your age-mix requirements.

## Financial

1. Utilize excess cash balances.

2. Cover cash deficiencies.

3. Increase the price earnings ratio (P/E).

4. Increase debt capacity.

5. Obtain new debt financing.

6. Improve credit standing.

7. Smooth out cyclical earnings and/or sales.

1. Acquire a firm that can employ excess funds more profitably than you can.

2. Acquire a firm with excess cash balances that you can profitably employ.

3. Acquire a firm with a higher P/E multiple than your firm. This should increase the P/E multiple of the combined firm over the current level of your firm.

4. Acquire a firm with mortgageable assets.

5. Acquire a firm that is highly leveraged. (This is one way for a firm with a poor credit rating to obtain debt financing at an acceptable interest rate.)

6. Acquire a firm with a credit rating superior to your firm.

7. Acquire a firm in an industry where earnings and/or sales are either more stable than or countercyclical to your industry.

---

* Two caveats regarding human resource acquisition objectives:

1. It is certainly not reasonable to acquire an entire company just to acquire the managerial expertise of its chief executive; it makes much more sense to simply hire the executive away from his current employer.

2. If an acquisition is contemplated to achieve human resource objectives, employment contracts for the human resource target group should be agreed on before the acquisition is closed. This is particularly important in a service industry, where the acquiree company's primary asset is usually its human capital.

| *Objective (Need)* | *Strategy (For Satisfaction)* |
|---|---|
| 8. Go public. | 8. Acquire a firm that is already registered with the SEC and is publicly traded. (This is sometimes called listing "through the back door" and is a way to avoid some of the costs and problems involved in an initial SEC registration.) |
| 9. Improve your listing on a stock exchange. | 9. Acquire a firm that is traded on the NYSE (if you are traded on ASE) or on the ASE (if you are traded on a regional exchange). |
| 10. Reduce corporate income taxes. | 10. Acquire a firm with a net operating loss carryforward, large unclaimed investment tax credits, or other tax shelters. |
| 11. Avoid distributing dividends (and avoid IRS penalties for excess accumulation of earnings). | 11. Acquire any firm (that meets other acquisition criteria) so that the acquisition demonstrates a use of accumulated earnings. |

## Legal

| | |
|---|---|
| 1. Develop patent protection on products (assuming it is not available on current products). | 1. Acquire a firm whose products are protected by patents. |
| 2. Develop a recognizable trademark. | 2. Acquire a firm with a famous trademark that you can apply to all of your products. (Usually this strategy is more time-effective and cost-effective than developing a trademark from scratch and hoping it catches on.) |
| 3. Obtain a land right, mineral right, lease, or leasehold (that some other firm is holding). | 3. Acquire a firm that holds the valuable right or lease. |
| 4. Avoid antitrust and industry concentration charges. | 4. Acquire a firm in an industry other than your own (which decreases your dependence on the concentrated industry) and in an industry that is more fragmented. |

## Operational

| | |
|---|---|
| 1. Reduce operating leverage and increase absorption of fixed costs. | 1. Acquire a firm with a lower degree of operating leverage that can absorb some of your firm's fixed costs. |
| 2. Utilize idle or excess plant capacity. | 2. Acquire a business that can operate in your current plant. |

| *Objective (Need)* | *Strategy (For Satisfaction)* |
|---|---|
| 3. Integrate vertically:<br>   a. backward<br>   b. forward | 3. Acquire a firm that has been a:<br>   a. supplier<br>   b. distributor |
| 4. Reduce inventory levels. | 4. Acquire a customer (but, obviously, not a use consumer) and adjust your inventory levels to match "customer" acquiree's orders. |
| 5. Increase procurement clout. | 5. Acquire a firm that uses the same raw materials as you do; a combined firm can purchase materials from a single source with more clout. |
| 6. Reduce indirect operating and/or fixed costs. | 6. Acquire a firm where duplicate operating costs (e.g., warehousing, distribution, etc.) and/or duplicate fixed costs (e.g., corporate and staff functional groups) can be eliminated. |

Note: Diversification in and of itself is saliently absent from the list of bona fide acquisition objectives; however, diversification through acquisition is a strategy to accomplish several of the marketing (e.g., increase absolute market size), financial (e.g., smooth out cyclical sales), and legal (e.g., avoid antitrust and industry concentration charges) objectives.

## APPENDIX 30-2   AN APPLICATION OF THE PRESENT-VALUE-OF-FUTURE-CASH-FLOWS PRICING TECHNIQUE

### Introduction

Acquiring Company has decided on a strategic plan for corporate diversification and has assembled a list of possible acquisition candidates. From that list, it was decided that Candidate Company has the best "fit." Acquiring must now determine the maximum price it should pay to buy out Candidate Company.

### Step 1

Candidate's comparative income statement and balance sheet, with five years of comparative data, are included as Figures 30-2.1 and 30-2.2, respectively.

### Step 2

Candidate's trended income statement and balance sheet, with five years of data, are included as Figures 30-2.3 and 30-2.4, respectively.

## Step 3

Candidate's common-size income statement and balance sheet, with five years of data, are included as Figures 30-2.5 and 30-2.6, respectively.

## Step 4

All accounts in Figures 30-2.3, 30-2.4, 30-2.5, and 30-2.6 are analyzed for trends, deviations from trends, or unusually high or low balances. On the common-size income statement, for instance, cost of sales is exhibiting a generally upward trend. On the common-size balance sheet, the cash and long-term debt accounts are exhibiting a generally upward trend.

## Steps 5 and 6

Figure 30-2.7 is a logarithmic time-series graph of candidate's net sales, net income, and earnings per share.

## Step 7

The historical growth rates for net sales and net income are 6.5 and 5.7 percent, respectively. These were obtained by using the formulas:

$$(1 + g)^{x4} = \frac{\text{sales in period } X4}{\text{sales in period } X0} \quad \text{and}$$

$$(1 + g)^{x4} = \frac{\text{net income in period } X4}{\text{net income in period } X0}$$

For illustrative purposes only, the five-year constant growth rate was calculated for each trended income statement and balance sheet account. These growth rates are included as the last column of Figures 30-2.3 and 30-2.4.

## Step 8

Figure 30-2.8 shows the historical cash flow for Candidate Company.

## Step 9

Figure 30-2.9 shows a financial ratio analysis for Candidate Company.

## Step 10

Figure 30-2.7 includes an extrapolation of the logarithmic time-series graph for a five-year forecast period.

## Step 11

Figures 30-2.10 and 30-2.11 are the pro forma income statement and balance sheet, respectively.

## Step 12

Figure 30-2.12 is a pro forma five-year cash-flow projection for Candidate Company, based on the pro forma income statement and balance sheet.

## Step 13

This step involves determining an appropriate risk-adjusted discount rate for discounting Candidate cash flows (for the five-year forecast period) and salvage value (at the end of the fifth forecast year). In this example, the beta-adjusted discount rate will be illustrated.

First, assume Acquiring's historical rate of return on assets is 13 percent. Second, assume Candidate's beta is 1.1. Candidate's beta could be determined from published sources (if the firm is large enough), from regression analysis (if the firm is listed), or from the surrogate beta of a similar firm in the same industry (obtained from either published sources or regression).

Using the beta-adjusted discount rate formula:

$$
\begin{aligned}
d &= R + B - 1.0\,(20) \\
&= 13.0 + 1.1 - 1.0\,(20) \\
&= 13.0 + (.1)\,(20) \\
&= 13.0 + 2.0 \\
d &= 15.0\%
\end{aligned}
$$

## Step 14

Figure 30-2.13 shows the pro forma cash flow of Candidate discounted at the beta-adjusted discount rate.

## Step 15

Figure 30-2.14 shows the determination of the salvage value of Candidate at the end of the five-year forecast period and the present value of the project.

### Summary

Acquiring should be willing to pay up to $12,691,000 to acquire Candidate (and still earn a risk-adjusted 15 percent annual return on its investment).

| | 19X0 | 19X1 | 19X2 | 19X3 | 19X4 |
|---|---|---|---|---|---|
| Gross Sales | $ 16,050 | $ 17,655 | $ 19,425 | $ 21,360 | $ 23,505 |
|   Sales Deductions | 1,050 | 1,155 | 1,275 | 1,395 | 1,545 |
| Net Sales | 15,000 | 16,500 | 18,150 | 19,965 | 21,960 |
|   Cost of Sales[1] | 10,500 | 11,880 | 13,245 | 14,580 | 16,245 |
| Gross Profit | 4,500 | 4,620 | 4,905 | 5,385 | 5,715 |
|   Selling and Administrative[2] | 1,500 | 1,575 | 1,650 | 1,725 | 1,800 |
|   Interest | 600 | 615 | 645 | 690 | 750 |
| Profit Before Taxes | 2,400 | 2,430 | 2,610 | 2,970 | 3,165 |
|   Taxes | 1,200 | 1,215 | 1,305 | 1,485 | 1,583 |
| Profit After Taxes | $ 1,200 | $ 1,215 | $ 1,305 | $ 1,485 | $ 1,583 |
| Dividends Paid | $ 600 | $ 608 | $ 653 | $ 743 | $ 792 |
| Average Number of Common | | | | | |
|   Shares Outstanding | 100,000 | 100,000 | 100,000 | 100,000 | 100,000 |
| Earnings Per Share | $ 12.00 | $ 12.15 | $ 13.05 | $ 14.85 | $ 15.83 |
| Dividends Per Share | $ 6.00 | $ 6.08 | $ 6.53 | $ 7.43 | $ 7.92 |

[1] Includes depreciation expense of $750 per year.
[2] Includes annual rental of $150 on long-term lease of office building (lease not capitalized in this example for simplicity).

FIGURE 30-2.1 CANDIDATE COMPANY INCOME STATEMENT SUMMARY FOR THE FISCAL YEARS ENDED JUNE 30th (IN $000)

| ASSETS | 19X0 | 19X1 | 19X2 | 19X3 | 19X4 |
|---|---|---|---|---|---|
| Current Assets | | | | | |
| Cash | $ 450 | $ 600 | $ 750 | $ 1,500 | $ 2,100 |
| Accounts Receivable-Net | 1,200 | 1,500 | 1,800 | 2,100 | 2,400 |
| Inventory | 1,800 | 1,950 | 2,400 | 2,850 | 3,300 |
| Prepaid Expenses | 300 | 450 | 600 | 750 | 900 |
| Total Current Assets | $3,750 | $4,500 | $5,550 | $ 7,200 | $ 8,700 |
| Plant, Property and Equipment | 6,000 | 6,000 | 7,500 | 9,000 | 10,500 |
| Less Accumulated Depreciation | 3,000 | 3,750 | 4,500 | 5,250 | 6,000 |
| Net Plant, Property and Equipment | 3,000 | 2,250 | 3,000 | 3,750 | 4,500 |
| Total Assets | $6,750 | $6,750 | $8,550 | $10,950 | $13,200 |
| **LIABILITIES AND SHAREHOLDERS' EQUITY** | | | | | |
| Current Liabilities | | | | | |
| Accounts Payable | $1,200 | $1,350 | $1,350 | $ 1,500 | $ 1,800 |
| Notes Payable | 750 | 150 | 1,050 | 900 | 1,350 |
| Accrued Expenses | 750 | 593 | 840 | 998 | 957 |
| Total Current Liabilities | $2,700 | $2,093 | $3,240 | $ 3,398 | $ 4,107 |
| Long-Term Debt | 1,500 | 1,500 | 1,500 | 3,000 | 3,750 |
| Shareholders' Equity | | | | | |
| Common Stock | 150 | 150 | 150 | 150 | 150 |
| Capital Surplus | 600 | 600 | 600 | 600 | 600 |
| Retained Earnings | 1,800 | 2,408 | 3,060 | 3,803 | 4,593 |
| | 2,550 | 3,158 | 3,810 | 4,553 | 5,343 |
| Total Liabilities and Shareholders' Equity | $6,750 | $6,750 | $8,550 | $10,950 | $13,200 |
| Working Capital | $1,050 | $2,407 | $2,310 | $ 3,802 | $ 4,593 |

FIGURE 30-2.2  CANDIDATE COMPANY CONSOLIDATED BALANCE SHEET FOR THE FISCAL YEARS ENDED JUNE 30th (IN $000)

| | 19X0 | 19X1 | 19X2 | 19X3 | 19X4 | 5-Year Constant Growth Rate |
|---|---|---|---|---|---|---|
| Gross Sales | 100% | 110 % | 121.0% | 133.1% | 137.1% | 6.5% |
| Sales Deductions | 100 | 110 | 121.0 | 133.1 | 137.1 | 6.5 |
| Net Sales | 100 | 110 | 121.0 | 133.1 | 137.1 | 6.5 |
| Cost of Sales | 100 | 113.1 | 126.1 | 138.9 | 154.7 | 9.2 |
| Gross Profit | 100 | 102.7 | 109 | 119.7 | 127 | 4.9 |
| Selling and Administrative | 100 | 105 | 110 | 115 | 120 | 3.7 |
| Interest | 100 | 102.5 | 107.5 | 115 | 125 | 4.5 |
| Profit Before Taxes | 100 | 101.3 | 108.8 | 123.8 | 131.19 | 5.7 |
| Taxes | 100 | 101.3 | 108.8 | 123.8 | 131.9 | 5.7 |
| Profit After Taxes | 100% | 101.3% | 108.8% | 123.8% | 131.9% | 5.7 |
| Dividends Paid | 100 | 101.3 | 108.8 | 123.8 | 131.9 | 5.7 |
| Earnings Per Share | 100 | 101.3 | 108.8 | 123.8 | 131.9 | 5.7 |
| Dividends Per Share | 100% | 101.3% | 108.8% | 123.8% | 131.9% | 5.7% |

FIGURE 30-2.3 CANDIDATE COMPANY TRENDED INCOME STATEMENT (19X0 AS BASE YEAR) FOR THE FISCAL YEARS ENDED JUNE 30th

| ASSETS | 19X0 | 19X1 | 19X2 | 19X3 | 19X4 | 5-Year Constant Growth Rate |
|---|---|---|---|---|---|---|
| Current Assets | | | | | | |
| Cash | 100% | 133.3% | 166.7% | 333.3% | 466.7% | 36.3% |
| Accounts Receivable—Net | 100 | 125 | 150 | 175 | 200 | 14.9 |
| Inventory | 100 | 108.3 | 133.3 | 158.3 | 183.3 | 12.9 |
| Prepaid Expenses | 100 | 150 | 200 | 250 | 300 | 24.6 |
| Total Current Assets | 100 | 120 | 148 | 192 | 232 | 18.3 |
| Plant, Property and Equipment | 100 | 100 | 125 | 150 | 175 | 11.9 |
| Less Accumulated Depreciation | 100 | 125 | 150 | 175 | 200 | 14.9 |
| Net Plant, Property and Equipment | 100 | 75 | 100 | 125 | 150 | 8.5 |
| Total Assets | 100% | 100% | 126.7% | 162.2% | 195.6% | 14.3% |
| LIABILITIES AND SHAREHOLDERS' EQUITY | | | | | | |
| Current Liabilities | | | | | | |
| Accounts Payable | 100% | 112.5% | 112.5% | 125% | 150% | 8.5% |
| Notes Payable | 100 | 20 | 140 | 120 | 180 | 12.5 |
| Accrued Expenses | 100 | 79 | 112 | 133 | 127.6 | 5.2 |
| Total Current Liabilities | 100 | 77.5 | 120 | 25.8 | 52 | 8.7 |
| Long-Term Debt | 100 | 100 | 100 | 200 | 250 | 20.1 |
| Shareholders' Equity | | | | | | |
| Common Stock | 100 | 100 | 100 | 100 | 100 | 0 |
| Capital Surplus | 100 | 100 | 100 | 100 | 100 | 0 |
| Retained Earnings | 100 | 133.8 | 170 | 211.3 | 255.2 | 20.3 |
| | 100 | 123.8 | 149.4 | 78.5 | 209.5 | 15.9 |
| Total Liabilities and Shareholders' Equity | 100% | 100% | 126.7% | 162.2% | 195.6% | 14.3% |
| Working Capital | 100% | 229.2% | 220% | 362.1% | 437.4% | 34.6% |

FIGURE 30-2.4 CANDIDATE COMPANY TRENDED BALANCE SHEET (19X0 AS BASE YEAR) FOR THE FISCAL YEARS ENDED JUNE 30th

| | 19X0 | 19X1 | 19X2 | 19X3 | 19X4 | 5-Year Average |
|---|---|---|---|---|---|---|
| Gross Sales | 107.0% | 107.0% | 107.0% | 107.0% | 107.0% | 107.0% |
| Sales Deductions | 7.0 | 7.0 | 7.0 | 7.0 | 7.0 | 7.0 |
| Net Sales | 100.0 | 100.0 | 100.0 | 100.0 | 100.0 | 100.0 |
| Cost of Sales | 70.0 | 72.0 | 73.0 | 73.0 | 74.0 | 72.4 |
| Gross Profit | 30.0 | 28.0 | 27.0 | 27.0 | 26.0 | 27.6 |
| Selling and Administrative | 10.0 | 9.5 | 9.1 | 8.6 | 8.2 | 9.1 |
| Interest | 4.0 | 3.7 | 3.6 | 3.5 | 3.4 | 3.6 |
| Profit Before Taxes | 16.0 | 14.8 | 14.3 | 14.9 | 14.4 | 14.9 |
| Taxes | 8.0 | 7.4 | 7.1 | 7.4 | 7.2 | 7.4 |
| Profit After Taxes | 8.0% | 7.4% | 7.2% | 7.5% | 7.2% | 7.5% |
| Dividends Paid | 4.0% | 3.7% | 3.6% | 3.7% | 3.6% | 3.7% |

FIGURE 30-2.5   CANDIDATE COMPANY COMMON SIZE INCOME STATEMENT (NET SALES AS BASE ACCOUNT) FOR THE FISCAL YEARS ENDED JUNE 30th

| ASSETS | 19X0 | 19X1 | 19X2 | 19X3 | 19X4 | 5-Year Average |
|---|---|---|---|---|---|---|
| **Current Assets** | | | | | | |
| Cash | 6.7% | 8.9% | 8.8% | 13.7% | 15.9% | 10.8% |
| Accounts Receivable—Net | 17.8 | 22.2 | 21.1 | 19.2 | 18.2 | 19.7 |
| Inventory | 26.7 | 28.9 | 28.1 | 26.0 | 25.0 | 26.9 |
| Prepaid Expenses | 4.4 | 6.7 | 7.0 | 6.8 | 6.8 | 6.3 |
| Total Current Assets | 55.6 | 66.7 | 65.0 | 65.7 | 65.9 | 63.7 |
| Plant, Property and Equipment | 88.9 | 88.9 | 87.7 | 82.2 | 79.5 | 85.4 |
| Less Accumulated Depreciation | (44.5) | (55.6) | (52.7) | (47.9) | (45.4) | (49.1) |
| Net Plant, Property, and Equipment | 44.4 | 33.3 | 35.0 | 34.3 | 34.1 | 36.3 |
| Total Assets | 100.0% | 100.0% | 100.0% | 100.0% | 100.0% | 100.0% |
| **LIABILITIES AND SHAREHOLDERS' EQUITY** | | | | | | |
| **Current Liabilities** | | | | | | |
| Accounts Payable | 17.8% | 20.0% | 15.8% | 13.7% | 13.6% | 16.2% |
| Notes Payable | 11.1 | 2.2 | 12.3 | 8.2 | 10.2 | 8.8 |
| Accrued Expenses | 11.1 | 8.8 | 9.8 | 9.1 | 7.3 | 9.2 |
| Total Current Liabilities | 40.0 | 31.0 | 37.9 | 31.0 | 31.1 | 34.2 |
| Long-Term Debt | 22.2 | 22.2 | 17.5 | 27.4 | 28.4 | 23.5 |
| **Shareholders' Equity** | | | | | | |
| Common Stock | 2.2 | 2.2 | 1.8 | 1.4 | 1.1 | 1.7 |
| Capital Surplus | 8.8 | 8.8 | 7.0 | 5.5 | 4.5 | 6.9 |
| Retained Earnings | 26.8 | 35.8 | 35.8 | 34.7 | 34.9 | 33.7 |
| | 37.8 | 46.8 | 44.6 | 41.6 | 40.5 | 42.3 |
| Total Liabilities and Shareholders' Equity | 100.0% | 100.0% | 100.0% | 100.0% | 100.0% | 100.0% |
| Working Capital | 15.6% | 35.7% | 27.0% | 34.7% | 34.8% | 29.6% |

FIGURE 30-2.6   CANDIDATE COMPANY COMMON SIZE BALANCE SHEET (TOTAL ASSETS AS BASE ACCOUNT) FOR THE FISCAL YEARS ENDED JUNE 30th

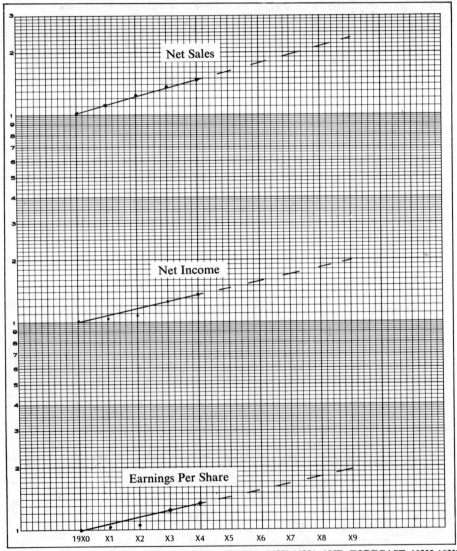

FIGURE 30-2.7  TREND SERIES GRAPH ACTUAL 19X0-19X4 AND FORECAST 19X5-19X9

| | 19X0 | 19X1 | 19X2 | 19X3 | 19X4 |
|---|---|---|---|---|---|
| **OPERATING CASH FLOWS** | | | | | |
| Net Sales Revenue | $15,000 | $16,500 | $18,150 | $19,965 | $21,960 |
| Change in Accounts Receivable | ( 300) | ( 300) | ( 300) | ( 300) | ( 300) |
| Cash Received from Operations | 14,700 | 16,200 | 17,850 | 19,665 | 21,660 |
| Cost of Sales | ( 10,500) | ( 11,880) | ( 13,245) | ( 14,580) | ( 16,245) |
| Selling and Administrative Expense | ( 1,500) | ( 1,575) | ( 1,650) | ( 1,725) | ( 1,800) |
| Interest Expense | ( 600) | ( 615) | ( 645) | ( 690) | ( 750) |
| Non-Cash Expense | 750 | 750 | 750 | 750 | 750 |
| Change in Inventory | ( 150) | ( 150) | ( 450) | ( 450) | ( 450) |
| Change in Prepaid Expenses | ( 150) | ( 150) | ( 150) | ( 150) | ( 150) |
| Change in Accounts Payable | 150 | 150 | 0 | 150 | 300 |
| Change in Accrued Expenses | 75 | ( 157) | 247 | 158 | ( 40) |
| Cash Disbursed for Operations | ( 11,925) | ( 13,627) | ( 15,142) | ( 16,537) | ( 18,385) |
| Operating Cash Flow Before Taxes | 2,775 | 2,573 | 2,708 | 3,128 | 3,275 |
| Taxes Paid | ( 1,200) | ( 1,215) | ( 1,305) | ( 1,485) | ( 1,583) |
| Net Cash Flow from Operations | 1,575 | 1,358 | 1,403 | 1,643 | 1,692 |
| **FINANCIAL CASH FLOWS** | | | | | |
| Dividends Paid | ( 600) | ( 608) | ( 653) | ( 743) | ( 792) |
| Cash Available for Investment | 975 | 750 | 750 | 900 | 900 |
| Capital Expenditures | — | — | ( 1,500) | ( 1,500) | ( 1,500) |
| Cash Flow Before Financing Transactions | 975 | 750 | ( 750) | ( 600) | ( 600) |
| **FINANCING TRANSACTIONS** | | | | | |
| Retirement of Short-Term Debt | ( 450) | ( 600) | — | ( 150) | — |
| Retirement of Long-Term Debt | — | — | — | — | — |
| Cash Flow Required to be Financed | — | — | ( 750) | ( 750) | ( 600) |
| Increase in Short-Term Debt | — | — | 900 | — | 450 |
| Increase in Long-Term Debt | — | — | — | 1,500 | 750 |
| Increase (Decrease) in Cash | $ 525 | $ 150 | $ 150 | $ 750 | $ 600 |

FIGURE 30-2.8  CANDIDATE COMPANY HISTORICAL CASH-FLOW STATEMENT FOR THE FISCAL YEARS ENDED JUNE 30th (IN $000)

| Ratio | |
|---|---|
| Liquidity | |
|   Current | Current Assets ÷ Current Liabilities |
|   Quick, or acid test | (Current Assets − Inventory) ÷ Current Liabilities |
| Leverage | |
|   Debt to total assets | Total Debt ÷ Total Assets |
|   Times interest earned | (Profit before Taxes plus Interest Charges) ÷ Interest Charges |
|   Fixed charge coverage | Income Available for Meeting Fixed Charges ÷ Fixed Charges |
| Activity | |
|   Inventory turnover | Sales ÷ Average Inventory |
|   Average collection period | Receivables ÷ Sales per Day |
|   Fixed assets turnover | Sales ÷ Year-End Fixed Assets |
|   Total assets turnover | Sales ÷ Year-End Total Assets |
| Profitability | |
|   Profit margin on sales | Profit after Taxes ÷ Sales |
|   Return on total assets | Profit after Taxes ÷ Total Assets |
|   Return on net worth | Profit after Taxes ÷ Shareholders' Equity |

| 19X0 | 19X1 | 19X2 | 19X3 | 19X4 | 5-Year Average |
|---|---|---|---|---|---|
| 1.39 | 2.15 | 1.71 | 2.12 | 2.12 | 1.90 times |
| .72 | 1.22 | .97 | 1.28 | 1.31 | 1.10 times |
| | | | | | |
| .62 | .53 | .55 | .58 | .60 | .58 percent |
| 5.00 | 4.95 | 5.05 | 5.30 | 5.22 | 5.10 times |
| 4.20 | 4.18 | 4.28 | 4.54 | 4.52 | 4.34 times |
| | | | | | |
| 8.70 | 8.80 | 8.34 | 7.61 | 7.14 | 8.12 times |
| 28.8 | 32.7 | 35.7 | 37.9 | 39.3 | 34.5 days |
| 5.00 | 7.33 | 6.05 | 5.32 | 4.88 | 5.72 times |
| 2.22 | 2.44 | 2.13 | 1.82 | 1.66 | 2.05 times |
| | | | | | |
| 8.00 | 7.36 | 7.19 | 7.43 | 7.21 | 7.44 percent |
| 17.8 | 18.0 | 15.3 | 13.6 | 12.0 | 15.3 percent |
| 47.1 | 38.5 | 34.3 | 32.6 | 29.6 | 36.4 percent |

FIGURE 30-2.9 CANDIDATE COMPANY FINANCIAL RATIO ANALYSIS BASED ON HISTORICAL FINANCIAL DATA

| | 19X5 | 19X6 | 19X7 | 19X8 | 19X9 |
|---|---|---|---|---|---|
| Gross Sales | $25,680 | $28,245 | $30,975 | $34,020 | $37,395 |
|   Sales Deductions | 1,680 | 1,845 | 2,025 | 2,220 | 2,445 |
| Net Sales | 24,000 | 26,400 | 28,950 | 31,800 | 34,950 |
|   Cost of Sales | 17,460 | 19,275 | 21,180 | 23,385 | 25,710 |
| Gross Profit | 6,540 | 7,125 | 7,770 | 8,415 | 9,240 |
|   Selling and Administrative | 2,190 | 2,400 | 2,640 | 2,895 | 3,180 |
|   Interest | 870 | 945 | 1,050 | 1,140 | 1,260 |
| Profit Before Taxes | 3,480 | 3,780 | 4,080 | 4,380 | 4,800 |
|   Taxes | 1,740 | 1,890 | 2,040 | 2,190 | 2,400 |
| Profit After Taxes | $ 1,740 | $ 1,890 | $ 2,040 | $ 2,190 | $ 2,400 |

| | |
|---|---|
| Dividends Paid | No longer relevant since all outstanding shares will |
| Earnings Per Share | be acquired by Acquiring Company and all earnings |
| Dividends Per Share | will be consolidated. |

FIGURE 30-2.10 CANDIDATE COMPANY PRO FORMA INCOME STATEMENT FOR THE FISCAL YEARS ENDED JUNE 30th (IN $000)

| ASSETS | 19X5 | 19X6 | 19X7 | 19X8 | 19X9 |
|---|---|---|---|---|---|
| Current Assets | | | | | |
| Cash | $ 1,770 | $ 1,890 | $ 2,055 | $ 2,235 | $ 2,445 |
| Accounts Receivable-Net | 2,520 | 2,775 | 3,045 | 3,345 | 3,675 |
| Inventory | 3,150 | 3,480 | 3,810 | 4,185 | 4,605 |
| Prepaid Expenses | 1,050 | 1,200 | 1,350 | 1,500 | 1,650 |
| Total Current Assets | 8,490 | 9,345 | 10,260 | 11,265 | 12,375 |
| Plant, Property, and Equipment | 11,160 | 12,345 | 13,560 | 14,835 | 16,170 |
| Less Accumulated Depreciation | 6,750 | 7,500 | 8,250 | 9,000 | 9,750 |
| Net Plant, Property, and Equipment | 4,410 | 4,845 | 5,310 | 5,835 | 6,420 |
| Total Assets | $12,900 | $14,190 | $15,570 | $17,100 | $18,795 |
| | | | | | |
| LIABILITIES AND SHAREHOLDERS' EQUITY | | | | | |
| Current Liabilities | | | | | |
| Accounts Payable | $ 1,920 | $ 2,115 | $ 2,310 | $ 2,550 | $ 2,700 |
| Notes Payable | 1,590 | 1,740 | 1,092 | 72 | — |
| Accrued Expenses | 960 | 1,065 | 1,555 | 1,275 | 492 |
| Total Current Liabilities | 4,470 | 4,920 | 4,557 | 3,897 | 3,192 |
| Long-Term Debt | 1,347 | 297 | — | — | — |
| Shareholders' Equity | | | | | |
| Common Stock | 150 | 150 | 150 | 150 | 150 |
| Capital Surplus | 600 | 600 | 600 | 600 | 600 |
| Retained Earnings[1] | 6,333 | 8,223 | 10,263 | 12,453 | 14,853 |
| | 7,083 | 8,973 | 11,013 | 13,203 | 15,603 |
| Total Liabilities and Shareholders' Equity | $12,900 | $14,190 | $15,570 | $17,100 | $18,795 |
| Working Capital | $ 4,020 | $ 4,425 | $ 5,703 | $ 7,368 | $ 9,183 |

[1] No dividends paid after acquisition; for illustrative purposes, profits will be retained by the new, merged firm.

FIGURE 30-2.11  CANDIDATE COMPANY PRO FORMA BALANCE SHEET FOR THE FISCAL YEARS ENDED JUNE 30th (IN $000)

| OPERATING CASH FLOWS | 19X5 | 19X6 | 19X7 | 19X8 | 19X9 |
|---|---|---|---|---|---|
| Net Sales Revenue | $24,000 | $26,400 | $28,950 | $31,800 | $34,950 |
| Changes in Accounts Receivable | ( 120) | ( 255) | ( 270) | 300 | 330 |
| Cash Received from Operations | 23,880 | 26,145 | 28,680 | 31,500 | 34,620 |
| Cost of Sales | ( 17,460) | ( 19,275) | ( 21,180) | ( 23,385) | ( 25,710) |
| Selling and Administrative Expense | ( 2,190) | ( 2,400) | ( 2,640) | ( 2,895) | ( 3,180) |
| Interest Expense | ( 870) | ( 945) | ( 1,050) | ( 1,140) | ( 1,260) |
| Non-Cash Expense | 750 | 750 | 750 | 750 | 750 |
| Change in Inventory | 150 | ( 330) | ( 330) | ( 375) | ( 420) |
| Change in Prepaid Expenses | ( 150) | ( 150) | ( 150) | ( 150) | ( 150) |
| Change in Accounts Payable | 120 | 195 | 195 | 240 | 150 |
| Change in Accrued Expenses | 3 | 105 | 90 | 120 | 783 |
| Cash Disbursed for Operations | ( 19,647) | ( 22,050) | ( 24,315) | ( 26,835) | ( 30,603) |
| Operating Cash Flow Before Taxes | 4,233 | 4,095 | 4,365 | 4,665 | 4,017 |
| Taxes Paid | ( 1,740) | ( 1,890) | ( 2,040) | ( 2,190) | ( 2,400) |
| Net Cash Flow From Operations | 2,493 | 2,205 | 2,325 | 2,475 | 1,617 |
| FINANCIAL CASH FLOWS | | | | | |
| Dividends Paid | — | — | — | — | — |
| Cash Available for Investment | 2,493 | 2,205 | 2,325 | 2,475 | 1,617 |
| Capital Expenditures | ( 660) | ( 1,185) | ( 1,215) | ( 1,275) | ( 1,335) |
| CASH FLOW TO ACQUIRING COMPANY | | | | | |
| Cash Flow Surplus/(Deficit) [1] | $ 1,833 | $ 1,020 | $ 1,110 | $ 1,200 | $ 282 |

[1] Although the Pro Forma Balance Sheet for Candidate Company indicates activity in the long-term and short-term debt accounts for the forecast period, it is assumed that these funds are borrowed from or through (or paid back to or through) the Acquiring Company.

FIGURE 30-2.12 CANDIDATE COMPANY PRO FORMA CASH-FLOW STATEMENT FOR THE FISCAL YEARS ENDED JUNE 30th (IN $000)

$$\text{Present Value of Cash Flows} = \sum_{1}^{n} \frac{\text{cash } t}{(1+d)^t}$$

where:
$t$ represents each respective time period, and
$d$ is the risk-adjusted discount rate.

$$PV = \frac{\$1,833}{(1+.15)^1} + \frac{\$1,020}{(1+.15)^2} + \frac{\$1,110}{(1+.15)^3} + \frac{\$1,200}{(1+.15)^4} + \frac{\$\ 282}{(1+.15)^5}$$

$$= \$1,594 \quad + \quad \$\ 887 \quad + \quad \$\ 965 \quad + \quad \$1,043 \quad + \quad \$\ 245$$

$$PV = \$4,736$$

Actually, the above cash flow was discounted at the rate of 15.0% *compounded monthly*. This is appropriate since cash flow is usually distributed throughout the year, rather than existing only at the end of the year. The following are the present value discount factors for a 15.0% discount rate, compounded monthly and compounded annually:

|  | *discount factor for 15.0% discount rate* | |
| --- | --- | --- |
|  | *compounded monthly*[1] | *compounded annually* |
| Year 1 | .861509 | .869565 |
| Year 2 | .742197 | .756144 |
| Year 3 | .639409 | .647516 |
| Year 4 | .550856 | .571753 |
| Year 5 | .474568 | .497177 |

[1] This method used in above illustration.

FIGURE 30-2.13   CANDIDATE COMPANY DISCOUNTED CASH FLOW (IN $000)

---

DETERMINATION OF "SALVAGE VALUE"

| | |
|---|---:|
| Expected earnings at the end of forecast year five—19X9 (from Figure 30-2.10): | $ 2,400 |
| Risk-adjusted discount rate for future earnings (see Step 13) | 15.0% |
| Future value of an income of $2,400 per year, discounted at 15.0%, at the end of year 19X9: | $2,400 ÷ 15.0% = $16,000 |

Present value of an income flow
discounted back to today (end of 19X4):

$$= \frac{\$16,000}{(1+d)^t} = \frac{\$16,000}{(1+.15)^5} = \$\,7,955$$

Thus, $7,955 represents the "salvage value" or the fair market value of Candidate at the end of 19X9, discounted back to the end of 19X4. Based on the value of the firm as the discounted flow of future earnings, this is what Acquiring Company should be able to sell Candidate for at the end of 19X9 (discounted to 19X4), *ceteris paribus*.

DETERMINATION OF PRESENT VALUE OF THE ACQUISITION

| | | |
|---|---|---|
| Present Value of the Acquisition | = | PV of the forecast cash flow + PV of "salvage" |
| | = | $4,736 (from Figure 30-2.13) + $7,955 |
| | | (from above) |
| Present Value of the Acquisition | = | $12,691 |

---

FIGURE 30-2.14.  CANDIDATE COMPANY DETERMINATION OF "SALVAGE VALUE" AND PRESENT VALUE OF THE ACQUISITION (IN $000)

# APPENDIX 30-3  ILLUSTRATIVE TIMETABLE OF AN ACQUISITION

| *Date* | *Event* |
|---|---|
| January 1 | Buyer's board of directors meets to approve proposed acquisition of seller. |
| January 2 | Seller's board of directors meets to approve proposed acquisition by buyer. |
| January 3-10 | Agreement in principle is drafted by buyer's counsel, reviewed by seller's counsel, and approved by both managements. |
| January 10 | Agreement in principle regarding acquisition is signed by buyer and seller. |
| | Buyer issues press release. |
| | Seller issues press release. |
| January 11 | Buyer's investigating team begins detailed investigation of seller. |
| January 31 | Buyer and its independent auditor conduct physical inventory of seller. |
| February 15 | Buyer's investigating team concludes detailed investigation of seller. |
| February 15-16 | Buyer management decides to continue with investigation, based on results of examination. |
| February 16-20 | Managements of buyer and seller meet to negotiate acquisition price. |
| February 20-25 | Managements of buyer and seller meet with counsel to decide on acquisition terms (e.g., method of payment, tax treatment). |
| February 26 | Seller prepares draft of proxy materials for special meeting of its stockholders. |
| February 28 | Buyer prepares draft of listing application for ASE. |
| March 1 | Buyer and seller officers meet with counsel to review agreement regarding acquisition terms and the draft of proxy materials. |
| March 5 | Special meeting of seller's board of directors to: |
| | 1. Approve the agreement, |
| | 2. Call special stockholders meeting to be held on April 15 to adopt the agreement, and setting record date therefor, and |
| | 3. Approve proxy material and appoint proxies. |
| March 10 | Special meeting of buyer's board of directors to: |
| | 1. Approve the agreement, |

| *Date* | *Event* |
|---|---|
| March 10 | 2. Approve the application for listing additional shares on the ASE, and |
|  | 3. Extend authority of the transfer agent and registrar to cover shares issuable in connection with the acquisition. |
| March 11 | Seller files preliminary proxy materials with SEC. |
| March 12 | Buyer and seller mail joint letter from counsel for buyer and seller to the Commissioner of Internal Revenue requesting tax ruling on the tax aspects of the proposed acquisition. |
| March 15 | Seller obtains SEC comments on proxy material. |
| March 16 | Seller can begin printing definitive copies of proxy materials. |
| March 22 | Seller can mail proxy material to SEC and holders of record of seller's stock. |
| March 23 | Buyer files listing application and supporting documents with ASE regarding additional shares to be issued to acquire seller. |
| April 5 | Seller should mail any follow-up letters deemed advisable to solicit further proxies of seller's stockholders. |
| April 15 | Special meeting of seller's stockholders to take the following action: |
|  | 1. Approve and adopt the acquisition, and |
|  | 2. Authorize such other matters as may be deemed advisable in connection with the acquisition. |
| April 15 | Buyer's counsel notifies ASE of stockholder approval. |
| April 20 | Board of governors of ASE approves listing application pending notice of issuance. |
| May 10 | Buyer and seller receive favorable tax ruling from the IRS. |
| May 15 | Management of buyer and seller meet to sign acquisition contract. |
| May 15 | Buyer issues press release. |

# 31

# Mergers and Acquisitions— Accounting and Tax Problems[1]

*Stanley H. Pantowich*

*Mel Levine*

---

[1] The authors acknowledge with thanks the contribution to this chapter of Stephen L. Key, a partner of Arthur Young & Company.

## INTRODUCTION

One corporation may acquire another through either a nontaxable or a taxable transaction. Within each category, the parties might agree to either a sale of assets or a sale of stock. The controller must evaluate the nontaxable and the taxable routes from both a tax and an accounting perspective. Obviously, the perspective of the controller will vary, depending on whether his corporation is interested in buying or selling. This chapter reviews the various tax and accounting implications that should be considered. In addition, it highlights the key points that particularly concern the corporate controller, regardless of whether he is acting for the buyer or seller. However, this discussion is not meant to be a substitute for consultation at every stage of the acquisition transaction with competent tax counsel, legal counsel, and accountants.

## THE TAX-FREE ACQUISITION

In income tax jargon, the tax-free acquisition is commonly referred to as a *reorganization*. Section 368 of the Internal Revenue Code (IRC) defines six basic categories of reorganization:

1. A statutory merger or consolidation. (This is known as a *type A reorganization*.)
2. The acquisition by a corporation of the stock of another corporation solely in exchange for all or part of its voting stock (or the voting stock of its parent corporation). The acquiring corporation must have control of the second corporation immediately after the acquisition. (This is known as a *type B reorganization*.) For purposes of this section, *control* means 80 percent of voting stock and each other class of stock.
3. The acquisition of substantially all the properties of a corporation in exchange for all or part of the acquirer's voting stock (or the voting stock of its parent corporation). The acquiring corporation must pay solely in voting stock, except that it

may assume liabilities of the acquired corporation, take property subject to liabilities, and under certain circumstances, pay a limited amount of money or other considerations. (This is known as a *type C reorganization.*)

4. A transfer by a corporation of all or part of its assets to another corporation (usually a new corporation), if the transferor, its shareholders (including its former shareholders), or both in combination are in control of the transferee corporation immediately after the transfer. The transaction is tax-free only if the stock or securities of the transferee corporation are distributed under the plan in a transaction that qualifies under Section 354, 355, or 356 of the IRC. (This is known as a *type D reorganization.*)

5. A recapitalization. (This is known as a *type E reorganization.*)

6. A mere change in identity, form, or place of organization, however effected. (This is known as a *type F reorganization.*)

Type A, B, and C reorganizations are commonly referred to as *acquisitive reorganizations.* In each of these types, two separate corporate entities are combined into one common organization (which may be a new corporation formed for the acquisition). Types D, E, and F are not considered acquisitive and are not discussed here. They more commonly involve a corporate separation, a reshuffling of corporate capital structure, or the transfer of a corporation's legal place of organization from one state to another.

## The Type A Acquisition—Buyer's Perspective

A type A reorganization is defined as a statutory merger or consolidation. In a *merger*, two or more corporations are combined into one of the original corporations. A *consolidation*, on the other hand, refers to a combination of two or more corporations into a new corporation. Since this type of reorganization is governed by law, the buyer must be aware that both the assets and liabilities of the acquired corporation are transferred to the acquiring corporation. Subsequent to the merger, the transferor (acquired) corporation no longer exists as a separate legal entity.

**Requisite Equity Interest.** In a type A reorganization (and in types B and C as well) the stockholders of the acquired corporation must have a continuing equity interest in the acquiring corporation. The shareholders of the transferor corporation must, therefore, acquire some interest in the acquiring corporation. Generally, the shareholders of the acquired corporation will *not* receive the requisite equity interest in the acquiring corporation if they receive (1) cash, (2) bonds, (3) an option to take cash or preferred stock, (4) short-term notes, or (5) bonds with voting rights in exchange for their stock interest.

The requisite continuing equity interest is met in a type A reorganization if the shareholders of the acquired corporation receive voting or nonvoting common stock or, alternatively, voting or nonvoting preferred stock. The fact that an exchange of nonvoting stock is permissible in a type A reorganization should be of significant importance to the buyer when he considers this acquisition method.

**Fifty Percent Test.** The requisite interest, discussed above, is commonly referred to as the *continuity-of-interest requirement*. In general, for purposes of obtaining an advance ruling from the Internal Revenue Service (IRS) on a type A reorganization, this continuity-of-interest requirement will be satisfied if the shareholders of the acquired corporation receive stock (voting or nonvoting) equal in value to 50 percent of the value of all the formerly outstanding stock of the acquired corporation. This 50 percent test applies to *total* stock holdings rather than to the stock of each shareholder. However, redemptions that are made either prior or subsequent to the exchange and that are part of the overall plan of reorganization are included in measuring the 50 percent requirement.

Since the continuity-of-interest requirement necessitates that the shareholders of the acquired corporation receive equity equivalent to only 50 percent of the value of all the formerly outstanding stock, their remaining consideration can consist of either cash or debt. Additionally, since the 50 percent test is applied in the aggregate, dissident shareholders can be paid entirely in cash.

**Automatic Transfer.** Another consideration from the buyer's perspective is the ease of transferability of assets. Following formal shareholder approval and the actual exchange of the acquiring corporation's stock for that of the acquired corporation, the remaining mechanical details with respect to transferred assets of the disappearing corporation are automatic. The transfer takes place as of the effective date of the merger "by operation of law."

**Business Purpose Requirement.** In a type A reorganization (as in a type B or C), the transaction must have a bona fide business purpose other than the avoidance of tax.

The IRS applies this business purpose requirement at the corporate level. Moreover, this business purpose requirement (as well as the continuity-of-interest and continuity-of-business-enterprise requirements) generally relates directly to the acquired corporation. However, the courts have been willing on occasion to accept either a corporate or shareholder purpose.

**Satisfying Legal Requirements.** In order to qualify as a type A reorganization, the transaction must be a merger or a consolidation effected pursuant to the corporation laws of the United States, a state or territory, or the District of Columbia. Thus, it is imperative that local state law requirements be satisfied.

## The Type B Acquisition—Buyer's Perspective

A type B reorganization is an acquisition of the stock of a corporation solely in exchange for the voting stock of the acquiring corporation or of a corporation that controls it (i.e., its parent corporation). In a type B reorganization, the acquiring corporation (or its parent corporation) must control the acquired corporation immediately after the exchange. Control consists of 80 percent of the voting stock and 80 percent of each other class of stock. The business purpose test and the continuity-of-business requirement that must be satisfied for a type A reorganization must also be met for a type B.

**Ease of Consummation.** A primary advantage of using a type B reorganization is its relative ease of consummation. This is especially true when the two parties involved are closely held companies. In a type B reorganization, shareholder approval, particularly of the acquiring corporation, is often not required. Moreover, dissenting shareholders are not entitled to appraisal rights. Because of the nature of the type B reorganization, the buyer may avoid the problems associated with the transfer of assets. Further, since under a type B reorganization the target corporation's corporate entity remains intact, a substantial amount of paperwork pertaining to a new corporate entity is eliminated.

**Rigid Stipulations.** As a direct trade-off to this relative ease of consummation is the inflexible criterion that the acquirer must use. The acquisition must be "solely for voting stock," and the IRS interprets this phrase literally. It has consistently taken the position that even the least amount of other consideration will negate a type B reorganization. However, the exchange of cash in lieu of fractional shares, if not separately bargained for, does not disqualify a type B reorganization. (In two recent court cases, the fact that a limited amount of cash was used by the acquiring corporation did not negate the tax-free status of the type B reorganization. However, in both of these cases, notwithstanding the cash involved, 80 percent of the stock of the target corporation was acquired "solely for voting stock.")

**Assumption of Liabilities.** Another business consideration to be weighed in a type B reorganization is that *all* the assets and liabilities of the target corporation are acquired, although the acquiring corporation does not directly assume the liabilities of the target. Rather, the liabilities remain with the target corporation in a new parent-subsidiary relationship. Nevertheless, the ultimate accountability for the liabilities rests with the acquiror.

**Multiple Transactions.** As previously noted, the continuity-of-interest requirement in a type B reorganization is 80 percent. That is, one corporation, by issuing only voting stock, must acquire 80 percent or more of the voting stock of another corporation. The acquiring corporation does not have to meet the 80 percent control requirement solely for voting stock in one transaction. However, the acquisition that brings it to the 80 percent mark *must* be solely for voting stock. Previous acquisitions, if totally unrelated, could even have been made for cash. Additionally, even if pursuant to a single plan, a type B reorganization may encompass a series of acquisitions.

The following example clarifies these latter points. ABC Corporation purchased 25 percent of the stock of XYZ Corporation for cash in 1970. In 1979, ABC, pursuant to a single plan, acquired in two separate transactions an additional 55 percent of the stock of XYZ in exchange solely for its voting stock. The 1979 exchange is tax-free, since ABC has 80 percent control of XYZ immediately after the exchange. Additionally, any subsequent acquisition of XYZ stock by ABC solely in exchange for voting stock of ABC would be tax-free.

The buyer must exercise a great deal of care in situations in which part of the stock of the target corporation is acquired for cash, and soon thereafter additional stock is acquired in a transaction that is intended by the parties to qualify as a type B reorganization. If the IRS were to apply the step-transaction doctrine, the B reorganization would be negated, and the transaction would be taxable.

In general, the *step-transaction doctrine* is essentially a substance-over-form analysis. It assumes that two or more steps are really related and should be combined as a single transaction. Recent activity by the courts (e.g., *Reeves*, 71 T.C. 69) has eroded the use of the step-transaction doctrine, but the prudent planner will take note of the possible implications of its application.

### The Type C Acquisition—Buyer's Perspective

In a type C reorganization, one corporation acquires *substantially all* the properties of another corporation (and assumes its liabilities) in exchange for all or part of the voting stock of the acquiring corporation or its parent. As discussed below, cash may be given under certain circumstances.

In contrast to either a type A or B reorganization, the acquiring corporation in a type C reorganization becomes responsible for only specified liabilities of the target corporation. In both types A and B the acquiring corporation, either directly or indirectly, becomes responsible for all the acquired corporation's liabilities. In a type C reorganization, the acquiring corporation can specifically negotiate for the named assets it wishes to acquire. The leeway given an acquiring corporation in a type C reorganization to "pick and choose" specified assets and liabilities is an important consideration.

**Voting Stock Requirement.** Under a type C reorganization (and in a type B, as well) the acquiring corporation must issue *voting stock* in exchange for "substantially all the properties" of the target company. However, if at least 80 percent of the fair market value of all the property (not just the acquired property) of the other corporation is acquired solely for voting stock, the balance of the property may then be acquired for cash or other property without disqualifying the transaction as a type C reorganization. If cash or other property is transferred together with voting stock, any liabilities assumed or to which the acquired property is subject will also be counted as other property in applying the 80 percent test. But such liabilities by themselves will not violate the solely-for-voting-stock requirement (i.e., the 80 percent test), regardless of the amount.

Again, an example should be helpful. ABC Corporation has assets with a gross fair market value of $1 million. It also has liabilities of $100,000. XYZ Corporation acquires $960,000 worth of the assets, which are subject to liabilities of

$100,000. In exchange for these assets, XYZ issues voting stock, assumes the $100,000 of liabilities, and pays $60,000 in cash. This transaction qualifies as a type C reorganization because at least 80 percent of the fair market value of all the assets of ABC ($800,000) were acquired solely for voting stock. However, if the assets of ABC were instead subject to $300,000 in liabilities, an acquisition of all the assets subject to the liabilities could be a type C reorganization only if no cash is given. Since the liabilities alone are 30 percent of the fair market value of the assets of ABC, any cash given in the exchange would disqualify the transaction. The liabilities are not counted unless cash or other property is used in part payment for the assets.

A few fine points should be noted. It has been held (*Helvering v. Southwest Consolidated Corp.*, 42 USTC 9248) that if the acquiring corporation assumes any liability whose exact nature and amount is "fixed and determined" in the reorganization, assumption of the liability may be considered equivalent to a payment of cash. Thus, if other liabilities were assumed and they exceeded 20 percent in value of the transferor's assets, the reorganization would be taxable. For example, the assumption of a liability to pay dissenters is treated as the payment of cash. However, the IRS has ruled that the assumption of liabilities for bona fide reorganization expenses of the acquired corporation for its shareholders will not violate the solely-for-voting-stock requirement of a type C reorganization (nor of a type B).

**Defining "Substantially All."** In a type C reorganization, "substantially all the properties" of the target company must be transferred to the acquiring corporation. The IRS has defined "substantially all" to mean:

1. At least 90 percent of the fair market value of the net assets; and
2. At least 70 percent of the fair market value of the gross assets of the transferor corporation at the date of the exchange.

For example, consider a target corporation with assets having a fair market value of $150,000 that are subject to $50,000 in liabilities. If the acquiring corporation exchanges its voting stock for assets of the target company with a fair market value of $100,000 (i.e., the net worth of the target), the transaction would not qualify as a type C transaction under the 90/70 percent test. Although the acquiring corporation received 100 percent of the net assets of the company, it only received 67 percent of the gross assets of the transferor corporation. Note that the transaction might still meet the substantially-all requirement pursuant to Rev. Rul. 57-518, 1957-2 C.B. 255. Under this ruling, the IRS indicated that the substantially all requirement of 368(a)(1)(C) would be met if assets are retained by the transferor corporation solely to meet its existing liabilities. But even under this alternative, if the percentage of gross assets transferred is too low, the transaction would not qualify.

The 90/70 percent test is IRS policy only, and does not bind the courts. The courts consider all the underlying facts of any particular case, including the nature of the assets transferred and retained and whether the liabilities of the business are assumed by the transferee or are to be paid out of the assets retained by the transferor. Nevertheless, from a planning perspective, it is wise to try to meet the safe harbor rules established by the IRS.

### Triangular Acquisition

A triangular acquisition (also known as a *subsidiary A merger*) involves a transfer of assets to, or an acquisition by, a subsidiary. In a triangular type A reorganization, the acquiring corporation is permitted to transfer all or part of the assets acquired into a controlled subsidiary without affecting the tax-free status of the transaction. The triangular acquisition or merger is really just a variation of the type A technique, in that assets of an acquired corporation are transferred directly to the acquiror's subsidiary in exchange for stock of the parent. This is in direct contrast to a normal type A reorganization, in which all the assets and liabilities are merged into the acquiring corporation.

A prime business consideration in deciding whether to take advantage of a triangular acquisition is the fact that (as in the type B or C reorganization) the shareholders of the acquiring corporation do not have to approve the transaction. Compare this with a straightforward type A reorganization, in which such shareholder approval is a prerequisite to the acquisition.

**Similar Requirements.** In most respects, the requirements for a subsidiary A merger are similar to those of a standard type A reorganization. Therefore, either voting or nonvoting stock may be used, the 50 percent continuity-of-interest test must be met, and the merger must be effected in conformity with local law.

Note that in a subsidiary A merger, the transaction will qualify for tax-free treatment even though under the plan of reorganization the parent corporation assumed some of the liabilities of the acquired corporation and the subsidiary assumes the remaining liabilities.

In a subsidiary A merger, *only* the stock of the parent corporation may be used in the exchange. If the acquiring corporation (i.e., the subsidiary) uses both stock of the parent and its own stock, the tax-free status will be negated.

One further technical requirement exists in a subsidiary A merger. Similar to a type C reorganization, the acquiring corporation must acquire "substantially all the properties" of the acquired corporation. The phrase "substantially all the properties" has the same meaning in this context that it has in a type C reorganization. Thus, 90 percent of the fair market value of the net assets and 70 percent of the fair market value of the gross assets must be acquired by the subsidiary.

Note that following a subsidiary A merger of an acquired corporation into a subsidiary, the subsidiary is free to transfer the newly acquired assets into a second-tier controlled subsidiary. This will not negate the tax-free status of the acquisition.

In planning a subsidiary A merger, it is important (as with all reorganizations) not to trigger the step-transaction doctrine. In such cases, the parties to the reorganization might receive some unexpected results.

**Treatment of Tax Attributes.** A subsidiary A merger is intended to achieve a similar result to that of merging an acquiring corporation into a parent corporation and then having the parent transfer the assets and liabilities of the acquired corporation to a controlled subsidiary. However, there may be substantive tax differences between those two alternatives.

In a direct merger into a parent corporation, the tax attributes of the acquired corporation pass to the parent. These attributes include net operating losses (limited to certain conditions), potential investment tax credit recapture, charitable contribution and investment tax credit carryforwards, earnings and profits, and so on. However, on subsequent transfer of the acquired properties to the controlled subsidiary, some of the acquired tax attributes may not be passed along. For example, if not pursuant to a single plan of reorganization, the previously acquired earnings and profits will remain with the parent on subsequent transfer of the acquired assets to its controlled subsidiary. In a subsidiary A merger, on the other hand, *all* the tax attributes of the acquired corporation are passed directly to the subsidiary.

### Reverse Triangular Acquisition

In a reverse triangular acquisition, a controlled subsidiary is merged into the acquired corporation. Again, the stock of the parent corporation is used as the medium of exchange. This type of acquisition is generally referred to as a *reverse subsidiary A merger*.

When this method is utilized, the legal corporate existence of the acquired company remains after the transaction is completed. This can be an important consideration if the acquired corporation has certain rights (e.g., easements) and/or licenses (e.g., government) that might prove troublesome to transfer. Additionally, grandfather rights of an acquired corporation are not lost in a reverse subsidiary A merger as they would be in a type A or C reorganization.

**Similarities With Subsidiary A Mergers.** The shareholders of the acquiring company in a reverse subsidiary A merger do not have to approve the acquisition. Another similarity is that in both types of mergers, all the assets and liabilities of the acquired corporation are assumed.

Following completion of the reverse subsidiary A merger, the acquired surviving company must hold "substantially all the properties" of the former subsidiary. Accordingly, the surviving corporation must meet the previously discussed 90/70 percent test established by the IRS.

**An Important Difference.** Despite the similarities between the reverse and straightforward subsidiary A mergers, there is one significant technical difference: In a reverse subsidiary A merger, the parent corporation must acquire control of the acquired corporation in exchange solely for its voting stock. This requirement brings into play the 80 percent continuity-of-interest test. The parent corporation, by issuing only voting stock, must acquire 80-percent-or-more control of another corporation. Although the parent does not have to meet the 80 percent requirement in one transaction, the acquisition that brings the parent's control to the 80 percent level must be in exchange solely for voting stock if the transaction is to maintain its tax-free status.

### Seller's Perspective

It is obvious that the seller must carefully weigh all the considerations that a buyer takes into account in any prospective tax-free reorganization. However, the seller must also decide the amount of continuing participation it wishes to have in the new business. The controller, whose function is central to the everyday affairs of the selling company, has a critical role in shaping the ultimate form of the transaction.

Specifically, the seller must decide:

1. Whether it wants to receive all stock or part stock and part cash in the tax-free exchange;
2. Whether it will accept continued responsibility for all or some of the liabilities of the corporation or, alternatively, prefers to "bail out" from them; and
3. Whether it wants to receive voting or nonvoting stock.

The first consideration directly affects the amount of control the shareholders of the acquired company will have in the new business. Clearly, the greater the amount of cash tendered, the less control the acquiree's shareholders will have in the surviving entity. However, the seller may require this cash for a variety of reasons (e.g., to pay off existing liabilities or as an incentive to win shareholder approval). The second consideration, "bailing out" from liabilities, is usually a one-sided dilemma. Under most circumstances, the seller prefers to rid itself of previously incurred liabilities. However, if for some reason it does not wish to or cannot avoid a specific liability, it should select the ultimate transaction method carefully. The third consideration, acceptance of voting versus nonvoting stock, also affects control.

Each acquisitive reorganization carries its own particular attributes, and is suitable in different circumstances and situations. After the parties to an exchange agree on the consideration and its form, they must find the best type of reorganization for their purposes. Failure to choose the appropriate type might subvert the intent of the parties.

Figure 31.1 summarizes the provisions of the five types of acquisitive tax-free reorganizations in terms of these selling considerations.

## TAXABLE ACQUISITIONS

A taxable acquisition of a corporation may be accomplished either through the purchase of assets or the purchase of stock. The following sections will analyze the key aspects of these alternatives.

| Consideration | A | B | C | Subsidiary A Merger | Reverse Subsidiary A Merger |
|---|---|---|---|---|---|
| 1. Amount of cash permitted with stock | 50%[a] | 20%[b] | 20%[c] | 50%[a] | 20% |
| 2. Specific liabilities can remain with seller | NO | NO | YES | NO | NO |
| 3. Nonvoting stock permitted | YES | NO | NO | YES | NO |

[a] The IRS has ruled that amount of cash cannot be greater than 50%.

[b] The IRS has ruled that no cash may be received.

[c] Assuming no liabilities are assumed.

FIGURE 31.1  SELLING CONSIDERATIONS FOR ACQUISITIVE TAX-FREE REORGANIZATIONS

## Acquisition of Assets—Buyer's Perspective

**Allocation of Purchase Price.**  A primary factor in an asset acquisition is that the tax basis of the assets are generally "stepped-up" to reflect their fair market at the time of acquisition.  IRS regulations require that the total purchase price paid by the buyer be allocated among the individual assets.  As a general rule, the purchase price is allocated to individual assets on the basis of relative fair market values.  However, in a number of cases assets have been allocated on the basis of the mutual agreement of both the buyer and seller conducting negotiations at arm's length.  The rationale that permits this method of allocation is that the interests of the respective negotiating parties are adverse.

The allocation of the purchase price among the assets is critical to both the buyer and seller.  From a planning perspective, the buyer wants to allocate the highest possible amount to ordinary income items such as inventory and accounts receivable.  High allocations will also be sought for depreciable assets, especially those that are susceptible to quick write-offs.  Alternatively, the buyer will seek the lowest possible allocation to assets such as goodwill or a franchise agreement, since assets of this nature are not subject to any write-offs.  (Note that the IRS may attempt to allocate a portion of the purchase price to nondepreciable going-concern value if the acquired assets have been enhanced from their presence as part of an integrated and established business operation.  This going-concern value has also been allocated by the IRS in a Section 334(b)(2) situation, discussed below.  See *Black Industries Inc.*, T.C.M. 1979-61; *VGS Corp.*, 68 T.C. 563.)

The seller will want to allocate the lowest possible amount to items such as covenants not to compete, since any gain recognized on them will be ordinary.

Additionally, the seller will also want to allocate a low purchase price to depreciable assets. The lower the allocation to depreciable assets, the lower the potential recapture of depreciation upon disposition.

**Unwanted Assets and Liabilities.** When the buyer considers an asset acquisition, it is also concerned with the ability to leave behind any or all of the liabilities of the acquired company. As a general rule, the buyer is protected from any preacquisition business liabilities that are not specifically assumed. However, the buyer must comply with the appropriate state Bulk Sales Act in order to ensure this protection.

In the course of an asset acquisition, the buyer can also leave behind any unwanted assets. Obviously, this is a significant advantage from a practical business viewpoint, since assets that are either outdated (e.g., modern technology has superseded them) or duplicative (e.g., the buyer might already have sufficient warehouse space and have no need for the seller's warehouse) can be left out of the negotiations.

**Recapture Costs.** The buyer has a distinct advantage in an asset acquisition in the area of *recapture*. Simply put, recapture involves the recognition of gain on the sale of depreciable property as ordinary income to the extent of previous deductions for depreciation. Since this gain would be subject to capital gain rates in the absence of the recapture rules, the imposition of these rules can be costly.

In a taxable acquisition of assets, the seller pays the tax on the recapture of depreciation. Under certain circumstances, this consideration alone may strongly motivate the buyer to require that the transaction take the form of an asset acquisition. Similarly, in an asset acquisition, the seller is also burdened with the costs of any investment tax credit recapture. It should be understood that these potential tax burdens of the seller have to be considered in negotiating the acquisition price. If the incremental tax brackets of the buyer and seller are unequal, there are opportunities for negotiating an advantage for both sides.

**Recognition of Dividend Income.** A recent advantage to the buyer arising from a taxable acquisition of assets resulted from the passage of the Tax Reform Act of 1976. Prior to this act, the selling corporation could avoid recognition of any dividends from a controlled foreign corporation by selling the stock of the foreign corporation to the acquiring corporation and then liquidating under Section 337 (one-year liquidation). Now if the selling corporation sells the stock of a controlled foreign corporation in a transaction to which Section 337 applies, the selling corporation must recognize as dividend income an amount equal to the excess of the fair market value of the stock of the foreign corporation over its basis, to the extent of the earnings and profits of the foreign corporation that were accumulated after 1962. The tax payable on the dividend income will be reduced by "deemed paid" foreign tax credits. If the transaction is a taxable stock acquisition, the seller is able to totally divorce itself from any dividend consequences on tendering the stock. The buyer inherits the problem.

Along similar lines, in an asset acquisition, the seller is left with the ultimate tax burden that arises from disposing of a Domestic International Sales Corporation (the tax on the untaxed portion of prior year's income). In a taxable stock acquisition, on the other hand, the ultimate tax liability is shifted to the buyer. LIFO reserves are similarly treated for acquisitions occurring after 1981.

**Investment Incentive.** A taxable acquisition of assets provides a certain degree of investment incentive. A purchaser of investment credit property is entitled to take up to $100,000 worth of used property into account in calculating the allowable credit. Assuming that the property has at least a seven-year useful life, the buyer will have a $10,000 tax credit. In an asset acquisition, the buyer may also be entitled to *bonus depreciation*. If the buyer acquires new or used depreciable personal property with a useful life of six years or more, an additional 20 percent depreciation deduction is permitted in the first year. This additional deduction is limited to $2,000. Although the tax savings generated by the potential bonus depreciation and the investment tax credit is small, it should not be ignored, especially by smaller businesses.

**Noncarryover of Tax Attributes.** In an asset acquisition, there is no carryover of tax attributes. This means that the possibility of carrying over any net operating loss is forfeited to the detriment of the buyer. However, this negative factor is mitigated because the opportunity to carry over a loss has been severely limited. (This subject is discussed later in this chapter.) On the positive side, earnings and profits of the acquired corporation will not be carried over to the acquiring corporation. In addition, the buyer can reevaluate such factors as accounting methods, useful lives of depreciable assets, and new methods of inventory accounting.

### Acquisition of Stock—Buyer's Perspective

An important factor influencing the buyer in a stock acquisition is the flexibility it permits in acquiring the stock of the target company. The purchaser can attain only partial ownership. This can be significant under circumstances where the purchaser may be able to effectively control the acquired company through a relatively small amount of stock ownership. As a general rule, the tax consequences to the buyer in the taxable acquisition of the acquired company's stock are less desirable than in a taxable asset acquisition. Some specific differences in tax consequences are discussed below.

**Assumption of Liabilities.** In an outright purchase of stock, the buyer acquires the existing entity, complete with all its liabilities. This is significant if the acquired company has known and unknown contingent liabilities. Care must be exercised to avoid "buying a lawsuit." When negotiating a stock purchase, the buyer should try to obtain *covenants of indemnity* from the seller that protect him from an unfavorable disposition of the contingent liabilities. However, even with these covenants, an asset acquisition has a clear advantage over stock acquisition in that, under the former method, the purchaser may be able to completely divorce itself from any or all liabilities.

**Basis Considerations.** In the taxable stock acquisition, the purchaser receives a cost basis in the *stock* that he acquires. This means that the buyer's cost basis in the stock is *not* reflected in the individual basis of the assets that are in the hands of the corporation. To the contrary, the corporate entity completely "shelters" the corporate assets from the transfer of stock. In an asset acquisition, however, the buyer's cost is immediately reflected in the basis of the assets held by the corporation. This particular attribute of a stock acquisition means that fair market value of the underlying assets of the acquired company may not be realistically reflected with this type of transaction.

Consider the following example. ABC Corporation has a tax basis of $100,000 in its underlying assets. X purchases the stock of ABC for $500,000, its fair market value. Following the acquisition, X will have a $500,000 cost basis in the stock of ABC. However, the basis of ABC's assets will remain $100,000. Accordingly, X will have no opportunity to write off $400,000 of the purchase price through depreciation. Additionally, in computing gain or loss on the sale of any of the individual assets, the true purchase price of the assets will not be considered.

The buyer should be aware that the above principle can sometimes work to its advantage. If in the above illustration the tax basis of the assets was $500,000 and the cost of the stock was $100,000 (the result, for example, of a history of losses), the purchaser might be entitled to a "windfall" (assuming the principal purpose of the acquisition was not the avoidance of income taxes). Specifically, he would have the opportunity to write off through depreciation deductions up to $400,000 of basis he did not pay for.

**Liquidation of the Controlled Subsidiary.** If the acquiring company does not want to operate the acquired company as its subsidiary, but would rather operate the business under its own corporate form, a *step-up in basis* can be achieved.

To do so, the newly acquired subsidiary would have to be liquidated pursuant to IRC Sections 332 and 334(b)(2) (hereafter referred to only as Section 334(b)(2)). Under this method of liquidation, the assets of the purchased subsidiary would be adjusted to reflect the purchase price of the stock. In order to qualify to use Section 334(b)(2), the following requirements must be met:

1. Eighty percent of the subsidiary's stock must be purchased within a twelve-month period; *and*
2. The plan to liquidate the subsidiary must be adopted within two years of the date when the 80 percent stock control was acquired.

If the requirements are met, the cost basis of the stock is allocated among the assets that are distributed in liquidation according to their respective fair market values. At first glance, the results attained with a Section 334(b)(2) liquidation appear identical to those achieved with an asset acquisition; however, there are two critical differences.

First, under an asset acquisition, there is some flexibility in the allocation of basis. Specifically, the IRS is often willing to accept allocation based on an arm's-length negotiation. Under Section 334(b)(2), no such flexibility exists. Rather, relative fair market values are the sole determining factors.

Second, the recapture of any depreciation or investment tax credits would be triggered on liquidation under Section 334(b)(2). Although this latter tax burden would fall directly on the subsidiary (the parent does not recognize any gain on the liquidation of a controlled subsidiary) it would indirectly become the liability of the purchaser, since it owns the liquidated company. The buyer would also bear the ultimate tax burden that would arise on liquidation of a subsidiary as a result of the disposition of the stock of a controlled foreign corporation or a DISC. Similarly, income equal to a LIFO inventory reserve would be triggered in a liquidation occurring after 1981.

Clearly, there are a variety of differences between an asset acquisition and a stock acquisition followed by liquidation of the controlled subsidiary pursuant to Section 334(b)(2).

**No Investment Credit.** The previous section dealing with an asset acquisition discussed the availability of limited investment incentives and noncarryover of tax attributes. In a stock acquisition, the relevant consideration in these respective areas are completely reversed. Specifically, there are no investment incentives, and the corporate tax history of the former business carries over to the new enterprise. The buyer must consider the possibility of contingent tax liabilities arising from an examination of the corporation's prior tax returns.

**Nonassignable Rights.** Despite the relative disadvantages of a taxable acquisition of stock as opposed to the acquisition of assets, one factor exists that may compel use of the former method. Conceivably, a corporation might have a valuable *nonassignable* legal right. For instance, the corporation may have an easement over a valuable piece of land or equitable title to a franchise. A stock acquisition might be the only available means of effectively transferring these nonassignable rights.

### Sale of Assets—Seller's Perspective

**Bargaining Considerations.** A significant drawback to a seller in any prospective sale of assets is that the seller is burdened with any preacquisition liabilities that are not specifically assumed by the buyer. In addition, since the legal entity (i.e., the corporation) survives a sale of assets, the seller has to reckon with any contingent liabilities that eventually materialize. Thus, the seller must enter the negotiations determined to pass along to the buyer as many liabilities as it can.

The seller must also enter negotiations intent on allocating as much of the purchase price as possible to items such as goodwill, and nondepreciable assets such as land. At the other end of the transaction, the buyer will be trying to shift the weight of the allocation towards inventory, accounts receivable, and depreciable assets. The buyer's success could prove to be costly to the seller.

**Seller's Special Tax Problems.** With the sale of assets, the corporate entity will survive. Accordingly, the seller must decide whether to liquidate the corporate shell or maintain its existence. Either alternative imposes special tax problems that must be considered by the seller.

As a general rule, the sale of assets by a corporation is a taxable event. Additionally, the liquidation of a corporation is also a taxable event. Thus, without the aid of a statutory exception, the sale of assets by a corporation followed by the liquidation and distribution of the sales proceeds to the shareholders would result in a double tax. However, the seller can avoid this double tax if the requirements of IRC Section 337 (one-year liquidation) are met. The tax, with certain exceptions, will then be imposed only at the shareholder level, and usually at capital gain rates.

In order to qualify under Section 337, the seller must meet the following requirements:

1. It must adopt a liquidation plan prior to the date of any sale of assets. The plan must authorize the distribution of all the corporation's assets in redemption of its stock.
2. All the assets of the selling corporation must be distributed within a twelve-month period beginning with the date of adoption of the liquidation plan.
3. Notice of the Section 337 liquidation must be filed with the district tax director.

If the requirements of Section 337 are met, the tax, subject to the exceptions noted below, will be imposed only on the shareholders. Note that these general exceptions can be either statutory or nonstatutory. In either case, however, the result will be the same—a tax will be imposed on both the corporation and the shareholder.

*Statutory exceptions.* The recapture of depreciation, whether it pertains to personal or real property, overrides the nonrecognition provision of Section 337. This depreciation will be recaptured at ordinary income rates. Similarly, if assets are sold prior to the end of their investment credit lives, the seller is required to repay investment tax credits. As previously noted, the seller of stock of a controlled foreign corporation can no longer use Section 337 to avoid nonrecognition of gain. The seller is now required to recognize as a dividend an amount generally equal to the gain on the sale but not exceeding the amount of undistributed earnings of the foreign corporation after 1962. In addition, previously deferred income of a DISC will have to be recaptured. (Note that although Section 337 provides for the nonrecognition of gain on the sale of inventory, this sale must take place in one transaction and to one person. Thus, the piecemeal sale of inventory *will* result in gain to the selling corporation.) However, for sales of inventory occurring after 1981, income attributable to the LIFO reserve will be triggered.

*Nonstatutory exceptions.* There are two broad categories of nonstatutory exceptions. First, the IRS generally takes the position that items previously expensed by the seller must be restored to income. Thus, items such as supplies, whose cost was previously deducted by the taxpayer, will have to be brought back into income. This restoration is based on what is commonly referred to as the *tax benefit theory*. A second category is subject to an IRS ruling whose ultimate disposition is still unclear. In this exceptions category, any reserve for bad debts set up by the seller will generally have to be restored to income. This ruling, however, is not beyond debate. There is some support for the position that receivables that are sold at net value (face value less reserve), as opposed to face value, should not result in any income. One solution is to wipe out or reduce the reserve by actual write-offs of doubtful accounts. Of course, such write-offs would have to be supported by evidence of worthlessness.

*Installment sale treatment.* Sellers of assets may effectively use the installment sale method for reporting income. In effect, gain is only taxed when cash is received. Recent legislative changes have given great flexibility to this technique. For example, a seller receiving 50 percent cash and "paper" for the balance of the selling price will recognize 50 percent of the gain immediately and the balance will be recognized when cash is received for the paper. The paper must provide for a minimum rate of interest (currently 6 percent), or a portion of the gain will be converted to interest income under the imputed interest rules of Section 483. Third party guarantees of the paper, such as bank letters of credit, will not disqualify the deferral; use of cash escrow agreements to secure the paper would have to be carefully designed to avoid immediate taxation of the paper. Contingent sales prices may be structured using the installment sale technique. For example, a deal could be struck that payment will consist of a fixed cash payment (either paid currently, deferred, or a combination thereof) and a contingent amount based on a percentage of the next three years' earnings. In fact, the whole of the purchase price could be based on contingencies. Again, gain is recognized only when cash is received.

**Retaining the Corporate Shell.** The seller can also decide to retain the corporate shell following the sale of the assets. Retaining the corporate entity is attractive in many cases, since the potential gain to be recognized by the shareholders on liquidation can be deferred until a more suitable time.

Consider the following example. X, the sole shareholder of ABC Corporation, has a $10,000 cost basis in the stock of the corporation. ABC has a cost basis in its assets of $100,000. ABC sells its assets to Y Corporation for $100,000. ABC recognizes no gain on the sale, since the selling price of the assets is equal to ABC's basis. However, if ABC were to liquidate the corporation following the sale, X would recognize a $90,000 gain (probably capital). By keeping the corporate entity in existence, X can defer the ultimate gain until a more suitable time (e.g., when X has a capital loss available). Thus, X can continue to earn income on the deferred tax.

If the assets are retained in the corporation, there is a good possibility that the corporation will become a personal holding company. In that case, in the years following the sale the corporation would be subject to the personal holding company surtax of 70 percent (in addition to the normal corporate tax) on undistributed personal holding company income. However, this tax burden can be substantially reduced through careful planning. First, if all personal holding company income is distributed currently, the 70 percent surtax will be avoided. Second, if the bulk of the corporation's investments are in domestic dividends, the normal effective corporate tax rate will be reduced to a minimum. This reduction is the result of the interplay of the corporate surtax exemption and the 85 percent dividend exclusion available to corporations.

Consider the following example. ABC Corporation receives $5 million from the sale of its assets. The sale proceeds are not distributed to its shareholders. Rather, the money is invested in securities that earn 10 percent. During the year, ABC has dividend income of $500,000 (personal holding company income), which it intends to distribute to its shareholders. Accordingly, the 70 percent personal holding company surtax is avoided. With respect to the normal corporate tax, 85 percent of the dividend income is nontaxable (IRC Section 243). The balance, $75,000, although included in taxable income, is taxed at the lowest rates. Accordingly, using 1980 tax rates, ABC's tax is $16,750. This is an effective tax rate of 3.35 percent ($16,750 ÷ $500,000). The highest effective rate on dividend income would be 6.9 percent (15 percent × 46 percent).

Note that in a taxable sale of assets or, alternatively, in a liquidation under Section 337, the seller is going to be saddled with paying the tax on recaptures. This aspect alone may compel the seller to seek another route or negotiate a better price.

### Sale of Stock—Seller's Perspective

**Advantages of Stock Sale to Seller.** As a general rule, a taxable sale of stock will have much more to offer the seller than will a taxable sale of assets.

*Liabilities bail-out.* Perhaps the biggest advantage to the seller is its ability to "bail out" of all responsibilities for liabilities. On selling the stock of the company, the seller passes all the underlying liabilities to the purchaser. For example, in a manufacturing company, there may be a significant number of warranties outstanding. Alternatively, in a service-oriented corporation, service commitments may still have to be fulfilled. In addition, pension plan liabilities, actual and contingent, may be very large; and outstanding tax liabilities or contingent liabilities can be significant. All such liabilities would be passed along to the purchaser of the stock. Obviously, in the negotiations, the buyer will seek covenants of indemnity from the seller in order to protect himself from unforeseen liabilities. However, even these covenants may prove to be unsatisfactory if the seller becomes financially insecure subsequent to the sale or negotiates a limit on its covenant, either in amount, or time, or both.

*Shifting recapture taxes to purchaser.* Another significant advantage to the seller in a stock sale is his ability to shift the payment of the recapture taxes to the buyer. The buyer will normally consider such taxes in his negotiations, but the possibility of a saving for both sides exists. This is especially true if the buyer intends to retain the assets until the end of their useful lives.

**Recognition of Capital Gain or Loss.** As a general rule, the gain (loss) recognized by the seller in a stock sale will usually be capital gain (loss). The gain (loss) recognized will be measured by the difference between the sales price and the seller's basis in its stock (usually cost). There are, however, some general exceptions to this rule. Ordinary income (or loss) will be recognized:

1. When consideration is received for management or consulting services.
2. When consideration is received for a covenant not to compete (but only if separately bargained for and clearly severable from goodwill).
3. On the sale of certain preferred stock (Section 306 stock). This exception will not be triggered in a complete termination of a shareholder's interest.
4. On the sale of a collapsible corporation (Section 341).

**Installment Sale Provisions.** If only cash is tendered in the exchange, the seller will recognize its total gain or loss in the year of the sale. However, if gain is to be recognized by the seller and the purchase price is to be paid out in installments, then such gain will be recognized only upon receipt of each installment unless otherwise elected. (The installment method is discussed in detail earlier in this chapter.)

## VARIATIONS OF TECHNIQUE

### Contingent Stock

Because of the uncertainties regarding the value of the acquiree that traditionally surround any corporate acquisition or merger, the parties may want to review the transaction after a period of time. They may retain this opportunity through a contingent stock arrangement.

Contingent stock is shares issued by the buyer to the acquired corporation when a specified contingency (subsequent condition) occurs after the transaction is consummated. As a general rule, the tax-free status of a reorganization will not be affected by utilizing contingent stock, if the following requirements are met:

1. All the contingent stock must be issued within five years from the date of reorganization. If the reorganization involves a series of exchanges, the stock must then be issued within five years of the initial exchange.

2. There is a valid business reason for using contingent stock. The IRS has ruled that a valid reason exists if, for example, there is difficulty in valuation and if the acquired corporation has substantial contingent liabilities.

3. The plan of reorganization states the maximum number of contingent shares that can be issued.

4. At least 50 percent of the maximum number of shares of each class of stock are issued in the initial distribution.

5. The contingency agreement is made expressly nonassignable, nonnegotiable, and nonmarketable, except by operation of law.

6. The acquired corporation's stockholders may only receive additional stock of the acquiring corporation or its parent. In other words, any accrued dividends on the contingent stock can only be paid in stock. Further, any interest that may come due must also be paid in stock. Such additional stock is counted in computing the 50 percent rule.

Although contingent stock arrangements can give rise to imputed interest, this interest does not constitute "boot," which would destroy the tax-free status of the reorganization. If the parties provide for interest at the specified minimum interest rate, the imputed interest rules can be avoided.

If a contingent stock arrangement is outstanding when the first acquiring company is in turn absorbed by another corporation, the stock of the new corporation cannot be substituted for the original contingent stock obligation. The problems posed by such a future reorganization can be avoided if the original plan of reorganization provides for an accelerated settlement of the contingent obligation before the subsequent transaction occurs.

One further point should be made. The pooling-of-interests method may not be used for a contingent stock arrangement that is related to specified earnings over a period of years or on a guarantee of the fair market value of the buyer's stock. In a type B or C reorganization, the contingent stock, when issued, must possess voting rights.

### Escrowed Shares

Instead of agreeing to issue contingent stock, the buyer may place the shares in escrow and arrange for the escrow agent to transfer them to the shareholders of the acquired corporation if specified conditions are satisfied by a designated date. If the condition remains unsatisfied, the escrow agent will return the shares.

The escrow arrangement is particularly useful under certain circumstances, because it is not subject to the stringent conditions required by a contingent stock arrangement. For example, if the acquired company has a shaky earnings history, the acquiring corporation may not feel comfortable making an initial distribution of 50 percent of the maximum shares, a requirement that does not exist in an escrow arrangement.

There is no five-year-issuance requirement for escrowed stock, since escrowed stock is considered issued when it is actually deposited in escrow. In a contingent stock arrangement, the stock is not considered to be issued until actually transferred to the sellers. An escrowed stock arrangement must grant the right to vote the stock if it is issued in a type B or C reorganization or in a reverse subsidiary A merger. (The stock issued in a type A reorganization or a subsidiary A merger need not carry voting rights.) This deemed issuance also dictates that the escrowed stock must carry with it the right of the escrowed shareholders to receive dividends. Since the stock is considered issued when deposited into escrow, the imputed interest rules are not applicable.

If the escrowed shares are forfeited as the result of a failure to attain the specified conditions, no gain or loss should result to either party if the shares are returned at their original purchase price. On repossession, the parties have not received any benefit or detriment from the change in value of these escrowed shares.

Note that the use of escrowed shares may be allowed under certain limited circumstances in conjunction with the pooling-of-interests method.

## AVAILABILITY OF NET OPERATING LOSSES

In any acquisition or merger, whether it be taxable or nontaxable, an important consideration is the availability to the acquiring company of the acquired company's net operating loss carryovers. The provisions relating to net operating loss carryovers were significantly changed by the Tax Reform Act of 1976. However, the effective date of the changes has been delayed. For taxable acquisitions, the new rules are effective for taxable years beginning after June 30, 1982. For tax-free acquisitions, the new rules are effective for plans of reorganization adopted on or after January 1, 1982. The controller is advised to consult tax counsel for an explanation of the full effect of the changes, especially when the Act gives certain taxpayers an option to choose between applying the old and new rules.

### Taxable Acquisitions Prior to the Tax Reform Act of 1976

Under the old law, for taxable stock acquisitions in a taxable year of an acquired corporation beginning before June 30, 1982 (the new effective date), an acquired company's net operating losses can be carried over in full. However, no carryovers are permitted in a taxable asset acquisition.

The entire net operating loss carryovers from prior taxable years to the taxable year or to subsequent taxable years is disallowed in its entirety if *all* the following conditions are met at the end of the taxable year:

1. One or more of the corporation's ten largest stockholders own at least 50 percentage points more of the fair market value of its outstanding stock than they owned at the beginning of the year or at the beginning of the prior taxable year.

2. The increase in (1) above is the result of either (a) purchase or (b) a decrease in the loss corporation's outstanding stock or the stock of another corporation owning stock in the loss corporation (except for redemptions to pay death taxes).

3. The loss corporation has not continued to carry on a trade or business substantially the same as that conducted before the change in ownership.

In computing the 50-percentage-point change, it is important to distinguish between an increase of 50 percentage points and a 50 percent increase. A percentage point is a measure of all outstanding shares of a corporation. A percent is a measure of the shares owned by a shareholder.

Consider the following example. X Corporation owns 8 percent of the fair market value of the stock of Y Corporation. X increases its stock ownership to 12 percent during the year. X has had a 50 percent increase in ownership, but its actual percentage-point increase is only four.

The requirement of carrying on substantially the same trade or business can be troublesome, since it is in the nature of a subjective test.

### Tax-Free Acquisitions Prior to the Tax Reform Act of 1976

As initially stated, the new law, as it pertains to tax-free acquisitions, is effective for plans of reorganization adopted on or after January 1, 1982. The old law applies to type A, C, D and F reorganizations. Type B reorganizations are not limited by these rules.

If a corporation having net operating loss carryovers participates in an applicable tax-free reorganization involving a transfer of substantially all the assets of a corporation, such losses are eliminated in whole or part if the shareholders of such loss corporation acquire less than 20 percent of the fair market value of the stock of the acquiring corporation. For each percentage point of stock ownership below 20 percent that these shareholders acquire, 5 percent of the acquired company's net operating loss is eliminated.

The following example illustrates the application of this rule. ABC Corporation has a net operating loss carryover from 1980 to 1981 of $1 million and net assets valued at 1/9th of the net assets of XYZ Corporation. XYZ merges into ABC during 1981. Following the merger, XYZ's stockholders own, as a result of the merger, 95 percent of the fair market value of ABC's outstanding stock. ABC's former shareholders own the remaining 5 percent. Since the stockholders of the loss corporation own less than 20 percent of the surviving corporation following the merger, ABC's net operating loss carryover must be scaled down. The 1981 net operating loss deduction would be $250,000, computed as follows:

| | |
|---|---:|
| Net operating loss carryover | $1,000,000 |
| Percentage of stock surviving corporation owned immediately after the merger by stockholders of the loss corporation below 20% | |
| (20% less 5%) | 15% |

| | |
|---|---|
| Percentage of stock owned below 20% multiplied by 5 | 75% |
| Required scale-down (75% × $1,000,000) | $750,000 |
| Available net operating loss | $250,000 |

As already mentioned, no scale-down is required in a type B reorganization. Thus, when a reorganization involves a corporation's acquisition of a controlling stock interest in another corporation by means of a stock-for-stock exchange, the net operating loss carryovers of the acquired corporation are available. Additionally, when the acquired company continues to operate as a separate company following the acquisition (as in a subsidiary A merger with the acquiring subsidiary formed solely for the acquisition), no scale-down is required. Thus, subsidiary A mergers will be useful in allowing this exception to be effective. Note that while the losses remain available, the utilization of the losses will be limited to postacquisition income of that subsidiary.

### Taxable Acquisitions After the Tax Reform Act of 1976

One of the principal changes of the 1976 law that is applicable to taxable purchases of stock of a loss corporation for its years beginning June 30, 1982, is the elimination of the all-or-nothing approach to net operating loss carryovers in the event of a taxable purchase. Thus, instead of having a situation in which the net operating loss is either allowed or disallowed in full when a corporation is purchased or there is a possible proportionate reduction of the carryover in an acquisition by reorganization, the new rules apply the proportionate reduction principle to both types of acquisitions.

**Scale-Down Provisions.** The new rule provides that the net operating loss carryovers of the acquired company will be scaled down if the following conditions are met on the last day of a corporation's taxable year:

1. One or more of the corporation's fifteen largest shareholders own in excess of 60 percentage points more of the fair market value of either the participating stock or all the stock of the corporation (whichever is greater) on the last day of its taxable year than they owned at the beginning of such taxable year or at the beginning of the first or second preceding taxable years.
2. The increase in percentage points is the result of:
   a. Purchase;
   b. An acquisition of an interest in a partnership;
   c. An exchange to which Section 351 applies;
   d. A contribution to the capital of the loss corporation;
   e. A decrease in the total outstanding stock of the loss corporation;
   f. A liquidation of an interest of a partner in a partnership; or
   g. Any combination of the transaction in (a) through (f).

These are the sole requirements for the application of the new rules. The continuity-of-substantially-the-same-trade-or-business rule, which had been troublesome in its subjectivity, has been eliminated.

**Reduction Schedule.** If the new rule is applicable, a scale-down of the net operating loss is required. For each percentage point that the increase exceeds 60 percentage points (up to 80 percentage points), the net operating loss carryovers are reduced by 3½ percentage points. For each percentage point of increase in excess of 80 percentage points, the carryovers are reduced by an additional 1½ percentage points.

Consider the following example. Buyer X increases his stock ownership by 96 percentage points. The reduction in the net operating loss carryover of the acquired corporation will be 94 percent, calculated as follows:

| | |
|---|---|
| Percentage-point increase above 60 and up to 80 (20 × 3½) | 70% |
| Percentage-point increase above 80 and up to 96 (16 × 1½) | 24% |
| Required reduction of carryover | 94% |

Note that the net operating loss from any year in which the acquiring company owns at least 40 percent of the total stock (number and fair market value) of the corporation for the last half of the year is allowed as a carryover in full. Suppose XYZ Corporation initially purchases 40 percent of a loss company's stock during the first half of 1981 and then buys an additional 30 percent in 1982. The loss carryovers to 1982 from 1980 and prior years will be reduced by 35 percent, because XYZ owns in excess of 60 percentage points more of the stock of the loss corporation than it owned at the beginning of the first preceding taxable year. However, the minimum-ownership rule will permit a loss incurred in 1981 to be carried over in full to 1982 and subsequent years, because XYZ will have owned the requisite 40 percent interest in the loss corporation during all of the last half of 1981.

Note that losses incurred in years after 1981 will also be allowed as carryovers in full, since the minimum-ownership requirement will also be satisfied as to those later years.

This 40 percent rule provides a planning opportunity. Specifically, a corporation acquiring the stock of a loss corporation should plan the acquisition to take place six months before year-end. Any net operating loss incurred during the acquisition year will thus be preserved. (For situations to which the above rule does not apply, see IRC § 382(a)(5).)

## Tax-Free Acquisitions After the Tax Reform Act of 1976

The new net operating loss rules in respect to tax-free acquisitions are effective for plans of reorganization adopted on or after January 1, 1982. The new rules apply to type A, B, C, D (under certain conditions), and F reorganizations if the following conditions are met:

1. Either the acquiring or acquired corporation has a net operating loss in the year of

the reorganization or a net operating loss carryover from a prior taxable year to the year of the reorganization, *and*

2. The shareholders of the loss corporation own (immediately after the reorganization) less than 40 percent of all the stock and the fair market value of the stock of the acquiring corporation.

If these conditions are met, a scale-down similar to that encountered in a taxable acquisition is required. For each percent of ownership below 40 percent and above 20 percent, the loss carryovers are reduced 3½ percentage points. For each percent of ownership below the 20 percent level, the carryovers are decreased an additional 1½ percentage points, as illustrated in this example. Two corporations effect a type C reorganization. The shareholders of the loss corporation receive 10 percent of both the fair market value of the stock and all the stock of the surviving corporation. The net operating loss carryovers will be reduced by 85 percent, computed as follows:

| | |
|---|---|
| Percentage-point decrease below 40 and above 20 (20 × 3½) | 70% |
| Percentage-point decrease below 20 and up to 10 (10 × 1½) | 15% |
| Required reduction of carryover | 85% |

Certain provisions of the new rules pertain specifically to type B reorganizations. Under the new rules, if the stock of a loss corporation is acquired in a type B reorganization, the percentage-of-ownership rules are applied by direct reference to the stock ownership of the loss company. Exchanging shareholders are treated as owning a percentage of the loss company's stock acquired by the acquiring company equal to the percentage of the acquiring company's stock received in the exchange. This percentage is then added to the percentage of the loss company's stock that its shareholders did not exchange.

Consider this example. P Corporation acquires 85 percent of the only class of loss corporation T stock for 20 percent of the only class of P stock in a B reorganization. Continuity of ownership would be 32 percent, consisting of the 15 percent of the T stock that was not exchanged and 17 percent of the T stock treated as owned by former T shareholders who now own P stock as a result of their exchange (20 percent × 85 percent). The loss carryovers of T Corporation would, therefore, be reduced by 28 percent.

While the old rules did not apply to an acquisition of at least 80 percent of the stock of a corporation solely in exchange for voting stock of an acquiring corporation or its parent, this transaction (a type B reorganization) now requires a scale-down as described above.

## ACCOUNTING FOR BUSINESS COMBINATIONS

In an acquisition, the acquiring corporation can structure the transaction in one of two ways: it can use the purchase method or it can pool the two businesses into a single entity. The method it chooses may significantly affect its book income and balance sheet (including stockholders' equity) after the acquisition.

Under the *pooling-of-interests method*, the acquiring corporation records the assets and liabilities of the acquired corporation at their historical book value on the acquisition date. All accounts of the two companies are combined, except that the capital stock of the acquiree disappears and the new stock issued to its stockholders is recorded.

Under the *purchase method*, the assets and liabilities of the acquired corporation are accounted for on the books of the acquiring corporation at their relative fair market values to the acquisitor at the date of acquisition. The acquired corporation's equity accounts are not carried forward. The purchase method may also give rise to the recording of *goodwill*. Basically, goodwill represents the excess consideration paid by an acquiring corporation over the net fair market value of the assets purchased and liabilities assumed. APB 17, *Accounting for Intangible Assets*, requires the purchaser to amortize goodwill over its useful life through an annual charge to earnings. However, such life may not exceed forty years. Amortization is generally required on a straight-line basis, unless another systematic method of amortization can be demonstrated to be more appropriate. The amortization of goodwill is nondeductible for tax purposes.

When the purchase price of an acquired corporation exceeds historical book value, the purchase method will result in lower future earnings than if the pooling method is used. This is a direct result of the requirement to allocate the excess purchase price to net assets acquired, which must be allocated or depreciated against earnings, and to amortize goodwill over a period not to exceed forty years. In a pooling, no goodwill is recognized, and assets and liabilities of the acquired company are recorded at historical carrying values.

### Theory of Purchase Accounting

Under the purchase method of accounting, the assets and liabilities of the acquired corporation are recorded on the books of the acquiring corporation at their relative fair market values. The basic underlying theory supporting the purchase method of accounting is:

1. Almost every business combination is an acquisition (as opposed to a true pooling of interests).
2. The purchase method clearly reflects a bargained transaction.
3. The purchase method accounts for the economic substance of the acquisition.

In respect to the first argument, one of the corporations in the transaction always assumes the dominant role, and the other company ceases to control its assets and operations. Thus, to treat the transaction merely as a pooling of the interests of two companies would be inconsistent with the true substance of the transaction.

The substance of the second argument is that the purchase method more clearly reflects the arm's-length bargaining of two independent parties. For example, dividend-paying capacity, acquisition of technical know-how, and acquisition of management are all considered. Thus, based on these arm's-length negotiations and the additional fact that one party to the transaction assumes the dominant role, all the elements of an outright purchase are present.

Other proponents of purchase accounting argue that the purchase method more clearly reflects the economic substance of the transaction for the following reasons:

1. The bargained purchase price of the assets (less liabilities), not their cost to a previous owner, should be recorded on the financial statements of the acquiring company.
2. The purchase method reflects fair market value of the consideration received for the stock issued, whereas the equity shown in the financial statements of an acquired company in a pooling does not reflect substantive values.

## Problems With Purchase Accounting

There are two significant problems with purchase accounting for business combinations: valuation and goodwill.

It is fair to say that valuation is a difficult concept. However, the problem of valuation is not peculiar to the purchase method of accounting. It arises in a variety of business and tax situations. Appraisal techniques have become increasingly more sophisticated in recent years, so the problem is not as difficult today.

The major objection to the recording of goodwill is that it is an imprecise valuation. Since goodwill is the result of the excess of the cost of the acquisition over the value assigned to net tangible assets acquired, its "value" merely represents a residue. As a practical matter, if the purchaser is willing to pay more for a company than the fair market value of its net assets, the excess must be for intangible factors, which are recorded as goodwill.

## Theory of Pooling-of-Interests Accounting

The pooling-of-interests method accounts for an acquisition as a change in ownership interests by recording an exchange of equity securities. The basic assumption underlying this method of accounting is that a business combination is brought about by an exchange of equity interests, which in substance is merely an arrangement between stockholder groups. Proponents of the pooling method argue that no new basis of valuing the respective assets of the combining companies should arise. Rather, the only tangible change is in the form of the corporation. Each of the stockholder groups continues to maintain its relative ownership interests, in addition to a proportionate risk in the new entity.

## Problems With Pooling-of-Interests Accounting

There are three problems often cited in any discussion of pooling-of-interests accounting: valuation, misstatement of equity, and impairment of comparability.

A valuation problem often advanced has to do with the concept of *instant earnings*. If assets are recorded at book value as the result of a pooling and their respective fair market values are in excess of book, then an immediate gain can be recognized if the acquiring company sells these assets subsequent to the combination. However, supporters of the pooling method claim that since the same gain could have been realized prior to the business combination by the acquired company, there is nothing wrong with the recognition of instant earnings.

Misstatement of equity is also considered by some to be a problem. Under the pooling method, at the time the acquisition is recorded, adjustments are required to be made to paid-in capital to account for the difference between the total par value of the outstanding common stock of the acquiring firm, prior to merger, and the par value of the common stock issued in the business combination. Thus, it is contended that the source of equity capital is distorted.

Critics of the pooling method contend that in most business combinations it is misleading to assume that the sum of the precombination earnings is comparable to total postcombination earnings. Such critics believe that comparability is impaired because a discontinuity has occurred.

### Criteria for Using Pooling

APB 16, *Accounting for Business Combinations*, sets forth the requirements that must be satisfied in order for the pooling method to be used. If a business combination satisfies *all* the requirements, it must be treated as a pooling. However, if one or more conditions are *not* satisfied, the combination must be treated as a purchase. A single method must be applied; part purchase, part pooling is not permitted.

There are three broad categories of conditions that must be met if a combination is to qualify for pooling:

1. Attributes of combining companies;
2. Interest of combining companies; and
3. Absence of planned transactions.

**Attributes of Combining Companies.** For a two-year period prior to the initiation of the plan of combination, the combining companies must have been independent of each other and have been autonomous. Thus, if either was a subsidiary or division of another corporation, this condition would not be met. The initiation of a plan of combination is defined as the earlier of (1) the date the principal terms of the plan are publicly announced or (2) the date of written notification to stockholders of a combining company of an exchange offer. The independence test is satisfied if each combining company does not own more than 10 percent of the outstanding voting common stock of the other combining company at the date that the plan is initiated *and* at the date the plan is consummated.

**Interest of Combining Companies.** The second broad condition involves the manner in which interests must be combined. First, the pooling combination must take place in a single transaction or within one year of the initiation of the plan.

Second, only common stock with rights identical to those of the majority of the outstanding voting stock of the acquiring corporation may be exchanged for substantially all the voting common stock interest of the acquired corporation. For purposes of this condition, "substantially all the voting common stock" means 90 percent.

However, in determining if the 90 percent test has been met, it is necessary to exclude shares of the acquired corporation (1) acquired before and held by the acquiring corporation and its subsidiaries at the date the plan is initiated; (2) obtained by the acquiring corporation and its subsidiaries after the date the plan is initiated, other than through the issuance of voting common stock of the acquiring corporation; or (3) outstanding after the consummation of the combination.

In testing for 90 percent, any shares of voting common stock of the acquiring corporation held by the acquiree company must be restated as an equivalent number of shares of the acquiree based on the ratio of the exchange of stock in the combination. This restated number is subtracted from the number of shares of voting common stock exchanged. This reduced number is then compared with 90 percent of the outstanding voting common stock of the seller.

Consider the following example. XYZ Corporation issues 96,000 shares of voting common stock in exchange for 192,000 shares of voting common stock of ABC Corporation based on a 1 to 2 exchange ratio pursuant to a plan of combination. ABC has 200,000 shares of voting common stock and at the plan initiation date owned 10,000 shares of XYZ voting common stock. The pooling method is not available in this situation. After being restated at the 1 for 2 ratio, 10,000 shares of XYZ are equivalent to 20,000 shares of ABC stock. This reduces the number of shares exchanged to 172,000, which is only equal to 86 percent of the stock of the combining company. Accordingly, the 90 percent test is not met.

**Absence of Planned Transactions.** Three points are significant. First, the acquiring corporation may not agree to reacquire or retire all or a portion of the common stock issued in the acquisition. Second, the acquiring corporation is not permitted to enter into any financial arrangement which benefits the former shareholders of the acquired corporation. Third, pooling is not permitted if the acquiring corporation plans to dispose of a significant portion of the assets of the acquired corporation within two years of the combination.

There are various other conditions, restrictions, and definitions relating to the common stock of the combining companies, which are listed in APB 16.

## SUMMARY

The accounting implications of a purchase or pooling transaction relative to mergers and acquisitions are significantly different. The method used can have a substantial effect on the future earnings of the combined entity. The corporate controller should prepare a forecast of earnings for some future period (e.g., five years) to illustrate for management the effect on earnings of each method. Although there are many factors that determine the structure of an acquisition, the accounting implications of the purchase and pooling method should be clearly understood by buyer's management before the form of the transaction is finalized. It is the controller's responsibility to see that management is aware of the avoidable alternatives, their financial and tax effects, and the problems inherent in each course of action.

Competent professional assistance for both the buyer and seller is absolutely necessary at each stage of a merger or acquisition.

## SUGGESTED READING

Bacon, Richard L. "Using Acquired Corporation's NOLs Restricted by 1976 Tax Reform Act." *Journal of Taxation*, Vol. 46 (February, 1977), p. 78.

Bittker, Borris I., and Eustice, James S. *Federal Income Taxation of Corporations and Shareholders.* 4th ed. Boston: Warren, Gorham & Lamont, 1979.

Brode, George Jr. "Planning to Use NOL Carryovers: Trafficking in Profit Corporations After 1977." *Journal of Taxation*, Vol. 47 (November, 1977), p. 258.

Crumbley, Larry D. "How to Choose the Most Advantageous Way to Combine Separate Business Interests." *Taxation for Accountants*, Vol. 15 (1975), p. 244.

Henke, Jeff. "The 'Substantially All' Requirement in Triangular 'A' Mergers." *Tax Adviser,* Vol. 6 (1975), p. 270.

Libin, Jerome B. "Recent Developments in Corporate Organizations and Reorganizations—Including a New Look for Sec. 382." *Taxes—The Tax Magazine,* Vol. 54 (1976), p. 876.

Walker, John F. Jr. "Planning Corporate Acquisitions so as to Preserve Available Tax Benefits." *Taxation for Accountants*, Vol. 20 (1978), p. 270.

# 32

# Divestments—Financial and Planning Considerations

*Harry H. Ness*

*Anthony C. Paddock*[1]

---

[1] The authors acknowledge with thanks the contributions to this chapter of John E. Stein-mueller of American Appraisal Associates, Inc.

## THE PLANNING PROCESS

In today's fluctuating business environment many corporate managers are forced to dispose of company subsidiaries or divisions for a variety of reasons. The subject of corporate divestitures is an interesting and complex one; in many ways it represents the other side of the merger and acquisition activities carried on for expansion or diversification. If a controller is to contribute actively to the divestiture process, he must clearly understand the basic corporate objectives of the divestiture as well as be able to identify the financial problems that can arise from this decision. These problems include not only the impact of a divestiture on the balance sheet and income statement of the parent company, but also the accounting and tax implications which generally differ from those of acquisitions. Management must consider every aspect of a potential divestiture if it is to choose the best form of transaction.

### Corporate Objectives

**Eliminating Unprofitable Operations.** There are many reasons for corporate divestiture of subsidiaries or divisions, but the most common is the elimination of marginally profitable or unprofitable operations. Lack of profit also explains why divestitures, by and large, are carried out in certain ways. If the divested activity is draining the parent company of management time and talent, as well as corporate profits, management is often under great pressure to sell the unit to an outside party.

**Incompatible Activities.** Other reasons motivate companies to eliminate certain activities; for example, management may decide to sell a unit not compatible with the overall structure of the company's business. Recently, a publishing company sold a subsidiary that makes plastic components for the telephone industry. In this situation, the unit that was sold was clearly an incompatible activity for the parent, but was attractive and reasonably priced for the purchaser who had a better relationship to the subsidiary's business.

Opportunities to successfully dispose of an operation that does not fit in with the parent's goals are usually greater than those where the subsidiary is unprofitable. The case for divestiture is less clear when a subsidiary is profitable but does not earn the rate of return that the parent's management believes is required. The company might be somewhat marginal given the overhead of the parent, but could be made considerably more profitable if acquired and operated by a third party.

**Government Regulations.** Another reason for divestiture is government regulation. For example, the passage of the one-bank holding company act forced many industrial companies to sell banks that they owned. Anti-trust cases and Federal Trade Commission consent decrees have also forced corporations to divest themselves of attractive subsidiaries. However, under these circumstances, sellers must recognize that the regulatory restraints involved may limit the market of interested purchasers. This is particularly true if the unit being sold, such as a bank, railroad company, airline, or broadcasting company, is itself directly regulated by the government.

**Parent Financial Problems.** Another strong incentive for divestiture occurs when the parent company becomes seriously enmeshed in financial problems. Unlike the situation of the unprofitable subsidiary, it is the parent's problems that create the divestiture necessity, usually to improve a tight cash position and/or to relieve the pressures imposed by large amounts of borrowed money. The time pressure involved in selling the subsidiary often leads to the parent's consent to take a smaller price for its unit than otherwise might be negotiated.

**Other Reasons to Divest.** There are a variety of other reasons that lead a corporation to divest itself of various operating units. A change in top management often leads to a change in general corporate goals and management style; subsidiaries or divisions that may have appeared attractive to previous management suddenly appear less desirable. A company that has decided to recentralize its management often finds that some of its activities can properly be run only on a decentralized basis, thus providing a strong reason for disposing of these units. At times, a divestiture through a spin-off may increase the combined value of the parent and subsidiary to the public. "Unwinding the corporate marriage" by distributing the business units acquired back to the original shareholders in exchange for the surrender of their stock in the purchased company is a valid business objective and can, under certain circumstances, be tax free for both parties. Divestiture is also used to end shareholder disputes. Assets or groups of assets constituting a business may be distributed to recalcitrant shareholders in order to eliminate them from the distributing company.

## PROBLEMS TO OVERCOME

### Proper Information

When a parent company structures a divestiture, it must consider a number of problems. One of these is determining what data is available for the unit to be sold. The data of many divisions, and even some subsidiaries, are so intertwined with the parent's own financial systems that it is time-consuming and expensive to separate out the information that allows the unit to be considered on its own.

### Defining the Saleable Package

Underlying the problem of proper information is that of determining what exactly the parent is putting up for sale or other disposition.

**Disposition of Assets.** The parent must first decide whether or not all the assets of the unit are to be sold. Clearly, if the unit is a free-standing, 100 percent-owned subsidiary that has been treated as a separate unit, the problems are considerably less than in the case of a division of a highly integrated company, where the business has not been considered a "stand-alone" activity for many years. Although most divestitures fall between these two extremes, the potential seller must carefully define exactly what is being offered for sale; for instance, will the parent retain the outstanding accounts receivable and if so, who is responsible for collecting those receivables on an ongoing basis? Another area of dispute could be the definition of the inventory to be sold; will the inventory risk be assumed by the buyer or will warranties and representations concerning its value and condition extend beyond the closing? Another consideration is whether patents and trademarks are to be sold with the operating unit and, also, whether all material contracts are assignable.

**Liabilities.** If only assets are being acquired, the purchaser often does not pick up the liabilities attached to the unit being sold. Therefore, the seller must carefully determine which liabilities it will retain after the sale. This planning applies particularly to contingent liabilities and liabilities (including certain lease obligations) that may not appear on the balance sheet of the business being sold. These liabilities can be onerous, but if the seller is willing to retain them as part of the transaction, documentation will be simplified, and the sale will be closed more rapidly.

Although accounts payable often remain with the seller, the largest liabilities in dollar amount are typically the outstanding debt obligations and/or quasi-equity incurred by the subsidiary being sold. The selling parent must decide whether it is willing to assume the debt obligations of the unit for sale or attempt to pass them to the buyer. It is even more difficult to make this determination in the case of the quasi-equity obligations—preferred stock, warrants, and stock options—that are outstanding if the purchaser is buying assets rather than a subsidiary corporation. A particularly thorny question is what to do about guarantees from the parent supporting the debt obligations and other liabilities of the unit. In the end, however, the question of liability retention is part of the price negotiation between seller and buyer.

## Tax Considerations

From a tax point of view, the purchaser generally prefers to buy assets, while the seller wants to sell stock. The seller who sells stock will be taxed on capital gain rather than on ordinary income and will have disposed of the entire corporation with all liabilities, known and unknown, contingent or otherwise. The purchaser of assets, on the other hand, can pick and choose which assets it desires, can avoid undersirable recapture of Federal income taxes, and generally can more easily assign the proper values to the assets it has purchased. (Tax considerations are further discussed in Chapter 33.)

## Compliance With Government Regulations

Another problem affecting the form and substance of divestitures is government regulation and compliance. If the parent or its subsidiary is a regulated industry, government approval often must be obtained before the transaction can be closed. Since the regulation process generally requires a great deal of time, the seller must be aware of this limitation when offering the company for sale.

## Labor Considerations

An increasing number of union contracts allow unions to participate in negotiations to dispose of a parent company's subsidiaries or divisions. Unions are legitimately concerned in the areas of severance benefits and the carry-over of pension rights and guarantees. Under ERISA the question of liability for pensions has become even more important and is a significant negotiating point in any discussion of divestiture.

## Marketing and Licensing Agreements

Marketing and licensing agreements can also present negotiating problems because of the importance of such agreements to the business operations. When these agreements are intertwined with the parent company's own business, it may be quite difficult to disentangle the unit in order to make it suitable for sale.

## Timing

One of the crucial factors in a successful divestiture is the choice of the proper time to proceed. If the timing can be controlled, divestitures should be initiated when the stock and capital markets are strong and buoyant and when the unit to be sold is showing strong growth and the outlook is optimistic. Unfortunately, the timing of most divestitures may not be controllable by the parent. Other factors then become secondary and must be subordinated to the time pressures involved. For example, although it is often preferable to obtain a prior private tax ruling on a proposed transaction, management may be compelled to consummate the sale, subject to a tax ruling, so the transaction is not delayed.

The seller who faces both time pressure and a strong "buyer's market" for its properties must move carefully but quickly to achieve its goal. The necessity to cut off an unprofitable operation as quickly as possible is often a factor that overrides other considerations—both financial and tax. In this case, it is important for the divesting company to understand the realistic range of value for the property to be sold. It is pointless to undergo a protracted effort to sell the company if the price objectives are unreasonable or if the outlook for the activity is so poor that few, if any, potential buyers would be seriously interested.

## Public Relations

Because of the nature of many proposed divestitures, the announcement of divestiture by the parent's management can often be a traumatic experience. Press relations must be handled carefully because potential buyers can easily be frightened by adverse publicity. Treading the fine line between selling the best points of the divesting unit and telling an honest, straightforward story about its problems is essential to a successful effort.

## DIVESTMENT ALTERNATIVES

The controller must bear in mind the seller's business objectives when he decides how to structure the financial aspects of the divestment.

### Retaining and Reducing the Operation

There are many ways to structure a divestiture. One obvious way is not to sell the company at all, but rather to retain the business and scale it down considerably. If the business is unsuccessful, scaling it down preserves the profitable lines of business and reduces the drain on the parent's resources. If it is not feasible to retain the business by reducing its scope, another alternative is to mothball the activity. It may be that merely shutting the operation down for a period of time can resolve problems and make the business attractive at a later date. This might apply, for instance, to wasting assets such as oil fields or gold mines. Mothballing is also a way to avoid certain government regulatory problems and should not be overlooked as a possible solution.

### Selling A Going Concern

Realistically, most divestitures are structured as a sale of the going business, i.e., the purchaser buys the equity control of a subsidiary rather than merely buying its assets. This permits a corporation to continue as a going business after sale, without having to put the assets into a different corporation. From the standpoint of the seller, a sale is by far the neatest way of disposing of a subsidiary. Similarly, a seller can dispose of a division by putting the assets and liabilities of the division into a new corporation, which it, in turn, sells. This method avoids the negotiating difficulties that arise from the disposition of the liabilities (both contingent and unknown) because the purchaser is taking all of the assets and liabilities that are normally subject to warranties by the seller.

**Payment Considerations.** Payment may take many forms—including cash, debt or equity securities of the purchaser, or debt in the divested unit. If voting stock is received, there may be no gain or loss recognized to the seller until such stock is converted to cash.

**Selling Assets.** The alternative is to sell the assets of the division or subsidiary without selling the corporate shell with its related liabilities. This approach has certain advantages as well as disadvantages to the seller. The buyer does not have to concern itself with contingent or unknown liabilities and will more easily (and perhaps more quickly) negotiate a fair purchase price. The seller can control what assets are to be put up for sale.

### Creating a Joint Venture

The joint venture represents a compromise solution. The business or division that the parent corporation wishes to divest may be set up as a separate corporation and outside parties may be persuaded to transfer cash or other assets to the parent in exchange for the stock of the new company. The parent corporation's interest in the new company has thus been diluted, and the parent has found a desirable way to raise funds and to phase itself out of the unwanted operation. The parent may withdraw from the new corporation by exercising options to have the new corporation redeem its stock or to sell to the new investors.

A joint venture is a method for partial withdrawal. It avoids complete divestment because it permits the parent to retain enough stock interest to participate in the new company if it should prosper. This method is particularly desirable where the corporation attempts to tap new markets in foreign countries by transferring patents and know-how concurrent with the foreign joint venturer's transferring market facilities and knowledge of existing business practices to the joint venture in the foreign country. The two corporations pool their common talent for the betterment of the whole.

### Leveraged Buyouts

Another variation is a leveraged buyout. In effect, the purchaser uses the unit's debt capacity to borrow money on the existing business in order to finance the purchase of the division or subsidiary. Although this purchase method has been given great publicity in the last few years, in many cases a number of factors make it inapplicable. The unit must first have sufficient debt capacity to enable the purchaser to borrow additional funds on its credit. Second, not only must the entity have a good credit rating on the basis of which the purchaser can borrow more money, but it must have prospects for a strong future cash flow in order to service both existing debt as well as the substantial new debt. In some situations, the first problem is solved because the seller is so anxious to dispose of the division or subsidiary that it will take long-term notes, secured only by the capital stock of the business sold, for the purchase price. The assets of the business can then be used to secure bank loans. But the need for a strong future cash flow for debt service will still remain. As an alternative, certain assets of the divested unit could be sold to provide part of the purchase price. (There are certain accounting problems associated with a seller financed leveraged sale that are covered in Chapter 33.)

### Sale to Employees

The sale of the unit to employees is another type of leveraged sale. In one such type, commonly called an *employee stock ownership plan (ESOP)*, the selling parent takes notes from a new trust secured by the contributions of the corporation and its stock. Contributions are paid into the trust, which in turn will ultimately pay off the notes to the parent. This structure provides a way to spin off operations that do not for one reason or another fit into the general corporate plan, and enables the existing employees to manage and operate the company with greater incentive than might otherwise be the case. In essence, the purchase price is paid by the future earnings of the divested unit. The sale can be structured so that the selling corporation can receive not only notes from the ESOP but also debentures or preferred stock from the corporation that may give the sellers a stake in the new company. As an alternative, the unit could be sold to the employees without using an ESOP.

### Distribution to Shareholders

Another divestment alternative is a spinoff to shareholders of the parent. The entity to be disposed of is set up as a separate corporation. Its stock is distributed, usually on a pro rata basis, to the parent's existing shareholders. If the parent is a publicly held corporation, the new corporation also immediately achieves a public market. This arrangement will work only where the divested company can stand alone with a complete management team in place.

There are special tax implications for a spinoff. The tax basis of the securities spun off to the existing shareholders is an allocated share of the tax basis of the shares of the parent held by the stockholders, based on the fair market value of both stocks. Thus, the tax basis of shareholdings in the parent company is considerably reduced, in an amount that depends on the value of the securities spun off. (The tax rules for spinoffs are reviewed in detail in Chapter 33.)

A parent may also dispose of an unwanted business unit by distributing its assets in kind to the shareholders. Such distribution may be pro rata to the shareholders or may be non-pro rata to a certain group of shareholders, in exchange for such shareholders' surrender of an amount of stock equal to the fair market value of the assets distributed. There is no gain or loss to the corporation in such transactions, for either tax or accounting purposes. Such distribution may be either a dividend (ordinary income) or a partial liquidation (capital gain) to the stockholders.

### Charitable Distributions

Yet another alternative is the donation of the unit to an eleemosynary organization, a charitable foundation or public charity; this results in a charitable deduction for the disposing corporation. Rather than wholly a donation, the sale may be a bargain sale or bootstrap sale, the sale proceeds to be paid from the future profits of the corporation.

### Liquidation

The parent has one last alternative—liquidation (by auction or negotiated sale), or abandonment of the real property, fixed assets, and intangibles of the unwanted business unit.

## VALUATION OF DIVESTITURES

Once the decision has been made to divest, and the company has analyzed what form the divestiture will take, the value of the divestiture must be determined, along with related tax and accounting ramifications. This determination usually involves many people in the parent company. The controller's department has accounting information about the unit's assets and can provide financial information and the related accounting considerations for prospective purchasers. The tax department is normally responsible for determining potential tax gains or losses, recapture liability on Section 1245 and 1250 property, and Investment Tax Credit payback. The corporate planning area might suggest possible markets for disposal of the entity or its assets. And outside expert consultants are sometimes used to establish fair market value.

The divesting company must understand that a particular asset or subsidiary can have numerous values; these values depend upon the purpose for the valuation and the methodology employed. The question of valuation as it relates to mergers and acquisitions is also discussed in Chapter 30.

### Valuation Considerations

In using the various valuation techniques, the seller must consider the viewpoint of potential buyers in order to determine a realistic price. The seller should set both a minimum amount it is willing to accept and the maximum amount it thinks the potential purchaser will pay. The range of values furnishes an area within which to negotiate a reasonable agreement.

**Fair Market Value.** The fundamental question is, "What will the unit being divested sell for in the marketplace?" There are many misconceptions as to what fair market value is. It is not an arbitrary multiple of earnings. It is neither the appraised value of all of the assets, plus an arbitrary formula for goodwill, nor, unless by coincidence, is it book value.

Fair market value may be defined as a range of prices within which an unbiased buyer, reasonably well informed about the property, and a willing seller will consummate a transaction when neither is under any compulsion to do so. As we have seen, however, divestments may not always occur free of compulsion. In such an arm's length transaction, value represents a multiple of the returns generally required by investors, taking into account the risk that they must assume. The greater the risk, the higher the required return on investment, and consequently, the lower the market value. The basic financial theory underlying all investment decisions, regardless of type of investment, is the risk-reward trade-off. For example, bonds with higher risk sell at higher interest rates; those with lower risk at lower rates.

Although both buyer and seller arrive at their estimates of a property's value using these risk and return yardsticks, the comparative negotiating skill of each party may cause the amount actually paid for an asset to vary. For example, a buyer may pay more than the objectively "right" price if the purchase gives it access to a strategic raw material or process, access to a particular market, or access to certain skills. On the other hand, the divesting company may accept less than it otherwise would if it is under pressure to terminate ownership quickly. In the last analysis, the finally determined price results from the objective facts, subjective judgments, and the negotiating skills of the parties.

## Classification of Risk

There are three basic risk classifications: financial risk, business risk, and investment risk.

*Financial risk.* Financial risk is associated with the company's financial structure, including its capitalization as well as its financial and operating ratios. Factors most indicative of high financial risk are high debt to equity ratio; low working capital and quick-asset ratios; and wide fluctuations in revenues and earnings, profit margins, and return on investment. The selling parent must be able to comment to a potential buyer on the reasons for the level of the divested unit's ratios in a way that is both understandable and convincing.

*Business risk.* Business risk is associated with the divesting company's industry and business environment. High business risk includes such factors as ease of entry into the marketplace, dependence upon one or a few customers or suppliers, and dependence upon one or a few key employees. Again, the seller must be able to describe, in a persuasive way, the benefits as well as the risks associated with the unit's business.

*Investment risk.* Investment risk is related to the trends and outlook for the stock market and interest rates.

## Approaches to the Valuation of a Going Concern

Three steps are required in order to determine a value for the going concern.

**Examination of Financial Statements.** A knowledgeable purchaser will want to examine the financial statements for at least the latest available five years. However, if the divested unit's business is cyclical, a period covering a full cycle should be studied because the shorter period may be heavily weighted at a particular point on the cycle. If financial statements have not been historically prepared on a regular basis, the company will have to furnish them on a reconstructed or pro forma basis.

Where necessary, the financial statements must be "normalized" to eliminate all unusual items of income or expense, including such items as overhead charges from the parent, or expenses absorbed by the parent, which would not apply under other circumstances. In addition, adjustments are necessary to account for assets or liabilities not being transferred.

**Examination of Comparable Companies.** Comparative publicly-held companies must be examined in order to gauge values reflected in the public securities markets. This can be a difficult process. Many times, major competition comes from closely held companies where little or no public data is available, or from subsidiaries or divisions of larger companies whose primary business involves unrelated products. While some of the latter companies may report on a product line basis, their market appraisal ratios are a function of the total company.

The best way to begin the search is to determine the subject company's *SIC code* (the Commerce Department Standard Industrial Classification code). A search of such sources as Dun & Bradstreet's *Million Dollar Directory,* Moody's *Manuals,* Standard & Poor's *Corporation Records,* and *Companies Filing Annual Reports With the SEC* provides a list of possible comparative companies. The valuator must then eliminate those companies that are not to be considered as comparable. Possible grounds for elimination include revenue or investment size, product line comparability, and factors affecting market price (merger or take-over rumors, etc.).

A study of financial statements similar to that made for the subject unit over a period of years should then be made for each of the selected companies. Note should be taken of significant differences in the accounting for inventories, depreciation, or other items which may have to be compensated for in a comparison of the companies' relative financial condition and operation performances.

*Measure of performance.* Many measures of performance can be used to compare the subject unit with comparable companies. Among the best known are the following:

- Operating profits before and after depreciation as a percent of sales;
- Net income before and after taxes as a percent of sales;
- Study of trends of pertinent operating items either expressed as an annual percentage increase or decrease or in terms of a percentage of sales;
- Net income as a rate of return on average common stock equity;
- Net income before taxes and interest as a return on average total assets;
- Leverage factor—measured by the relationship of total assets to common stock equity; and
- Liquidity ratios (current and quick asset ratios).

The above list is by no means all inclusive. Each industry has its particular measures, all of which are helpful in assessing risk relative to the subject company as compared with similar operations. (See Chapter 16 on monitoring techniques for other ratios.)

**Investor Appraisal Approach to Value.** The investor appraisal is useful in determining the value of an industrial unit that can stand on its own and that has either had a record of profitability, or can be made profitable. The key in this approach is to make qualitative and quantitative comparisons between the subject unit and similar publicly owned companies.

A number of ratios—price-earnings ratios, dividend yields, ratios of market price to book value—can be generated from the comparative company data to provide ready-made yardsticks to indicate how investors appraise companies that can be considered as similar. Generally, companies with demonstrated growth and a strong record of profitability tend to sell at higher price-earnings multiples and ratios of market to book value and have lower dividend yields than companies with lesser sustained profitability. Although the dividend yield is often significant in determining the value of a minority and noncontrolling interest, it is usually of little importance in determining the value of an entire company or unit, as the purchaser can set whatever reasonable dividend policy might suit his requirements. The market price ratios should be computed on a year-to-year basis for at least the latest five-year period and on a basis current to the date of the analysis (e.g., average prices in the latest months).

The stage has now been set to develop the value of the subject company. By matching comparable financial analysis data of the subject company with that for the comparatives, a determination can be made as to how that company measures up against the comparatives in terms of operating results and financial condition— better (by how much), worse (by how much), or about on a par with the comparative company average. After weighing the differences in the nature of business and operating characteristics between the subject company and the comparative companies (and any idiosyncrasies affecting the subject company), indications of the subject's value can be obtained by applying: (1) appropriate price-earnings ratios to the earnings for the subject company; and (2) the appropriate ratio of market price to book value to latest year-end book value. With the latter, the magnitude of the applicable ratio will depend on the subject company's rate of earnings on equity. Generally, the higher the rate of return, the higher the company's stock is appraised in the market place.

*Price-earnings approach.* In the price-earnings approach, a judgment must be made as to the probable level of earnings (expected in the foreseeable future), of the unit to be divested. Based on the comparisons of the subject unit's performance with comparative companies, a further judgment is made relative to the applicable price-earnings multiple.

Figures 32.1 and 32.2 show pertinent earnings and price-earnings relationships based on average annual prices and average price for a current valuation period, respectively, for a group of small tool manufacturers. Figures 32.3, 32.4, 32.5 and 32.6 compare the performance of the subject unit with that of the selected comparative companies.

Examination of these figures leads to the following observations regarding the subject unit and the comparative companies:

- The subject unit's margins at all levels were generally well above all of the comparative companies, except American Tool Corporation.

- The subject unit's rate of return on average total assets was well above the comparatives' median in every year.

- The subject unit's rate of return on average common stock equity exceeded the median rate during most of the period.

- Over the period studied, the subject unit was less leveraged (had a lower ratio of total assets to common stock equity) than any of the comparatives. The subject unit's management policy has been to finance from within.

- With respect to growth in income, the quality of the subject unit's performance was not as consistent or as strong as the median of the comparatives.

- The unit's working capital condition, as evidenced by current and quick-asset ratios, was better than that of the comparatives throughout most of the period.

In arriving at the price-earnings multiples applicable to the subject unit's earnings, the appraiser brings into play all relevant factors, in the present case including the trend and outlook for earnings, the earlier mentioned performance observation, and the price-earnings history of similar companies. Figure 32.7 is an example of three different bases for computing indicated values.

| Company | 19X5 | 19X6 | 19X7 | 19X8 | 19X9 |
|---|---|---|---|---|---|
| | *Primary Earnings Per Share (as reported)* | | | | |
| American Tool Corporation | $0.61 | $0.71 | $0.98 | $1.14 | $1.65 |
| Delta Corporation | 1.50 | 1.48 | 2.29 | 2.75 | 3.50 |
| The United States Corporation | −0.70 | −0.41 | 1.02 | 1.16 | 1.72 |
| The XYZ Corporation | 0.90 | 1.23 | 2.31 | 2.48 | 2.56 |
| Median | $0.76 | $0.97 | $1.66 | $1.82 | $2.14 |
| | *Price-Earnings Multiples Based on Above Primary Earnings and Average Annual Market Prices* | | | | |
| American Tool Corporation | 27.3 | 20.7 | 16.6 | 12.8 | 10.8 |
| Delta Corporation | 9.6 | 8.0 | 7.9 | 7.6 | 7.0 |
| The United States Corporation | DEF | DEF | 2.7 | 5.6 | 7.2 |
| The XYZ Corporation | 4.5 | 4.7 | 6.3 | 7.6 | 9.8 |
| Median | 18.4 | 14.3 | 7.1 | 7.6 | 8.5 |

*Sources:* Company reports; SEC Forms 10–K; Standard & Poor's Stock Reports, Corporation Records, and Stock Guide. Computations by Standard Research Consultants.

FIGURE 32.1   COMPARATIVE COMPANIES: EARNINGS AND PRICE-EARNINGS MULTIPLES

| Company | Primary Earnings Per Share | | | | Per Share | | |
| --- | --- | --- | --- | --- | --- | --- | --- |
| | 5-Year Average (a) | 3-Year Average (b) | Latest Year | Latest 12 Months To | Dividend Rate(c) | Tangible Book Value(d) | Average Market Price(e) |
| American Corporation | $1.02 | $1.26 | $1.64 | $1.89  4/30/X0 | $0.80 | $ 6.86 | $22.50 |
| Delta Corporation | 2.30 | 2.85 | 3.50 | 4.24  4/30/X0 | 1.24 | 22.75 | 32.51 |
| The United States Corporation | 0.56 | 1.30 | 1.72 | 1.91  4/30/X0 | 0.20 | 12.90 | 13.50 |
| The XYZ Corporation | 1.90 | 2.45 | 2.56 | 2.56  4/30/X0 | 0.32 | 13.51 | 20.94 |

*Price: Earnings Multiples Based on Above Earnings and Average Market Price for Current Period*

| Company | 5-Year Average (a) | 3-Year Average (b) | Latest Year | Latest 12 Months To | Indicated Dividend Yield | Market Price(e) to Tangible Book Value(d) | Return on Average Common Equity |
| --- | --- | --- | --- | --- | --- | --- | --- |
| American Corporation | 22.1 | 17.9 | 13.7 | 11.9 | 3.6% | 328% | 26.2% |
| Delta Corporation | 14.1 | 11.4 | 9.3 | 7.7 | 3.8 | 143 | 16.0 |
| The United States Corporation | 24.1 | 10.4 | 7.8 | 7.1 | 1.5 | 105 | 14.9 |
| The XYZ Corporation | 11.0 | 8.5 | 8.2 | 8.2 | 1.5 | 155 | 20.7 |
| Median | 18.1 | 10.9 | 8.8 | 8.0 | 2.6% | | 18.4% |

*Notes:* (a) 19X5–X9. (b) 19X7–X9. (c) Latest indicated annual rate at the valuation date. (d) Latest year available at the valuation date. (e) Average market price in the current period.

*Sources:* Company reports; SEC Forms 10–K; Standard & Poor's Stock Guide, Corporation Records, Dividend Record; Barron's and the Wall Street Journal. Computations by Standard Research Consultants.

FIGURE 32.2   COMPARATIVE COMPANIES: INVESTOR APPRAISAL RATIOS AT VALUATION DATE

**Operating Income Before Depreciation — As a Percent of Operating Revenues**

| Company | 19X5 | 19X6 | 19X7 | 19X8 | 19X9 |
|---|---|---|---|---|---|
| American Tool Corporation | 16.2 | 17.5 | 19.5 | 20.0 | 23.4 |
| Delta Corporation | 10.9 | 12.0 | 13.1 | 14.7 | 15.3 |
| The United States Corporation | 4.8 | 5.0 | 11.1 | 11.4 | 11.5 |
| The XYZ Corporation | 13.6 | 15.6 | 18.8 | 15.6 | 16.7 |
| Median | 12.3 | 13.8 | 16.0 | 15.2 | 16.0 |
| Subject Unit | 30.6 | 15.6 | 22.6 | 24.9 | 21.3 |

**Operating Income After Depreciation — As a Percent of Operating Revenues**

| Company | 19X5 | 19X6 | 19X7 | 19X8 | 19X9 |
|---|---|---|---|---|---|
| American Tool Corporation | 14.3 | 15.3 | 17.3 | 17.9 | 21.3 |
| Delta Corporation | 8.0 | 8.5 | 10.3 | 12.0 | 12.8 |
| The United States Corporation | 1.5 | 1.3 | 8.1 | 8.7 | 9.6 |
| The XYZ Corporation | 11.3 | 12.9 | 16.9 | 13.5 | 13.9 |
| Median | 9.7 | 10.7 | 13.6 | 12.8 | 13.4 |
| Subject Unit | 30.3 | 15.1 | 22.1 | 24.5 | 20.8 |

**Income Before Income Taxes(a)**

| Company | 19X5 | 19X6 | 19X7 | 19X8 | 19X9 |
|---|---|---|---|---|---|
| American Tool Corporation | 13.8 | 14.3 | 16.5 | 17.2 | 20.8 |
| Delta Corporation | 6.6 | 7.2 | 10.3 | 10.4 | 10.7 |
| The United States Corporation | −4.0 | −2.9 | 5.4 | 6.2 | 7.2 |
| The XYZ Corporation | 9.8 | 11.8 | 16.0 | 12.4 | 12.0 |
| Median | 8.2 | 9.5 | 13.2 | 11.4 | 11.4 |
| Subject Unit | 32.1 | 16.7 | 23.6 | 25.9 | 22.0 |

**Income After Income Taxes(a)**

| Company | 19X5 | 19X6 | 19X7 | 19X8 | 19X9 |
|---|---|---|---|---|---|
| American Tool Corporation | 7.6 | 8.1 | 9.0 | 8.8 | 10.4 |
| Delta Corporation | 3.5 | 3.7 | 4.9 | 5.1 | 5.5 |
| The United States Corporation | −1.9 | −1.4 | 2.9 | 3.3 | 4.2 |
| The XYZ Corporation | 5.2 | 6.1 | 8.2 | 6.8 | 6.7 |
| Median | 4.4 | 4.0 | 6.6 | 6.0 | 6.1 |
| Subject Unit | 16.0 | 8.7 | 11.6 | 13.1 | 11.5 |

*Notes:* (a) Before minority interests, equity in net income of unconsolidated subsidiaries, and extraordinary items.
*Source:* Company reports and SEC Form 10–K. Computations by Standard Research Consultants.

FIGURE 32.3   SUBJECT UNIT VERSUS COMPARATIVE COMPANIES:   PROFIT MARGINS 19X5-19X9

| Company | 19X5 | 19X6 | 19X7 | 19X8 | 19X9 |
|---|---|---|---|---|---|
| | | Operating Revenues(b) | | | |
| American Tool Corporation | 72 | 81 | 100 | 120 | 146 |
| Delta Corporation | 87 | 83 | 100 | 113 | 133 |
| The United States Corporation | 102 | 86 | 100 | 101 | 116 |
| The XYZ Corporation | 62 | 72 | 100 | 130 | 137 |
| Median | 80 | 82 | 100 | 117 | 135 |
| Subject Unit | 92 | 76 | 100 | 132 | 158 |

| Company | 19X5 | 19X6 | 19X7 | 19X8(a)(b) | 19X9 |
|---|---|---|---|---|---|
| | | Operating Income(a)(b) | | | |
| American Tool Corporation | 62 | 71 | 100 | 121 | 176 |
| Delta Corporation | 67 | 71 | 100 | 125 | 154 |
| The United States Corporation | 19 | 14 | 100 | 109 | 138 |
| The XYZ Corporation | 42 | 56 | 100 | 104 | 110 |
| Median | 52 | 64 | 100 | 115 | 146 |
| Subject Unit | 125 | 52 | 100 | 146 | 149 |

*Income Before Extraordinary Items*

| Company | 19X5 | 19X6 | 19X7 | 19X8 | 19X9 |
|---|---|---|---|---|---|
| American Tool Corporation | 61 | 72 | 100 | 117 | 169 |
| Delta Corporation | 62 | 64 | 100 | 120 | 152 |
| The United States Corporation | DEF | DEF | 100 | 114 | 169 |
| The XYZ Corporation | 39 | 53 | 100 | 108 | 112 |
| Median | 50 | 59 | 100 | 116 | 161 |
| Subject Unit | 126 | 57 | 100 | 149 | 157 |

*Notes:* (a) After depreciation. (b) 19X7 Base Year = 100.
*Sources:* Company reports and SEC Form 10–K. Computations by Standard Research Consultants.

FIGURE 32.4   SUBJECT UNIT VERSUS COMPARATIVE COMPANIES: TRENDS IN REVENUES AND INCOME, 19X5-19X9

| Company | Return on Average Total Assets(a) | | | | | Return on Average Common Stock Equity(b) | | | | |
|---|---|---|---|---|---|---|---|---|---|---|
| | 19X5 | 19X6 | 19X7 | 19X8 | 19X9 | 19X5 | 19X6 | 19X7 | 19X8 | 19X9 |
| American Tool Corporation | 20.8% | 20.2% | 24.2% | 25.3% | 31.1% | 16.8% | 17.6% | 21.3% | 21.4% | 26.2% |
| Delta Corporation | 12.4 | 11.6 | 17.7 | 18.2 | 19.2 | 9.5 | 8.8 | 12.8 | 14.1 | 16.0 |
| The United States Corporation | .0 | 1.4 | 11.1 | 12.1 | 14.9 | −7.1 | −4.5 | 10.8 | 11.2 | 14.9 |
| The XYZ Corporation | 19.6 | 22.3 | 32.9 | 25.5 | 20.8 | 16.4 | 19.3 | 29.1 | 24.6 | 20.7 |
| Median | 16.0% | 15.9% | 21.0% | 21.8% | 20.2% | 13.0% | 13.2% | 17.1% | 17.8% | 18.4% |
| Subject Unit | 41.8% | 18.4% | 30.4% | 37.3% | 33.7% | 24.4% | 11.2% | 19.0% | 25.0% | 22.1% |

| Company | Total Assets to Common Stock Equity | | | | |
|---|---|---|---|---|---|
| | 19X5 | 19X6 | 19X7 | 19X8 | 19X9 |
| American Tool Corporation | 1.6 | 1.7 | 1.7 | 1.8 | 1.7 |
| Delta Corporation | 1.9 | 1.8 | 1.8 | 1.8 | 1.8 |
| The United States Corporation | 3.2 | 2.8 | 2.6 | 2.4 | 2.2 |
| The XYZ Corporation | 1.9 | 1.8 | 1.8 | 2.0 | 2.0 |
| Median | 1.9 | 1.8 | 1.8 | 1.9 | 1.9 |
| Subject Unit | 1.2 | 1.2 | 1.3 | 1.3 | 1.2 |

*Notes:* (a) Income before income taxes plus interest expense as a percent of average total assets; (b) Income available for common stock equity before extraordinary items as a percent of average common stock equity.

*Sources:* Company reports and SEC Form 10–K. Computations by Standard Research Consultants.

FIGURE 32.5   SUBJECT UNIT VERSUS COMPARATIVE COMPANIES: RATES OF RETURN AND LEVERAGE FACTOR, 19X5-19X9

| Company | 19X5 | 19X6 | 19X7 | 19X8 | 19X9 |
|---|---|---|---|---|---|
| | | | *Times* | | |
| | | | *Working-Capital Ratios* | | |
| American Tool Corporation | 3.1 | 3.2 | 3.0 | 2.7 | 2.6 |
| Delta Corporation | 2.0 | 2.9 | 2.8 | 3.0 | 2.9 |
| The United States Corporation | 1.8 | 3.1 | 3.3 | 3.6 | 3.2 |
| The XYZ Corporation | 2.3 | 3.3 | 2.6 | 3.6 | 3.7 |
| Median | 2.2 | 3.2 | 2.9 | 3.3 | 3.1 |
| Subject Unit | 5.2 | 4.6 | 3.3 | 3.4 | 4.7 |
| | | | *Quick-Asset Ratios* | | |
| American Steel Corporation | 1.2 | 1.6 | 1.6 | 1.5 | 1.4 |
| Delta Corporation | .9 | 1.6 | 1.7 | 1.8 | 1.7 |
| The United States Corporation | .5 | 1.0 | 1.5 | 1.6 | 1.2 |
| The XYZ Corporation | .8 | 1.7 | .9 | 1.6 | 1.3 |
| Median | .9 | 1.6 | 1.6 | 1.6 | 1.4 |
| Subject Unit | 4.1 | 3.2 | 2.5 | 2.6 | 3.5 |

*Sources:* Company reports and SEC Form 10–K. Computations by Standard Research Consultants.

FIGURE 32.6   SUBJECT UNIT VERSUS COMPARATIVE COMPANIES: WORKING-CAPITAL CONDITION, 19X5-19X9

*Dividend approach.* While there is little a noncontrolling stockholder can do to influence dividend policy, a controlling stockholder, guided by good business judgment, can institute a dividend policy that might suit his and/or the company's requirements. In this case, as we are considering the divestiture of an entire division or subsidiary, a dividend approach would not yield a meaningful value.

*Return on equity approach.* Book value in and of itself has little bearing on the determination of the fair market value of a successful industrial company. The rate of earnings on book value is more significant. Figure 32.8 tabulates the comparatives' latest available year-end (12/31/79) rate of return on average common stock equity, 1979 ratios of market to book value, and the ratio of current average market price to latest available book value.

The comparative companies earning at similar rates were currently selling at market to book ratios ranging between 155 percent and 328 percent. The company earning at the higher rate generally has historically earned at higher annually

| Fiscal Year Ended December 31 | Net Earnings ($000) | Applicable Multiple (Times) | Indicated Value ($000) |
|---|---|---|---|
| 19X5 | 380 | | |
| 19X6 | 412 | | |
| 19X7 | 456 | | |
| 19X8 | 681 | | |
| 19X9 | 714 | 7.5 | 5355 |
| | | | |
| 19X0 | 750 (estimated) | | |
| 5-year (19X5-X9) Average | 529 | 10.0 | 5290 |
| 3-year (19X7-X9) Average | 617 | 8.5 | 5245 |
| Projected | 750 | 7.5 | 5625 |

FIGURE 32.7   BASES FOR COMPUTING INDICATED VALUES

increasing rates. An appropriate ratio of market to book value might be 160 percent. This rate would indicate a market value of $5,768,000 when applied to an assumed book value of $3,605,000.

*Summary of indicated values—Going concern approach.* Using the two approaches, the appraiser thus has a range of values of between $5,290,000 and $5,768,000. These values are equal to the total value of all the shares (or the entire company), assuming the shares were freely and actively traded in a recognized securities market. However, as the appraiser would be determining the value of an entire company or division, he would also consider the factor of control.

*Other considerations of the seller.* In setting its minimum price, the seller should also consider the following factors:

- The extent and value of assets not required for the normal operation of the subject company's business (e.g., excess real estate and excess working capital);
- Assets and/or liabilities, if any, that will not be involved in the transaction;
- The parent's investment; and
- The impact on the parent's business, customers, competition, tax position, and accounting methods.

*Other considerations of the purchaser.* The potential purchaser generally sets a mental maximum price to determine the feasibility of proceeding with the acquisition. Before entering negotiations with a potential purchaser, the seller management must take into account the factors that a buyer will consider:

- The structure of the deal;
- The effect on the purchaser's financial condition, operations, operating results, and

growth posture, noting the extent to which there may be a short-term dilution in earnings and book value;

- The benefits of expanding the purchaser's products, services, and markets through acquisition, as opposed to the time and cost to accomplish the same result through start-up or internal expansion;

- The tax benefits to the buyer that may result through the transaction (e.g., tax loss carry-forward, if any) and/or the manner in which the transaction is treated;

- The magnitude of the premium or discount that may be applied, especially where the investment market is valuing common stocks of comparative companies at atypically high or low investor appraisal ratios;

- The time and cost of obtaining community and/or seller company personnel acceptance of new ownership; and

- The additional debt capacity of the divested unit available to the buyer.

| Company | Latest Available Year-End Date | 19X9 Return on Average Common Stock Equity | 19X9 Market Price to Book Value | Ratio of Average Current Price to Latest Available Book Value |
|---|---|---|---|---|
| | | % | % | % |
| The United States Corporation | 12/31/X9 | 14.9 | 96 | 105 |
| Delta Corporation | 12/31/X9 | 16.0 | 107 | 143 |
| The XYZ Corporation | 12/31/X9 | 20.7 | 186 | 155 |
| American Tool Corporation | 12/31/X9 | 26.2 | 258 | 328 |

The following tabulation sets forth similar information based on average data for the 1975–79 period.

| Company | 19X5–X9 Average Return on Average Common Stock Equity | 19X5–X9 Average Ratio of Market to Book Value | Ratio of Average Current Price to Latest Available Book Value |
|---|---|---|---|
| | % | % | % |
| The United States Corporation | 5.1 | 47 | 105 |
| Delta Corporation | 12.2 | 94 | 143 |
| American Tool Corporation | 20.7 | 324 | 328 |
| The XYZ Corporation | 22.0 | 134 | 155 |

FIGURE 32.8  COMPARATIVE COMPANIES' RATES OF RETURN

*Final determination of sales price.* If, after weighing the foregoing factors, the parties are still within each other's parameters of value, the agreed upon price ultimately reflects the negotiating abilities of the parties and the extent to which each is aware of the other's needs and objectives, as well as the benefits accruing to each as a result of the transaction. The magnitude of any concession will depend on the seller's evaluation of the benefits that would accrue to the purchaser, and how far it thinks it can go, giving weight to the circumstances.

**Net Asset Value Approach.** A second method of determining value is the *net asset value* approach. Asset values are most applicable where corporate liquidations are likely to occur: in valuing investment or holding companies, with certain natural resource companies, and with companies where earning power is so low that an earnings approach may not yield results that indicate approximate value.

The asset value approach is the primary approach in the valuation of going concerns, where earnings are low relative to assets (such as investment companies and real estate holding companies) and in liquidations. In other situations, such as those involving natural resource companies, the asset approach is a supplementary approach that may be used with those employed in the investor appraisal approach.

Whenever the asset approach is used, net asset value (common stock equity restated to reflect the market value of assets) must be discounted to reflect the fact that many assets cannot be liquidated without some cost. When liquidation is contemplated, deductions should be taken for such factors as:

- Contingent liabilities (termination of contracts or leases, severance pay, IRS or state tax claims, product litigation claims, pensions, etc.);
- Commissions and other expenses necessary to dispose of assets;
- Tax consequences of the liquidation (discussed in Chapter 33); and
- The reduction in value resulting from the receipt of funds after what may have been a long liquidation process.

**Discounted Cash Flow.** The *discounted cash flow* method (discussed in detail in Chapter 30) deals with valuation for mergers and acquisitions. DCF analysis is commonly utilized in merger and acquisition pricing studies where detailed projections of future cash flows can be made, based on the historical record of the acquired company. In calculating DCF, the analyst estimates the future cash flows (net income plus non-cash items like depreciation) expected to result from the purchase. The cash flows are then discounted by a rate that represents the cost of capital involved (the return required to justify the investment at a given risk level). The rate of discount must also reflect the opportunity cost that a purchaser must accept (the cost of electing one investment opportunity versus another).

The higher the risks involved in the entity to be divested, the higher the discount rate used on future cash flows. Discounting involves computing *present value*, or how much a dollar to be earned at a given point in the future is worth today, assuming a compound rate of return on the purchase price. Techniques used to refine this approach can include determining a *terminal value* or *residual value* of the assets at the end of the period of time represented by the discounted cash flow. This terminal value represents the estimated value of the assets that the company will retain at the end of the cash flow period.

*Limitations on DCF use.* Although the discounted cash flow approach is highly technical and challenging, several serious problems limit its usefulness in valuing entities to be divested. The first problem is whether reasonably accurate detailed cash flow projections can be constructed for a long period, preferably at least seven to ten years. In the case of a potential divestiture, particularly if the entity is marginally profitable or nonprofitable, it may be difficult to use the earnings history of the divestiture to develop projections useful in setting the selling price.

The second limitation is the fact that the selling parent is not in a position to make the proper assumptions concerning projections without knowing the business methods and philosophy of a potential buyer. The potential buyer may view the future earnings of the company very differently.

The final problem is related to the first two and concerns the appropriate discount rate to be used for the entity to be divested. A seller is likely to have an optimistic bias toward the risks involved in the business to be sold and will choose a discount rate too low to be applied to expected future cash flows.

To summarize, the controller of a parent company making the divestment will find the discounted cash flow method of limited usefulness in arriving at a reasonable offering price. A more realistic approach in determining fair market value utilizes the more traditional methods discussed earlier.

## Liquidation of Assets

An alternative to divesting a "going concern" is to sell or liquidate individual assets. To choose the alternative that will maximize potential compensation, the market value of these assets must be determined. Management must first decide which assets are to be sold.

Certain assets that are easily recognizable and that contribute to an on-going business operation are generally stated on the balance sheet. These include those assets that comprise the working capital position of a company (cash, near-cash, inventories, etc.) and those assets that comprise the fixed asset portion of the company's balance sheet (land, buildings, machinery and equipment, etc.). However, intangible assets not generally valued in a company's balance sheet are frequently overlooked. In the case of an equity being divested because it is either unprofitable or marginally profitable, there may be very little, if any, intangible value. However, if an operation is profitable, a portion of those earnings may be directly attributed to intangibles such as patents, license agreements, leasehold interest, secret formulas, copyrights, product drawings, and goodwill.

In the valuation of intangible assets, several approaches are used, among which the more significant are as follows:

- Replacement cost;
- Fair market value; and
- Liquidation value.

Although these terms are familiar to controllers because they are the terms commonly used when discussing areas such as accounting (book and tax), insurance, and buying or selling, they are very often misused. For example, some will try to determine the value of an asset for sale by using the cost of reproduction new, an approach to value generally used for insurance.

Since so many values can be associated with a single asset, these approaches are further broken down below. When considering a liquidation, the definitions are of particular importance.

**Replacement Cost.** Replacement cost, or cost of replacement new, is the amount necessary to replace an asset with a modern one of equivalent capacity and utility. It is important to remember that the insurance industry uses the term replacement cost, but means reproduction cost.

**Fair Market Value.** Market value for continued use is the amount at which the property might exchange between a willing buyer and a willing seller. They both have full knowledge of the facts and both plan to retain the facilities at their present location, for continuation of the operations as part of an existing business enterprise. Market value for sale in the open market is the amount that might be realized from piecemeal disposition of the property in the secondhand market, allowing a reasonable period in which to complete the transaction.

**Liquidation Value.** Liquidation value, also used to describe value when the seller has an unduly compelling reason to sell, is the amount that might be realized from piecemeal disposition of the assets in the secondhand market over a relatively short period of time.

The type of operation in which these assets are employed determines liquidation values received; they can be surprisingly low. Certain assets may have no value, and may, in fact, cost the divesting company to have them picked up and taken away. Depending on the urgency with which the disposition must take place, the liquidation is considered *orderly* or *forced* (also known as *auction*), which, in turn affects the amount realized from the sale of these assets. In an orderly liquidation, a three to six month period is generally allowed for sale. The company has time to advertise, entertain bids, and develop some plan for liquidation. Even with the luxury of this time period, a divesting company may receive as little as 20 cents on the dollar for its assets. In a forced liquidation, a company is generally allowed only a short period of time to sell its assets. In most cases, assets sold at auction net a company as little as 10 cents on the dollar.

While liquidation values are extremely low, it is important to understand the buyer's strategy when it bids on these assets. In many cases, a buyer who is a machinery dealer will bid on all the machinery and equipment even though some of the pieces have no value. He does so because the overall price may be less than the auction price for individual items.

Three measures are used to value individually the assets which are to be sold, although all might not apply to each asset. The *cost approach* refers to the cost to replace or reproduce the asset depreciated for physical, functional, and economic obsolescence. The *market approach* takes into account the price of similar assets "in the market place" and considers such factors as age and condition. The *income approach* stresses the earnings stream that would be generated by a particular asset or property.

**Liquidation Process.** While many elements enter into negotiating the liquidation of assets, certain conditions should always be considered. If a company is divesting itself of an unprofitable business that is a going concern, the minimum value that should be accepted for that business is the liquidation value of those assets. If no one is willing to purchase the business operations for a sum higher than the liquidation value of the assets, it would be more prudent for the company to sell the assets in a piecemeal fashion. This might mean selling off the inventories, putting the real estate up for sale on the open market, and bringing in the used equipment dealers to bid on the machinery and equipment.

If the business entity to be divested is a profitable one, then these assets can be sold at their highest fair market value. No one will pay more for a tangible asset (e.g., a machine tool) than it would cost to buy a similar one in the open market and have it made ready for operation (freight and installation).

There may be a premium over that value that a buyer would be willing to pay, based on the earnings he can expect from the assemblage of all the assets, including the intangible assets. Since liquidation value is the minimal value one would expect to receive when divesting an asset or assets, the following specific factors must be considered in valuing each type of asset.

*Factors in the case of real estate.*

- Location, size and utility of the land;
- Size, condition, and utility of the buildings, compared to new facilities;
- Sales, asking prices, and rentals of similar vacant sites and improved properties in the vicinity; and
- Highest and best use of the land and the total real estate.

*Factors in the case of personal property (machinery and equipment).*

- Extent, character, and utility of the property;
- Cost of reproduction new of the individual items in accordance with current market prices for labor, materials, and manufactured equipment, but exclusive of freight and installation;
- Age, condition, past maintenance, and present and prospective service ability in comparison with new units of like kind;
- Current prices a dealer in used equipment or an alternate user might pay for similar items or property in like condition;
- Amount that might be realized through auction sale with buyers assuming the cost of dismantlement and removal; and
- A reasonably short period of time in which to complete the transactions.

A company does not usually have in-house all of the information necessary to determine both fair market and liquidation values. Accounting values or insurance values are certainly no indication of fair market values or liquidation values. Depending on the number of assets to be divested and the company's investment, management should consider using a professional appraisal/valuation counsel to assist in determining the appropriate values.

## SUGGESTED READING

Bing, Gordon, *Corporate Divestment.* Houston: Gulf Publishing Company, 1978.

Bishop, John A., Rosenbloom, Arthur H., and Standard Research Consultants, *Federal Tax Valuation Digest.* 1979 edition. Boston: Warren, Gorham & Lamont, Inc.

*C.F.A. Readings in Financial Analysis.* 3rd ed. Homewood, Illinois: Richard D. Irwin, Inc., 1975.

Cohen, Jerome B., Zinbarg, Edward D., and Zeikel, Arthur, *Investment Analysis and Portfolio Management.* Revised ed. Homewood, Illinois: Richard D. Irwin, Inc., 1977.

Desmond, Glenn M. and Kelley, Richard E. *Business Valuation Handbook.* California: Valuation Press, Inc., 1977.

Hawkins, David F., *Financial Reporting Practices of Corporations.* Homewood, Illinois: Dow Jones-Irwin, Inc., 1977.

# 33

# Divestments—Tax and Financial Accounting Problems

*Gilbert D. Bloom and Donald J. Moulin*

## TAX ACCOUNTING IMPLICATIONS

### Reorganizations

After reaching the decision to divest, either on a going concern basis or as a liquidation, and after determining the time table, the parent company must search out potential buyers. (See Chapter 30.)

When the selling parent enters into negotiations with the potential buyer, it must consider three interrelated questions:

- What is its negotiating position with regard to the fair asking price for the divestment?
- How can the divestment be structured so as to maximize tax benefits from the sale while still retaining its acceptability to the buyer?
- How should the accounting aspects of such a transaction be treated, and how will this treatment affect the value of the proceeds received from the sale?

The first question, valuation, has been discussed in Chapter 32. The second question deals with the tax impact on the structure of the transaction. There are two basic forms of sale in which tax considerations play an important role: (a) tax-free reorganizations and (b) taxable transactions. To avoid a tax upon the sale of the unit, the tax code sets forth fairly rigorous requirements. Described below are the rules that must be met for tax-free reorganizations where: (1) the stock of a subsidiary is sold in exchange for stock of another corporation; and (2) where assets are sold in exchange for the purchaser's stock.

**Tax-Free Transactions: Stock for Stock.** The disposition of stock of a subsidiary will be tax-free to the selling corporation if the selling corporation receives, in exchange, voting stock of the acquiring corporation. A tax-free stock for stock exchange may be desirable to both parties where the selling corporation has a substantial unrecognized gain in the divested subsidiary, the buyer is cash poor and does not wish to incur debt, and the seller desires an equity stake in the buyer so as to indirectly profit from the future operations of the divested subsidiary.

When the value of the divested unit is not determined at the time of the sale, the seller may arrange to receive a minimum amount of the stock for the sale of the subsidiary and defer the balance for a number of years until a more measurable indicator arises or until some external event occurs. The tax rules require the down payment to equal at least 50 percent of the maximum price. For example, if the parties agree that the subsidiary is worth at least $5 million, the purchaser delivers $5 million of its voting stock on the date of the closing. The acquiring corporation can agree to deliver additional shares of the acquiring stock totalling up to $5 million within the next five years, depending on the future market performance of the acquiring corporation, on the future profitability of the divested subsidiary, or on other external factors which would influence value. The current receipt of the voting stock and all subsequent receipts of additional shares of voting stock within the five-year period will be tax-free.

While the selling corporation cannot receive any consideration other than voting stock from the acquiring corporation, the selling corporation can receive other property, including cash, from the divested subsidiary as long as the cash or other property comes from the subsidiary and not directly or indirectly from the acquiring corporation. In this manner, the selling corporation may receive non-qualified property. Thus, in an attempt to reduce the value of the subsidiary being disposed of, a large dividend of cash or other assets may be declared from the subsidiary to the selling corporation prior to the selling corporation's disposition of the subsidiary stock. The seller can thus preserve the tax-free nature of the transaction.

The selling corporation should protect itself by making sure that the exchange agreement includes representations from the acquiring corporation that the latter will not liquidate the subsidiary acquired. If a liquidation of the subsidiary takes place as part of the plan of the stock-for-stock reorganization, the Internal Revenue Service may argue that an asset acquisition, rather than a substantive stock-for-stock exchange, has occurred. While an asset acquisition solely for voting stock may qualify as another type of reorganization ("C" type reorganization), the "C" type reorganization requires that substantially all the assets be transferred to the acquiring corporation. If a substantial dividend is received by the selling corporation from the subsidiary as part of the plan to reduce the size of the subsidiary, then the "substantially all" requirement may be impaired, thus rendering the transaction taxable.

**Tax-Free Treatment: Stock for Assets.** The transfer by the subsidiary of the selling corporation of substantially all its assets to the acquiring corporation can qualify as a tax-free merger of the subsidiary into the acquiring corporation ("A" type reorganization), or as a transfer by the subsidiary of substantially all its assets to the acquiring corporation solely for voting stock of the acquiring corporation ("C" type reorganization).

Note that the selling corporation wishing to dispose of the assets of a division may not utilize any of the tax-free reorganization techniques.

*A subsidiary is required.* To qualify for tax-free treatment, the assets must be in a subsidiary rather than a division of the selling corporation, because a merger requires that all of the assets of an existing corporation be transferred. A "C" type reorganization requires that substantially all of the assets of that corporation be transferred, and a stock-for-stock or "B" type reorganization requires that the assets be transferred by reason of the stock being transferred. Since a reorganization is impossible if a division in a larger corporation is disposed of, it is imperative that the assets to be disposed of be in an existing subsidiary. (The Internal Revenue Service may argue that the momentary transfer of assets from the selling corporation to a newly created subsidiary, in anticipation of disposing of the stock of the subsidiary, will render the transaction taxable on the theory that there is no substance to the creation of a corporation and its immediate disposition. While taxpayers have been successful in court in combating such argument, prudence would dictate that the subsidiary be created significantly in advance of any attempted disposition of the subsidiary's stock or assets.)

*A straight merger is preferable.* Of the two types of asset reorganizations (the "A" and "C" types), it is clearly easier for the seller to comply with the terms of the merger, or "A" type. All that is necessary is that the subsidiary be merged in accordance with applicable state law. Although the rules concerning acquisitions are inapplicable to transactions between U.S. and foreign corporations or wholly between foreign corporations, any type of stock consideration may be used in an "A" type reorganization as long as legitimate equity is transferred. The equity may be voting stock, nonvoting stock, convertible stock, preferred or common, and a generous amount of nonstock consideration, such as cash or other property, as long as the nonstock consideration does not exceed 50 percent of the total consideration. In a "C" type reorganization, on the other hand, the rule governing the "B" type reorganization, that solely voting stock of the acquiring corporation must be transferred, generally applies. The only exception to this rule is minor and applies to cases in which an insignificant amount of liabilities are assumed by the acquiring corporation. The acquiring corporation may give up to 20 percent of the purchase price in the form of other property, plus the liabilities assumed. However, this limited exception does not apply to any normal subsidiary whose assets are not more than five times greater than its liabilities (i.e., assumed liabilities equals or exceeds 20 percent of total assets).

One of the pitfalls of the "C" type reorganization definition is that substantially all the assets of the subsidiary must be transferred. Thus, substantial dividend distributions, redemption distributions, or prior spin-off transactions that are considered by the Internal Revenue Service to be part of the present plan of reorganization, may preclude the use of the "C" type reorganization. All of the rules relating to the definition of voting stock applicable to a "B" type reorganization are equally applicable to a "C" type reorganization. (See Chapter 31 for a more detailed explanation of the tax rules for mergers and acquisitions.)

**Reorganization Techniques: Advantages and Disadvantages.** From the selling corporation's point of view, the merger technique is probably the most advantageous in that it permits it to acquire up to 50 percent of the total consideration in nonstock consideration coming directly from the acquiring corporation. In the merger, assets are easily disposed of and the acquiring corporation accepts all of the liabilities. Since the acquiring corporation takes all assets and assumes all liabilities by operation of law, the merger eases negotiations as to the type of assets to be acquired and reduces recording problems with various land records offices, personal property filings, and other state regulatory bodies. However, both seller and buyer must obtain shareholder approval. This can be a major disadvantage where the buyer is a public company and desires to acquire the assets directly. Where the buyer creates a new wholly owned corporation to acquire the assets of the seller in a merger, buyer shareholder approval is unnecessary since the buyer is the new corporation and its shareholder is its parent corporation.

The acquiring corporation may be reluctant to take on all liabilities of the subsidiary, known or unknown, contingent or otherwise. The generous use of nonstock consideration is of no benefit to the buyer since a "step-up" in the basis of the assets for tax purposes is denied even if 50 percent of the consideration is cash. In such cases, the "C" type reorganization, although more restrictive as to the nonstock consideration to be used in a merger, at least permits the acquiring corporation to negotiate for which assets are to be taken and which liabilities are to be assumed.

Where it is imperative that the validity of the corporation is kept intact to avoid renegotiation of contracts or the regranting of regulatory approval, the "B" type reorganization is the tax-free method that preserves the integrity of the corporation. Since the stock of the subsidiary is merely being exchanged, all the attributes of the subsidiary survive the reorganization and all attributes and liabilities remain with that corporation.

In each of the reorganizations, the earnings and profits, accounting methods, depreciation methods and other tax attributes become the property of the acquiring corporation. One of the significant attributes is net operating loss and capital loss carryovers. These carryovers survive by operation of the reorganization rules, but may be scaled down by other rules that require the selling corporation stockholders to receive significant amounts of common stock (20 percent until 1982 and 40 percent thereafter) in the acquiring corporation. (See Chapter 31 for a more detailed review of the rules for net operating loss and capital loss carryovers.)

### Divestment by Distributions to Shareholders

If the selling corporation decides to divest a subsidiary corporation to its existing stockholders by distributing either the subsidiary's stock or assets rather than to sell it to a third party, the corporation must closely examine the tax implications.

**Spin-Off.** A transfer of business assets in a subsidiary to the shareholders of the distributing corporation may qualify for tax-free treatment, provided the corporation meets certain rigid standards of prior business history.

*Active trade or business concepts.* If the business to be distributed constitutes an active trade or business and was held by the selling or distributing corporation for at least five years, then the transaction can be accomplished tax-free to the distributing corporation and its shareholders. The active conduct of a trade or business is defined as the participation in activity which involves significant management and supervisory endeavors as distinguished from passive activities or activities performed by independent contractors or third parties. Marketing, manufacturing, and construction by their very natures are active businesses. For other enterprises, such as a real estate function, the existence of employees who work full-time and provide management and supervisory control of a business provides activity sufficient to qualify the transaction as a spin-off. This level of activity must have been maintained for at least five years. The level of activity, even if significant, is not considered operative until the corporation has income as well as expense. Drilling for oil is not considered a qualified activity until oil is found and income has been generated. Note, however, that while the trade or business must have been in existence for at least five years, the distributing corporation need not have conducted the business (directly or through a subsidiary) for the entire five-year period if the distributing corporation acquired the business in a nontaxable manner during the five-year period. The distributing corporation can "tack on" the predecessor's history if the trade or business was acquired in a nontaxable manner (generally, a reorganization where no boot or other property was given in exchange for the stock) during the five-year period. It is important not only that the subsidiary to be distributed be engaged in the conduct of a five-year trade or business but also that the retained business in the distributing corporation be so engaged.

Based on case law, the IRS has concluded that the five-year business history must be found in the company to be spun-off as well as in the distributing corporation after, but not necessarily before, the date of the distribution. For the prior five-year history, it is sufficient that one trade or business has been operated as long as there are two trades or businesses after the distribution. Thus, a department store operating ten years in the downtown city and three years in the suburbs may be considered one business due to common facilities and common management. A corporation containing the suburban location constitutes a separate trade or business after the distribution of its stock, just as the downtown operation constitutes a separate business after the distribution. The suburban location need not have been in existence for a full five years so long as the downtown facility has been operating for five years, the suburban location's growth was a natural outgrowth of the downtown location, and the suburban store and the downtown store had common facilities, employees, and management during its period of existence. If the suburban location was different in style and method of operation and had no relationship to the downtown operation, each location must achieve a full five-year history.

*Valid business purpose concept.* An equally important requirement for tax-free distributions under spin-off rules is that the stock be distributed pursuant to a valid business purpose. Unlike other areas of corporate tax law, where business purpose can be satisfied in a perfunctory manner, a strong, compelling, and immediate corporate business purpose must be met before the spin-off rules can be satisfied. Shareholder business reasons, such as estate planning or saving withholding taxes at the shareholder level on foreign distributions do not qualify; nor do corporate business purposes, such as isolation of liabilities, separation of risks, or any other business purpose that could generally be satisfied by the mere creation of a subsidiary.

The key element characterizing a good corporate business purpose is compulsion by a third party. Examples of such compulsion include the following:

- Required divestiture;
- Credit limitation imposed by banks (if the corporation is not a subsidiary, its loan limit will be independently determined and not limited by a combined parent-subsidiary limitation);
- Desire to sell stock to employees of the parent and the subsidiary without giving one group of employees an indirect interest in the corporation in which they have no interest;
- Avoidance of union problems (a union in the parent will push for a unionized subsidiary but if the two corporations are commonly owned brother-sister corporations, they will be treated as separate by the unions);
- Distribution of nonutility assets to prevent a public service commission from determining profitability of the utility by use of the extraneous assets; and
- Protection of assets from an immediate threat of nationalization.

Having satisfied the active trade or business requirement and the strong and compelling business purpose requirement, it is incumbent on the distributee shareholders to hold onto the stock of the spun-off corporation and to neither plan to sell or exchange it in a taxable transaction, nor to indicate any intent to liquidate the company. The transaction must not be used as a device to distribute earnings and profits by indirectly substituting the spin-off distribution for what would normally be a dividend distribution. The strong business purpose, along with the intention to hold onto the stock, indicates the absence of a motive to indirectly distribute earnings and profits.

If the distribution of the stock of the spun-off company to the shareholders is to be tax-free, it can be pro rata or it can be non-pro rata to a specific group of shareholders, i.e., in exchange for all their stock in the distributing corporation, thus eliminating them from the company. Where the transaction is non-pro rata, the distribution must result in a fair market value exchange. It is not inconsistent with a spin-off distribution to have the shareholders, at a separate meeting at some time after the distribution, vote on disposing of the stock in a tax-free transaction. Thus, after the distribution of the subsidiary is made to the shareholders and the shareholders have legitimately taken title to the shares, a separate meeting can be convened and a separate vote taken on an offer by a third party to have the shareholders exchange the stock of the spun-off corporation for the stock of an acquiring corporation.

While it is not mandatory that the distributing corporation distribute all of the stock, at least 80 percent of the stock of the subsidiary must be distributed to the shareholders and a strong reason must be established for retention of the difference between what is distributed and 100 percent. The stock must not have been retained in order to influence the control or operation of the spun-off corporation. Providing future stock options or collateralizing existing loans are, however, considered valid business reasons.

**Partial Liquidations.** Rather than distribute the stock of a subsidiary containing an active trade or business, the distributing corporation may distribute the assets of such active trade or business "in kind" to the shareholders. Such a distribution cannot qualify for tax-free treatment, but can qualify for capital gain treatment to the shareholders. The measure of the capital gain is the fair market value of the assets received over the basis in the stock surrendered. If a partial liquidation reduces the size of a corporation by 30 percent, then 30 percent of the shares, and their corresponding basis, will be surrendered. The distinguishing factor between a normal dividend and a partial liquidation distribution is the quantum of the distribution. A significant reduction in the size of the business, which reduces the number of employees, the gross income, and the gross assets by approximately 15 percent will result in a partial liquidation distribution. Whereas normal recurring liquid asset distributions would not have any effect on the level of activity, a partial liquidation distribution is a significant contraction of the corporation's business. The distribution of the assets to the shareholders can then be disposed of at no cost to the corporation. The receipt of the distribution results in a taxable transaction to the shareholders equal to the fair market value of the assets. The tax effect on the shareholders depends on their basis in the shares and their holding period. Obviously, a partial liquidation distribution is feasible only in cases where the corporation does not have many shareholders, thus precluding the feasibility of making "in kind" distributions.

**Redemption Distributions.** A divestment of assets may take the form of a *redemption distribution.* One or more shareholders may receive assets or subsidiary stock in exchange for all or part of their stock in the corporation. These shareholders would probably accept the assets or subsidiary stock if they presently operate the business associated with these assets. They may have previously exchanged their business for stock in the corporation and have continued their employment in the business. The "marriage" may now be dissolved by their taking back the business in exchange for the stock.

*Reduction in corporation's outstanding shares.* In another context, the redemption distribution need not be made to an existing shareholder, but may be made to shareholder(s) who become such in contemplation of receiving a corporate distribution of assets or stock. A corporation that desires to sell a subsidiary, and at the same time wants to reduce its outstanding shares can, in effect, dispose of the subsidiary tax-free. Assume that X corporation has a wholly owned subsidiary (Y) that has failed to meet management's expectations as to earning levels. X wants to "sell" Y to Corporation Z, which has expressed an interest in purchasing Y for cash. In addition, X has noticed that the market price of its traded stock is unrealistically low and believes that it is a propitious moment to reduce its outstanding shares. Pursuant to an agreement between X and Z, Z makes a cash tender offer for X's stock equal to the value of Y. When Z acquires sufficient shares of X, Z exchanges the shares with X for Y's stock. For tax purposes, X would be justified in treating the disposition of Y as a tax-free redemption. Z would have to comply with the tender offer rules of the Securities and Exchange Commission.

*Contraction of shareholder's interests.* While partial liquidation distributions are contractions at the corporate level, redemption distributions are contractions at the shareholder level. That is, they are generally made to one or more, but not all, of the shareholders and they significantly reduce that shareholder's interest in the enterprise. Thus, redemptions contemplate a surrender by the shareholder of the stock back to the corporation. Partial liquidating distributions are generally pro rata and, therefore, have no effect on the shareholder's stake in the enterprise. Redemption distributions, in order to qualify for capital gain treatment, require a contraction of the shareholder's stake in the enterprise. Any reduction in the shareholder's stake in the enterprise, regardless of how small, will qualify for capital gain treatment if the distribution is to a small minority shareholder who reduces his interest and whose actions have no effect upon the policies of the corporation. A general safe harbor rule would be a 20 percent reduction in such shareholder's interest. Thus, if a shareholder held 16 percent of the stock in a  corporation before the transaction and, after his redemption held 12 percent of the stock, the transaction would qualify as a capital gain redemption.

**Dividend Distributions.** A seller corporation generally will divest by a dividend "in kind" to the corporation's shareholders when all other possible distributions to shareholders are inapplicable. A distribution of assets is considered a dividend only when the distribution cannot qualify as a spin-off, a partial liquidation, or a redemption. It should be noted, however, that dividend distributions from domestic corporations are taxed more favorably to corporate shareholders than to individual or noncorporate shareholders. Corporate shareholders would prefer to receive a dividend distribution rather than a capital gain, partial liquidation, or redemption distribution because only 15 percent of the dividend is taxable, and it is included in income at the lesser of two values: (a) the fair market value of the property, or (b) the adjusted basis for the property in the hands of the distributing corporation increased by gain recognized in the transaction, immediately before the distribution. A dividend will be taxed at ordinary income tax rates to the extent that there are sufficient earnings and profits to cover the fair market value of the distribution.

**Effect of Distributions on the Corporation.** Generally, distributions as spin-offs, partial liquidations, redemptions, or dividends have no tax effect upon a corporation making the distribution, or upon its shareholders. However the following exceptions should be noted:

- Recapture of investment tax credits in all four types of distributions;
- Depreciation recapture on partial liquidations, dividends, and redemption distributions;
- Distributions of appreciated property (other than stock of a 50 percent owned subsidiary) in redemptions not qualifying as a complete termination of interest of at least a 10-percent shareholder;
- Redemption distributions of LIFO inventory; and
- Partial liquidation and redemption distributions of installment obligations.

## Taxable Transactions

**Sale of Assets by a Parent.** The sale of assets by a corporation results in a capital transaction or ordinary income or loss depending on the character of the assets sold. If the corporation sells land or stock, which are capital assets, it will sustain a capital gain or loss (either long-term or short-term depending on the holding period). If it disposes of inventory or trade receivables, the sale will give rise to ordinary income or loss. The parties must thus agree to the items being sold and allocate a purchase price to the assets that is generally satisfactory to both sides. If the sale of a going concern includes an inherent goodwill factor, the selling corporation should specifically allocate a portion of the purchase price to goodwill; otherwise, the buyer will usually not allocate any specific amount to goodwill. If the agreement includes a covenant in which the seller agrees not to compete, the covenant is ordinary income and should be specifically valued. If the covenant is not specifically valued, the Internal Revenue Service may decide the proper allocation of the sales price or may determine that it has no value at all.

**Sale of Assets by a Subsidiary.** Assets sold by a subsidiary corporation to a third party are taxable in the same manner as if the parent corporation had sold the assets. Generally, when a corporation sells all of its assets and liquidates, no gain or loss is recognized to the corporation on the sale if it makes the proper election under the tax laws and the subsequent liquidation is to individual shareholders. When a subsidiary sells its assets and liquidates into its parent corporation, the subsidiary recognizes gain or loss on the transaction. Subsequent liquidation by the subsidiary to the parent corporation (with the proceeds of sale being transferred to the parent) is a tax-free transaction.

A parent may completely liquidate a controlled subsidiary tax-free and receive all of the subsidiary assets; the parent may then choose which assets to retain and which assets to dispose of. In determining capital gain or loss or ordinary income or loss, the parent's basis in the subsidiary assets will generally be the same basis that the subsidiary had in its own assets. An exception to the carry over basis of the assets occurs where the parent purchased control of a subsidiary within a twelve-month period and completely liquidates it within two years after acquiring control. In such a case, the parent's basis in the subsidiary assets is equal to the parent's cost of the subsidiary's stock allocated (with appropriate adjustments) among the assets in proportion to the fair market value of the assets.

The sale of certain items by the corporation will give rise to ordinary income or additional tax, notwithstanding the fact that capital assets are sold or a nontaxable liquidation is elected. Thus, the recapture of depreciation on certain personal and real property, along with investment credit recapture on early disposition of property, will be "triggered" by the selling corporation at the time of the sale.

**Sale of Stock With a Deemed Dividend Election.** The sale by a parent corporation of the stock of one of its subsidiaries generally results in a capital gain or loss. The capital gain can be reduced and the loss increased by making a "deemed dividend election" if the corporation files a consolidated return. Such an election permits the parent to increase its basis in the subsidiary stock by an amount equal to the subsidiary's earnings and profits accumulated during: (1) pre-1966 consolidated return years, and (2) all years in which the subsidiary was a member of the group but separate returns were filed (provided such years were not separate return limitation years).

**Stock Sales Through Pre-Sale Distributions.** The purchase price of the stock of an existing subsidiary can be reduced by distributions of assets from the subsidiary to the parent corporation prior to the parent's selling the subsidiary stock. Such a distribution could also be advisable if certain assets are desired by the parent corporation or specifically not desired by the buyer. These pre-sale distributions may be taxed as dividend income, subject to the favorable 85 percent dividends received deduction, and result in a maximum corporate tax of approximately 7 percent (46 percent times 15 percent). The Internal Revenue Service will recognize these initial distributions from the subsidiary to the parent even though the parent may realize substantial tax savings by converting an otherwise capital gain into dividend income. This favorable result is not achieved if the parent and subsidiary file a consolidated tax return because the distribution from the subsidiary to the parent reduces the parent's basis in the subsidiary's stock and the subsequent sale of the subsidiary stock results in the same amount of capital gain that otherwise would have been paid. However, the parent's basis in the stock of a subsidiary included in a consolidated return would generally be higher than for a separate return subsidiary.

**Sale of Stock Through Installment Payments.** A sale of stock may be consummated and the entire purchase price paid immediately, or the payment can be stretched out over years. Where the sales price is to be paid in the future, the taxpayer is now required to use the installment reporting method for Federal income tax purposes unless a special election is filed with the tax return for the year of the sale. On the installment reporting method, each payment is income based on a ratio, the numerator of which is the gain on the sale and the denominator of which is the selling price. A deferral of the purchase price that does not provide for interest or that provides for a nominal rate of interest results in the Internal Revenue Service treating part of each payment as imputed interest.

While it is not usually a problem, it should be noted that the buyer is limited by law to an annual interest deduction of $5 million on debt incurred to purchase the stock or two-thirds of all the operating assets (excluding cash) of another corporation.

**Exceptions to Capital Gain Treatment for Stock Sales.** Exceptions to the general rule that the sale of stock results in capital gain or loss treatment are found where the stock sold represents stock in a collapsible corporation. A collapsible corporation is one that is "formed or availed of principally for the manufacture, construction, or production of property with a view toward converting ordinary income into capital gain." Thus, if a subsidiary is established to subdivide and sell real estate and the corporate stock is disposed of before a substantial part of the income has been realized, the proceeds of that sale may be treated as ordinary income. Another major exception to capital gain treatment for stock sales is a sale of stock in a "controlled foreign corporation." A controlled foreign corporation is one in which at least 51 percent of the stock is controlled by U.S. persons who individually own at least 10 percent of the stock. The sale of the stock results in dividend income, subject to foreign tax credits, to the extent of the earnings and profits of the foreign corporations.

**Divestments to Charity.** A transfer of assets or stock to a charitable organization may give rise to a corporate charitable contribution. The Internal Revenue Service has acquiesced in cases where stock of a subsidiary has been donated to a charitable organization and pursuant to an understanding, but not a binding commitment, the stock is then redeemed by the subsidiary. The corporation's charitable contribution is limited to 5 percent of corporate taxable income computed without regard to the charitable deduction and certain other deductions. A corporation may carry forward for five years any excess charitable contributions, subject each year to the 5 percent limitation.

**Joint Venture Dispositions.** The transfer by the parent corporation of assets or stock to a new company concurrent with another party's transferring assets to the new company is a tax-free transaction. The parent has diluted its interest in the new company, possibly as a prelude to eventual divestiture. However, if the new company is profitable, the parent may retain its stock. This method may be used as a "hedge," an attempt to spread the risk of the business, or to bring new capital that is needed in the corporation. Under these circumstances, there will be no tax consequences until the transferor corporation is retired from the enterprise. The redemption of stock which does not significantly reduce the parent corporation's control or influence in the company will be treated as a dividend until the last redemption that completely terminates the parent's interest in the new company. The last redemption will be treated as a capital gain.

## FINANCIAL ACCOUNTING FOR DIVESTMENTS

The accounting aspects of a divestiture must be considered in the decision-making process that precedes it. The form and structure that are to be used for the sale or liquidation impact the financial statements of the seller as well as the price tag to be put on the unit and the tax implications. All of these aspects are closely intertwined.

### Disposal of a Segment of Business

A divestment may be consummated by a sale, an exchange (a reciprocal transfer), a nonreciprocal transfer (including a liquidation, as covered later in this chapter), or an abandonment. Any of these methods may constitute a disposal of a segment of a business as discussed in APB Opinion No. 30. A "segment of a business" in this context refers to a component of an entity whose activities represent a separate major line of business or class of customer. A segment may be in the form of a subsidiary, a division, or a department, and in some cases a joint venture or other nonsubsidiary investee, provided that its assets, results of operations, and activities can be clearly distinguished, physically and operationally and for financial reporting purposes, from other assets, results of operations, and activities of the entity. If the results of operations of the segment being sold or abandoned cannot be separately identified from those in the remainder of the organization, this fact strongly suggests that the transaction should not be classified as a disposal of a segment of a business. (See paragraph 13 of APB Opinion No. 30.) (A segment of a business for purposes of accounting for a disposal is separate and distinct from the industry segments and lines of business disclosure requirements included in Regulation S-K of the Securities and Exchange Commission and from the industry segment concept set forth in FASB Statement of Financial Accounting Standards No. 14, *Financial Reporting for Segments of a Business Enterprise.)*

If a divestment meets the criteria for disposal of a segment of a business, the financial statements must conform to the accounting rules for discontinued operations as set forth in APB Opinion No. 30.

**Reporting Discontinued Operations.** The term "discontinued operations" refers to the operations of a segment of a business as defined above that has been sold, abandoned, spun-off, or otherwise disposed of or, if it is still owned and operating, is the subject of a formal plan for disposal. The results of continuing operations should be reported separately from discontinued operations and any gain or loss from the disposal of a segment of a business should be reported in conjunction with the related results of discontinued operations and not as an extraordinary item. Paragraph 8 of APB Opinion No. 30 illustrates how to report discontinued operations:

| | | |
|---|---|---|
| Income from continuing operations before income taxes .............. | $xxxx | |
| Provision for income taxes ............................................................. | xxx | |
|     Income from continuing operations ........................................... | | $xxxx |
| | | |
| Discontinued operations (Note —): | | |
|     Income (loss) from operations of discontinued Division X (less | | |
|         applicable income taxes of $................) ................................. | $xxxx | |
|     Loss on disposal of Dixision X, including provision of $ ............. | | |
|         for operating losses during phase-out period (less applicable | | |
|         income taxes of $..................) ............................................... | xxxx | xxxx |
|     Net Income ................................................................. | | $xxxx |

*Measurement date and disposal date.* For purposes of reporting discontinued operations, the *measurement date* of a disposal is the date on which management, having authority to approve the action, commits itself to a *formal plan* to dispose of a segment of a business, whether by sale or abandonment. The plan of disposal should include, as a minimum:

- Identification of the major assets to be disposed of;
- The expected method of disposal;
- The period expected to be required for completion of the disposal;
- An active program to find a buyer if disposal is to be by sale;
- The estimated results of operations of the segment from the measurement date to the disposal date; and
- The estimated proceeds or salvage to be realized by disposal.

The *disposal date* is the date of closing the sale, if the disposal is by sale, or the date that operations cease, if the disposal is by abandonment. (See Paragraph 14 of APB Opinion No. 30.) If the disposal is by exchange, the disposal date would be the date of the closing of an exchange. If the disposal is a nonreciprocal transfer, the disposal date would be the date the transfer is made.

*Reporting income or loss from operations of a discontinued segment.* The operations of a segment that has been or will be discontinued should be reported separately as a component of income before any extraordinary items and the cumulative effect of accounting changes, as previously indicated. The line item under discontinued operations in the income statement for reporting the income or loss from operations of a discontinued segment should include only the results of operations to the measurement date as previously defined. The comparable amount in prior period financial statements should be reclassified as discontinued operations in any comparative financial statements. The reporting of the results of operations of a discontinued segment from the measurement date to the disposal date should be included in the determination of gain or loss on the disposal.

*Reporting and determining the gain or loss on disposal of a segment.* If a loss is expected from the proposed disposition of a segment, the estimated loss should be provided for at the measurement date. If management expects a net loss from operations to be incurred between the measurement date and the expected disposal date, the computation of the gain or loss on the disposal should include an estimate of such operating loss. If income is expected to be produced from operations between the measurement date and the disposal date, the computation of the gain or loss should include the estimated income, to the extent of the estimated loss from the disposal otherwise recognizable. However, any net gain anticipated on the disposal should not be recognized until realized, which ordinarily would be the disposal date. In measuring the gain or loss from a disposal of a segment of a business, only such costs and expenses that are clearly the direct result of the decision to dispose of the segment and are clearly not the adjustments of carrying amounts or costs, or expenses that should have been recognized on a going-concern basis prior to the measurement date, should be included in determining the gain or loss on disposal. Accordingly, the results of operations before the measurement date should not be included in the gain or loss on disposal. Examples of costs and expenses directly associated with the decision to dispose include items such as severance pay, additional pension costs, employee relocation expenses, and future rentals on long-term leases to the extent they are not offset by sublease rentals.

If the disposal of a segment spans more than one accounting period, the gain or loss previously reported should not be restated unless the criteria for a prior period adjustment are met, that is, correction of an error. Adjustments occurring in subsequent accounting periods should be reported as a change in estimate and classified separately in the current period in the same manner as the original item was presented.

*Contingent consideration.* If the expected consideration to be received on the disposal is contingent on future events, the gain or loss reported should include only the consideration that is clearly established and is assured of collection. The contingent consideration should be recognized at the time it is realized. If the contingency is in reality one that affects the consummation of the disposal rather than merely the amount of consideration or sales price, then it is doubtful that the requirement for a formal plan of disposal meeting the criteria for a disposal of a business has been met. Accordingly, the accounting for discontinued operations would not be appropriate.

*Disclosure requirements.* In addition to the disclosure on the income statement set forth in the example presented earlier, the following earnings per share disclosures should be made by public companies:

- Earnings per share should be presented for continuing operations and net income on the face of the income statement.
- If earnings per share data for the results of discontinued operations and gain or loss from disposal of a business segment are presented, they may be included on the face of the income statement or in a related note to the financial statements.

The notes to the financial statements should disclose the following:

- Revenues applicable to the discontinued operations for all periods presented; and
- Financial statements covering the period including the measurement date should disclose: (1) the identity of the segment of business that has been or will be discontinued; (2) the expected disposal date, if known; (3) the expected manner of disposal; (4) a description of the remaining assets and liabilities of the segment at the balance sheet date; and (5) the income or loss from operations and any proceeds from disposal of the segment during the period from the measurement date to the date of the balance sheet.

For the accounting period subsequent to the measurement date and including the period of disposal, the notes to the financial statement should disclose information listed in (1), (2), (3), and (4) above and also the information listed in (5) above compared with the prior estimates.

## Divestments That Do Not Constitute a Disposal of a Business Segment

A company may divest of a portion of a business that does not meet the definition of a segment of a business as described in the preceding discussion. In such a situation, the gain or loss on the sale of the portion of a business should be determined using the same measurement principles as if it were a segment of the business. The amount of the gain or loss from the disposal should be reported as a separate component of income from continuing operations. This presentation fits the criteria of Paragraph 26 of APB Opinion No. 30. In such a situation, the gain or loss should not be reported on the face of the income statement net of income taxes. In addition, earnings per share information should not be disclosed on the face of the income statement. Of course, revenues and related costs and expenses of the portion of the business prior to the measurement date should not be segregated on the face of the income statement, but may be disclosed in the notes to the financial statements. Disclosures similar to those required for a disposal of a segment of business are recommended to be disclosed in the notes to the financial statements of a company having a divestment not qualifying as a disposal of a segment of the business.

### Accounting for Leveraged Divestments

Care must be exercised in accounting for divestments that are highly leveraged. The accounting for the leveraged divestment is no different than the accounting for leveraged sales. Before it is appropriate to recognize the gain on such sales, there must be assurance that the consideration will be received and that the resulting gain will in fact be realized. This is particularly important for publicly owned organizations. The Securities and Exchange Commission ("SEC") has been concerned with leveraged disposals and in June, 1979, the SEC issued Staff Accounting Bulletin (SAB) No. 30 entitled "Accounting for Divestiture of a Subsidiary or Other Business Operation" (included in the codification of the Staff Accounting Bulletins at Topic 5:M). This SAB discusses the staff's view regarding: (a) circumstances that indicate a divestiture has not taken place for accounting purposes in connection with the sale of a subsidiary or other business operation, and (b) the appropriate accounting and reporting treatment for such transactions.

**Circumstances Indicating No Accounting Divestiture.** When the economic substance of a transaction indicates that the seller retains the usual risks of ownership, SAB No. 30 recommends that a sale of a subsidiary or other business operation should not be recorded as a divestiture for accounting purposes.

According to the SAB, the following circumstances indicate that risks of ownership have not been transferred to the buyer:

- Continued involvement by the seller in the business as evidenced by:
  - Effective veto power over major contracts or customers,
  - Significant voting power on the board of directors, or
  - Other involvement in the continuing operations of the business, entailing risks or managerial authority similar to that of ownership;
- Absence of significant financial investment in the business by the buyer (e.g., a token down payment);
- Repayment of debt (which constitutes the principal consideration in the transaction) dependent on future successful operations of the business; and
- Continued necessity for debt or contract performance guarantees by the seller on behalf of the business.

**Accounting for Sales Not Considered a Divestiture.** The accounting treatment discussed by the SEC's staff for situations where the sale of a business does not constitute a divestiture for accounting purposes is based on the staff's view that elimination of the operating results of the business from the financial statements of the seller may be misleading. The staff believes the following accounting treatment is appropriate where risks of ownership have not been transferred:

- Assets and liabilities of the business should remain on the seller's balance sheet and be appropriately segregated; and
- Operating losses of the business, where realization of the sale price is wholly or principally dependent on the operating results of such business, should be reflected in the financial statements of the seller.

The SAB also addresses the issue of when gain or loss should be recognized after it has been determined that divestiture for accounting purposes has not occurred. The staff states that gain should not be recognized until:

- The circumstances that precluded treatment of the transaction as a divestiture have changed sufficiently to permit recognition of the gain; and
- Any major uncertainties as to the ultimate realization of profit have been removed and the consideration received in the transaction can be reasonably evaluated.

Of course, a loss on a divestiture should always be recognized as soon as it can be reasonably foreseen and measured.

The SAB also furnished guidance in determining whether the consideration to be received is reasonably assured of collection and the resulting profit recognition is appropriate. The following circumstances raise questions about the propriety of profit recognition at any time subsequent to the transaction:

- Evidence of financial weakness of the buyer;
- Substantial uncertainty as to the amount of future costs and expenses to be incurred by the seller; and
- Substantial uncertainty as to the amount of proceeds to be realized because of the form of consideration received. Examples include non-recourse debt, notes with optional settlement provisions, purchaser's stock, or other non-monetary consideration that may have indeterminable value.

The SAB includes an example of a leveraged sale to employees and circumstances where the payments by the buyer are not obligatory unless the operation divested by the seller is or becomes profitable. These conditions would indicate that divestiture accounting may not be appropriate.

### Accounting for Other Divestment Methods

The accounting for a spin-off to shareholders or other nonreciprocal transfer of both monetary and nonmonetary assets is described later in this chapter. The accounting for divestments constituting a sale would be the same as the accounting for any other sales of a company's assets. If the sales are material, consideration should be given to presenting the sale as a separate item of continuing operations of the business. Disclosures should be made in the notes to the financial statements similar to the information suggested to be disclosed in accounting for a disposal of a segment of business. Of course, only the pertinent information need be disclosed.

### Accounting Aspects of Divestiture Without Consideration

The accounting for a liquidation or a divestiture without consideration depends upon the nature of the transaction. In this context, a liquidation is defined as a transfer of assets or net assets for which no assets are received or relinquished in exchange. The accounting profession calls this form of transaction a *nonreciprocal transfer,* which is a transfer of assets and services in one direction, either from an enterprise to its owners (whether or not in exchange for their ownership interests) or another entity, or from owners or another entity to the enterprise. (See Paragraph 3(d) APB Opinion No. 29.)

These transfers may include a distribution to owners of the capital stock of subsidiaries, the net assets following a complete or partial corporate liquidation, or plans of reorganization to dispose of a segment of a business. These plans are sometimes referred to as spin-offs, split-ups, or split-offs.

**Accounting for a Nonreciprocal Transfer.** The accounting for a nonreciprocal transfer differs according to the circumstances. The following questions must be answered:

- Are the net assets monetary or nonmonetary?
- If the net assets are nonmonetary, is the transfer to owners or nonowners?
- If the distribution is a transfer of nonmonetary assets to owners, does it constitute a spin-off or other form of reorganization or liquidation?
- If the net assets being transferred are nonmonetary, is the fair value of the assets determinable within reasonable limits?

*Monetary or nonmonetary assets.* The following definitions are taken from Paragraph 3 of APB Opinion No. 29:

- Monetary assets and liabilities are assets and liabilities whose amounts are fixed in terms of units of currency by contract or otherwise. Examples are cash, short- or long-term accounts and notes receivable in cash, and short- or long-term accounts and notes payable in cash.
- Nonmonetary assets and liabilities are assets and liabilities other than monetary ones. Examples are inventories; investments in common stock; property, plant, and equipment; and liabilities for rent collected in advance.

If the net assets transferred are monetary, the general rule is that the transfer should be recorded by the transferor at the fair value of the net assets being distributed. Generally, the fair value of monetary assets will be the carrying amount, but if it is not, the difference between the carrying amount and the fair value of the assets should be recognized as a gain or loss.

If the assets are nonmonetary, the other questions must be addressed, as discussed below.

*Transfer to owners or nonowners.* If the transfer is to nonowners, the general rule is that the transfer should be recorded at the fair value of the nonmonetary assets, and gain or loss should be recognized by the transferor. If the transfer is to owners, the transaction will be accounted for at recorded cost or fair value depending on the circumstances. Nonreciprocal transfers of nonmonetary assets to owners should be accounted for at fair value only if the fair value of the nonmonetary assets distributed is objectively measurable and would be clearly realizable to the distributing entity in an outright sale at or near the time of the distribution. (See Paragraph 23 of APB Opinion No. 29.) Unless these criteria are met, the general rule is that nonreciprocal transfers of nonmonetary assets to owners should be accounted for at the recorded amount of the net assets transferred. The recorded amount of assets is original cost less adjustments for depreciation or amortization or adjustments to recognize any permanent impairment of value.

*Distribution in a spin-off, other reorganization or liquidation.* If the distribution of nonmonetary assets to owners is a spin-off or other form of reorganization, or liquidation, it should be accounted for at the recorded amount of the nonmonetary assets distributed. A pro rata distribution to owners of shares of a subsidiary or other investee company that has been or is being consolidated or that has been or is being accounted for under the equity method is considered to be equivalent to a spin-off. (See Paragraph 23 of APB Opinion No. 29.)

*Determining fair value.* The fair value of a nonmonetary asset transferred in a nonmonetary transaction should be determined by referring to estimated realizable values in cash transactions of the same or similar assets, quoted market prices, independent appraisals, and other available evidence. If the parties in a nonmonetary transaction could have elected to receive cash instead of the nonmonetary assets, the amount of cash they could have received may be used as evidence of the fair value of the nonmonetary assets transferred. When there are major uncertainties about the realizability of the value that would be assigned to an asset being transferred in a nonmonetary transaction, fair value should be regarded as not determinable within reasonable limits. If the fair value of a nonmonetary asset transferred is not determinable within reasonable limits, the recorded amount of the nonmonetary asset transferred may be the only available measure of the transaction. (See Paragraphs 25 and 26 of APB Opinion No. 29.)

*Transfer to persons under common control.* Of course, the preceding discussion of nonreciprocal transfers does not apply to a transfer to a company or person under common control. For example, a transfer from a parent company to a subsidiary or from one subsidiary to another subsidiary having the same parent or from a corporate joint venture to its owners would be accounted for at the recorded amount even though the criteria described previously are met.

*Disclosure requirements.* If a liquidation, spin-off, or other nonmonetary transaction has occurred or is planned, the financial statements for the period should disclose the nature of the transaction, the basis of accounting for the assets transferred, and gain or loss recognized on the transfer. (See Paragraph 28 of APB Opinion No. 29.)

## SUGGESTED READING

Bierman, Jacquin, and Fuller, James. "Partial Liquidations Under Section 346: Corporate Effects and Special Problems." *Journal of Taxation* (May, 1975).

Crumbley, Larry. "How to Choose the Most Advantageous Way to Combine or Separate Business Interests." *Taxation for Accountants* (October, 1975).

Dean, Stephen, and Egerton, Charles. "Acquisitive Reorganizations: The Other Method of Buying or Selling a Corporate Business." *University of Florida Law Review* (Summer, 1975).

Higgins, Stephen. "Gain on Corporate Sales During Liquidation Can Be Avoided by 12-Month Liquidation Rules." *Taxation for Accountants* (March, 1976).

Holden, James, and McAndrews, Joseph. "The Sale and Purchase of a Corporate Business in a Taxable Transaction." Tulane Twenty-Fourth Annual Tax Institute (1974).

Llewellyn, Don, Lewis, Barbara, and Majors, Stan. "Selling a Close Corporation: Should Stock or Assets Be Sold for Maximum Tax Benefits." *Taxation for Accountants* (August, 1976).

# 34

# Capital Expenditures

*David R. Shelton*

## INTRODUCTION

Capital investments can generally be defined as investments which yield benefits in future years. For many companies, capital investment decisions are the most important of financial decisions. They shape the amount and mix of the firm's assets for years to come. And the investments often involve large dollar amounts with irreversible commitments of those dollars.

The concept of capital investment is an economic concept. The relevant question is: are future period benefits involved? The classification of an expenditure as a capital investment (as opposed to an operating expense), will usually parallel the company's accounting policies that direct certain expenditures to be capitalized. But this is not necessarily so. For example, expenditures for research and development programs and advertising campaigns can, in most cases, be properly defined as capital investments. Such expenditures, however, are usually expensed for accounting purposes.

A capital investment can typically be described as falling into one of the following categories:

- Product expansion or enhancement;
- Building and equipment replacement or expansion;
- Acquisition of another company;
- Exploration for resources;
- Research and development; and
- Others, such as major advertising programs.

While the investment usually involves an outlay of funds in one of these areas, investments shouldn't be thought of as only cash outlays. Asset disposal and divestment decisions that will produce cash inflows are also capital investment decisions because future period benefits are involved.

### The Capital Investment Function

There are six basic steps when making a capital investment. First, the investment idea must be generated. Second, financial and general business aspects of the idea are developed. Third, the economics of the project are analyzed. Fourth, the investment decision is made. Fifth, outlays for the approved project must be controlled. And sixth, the project is reviewed after its completion—the post-completion audit review.

Although it is possible to list and discuss each of these steps separately, they are interrelated. Futhermore, and perhaps more importantly, they must conform to the overall objectives and strategies of the company and to the company's day-to-day operations. This leads to the fundamental requirements for an effective capital investment function.

**Primacy of Overall Corporate Strategies.** The overall objectives and strategies of the company should be given importance over any of the capital investment steps. A random scattering of individual investments cannot be viewed in isolation. Broader issues about what lines of business the company is in and how the investment affects those businesses will ultimately determine whether or not the company meets its objectives.

The primacy of corporate strategy may sometimes lead to contradictions. For example, if senior management is committed to a product line, and if equipment that is critical to its production urgently needs replacement, the equipment should be replaced, even if the expected economic return on the equipment investment is substandard. If the replacement is not made—and soon—the company may lose orders, may lose its market share, and, as a result, the overall strategic commitment could be thwarted. Similarly, an investment offering an acceptable return should probably be rejected if it doesn't support the firm's long-range plans, particularly if it might divert resources from investments that do support those plans.

**Practicality and Flexibility.** The performance of the capital investment steps should be both flexible and practical. Management should constantly be aware of the trade-offs between costs and benefits and of the relative importance of the various steps in the investment process. For example, increased effort to develop an investment proposal detail may not be worthwhile if the basic merits of the proposal are obvious. In a like manner, management should not become so preoccupied with sophisticated economic analysis that it loses sight of the greater importance of idea generation and proposal development. Without ideas, there will be nothing to analyze. Without good input, the most rigorous analysis cannot provide meaningful output.

**Needed Balance.** The capital investment process is both an art and a science. Management judgment, subjective by nature, determines in the end the success of the process. Along the way, however, application of sound economic concepts and methods of quantitative analysis can be helpful in forming sound judgments. In short, an effective capital investment function is one that is conceptually and technically sound, but pragmatic and consistent with the company's long-range plans.

## FUNDAMENTAL INVESTMENT CONCEPTS

Discussion of investment concepts is a good starting point for understanding the capital investment function. Some of the concepts involve broad issues about which there is no consensus—no one answer. The following brief review will help ensure a common ground for subsequent discussion about the investment process.

### Return on Investment

The return on an investment is determined by the cash received from the investment in excess of the cash expended for it, and by the timing of these cash flows.

In a world free of inflation and uncertainty, an investor would know exactly what the amounts and timing of an investment's cash flows are going to be. The price he would be willing to pay for the investment (i.e., the return he would require) would simply depend upon his marginal preference for a dollar now, versus later, or, in other words, upon the time value he places on money.

The return required in this perfect world is commonly called the "real" rate of return on capital. Unfortunately, we do not live in a trouble-free world. There *is* inflation and there *is* uncertainty.

In arriving at an acceptable return, the typical investor will add some inflation premium to his real rate of return. Assuming he is averse to risk, he will also require additional compensation by attaching a risk premium to the return. The greater the uncertainty, the greater the premium.

In summary, the return on investment required by an investor can be thought of as:

$$\begin{matrix} \text{Required} \\ \text{Return} \end{matrix} = \begin{matrix} \text{Real} \\ \text{Return} \end{matrix} + \begin{matrix} \text{Inflation} \\ \text{Premium} \end{matrix} + \begin{matrix} \text{Risk} \\ \text{Premium} \end{matrix}$$

### Objective of Business Investment

The maximization of shareholder wealth is commonly accepted as a firm's basic objective. This objective should underlie all capital investment decisions. The relationship between shareholder wealth and investment decisions is, in itself, however, too nebulous to use in decision making. The concept of cost of capital provides the necessary linkage between shareholder wealth and decisions about individual investments.

**Cost of Capital and the Investment Decision.** The cost of capital is the mirror image of the return required by an investor. If the market prices a stock such that a 15 percent return on investment is expected by an investor, then the company's cost of equity capital can be said to be 15 percent.

To see how the cost of capital relates to an investment decision, it is useful to look at how shareholders obtain a return on investment.

As with any investment, a shareholder's return from buying stock is determined by the amount and timing of net cash received. An individual investor's return for a particular period consists of dividends received plus or minus the change in the stock price. Over the long term, however, the return to a company's shareholders as a group consists solely of dividends. Book earnings are relevant to the shareholder group only as an indicator of future dividends. Shareholders benefit not from earnings per se, but from the dividends the earnings make possible.

Given that cash dividends are all the company's group of shareholders can expect to receive from its investment, the maximization of shareholder wealth objective can be restated: the firm should strive to maximize the present value of cash flows available to shareholders, discounted at the rate of return required by the shareholders.

The relevant financial information about a particular corporate investment thus is cash flows available to shareholders. The acceptability of the investment is determined by discounting these new cash flows at the cost of equity capital. If the present value is equal to or greater than zero, then the return is sufficient to satisfy the shareholder return requirement.

### Investment Versus Financing Decision

Most companies use debt as well as equity to raise capital. The cash inflows and outflows arising from debt financing (i.e., principal and interest) affect the cash available to shareholders and must be considered in assessing return on equity investment. This does not mean, however, that the cash flows of debt financing arranged coincidentally with an investment, such as a mortgage, should be the debt flows considered in the investment analysis.

It is generally appropriate to think of the firm's total capital as a pool of capital; the funding of individual investments comes from this pool. Financing that is chronologically related to a particular investment simply maintains the overall mix of capital in the capital structure. It follows that investment and specific financing decisions should be treated separately. The pattern of debt flows to be incorporated in investment analysis should be premised on the overall amount and cost of debt in the capital structure—not the amount or cost of a particular financing.[1]

---

[1] There are certain situations in which it may be appropriate to consider specific financing along with the investment decision—if a unique financing opportunity is available for the investment. Tax exempt revenue bond financing is an example. The "bargain" financing effectively acts as an investment subsidy. It can be persuasively argued that the cash benefits over conventional financing should be incorporated into the analysis.

### Marginal Capital Structure and the Investment Decision

The capital structure relevant to the investment decision is the *marginal capital structure*—the mix of capital securities the firm anticipates using to raise capital in the future. The costs of capital, relevant to the investment decision, are similarly the marginal costs.

The marginal capital structure and costs will very possibly differ from the present or past structure and costs. If a company uses the marginal data it can continually raise and invest capital. The continual matching of returns required on new investments with the types and costs of new capital will ensure that the firm's overall economic return and cost of capital are kept in balance.

**Costs of Capital Structure Components.** Although an in-depth cost of capital discussion is beyond the scope of this chapter, two observations should be noted.

First, the marginal costs of most types of capital are relatively easy to estimate. One example is the effective interest rate for debt instruments as adjusted for transaction costs. The type of capital whose cost is most difficult to determine is common equity.

It is one thing to say that the cost of equity is simply the return required by shareholders (as suggested earlier). It is quite another to isolate this required return. Although much has been written on the subject, there is no consensus. There is no one "correct" way to compute the cost of equity.

But the cost of equity is an important issue. Satisfying it with the company's return on investment is synonymous with meeting the company's objective—maximization of shareholder wealth. Management should, therefore, be familar with the issues surrounding the cost of equity controversy. Armed with this background, a reasonable estimate of the equity cost can be made. Most corporate finance texts provide a good source of background material for this purpose.

The second observation is that the tax effects of an investment's cash flow streams vary. To properly capture the impact of these variations, it is generally appropriate to deduct taxes from the cash flows. This in turn dictates that the costs of capital against which the cash flows are being measured be tax affected. In other words, the tax savings associated with a given type of capital cost should be subtracted from the pretax cost.

### Overall Cost of Capital

The idea of an overall cost of capital is an outgrowth of the concept of *pool of capital*.

The overall cost of a firm's capital can be expressed as the average cost of its different types of capital securities, weighted by their respective portions in the capital structure. By discounting the cash flows available to all investors (i.e., pre-interest, or operating, cash flows) at the weighted average rate, the acceptability of the investment can be determined. If a project generates a return equal to or greater than the average return required by components of the capital structure, then all the components' return requirements have been satisfied.

**Weighted Average Computation.** The computation of weighted average cost of capital is straightforward.

| Type of Capital | Capital Structure | Weighting Factor | × | After Tax Cost | = | Weighted Cost |
|---|---|---|---|---|---|---|
| Short-Term Debt | 10% | .1 | | 4.0% | | .4% |
| Long-Term Debt | 30 | .3 | | 5.0 | | 1.5 |
| Preferred Stock | 10 | .1 | | 8.0 | | .8 |
| Deferred Taxes | 10 | – | | – | | – |
| Common Stock | 40 | .5 | | 15.0 | | 7.5 |
| | 100% | 1.0 | | | | |
| | | | | Weighted Average | | 10.2% |

It is significant to note that although deferred taxes appear in the company's capital structure, they are not included in the weighted average computation. This is because deferred taxes are not a source of new capital. They are simply the result of a delay in the payment of income taxes based on financial income.

Tax deferral benefits associated with a new investment will normally be incorporated into the investment's projected cash flows. To also treat the investment's deferred tax benefits as a source of capital for funding the investment would be double counting.

## Cost of Capital Versus Cost of Equity

Application of the weighted average cost of capital concept to investment analysis entails analysis of the investment's operating cash flows. Flows associated with the capital structure, such as interest payments, are not considered. Conclusions are reached in terms of return on total capital investment.

In contrast, application of the cost of equity concept combines debt flows with the investment's operating cash flows to arrive at net cash available to shareholders. Conclusions are reached in terms of return on equity investment.

Aside from minor arithmetic differences, the weighted average cost of capital and equity cost of capital concepts generally lead to the same investment analysis conclusions. Most companies rely upon the weighted average cost of capital concept because it is easier to apply—debt flows can be ignored. However, here the return on equity approach is recommended.

For one thing, the equity approach is more directly aimed at the basic objective of the firm—return on shareholder investment. This tends to improve the understandability of investment analysis. A second advantage lies in the fact that the equity approach is amenable to handling the effects of a varying capital structure—

where the mix of the firm's capital can not be assumed to be constant over the investment life. The overall cost of capital approach is inadequate in such cases because a constant capital structure is implicit in the approach.

### Cost of Capital for a Division of a Firm

Some multidivision companies subdivide the firm's pool of capital into separate division or subsidiary pools. Major projects that essentially stand on their own (such as joint venture and independent projects of the type characterized by project financing) are sometimes also handled this way.

The subdivision requires a determination of the target capital structures and the marginal costs of capital for the divisions. The merit of making this effort increases as a company becomes more complex and its lines of business more diverse.

Throughout this chapter, company, division, and special project costs of capital should be thought of as interchangeable terms.

### Stock Price and Book Results

The yardstick by which management performance is measured against the maximization of shareholder wealth objective is the price of the company's stock. To the extent that management successfully meets the objective by obtaining acceptable investment returns, the stock price will, over the long run, stay constant or rise. If management is unsuccessful, the price will fall.

It is sometimes countered that stock price may be an appropriate performance measure for publicly traded companies, but not for closely held ones. However, every firm's equity has a price (except possibly in cases of bankruptcy), whether indicated by active market trading or indicated by the price an owner could obtain from a willing buyer. The concept of stock price as a management performance measure holds for closely held as well as publicly traded companies.

A stock's price is theoretically determined in efficient capital markets by evaluation of the company's projected cash flows and the risks inherent in those projections. There is considerable evidence to suggest that the capital markets are efficient —but they are not totally efficient. The fact that book results regularly affect stock price over the short term has implications for capital investment.

A project with a high economic return should, in theory, be adopted, even if it will produce large book losses early in its life. A probable short term consequence, however, is that the market will erroneously lower its dividend expectations and the price of the stock will fall.

In the long term, market misinterpretations of this sort are correctable. Management can help ensure this through efforts to educate and communicate with investors about the economics of the company's business(es). But even given this, both management and the current group of shareholders have finite lives. To the extent book income has informational impact on market expectations, it can and frequently should be given consideration. Management may justifiably decide upon some trade-off between long-term economic performance and shorter term accounting performance.

There may also be some economic rationale for this trade-off. If the market's expectations are improved by the informational content of the book results, the firm's cost of new capital may be at least temporarily lowered, allowing it to take advantage of projects it might otherwise have to pass up. For example, the company's marginal cost of debt might be lowered, allowing the company to accept projects previously unacceptable because their returns were below the hurdle rate.

Cash flows are the underlying determinant of return on investment. The real world importance of book results cannot, however, be ignored in making investment decisions, especially when the effect on book income is sizable.

## INVESTMENT STEP ONE: THE GENERATION OF IDEAS

The generation of investment ideas can take place in many areas of a company. The proposal to acquire another company might come from a division manager, or plant engineers may suggest automation to reduce labor costs. Certain expenditures can also be prompted by external forces, such as environmental regulations. Ultimately, however, the successful generation of investment ideas is the responsibility of senior management.

Although senior management obviously cannot be the source of all ideas, it can directly support innovative thought throughout the company. It should be receptive to new ideas, encourage and reward creativity, hire efficient and reliable staff, and actively support research and development.

The controller must support senior management efforts to encourage new ideas. He can do so by ensuring that the company's long-range plans, investment objectives, and capital allocations are properly explained to operating managers. He should formalize capital investment procedures so that misunderstandings are minimized but the procedures are kept flexible and practical so that the approval process does not become onerous to operating management.

The controller should also support a heathy attitude toward risk and return, being aware that too much risk aversion may unreasonably eliminate all available investment opportunities. He can do this by cooperating in the development of investment proposals, offering positive suggestions, and exhibiting leadership as well as critical review.

And finally, the controller should make certain that the capital investment function is properly coordinated with the company's strategic plans.

## INVESTMENT STEP TWO: DEVELOPMENT OF THE PROPOSAL

Once an idea has been generated, proposal development becomes the heart of the investment process. No amount of rigorous, complex, and sophisticated analysis can compensate for poor proposal input.

The effort required to develop an investment idea will vary with the circumstances. If a new type of investment is proposed, more development of data is necessary than if the project is similar to earlier projects. Projects that involve complex technology probably require considerable developmental effort. But a proposal to replace an asset critical to a line of business committed to by the company probably requires little development. Such "basic upkeep" or "must do" investments, like the replacement of a worn-out conveyor in an assembly line, are usually vital to a bigger investment—in this case, the assembly line itself. Unless it is appropriate to reconsider the investment in the assembly line, extensive development of the conveyor investment proposal would not be worthwhile.

### Procedures for Proposal Review

The amount of development needed also depends upon the project's cost. Normal company investment review procedures usually require that the higher the cost, the higher the level of review must be, and the more carefully the development must be planned. Most companies use multiple review levels, with the final approval point determined by the cost of the project.

Proposal review procedures vary from firm to firm. But there are two things that all review procedures should have in common: they should be both formalized and flexible. The balance is delicate. Formalization improves efficiency and internal control and helps avoid misunderstandings that hinder the generation of ideas and that eventually lead to political problems within the firm. On the other hand, excessive rigidity and paper work requirements discourage new ideas.

**Gathering Data.** Four types of information should be included in an investment proposal: business background, technical data, preliminary screening of alternatives, and financial data. The specific items of information needed and the format in which they should be presented vary with the nature of the proposal and the company, particularly for the first three types of information.

*Business background.* Business background should include such things as the nature of the project, markets to be served, how the proposal fits into strategic and tactical business plans, and how the investment relates to the division's capital budget as well as to other development proposals.

*Technical data.* Factors such as building dimensions and machine output must also be considered. Sufficient study must be done to ensure that the project is technologically feasible.

*Preliminary screening of investment alternatives.* While several alternatives might, to varying degrees, satisfy the same investment objective, preliminary cost and benefit review may indicate that certain of the investment possibilities are clearly inferior to others and obviously do not warrant further investigation. The final proposal should indicate that such alternatives were considered, as well as why they were rejected.

**Financial Data.** The key financial data to be developed for an investment proposal is the investment's projected cash flows. For reference, comparisons to the cash flow results of other similar types of investments should be made. The book income effects of a proposed investment, particularly a large one, can also be important. The effect of the investment on book income, however, should almost invariably be secondary to the role of cash flow.

The cash flow and income data relevant to an investment decision are the incremental, or marginal, cash flows and income provided by the investment. In other words, the differences between the cash flows and net income of the company, with and without the project, are relevant, not the absolute results of the proposal itself.

The types of cash flows to be considered can typically be categorized as investment outlays, operating flows, tax effects, and residual values. Cash flows related to debt financing may also be considered, depending upon whether return on equity or on total investment is being evaluated.

In some situations, it may be unrealistic to make cash flow and book income projections. Research and development (R & D) expenditures are perhaps the best example. But even here, financial data are not irrelevant to R & D investment decisions. R & D proposals can contain three types of financial data: (1) the costs and benefits of past projects of this type; (2) spending projections that permit management to control actual spending effectively; and (3) some quantitative or qualitative analysis of investment benefits despite the difficulty inherent in projecting benefits.

The following example of a more typical investment for which projections can reasonably be made demonstrates in detail the projection of incremental cash flows.

Firm ABC is considering the automation of a packaging operation. The automation is expected to both reduce labor costs and support a sales increase due to greater production capacity. Management estimates that the impact on pretax operating income (i.e., before depreciation and interest expense) will be $50,000 in Year 1, $100,000 in Year 2, $150,000 in Years 3 and 4, and $200,000 in Years 5 through 7.

The automation will require the investment of $500,000 for the purchase and installation of new equipment. Additional capital spending of $100,000 will be required for a major overhaul at the end of Year 4. The company estimates the useful life of the system to be seven years, and the salvage value at termination to be $75,000. Book depreciation will be straight line. For tax purposes, the equipment will be depreciated over seven years (three years for the Year 4 investment), using sum-of-the-years'-digits accelerated depreciation. The initial equipment purchase will qualify for a 10 percent investment tax credit (ITC), which can be immediately used by the company. The Year 4 spending will be eligible for only one-third of the 10 percent ITC because of ITC limitations on assets with less than seven year lives.

In addition to the investment in equipment, the sales increase is expected to require a $40,000 one-time increase in working capital.

If the company buys the new equipment, it will be able to dispose of several older machines at a current market value of $80,000. These machines are being depreciated over twelve years for tax purposes, and currently have a tax basis of $53,-846. It is estimated that they would have a salvage value of $40,000 in seven years.

It is further assumed that the marginal income tax rate over the next seven years will be 46 percent.

The cash flow projections for the example are summarized in Figure 34.1. The column totals indicate the net annual and cumulative increase or decrease in cash available to the firm.

The cash required for the initial equipment purchase was determined as follows:

| | | |
|---|---|---|
| New equipment cost | | $500,000 |
| less: Disposal of old machinery: | | |
| Market value | $80,000 | |
| Tax on disposal* | (12,031) | |
| | | 67,969 |
| Net Cash Required | | $432,031 |
| | | |
| *Market value | $80,000 | |
| less: Tax basis | (53,846) | |
| Taxable gain | 26,154 | |
| Tax @ 46% | $12,031 | |

The operating cash flows are shown after-tax. That is, the projected pretax savings were multiplied by $(1 - .46)$, or 54 percent. The residuals are net of tax on taxable gains. Because the tax basis at the end of Year 7 will be zero for both the old and new equipment, the realizable values are fully taxable. As shown in the above initial disposal computations, the effective tax rate on equipment gains is the ordinary income tax rate—to the extent the disposal value is less than the original tax basis. Thereafter, it would be the capital gains rate.

The incremental depreciation tax shelter in Figure 34.1 was computed as shown in Figure 34.2.

### Specifics of Cash Flow Projections

Certain generalizations can be made about cash flow projections, but the specifics will, of course, vary from investment to investment.

**Effect on the Company.** The projections should consider all indirect as well as direct cash flow effects on the company. The relevant cash flows are the changes in the company's total cash flows, arising as a result of the investment. Relevant cash outlays should, therefore, include outlays appurtenant to the investment as well as for the investment itself. (Equipment installation costs and additional working capital investment are typical of appurtenant investments.)

The impact upon cash flows of existing investments should also be included in the projections. For example, if investment in a new product line is expected to stimu-

## PROPOSED PACKAGING AUTOMATION
## INCREMENTAL CASH FLOW PROJECTIONS

Inflows (Outflows)

| | Present | | | | Year | | | |
| --- | --- | --- | --- | --- | --- | --- | --- | --- |
| | | 1 | 2 | 3 | 4 | 5 | 6 | 7 |
| *Investment Outlays* | | | | | | | | |
| Equipment—initial | (432,031) | | | | | | | |
| Equipment—year 4 | | | | | (100,000) | | | |
| Working capital | ( 40,000) | | | | | | | |
| *Operating Cash Flows, after tax* | | 27,000 | 54,000 | 81,000 | 81,000 | 108,000 | 108,000 | 108,000 |
| *Depreciation Tax Shelter* | | 50,432 | 43,388 | 36,354 | 29,319 | 45,284 | 30,582 | 15,881 |
| ITC | 50,000 | | | | 3,333 | | | |
| *Residuals* | | | | | | | | |
| New Equipment, net of tax | | | | | | | | 40,500 |
| Old Equipment, net of tax | | | | | | | | (21,600) |
| Working Capital | | | | | | | | 40,000 |
| Total Incremental Cash Flows | (422,031) | 77,432 | 97,388 | 117,354 | 13,652 | 153,284 | 138,582 | 182,781 |
| Cumulative Cash Flows | | (344,599) | (247,211) | (129,857) | (116,205) | 37,079 | 175,661 | 358,442 |

FIGURE 34.1 CASH FLOW PROJECTIONS

late sales of an existing product, the resulting increase in revenues from the existing product should also be considered. If the company has a tax shelter that must be delayed or may be lost, and the investment is expected to generate taxable income that allows that tax shelter to be used immediately, the incremental tax benefits should be incorporated into the cash flow projection. The impacts of such synergistic benefits are frequently difficult to estimate. Nevertheless, efforts should be made to quantify them or, at the least, they should be considered qualitatively.

**Interdependence of Investments.** In cash flow projections, it must be taken into account that many investments are interdependent. For example, the separate proposals to acquire land, buildings, and equipment for a new plant are integrally related. A proposal to purchase a new fleet of delivery trucks and a proposal to build a new warehouse may also be interdependent. The benefits derived from the truck fleet could be dependent upon the warehouse location and vice versa. Interdependent investments should be analyzed as one project. In the case of the truck fleet and warehouse proposals, the two proposals should be looked at in conjunction with each other. The cash flow projections for the various alternatives should be prepared in combination (e.g., old fleet and old warehouse, old fleet and new warehouse, and so on).

**Treatment of Cost Amounts and Timing.** For the purposes of cash flow analysis, cost reductions resulting from an investment represent cash inflows, just as revenues represent inflows. Investment alternatives sometimes in fact present no differences in cash benefits to the company other than differences in the amount and timing of expenditures. This frequently is true when a firm is deciding whether to make or buy an asset or deciding whether to replace or upgrade a piece of equipment. Proper treatment of cost reductions is obviously critical in such instances.

**Opportunity Costs.** Foregone opportunities to receive cash inflows represent cash outflows. They are called *opportunity costs*. The foregoing Year 7 disposal value of the existing machinery as shown in Figure 34.1 (cash flow projections) is an example of an opportunity cost.

**Tax Considerations.** The potential tax benefits of an investment, along with the company's ability to use them, can be important determinants of the investment's economic return. In the project example, it was assumed that the maximum benefits available from the new equipment could be utilized by the company. However, assume the company is in an ITC carryforward position and management has estimated that new ITC generated cannot be used to offset current tax liability for three years. Given these circumstances, the cash flow projections should be adjusted to show the $50,000 ITC on new equipment arising in Year 3, not at the time of initial investment.

**Effects of Inflation.** An inflation premium is implicitly incorporated in the return required by investors. Consistency requires that anticipated inflation also be

## PROPOSED PACKAGING AUTOMATION
### Incremental Depreciation Tax Shelter Projections

| | | | | Year | | | |
|---|---|---|---|---|---|---|---|
| | 1 | 2 | 3 | 4 | 5 | 6 | 7 |
| Depreciation on Initial New Equipment | 125,000 | 107,143 | 89,286 | 71,429 | 53,571 | 35,714 | 17,857 |
| Add: Depreciation on Year 4 New Equipment | — | — | — | — | 50,000 | 33,333 | 16,667 |
| Less: Depreciation on Old Equipment | (15,385) | (12,821) | (10,256) | (7,692) | (5,128) | (2,564) | — |
| Total Depreciation | 109,615 | 94,322 | 79,030 | 63,737 | 98,443 | 66,483 | 34,524 |
| × Tax Rate | .46 | .46 | .46 | .46 | .46 | .46 | .46 |
| TAX SHELTER | 50,423 | 43,388 | 36,354 | 29,319 | 45,284 | 30,582 | 15,881 |

FIGURE 34.2  TAX SHELTER PROJECTIONS

reflected in the cash flow projections. Because inflationary impacts are difficult to anticipate, many firms consciously ignore inflation in cash flow projections. It is sometimes argued that the exclusion of inflation from cash flow projections systematically provides a conservative bias.

The exclusion of inflation from cash flow projections may be practical and appropriate in many instances. However, in a period of relatively high inflation, this exclusion can lead to some serious errors. Particularly for large and long-lived investments, some effort should be made explicitly to anticipate the effects inflation will have on the investment's various cash flow streams.

**Analysis Horizon.** It would be possible to project indefinitely the cash flow implications of a given investment. However, practicality requires that we stop somewhere. The investment analysis should generally be limited to the useful life of the proposed investment. Any asset value remaining at the end of that period (e.g., value as scrap or for resale) should be included as an inflow at that time.

An exception to this general rule is the case of mutually exclusive investments with significantly different useful lives. In such instances, it may be appropriate to extend the analysis period of the shorter-lived investment to equal that of the longer-lived one, or vice versa. The purpose is to equate the longer term investment implications of the alternatives. For example, if two machines of unequal life are being considered for a particular production line task, what action to be taken when the shorter lived equipment wears out should be considered. Considerations of this sort become increasingly relevant in periods of high inflation.

# INVESTMENT STEP THREE: METHODS OF ANALYSIS

## Return Analysis

Three basic methodologies can be used to analyze capital investments—accounting return, payback, and discounted cash flow (DCF). DCF is conceptually superior to the other approaches, although the others do have certain advantages. A firm may find it appropriate to use more than one of the methods in its capital investment analyses.

**Accounting Rate of Return.** In its simplest form, the accounting return on an investment is:

$$\text{Return} = \frac{\text{Increase in Firm's Avg. Annual Net Income}}{\text{Initial Investment}}$$

A variation of this computation uses the average book value of the investment over its life in the denominator of this ratio. In either case, the computed return is compared to a standard. If it meets the standard, the project is accepted; if not, it is rejected.

Assume a firm is considering a $100,000 equipment purchase to increase production capacity. The equipment is expected to have a life of five years and will increase book income by an average of $20,000 per year. The accounting rate of return would be:

$$\text{Return} = \frac{\$ 20,000}{\$100,000}$$

$$= 20\%$$

If the average equipment investment were used, rather than the initial investment, the average return, assuming no residual value, would be:

$$\text{Average Return} = \frac{\$ 20,000}{\$ 50,000}$$

$$= 40\%$$

The principal advantage of the accounting return approach is that it is founded upon accrual accounting concepts and utilizes readily available accounting data with which operating management is familiar. It also provides needed consistency with management performance evaluation standards, typically accounting based.

The principal disadvantages of the accounting approach are that it does not take account of cash flows and that it ignores the time value of money. Consider, for example, two competitive equipment investments with the following characteristics:

|  | Equipment A | | Equipment B | |
|---|---|---|---|---|
|  | Book Income | Cash Flows | Book Income | Cash Flows |
| Initial Purchase | $ — | $(100,000) | $ — | $(100,000) |
| Year 1 | 10,000 | 40,000 | 15,000 | 20,000 |
| Year 2 | 15,000 | 30,000 | 15,000 | 20,000 |
| Year 3 | 20,000 | 30,000 | 20,000 | 25,000 |
| Year 4 | 25,000 | 20,000 | 25,000 | 25,000 |
| Year 5 | 30,000 | 20,000 | 25,000 | 50,000 |

The accounting return is the same in both cases—20 percent on initial investment, indicating that the investments would be equally advantageous. However, the timing of cash flows—the determinant of economic return—clearly indicates that Equipment A is the better choice.

**Payback.** The payback approach asks how much time is required for the initial investment outlay to be recouped by cash flows from the project:

$$\text{Payback Period} = \frac{\text{Initial Investment}}{\text{Annual Cash Flows}}$$

For example, the payback period for an investment costing $12,000 that will produce annual cash flows of $2,000 over 10 years would be:

$$\text{Payback Period} = \frac{\$12,000}{\$\,2,000}$$

$$= \quad 6.0 \text{ years}$$

If the payback standard of the company is 7 years, acceptance of the project is indicated.

Payback computation for projects that generate uneven cash flows is slightly more complicated. In the preceding accounting return example, $90,000 of the $100,000 investment in Equipment B would be recovered by the end of Year 4. The total payback period would then be computed as: 4 years plus $10,000/$50,000, or 4.2 years.

The payback approach is a step forward from the accounting return approach insofar as fundamental investment concepts are concerned. It is concerned with cash flows, not book income. And it does, to some extent, consider the time value of money. A project with total cash flows skewed toward the earlier years will have a faster payback than one with cash flows skewed toward the later years. Another advantage of payback is the fact that the approach is straightforward and easy to apply. Furthermore, it incorporates some consideration of liquidity risk. The lower the payback period, the less time the initial cash outlay is exposed to loss; hence, the lower the risk.

Liquidity risk is somewhat different from basic investment risk, which is concerned with potential variability in investment return. Liquidity risk may be of particular significance to a company under liquidity pressure. If this is the case, a modification to the payback approach may be of even further use—the computation of *bail-out period*. The bail-out period tells the company how soon it can bail out of a project without cash loss. It is determined by simply adding the estimated salvage value of the investment, at various points in its life, to the projected cash flows of the investment; the payback period is then computed. In the case of Equipment A in the accounting return example, the bail-out period would be one year if the investment were projected to have an after-tax salvage value of $60,000 at the end of Year 1.

The major difficulties with the payback approach lie in the fact that it doesn't consider the timing of cash flows within the payback period and that it doesn't consider the cash flows at all after the payback period. In the following example both investment opportunities have a payback period of three years; yet Investment X is clearly preferable.

|  | Investment X | Investment Y |
|---|---|---|
| Initial Investment | $(30,000) | $(30,000) |
| Year 1 | 15,000 | 10,000 |
| Year 2 | 10,000 | 10,000 |
| Year 3 | 5,000 | 10,000 |
| Year 4 | 5,000 | — |
| Year 5 | 5,000 | — |

**Discounted Cash Flow (DCF).** Internal rate of return and present value analysis are the two most commonly used DCF methods. Both are conceptually superior to the accounting return and payback methods because they explicitly consider the time value of the cash flows in each year of the investment's life.

*Present value analysis.* In present value analysis, each future period's net cash flows are discounted to their present value.[2] The discount rate used is either the company's weighted average cost of capital or its cost of equity capital, in which case debt flows will be included in the investment cash flows. The discount rate is properly thought of as a hurdle rate. If the present value of the future cash flows is equal to or greater than the initial cost of the investment, then the investment has an economic return equal to or greater than the cost of capital. The hurdle has thus been satisfied, and the project should be accepted. On the other hand, if the discounted value of the cash flows is less than the investment cost, the return is substandard and the investment should be rejected.

*Net present value.* The present value of an investment's future cash flows less its initial cost is called the investment's *net present value*. It may be helpful to view the net present value as the increase or decrease in initial investment cost that will adjust the return on investment to the minimum required return (i.e., cost of capital). This view is particularly applicable when the investment price is subject to negotiation. However, a more fundamental view of the project's net present value is that it represents the increase or decrease in investor wealth provided by the investment.

The present value procedure can be demonstrated using the cash flow data for Equipment A in the accounting return example. Assuming a 12 percent hurdle rate, the Equipment A cash flows would be discounted as follows:

---

[2] Selected compound interest formulas:
  Where:
$$r = \text{interest rate per period}$$
$$c = \text{cash flow per period}$$
$$n = \text{total number of periods}$$
*Present Value*
• Present value of $1 to be received at the end of period n.
$$\frac{1}{(1+r)^n}$$
• Present value of a stream of periodic cash flows to be received at the end of the respective periods.
$$\sum_{t\text{-}0}^{n} \frac{c}{(1+r)^t}$$

*Internal Return*
• Internal rate of return on investment.
$$\sum_{t\text{-}0}^{n} \frac{c}{(1+r)^t} = 0$$
*Terminal Value*
• Future value of $1 to be received at the end of period n.
$$(1+r)^n$$
• Future value of a stream of periodic cash flows to be received at the end of the respective periods.
$$\sum_{t\text{-}0}^{n} c(1+r)^{n\text{-}t}$$

| Year | Cash Flows | × | Present Value Factor | = | Present Value |
|------|-----------|---|----------------------|---|---------------|
| 1 | $40,000 | | .8929 | | $ 35,716 |
| 2 | 30,000 | | .7972 | | 23,916 |
| 3 | 30,000 | | .7118 | | 21,354 |
| 4 | 20,000 | | .6355 | | 12,710 |
| 5 | 20,000 | | .5674 | | 11,348 |

|  |  |  |
|--|--|--|
| Total Present Value | | $105,044 |
| less: Cost of Investment | | (100,000) |
| Net Present Value | | $ 5,044 |

The discounted value of the cash flows is greater than the $100,000 cost of the equipment, so Equipment A is thus an acceptable investment opportunity. On the other hand, similar computations for Equipment B indicate a net present value of ($4,145). The return on B does not meet the hurdle rate, so it should be rejected.

*Adjusting for varying discount periods.* We have assumed for the sake of simplicity that the annual cash flows from the Equipment A and B investments are received at the end of each year. It is more likely that the benefits would be received throughout the year. More precise analysis to reflect this could be accomplished by subdividing the projection periods and adjusting the discount rate accordingly. We might, for example, break the years up into quarters and adjust the discount rate from a 12 percent annual rate to a quarterly rate of 3 percent:

| | | | Cash Flows | × | Present Value Factor | = | Present Value |
|--|--|--|-----------|---|----------------------|---|---------------|
| Year 1 | Quarter | 1 | $10,000 | | .9709 | | $9,709 |
| " | " | 2 | 10,000 | | .9426 | | 9,426 |
| " | " | | – | | – | | – |
| " | " | | – | | – | | – |
| " | " | | – | | – | | – |
| Year 5 | Quarter | 4 | 5,000 | | .5537 | | 2,769 |

|  |  |  |
|--|--|--|
| Total Present Value | | $108,565 |
| less: Cost of Investment | | (100,000) |
| Net Present Value | | $ 8,565 |

Although the amount differs, the net present value is still positive.

This difference highlights the fact that the present value calculation varies with the basic discount period. The accept/reject decision can, in fact, be different, depending upon the discount period selected. Acceptance might be indicated by a calculation discounted on a monthly basis and rejection indicated by an annual discount calculation. In general, the shorter the discount period, the more precise the analysis answer; however, monthly discounting is usually the shortest practical period.

*Adjustment for varying discount rates.* The firm in our example is considering either Equipment A or Equipment B as alternative possibilities for one purpose—to increase production capacity. If it invests in one, it won't invest in the other. They are mutually exclusive. The superiority of A over B was clear-cut when a 12 percent discount rate was assumed. Investment in B produced a negative net present value. But if the hurdle rate had been 9 percent, A's advantage would have been less obvious. Discounting annually, the net present values of A and B would have been $12,280 and $4,694, respectively. This demonstrates that the discount rate selected can lead to sharply varying results. The higher the discount rate, the lower the influence of distant cash flows. Equipment B switched from a "rejection" at 12 percent to a possible "acceptance" at 9 percent; the lower discount rate gave greater weight to its higher cash flows in later years.

The relative profitability of one investment over another can, in fact, be reversed with changes in the discount rate. This is most likely to happen if there are large differences in later year cash flows of the investments' lives. For example, consider the following:

| Time Period | Project Y | Project Z |
|---|---|---|
| 0 | $ (90,000) | (90,000) |
| 1 | 75,000 | 85,000 |
| 2 | 75,000 | 85,000 |
| 3 | 75,000 | 85,000 |
| 4 | (120,000) | (155,000) |
| | | |
| Net Present Value @ 14% | $ 13,073 | 15,566 |
| Net Present Value @ 6% | 15,425 | 14,432 |

At a higher discount rate, Project Z appears more profitable; Project Y appears more profitable at a lower discount rate.

*Profitability indexing.* A modification of present value analysis is sometimes used to facilitate investment review. A profitability index that ranks projects according to relative profitability is arrived at by dividing the present value of cash flows from the investment by the present value of investment cost.

The present value of investment cost consists of the initial cost of the project, plus the present value of subsequent period outlays which constitute an integral part of the investment. In the Equipment A and B example, where a 12 percent discount rate was used, the index for A is 1.05; for B it is .96. The profitability index method thus gives the same accept/reject answer in this instance that the net present value computations did.

However, a profitability index can be misleading in some mutually exclusive investment cases. Assume that Equipment B cost only $60,000, but had a present value of cash benefits of $64,000. The comparison with A would be as follows:

|                        | A          | B         |
| ---------------------- | ---------- | --------- |
| PV of Cash Flows       | $105,044   | $64,000   |
| Investment Cost        | $100,000   | $60,000   |
| Profitability Index    | 1.05       | 1.07      |
|                        |            |           |
| Net Present Value      | $   5,044  | $  4,000  |

The profitability index says to select B, but the net present value comparison indicates A. Equipment A would be the better selection because the net present value, and hence, investor wealth, is greater with A than with B. The profitability index is misleading in this instance.

*Internal rate of return analysis.* An investment's internal rate of return is equal to the discount rate that will produce a present value of cash inflows equal to the present value of cash outflows. The internal rate of return can be properly thought of as a special case of the present value approach—the case where the net present value is equal to zero.

Determination of the internal rate of return involves trial and error testing of various discount rates. A series of present value computations is performed, converging on the discount rate that produces a net present value of zero. The evolution of computers and calculators has fortunately facilitated this task.

Returning to the example of Equipment A and Equipment B, the internal rate of return for A is 14.31 percent, and the return for B is 10.54 percent. As expected from the earlier present value analyses, the return is greater from Equipment A than from Equipment B.

Once a project's internal rate of return has been determined, it can be compared to the applicable hurdle rate. If the return exceeds the hurdle rate, the project should be accepted; if the return is below the hurdle, it should be rejected. Similarly, the investment with the highest interest return should usually be accepted in cases of mutually exclusive proposals.

*Present value versus internal rate of return.* Present value and internal rate of return analyses generally lead to the same conclusions. There are, however, advantages and disadvantages to each method.

One advantage of the internal rate of return approach lies in the fact that analysts need not specify a discount rate as they must when using present value analysis. Since the determination of an appropriate cost of capital, particularly the cost of equity, can be controversial, the ability to rank investment proposals without this computation can be an advantage. At the same time, some knowledge of the cost of capital is necessary if one is to determine the threshold of acceptable internal rates of return. The internal return method, therefore, is not a solution to the problem of computing the cost of capital.

Another frequently cited advantage of internal return analysis is that it is more straightforward than present value analysis; it deals in return percentages and is therefore apt to be more comprehensible to management. On the other hand, it may be argued that the two methods are really one and the same (i.e., internal return is simply a special case of present value), and if one method can be understood by management, then the other can also.

A major shortcoming of the internal rate of return method is the problem of multiple solutions—there may be several possible internal returns when cash flow signs reverse during the life of the project. In other words, more than one discount rate may lead to a net present value of zero.[3] This is not a problem with the present value approach because the discount rate is specified.

*Terminal value techniques.* It is frequently pointed out that the internal return method implicitly assumes that management reinvests cash flows from the project at a return equal to the internal rate of return. This is not exactly true; technically, there is no reinvestment assumption implicit in the internal rate of return.

Technicality notwithstanding, a project's economic benefit to the firm may be misstated by the internal rate of return if reinvestment returns near the internal rate are not available. An internal return above the hurdle rate will always show whether a project is acceptable or not. But when mutually exclusive investments with internal returns above the hurdle rate are compared, and when reinvestment opportunities equal to or near these rates are not available, the ranking of desirability according to the investments' internal returns may lead to spurious conclusions.

A firm can be thought of as a pool of investment funds, with cash constantly flowing into and out of the pool from earlier investments, either as dividends or new investments. A firm's underlying value is equal to the net present value of all future cash flows into this pool. When analysts look at mutually exclusive investment opportunities, they may find that an investment with a lower internal rate of return will actually contribute to a higher present value of the firm's total cash inflows than one with a higher internal return. This occurs because the cash flow characteristics of the lower return investment may, given the reinvestment opportunities available to the firm, facilitate better reinvestment of the company's pool of funds. The following example illustrates the point.

Assume a company is confronted with two mutually exclusive investment opportunities having the following projected cash flows:

---

[3] The number of possible returns will depend upon the number of times the cash flow sign reverses and the relative magnitudes of the cash flows involved in the sign reversals. There are methods for detecting the existence of multiple solutions, which essentially consist of following the net present value curve generated by discounting at different rates.

| Time Period | Project One | Project Two |
|:---:|:---:|:---:|
| 0 | $(10,000) | $(10,000) |
| 1 | 4,500 | — |
| 2 | 4,500 | — |
| 3 | 4,500 | 15,250 |
| Internal Rate of Return | 16.6% | 15.1% |
| "Terminal Value" with Reinvestment @ 10% | $14,895 | $15,250 |

Project One has the higher internal rate of return and appears preferable to Project Two. However, if it is known that opportunities available for reinvestment of cash flows will generate only 10 percent returns, the relative desirability of the two projects changes. When the projects' cash flows in Periods 1 through 3 are compounded forward at 10 percent, a larger terminal (or future) value for Project Two is produced than for Project One—$15,250 versus $14,895. In effect, the terminal values tell us that the company's pool of funds will, given 10 percent reinvestment opportunities, be larger if Project Two is selected than if Project One is selected.

Terminal value analysis can be carried further to test the implications of different reinvestment rates. It might be particularly useful to determine the breakeven reinvestment rate. In the above example, it is 12.45 percent. At reinvestment rates above this level, Project One will have the greater terminal value; below this level, Project Two will produce a higher value.[4]

In Projects One and Two, the initial investment amounts are conveniently the same. This will, of course, not always be the case. To handle cases where the initial investments differ, the future values of the initial investment outlays themselves can be determined and netted from the terminal values. The result is the net terminal value, or net future value. The project with the higher net terminal value will be the preferred project.

In terminal analysis, still another way to compare projects with different initial investment levels is to compute the internal returns generated by the terminal values, relative to the initial investment amounts. With available reinvestment opportunities already explicitly considered in computing the terminal values, the ranking of these internal returns will give the right answer. In the above example, the returns computed in this way for Projects One and Two are 14.2 and 15.1 percent respectively, confirming the preference for Project Two.

Terminal value analysis, in one form or another, can thus solve the reinvestment opportunity problem inherent in internal rate of return analysis. Similarly, it can be

---

[4] The computation of the break-even reinvestment rate generally involves trial and error, which is tedious unless a computer does the work. There is, however, a shortcut. It entails subtractions of the higher ROI investment's cash flows from those of the lower ROI investment and solving for the internal return of these net cash flows.

used to test multiple returns for reasonableness. The obvious drawback to terminal value analysis is that it requires additional computations. So long as the discount rate used reflects the reinvestment returns available to the firm, present value analysis avoids the entire reinvestment problem.

**Summary Evaluation of Analysis Methods.** Certain general and summary observations can be made about the three approaches to analyzing capital investments: accounting return, payback, and discounted cash flow.

First, the present value and internal rate of return methods are conceptual equals. However, certain qualitative advantages of internal return must be weighed against its substantial and potentially misleading mechanical difficulties.

Second, the DCF approach is conceptually superior to accounting return and payback, and it should be a company's principal method of economic investment analysis. It ensures direct linkage between the maximization of shareholder wealth objective and the individual investment decision. Accounting return and payback, however, do have certain advantages. It may be appropriate for the company to use one, or possibly both of these approaches in conjunction with DCF.

Third, accounting return, payback, and DCF approaches are all adaptable to either the return on equity or the return on total investment approaches to investment analysis.

Fourth, it is useful to note the underlying relationship between DCF and accounting returns. There is a positive relationship that may not be easy to demonstrate. The controller or financial manager who has recommended investments expected to yield certain economic returns may well be asked to explain why the company's book returns are significantly different from the DCF returns promised.

The accounting return for a particular investment, as well as for the company as a whole, varies with the types of accounting policies adopted; these policies generally do not reflect the true economics of the investment as measured by DCF techniques. Because of these differences, a firm's book return rarely matches its economic return for any one accounting period. However, over time and in the absence of other factors, the total book return of a company will tend to grow closer to the overall economic return on the company's investments.

These observations lead to several conclusions about the relationship between DCF and accounting returns. First, the book return may fluctuate widely around the DCF return over shorter periods of time, with the magnitude of the fluctuation dependent upon specific accrual accounting policies of the company. Second, to the extent that the firm reinvests all its cash flows in similar types of investments, the book return and DCF returns of the firm will, over the longer term, tend to converge. Third, if the firm reinvests only part of its cash flows in similar investments while paying a portion of earnings as dividends, convergence of the book and DCF returns will be permanently delayed. The book return will tend to converge on a return greater than the DCF return. And fourth, it follows that an increase in the economic returns on a company's investments will, over the long term, tend to increase the company's accounting returns.

## Real World Constraints

It has thus far been implied that the firm can and should take advantage of all investment opportunities that provide an economic return equal to or greater than its cost of capital. This is not possible, however, in the real world. The firm may have capital budget limitations, face operating constraints, or may deem it necessary to consider book accounting results. The introduction of such constraints adds to the complexity of investment decisions.

**Capital Budget Constraints and Capital Rationing.** Capital rationing is the process of selecting the most beneficial combination of projects when capital budget constraints require that some acceptable projects be foregone. The projects that "benefit" the firm most are defined as those that yield the greatest net present value.

Assume that a firm with a $240,000 capital budget has the following five investment opportunities:

| | Project | | | | |
|---|---|---|---|---|---|
| | *1* | *2* | *3* | *4* | *5* |
| Initial Investment | $80,000 | $140,000 | $100,000 | $250,000 | $30,000 |
| Net Present Value | 40,000 | 50,000 | 20,000 | 80,000 | 15,000 |
| Profitability Index | 1.50 | 1.36 | 1.20 | 1.32 | 1.50 |

All of the projects have positive net present values and are therefore acceptable investment opportunities. However, it is clear that not all of the projects can be undertaken.

If the projects are capable of unlimited subdivision (i.e., parts of projects can be accepted), the group of investments offering the greatest benefit to the company could be determined by simply taking the projects in descending profitability index order:

| *Project* | *Initial Investment* | *Profitability Index* | *Net Present Value* |
|---|---|---|---|
| 1 | $ 80,000 | 1.50 | $ 40,000 |
| 5 | 30,000 | 1.50 | 15,000 |
| 2 | 130,000 | 1.36 | 46,429* |
| | $240,000 | | $101,429 |

\* ($130,000/140,000) 50,000 = $46,429

But investments usually cannot be subdivided. If this were true for the example, management would do best to select Projects 1 and 2, with combined initial investment and net present value of $220,000 and $90,000, respectively.

Capital rationing choices can become complex. Some investments may be deferable, while others are not. This means that projected capital spending as well as capital budget limitations for more than one period ahead *are relevant*.

Furthermore, some projects may be capable of subdivision while others are not. In sorting through such complexities, management should try to select that combination of projects that, in view of current and future spending plans and budget constraints, is expected to produce the highest net present value.

*Capital rationing and the hurdle rate.* The question of reinvestment opportunity available to the firm can be ignored in the absence of capital rationing. It is assumed that all investments with return equal to or greater than the company's cost of capital are accepted, and any funds left over are returned to the shareholders. In other words, the cost of capital is synonymous with the reinvestment opportunity cost. In the case of capital rationing, however, investments must be cut off at a point above the cost of capital. Specific reinvestment opportunity costs become relevant and must be used as the hurdle rate.

*Capital rationing policies.* A few words should be said about capital rationing in general.

Because it implies the rejection or deferral of capital investments offering returns equal to or above the cost of capital, capital rationing is contrary to the objective of the firm. If internally generated capital is insufficient to fund all the acceptable investment opportunities available, then theoretically, new capital should be raised externally.

This is, of course, more easily said than done. A company can't efficiently issue new securities every time internal capital generation appears to be inadequate. Furthermore, the company's strategic plans may limit spending for certain lines of business. At the same time, excessively rigid capital budget constraints, combined with a permanent capital rationing posture, may well indicate that management is not achieving the firm's objective of maximizing shareholder wealth.

**Operating Constraints.** Operating constraints consist of such factors as limitations on raw material or labor availability. As with capital rationing constraints, their integration into the analysis of capital expenditures can be complex. Management must again consider deferring or subdividing projects, in terms of the expected duration of such constraints.

**Book Accounting Limitations.** Although the expected economic return should be of primary importance to the investment decision, it may be appropriate to consider the investment's book implications. To briefly reiterate an earlier discussion, the capital markets are not totally efficient. They may react to book results rather than to the underlying economics. Some management concern about book results (e.g., earnings per share) may, therefore, be justified. And this concern may lead to the imposition of accounting constraints (e.g., no book losses allowed) upon the company's investments.

**Quantitative Techniques.** The quantitative methodology most readily used to incorporate real world constraints into investment decisions is *linear programming*.

Linear programming is a method of optimizing a certain function (e.g., maximization of present value or minimization of costs) given a set of constraints. It is, in essence, a means of allocating resources, such as capital or labor, that are in scarce supply.

At its simplest, linear programming is relatively easy to apply. However, as the number of variables expands, application quickly becomes complex and requires the use of a computer.

A technical shortcoming of linear programming is its difficulty in integrating probability analysis. For example, based upon their probabilities of occurrence, it is difficult to analyze various capital rationing possibilities.

Simulation is a quantitative approach that does not provide *an* optimal solution, but that does overcome some of the impracticalities of linear programming. Simulation will be discussed further in the next section on risk analysis.

### Risk Analysis

It has thus far been assumed that the investment's risk is approximately equivalent to that of the company as a whole. The concern has consequently been with aggregate return benchmarks, such as the overall cost of capital. But when the investment amount is large and/or risk characteristics are materially different from those of the firm as a whole, it is worthwhile to look closely at the investment's unique risk characteristics.

In practice, management usually incorporates, subconsciously if not consciously, some form of specific risk evaluation into investment decisions. It may reject an investment with a projected internal return above the hurdle rate because it intuitively feels that the project is too risky. Or management may increase the hurdle rate because it believes that perceived risks warrant an additional risk premium.

Risk evaluation is necessarily judgmental in nature. However, methodology for quantifying investment risk has become considerably advanced in recent years. Familiarity with the measurement concepts and, in some instances, formal application of quantitative risk analysis, can provide valuable insight.

Certain of the risk measurement concepts and techniques can be adequately explored only in financial or statistical texts. The following is a brief discussion of the more basic ones.

**Investment Risk—A General Definition.** An investor is confronted with not just one, but many possible returns on investment. These possible returns can be thought of as arrayed in a probability distribution, like a bell-shaped distribution curve. The investor's probable, or expected, return is the average of the various possiblities in the distribution, weighted by their probabilities of occurrence.

Investment risk is defined as the dispersion of the possible returns around the probable return. That is, it is the potential variability of the return from the expected return. In the context of a distribution curve, the broader the curve, the greater the dispersion; hence, the greater the investment risk.

**Tools for Measuring Risk.** Risk measurement entails analysis of possible outcomes to determine the probabilities that the various outcomes will occur. Armed with these probabilities, management can quantify its judgments as to the likelihood of investment success. Risk measurement, in short, involves the substitution of calculated risks for undefined uncertainty.

*Quantitative risk tools.* The basic tools of quantitative risk measurement are *expected value* (or *expected outcome*) and *standard deviation.* Expected outcome is the average of the various possible outcomes weighted by their probabilities of occurrence. Standard deviation is a statistical measure that quantifies the degree of dispersion, or variability, of the possible outcomes around the expected value. The higher the dispersion, the higher the standard deviation. Mathematical definitions of expected value and standard deviation may be found in any introductory statistics text.

Without going into the details of calculations, the following simplified example demonstrates the application of risk measurement to investment analysis.

Assume that a company is reviewing a $40,000 investment that has a two-year life. Management has concluded that Year 1 results will in no way affect Year 2 results (a simplifying although probably unrealistic assumption) and that the following cash flow possibilities exist:

| Year 1 | | Year 2 | |
|---|---|---|---|
| Probability | Cash Flow | Probability | Cash Flow |
| .10 | $15,000 | .20 | $25,000 |
| .20 | 20,000 | .60 | 30,000 |
| .40 | 25,000 | .20 | 35,000 |
| .20 | 30,000 | | |
| .10 | 35,000 | | |

(This initial step in risk measurement—assessment of outcome probabilities—is particularly important. The usefulness of subsequent analysis depends upon the reasonableness of management's assessment of probabilities.)

The expected value of Year 1 cash flows (the average outcome weighted by probabilities of occurrence) is $25,000; it is $30,000 for the Year 2 cash flows. The standard deviations of the Year 1 and Year 2 cash flows can be computed as $5,477 and $3,162, respectively.

The expected value of the investment's net present value can also be computed. The computation is similar to a normal net present value calculation, except that the Years 1 and 2 "expected value" cash flows are discounted instead of discrete cash flows. In addition, for purposes of risk analysis, the expected values are discounted using a "risk free" rate of return (e.g., return on government securities) instead of the firm's cost of capital. The risk free rate is appropriate because the cost of capital includes a risk premium. Since risk is the factor being explicitly evaluated in risk analysis, to use the firm's cost of capital in the analysis would be to double count the impact of risk.

Assuming a risk-free after-tax discount rate of 5 percent, the expected net present value of the $40,000 investment is $11,020. The potential variability (i.e., dispersion) of possible outcomes can then be assessed by determining the standard deviation of the present values. It is $5,953. For purposes of comparison to other investments, the "coefficient of variation" might also be determined. It provides a kind of risk index that is the standard deviation divided by the expected value. In this case, the coefficient is 54.0 percent (i.e., $5,953/$11,020).

Additional insight might be gained by turning to probability distribution tables.

Assuming that risk is normally distributed (usually a reasonable assumption), 68.5 percent of the expected outcomes will be within the range defined by the expected value plus or minus one standard deviation. The percentage of outcomes within two standard deviations is 94.4 percent; within three standard deviations, 99.7 percent. Thus, in the example ($11,020 expected net present value; $5,953 standard deviation), management can be 94.4 percent confident that the net present value will fall between $22,926 and ($886).

Perhaps more relevant is downside risk. Zero net present value is the minimum acceptable. In this instance it is 1.85 standard deviations below the expected outcome. Management can therefore be confident that the net present value will not be below zero—that the investment return will be acceptable.

*Real world applications.* Statistical analysis can be used with investment analysis approaches other than present value, internal return, for example. In all cases, however, application of quantitative risk measurement quickly becomes too complex to be practical if certain significant simplifying assumptions are not permitted. For example, additional complexity occurs when it cannot be assumed that the distribution of possible outcomes is normal, but is "skewed" toward higher or lower values. It also occurs when time periods cannot be assumed independent of each other (as was assumed in the example). And this is generally the case—the results in later years are related to what happens in earlier years.

*Simulation analysis.* Simulation can offer a viable quantitative alternative to pure statistical measurement of risk. It involves the combination of different factors in different ways. When these combinations are done in sufficient number, and probabilities of occurrence and interperiod dependencies are properly incorporated, the resulting scenarios realistically portray the potential investment outcomes, together with their likelihoods of occurrence. Evaluation of such scenarios provides a helpful guide to assessing the riskiness of complicated real world situations.

Simulation analysis can perhaps best be described as "what-if" analysis. It answers the question of "what" will happen "if" certain things occur. Simple analyses can be performed manually, although the computer is necessary as the number of calculations sharply increases with the number of "if" variables.

*Sequential decisions.* The decision process becomes more intricate when a series of interdependent decisions is involved. Analysis of the immediate question should somehow reflect the implications of potential subsequent developments.

Sequential decision analysis is a systematic approach for evaluating such decisions. It involves a decision tree format with examination of relevant probabilities at each decision point on the tree, working backward from the last toward the immediate decision.

*Non-statistical risk tools.* It is frequently sufficient for management to be aware of possible outcomes and to arrive intuitively at judgments about risk. Short of elaborate risk measurement, simplified simulation, sequential decision, or breakeven analysis can be useful in making such judgments.

For example, an investment proposal might be analyzed under three scenarios— best guess, more optimistic, and more pessimistic. The results of these three scenarios may be all that is necessary to provide confidence in making the investment decision. The pessimistic case is likely to be of particular interest because it represents the investment downside risk. It may, in fact, be sufficient to evaluate only the best guess and pessimistic cases.

**Relevant Risk and the Investment Decision.** The measurement of an investment's risk with tools such as those just described is one question. Evaluation of the risk to determine how much of the risk is actually relevant to the investment decision is another. And it is a controversial question. By way of brief summary, there are three basic views.

*Total firm risk approach.* The first view is that the relevant risk is the investment's impact on the firm's total risk. This view is derived from general portfolio theory which says that a company's investments constitute a portfolio, and diversification within this portfolio leads to offsetting of risks.

The total firm risk approach implies analysis of the proposed investment within the context of all the company's existing and expected investments. The risk premium component of the firm's cost of capital is adjusted for the marginal impact of the investment on the firm's overall risk; this adjusted cost of capital is used for the investment analysis.

The approach has considerable conceptual merit, but implementation problems. Short of undertaking extensive analysis of all existing and proposed investments each time an investment is contemplated, management's estimate of the marginal risk impact of a particular investment must be, for the most part, subjective.

*Systematic risk approach.* The systematic risk approach is founded on the Capital Asset Pricing Model (CAPM). The essence of the model is that a common stock's investment risk can be divided into two parts—systematic risk and unsystematic risk. Systematic risk cannot be diversified away by the investor because it is related to the stock market as a whole (the system). The chance of a recession is an example of systematic risk. It will affect the entire market. Unsystematic risk is, on the other hand, diversifiable because it includes risks unique to the firm—for example, exposure to technological obsolescence. It follows that systematic, but not unsystematic, risk is relevant to the investor.[5]

CAPM evolved as an explanation for common stock prices. However, the model has been expanded to other capital investments. Furthermore, the systematic risks of individual investments of a company are independent of the overall systematic risk of the company and its stock. In other words, each investment has its own unique systematic risk and its own unique cost of capital. And the model suggests that an investment should be evaluated against its unique cost of capital.

Like the total firm approach, CAPM has theoretical appeal. But also like the total firm approach, the methodology is generally impractical for capital investment analysis. In most cases it is too difficult to arrive objectively at an estimate of a project's systematic risk.

*Project risk approach.* The third view of investment risk is that the relevant risk relates only to the project itself. The approach maintains that the firm's cost of capital is an appropriate general benchmark against which to measure investments; it reflects the return that investors require of the firm, given the firm's current overall investment risk. The question of what risk is involved in a particular investment achieving this benchmark, and how the investment's risk might interact with the overall risk of the firm can then be considered separately. For example, management can intuitively decide that a 20 percent chance of a substandard return is acceptable.

*Recommended approach to risk.* The project risk approach is considered to be the weakest conceptually of the three views. It does not directly relate the effect of the investment's risk on either the overall risk of the firm (total firm approach) or on the returns required by investors (systematic risk approach). It is, however, the most pragmatic. It also avoids a potential problem inherent in the other approaches.

The effort to determine a project's systematic risk or impact upon the firm's total portfolio risk tends to result in subjective adjustments to the cost of capital. This can be dangerous. Valuable specific information about the potential variability of the project's cash flows may be overlooked.

Pros and cons aside, the three perspectives on relevant risk are not mutually exclusive. The most practical solution is generally to employ the project risk approach—but to be intuitively aware of total firm and systematic risk implications.

**Risk Analysis in Summary.** Risk analysis has esoteric connotations. Furthermore, thinking about specific probabilities is uncomfortable, a natural reaction to

---

[5] CAPM provides a statistical measure of systematic risk called beta (b). It is derived from analysis of the historic relationship between variability in a particular stock's return and variability in the total stock market return.

uncertainty. These factors often discourage management about risk analysis. Yet estimate of risk is essentially rational and is unavoidable in a world of uncertainty. It is, in fact, invariably performed by management in some form, if not consciously, then subconsciously.

On balance, risk analysis should be systematized in the investment function. It should at least provide needed discipline in the evaluation of an investment. The exact form in which it is systematized must be flexible and sensitive to the costs and benefits of additional analysis. In some instances, sophisticated statistical computations may be warranted. In others, a brief "what-if" consideration of downside risk may suffice.

### Perspective

Quantitative analysis contributes needed *objectivity* and *discipline* to the investment process. It also facilitates synthesis of larger amounts of data than is otherwise possible. There are, however, pitfalls to be avoided.

**Potential Pitfalls.** First, there is a tendency for increasingly sophisticated analysis to become an end unto itself. This can draw attention away from the more fundamental investment steps of idea generation and proposal development.

Second, spurious conclusions can be reached if analysis limitations and nuances of methodology are not appreciated. For example, an ROI result can be misleading if it differs significantly from available reinvestment returns.

Third, analysis takes time and money. Cost-benefit trade-offs may make simulation worthwhile for a major project, but not a minor one.

Fourth, inflexible application of analysis methodology can produce irrational results. For example, rigid application of the firm's hurdle rate might lead to no further investment in a struggling division, further compounding the division's problems. This is irrational so long as senior management is strategically committed to the division. The hurdle rate should be lowered for operating purposes until such time as senior management changes its mind.

Fifth, management must not close its mind to alternative analysis concepts and techniques. As evidenced throughout this chapter, there is often no generally agreed upon "correct" way of analyzing investments. It may, in fact, be appropriate to adopt several analysis techniques within one company (e.g., both present value and ROI analysis).

## INVESTMENT STEP FOUR: THE DECISION

It was suggested at the outset of this chapter that capital investment decision making is more an art than a science. There is no substitute for management judgment. Quantitative tools and methods of analysis simply provide input into those judgments.

Some investment proposals are clear cut and should obviously be accepted. They are consistent with the company's long-range plans, expected returns are well above the hurdle rate, and the degree of risk is acceptable. Or the strategic requirement may be so strong as to make quantifiable economic returns largely irrelevant. But many investment opportunities fall into gray areas. It is impossible to make generalizations about decisions concerning these investments. The proper answer depends upon the company's unique characteristics and management's assessment of current and expected circumstances. In short, it depends upon management judgment.

### Decision Guidelines

Internal control requires that administration procedures be promulgated to cover capital expenditures. Although specific criteria for investment decisions cannot be set forth in a way that will satisfactorily cover all investment proposals, general accept/reject guidelines can be established. These guidelines, with explanations of the rationale behind them, are usually worthwhile supplements to control procedures. They educate management, develop a positive attitude toward the investment function, and avoid misunderstandings.

The benefit of management education is self evident. A positive attitude toward investment and investment risk is necessary for creativity and the ongoing generation of ideas. Clear delineation of senior management views on risk averts wasted effort on the part of line management. However, the explicit promulgation of company philosophy should avoid the appearance of excessive risk aversion. This leads to a dearth of new ideas. Misunderstandings that result from inadequately understood investment ground rules can also be counterproductive. Witness the frictions that can develop when a "critical" division appropriation request is rejected by the corporate office.

In summary, formal investment procedures and explanation of investment guidelines are important. But they should not be too formal, too voluminous or too complex for general management's understanding. Excessive rigidity and complexity can be counterproductive.

Following is a partial listing of types of investment guidelines that can be useful to operating management. Once such guidelines have been developed, they should, like the company's goals and strategies, be regularly reviewed and revised as necessary.

**Division and/or Line of Business Capital Budgets.** A company's overall capital budget and the allocation of that budget will depend upon the firm's financial position, its management philosophy regarding capital rationing, and its corporate goals and strategic plans. These areas are largely the responsibility of senior management, and disclosures may, of necessity, be limited. However, to the extent practicable, management should convey such information to operating divisions.

**Relevant Business Planning and Financial Information.** The kinds of data considered relevant to investment decisions must be explained to operations management if unnecessary data collection and analysis effort are to be avoided. Generally speaking, the more important the strategic implications of the investment, the less important the financial data.

**Degree of Proposal Development.** Guidelines regarding the degree of proposal development should be explained. Initial investment size is commonly used as a means of stratifying investment proposals. The lower the investment amount, generally the less the proposal development required. Again, however, such stratification should be flexible as to strategic implications.

**Format for Presentation of Investment Proposals.** Efficiency can be improved if predetermined formats for proposal presentation are established. The format might simply consist of a form cover sheet, to be followed by the full text of the proposal. The form might consist of a summary of the information typically required—the nature and purpose of the project, a summary of projected financial data, DCF return and/or payback period, etc., (see Figure 34.3), or the form might be more extensive. The danger of detailing required proposal data too specifically is that the process may become too formal and complex.

**Economic Risk and Return Measurement.** Both the analysis methodologies and the cut-off levels (e.g., minimum hurdles rates and measures of downside risk) that the company adopts are examples of economic measurement guidelines to be explained to operating managers. Since this kind of information has a tendency to be academic in nature, it is particularly important to simplify the guidelines so that they are understandable to general management. In addition, operating divisions should be told what analyses they are expected to prepare and what analyses will be done at the corporate level.

### Decision Making Level

Internal control typically mandates multiple approvals of an investment decision. The number and specific levels of such approvals are usually related to the size of the investment. The exact approval hierarchy depends upon both the firm and the circumstances.

In general, efficiency mandates that some approval authority be relegated to middle and lower management levels. Although capital investment decisions are important, senior management cannot be intimately involved with each and every decision. The level at which the decisions should be made depends upon an assessment of risks and benefits.

The risk of poor decisions may be increased when less experienced or unproven managers make investment decisions. At the same time, efficiency is improved, and lower level managers learn from the decision-making process. Furthermore, as lower level managers participate in the capital investment process, they become more personally involved. This personal involvement stimulates the generation of future investment ideas and gives operating management a vested interest in seeing that new investments perform well.

| | | A/R Control Number _____ |
| --- | --- | --- |
| | | Budget Proposal Number _____ |
| _____ | | |
| *Affiliate* | | Date _____ |

| | Item | Capital | Expense | Total | PLANNED SPENDING SCHEDULE |
| --- | --- | --- | --- | --- | --- |
| **F U N D S** | | | | | |
| | Total Request | | | | |

**DESCRIPTION OF FUND USE AND OBJECTIVE:**

**F O R**

| | | | Yr. | Incremental Cash Flow | Incremental IBT |
| --- | --- | --- | --- | --- | --- |

*Asset Acquisition*

[ ]  Profit Oriented:
  Investment NPV  @ _____%  $_____
  Equity NPV      @ _____%  $_____
  ROI                        _____%
  ROE                        _____%
  Payout                     _____Yrs.

[ ]  Basic Upkeep

[ ]  Intangible

**J U S T I F I C A T I O N**

*Asset Retirement*
  Net Book Value $_____    Net Disposal Realization $_____    Book Gain (Loss) $_____

Investment Risk

General Comments

| Title | Reviewed By [Staff] Signature | Date | Title | Approved By [Line] Signature | Date |
| --- | --- | --- | --- | --- | --- |

**FIGURE 34.3  APPROPRIATION REQUEST COVERSHEET**

# INVESTMENT STEP FIVE: CONTROL OF PROJECTS

Once an investment has been approved, the investment transaction is initiated. If the project is long-term and/or involves many separate transactions, the process can be quite drawn out. Control over investment spending becomes increasingly important as project size, timing, and complexity increase.

Control over investment transactions is actually a subject of internal control. (See Chapter 17.) However, two particularly relevant issues will be cited here. The first issue has to do with tracking project spending. The second involves actions resulting from sizable cost overruns.

## Tracking Project Spending

Management must control investment spending to ensure that funds are properly used and to avoid surprises before it is too late. The actual cost of an investment almost invariably differs from original estimates, varying usually on the high side. The longer the time horizon involved, the more the likelihood of this being true. It is important to know when and why such variances from plan are occurring.

**Cost Status Reports.** Some form of cost status reports must be used to control investment spending. Such reports may be required weekly or monthly, depending upon the circumstances and size of the project. They should compare the spending originally forecast to the actual spending to date for each significant spending category. The reports should relate the project's physical status to spending. A report saying that 80 percent of the budgeted investment has been expended could be misleading if it neglected to indicate that the project is only 50 percent complete. Another way of ensuring that the reports are useful is to require projections of remaining spending in the status report. A revised forecast of total spending can then be compared to the original budget.

**Numerical Control System.** If a firm has a number of investment projects, it may be useful to adopt a numerical control system to relate investment proposals and spending status reports. For example, a numbering system would identify a project by division and specific project. Such a control system not only decreases confusion and errors but provides identification for future reference.

## Reviewing Cost Overruns

Cost overruns are inevitable. If they are small in relationship to the project, they can generally be ignored. As soon as a significant overrun appears likely, however, the entire project should be closely reviewed. Many companies require that all expected overruns above a certain level be treated as new investment proposals. This level may be defined as an absolute amount and/or as some percentage of the original budget.

# INVESTMENT STEP SIX: POST-COMPLETION AUDIT REVIEW

The post-completion audit review involves the comparison of investment performance with original expectations. A common perception of this review is that it seeks to identify investments that have not lived up to expectations. It has the negative connotation of assigning somewhere and to someone responsibility for poor investments. Unfortunately, this negative view may obscure the review's more important positive objectives: to improve future investment decisions and to identify remedial steps for projections that are currently having problems.

Information gleaned through post-completion audit reviews of completed investments helps evaluate future investment proposals. And if managers realize that their investment proposals will be reviewed against results, they will become more circumspect in proposing investments. In addition, the review's identification of successful investments encourages further utilization of such projects and their managers in other areas of the company or in new markets. For example, the discovery that a new product line's performance has exceeded expectations might hasten its introduction into new markets.

The post-completion audit review's role in identifying remedial actions for problem projects it not so obviously positive as its role in improving future investment decisions. But it is truly a positive attribute of the post-completion audit review. The question to be answered is simple: In view of the current facts and problems, what should be done to maximize the return on shareholder capital? In some instances, the answer may call for operating changes or additional investment. In other instances, it might suggest disposal of the investment.

## Problems of Post-Completion Audit Review

Management frequently encounters two obstacles in the post-completion comparison of actual investment performance to original performance expectations. The first obstacle is that actual performance may be measured differently than the expected performance was measured. For example, DCF techniques may originally have been used to evaluate the investment proposal; but actual investment results are being recorded on an accrual accounting basis. The two types of measures are not directly comparable.

The second obstacle often confronted by the post-completion audit review is that the specific investment's performance is not being tracked by the firm's financial reporting system. For example, a piece of equipment may be an integral part of a plant and therefore may not be accounted for separately.

Despite these obstacles, certain measures common to both expected and actual performance can almost always be found (e.g., investment cost, machine output, labor costs). Above all, management must take care to ensure that the actual and expected performance measures are fully comparable; or if not, to be aware of what the differences are. An erroneous audit conclusion derived from improper performance comparison can do more harm than good.

### Administration of the Post-Completion Audit Review Function

Post-completion audit review policies necessarily vary from company to company. One common practice, however, is to review only certain investments; the review of all projects would be impractical. Dollar size is usually the criterion for selecting the investments to be reviewed. For example, all investments above a certain dollar amount and only selected projects below this amount may be subject to review.

As with investment decision making, it is important to have clearly delineated objectives and guidelines for the post-completion audit review. It is generally helpful to use a standard review coversheet, illustrated in Figure 34.4.

The timing of the initial post-completion audit review requires the balancing of two considerations. The review should be completed as soon as possible so that any problems or useful insights will be identified sooner rather than later. But a project must settle down before a meaningful review can be made.

The post-completion audit review is commonly referred to in the singular, as if each investment should receive one and only one review. This is not necessarily true. Two or more reviews may be warranted, especially for large or complex projects.

### Accounting as an Ongoing Audit Review Function

It is useful to think of the company's general accounting function as an ongoing post-completion audit review. An investment may retain its separate identify for management and financial reporting purposes, or it may lose its identity by being merged into a larger investment. Regardless, the investment is continually being reviewed. In a very real sense, the post-compltion audit review blends into the ongoing line of business review. Looking forward, it becomes part of the basis for shaping the firm's future strategic plans. It completes the full circle of the capital investment function.

## SPECIAL CAPITAL INVESTMENT SITUATIONS

Some situations arise that pose unique capital investment considerations. Although space does not permit an in-depth treatment of these issues, certain comments may prove helpful. In some cases, the reader is referred to other chapters for a more detailed discussion.

### Asset Disposal

The decision to dispose of a capital asset is a capital investment decision if future period cash flows will be affected. Disposal can, in fact, perhaps best be thought of as the negative acquisition of an asset. Evaluation of the disposal decision should be

---

        A/R Control Number _____

_____    Date Approved _____
          Affiliate              Amount Approved _____

DESCRIPTION OF FUND USE AND OBJECTIVE

---

*Spending*

| Item | Planned | Actual | Variance (Over)/Under Amount | % | Completion Date |
|------|---------|--------|--------|---|-----------------|
| | | | | | Planned _____ |
| | | | | | Actual _____ |
| | | | | | |
| | | | | | |
| | | | | | |
| | | | | | |
| Total | | | | | |

---

*Justification*

                              Planned       Current Estimate

[ ]   Profit Oriented

     Investment NPV @ _____%      $_____      $_____
     Equity NPV     @ _____%
     ROI                         _____%      _____%
     ROE                         _____%      _____%
     Payout                    _____Yrs.      _____Yrs.

[ ]   Basic Upkeep

[ ]   Intangible

---

| Year | *Incremental Cash Flow* Planned | *Actual/Cur. Est.* | *Incremental IBT* Planned | *Actual/Cur. Est.* |
|------|---------|-------------|---------|-------------|
| | | | | |
| | | | | |
| | | | | |
| | | | | |
| | | | | |
| | | | | |
| | | | | |

COMMENTS

---

FIGURE 34.4   APPROPRIATION POST-COMPLETION AUDIT REVIEW

similar to evaluation of the proposal to acquire a new asset. The cash flows relevant to the decisions are the fair market value of the asset (less any selling costs) and net future cash benefits to be derived from continued ownership.

If the firm were to dispose of the asset, it could receive cash equal to the asset's fair market value, net of selling costs. Continued ownership means foregoing the opportunity to receive this cash. The future cash benefits of continued ownership should be compared to the sale proceeds foregone in an analysis similar to the comparison of the expected future benefits of an asset being acquired to its cost. The cash flows from the retained asset can be discounted at the applicable hurdle rate. A positive net present value would indicate that continued ownership is preferable; a negative net present value would indicate that disposal is preferable.

Management is sometimes reluctant to dispose of an asset prior to the end of the useful life originally anticipated. This reluctance may be a defensive reaction because management was involved in the earlier acquisition decision. Such emotional reactions should be avoided, and management should make those decisions that are in the current best interests of the shareholders.

Management should continually be aware of disposal alternatives in the day-to-day management of the company. It may even be worthwhile to formalize a review of investment assets so that disposal options are systematically considered. The approach is somewhat akin to zero based budgeting. Similarly, it may be appropriate to incorporate early disposal possibilities into the economic analysis of investment proposals. As discussed regarding payback and the bailout factor, early disposal provides a hedge against downside risk.

### Acquisition and Divestment of Companies

Although acquisition and divestment strategies and procedures are the subjects of other chapters, it should be emphasized here that the decision to acquire another company is a capital investment decision. Future period cash flows are involved. A company's decision to divest tself of a subsidiary company or line of business is also a capital investment decision. The fundamental objective of an acquisition or divestment should be the same as for an nvestment decision—to maximize shareholder wealth. And the criteria for making the decision should be the same as for any capital investment decision—assessment of strategic implications and evaluation of risks and returns. (See Chapters 30 and 32 for a full discussion of the concepts, policies, techniques, and implications that relate to acquisitions and divestments.)

### Foreign Capital Investments

With foreign investments, certain problems are encountered that are not encountered with domestic investments—foreign exchange exposure, foreign political risk, and multinational taxation. The foreign exchange and taxation issues can be particularly complex. Rather than address the issues here, several pertinent references are mentioned in the suggested reading.

## Lease Versus Buy Decisions

The lease versus buy decision is a financing decision decided *after* the decision to invest has been made. The purpose is to determine which financing alternative offers the lower cost.

Lease versus buy analysis has probably generated as much controversy as any subject in corporate finance. Although certain issues remain unsettled, a conceptually sound and workable approach is possible. (The lease versus buy decision, as it affects real estate planning and control, is discussed in Chapter 36.)

**Lease Characteristics.** An asset represents a bundle of future economic benefits. A lease is an agreement to acquire certain of these benefits for a specified period of time. In this respect, a lease represents an investment. Simultaneously, however, the lease provides 100 percent financing of the benefits acquired. And a lease is, in this sense, a form of financing.

For day-to-day management and accounting purposes, leases are typically classified into one of two categories—*finance leases* and *operating leases*. (Finance leases are also sometimes referred to as *capital* leases.) In general, finance leases include those agreements in which a substantial portion of the benefits, responsibilities, and risks of asset ownership are passed to the lessee in a noncancellable commitment. Operating leases include all nonfinance leases.

Management usually gives finance leases the same attention that asset purchases receive. For example, the investment aspects of the lease are analyzed like a purchased asset. The lease is also likely to be capitalized on the company's balance sheet in accordance with FASB Statement 13, just as a purchased asset would be capitalized. (See Chapter 4 for a discussion of lease capitalization accounting.)

Operating leases, however, tend to be given less attention than asset purchases. Operating lease decisions are often made by operating managers; they are treated strictly as routine operating decisions, like raw material purchases. Even when operating leases are reviewed by the financial staff (e.g., because the dollar commitment is large), the review is frequently limited, with little consideration paid to the investment implications involved. Furthermore, operating leases are not capitalized on the balance sheet itself, but are instead included in footnotes to the company's financial statements.

The finance versus operating leases distinction is neither legal nor economic—it is simply a practical way of segregating leases according to their materiality. The segregation is, in fact, somewhat arbitrary. Acquisition of an asset's future benefits can be viewed as a continuum. A finance lease tends to be near the ownership end of the spectrum, where all benefits are acquired. An operating lease tends toward the other end, with only a small portion of the benefits acquired. The decision about where to draw the finance versus operating line is subjective.

The arbitrariness of the distinction between operating and finance leases is often not understood or is overlooked by management. Because the distinction determines the amount of attention a lease proposal receives, significant error can result. For example, a company may rent a warehouse for years under a series of short-term leases. Although ownership would be much less expensive over the long term, the question is not adequately addressed because lease renewals are routinely handled by the local division manager.

The financial data relevant to the lease versus buy decision are the magnitude and timing of cash flows arising from the financing alternatives. As with investment analysis, DCF techniques are generally the most appropriate way to evaluate these flows. Operating considerations, such as uncertainty about technological obsolescence and the ability to realize residual value, may also be relevant. They can be incorporated into the lease versus buy analysis by using techniques similar to those with which risk analysis is incorporated into investment proposals.

The fact that certain cash flows relevant to the investment decision (tax depreciation and residual value, for example) are necessarily related to the lease versus buy financing decision is sometimes confusing. In this regard, it is useful to restate the purpose of lease versus buy analysis: to determine if the nominal financing cost of the lease is sufficiently lower than the cost of conventional borrowing to offset the ownership benefits that are foregone when leasing.

**Relevant Cash Flows.** The cash flows relevant to the lease versus buy decision can be grouped into five categories:

- The initial investment required if the asset is purchased;
- The principal and interest payments that will be incurred if the asset is purchased and financed with conventional borrowings;
- Lease payments. The portions of these payments that represent nonfinancing services, such as maintenance services under a full service lease, should be subtracted. It is relatively easy to exclude the costs if the lessor unbundles pricing. Otherwise, the costs must be estimated.
- The residual value of the asset at the expiration of the financing term. If the asset is purchased, it will probably have some terminal value that will accrue to the owner. A lessee can obtain this value only by paying for it.
- Depreciation tax shelter, ITC, and the tax effects of the other cash flow categories. Examples of these flows are the tax shield provided by lease payments and the taxes due on the projected residual value of an owned asset.

**Cash Flow Disequilibrium Problem.** A cash flow disequilibrium must be recognized in lease versus buy analysis. The lease payments represent the cost of 100 percent financing, while the debt flows that would be present if the asset were purchased may represent the financing cost of less than 100 percent financing. A direct comparison of the lease and conventional debt cash flows may consequently ignore the different impact the alternatives will have on the company's overall capital structure.

For example, assume the firm's target (and actual) debt to equity ratio is one-to-one. If management decides to purchase the asset, it would presumably finance the purchase evenly with debt and equity. This procedure would preserve the target debt to equity ratio.

On the other hand, if it is decided to lease the asset, the amount of financing is 100 percent. It will be necessary to displace (i.e., repay) debt elsewhere in the company in order to retain the one-to-one ratio. The debt displacement will initially require cash outflow. But it will provide cash savings in subsequent periods equal to the debt service that would have been required on the prepaid debt. Both the initial and future period displaced debt cash flows must be considered when evaluating the lease alternative in order to put the lease and buy financing alternatives on common ground.

The concept that a lease creates the need to displace debt elsewhere in the company has only recently been acknowledged. A reason to lease often cited was that leases do not require equity. The recognition of the underlying reality of leasing has, however, shown that a leased asset does require equity. A lease is simply another type of debt instrument used to raise funds for the company's pool of capital. If a company overborrows with 100 percent lease financing, it must use equity to displace debt elsewhere; this is to keep the capital structure in balance.

*The 100 percent financing solution.* The commonly suggested solution to the lease and buy disequilibrium problem is to assume that the amount of financing under the buy alternative is equal to the purchase price of the asset (i.e., 100 percent financing). It is further suggested that the amortization of the debt should be assumed to parallel the lease amortization. For example, if the lease payments are level payment, the debt amortization should be treated as level payment; if the lease payments are made in advance, the debt payments should be treated as in advance. These assumptions ostensibly equalize the amounts of financing implicit in the lease and buy alternatives, thus neutralizing the different impacts of the financing alternatives on the company's capital structure.

The problem with this solution to the disequilibrium is that it assumes an asset has the same value to the investor, regardless of whether it is purchased or leased. As a corollary, it assumes the debt capacity of an asset in the hands of an investor is the same, again regardless of whether it is acquired through purchase or lease.

When an asset is purchased, all its potential cash flows are acquired. But when the asset is leased, only the rights to the operating cash flows are typically acquired, with the lessor retaining ownership of the tax shelter, as well as the residual, and perhaps a part of, the operating cash flows. To the extent certain of the asset's future cash flows are retained by the lessor, the value of the economic benefits acquired is lower if the asset is leased than if it is purchased. Furthermore, given that the firm's debt capacity is determined by the future cash flows from its investments, the company's debt capacity is less if the asset is leased than if purchased.

It follows that the assumption that the asset will be purchased with 100 percent conventional borrowings does not fully neutralize the different impacts of the financing alternatives on the company's capital structure. The value of the purchased asset is greater than the leased asset. The 100 percent conventional borrowings therefore represents contractual debt greater than the debt implicit in the lease obligation.

*Quantifying displaced debt cash flows.* Another solution to the cash flow disequilibrium problem in lease versus buy analysis is to assume conventional financing under the buy alternative in accordance with the firm's target capital structure, and to explicitly quantify the displaced debt cash flows related to the lease. These displaced debt cash flows can then be combined with the leasing cash flows. The amount of initial debt displacement required is included in the lease alternative as a cash outflow. The future interest and principal payments avoided because debt was prepaid are treated as inflows.

The displaced debt approach avoids the shortcomings of assuming the conventional debt equal to the asset cost. The objective is to make the amounts of financing implicit in the lease and buy alternatives the same *proportion* of acquired asset value; that is, the same percentage financing. This effectively neutralizes the different impacts on the company's capital structure of the financing alternatives.

*An example.* An example will better demonstrate both the cash flow disequilibrium problem and the two approaches to solving it. Assume that a company has decided to acquire a $900,000 piece of equipment having an expected useful life of seven years. Other relevant data include the following:

| | |
|---|---|
| Tax Depreciation | 7 years sum-of-the-years-digits (SYD) |
| Investment Tax Credit (ITC) | $90,000 credit (10%) to be realized at the end of Year 3—delay because of ITC carryforward. |
| Proposed Lease Term | 7 equal annual payments of $135,000, payable in advance. |
| Residual Value | 10% residual, fully taxable at ordinary FIT rate, due to depreciation recapture. |
| Capital Structure | Target capital structure is a one-to-one debt to equity ratio. |
| Marginal (or Incremental) Borrowing Rate for Secured Debt | 10% |
| Marginal Income Tax Rate | 46% |

Figures 34.5 and 34.6 both show the relevant cash flows under the buy and lease alternatives.

Figure 34.5 handles lease versus buy disequilibrium by assuming the asset purchase will be financed with debt equal to the cost of the asset; that is, 100 percent financing. This is the commonly suggested solution to the disequilibrium problem. The borrowings are assumed to be level payment (i.e., mortgage type) and payable in advance—a pattern identical to the lease financing.

In contrast, Figure 34.6 handles the disequilibrium problem by assuming conventional financing under the buy alternative to be equal to 50 percent of the asset book value (one-to-one capital structure), and by explicitly computing the displaced debt flows attributable to the lease financing. The displaced debt levels were computed as 50 percent of the net present values of the lease at the ends of the various periods.

|  | Year | | | | | | | |
|---|---|---|---|---|---|---|---|---|
|  | 0 | 1 | 2 | 3 | 4 | 5 | 6 | 7 |
| *Ownership Cash Flows* | | | | | | | | |
| Investment in Equipment | (900,000) | | | | | | | |
| Debt: | | | | | | | | |
|   Initial Borrowing | 900,000 | | | | | | | |
|   Principal Repayment | (168,059) | ( 94,865) | (104,351) | (114,787) | (126,265) | (138,892) | (152,781) | |
|   Interest Expense | | ( 73,194) | ( 63,708) | ( 53,272) | ( 41,794) | ( 29,167) | ( 15,278) | |
|   Interest Tax Shelter | | 33,669 | 29,306 | 24,505 | 19,225 | 13,417 | 7,028 | |
|     Total | 731,941 | (134,390) | (138,753) | (143,554) | (148,834) | (154,642) | (161,031) | |
| Depreciation Tax Shelter | | 103,500 | 88,596 | 74,106 | 59,202 | 44,298 | 29,394 | 14,904 |
| ITC | | | | 90,000 | | | | |
| Residual, net | | | | | | | | 48,600 |
|     Total | (168,059) | ( 30,890) | ( 50,157) | 20,552 | ( 89,632) | (110,344) | (131,637) | 63,504 |
| *Leasing Cash Flows* | | | | | | | | |
| Lease Payments | (135,000) | (135,000) | (135,000) | (135,000) | (135,000) | (135,000) | (135,000) | |
| Tax Shelter | | 62,100 | 62,100 | 62,100 | 62,100 | 62,100 | 62,100 | 62,100 |
|     Total | (135,000) | ( 72,900) | ( 72,900) | ( 72,900) | ( 72,900) | ( 72,900) | ( 72,900) | 62,100 |

FIGURE 34.5   LEASE VERSUS BUY WITH 100% OWNERSHIP DEBT

The present values of the lease were determined by discounting at the company's marginal borrowing rate of 10 percent.[6] The initial displacement represents an outflow—funds used to repay debt elsewhere. To the extent debt is repaid elsewhere, interest and principal otherwise payable is avoided—inflow.

It should be noted that in both figures, the tax benefits attributable to lease and interest payments paid in advance are delayed one year. Assuming the company is an accrual basis taxpayer, the deductions could not be taken until the liability has been accrued.

**Choosing the Discount Rate.** After relevant cash flows have been determined for the lease and buy alternatives, they must then be valued. The question is: What rate or rates should be used to discount the cash flows?

There is no consensus about the answer to this question. Some maintain that the appropriate rate is the company's marginal borrowing rate. Others suggest using the firm's overall cost of capital, and still others an equity rate. Arguments can also be made for using different rates for the different components of the cash flow streams. And finally, it is often suggested that an internal return approach should be used because agreement simply cannot be reached on a discount rate.

**Suggested Discounting Method.** In view of the ongoing controversy about the appropriate way to value lease versus buy cash flows, it would be presumptuous to recommend a *correct* approach. The following is, however, suggested as a conceptually reasonable and practical method of discounting cash flows in lease versus buy analysis.

It is suggested that the company use net present value analysis with its marginal after-tax cost of debt as the discount rate.

The rationale for using a debt discount rate is twofold. First, the major consideration in determining the discount rate to be used in a financing decision is the risk characteristics of the cash flows involved. (Capital rationing is an exception where reinvestment opportunity cost is relevant; this will be covered shortly.) Except for residual cash flows, lease versus buy cash flows tend to be relatively certain, similar to the certainty of debt flows. A company's marginal borrowing rate thereby offers a good general benchmark from which to evaluate the lease versus buy decision.

Second, to the extent management lacks confidence in the residual, and perhaps tax shelter cash flows, the uncertainty can be dealt with separately. For example, a break-even residual can be computed, or the sensitivity of results to tax shelter utili-

---

[6] The company's lease payment obligation is a senior contractual obligation of the company, substantially the same as any other of its senior debt obligations. It can be reasonably assumed that an investor would value lease payments similarly to debt service flows on comparable conventional debt instruments. The amount of debt implicit in the lease can therefore be estimated by discounting the lease payments at the company's marginal borrowing rate for conventional debt. Furthermore, because the economic benefits acquired through lease are, by definition, equal to the debt implicit in the lease, the value of the economic benefits acquired by lease will be simultaneously determined.

| | | | | Year | | | | |
|---|---|---|---|---|---|---|---|---|
| | 0 | 1 | 2 | 3 | 4 | 5 | 6 | 7 |
| *Ownership Cash Flows* | | | | | | | | |
| Investment in Equipment | (900,000) | | | | | | | |
| Debt: | | | | | | | | |
| Initial Borrowing | 450,000 | | | | | | | |
| Principal Repayment | | ( 57,857) | ( 57,857) | ( 57,857) | ( 57,857) | ( 57,857) | ( 57,857) | (102,858) |
| Interest Expense | | ( 45,000) | ( 39,214) | ( 33,429) | ( 27,643) | ( 21,857) | ( 16,072) | ( 10,286) |
| Interest Tax Shelter | | 20,700 | 18,038 | 15,377 | 12,716 | 10,054 | 7,393 | 4,732 |
| Total | 450,000 | ( 82,157) | ( 79,033) | ( 75,909) | ( 72,784) | ( 69,660) | ( 66,536) | (108,412) |
| Depreciation Tax Shelter | | 103,500 | 88,596 | 74,106 | 59,202 | 44,298 | 29,394 | 14,904 |
| ITC | | | | 90,000 | | | | |
| Residual, net | | | | | | | | 48,600 |
| Total | (450,000) | 21,343 | 9,563 | 88,197 | ( 13,582) | ( 25,362) | ( 37,142) | ( 44,908) |
| *Leasing Cash Flows* | | | | | | | | |
| Lease Payments: | | | | | | | | |
| Payments | (135,000) | (135,000) | (135,000) | (135,000) | (135,000) | (135,000) | (135,000) | |
| Tax Shelter | | 62,100 | 62,100 | 62,100 | 62,100 | 62,100 | 62,100 | 62,100 |
| Total | (135,000) | ( 72,900) | ( 72,900) | ( 72,900) | ( 72,900) | ( 72,900) | ( 72,900) | 62,100 |
| Displaced Debt: | | | | | | | | |
| Initial Displacement | (293,980) | | | | | | | |
| Reduction in Displacement | | 38,102 | 41,912 | 46,103 | 50,714 | 55,785 | 61,364 | |
| Interest Saved | | 29,398 | 25,588 | 21,397 | 16,786 | 11,715 | 6,136 | |
| Reduction in Interest Tax Shelter | | ( 13,523) | ( 11,770) | ( 9,843) | ( 7,722) | ( 5,389) | ( 2,823) | |
| Total | (293,980) | 53,977 | 55,730 | 57,657 | 59,778 | 62,111 | 64,677 | |
| Total | (428,980) | ( 18,923) | ( 17,170) | ( 15,243) | ( 13,122) | ( 10,789) | ( 8,233) | 62,100 |

FIGURE 34.6  LEASE VERSUS BUY WITH DISPLACED DEBT

zation can be tested. This is essentially the same as the project risk approach suggested earlier for investment decision risk analysis.

The idea of different discount rates to reflect the varying degress of cash flow certainty (for example, one rate for lease payments, another for the residual, and so on) at first seems a viable alternative to choosing just one discount rate, such as the after-tax debt rate. The concept is an outgrowth of the Capital Asset Pricing Model (CAPM). However, as in the CAPM investment application, the model tends to detract from useful consideration of specific cash flow variability such as the project risk approach provides.

There are three reasons for recommending net present value analysis over internal return for lease versus buy. The first is the possibility of multiple rates of return with internal return analysis. Second, internal return does not facilitate risk analysis (such as break-even residual value) as well as present value. Third, the internal return approach does not eliminate the need to specify a discount rate benchmark. The lease internal return is generally compared to the debt rate to determine which is cheaper—meaning that the debt rate is implicitly assumed as the benchmark. This also points out an inconsistency. The cash flows in the lease alternative are in essence being valued (or discounted) at the internal rate of return while the debt alternative flows are being discounted at another rate, the debt rate.

**Capital Rationing.** As is the case with investment decisions, capital rationing presents a situation in which reinvestment opportunity costs of the company are relevant to the lease versus buy decision. An ongoing policy of capital rationing is, in theory, difficult to justify. In practice, however, relatively permanent capital rationing constraints are often found. When such constraints are in existence, the opportunity cost of equity types of investment should be used as the discount rate for analyzing lease versus buy decisions. The premise is that in such situations the cash flow differences between the financing alternatives will, in fact, be invested or disinvested by the company as equity capital.

**Application of the Suggested Discounting Method.** Four observations may prove useful to the application of the suggested lease versus buy methodology. First, so long as the discount rate is constant, cash flows are additive for discounting purposes. This means that if one discount rate (for example, a debt discount rate) is used for all lease and buy cash flows, the component cash flows can either be discounted separately or in various groupings, such as total lease versus total ownership flows or lease less ownership flows. The result will be the same with all approaches. This characteristic can be particularly helpful in evaluating the sensitivity of lease versus buy results to changes in projections, such as the timing of tax benefits and the residual value.

Second, the present value of ownership debt flows and leasing, plus displaced debt flows, will equal zero when discounted at the after-tax cost of debt. This means that, except in capital rationing situations, the computation of displaced debt is unnecessary, and the lease versus buy analysis is reduced to a comparison of:

| Ownership flows | vs. | Leasing flows |
|---|---|---|
| Purchase price | | Lease payments, net |
| Depreciation tax shelter | | |
| Residual value, net | | |

Third, where the objective of investment analysis is to maximize the net present value, the objective of lease versus buy analysis is to minimize the net present value —to minimize cost. For example, the present value of the ownership outflows in Figure 34.6 is $(434,488), greater than the $(457,357) present value of the lease flows. Ownership is preferable.

Fourth, the residual value which will cause the lease and buy present values in the example to break even is $28,802 (after adjustment for tax effects). If it is likely that the residual will be above this amount (as projected), ownership is preferable. If not, leasing will be preferable. It is important in assessing the residual possibilities that management keep in mind that a debt discount rate was used. This implies a relatively high degree of certainty, so estimates about residual realization should tend to be conservative.

**Analysis Horizon.** In evaluating both the investment and financing implications of lease proposals, the initial lease term generally offers a reasonable analysis horizon. For shorter term leases, however, this may not be sufficient. Such a short horizon may not adequately take into account the long-term investment implications involved.

It was suggested in "Investment Step Two: Development of the Proposal" (regarding mutually exclusive investments) that it may be appropriate to extend the analysis horizon beyond an investment's life. This might have particular merit in periods of high inflation because of concern about the cost of replacing assets.

This same suggestion may be applicable to lease analysis, especially where the initial lease term is relatively short. For example, the analysis of a three year lease proposal might be extended to six years, with assumptions made about lease renewal. The alternative is to ensure that future implications are fully reflected in the ownership residual value at the end of three years.

It has thus far been assumed that the asset will be sold at residual value under the buy alternative. It may alternatively be more appropriate to assume that the asset will be purchased at the lease expiration. The purchase price (residual value) and the subsequent tax and other ownership benefits would then be included in lease alternative cash flows.

**Lease Only Decisions.** Circumstances in which an asset can only be leased present a unique investment problem. Public facilities are a common example of this type of situation. The asset cost normally used in making the investment decision is not known; the investment and financing decisions are, in fact, one and the same.

There is no completely satisfactory solution to this problem. What appears to be the best approach involves three steps. The first step is to estimate a purchase, or cash equivalent value of the asset to be acquired. This can be done in the manner suggested for determining the asset value and debt obligation implicit in a lease; that is, by discounting the lease payments at the company's marginal borrowing rate.

The second step is to analyze the proposal as an investment, with the purchase price assumed to be equal to the cash equivalent price determined in step one. The procedure should be the same as that followed for normal investment analysis. For example, the applicable hurdle rate should be used as the discount rate. However, some of the cash flows normally involved in the investment analysis won't be present; for example, depreciation tax shelter. Particular care should be taken that the lease payments are *not* included in the investment cash flows. Lease payments are a part of the cost of financing, and the cost of financing is already included in the discount rate. To include the lease payments in the investment cash flows would be double counting.

The third step is actually not a separate step. If the investment decision is a positive one, the financing decision is made by default. Leasing is the only available financing.

**Operating Uncertainties.** There are frequently operating uncertainties involved in the lease versus buy decision. These uncertainties can generally be grouped into three categories—asset requirements, technological obsolescence, and the value of services to be provided by the lessor.

*Asset requirements.* The best way to cope with asset requirements such as uncertainty about size and/or location needs for office or warehouse space may be to extend the analysis period to one that management believes more practical for projecting its asset needs. At a minimum, the analysis horizon should be equal to the initial lease term.

*Technological obsolescence.* Technological obsolescence can affect the company in many ways. The specific implications can be affected by the lease versus buy decision. For example, if an asset is owned, the owner bears the risk that the asset residual value may be reduced by obsolescence. In addition, some lessors, particularly manufacturers, sometimes provide a guarantee to upgrade equipment free of charge if new products become available. An asset owner would have to bear the cost of such upgrade. In other instances, the lease can work to the lessee's disadvantage if technological change occurs—the lease may be a noncancellable one, making it impossible for the lessee to extricate himself from the commitment to old equipment. If the equipment were owned, it could be sold and new equipment purchased.

Uncertainty about technological obsolescence is particularly difficult to quantify. It involves not only the assessment of obsolescence possibly occurring, but also estimates of when future investment decisions will be made. Some of the investment possibilities may not even exist at present because the technology is unknown.

*Value of lessor-provided services.* The third category of operating uncertainties involves concern about being able to duplicate services offered by the lessor. The most straightforward way to incorporate this concern into lease versus buy analysis is probably to pay particular attention to the value placed upon the lessor's services when adjusting the lease payment stream for nonfinancing services. The higher the value placed upon the lessor's nonfinancing services, the more the lease payments should be reduced.

Risk analysis can be useful in evaluating the implications of all three operating risk categories. Simulation and present value break-even analysis can be particularly helpful. Probability and sequential decision analysis may also be appropriate for larger transactions.

## SUGGESTED READING

Bierman, Harold, Jr., and Smidt, Seymour. *The Capital Budgeting Decision*, 4th ed. New York: Macmillan, 1975.

Bower, Richard S. "Issues in Lease Financing." *Financial Management,* (Winter, 1973), pp. 25-34.

Donaldson, Gordon. "Strategic Hurdle Rates for Capital Investment." *Harvard Business Review* (March-April 1972), pp. 50-58.

Feinschreiber, Robert. *International Tax Planning Today.* Greenvale, New York: Panel Publishers, 1977.

Horngren, Charles T. *Cost Accounting, a Managerial Emphasis.* Englewood Cliffs, New Jersey: Prentice-Hall, Inc., 1977.

Moore, Michael L., and Bagley, Ronald N. *U.S. Aspects of Doing Business Abroad.* New York: American Institute of Certified Public Accountants, Inc., 1978.

Shapiro, Alan C. "Capital Budgeting for the Multinational Corporation." *Financial Management* (Spring 1978), pp. 7-16.

Van Horne, James C. *Financial Management and Policy.* Englewood Cliffs, New Jersey: Prentice-Hall, 1977.

Weston, J. Fred. "Investment Decisions Using the Capital Asset Pricing Model." *Financial Management* (Spring 1973), pp. 25-33.

Weston, J. Fred, and Brigham, Eugene F. *Essentials of Managerial Finance.* Hinsdale, Illinois: The Dryden Press, 1979.

# Part VIII

## Administrative Functions

# 35

# Risk Management

*Matthew Lenz, Jr.*

## PRINCIPLES AND TECHNIQUES

One of the corporate functions for which the controller or treasurer frequently has oversight responsibility is insurance, or risk management. This function, once looked upon as the simple, part-time responsibility of the treasury department, is now recognized as having advanced far beyond that stage. The cost of insurance, as well as other risk treatment techniques, has become a significant factor in the budget of many firms, and now approaches 0.6 percent of revenues.[1] In addition, insurance

---

[1] Jay M. Bedell, Bernard M. Brown, and Charles F. Moody, Jr., *Cost of Risk Survey* (Darien: Risk Planning Group, Inc., 1980).

has become a very complex area, with many options available. A large corporation requires a full-time professional to keep abreast of the rapidly changing laws, judicial interpretations, and current social expectations and publications.

Professional insurance managers recognized quite some time ago that insurance was not the only method of managing corporate exposures to loss, that it was frequently not the best method, and, in fact, that it was often the most expensive. This recognition led to the birth of the now robust, but still developing, discipline of risk management. Risk management uses insurance as just one technique for the funding of risk. Since the risk manager most commonly reports to the controller or treasurer, those officials should know something about the discipline.

Risk management has been defined as the identification, analysis, and evaluation of risk and the selection of the most advantagous method of treating it.[2] The risk manager's major concern is to protect the firm's assets from economic loss and to preserve its earning ability. This should be done in the most cost-effective way by seeking to minimize the total cost of risk, a concept introduced by Douglas Barlow of Massey-Ferguson Company in the early 1960s.

There are four elements to the cost of risk:

- Insurance premiums,
- Uninsured losses,
- Loss control costs, and
- Administrative costs.

These elements are highly interrelated—as the level of risk retention (and therefore uninsured losses) increases, the cost of insurance premiums should decrease. As risk retention increases, the loss control effort usually also increases and frequently further decreases insurance premiums. An increase in any of the first three elements will usually cause an increase in administrative costs. The model is dynamic, and reducing its sum to a minimum is not a simple task.

## THE PROCESS OF RISK MANAGEMENT

While many aspects of risk management are highly subjective, and there is much opportunity for creativity and individual expression, general agreement exists that the process of risk management consists of four steps, taken in the following sequence:

- Identification,

---

[2] Matthew Lenz, Jr., *Risk Management Manual* Vol. I (Santa Monica: The Merritt Co., 1971), p. 1.

- Evaluation,
- Management, and
- Monitoring.

## Identification

This step determines what can happen to create a loss to an asset[3] or to reduce the earning ability of the firm. The risk manager must be able to identify all property the firm owns, leases, or otherwise uses. He must know everything the firm does, how it is done, what it uses, how, where, and by whom its products and services are distributed, and what its plans are. In short, he has to know everything about everything. A knowledge of law is extremely valuable because the potential legal liability inherent in much of a firm's activities represents the largest single exposure to loss.

The identification process is a continuing one. It requires a constant flow of information from all levels of management and from all departments. In addition, the risk manager must visit the firm's physical facilities regularly to actually see how it is functioning. Contracts, leases, and advertising copy ideally should be submitted for risk review before being acted upon. If this is done, risks can be identified before, rather than after, the fact. No major changes in operations or physical facilities should occur until the risk manager has been notified. The risk implications in the change can then be identified and acted upon. The risk manager should also be part of the team evaluating a proposed merger or acquisition so that he has an opportunity to identify and estimate the cost of any unexpected risks.

## Evaluation

Once a "laundry list" of exposures to loss has been developed, the risk manager must evaluate the various exposures to see which are significant and which can be ignored. Since what is "significant" is a matter of individual interpretation, the board of directors should adopt a written corporate statement of risk management philosophy. The risk manager and controller or treasurer should participate in its preparation, but to be effective, it must be the board's statement. It should be narrow enough to provide real direction, yet broad enough to allow the risk manager some discretion. It should be flexible enough to allow for changing conditions, or, if not, it should be reviewed regularly by the board to make whatever adjustments become necessary. It should spell out the company's official position on the retention of risk, the purchase of insurance, the implementation of safety rules, and other risk-related matters.

The individual exposures to loss have to be evaluated within the parameters of the corporate statement of philosophy. The evaluation determines the odds of the

---

[3] The term *asset* is used in the broadest possible sense to include real and personal property, bank accounts, licenses, franchises, good will, credit, and anything else of a tangible or intangible nature whose loss or damage will affect the net worth or going-concern value of the firm.

occurrence of the loss associated with each risk (or exposure), the probable frequency of loss, and the probable severity of a loss, should it occur. From these estimates, risks can then be classified by any number of different systems, the purpose of each being to determine which risks require attention and which can be ignored. The end result of the evaluation process is a refined list of exposures to loss, all of which then have to be managed.

## Management

The management of risk is a four-step process, with each risk filtered through each step in sequence. The steps, in order of priority, are:

1. Avoid or eliminate,
2. Minimize,
3. Retain, and
4. Transfer.

**Avoid or Eliminate.** The best thing to do with risk is to get rid of it. Avoidance and elimination are simply two versions of the same step. Which step is taken is a function solely of the timing of involvement. If a new building is planned and the risk manager is able to review the blueprints, he can avoid certain risks (such as non-fire resistive ceiling tiles) by having the plans changed. On the other hand, if an existing building with improper tiles is purchased, the exposure can be removed only by eliminating the tiles because they are already there.

While this step is the most desirable way to manage risk, it is by its nature the least feasible because it is frequently impossible to eliminate functions or operations. There are times, however, when dropping a product line causing a disproportionate share of product liability losses makes a great deal of sense. Some hazardous functions, such as paint spraying, if a minor part of an operation, can frequently be contracted out.

**Minimize.** Many risks do lend themselves to some form of control. Most routine loss prevention activities—such as automatic sprinkler systems, burglar alarms, and accounting controls—fit into this category. Most of the dollars of the loss control element of the cost of risk will be spent here, and it is here that the greatest impact on the reduction or prevention of loss can be made.

Loss control, however, is not always routine. A case in point is a bank in New York City which installed and maintained an escalator in a subway station, making it easier for people to get to its "walk-up" teller windows. The bank soon began receiving an inordinate number of slip and fall claims. Thorough inspection revealed nothing wrong with the equipment or the manner in which it was functioning. A detailed analysis of the claims showed that the overwhelming majority of the accidents were occurring between 10:00 and 11:00 A.M. and between 3:00 and 4:00 P.M. The risk manager then remembered that senior citizens were able to travel at half price between the hours of 10:00 A.M. and 4:00 P.M.; it was logical that the first and last hours of that period would have the heaviest traffic. The problem was obvious—while the escalator speed was proper for a normal population mix, it was too fast for a population with a preponderance of senior citizens. The mechanism was reprogrammed to operate more slowly during those two critical hours, and the accident rate quickly dropped to normal.

**Retain.** Once all the risks that can be eliminated have been disposed of and the remaining ones have been reduced as much as possible, the question of which risks can be retained[4] must be answered. The board of directors should already have included pertinent guidelines in its statement of risk management philosophy, and much of the discussion which follows applies to making that decision.

*Why retain risk?* The question is often asked: "Why should I retain risk when insurance is available to protect me?" There are a number of different answers possible. The controller frequently finds that he can make much better use of the funds. Insurance is not inexpensive; most property-casualty insurers operate on an expense ratio of from 30 to 35 percent. Where potential losses can be predicted with an acceptable degree of accuracy, and where their size falls within an acceptable dollar limit, it is much less expensive for a firm to pay its own losses. Having an insurance company do it means simply trading dollars in addition to paying a fee of 30 to 35 percent for the privilege. If the expected claims or losses are budgeted as a regular expense, they can be paid out of working capital. That means that until the loss occurs, the firm has full use of the funds, whereas insurance premiums, paid at the beginning of the policy year, are at work in the insurer's portfolio until needed.

Insurance is sometimes not available because of market conditions. The firm then has no choice but to retain a risk. In the past several years, some firms were unable to obtain product liability insurance because of the rapidly changing social and judicial attitudes concerning responsibility for injuries caused by using a manufactured product. Some doctors and hospitals have found it impossible to buy professional liability insurance in recent years, and have been forced to retain risk they would rather insure.

Insurance may be available, but at a cost considered exorbitant. Insurance rates are set on a class basis, as an insurance company needs a large body of data to give its statistics credibility. An individual entity, whose record is far better than the average for its class, may find the quoted rates unacceptable. Sometimes a firm may find an insurer that, on the basis of the entity's record, is willing to offer the insurance at an acceptable rate. Frequently, however, that does not happen and the company retains its own risk.

---

[4] The term *self insured* is frequently used in this context. It is really a meaningless term since insurance, by definition, requires either a pooling of the risks of several entities, or a transfer of risk to another entity. By definition, then, *self insurance* is an impossibility. The FASB has said that self insurance is no insurance. The proper term is retention, or retained risk. The term *assumed* will also be seen. This, too, is incorrect as *assume* means to take on something which the entity did not have before. What is meant here is to keep that risk which already exists.

Retention is sometimes practiced as a control mechanism when a firm or conglomerate is operated on a profit center basis. A particular division or unit manager may be reluctant to spend money or time on proper loss prevention and safety activities, rationalizing that if a loss occurs, the insurance will pay for it. If the insurance program is administered from corporate headquarters, a deductible can be imposed on the unit, a deductible high enough to convince the manager that it will be to his own best interest to spend some time or money on the recommended loss control measures.

*Funding techniques.* Once a retention program has been decided upon, plans must be made to fund the exposure. The funding can be either the *pre-loss* or *post-loss type.*

*Cash reserve fund.* One system of pre-loss funding is the establishment of a cash reserve fund, with real dollars set aside for contingencies. This system is almost nonexistent today since the reserves have to be set up with after-tax dollars.

The most common method of funding is to budget the expected losses and when they do occur, to treat them as current expenses. This avoids the after-tax dollar problem and allows the money to be used as working capital until needed.

Another technique is to establish a standby guaranteed line of credit for the amount of funds expected to be necessary for other than routine, high frequency losses. A modest maintenance fee is paid until the funds are actually drawn; the prevailing rate of interest is then paid.

The insurance mechanism is used for some casualty exposures. Under a plan known as a *paid loss retro* plan, a policy is written with a modest deposit premium, the final premium consisting of actual paid losses and a service fee. In most jurisdictions, a letter of the insurer requires a letter of credit to guarantee payment of the ultimate cost. The state of California has recently required a promissory note with an interest charge of one-half to one percent over the rate for Treasury bills to compensate the insurer for the loss of use of funds. Such a requirement obviously reduces the desirability of the plan, and insurers and brokers are trying to design ways to lessen the impact of the rule. The Internal Revenue Service has also attacked the plan, contending that there is no real transfer of risk to the insurer, without which the "premiums" cannot be deducted as an expense. At this time, the issue is still unresolved.

A favored technique in recent years has been to form a *captive insurance company.* A *pure captive* is an insurance company organized by a commercial or industrial company solely to insure the risks of its parent. Among the reasons for forming a captive are:

- To fund a retention program;
- To provide broader coverage than is available in the normal market place; and
- To reduce the cost of insurance.

With a captive insurer, a firm has access to the worldwide reinsurance market, which, generally speaking, is not hampered by the rate and form regulations controlling the primary insurance market. A firm can therefore write a policy in very broad language in its own insurance company and reinsure 90 to 95 percent of it in the reinsurance market, usually at very competitive rates. Most captives are formed outside the United States (Bermuda is a favored haven, with about 1,200 captives) to avoid the regulations mentioned above, the high capital and surplus requirements of most states, and the statutory requirement of participation in residual pools such as the Automobile Insurance Plan and the F.A.I.R. plan for fire insurance. There are also, of course, tax advantages in having the captive domiciled outside the United States—especially for premiums received from foreign subsidiaries. While the tax factor is usually considered when deciding on a captive, it should not be a main element in the decision. The IRS is fighting the deductibility of premiums paid to a single parent pure captive, contending that the parent and the captive are part of the same economic family and that no risk transfer is involved. The judicial record is mixed, and no firm answers are available. If a captive is formed primarily for the presumed tax advantage (which can disappear overnight), it could be a very expensive undertaking. The decision should be based entirely on other considerations, with the tax advantage, if available, considered as an extra bonus.

A firm can sometimes obtain the advantage of a captive without actually forming one. The Aneco Insurance Group, for example, operates what it calls the Insurance Profit Center (IPC) which, through a complicated process involving the purchase of non-voting preferred shares in one of its companies, allows a company to "rent" the captive for the period of its need.

*How much retention?* Once a decision has been made to accept the concept of risk retention, the next question to be answered is, "How much?" Literature is replete with formulas for determining the "optimum" size of the deductible. The mere fact that there are a number of different formulas from which to choose suggests that none are really absolute; this aspect of risk management amply illustrates the truth of the statement that risk management is an art rather than a science. There are three general problems, one or more of which can be found in virtually all of the formulas: (1) data are required which are not available; (2) the statistical analysis is based on false assumptions regarding the nature of the data; and (3) the data required are so subjective that the mathematical manipulation is an exercise in gamesmanship.

There are a number of rules of thumb methods in use, all of which are totally subjective and none of which have any universal application. Each is based on a different aspect of a firm's financial structure and probably says more about the financial philosophy of the originator than it does about the proper amount of retention. Some of the more common are:

- *Working capital.* Retain one to five percent. This rule of thumb is based on the premise that working capital is a measure of liquidity.
- *Earnings and surplus.* Retain one percent of retained earnings plus one percent of

the average pretax profit for the past five years. This method is based on the fact that surplus is the real source of the money.

- *Sales.* Retain one to five percent. This method assumes that there is a direct, proportional relationship between sales and losses. This may be true for product liability, but would hardly seem to be true for other exposures, such as fire or embezzlement, for example.
- *Earnings per share.* Retain just below the point at which stockholders or the financial community would become upset.
- *Premium savings.* This is a poor criterion, as it has no relation to a firm's ability to retain risk, and because it can be manipulated by the underwriter. There would also be no consistency between different kinds of coverage.
- *Thresholds.* A number of different thresholds have been suggested, with the limit of retention fixed just below the threshold. Three such thresholds are:
  – Financial pain. At what point will pain become excessive?
  – Psychological acceptance. At what point will the chief executive officer object?
  – Auditor's footnote. At what level of uninsured loss would the outside auditor feel constrained to put a footnote on the income statement?

The best method is probably to make a detailed study of losses for the past five or ten years, with losses aggregated in ranges. Based on that past record, some probability estimates can be made for the coming year. (This does not mean blindly accepting the premise that history will be repeated. Modifications should be made based on changed, or changing conditions, the expected effect of increased loss control measures, etc. This approach is admittedly subjective, but is probably more realistic than assuming that the history of the past five years will be repeated next year.)

Insurance quotes or premium estimates should be developed for different levels of retention. Estimates should be made of loss control and administrative costs. All of these figures should then be plugged into the cost of risk equation, and the combination which produces a minimum cost will indicate the proper retention level. (If the data are graphed, a U-shaped curve will usually indicate that beyond a certain point, increased retention is uneconomical.)

The retention indicated by the graph or matrix has to be tempered by considerations of the attitude toward risk of the chief financial officer and the chief executive officer, of the firm's liquidity, and of its cash flow patterns. Losses occur at random, and a severe loss may well occur at the firm's lowest ebb of cash flow. A retention based just on cost of risk considerations may create a serious problem if there is no cash available to pay for the loss.

The retention limit finally determined constitutes an annual aggregate figure, not a per policy deductible. To arrive at an acceptable per policy retention, provisions must be made to either buy annual aggregate stop-loss insurance, or to break down the aggregate figure by kinds of exposure and number of expected losses.

**Transfer.** Obviously, not all risk can be retained. The potential loss may be too large, or a contract or law may require an insurance contract, or the risk management principle "Don't risk a lot for a little"[5] may come into play. Whatever the reason, a fair amount of risk must usually be transferred.

*Non-insurance risk transfers.* In planning a transfer of risk, the first thought should be to try to do it without buying insurance, because insurance costs money. Opportunities for this kind of transfer are limited, but they should be sought because the only impact they have on the cost of risk is a slight addition to the administrative cost element.

The most commonly used noninsurance risk transfer technique is the *hold harmless agreement.* This can only be used where the political or economic situation gives a firm the power to force another entity to assume some of its liability. It is frequently found in a lease situation where a tenant agrees to hold a landlord harmless for injuries occurring to people in and around the building. Subcontractors will usually agree to hold a prime contractor and/or the general contractor harmless on a construction or installation job. Almost anyone doing any work for a governmental agency is required to give a very broad hold harmless agreement to the agency.

Reliance on hold harmless agreements can be dangerous. Courts have frequently declared them null and void on the grounds that they are against public policy. Such decisions have usually involved very broad language in which the indemnitor assumed all liability, even including sole negligence of the indemnitee. But the problem is that after a loss, any agreement is subject to challenge and one can never be sure of what a court is going to decide. Another problem lies in the fact that the agreement is only as strong as the entity giving it. Hold harmless agreements should generally be backed by insurance policies which clearly indicate coverage for the liability assumed by the agreement.

Another type of noninsurance transfer is a *warranty on goods manufactured,* used to limit the firm's liability by specifying those things for which it is liable. Once again, this is a type of protection that can be overturned by the courts, and that must therefore be used judiciously.

A relatively new technique, applicable in a small number of cases, is buying *currency futures.* Obviously this technique is applicable only for international operations. It was used to excellent advantage following the severe fire suffered by Ford Motor Company in Cologne, Germany. Reserves in dollars were established by the various insurance companies shortly after the loss. By the time the claim was actually settled—nearly a year later—the value of the Deutsche mark had gone up roughly 25 percent vis-a-vis the dollar, and most insurers found their reserves inadequate. At least one company had, however, purchased a futures contract for marks and did not suffer. The same technique can be used by a risk manager with a risk retention program.

---

[5] This principle was first expounded by Bob Hedges and Robert Mehr in their pioneer text *Risk Management in the Business Enterprise,* published by Irwin in 1963. It suggests that even if a risk is within the firm's retention limit, if the cost of insurance is extremely low (e.g., fire insurance on a sprinklered, fire resistive office building), it makes sense to buy the insurance.

*Insurance.* The major risk transfer technique is, of course, insurance. Insurance is available for losses caused by almost any exposure that will have been identified, but it would obviously not be good management to buy it all.

Nonlife insurance is usually divided into two broad categories—*property* and *casualty* (also known as liability). Property coverages provide protection against loss to physical properties such as buildings, machinery, equipment, inventory, and vehicles. Insurance for direct loss may be on either a *named peril* or *all risk* basis. In a named peril policy, the perils (loss-causing agents such as fire, wind, explosion, theft) are specifically enumerated. If a cause of loss is not listed in the policy, the loss is not covered. The list of perils can be short (the standard fire policy covers loss caused by fire, lightning, and removal from premises endangered by fire) or long (a broad named peril form may include nineteen or twenty perils). The so-called all risk form covers all direct loss or damage except for those perils specifically excluded. In this form, if the peril is listed the loss is *not* covered. Here again, the list can be quite short or quite extensive; in this case, the shorter the better. Informal polls of corporate risk managers from all over the country have for several years consistently shown an almost exact 50–50 split as to how they purchase coverage.

The *valuation clause* in the standard property policy uses *actual cash value* as the measure of loss. The definition of actual cash value is argued regularly, but the generally accepted meaning is replacement cost new at the time of loss, less actual physical depreciation. The courts in California seem to equate actual cash value with market value, and a recent decision in Indiana defined it as the amount of money necessary to rebuild the property. Current decisions have therefore to be checked in all states. An endorsement is available in every state to convert the valuation to replacement cost, but this ignores the factor of depreciation. There are some restrictions in using this form, but they are minor. While the coverage provided by this language is broader, it does carry the obligation to buy more insurance. Again, informal polls of risk managers consistently show a 50–50 split on preference for actual cash value coverage versus replacement cost coverage.

There are many indirect, or consequential losses, which can flow from loss or destruction of property, and most of them are not covered by a direct damage policy. Such losses would include loss of rents, loss of sales, loss of tolls (e.g. the Tampa, Florida bridge knocked down by a freighter), loss of production, increased cost of doing business, loss of value to a set if one piece is destroyed, and so on. All of these potential losses can be covered by separate policies, or in some cases, by endorsement to a direct damage policy.

Casualty insurance includes *liability, workers' compensation*, and *automobile liability* as its main elements. Workers' compensation is a statutory coverage, with rigidly prescribed policy language. Liability insurance can be written on a very narrow basis or on what is called a *comprehensive form.* Even the comprehensive form has many restrictions, and much can be done to broaden it. It is obviously beyond the scope of this chapter to suggest all the refinements that can be made. Suffice it to say that no firm should ever accept a standard policy (even a company's "special" package policy) without modification, and if a broker can't suggest several improvements in language, he should probably be replaced.

The casualty field has more room for imaginative rating plans than does property insurance, because the regulation is less strict and the rating bases are more flexible. Composite rating plans can be developed to provide a single rating base for several different coverages. Retrospective rating plans reward a firm for better than expected loss experience, but can also penalize it for poor experience. Plans can be designed that virtually permit a company to have its premium be simply the sum of the loss payments plus an administration fee to the insurer.

Insurers do not have complete freedom to write the coverage or charge the premiums they want. Insurance is a heavily regulated industry, with authority vested in the states. The degree and style of regulation varies from one state to another. For coverage not available in the regular market, a broker can go to the *excess* or *surplus line* market, which consists of companies not licensed in the state, companies abroad, and Lloyds of London. This is a specialty market, which frequently provides innovative coverage. Care has to be exercised in using it, however, since the companies are not supervised by state regulatory authorities.

### Monitoring

No risk management plan, regardless of how carefully thought out, can ever be considered final. Laws change, thus creating new liabilities. Juries and courts put new interpretations on old laws, thus changing (sometimes retroactively) the rules under which the firm operates. The economy changes, requiring reevaluation of physical properties and earning abilities. The firm's earnings may increase or decrease; its plans for expansion may be accelerated or contracted, or a dozen other things may happen that could affect its cash flow. Inflation can affect the value of the dollar, making today's retention limit seem silly. Some loss control measures may not work, or may be less cost effective than anticipated. New technology may make a type of loss control obsolete. New products will create new exposures to loss. The litany is endless, but the point is clear: any risk management program needs constant review and evaluation. The cost of risk must be watched constantly. It should be converted to a percentage of sales, or payroll, or units manufactured, or some other dynamic criterion to provide a relative cost of risk over time.

The risk manager must receive a steady flow of information from all units of the organization so that he can instantly be apprised of any new developments that might affect the plan. He must constantly review accident and loss records to see if any trends that might require special action are developing. He must know what changes in operations are planned so as to determine whether or not current strategies are adequate for whatever new exposures will be created. He must constantly test the insurance market as prices there change in reaction to many variables, and a change in insurance cost can affect the optimum mix of the components of the cost of risk.

Risk management is a dynamic function requiring regular feedback, constant evaluation, and an ability to shift emphasis when indicated.

## EVALUATION OF THE RISK MANAGER

One of the perennial problems of the discipline is how to evaluate the performance of the risk manager. Since risk management is an art with relatively few absolutes, objective criteria are virtually nonexistent. Some years ago, a group of risk management consultants attempted to develop a list of objective standards for a risk management program. This would have enabled them to issue a "certified" audit, comparable in significance to a certified financial statement. After several fruitless meetings, the scheme was abandoned because it was realized that there is no one right way to plan a program. The same situation exists in attempting to evaluate the risk manager. There are frequently many ways of solving a problem, and a manager's personal value system will also frequently play a part in selecting from among the alternatives.

The risk manager of a Fortune 500 company had an interesting problem a few years ago. He discovered that the firm's outside auditor was evaluating the effectiveness of his department on the ratio of insurance recoveries to insurance premiums paid: the higher the ratio, the more effective his operation. Since he was spending a great deal of his time and budget on loss control activities, he was working toward having no losses. He had also increased the firm's retention of risk considerably, so that insurance would come into play only in the event of a fairly large loss. Yet the more he accomplished his stated objective, the less effective he was considered by the auditor!

The cost of risk concept can perhaps act as one measure of a risk manager's effectiveness. Industry figures were not available until early 1980 when Risk Planning Group of Darien, Connecticut released its study (referred to earlier). The study is limited in scope, and since all companies do not report their expenses in a uniform manner the results are unfortunately distorted. It is a start, however, and future studies will probably improve upon this first effort. Through such studies, a firm's cost of risk could be compared with others in the same industry. Absolute figures would be meaningless, of course, but the cost of risk expressed as a percentage of sales would have some meaning. The comparison would always have to take into consideration any restraints imposed upon the risk manager because of executive risk aversion, cash flow or liquidity problems, or for any other reason.

Any attempt at evaluation should start with a definition of the objectives of the department. This could then lead to the establishment of measurable performance criteria. Most risk managers would welcome and participate in such an exercise because it would provide top management with a better understanding of the function. As long as all concerned recognize the subjective nature of the job, criteria for evaluation can be agreed upon.

## SELECTION CRITERIA

A risk management system can be thought of as having four major components: the risk manager, a broker, an insurance company, and a consultant. Not every system uses all four; the absolute minimum would be to have a risk manager (or someone performing that function on either a full or part-time basis) and an insurance company. Since there are many risk manager aspirants, and an untold number of brokers, insurance companies, and consultants, the problem of choice can be difficult. No checklist of criteria is infallible and, as with all personnel selection, subjective evaluation and personal chemistry will always play a large part. Each component does have some basic requirements that should be met by a candidate. The following sections review the factors to be considered in the selection process.

### Risk Manager

**Background.** Historically, new risk managers came from either an insurance company or insurance brokerage background. That is still true for the majority of new risk managers, but since risk management has been recognized as a discipline in its own right, people are now being graduated with degrees in insurance and risk management at both the baccalaureate and master's levels. Many of these graduates are beginning to work as assistant risk managers, thus bypassing the insurance apprenticeship. There is much to be said for either route. Insurance will probably always remain the largest component of the cost of risk and will continue to be the major vehicle for funding risk. A solid working knowledge of the intricacies of insurance will always be important, and an understanding of the thinking process of the underwriter can be invaluable. The shortcoming of the insurance background lies in the fact that the person may become imbued with the thought that insurance is the best answer to all problems, rather than thinking of it as a last resort mechanism. Generally, however, the advantages outweigh the disadvantages.

Many risk managers are attorneys. This is an advantage, since the major exposure faced by most firms is that of legal liability, which has no dollar limit. While a law degree is by no means essential (most firms have their own legal counsel, either in-house or on retainer), some knowledge of contract and negligence law is important.

Since there is a definite trend toward greater retention of risk, the risk manager should know something about statistical analysis to be able to assist in determining proper limits of retention, and something about money management to be able to administer a program. He should understand the concept of discounted cash flow and the meaning of net present value in order to choose among alternative methods of risk treatment.

To handle risk management in a large firm, the candidate should have three to five years experience as a risk manager, preferably in the same industry, although that is by no means essential. For a medium-sized firm, three to five years experience as an assistant risk manager would be acceptable. A small firm hiring its first risk manager would probably be safe in hiring someone directly from an insurance company or brokerage house, assuming he has diversified experience and a demonstrated high level of competence. Naturally, hiring someone with experience in a risk management department would be preferable.

**Attitude.** Attitude is probably one of the most important considerations. It is vital that the risk manager have a solid understanding of the concept of risk management and the role of insurance. Imagination, creativity, a willingness to experiment, to try the unorthodox, are personal characteristics that should be sought.

**Education.** The ideal educational background is probably an undergraduate degree in insurance from institutions such as The College of Insurance in New York, Georgia State University in Atlanta, or Temple University in Philadelphia, followed by an M.B.A. in finance from any good graduate business school. The professional designations of Chartered Property Casualty Underwriter (CPCU) and Associate in Risk Management (ARM) are highly desirable. The CPCU designation is awarded by the American Institute for Property and Liability Underwriters, Incorporated, upon satisfactory completion of ten essay examinations in insurance, risk management, law, economics, management, accounting, finance, and insurance company administration. A three year experience requirement also exists. The ARM designation is awarded by the Insurance Institute of America after satisfactory completion of three essay examinations in the process of risk management, loss control, and risk funding.

### Broker

The type of broker needed will vary considerably with the size, complexity, and geographical spread of the firm.

The term *broker* is used here in the sense of insurance intermediary and includes *agents*. There is a legal distinction between agents and brokers, in that agents have contracts with insurance companies and, by law, represent those companies. A broker, on the other hand, is the representative of the insured. Agents generally operate in a local area. Many brokers have branches over a wide regional area; some are national in scope and a few are international. The so-called "alphabet houses" (because they are known by their initials) have become financial conglomerates. Through their various subsidiary organizations they can offer a full range of services, including loss control, engineering, insurance, captive company management, claim analysis, retention studies, and so on. In some states, such as New York, an intermediary can be both an agent or broker. At the other extreme, some states, such as Wyoming, do not permit brokers.

**General Background.** In selecting a brokerage firm, a controller should look for one that has been in business at least five years and has established a record of stability. He should select one that handles primarily commercial accounts and preferably some accounts in his industry. The controller should also examine the average size of the brokerage firm's accounts. His company should not be the smallest, as it will not have much clout. It should not be the biggest because the account might be too complex to handle; somewhere in the upper third is probably ideal. The firm should be willing to give the controller the names of some of its major clients as references so he can check on its competence and quality of service.

**Staff.** A principal should be assigned to the company account and the controller should know who that would be. In a big brokerage firm, a vice president should be assigned as account executive. The controller should know what other accounts are handled by this account executive—they should certainly include others of similar size and complexity. The qualifications of the account executive's assistant, or alternate, in case the designated executive is unavailable when needed, and those of the backup staff are also important, because they frequently handle the service on routine matters.

**Services.** Not every firm needs all the services offered by a large brokerage house. The controller should determine what services are needed, and should draw up a list of the minimum requirements that a brokerage firm candidate must satisfy.

**Insurance Companies.** The insurance companies with which a broker does business can be an important factor. If the firm has special needs that only a few insurers can meet, obviously, the broker has to do business with one of them. Different companies have different reputations for underwriting stability, pricing, engineering services, accuracy, and claim handling. The firm should avoid brokers that deal primarily with companies rating at the lower end of the scale on these criteria. A broker dealing only with top flight companies will usually be a better broker. Companies are conscious of, and jealous of, their reputations and do use care in determining with whom they will do business.

**Adaptability.** The attitude of the brokerage principals toward the concept of risk management is vital. A firm only interested in selling insurance should obviously be avoided. The brokerage executives must understand the idea of the cost of risk and be willing to work toward its minimization. Like the risk manager with whom they will be working, they must be imaginative, creative, and willing to try the unorthodox. They must also recognize that the interests of the firms they represent have to be paramount in any dispute with the insurance company. This may create a problem for an agent, who, by law, represents the company, but this issue must be faced before a problem arises.

**Compensation.** One of the problems with the insurance distribution system is that the intermediaries are compensated by retaining a percentage of the premium as commission. This creates an immediate conflict of interest between the producer, whose interest is best served by maximizing insurance premiums, and the client, who wants to minimize them. The problem weaves its way through the whole process of selection of risk treatment technique, selection of company, and selection of rating system. It is an anachronistic system, producing the anomaly that the more the broker works to truly serve a client's best interest, the less compensation he receives. One way out of this dilemma is a fee system, in which a formula is agreed upon (usually a flat fee or an hourly rate) to pay for the broker's service. The broker no longer is compelled to rely on commission from the sale of insurance to provide an income, and is also able to deal with those insurance companies that do not pay commissions. All but one of the large brokerage houses will use the fee system, and many smaller offices are now beginning to use it. There is a legal problem in some states about paying fees, so local laws must be checked.

Another indirect factor affecting the broker's compensation is how long an account is retained. The first-year expense frequently exceeds the commission income, and the broker only begins to make money in the second and subsequent years. A firm that shops its insurance every year or two will soon find no bidders, or at least none of the desired quality. A firm should guarantee a broker (and insurer) a tenure of at least three, and preferably five, years for them to make a maximum commitment. Obviously, the guarantee will be contingent on satisfactory service and continued good pricing.

**Geographical Scope.**  A firm with only one location need not be concerned with the branch office system of its broker.  An accident occurring elsewhere can be handled adequately by the insurer's claim representative at that location, and the broker can contact the risk manager at the plant site.  A firm with widespread operations, however, should have a broker capable of making on-site visits and inspections and applying local pressure where necessary.  This could be especially important for a firm doing an international business in which the laws and customs can be vastly different.

### Insurance Company

The insurance company is the link in the chain that provides the financial security, and its selection is therefore of the utmost importance.

**Financial Strength.**  The first consideration in the selection of a company is its financial integrity.  Ratings are published by Alfred M. Best Company of Oldwick, New Jersey.  They have been used for years and can be relied upon.  The ratings are in two parts.  The first part is a simple measure of size, determined by the surplus to policyholders and conditional or technical reserves plus equities in unearned premium and loss reserves.  The ratings range from Class I, $250,000 or less, to Class XV, $100 million or more.  Policyholder's ratings are also assigned, ranging from "C," fair, to "A+," excellent.  The rating is based on the editor's judgment of five factors: competent underwriting, cost control and efficient management, adequate reserves for undischarged liabilities, net resources adequate to absorb unusual shock, and soundness of investments.

**Underwriting.**  Another major consideration is underwriting consistency—the reputation of the company for providing a market regardless of the ups and downs of the underwriting cycle.  Some companies will provide coverage when the market is on the upswing, but will cancel or refuse to renew as soon as the cycle turns down.  Such companies should be avoided.  The underwriting philosophy of the company should also be examined.  Some companies write strictly "by the book," with individual underwriters having very little discretion or opportunity to use any imagination.  Other companies encourage their underwriters to try to find ways to write any account through the use of special endorsements, special rating plans, or by suggesting physical or operating changes.  Some underwriters are far more willing than others to consider special policy language to meet unique conditions or to broaden standard policies.

**Claim Handling.** The controller should carefully check out the company's reputation for claims. Are its adjusters (staff or independents) competent? Are they readily available? Do they have people on staff with knowledge of each account's unique problems, if any, regarding raw materials, special equipment, unusual shipping or storage conditions, or whatever? Is the loss department willing to go through a simulated adjustment and indicate in advance what documentation will be needed if a loss occurs? Does the claim department interpret policy conditions the same way the underwriting department does? (It is surprising to note how often these two departments look at things differently. A meeting of adjuster, underwriter, broker, and risk manager—to clarify possible points of difference before a loss occurs—would be time well spent.) What arrangements does the company have for accidents occurring out of town—are local adjusters available? What kind of loss statistical data is the company willing to provide, and how often? What analysis will the loss department make of the loss record? Does it have loss control specialists to make recommendations?

**Services.** Many of the services that automatically came with an insurance policy are no longer included because of the trend to greater retention on the part of insureds. However, many companies have "unbundled" their services, and they are available from the companies or their subsidiaries organized for that purpose. This enables a firm to buy only those services it really needs. Some companies do still provide some services, however, and the situation would have to be determined separately for each company. Some of the services which may be available, gratuitously or for a fee, are safety engineering, fire prevention engineering, loss analysis, administration of retained risks (especially workers' compensation), rehabilitation of injured workers, motor vehicle fleet safety programs, and captive insurance company management.

**Geographical Scope.** A multilocation firm would be interested in the branch office locations of the insurer. This would help to determine whether engineering and claim service would be quickly available when needed. If branches are not located in or near the cities or towns where the firm has its units, does the company have arrangements with independent engineers and adjusters, and, if so, who are they? Since these people are independent entrepreneurs, their reputations in their local communities should be checked out.

**Payment Policy.** Since the cost of money is becoming an ever more critical concern, the payment requirements of an insurer should be reviewed. Obviously, the longer the payment can be delayed, the better. Quarterly or monthly payment schedules can often be arranged at little or no cost. Frequently, on casualty business such as liability or workers' compensation, arrangements can be made for the firm to retain the money normally put into loss reserves, thus providing the insurer with a letter of credit for its protection. Since some reserves often remain in place for many years, this can be a significant factor in the total cost of insurance. All avenues for delaying payments and retaining funds should be explored, especially in a "soft" market, when, for competitive reasons, insurers are more willing to make concessions.

**Local Conditions.** All of the criteria listed above should be checked against local conditions. Insurance companies all have global reputations, but the impact on a particular insured is based upon the actions of the local manager and staff. While a local official cannot obviously deviate drastically from official policy, people in one branch are sometimes more competent or imaginative, or more willing to listen to suggestions, or more interested in finding solutions to unique problems than people in another branch. While the overall reputation is important, weight should be given to the local environment.

## Consultant

A consultant is included as part of the system, not because everybody does, or should, use one, but because more firms are using them than formerly, and because they can play an important role. There are five major ways in which consultants can be used in the risk management process: to make a one-time analysis, to review a special, nonrecurring problem, to make an audit, to maintain oversight of a continuing program, or as a surrogate risk manager.

**One-Time Analysis.** When a new controller or treasurer steps into an organization and is given responsibility for the risk management-insurance function, it might be wise to have an objective, external opinion of the adequacy of the program being inherited. This would be especially important if there is no full-time professional risk manager on staff, because that generally means that a great deal of the responsibility has fallen on the broker—who may have a built-in conflict of interest. The consultant, who should be selected with the same care and on the basis of most of the same criteria as the broker, does not have that interest conflict and can give the controller an unbiased view of the adequacy and effectiveness of the existing program.

**Solving Special Problems.** Occasionally, a problem arises that the in-house staff cannot solve, either because it lacks expertise, or time, or sometimes the required objectivity. In such cases, the services of a consultant are clearly indicated. Examples of such studies are: determination of retention limits; a feasibility study on the "self-insuring" of worker's compensation insurance; a feasibility study on the formation of a captive insurance company; an analysis of loss experience to determine trends and recommend steps to improve the experience; an analysis of competing insurance proposals—the list is endless.

**Audit.** Virtually every public firm, most closely held corporations, and many nonprofit organizations have their financial records audited by outside public accounting firms. The staff accountants do not look upon such audits as a questioning of their competence or integrity. They generally welcome the audit as a means of substantiating the fact that they are doing a capable job, and as a means of gaining expert advice and assistance. An increasing number of firms are having an annual audit of the risk management function for the same reasons they have an accounting audit. When it is undertaken with the cooperation of the risk manager, such an audit provides management with a valuable external opinion on the efficiency of its program.

**Continuing Oversight.** Some firms without a full-time risk manager on staff keep a consultant on retainer, frequently the consultant who made the initial analysis and drafted the program. By having the consultant committed to a minimum number of hours of conference and periodic reviews of policies, loss data, etc., the firm is assured of continued implementation of the program. The number of conference hours and the frequency of reviews can be adjusted according to need.

**Surrogate Risk Manager.** The ultimate extension of the above concept occurs when the consultant actually acts in the capacity of risk manager. A number of consultants have many clients who are not large enough to require a full-time professional staff member. Based on each firm's need, the consultant is on the scene once a month, once a week, once a quarter, or whenever it is necessary. He performs all the functions of an in-house risk manager—he negotiates with the broker, reviews policies, approves premium payments, files and collects claims, makes reports to management, and does all the other things a risk manager would do. His fee obviously varies with the amount and complexity of the work he does, and the firm controls that decision. This system provides an orderly transition from virtually total reliance on a broker to having a risk manager on staff. It is a growing method of operation and one that can be very valuable.

## SUGGESTED READING

Bickelhaupt, David L., *General Insurance*, 10th edition. Homewood, Illinois: Richard D. Irwin, Inc., 1979.

Lally, Edward P., *Self-Assumption, Self-Insurance and the Captive Insurance Company Concept*. New York: Risk and Insurance Management Society, 1975.

Lenz, Matthew, Jr., *Risk Management Manual*. Santa Monica: The Merritt Co., 1971. (Bi-monthly supplements).

Mehr, Robert I., and Cammack, Emerson, *Principles of Insurance*, 7th ed. Homewood, Ill.: Richard D. Irwin, Inc., 1980.

Mehr, Robert I., and Hedges, Bob A., *Risk Management Concepts and Applications*. Homewood, Ill.: Richard D. Irwin, Inc., 1974.

*Risk Management,* New York: Risk and Insurance Management Society. (Official monthly RIMS publication.)

*The National Underwriter* (Property and Casualty Insurance Edition). Cincinnati: The National Underwriter Co. (Weekly news magazine.)

Williams, C. Arthur, and Heins, Richard M., *Risk Management and Insurance,* 4th ed. New York: McGraw-Hill Book Company, 1980.

# 36

# Real Estate Planning and Control

*Robert L. Collins and S. Bleecker Totten*

## AN OVERVIEW

An expert in corporate real estate transactions requires knowledge in several critical areas: legal, financial, appraisal, tax, political, accounting (just to name a few), and—most important of all—in-depth knowledge of a particular business and its requirements. Real estate experts are, however, rarely found in any company, because real estate transactions in and of themselves do not occur with the same frequency as other types of business transactions. Once they are completed and entered on the books they are given little, if any, further thought.

Regardless of this, all organizations must be concerned in some manner with real estate. In many companies, real estate represents a substantial corporate asset. When a company moves in the direction of a real estate transaction, someone in the company must activate and coordinate the significant inputs from necessary experts before the transaction goes too far. This approach not only saves time and money, but could avert a financial disaster. The fact that every real estate transaction involves a financial implication of some magnitude means that sound real estate decisions are crucial to corporate profitability.

### The Controller's Role in Real Estate

The real estate business is complex and can entrap the unwary and the amateur. Many executives fall into the trap of believing they are experts in real estate and are often guilty of allowing their company's real estate holdings to be given short shrift.

**Assuming General Responsibilities.** Real estate propositions presented to the company are generally approved or disapproved without appropriate analysis, and sometimes without much review or discussion. The following illustrates the lack of ongoing interest in, or attention paid to, real estate holdings in many companies.

A company leases 50,000 square feet of space for ten years at a base rental of $500,000 per year, and agrees to pay tax and operating cost escalation. After the lease is executed, the $500,000 annual base rent is budgeted and, once in the system, it is ignored, generally on the assumption that the material aspects are fixed for ten years. In time, the firm will receive escalation statements from the landlord and will review, approve, and pay them. But who reviews them? Who understands them? In many cases controllers do not and attorneys do not, and often they do not even know the right questions to ask. Those who actually process invoices for payment cannot be expected to understand the escalation factors inherent in most landlords' invoices. Errors in billings are therefore difficult to detect and can amount to substantial sums.

If the real estate responsibility is assigned to a junior staff member or if it is the minor responsibility of an executive who lacks the proper expertise, chances are excellent that the company is wasting a primary corporate asset and that real dollars are lost each year. Although the controller may not have direct operating responsibility for real estate operations, he must try to overcome the tendency on the part of many companies to underestimate the importance of the company's real estate holdings. He must take an active part in its real estate transactions, however infrequent they may be.

**Involvement in Decision Making.** Whenever a company wishes to acquire or dispose of real property, the controller should be involved in the decision-making process at an early stage, certainly before irrevocable decisions are made. Even tentative decisions in such areas as site selection and building design have financial implications. Although they are not irreversible, they can be difficult to overturn.

If a firm is considering a corporate relocation, for example, and the proper geographical site has been selected and decisions reached with regard to the size of the facility, the controller should assist in considering a multitude of other factors, such as labor supply, transportation, utilities, and postal services. He must then approach management with a two-pronged cost analysis that involves:

- The *one-time* cash and expense impact of the relocation, including the cost to acquire the site, construct and equip the facility, accomplish the physical move, install telephones, and relocate employees; and
- A comparison between ongoing costs at the present facility and those at the new location.

Management is then able to determine whether it can afford the relocation in the first place and what such a move will do to the company's future earnings.

**Asking the Right Questions.** The controller must be sure that the financial considerations involved in any relocation are taken into account, as well as business implications that conceal serious financial implications. For example, will the new site affect inventory taxes? Should the company be located in a free trade zone? Are industrial development funds available from local, state, or federal governments? What are the real (not statistical) labor costs in the new area? Is the company vulnerable to a limited transportation supply? What are the real costs of utilities? Asking the right questions builds the foundation for proper decisions.

### The Importance of Planning Ahead

Planning ahead for housing requirements prevents expensive panic decisions and keeps normal business operations free from unnecessary disruptions. Before a new site is selected, the following two steps should have occurred:

1. A projection of current and future facility requirements for the next ten years and approval of these projections of the operating units by management; and
2. Workflow studies to seek optimum massing and layout of the facility.

With these data, the progress toward site selection and building size becomes more logical. The data help answer such difficult intermediate questions as: How much expansion space should be provided? Should operations be split and located at separate sites? Should construction be planned to provide for building expansion at a later date?

Planning ahead also prevents chaos and panic when the company considers leasing. Just as it is naive to expect that a building can be erected overnight when a company needs more space, it should be just as obvious that leased quarters cannot be had merely for the asking. The leasing process includes determination of space layout and design; lease negotiations; legal review; and a physical move and communications installation, all of which are time consuming and costly. Good planning reduces the time and expense involved and avoids significant cost penalties caused by, for example, a block of 10,000 square feet of leased space sitting vacant for two months because of poorly coordinated installation of new telephones and equipment.

In planning ahead, management should consider such elements as the current rental market in its area. If it is on the upswing, if the company wants to remain where it is, and if the lease has only a short while to run, it may be desirable to open negotiations and lock into a rental rate before it goes higher. If there is demand for rental or owned space in this location and it is believed that another area is more desirable for the company's operations, planning should commence immediately to take advantage of the existing high rent market by recommending subleasing or selling before demand subsides.

The formal process of planning ahead should be ongoing. Reasonably frequent projections of employees and space needs should be made, option dates within existing leases should be examined, and vigorous discussion should take place concerning the desirability of the company's current location.

### Use of Consultants

As indicated earlier, most small to medium-sized companies are only periodically involved in real estate transactions, and thus rarely develop considerable real estate expertise. Even larger companies with real estate departments find it difficult to hire a complement of experts who understand all the myriad aspects of real property transactions. Consequently, when the need arises it is often the wisest course of action to hire, on a temporary basis, the best real estate consultant available.

When a corporation is involved in a real property transaction and decides to engage a consultant, whether architect, attorney, or real estate broker, it should try to define, in general, the questions to be asked, and should then seek the consultant who can best answer these questions. It should be clearly understood what services the consultant will (and will not) provide. Establishing these guidelines at the outset makes the relationship with the consultant professional and efficient and encourages the rapid flow of information. Another important point to remember in the selection and use of consultants is that fees must be agreed upon before any work is begun.

**Professional Organizations.** There are professional real estate organizations that can be approached for assistance. For example, NACORE (National Association of

Corporate Real Estate Executives) was formed specifically to provide this kind of liaison and dissemination of real property knowledge among corporate executives. In addition, controllers can seek advice from local economic development commissions, appraisers, brokers, architects, public utility companies, and so on. Whom they consult depends on the specific type of information needed.

In the area of consultation, the controller should determine the financial risk the company is taking or the obligations it assumes as a result of the real property transaction. With that exposure as a guide, he should determine a reasonable consulting fee. Needless skimping on the fee amount can be foolish. Some brokers provide consulting services for the commission attained from the sale of real property; others charge an hourly rate or a flat fee.

**Real Estate Brokerage Fees.** In industrial and commercial real estate transactions, particularly if the company is an owner or a landlord, real estate brokerage fees are a substantial expense item. Who is responsible for real estate commissions? When and how are they earned? How much are they and are they calculated by taking a percentage of the selling price or of total lease commitments? Are items of personal property or allowances for alterations included in the calculation of a commission? Are there written agreements with the broker? The most important questions for the controller to determine at the outset are when is the company obligated to pay a broker a commission, and how is it calculated? Care should be taken when seeking space and a real estate broker shows the property; if it is leased or bought through a second broker, someone may be obligated for *another* commission to the first broker who showed the property. The converse is also true. A company may be obligated to pay commissions twice if it sells or leases space through one broker when another procures the prospective tenant or purchaser.

**Legal Services.** Once a site has been selected and the price and other essential terms have been negotiated, the remaining terms and conditions are often negotiated by an attorney rather than the corporate executive charged with responsibility for the project. A common fault of many real estate negotiations is the lack of preplanning and coordination among the in-house staff (real estate, tax, insurance, finance, and legal). This problem ultimately affects the attorney-client relationship, regardless of whether the company uses in-house counsel or engages an outside attorney.

If an outside attorney is retained, the controller must remember that the attorney is working as a consultant. His advice should be solicited and respected and he should explain the legal ramifications of the terms and conditions of the contract. But the controller and other top management must be the negotiators of the business terms and conditions. They must make final judgments, perhaps even countermanding the written or verbal advice of counsel. In short, a good attorney is an absolute necessity, but should never be allowed to assume the role of negotiator and final arbiter of the business terms.

**Financial Experts.** A word involving consultants in the controller's area of expertise is appropriate. Negotiations lead to, and contract terms reflect, complicated financing techniques and conditions. Failure to admit a lack of understanding in such an area could lead to approval of disastrous terms. Here again, a consultant should be engaged (if necessary) to explain fully and clearly the implications of all financial considerations.

## Accounting Trends

In recent years, the philosophy of financial reporting for public companies has changed from a historical narrow basis to a much broader current one. One general trend is toward more detailed information, more disclosure, and the forecasting of future results. Stricter requirements than the furnishing of information only once a year are also expected. Requirements that affect real estate accounting have come mainly from the Financial Accounting Standards Board (FASB), and the American Institute of CPAs (AICPA), but the SEC has also been moving in this direction.

A second significant trend is that of increased corporate accountability. The Foreign Corrupt Practices Act (FCPA) began as an attempt to make it illegal to bribe companies and expanded to include requirements that public companies maintain accurate books and records and provide adequate internal accounting controls. (See Chapter 18.)

Finally, data requirements will continue to grow in the areas that affect energy and the physical environment. The controller must continue to play an active role in meeting these requirements. Following is a brief summary of the most significant accounting pronouncements directly affecting real estate matters.

**SFAS No. 13—Accounting for Leases.** Long-term leases for real property may no longer escape balance sheet disclosure. If balance sheet ratios are important to the company before entering into a material lease, the controller should research this FASB statement, which specifies the conditions under which a lease must be capitalized. (See Chapter 4.)

**SFAS No. 34—Capitalization of Interest Cost.** This statement requires interest costs during the construction period to be capitalized as part of the cost for any facility built for the company's use. The amount of interest required to be capitalized may be the actual amount based upon a loan specifically earmarked for that facility, or it may be an estimated, allocated amount because the company borrowed from one or several sources without specifically earmarking the construction loan as such.

**Accounting for Retail Land Sales.** This accounting guide, developed by a special committee of the AICPA, discusses special problems that may be encountered in recording retail land sales and provides guidance and recommended procedures for dealing with them. Controllers of non-real estate companies will normally not be concerned with retail land sales, but some of the problems covered in the guide would be helpful to a company if it decided to develop and sell a portion of its land.

**Statements of Position.** These SOPs are issued by the AICPA's Accounting Standards Division as recommended methods of accounting for specific industries or problem situations. The FASB has approved most SOPs as a preferable accounting principle for companies that want to change from another accounting method. The following SOPs are related to real estate accounting:

- 75–6, Questions Concerning Profit Recognition on Sales of Real Estate;
- 78–3, Accounting for Costs to Sell and Rent, and Initial Rental Operations of, Real Estate Projects;
- 78–4, Application of the Deposit, Installment, and Cost Recovery Methods in Accounting for Sales of Real Estate;
- 78–9, Accounting for Investments in Real Estate Ventures; and
- 80–3, Accounting for Real Estate Acquisition, Development, and Construction Costs.

# THE BUY-LEASE DECISION

## General Considerations

From a purely economic standpoint, it is usually advantageous for a company to own a property rather than to lease it. This assumes that appreciation in the property (and its deferred tax status) is the single most important financial factor that can be realized from long-term use of property. Investment tax credits, rehabilitation credits, and the impact of other taxes, however, all must be taken into consideration before the lease or purchase decision can be made.

Sometimes, however, a company has no option to buy. If the firm must remain in a specific location, if a suitable site is not available for sale, if the firm cannot build for a variety of reasons, or if the firm cannot count on remaining in a particular location for too long a period, ownership may not be a viable choice. Under such circumstances, leasing becomes attractive. The following are some of its most obvious advantages:

- Large up-front cash outlays on loan obligations to finance the cost of the property (except, in some cases, for the preparation of leased space) are not necessary.

   If the lease complies with SFAS 13 requirements for an operating lease, loan restrictions on new debt financing based on the firm's debt-equity ratio may be avoided.

- There is generally no dispute as to the tax deductibility of rental costs versus depreciation provisions.

- Rental costs may be geared to a company's forecasted economic condition either through a graduated lease (where rental costs are lower in the early years and higher in the later years) or a percentage lease (which adjusts rental costs to gross income).

- If owned property is a factor in the calculation of franchise or income taxes, then the allocation formula for such taxes would be reduced. However, most state allocation formulas include a multiple of rent as a property factor.

On the other hand, leasing has some important disadvantages:

- When the lease terminates, the firm loses all right to the property.
- Housing cost may be greater, since rental costs include a return to the landlord and may reflect more expensive debt financing.
- It may be more difficult to dispose of rented space than it is to sell owned property.
- Operating flexibility may be limited, since the rented premises are occupied under restraints imposed by the lease.

Because real-property decisions represent substantial commitments and obligations, the data and authority for making and controlling such decisions should be centered in one company department or executive. The controller is often in the best position to ensure that the company avoids potential default problems, an over supply of space, or other exposure in an often underestimated but significant area of costs.

In the final analysis, it must be recognized that the most rational lease-buy decision soundly based on a set of logical, economic facts will not always prevail. Subjective considerations, imposed by corporate boards or top-level executives, must be considered and can frustrate the decision process. The possibility that his recommendations may not be followed should not deter the controller from taking the necessary steps. If management then overrides his findings, it does so with full knowledge of the costs and dangers.

### The "Buy," "Build," and "Sell" Decisions

**Valuation of Property.** When a company selects a site and decides to purchase, it should be interested in the cost of the property, how the price was arrived at, and the going price per acre for land in the area. If, because of extenuating circumstances, the corporation agrees to pay $1,000 or $20,000 per acre in an area where land has generally been selling for $10,000 per acre, the justification for paying the price indicated should be fully documented. If the land was "stolen" for $1,000 per acre, the IRS may think the company is loading the depreciable portion of the asset. If it was bought for $20,000 per acre, the company's stockholders may demand an explanation.

If one is available, the record should include a current market-value appraisal for the property. The controller should review the appraisal, the appraiser's qualifications, and the date the value was determined. (An appraisal is also an excellent technique for protecting the company if it is selling property.)

If an appraiser belongs to one of the national professional appraisal organizations, it is usually a better indication of his qualifications than if he lacks a professional affiliation. In place of a formal appraisal, a broker may be able to supply a list of recent sales of comparable properties in the area. Another rough method of determining value is the latest assessed valuation of the property for tax purposes. However, this method is not without its pitfalls; it may, for example, be assessed at only a percentage of its true value.

**Zoning and Environmental Considerations.** The question of zoning generally enters the picture early in the process of selecting a site for relocation. Zoning problems are determined by the type of building and business (e.g., office, warehouse, light/heavy manufacturing) planned. The company ordinarily should not attempt to place a heavy manufacturing installation in a research or office zone unless there are specific reasons for doing so.

If the facility is to be built in a suitable zone, or one in which a variance can be obtained, it is not difficult to determine from a meeting with local officials whether or not the installation will be welcome in the community. If the atmosphere appears unfavorable, and unless there is a compelling reason to locate there, it might be less expensive in time, money, and image to seek another area. If possible, management should select two areas for relocation before any agreements are signed (other than perhaps an option), and proceed in both areas simultaneously. In any event, zoning problems should be resolved prior to the final acquisition of a site. To that end, the final contract of sale should include a condition precedent to cover zoning.

If management is acquiring an existing facility, it should research the zoning and building codes. Are property lines properly set back? Is the property being purchased under a nonconforming use restriction? Will an inordinate amount of money have to be spent to bring the facility up to local building codes? More importantly, what are the company's long-range plans for this facility? Does it expect to increase its size? If so, is there sufficient vacant land to meet the land-to-ground coverage requirements—including setbacks, parking, and landscaping? Could expansion of a nearby highway require part of the land, and if so, how would this "taking" affect the use of the property? Does the certificate of occupancy restrict the use of the facility? It would be embarrassing, to say the least, to acquire a building and then discover that it cannot be used for the desired purposes.

Prior to any acquisition of land, the environmental considerations and their implications should be clearly understood. The ground rules change daily, but the basic questions are: Will an environmental impact report be required, and if so, who will prepare it? What is the cost, and how long will it take? If an environmental report is required, is there any way to assess the likely results? The response to this last question is best obtained from experts. Seeking immediate advice on this subject can save much money, energy, and time.

**Negotiations.** Webster's dictionary defines *negotiation* as "to carry on business" or "conferring, discussing or bargaining to reach agreement." The primary qualification of a good negotiator is wide experience in the area. Smaller corporations often lack such experience, particularly in real estate dealings. In a typical transaction, if a company needs a sales office, it may send someone from headquarters, the manager of a nearby office, or even a local broker to seek the space. A lease is frequently prepared by the landlord and sent to the company's attorney, whose task is to negotiate and reach agreement. A multitude of business decisions must be made: Who pays for construction? When does rent commence? What is the base year for tax and operating escalation? What are the subleasing and assignment rights?

If the company attorney has not had a great deal of experience with leases or does not have the background experience in the company to make the correct business decisions, he is probably not in a good position to negotiate in the company's interest. If the company does not have qualified lease negotiators on its staff, engaging sound representation and advice can be a wise investment. Most real-property leases are material obligations in terms of liability exposure and dollar value of the lease.

There is no magic to negotiating. The prepared negotiator often practices brinksmanship, but he knows market conditions, how badly the company needs the space, what it can afford to pay, and whether or not the lessor needs the lease to help satisfy his mortgage requirements. With a skilled, well-informed negotiator, and assuming reasonableness from both parties, an agreement can almost always be reached.

Whether the company's negotiator is a staff or an outside attorney, he should be instructed not to break off negotiations without a thorough review of final positions with a senior level member of the organization.

**Financing Techniques.** Prior to entering into a contract to purchase vacant land, land and building, or some other interest in real property, the controller must know the approximate cost and how it will be paid. If the company is cash-rich, it may want to pay for the land and/or building out of its own pocket. But, even if his organization can pay in cash, and ultimately decides to do so, the controller should research and report on the availability of external financing. In some instances, loans for real property needs can include operating equipment costs and consulting fees. It might even be possible to finance some projects up to 100 percent of cost.

*Bank financing.* The most obvious source of needed capital to finance a purchase of real property is the firm's banking institution. A visit to the bank's loan officer and a discussion of the bank's lending criteria will indicate whether the bank can provide the amount needed, whether it is willing to make the loan, and what its terms are.

*Mortgage brokers.* Raising funds from other institutional lenders (e.g., insurance companies, pension funds) is a somewhat more complicated and impersonal process. Because of the complex negotiations that may be involved, the amount of paper work, and time pressures, it often makes sense to engage an agent to smooth the borrowing process. Such agents, generally called "mortgage brokers," have sources of funds other than institutional lenders—venture capital firms, corporate finance subsidiaries, even individuals. Mortgage brokers may have minimum fees, ranging upward from $20,000. Beyond that minimum, the fee can start as high as five percent of principal, but scales down as the loan amount increases. Generally speaking, an agent's fee is contingent on completion of financing, but some charge a portion in advance to cover the time and costs they incur while preparing the financing memoranda required by large lending institutions.

*Sale-leasebacks.* Another common financing vehicle is the conversion of nonliquid assets, such as real property, into liquid assets through what are commonly called "sale-leaseback" arrangements. A company may sell the office building and/or the land upon which the building is located to an investor, and then lease them back for a specified period. There is little change in the company's situation except for the transfer of cash and the ownership of the property. In short, in exchange for cash up front, the company gives up ownership and agrees to rent over a fixed period of time. It may make particular sense for the company to sell and lease back the building after the building has been completely depreciated.

Sale-leaseback arrangements can involve land as well as improvements. For a business, land is not a tax depreciable asset. But by selling it and paying rent, it converts the cost to deductible rent expense. However, SFAS No. 13 generally requires a sale-leaseback transaction to be capitalized for accounting purposes.

*Government development funds.* Are state funds available and, if so, can they be obtained less expensively than conventional financing sources? State economic development funds are known by different names in the various states, and the ground rules differ considerably from state to state.

In addition to state funds, there are a number of other sources for funds at the local and federal government levels—HUD Urban Development Action Grants, the Commerce Department's Economic Development Loans, and the Small Business Administration loan program. If their conditions can be met, the difference in financing cost, as compared to conventional loans, can save a company a great deal of money.

**Purchase Contracts.** A purchase contract is a legal document insofar as it deals with the rights and obligations of the parties and the conversion of all agreements into legal language. Once the parties have negotiated the purchase or sale, the financing terms, zoning, building code compliances, and other business items, the company's in-house attorney or outside counsel, together with the firm's real estate representative, must ensure that the organization is protected. Nothing should be signed—not even a letter—without his prior approval.

The attorney should be familiar with practices in the state in which the property is being bought and should be able to deal with such questions as the following: Is the firm receiving or giving a warranty deed, a bargain and sale deed with or without covenants against the grantor's acts, or a quit-claim deed? Is title insurance necessary? What does a title search on the property disclose? Are there any easements or other encumbrances? Are the essential elements contained in the contract in order to make the agreement binding? Is "time of the essence" included as a stipulation and what does this mean? What about the agreement to pay brokerage commissions? Are there mortgage, zoning, or other contingencies? The possible variations are great, but the message should be clear. An attorney is required and should be consulted in the beginning in order to prevent costly mistakes and complications.

The following checklist gives some typical questions that should be asked regarding contract terms and conditions:

1. Purchase of Vacant Land.
   - What is the cost of the land, and financing arrangements, if any?
   - What is the closing date (when is cash needed)?
   - What are the survey costs?
   - What are the title insurance costs?
   - What are the attorneys' fees?
   - If construction is contemplated, what is the cost of test borings?
   - How much are the real property taxes?
   - What are the escrow fees, if any?
   - Are there state or local transfer taxes?
   - Is any other cash required at closing?
2. Purchase of Land With a Building.
   - All costs listed above.
   - Is title closing contingent upon receiving mortgage money or economic development funds of some type?
   - What if these funds cannot be obtained?
   - Will these funds be obtained at closing?
   - If the building is occupied by other tenants, what are the provisions for transfer of security deposits and rents? Are there any other steps necessary to satisfy the terms of existing leases?
   - What portion of the purchase price should apply to land, and what portion to the building?
   - Have the local tax authorities been notified of transfer of title?

**Construction.** Hiring an architect and a general contractor and then having a new building erected sounds like a simple process; it is not. If care is not taken to select a qualified team and to draw up tight contracts, the company will find that it is spending a great deal more time and money than it originally estimated. On the other hand, a well-planned and coordinated project can meet management goals not only with regard to time parameters but within budgeted costs as well.

*Selecting a team.* An architect or general contractor who has worked exclusively on residential buildings should obviously not be selected to construct a commercial office building. The project should be discussed with several candidates, time should be taken to review some projects they have completed, and their capabilities should be discussed with other organizations for whom they have worked.

The architect, recruited early in the selection process, prepares preliminary plans, specifications, and cost estimates. When these have been approved in concept, final plans and specifications are prepared, and bids are solicited from general contractors. The contracts are then awarded and construction begins.

*Construction contracts.* The American Institute of Architects (AIA) has developed contract forms for both architects and general contractors. These forms cover all kinds of arrangements, such as a fixed price, a bid price, or a negotiated price (e.g., cost plus with a fixed percentage for the general contractor; cost plus with a fixed fee for the general contractor; guaranteed maximum price; and an incentive contract). Whatever type of contract selected, the terminology used should be thoroughly understood. For example, does a fixed fee include the general contractor's overhead for items such as insurance, consumable small tools, rent, and utilities?

Regardless of the type of contract selected, it should be reviewed carefully with the attorney so that all parties understand what (and when) the contract obligates the organization to pay. Mistakes can often be costly, and quite frequently end in arbitration or litigation, which delay the construction project.

*New management techniques.* New management techniques are emerging today that differ from traditional procedures.

1. *Construction management.* A construction manager is added to the team some time prior to selection of an architect, but in any event no later than the architect. The construction manager becomes involved on behalf of the company in the specifying of materials, since he knows their costs and availability, in scheduling subcontractors, and in coordinating the multitude of parts and materials that must come together at the right time and in the right order.

2. *Fast tracking.* Fast tracking can be used when time is not available to prepare complete plans and specifications and take bids on the entire project and/or when cost escalation is rampant. This method puts tremendous pressure on the owner and architect to make decisions without the benefit of completed proposals, designs, and cost estimates. For example, excavation plans may be prepared and excavation undertaken while the plans for the foundation and drainage are incomplete. Such an approach has risks, but it also reduces the timing of the construction cycle at a time when costs are rising rapidly.

3. *Life cycle costs.* New procedures are being developed to evaluate alternatives in terms of the life cycle costs of the building. For example, since the cost of energy is so high, building components and systems should be evaluated not only in terms of the initial cash outlay, but also in terms of what their installation will cost or save over their useful life in the building.

**Selling Real Property.** When a company decides to sell some of its real property, one important question to ask is whether anyone has determined that the property is excess and that such disposition will not adversely affect the long-range needs of the company.

Assuming the need to sell is real, a reasonable market value for the property must be determined by having the property appraised. The appraiser may see that a prospective buyer's higher and better use can produce a better selling price than the owner presently perceives; or perhaps he will appraise it from a "reproduction" or an "income production" point of view, which could make its value to others greater than to the seller.

A professional appraiser (e.g., an MAI, or Member of the American Institute of Real Estate Appraisers) qualified to appraise commercial/industrial property should preferably be retained. The appraiser should be given specific instructions as to the type of appraisal required. For example, the management may want to know the present-day market value of vacant land in its "as is" condition even though it conflicts with a "highest and best use" determination. Why? Because it may cost a great deal of money to change zoning or to obtain a variance in order to make the land suitable for its highest and best use, and management doesn't want that involvement to interfere with a prospective sale.

After obtaining the appraised value, property is normally listed with a broker, such as a member of the Society of Industrial Realtors (SIR) or some other experienced commercial or industrial broker. The asking price should be stipulated in writing; also, terms (e.g., all cash, purchase money mortgage, other type of paper); duration of the listing with the broker; who pays for advertising and promotion; brokerage commission rates and how and when they are to be paid; and whether or not the broker is expected to assume certain responsibilities for the property at company expense.

After the property is listed, there should be regular contact and follow-up between the controller or his representative and the broker. If the broker is given all the details of a sale (such as items of personal property to be included as well as the terms that might be acceptable) the broker is in a better position to screen potential purchasers and expedite the sale.

**The Business Condominium.** The business condominium form of real-property ownership is gaining in popularity as an extension of its success in the residential market place. In office buildings, shopping centers, and even parking garages, ownerships of partial units of a greater whole are being sold. Condominium sales of business properties are popular because there is sometimes a greater market for selling parts of a building instead of the entire structure to one buyer, and sale of the parts often generates more value than the whole. In addition, in many condominium arrangements the seller retains management of the business property from which he generates a profit.

Wholly apart from balance sheet considerations, the most significant advantage to the business condominium buyer is the potential for appreciation of the property and better control over cost increases. However, like purchases of real estate anywhere, there is no guarantee that the property will appreciate. The same prudence exercised in the purchase of undivided ownership of real estate should be exercised in the purchase of business condominiums.

## The "Lease" and "Sublease" Decisions

**Types of Leases.** Although there are many variations, the three most common types of leases are gross leases, net leases, and percentage leases.

*Gross leases.* Under gross lease agreements, a number of services provided by the lessor are included in the rental consideration paid by a tenant. These can include all building operating costs, real estate taxes, cleaning, utilities, general maintenance, and landscaping; however, cost for replacement of capital items is usually excluded from rent. The base rental rate is usually fixed for the term of the lease, although it may be graduated upwards during the lease term; increases in the lessor's costs, usually after the first (base) year, are charged to the tenant in the same ratio that his space bears to all space in the building.

*Net leases.* Many owners like to add, for emphasis and clarity, several "nets" to this description. These are the direct opposite of gross leases. In exchange for a flat (or graduated) term-of-lease rental rate paid to the lessor, the tenant assumes responsibility for *all* costs in connection with the property. These costs include real estate taxes, insurance, maintenance, and building operation. Generally, no escalation charges are payable to the lessor unless provision has been made to increase the lessor's return on investment resulting from fluctuations in the economy. The area subject to most negotiation and dispute is the responsibility for the structural shell and major building systems, and under what conditions either lessor or tenant would be responsible for repairing or replacing them.

*Percentage leases.* These leases protect, to some degree, the lessor's return on investment in a rising economy. They require tenants to pay (usually in addition to a minimum rent amount) a percentage of the tenant's sales as additional rent. Such leases are most common in shopping centers and individual stores, and the merchant is usually also required to pay his share of certain increases in the lessor's cost of operating the premises as well as real estate taxes above specified base amounts. Although merchants object to sharing their sales successes with lessors, such arrangements can be advantageous when sales are slumping or during store start-up periods.

**Rent or Other Concessions.** When a firm seeks space from a lessor, it almost goes without saying that the lessor's initial asking price is higher than he expects to get. However, although the lessor may not reduce the rental rate below a certain level, he may be willing to grant other concessions which may be even more valuable than a lowered rent. For example, he might pay for specified costs of preparing the lessee's initial installation, he might offer free rent for the first month or months of the lease, he might grant first right of refusal on contiguous or nearby space in the premises, he might agree to a graduated rental rate where the lessee pays less rent in the early years and more in the later years, or he might agree to additional parking spaces. In short, the controller should be aware that "concessions" may be available in these side areas.

*Options.* Among the most potentially valuable of concessions are options that permit the option holder to tie up land and/or buildings until he decides whether to buy. They can consequently be hardest to get. The company may seek an option to renew its lease at expiration or to cancel during the term, all at an agreed-on cost. Or, it may negotiate an option for additional space in the building when other leases expire, or perhaps even the right to purchase the property at a specified time either at a fixed price or at a price to be established by an appraiser or other disinterested person. The future value of these options is generally not known when they are negotiated, and the company is not obligated to exercise them. They are, however, good hedges against future problems and may even become extremely valuable with the passage of time.

How much a company receives in concessions of any kind depends on the persuasive powers of its negotiating team, the strength of its bargaining position based on size-of-lease in that lessor's premises, and the company's reputation. If the firm is a major tenant, its bargaining power is greatly increased.

**Length of the Lease Term.** If the company has any control over the term at all, this decision is probably one of the most difficult and meaningful ones to make when entering into a lease. The company should start with some predetermined idea of the space it needs to meet future expansion requirements. With such estimates in hand, these requirements can be accommodated in several ways.

- Lease more space than is required and sublease the balance (to more than one subtenant) with staggered sublease expiration dates.
- Try to get options on adjustment space or on space within the same building, or gamble that space later required for expansion will be available when needed.

If the firm is entering into a long-term lease, it should consider whether the area can satisfy its future business requirements and whether it will continue to be desirable for its business. If the answer to either question is not firmly positive, the lease may become a burden in the long run. On the other hand, in a rising economy, or in an area that is on the upswing, a long-term lease at a fixed rental rate can be a valuable asset. If possible, the company negotiator should secure a right to cancel the lease at certain specified periods during the term (but he should expect the landlord to extract some price in return for such a concession). If the lease term is short, it may be possible to hedge against future problems or space needs by getting renewal options at lease expiration, or options on other space in the building when available.

The major purpose of such tactics is to gain flexibility, whether the lease term is short or long. Predicting the future is difficult, and it is a major advantage to secure built-in alternatives for expanding or relocating, without substantial financial risk or burden.

**Escalation.** Escalation clauses in lease contracts represent a lessor's desire to recover future increases in operating costs during the term of the lease, thereby guarding against erosion of his return on investment. This is such a widely accepted practice that it is virtually impossible to find a commercial lease without an escalation clause.

Generally, there are two kinds of escalation recoveries: on operating costs and on real estate taxes. In a typical lease, the escalation clause will say that as operating costs increase each year beyond a stipulated "base year," the tenant will pay a portion of these increases in the ratio his space bears to the entire building area. At the close of each fiscal period, the lessor will justify his increased costs to the tenant by submitting a certified accounting statement and tax statements, or will make his books available for the tenant's inspection.

Although conceptually simple, the application is much more difficult in practice, and is often tangled and obscure. Lessors recognize that there are simpler ways to "recover" escalation costs, and most if not all of these ways bear no correlation to the actual cost increases. Although landlords attempt to promote escalation clauses based on such factors as porters' wage increases, a more widely used method is to tie increases to the Consumer Price Index. In the past fifteen years, alternative methods may have permitted many lessors to recover considerably more than their actual increases in operating costs.

Escalation bills are often paid automatically and with a minimum of scrutiny, despite the fact that lessors' billings for escalation costs can be replete with errors. This occurs because the language of escalation clauses has become so complicated or because the tenant's accounting personnel do not have access to the lease. The controller should be certain that adequate controls are in place for payment of escalation invoices. They should be reviewed by a competent authority in the company or by experts outside the company who have been retained to review such statements. Just as utility and traffic rate analysts review billings for a fee based on the amounts they save for their clients, organizations review escalation statements for a fee based solely on participation in company savings.

**Space Measurement.** When leasing space, ambiguous terms may be encountered, particularly in the description of a leaseable area, most often quoted in terms of square feet. It is important to understand that there is a difference, and sometimes a significant difference, between such terms as "net usable" (or "walk-on" area) and "rentable" area. The first term generally describes the space in which the business operation is physically housed, and the second term refers to the larger area actually leased. Rentable square feet generally includes additional areas that service and support the work space: corridors, washrooms, and all or a portion of mechanical equipment rooms. As every controller knows, the terms mark-up and mark-down can refer to the same price. In much the same way, lessors use two dissimilar terms to describe the relationship between the net usable and rentable area. One thousand square feet of usable space and 250 square feet of support space produce a *gross factor* (the relationship of 250 square feet to 1,000 square feet) of 25 percent; that is, the lessee pays 25 percent for support space. However, a lessor can obtain a different percentage by calling the 250 square feet a *loss factor*. He is renting 1,250 square feet, 250 square feet of which is support space, and out of the 1,250 square feet the tenant has lost only 20 percent. In short, the lessor can describe the 250 square feet at the lower percentage when extolling the merits of the property to a prospective tenant.

The larger the building, the more complex the measurement of unusable support space included in rentable cost. It can include elevator, air, telephone, and venting shafts; vaults; and so on. Thus, when large blocks of space and material lease dollars are involved, experts should be employed to assist in developing exact area measurements. Over the term of a lease obligation, their findings may more than pay for their services.

The controller should understand, before any lease is executed, exactly how much space he must pay for that cannot be used for work operations. Such data helps him to compare the work and cost efficiency of one building to another.

**Utilities.** Another obvious consideration in selecting any location is the utilities needed to service the company's operations as well as the cost of these utilities. Less obvious is the growing practice of *electric rent inclusion,* whereby the lessor pays for electricity entering his premises through a single meter and then "sells" the electricity to tenants. When provision for this practice is included in the lease, there are two areas to explore before signing. The first is to examine the base cost established for utility use; the second is to consider carefully the basis by which the cost of utilities will escalate during the lease term. The only fair way to determine the reasonableness of base cost is to seek data from tenants of comparable size and power needs in that or other locations. Since there are so many methods used to escalate utilities costs, it is difficult to determine the fairness of a specific method other than by using judgment and common sense. So long as the base is equitable, a not unreasonable solution is to agree to pay any rate increases imposed on and actually paid by the lessor. Generally, however, there is room to negotiate such utility costs with lessors before the lease is signed.

**Miscellaneous Landlord Services.** It is important to specify clearly at the outset of negotiations exactly which services the lessor will provide, the level of such services included in the base rent, and the services for which there will be an additional charge. For example, lessors of multitenant buildings will usually provide and pay for a certain level of cleaning in the tenant's space. They will also generally do the cleaning through their contractor.

The lease should then be examined carefully to determine if some areas are excluded from the lessor's cleaning obligation and if there may be levels of service needed that he does not provide. It is usually less expensive to arrange for the lessor's cleaning contractor to expand his services to meet a tenant's requirements than it would be for a tenant to hire another contractor to perform additional services. Other services often excluded or limited in the lease in some manner could involve trash removal (e.g., they may not remove "wet trash" except at added cost), vending services, and elevator services. The controller should secure at the outset the schedule of the lessor's charges for services other than those provided in the base rent.

**Overtime and Holiday Use of Premises.** Before a lease is signed, the two parties should clearly understand not only what the tenant firm will use the premises for (as defined clearly in the "use" clause), but *when* the tenant intends or needs to use these premises. Most leases indicate that a building will be open during "normal business hours" and on "normal business days." If the business must operate during hours other than those of, say, 9:00 A.M. through 5:00 P.M., on weekends, or on certain holidays when the building would normally be closed, the matter is subject to negotiation and financial adjustments. If the lessor is willing to operate his premises on days other than those indicated in the lease, he will charge for the service. This could be expensive and could involve such services as operation of elevators; heating, ventilating, and air conditioning; cleaning services; and utilities. These charges and payments are normally not included in the escalation computation, but the landlord will prospectively increase such charges as costs increase.

The tenant firm must first consider if it can amend the hours or days of operation. If not, the schedule of charges and the cost burden for such overtime/holiday use of the premises must be determined. The cost penalty for occupying some premises on an "overtime" basis could be so great that it will prevent the firm from signing the lease.

**Space Preparation and Work Letters.** What is the value of the work supplied by the landlord to prepare the space for the initial move-in? What is the tenant's additional out-of-pocket cost to make the space ready for occupancy? Do such estimates include the cost for architects, engineers, and general contractors; the cost of the physical move; the cost to install telephones and/or any other telecommunications or essential electronic hardware?

Landlords will often offer to do and/or pay for a certain amount of work for a tenant in new premises as an inducement to the tenant to enter into the lease. Such concessions can take many confusing forms, but the tenant must know the dollar value of a space preparation allowance. Only then can it determine its net space preparation cost, assuming it wants more work done than the lessor is willing to provide.

The *work letter* in a lease embodies the agreement between the landlord and tenant as to work which the landlord is required to perform and for which he is not entitled to additional compensation over and above the agreed rental. The document also covers the building standard and the tenant's requirements in excess of the building standard, as well as other special construction items. Appendix 36–1 is a checklist of items to consider in negotiating a work letter included in a lease agreement.

As the checklist illustrates, a typical work letter also elaborates on the mechanics of preparing plans for the interior, the time within which the work is to be performed, and the time schedule for the production of plans. It often sets out types, quality, and quantities of materials, and what the landlord is prepared to do, but it often does not have a dollar value attached to the work. The tenant must be careful to get permission to use substitute materials if he wishes to do so. But it is more important to ensure that the landlord contributes the dollar value of that work letter if substitutions are made. In order to determine the landlord's contribution if the tenant seeks only partial substitutions, the tenant must know the unit value of each item that the landlord provides.

During the term of the lease, the tenant should have the right to make reasonable alterations to its premises. Although landlords generally try to limit this right to prevent any adverse effects on the building's major systems, the tenant's negotiator should try not to let the lease mandate that the lessor's contractor be used.

**Holdovers and Lease Extensions.** "If tenant retains possession of the demised premises at the end of the lease term, tenant shall pay the landlord the monthly rent, at double the rate payable for the month immediately preceding said holding over, for each month or part thereof, and, in addition thereto, tenant shall pay landlord all damages, consequential as well as direct, sustained by reason of tenant's retention of possession." The above provision from an actual lease could conceivably result in bankrupting the tenant company unless it is able to move to its new location punctually and smoothly. Assume Company A decides to move. A new lease has been negotiated, but all moving companies go out on strike. The building is effectively closed, and Company A cannot make its move. Its present lease expires, and it holds over. According to the lease, what are the consequences to Company A?

1. First, Company A's rent doubles and the landlord can add additional tax and operating expenses, with an immediate impact on Company A's bottom line.
2. More importantly, Company A has agreed to be liable for consequential damages, which could be significant. Company B occupies 50,000 square feet of contiguous space and has signed a lease with the landlord to take over Company A's 10,000 square feet when Company A's lease expires; without this space, Company B cannot operate. The landlord cannot deliver the 10,000 square feet, thus causing Company B to cancel its lease with the landlord. What kind of deal had Company B negotiated for Company A's 10,000 square feet? Would it have paid a premium rent? What are the landlord's losses? They could be astronomical, but Company A has agreed to be liable.
3. The landlord at Company A's new premises has completed the preparation of its space, its rent commences, but it cannot move in. Company A has doubled its rent at the existing space and is now paying rent at the new location. One strike has tripled its rent bill.

In summary, few companies can afford the known obligations of holding over, even without considering the possibility of consequential damages. The controller must get a careful explanation of the clause from the company attorney and must make a business decision as to how to instruct the negotiator with regard to seeking changes. Most landlords are willing to negotiate the holdover clause, but they won't bring it up unless the tenant does.

**Restoration Clauses.** Although restoration clauses may seem insignificant, they may represent future problems. If the landlord, at his sole option, by giving the tenant written notice, can require the tenant at its sole cost and expense to restore the premises to their original condition, the tenant may have a time bomb ticking away in his lease.

It can be difficult even with short-term leases to determine exactly what "original condition" means. Pertinent issues include the following: How long has the lease been running at this point? Who determined the condition of the premises at the inception of the lease? Did the landlord improve the premises at his cost and expense as part of the consideration for the tenant to lease the premises, or did he offer the tenant an alteration allowance? Did the tenant pay for any other improvements to the premises? In order to avoid litigation, the vacating company often negotiates a monetary settlement with the landlord. Such a settlement could indeed be expensive, particularly if a large block of space is involved. Much thought and consideration must thus be given to the restoration clause and to the best position for the corporation. If the company negotiator can arrange to have the clause excluded, he should by all means do so. In the event that he cannot eliminate the clause, he should try to couch it in more explicit terms or put a dollar limit on the value of such restoration.

**Negotiating Responsibilities.** A checklist of items to be considered in negotiating and reviewing a lease is presented in Appendix 36-2. As a generalization, the business terms and conditions of a lease should be handled by knowledgeable company representatives, and attorneys should handle the legal matters. Although this division of responsibility seems clear-cut and reasonable, negotiating responsibilities can never be clearly defined. If clauses are couched in legal language that the controller does not fully understand but that he suspects may result in monetary obligations by way of a court proceeding, he is neglecting his responsibilities if he does not become involved. Conversely, dollar requirements and limitations spelled out must be converted into proper legal language by an attorney. In both cases, each must review the steps taken by the other prior to lease execution. Every clause in a lease is important, and cooperative interaction between company representatives is an absolute necessity. As a side benefit, such diligent interaction prior to execution of the lease reveals possible alternative negotiating positions. As a result, decisions concerning clauses that involve risks can be made more intelligently.

**Tickler File for Lease Dates.** A tickler file on all important lease-related dates should be maintained. Leases are generally loaded with future obligations of varying types, and missing an important date (e.g., to exercise an option) can be expensive and even disastrous. Consequently, after each lease is executed it should be carefully reviewed and the important dates recorded in a tickler file.

**Subleasing and Assignment.** Landlords generally don't want to permit the tenant to sublease, and the tenant wants the right to sublease (or assign) at all costs. The landlord will sometimes give in to this extent: "The tenant cannot sublease or assign

. . . without the landlord's prior written consent." In such a case, the tenant's negotiator should try to add "which consent will not be unreasonably withheld or delayed."

If the landlord permits the tenant to sublease or assign, but insists he take all resulting profits (a common request), the tenant should be sure to define "profit" specifically enough to exclude brokerage commissions (if any), alterations the tenant may provide for the subtenant, and down time on the space if it remains vacant while the tenant arranges to sublease or assign it. The lease should provide that "profit" is calculated on the entire space to be sublet, not only on a portion thereof. The lessor might otherwise end up siphoning off dollars from one segment while the tenant is still paying for another.

Provisions that allow the assignment of leases and the subletting of space should be in the original lease. Clauses that allow some flexibility in the use of space when it is no longer needed have a large financial impact on the organization if management has to dispose of the lease cost in some way. It is important to note, however, that even if the firm is successful in subleasing or assigning, it is unlikely that the landlord will release it from its obligation. The prudent course is to seek a creditworthy subtenant for the space and to try to get such a release from the landlord. It may be worth a cash settlement to obtain a release to dispose of a headache that can last for years.

## OTHER REAL PROPERTY CONSIDERATIONS

### Investment Properties

Any company whose main business is *not* real estate investment but that wants to invest some idle cash in real estate property should seek professional expertise consistent with the investment amount. Casual investments should not be undertaken lightly, and they should follow the same rules that apply to gambling: risk no more than you can afford to lose. All income-producing properties may lose their income stream somewhere during the life of the project; non-income-producing properties may never produce income; and even land purchased in some remote area for appreciation, on which the company expects to pay low real estate taxes, may end up the target of conservationists, in litigation of one kind or another, or entangled in thorny assessment problems.

There is, however, one investment opportunity most companies can avail themselves of, and that involves the property (purchased or leased) that they occupy in the course of operating their business. When the selection is made, in addition to examining the property's ability to satisfy business requirements, management should look at the potential of the location to increase in value at some future time. Is the property located in an expanding population corridor? Does it have attractive features that may make it valuable for resort or retirement village purposes? Is it situated near a body of water and are there riparian rights that may be marketable? The air rights also may be valuable and saleable. The firm needn't own the property to take advantage of appreciation, but it helps. A long-term lease can also be a valuable asset, especially if a developer needs the site and is compelled to buy out the lease in order to make his project a reality.

## Real Estate Taxation

**Disputing Increased Valuations.** The accounting records of many companies show the historical cost of their assets as capitalized on their books. These generally include real property (but also include personal property), upon which many tax valuations are based. The problem with such records is that they often do not truly reflect assets in use at any particular point in time. Some assets may be rebuilt, others abandoned; some may have been divided and used in parts; and others may have mysteriously disappeared when an inventory was taken and reconciled with the book record. Companies often significantly overpay property taxes, even when they conscientiously report correct values as the bases for tax calculations and these values agree with their accounting records.

In addition, it pays management to keep an eye on increases in taxation in its business area. It should periodically check on taxes paid by other businesses and should try to establish reasonable comparability. Questions can be raised with the taxing authorities if significant inequities are detected. If the complexities of arguing its situation are too time consuming and perhaps beyond the controller's experience, there are many good valuation consultants who, for a relatively low fee, will do the job.

Finally, assets on the books should be segregated by acquisition date within each asset type and, if necessary, by location. And, in the event of multiple locations, asset movement between or among locations should be accurately recorded.

**Tax-Free Exchanges.** Instead of selling property and perhaps paying a tax on the gain, management may be able to exchange one property for another and defer payment of taxes on that gain. However, because of the pitfalls and complexities involved in certain exchanges, all the homework should be done on an exchange prior to entering into a contract. A gain may appear to be postponed when it actually is not. Consequently, the firm may unexpectedly be subject to taxes. All relative accounting and tax regulations should be researched. The holding period of the property to be exchanged is important, as is the type of property for which it is being exchanged and the terms of the agreement. Note that receiving cash in addition to exchanging property does not necessarily prevent the transaction from qualifying as a tax-free exchange. This is another area of specialization where investment in an accountant's or attorney's advice can pay good dividends. If the potential taxable gain on an exchange is significant, it may pay to request an advance ruling from the Internal Revenue Service.

**Installment Purchases and Sales.** Accounting practices for purchase of real property on an installment basis are reasonably cut-and-dried and should be familiar to most controllers. Special care should be taken, however, when entering into a lease, that what seems to be a lease is not really an installment purchase under SFAS No. 13. In such a case, what is believed to be a lease may require recognition on the balance sheet as though it were a purchase.

Recording sales of real property on an installment basis can be a little trickier, and in general there are two methods of doing so. Under the *installment method* each principal collection may be apportioned between the cost recovered and the profit recognized in the same ratio as cost and profit are presumed to constitute sales value. (Interest on the related receivable is properly recorded as income when received.)

Under the *cost recovery method*, when a sale has occurred for accounting purposes but no profit should be recognized until all costs are recovered (for a variety of specified reasons), the cost recovery method must be used. (In actuality, the cost recovery method can usually be used as an alternative to the installment method.) Profit is not recognized until collections exceed the cost of the property sold.

Care must also be taken to ensure that a real estate transaction is not really a financing arrangement as opposed to a true sale of real property. This generally occurs where the seller must repurchase the property at an amount higher than the payments to be received. Indeed, an *option* to repurchase may be in the same class as an *obligation* to repurchase, and the firm may therefore not be able to record a sale if it has retained such an option.

Since the possibilities for variations on the theme in an installment sale are almost limitless because of the many pitfalls involved, when an installment sale is contemplated the controller should carefully review all accounting and tax guidelines prior to entering into any agreement of sale, or should seek advice if he is not versed in this area.

**Commercial Rent and Occupancy Taxes.** There is a growing trend in many municipalities to raise additional tax revenues by imposing taxes on the businesses that pay rent, in addition to real estate taxes on those who own properties. (It is inequitable to some degree, since most landlords pass their increased costs of real estate taxes on to tenants via escalation.) For example, New York City imposes a commercial rent tax on business tenants (between six and seven percent of total rental obligation for larger tenants).

Taxes of this magnitude become important considerations in determining just how rental obligations are treated in the lease. If certain portions of rental costs (e.g., cleaning the premises) can be carved out of the lease and put in separate agreements, and payment of such costs is thus not considered rent at all, then this tax can be reduced.

Such local rent taxes should be carefully researched for other possible tax savings. The firm may be entitled to a reduction in the tax if, for example, a portion of the premises is vacant during the tax year.

**Investment Credit.** Improvements of rented premises (in addition to portions of new building construction) may be eligible for investment tax credit. As of October

31, 1978, a company may reduce its tax bill by 10 percent for amounts expended on rehabilitating an old building (plan, office, or warehouse) that has been in use for over twenty years. It appears that the company does not have to own that building in order to claim the credit. Nevertheless, the allocation of the investment credit, as between the owner and the tenant, should be clearly noted in the lease or in a separate document in order to avoid a dispute at tax time. An additional 10 percent investment tax credit is also allowed for energy saving improvements.

## SUGGESTED READING

Arnold, Alvin. *Modern Real Estate and Mortgage Forms: Basic Forms and Agreements,* Rev. ed. Boston: Warren, Gorham & Lamont, Inc., 1978.

Arnold, Alvin, Benton, Donald, and Lopatin, Robert. *Modern Real Estate and Mortgage Forms: Checklists.* Boston: Warren, Gorham & Lamont, Inc., 1979.

Bagby, Joseph R. *Real Estate Financing Desk Book.* Englewood Cliffs, N.J.: Prentice-Hall, Inc., 1977.

Friedman, Milton R. *Friedman on Leases.* New York: Practicing Law Institute, 1978.

Kusnet, Jack, and Lopatin, Robert. *Modern Real Estate Leasing Forms.* Boston: Warren, Gorham & Lamont, Inc., 1980.

*Real Estate Review Portfolio Series.* Boston: Warren, Gorham & Lamont, Inc. (annual updates).

Weimer, Arthur M., Hoyt, Homer, and Bloom, George F. *Real Estate,* 7th ed. New York: The Ronald Press Co., 1978.

Wendt, Paul F. and Cerf, Alan R. *Real Estate Investment Analysis and Taxation,* 2nd ed. New York: McGraw-Hill Book Co., 1979.

## APPENDIX 36-1  REAL ESTATE WORK LETTER CHECKLIST

[  ]  Tenant's Plans and Specifications

- Who prepares architectural and mechanical "working" drawings and what they are to contain
- Delivery schedule for plans
- What landlord approvals are required
- Tenant changes in plans once they are delivered to landlord

[  ]  Landlord's Plans and Specifications

- Nature and type of working drawings landlord must prepare
- What trades these must cover (electrical, plumbing, HVAC)
- To what extent landlord can make changes in plans for shell, core, and tenant areas
- Definition and limitations of material substitution by landlord

[  ]  Landlord's Work

- Schedule of items landlord will furnish (standard of the building)

[  ]  Tenant Requirements in Excess of Standard of the Building

- Tenant substitutions
- Limitations on substitutions
- Construction causing delay in completion of landlord's work or in commencement of lease date
- Extent to which landlord and government may permit changes
- Any impairment of landlord's ability to fulfill occupancy dates
- Any effect on completion of space for other tenants
- Logistics of extra work: when plans must be submitted, who may perform extra work, and rules for tenant bringing in contractor
- Method of estimating and pricing work
- Theory of substitutions: Must substitution be of like kind and quality and serve the same function as item replaced?
- Any credits for omitted items of standard work, methods of crediting substitutions, and basis for establishing credits
- Time of payment for extra work
- Certification of completion: Who decides work is complete?

[  ]  Schedule of Delivery of Tenant's Plans

- Special floor loading, floor openings, air conditioning, plumbing, electrical loads, and telephone equipment
- Location of partitions, doors, ceilings, and outlets

- Locations, loads, and dimensions of telephone equipment rooms, air conditioning, plumbing, and cabinet work
- Nonstandard ceiling heights and materials
- Decorating plans (floor coverings, drapes, and wall coverings)
- Consequences of failure to meet schedules for plan submissions

[ ] Delays in Landlord's Work

- Due to landlord's negligence or inability
- Due to force majeure (acts of God, strikes, insurrection)
- Because of tenant's failure to furnish plans when due, extra work, changes in plans subsequent to submission to landlord, subcontractors' inability to perform
- Effect on tenant's occupancy dates, landlord's completion dates, rental commencement dates; and losses, costs, and damages caused by such delays by either party

[ ] Tenant's Entry Prior to Commencement Date

- Performance of tenant's work by his own contractors
- Methods which will not conflict with landlord's completion of balance of building and/or work in other tenants' spaces; possibilities of union disputes; use of and charges for landlord's hoisting equipment; scheduling use of such equipment

[ ] Entry After Substantial Completion

- Understanding as to what constitutes completion or "substantial" completion for the purposes of rental commencement
- Agreement as to what constitutes constructive eviction

Courtesy of Albert I. Rubenstein, Esq., Attorney and Real Estate Consultant.

## APPENDIX 36-2   CHECKLIST FOR COMMERCIAL LEASE ANALYSIS

(1) *Type of building.*

(2) *Landlord:*
- ☐ Capacity: individual; executor; partnership; or corporation.
- ☐ If executor, has a court order approving the lease been issued?

- ☐ If partnership, have all partners signed? ☐ Partnership agreement necessary?
- ☐ If corporation, have company minutes authorizing lease been attached?
- ☐ If corporation is closely held, have principal owners signed individually?
- ☐ If subsidiary, is parent company signing or guaranteeing lease?

(3) *Tenant:* (same as item (2)).

(4) *Premises:*
- ☐ Address.
- ☐ Legal description.
- ☐ Has a plot plan been made part of the lease?
- ☐ Any outside parking been made part of the lease?

(5) *Term:*
- ☐ ............... years, ............... months, ............... days.
- ☐ Begins.
- ☐ Terminates.
- ☐ If lease begins at a time to be determined, what is the latest date for commencement?
- ☐ What is the contingency on which commencement depends?
- ☐ What is latest date that lease can terminate?
- ☐ Does lease contain options to renew?
- ☐ When must option be exercised?
- ☐ Under what circumstances may landlord cancel this lease?
- ☐ Under what circumstances may tenant cancel this lease?

(6) *Rental:*
- ☐ Total minimum rent due under the lease.
- ☐ Payable monthly, annually, etc.
- ☐ Amount of installment.
- ☐ Where payable?
- ☐ Advance rent or security deposit—how is this to be used, can lender reach it?

☐ Reevaluation clauses: at what intervals; formula for determining new rent.

☐ Does tenant have to pay landlord any payment other than rent?
  - Equipment.
  - Parking Costs.
  - Advertising.
  - Maintenance.

☐ Who pays heating costs?

☐ Who pays cooling costs?

☐ Who pays lighting costs?

☐ Who pays water costs?

☐ Does tenant pay any part of real estate taxes?

☐ Does tenant pay any part of future assessments?

☐ Is there a clause preventing the reduction of rent or changes in lease terms without consent of lender?

☐ Has tenant been provided with additional equipment, or are there any terms or circumstances that indicate that the rental should be considered as out of the ordinary?

☐ Has tenant contracted to spend money on construction, etc.?

☐ Who pays cleaning costs?

☐ Does lease include any free period?

(7) *Percentage Rentals:*

☐ Is there a minimum rent?

☐ Is there a maximum rent?

☐ What is the percentage rate?

☐ Does this percentage apply to all of the gross?

☐ Are there any items not included?

☐ Are there any items which have to be computed at a different rate?

☐ Is the excess rent computed monthly, quarterly, annually, etc.?

☐ Is there any adjustment that has to be made quarterly, annually, etc.?

☐ What items may tenant use to offset excess rent payments?

☐ At what intervals is tenant to report his sales volume?

☐ Does landlord have the right to inspect all of tenant's records?

☐ Does landlord have the right to have tenant's records audited?

☐ Who pays for audit in event error is found?

☐ Is there any penalty in event tenant has been proved to be reporting too little volume?

☐ Is tenant required to remain open certain hours?

☐ Any restriction on tenant opening other stores within certain radius?

☐ Has landlord agreed to prohibit certain businesses that might compete with tenant from property under his control?

☐ Has landlord agreed to prohibit other tenants from selling certain items?

☐ Does percentage apply to concessionaires?

☐ Is there a recapture clause in event sufficient excess is not earned?

☐ Are there clauses that require tenant to adequately staff and stock store?

(8) *Real Estate Taxes:*

☐ Who pays real estate taxes?

☐ Does lease provide for tenant to pay own personal property taxes?

☐ If tenant pays real estate taxes what part for first and last year of lease?

☐ Are tax receipts to be presented?

☐ May tenant contest amount of taxes?

☐ If tenant pays only part of taxes, how is his share determined?

(9) *Maintenance and Repairs:*

☐ Is the lease specific?

☐ Who is responsible for roof, walls, floors and foundations, heating and cooling, electrical, elevator, plumbing, glass, appurtenances, sidewalks, etc.?

☐ Who is responsible for compliance with new requirements of local authorities?

☐ Does landlord have to approve all changes and alterations?

☐ Are plans and specifications to be submitted?

(10) *Insurance:*

☐ Who pays for fire insurance?

☐ Who pays for other insurance?

• Public liability (personal injury and property damage).

• Plate glass.

• Elevator.

• Boiler.

• Rental income.

• Workmen's compensation.

• Earthquake.

☐ What amount of insurance is to be carried?

☐ Who is to determine amount?

☐ How can amount of insurance be changed?

☐ Is landlord or tenant to approve insurance carrier?

☐ To whom is loss payable?

☐ How are funds to be handled?

☐ Is landlord required to rebuild?

☐ Is tenant required to rebuild?

☐ Who is to provide deficiency if any?

☐ Does lease provide for landlord/tenant to provide other with copy of policy?

☐ If so, is it provided for new policy to be in other's hands about thirty days before old policy expires?

(11) *Rebuilding If Damage or Destruction:*
☐ Under what circumstances must landlord or tenant rebuild?
☐ Has any time limit been set for rebuilding?
☐ Under what circumstances may landlord or tenant avoid rebuilding?
☐ In the event of injury or destruction, may landlord or tenant terminate lease?
☐ Is any abatement of rent provided for?

(12) *Construction of New Building or Major Improvements:*
☐ When is construction to begin?
☐ When is construction to be completed?
☐ Does landlord have to approve contractor?
☐ Any penalty for delay or bonus for earlier completion?
☐ Does the lease call for a lien and completion bond?
☐ If tenant is to build, has he finalized his financing, and/or does he have his building funds in a separate account?
☐ Have the plans and specifications been made part of the lease?
☐ Have the plans and specifications been approved by the proper parties?
☐ Has a building permit been issued on the basis of the approved plans?
☐ Who is to carry insurance during the construction?
☐ Who receives title to completed building and when does title pass?
☐ Can lease be canceled if building not complete by certain date?
☐ Is lease term extended by delay in completing building?

(13) *Security Deposits:*
☐ Is deposit required of tenant?
☐ If lease is now executed, was the deposit paid?
☐ What form is deposit to take: cash? stock? bonds?
☐ Who gets the income from the deposit?
☐ Can tenant substitute different bonds with bonds of like value?
☐ Can landlord obtain additional deposit if stocks decline?
☐ What happens to deposit if tenant defaults?
☐ What happens if tenant or landlord goes bankrupt?

(14) *Liens:*
☐ Is tenant to notify landlord at commencement of any work done at premises?

(15) *Advances by Landlord:*
☐ Does lease provide for landlord to pay taxes, insurance, etc.?
☐ If landlord has to advance funds on tenant's behalf, is there any interest or penalty called for?

(16) *Mortgage of Reversion (Fee) Interest:*
☐ Must landlord give tenant notice?
☐ Is the lease recorded?
☐ Does tenant agree to subordinate to a subsequent mortgage?
☐ Is there any limit placed on the amount that landlord may encumber for?
☐ Has tenant the right to pay on the loan if landlord defaults?
☐ If tenant makes such payment does it apply on his rent account?
☐ Has tenant agreed to subordinate only providing that he may not be disturbed so long as he keeps his lease in order?

(17) *Default of Tenant:*
☐ Does tenant have grace period to cure default?
☐ Is nonpayment of rent treated differently than other defaults?
☐ Must landlord serve notice of default? If so, how?
☐ In the event of tenant's default, may landlord reenter and terminate any subleases?

(18) *Lien for Rent:*
☐ Does landlord have lien on any tenant's property for delinquent rent?

(19) *Reentry:*
☐ Does landlord have the right to reenter, if tenant defaults?
☐ What provision has been made re tenant's property if abandoned on premises?

(20) *Assignments and Subleases:*
☐ Are new construction or major improvements to be completed before any assignment?
☐ Is assignee to assume all liability under lease?
☐ Is original tenant to remain liable under the form of assignment?
☐ May subleases be made without consent?
☐ Is landlord's consent required to all assignments?
☐ Can subleases be made that adversely affect lender?

(21) *Mortgage of Leasehold:*
☐ Is landlord's consent required?
☐ Does mortgage instrument provide for landlord to be notified in case of default?
☐ Does mortgage provide for landlord to take over tenant's position if he so desires?
☐ Can landlord make payment for tenant if tenant defaults, without assuming responsibility for the loan?
☐ Has the income from subleases been assigned?

(22) *Condemnation:*
☐ If less than 100 percent taken, is there abatement of rent?
☐ Can tenant terminate?

☐ Can landlord terminate?

☐ Does remainder have to be remodeled?

☐ Does tenant share in award?

☐ Does landlord bar tenant from sharing in award but arrange to compensate tenant for any new construction or major improvements out of landlord's award?

☐ How is tenant's share to be computed?

☐ Is landlord required to stand suit or may he negotiate a settlement with condemnor?

(23) *Option to Purchase:*

☐ When must option be exercised?

☐ What procedure must be followed?

☐ What is the sale price?

☐ How is the sale price to be determined?

☐ How is the purchase to be financed?

(24) *Signs:*

☐ May tenant erect signs on roof, wall?

☐ Is landlord's consent required before tenant erects signs?

☐ Does landlord have control over window signs?

(25) *Co-tenancy:*

☐ Are there any clauses requiring other tenants to take possession before this lease becomes effective?

☐ Can the lease be canceled in event other tenant's vacate?

(26) *Zoning:*

☐ Is the lease dependent on certain zoning being obtained?

(27) *Parking:*

☐ Does landlord agree to provide tenant with a minimum amount of exclusive parking?

(28) *Fixtures:*

☐ May tenant remove certain fixtures?

# 37

# Controlling Energy Costs

*Robert O. Redd*

## INTRODUCTION

The effectiveness of an energy management program depends on the long-term continuing support and involvement of a company's top executives. Energy planning and control is essential to the strategic planning for every company, and must be an ongoing concern of everyone in the organization. As well as current profitability, energy costs and availability affect a company's product life cycles, new factory locations, distribution networks, and overall marketing plans. The availability and future costs of energy will determine the survival of many companies.

As an example, consider the frozen food industry. Food is first cooked, then repackaged and frozen. The product must remain under refrigeration throughout the supply chain. Frozen food processing requires a great deal of energy and may force some types of frozen foods to become so highly priced, in comparison with others, that the market will disappear.

Or, a trucking company may mainly use large vehicles to deliver goods, even though the majority of its trucks leave the terminal only partially full. Despite the capital costs, higher gasoline costs may make it worthwhile to buy and maintain a separate fleet of smaller vehicles to handle these smaller loads.

### The Controller's Role

The controller should apply the same principles of planning, budgeting, and control used in financial management to energy management. As a member of the management team, he plays an important role in initiating, planning, and executing energy programs. He must determine areas of opportunity for energy savings, and must decide whether corrective action makes financial sense. He does not make these decisions alone, but is an essential member of an energy committee, and as such, provides this group with continuity and direction.

### The Energy Team

The energy committee is the master control group responsible for the planning of the corporate energy program. It could include the following management personnel:

- Chief executive officer,
- Corporate controller,
- Chief of manufacturing, and
- Plant engineer or maintenance chief.

Numerous other job titles might be involved, depending on the type of business the company does. These titles could include:

- Vice president for product development,
- Research chief,
- Purchasing manager,
- Office manager, and
- Building superintendent.

This is the master control group for the planning of corporate energy programs. All information regarding consumption and requirements for energy should be directed to this group. The team is responsible for the following activities:

- Setting conservation goals;
- Developing appropriate plans of action; and
- Acting as a conduit for the dissemination of directives and information.

The committee should be coordinated by a top management representative at each plant location. This representative should have the authority to resolve the tough energy-related trade-offs that may be necessary to carry out energy programs, such as changing plant work schedules, dropping products, or revamping maintenance and product distribution systems.

### Energy Usage Data

For purposes of analyzing and reporting, energy usage data must utilize a convenient measure of energy. Most firms will probably find the BTU (British Thermal Unit) the most convenient measure.[1] Or, in another instance, a transportation firm may convert all energy use into gasoline equivalents.

In this chapter, examples will be given in terms of BTUs. All energy use—whether in the form of oil, gas, electricity, coal, steam, or any other energy source—will be converted into BTUs used. This allows for a simple way of comparing the costs; for example, heat exchangers using purchased steam as opposed to a gas-fired boiler. Utilizing BTUs also allows a measure of the true heat value of variable quality fuels such as coal. Some coal produces only 3,000 BTUs per pound, while other coal may produce 7,000. Clearly, measuring energy use in "tons of coal" can lead to erroneous conclusions about energy consumption.

## ENERGY BUDGETING

A separate energy budget should be established for each company location. This will reflect the overall energy consumption of the plant or office at various activity levels and will take into account current procedures and equipment.

### Bill Analysis

The controller first collects all utility bills for the past two years and analyzes the company's utility history, documenting usages and costs (See Figure 37.1). This figure summarizes changes in consumption, month by month, and enables the controller to analyze activity levels and determine the historical trends. This data can be useful in highlighting any seasonal changes in usage, particularly for space heating or for manufacturing processes that take place out-of-doors, common at large steel fabrication plants. (For purposes of analysis, this data should be converted from electric billings to BTUs.)

---

[1] A BTU is the amount of heat required to raise the temperature of one pound of water by one degree Fahrenheit.

## ENERGY HISTORY
### ELECTRICAL

| | Usage—Kwh | | % | Demand—Kw | | % | Fuel Adj Factor | | Total Cost—Dollars | | % |
|---|---|---|---|---|---|---|---|---|---|---|---|
| | 19X6–X7 | 19X7–X8 | Change | 19X6–X7 | 19X7–X8 | Change | 19X6–X7 | 19X7–X8 | 19X6–X7 | 19X7–X8 | Change |
| Nov. | 303,300 | 340,500 | 12.3 | 594 | 920 | 54.9 | .00066 | − .00008 | $ 4,473 | $ 10,859 | 142.8 |
| Dec. | 319,000 | 280,000 | −12.2 | 612 | 870 | 42.2 | .00871 | − .00229 | 13,045 | 8,626 | −33.9 |
| Jan. | 287,900 | 247,000 | −14.2 | 594 | 547 | − 8.0 | .00306 | − .00019 | 7,777 | 7,835 | 0.7 |
| Feb. | 281,300 | 282,000 | 0.2 | 594 | 580 | − 2.4 | .00001 | − .00029 | 8,695 | 8,633 | − 0.7 |
| March | 291,500 | 280,000 | − 3.9 | 476 | 630 | 32.4 | .00212 | + .00087 | 9,655 | 7,627 | −21.0 |
| April | 280,900 | 337,000 | 20.0 | 648 | 630 | − 3.0 | .00170 | .00087 | 9,309 | 10,162 | 9.2 |
| May | 285,400 | 375,000 | 31.4 | 648 | 680 | 5.0 | .00150 | − .00024 | 9,367 | 11,132 | 18.8 |
| June | 320,300 | 371,000 | 15.8 | 666 | 680 | 2.1 | .00248 | − .00040 | 10,643 | 10,401 | − 2.3 |
| July | 308,800 | 339,000 | 9.8 | 684 | 680 | − 0.6 | −.00038 | − .00174 | 9,448 | 9,724 | 2.9 |
| Aug. | 318,600 | 354,000 | 11.1 | 666 | 680 | 2.1 | .00085 | − .00112 | 10,052 | 10,295 | 2.4 |
| Sept. | 370,400 | 304,000 | −17.9 | 684 | 680 | − 0.6 | .00187 | − .00198 | 11,799 | 8,851 | −25.0 |
| Oct. | 302,000 | 280,000 | − 7.3 | 666 | 630 | 5.4 | .00602 | − .00006 | 11,275 | 8,768 | −22.2 |
| | 3,669,400 | 3,789,500 | 3.3 | | | | | | $120,538 | $112,913 | − 6.3 |

FIGURE 37.1 UTILITY HISTORY

**Budget Preparation**

After the utility analysis has been completed, the controller should prepare an energy budget (an example is provided in Figure 37.2). The energy budget displays the expected energy consumption and relates it to *degree days*, a measure of the weather in the surrounding area. (A degree day is the amount of temperature variation between 65 degrees and the average temperature for a specific day. For example, if the average temperature during a day in February was 45 degrees, that day would be a 20 degree day.) These amounts are totalled daily for the year and published by the National Oceanic and Atmospheric Administration. Local figures are often available from residential fuel-oil dealers or from NOAA offices at large airports.

The energy content of production units should be developed in BTUs and used as the basis for budgeting the company's production energy requirements.

In some manufacturing concerns, the development of energy budgets involves complex computations; in this case, the use of BTU accounting can be advantageous. (BTU accounting is discussed later in this chapter.)

**Budget Reviews**

The completed budget should be reviewed with the plant manager or production chief. This will assure that it is reasonable both in relation to past experiences and to expected activity level of the company. Graphs displaying the pattern of consumption during the past are also useful. Figure 37.3 depicts typical electricity usage for an electrical consumption pattern in most commercial or office buildings. Note the substantial increase in consumption in the summer, due to the office air-conditioning system load. If the graph shows a high consumption level during the entire year, however, the heating controls may be ineffective and the air-conditioning system out of control. (It is not uncommon in office buildings for heating and air conditioning systems to be operating at the same time.) Graphs can also be used to monitor usage, thus showing management if energy consumption is trending away from budget.

## ORGANIZING FOR ENERGY MANAGEMENT

**Analyzing Energy Usage**

By carefully analyzing the overall energy usage, the energy committee can develop a general understanding of the energy consumption pattern of the company. Data should be collected and summarized in a graphic display showing where energy is being expended. Figure 37.4 illustrates an overview analysis of energy consumption for a typical bakery. There are two categories of fuel consumed; one

ENERGY BUDGET

_____ YEAR

BUILDING _____

| Month | Htg./Cool. Degree Days (2) | Electricity | | | | | | | | Purchased Steam | | | | | | | Oil | | | | Fuel Check Gas ☐ Coal ☐ Other ☐ | | | | Fuel/ Deg. Days (22) | Total Energy BTU (23) |
|---|---|---|---|---|---|---|---|---|---|---|---|---|---|---|---|---|---|---|---|---|---|---|---|---|---|
| | | % p1 (3) | KWH (4) | KWH/ Deg. Days (5) | KW Demand Actual (6) | KW Demand Billed (7) | Cost Total (8) | Cost Per Ut. (9) | M (lbs.) (10) | M(lbs.)/ Deg. Days (11) | lbs/hr Demand Actual (12) | lbs/hr Demand Billed (13) | Cost Total (14) | Cost Per Unit (15) | Quant. (Gal.) (16) | Cost Total (17) | Cost Per Unit (18) | Quant. (19) | Cost Total (20) | Cost Per Unit (21) | | |
| (1) | | | | | | | | | | | | | | | | | | | | | | |
| Jan. | / | | | | | | | | | | | | | | | | | | | | | |
| Feb. | / | | | | | | | | | | | | | | | | | | | | | |
| March | / | | | | | | | | | | | | | | | | | | | | | |
| 1st Quarter | | | | | | | | | | | | | | | | | | | | | | |
| April | / | | | | | | | | | | | | | | | | | | | | | |
| May | / | | | | | | | | | | | | | | | | | | | | | |
| June | / | | | | | | | | | | | | | | | | | | | | | |
| 2nd Quarter | | | | | | | | | | | | | | | | | | | | | | |
| July | / | | | | | | | | | | | | | | | | | | | | | |
| Aug. | / | | | | | | | | | | | | | | | | | | | | | |
| Sep. | / | | | | | | | | | | | | | | | | | | | | | |
| 3rd Quarter | | | | | | | | | | | | | | | | | | | | | | |
| Oct. | / | | | | | | | | | | | | | | | | | | | | | |
| Nov. | / | | | | | | | | | | | | | | | | | | | | | |
| Dec. | / | | | | | | | | | | | | | | | | | | | | | |
| 4th Quarter | | | | | | | | | | | | | | | | | | | | | | |
| Total Per Year | | | | | | | | | | | | | | | | | | | | | | |

Building Data

Gross Area (ft.)² _____ Gross Volume (ft.)³ _____

General Notes _____

Annual Energy Consumption in BTU's

| | Quantity | | Conversion Fac. | BTU/Yr |
|---|---|---|---|---|
| 1. Electricity | _____ | kwh | 10,200 | _____ |
| 2. Purchased Steam | _____ | (M)lbs | 1,000,000 | _____ |
| 3. Natural Gas | _____ | MCF | 1,030,000 | _____ |
| 4. Oil | _____ | Gallons | #2-138,700 #6-149,700 | _____ |
| 5. Other Fuel | | | | _____ |
| | | | 6. Total | _____ |

Energy Utilization Index

$$EUI = \frac{\text{Total Energy Consumption BTU's/Yr}}{\text{Gross Area (ft.)}^2}$$

= _____ = _____ BTU's/ft²/Yr ÷ 100,000

= _____ = _____ THERMS

FIGURE 37.2 ENERGY BUDGET

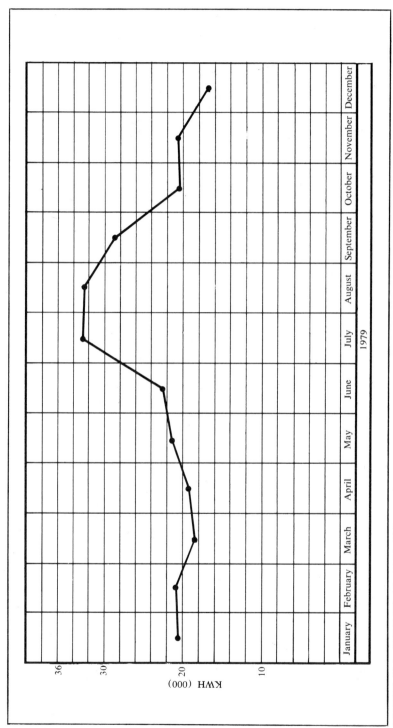

FIGURE 37.3  ENERGY CONSUMPTION GRAPH—ELECTRICAL

is gas—15,700 million BTUs. The second is steam boilers—14,200 million BTUs. The gas for heating and washing is broken down into the following components:

| Usage | Million BTUs |
|---|---|
| Heating | 5,400 |
| Fryer | 600 |
| Pan washers | 2,100 |
| Ovens | 7,600 |

Note that the consumption of fuel in the ovens is then broken down even further. In this case, 4,300 million BTUs is attributable to losses from energy leaks through the oven's insulation, including losses sustained when the oven door is open, as well as losses up the oven's flue. Only 3,300 million BTUs are actually used in baking the product.

Such numbers are often available from equipment manufacturers. Or, on larger custom equipment, it may be worthwhile to hire a consultant to use sophisticated monitoring devices to measure heat losses accurately.

## Reducing Consumption

The energy management group can now direct its attention to reducing the loss. In this example, it might be worthwhile to install a device to recapture heat wasted in the flue and use it to help heat either the building or the washing water. Perhaps the oven door is being kept open unnecessarily; correcting this might require an employee training program or an adjustment in production schedules.

This type of analysis provides a perspective on where energy is wasted and how, with better equipment, it might be recovered. The controller, with the help of the plant engineer and other appropriate personnel, can request funds to reduce energy consumption. The requests must define the cost and benefits expected; for example, from the installation of conservation equipment. The manufacturing representative can initiate employee training programs. Marketing and product designers can analyze their areas of responsibility to determine how they might also reduce consumption.

## A Master Plan

In many companies, the energy committee will find it important to formulate a five-year energy plan. This should take into account the best information available regarding the *availability* of energy resources, the estimated *cost* of these resources, and the *impact* of predicted governmental regulations. The master plan should also consider the additional capital and engineering talent needed to implement proposed changes in facilities, changes that may become necessary as energy costs increase.

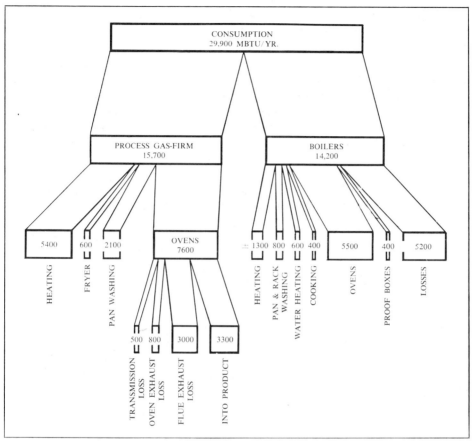

FIGURE 37.4 OVERALL CONSUMPTION CHART FOR A BAKERY

## UTILITY BILL ANALYSIS

The following procedures are used to analyze utility bills.

### Electric Power

Electric power is billed in terms of kilowatt hours of energy consumed, as well as by a demand factor. In addition, the electric power bill usually includes a fuel adjustment charge with local taxes, also calculated according to how many kilowatt hours of energy are consumed. Manufacturers will often have a "power factor" charge as well. The following definitions of charges will be helpful.

**Energy Charge.** The energy charge is for the kilowatts of energy actually consumed during the time period included in the bill. This charge is calculated on the basis of cents per kilowatt per hour.

**Demand Charge.** The demand charge is the amount charged for the user's peak electricity demand for time periods during the peak hours; these periods are usually divided into fifteen minute increments. This payment is not for energy delivered, but is for the utility's guarantee that such levels of capacity will be available on demand. The demand charge often represents 30 to 40 percent of the total bill for a manufacturing plant. It is possible to reduce the demand charge by shedding unrequired loads during critical demand peaks. To reduce the demand charge, this must be done every day of every month, because the demand charge rates usually include a *ratchet clause* that states: "In any twelve-month period a peak is reached, 80 percent of this peak demand will apply for the entire twelve months."

**Fuel Adjustment Charge.** This charge is applied to allow the utility to compensate for cost increases in fuel purchased between rate adjustment periods.

**Power Factor.** The utility makes this charge if the company has excessive inductive loads that cause a lag in the current and create inefficient electrical performance. If the controller identifies a power factor charge on the bill, he should contact the plant engineer to evaluate the cost of correcting the situation by adding capacitors.

**The State Sales Tax.** In many states, the energy required for processing is not taxed by the state, but heating and similar energy needs *are* subject to the tax. Therefore, the full energy bill may not be subject to sales tax. (This policy is based on the theory that energy is a part of the product and is resold with the final product, at which time the sales tax is paid.) If sales tax is charged on the bill, the controller should determine whether or not the tax is applicable.

**Analyzing Alternatives.** A number of alternative electrical rates are available through most utilities, and special rates can be established where very high consumption is involved. The plant engineer should analyze these alternatives to see if the company's bills can be reduced. A company also has the option of purchasing primary current, 12,000 volts, instead of secondary current, 480 volts. The cost of primary current is usually lower than that of secondary. Although a change to primary current requires the installation of transformers, the cost of this equipment is usually recovered in two to four years.

### Gas and Other Fuels

Gas is metered and billed in MCF (one thousand cubic feet) or in therms. These values can be readily identified on the billing and converted to BTUs.

Oil usage is metered in gallons, and meters should be installed on each large oil-consuming unit. Reliance on overall usage is not satisfactory because the service periods of individual units, with their individual efficiencies, can possibly be hidden. Steam from outside utilities is metered by condensate or flow meters and billed on the basis of pounds used.

## ENERGY AUDIT TECHNIQUES

The controller should encourage periodic energy audits by a qualified person (or team, depending on the size of the plant) at least once per year. An energy audit analyzes all the energy consumption and usage in individual buildings or factories. Every energy use is challenged by the "auditors" to determine what measures can be taken to reduce energy consumption. Most companies and consultants find it possible to reduce consumption between 20 and 40 percent if the following procedures are followed:

- Identification of present operating conditions, specific energy leaks, and inefficient equipment;
- Calculation of specific cost savings derived from corrective action in each case; and
- Establishment of priorities, taking into account cost and time factors.

Although the initial calculations are time-consuming, it is important to pinpoint raw materials and manufacturing processes that use large amounts of energy. Some energy waste can be corrected quickly and cheaply through equipment maintenance and operational changes; other waste requires time and capital expenditures to acquire new equipment and supplies.

### Monitoring Activities

**Lighting.** The plant engineer reviews the lighting levels throughout the facilities and determines whether they are appropriate for the work being done. In 1976, the Federal Energy Administration (now part of the Department of Energy) established lighting levels appropriate for various tasks. (Figure 37.5 illustrates the lighting levels FEA recommended for various working conditions.) These lighting levels are substantially lower than those found in most offices. The reduction in lighting levels can also have a substantial effect on the air conditioning requirements of a building because lighting fixtures increase the heating load during the summer.

**Heating and Ventilation.** The engineer should then analyze the heating and ventilating system to determine whether it is appropriate. He will review the building structure, boilers, insulation thicknesses, and the possible use of equipment to recover heat from processes that would otherwise waste this heat. At the completion of this analysis, the engineer must prepare a summary report describing everything that can be done to reduce energy consumption and the steps necessary to implement this conservation program. It is the controller's task to assist management in the development of financial resources necessary to implement the recommendations.

| Location<br>*Interior Areas* | Measured Average<br>Footcandles* |
|---|---|
| General work and circulation areas | 25 — 35 |
| Hallways and corridors | 5 — 15 |
| Service or public areas | 12 — 18 |
| Work stations—normal | 40 — 60 |
| Work stations—prolonged and visually difficult | 60 — 90 |
| Work stations—prolonged and visually critical | 80 — 120 |
| Auditoriums | 20 — 40 |
| Cafeterias | 20 — 40 |
| Conference rooms | 25 — 35 |
| Kitchens | 30 — 70 |
| Mechanical rooms | 5 — 15 |
| Storage areas—general | 5 — 15 |
| Storage areas—fine detail | 25 — 35 |
| Toilets | 15 — 30 |
| *Exterior Areas* | |
| Building entrances—active | 5 |
| Building entrances—inactive | 1 |
| Parking lots used at night | 1 |
| Roadways between or along buildings | 1 |
| Roadways at entrances or intersections | 2 |
| Truck aprons | 5 |
| Railroad sidings—active | 5 |
| Process area—general | 5 |
| Process area with operating equipment | 10 |

\* A footcandle is the amount of light available from a standard candle one foot away. This is a standard unit of measure for lighting levels.

*Note:* In some areas, local codes forbid low lighting levels in passageways and doors used in emergencies; they may require higher levels set by the Illuminating Engineering Society, at least for emergency lamps.

FIGURE 37.5   RECOMMENDED FEDERAL LIGHTING LEVELS

## LIFE CYCLE COSTING

Numerous methods have been developed to evaluate the advisability of capital expenditures. In the past, decisions were often made on the basis of initial cost and payback periods. Since energy costs have increased, companies now consider operating costs as well as initial costs. Figure 37.6 illustrates the effect of this technique, expressed as *Life Cycle Costing*. In this example, the proposed equipment has an initial cost of $50,000. After taking the investment credit and energy tax credit, the cost of the equipment will then be $40,000. Its use will result in annual savings estimated at $14,000 in the first year, increasing to $27,282 in the eighth year. Changes in energy and maintenance costs are factored into the computation. Each

| | | | | Year | | | | | |
|---|---|---|---|---|---|---|---|---|---|
| | 0 | 1 | 2 | 3 | 4 | 5 | 6 | 7 | 8 |
| 1. Initial cost | $(50,000) | — | — | — | — | — | — | — | — |
| 2. Investment tax credit | 5,000 | | | | | | | | |
| 3. Energy tax credit | 5,000 | | | | | | | | |
| 4. Property tax credit | | ( 250) | ( 213) | ( 201) | ( 180) | ( 162) | ( 148) | ( 132) | ( 125) |
| 5. Operating energy cost * | | ( 2,570) | ( 2,827) | ( 3,110) | ( 3,420) | 3,762 | ( 4,139) | ( 4,553) | ( 5,008) |
| 6. Maintenance cost ** | | ( 576) | ( 616) | ( 659) | ( 705) | ( 755) | ( 807) | ( 864) | ( 924) |
| 7. Annual savings | 14,000 | 14,000 | 15,400 | 16,940 | 18,634 | 20,497 | 22,547 | 24,801 | 27,282 |
| 8. Life cycle cost | (40,000) | 10,604 | 11,744 | 12,970 | 14,324 | 15,848 | 17,453 | 19,252 | 21,225 |
| 9. Present value @ 10% | (40,000) | 9,640 | 9,705 | 9,744 | 9,786 | 9,821 | 9,851 | 9,879 | 9,901 |

10. Sum of present value = $38,327

\* Energy costs increasing at the rate of 10% per year.
\*\* Maintenance costs increasing at the rate of 7% per year.

FIGURE 37.6  LIFE CYCLE CAPITAL INVESTMENT ANALYSIS

year, the net effect for the procured equipment is computed and discounted by ten percent, thus reflecting the cost of invested money. Considering increasing energy costs and maintenance, the present value of the cash flow for the eight years would be $38,327. In this case, the project might not be worthwhile, but future higher energy costs could improve the project's economic attractiveness.


## BTU ACCOUNTING

The development of energy budgets, as described earlier in this chapter, is a straightforward matter in an office building or department store. When product manufacturing is involved, however, the matter becomes much more complex. A portion of the energy budget is fixed, since a minimum amount of heat is needed to prevent freezing, to keep workers comfortable, and so on. A major portion of the processing energy is variable, however, depending on the amount of product being produced. The controller must identify that portion of the energy consumption that is fixed and that portion that is variable. He can then develop a projection of consumption by product and product volume.

To facilitate this process, a BTU standard should be computed for each product being manufactured. Figure 37.7 shows a typical BTU standard for a batch of chemical products. This BTU standard is expressed in millions of BTUs per pound of product produced (the right-hand column on the exhibit). In this instance, the total BTUs per pound is 0.0328. It is further broken down into the energy content of raw materials and an energy-by-utilities category. At the completion of the

Product A
Production (capacity) 13,000,000

| Description | Std lbs | MMBtu/lb raw material | Btu | MMBtu/lb |
|---|---|---|---|---|
| Product B | 13,000,000 | .034400 | 447,200 | .0344 |
| Product C* | −7,583,000 | .005025 | −38,105 | −.0029 |
| Total Raw Material | | | 409,097 | .0315 |
| Utility 1 | 7,000 | .920000 | 6,440 | .0005 |
| Utility 2 | 1,500 | 1.311333 | 1,966 | .0002 |
| ⋮ | ⋮ | ⋮ | ⋮ | ⋮ |
| Utility 8 | 4,000 | .077727 | 341 | |
| Total Utilities | | | 16,770 | .0013 |
| Account Total | | | 425,867 | .0328 |

Note: This report displays the energy standard for product A.
* Product C is recovered and reused.

FIGURE 37.7  BTU STANDARD

Product A

## Raw Material and Conversion BTU Consumed
## Production 12,067,434

| Description | Std Btu unit | Unit ratio | Actual MMBtu | Btu/ prod | Btu Standard for Batch MMBtu | Btu/ prod | MMBtu Over/Under |
|---|---|---|---|---|---|---|---|
| Product B | 34,400 | 1.000000 | 415,120 | 34,400 | 415,120 | 34,400 | 0 |
| Product C* | 5,025 | −.591545 | −35,914 | −2,976 | −35,381 | −2,931 | −533 |
| Total Raw Material | | .408455 | 379,206 | 31,425 | 379,739 | 31,469 | −533 |
| Utility 1 | 920,000 | .000773 | 8,584 | 711 | 5,976 | 495 | 2.606 |
| Utility 2 | 1,311,333 | .001435 | 22,720 | 1,882 | 1,025 | 151 | 20,895 |
| .... | .... | | .... | | .... | | .... |
| Utility 8 | 77,727 | .000187 | 175 | 16 | 310 | 26 | −143 |
| Total Utilities | | | 34,528 | 2,861 | 15,569 | 1,290 | 18,959 |
| Raw Material Total | | | 379,206 | 31,425 | 379,739 | 31,469 | −533 |
| Conversion Total | | | 34,528 | 2,861 | 15,569 | 1,290 | 18,959 |
| Account Total | | | 413,734 | 34,286 | 395,308 | 32,759 | 18,426 |
| 1972 base period: Raw material total | | | 29,453 | | | | |
| Conversion total | | | 2,420 | | | | |
| Account total | | | 31,873 | | | | |

−533 } Excessive Usage
18,959 } This Batch
18,426 }

*Note:* This report displays the actual energy usage versus standard.

* Product C is recovered and reused.

FIGURE 37.8  ACTUAL BTU USAGE REPORT

batch, the actual consumption has been reported and compared to standard. Figure 37.8 shows the production results. In this case, the batch required more energy than was expected; this is reflected in the summary report as an 18,426 BTU variance.

Although the implementation of BTU accounting involves the initial expense of installing additional meters throughout the plant, the variance reporting information can be used by management to determine whether personnel and processes are being effectively controlled. By using BTU accounting, one heat treating company reduced the number of its operating furnaces by 30 percent. It accomplished this by scheduling the loads into the furnaces rather than by operating the furnaces as loads appeared.

Data developed in this way can also be useful in corporate strategic planning. Decisions regarding new plant locations, new products or processes should be evaluated on the basis of energy consumption and availability. Pricing strategy may also be strongly influenced by changes in energy costs as oil becomes both higher in price and harder to buy.

## SUGGESTED READING

Bailey, James E., ed., *Energy Systems: An Analysis for Engineers and Policy Makers.* New York: Marcel Dekker, 1978.

*BOCA Building Code: Basic Energy Conservation Code.* Chicago, Illinois: Building Officials and Code Administration, International, 1978.

Collins, Robert L. "Energy Management and Post-Audits." *Journal of Property Management,* (Sept/Oct 1979).

Considine, Douglas M., *Energy Technology Handbook.* New York: McGraw Hill Book Company, 1977.

Loftness, Robert L., *Energy Handbook.* New York: Van Nostrand Reinhold, 1979.

*Managing Industrial Energy Conservation.* New York: American Management Association, 1977.

Roose, Robert W., ed., *Handbook of Energy Conservation for Mechanical Systems in Buildings.* New York: Van Nostrand Reinhold, 1978.

Shinskey, Francis G. *Energy Conservation Through Control.* New York: Academic Press, Incorporated, 1978.

Wilson, Richard, "Financial Methods for Making Energy Management Decisions." *Journal of Property Management,* (May/June 1979).

# Part IX

## Government Reporting and Regulations

# 38

# Federal Taxes— Planning and Control

*Steven A. Braun*

## RESPONSIBILITY FOR TAX PLANNING AND MANAGEMENT

With tax rates at their current levels, federal, state, and local governments have large priority claims on business income. An increasing body of overlapping and sometimes inconsistent laws, regulations, opinions, forms, and procedures affect every corporation's financial operations and planning. The nature of our tax system and the interaction between federal, state, and local authorities present U.S. businesses with increasingly involved and bewildering problems of tax administration.

While many executives agree that tax planning is an important aspect of corporate tax management, there is no universal agreement as to what tax planning means. Many define it as reaching the most advantageous tax position from which to make important operating decisions. Others believe that tax planning is an element of long-range planning and involves the identification and evaluation of future tax problems. Actually, good tax planning includes both.

Tax planning and management are major concerns of both financial and operating executives, because taxes are directly related to business profits and growth. A majority of corporations assign overall responsibility for the tax function to the controller or treasurer, who may be assisted by a separate tax department. The company's size and the complexity of its tax requirements usually determine the structure of the company's tax management function. Large companies usually need a separate tax department, whereas small companies may require only the services of a single tax specialist. Companies with little in-house tax expertise may have all their tax services performed by independent tax professionals such as certified public accountants.

Senior corporate management is generally concerned with two areas of tax management: tax planning and complying with tax laws and regulations. Other areas of involvement for tax personnel include minimizing the company's tax liabilities, advising management on tax problems, and conducting related research.

The compliance function—meeting corporate tax obligations—is the responsibility most frequently handled by corporate tax personnel. Their primary concern is to avoid friction with the IRS and to see that no additional payments and interest charges are assessed because of violations. Because of the complexity of our tax laws, considerable judgment and expertise must be exercised in preparing tax returns for the various taxing authorities. The preparation and filing of tax returns is not a routine process but a substantial managerial task that involves:

- Meeting estimated payment requirements;
- Making timely elections;
- Preparing required tax returns;
- Properly executing tax and related forms; and
- Filing required returns.

## COORDINATING THE TAX FUNCTION

The impact of taxes permeates all operations of a company. For successful tax planning, a "tax awareness" must be developed within the total organization, including its board of directors, high-level operating and financial management, operating and financial departments, and outside advisers. All groups within the organization must realize that most company transactions have tax implications. Tax personnel should be consulted before any important contract is signed or unusual transaction completed.

### Initiating Tax Planning

In small-to-medium-sized firms in which the controller has the responsibility for overseeing the tax function, he should also have the authority to initiate corporate tax planning. This planning must be compatible with the overall corporate strategy and business operations of the company. Since tax planning is effective only when the controller is aware of transactions *before* they occur, the tax planner should properly have access to top management in both the financial and operating areas. In most instances, obtaining the most desirable tax result is difficult, if not impossible, when planning is done *after* the transaction has occurred.

### Effective Working Relationships

To most effectively execute tax planning and prepare tax returns, the controller and his tax personnel must have a good working relationship with various corporate officers and departments.

**Treasurer.** In companies in which the tax executive is not a member of the treasurer's department, he must maintain a line of communication with the treasurer regarding tax bill due dates and the funds needed to pay them. While most companies provide for automatic notification as part of the budgetary process, a periodic updating of the notification procedures is beneficial.

**Corporate Counsel.** Since the corporate counsel is involved in the preparation and execution of all corporate documents, he should carefully consider the tax consequences involved in the signing of contracts or other documents and in the formation of divisions or subsidiaries. Each agreement should be examined in terms of its tax implications to make sure that no unforeseen complications arise. If this process is performed prior to the signing of any contracts or the formation of any companies, any required changes can be promptly effected.

**Accounting Department.** Tax returns are prepared from financial and accounting information obtained by the tax staff from the accounting department. (In many companies, tax personnel are members of the accounting department.)

**Engineering Department.** In companies with large amounts of depreciable assets, tax personnel should work closely with the company's engineering department. The engineer's technical expertise is important in determining useful lives of depreciable assets and in classifying assets for investment credit purposes.

**Outside Advisers.** Effective tax planners also make use of outside tax advisers such as certified public accountants and legal counsel. For maximum effectiveness, these advisers must be aware of any special tax problems or transactions as well as the company's overall tax philosophy. Since many companies prefer to take either an aggressive or a conservative tax position, it is important that the advice given by the outside consultants be consistent with the company's overall outlook and attitudes. The liaison occurs at the senior financial staff level and at lower staff levels as well.

Companies differ in the extent to which they utilize outside advisers and in the kind of advisers they select. Many routinely consult their outside accountants on all tax matters, whereas others use them only for substantive problems. Attorneys, of course, are consulted mainly in situations that involve legal questions or litigations. However, many companies will initially consult with legal counsel rather than their accounting firm. The route taken is generally determined by the background of the individual tax executive.

### Utilizing Outside Training Sources

The controller and his tax personnel should consider attending the training sessions given by the large accounting firms for their own staff. Many accounting firms make these training courses available to client personnel. Periodic newsletters from accountants and attorneys also supply valuable information.

## TAX PLANNING AND CORPORATE STRATEGIES

The key to effective tax planning is the ability to rethink operating strategies and restructure transactions to obtain the best tax benefits. An effective tax planner should not be content with the status quo but should recommend appropriate changes to obtain better tax results.

Given that proper tax planning is only effective when compatible with the overall corporate strategy, there are several areas in which effective planning can reduce corporate tax liability.

### Choosing Favorable Accounting Methods

All companies, whether privately or publicly held, are interested in increasing financial statement earnings and reducing taxable income. Public corporations seek high financial earnings because high earnings have a favorable effect on the market price of their stocks, on the opinion of financial analysts, and on their ability to market future securities. Privately held companies want high financial statement earnings so that bankers and other lenders regard them as better credit risks and give them more favorable credit terms. Higher financial earnings may also be important if privately held companies plan to go public.

Corporations can maximize earnings while minimizing taxes by using different accounting methods for financial and tax reporting. There are many instances where proper financial reporting does not necessarily dictate the accounting method to be used for tax purposes. For example, companies that do not use inventories in the determination of income can report on the basis of cash receipts and disbursements for tax purposes but use the accrual method of accounting for financial statements. Companies eligible to use the percentage-of-completion or completed-contract method for tax purposes may use the accrual method in financial statements. In most situations, the accrual method will recognize income more quickly than the cash-basis and long-term-contract methods.

### Electing a New Accounting Method

If a company decides to elect a more favorable tax accounting method, it may request a change in its overall method of accounting within 180 days of the beginning of the year of change by filing Form 3115 with the Commissioner of the Internal Revenue Service. At the present time, the Commissioner will generally grant permission to change to a method that accurately reflects taxable income. The effect of the change can be taken into income over either a ten-year period or the number of years the company has been in existence if less than ten years. This provision is beneficial, since there is also a ten-year payout of any additional tax due without interest. Unfortunately, however, in many instances the IRS has taken the position that, in order to make a change for tax purposes, the company must also change the accounting method it uses for financial reporting purposes. This ruling, of course, defeats the purpose of the change.

The financial conformity requirement, however, does not apply when a new company is being formed. Management is allowed to select the most beneficial tax accounting method, as long as it properly reflects income under the Internal Revenue Code and Regulations, and to use a different method for financial reporting. When new companies are established within the corporate group, the controller should attempt to obtain the most favorable tax accounting method available.

### Accounting for Specific Items

If the adoption or change of an overall accounting method is not possible or desirable, a company may be able to select different methods of accounting for specific items. The most significant of these areas are inventory and fixed asset accounting.

**Inventory Accounting.** In a period of rising inflation, the use of the *last-in, first-out* (LIFO) method of inventory accounting should be considered. In effect, LIFO charges the cost of the latest goods acquired against the current year's sales. This is in contrast to the most commonly used method of inventory accounting, known as *first-in, first-out* (FIFO), in which the earliest costs are charged against the current year's sales. In an inflationary economy, the latest cost is generally higher, and the use of the LIFO method reduces gross profits and taxable income. However, if companies use the LIFO method, IRS regulations require them to use LIFO for financial statement purposes as well. If this conformity requirement is violated, the IRS can refuse to allow the company to use the LIFO method, and its tax advantage would be lost.

For many years this conformity requirement was the major disadvantage in changing to the LIFO method. However, disclosure requirements have recently become more liberal. Although the LIFO method must still be used for financial reporting if it is used for tax reporting, shareholders, creditors, and financial analysts can be given information to indicate the tax benefits of using LIFO as well as the increased earnings that would have been reported had the company continued on the FIFO method. (Public companies should check current SEC rules on LIFO/FIFO reporting restrictions.)

Unlike other accounting method changes, the total reduction in income when changing to the LIFO method is taken into account in the year of change. In effect, an interest-free loan is thereby granted to the company by the federal and, in most cases, state governments. The LIFO method can be adopted after the company's year-end, and does not have to be made effective until the financial statements are issued and tax returns are filed. (See Chapter 3 for a complete discussion of the LIFO inventory method.)

A Supreme Court decision (*Thor Power Tool Co. v. Comm'r*, 99 S. Ct. 773 [1979]) affects how a company values its inventory on a FIFO basis. In this case the Supreme Court held that the amount of inventory that exceeds current demand cannot arbitrarily be written down by a company. The fact that the write-down is good accounting practice is not an acceptable rationale, since the inventory method must also clearly reflect income under IRS regulations. As a result of the Supreme Court decision, the IRS issued regulations requiring all companies using an inventory method similar to Thor Power Tool to change to an acceptable tax method without requiring the usual permission from IRS. The inventory adjustment resulting from the change in method can be added to taxable income over ten years from the year of change.

**Fixed-Asset Acquisitions.** Many companies use accelerated methods of depreciation for tax purposes and depreciate their assets on a straight-line basis for financial statements. Even with the deferred tax implications, this procedure has a beneficial impact on the financial statements, because deferred taxes related to depreciation are a long-term liability whereas the taxes that would be due are a current liability. The change in classification reflects a better financial position for the company.

## Aggressive Tax Positions

Aggressive tax positions in the areas of depreciation, investment credit, and capitalization can significantly benefit a company's cash flow.

**Depreciable Lives.** A company can take an aggressive position on the depreciable lives of its fixed assets. While most companies usually depreciate assets over the lives set forth by the IRS, shorter lives can be used under extenuating circumstances if the taxpayer can prove that the shorter life is the asset's useful life.

Shorter depreciable lives for real property can be achieved by the use of the *component method* of depreciation. Under this method, a building is broken down into its structural components, such as shell, electrical system, heating and air conditioning, and roof. Shorter useful lives are then assigned to those components that will wear out in less time than the building shell. The allocation of the construction cost among the various components must be supported by construction contracts, invoices, or a reliable appraisal. While the IRS will accept the component method, it requires that the useful life of the building shell be longer than the IRS guidelines, since the latter reflect composite depreciable lives. This proviso notwithstanding, the use of component depreciation generally results in sizable tax benefits. (See Chapter 5 for a detailed discussion of depreciation methods.)

**Investment Credit.** The same aggressive tax planning techniques apply to claiming investment credits. A careful analysis of acquisitions, plant construction, and equipment can yield additional investment credit property. However, in attempting to maximize investment credit and depreciation, tax planners should be aware that using shorter depreciable lives may reduce the amount of investment credit they can claim.

**Capitalization Versus Expensing.** An aggressive position on the question of capitalization versus expensing of additional assets can also be beneficial. Many companies adopt an accounting method whereby additions of small items are expensed rather than capitalized and depreciated. The extent to which they may expense these items depends on the amount and type of the company's normal capital acquisitions. If most of the items purchased are of small dollar value, the IRS will probably object to this accounting method. However, in companies where the quantity of such items is small compared to most of the capital assets acquired, the IRS would probably not object.

**Vacation Payroll.** A significant tax benefit can also be achieved by changing the method of deducting vacation payroll. A number of companies deduct vacation payroll as it is paid to the employees. However, most vacation pay is vested. In other words, if an employee leaves before the vacation is taken, the unused vacation pay is generally paid to the employee. Since this is a fixed liability, the company can deduct the vested portion of the vacation pay when the liability arises. In the year that the change is made, a double deduction can be claimed—the vacation pay actually paid in the year plus the accrued portion. Permission is required to change to this method and must be requested within 180 days of the beginning of the year of change. A new accounting rule requires companies to use the accrual method for financial statement purposes. Unless the tax method is similar, there will be an unfavorable tax effect.

### Tax Strategies in the Investment of Company Funds

The controller should have a voice in the investment strategy of the company. A company with surplus funds has several alternative investment vehicles. (See Chapter 25 for a detailed discussion of surplus fund investment.) However, the tax effect on the income earned by these investments varies widely, and these tax effects can change the rate of return. Interest-bearing obligations such as corporate bonds, certificates of deposit, and treasury bills are taxable at regular rates for federal and (except for treasury bills) state tax purposes. Tax-exempt obligations are not taxable for federal purposes and may be tax-exempt for state purposes as well. Even though the interest rate on tax-exempt securities is lower than on taxable interest-bearing securities, their net after-tax return may be greater, depending on the interest rates being paid and the company's tax bracket.

Dividend-paying stocks are tax shelters for corporations. All corporations receive an 85 percent dividend-received deduction. Assuming a 50 percent tax rate, the effective tax on dividend income is 7.5 percent. This makes high-yield dividend-paying stocks very attractive investment vehicles for corporations. An investment portfolio can also be used as collateral for loans and thereby reduce the effective cost of borrowing money. With dividends taxed at 7.5 percent and interest deductible at a rate of 50 percent, the leverage is significant.

A word of caution: an aggressive investment program can bring privately held companies and relatively closely held public companies under IRS scrutiny with regard to the *accumulated earnings tax*. This tax (in addition to the regular income tax) is assessed on funds that are intentionally retained in the corporation to avoid paying dividends to shareholders. The ability to invest excess funds in marketable securities indicates to examining agents that funds are being accumulated that could possibly be paid out as dividends.

### Tax Implications of Foreign Transactions

For effective tax planning, the controller should be aware of the tax implications of foreign transactions. Companies operating internationally have significant opportunities for successful and creative tax planning. They can use a Domestic International Sales Corporation (DISC), foreign corporations, and tax-haven corporations to reduce their effective tax rates. This is one area in which many companies use outside accountants and/or legal counsel to good advantage.

### Year-End Tax Planning

It is important that tax planning be done on a systematic basis. Year-end tax planning should be required in all companies and should take place at least two months prior to year-end. At that time, the controller should meet with outside consultants and other concerned corporate personnel.

The actual operating results of the company to date should be reviewed to determine the estimated taxable income for the year. This data should be compared to

| LINE NO. | | (1) SALES 6000 | (2) COST OF GOODS SOLD 6100 | (3) SELLING EXPENSES 6200 | (4) ADMIN. EXPENSES 6300 | (5) OTHER INCOME 6500 | (6) OTHER DEDUCTIONS 6600 | (7) OTHER | (8) TOTAL | (9) INDEX | (10)(11) SCHEDULE M-1 DESCRIPTION | (12) AMOUNT | (13) TAX RETURN |
|---|---|---|---|---|---|---|---|---|---|---|---|---|---|
| 1 | Net Sales | | | | | | | | | | | | |
| | Opening inventory | | | | | | | | | | | | |
| | Purchases | | | | | | | | | | | | |
| | Salaries and wages | | | | | | | | | | | | |
| | Other costs | | | | | | | | | | | | |
| | Subtotal | | | | | | | | | | | | |
| | Ending inventory | | | | | | | | | | | | |
| 2 | Cost of goods sold | | | | | | | | | | | | |
| 3 | Gross profit | | | | | | | | | | | | |
| 4 | Dividends | | | | | | | | | | | | |
| 5 | U. S. interest | | | | | | | | | | | | |
| 6 | Other interest | | | | | | | | | | | | |
| 7 | Rent | | | | | | | | | | | | |
| 9 | Net gains (losses) | | | | | | | | | | | | |
| 10 | Other income | | | | | | | | | | | | |
| 11 | Total income | | | | | | | | | | | | |
| 12 | Comp. of officers | | | | | | | | | | | | |
| 13 | Salaries and wages | | | | | | | | | | | | |
| 14 | Repairs | | | | | | | | | | | | |
| 15 | Bad debts | | | | | | | | | | | | |
| 16 | Rents | | | | | | | | | | | | |
| 17 | Taxes | | | | | | | | | | | | |
| 18 | Interest | | | | | | | | | | | | |
| 19 | Contributions | | | | | | | | | | | | |
| 21 | Amortization | | | | | | | | | | | | |
| 22 | Depreciation | | | | | | | | | | | | |
| 24 | Advertising | | | | | | | | | | | | |
| 25 | (a) Pension and P.S.T. | | | | | | | | | | | | |
| | (b) Other plans | | | | | | | | | | | | |
| 26 | Other deductions | | | | | | | | | | | | |
| 27 | Total deductions | | | | | | | | | | | | |
| | Totals per audit | | | | | | | | | Net Schedule M-1 adjustments | | | |
| | | | | | | | | | | Taxable Income (Cols. 12 & 13) | | | |
| | | | | | | | | | | Net book income before F.I.T. | | | |
| | | | | | | | | | | Federal income tax | | | |
| | | | | | | | | | | Dividends paid | | | |
| | | | | | | | | | | Retained earnings - beginning | | | |
| | | | | | | | | | | Retained earnings - ending | | | |

Form A-346

FIGURE 38.1  CORPORATE INCOME TAX RETURN PRIMARY GROUPING SHEET

the forecast of taxable income, with any significant differences reconciled. At the same time, participants should review any unusual transactions that occurred during the past year, in order to determine their tax impact as well as the need for any restructuring to achieve desired tax results. Many companies use a checklist to ensure that all significant problem areas are reviewed. (Appendix 38-1 is an example of such a checklist.) It is important for the group to rethink current tax strategies so as to achieve the lowest tax burden for the year. This planning conference should also act as the basis for next year's tax planning.

## TAX RETURNS AND TAX ACCRUALS

### Preparation

Tax returns and financial statement tax accruals are prepared either by the company or by the company's outside public accountants. Companies with in-house tax expertise or sophisticated accounting departments generally prepare both tax returns and tax accruals and have them reviewed by the outside public accounting firm. Companies that have less tax sophistication generally have their returns and accruals prepared by their accounting firm. These returns should be reviewed by the company's controller or other financial officers. No matter who prepares the return, ultimate responsibility for preparation and filing rests with management.

The use of *grouping sheets* (see Figure 38.1) is strongly recommended. These working papers provide an audit trail between the financial statement and the tax returns. In situations where the outside accounting firm prepares the tax return, the accounting department generally prepares the grouping sheets.

Formal tax-accrual grouping sheets (see Figure 38.2) should also be used. This worksheet is used to convert financial statement income before taxes into taxable income, and to calculate the accrual and expense that appears on the financial statements. Figures 38.3 through 38.5 provide backup data for the working paper shown in Figure 38.2 as well as disclosure information relating to tax expense that is required in reports to the SEC by a public company.

### Calculation of Accruals

There are two theories on the calculation of tax accruals. Some companies use exact calculations; others include an amount for disallowances within their provision. There are advantages and disadvantages to both methods. If exact calculations are used and subsequent disallowances are made that result in additional taxes, the effect will appear in the financial statements in the year the liability arises. Companies that use provisions for possible disallowances charge the assessment against that liability. However, this may indicate to an examining agent that questionable areas exist and may act as an incentive for them to find deductions to disallow.

**Timing for Review and Extension Requests**

If the tax returns are prepared by an outside accounting firm, the firm should transmit the returns to the company at least two weeks prior to the filing date. This is adequate time for the financial and executive officers to review the returns, sign them, and file them with the proper taxing authority. The same timing should apply to extensions. Very often companies prepare extension requests at the last moment and file them with the required tax payments. This is not to the company's benefit. Tax personnel must determine tax liabilities for an extension with the same care as they prepare tax returns, because the underpayment of tax on an extension can result in substantial tax penalties. For example, corporations are allowed to pay their tax liability in two installments—half on the normal due date and the rest three months later. In requesting a time extension (Form 7004) for a corporate tax return, half the year's tax liability must be paid. If a proper calculation isn't made and less than one half of the final liability is paid, the IRS will not allow the extension and the two-payment provision. The company will then be assessed interest and penalties for the late filing of the return and the late payment of the tax liability.

**Centralization of Controls**

Most companies with significant in-house tax expertise agree that control of the tax compliance function and policy making should be maintained at corporate headquarters. The corporate headquarters should administer the payment and filing of federal taxes. While it may be possible to decentralize to a degree and assign the responsibility for the filing of state and local taxes to the various subsidiary companies involved, control should be centralized as much as possible.

When centralization is practiced, administrative costs are reduced, and fewer tax personnel are needed. Information flows to other departments, and among tax department personnel, faster and more efficiently. One of the most effective ways to maintain centralized control is through the use of tax calendars. Also, tax returns should be continually reviewed by corporate tax personnel.

**Useful Aids and Techniques**

**Tax Calendars.** The tax calendar is used for advance notification of due dates for filing reports, making tax payments, filing appeals, and attending to other compliance functions. The tax calendar is arranged by months; an effective tax department usually operates with a two-month lead time. Tax calendars generally are card files, although loose-leaf sheets or computer print-outs are also used.

If cards (see Figure 38.6 for an example) are used, they should contain enough information to indicate to the controller what must be done, when it is to be done, what tax is involved, and who is responsible. The cards are usually filed by month. At the beginning of each month the cards are extracted from the file, and a list is made and distributed to tax personnel. As each return is filed, the date of filing is noted on the card and the card is refiled into the monthly file. If the due date of the

*General*

This workpaper is used to document changes in the deferred tax asset or credit balance for five years and to summarize the reconciliation of book to taxable income. A separate workpaper should be used for each type of deferred tax balance (Federal, State, Local, Foreign).

*Income Tax Reconciliation*

(A) **Earnings (Loss) per books should be entered net of other income taxes that may be deducted in computing taxable income. For example,** in the federal income tax reconciliation, earnings per books should be entered net of deductible state income taxes.

(B) Each difference between earnings (loss) per books and taxable income must be identified as either a permanent difference or a timing difference. Permanent differences (AC Section 4091.32) arise from statutory provisions under which certain revenues are exempt from taxation or certain expenses are not deductible in determining taxable income. Since permanent differences will not reverse in subsequent years, no deferred taxes are provided. Although certain differences are easily identified as permanent (i.e., interest received on municipal obligations), it is often difficult to distinguish between permanent and timing differences. APB Opinion Nos. 23 and 24 (AC Sections 4095 and 4096) provide guidance in several special areas. FASB Interpretation No. 22 (AC Section No. 4091-1) restricted the indefinite reversal criteria set forth in APB Opinion No. 23 to the transactions specifically mentioned in APB Opinion No. 23. Therefore, it is not acceptable to use the indefinite reversal criteria as justification for treating other timing differences—even those not expected to reverse until some indefinite future period—as permanent differences.

(C) **The timing differences listed in the** income tax reconciliation should correspond to those comprising the deferred tax balance on the bottom portion of this workpaper. The deferred tax effect of each timing difference should be entered on the bottom portion of this workpaper. In general, the deferred tax effect of a timing difference should be measured by the difference between income taxes computed with and without inclusion of the transaction creating the difference between taxable income and pretax accounting income (AC Section 4091.35). However, if tax carryforwards arise, this computation may be different and Form 1-262 (Fig. 38.3) should be used for guidance. Furthermore, if there is more than one timing difference in a period when there are earnings per books and a taxable loss, it is necessary to establish the order in which the timing differences are included in the "with and without" computation. Since the timing differences reverse in different periods, the order affects the deferred taxes computed in the future and, accordingly, such order should be documented and followed consistently.

If the gross change method is used,

each timing difference must be identified as either originating or reversing in the column headed "O/R." Under both the net change and gross change methods, the deferred tax effect of originating differences should be computed in accordance with tax rates currently in effect. Under the gross change method the deferred tax effect of reversing differences is computed using tax rates in effect when the timing differences originated (AC Section U4091.065). If the timing difference originated over several years, the deferred tax effect of reversing differences may be computed using either the first-in, first-out or average rate assumptions (AC Section U4091.066 and .067). Under the net change method, the deferred tax amortization of net reversing differences should be computed using tax rates currently in effect (AC Section 4091.068). However, under both methods, the deferred tax amortization of reversing differences may not exceed the amounts previously provided.

(D) Net operating loss (NOL) carryforwards used should ordinarily agree to the amounts entered on tax returns. If a net operating loss carryforward is used it may be necessary to adjust the deferred tax balance as explained in the instructions to Form 1-262 (Fig. 38.3). **As explained in the** instructions to Form 1-263 (Fig. 38.4), the tax benefit resulting from the realization of a carryforward of a prior period net operating loss is usually reported in the financial statements as an extraordinary item.

(E) In the federal tax reconciliation, the taxable income (loss) should agree to the amount entered on line 30 of U.S. Form 1120.

(F) Enter the tax effect and the year-end deferred tax balance pertaining to each type of timing difference. It is necessary to complete the income tax reconciliation on the top of this workpaper before the annual deferred tax entry can be determined. If the gross change method (AC Section U4091.057 to .060) is used, each originating and reversing timing difference should be listed separately. However, if the net change method (AC Section U4091.057 to .060) is used, originating and reversing amounts of similar types of timing differences may be grouped together. For example, under the net change method, all timing differences between accounting depreciation and tax depreciation may be grouped together even though these differences pertain to different types of assets acquired in different years.

(G) If tax carryforwards arise, it may be necessary to adjust the deferred tax balance. Tax carryforwards and related deferred tax adjustments should be documented on Form 1-262 (Fig. 38.3). The most common tax carryforwards are net operating losses, unused investment tax credits, contributions, capital losses, and foreign tax credits.

(H) Any other adjustments to the deferred tax balance should be explained on a separate workpaper.

**FIGURE 38.2 INSTRUCTIONS**

INCOME TAX RECONCILIATION

DEFERRED TAX BALANCE

Reference

(A) Earnings (loss) per books

(B) Permanent differences
1.
2.
3.
4.

(C) Timing differences
1.
2.
3.
4.
5.
6.
7.
8.
9.
10.
Taxable income before NOL carryforward
NOL carryforwards used

(D)

(E) Taxable income (loss)

(F) Effect of Timing Differences
1.
2.
3.
4.
5.
6.
7.
8.
9.
10.

(G) Adjustments
Due to carryforwards

(H) Other
Balance

Column headings (Income Tax Reconciliation): WP | O/R | 19__ | WP | O/R | 19__ | WP | O/R | 19__ | WP | O/R | 19__

Column headings (Deferred Tax Balance): Balance Dr (Cr) / 19__ | Deferred Tax Dr (Cr) / 19__ | Balance Dr (Cr) / 19__ | Deferred Tax Dr (Cr) / 19__ | Balance Dr (Cr) / 19__ | Deferred Tax Dr (Cr) / 19__ | Balance Dr (Cr) / 19__ | Deferred Tax Dr (Cr) / 19__ | Balance Dr (Cr) / 19__

FIGURE 38.2   PERMANENT FILE—DEFERRED TAX WORKPAPER

*General*

This workpaper is used to document changes in the tax carryforwards for five years and to assist in computing any related adjustments to the deferred tax balance. A separate workpaper should be used for each tax jurisdiction (Federal, State, Local, Foreign) in which there are carryforwards.

*Tax Carryforwards*

(A) Enter the carryforward arising, carryforward realized, carryforward expired, and year-end carryforward balance for each type of tax carryforward. Applicable income tax laws, many of which seem to change frequently, provide information concerning the availability, use, and expiration of tax carryforwards. The instructions to the bottom section of this workpaper should be reviewed to determine if these carryforwards require any adjustments to the deferred tax balance.

*Deferred Tax Adjustments*

(B) Where timing differences exist, the amount of carryforwards available for accounting purposes will differ from the amount of carryforwards available for tax purposes. In such cases, supporting documentation should include the differences between book and tax amounts. When the tax benefits of carryforwards are later realized, consideration should be given to the necessity of adjusting the deferred tax accounts for the tax effects of timing differences that were not previously recorded.

(C) Refunds of prior year taxes resulting from carryback of a tax loss should be recognized in the loss year and the deferred tax effects of any timing differences should be recorded in the normal manner as explained in instruction F to Form 1-261 (AC Section 4091.43). It is necessary to eliminate existing deferred tax charges that arose during the carryback period, when a carryback refund is later realzed. If the loss results in a carryforward, however, the tax benefit of the carryforward is usually not recognized until it is actually realized. However, the tax benefit of a loss carryforward may be recognized in the loss year in the unusual case where realization is "assured beyond any reasonable doubt." AC Section 4091.44 to .46 and U4091.83 to .87 discuss criteria for determining whether the tax benefit of a loss carryforward is "assured beyond any reasonable doubt." In the usual case where the tax benefit of the loss carryforward is not recognized in the loss year, the tax benefit resulting from subsequent realization is reported as an extraordinary item in the financial statements (Form 1-263). Furthermore, when the tax benefit of the loss carryforward is not recognized in the loss year, it may not be appropriate to record deferred taxes on timing differences during the loss year and adjustments to the existing deferred tax balances may be necessary, as follows:

- If there are net deferred tax credits, they should be eliminated to the extent of the lower of (a) the tax effect of the loss carryforward or (b) the amortization of the net deferred tax credits that would otherwise have occurred during the carryforward period. To the extent that the loss carryforwards are subsequently realized, the amounts eliminated (which would not have already reversed) should be reinstated at the tax rates then in effect (AC Section 4091.47 and U4091.092).

- If there are net deferred tax charges and realization of the tax loss carryforward is not "assured beyond any reasonable doubt," it may also not be appropriate to continue to carry the remaining net deferred charges as an asset. In these situations, the remaining net deferred tax charges should be evaluated as to realizability in the same manner as are other assets (AC Section U4091.095). If they are not considered realizable, the remaining net deferred tax charges should be eliminated by a charge to expense.

(D) If investment tax credits arising in the current year are carried back to prior years, the tax benefit of the carryback should be recognized as a reduction of current year tax expense. Unused investment tax credits arising in the current year or carried forward from a prior period should be recognized as deferred tax adjustments to the extent the benefit would have been realized if taxes payable had been based on pretax accounting income, as adjusted for permanent differences. If deferred tax accounts exist when unused investment tax credits arise, deferred tax adjustments may be required, as follows:

- If there are net deferred tax credits, they should be eliminated at the lower of (a) the amount of the carryforward benefit or (b) the amount of the deferred tax credits reversing during the carryforward period, disregarding any timing differences that may originate during the carryforward period. To the extent that these unused investment tax credit carryforwards are subsequently realized, deferred taxes eliminated, net of amounts that would otherwise have reversed, should be reinstated at the tax rates then in effect (AC Section U4091.110 and .111).

- If there are net deferred tax charges, it may not be appropriate to continue carrying the remaining net deferred tax charges as an asset. In these situations, the remaining net deferred tax charges should be evaluated as to realizability in the same manner as other assets. If they are not considered realizable, the remaining net deferred tax charges should be eliminated by a charge to expense (AC Section U4091.112).

(E) Other unused tax credits and deductions are treated in the same manner as net operating losses (AC Section 4091.52).

(F) The total deferred tax adjustments resulting from carryforwards are entered on Form 1-261 (Fig. 38.2).

**FIGURE 38.3   INSTRUCTIONS**

TAX CARRYFORWARDS (A)*

| Year | Workpapers | Net Operating Loss | Invest-ment Tax Credit | Contri-bution | Capital Loss | Foreign Tax Credit | Other |
|---|---|---|---|---|---|---|---|
| Balance / 19___ | | | | | | | |
| Carryforward Arising | | | | | | | |
| Realized | | | | | | | |
| Expired | | | | | | | |
| Balance / 19___ | | | | | | | |
| Carryforward Arising | | | | | | | |
| Realized | | | | | | | |
| Expired | | | | | | | |
| Balance / 19___ | | | | | | | |
| Carryforward Arising | | | | | | | |
| Realized | | | | | | | |
| Expired | | | | | | | |
| Balance / 19___ | | | | | | | |
| Carryforward Arising | | | | | | | |
| Realized | | | | | | | |
| Expired | | | | | | | |
| Balance / 19___ | | | | | | | |
| Carryforward Arising | | | | | | | |
| Realized | | | | | | | |
| Expired | | | | | | | |
| Balance / 19___ | | | | | | | |

DEFERRED TAX ADJUSTMENTS (B)*

| Year | Reference * Workpaper | (C) Net Operating Loss | (D) Invest-ment Tax Credit | (E) Contri-bution | (E) Capital Loss | (E) Foreign Tax Credit | (E) Other | (F) Total Adjustment |
|---|---|---|---|---|---|---|---|---|
| 19___ | | | | | | | | |
| 19___ | | | | | | | | |
| 19___ | | | | | | | | |
| 19___ | | | | | | | | |
| 19___ | | | | | | | | |

FIGURE 38.3  PERMANENT FILE—TAX CARRY FORWARDS

*General*

This workpaper is used to summarize the (1) components of the current year income tax provision and (2) balance sheet classification of the deferred tax accounts. Totals from this workpaper should agree to lead schedules. See Instruction G for information that may require financial statement disclosure.

*Earnings Statement Summary*

(A) The blank line should be used for foreign taxes if any, or to segregate the effects of tax credits (i.e., investment tax credits) if such segregation is deemed desirable.

(B) Enter taxes estimated to be payable for the current year or, if applicable, the refund of prior year(s) taxes resulting from carryback of net operating losses and other items.
The total current tax expense/(benefit) must be allocated between (a) income/(loss) from continuing operations before extraordinary items, (2) gain/(loss) from discontinued operations, (3) extraordinary items, and (4) other items reported separately—principally direct entires to stockholders' equity accounts and the cumulative effect of changes in accounting principles. If there are no discontinued operations, extraordinary items, or other items reported separately, the entire current tax expense/(benefit) is allocated to income/(loss) from continuing operations before extraordinary items. However, if any of these items exist, the current tax expense/(benefit) allocated to continuing operations is the amount that would have been determined by excluding from pretax accounting income/(loss) all transactions that are reported separately. The difference between the total current tax expense/(benefit) and the amount allocated to income/(loss) from continuing operations before extraordinary items is then allocated to each item reported separately (AC Section U4091.115 to .118).

(C) Enter the deferred tax expense/(benefit) resulting from timing differences, tax carryforward adjustments, and other adjustments. These amounts are obtained from the separate Form 1-262 (Fig. 38.2) for deferred federal, state, local, and foreign income taxes. The components of the deferred tax expense/(benefit) should be allocated between income/(loss) from continuing operations before extraordinary items and each discontinued operation, extraordinary item, and other separately reported item.

(D) When a net operating loss carryforward that was not recognized in the loss year is subsequently realized, the tax benefit is reported as an extraordinary item (AC Section 4091.60). However, the amount reported as an

extraordinary item is reduced to the extent of net deferred tax credits that must be reinstated (AC Section U4091.092). Net deferred tax credits eliminated during the year the loss carryforward arose, as well as credits related to originating timing differences not recognized during the loss year, should be reinstated (net of amounts that would otherwise have reversed) at the tax rates in effect when the loss carryforward is realized.

*Balance Sheet Classification of Deferred Tax Accounts*

(E) Components of the deferred tax balance should be presented on the balance sheet in two categories—one for net current amounts and the other for net noncurrent amounts. The deferred tax credit or charge related to each timing difference listed on Form 1-261 (Fig. 38.2) should be allocated between current and non-current based on the classification of the asset of liability causing the timing difference (AC Section U4091. 125). If the assets and liabilities causing a specific timing difference are classified as both current and noncurrent (i.e., installment receivables), the net deferred tax credit or charge should be allocated between current and noncurrent in the same proportion as the underlying assets or liabilities.

(F) If the tax benefit is recognized as an offset to deferred tax credits, such benefit should be allocated between current and noncurrent deferred taxes in proportion to net current and net noncurrent deferred tax balances.

*Disclosure*

(G) The following information should be disclosed (AC Section U4091.127):
  • Amounts of any operating loss carryforwards not recognized in the loss period, together with expiration dates. Amounts that, upon realization of the operating loss, would be credited (reinstated) to deferred tax accounts must also be disclosed.
  • Significant amounts of any other unused deductions or credits, together with expiration dates.
  • Reasons for significant variations in the customary relationships between income tax expense and pretax accounting income, if they are not otherwise apparent from the financial statements or from the nature of the business.
In addition, it is recommended that the nature of significant differences between pretax accounting income and taxable income be disclosed (AC Section 4091.62). Further, the SEC requires additional disclosures for registered companies. The information required for the SEC income tax disclosures can be accumulated on Form 1-264 (Fig. 38.5).

**FIGURE 38.4   INSTRUCTIONS**

STATEMENT OF EARNINGS SUMMARY

| *Reference | Workpapers | Operations | Dis-continued Operations | Extra-ordinary Item(s) | Other | Total |
|---|---|---|---|---|---|---|
| (A) | | | | | | |
| (B) Current Tax Expense/(Benefit) | | | | | | |
| Federal | | | | | | |
| State and Local | | | | | | |
| (describe) | | | | | | |
| Total current | | | | | | |
| (C) Deferred Tax Expense/(Benefit) | | | | | | |
| Effect of timing differences | | | | | | |
| Federal | | | | | | |
| State and Local | | | | | | |
| (describe) | | | | | | |
| Tax carryforward adjustments | | | | | | |
| Federal | | | | | | |
| State and Local | | | | | | |
| (describe) | | | | | | |
| Other adjustments | | | | | | |
| Federal | | | | | | |
| State and Local | | | | | | |
| (describe) | | | | | | |
| Total deferred | | | | | | |
| (D) Extraordinary tax benefit resulting from carryforward of prior year(s) operating loss | | | | | | |

BALANCE SHEET CLASSIFICATION OF DEFERRED TAX ACCOUNTS

| *Reference | | FEDERAL Current Dr (Cr) | FEDERAL Noncurrent Dr (Cr) |
|---|---|---|---|
| (E) | Timing Differences | | |
| | 1. | | |
| | 2. | | |
| | 3. | | |
| | 4. | | |
| | 5. | | |
| | 6. | | |
| | 7. | | |
| | 8. | | |
| | 9. | | |
| | 10. | | |
| (F) | Tax carryforward adjustments | | |
| | Other adjustments | | |
| | Total | | |

| *Reference | | OTHER Current Dr (Cr) | OTHER Noncurrent Dr (Cr) |
|---|---|---|---|
| (E) | Timing Differences | | |
| | 1. | | |
| | 2. | | |
| | 3. | | |
| | 4. | | |
| | 5. | | |
| | 6. | | |
| | 7. | | |
| | 8. | | |
| | 9. | | |
| | 10. | | |
| (F) | Tax carryforward adjustments | | |
| | Other adjustments | | |
| | Total | | |
| | Total Deferred Tax Balances | | |

**FIGURE 38.4   INCOME TAX SUMMARY**

### General

This workpaper is used to accumulate income tax information that must be disclosed by companies registered with the SEC (Regulation S-X, Rule 4.08(g). Registrants must disclose this information in addition to the required general disclosures (AC Section 4091.62) which are summarized in Instruction G to Form 1-263 (Fig. 38.4). Information needed to complete this workpaper is obtained from Form 1-261 (Fig. 38.2) and Form 1-263 (Fig. 38.4).

### Income Tax Expense/(Benefit)

(A) Summarize the current and deferred income tax expense/(benefit) applicable to Federal, State, Local, and Foreign income taxes. If State and Local or Foreign income taxes are less than 5% of the total current and total deferred tax expense/(benefit), such amounts need not be separately disclosed but may be combined and identified as other.

### Deferred Tax Expense/(Benefit)

(B) Summarize the components of the deferred tax expense/(benefit). The total from this summary should agree to the total deferred tax expense/(benefit) entered above (see Instruction A). Each timing difference or tax carryforward adjustment from Form 1-261 (Fig. 38.2) that has a deferred tax effect in either the current or prior year in excess of 5% of the amount computed by multiplying the pretax accounting income/(loss) by the applicable statutory tax rate should be listed as a separate component on this summary. Timing differences less than 5% of such amount may be combined and identified as other.

### Reconciliation to Statutory Tax Expense/(Benefit)

(C) Reconciliation of the actual tax expense/(benefit) to the amount computed by multiplying the pretax accounting income/(loss) by the applicable statutory tax rate. For U.S. companies, the Federal income tax rate should be used as the statutory rate. For Foreign registrants, the income tax rate in the entity's country of domicile should be used as the statutory rate. If a statutory rate other than the Federal rate is used, the statutory rate used and basis for such rate should be disclosed.

(D) Individual items comprising the difference between the statutory tax expense/(benefit) and the actual tax expense/(benefit) should be listed if they exceed 5% of the statutory tax expense/(benefit). Items amounting to less than 5% of the statutory tax expense/(benefit) may be combined and identified as other. However, if no individual reconciling item amounts to more than 5% of the statutory tax expense/(benefit) and the total difference to be reconciled is less than 5%, no reconciliation need be provided unless such information would be significant in appraising the trend of earnings. The reconciliation may be presented in dollar amounts, percentages, or both dollar amounts and percentages. If percentages are presented, all amounts should be stated as a percentage of pretax accounting income/(loss).

(E) Actual tax expense/(benefit) should agree to the total current and deferred taxes presented in the income tax summary on the top left section of this workpaper (see Instruction A).

### Other

(F) If cash outlays for income taxes in any of the three succeeding years are expected to substantially exceed income tax expense for such years, disclosure is required of the approximate amount of such excess year(s), and reason(s) for the excess.

FIGURE 38.5  INSTRUCTIONS

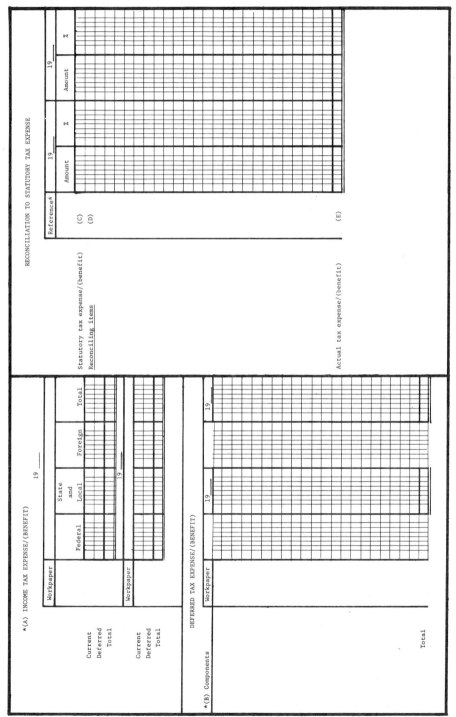

FIGURE 38.5   PUBLIC COMPANY INCOME TAX FOOTNOTE DISCLOSURE

tax return is extended, the card is marked and placed under that monthly tab. The card acts as a permanent record of mailing dates. Cards of different colors should be used—one color for federal returns, others for the various state and local tax returns.

Some companies use loose-leaf calendars that list all the tax returns to be filed for a single day or for a single month.

**Ticker Files.** Most tax calendars are used for recurring items. However, throughout the year there are several nonrecurring projects and filings that must be handled. These can be kept track of by the use of a tickler file. This tickler file is kept on a monthly basis. At the beginning of the month the cards (see Figure 38.7 for an example) are distributed to the proper individuals. Control over these cards is maintained by duplicate copies or a listing. When the work has been performed and indicated on the card, the card is destroyed.

**Tax Manuals.** Two types of loose-leaf tax manuals should be permanently maintained. The first manual should be broken down by companies (or divisions, if applicable) and should indicate all the tax returns to be filed by each company and their due dates. The second manual consists of technical information on the different taxes for which the company is responsible. Generally, separate sheets are utilized for each type of tax. This type of tax manual includes the following topics:

- Name of tax;
- Nature of tax;
- Taxable and nontaxable items;
- Exemptions;
- Basis and rate of tax;
- Collection of tax;
- Methods of obtaining refunds and statute of limitations;
- Penalties;
- Sources of information; and
- Methods of paying tax.

The manual may be arranged to suit the needs of the company. Federal tax information may be placed in front, with information on various state and local taxes placed alphabetically behind it. Or, in corporate groups or divisional groups, the information may be kept by various companies or divisions.

It is important that these tax manuals be kept current. This is a difficult job because of the ever-changing nature of taxes, but one that must not be overlooked.

**Tax Services.** Due to the complexity of the various taxing systems, companies should consider subscribing to a loose-leaf tax service published by one of the major tax publication companies. These services, which are available for all federal, state, and local taxes, cover the law, regulations, rulings, and court decisions applicable to each tax. In addition, they offer explanations written by the editorial staff of the

| Code No. | COMPANY | RETURN | FYE MO. | DUE DATE | PTR NO. |
|---|---|---|---|---|---|
| MAIL TO: | | | | | No of Copies |

| DATE | | PERSON RESPONSIBLE | DATE | | PERSON RESPONSIBLE |
|---|---|---|---|---|---|
| REVIEW | MAILED | PAID | | REVIEW | MAILED | PAID | |

FIGURE 38.6 SAMPLE CARD FOR A TAX CALENDAR FILE

publication on various aspects of taxation. The type and complexity of loose-leaf service used depend on the sophistication of the company's tax personnel and its use of outside consultants.

**Tax Filing Systems.** Separate files should be maintained for tax returns, research projects, tax memorandums, and tax correspondence. Each file should be designated by a code number and entered on a master card file.

All tax returns should be placed in files designated with a "T" number on the filing card. Each year's returns for each company should be filed separately. Separate files should be maintained for federal, state, and local tax returns. A corporate return file should include the following information:

- Tax return grouping sheets;
- Tax working papers;
- Tax department review notes;
- A copy of the complete return;
- Copies of estimated tax calculations; and
- Copies of extension requests and related filing instructions.

Alphabetical *general tax files* should be established in the tax department for each company. They should contain copies of both internal and external tax correspondence. The files should be assigned a code number (with "GTF") and be entered on the card file. If a tax research project or revenue agent's examination is expected to generate a large file, a special file designated "S" should be established. All documentation related to the specific project should be placed within this file.

It is also useful to maintain master files of blank federal and state tax forms for each year. In addition to the forms, copies of the instruction booklets for all returns for each of the years should also be filed.

| |
|---|
| Follow-up date _____ |
| Company _____ |
| This card prepared by _____ |
| Action required |
| |
| |
| |
| Action required by _____ |
| Deadline _____ |

FIGURE 38.7 SAMPLE CARD FOR A TICKLER FILE

### Training Personnel

Selected persons should be trained in taxation. The level of training will depend on the company's tax requirements and the sophistication of its staff. Training can be achieved through various means. If the company uses the services of a large certified public accounting firm, the firm's own training programs may be open to client personnel. In addition, there are many private and professional organizations that offer training programs. It is important that tax personnel keep up to date on new tax laws, regulations, and techniques.

## HANDLING TAX EXAMINATIONS

A company benefits when its tax personnel have continuing cordial relations with various tax authorities; membership in local organizations that maintain relations with both federal, state, and local tax authorities is a good idea. A friendly relationship with tax authorities offers a means of obtaining their viewpoints on current matters.

During the course of a tax examination, the examining agent should be treated as a professional. When the agent arrives on the premises, he should be greeted by the controller and introduced to the individual with whom he will be working. (This person differs with each company. In many companies the controller himself or a member of his staff will have that function. In others, it may be a member of the tax department, an outside accountant, or an attorney.) In those companies where the outside public accountant or attorney will be handling the examination, he should be available on the initial day to meet the agent. The agent and his principal contact with the company should discuss the limits of the examination and the procedures that will be followed.

In situations in which the examination is handled by a member of the controller's department or the company's tax staff, the outside accountant or attorney is brought into the discussions if it appears that an assessment will be made. This individual may meet with the examining agent or act as an adviser. It is important that there be a close working relationship between the controller and his outside consultant in these situations.

Before the initial contact with the agent, the controller and the outside consultants should review the tax return and significant problem areas. At this meeting, they should determine the strategy for handling the tax examination.

Agents require that powers of attorney be presented before they will discuss the examination with company personnel or outside consultants. The power of attorney should indicate that the company's chief financial officer or tax executive, a member of the outside accounting firm, and a member of the outside law firm are empowered to represent the company. In order to maintain control over the examination, only one individual should deal with the agent, and all questions and information submit-

Taxpayer

Address

City, Village or P.O.     State

Form no.     Taxable year

Date filed     District filed in

### NOTICE OF TAX EXAMINATION

Date first notified

By (Agent)

Division

Address

Phone     Ext.

Appt. made for:

    Hour _____

    Date _____

    At _____

Subsequent examination dates:

_____

_____

_____

_____

### WAIVERS SIGNED (FORM 872)

By client on _____

Statute extended to _____

Then re-extended again by
    taxpayer on _____

Until _____

### AGREEMENT FORM 870 EXECUTED

By taxpayer on _____

Delivered or mailed to dept. on

_____

Net income per return ............$_____

Net income as agreed to ........ _____

Net adjustment (see over) ....$_____

Additional tax ......................$_____

Negligence penalty ................ _____

Fraud penalty .........................  _____

Interest from _____

    To _____    $_____

Total due .............................$_____

### PROTEST RECORD

Protest filed on _____

Conference held on _____

With conferee _____

At _____

Case disposition as follows:

_____

Other notes:

_____

_____

FIGURE 38.8  TAX EXAMINATION DATA AND FOLLOW-UP SHEET

AGENTS' REPORT DATE_____RECEIVED ON _____

EXPLANATION OF CHANGES IN NET INCOME BY THE UNITED STATES TREASURY DEPT.

UNALLOWABLE DEDUCTIONS AND ADDITIONAL INCOME

ITEM

| | | |
|---|---|---|
| | | |
| | | |
| | | |
| | | |
| | | |
| TOTAL | $ | |

NON-TAXABLE INCOME AND ADDITIONAL DEDUCTIONS

ITEM

| | | |
|---|---|---|
| | | |
| | | |
| | | |
| | | |
| TOTAL | $ | |
| NET ADDITIONAL INCOME | $ | |

| Journal entries to be put on books as at | Dr. | Cr. |
|---|---|---|
| | | |
| | | |
| | | |
| | | |
| | | |
| | | |

Changes reported to state _____     Refund claim to be filed

By letter on _____         For_____

By form no. _____        Notes:_____

   On _____

Additional state tax ...............$ _____

Penalties ...............................$ _____

FIGURE 38.8  CONTINUED

ted should be routed through him. This individual should maintain a record of questions asked by the agent, the answers given, and the information submitted.

The importance of giving accurate information to the agent can not be overemphasized. Incorrect, improper, or poorly prepared information always raises questions in the agent's mind as to its validity. It is also important to comply with the agent's request for information on a timely basis. Delayed compliance will also raise questions regarding the accuracy of the submitted information.

Once the agent has completed his examination, the controller should discuss the results with him. If any significant issues should arise, all decisions should be deferred until they can be discussed and reviewed with outside consultants and senior management. All concerned parties should then meet to determine whether or not to accept the agent's findings, the appeal procedures to be used, and any possible litigation. The agent should then be informed of the company's decision. When the company receives the agent's report, a summary should be prepared (Figure 38.8), submitted to all concerned parties, and properly filed.

## CONCLUSION

Good tax planning and careful tax return preparation should generally minimize disallowances of deductions and shorten the time required for the agent to complete his examination of the tax return. It is also helpful to have all necessary records available in an organized fashion so that information can be quickly provided. A display of organization and efficiency can go a long way toward impressing a tax agent that the company has filed a complete and accurate tax return.

## SUGGESTED READING

Bittker, Boris I. *Federal Taxation of Income, Estates and Gifts.* Boston: Warren, Gorham & Lamont, Inc., 1981.

Bittker, Boris I., and Eustice, James S. *Federal Income Taxation of Corporations and Shareholders.* Boston: Warren, Gorham & Lamont, Inc., 1979.

Cavitch, Zolman. *Tax Planning for Corporations and Shareholders.* New York: Matthew Bender & Co., Inc., 1974.

Fisher, David I., Shattuck, Carol H., and Walsh, Francis J. Jr. *Managing the Corporate Tax Function.* New York: The Conference Board, 1971.

# APPENDIX 38-1  CORPORATE TAX PLANNING CHECKLIST

|  | *Yes* | *No* | *N/A* |
|---|---|---|---|

## Cash

1. Consider exposure to the accumulated earnings penalty tax—levy can be avoided by

|  | Yes | No | N/A |
|---|---|---|---|
| • Proving cash is accumulated for business needs. | ☐ | ☐ | ☐ |
| • Electing Subchapter S status. | ☐ | ☐ | ☐ |
| • Dividends payments. | ☐ | ☐ | ☐ |
| 2. If inadequate cash is a problem, consider a sale leaseback. | ☐ | ☐ | ☐ |
| 3. Should consideration be given to making charitable contributions from appreciated property? | ☐ | ☐ | ☐ |
| 4. Are there any contested items that should be settled or paid this year in order to achieve deductibility? | ☐ | ☐ | ☐ |

## Accounts Receivable

| | Yes | No | N/A |
|---|---|---|---|
| 1. Consider switching to the installment reporting method for sales on time and consider selling receivables before the switch is made. | ☐ | ☐ | ☐ |
| 2. To increase bad debts deduction, | | | |
| • Change to reserve method. | ☐ | ☐ | ☐ |
| • Deduct partially worthless debts. | ☐ | ☐ | ☐ |
| 3. Companies deriving income from long-term contracts should consider switching to the completed contract method. | ☐ | ☐ | ☐ |
| 4. Check the interest on receivables between affiliated companies. | ☐ | ☐ | ☐ |
| 5. Formalize the stockholders' obligations to the corporation by a note with interest. | ☐ | ☐ | ☐ |
| 6. Should a bad debt reserve be set up for dealer reserves or for trade receivables sold with recourse? | ☐ | ☐ | ☐ |

## Inventories

| | Yes | No | N/A |
|---|---|---|---|
| 1. Switching from FIFO to LIFO minimizes taxable profit. | ☐ | ☐ | ☐ |
| 2. Is the corporation including in inventory overhead costs that should be charged to expense? | ☐ | ☐ | ☐ |

## Securities and Investments

| | Yes | No | N/A |
|---|---|---|---|
| 1. Can large capital gains be postponed until net operating losses have been fully utilized? | ☐ | ☐ | ☐ |

| | Yes | No | N/A |
|---|---|---|---|
| 2. Consider the following changes: | | | |
| • Switch to tax-exempt securities. | ☐ | ☐ | ☐ |
| • Switch to dividend-paying stock. | ☐ | ☐ | ☐ |
| • Switch to partially tax-free dividends. | ☐ | ☐ | ☐ |
| 3. Corporation's switch of securities at a loss can bring tax refund. | ☐ | ☐ | ☐ |
| 4. To avoid personal holding company tax, corporations should consider shifting investment or paying dividends. | ☐ | ☐ | ☐ |

**Property, Plant, and Equipment**

| | Yes | No | N/A |
|---|---|---|---|
| 1. In maximizing depreciation deduction for the client, consider | | | |
| • A rapid depreciation method. | ☐ | ☐ | ☐ |
| • Additional first-year depreciation deduction up to $2,000. | ☐ | ☐ | ☐ |
| • A short useful life under the class system. | ☐ | ☐ | ☐ |
| • Beginning depreciation before the property is acquired. | ☐ | ☐ | ☐ |
| • Ignoring salvage value in figuring depreciation. | ☐ | ☐ | ☐ |
| 2. The client may prefer regular, stable depreciation to rapid depreciation. | ☐ | ☐ | ☐ |
| 3. In utilizing the investment tax credit, be alert to the fact that | | | |
| • The investment tax credit reduces the true costs of equipment purchases. | ☐ | ☐ | ☐ |
| • Under the Revenue Act of 1978, the full credit is allowed for pollution-control facilities even when five-year amortization is elected. | ☐ | ☐ | ☐ |
| • The credit is available for qualified rehabilitation expenditures (depreciable rehabilitation costs incurred in connection with a building placed in service twenty years earlier) for all types of depreciable buildings except those used for residential purposes. | ☐ | ☐ | ☐ |
| • There is an additional 10 percent credit for investing in alternative energy property, specially defined energy property and equipment for recycling, producing shale oil, and natural gas from geopressured brine. | ☐ | ☐ | ☐ |
| 4. Certain long-lived items may be written off over a sixty-month period. | ☐ | ☐ | ☐ |
| 5. A lessee of equipment should negotiate for any valuable investment credit. | ☐ | ☐ | ☐ |
| 6. When the client is constructing a building, consider capitalizing taxes, interest, and carrying charges. | ☐ | ☐ | ☐ |
| 7. If the client plans to sell property, he should | | | |
| • Put off sale until he has held it more than a year. | ☐ | ☐ | ☐ |
| • Consider taking profits in one year and losses in another. | ☐ | ☐ | ☐ |

|  | Yes | No | N/A |
|---|---|---|---|

8. If a client plans to sell a building, he should
- Postpone sale until he has held it more than a year.  ☐ ☐ ☐
- Consider borrowing on it instead of selling it.  ☐ ☐ ☐
9. If the client plans to sell equipment on which he took an investment credit, further timing factors are involved.  ☐ ☐ ☐
10. Instead of selling property, consider trading it, tax-free.  ☐ ☐ ☐
11. Tax on property that was condemned, stolen, or destroyed is avoided by replacing it with like property.  ☐ ☐ ☐
12. "Loss" property should sometimes be abandoned instead of sold.  ☐ ☐ ☐

## Intangible Assets

1. Many intangible assets may be amortized.  ☐ ☐ ☐

## Accrued Liabilities

1. Bonus can be deducted this year though not determined or paid until next year.  ☐ ☐ ☐
2. Some accrual method companies should consider changing to a "vested" vacation plan.  ☐ ☐ ☐
3. Tax trap: payables to related persons.  ☐ ☐ ☐
4. Tax trap: Eliminating an old account payable.  ☐ ☐ ☐

## Deferred Income

1. Tax can be deferred on advance payments for goods and services.  ☐ ☐ ☐

## Notes and Bonds Payable

1. Consider tax incentives favoring debt over stock capitalization for corporation.  ☐ ☐ ☐
2. Formalize debt obligations to protect corporation's interest deduction.  ☐ ☐ ☐
3. Redistribution of debt or stock may be advisable.  ☐ ☐ ☐

## Dividends and Distributions

1. Time dividends to suit stockholders' tax convenience by
- Deferring tax.  ☐ ☐ ☐
- Avoiding bunched income.  ☐ ☐ ☐
- Offsetting losses.  ☐ ☐ ☐

| | Yes | No | N/A |
|---|---|---|---|
| 2. For a corporate stockholder, an operating loss may be desirable in a year in which large dividend will be received. | ☐ | ☐ | ☐ |
| 3. With a dividend in property, corporate assets can be passed through to the stockholders free of corporate tax; special tax favoritism applies to dividends to stockholder-corporations. | ☐ | ☐ | ☐ |
| 4. Tax trap: Converting retained earnings to stock dividends. | ☐ | ☐ | ☐ |
| 5. Protect stockholder's deduction for stock losses. | ☐ | ☐ | ☐ |
| 6. Consider electing tax-free corporate status under Subchapter S. | ☐ | ☐ | ☐ |

### Earnings and Profits

| | Yes | No | N/A |
|---|---|---|---|
| 1. Are all IRS adjustments accurately reflected in the corporate books? | ☐ | ☐ | ☐ |
| 2. Are any tax years presently under audit by IRS? | ☐ | ☐ | ☐ |
| 3. Are any refund claims presently pending before IRS? | ☐ | ☐ | ☐ |
| 4. If any tax deficiencies have been paid within the past two years, consider filing protective refund claims. | ☐ | ☐ | ☐ |

### Employee Benefits

| | Yes | No | N/A |
|---|---|---|---|
| 1. Should the corporation | | | |
| • Adopt a pension or profit-sharing plan? | ☐ | ☐ | ☐ |
| • Revise an existing pension or profit-sharing plan? | ☐ | ☐ | ☐ |
| • Consider group life insurance? | ☐ | ☐ | ☐ |
| • Consider health and accident insurance? | ☐ | ☐ | ☐ |
| • Consider a medical-reimbursement plan? | ☐ | ☐ | ☐ |
| • Consider disability benefits? | ☐ | ☐ | ☐ |
| • Adopt a sick-pay plan? | ☐ | ☐ | ☐ |
| • Pay death benefits? | ☐ | ☐ | ☐ |
| • Defer compensation? | ☐ | ☐ | ☐ |
| • Consider stock options? | ☐ | ☐ | ☐ |
| • Consider split-dollar insurance? | ☐ | ☐ | ☐ |
| • Consider changes in officer compensation? | ☐ | ☐ | ☐ |
| 2. Should a change in the accrual method of accounting for nonvested vacation pay be considered? | ☐ | ☐ | ☐ |

### Corporate Structure

| | Yes | No | N/A |
|---|---|---|---|
| 1. Is there a possibility of forming one or more subsidiaries? | ☐ | ☐ | ☐ |
| 2. Consider splitting up the corporation into two entities by | | | |
| • A transfer of assets. | ☐ | ☐ | ☐ |

|  | Yes | No | N/A |
|---|---|---|---|
| • A transfer of business function. | ☐ | ☐ | ☐ |
| • A transfer of a separate branch or location. | ☐ | ☐ | ☐ |
| 3. Are there any related loss companies with which the company could be merged? | ☐ | ☐ | ☐ |
| 4. Consider spinning off a separate business within the corporation under I.R.C. § 355. | ☐ | ☐ | ☐ |
| 5. If the acquisition of a corporate business is contemplated, has consideration been given to | | | |
| • Retaining the tax basis of the assets acquired? | ☐ | ☐ | ☐ |
| • A stepup basis for the assets acquired? | ☐ | ☐ | ☐ |
| • Retaining any tax benefits enjoyed by the acquired corporation, such as net operating losses, deficit in retained earnings, etc.? | ☐ | ☐ | ☐ |
| 6. Consider forming an affiliated group by contributing stock of related companies to | | | |
| • Use losses of related companies. | ☐ | ☐ | ☐ |
| • Facilitate the future liquidation of collapsible corporations. | ☐ | ☐ | ☐ |
| • Supply capital for a related company. | ☐ | ☐ | ☐ |
| • Solve an unreasonable accumulations problem through intercompany dividends. | ☐ | ☐ | ☐ |

## Record Keeping and Retention

| | Yes | No | N/A |
|---|---|---|---|
| 1. Do the corporation's records of travel and entertainment expenses provide sufficient substantiation to comply with the Internal Revenue Code and Treasury regulations? | ☐ | ☐ | ☐ |
| 2. If there is an EDP installation, does the corporation meet the record-retention requirements established by IRS for punched cards, magnetic tapes, disks, etc.? | ☐ | ☐ | ☐ |
| 3. Have the corporation's EDP record-retention policies been evaluated by IRS, and if so, has a written agreement as to their adequacy been entered into with IRS? | ☐ | ☐ | ☐ |
| 4. Is the company considering adoption of a microfilm system for its summary records, for which permission must be obtained from IRS? | ☐ | ☐ | ☐ |

## General

| | Yes | No | N/A |
|---|---|---|---|
| 1. Should the form of organization be changed by | | | |
| • Adding a new corporation? | ☐ | ☐ | ☐ |
| • Reducing the number of corporations? | ☐ | ☐ | ☐ |
| • Forming one or more joint ventures? | ☐ | ☐ | ☐ |

2. Should the corporation change its accounting period?    □    □    □

3. Consider the following changes in accounting method or accounting elections:

- Change overall method.    □    □    □
- Change from completed contract to percentage of completion.    □    □    □
- Amortize organizational expenses.    □    □    □
- Capitalize taxes and carrying charges.    □    □    □
- Elect to treat research-and-development expenditures as deferred expense or treat as a current deduction.    □    □    □
- Elect or terminate Subchapter S status.    □    □    □

# 39

# State and Local Taxes— Planning and Control

*Gary Dudley*

*Michael F. Klein*

## THE CONTROLLER'S ROLE

The wide range of state income tax rates have a direct bearing on the after-tax profits and cash flow for a business enterprise (see Figure 39.1). The states are not consistent in their approach to taxation, and differences in state law require a detailed investigation of the applicable laws when analyzing various alternatives. The controller's role in planning multiple state operations, therefore, cannot be understated. He must have a thorough knowledge of the various states' income tax laws or employ outside accountants who have that information.

### MAXIMUM STATE CORPORATE INCOME TAX RATES, LISTED IN ALPHABETICAL ORDER (A)

| | *Maximum Tax Rate* | | | *Maximum Tax Rate* | |
|---|---|---|---|---|---|
| *Alabama | 5.0% | | Minnesota | 12.0% | |
| Alaska | 9.4 | (B) | Mississippi | 4.0 | (C) |
| *Arizona | 10.5 | (C) | *Missouri | 5.0 | |
| Arkansas | 6.0 | (C) | Montana | 6.75 | |
| California | 9.6 | | Nebraska | 4.675 | (C) |
| Colorado | 5.0 | | New Hampshire | 8.0 | |
| Connecticut | 10.0 | | New Jersey | 9.0 | |
| Delaware | 8.7 | | New Mexico | 5.0 | |
| Dist. of Columbia | 9.9 | (D) | New York | 10.0 | |
| Florida | 5.0 | | North Carolina | 6.0 | |
| Georgia | 6.0 | | *North Dakota | 8.5 | (C) |
| Hawaii | 6.435 | (C) | Ohio | 8.0 | (C) |
| Idaho | 6.5 | | Oklahoma | 4.0 | |
| Illinois | 6.85 | | Oregon | 7.5 | |
| Indiana | 6.0 | | Pennsylvania | 10.5 | |
| *Iowa | 10.0 | (C) | Rhode Island | 8.0 | |
| Kansas | 6.75 | (C) | South Carolina | 6.0 | |
| Kentucky | 6.0 | (C) | Tennessee | 6.0 | |
| *Louisiana | 8.0 | (C) | Utah | 4.0 | |
| Maine | 6.93 | (C) | Vermont | 7.5 | (C) |
| Maryland | 7.0 | | Virginia | 6.0 | |
| Massachusetts | 9.5 | (E) | West Virginia | 6.0 | |
| Michigan | 2.35 | | Wisconsin | 7.9 | (C) |

(A) States not levying tax on income or based on income: Nevada, South Dakota, Texas, Washington, and Wyoming.

(B) Rate includes Alaska 4% surtax.

(C) State uses graduated rates. Rate shown is the maximum.

(D) Rate includes District of Columbia 10% surtax.

(E) Rate includes Massachusetts 14% surtax.

* States allow some form of deduction for federal income taxes.

FIGURE 39.1  1980 STATE CORPORATE INCOME TAX RATES

## Planning for Multiple Jurisdiction Operations

An existing business that is expanding operations into a new state should decide whether or not to form a new subsidiary and should weigh the need for new accounting procedures after analyzing such factors as whether or not net operating loss carrybacks are allowable, whether separate accounting is available, and what factors are used for apportionment. Some states allow consolidated returns, which in effect may allow a corporation to offset the losses of their affiliates before applying apportionment factors.

The controller should also know the nature of the tax base of each state in which the company operates. For instance, there is no income tax in Texas; however, there is a capital-stock tax based on capital employed in the state. Pennsylvania has both types of taxes and one of the heaviest rates of income tax. The controller must deal with many such differences in various state laws.

In order to plan effectively to minimize the state income tax burden, the controller must be aware not only of the impact of various state laws but also of the provisions of the Uniform Division of Income for Tax Purposes Act and the Multistate Tax Compact. He must be prepared to use this information effectively as management formulates policy and implements its decisions.

## Tax Planning as Part of Management Strategy

Unfortunately, management often makes business decisions without considering their impact on state and local income taxation. Many firms that pay attention to the federal law neglect the implications of state tax laws that, because of their complexity and inconsistency, defy quick analysis. A controller must be ready to provide management with meaningful information on the various alternatives under review in order to minimize the corporation's overall state and local tax burden. He might be asked such questions as: Does a firm's employment of a salesman in a new state necessitate subsequent filings of tax returns in that state? Is the firm considering a new plant in a state with a high income tax rate that uses property as one of its main determinates of apportionment? How does each state in which the firm does business treat depreciation methods and calculations compared to what is allowed by the Internal Revenue Service?

## Planning for Proper Record-Keeping Controls

Once it has been established that a company is legally doing business in a particular state and must file the related income and/or franchise tax returns, an accounting system should be designed to gather the information and minimize the compliance effort. An effective approach is to analyze the information that will be required for apportionment factors and design the books of original entry accordingly. Gathering information throughout the year saves hurried last-minute efforts in preparing state returns.

Some companies design their general ledger specifically to capture information on sales, property, and payroll by states. This information can be found in such sources as payroll tax returns or, possibly, property tax returns. The proper record-keeping controls are also essential to substantiate amounts when the returns are examined by the state authorities. (Record-keeping controls are discussed in more detail later in this chapter.)

### Use of Outside Accountants

A controller cannot be expected to stay technically up to date in all areas of the various state laws. Selective use of outside accountants to review proposed major actions by management may produce substantial tax savings. Outside accountants can also be used effectively to conduct multistate tax studies in an attempt to minimize the company's overall income tax burden. These tax studies involve analyzing the best locations for company assets, proposed expansion into new states, ways to minimize the capital base in states using capital as the tax base, and the different state tax-reporting alternatives. The use of outside accountants for tax reporting and their engagement in connection with tax examinations are discussed later in this chapter.

Whenever outside accountants are used on a project, an *engagement letter* between the parties should outline the scope of the project and specify the agreed-on fees. Usually the cost of such a project is more than justified in terms of annual savings of state and local income taxes.

## STATE JURISDICTION REQUIREMENTS

### Constitutional and Federal Law Requirements

The most significant limitation on states' powers to tax is the commerce clause of the United States Constitution. Article 1, Section 8, Clause 3, states that Congress shall have the power "to regulate commerce with foreign nations, *and among the several states* [emphasis supplied], and with the Indian tribes."

The early cases have established that any taxation that imposes a substantial burden on interstate commerce constitutes an attempted regulation of that commerce by the state and consequently is invalid. A further series of cases extended this doctrine by stating that such a tax, at least when not apportioned to the activities carried on within the state, burdens commerce in the same manner and to the same extent as a tax for the privilege of engaging in interstate commerce. It would thus expose the taxpayer to multiple tax burdens, each measured by the entire amount of the commerce—an amount to which the local commerce is not subject.

Later cases, however, stated that the commerce clause does not prohibit all state taxation affecting interstate commerce; certain types of legislation are permitted. Net earnings from interstate commerce are subject to tax, and if the commerce is carried on by a corporation, a franchise tax may be imposed, measured by the net income from business done within the state. This net income includes that portion derived from interstate commerce that may be attributable (by a fair method of apportionment) to the business done within the state.

Further limitations on the states are contained within the Constitution. The Fourteenth Amendment extended the limitations of due process of law on the states and is enforceable by the federal courts. While a corporation is not a citizen within the meaning of the privileges and immunities clause, it is a person within the meaning of the equal-protection clause.

The United States Supreme Court ruled in 1959 that a nondiscriminatory state tax levied directly on the net income of a foreign corporation engaged exclusively in interstate commerce, and fairly apportioned to local activities within the taxing state forming sufficient presence to support it, does not violate the due-process and commerce clauses of the Constitution.

Later that year, Congress imposed the Interstate Income Law (Pub. L. No. 86-272), which sought to limit the local activities that give a state the right to impose a net income tax on a foreign corporation. Specifically, this law protects companies engaged in interstate commerce from a tax levied on or measured by net income when the only activities of such companies in the state consist of either or both of the following:

- Solicitation of orders by a company's representative when such orders are sent outside the state for approval or rejection and, on approval, are filled by shipment or delivery from a point outside the state; and
- Solicitation of orders for sales, or the making of sales, or the maintenance of an office in the state by one or more independent contractors.

This law offers a company no protection against sales, use, gross receipts, and capital-stock taxes; qualification fees; and other types of taxes levied by the fifty states. Only those taxes measured by net income are protected.

Since the Interstate Income Law was passed in 1959, court rulings in significant cases brought before the Louisiana, Oregon, and Missouri Supreme Courts upheld the validity of this law.

### Sales and Use Taxes

In general, sales taxes are either imposed directly on sales or measured by sales. Taxes imposed directly on sales are commonly known as *consumer's sales taxes,* since the tax is based on the purchase price of each item sold and is paid by the retail purchaser. Taxes measured by sales are known as *occupation* or *license taxes.* Sales taxes are usually intended to be single-turnover taxes, that is, each article is taxed only once. Sales for resale are usually not taxed. Generally, sales of raw materials to be incorporated into a finished product destined for ultimate sale to the consumer are not taxed; but sales of tools, coal, or other material used or consumed in manufacturing, not incorporated into the product to be sold, are taxable.

In general, the *use* or *compensating tax* supplements the sales tax and is imposed either as a separate tax or as an extension of the base of taxes otherwise imposed on sales. Use taxes are usually levied on the storage, use, or consumption within the state where tangible personal property is purchased, and refer to property on which the sales tax has not been paid. The measure of the use tax is substantially the same as that of the sales tax, inasmuch as the same class of property is affected. However, a state's use-tax base may not be broader than its sales-tax base.

Whether a sales-type tax constitutes an undue burden on interstate commerce is the primary concern in determining its validity under the federal Constitution. A long line of decisions seems to settle beyond any doubt that a tax cannot be imposed on or with respect to gross receipts from interstate commerce.

However, in *McGoldrick v. Berwind-White Coal Mining Co.*, 309 U.S. 33 (1940), a considerable departure from these doctrines was made. The court held that the sale of coal delivered from a Pennsylvania mine to points in New York City on the basis of contracts entered into in New York City is subject to New York City sales tax. There is no discrimination against interstate commerce, since a like tax is imposed on sales within the city. Likewise, in *McGoldrick v. Felt & Tarrant Manufacturing Co.*, 309 U.S. 70 (1940), the court held that sales in New York City solicited by salesmen through orders subject to acceptance outside the state, and to be filled outside the state and delivered directly to purchasers in the city, are subject to a city sales tax.

The imposition of a use tax has enabled the state to circumvent somewhat the restrictions of the commerce clause in the federal Constitution. In *Henneford v. Silas Mason Company, Inc.*, 300 U.S. 577 (1937), the Washington use tax was sustained. The court held that the tax was not on the operations of interstate commerce but on the privilege of use after commerce is finished.

Experience shows that states have used the use tax as a method of taxation, especially if a sales tax has not been paid. The District of Columbia, and all states with sales and use taxes except Arkansas and West Virginia, allow a use-tax credit for sales taxes paid on the same property in another state, though reciprocity may be required. Arkansas, however, has adopted the Multistate Tax Compact, which contains provisions allowing a credit against a use tax for amounts paid as sales tax on the same property in another state or one of its subdivisions. In Nevada no credit is allowed by law, but other sales-tax states will excuse Nevada residents from sales tax if they submit affidavits that they are returning to Nevada and will be liable for Nevada use tax.

### Review of State Allocation Rules

**Accounting Methods.** State allocation rules measure the amount of income each state may tax. There are two general methods for determining the proportion of income to be taxed to a particular state:

- Separate accounting, and
- Unitary accounting.

*Separate accounting.* The separate accounting method requires that a business entity keep books for each state showing income and expenses allocable to transactions taking place in that state. In addition, the firm must demonstrate that there are no interdepartmental sales or purchases, no centralized management services, and no central accounting functions and that several other stringent requirements are met. The multistate business that takes advantage of the economic savings of operations such as centralized management and centralized payroll often will find it impossible to use separate accounting for state income tax purposes. Most states require such companies to use the unitary method.

*Unitary accounting.* The unitary business is one in which operations contribute toward or depend on operations outside the state. The theory behind the unitary method is that the portion of a company's consolidated income produced in a state is directly related to property, payroll, and sales within that state. The most widely used method of determining the business income attributable to a particular state is an apportionment formula using those three factors. This degree of uniformity in allocation arises from the adoption of the Uniform Division of Income for Tax Purposes Act (UDITPA) and the Multistate Tax Compact (Compact), both of which treat methods of income allocation and apportionment in substantially the same way.

**UDITPA (Allocation and Apportionment).** The Uniform Division of Income for Tax Purposes Act (UDITPA) provides a model apportionment formula for interstate income for states levying taxes on, or measured by, net income. The Act, approved by the National Conference of Commissioners on Uniform State Laws in 1958, provides that taxable income be apportioned by multiplying the unitary taxable income figure by an apportionment ratio that is the average of three factors.

*The property factor.* The property factor is a fraction whose numerator is the average value of the taxpayer's real and tangible personal property owned or rented and used in a state during the tax period and whose denominator is the average value of the taxpayer's real and tangible personal property owned or rented everywhere and used during the tax period. Property owned by the taxpayer is valued at its original cost, and property rented by the taxpayer is valued at eight times the net annual rental rate. The average value of the property is generally determined by averaging the values at the beginning and end of the tax period.

*The payroll factor.* The payroll factor is a fraction whose numerator is the total compensation paid in a state during the tax period and whose denominator is the total compensation paid everywhere during the tax period.

*The sales factor.* The sales factor is a fraction whose numerator is the total sales of the taxpayer in a state during the tax period and whose denominator is the total sales of the taxpayer everywhere during the tax period. Sales of tangible personal property occur within a state if the property is delivered or shipped to a purchaser (other than the United States government) within the state, regardless of the FOB point or other conditions of the sale, or if the property is shipped from an office, store, warehouse, factory, or other place of storage in this state and (1) the purchaser is the United States government or (2) the taxpayer is not taxable in the state of the purchaser.

**Nonbusiness Income.** Nonbusiness income under UDITPA is subject to specific allocation rather than formula apportionment. Nonbusiness income includes capital gains, rents, royalties, interest, and dividends that are separable from unitary business income. Such income is generally assigned to the state in which the income-producing property is located or to the state in which the company is considered to have its commercial domicile.

Certain states (Kansas and Illinois, for example) now take the position that all income is business income. They argue that passive investment income, which would normally be allocable to the state of commercial domicile, is business income subject to apportionment because that income finances the taxpayer's business activities in a particular state. This tax position can be an area of abuse within the states, because the state of commercial domicile will normally want nonbusiness income to be allocated to it. Thus, in effect, a multistate corporation can be taxed more than 100 percent on its passive investment income. The concept of nonallocation of passive investment income is that such income is a separate accounting item not subject to apportionment.

The United States Supreme Court, in *Mobil Oil Corp.*, 445 U.S. 425 (1980), upheld imposition of Vermont's corporate income tax on foreign source dividend income received by the taxpayer from subsidiaries and affiliates doing business abroad. The Court found that dividends were not exempt from a fairly apportioned Vermont income tax, and rejected the contention that the taxpayer's subsidiaries and affiliates engage in business activities unrelated to the taxpayer's sale of petroleum products in Vermont.

However, in *ASARCO, Inc.*, 445 U.S. 939 (1980), the United States Supreme Court vacated the case and remanded it to the Idaho Supreme Court for further consideration in light of the *Mobil Oil Corp.* ruling. The Idaho Supreme Court had ruled that investment income of a multistate or multinational corporation was properly categorized as business income subject to formula apportionment rather than as investment income allocable entirely outside Idaho.

**Other Considerations and Planning.** Many states that have not adopted UDITPA or the Multistate Tax Compact use other three-factor formulas. (Figure 39.2 illustrates the income apportionment methods accepted by the various states.) However, some states may value property at net book value rather than cost. A sales factor may be given a different weight (such as 50 percent in New York State). Also, a particular state may not have a *purchaser throwback rule*, whereby shipments originating in one state and shipped to another state where they are not taxed are then subject to tax as part of the sales factor in the origination state.

There are definite planning opportunities, therefore, in managing the operations

| | Apportionment Method Accepted[1] | | | |
| | Method Prescribed By | | Other 3-Factor Apportionment Formulas | Other Rules |
| | UDITPA[2,3] | Multistate Tax Compact[3] | | |
|---|---|---|---|---|
| Alabama | X | | | |
| Alaska | X | X | | |
| Arizona | | | | X |
| Arkansas | X | X | | |
| California | X | | | |
| Colorado | | X | | |
| Connecticut | | | X | |
| Delaware | | | X | |
| Dist. of Columbia | X | | | |
| Georgia | | | X | |
| Florida | | | X | |
| Hawaii | X | X | | |
| Idaho | X | X | | |
| Illinois | X | | | |
| Indiana | X | | | |
| Iowa | | | | X |
| Kansas | X | X | | |
| Kentucky | X | | | |
| Louisiana | | | X | |
| Maine | X | | | |
| Maryland | | | X | |
| Massachusetts | | | X | |
| Michigan | X | X | | |
| Minnesota | | | X | |
| Mississippi | | | | X |
| Missouri | | X | | |
| Montana | X | X | | |
| Nebraska | X | X | | |
| New Hampshire | | | X | |
| New Jersey | | | X | |
| New Mexico | X | X | | |
| New York | | | X | |
| North Carolina | X | | | |
| North Dakota | X | X | | |
| Ohio | | | X | |
| Oklahoma | X | | | |
| Oregon | X | X | | |
| Pennsylvania | X | | | |
| Rhode Island | | | X | |
| South Carolina | X | | | |
| Tennessee | X | | | |
| Utah | X | X | | |
| Vermont | | | X | |
| Virginia | X | | | |
| West Virginia | | | | X |
| Wisconsin | | | X | |

[1] Only states assessing a corporate income tax are listed.

[2] Uniform Division of Income for Tax Purposes Act.

[3] Provisions of the UDITPA and the Multistate Tax Compact are identical to each other in respect to formula apportionment.

FIGURE 39.2 INCOME APPORTIONMENT METHODS

of a multistate business. For instance, if a purchaser throwback rule exists in a given high-tax-rate state, increased sales may be allocated to that state. If a firm sells a considerable amount in a low-tax-rate state, the firm may find it worthwhile to increase its shipments from that particular state, incur taxes there, and thus reduce the factor in the high-rate state. Also, to the extent possible, property and payroll should be located in lower-rate states.

**Unitary Concepts and Multiple Corporations.** Some states (notably California, Oregon, and Alaska) are successfully applying the unitary method to an entire business group although few of the group's operations are located there. To the extent related companies have unitary operations, they may be required to file a "combined" report, which results in world-wide income being a part of the income apportionment base. A number of other states, including Idaho, Utah, Colorado, North Dakota, and Montana, are beginning to implement unitary accounting.

## MULTISTATE TAX COMPACT

### Background

The Interstate Income Law, as previously noted, was enacted in 1959 to prohibit a state from imposing a net income tax derived from interstate commerce when the only business activity conducted in the state consisted of solicitation of orders for the purchase of tangible personal property. In 1965 a Special Subcommittee on State Taxation of Interstate Commerce introduced an interstate taxation bill that was a product of more than five years of study and hearings. Hearings on that bill revealed that both the states and the business interests objected to its provisions. Since 1966 many versions of the interstate taxation bill have been introduced, but none have been enacted.

As an alternative to these interstate taxation bills pending in Congress, the Council of State Governments proposed a Multistate Tax Compact. The Compact, offered for adoption by the states, contains solutions to the problems of state taxation of interstate commerce based on state action rather than on federal restriction of state taxing powers.

The Multistate Tax Compact was entered into by a number of states to:

- Facilitate proper determination of state and local tax liability of multistate taxpayers;
- Promote uniformity and compatibility in state tax systems;
- Facilitate taxpayer convenience and compliance in the filing of tax returns and in other phases of tax administration; and
- Avoid duplicative taxation.

The Multistate Tax Commission was then created to carry out the Compact. Each member state can request that the Commission perform an audit on its behalf.

The Commission may seek compulsory process, which may be its only power, in the courts of any state specifically permitting such procedure. Individual states retain complete control over all legislative and administrative action affecting tax rates, the composition of the tax base, and the means and methods of determining tax liability and collecting any tax due. Each member state is free to adopt or reject the Commission's rules and regulations and to withdraw from the Compact at any time.

### Pertinent Provisions

**Division of Income.** Article IV, Division of Income, substantially adopts the Uniform Division of Income for Tax Purposes Act (UDITPA), the provisions of which have been detailed previously in this chapter.

**Sales and Use Tax.** Article V, Elements of Sales and Use Tax Laws, provides that each purchaser liable for a use tax on tangible personal property is entitled to full credit for the combined amount or amounts of legally imposed sales or use taxes paid by him to another state and any of its subdivisions with respect to the same property. Also, whenever a vendor receives and accepts in good faith from a purchaser a resale or other exempt certificate or other written evidence of exemption authorized by the appropriate state or subdivision taxing authority, the vendor is relieved of liability for sales or use tax with regard to that purchaser.

**Multistate Tax Commission.** Article VI creates the Multistate Tax Commission, composed of the tax administrators from all the member states. Under this article, the Commission is authorized to:

- Study state and local tax systems;
- Develop and recommend proposals for an increase in uniformity and compatibility of state and local tax laws in order to encourage simplicity and improvement in state and local tax law administration;
- Compile and publish information that may assist member states in implementing the Compact and assist taxpayers in complying with state and local tax laws; and
- Do all things necessary and incidental to the administration of its functions under the Compact.

Articles VII and VIII detail more specific powers of the Commission. Under Article VII, the Commission may adopt uniform administrative regulations in the event two or more states have uniform provisions relating to specified types of taxes. These regulations are advisory only. Each member state has the power to reject, disregard, amend, or modify any rules or regulations promulgated by the Commission. They have no force in any member state until that state adopts the regulations in accordance with its own law.

**Audits.** Article VIII, Interstate Audits, applies only to those states that specifically adopt the article by statute. It authorizes any member state or its subdivisions to request that the Commission perform an audit on its behalf. The Commission, as the state's auditing agent, may seek compulsory process in aid of its auditing power in the courts of any state that has adopted Article VIII. Information obtained by the audit may be disclosed only in accordance with the laws of the requesting state. Moreover, individual member states retain complete control over all legislation and administrative action affecting the rate of tax, the composition of the tax base (including the determination of the components of taxable income), and the means and methods of determining tax liability and collecting any taxes due.

**Withdrawal.** Article X permits any party to withdraw from the Compact by enacting a repealing statute.

### Effect on Corporate Tax Strategy

A controller of a multistate corporation must determine which of those states participate in the Multistate Tax Compact. Within the Compact states, at least, he should be assured that the apportionment factors of property, payroll, and sales will be computed on a consistent basis. Most important, within these particular states, firms should find consistent treatment of definitions of business and nonbusiness income for allocation of income to the state of commercial domicile.

### Need for Accurate Records

Because so many firms conduct multistate operations and have centralized management, separate accounting should not be necessary or even allowed within the Compact states. However, companies should keep accurate records detailing the various apportionment factors and should tie these records into the company balance sheet.

It is easy to keep records of the location of property. However, all sales should be enumerated as to destination and shipping point. (Sales belonging to a Compact state are those sales of merchandise or materials delivered or shipped to a purchaser within the particular state, and those sales shipped from within this particular state if the purchaser is the United States government or is located in a state in which the seller is not taxed.)

The other factor, the payroll factor, is based primarily on the particular state in which the person performing the services is located. If a company has property and payroll within a particular state, it would probably be considered as doing business within that state and to be taxable on that basis.

### Consistent Tax Treatment Among the Various States

One of the purposes of the Compact is to assure consistent tax treatment among the various Compact states. Thus, it may be beneficial for a firm to utilize the Multistate Tax Commission audit to ensure that it is being taxed consistently among Compact states, and that it is avoiding the duplicate taxation that could occur if items of income are interpreted differently by individual state auditors. For example, if the state of a firm's commercial domicile insists that investment income be allocated to that particular state, all other income should be apportioned by the three-factor formula. In another instance, another state may interpret a firm's nonbusiness income as business income, thus apportioning more business income to that state by the three-factor formula. If the nonbusiness income was allocated to the state of commercial domicile, the state that does not have commercial domicile would have a smaller business-income base subject to apportionment. In other words, a joint audit by the Commission may avoid duplicate taxation of the nonbusiness income. It is important to note, however, that Article IX of the Compact does permit a taxpayer who follows the provisions of Article IV for apportionment to secure arbitration of an apportionment or allocation, if he is dissatisfied with the final administrative determination of the tax agency of a state or subdivision in that regard on the grounds that it would subject him to double or multiple taxation by two or more party states or their subdivisions.

The following states were members of the Multistate Tax Compact in 1980: Alaska, Arkansas, California, Colorado, Hawaii, Idaho, Kansas, Michigan, Missouri, Montana, Nebraska, Nevada, New Mexico, North Dakota, Oregon, South Dakota, Texas, Utah, and Washington. The following states are associates of the Compact: Alabama, Arizona, Delaware, Georgia, Louisiana, Massachusetts, Minnesota, Ohio, Pennsylvania, and West Virginia. The Multistate Tax Commission has issued regulations that have been adopted in varying form by Alaska, Arkansas, California, Colorado, Idaho, Montana, Nebraska, New Mexico, North Dakota, Oregon, and Utah.

The United States Supreme Court, in a decision dated February 21, 1978 (*United States Steel Corp. v. Multistate Tax Commission,* 434 U.S. 452 [1978]), upheld the constitutionality of the Multistate Tax Compact, refusing to "read literally" the provision in the Constitution that requires congressional approval of "any agreement or compact" between states.

Regarding the Multistate Tax Compact, Justice Powell saw nothing on its face or in its effects that would violate the compact-approval clause. No provisions in the Compact, he said, would enhance the political power of the member states in a way that would encroach on the supremacy of the United States. While there may be some increase in the bargaining power of the member states as against the corporation subject to their respective taxing jurisdictions, the Compact does not enhance the power of the member states as against the federal government. The Compact does not authorize the member states to exercise powers that they individually could not. Moreover, each state is free to withdraw at any time.

Thus, the Multistate Tax Compact has been passed. It is currently accepted by the states indicated above, and has been approved by the United States Supreme Court. Corporate tax strategy must take its provisions into account when dealing with multistate taxation.

## TAX REPORTING

As a company expands its business to more and more states, it becomes increasingly aware that the complexity of state tax reporting regulations requires efficient organization. A controller must be sure that he receives proper and prompt notification when the company qualifies to do business in a new state and is required to file income tax returns in that state. Most states issue an income tax identification number when a new certificate of authority is issued, and will follow up if returns are not filed. Even if the company ultimately does not conduct business in the state, it should file a "no activity" return with the state's Department of Revenue.

The controller must also consider how he will keep up to date with the technical details of the state laws to which his company is subject. A number of the large publishing houses offer a complete volume on individual state's income, franchise, sales, property, payroll, and miscellaneous taxes, which furnishes adequate information for the controller's needs. The publishing houses also provide an all-states volume, which provides concise summaries for the various tax provisions in each state and is useful if the corporation has only a little activity in a state. Both of these volumes are updated periodically, and the publishing houses also provide monthly reports reviewing the latest law developments in the states. The controller or his assistant should review this information regularly for matters that may affect the company.

### Preparation and Use of a Tax Calendar

As seen above, the states are striving for a degree of consistency in apportionment. Filing dates and requirements, however, remain quite varied. Some states, such as California and Nebraska, require the filing of returns on the same date that the company's federal tax return is due. Other states lag a month behind. Florida has decided to give companies four months after year-end in which to file a return, and others have picked alternative dates. Since penalties for late filing of state income tax returns and underpayments of estimated tax payments are significant, a controller needs some kind of assistance in meeting the due dates for the various jurisdictions in which he files.

A *tax calendar* is one such aid that is frequently used. The calendar is a chronological listing of the filing due dates for returns, extensions (if requested), and estimated tax payments. Usually, a state tax calendar is combined with a federal tax calendar and would include filing dates for franchise returns, property tax returns, sales tax returns, and payroll tax returns. Since the calendar is effective only if it contains complete information, due dates in the various categories must be added as soon as they are known.

After the tax calendar is prepared, pertinent information is recorded as the returns are filed. If an extension rather than a return is filed, the extended due date is then entered into the calendar so it will not be missed. The calendar can also be used effectively to list backlogged compliance work and to budget the staff's work load. To be used properly, a tax calendar should be reviewed on a weekly, if not a daily, basis.

### Use of a Tickler File

A tax calendar may require frequent updating as the company enters new states or encounters changes in compliance requirements. To handle these changes more efficiently some companies use a *tickler file* as a reminder to make tax payments.

This file can be used independently, or together with the tax calendar, and consists of a group of index cards. Some companies will use two sets of cards, one arranged by state and giving the history and dates of returns filed in each state, the second placed in chronological order by due dates. Like the tax calendar, a tickler file is useful only if it is reviewed on a frequent (daily) basis. (See Chapter 38 for a discussion of these aids in tracking federal tax payments.)

### Use of Outside Accountants

There is no general rule governing outside accountants' involvement in a company's state and local income tax returns. When a firm considers hiring outside accountants, it should take into account the controller's and staff's expertise in multistate taxation, the outside accountants' familiarity with the company's operations and its books and records, the number and complexity of the state returns that must be filed, the man-hours that are required to handle the work, other demands upon the controller's time, and finally, the accountants' fees. If the firm decides to engage outside accountants, it may do so in several ways.

**Selective Consultation.** If the controller has expertise in preparing state taxes and has the time available, he may use outside accountants only for special questions of law or reporting. Under this arrangement, the controller must stay current in the technical aspects of state income tax law.

**Review of Returns.** The company may reduce its professional fees but still profit from professional advice on tax planning by having the outside accountants review each state income tax return after it is prepared by the controller or his staff. The returns should be reviewed in sufficient detail to enable the outside accountants to sign the return with the controller. If the company engages outside accountants for this type of review, it must make sure the accountants understand the assumptions and positions taken by the controller in the preparation of the return. Outside accountants charge considerably lower fees for this service than for complete preparation of returns.

**Complete Preparation.** If the controller has had limited experience in multistate taxation or lacks the time required to prepare the returns, the company should consider engaging outside accountants for the preparation of all federal, state, and local income tax returns. This is often the approach taken by companies not large enough to justify their own tax department or with limited accounting staffs. Although this may seem to be the most expensive approach, it may in fact be cost-effective, because the outside accountants' experience with the returns enables them to work efficiently and their audit working papers usually contain most if not all of the information required to complete the returns.

Each year before any outside accountants are hired, the controller may request a fee estimate or other information on the firm's arrangements for preparation of the returns. These charges should be evaluated to determine the costs of each type of service.

## TAX EXAMINATION

### Preparation for the Examination

State tax examinations are becoming more commonplace as a result of increased emphasis on the Multistate Tax Compact and because of such issues as nonbusiness versus business income. State and local examinations usually are not as arduous or complex as those conducted by the Internal Revenue Service, but their importance cannot be underestimated. Substantial tax liabilities can be incurred, depending on methods of accounting, apportionment factors, or whether a taxable location is or is not being operated within a state. In the following discussion of a state or local authority's conduct of an examination, controllers should keep in mind that states differ in their approaches to examinations and audit procedures.

**Accurate Records.** Although it seems obvious that all taxpayers should have accurate records to support the data contained in their federal, state, and local income tax returns, it is surprising how often these records are inadequate or incorrect. Frequently this deficiency occurs because the controller must operate under severe time constraints. During critical periods when tax returns come due, the controller must deal with internal auditors, outside accountants, IRS agents, and most importantly, other management functions. The key to adequate documentation lies in preparing accurate records and working papers as the tax returns are prepared. The controller cannot reasonably expect to recall all decisions and sources of information when the examiners arrive two years later. A special tax working paper file should be established each year to maintain appropriate information in the event of an audit.

Taxing authorities generally give advance notice of their arrival and provide a detailed list of the documents they will want to see during the course of the examination. This notice gives the controller an opportunity to review the specific records requested. During this review some problem areas can be anticipated and possibly avoided. Basics such as tracing amounts from the general ledger to the tax return, reconciling book/tax differences, and reconciling allocation factors should be completed or corrected if there was not sufficient time to do so when the returns were originally prepared. Additionally, the controller can delete suggestive or subjective comments or opinions in the various source materials.

It is in the interest of the company and the controller to have the documents ready when the examiners arrive. If, through unavoidable circumstances, a controller is not ready for an examination, he should contact the examining agency and request an alternate examination date. Reasonable requests for postponements avoid the unforeseen surprises that can occur when agents are given access to records that have not been reviewed in advance.

Accurate documentation, promptness, and cooperation foster favorable impressions and a good relationship with the agent. Conversely, any refusal to cooperate or a presentation of shoddy, inaccurate records creates a natural assumption on the part of the agent that problem tax-exposure areas exist.

**Substantiation of Allocation Factors.** Most states do not have the funds to provide an agent force to conduct full tax examinations. In fact, many states rely on the Internal Revenue Service to audit and verify a company's federal taxable income, which is often used as the basis for its state income tax return. The states do have the authority to challenge items in a federal return and make adjustments, but in practice they don't often do it. In most cases, a state examiner will spend his time challenging the compilation and accuracy of allocation factors, the treatment of nonbusiness income, and the special handling of items treated differently under state and federal law.

Since most states use some kind of three-factor apportionment formula, the company should have the proper support data for each of the three factors of the formula. The payroll information can most likely be found and supported by examining the various states' unemployment tax returns or wage-withholding reports. The amounts allocated to the various states should be totaled and cross-checked with the total wages reported to the Internal Revenue Service on the federal payroll form, Form 941. Reconciling items between the payroll tax returns and the income tax returns may include certain accruals for bonuses and vacation pay.

The property factor involves property both owned and rented. Many companies find the easiest approach to gathering and substantiating property factors is by clearly identifying them in their general ledgers when they record the transactions. The property can be segregated by state by using separate state subcodes within the general ledger account number. Rental expense can be designated in the same way and identified in the books of original entry.

Sales factors used in the three-factor apportionment formula often require more detailed analysis work. Proper identification may involve a manual tabulation or, if possible, a computer sales analysis run by customer number with a special designation or subcode for each state.

Procedures used to gather apportionment factors are as varied as the businesses subject to multistate taxation. It is important that each company gather the needed information carefully, fully document the transactions, and ensure that its procedures are consistent with prior years'.

The examiners will be especially interested in the use of any special deductions or allocations to states, such as nonbusiness income amounts or sales allocations to states with only a sales office. The controller should, of course, include in the file appropriate details as to how the amounts were computed, but it would also be appropriate to maintain a reference to the authority relied on for any special treatment.

## Use of Outside Accountants

The primary advantages of a company's using outside accountants to deal with the state examiner are to save time and to benefit from the accountants' expertise. Experienced accountants know what the agents are looking for and what facts they need to complete their work. They are also aware of the issues raised in state examinations and can generate the needed documentation. When engaging outside accountants, however, the controller should make specific inquiries as to their prior experience in dealing with the taxing authority conducting the investigation.

Time savings are significant only if the accountants were involved with the initial preparation of the return. If they were not, the controller may spend as much time explaining a position taken in the return to the outside accountants as he would have to the examiners.

The major disadvantage of hiring outside accountants may be the cost. The potential tax liability in a state in which little business is conducted may be minimal, or at least less than the projected time charges of an outside accountant hired to handle the matter. When engaging outside accountants, the controller should request a brief summary of what the accountants consider the potential issues in the examination and the related tax exposure. It may be worthwhile to pay a small fee for this study and avoid a larger fee to protect the company from what may be a nominal tax assessment.

In sum, the advantages of using outside accountants should be evaluated in light of other demands on the controller's time, the complexity of the state return, and an evaluation of the tax exposure and costs.

## SUGGESTED READING

"An Analysis of the Supreme Court's U.S. Steel Decision Upholding Multistate Tax Compact." *Journal of Taxation*, June, 1978, p. 368.

"Multistate Compact Can Mean Harsher Tax Audits by the Member States." *Taxation for Accountants*, October, 1979, p. 226.

*Topical Law Reports State Tax Guide.* (Loose-leaf service with periodic update.) Chicago: Commerce Clearing House.

# 40

# Payroll Taxes—Planning and Control

*Edward Mendlowitz*

## INTRODUCTION

### Increasing Cost of Payroll Taxes

**Federal Payroll Taxes.** Federal payroll taxes consist of Social Security (Federal Insurance Contributions Act [FICA]) and Federal Unemployment Insurance (FUI).

The FUI is filed annually, with the tax paid in quarterly deposits. This tax has been fairly stable and is among the lowest of the various payroll taxes. In 1980, the

FUI rate was 3.4 percent. Since this was offset by a credit of 2.7 percent for state taxes paid, the effective rate was 0.7 percent. This rate was paid on the first $6,000 of covered wages.

Social Security, or FICA, is the highest payroll tax. This tax has to be paid as frequently as eight times a month if necessary, and is reported on a quarterly tax return. Since large amounts of tax money are involved in any organization with a number of employees, and FICA lends itself to some planning opportunities, the controller must be familiar with its requirements. FICA rates and base are scheduled to rise through 1990. Figure 40.1 is a schedule of the FICA rates since inception in 1937. It is doubtful that anyone would have believed in 1949 that the amount of the tax would increase by 658 percent in 32 years.

**State Payroll Taxes.** State payroll taxes consist primarily of unemployment insurance and disability insurance. These are sometimes collected together by the state, but can also be administered separately with the state collecting the unemployment insurance and private insurance policies used for the disability coverage. Worker's compensation insurance is another state dictated "tax." The states can also "tax" by instituting a myriad of compliance procedures, such as listings of employees' names, social security numbers, and wages for social welfare boards as well as detailed analyses of payroll records for unemployment insurance purposes.

### Importance of Planning

Payroll taxes, including worker's compensation insurance, can exceed 20 percent of an employer's covered payroll (before including voluntary company benefits such as medical or group life insurance and union costs if applicable). The 20 percent figure does not apply to all types of companies and industries, but is so high as to warrant a controller's careful thought, planning, and control. The controller must understand all the payroll tax requirements for his jurisdictions in order to keep the firm's taxes at the minimum level possible, as well as to comply with the various states' record keeping statutes.

Careful planning is essential in order to avoid the numerous late filing penalties, interest assessments, and very high personal penalties for non-payment and non-compliance with the laws. The controller must ensure that the firm's bookkeeping systems are suited to the proper recording of the payroll transactions so that reporting is prompt and accurate.

### Controller's Role in Payroll Tax Planning and Control

While many, if not all, of the reporting procedures connected with payroll tax planning and control are carried out by bookkeepers, clerks, and other accounting personnel, the planning process begins, and usually ends, with the controller. The controller oversees the entire process, tying together the various dangling strings. The controller must review and question the computation and payment of a given tax and must also supervise its administration. He must see that the proper information is gathered so that compliance procedures are followed. The controller must be able to assure senior management that this area is completely under control.

Whenever the company decides to set up operations in a new state or other taxing jurisdiction, the controller should investigate the local payroll taxes to determine how to keep such taxes at a minimum. He must alert management if he finds that the local taxes are higher than those included in the budget for the new operation.

| Year(s) | Rate for both employee and employer | Maximum amount of payroll subject to FICA | Tax | Combined tax for both employee and employer |
|---|---|---|---|---|
| 1937-1949 | 1.00% | $ 3,000 | $ 30.00 | $ 60.00 |
| 1950 | 1.50 | 3,000 | 45.00 | 90.00 |
| 1951-1953 | 1.50 | 3,600 | 54.00 | 108.00 |
| 1954 | 2.00 | 3,600 | 72.00 | 144.00 |
| 1955-1956 | 2.00 | 4,200 | 84.00 | 168.00 |
| 1957-1958 | 2.25 | 4,200 | 94.50 | 189.00 |
| 1959 | 2.50 | 4,800 | 120.00 | 240.00 |
| 1960-1961 | 3.00 | 4,800 | 144.00 | 288.00 |
| 1962 | 3.125 | 4,800 | 150.00 | 300.00 |
| 1963-1965 | 3.625 | 4,800 | 174.00 | 348.00 |
| 1966 | 4.20 | 6,600 | 277.20 | 554.40 |
| 1967 | 4.40 | 6,600 | 290.40 | 580.80 |
| 1968 | 4.40 | 7,800 | 343.20 | 686.40 |
| 1969-1970 | 4.80 | 7,800 | 374.40 | 748.80 |
| 1971 | 5.20 | 7,800 | 405.60 | 811.20 |
| 1972 | 5.20 | 9,000 | 468.00 | 936.00 |
| 1973 | 5.85 | 10,800 | 631.80 | 1,263.60 |
| 1974 | 5.85 | 13,200 | 772.20 | 1,544.40 |
| 1975 | 5.85 | 14,100 | 824.85 | 1,649.70 |
| 1976 | 5.85 | 15,300 | 895.05 | 1,790.10 |
| 1977 | 5.85 | 16,500 | 965.25 | 1,930.50 |
| 1978 | 6.05 | 17,700 | 1,070.85 | 2,141.70 |
| 1979 | 6.13 | 22,900 | 1,403.77 | 2,807.54 |
| 1980 | 6.13 | 25,900 | 1,587.67 | 3,175.34 |
| 1981 | 6.65 | 29,700 | 1,975.05 | 3,950.10 |
| 1982-1984** | 6.70 | * | | |
| 1985** | 7.05 | * | | |
| 1986-1989** | 7.15 | * | | |
| 1990** | 7.65 | * | | |

  \* Special escalator clauses go into effect based upon increases in cost of living indexes.
\*\* Based on current law—subject to change.

FIGURE 40.1   SCHEDULE OF FICA RATES

If the controller lacks the time or the expertise to adequately plan and control the firm's payroll taxes, he should seek advice from the company's independent accountant.

This chapter discusses the various types of payroll taxes and gives specific tax savings ideas for each.


## SOCIAL SECURITY TAXES

### Coverage

Generally speaking, every employee is covered, with the exception of those working for the Federal government, nonelecting municipalities, and nonprofit organizations. Retired persons collecting social security are covered when they work. Self-employed individuals are also subject to FICA tax, but they pay at a special rate falling between the employee rate and the combined rate. For 1981, the self-employed rate is scheduled to be 9.3 percent on the first $29,700 of net self-employment income.

Director's fees paid to outside directors are usually treated as fees and not as payroll, thereby removing them from the corporation's payroll tax reporting requirements. However, the director is then subject to his own self-employment tax, if necessary. This generally applies to directors who are retired from their regular employment.

### Definition of an Employee

Section 3121 (d) of the Internal Revenue Codes gives the following definition of an employee:

"The term 'employee' means:
1. Any officer of a corporation; or
2. Any individual who, under the usual common law rules applicable in determining the employer-employee relationship, has the status of an employee; or
3. Any individual (other than an individual who is an employee under paragraph 1 or 2) who performs services for remuneration for any person. . . . If the contract of service contemplates that substantially all of such services are to be performed personally by such individual; except that an individual shall not be included in the term 'employee' under the provisions of this paragraph if such individual has a substantial investment in facilities used in connection with performance of such services (other than in facilities for transportation), or if the services are in the nature of a single transaction not part of a continuing relationship with the person for whom the services are performed."

**Independent Contractors.**  In some industries, such as real estate and the garment industry, it is standard practice to treat certain employees as independent contractors. In others, it is done selectively to exclude specified people from employee fringe benefit programs. It is generally an advantage to treat someone as an independent contractor. The employer (used here as a descriptive term to signify the receiver of the service) usually pays independent contractors gross amounts with no taxes withheld and does not cover them for social security or unemployment insurance. (Some states may consider independent contractors as subject to unemployment insurance and disability income requirements, irrespective of their treatment for federal social security tax purposes.)

Independent contractors generally have their own businesses and perform services for more than one company. Obvious examples are lawyers, CPAs, plumbers, and repairmen. Less obvious examples are salespeople carrying two complementary lines or real estate people who work for only one company, but only when they want to, and only on commission.

*Criteria.* It is not sufficient for two parties merely to agree that one is working as an independent contractor. The following common law tests determine whether an individual performing a service is an independent contractor rather than an employee:

- Is the individual hired to achieve a specific result and does he then function without any direct control from the employer?
- Is the service performed on a per job or project basis and not on a time basis?
- Do the skills required need special training that is usually engaged on a when-needed basis?
- Are special or costly equipment or tools needed?
- Is the work to be performed off the employer's premises?
- Are assistants engaged by the independent contractor?
- Is the fee or payment based upon a variable rate rather than a fixed or time rate?

The seven tests stated above have to be evaluated on a case-by-case basis, considering the individual situation and the intent of the parties. Inasmuch as there are many situations in which the employer has the right to control the manner in which the service is performed for both employees and for independent contractors, the nature of the engagement must be explored. Does the employee regularly perform the same project in the same manner or does he perform it on an as-needed basis? Does the employer have to engage the employee on each occasion, or does he employ the individual on a continuous basis, with the understanding that the latter will perform that particular service when it has to be done?

The method of payment is also important, but is not completely conclusive by itself. A computer programmer can be employed on a per job or project basis, but that job or project might last for two years. Is it fair to say that this person is an independent contractor because he is not employed on a time basis? Probably not. There are also many instances when an employer will require the use of costly or special equipment. A plumber can be required to have his own tools and equipment even when he is "employed."

In some situations, the distinction is easily made. Where the independent contractor has a business, has his own office or place of business, is registered as a business with the local authorities, works for many different companies, and has the ability to pick and choose the situations in which he wants to work, the independent contractor relationship is more obvious. It is important to evaluate each situation carefully because the firm can be adversely affected if a person treated as an independent contractor is later deemed by the IRS to be an employee.

One such problem is that the firm will be liable for the person's withholding taxes if that person does not pay his own taxes. The government can then require the firm to pay to the IRS the amounts that would have been withheld had the payments been "properly" treated.

When a company engages independent contractors, it must be aware that they are not covered by worker's compensation insurance. If they are hurt on the job, they have the right to sue the firm for which they are working. Other problems may occur when a person treated as an independent contractor attempts to collect unemployment insurance and social security at a later time. This can cause the firm problems in tax audits and research of old records. It is advisable to file a Form 1099 each year; this puts each independent contractor on notice that he does not have employee status. This step, however, is not always sufficient.

The IRS is presently reviewing its policies on independent contractor treatment. Its current position should be determined before a firm decides to hire anyone whose status as an independent contractor is doubtful.

### Common Paymaster Procedure

If an individual is employed by more than one employer, duplicate payroll taxes, including FICA, will be paid by both employer and employee. Employees can indicate any overpayment when they file their individual income tax returns, and can receive a refund. The employer can never get its excess portion back.

If a number of different corporations are part of an affiliated or related group, one of the corporations can become a *common paymaster* for the group and pay only one FICA and FUTA tax for each employee who works for more than one company within the group. Any one of the corporations can act as a common paymaster, or a new corporation can be formed whose sole purpose is to serve as a common paymaster. The common paymaster does not have to pay salaries to all of the employees of each corporation, but can selectively choose which employees it will pay, with the rest of the employees paid under normal procedures by their respective corporations. The common paymaster may choose to pay one check to each employee or to give each employee a number of checks that cover the same payroll period. This can be decided at the option of the company. More than one common paymaster may be permitted for a group. The only real requirement for common paymaster procedures is that the employee work concurrently for at least two corporations.

The common paymaster has the primary responsibility for the payment of withholding taxes and other employment taxes for the salaries that it pays. In addition, each of the other corporations using the common paymaster is jointly and severally liable for all of the taxes.

The common paymaster procedure is authorized by IRC Section 3121(s). Some states have adopted the federal procedures. The controller should check with each state within which the firm operates as to the applicability of the common paymaster procedures.

If a company is sold during a given year, the new owner of the firm can use a continuing FICA and FUTA base for the entire year, irrespective of any changes in legal entity, identity or form, provided it engages the same employees and continues the business. The new owner should also be able to maintain the same experience rating for state unemployment insurance taxes which could provide a lower tax rate.

### FICA Savings Techniques

**Sick Pay Plans.** Wages paid under a sick pay plan are not subject to FICA tax. If the employee makes less than the FICA maximum wage base (excluding the sick pay) there will be a savings.

Records must be maintained of the days the employee was absent. If a company has had a sick pay plan in effect, but has incorrectly deducted and paid FICA tax on these payments, refunds can be claimed for three years after the filing date of the return that included the sick pay.

Setting up a sick pay plan is a relatively simple affair. The plan should state company policy regarding sick pay, should be in writing, and should be communicated to the employees.

If the company pays employees sick pay but has never had a written plan, it may still be possible to obtain refunds for the amounts incorrectly deducted. If the employees "knew" they would be paid for sick days, then the company can claim that it had a plan, albeit not a written one. The company should immediately stop collecting and paying FICA tax on sick pay.

**IRS Refund Policy.** In general, the period for requesting refunds from the IRS is the greater of three years from the date the return was filed or the due date of the return. The same policy applies to refunds for FICA taxes.

**FICA-Exempt Fringe Benefits.** Not all compensation paid to employees is subject to FICA. Following is a listing of certain compensation items not subject to FICA:

- Income attributed to employees from company paid group term and pension life insurance;
- Income from certain split dollar life insurance payments;
- Widow's death benefit;
- Achievement and suggestion awards to employees, up to $100 per year;
- Gifts to employees, up to $25 per year;
- Moving and relocation expense reimbursements;

- Accident and health insurance premiums;
- Medical insurance premiums and medical expense reimbursements;
- Pension and profit sharing plan contributions and distributions;
- Interest free loans;
- Legal insurance plans;
- Personal problem counseling services;
- Certain expense reimbursements;
- Right to purchase personal items at discount prices;
- Special awards made in recognition of charitable, religious, educational or literary accomplishments. A condition is that the recipients be selected without any action on their part and there is no requirement for the performance of any future services; and
- Personal use of a company car.

## UNEMPLOYMENT INSURANCE TAXES

### Experience Ratings

There are as many unemployment insurance laws and procedures as there are states. The *experience rating*, however, is common to all.

The experience rating determines the amount of unemployment taxes a company has to pay. To each state's basic rate, a formula based upon the amount of benefits paid out of the company's "account" is applied. The resulting rate is added to (and sometimes subtracted from) the basic rate. It is not uncommon for rates to vary by 50 to 75 percent from one company to another. The purpose of the rates is to replenish or maintain an "account" deemed adequate to meet expected unemployment insurance benefits to be paid to a company's ex-employees.

Each state also has a wage base to which the experience rating is applied. An employee's wages in excess of that amount are not subject to the unemployment insurance tax. Most states use the FUI wage base of $6,000.

The *account* is a bookkeeping record maintained by the Unemployment Insurance Fund or Board. It does not necessarily represent actual dollars or claims that a company has paid or charged to the fund.

### Maintaining or Improving a Rating

**Disputing Claims.** Since all claims paid to ex-employees are charged to the employer's account, a careful review of all claims is mandatory. If an employer wishes to challenge a claim, timeliness is a must. An unjustified benefit of $100 per week for 26 weeks will potentially reduce the company's account by $2,600 and increase its experience rating, and eventually, its U.I. tax rate.

The challenge should be made on the first claim notification form sent by the Unemployment Insurance Fund, and answers to all questions should be well documented. It usually does not take much time to prepare a challenge, provided adequate payroll records are maintained. Of course, if a claim is justified, no challenge should be made.

In addition to challenging all questionable claims, the controller should see that all charges against the firm's account are reviewed. The states do make mistakes. Eliminating a mistaken charge will save taxes in the long run. Some states permit firms to reduce U.I. taxes by applying for relief if a former employee has been laid off by a later employer.

Still another way of keeping taxes down is to be aware of the fact that under state law some termination procedures affect employee eligibility for benefits. A firm can often save considerable sums by knowing how to terminate an employee.

**Contributions to Rating Account.** Some states permit companies to make voluntary additional contributions to the Unemployment Insurance Fund or Trust. Such contributions can place an account in a lower "bracket," thereby reducing the entire annual rate. A rate reduction of one percent on an eligible payroll of $1 million is a savings of $10,000. If the voluntary payment necessary to reduce the rate is less than $10,000, a savings will result.

**Other Rate Reducing Techniques.** Unemployment Insurance Account transfers are permitted from acquiree to acquiror corporations in some states. Affiliated groups can also elect to be treated under one combined experience rating. Each state has different rules. The controller must carefully study the regulations of each applicable state for possible rate reducing techniques.

**Using Outside Experts.** Many independent consultants provide help in keeping the unemployment insurance tax at a minimum. Some work for a fee, either per month or per transaction, and some work on a commission basis. Some of these services are peripheral to payroll preparation services and are quite inexpensive. The controller should investigate the use of an outside service or consultant.

## OTHER PAYROLL RELATED MATTERS

### Worker's Compensation

Worker's compensation is primarily a "payroll tax," although worker's compensation insurance sometimes covers independent contractors and other non-employee individuals performing services for a company. The premiums are based on rates for a given industry and work classification and payroll up to a maximum amount. Rates can vary from less than one-half of one percent to over 10 percent. A slight shifting of classification may often result in a four to five percent change in rate. Each state has different determining factors. The employer should review every rate category as well as every employment classification.

**Audits.** Worker's compensation audits are generally conducted on a regular basis, approximately once every year. The record keeping needed to facilitate these audits involves listing employees by the proper work classification as well as including a detailed listing of any overtime payments.

Worker's compensation costs are primarily based on salaries, without overtime premiums. In some instances, categories of workers in the same plant or factory can be broken down so that lower rates will be charged on certain workers (e.g. clerks or supervisors). If there is no such breakdown, the auditor usually presumes that the worker's function belongs in the category that has the highest rate.

After an auditor finishes he usually leaves a copy of his report with the company. The controller should review this report immediately—if possible with the auditor —so that categories of payroll may be shifted from a higher to a lower rate if there has been an incorrect classification. The insurance companies generally make their assessments soon after they receive the results of the audit. Any delay in reviewing the audit report makes it difficult to reduce the firm's bill for worker's compensation. Another reason to review the audit promptly is that the next year's estimated payments are usually based on the prior year's payments. If an assessment has been made, even though the controller is able to get it reduced, it will probably be too late to reduce the estimated payment for the subsequent year.

### Disability Insurance

Some states include disability insurance with the unemployment insurance reporting, while other states require companies to purchase disability insurance from private insurers. In the latter case, if a company is unable to obtain private insurance, the state usually arranges for insurance to be provided either by a pool or by a quasi-governmental insurance company.

Rates for disability insurance are usually uniform for all categories of employees. The controller should, however, check several insurance companies since not all charge the same rates.

### Targeted Jobs Tax Credit

**The Credit Program.** The Targeted Jobs Tax Credit (TJTC) program offers tax savings to an employer for each targeted worker hired and requires a minimum of paper work. Under the program, new employees (hired after September 26, 1978) from one of the several eligible groups may qualify for a credit against federal income taxes for a percentage of wages up to $3,000 per person for the qualified first year's wages and up to $1,500 for the qualified second year's wages. The actual amount of the credit varies depending on the company's tax bracket, other business deductions, and the salary of the new employee.

Local agencies handle most of the administrative details. They screen potential employees to determine their eligibility and give them vouchers for presentation to employers. When an eligible worker is hired, the voucher is sent to the State

Employment Security Agency, which certifies it and sends back all the documentation needed for tax purposes.

**Qualified Groups.** The following groups qualify for this tax credit:

- Vocational rehabilitation referral individuals;
- Economically disadvantaged youths;
- Economically disadvantaged Vietnam-era veterans;
- SSI recipients;
- General assistance recipients;
- Youths participating in cooperative education programs; and
- Economically disadvantaged ex-convicts.

In most cases, the employee must have been hired after September 26, 1978. The credit applies only to wage costs incurred between January 1, 1979, and December 31, 1980, and is limited to 90 percent of the employer's Federal tax liability.

**Electing the Credit Option.** To the extent that the employer reduces its Federal income taxes by a TJTC, it must reduce the amount of payroll deducted on its tax return by an equivalent amount. This reduces the effect of the tax credit by an amount based on the company's tax bracket (17 to 46 percent).

The targeted jobs tax credit is elective, so it should not be taken if the result is not favorable. Some states require an employer who elects a TJTC to use the lower payroll amount for state purposes, without the benefit of any state tax credit; other states allow the full payroll to be deducted. It is important both to check each state's rules before deciding whether or not it is worth electing the tax credit, and to determine if the credit has been expanded or extended.

## REPORTING AND PAYMENT

### Use of a Tax Calendar

A tax calendar is essential to ensure that reports are filed promptly. It should list every tax due during the year, with the due dates and approximate amounts. This is especially important when the company does business in many states, and each state has slightly different due dates. Although many states automatically send forms just before taxes are due, the responsibility for timely filing rests with the taxpayer, whether or not the forms are received from the state.

Federal tax payments are usually not submitted when the forms are filed. State payments usually accompany the forms. Figure 40.2 is a schedule of the major payroll taxes and their due dates.

| Return | Filing Frequency | Due Date |
|---|---|---|
| Federal Form 941 – Employer's Quarterly Federal Tax Return | Quarterly | Last day of month following end of quarter. The filing period is extended 10 days past that if taxes are paid in full on a timely basis. |
| Federal Form 940 – Employer's Annual Unemployment Tax Return | Annually | January 31. If tax is timely paid then due date is February 10. |
| State Unemployment Insurance | Quarterly | Last day of month following end of quarter |
| State Disability Insurance | Quarterly, semi-annually or annually | Last day of month following end of reporting period |
| State Withholding Tax | Semi-monthly or less frequently | Last day of month following end of monthly or quarterly reporting period |
| W–2's Sent to IRS | Annually | February 28 |
| W–2's Given to Employee | Annually or within 30 days after terminated employee requests a W–2 | January 31 |
| Copy of W–2's mailed to State | Annually | Varies |
| Copy of W–2's mailed to City | Annually | Varies |
| Federal Form 1099 – Various information returns to independent contractors and recipients of miscellaneous income of $600 or more, plus summary Form 1096 and a copy of all Forms 1099 to IRS | Annually | February 28 |

FIGURE 40.2 SCHEDULE OF MAJOR PAYROLL TAXES AND DUE DATES

## Rules for Deposit of Federal Withholding and FICA

The IRS requires timely payment of withheld employee taxes and employer FICA taxes. The payment should be made directly to a depository agent or bank with Federal Tax Deposit (FTD) Form 501. The amount of taxes due determines how frequently funds must be deposited.

New regulations are effective for wages paid in 1981 and in subsequent years. In general, deposit requirements are explained in the instructions for Form 941. Figure 40.3 summarizes the 1981 regulations.

No penalties are imposed provided that at least 95 percent (90 percent in 1981) of this liability is deposited on time. The remainder is due on specific dates thereafter.

Generally speaking, a company becoming eligible for the first time for the "eighth-monthly" payment requirements will be permitted to waive those requirements for the first month it accumulates $3,000. A single monthly deposit can be made. Thereafter, the eighth-monthly rules must be met.

## Rules for Deposit of FUTA

If the amount of tax due for any quarter exceeds $100, that amount must be deposited by the last day of the first month following the end of the quarter. These are deposited with FTD Form 508.

---

*Income Tax Withheld and Social Security Taxes*

| *Amount of Undeposited Taxes* | *Deposit Due by* |
|---|---|
| $3,000 or more undeposited taxes by end of any eighth-monthly period (a period ending on the 3rd, 7th, 11th, 15th, 19th, 22nd, 25th and last day of any month) | 3rd banking day after the end of eighth-monthly period in which undeposited taxes reach $3,000. Banking days do not include Saturdays, Sundays, and legal holidays. |
| $500 or more but less than $3,000 undeposited taxes by last day of month (including last month of quarter) | 15th day of following month |
| Less than $500 undeposited taxes by last day of third month of calendar quarter | Deposit by last day of following month or pay with return |

FIGURE 40.3   SUMMARY OF 1981 REGULATIONS

### Penalities for Non-Payment of Withheld Taxes

Costly penalties are imposed for underpayment and nonpayment of withheld taxes:

- A penalty of 5 percent is imposed for failure to meet FTD requirements;
- A penalty of 5 percent per month (up to 25 percent) is imposed for late filing; and
- A penalty of one percent per month (to be adjusted annually) is assessed for late payment.

In addition, a penalty of 100 percent of any unpaid withholding tax is imposed on each *responsible party*. This term is broadly interpreted to include anyone who in any manner could direct payment of any business funds. This means that a controller who signs checks, even if he has no stock ownership or other ownership interest, could be personally liable for unpaid withholding taxes.

**Controller's Responsibility.** In situations where withholding taxes are not being paid, the controller should take immediate steps to withdraw his signature from the check signing privileges on file with the bank. This will not, however, relieve the controller of the responsibility for payment should the amounts that have already not been paid remain unpaid. The IRS and state governments are usually aggressive in collecting the trust fund money, and even if a subsequent investigation discloses that the controller is not personally liable, the experience can be costly and unpleasant. The controller should remove his signature when he suspects that the taxes cannot be paid on time; he should not wait until they are overdue.

## SUGGESTED READING

"Employer's Tax Guide," *Publications of the IRS* (3-volume Service, updated annually). Englewood Cliffs, N.J.: Prentice-Hall, Inc.

Keeling, B. Lewis. *Payroll Records and Accounting.* Cincinnati, Ohio: South-Western Publishing Co., 1976.

*Payroll Guide* (loose-leaf service, updated annually). Englewood Cliffs, N.J.: Prentice-Hall, Inc.

*State Tax Handbook* (annual update). Chicago, Ill.: Commerce Clearing House.

Wigge, B.F. and Wood, M. *Payroll Systems and Procedures.* New York: McGraw-Hill Co., 1970.

# 41

# Government Contract Requirements

*Franklin R. Johnson*

## INTRODUCTION

In accounting for government contracts, the controller will be confronted with a myriad of rules, regulations, and laws. If the transactions are to be profitable, the controller must effectively create an environment of peaceful coexistence between company objectives and desires and the seemingly contradictory instructions of the government. This will entail his learning a new language that includes terms such as *allowable, compliance, procurement regulation,* and *public law.* It will also entail searching out helpful sources of information and identifying the procedures his firm is expected to follow.

This chapter provides the controller with an overview of the government-contracting process and highlights some of the key differences between dealing with the government and dealing in the commercial marketplace. While the discussion that follows does not eliminate the need for a comprehensive review of the detailed rules and regulations, it is designed to provide the controller with sufficient information to design systems and procedures that will adequately satisfy both the government's and the company's needs.

## THE GOVERNMENT-CONTRACT ENVIRONMENT

Because the government-contracting process operates under a system of public laws and regulations, the controller must have a working knowledge of these rules. He must also be aware of their potential impact, not only on the company's actions and decisions, but on the government representatives as well.

### Regulations

Under the generic category of regulations are public laws and procurement regulations. Laws passed by Congress may require certain financial treatment or considerations. These laws are binding not only on companies awarded the contracts that come under the purview of these laws, but also on government officials. One such law established the Cost Accounting Standards Board, which has subsequently issued seventeen standards for cost accounting in areas not considered to have been sufficiently defined by other regulations or accounting practice. The Board's standards are designed to achieve uniformity and consistency in cost accounting practices.

Procurement regulations generally fall within two categories: civilian or military. The civilian agencies of the government operate under the Federal Procurement Regulations (FPRs). The military departments' (Army, Navy, Air Force, or Defense Logistics Agency) procurement regulations are known as the Defense Acquisition Regulations (DARs). They were previously known as the Armed Services Procurement Regulations (ASPRs). These regulations may be further supplemented by implementation regulations issued by the individual departments.

**Uniformity in Regulation.** Congress has created the Office of Federal Procurement Policy (OFPP) and charged it with promoting economy, efficiency, and effectiveness in federal procurement. OFPP is currently directing the drafting of a single set of regulations to replace the FPRs and DARs. These new regulations will be known as Federal Acquisition Regulations (FARs).

**Regulations and the Contract.** In some instances the regulations specify the type, form, and content of a government contract that must be used for a given type of procurement. Likewise, the contract will generally refer to certain mandatory clauses required by the regulations. The regulations and the contract are thus impossibly intertwined, as shown in a decision rendered by the Court of Claims in *G. L. Christian and Associates v. United States.* The court stated that a clause mandated by procurement regulations was to be considered part of the contract, even though the clause was not specifically included in the contract. Therefore, it is imperative that a controller thoroughly understand the regulations as well as the specific terms of the contract.

**Obtaining the Regulations.** Controllers may obtain copies of the Defense Acquisition Regulations, Federal Procurement Regulations, and Cost Accounting Standards by writing to the Superintendent of Documents, U.S. Government Printing Office, Washington, D.C. 20402.

### Contract Administration Personnel

The *contracting officer* is the most important government representative that controllers will encounter in the course of financial negotiations. In the regulations he is described as the "exclusive agent" to act on behalf of the government "in accordance with agency (department) procedures." The contracting officer is generally the only person who can enter into or authorize a change in a contract.

When dealing with the Department of Defense, a controller may be exposed to both a *procurement contracting officer* (PCO) and an *administrative contracting officer* (ACO). This role distinction does not exist in civilian agencies. The PCO is involved in the original contract award and, often, with any subsequent changes. ACOs are assigned to contractors and are generally responsible for administering all of an individual contractor's government contracts.

The controller should exercise prudence in negotiating with the contracting officer, whose primary responsibility is to obtain the product and service at the most favorable cost to the public. At best, a controller should expect the contracting officer to be fair and reasonable. The controller should not expect the contracting officer to be his advocate.

A contracting officer has many resources at his disposal. Legal, technical, audit, and financial analysts, among others, assist him during all phases of negotiation. A controller should avail himself of similar experts when confronted with potential problems.

The technical representative reviews the day-to-day technical performance of the contractor, whereas the auditor is responsible for the financial aspects of the contract. While the contracting officer may request the auditor's assistance, the auditor is not part of the contracting officer's staff. He is expected to be independent, and usually reports to a different organizational level within the agency or department. This reporting relationship—and the normally limited accounting expertise of contracting officers—makes it difficult for contracting officers to disagree with auditors, particularly on accounting issues.

Contract audits are conducted much differently than audits of financial statements, which determine that financial statements are fairly stated and presented. Any exceptions encountered by a contract auditor will result in costs being questioned. The contracting officer then will review the questioned items and consider them in his negotiations with the company.

### Government Procurement Methods and Contract Types

**Procurement Methods.** In the broadest sense, government procurement methods may be divided into two categories: formal advertising and negotiation.

*Formal advertising.* The government's policy is to use formal advertising whenever "feasible and practicable." In reality, this method is widely practiced to procure "off-the-shelf" items and other products for which the government's requirements can be stated in clear and unambiguous specifications. Formally advertised contracts are usually awarded on a firm, fixed-price basis, but they may also include escalation clauses. Formally advertised, firm, fixed-price contracts do not require that the contractor submit cost detail, nor do they often result in a government audit.

*Negotiation.* Procurement by negotiation is usually initiated by a request for proposal (RFP), which sets out the government's requirements and criteria for evaluating the offers. The negotiation method is used when the product or service is considered to be of a unique or one-time nature. The results required are specified, and the contractors are requested to describe the techniques they will use to accomplish them. The proposals are frequently subjected to reviews by government auditors and negotiations between the contractors and the government contracting officer before an award is made.

**Contract Types.** Government procurement regulations permit a wide range of negotiated contract types under two general categories: fixed price and cost reimbursement.

*Fixed price.* The amount of a firm, fixed-price negotiated contract is arrived at following the government's audit and/or other review of the contractor's proposal and the subsequent negotiations.

After it awards the contract, the government establishes its right to audit the costs of firm, fixed-price (as well as other) negotiated contracts by means of standard contract clauses. During performance of the contract (or after its completion), the government will audit it to determine whether the cost or pricing data submitted in support of a proposal was in fact accurate, complete, and current. When the government finds that the data was "defective" (inaccurate, incomplete, or noncurrent), the government contract clause permits it to reduce the contract price to what it would have been if the contractor's data had been accurate, complete, and current—even if the defect was inadvertent.

*Cost reimbursement.* The most commonly used cost-reimbursement contract is the *cost-plus-a-fixed-fee* (CPFF) contract, which provides for reimbursement of allowable costs plus a fee. Once negotiated, the fee does not vary with the actual cost unless the government changes the scope of the work.

## Subcontractors

As a general rule, the procurement regulations and their inherent cost accounting ramifications apply to any subcontractor that is engaged by a prime contractor on other than a competitively awarded firm, fixed-price basis. The government will hold the prime contractor responsible for any failure of a subcontractor to comply with procurement regulations, public law, or other mandatory contract clauses.

## Profit or Fee

In establishing a profit or fee objective for negotiated contracts that are priced on the basis of cost analysis, the Department of Defense requires the application of a structured formula to a number of specific evaluation criteria. These criteria might include such special factors as the contractor's effort (the types of costs to be incurred), the contractor's risk, and the investment in facilities.

## Renegotiation of Profit

Presently, the Vinson-Trammell Act of 1934 is the only basis on which the government can recapture contractor profits. However, this legislation only applies to contracts over $10,000 that involve the construction or manufacture of a new naval vessel, military aircraft, or portions of either. The limitation is 10 percent for naval vessels and 12 percent for military aircraft.

## Disputes

The Contract Disputes Act of 1978 (Pub. L. 95-563, 92 Stat. 2382 [1978]) recognizes that differences will arise between contractors and the government. Generally, the contracting officer, as the authorized representative of the government, will render a final decision. If the company disagrees with this decision, it must appeal to the agency's Board of Contract Appeals within ninety days or to the Court of Claims within twelve months. Otherwise, the contracting officer's decision will be contractually binding and cannot be appealed.

A key difference between dealing with the government and another company is that under the contract disputes clause the contractor may be required to proceed diligently with performance of the contract in accordance with the contracting officer's decision. To stop work in face of the dispute may result in the government's terminating the contract for default. Another provision of the Contract Disputes Act states:

> If a contractor is unable to support any part of his claim and it is determined that such inability is attributable to misrepresentation of fact or fraud on the part of the contractor, he shall be liable to the government for an amount equal to such unsupported part of the claim in addition to all costs to the government attributable to the cost of reviewing said part of his claim.

### Preference for Government Contracts

To assist in the achievement of social goals, laws or regulations may provide that certain types or classes of contracts be awarded in a less than totally competitive manner. In some cases, public law or regulations might encourage the award of prime and/or subcontracts to small business organizations or minority-owned businesses. In other cases it may impose a mandatory requirement for such action.

One of the responsibilities of the Small Business Administration (SBA) is to assist small firms in obtaining a fair share of contracts and orders for supplies and services for the government as well as a fair share of property being sold or leased by the government. The Defense Acquisition Regulations provide assistance to the SBA in achieving this goal by stating that it is Department of Defense policy to award a fair share of its procurements to small business concerns. This may be accomplished by restricting all or part of an award to only small business concerns. The government will also include in certain prime contracts a clause that "the contractor agrees to accomplish the maximum amount of subcontracting to small business concerns that the contractor finds to be consistent with the efficient performance of this contract."

The same benefits that apply to small business concerns in terms of setting aside contract awards may also apply to *labor surplus area* concerns. Labor surplus areas are areas of persistent or substantial labor surplus and sections of concentrated unemployment or underemployment.

### Summary

Whenever a contractor's costs are subject to government review, the government will use the applicable regulations—such as DARs, FPRs, Cost Accounting Standards, and supplemental agency regulations—as the basis for evaluating costs. Government review may cover fixed-price as well as cost-reimbursement contracts. The data examined may include cost or pricing data submitted prior to the award of the contract and/or actual contract cost performance data.

The single overriding prerequisite for satisfactory experience with government contracts is a thorough knowledge of the applicable regulations. With this knowledge, the controller's relationship with the contracting officer, the technical representative, and the government auditor will be much easier to understand. Also, a careful reading of the regulations will demonstrate the necessity for having a sound cost accounting system before undertaking a government contract. In addition, it is essential that a controller have a working knowledge of commonly encountered terms, such as *allowability, reasonableness,* and *allocability*, which are discussed later in this chapter.

## THE CONTRACTING CYCLE

The contracting cycle has three distinguishable phases—the proposal phase, the performance phase, and the billing phase. The controller must grasp the interaction of the parties involved in this cycle if he is to understand government contracting.

### Proposal Phase

The process of soliciting offers for other than "off-the-shelf" items usually begins with a government agency or department issuing a Request for Proposal (RFP). Controllers can learn about RFPs by asking to be included on an agency's mailing list or by reading the announcements of RFPs in publications such as the Commerce Business Daily, which is designed for that purpose. Often, the technical or contracting personnel of the agency that is requesting the bids will hold bidders' conferences to provide an opportunity for interested contractors to ask questions.

The contracting officer may request evaluations of both the cost and technical aspects of the proposals submitted to determine the firm that will be awarded the contract or, as frequently happens, to narrow the field to two or three candidates. If the latter course of action is chosen, the agency requests the bidders to make a "best and final offer." This serves to heighten competition, because the finalists believe that a downward revision of their price, or some other pricing concessions, may place them in a better position to receive the final award. After the agency evaluates the "best and final offers," it awards the contract.

### Performance Phase

While fulfilling a government contract, the controller will deal almost exclusively with the technical and audit personnel. In fact, the number of times the controller will deal with the contracting officer depends on the problems he encounters and the number of changes he proposes in the timing or scope of the work. Whenever such changes occur, the controller should ask the contracting officer for a change in the contract.

Controllers are well advised to review carefully all of a contract's terms and conditions. The controller cannot judge if items are major or minor unless he has at least a reasonable understanding of their significance. If he identifies the appropriate administrative controls that will ensure compliance, he will be in a position to effectively monitor the contract's progress and anticipate problems before they become critical. It does little good for a controller to say: That's the way we operate our business, if in fact the company has entered into a contract that mandates a change in operation. It's wise to realize from the outset that when one deals with the government, one is not in a "handshake" environment.

### Billing Phase

Billing in the government environment varies from the customary billing procedures of private business. The firm must submit more copies of the bills, in more detail. And the government may process the payments much more slowly. Before submitting bills, controllers with little experience should check with the contracting officer and the agency's disbursing section to see if they are proceeding in an acceptable manner. Also, they should keep the technical representative abreast of the status of billings, since he may be required to approve them before payment.

Under *fixed-price contracts*, the government agency pays the contractor when it receives the invoices for the goods or services provided or when the contractor has achieved the measurable goals written into the contract.

Under *cost-reimbursement contracts*, the controller submits reimbursement vouchers for payment. For most established contractors, the government provisionally approves these vouchers before payment. For direct costs, the controller should submit the bill when the firm incurs the actual expense. For indirect costs, the controller should use the rates negotiated for provisional billing purposes. However, the government may adjust these rates when it establishes the final overhead rates, which are based on subsequently incurred actual costs. During the life of the contract, government auditors may perform occasional audits of the contractor's books and records to establish the allowability of the direct and indirect costs that are charged to the contracts and billed on the reimbursement vouchers.

## FACTORS AFFECTING THE ALLOWABILITY OF COST

The profitability of a contract with the government is predicated on recovery of costs incurred in performing under the contract, plus a fee or profit. Not all costs incurred may be recoverable. Procurement regulations provide that the following criteria will be used to determine if given costs are recoverable, or as referred to in procurement language, *allowable*:

- Reasonableness,
- Allocability,
- Limitations in the contract itself,
- Limitations or exclusions set forth in the regulations (DAR/FPRs),
- Cost Accounting Standards (CASs) if applicable, or
- Generally accepted accounting principles (GAAP).

## Application of the Criteria

Generally, the last four items listed above are attempts to further establish specific parameters of reasonableness and allocability. It is only in those instances in which the remaining criteria do not provide specific guidance that subcontractors and the government are forced to deal with the broad and subjective aspects of the first two criteria—reasonableness and allocability.

**Reasonableness of Cost.** Here is how the DAR/FPRs define reasonableness:

A cost is reasonable if, in its nature or amount, it does not exceed that which would be incurred by an ordinarily prudent person in the conduct of competitive business. The question of the reasonableness of specific costs must be scrutinized with particular care in connection with firms or separate divisions thereof, which may not be subject to effective competitive restraints. What is reasonable depends upon a variety of considerations and circumstances involving both the nature and the amount of the cost in question. In determining the reasonableness of a given cost, consideration shall be given to: (a) whether the cost is of a type generally recognized as ordinary and necessary for the conduct of the contractor's business or the performance of the contract; (b) the restraints or requirements imposed by such factors as generally accepted sound business practice, arm's-length bargaining, federal and state laws and regulations, and contract terms and specifications; (c) the action that a prudent businessman would take in the circumstances, considering his responsibilities to the owners of the business, his employees, his customers, the government and the public at large; and (d) significant deviations from the established practices of the contractor which may unjustifiably increase the contract cost.

Reasonableness involves several considerations, including economic, business, and legal aspects. But, because of its subjective nature, determination of reasonableness often results in complex controversies. To avoid some of these, the government frequently includes in the contract terms advance understandings that are applied to the term "reasonableness." For example, when per diem allowances for traveling staff are charged to government contracts, they are sometimes limited to a specific rate.

**Allocability of Cost.** For a cost to be allocable it must bear a causal and/or beneficial relationship to the performance of work under a government contract. To be allocable a cost must:

- Have been incurred specifically for the government contract;
- Have benefited both the government contract and other work of the company and be split in reasonable proportion to that benefit; or
- Have been necessary to the overall operation of the business.

In matters concerned with the allocation of cost, the controller must recognize that the contract is the overriding legal document. It contains language that incorporates pertinent provisions of the DAR/FPRs and other applicable government regulations. Any dispute between the government and the company is usually resolved by referring to its terms.

Contracts often include specific clauses that the agency uses to further clarify cost determination or to establish an advance understanding with the company. These contract provisions frequently concern unique circumstances or conditions that may surround a particular project. Such clauses are usually intended to provide definitive guidance on the nature and/or amount of reimbursement allowable within a specific cost area. These special provisions supersede the conditions imposed by cost clauses from either the FPRs or a department's or agency's implementation regulations. In addition, the special provisions are generally more restrictive about cost reimbursement than either of the latter restrictions.

The government contracting officer has a reasonably wide degree of latitude in negotiating contracts. Chiefly because of his interest in obtaining the best possible price for the government, the contracting officer may insist that clauses be included that place restrictions beyond the DAR/FPR provisions on reimbursable contract costs. However, these items are subject to negotiation and can be used by either party. To effectively bind the government, the controller should insist on advance understandings during contract negotiations and include them in basic contract terms.

The controller should ensure that the parties reach these understandings before any costs are incurred, although a contracting officer may not permit recovery of costs that are expressly unallowable in the DAR/FPRs. Controllers should not hesitate to propose advance understandings when they expect to incur costs that are unusual in nature or amount.

After the controller examines a contract to determine whether the government has modified DAR/FPR cost principles and procedures in any respect or whether any other limitations have been placed on individual costs, he must consider the other DAR/FPR criteria. The selected costs provision of the regulations is particularly significant. This provision discusses fifty cost elements or types of expenses in detail and provides substantial guidance on their allowability. Appendix 41-1 contains a listing of the fifty selected costs specifically addressed in the DAR/FPRs. This guidance ranges from the complete definition of the cost element and a full discussion of the conditions under which the government may allow costs, to a simple statement that the government does not allow the cost. Controllers should be aware, however, that failure to treat any item of cost under selected costs does not imply that it is either allowable or unallowable.

Most active businesses would expect to incur some of the expenses that are unallowable under the selected costs section of the DAR/FPRs. Included among these unallowable costs are:

- Bad debts,
- Contributions and donations,

- Entertainment costs,
- Interest,
- Organization or reorganization costs, and
- Federal income taxes.

The controller must be aware of these unallowable costs in determining the effective profit on a particular government contract. Although these costs may represent necessary business expenditures, they are not directly recoverable under the contract.

Unless there are other specific provisions, both the FPRs and DARs state that cost must be determined and allocated on the basis of "standards promulgated by the Cost Accounting Standards Board, if applicable, otherwise, generally accepted accounting principles (GAAP) and practices appropriate to the particular circumstances." The Cost Accounting Standards Board (CASB) standards presently describe the method of accounting to use for certain costs in areas such as allocation of home office expenses, capitalization and depreciation of tangible assets, pension expense, and deferred compensation. The CASB has been discontinued but its rules still apply to government contract costs.

Presently, the principal situations in which the standards do not apply include: (1) firms that meet the Small Business Administration's criteria of a small business, (2) companies that have never received a government contract in excess of $500,000, (3) educational institutions, (4) hospitals, and (5) state and local governments. Also, in the event that CAS-covered contracts (as defined by the regulations) aggregate less than $10 million and also less than 10 percent of total sales for a fiscal period for a single business unit, only Standards 401 (Consistency in Estimating, Accumulating, and Reporting Costs) and 402 (Consistency in Allocating Costs Incurred for the Same Purpose) must be applied. Furthermore, a contractor that has solely nondefense contracts need only comply with Standards 401 and 402.

Generally accepted accounting principles include the opinions and pronouncements of the American Institute of Certified Public Accountants (AICPA) and the Financial Accounting Standards Board (FASB). Many of these principles are unwritten, however, so there is often controversy over what constitutes "generally accepted." Nonetheless, GAAP provides a framework that businesses use to prepare general purpose financial statements. However, neither the AICPA nor the FASB has widely pursued intraperiod accounting for cost, nor have they substantially addressed allocation of cost to specific jobs or projects.

### Direct and Indirect Expenses

After a controller determines that a specific type of cost appears to meet the criteria for allowability, he must separate the allowable costs into the direct and indirect categories. A *direct cost* is one that is identified specifically with a contract and is charged to that contract. An *indirect cost* is allocated on some acceptable basis to all efforts (contract and other cost objectives) that benefited from the cost during the period. This distinction is necessary to determine the allocability of cost.

## Other Cost Determination Factors

**Limitation-of-Cost Clause.** The limitation-of-cost clause, which is found in cost-reimbursement contracts, establishes the contractor's responsibility to notify the contracting officer when actual costs vary significantly from the estimated cost in the contract. This clause generally provides that:

- The total cost to the government cannot exceed the estimated cost of the contract. The contractor must notify the government in writing when it has reason to believe that:
  a. The cost it will incur in the next sixty days, when added to all previous costs, will exceed 75 percent of the estimated costs, and
  b. The total cost will greatly surpass or fall short of the estimated cost.
- The government is not obligated to reimburse the contractor for costs incurred in excess of the estimated cost of the contract, and the contractor is not obligated to continue performance if continuing will result in costs that will exceed estimated costs.
- If the contractor stops performance before completing the contract task because he has incurred costs equal to or in excess of estimated costs, and the government elects not to increase the estimated cost, the government must pay the full fee originally proposed even though the task may not be completed.

**The Changes Clause.** Government contracts (unlike commercial contracts, which normally require bilateral agreement for modifications) contain a change clause, under which the contracting officer may, at any time, unilaterally make alterations in drawings, designs, or specifications by written order—as long as the changes are within the contract's general scope. The government will make equitable adjustments in contract price and/or delivery schedules, and the contractor must comply with such orders. However, the contracting officer must direct and sign these changes. The contractor must comply with other requirements in the clause, particularly that he must assert an adjustment claim within thirty days after he receives notification of the change. The inability of the contracting parties to agree on the proper equitable adjustment for a change has often resulted in considerable controversy and a number of appeals to boards or the courts. To substantiate a proposal for an equitable adjustment, the contractor must maintain detailed documentation and cost data for the changed and unchanged work.

**Supporting Data.** To be awarded a negotiated cost-reimbursement or fixed-price contract that is expected to exceed $100,000, the company must support its proposal by submitting written cost or pricing data in the procurement agency's prescribed format. This does not apply if the price is set by law or regulation, based on adequate price competition or on the established catalogue or market price of commercial items that are sold in substantial quantities to the general public. Also, the government, through the prime contractors, may require subcontractors to make similar submissions. A subcontractor must make these submissions when its estimate is either: (1) $1 million or more, or (2) more than $100,000 and more than 10 percent of the prime contractor's proposed current price.

The cost of pricing data generally include the proposed profit and a cost breakdown by cost element, for example, direct material and direct labor or other direct costs, overhead, and general and administrative expenses. The procurement agency's auditors usually analyze the data and submit an advisory report to the contracting officer, along with an opinion about the propriety of the estimated costs. The contracting officer reviews the company's cost submission and the related audit report, together with any other information, including technical matters, that the contractor submits in response to the proposal. These data form the basis for the negotiation of the final contract price.

The contractor must submit a certificate of current cost or pricing data as close as possible to the date when the parties conclude negotiations and agree on a contract price. In accordance with public law, the company must certify that the submitted cost data were accurate, complete, and current on that date.

**Termination.** For its own convenience (or best interest) or because of a contractor's default, the government has the right to terminate a contract. There are significant differences in settlement claims between *termination for convenience* and a *termination for default* on fixed-price contracts. The termination for convenience clause sets forth the procedures and basis for settlement in considerable detail. It also has a specific set of cost principles that apply to such a settlement. A termination for default has onerous implications that expose a contractor to any additional expense the government may incur if reprocurement from another contractor results in additional costs.

After a contractor receives a written notice of termination for convenience, it must stop work, mitigate any cost to the government, and promptly submit a settlement proposal. The government must pay the contractor for costs it incurred for the work performed and for its preparation of the terminated portions of the contract, including an allowance for profit on the prepared portions. The government will reimburse settlement expenses, including accounting, legal, clerical, and similar costs that are associated with the administration of terminated portions of the contract. It is often worthwhile for controllers to engage outside help to assist them in preparing termination claims.

### Summary

Most of the confusion that usually arises in any discussion of the allowability of cost comes from the failure to consider each of the determining factors or criteria. Experienced controllers can readily apply the criteria to a wide range of expense categories. If newcomers carefully consider each of the criteria specified above, they will have a much clearer understanding of how the government determines allowability.

When controllers subject all the costs they incur to this review, they should end up with two groups of expenses—allowable and unallowable. Unfortunately, there is little that can be done to recover unallowable costs except to consider them when negotiating the fixed fee or profit factor in a contract.

## ACCOUNTING SYSTEMS

When evaluating the adequacy of his firm's accounting systems and procedures as they relate to government-contract requirements, the controller should focus on those aspects of cost systems that are necessary to meet the requirements of government contracting. In the context of cost systems for government contractors, costs typically are captured on a contract-by-contract basis.

When government-contract activity is insignificant in relation to overall operations, some controllers have found it most practical to accumulate government-contract costs on worksheets, which they can then reconcile with the formal accounting records. However, if a company expects government-contract activity to represent a significant portion of its ongoing business, it should accumulate government-contract costs more efficiently.

### Government Requirements

A company performing under a cost-reimbursement contract has a clear need to maintain a cost system that is responsive to government cost accounting regulations. A company performing under a fixed-price contract has a similar, but frequently less demanding, need.

Government cost-reimbursement contracts usually contain a clause similar to the following:

> The contractor shall maintain books, records, documents, and other evidence and accounting procedures and practices, sufficient to reflect properly all direct and indirect costs of whatever nature, that are claimed to have been incurred and anticipated to have been incurred in the performance of this contract.

The regulations do not specify that the contractor maintain any specific type of accounting system. Rather, they state: "Any generally accepted method of determining or estimating costs that is equitable under the circumstances may be used." Thus, controllers can be flexible in designing these systems.

### Controls

Controllers should also pay particular attention to the quality of the existing system of internal controls, because government-contract auditors will examine it closely when auditing contract costs.

A controller should especially want to develop a sound budgetary process. (See Chapter 12 on preparation and use of budgets.) Aside from the control a budget system provides over the business as a whole, a well-developed budget assists controllers in preparing cost proposals for government contracts. Management can use a properly prepared budget as the basis for projecting overhead rates and as the basis for negotiating provisional overhead rates for progress billing on cost-reimbursement contracts.

## Chart of Accounts

A company's chart of accounts is its principal means of classifying accounting transactions to prepare financial statements and cost reports. Many companies classify their costs by natural expenses classification, such as labor, accounting, legal, and travel. With little modification, this concept can be adapted for use on government-contract costing. If the chart of accounts were to group expenses by the three areas discussed under the allocability of cost, the chart of accounts could provide contract cost allocations. For example, a 500-series expense code could represent those costs charged directly to a contract, and a 600-series could represent costs incurred as the result of two or more contracts or jobs undertaken for the overall operation of the business. The only remaining requirement would be to identify each 500-series cost with a particular job or contract and appropriately allocate the 600-series accounts.

## Direct and Indirect Expenses

*Direct costs* represent expenses incurred solely as the result of an individual or specific contract effort. Conversely, *indirect costs* are typically those that are not exclusively identifiable with any single contract activity and that benefit two or more cost objectives (e.g., contracts and activities).

Often, controllers do not sufficiently review and evaluate cost characteristics to determine whether they should treat the costs directly or indirectly. All too frequently, their desire to develop a simple system—or avoid changes to an existing system—discourages them from considering alternatives that may yield fuller, or more equitable, cost recovery. If the incidence of a particular expense—like travel —is higher on government cost-reimbursement work than on fixed-price government and commercial business, allocation of this cost to indirect rather than direct expense will likely result in lower charges to the cost-reimbursement contracts and, consequently, a lesser recovery of travel expense.

A controller must consistently apply the accounting method he adopts for indirect costs to all government and commercial contracts. And he must treat the entire amount of any cost element for all contracts in the same fashion. Costs must be treated consistently, not only on a year-to-year basis, but also within an accounting period. The government allows procedural changes, but the burden of their justification rests with the contractor. Thus, a controller cannot charge travel applicable to one contract as a direct expense, and at the same time charge travel attributable to other contracts as an allocable, indirect expense. The first contract would then absorb not only its direct travel expense, but also a proration of the expense applicable to all the other contracts. This practice is known as *double counting* and is prohibited by the Cost Accounting Standards.

Once the controller has identified those costs that the government considers indirect, he must adopt an appropriate basis for distributing them to cost centers and/or individual contracts. For example, many personal-service contractors distribute the aggregate of their indirect costs on the basis of direct labor dollars. The Cost Accounting Standards generally provide criteria for the allocation of indirect expenses.

In summary, the controller should carefully review the nature of the company's expenses to determine whether they benefit more than one cost objective, and he should allocate such costs as indirect rather than direct expenses. The controller should make a sufficiently comprehensive review that he can select the appropriate number of cost pools and the appropriate bases on which to allocate indirect expenses.

### Individual Project Cost Records

Controllers should maintain individual cost records for each contract or substantive project undertaken and should arrange these records in a way that permits efficient and timely accumulation of both cost and billing information.

The controller should summarize direct costs by category so that when he totals the direct costs of all projects, the composite will agree with the general ledger control accounts. The controller should complete the individual project cost records by allocating indirect expenses to each job, based on the agreed-on provisional overhead rate. He should prepare billings for cost-reimbursement contracts (or fixed-price contracts with provisions for progress payments) directly from the information shown in the individual project cost records. On a monthly basis, he should total the provisional overhead charges on each project for the month as well as for the year to date. This process allows him to compare these totals to the actual indirect costs included in the general ledger control accounts for allowable overhead expenses. If the actual overhead varies significantly from the provisional charges, the controller should consider the causes. Also, he should review the steps that he might take to reduce overhead or to request adjustments in the provisional rate.

The controller also can use individual project cost records to analyze periodically the potential for cost overruns during performance of the contract. The controller should compare the costs incurred to date—plus his estimates of costs that he will incur in completing the contract—with contract cost ceilings. This will enable him to notify contract officers on a timely basis if cost overruns become evident on cost-reimbursement contracts. Or, in the case of a fixed-price contract, the comparison will provide the basis for recording lower profits or losses.

## Forms and Documentation

The controller must maintain documentation to support all charges to individual projects. Approved time sheets and payroll records that show chargeable rates will suffice for a company's payroll, and executed contracts and paid invoices will be adequate for subcontractors and consultants. In the case of other direct charges, similar data must be collected. The following list illustrates appropriate documentation:

- *Travel expenses*—approved employee expense reports with appropriate supporting documentation;
- *Long-distance telephone and telegraph*—charge slips detailing the time and purpose of the call and telephone bills;
- *Direct materials*—approved purchase orders and a paid invoice or requisition form; and
- *Reproduction costs*—charge slips detailing the cost and number of copies.

The controller should code all these documents with the proper general ledger account and the contract's project number. These expenses can then be summarized by project and used to support charges to individual contracts.

Every employee, including officers, who works directly on a contract should complete detailed time records, to ensure proper support for the allocation of staff time to contracts and other activities.

## Accounting Procedures Manual

The controller should describe accounting and operational procedures in an accounting procedures manual so that employees can become familiar with company policies and management can uniformly apply them. Written procedures, instructions, and assignments of duties will prevent duplication of work, overlap of functions, omission of functions, and confusion. Another advantage is that the government auditor will find it easier to review the company's internal controls and may request less detail during the course of the audit.

## Summary

The previous accounting system discussion highlights the importance of:

- Assuring compliance with contractual provisions and applicable government procurement regulation;
- Providing an adequate system of internal (administrative and accounting) controls;
- Establishing a workable and flexible chart of accounts;
- Maintaining the appropriate separation between direct and indirect expenses;

- Adopting acceptable and realistic procedures for the allocation of expenses to cost objectives;
- Implementing the use of appropriate project cost records;
- Providing a proper level of supporting documentation for such items as travel, reproduction, telephone, and labor costs incurred; and
- Publishing and utilizing appropriate accounting and operational policies and procedures.

The problems that controllers encounter in government contracting frequently result from fundamental weaknesses in accounting systems and a lack of adequate documentation of procedures and controls. The controllers' system need not be costly or complex, but it should provide an appropriate basis for reporting and evaluating incurred costs. With proper planning and some assistance from independent accountants, controllers can handle government contracts with a minimum of difficulty.

## SUGGESTED READING

*Government Contracts Reporter.* New York: Commerce Clearing House (weekly loose-leaf service).

Price Waterhouse & Co. *Accounting for Government Contracts—An Introduction.* New York: 1979.

———— . *Cost Accounting Standards—A Guide to the Background, Objectives, Operations and Pronouncements of the Cost Accounting Standards Board.* New York: 1976.

————. *1976 Survey of Financial Reporting and Accounting Practices of Government Contractors.* New York: 1976.

Trueger, Paul M. *Accounting Guide for Defense Contracts.* New York: Commerce Clearing House, 1971.

## APPENDIX 41-1   SELECTED COSTS TREATED IN THE DEFENSE ACQUISITION REGULATIONS AND THE FEDERAL PROCUREMENT REGULATIONS

| | |
|---|---|
| Advertising costs | Compensation for personal services |
| Automatic data processing equipment (ADPE) leasing costs | Contingencies |
| Bad debts | Contributions and donations |
| Bidding costs | Depreciation |
| Bonding costs | Dividends |
| Civil defense costs | Economic planning costs |

Employee morale, health, welfare, food service, and dormitory costs and credits

Entertainment costs

Fines and penalties

Fringe benefits

Idle facilities and idle capacity

Insurance and indemnification

Interest and other financial costs

Labor relations costs

Losses on other contracts

Maintenance and repair costs

Manufacturing and production engineering costs

Material costs

Organization costs

Other business expenses

Page charges in scientific journals

Patent costs

Pension plans

Plant protection costs

Plant reconversion costs

Precontract costs

Preservation of records

Professional and consultant service costs— legal, accounting, engineering, and other

Profits and losses on disposition of plant, equipment, or other capital assets

Recruitment costs

Relocation costs

Rental costs (including sale and leaseback of property)

Research and development costs

Royalties and other costs for use of patents

Selling costs

Service and warranty costs

Severance pay

Special tooling and special test equipment costs

Taxes

Termination costs

Trade, business, technical, and professional activity costs

Training and educational costs

Transportation costs

Travel costs

## APPENDIX 41-2   SELECTED ACRONYMS USED IN U.S. GOVERNMENT PROCUREMENT

ACO          Administrative Contracting Officer

ASBCA        Armed Services Board of Contract Appeals

ASPR         Armed Services Procurement Regulations

B&P          Bid and Proposal Costs

CAS          Cost Accounting Standards

CASB         Cost Accounting Standards Board

CPIF         Cost Plus Incentive Fee

CWAS      Contractor Weighted Average Share

DAR      Defense Acquisition Regulation

DCAA      Defense Contract Audit Agency

DCAS      Defense Contract Administration Services

DLA      Defense Logistics Agency (formerly DSA—Defense Supply Agency)

DOD      Department of Defense

DOT      Department of Transportation

DAC      Defense Acquisition Circular

ERDA      Energy Research and Development Agency

FAR      Federal Acquisition Regulations

FPIF      Fixed-Price Incentive Fee

FPR      Federal Procurement Regulations

GAO      General Accounting Office

GSA      General Services Administration

HEW      Department of Health Education & Welfare

IR&D      Independent Research and Development

NASA      National Aeronautics and Space Agency

PCO      Procuring Contracting Officer

T&M      Time and Material

# 42

# Regulatory Requirements

*Gilbert Simonetti Jr.*

## INTRODUCTION

In a 1979 report to the President and Congress, the Office of Management and Budget (OMB) estimated that the federal government imposes almost 5,000 reporting requirements, representing a reporting burden on the public of almost 786 million hours. The information generated by these reporting requirements is put to a wide variety of uses by the government, including development of regulatory policies, determination of regulatory compliance, determination of licensing, and measurement of the national economy and trade patterns.

While most government reporting requirements apply to individuals or to specific industries or product lines, in recent years new programs cut across industry lines and require all businesses to report certain financial and operating information. In part, this is a reflection of a newer type of government regulation that sets economic, environmental, and social standards for all businesses, rather than the more traditional regulation of a single industry represented, for example, by Interstate Commerce Commission supervision of the trucking and railroad industries.

This chapter discusses several of the principal federal financial reporting programs that cut across industry lines. The focus is on financial reporting, since this aspect of federal regulation is likely to be most relevant to the duties of a corporate controller. The chapter also covers the general rules under which the reporting requirements are developed. Since some of the information required by the government is considered sensitive, if not proprietary or a trade secret, methods of preventing sensitive business information from getting into the hands of a firm's competitors are also described.

Clearly this chapter is not an exhaustive account of all federal reporting requirements. For one thing, there are too many and they are too complex. For another, the scene changes continually with new programs being created and old ones being terminated. Each controller must identify both the general reporting requirements that apply to all firms and the specific rules that apply to his own industry. (See Chapters 10 and 22 for SEC and public offering requirements that pertain to all public companies.)

# THE AGENCIES

## Bureau of Economic Analysis

The Bureau of Economic Analysis (BEA) prepares, develops, and interprets the economic accounts of the United States. Much of the data used for the BEA's analyses are gathered by other agencies of government (primarily the Bureau of the Census). However, the BEA collects some original information relating to foreign investment in the U.S., investments by American companies abroad, balance of payments, and domestic plant and equipment spending.

## Bureau of the Census

The Bureau of the Census is the principal statistical agency of the federal government. Its major function, the census of population, is authorized by the U.S. Constitution. Additionally, the Census Bureau conducts, at five-year intervals, censuses of agriculture, manufacturers, mineral industries, distributive trades, construction industries, and transportation.

The bureau on a more frequent basis also conducts special surveys of many of the industries covered in the various censuses. For example, it compiles export statistics from shippers' export declarations and publishes this and other trade data in aggregate form, and issues current reports on manufacturing, retail and wholesale trade, selected services, construction, and other subjects.

### Federal Trade Commission

The Federal Trade Commission (FTC) is one of the oldest of the independent regulatory agencies. It also has perhaps the broadest jurisdiction of any regulatory agency in government. Generally, the FTC is responsible for ensuring the health of our competitive economy by preventing "unfair methods of competition" and "unfair or deceptive acts or practices" in commerce. A number of acts assigning specific responsibilities to the FTC have been passed since the Federal Trade Commission Act of 1914, including the Wool Products Labeling Act, the Fair Packaging and Labeling Act, the Truth-in-Lending Act, and the Fair Credit Reporting Act.

The FTC is also responsible for economic and statistical studies of conditions and problems affecting competition in our economy. Some of these studies are made at the request of Congress or the commissioners of the FTC, to shed light on particular problems. Some are prepared regularly, on a quarterly or annual basis, to give an ongoing picture of trends in business and the economy. It is this latter responsibility that provides authority for the financial reporting programs described later in this chapter.

## HOW REPORTING REQUIREMENTS ARE DEVELOPED

Most major reporting requirements can be traced to legislation passed by Congress. Usually the requirement will be phrased in fairly general terms in the legislation. After enactment it is up to the responsible agency to develop the specific reporting requirements. There are general statutory guidelines that agencies must follow in developing these requirements.

### Administrative Procedures Act

The Administrative Procedures Act of 1946 (APA) sets out the basic minimal procedures that any agency of government must use in developing rules and regulations. Individual agencies have developed their own procedural variations for policy making, but they must at least abide by the steps required by the APA.

An agency must give public notice that it intends to develop a rule. This announcement must appear in the Federal Register (available by subscription from the Government Printing Office) as a *notice of proposed rulemaking* (NPR). The NPR gives the legal authority for the proposal, the text of the proposed rule, background information that helps translate the text into layman's language, and the name and phone number of a contact in the agency for further information.

This procedure gives the public a chance to participate in the rulemaking. In some cases the agency will conduct hearings, at which a company can testify as to the rule's impact. In all cases, a firm can submit written comments, which the APA requires the agencies to consider. In most cases a company has at least thirty days after the NPR is issued to develop and submit its comments. Often the comment period will be longer.

After the agency staff has received and digested all public comments, a *final rule* will be published in the *Federal Register*. In a group decision-making agency (e.g., the five commissioners of the Federal Trade Commission), a public vote must be taken in an open meeting before the final rule can be issued. The final rule must be published at least thirty days before the effective date of the rule, unless the agency has good cause to make it effective sooner.

Once the rule is in effect it carries the force of law and is printed in the Code of Federal Regulations.

## Federal Reports Act

The Federal Reports Act (FRA), as amended, governs the information-gathering activities of most federal agencies. The following agencies and branches of government are *not* required under current law to have their information-gathering methods approved: Congress and the Judiciary, the General Accounting Office, the Federal Election Commission, and the governments of the District of Columbia and the Territories and Possessions of the United States.

The FRA requires agencies to keep their reporting burden minimal and to be sure that the information they demand is needed, is useful and is not available elsewhere. The coverage of the Act is not limited to fill-in-the-blank questionnaires. Whenever an agency wants answers to identical questions from ten or more persons or firms, the plans and forms to be used in the data collection must first be approved by the Office of Management and Budget (OMB). This also applies to information gathered by letters, telegrams, and telephone surveys.

In the approval process at OMB, agencies are required to submit copies of the proposed reporting form or record-keeping requirement, a justification of why the information is needed, and a description of how it will be used. Additionally, the agencies must describe the types of individuals, businesses, or groups that will be subject to the request. Finally, the agencies must estimate the reporting burden that will be imposed as a result of the requirement. The files at OMB containing these agency submissions are open to the public and provide a wealth of information on federal reporting requirements.

When a federal reporting form or questionnaire is approved by OMB, it is given a clearance number, which is printed on the form. The form will also be given an expiration date. The government cannot compel a firm to respond if the form has no clearance number or if the expiration date has lapsed.

Opportunities exist for a firm to offer its views on the scope and content of federal information gathering. When agencies submit proposed reporting forms to OMB for clearance, a notice appears in the Federal Register and a period must be provided for public comment before clearance approval is granted. There have been several cases in which businesses and trade associations have argued successfully for the modification of agency reporting forms and requirements. For example, the Federal Trade Commission (FTC) proposed a questionnaire in 1978 that requested information from about 500 businesses on their compliance with new FTC rules on consumer product warranties. Complaints from the business community that the reporting requirement was burdensome and that much of the information sought was already available elsewhere on the public record resulted in the FTC proposal being scaled down considerably.

Since all reporting forms have expiration dates, opportunity exists to reshape burdensome requirements when the forms are up for reauthorization. When an agency requests reauthorization of a reporting requirement, a notice appears in the Federal Register.

The Federal Reports Act and the Administrative Procedures Act provide business with the statutory tools to participate in the regulatory policies and reporting requirements that it must cope with in day-to-day operations. Clearly such participation requires an investment of time and resources, but OMB has revealed a sensitivity to these problems by saying, in connection with new paperwork management proposals, "the attitude is developing that the public's time and patience for complying with Federal reporting requirements is not limitless."[1]

## CONFIDENTIALITY OF SUBMITTED INFORMATION

There is no comprehensive, consistent federal policy governing the release of confidential information submitted to the government. The Commission on Federal Paperwork, as part of its research effort, identified over 200 statutes that regulate the use and disclosure of specific confidential information collected by the federal government.[2] The commission found that some statutes prohibit disclosure, some give the head of an agency the discretion to release confidential information, some permit release to other government agencies, and some permit release only if identifiable information is removed.

There is one general statute that provides a measure of protection for sensitive business information that is submitted to the federal government: the Freedom of Information Act. However, the protection offered is limited. Moreover, each federal agency can interpret and administer the statute as it sees fit, and there is considerable variation in interpretation.

If a controller is concerned about the confidentiality of any information regarding his firm's operations that he submits to the federal government, he would be well advised to be sure his corporate counsel is knowledgeable about the specific practices and policies of the agencies with which he deals. This is an area of the law and

---

[1] Office of Management and Budget, Notice of Proposed Rulemaking, *Federal Register,* Vol. 45 (January 11, 1980) p. 2586.

[2] Commission on Federal Paperwork, "Confidentiality and Privacy," July 29, 1977, p. 2.

public policy that is currently evolving. Unfortunately, one cannot now assume that sensitive information submitted to the government will be kept out of the hands of competitors, unless there is a statutory pledge of confidentiality such as that granted census data. The Commission on Federal Paperwork summed up the relevant law and recent court cases by saying, "No agency can rely on its administratively bestowed confidentiality pledges to withhold information unless there is specific statutory authority to keep that information confidential."[3]

### Freedom of Information Act

Federal policy, as reflected in the Freedom of Information Act of 1966 (FOIA), holds that all government information should be available to the public unless there is a reason to withhold it. FOIA lists nine specific reasons an agency can withhold information. The FOIA does not apply to matters that are:

1. a. Specifically authorized under criteria established by an executive order to be kept secret in the interest of national defense or foreign policy, and
   b. are in fact properly classified pursuant to such executive order;
2. Related solely to the internal personnel rules and practices of an agency;
3. Specifically exempted from disclosure by statute (other than Section 552b on this title), provided that such statute:
   a. requires that the matters be withheld from the public in such a manner as to leave no discretion on the issue, or
   b. establishes particular criteria for withholding or refers to particular types of matters to be withheld;
4. Commercial or financial information and trade secrets obtained from a person that are privileged or confidential;
5. Interagency or intraagency memorandums or letters that would not be available by law to a party other than an agency in litigation with the agency;
6. Personnel, medical, and similar files the disclosure of which would constitute a clearly unwarranted invasion of personal privacy;
7. Investigatory records compiled for law enforcement purposes, but only to the extent that the production of such records would:
   a. interfere with enforcement proceedings,
   b. deprive a person of a right to a fair trial or an impartial adjudication,
   c. constitute an unwarranted invasion of personal privacy,
   d. disclose the identity of a confidential source and, in the case of a record compiled by a criminal law enforcement authority in the course of a criminal investigation, or by an agency conducting a lawful national security intelligence investigation, confidential information furnished only by the confidential source,
   e. disclose investigative techniques and procedures, or
   f. endanger the life or physical safety of law enforcement personnel;
8. Contained in or related to examination, operating, or condition reports prepared

---

[3] Ibid., p. 30.

by, on behalf of, or for the use of an agency responsible for the regulation or supervision of financial institutions; or

9. Geological and geophysical information and data (including maps) concerning wells.

The business-records exemption (4 above) is the part of the Act most relevant to this chapter. It is essential that controllers understand that this exemption is discretionary. In other words, the FOIA does not *require* an agency to withhold information covered by this exemption, but rather it *permits* the agency to do so.

The FOIA does not provide federal agencies with much specific procedural guidance. It allows agencies to charge those who request government information "reasonable" fees for searching out and duplicating the records. It requires agencies to respond to an FOIA request within ten working days. If an FOIA request is refused, the Act requires the agency to give the reasons for the adverse decision and to notifiy the requester of his rights to appeal the adverse decision to the agency head. If an appeal is filed, the Act requires the agency to decide on the appeal within twenty working days. If the appeal is denied, the requester has the final option of bringing suit in federal district court to force disclosure of the information sought.

Most government agencies have formally designated a Freedom of Information Act officer. This person receives FOIA requests directed to his agency and coordinates the agency's response. Generally, the FOIA officer forwards the request for information to the section of the agency that is working on the material to which the information sought is related. For example, in a regulatory agency, the attorney working on a case that is the subject of an FOIA request would generally be the individual who decides whether or not to release the information. Of course this decision is subject to appeal.

**Policy of Notification.** There is no FOIA provision that requires a federal agency to notify a company that information or records it has submitted have been requested by another party under the FOIA. Some agencies have adopted a policy of notification, but the heavy volume of FOIA requests limits the possibility of blanket notification policies. A former commissioner of the Food and Drug Administration, Donald Kennedy, testifying on his agency's restrictive notification policy, under which the FDA will consult with the submitter of information only when the confidentiality of the records is "uncertain," said:

Nor do we feel that providing notice in advance of every disclosure would provide benefits justifying the time and expenses involved. If the public is to have prompt access to Agency records, the disclosure process cannot be encumbered with elaborate procedures that give private persons, with an interest in confidentiality in opportunity to negotiate each disclosure decision.[4]

---

[4] Hearing before Committee on Government Operations, U.S. House of Representatives, 95th Congress, First Session, "Business Record Exemption of the Freedom of Information Act," October 3 & 4, 1977, p. 94.

The Environmental Protection Agency also has a limited notification policy. EPA regulations require the agency, when requesting sensitive information, to inform a company that it must make its claim for confidential treatment at the time the information is submitted. If the company does not make such a claim of confidentiality at the proper time, EPA may later release the information without further notification.

**Asserting Claims for Confidential Treatment.** There is no government-wide procedure for asserting a claim for confidential treatment of sensitive information submitted to a government agency. Until an overall policy and specific procedures are developed, companies should always indicate page by page which sections of documents submitted to the government are considered sensitive and those for which confidential treatment is requested. Remember, though, that any request for confidential treatment can be disclosed under the FOIA.

**Criteria for Evaluating Claims.** The legislative history of the FOIA does not provide adequate criteria for agencies to use in deciding whether sensitive business information should be granted confidential treatment. The courts have evolved two tests to apply to a request for confidential treatment: "Commercial or financial information is confidential under exemption 4 if disclosure is likely to have either of the following effects: (1) to impair the government's ability to obtain necessary information in the future; or (2) to cause substantial harm to the competitive position of the person from whom the information was obtained."[5] The Committee on Government Operations of the U.S. House of Representatives, which has jurisdiction over the FOIA, found that the *substantial competitive harm test* is determined by the courts on a case-by-case basis, because "each case seems to be heavily dependent on independent factual circumstances."[6]

**SEC Rules**. The Securities and Exchange Commission has adopted confidentiality rules that clarify the first test for granting confidential treatment. Most government requests for confidential business information are authorized by law; the agency can compel a business entity by subpoena to produce the data. With such legal authority behind a reporting requirement, confidential disclosure could not impair the government's ability to obtain similar information in the future. However, the SEC points out in its notice of rulemaking:

> The Securities and Exchange Commission must carefully weigh competing interests in fulfilling its obligations to disclose records to the public under the FOIA while preserving the legitimate confidentiality of the corporations and individuals who submit information to the Commission.[7]

---

[5] Twenty-fifth Report by the Committee on Government Operations, U.S. House of Representatives, "Freedom of Information Act Requests for Business Data and Reverse-FOIA Lawsuits," House Report 95-1382, July 20, 1978, p. 20.

[6] Ibid., p. 20.

[7] Securities and Exchange Commission, "Confidential Treatment Procedures Under the Freedom of Information Act" Rel. No. 33-6241, September 19, 1980.

### Disclosure As a Business Tool

While the foregoing discussion of the FOIA has emphasized the issue of confidentiality, it should be noted that the basic intent of the Act is disclosure. Disclosure is a tool that a company can use to understand better the markets in which it operates. There is no reason management should not request information that it believes is in government files. There is no requirement that it justify its request or explain what it wants to do with the information. In fact, there is no reason a company must be identified as the requester, since it is common for an intermediary such as a law firm to file the actual request. If a controller decides to use the FOIA to further his firm's interests, he can obtain a copy of *A Citizen's Guide On How To Use the Freedom of Information Act and the Privacy Act In Requesting Government Documents* from the Government Printing Office.

## FINANCIAL REPORTING PROGRAMS

The major federal reporting and record-keeping requirements that follow cut across industry lines. These descriptions indicate the scope and nature of government data requirements but do not attempt to address the literally thousands of industry-specific and product-specific requirements. The information for these program descriptions came from the report review and clearance files of the Office of Management and Budget and General Accounting Office.

### Bureau of Economic Analysis

**Form BE-456.** Form BE-456, Plant and Equipment Expenditures Survey (Nonmanufacturing), is part of a larger survey used for the BEA's quarterly sample of capital investment programs, which has been conducted since 1947. More comprehensive benchmark surveys are conducted approximately every five years. The survey is designed to obtain sample data used in preparing estimates of actual and planned investment in new structure and equipment for nonagricultural business firms, professionals, and nonprofit organizations.

The BEA uses the data to help prepare estimates of the gross national product. The data are also used for analyses by the Counsel of Economic Advisors, the Treasury Department and the Federal Reserve Board. The aggregate results of the survey are published quarterly in Department of Commerce news releases and in the *Survey of Current Business*, a journal published by the BEA.

The survey covers 6,000 business firms each quarter. The BEA has found through experience that most business firms either maintain or can readily obtain information on capital investment. Therefore, the BEA estimates that the time required to complete each survey form should not exceed thirty minutes.

Since this program is voluntary and many businessmen consider capital expenditure plans to be confidential, respondents are assured that information supplied "will be accorded confidential treatment and will not be used for purposes of taxation, investigation, or regulation."

**Form BE-452.** Form BE-452, Plant and Equipment Expenditure Survey (Manufacturing and Utilities), is the companion to Form BE-456 and has identical purposes, procedures, and provisions for confidentiality. However, this survey is sent to a smaller sample of 3,000 manufacturing firms and utilities.

**Form BE-13.** Form BE-13, Report on a Foreign Person's Establishment, Acquisition or Purchase of the Operating Assets of a U.S. Business Enterprise, Including Real Estate, is a mandatory reporting program authorized by the International Investment Survey Act of 1976. It is designed to obtain operating and financial information on U.S. businesses that are established or acquired by foreign persons or businesses. To a limited extent the program collects information on the foreign entity. The reporting form seeks such information on the U.S. business as capital and debt structure, assets, plant and equipment expenditures, sales and income, and the number of employees and their compensation.

The reporting requirement is triggered when a foreign concern acquires directly, or indirectly through an existing U.S. affiliate, a 10 percent or more voting interest in a U.S. business enterprise. Filing of the BE-13 form is required within forty-five days of the transaction unless the acquisition is real estate held exclusively for personal use and not for profit-making purposes. Such real estate transactions are exempt. An acquisition costing less than $500,000 is also exempt from the reporting requirement. However, if the new U.S. affiliate owns 200 acres or more of U.S. land, the transaction must be reported regardless of total value. There is, in addition, a reporting requirement for agents and other intermediaries who assist in transactions, which will be described later in this section.

The Bureau estimates that about 400 reports should be filed each year. To enforce the reporting of appropriate transactions the Bureau relies on the identification efforts of the Commerce Department's Office of Foreign Investment in the United States and regularly monitors newspaper and trade journal reports.

Aggregate data from the reports is periodically published in the BEA's *Survey of Current Business*. It is used for analysis by the International Monetary Fund, the Council of Economic Advisors, the Departments of State and Treasury, and the Federal Reserve Board.

The BEA estimates the average reporting burden for completing the report to be two hours. Since the data required is obviously sensitive, the BEA gives assurances of confidentiality. No identifiable information can be released without written permission of the person who filed the report. "Whoever fails to report may be subject to a civil penalty not exceeding $10,000 and to injunctive relief commanding such person to comply, or both."

**Form BE-14.** Form BE-14, Report by a U.S. Person Who Assists or Intervenes in the Acquisition of a U.S. Business Enterprise by, or Who Enters Into a Joint Venture With, a Foreign Person, is a reporting requirement designed to help the

BEA identify transactions for which the BE-13 report should be filed. The BE-14 report is to be completed either by a U.S. citizen who has entered into a joint venture with a foreigner to establish a U.S. business or by a U.S. intermediary to a transaction in which a foreigner acquires 10 percent or more voting interest in a U.S. business. Intermediaries include, but are not limited to, real estate brokers, business brokers, brokerage houses, and lawyers.

The BE-14 form must be filed within forty-five days of the transaction, but only when there is reason to believe or suspect that the acquiring party may be foreign. The penalties for noncompliance, exemptions, and provisions for confidentiality are the same as for the BE-13 program.

**Form BE-15.** Form BE-15, Annual Survey of Foreign Direct Investment in the United States, is a reporting program designed to provide economic policy makers with the same sort of detailed operating and financial data on an ongoing basis that the BE-13 reports provide for new investment in the United States. Additionally, BE-15 requires a breakdown of employees; land and mineral rights (owned and leased); and property, plant, and equipment by state of location. A U.S. business could be subject to this reporting requirement if a foreign concern owns 10 percent or more of its voting interest.

The BE-15 survey goes to a sample of 1,800 of the 7,500 businesses that the BEA estimates could be covered by the program. (Banks are not covered by the requirements of this program.) All eligible businesses must report in a similar benchmark survey, which is conducted once every five years. The U.S. affiliate is not required to file form BE-15 if it does not own 200 acres or more of U.S. land and if each of the three following items for the U.S. affiliate (not the foreign parent's share) was less than $5 million during the reporting period: total assets, net sales or gross operating revenues (excluding sales taxes), and net income after provision for U.S. taxes. If any of the three items was more than $5 million the report must be filed.

The BEA estimates that the BE-15 form should take an average of three hours to complete. Companies operating in several states could require more time, because certain information must be broken down by states. The International Investment Survey Act of 1976, which authorized this and other BEA reporting programs, provides assurances that information submitted will remain confidential.

**Form BE-133C.** Form BE-133C, Schedule of Expenditures for Property, Plant, and Equipment of U.S. Direct Investments Abroad, provides government economic policy makers with information on the nature and location of foreign investments by U.S. companies. It requests actual and estimated property, plant, and equipment expenditures by country of operation.

Only those foreign affiliates in which the U.S. company owns a 50 percent or more interest must be reported. A firm need not report a foreign affiliate if the affiliate is inactive or if each of the following three items of the affiliate is less than $8 million: total assets, annual sales (revenues), and annual net income after taxes.

The International Investment Survey Act made response to the BE-133C questionnaire mandatory, because when this survey was originally conducted on a voluntary basis, a poor response rate yielded unreliable data. As with other BEA surveys, the information sought is for analytical and statistical rather than regulatory or legal purposes.

The BEA sends this survey annually to 1,800 companies out of an estimated total of 5,900 companies that could be covered. BEA finds from experience that the BE-133C form should take about an hour to complete. The information provided by a business entity on this form is given confidential treatment.

**Form BE-10.** Form BE-10, Benchmark Survey of U.S. Direct Investment Abroad, is the report form of a survey conducted every five years to provide a complete picture of U.S. direct investment abroad, changes in investment patterns, and return on investments. It also requires information on certain aspects of the operations of multinational companies and their foreign affiliates, such as balance sheets, income statements, employment, trade, and technology transfers. The BE-10 form is sent to all companies having direct or indirect ownership of 10 percent of the voting interest of a foreign business. The BEA estimated in 1979 that about 5,900 companies should be covered by the reporting requirements.

The report form asks relatively detailed questions about the capital and debt structure of the business; sales and income; investment transactions between the U.S. company and its foreign affiliates; labor costs; property, plant, and equipment expenditures; and so on. It is broken into two separate parts: BE-10-A for the U.S. company and BE-10-B for the foreign affiliate. Form BE-10-B does not have to be filed for affiliates whose total assets, net sales or gross operating revenues excluding sales taxes, and net income after income taxes are each less than $250,000. Also, in order to be exempt, the foreign affiliate cannot own another foreign affiliate that would be required to file BE-10-B.

Since a Form BE-10-B is required for each qualifying foreign affiliate, the reporting burden for this program varies according to the extent of a firm's foreign operations. The last time the survey was conducted (in 1977), the BEA estimated the average time required to complete the report to be 125 hours.

As with other reporting programs authorized by the International Investment Survey Act, the data generated by the BE-10 program is used only for economic and statistical analysis. The information is given confidential treatment.

### Bureau of the Census

**Form MA-100.** Form MA-100, Annual Survey of Manufactures, is the report form of the annual survey of manufactures, conducted since 1949 to supplement the more comprehensive census of manufactures, which is conducted at five-year intervals. The survey gathers information on employment and payrolls, hours and wages of production workers, value added by manufacture, cost of materials, value of shipments by class of product, expenditures for new plant and equipment, inventories, assets, energy consumption, and rental payments for buildings and equipment.

The information from this program is used for the Federal Reserve Board's index of industrial production and for the BEA's estimates of the gross national product. Additionally, the Department of Energy uses the data to measure the use of energy in producing manufactured products and the Small Business Administration does special analytical tabulations regarding the characteristics of small business. Private companies, research organizations, and trade associations make extensive use of this data for market analysis and production planning.

The MA-100 form is sent annually to a sample of 60,000 businesses out of a possible total of 350,000 business establishments. The Census Bureau sends a short form to about 9,000 single-establishment companies, generally to those with ten or fewer employees, and to a sample of single-establishment companies that have just started operations. The other companies in the sample receive a long form, which the bureau estimates should require about four hours to complete. The short form is estimated to require two hours to complete.

The statistics are published in aggregate form by industry and by area with area detail (state, standard metropolitan statistical area, county, and city). Special reports based on the data are also published.

Response to the survey is mandatory, and the information submitted is given confidential treatment. In fact, the law provides that copies of the survey retained in a firm's files are immune from legal process.

**Form MQ-C1.** Form MQ-C1, Survey of Plant Capacity, collects information on plant capacity utilization rates, absolute measures of capacity, reasons for underutilization, actual time in operation for the plant, the length of time it would require for a plant to reach capacity, and how long this maximum could be maintained.

The data is used by government agencies, private companies, trade associations, and consulting organizations to measure inflationary pressures and capital flows, to understand productivity determinants, to forecast economic trends, and to analyze industry trends and averages. The aggregate data are published annually as part of the Census Bureau's *Current Industrial Reports* series.

The MQ-C1 form is sent to a sample of 9,000 manufacturing establishments, including all major industry groups. Based on telephone conversations with past respondents, the Census Bureau estimates that the form requires an average of one and one-half hours to complete.

The report is mandatory. The information is given confidential treatment.

**Forms B-151, B-152, and B-153.** These are the reporting forms for the survey of retail trade, which has been conducted annually since 1951. It seeks data on total retail sales, end-of-year inventory and sales-stock ratios. Also, the report asks whether the inventory valuation method used was last-in, first-out (LIFO) or a method other than LIFO.

The survey is sent to a sample of 32,000 retail establishments. The probability of a firm's being included in the sample depends on the volume of its sales. All large retail operations are included on a regular basis, and smaller firms are surveyed on a random basis.

Based on experience, the Census Bureau estimates that this report should not take longer than twenty minutes to complete. The statistics generated by this reporting requirement are published as part of the *Current Business Reports* issued by the Census Bureau.

This reporting program is mandatory. The reports and data reported may be seen only by Census Bureau employees who have been sworn to secrecy and may be used only for statistical purposes.

**Forms 7525-V, 7525-V-Alternate (Intermodal), and 7525-M (Summary).** For each shipment of goods from this country, exporters or their agents must file Forms 7525-V and 7525-M, Shipper's Export Declaration (SED), with customs officials. The SED provides a description of the commodity being shipped; its size, value, and number of units; and the names of the exporter and consignee. The SED also identifies the carrier, ports of loading and unloading, and inland routing.

The standard and the alternate (intermodal) reports require identical information; only the format differs. Shippers can use whichever is most convenient.

After the SED is filed with customs officials, it is sent to the Census Bureau for statistical analyses. The agencies estimate that the form can be completed in about ten minutes, but a separate form must be filed for each shipment. For exporters who make numerous shipments of essentially the same commodities out of one port of export to one country of destination, a summary declaration is available. These exporters must apply to the Census Bureau for authorization to use the summary form, which requires essentially the same information as the other SED forms but is filed with customs on a monthly basis.

At this writing, the confidentiality of the data reported on SED forms is in dispute. Clearly some of the information reported on the SED, such as the price of products shipped and the name of the ultimate consignee (e.g., a customer list), is sensitive business information. The 1978 amendments to the Export Administration Act provided temporary protection against disclosure of information reported on SEDs resulting from Freedom-of-Information-Act requests, but this protection provision expired in June 1980. Congress and the Commerce Department were considering whether authority to grant confidential treatment to SEDs might be available under other statutes or whether new legislation might be necessary.

It is obvious that controllers and corporate counsel must be aware that policies and procedures governing treatment of sensitive business information are subject to change, and should carefully monitor federal policies regarding reporting and disclosure of corporate data.

**Federal Trade Commission**

**Form LB.** Form LB, Line-of-Business Report, is part of one of the more controversial and burdensome federal data-collection programs that have evolved in recent years. The purpose of the program is to obtain detailed economic and statistical information, broken down by product line, from the largest manufacturing companies. The FTC determined that the information generated by the LB program was needed because of the sharp upward trend of corporate diversification and the increase in corporate mergers.

The underlying need for the data is the FTC's statutory requirement to investigate the extent of competition in the U.S. economy. In the supporting statement accompanying the request for clearance of the original LB form, the FTC gave additional reasons for the program:

> Access to [these] statistics . . . will enhance the Commission's insight into how well competition is functioning in the nation's major industries, and hence allow it to allocate its enforcement resources in the most effective manner. It will provide a data base of unprecedented richness for economists studying pricing behavior, economies of scale, investment flows, and the sources of technological progress. With it industrial decision makers will be better able to identify industries in which competitive entry has been insufficient, thereby fostering a more rational allocation of manufacturing industry resources.[8]

The LB report requires financial performance information, broken down by line of business, on five items: (1) sales or receipts, (2) direct cost of sales and operations (including cost of materials, inventory adjustments, labor costs, depreciation, and other factory costs), (3) direct media advertising expense, (4) direct research and development expense, and (5) direct net plant, property, and equipment.

The LB report is required of 475 of the largest manufacturing companies. The selection process is not random, since the FTC seeks to have balanced coverage of size and industry category. Additionally, the FTC selected at least four companies for each industry category to avoid the possibility of identifying any one company's data.

The LB reports are confidential, and access to the reports is restricted to specified sections of the FTC. The aggregate data are published as a statistical report by the Bureau of Economics of the FTC. The FTC estimates that a respondent, on the average, requires 960 hours to complete the LB report.

**Forms MG and TR.** Form MG, Quarterly Financial Report (Manufacturing, Mining, and Wholesale Trade), and Form TR, Quarterly Financial Report (Retail Trade), are used by the Federal Trade Commission to collect profits data and balance sheet data from a sample of the manufacturing, mining, and trade sectors of the economy. The data are used by the FTC and other federal agencies as a leading economic indicator, an early estimate of GNP and national income, and for other economic analyses.

The sample of companies that must respond to this mandatory reporting program is drawn from Internal Revenue Service records of all manufacturing, trade, and mining companies that file corporate income tax returns. The IRS weights the sam-

---

[8] Federal Trade Commission, "Proposed Revision of Form LB, Supporting Statement," April 12, 1975, p. 1.

pling rate according to companies' asset levels, so that smaller companies have less chance of being included in the survey and larger companies have a greater chance.

Once a company has been included in the QFR sample, it remains subject to the reporting requirement for eight quarters. The report is due twenty-five days after the end of each quarter. The FTC estimates the QFR reporting burden should average one and three-quarters hours for each quarterly report filed by a respondent.

The QFR data is confidential. In the confidentiality guidelines for the program the FTC states: "Under no conditions are the individual company reports to be inspected or otherwise used for taxation, regulation or investigation or in any Commission adjudication or in connection with any investigation for the purpose of initiating adjudicative proceedings."

**Premerger Notification Report.** The premerger notification program is conducted jointly by the FTC and the Antitrust Division of the Justice Department. The information collected permits antitrust agencies to review quickly proposed large corporate mergers for anticompetitive implications.

The report is required whenever a company with assets or sales of $100 million or more acquires a company with assets or sales of $10 million or more. Reporting is also required if a $10 million company plans to acquire a $100 million company. A report would also be required if the acquisition involves assets or stocks amounting to at least 15 percent of the total assets or stock of the acquired firm.

The reporting form requires:

- Information identifying parties to the intended acquisition and the manner in which the acquisition will take place;
- Information about the reporting firm, its product lines, its corporate structure and investments interests, and its history of acquisitions;
- Information on the acquired firm if it produces the same or similar products as the acquiring firm;
- Various reports and documents, including a copy of the merger agreement; and
- Information regarding buyer-seller relationships between the parties.

When the Premerger Notification Report is filed, a waiting period must be observed before the proposed transaction can be completed. This waiting period gives antitrust agency staff time to review the documents. An additional waiting period may be required if the original filing is deficient or if more information on the deal is needed.

While the information generated by the premerger notification program can be used for antitrust litigation, it is exempt from disclosure to the public under the Freedom of Information Act. It could become public if made part of the record in an administrative or judicial proceeding. Also, premerger information can be made available to Congress. The FTC estimates that the report should require an average of fifty hours to complete for each transaction that is covered.

## SUGGESTED READING

Commission on Federal Paperwork. *Confidentiality and Privacy.* Washington, D.C.: U.S. Government Printing Office, July 29, 1977.

———. *Segmented Financial Reporting.* Washington, D.C.: U.S. Government Printing Office, June 10, 1977.

Committee on Government Operations. *Freedom of Information Act Requests for Business Data and Reverse-FOIA Lawsuits.* U.S. House of Representatives, H. Rept. 95-1382, July 20, 1978.

———. *A Citizen's Guide on how to Use the Freedom of Information Act and the Privacy Act in Requesting Government Documents.* U.S. House of Representatives, H. Rept. 95-793, November 2, 1977.

Office of the Federal Register. *United States Government Manual.* Washington, D.C.: U.S. Government Printing Office, 1980.

# Part X

# Management Liaison Functions

# 43

# Working With Executive Management

*Jerry L. Ford*

## THE MANAGEMENT TEAM

The term executive management refers to that management whose responsibilities, authority, and status establish them as the leadership corps of the company. They are in charge of major groups of units within the organization, and hold such positions as chief executive officer, president, vice president, division head, and so on. Some executives are also corporate officers, elected as such by the board of directors. Holding top-level positions, they are the decision makers, the planners, the action takers, the bearers of fiduciary responsibility, and the risk takers.

## THE CONTROLLER'S ROLE

### Primary Responsibilities

In most small to medium sized companies, the controller has primary responsibility for financial planning and management. He heads all corporate activities in areas related to profit measurement and control and must consider company policy, objectives, needs, and available resources. Since his functions cover a broad field and relate to the activities of all departments, he sometimes acts in an advisory capacity, making recommendations that must be carried out by the executives in charge of the departments concerned. He is, therefore, an integral member of the management team. In addition to his role in many companies as chief financial officer, he provides top management with the financial data needed for current and long-range planning, alerts it to possible tax issues, FCPA problems and accounting problems relating to any planned new projects, and helps reduce costs in all areas. He is often a member of key executive committees and is top management's liaison with the audit committee and the outside auditor, as well as with the investment community. (See Chapters 44 and 45.)

### Exercising Leadership

Because the controller's responsibilities cut across departmental lines, he often coordinates and heads corporate activities. In most companies, he reports directly to the president or chief executive officer, and, in some cases, to the board of directors or a committee of the board.

In order to exercise effective leadership within the corporation, the controller should set aside adequate time to get to know company personnel, particularly those in the operational divisions, with a view to understanding their operations and how they integrate their activities. Although some executives carry out purchasing, production, and marketing functions with some degree of independence, many rely heavily on the controller's department to monitor their activities and to warn them of deviations from budget or plan. For many years, operating and financial managers stood apart and assumed that each could carry on his own activities without excessive overlap into the other's functions and operations. The controller can play an important role in eliminating the problems that arise through this isolation.

The controller should also encourage interest, on the part of operating management, in how his financial organization functions. This should be done with a view to promoting sensitivity to financial matters and the factors that may cause financial change. As the controller expands his role in the organization by taking on and fulfilling increased responsibilities, others on the management team view with increasing respect his input into the organization as well as the recommendations made by his staff. An ongoing constructive relationship promotes a working atmosphere conducive to better service and more accurate financial analyses.

## Understanding the Business

One of the most important tools available to the controller in the role of corporate planner and coordinator is an understanding of corporate objectives and strategies. The more the controller understands about the business, the more he is able to communicate with other members of the management team and thus provide meaningful data for their planning and operations. Some questions that a controller should be able to answer about his company's operations are listed below.

1. How sensitive is the business to changes in the economy and the market place?
2. How important is technology to the success of the business?
3. What are the critical points in the manufacturing process or the production of services?
4. What peculiar problems exist at each location or region?
5. What data are necessary for operations management to control the business?
6. What steps are necessary between the receipt of an order and the shipment of product?
7. How sensitive is the business to a single supplier or to a few significant customers?
8. What is the makeup of the customers who buy the product or services?
9. How does management treat its employees?

With good insight into his own firm's needs and objectives, the controller provides the following benefits:

- His interpretation of financial data is based on knowledge of how operating conditions affect financial transactions.
- The services he provides are based on an understanding of business needs.
- His analysis of capital expenditure proposals is based on background knowledge of company resources and alternatives.
- His advice to management regarding the financial effect of new circumstances and changes in operations is helpful and informed.
- He is a source of information for the president on matters regarding new opportunities for increased profitability.

This list varies according to the organization, structure, and market area of various companies. Each company is subject to, and influenced by, its own business environment. Through personal relationships with management and personal visits to subsidiaries and divisions, a controller becomes aware of sensitive conditions and concerns.

## Integrating Financial and Tax Rules for Planning

The controller's role in operational planning is to ensure that top management formulates operational goals, policies, and strategies that take into account financial and tax problems and considerations. He may also help top management evaluate the planning of lower management levels (primarily line managers) in these areas.

An efficient controller keeps management apprised of the most effective ways to maximize, within the limits of prudent risk exposure, the profitability of the firm. As they arise, he also notifies management of pertinent tax issues that may have adverse tax impact upon the corporation, its officers or shareholders, or conversely, recommends shifts of income, deductions, or changes in the treatment of assets that will work to the corporation's advantage.

### Reducing Line Versus Staff Problems

The terms *line* and *staff* relate to organizational concepts used by management to segregate those with direct responsibility for the product or services of the organization (i.e., production and marketing) from those that help the line accomplish the firm's objectives (i.e., personnel, accounting, maintenance, etc.). Unfortunately, the line/staff issue quite often creates misunderstandings that lead to confusion, personnel frictions, and operational difficulties.

Regardless of official job titles, every organization has both line and staff personnel. Assume, for example, that Division ABC of the XYZ Company has a rather typical organization, with managers responsible for sales, manufacturing, finance, personnel, and administration. In this division, there is no doubt that the manufacturing manager is the line manager and that the financial manager is the staff manager. In another corporation, there are five divisions with each division operating under a separate company structure and performing as a separate manufacturing organization. In this case, the manufacturing managers of each of the divisions are line managers. However, the financial managers of each division may also be considered line managers since they are part of the line organization. At the corporate level, the financial group is considered staff. When either line or staff managers assume that they are the most important elements in the organization, a problem begins to surface. Controversy also occurs when line managers distrust staff and resent advice or criticism.

A controller deals with line/staff controversy by recognizing how the issue affects personnel. He must regularly and subtly remind line managers of the fact that his department functions to help them do their job more efficiently. Petty criticism should be avoided, and reports should be reviewed with managers before they are sent to corporate management. The problem is a continuing one and requires regular attention by the controller.

### Interpretation of Financial Data

Financial data are useful only if they are understood. If top management misunderstands financial information, its conclusions are faulty and it makes poor decisions.

The financial data the controller must interpret may be the company's own data or it may be data from outside, such as a financial statement from a major customer requesting credit authorization, data relative to a merger from the candidate company, or data from a potential supplier regarding his suitability as a major vendor.

The criteria used to evaluate or interpret internal data may differ from that used to interpret external data.

**External Financial Data.** The controller should first identify areas of missing or inadequate data. Where additional efforts must be made to supplement existing data, the controller should make the necessary outside contacts before giving his analyses to management.

It is important that the controller summarize the financial data available rather than ask operating or top management to wade through unevaluated details. If the controller summarizes the facts and significant relationships and presents the information in meaningful terms, top management can review it and take appropriate action quickly and efficiently.

**Internal Financial Data.** Internal financial data may be divided into two categories:

- Financial data relating to the organization or to a specific department; and
- Financial data relating to a project or to a particular transaction.

Financial results that relate to the organization as a whole are important to management in the decision-making process. Data must be presented in a way that is easily understood and utilized by the management team. Specific formats, methods, and procedures are presented elsewhere in this book.

Financial data concerning projects or transactions influence the choice of alternative courses of action. It is important that all of the alternatives be identified in order to be evaluated. It is often up to the controller and his staff to interpret the meaning of these alternatives and to describe how each may affect the financial results and objectives and strategies of the company.

Financial analysis techniques help in the decision-making process. In some cases, it may be appropriate to use modern data processing techniques to analyze data or to prepare financial models for "what if" forecasts. (See Chapter 11.) The controller must know when to use such techniques and how to interpret the results for management's use in making decisions.

## ALERTING MANAGEMENT TO PROBLEMS

Controllers are often accused of putting out fires rather than planning for the future. Fighting fires is often essential, but the more top management plans and looks to the future, the fewer fires will have to be extinguished. The controller is a key person in the planning process and is therefore primarily concerned with reducing problem areas.

There are many examples of planning that "pays off" if the controller takes the lead. The controller should alert management to problems arising in the complexities of estimating the savings involved in producing a new product. The savings may vary because of the use of accelerated depreciation, varying production levels, changes in tax rates, and other related items. The significant point is that the controller must be sure management clearly understands the assumptions used.

Increased direct and indirect costs of labor, raw materials, and maintenance must constantly be monitored because of their effect on investment decisions, forecasts, and schedules. New accounting standards and rules often affect company policies, operations, procedures, and reports. Here, too, the controller and his staff are responsible for alerting management to proposed and actual changes, and must help to make the necessary adjustments.

## Advance Tax Planning

Advance tax planning requires an awareness of possible tax problems and opportunities and the proper actions needed to improve the company's tax position. The prime responsibility for tax planning is often placed in the hands of a tax specialist, and the latter's relationship with the controller is an important one. Some controllers have full tax responsibilities while others have more indirect control. Regardless of his role in his organization, the controller must be aware of IRS rulings and make policy decisions with a full understanding of their tax consequences.

The following transactions and activities are likely candidates for advance tax planning (see Chapters 38, 39, and 40 for specific tax planning techniques):

- Depreciation. Integrating useful lives with the investment tax credit to obtain maximum tax advantage. Planning fixed asset purchases for maximum depreciation in the year of purchase.
- Shifting of revenues or expenses between fiscal years to take advantage of new tax laws and/or tax brackets.
- Local tax problems. Keeping allocation formulas and income low in high tax areas and vice versa.
- LIFO inventories. Planning year-end inventory levels to prevent disposition of a low cost layer.

The controller must always remember that tax planning is not done in a vacuum. All tax planning must be integrated with business decisions and the business decision always has priority. Once the basic business policy has been decided upon, the controller and the tax specialist should recommend alternative methods for reducing taxes; these should be methods that won't affect the business decision.

## Review of Financing Alternatives

The process of preparing operating and capital budget will normally alert the controller to the need for new financing or other sources of funds. (See Chapter 21.) Short-term cash forecasts may also indicate the need for interim financing. In either case, the controller should prepare a report for executive management listing the possible sources of funds, the effective cost, and the advantages and disadvantages of each source. The rapidly fluctuating interest rates of recent years have put a premium on advance planning and the ability to move fast when the market looks favorable.

The controller who has prepared his groundwork in advance and has obtained management's preferences for financing methods will be in a position to save the company substantial interest costs by being able to move quickly when favorable financing opportunities become available. The key to successful financing is advance planning, working closely with bankers and other financing sources, and keeping management advised of current developments.

## Planning for New Laws

In today's consumer- and environment-oriented atmosphere, business is faced with regularly changing rules and requirements. The controller cannot be responsible for keeping track of all laws that may affect the company's operations, but he should be aware of those that are within the financial area. New accounting rules, disclosure requirements, and governmental reporting requirements are areas that fall within the controller's purview. He should also regularly check with corporate counsel and line management regarding new or proposed laws or regulations—such as environmental requirements or restrictions on advertising—changes that would have a financial impact.

The controller's duty is to keep top management informed of pending laws, rules and regulations, and their estimated financial impact on the company. Whenever feasible, the controller should also present alternative courses of action that may mitigate the effect of the new laws or regulations.

## SPECIAL AREAS

There are several special areas in which the controller's expertise can be valuable to management. The controller should make an effort to be involved in the planning for these special situations.

## Anti-Trust Problems

Anti-trust problems are often overlooked or disregarded until a lawsuit is commenced or a Federal agency raises the issue. By that time it may be too late to prevent a costly legal action, but it is still necessary to prepare information and arguments that will help the company win its case. Obviously, the best course of action is to be aware of the anti-trust laws and requirements and to be alert to prohibited transactions.

It is important for the controller to know something about anti-trust regulations in order to recognize possible anti-trust violations and to know when it is appropriate to seek the advice of outside counsel. The controller should also discuss the matter with other members of the management team in order to fully understand the problem transactions. Certain types of records must be maintained in order to protect the company against potential claims; the recordkeeping should be reviewed with corporate counsel to ensure that it complies with the requirements of the law.

**Anti-Trust Laws and Regulations.** The controller should be aware of the general provisions of the Sherman Act, the Clayton Act, and the Federal Trade Commission Act. In general, these acts describe and prohibit unfair competition and unfair business behavior and define rules of competition. The anti-trust laws are enforced by the government through the Federal Trade Commission and the Justice Department.

Anti-trust regulations come into play when a company sets prices, creates distributors, enters supply contracts, establishes licensing agreements, or enters into "deals" regarding competitors, suppliers, and customers. It is important to realize that anti-trust problems often arise from an executive's ignorance of the rules, rather than from any illegal intent. Awareness of the anti-trust prohibitions is one of the critical tools for management to use in staying out of anti-trust problems. Remember, any anti-trust situation becomes a cost and cash drain to the company, either through litigation, research, administrative burden, or operating cost.

## Inflation and Long-Term Planning

Inflation as a factor in business planning will probably have to be considered for quite some time. Different countries have different inflation rates, but, in nearly all cases, inflation rates are significant enough to warrant the use of techniques for reporting financial results in an inflationary economy. Management is generally aware of the fact that current dollars do not have the same purchasing power as either prior or future dollars. However, the magnitude of the inflation effect on the results of operations and long-term budgets is often not apparent until, for purposes of comparison, the figures are converted to a base year standard.

It is the controller's job to include a reasonable inflation factor in long-term budgets or forecasts. He should also convert the current and prior year results of operations to either a constant dollar basis (through use of an index) or to a current cost basis so that they will be comparable. Unless management has inflation-adjusted financial data as a basis for decision making, it cannot arrive at informed decisions. Mental inflation estimates are not a substitute for adjusted financial results. The inflation accounting method used is not important as long as management understands it and uses it constantly.

## Market Research Analysis

Many companies spend significant amounts for market research and base important marketing decisions on the results, without fully evaluating the methodology and results of the research. While market research is not within the normal province of the controller, he can assist management to evaluate the usefulness of the research results. The controller should review the assumptions used for their relation to the company's operations and for the validity of the information gathering methods. He should have his staff review the computations and arithmetic in the reports to see that, where applicable, all of the figures tie in to each other. It is not unusual to find conclusions in a marketing report that are based on incorrect computations or faulty assumptions.

There may be other special areas in which the controller can assist management in its decision-making function. The above examples apply to most businesses, but the controller should be alert for situations in his own company where his financial expertise and logical mind can be useful to top management.

## DEVELOPING MANAGEMENT CONTROLS

Management control may be defined as management's awareness and ability to manage the business to obtain anticipated results within prescribed parameters. The controller must not only provide the basic data for management control, but must also interpret the results, analyze the problems, and work with top management to develop and implement solutions to perceived problems.

It is also important that the controller's staff be organized to provide the time needed to analyze special situations and conditions so management can be alerted to potential problems or inadequate results. This monitoring process assists in management control and reduction of costs, with the result being increased profits.

### Interplay With Management

While the controller provides financial analyses for management review, management must determine the need for cost cutting and the areas of operations that will be affected. Once management's decisions and policy have been communicated to line management, the controller must monitor results and report to management any variances from objectives, and, where possible, the reasons for the variances.

The controller should be alert to situations in which a cost reduction program affects employee morale and productivity. This effect should come to the controller's notice, through relationships with line management, before it becomes apparent in the financial results. The controller can provide a valuable service to top management by being a conduit between line management and corporate staff; his neutral position and his ability to check line management's complaints with production and financial results make this possible.

## COMMUNICATING WITH EXECUTIVE MANAGEMENT

Managers exchange information in different ways depending on their personalities and what they expect from communications. The following advice should be helpful to the controller in communicating with personnel at all levels, but can be particularly effective when working with executive management in the areas of planning objectives, and control.

### Awareness of the Audience

It is important to keep the audience's personal interests in mind and to think about the person or group at the other end of the communication stream. What are their management styles? What are their special interests? How do they like to operate? How do they think? What is their technical level? What responsibilities do they assume in the firm? What role does the controller intend to play, and most important, what message does he want to communicate?

If the controller is communicating upward in the organization, he is often presenting information or answering questions. Upward discussions are usually more formal than those directed towards subordinates in the organization. It is important to recognize and adjust to top management's style and to anticipate rather than react to their responses.

### Adequate Preparation

The controller should think through what he wants to accomplish before he begins to communicate. Before any discussion with executive management he should decide whether he's trying to sell a proposal, get information, alert management to a future problem, present financing alternatives, or lay a foundation for future discussions. If the controller is presenting an unfavorable financial report, he should prepare it carefully so that he is communicating not just the end result, but also the reasons for, and the background of, the bad financial news, accompanied by some suggestions for action.

On the other hand, if the financial news is good, the controller should emphasize its implications and indicate how these results relate to other company activities and decisions.

### Letters to Management

Clear, written communications are essential to an efficient management information system, particularly in a large organization. Controllers often prefer verbal rather than written communications when working with executive management, but there is no substitute in a complex organization for concise, clear, and carefully organized letters and memoranda. The controller should use the following recommendations to improve the quality and efficiency of his written communications:

- Plan carefully before writing. Decide upon one single objective, a key finding, or a key recommendation or proposal.

- Be sure that there are adequate data to support the conclusions.
- Use lists to present any series of facts, causes, procedures, or alternatives in order of importance.
- Anticipate questions and incorporate the answers into the arguments.
- Use short words, sentences, and paragraphs. Sentences should generally be twenty words or less and should contain active action verbs whenever possible.
- Keep the letters short and to the point. Simple, concise, one page letters are more likely to be read in full than longer ones.

### Meetings with Management

The effectiveness of meetings with executive management depends on preparation and attention to detail.

**Preparation.** The following factors should be taken into consideration when planning a meeting:

- Is it necessary? Never try to accomplish in a group meeting what one or two individuals can accomplish on their own.
- What is its purpose? The objective of the meeting should be clearly defined and communicated in advance to the participants.
- Who should attend? Those invited should be in a position either to contribute information, to join in problem solving, or to benefit from the exposure.

**Procedures.** Effective meetings proceed on the basis of a carefully planned sequence of steps that consider the subjects and issues to be covered:

- The basic problem or issue is presented, with an analysis of what the group is to accomplish.
- The facts are discussed, and the floor is opened to questions and comments.
- Alternative solutions are listed (in problem-solving conferences), with the advantages and disadvantages of each.
- A summary of the group's thinking is presented. This summary may include a specific decision or a program of follow-up action, or it may merely restate the main points of the meeting and the understandings derived from it.

## SUMMARY

Controllers who learn how to work effectively with executive management will not only find their jobs easier and more satisfying, but will quickly move up the corporate ladder. In the past decade, a substantial percentage of chief executive officers of public companies were once controllers or treasurers.

## SUGGESTED READING

Christensen, C. Roland, Berg, Norman A., and Salter, Malcolm S. *Policy Formulation and Administration*, 7th ed. Homewood, Illinois: Richard D. Irwin, Inc., 1976.

Drucker, Peter F. *Management: Tasks, Responsibilities, Practices.* New York: Harper & Row, Publishers, Inc., 1974.

Harriman, Bruce. "Up and Down the Communications Ladder," *Harvard Business Review*, Vol. 52, No. 5 (September/October 1974), pp. 143-151.

Rogers, Everett M. and Rekha Agarwala-Rogers. *Communication in Organizations.* New York: The Free Press, 1976.

Uyterhoeven, Hugo E.R., Ackerman, Robert W., and Rosenblum, John W. *Strategy and Organization: Text and Cases in General Management.* Rev. ed. Homewood, Illinois: Richard D. Irwin, 1977.

# 44

# Working With the Outside Auditor and the Audit Committee

*C. Richard Baker*

## INTRODUCTION

The controller plays a central role in developing a fruitful relationship between a company and the company's outside auditors. The extent to which the auditors will be able to perform a cost-effective and useful audit depends largely on the involvement of the controller and the chief accounting officer. In addition, the role of the controller as a liaison between outside auditors, internal auditors, and the audit committee of the board of directors is expanding as the principal focus of the outside auditor shifts from reporting to company management to reporting to the board of directors.

## WORKING WITH THE OUTSIDE AUDITOR

The audit of an entity by an outside audit firm can be performed expeditiously if management understands its significance and plans it carefully. With organization, audit cost can be reduced, the audit can be performed with minimum disturbance to personnel, and the results can add to the effectiveness and quality of the firm's accounting, record-keeping, and other functions.

### Preparing for the Annual Audit

**Audit Costs.** Many factors enter into the cost of an *annual audit*, including:

- The size of the corporation;
- The complexity of its operations;
- The sophistication, efficiency, and quality of the accounting and clerical departments; and
- The extent of computerization.

When assessing audit costs, companies are concerned principally with the fees charged by the CPA firm, but there are other hidden costs that are significant. Such hidden costs include the time the controller and other company personnel require to provide auditors with information and data, the time of executives involved in audit and accounting discussions, and similar matters. (The time of clerical personnel involved in preparing records and documents for the auditors and in assisting them throughout the audit is usually not recorded separately.)

The wide variation in cost figures suggests that controllers must take a hard look at the audit activity with an eye to reducing the cost and increasing the value obtained. Since the time charge for the work of the independent auditor's staff is estimated at approximately two and one-half to three times the salaries paid to the staff, a company should take every step to reduce the number of hours outside accountants require to perform their duties.

Audit costs have been increasing because of several factors that are beyond the control of the CPA firm and the audited company. The most significant factor has been the increase in salaries that audit firms must pay competent professional staff. Also, the increasing number of pronouncements on auditing standards, accounting principles, and SEC rules has added to auditing requirements. In some cases, the proliferation of computerized records has added to the auditor's workload. This workload increase is compounded by the fact that computers do not always leave a hard-copy audit trail. While programs can be established to furnish such trails, many computer supervisors believe that they merely add to computer costs.

**Staffing.** Before the audit begins, management should discuss staffing of the audit with the CPA firm to make certain that the composition of the CPA's auditing staff by rank is appropriate to the scope of the examination. The CPA firm has final authority in this regard. However, management should supply its complete organizational chart, with personnel names, titles, and responsibilities, so that the auditors know the position of the persons with whom they are talking and the weight to be given to the information supplied.

**Preparing In-House Personnel.** Before the audit begins, the controller should meet with the accounting and clerical staff to discuss the scope and needs of the audit and how the company is organized to handle it. The discussion should emphasize that the audit is a cooperative team effort involving the company's accounting department and the outside auditor and that its purpose is to obtain an opinion from the outside CPAs on the financial statements, not to search for defalcations or inefficiencies in the administrative or accounting departments.

**Liaison With The Auditor.** During the auditor's examination, questions arise, discussions are required to obtain facts regarding unusual transactions, and many matters must be explained. The work of an organization can be disrupted if auditors must search for the person best qualified to furnish the needed information. If the wrong person is asked and incorrect or incomplete information is received, time is wasted in correcting the inadequate or erroneous recording of data in the audit working papers. To prevent such errors and to facilitate the flow of accurate communication, one or two knowledgeable people from the controller's staff should be appointed to maintain liaison with the auditor and obtain information from the proper sources.

Conversely, the auditor should funnel all significant questions to the client through one or two members of its staff, preferably the audit manager or the in-charge staff person. Such a procedure also saves time, and avoids unnecessary questions. However, the auditor must not be restricted from access to all records and all personnel. Such restrictions would be considered an unacceptable limitation on the scope of the audit.

**Providing Appropriate Facilities.** Controllers should bear in mind that the outside auditor's time is costly, and that the audit should be completed as quickly as possible. Too often, time is wasted because outside auditors are treated as second-class citizens and are housed in a corner of the company's general office or crowded into a small office with inadequate lighting and facilities, far from the source of the data with which they must work. It is economical to provide auditors with appropriate working quarters and tools and to position them adjacent to any accounting or clerical personnel who will be called upon to assist them.  If adding machines and calculators are not available, they should be rented.

The auditor's facilities should be available for overtime and weekend work.  In addition, some of the company's accounting staff should be present to provide assistance during these periods.

### Audit Planning and Procedures

**Planning the Audit.**  The audit itself should be planned with the same care that is used in planning and budgeting other operations.  The development of an audit plan is a joint venture in which top personnel from the controller's staff and the CPA firm should participate.  The company's audit committee should also be involved.  At this point, the controller should assign responsibility for liaison with the auditor to an appropriate individual—the assistant controller, the chief accountant, or a senior staff member.

It is best to start the initial planning of the following year's audit shortly after the completion of the current audit.  Mistakes and problems are then fresh in the minds of all participants, and plans can be made to avoid them.  Furthermore, the auditor's working papers are readily available to help in making decisions on the details and working paper schedules for the succeeding year.

Management should bear in mind that the early plan is a preliminary one and that the final plan can be developed toward the end of the year on the basis of conditions then existing.  At that time, personnel and dollar budgets for the audit can be developed, discussed, and agreed on with the auditor.

The audit timetable and schedule, approved by the auditor and the company, would include:

- A list of the various working papers, schedules, and activities.
- An indication of whether the work is to be done by the auditor or by the company. (If the work is to be done by the company, the individuals responsible for its completion should be named.)
- A timetable for completion of the final working papers, schedules, and documents.
- An indication that the work has been done, by whom, and when.

**Budgeting.**  Management should budget the audit engagement in the same way it budgets any other corporate activity, and should base this budget on conditions existing at the time of the audit.  The amounts of specific items can be determined on the basis of the prior year's activities.  The auditor should provide a budget that allots a portion of the total audit fee to each subsidiary, division, or subdivision of the company based on personnel hours, rates for staff classifications, and out-of-pocket expenses.  Some auditing firms not only help to prepare such a budget and furnish it to the client but may also analyze the budget by various categories, such as balance sheet and profit and loss accounts, tax return preparation, and preparation of SEC reports.

When the controller reviews the budget with the auditor, he may sometimes effect economies by assigning some work previously done by the auditor to the company's internal auditing department.  However, in reducing budget items, management should never jeopardize the outside auditor's ability to determine that auditing standards have been met and that the financial statements have been prepared in accordance with generally accepted accounting principles that have been consistently applied.

**Audit Working Papers.**  To demonstrate compliance with the standards of field work, the auditor retains a file of working papers, which includes schedules prepared by the auditor or the client, copies of letters and other documents, confirmation requests and replies, and other evidentiary matters.  Many of these papers can be prepared or obtained by the controller's staff and furnished to the auditors, who review the data, indicate the work they have performed thereon, and retain the papers in their files.

Because the per diem cost of the CPA staff is high compared to the salaries of employees on the controller's staff, companies should cut costs by preparing schedules, obtaining documents, and preparing computer print-outs for the auditor's working paper review.  The auditor can then check to see that entries, additions, footings, and computations of various kinds are accurate and are properly recorded.

A controller may also reduce audit costs by hiring temporary help and assigning them to the auditor to perform computational work under the direction and control of the audit supervisor.

**Advance Work.**  The timely completion of an audit depends to a great extent on the amount of work done by the controller's staff before the arrival of the auditor. Costs can be reduced substantially by creating audit packages that are sent to each division and subdivision of the company, that designate the required audit working papers, and that provide instructions for uniform preparation.

Adequate use of internal control and internal audit reports prepared by the internal audit staff is also helpful.  An internal auditing department is usually charged with activities beyond the scope of the outside auditor's program.  The internal auditor can prepare documents and include in the internal audit reports comments about internal control in each of the divisions being audited.  The outside auditor can examine these reports, evaluate the extent of accounting and control procedures within the company, and reach conclusions about the quality of the financial records.  The firm can also use these reports to plan its audit programs, minimizing detailed audits in areas reviewed by the internal group.

**Interim Work.**  Audit programs can be divided into two segments: (1) a test of the transactions, which is a test of internal control and the quality of the client's records; and (2) the balance sheet audit, which establishes the validity of the amounts on the balance sheet and in the income statement.

Much of the testing of transactions, and some analytical work on the balance sheet audit, is frequently accomplished two, three, or more months before the end of the company's fiscal year. This reduces the time and amount of work between the close of the fiscal year and the issuance of the audited report.

This two-step approach should be encouraged. It spreads the burden of dealing with the auditor over two periods: an interim period, in which there is little pressure from timing requirements, and a final period, after year-end, in which the audit must be completed. The auditor can accomplish a great deal during the interim period and minimize the amount of work necessary to complete the transaction testing through the balance sheet date.

The interim program could also be used to complete the audits for branches, divisions, and subsidiaries one or two months prior to the end of the fiscal year. The auditor would not make a subsequent detailed examination of the transactions occurring between these audits and year-end but would reserve analysis for items of an unusual nature or amount.

Some companies have the audit performed at the end of the eleventh month of the year. As soon as the trial balance for the full year is obtained from the books, they then have the auditor quickly review the final month's transactions and issue its report. Again, only items of an unusual nature or amount are examined. Of course, this practice requires the auditor to have confidence in the integrity and quality of the accounting records and the internal control. This procedure is especially practical for public companies that want to furnish their annual reports to stockholders promptly after the close of the year.

**Special Work.** If work other than the audit, such as management advisory services or specialized tax work, is contemplated during the audit period, management should consider postponing such activities until after the audit is completed. In any event, such work should be separately costed and billed.

### Subsidiaries, Divisions and Branches

Delays in the completion of the audit can result from failure to plan appropriate audit steps for outlying divisions, branches, or subsidiaries. These audits must be timed so that the required information is received promptly and in a format that can be combined and consolidated quickly and accurately with home or corporate office accounts.

In some circumstances, the CPA firm, lacking an office at the location of the subsidiary or division, may utilize a correspondent auditor. In other cases, the client may want to use a local auditor because of the local political situation or, more frequently, to save travel costs when the principal auditor does not have a local office. Under these circumstances, it may be difficult for the principal CPA to plan and coordinate the program. Each case must be evaluated in the light of the local circumstances, the size of the subsidiary in relation to the whole, and the amount of control exercised by the principal CPA over the program and performance of the correspondent auditor.

If divisions or subsidiaries lack complete complements of staff and accounting records for internal reports, such activities might be transferred to the home office or to regional offices. The consolidation of these accounting activities could reduce corporate overhead and, in many instances, audit costs as well. This type of reorganization could also result in collateral improvement in clerical records, accounting procedures, and managerial controls.

Further problems arise when an audit of a consolidated foreign subsidiary is required. Auditing procedures and accounting principles and practices vary greatly between countries. Each situation should be reviewed in the light of prevailing circumstances, the capabilities of the foreign auditor, and local auditing principles and practices, and the CPA firm must be satisfied with the arrangements. Advance planning and precise instructions can prevent many troublesome problems.

## Cyclical Audits

If there are a number of distant entities, it may be desirable to establish audits for them on a cyclical basis. The decision to use cyclical audits generally rests with the audit firm, which must be satisfied that the audit is of sufficient scope so that it is able to attest to the fairness of the financial statements taken as a whole.

The cycles can be arranged so that those entities that are significant units (whether they are subsidiaries, divisions, branches, warehouses, or other subdivisions of the company) are audited with sufficient frequency. Smaller units can be reviewed on the basis of the internal audits or internal control procedures and can be audited by the CPA infrequently or not at all.

A cyclical procedure could also be applied to the testing of certain types of accounts, and the transactions in these accounts could be examined by the auditor only every other year or every third year. This practice should be adopted only at the discretion of the auditor, who must have confidence in the quality of corporate records, internal control, and internal auditing activities.

If the controller makes periodic reviews of internal control on a cyclical basis, each clerical and control operation can be examined at least once a year. Companies large enough to maintain an internal auditing staff usually include such a procedure in the internal auditing function. The outside audit firm should have access to the results of such reviews to help it evaluate the company's control procedures.

## Inventory Auditing

Inspection and auditing of inventories usually requires more time than any other portion of the audit. Good housekeeping and the physical maintenance of inventories in an orderly fashion throughout the year can reduce inspection time. Properly planned inventory taking, with good written instructions and preinventory meetings between assigned plant personnel and a representative of the audit firm, also helps to make counts efficient and accurate. Perpetual inventory records and controls, with frequent internal audit test counts, can often be relied on to meet the auditor's standards with a minimum of inspection and observation.

If inventories are located at outlying locations, divisions, and subsidiaries, the independent auditor may consider whether observation at every location is required each year. Cyclical counts at different locations on a controlled basis often suffice, particularly if good internal control and inventory records exist.

The techniques of statistical sampling should be explored and used if inventories are substantial and complete counts would be costly and time consuming. Statistical sampling can often reduce audit time and provide a high degree of reliability.

After the audit firm has satisfied itself concerning the quantities involved, it must ascertain that the clerical activities involved in recording the inventory and the unit-pricing methods are consistent and meet the lower-of-cost-or-market test.

When inventories are stated on a last-in, first-out (LIFO) basis, schedules of conversion to this method of pricing can be prepared for review. Since internal interim records are generally maintained on a basis other than LIFO (usually FIFO or average cost), the year-end conversion must be consistent with the method used in the prior year.

The significant amount of auditing time required for this phase of the audit suggests an early start. Many companies take physical inventories one, two, or three months before the end of the fiscal year, and the auditor examines the records as of this early date. The total inventory amounts are then updated to the year-end balance sheet date by adding and subtracting the totals of transactions for the short interim period.

**Unusual Transactions**

One of the time-consuming aspects of an audit is the examination of a significant transaction or the review of a change in an accounting policy or procedure. Time, money, and effort can be saved if such transactions or changes are discussed with the auditor before they are put into effect. Otherwise, a transaction may be recorded in a manner that is not in accordance with generally accepted accounting principles, or the auditor's opinion may be qualified because the principles have not been applied on a basis consistent with that of the prior year.

**Clerical and Accounting System Changes**

It is wise to consult with the outside auditor's management advisory staff when a significant change in accounting or clerical procedures is contemplated or when a feasibility study and installation of data processing equipment are under way. These changes may affect the internal accounting controls and thus bear directly on the audit program. The auditor may suggest procedures that would maintain controls without impairing the results desired by management. The experience and knowledge that the auditor's management advisory staff have gained from the examination of many systems can help the company avoid costly errors or add to the contemplated improvements from the changed procedure or installation.

## Internal Control

The auditor relies on existing internal control to determine the extent of tests and the auditing procedures to be applied. Good internal control procedures reduce external audit costs. Conversely, if internal control is weak, auditing tests must be extensive.

At the beginning of the audit the outside auditor generally reviews the company's internal control procedures and evaluates them to determine their adequacy for audit purposes. The auditor then performs compliance tests to learn whether the procedures are being followed, and judges their effectiveness. The tests generally include a study of the paper flow and the recording of the transactions. They may be applied for selected types of transactions, for limited periods of time, or for all transactions on a cyclical basis.

Since the procedures include preparation of schedules as evidence of the tests and an examination of the documents underlying the transactions, the controller should obtain as much information as possible concerning the audit program and the required working paper schedules. In many instances, if the company's staff can prepare these schedules and make documents available, the amount of time required by the auditor is reduced, without impairing his effectiveness and independence.

## Computer Auditing

The advent of computers and computerized accounting has had its impact on auditing techniques and procedures. (See Chapter 11 for a discussion of the use of computers for financial accounting and reporting.) Auditing needs should be considered during the programming of such installations, and the controller should consult the outside auditor before data processing procedures and programs are made final. Provision can be made for the auditor to use the equipment for the tests required to meet field work standards. Preplanning these audit requirements usually adds little or no cost to the installation, whereas costly revisions may be necessary if the system must be reprogrammed later to accommodate the requirements.

Many CPA firms have programs for the audit of computerized records through the use of the client's equipment, their own computers, or a service bureau. These audit programs require the use of the company's tapes and programs, which therefore must be retained for use at audit time. Furthermore, accounts receivable and other large-quantity confirmation requests are often prepared by the computer. In addition, the auditor may require copies of some of the company's regular printouts.

As part of the audit plan, management should determine the extent to which the company's computer is to be used in preparing documents and performing audit tests for the CPA firm. The computer supervisor should be involved in planning this work so that programs and timetables can be developed.

## WORKING WITH AUDIT COMMITTEES

An effective audit committee lends an important dimension to management's perspective on corporate operations. Audit committees composed of outside directors sharpen the distinction between corporate management, which runs operations, and the board, which monitors management's performance and establishes broad policy on the shareholders' behalf.

In light of the increased challenges relating to the Foreign Corrupt Practices Act and protection of assets, the independent audit now assumes critical importance. The use of audit committees gives directors and the controller valuable insight into the audit function and related financial controls.

The controller is management's liaison with the audit committee. He performs the following functions:

- Provides the committee with current financial data;
- Keeps the committee informed of management's plans and forecasts; and
- Reviews public announcements on financial matters.

### Common Policy and Procedural Issues

Because audit committees have developed without reference to a universally accepted set of rules, their structure and activities vary. The procedures may be informal or formal, the program loosely or tightly structured, and the reviewed activities confined narrowly to the annual independent audit or broadened sufficiently to include other matters. Although audit committee practices vary significantly from company to company, certain questions of policy and procedure are common to all companies:

- What relationship should the committee assume to the outside auditor? What role does the controller play?
- What kind of information should the committee seek from the outside auditor? How can the controller facilitate access to such information?
- What information should the committee seek from the internal auditors? How can the controller ensure that this information is pertinent and accessible?
- How intensive should the audit committee's investigations be?
- What staff and facilities can audit committees use to accomplish their purposes? How can the controller expedite their operations?
- What functions can audit committees perform aside from reviewing the annual independent audit? For example, should they be involved in the budgeting process? What role should the controller play?

Minimal audit committee functions include participating in the selection of the independent auditors, reviewing their prospective audit approach, and reviewing their findings. Even a minimal program allows wide latitude in the relative intensity of the committee's involvement. Other responsibilities could be incorporated into the audit committee's functions, such as reviewing internal audit activities, considering accounting policies selected by management, and reviewing internal accounting controls and related matters of asset security.

## Benefits of Audit Committees

A relationship between the outside auditor and management arises as a natural consequence of an audit. The existence of a nonofficer committee of the board of directors with audit review functions inhibits any tendency for this relationship to affect the auditor's independence.

Objectivity, moreover, is not only a question of overall attitude towards management decisions on financial matters. It also involves specific factors that audit committees can incorporate into their review procedures to bring important points to the surface. Committees might, for example, investigate the following conditions, all or any of which could affect the outside auditor's report:

- Lack of cooperation between management and the outside auditor;
- The outside auditor's inability to obtain important information;
- Limitations imposed on the scope of the auditor's examination;
- Management's failure to disclose important information in the financial statements;
- Disagreement as to valuation; and
- Failure to adhere to generally accepted accounting principles.

These conditions, if material, could lead to a qualified or negative auditor's report. Both the outside auditor and the controller will be particularly sensitive to the development of any such condition if they know that the audit committee is going to review the audit report and question the auditor before the report is issued to the public. Moreover, the effort to anticipate and prepare for directors' questions intensifies and broadens the auditor's review of the company's affairs. Both the auditor and the controller are encouraged to take a more aggressive and critical approach toward solving problems that they might otherwise be inclined to accept.

## Committee Structure and Functions

The potential benefits of audit committees depend on careful planning and organization of their activities. This planning begins with the selection of committee members.

**Size.** Most audit committees range in size from two to six members. As a general rule, audit committees should consist of at least three members, one serving as chairman.

**Composition.** About 30 percent of current committees have company employees —usually senior officers—as members. Generally, these officers are included on the strength of their personal qualifications and their ability to act collectively as a pipeline to management. Most boards, however, have enough nonemployee talent, including, but not limited to, business and financial expertise, to create an audit committee comprised solely of outside members. Generally, committees should have a majority of outside directors to maintain the independent point of view that is so crucial to the committee's effective functioning.

Unquestionably, a knowledge of business and finance is a distinct advantage to audit committee members. However, other factors also carry weight; for example, at least one member should be able to preside over meetings and to direct the discussion along constructive lines. Other important attributes for membership are the amount of time members can devote to duties and their motivation, inquisitiveness, persistence, and disposition towards critical analysis.

Finally, management should not minimize the desirability of diversity in outlook among committee members. A uniform point of view could lead to overemphasis in one direction.

Because investors have a special interest in the functioning of audit committees, committee members should be identified by name in the annual report.

**Term of Office.** Most audit committee members serve for one year. In determining an individual member's term of office, the board must weigh two opposing considerations:

- *Continuity.* Committee members need a minimum period of familiarization to operate efficiently.
- *Freshness.* Newly designated committee members automatically bring a fresh viewpoint to the committee's examinations.

A committee of several members with staggered terms of office might keep these considerations in balance.

**Responsibilities.** The audit committee must assist the board of directors in fulfilling its fiduciary responsibility relating to corporate accounting and reporting practices. The SEC and the courts are placing increased emphasis on the importance of the audit committee's role in this area. The audit committee must also maintain direct and separate lines of communication between the board of directors, the company's controller, and the outside auditor.

**Scope of Activities.** Although the audit committee's chief focus is the annual audit, many other activities fall within its purview. The committee's relationship with the controller and the auditor enables it to develop information and understanding that can significantly strengthen the board's command of company operations and enable the committee to undertake useful activities of its own.

Working with the controller and the auditor and on its own, the committee can investigate such matters as:

- The existence and quality of the company's system of internal accounting control;

- The quality and depth of staffing in the company's accounting and financial departments;
- The impact on the company's financial statements of proposed changes in generally accepted accounting principles;
- The quality of the company's internal audit program, or, if none exists, the desirability of establishing such a program;
- Fraud-detection measures and illegal acts; and
- The desirability of establishing a conflict-of-interest program administered by the audit committee itself.

The controller should meet with the committee and with the auditor to determine which programs should be established on a recurring basis and which programs could be beneficially conducted on an *ad hoc* basis.

The controller and the audit committee may also work together on the following types of projects:

- Reviewing the independent auditor's management letter recommending specific operational controls for management attention;
- Discussing implementation of the independent auditor's recommendations;
- Evaluating performance and staffing of accounting and financial departments;
- Discussing internal audit findings with the internal auditor;
- Discussing the adequacy of internal audit staff with the internal auditor; and
- Reviewing the company's budget and long-range financial planning each year.

While many of these activities relate to the company's financial statements and the systems involved in their preparation, most are also germane to profitability. Thus, they provide the board of directors with further understanding of both the degree of security of assets and overall management efficiency.

**Preparation for Meetings.** The controller can help committee members get the maximum benefit from audit committee meetings by providing information and background material in advance on the topics to be covered at the meetings. To assure adequate preparation by all parties, a written agenda, together with pertinent background material, should be drawn up for each meeting and circulated in advance to committee members and, where appropriate, the outside auditor, representatives of management, and the internal auditor. Careful planning and advance distribution of information and a prepared presentation from each participant should enable a typical committee to meet only once a year.

The agenda need not be the same each year. On the contrary, a policy of year-to-year uniformity can be severely restrictive: Investigative needs change annually. The agenda, therefore, may be drawn up to emphasize finance one year, internal control another year, and operational weaknesses a third year. To leave a clear trail and record of the audit committee's deliberations, decisions, and actions, minutes should be recorded and filed for future reference.

**Relationship With The Auditor**

**Selection.** Although the controller generally plays an important role in the selection of the auditor, the audit committee is also concerned with the selection process. As a rule, the controller and the audit committee consider several auditing firms.

Unquestionably, the ability, integrity, and even the personality of the partner or partners assigned to the audit are of great importance. Therefore, management should consider the personal qualities of key people in choosing one firm over a competitor firm. (Auditing firms that are interested in an engagement generally send representatives to interview key company financial and accounting personnel and visit company facilities in different locations.)

**Rotation.** Those who advocate periodic rotation of audit firms believe that the change:

- Reinforces the objectivity of the audit by discouraging overly close auditor-management relationships;
- Preserves a fresh auditor viewpoint; and
- Reduces the likelihood that the audit firm will not detect crucial items because it fails to recognize a change in conditions.

Countering these advantages, however, are certain significant drawbacks. A newly appointed firm must incur extra audit expenses to accumulate the information needed to become familiar with the company's operations and special industry characteristics. Furthermore, rotation can sometimes lead to a loss of continuity and a lack of familiarity with accounting principles used in prior periods. The corporation also incurs additional costs as a result of rotation—executives and staff must spend time familiarizing the new auditor with the company's business controls and procedures.

A client may preserve the advantages of rotation without forfeiting the advantages of continuity if the auditing firm's internal policies permit. Thus, an audit committee can explore:

- Rotating all personnel involved in audit activities; and
- Revising audit programs to keep auditing relevant to current conditions.

When a change of auditor occurs, it is preferable for the audit committee to meet with both management and the exiting auditor to obtain their views on the change. In this way, the committee can make sure there are no unstated differences that could have an effect on future relationships and may also gain insights that may be useful in avoiding future difficulties.

The Securities and Exchange Commission requires that, on selection of a new auditor, the registrant furnish a letter advising the commission whether there have been any recent disagreements with the former auditor on accounting or auditing matters. The registrant must also send the commission a letter from the former auditor stating its agreement (or disagreement) with the registrant's letter.

## Establishing an Internal Audit Department

The internal audit function identifies problems and possible solutions that may not be of major direct concern to the independent auditor. Since an internal audit department is such an important element of the internal control system, the audit committee or the entire board of directors may want to promote the establishment of such a department if none exists. (See Chapter 19 on internal auditing organization and planning.)

Since approaches to the internal audit function vary widely, audit committees should explore internal audit department operations to determine how internal and independent auditors can work together more effectively.

## Preaudit Interviews

The audit committee determines whether preaudit interviews with the independent auditor and with company officers are desirable. Preaudit interviews are useful to the committee not only in setting objectives in areas such as internal audit, fraud detection, and conflicts of interest but also in initiating measures to implement them. For example, an audit committee concerned about the potential for abuses in the use of the computer might ask the auditor to expand the scope of its examination by adding intensive tests of the integrity of the system.

Following the interview with the auditor, the committee may wish to interview individual representatives of company management, such as the financial vice president, controller, treasurer, other financial officers, and the internal auditor. Management interviews emphasize such areas as accounting policies, internal control, financial performance, efficiency, fraud detection, and conflict of interest, as well as management's views on matters covered by the independent auditor's management letter. The committee then identifies potential areas of investigation and determines whether to explore them directly or have management ask the auditor (either independent or internal) to investigate.

## Postaudit Interviews

Whatever other activities the audit committee undertakes, a comprehensive review of the year's financial statements is one of its principal functions. When the audit has been completed and the financial statements are ready for publication, the committee meets with the independent auditor (and possibly management as well).

In such postaudit interviews, the committee has four separate considerations:

- The financial statements themselves, and all their implications for the board, management, and stockholders;
- Interim and other unaudited data;
- The internal control considerations and the auditing procedures that make up the independent auditor's examination of the financial statements; and
- Any significant problems that arose in the examination or in applying generally accepted accounting principles.

Listed below are some representative questions that the committee might ask the auditor and management during the postaudit interviews:

- How do the company's accounting, financial, and operational controls compare to those prevailing in this or in other industries? Are other companies giving more or less information in the financial statements and elsewhere in the financial report?
- Do the company's systems and procedures provide a reliable basis for its quarterly reports to shareholders?
- Are there any material commitments of cash that are not disclosed?
- Has the value of marketable securities changed significantly since year-end?
- How does the average age of accounts receivable at year-end compare with the preceding year? How is the allowance for doubtful accounts determined? How does the present allowance compare to the change in the current year's receivables? Is the collectibility of any large individual amount in question? Are any amounts due from officers or employees?

**Audited and Interim Statements**

**Audited Financial Statements.** In reviewing the financial statements with the independent auditor, audit committees should be especially alert to areas that involve judgment in valuing assets and measuring liabilities. In the course of examining the financial statements, the auditor reviews management's decisions as to appropriate accounting treatments. Since these decisions involve judgments as to present and future conditions and their potential effects on matters such as asset realization, audit committees should be alert to situations where variations in judgment could have financial impact. The controller will, of course, have significant responsibilities for these situations. Representative areas and pertinent questions include the following:

- Inventory valuations. How are obsolete and slow-moving items treated?
- Provision for doubtful accounts receivable. What would be the effect of a credit crunch?
- Depreciation of property or plant. Do useful-life assumptions reflect technical obsolescence?
- Treatment of intangible assets, such as goodwill and deferred expenses. How does company practice differ from that followed by others in the industry?
- Significance of contingent liabilities and future commitments. Is a change in foreign currency exchange rates likely to increase corporate liabilities? Have hedges been placed?

**Unaudited Information.** The current scrutiny being given to unaudited information in general, and to interim financial statements in particular, makes this an area of interest to audit committees because of their responsibility for information communicated to outsiders and their concern with events affecting their companies.

Many audit committees conduct reviews of interim and other unaudited data. They question management, the internal auditor, and the independent auditor with regard to the following:

- Have generally accepted accounting principles been consistently applied in accordance with guidelines contained in Accounting Principles Board Opinion No. 28 on interim reporting?
- Are the company's financial and operating controls functioning and can they be expected to continue to function properly?
- Can changes in financial ratios and relationships reported in the interim financial statements be reasonably explained by reference to changes in the company's operations and financing practices?
- Are unusual and extraordinary items and seasonal variations in sales, costs, and expenses adequately disclosed and explained?
- Does the financial summarization contain adequate disclosures, particularly regarding matters such as commitments, contingent liabilities, and unusual risks and uncertainties?

Limited reviews of interim information by the independent accountant can play an important role in helping audit committees discharge their responsibilities with respect to such statements. The controller, as the principal member of management responsible for the preparation of interim financial statements, should review such statements with the audit committee.

## Overview of Internal Control

**Internal Control.** The committee members' concern with internal control is twofold. They must consider it from the point of view of the independent auditor's requirements as well as from the point of view of their own responsibilities. Areas of concern may include:

- System of asset protection;
- Adequacy of accounting system;
- Propriety in recording of transactions;
- Reliability of accounting records; and
- Accuracy and completeness of financial reports.

Committee members generally study these areas with the independent auditor and internal auditor where applicable.

**Management Letters.** The committee should obtain copies of recent reports to management on audit findings (sometimes referred to as *management letters*). Such reports commonly cover deficiencies in internal controls noted during the course of an audit and incorporate suggestions for improving controls. The prior year's management letter can provide clues to areas that may be of particular concern and to significant matters that should be followed up in the forthcoming audit. (While management letters are usually quite detailed, the more significant comments are frequently summarized for the audit committee so that its members are not burdened with reviewing less important matters.)

### New Areas of Concern

**Forecasts.** As the SEC and the accounting profession become increasingly concerned with financial forecasts, audit committees will devote increased attention to this area and will work closely with the controller's department, which generally participates in or directs the preparation of forecasts and budgets. Audit committees could also become involved in the formulation of longer-term financial forecasts submitted to lending institutions.

**Special Investigations.** The involvement of audit committees in special inquiry and investigative functions for boards of directors is a recent development. The use of corporate funds for political contributions or other illegal payments to public officials within or outside the United States is an area of particular concern.

### Reporting to the Board

Audit committees are normally required to report their activities to the board of directors, though the formality, detail, and frequency (some boards require interim reports) of reporting varies. The following topical breakdown shows the areas generally included in reports to the board:

- Selection of the auditor;
- Approval of audit fees;
- Financial statements;
- Accounting and financial policies;
- System of internal control;
- Effectiveness of accounting and internal audit operations and personnel; and
- Other matters specific to individual companies.

Reports to the board usually comprise an overall summary of the committee's activities for the year and a series of recommendations. Sometimes the reports are in writing, in which case they are often supplemented by minutes of the audit committee meetings. More commonly, the audit committee reports orally to the board and responds to questions from board members. Written agendas, together with any written background material, may provide a framework for the report.

## SUGGESTED READING

Brownstein, Howard. "Audit Committees and Lawyer-Auditor Conflicts." *Directors & Boards*, Vol. 1 (Spring, 1976), pp. 49-60.

Caplin, Mortimer. "Outside Directors and Their Responsibilities: A Program for the Exercise of Due Care." *Journal of Corporation Law*, Vol. 1 (Fall, 1975), pp. 57-82.

Choka, Allen D. "New Role of the Audit Committee." *Practical Lawyer,* Vol. 23 (September 1, 1977), pp. 53-60.

Corey, Gordon R. "Some New Comments on the Directors' Audit Committee and the Audit Functions." *Internal Auditor*, Vol. 34 (October, 1977), pp. 25-30.

Davies, Donald H. "Controls vs. Control." Internal Auditor, Vol. 33 (August, 1976), pp. 17-25.

Hardy, John W. "Audit Committee Practices." *CPA Journal*, Vol. 47 (September, 1977), pp. 9-12.

Loebbecke, James K. "Audit Planning and Company Assistance." *CPA Journal,* Vol. 47 (November, 1977), pp. 31-34.

Morison, Arthur. "Independence of the Auditor." *CPA Journal*, Vol. 47 (December, 1977), pp. 33-36.

# 45

# Working With the Investment Community

*Winthrop C. Neilson*

*Thomas C. Franco*

## THE INVESTOR AUDIENCE

For publicly held corporations, a major portion of the responsibility for communication with investors falls to the corporate controller. The extent of this responsibility varies widely, depending on the emphasis placed by management on investor relations as well as the kind of communications support provided by the company's public relations staff.

Many controllers are actively involved in written communications to investors, and many meet with the financial community. To develop effective investor communications, the controller should consider several basic audiences. The audiences with which the controller is most concerned are divided into several broad categories:

- Individual stockholders;
- Professional investors;
- The press;
- Employee stockholders; and
- Foreign investors.

### Individual Stockholders

From a high point of around 32 million, the number of small stockholders has shrunk steadily. According to latest statistics, they now number around 25 million. These investors have grown suspicious of common stock, primarily because of declining stock values, particularly in the face of inflation. This dissatisfaction has not been dispelled by the quality of the information they receive from both corporations and stock brokers.

Small stockholders are practical, and are primarily interested in earnings per share, the earnings outlook (though not necessarily projections), and dividends. They are suspicious of public relations gimmicks and want a true picture, presented briefly and clearly, and a sense of corporate direction. Contrary to popular belief, the average stockholder, if approached properly, tends to be loyal to management.

Annual and interim reports continue to be the forms of corporate literature most often received by individuals. Other communications include enclosures with the dividend check, the proxy statement, and literature concerning the annual meeting. Many corporations send out welcome letters to new stockholders. And, in recent years, some managements have taken to writing special letters to their stockholders on subjects of particular importance, such as public issues affecting business.

Corporations prefer individual investors over institutional investors. Individuals tend to be long-term holders, and their movement in and out of a stock does not create violent gyrations in the market place, as is the case with the trading of large holdings by institutions. Individuals also have a track record of supporting management at proxy time, often accepting recommendations at face value. On the other hand, individuals are difficult to communicate with, not only because their numbers are shrinking and they are scattered geographically, but also because they lack financial sophistication and frequently misunderstand stock market mechanics.

### Professional Investors

This group encompasses a wide range of investors, from large institutions and mutual funds to the more speculative brokerage accounts. Institutional interest can mean a higher price/earnings ratio if a company's financial position is sound and the industry is attractive to investors. However, controversy arises within corporate management about the relative merits of institutional ownership.

From the standpoint of communications, institutions are unquestionably easier to reach than individuals. They are tuned to corporate and financial terminology. But the disadvantages connected with institutional stock ownership are formidable. Unlike individuals, institutions disrupt stock prices when they buy and sell, they have no corporate loyalty beyond bottom-line statistics, they usually hide ownership behind nominee names, and they are much more selective in proxy voting. In most large companies, institutions hold a controlling position even though they rarely vote as a block. So it's not entirely surprising that individual investors distrust institutions and fear that they receive preferential treatment.

## The Press

The press plays a vital role in any investor relations program because of the disclosure requirements that all publicly held corporations face. Companies are required to disseminate any material information as it becomes available. Any information affecting the value of the stock is considered material.

The most common material disclosures that the controller should concern himself with include earnings statements, dividend declarations, company forecasts, merger announcements, major new-product developments, major capital program announcements that require outside financing, and labor contracts. The major exchanges, as well as the Securities and Exchange Commission, require that material information be released quickly and widely and be available to anyone trading in the stock.

The press is the primary disseminator of material information. Such information should not be discussed with members of the financial community until there has been verification that the news has appeared on either a major newswire or in a comparable publication. To supplement this press activity the company's stockholders and key members of the financial community who follow the company should also receive copies of the release. As a matter of prudent practice, no company official should trade in the stock until at least 48 hours after this information has been disseminated.

## Employee Stockholders

Corporations are increasingly interested in employee stockholders. In many instances, employees are more concerned about corporate progress than the average investor because of their direct stake in the company. Employees tend to be extremely loyal unless the corporation is undergoing major problems. Most employees hold on to their shares and can be counted on to support management in the event of a hostile tender offer.

On the other hand, some managements raise moral questions about the fairness of having an individual tie up his life savings in the company that provides his major source of income. If the stock price falls, many employees may become doubtful about management's competence and the quality of the company itself. There have been isolated instances when employee stockholders have challenged management on the assumption that as stockholders they have additional rights (which, in fact, they do).

Corporations that encourage employees to own stock often prepare special annual reports for their employees or hold employee meetings around the country to explain problems and new developments facing the company.

### Foreign Investors

The foreign investor is more sophisticated than his American counterpart. Technically most foreign investors fall into the category of institutional holdings. Yet companies face additional problems in servicing overseas stockholders. Because many foreigners lack familiarity with such matters as proxies, and because many exchanges trade American shares in the form of unregistered-bearer shares (thereby making it difficult to locate stockholders), the response time on stockholder communications may be unusually long.

Some corporations actively seek this type of stockholder, however, believing that foreign involvement provides new areas for marketing securities, spreading out the company's ownership, and increasing the company's visibility.

## THE CONTROLLER'S ROLE IN COMMUNICATIONS

The controller plays a vital role in shareowner relations. This role obviously varies from company to company. In some instances, it is limited to putting together the bare-boned statistics or checking the figures in the annual and interim reports. In other cases, the controller has major responsibility for written communications, including the drafting of the annual and interim reports. In still other cases, controllers become intimately involved in all investor relations planning.

### Structuring the Annual Report

Until recently, few items were mandated for this stockholder report. (See Chapter 9 for a detailed discussion of financial details required in such reports.) In fact, the most commonly used format evolved because most companies found it the most effective. Yet there is little sacred about this format. Some critics claim the annual report is the poorest of all corporate communications in terms of readership presentation. Others state it is the only communication that is read more intensely before it is published than afterward.

In structuring the report, the first concern is the emphasis that should be placed on reaching each of the two key audiences—the individual stockholder and the professional investor. This raises the broader concern of the firm's investor relations goals in terms of the type of investor the company is seeking and the importance (taking into account the current shareowner breakdown) of each group to the company.

Some corporations aim the major portion of their report to individuals and then develop supplemental statistical reports for the more sophisticated investor. The annual report should be a balanced response to the needs of the firm's major share-owner audiences.

For the most part, individual investors appreciate simplicity. The plethora of information they receive causes confusion. In contrast, professional investors depend on annual reports for detailed information that often goes beyond the under-standing of individuals. These two audiences are so obviously at odds that it has even been suggested that corporations print two separate reports, one for individu-als, the other for professionals.

**Format and Contents.** Annual reports are broken down into several sections. Although a few enterprising companies have deviated from the normal format in an effort to increase readership and understanding at less sophisticated levels, the basic format is:

- The cover;
- The corporate profile;
- The financial highlights;
- The stockholders letter; and
- The directors page.

*Cover.* The cover should serve three basic purposes: (1) identify the company and the year covered, (2) indicate the nature of the company business, and (3) be dramatic enough to attract the reader's attention. Besides glossy picture covers, some companies use charts and quotations from the text. A few companies restrict the graphics to logos, or print just the company name, but generally speaking, a dull cover presents a picture of stodginess.

*Corporate profile.* Ideally, the corporate profile appears on the inside front cover and page one. Often it is accompanied by appropriate financial charts and pictures. This section offers the individual a quick capsule of what has happened during the year as well as a recap of the company's major activities.

Most corporate profiles run only two or three paragraphs. They outline products and the markets served. Sometimes there is a brief historical overview. There is a trend to have the cover caption expanded into part of the profile.

*Financial highlights.* Financial highlights should be just that—highlights. The key figures are sales, operating earnings (optional), taxes, net income, net income per share, and number of shares outstanding, usually on a weighted average basis for the year. Other possibilities include book value per share, number of employees, and number of stockholders. Many corporations put in other figures, such as depre-ciation, total assets, working capital, capital expenditures, and ratios (e.g., current assets to current liabilities.) However, these figures are not meaningful in the absence of complete balance sheet figures.

The controller should make sure that the normally unaudited highlights on these first two pages jibe with other figures in the report. The outside auditors are also required to check these figures against the audited financial statements. Unusual circumstances, such as foreign taxes or loss carryforwards in footnotes, should be explained. The controller should consider using the two front pages for mandated quarterly figures, since they are of interest to individuals who often don't read the financial section, where this information generally appears.

*Stockholders letter.* Traditionally, this letter has been treated as the most important part of the annual report from a public relations point of view, although a few companies have adopted alternative approaches such as a memo, a news capsule, or even an interview with the president.

It is the rare chief executive who doesn't personally agonize over the letter's contents. While many stockholders don't look at this message as a true message, at least not in the terms corporations do, the letter is read by more individual investors than any other section of the report. The professional is also interested in it, particularly in terms of "management tone." However, the analyst will concentrate on the other text for in-depth analysis, or for what is sometimes referred to as the "bad news."

The size of the letter varies from short one-pagers to the entire report. The longer the letter, the less likely it is to be read, so it is best confined to a brief overview of what happened to the company over the past year, with some suggestions (not projections) for the future. Only one or two paragraphs should go into the specific figures. There is no need in the text to repeat what the highlights show. Interpretation of trends, a brief discussion of important operating events, the dividend action (a major consideration for investors, but one that is frequently omitted), capital programs, new products, competitive pressures, marketing products, research and development, public issues affecting the company, and the future outlook are frequent topics.

The controller should assist the writer in charge of the management analysis and check for accuracy in both the figures and the interpretation. SEC rules require a management analysis as part of the annual report.

*Directors page.* The directors and officers page is another important information item. It is mandated by the SEC that the principal occupation or affiliations of outside directors be listed. Some companies also list each director's age and length of service, and most companies show the committees on which each serves. The list of officers is very straightforward. Normally, the names appear on the back page, often accompanied by photographs. The small investor is not concerned with photographs, but the professional investor is, partly to see the officers' ages, partly to be able to identify certain executives in the event he meets them.

*Other information.* Stockholders must be notified that the Form 10-K is available upon request; however, most of the required 10-K information is now required in the stockholders report. Other items usually shown on the back page include the transfer agent, the registrar, the corporation's address and phone number, and the person or persons to contact for further information. The latter items are important stockholder concerns and should not be omitted.

Many corporations add to the annual report an invitation to the annual meeting. If an invitation is placed in the annual report, it should be placed in the front of the report, and couched in friendly rather than legal or perfunctory language.

**Coordination With Outsiders.** Outsiders are involved in the issuance of every annual report, some by necessity, others by choice. It is important that they be kept up to date and made aware of the pressures under which the report is being produced.

*The auditors.* Auditors are an essential part of the annual report team. They should be made aware of the printing schedule early so that they have sufficient time to prepare material. On occasion, annual reports have run into serious production problems because the auditors have been late turning in their work. This, in turn, has resulted in expensive overtime costs.

*The printers.* The annual report project should be bid out to several printers and should not be awarded on the basis of cost alone but on the basis of the printing firm's professionalism, its ability to move quickly, and its accessibility. The controller, along with the rest of the annual report team, should make his decision after looking at several examples of annual reports and talking to other companies about their printing experiences.

The annual report project, no matter how well it is planned, often turns out to be a pressured task. Figures come in at the last minute. Text changes are frequent. Pictures don't work out the way they should. The printers must be aware of these unusual problems and be able to react quickly. The closer a company is to its printer, the easier the logistics become. For this reason, if a company is located in a small city, a good local printer is often preferable to one in New York or Chicago. In addition, local printers are usually cheaper and more willing to put in the necessary overtime. If they are inexperienced, however, they must be supervised closely.

It is difficult for the controller to estimate how much a good annual report will cost. Figures are misleading, because large companies spend less on a volume basis than do small companies. The price for each copy of a report ranges from $1.00 to $3.00, but there are too many factors involved, including geographic variations, to come up with an accurate figure. Although the printer should estimate costs in advance, extra charges are incurred by changes made by the author (i.e., changes in the text after it has been set in type) and by overtime if the schedule is not met. It is not unusual for this secondary figure to run as high as the original budgeted cost.

*Art designers and photographers.* Most corporations use outside designers and should choose them by using the same cost and selection rules they use when choosing a printer. Designers can be quite expensive, and it is usually cheaper to have the printer handle the art work and designing tasks. Unfortunately, however, the printer's in-house designer may not be the most creative artist available. Sometimes, companies rely on their regular advertising firm for this service.

When working with photographers, the controller should make certain that the schedule for taking pictures provides ample time for photograph development. Preparation of pictures for printing must be coordinated closely with the needs of the printer.

*Outside writers or production firms.* Many corporations hire outside firms to assist them with the annual report in order to simplify the task or make the report more professional. Others may ask their investor relations or public relations firm to write the entire report.

There are advantages and disadvantages to seeking outside help. In most instances, it is more difficult to originate reliable text, because outsiders are not familiar with company operations. On the other hand, outsiders can be more objective. They can best be used as consultants to lend perspective to company-originated ideas. As consultants, they can also comment on the material to be included in the annual report and assist in the rewriting or editing of the original text. Professional outsiders are aware of current trends and are well versed on regulatory requirements. An experienced outsider also knows what short cuts can be taken to streamline production.

*Transfer agent and mailing.* The controller should coordinate the annual report mailing schedule with the department or outside agent that is responsible for maintaining shareholder records. It is important to alert the transfer agent well in advance as to the target mailing date.

The annual report must be mailed with or prior to the proxy statement, because stockholders technically should receive the report before or with the proxy. To satisfy this requirement, most companies mail their annual reports third class several days before the proxy is sent out. Finally, the SEC requires that the annual report be mailed to stockholders no later than 90 days after the end of the fiscal year. If there is an unavoidable delay, the company can ask the SEC for an extension.

## Other Stockholder Communications

In recent years, corporate communications to investors have grown in importance and quality. There is a great deal of corporate flexibility in how detailed or limited to make these special communications.

**Interim Reports.** Interim reports consist of two basic items—a message to the investors and an abbreviated income statement. Increasingly, corporations are also presenting a short, unaudited balance sheet. Arguments for including the balance sheet surfaced after the bankruptcy of several major corporations. Investors now want to see the company's financial position, including trends, more than once a year. (The quarterly Form 10-Q filed with the SEC requires a full condensed financial statement, so the information is available.)

The controller's role focuses on the more difficult balance sheet. It is his obligation to work with the writers, alerting them to important developments, particularly short-term ones, so that they are interpreted accurately to the reader.

The most common complaint about interim reports is their lack of timeliness. Many are printed two to three weeks after the quarterly earnings press release. Investors who have already read this information in the financial news feel they are receiving secondhand information. To avoid such criticism, some corporations send out their interim reports with the press release. This obviously puts a greater burden on the financial department, particularly if the reports include detailed information in addition to the income figures. However, in terms of good stockholder communications, the added burden is worthwhile.

Financial information presented in the income statement includes sales, net income before and after taxes, discontinued operations, extraordinary items, and per-share figures. The balance sheet includes normal items such as current, fixed, and other assets; current and long-term liabilities; and stockholders' equity.

**Fact Books.** In those industries in which there is a great deal of complicated financial information, such as insurance, banks, railroads, and utilities, fact books are very useful for the professional investor. They should, however, be developed as statistical supplements. Graphics, beyond good typing and a reasonable amount of white space, are not a key factor. Putting together such a book usually falls on the shoulders of the controller.

**Dividend Enclosures.** Dividend enclosures receive a high degree of readership, because all stockholders are interested in their checks and are likely to read the information that accompanies them. The most useful way to utilize this stockholder exposure is to express some particular company point of view. These enclosures are also used to sell dividend reinvestment plans.

**Employee Annual Reports.** There are no mandated requirements in employee annual reports. They provide management with the opportunity to convey a special message to employee stockholders in an effort to make them feel part of the team. The reports should emphasize that employee productivity means higher profits, which in turn will be reflected in the price of the stock. The controller has an excellent opportunity to explain to the employees, in simplified textbook terms, just what the various statistics mean, particularly in such items as cost of goods sold, administrative expenses, taxes, the need to pay dividends, and the role of capital expenditures.

### Communicating With Potential Investors

One of the controller's key roles is handling communications to the professional investment community. One of the important components that has to be considered is coordinating a program so that it applies to all potential investors, that is, to both institutions and individuals.

This is usually accomplished through a two-pronged approach: meetings sponsored by the company and meetings sponsored by analyst societies or other professional groups within the financial community.

**Company-Sponsored Meetings.** The first approach establishes a program of financial community meetings with analysts and portfolio managers in various financial centers in which the company believes there is investment interest. In identifying appropriate financial centers, the controller should keep the following in mind:

- Areas where the total number of stockholders is large;
- Areas where there is a high level of general shareownership relative to the population;
- Cities or regions that have resisted the national trend of declining shareownership;
- Areas where the company's business and products are regarded as a favorable investment; and
- Areas where the company has operations and high visibility.

The meeting process includes selection of the proper audience, presentation of the company story, and a follow-up survey of audience reaction. Often an outside investor relations firm is hired to assist the controller in identifying the proper mix of brokerage firms and institutional analysts invited to meetings. They can also help to target key cities.

The information provided at these sessions includes industry trends, ratio objectives, interpretation of performance, outlook, capital expenditures, unusual fluctuations, and quality of earnings expected. Other areas of interest are markets, product development, quality of management, competition, divisional breakdowns, fastest- and slowest-growing areas of the company, industry perspectives, dividend policy, effects of foreign currency translation, and acquisition programs.

**Meetings With Professional Societies.** Another approach is to appear before analyst societies or other professional groups within the financial community. Since the company has no control over the audience in these cases, meetings tend to be more of a platform for the press than a good give-and-take between management and the analysts. Exceptions are meetings with analyst splinter groups (small groups of industry specialists who meet to hear companies for which they are collectively responsible), which tend to be informative and provocative.

Appearances before broker groups have recently become popular. Corporations acting as sponsors, often getting outside help from an investor relations firm, find this an effective way of reaching potential individual investors.

### Stockholder Analysis

Analyzing stockholder lists reveals strengths and weaknesses in the event of a hostile tender offer but is also useful for proxy solicitation and investor relations planning. The controller generally shares this responsibility with the corporate secretary's department.

**Transfer Agents.** The transfer agent's lists are called *social breakdowns* and are normally divided into eight categories. However, these categories are best condensed into three: those who own stock directly in their name (individually); those who own it in a broker's name (brokers); and companies, banks, or mutual funds who own stock in a designated name (nominees).

Several nominees are affiliated with the various stock exchanges. CEDE (N.Y.S.E. and Amex), Kray & Co. (Midwest), and PAC & Co. (Pacific) appear on the transfer agent's social breakdown of stockholders as nominees. But they are really nominees for the brokerage firms and therefore should be classified as such. Therefore, the controller should attempt to properly identify these "nominees." He will see that for the most part they carry brokerage firm names, although some banks, particularly New York banks, may be included. The brokers listed should then be added to the broker list, the banks to the nominee list.

**Stockholder Lists.** Lists of stockholders should be reported to management quarterly, if not monthly. It is useful to analyze these lists in terms of the strength of the investor types represented. Generally speaking, the greater the number of individual investors, the more conservative the list, and the more stable and loyal the stockholders. The more broker accounts, the more speculative the company is considered. Finally, the greater the nominee holdings (institutions), the greater the professional interest in the company as a quality holding.

## Other Investor Relations Responsibilities

**Engaging Investor Relations Counsel.** Many corporations hire outside counsel to assist them in their shareowner relations activities. Basically, counsel assists in developing program objectives and coordination, organizing the financial community meetings, preparing written communications, and formulating the press and individual stockholder programs.

The financial department is often charged with selecting appropriate counsel. The key criterion for its choice should be the firm's professionalism and track record. And, of course, the investor relations firm's client list should be inspected. The quality of the companies often shows the quality of the firm itself. Several firms should be interviewed, and members of the financial community should be sought out for their views.

Costs for these services vary extensively. Some firms charge by the hour, whereas others prefer a flat retainer fee over an established period of time. A predetermined retainer fee ensures that there are no hidden charges, and is preferable from a budgetary point of view.

**Tender Offers.** All publicly held corporations are susceptible to tender offers. A prudent management team undertakes a contingency program to ascertain its vulnerabilities and prepare a response if it is approached from an unwanted source. Outsiders are definitely needed to advise on this question. Many companies hire these experts ahead of time as part of a contingency plan, although some wait until a problem arises.

Key members involved in tender-offer defense are the corporate counsel, investment bankers (although they come in after the fact) and the proxy solicitor, who is also normally a stockholder relations expert. Internally, the management team includes the chief executive, the corporate secretary, and of course, the controller. If the company has strong in-house investor relations or public relations personnel, they should also be included.

**Proxy Matters.** The controller normally does not get involved with the proxy process, because the responsibility belongs to the corporate secretary. However, preparation of the proxy material should be coordinated with that of the annual report. Moreover, the report has to be out well in advance of the annual meeting. First-quarter figures are often released at the annual meeting.

**Reporting to the Board.** The role of investor relations is often not fully understood by the board of directors, an ironic situation when one remembers that they are supposed to represent stockholders. It is important to develop a regular procedure for reporting to the board (as well as top management) on the status of the investor relations program. Items to be included in such a report are stockholder attitudes, financial community attitudes, program objectives and how they are being met, stock price activity, how the company's price/earnings ratio compares to that of competitors, and acquisition and tender concerns. The report must convey the importance of the program in fulfilling the company's responsibility to its stockholders.

## SUGGESTED READING

American Society of Corporate Secretaries. *Communicating With Shareholders Through the Annual Report.* New York: 1979.

Berg, Steven. *Communicating With Today's Investment Decision Makers.* New York: Corporate Shareholder Press, 1978.

New York Stock Exchange. *Public Attitudes Towards Investing—Marketing Publications.* New York: 1978.

Robinson, J. William. "To Counter Tender Offers, TLC for Shareholders." *Harvard Business Review*, January-February, 1976.

# Index

# Contents